PRINCIPLES OF
MARKETING
8th CANADIAN EDITION

PHILIP KOTLER
NORTHWESTERN UNIVERSITY

GARY ARMSTRONG
UNIVERSITY OF NORTH CAROLINA

PEGGY H. CUNNINGHAM
DALHOUSIE UNIVERSITY

VALERIE TRIFTS
DALHOUSIE UNIVERSITY

Pearson Canada
Toronto

Library and Archives Canada Cataloguing in Publication

Principles of marketing / Philip Kotler . . . [et al.]. — 8th Canadian ed.

Canadian ed. written by Philip Kotler, Gordon H. G. McDougall. 3rd Canadian ed. written by Philip Kotler . . . [et al.]. 4th–7th Canadian eds. written by Philip Kotler, Gary Armstrong, Peggy H. Cunningham.

Includes bibliographical references and index.

ISBN 978-0-13-508457-1

1. Marketing—Textbooks.   2. Marketing—Management—Textbooks.   I. Kotler, Philip II. Title.

HF5415.P75 2011   658.8   C2009-906672-6

ISBN 978-0-13-508457-1

Vice-President, Editorial Director: Gary Bennett
Editor-in-Chief: Nicole Lukach
Acquisitions Editor: Nick Durie
Sponsoring Editor: Don Thompson
Marketing Manager: Leigh-Anne Graham
Developmental Editor: Paul Donnelly
Production Editor: Cheryl Jackson
Copy Editor: Leanne Rancourt
Proofreader: Laurel Sparrow
Production Coordinator: Andrea Falkenberg
Compositor: MPS Limited, A Macmillan Company
Photo and Permissions Researcher: David Strand
Art Director: Julia Hall
Interior Designer: Miriam Blier
Cover Illustration: Miriam Blier

5 6 7 8   15 14 13 12

Printed and bound in the United States of America.

*To Kathy, Betty, Mandy, Matt, KC, Keri, Delaney, Molly, Macy, and Ben;
and Nancy, Amy, Melissa, and Jessica.*

—P.K. & G.A.

To Paul, Krista, and Tilley, who have been my joy, strength and support.

—P.C.

To John, Andrew, and Aiden.

—V. T.

About the Authors

Philip Kotler is the S. C. Johnson & Son Distinguished Professor of International Marketing at the Kellogg School of Management, Northwestern University. He received his master's degree at the University of Chicago and his PhD at MIT, both in economics. Dr. Kotler is the author of *Marketing Management* (Pearson Prentice Hall), now in its thirteenth edition and the most widely used marketing text book in graduate business schools worldwide. He has authored dozens of other successful books and has written more than 100 articles in leading journals. He is the only three-time winner of the coveted Alpha Kappa Psi award for the best annual article in the *Journal of Marketing*.

Professor Kotler was named the first recipient of two major awards: the Distinguished Marketing Educator of the Year Award, given by the American Marketing Association and the Philip Kotler Award for Excellence in Health Care Marketing, presented by the Academy for Health Care Services Marketing. His numerous other major honours include the Sales and Marketing Executives International Marketing Educator of the Year Award; the European Association of Marketing Consultants and Trainers Marketing Excellence Award; the Charles Coolidge Parlin Marketing Research Award; and the Paul D. Converse Award, given by the American Marketing Association to honour "outstanding contributions to science in marketing." In a recent *Financial Times* poll of 1000 senior executives across the world, Professor Kotler was ranked as the fourth "most influential business writer/guru" of the twenty-first century.

Dr. Kotler has served as chairman of the College on Marketing of the Institute of Management Sciences, a director of the American Marketing Association, and a trustee of the Marketing Science Institute. He has consulted with many major U.S. and international companies in the areas of marketing strategy and planning, marketing organization, and international marketing. He has travelled extensively throughout Europe, Asia, and South America, advising companies and governments about global marketing practices and opportunities.

Gary Armstrong is the Crist W. Blackwell Distinguished Professor of Undergraduate Education in the Kenan-Flagler Business School at the University of North Carolina at Chapel Hill. He holds undergraduate and master's degrees in business from Wayne State University in Detroit, and he received his PhD in marketing from Northwestern University. Dr. Armstrong has contributed numerous articles to leading business journals. As a consultant and researcher, he has worked with many companies on marketing research, sales management, and marketing strategy.

But Professor Armstrong's first love has always been teaching. His Blackwell Distinguished Professorship is the only permanent endowed professorship for distinguished undergraduate teaching at the University of North Carolina at Chapel Hill. He has been very active in the teaching and administration of Kenan-Flagler's undergraduate program. His administrative posts have included Chair of Marketing, Associate Director of the Undergraduate Business Program, Director of the Business Honors Program, and many others. He has worked closely with business student groups and has received several campuswide and Business School teaching awards. He is the only repeat recipient of the school's highly regarded Award for Excellence in Undergraduate Teaching, which he has received three times. Most recently, Professor Armstrong received the UNC Board of Governors Award for Excellence in Teaching, the highest teaching honour bestowed by the 16-campus University of North Carolina system.

Peggy Cunningham is the Acting Dean of the Faculty of Management, and the R. A. Jodrey Chair in the Faculty of Management at Dalhousie University. She joined Dalhousie University in January 2009 after serving as a professor at Queen's School of Business for 19 years. Dr. Cunningham has also worked in the U.K., Germany, China, and the U.S. Her teaching and research focus on brand management, ethics, corporate social responsibility, and partnerships within the field of marketing. Her research is published in a number of journals including the *Journal of the Academy of Marketing Science,* the *California Management Review,* and the *Journal of International Marketing*. Professor Cunningham is also an acclaimed teacher. Her awards include the PriceWaterhouseCoopers Leaders in Management Education award, the Academy of Marketing Science's Outstanding Teacher, and the Frank Knox Award for Teaching Excellence. She has written over 40 cases, and she is the co-author of three marketing textbooks.

Valerie Trifts is an Associate Professor of Marketing at Dalhousie University School of Business. She received her undergraduate business degree from the University of Prince Edward Island, her MBA from Saint Mary's University, and her PhD in Marketing from the University of Alberta. Her primary research interests are in the area of consumer information search and decision making. Specifically, she is interested in how firms can benefit from strategically providing their customers with information about competitors, as well as exploring individual difference variables that influence search behaviour. She integrates her research into a variety of courses she teaches, which include introduction to marketing, consumer behaviour, Internet marketing, and marketing research at both the undergraduate and graduate levels. Her research has been published in *Marketing Science* and the *Journal of Consumer Psychology*, presented at numerous academic conferences, and funded by the Social Sciences and Humanities Research Council of Canada.

Brief Contents

Contents

PART 3 Designing a Customer-Driven Strategy and Mix 238

Preface

The Eighth Canadian Edition of *Principles of Marketing:* Creating More Value for You!

The goal of every marketer is to create more value for customers. So it makes sense that our goal for the eighth Canadian edition is to continue creating more value for you—*our* customer. Our goal is to introduce you to the fascinating world of modem marketing in an innovative yet practical and enjoyable way. We've redesigned the book to make it easier to learn and study from, and we've added MyMarketingLab, our online personalized study and assessment tool.

Marketing: Creating Customer Value and Relationships

A recent survey of top marketers showed that they all share a common goal: putting the consumer at the heart of marketing. Today's marketing is all about creating customer value and building profitable customer relationships. It starts with understanding consumer needs and wants, deciding which target markets the organization can serve best, and developing a compelling value proposition by which the organization can attract, keep, and grow targeted consumers. If the organization does these things well, it will reap the rewards in terms of market share, profits, and customer equity.

Five Major Value Themes

From beginning to end, the eighth Canadian edition of *Principles of Marketing* develops an innovative customer-value and customer-relationships framework that captures the essence of today's marketing. It builds on five major value themes:

1. *Creating value for customers in order to capture value from customers in return.* Today's marketers must be good at creating customer value and managing customer relationships. Outstanding marketing companies understand the marketplace and customer needs, design value-creating marketing strategies, develop integrated marketing programs that deliver customer value and delight, and build strong customer relationships. In return, they capture value from customers in the form of sales, profits, and customer loyalty.

   This innovative *customer-value framework* is introduced at the start of Chapter 1 in a five-step marketing process model, which details how marketing *creates* customer

Marketing: Creating and Capturing Customer Value

Figure 1.1 A Simple Model of the Marketing Process

value and *captures* value in return. The framework is carefully explained in the first two chapters and then fully integrated throughout the remainder of the text.

2. *Building and managing strong, value-creating brands.* Well-positioned brands with strong brand equity provide the basis upon which to build customer value and profitable customer relationships. Today's marketers must position their brands powerfully and manage them well. They must build close brand relationships and experiences with customers.

3. *Measuring and managing return on marketing.* Marketing managers must ensure that their marketing dollars are being well spent. In the past, *many* marketers spent freely on big, expensive marketing programs, often without thinking carefully about the financial returns on their spending. But all that has changed rapidly. "Marketing accountability"—measuring and managing return on marketing investments—has now become an important part of strategic marketing decision making. This emphasis on marketing accountability is addressed throughout the eighth Canadian edition.

4. *Harnessing new marketing technologies.* New digital and other high-tech marketing developments are dramatically changing how consumers and marketers relate to one another. The eighth Canadian edition thoroughly explores the new technologies impacting marketing, from "Web 2.0" in Chapter 1 to new-age digital marketing and online technologies in Chapters 15 and 17 to the exploding use of online social networks and customer-generated marketing in Chapters 1, 5, 14, 17, and elsewhere.

5. *Sustainable marketing around the globe.* As technological developments make the world an increasingly smaller and more fragile place, marketers must be good at marketing their brands globally and in responsible and ethical ways. New material throughout the eighth Canadian edition emphasizes the concept of sustainable marketing—meeting the present needs of consumers and businesses while also preserving or enhancing the ability of future generations to meet their needs.

New in the Eighth Canadian Edition

We've thoroughly revised the eighth Canadian edition of *Principles of Marketing* to reflect the major trends and forces impacting marketing in this era of customer value and relationships. Here are just some of the major changes you'll find in this edition.

- The eighth Canadian edition has a completely new learning design! The newly designed chapter-opening layout helps to preview and position the chapter and its key concepts. Redesigned figures help students to simplify and organize chapter material. End-of-chapter features help to summarize important chapter concepts and highlight important themes, such as marketing technology, ethics, and financial marketing analysis. In all, the new design facilitates student understanding and eases learning.

- Throughout the eighth Canadian edition, you will find important new coverage of the rapidly changing nature of customer relationships with companies and brands. Today's marketers aim to create deeper consumer involvement and a sense of community surrounding a brand—to make the brand a meaningful part of consumers' conversations and their lives. New relationship-building tools include everything from blogs, websites, in-person events, and video sharing, to online communities and social networks, such as MySpace, Facebook, YouTube, or a company's own social networking sites.

- A revised Chapter 4 pulls marketing together under an important new sustainable marketing framework. It shows how sustainable marketing calls for socially and environmentally responsible actions that meet both the immediate and the future needs of customers, the company, and society as a whole.

- Increasingly, marketing is taking the form of two-way conversations between consumers and brands. The eighth Canadian edition contains new material on the exciting trend toward consumer-generated marketing, by which marketers invite consumers to play a more active role in providing customer insights (Chapter 5), shaping new products (Chapter 10), developing or passing along brand messages (Chapter 15), interacting in customer communities (Chapters 6, 15, and 17), and other developments.

- This edition provides new and expanded discussions of new marketing technologies, from "Web 2.0" in Chapter 1 to neuromarketing in Chapter 6 to RFID in Chapter 12 to the new-age digital marketing and online technologies in Chapters 1, 14, 15, and 17.

- In line with the text's emphasis on measuring and managing return on marketing, we've added end-of-chapter financial and quantitative marketing exercises that let students apply analytical thinking to relevant concepts in each chapter and link chapter concepts to the text's innovative Appendix 3: Marketing by the Numbers.

- The eighth Canadian edition provides refreshed and expanded coverage of the explosive developments in integrated marketing communications and direct and online marketing. It tells how marketers are incorporating a host of new digital and direct approaches to build and create more targeted, personal, and interactive customer relationships. No other text provides more current or encompassing coverage of these exciting developments.

Real Value Through Real Marketing

Principles of Marketing features in-depth, real-world examples and stories that show concepts in action and reveal the drama of modern marketing. In the eighth Canadian edition, every chapter opening vignette and "Real Marketing" highlight has been updated or replaced to provide fresh and relevant insights into real marketing practices.

- Bullfrog Power shows how an innovative new company can address isues related to sustainabiility while stretching a limited marketing budget through powerful public relations techniques.

- Dove's Campaign for Real Beauty tells the story of how a viral ad created by a Canadian agency took the world by storm.

- lululemon is a Canadian branding success story.

- Apple founder Steve Jobs used dazzling customer-driven innovation to first start the company and then to remake it again 20 years later.

- Nike gives consumers more than just good athletic gear. It markets a way of life, a sports culture, and a just-do-it attitude.

- McDonald's now sells more burgers and fries outside North America than within.

- Costco Canada tells the tale of how the war with other discounters can be won.

- Design consultancy ZIBA's new-product designs don't start in the research lab—its first design step is to research consumers and get to know them—*really* get to know them.

- Starbucks has brewed up an ambitious—perhaps overly ambitious—growth strategy to maintain its lead in an increasingly overcaffeinated marketplace.

- McCain shows how a firm born in the Atlantic provinces has grown into a global firm that dominates many food categories.

- Dunkin' Donuts targets the "Dunkin' Tribe"—not the Starbucks snob, but the average Joe.

- Once little-known, GEICO used an industry-changing advertising campaign featuring a likable spokes-lizard, an indignant clan of cavemen, and an enduring tagline to become an industry leader.

Each chapter is packed with numerous real, relevant, and timely examples that reinforce key concepts and bring marketing to life.

Valuable Learning Aids

A wealth of chapter-opening, within-chapter, and end-of-chapter learning devices help students to learn, link, and apply major concepts:

- *Chapter Preview.* As part of a new, more active and integrative chapter-opening design, a brief section at the beginning of each chapter previews chapter concepts, links them with previous chapter concepts, and introduces the chapter-opening story.
- *Chapter-opening marketing stories.* Each chapter begins with an engaging, deeply developed, illustrated, and annotated marketing story that introduces the chapter material and sparks student interest.
- *Objective outline.* This chapter-opening feature provides a helpful preview outline of chapter contents and learning objectives.
- *Real Marketing highlights.* Each chapter contains two highlight features that provide an in-depth look at real marketing practices of large and small companies.
- *Reviewing the Objectives and Key Terms.* A summary at the end of each chapter reviews major chapter concepts, chapter objectives, and key terms.
- *Discussing the Concepts and Applying the Concepts.* Each chapter contains a set of discussion questions and and a set of application exercises covering major chapter concepts.
- *Focus on Technology.* Application exercises at the end of each chapter provide discussion of important and emerging marketing technologies in this digital age.
- *Focus on Ethics.* Situation descriptions and questions highlight important issues in marketing ethics at the end of each chapter.
- *Marketing by the Numbers.* An exercise at the end of each chapter lets students apply analytical and financial thinking to relevant chapter concepts and links the chapter to Appendix 3: Marketing by the Numbers.
- *Company Cases.* All new or revised company cases for class or written discussion are provided at the end of each chapter. These cases challenge students to apply marketing principles to real companies in real situations.
- *Video Cases.* Short cases and discussion questions appear at the end of every chapter, to be used with the set of four- to six-minute videos that accompany this edition (on MyMarketingLab).
- Eight additional video cases, based on CBC programs, can also be accessed via MyMarketingLab. These segments comprise the **CBC/Pearson Canada Inc. Video Library**, which is available on DVD.
- *Comprehensive Case.* Appendix 1 is the compelling story of the ZENN Motor Company, which shows how this Canadian company uses new technologies to address one of the major causes of climate change. The firm has used a wide range of marketing tactics as it has grown, and the case illustrates many of the major concepts from the book. Questions at the end of the case help students better understand how to apply the concepts and analyze the situation faced by ZENN.
- *Marketing Plan.* Appendix 2 contains a sample marketing plan that helps students to apply important marketing planning concepts.
- *Marketing by the Numbers.* Appendix 3 provides students with a comprehensive introduction to the marketing financial analysis that helps to guide, assess, and support marketing decisions.
- *Careers in Marketing.* Appendix 4 shows students how to conduct a job search specific to their needs, describes marketing career paths open to them, and suggests other information sources.

More than ever before, the eighth Canadian edition of *Principles of Marketing* creates value for you—it gives you all you need to know about marketing in an effective and enjoyable total learning package!

For the Student

A successful marketing course requires more than a well-written book. A total package of resources extends this edition's emphasis on creating value for you. The following aids support *Principles of Marketing*.

MyMarketingLab (www.pearsoned.ca/mymarketinglab) gives you the opportunity to test yourself on key concepts and skills, track your own progress through the course, and use the personalized study plan activities—all to help you achieve success in the classroom. Features include:

- Personalized study plans. Pre- and post-tests with remediation activities help you understand and apply the concepts where you need the most help.
- Self-assessments. Pre-built self-assessments allow you to test yourself.
- Interactive elements. A wealth of hands-on activities and exercises let you experience and learn firsthand, whether it's with the Pearson eText in which you can search for specific keywords or page numbers, highlight specific sections, enter notes right on the eText page, and print reading assignments with notes for later review, or with other materials including video cases, end-of-chapter activities, glossary flashcards, discussion boards, and much more.
- MyLab On the Go—Study anytime, anywhere with audio chapter summaries, glossary flashcards, and chapter quizzes specifically created for downloading to your iPod.

Find out more at www.pearsoned.ca/mymarketinglab.

For the Instructor

Instructor resources are password protected and available for download via http://vig.pearsoned.ca. For your convenience, many of these resources are also available on the **Instructor's Resource CD-ROM** (ISBN 978-0-13-214223-6).

- **Instructor's Manual.** View this resource chapter-by-chapter or download the entire manual as a zip file.
- **TestGen and MyTest.** For your convenience, our testbank is available in two formats. TestGen is included on the Instructor's CD-ROM and MyTest is available through MyMarketingLab. Both represent a powerful assessment-generation program that helps instructors easily create and print quizzes, tests, and exams, as well as homework or practice handouts.
- When it comes to **PowerPoint® Presentations,** Pearson Canada knows that one size does not fit all. That's why we offer instructors more than one option.
    - **PowerPoint® BASIC.** This simple presentation includes basic outlines and key points from each chapter. BASIC was designed for instructors who prefer to customize PowerPoint slides and want to be spared from having to strip out embedded files or other media-rich features. The BASIC PowerPoint slides are also available to students in MyMarketingLab.
    - **PowerPoint® MEDIA RICH (on IRCD only).** This media-rich alternative includes basic outlines and key points from each chapter, plus advertisements and images from the text, discussion questions, weblinks, and embedded video snippets from the accompanying video library. It's the best option if you want a complete presentation solution. Instructors can further customize this presentation using the Image Library featured on the Instructor's Resource CD-ROM.

- **Instructor PowerPoint® Slides with Classroom Response System (CRS).** This set of slides offers the same content as the "Instructor PowerPoints," but with the added feature of 10–20 CRS question/answer slides offered throughout each chapter. These text-specific Q&A-style slides are designed for classrooms using "clickers" or classroom response systems.
- **Image Library (on IRCD only).** The Image Library provides access to many of the images, ads, and illustrations featured in the text. It is the ideal resource for Power-Point customization.
- **CBC/Pearson Canada Inc. Video Library.** Pearson Canada Inc. and the CBC have worked together to bring you eight segments from such notable CBC programs as *Venture, Marketplace,* and *Undercurrents.* Designed specifically to complement the text, this case collection is an excellent tool for bringing students into contact with the world outside the classroom. These programs have extremely high production quality, present substantial content, and have been chosen to relate directly to chapter topics. (Please contact your Pearson Canada Inc. sales representative for details. These videos are subject to availability and terms negotiated upon adoption of the text.)

CourseSmart   CourseSmart is a new way for instructors and students to access textbooks online anytime from anywhere. With thousands of titles across hundreds of courses, CourseSmart helps instructors choose the best textbook for their class and give their students a new option for buying the assigned textbook as a lower cost eTextbook. For more information, visit www.coursesmart.com.

Technology Specialists   Pearson's Technology Specialists work with faculty and campus course designers to ensure that Pearson technology products, assessment tools, and online course materials are tailored to meet your specific needs. This highly qualified team is dedicated to helping schools take full advantage of a wide range of educational resources, by assisting in the integration of a variety of instructional materials and media formats. Your local Pearson Canada Inc. sales representative can provide you with more details on this service program.

Acknowledgments

Many reviewers at other colleges and universities provided expert comments and suggestions. We are indebted to the following colleagues who reviewed for this edition:

Cathy Ace, Simon Fraser University

Raymond Bilodeau, Northern Alberta Institute of Technology

Peter Burgess, George Brown College

Jen Cherneski, Grant MacEwan University

Brock Valentine Cordes, University of Manitoba

Susan C. Graham, University of Prince Edward Island

Ingrid Kajzer Mitchell, Royal Roads University

Lea Prevel Katsanis, Concordia University

Geoffrey Malleck, University of Waterloo

David Moscovitz, Concordia University

Sandra Mudd, CGA-Canada

Beth Pett, Niagara College

Ray Rodda, Cambrian College

We also owe a great deal to the members of our team at Pearson Canada Inc., whose work was indispensible to the preparation of this edition: Don Thompson, Sponsoring Editor; Paul Donnelly, Developmental Editor; Cheryl Jackson, Production Editor; and Andrea Falkenberg, Production Coordinator. Thanks also to Leanne Rancourt, Copy Editor, for her fine work.

Finally, we owe many thanks to our families—Kathy, Betty, KC, Keri, Delaney, Mandy, Matt, and Molly; Nancy, Amy, Melissa, and Jessica; Paul, Krista, and Tilley; John, Andrew, and Aiden—for their constant support and encouragement. To them, we dedicate this book.

Philip Kotler
Gary Armstrong
Peggy Cunningham
Valerie Trifts

CHAPTER

1

Marketing: Creating and Capturing
Customer Value

PREVIEWING
THE CONCEPTS

In this chapter, we introduce you to the basic concepts of marketing. We start with the question, "What *is* marketing?" Simply put, marketing is managing profitable customer relationships. The aim of marketing is to create value *for* customers and to capture value *from* customers in return. Next, we discuss the five steps in the marketing process—from understanding customer needs, to designing customer-driven marketing strategies and programs, to building customer relationships and capturing value for the firm. Finally, we discuss the major trends and forces affecting marketing in this age of customer relationships. Understanding these basic concepts and forming your own ideas about what they really mean to you will give you a solid foundation for all that follows.

Let's start with a good story about marketing in action at Procter & Gamble, one of the world's largest and most respected marketing companies. P&G makes and markets a who's who list of consumer megabrands, including the likes of Tide, Crest, Bounty, Charmin, Puffs, Pampers, Pringles, Gillette, Dawn, Ivory, Febreze, Swiffer, Olay, CoverGirl, Pantene, Scope, NyQuil, Duracell, and hundreds more. P&G began manufacturing products in Canada in 1915, and in 2007 the company was named as one of the top 100 employers in Canada. It's also the world's largest advertiser, spending an eye-popping $8.2 billion each year on advertising worldwide, "telling and selling" consumers on the benefits of using its products. But look deeper and you'll see that this premier marketer does far more than just "tell and sell." The company's stated purpose is to provide products that "improve the lives of the world's consumers." P&G's products really do create value for consumers by solving their problems. In return, customers reward P&G with their brand loyalty and buying dollars. You'll see this theme of creating customer value to capture value in return repeated throughout the first chapter and throughout the text.

Creating customer value and building meaningful customer relationships sounds pretty lofty, especially for a company like P&G, which sells seemingly mundane, low-involvement consumer products such as detergents and shampoos, toothpastes and fabric softeners, and toilet paper and disposable diapers. Can you really develop a meaningful relationship with a laundry detergent? For P&G, the resounding answer is *yes*.

For example, take P&G's product Tide. Introduced in Canada in 1948, Tide revolutionized the industry as the first detergent to use synthetic compounds rather than soap chemicals for cleaning clothes. Tide really does get clothes clean. For decades, Tide's marketers have positioned the brand on superior functional performance, with hard-hitting ads showing before-and-after cleaning comparisons. But as it turns out, Tide means a lot more to consumers than just getting grass stains out of that old pair of jeans.

P&G's true strength lies in the relationships that it builds between brands and customers: "Tide knows fabrics best."

For several years, P&G has been on a mission to unearth and cultivate the deep connections that customers have with its products. Two years ago, P&G global marketing chief Jim Stengel mandated that the company's brands must "speak to consumers eye-to-eye" rather than relentlessly driving product benefits. "We need to think beyond consuming . . . and to really directly understand the role and the meaning the brand has in [consumers'] lives," says Stengel. Behind this strategy lies the realization that competitors can quickly copy product benefits, such as cleaning power. However, they can't easily copy how consumers *feel* about a brand. Consequently, P&G's true strength lies in the relationships that it builds between its brands and customers.

Under this mandate, the Tide marketing team decided that it needed a new message for the brand. Tide's brand share, although large, had been stagnant for several years. Also, as a result of its hard-hitting functional advertising, consumers saw the Tide brand as arrogant, self-absorbed, and very male. The brand needed to recapture the hearts and minds of its core female consumers.

So the team set out to gain a deeper understanding of the emotional connections that women have with their laundry. Rather than conducting the usual focus groups and research surveys, however, marketing executives and strategists from P&G and its longtime ad agency, Saatchi & Saatchi, went into a two-week consumer immersion. They tagged along with women in North American cities as they worked,

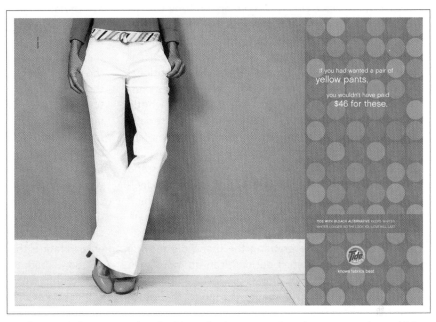

P&G is on a mission to unearth and cultivate the deep connections that customers have with its products. Can you really develop a meaningful relationship with a laundry detergent? For P&G, the resounding answer is *yes*.

shopped, and ran errands, and they sat in on discussions to hear women talk about what's important to them. "We got to an incredibly deep and personal level," says a Tide marketing executive. "We wanted to understand the role of laundry in their life." But "one of the great things," adds a Saatchi strategist, "is we didn't talk [to consumers] about their laundry habits [and practices]. We talked about their lives, what their needs were, how they felt as women. And we got a lot of rich stuff that we hadn't tapped into before."

For members of the Tide team who couldn't join the two-week consumer odyssey, including Saatchi's creative people, the agency videotaped the immersions, prepared scripts, and hired actresses to portray consumers in an hour-long play entitled *Pieces of Her*. "They were actually very

OBJECTIVES

1. Define marketing and outline the steps in the marketing process.

2. Explain the importance of understanding customers and the marketplace, and identify the five core marketplace concepts.

3. Identify the key elements of a customer-driven marketing strategy and discuss the marketing management orientations that guide marketing strategy.

4. Discuss customer relationship management and identify strategies for creating value *for* customers and capturing value *from* customers in return.

5. Describe the major trends and forces that are changing the marketing landscape in this age of relationships.

good actresses who brought to life many dimensions of women," says the Saatchi executive. "It's difficult to inspire creatives sometimes. And [their reaction to the play] was incredible. There was crying and laughing. And you can see it in the [later] work. It's just very connected to women."

From the customer immersions, the marketers learned that, although Tide and laundry aren't the most important things in customers' lives, women are very emotional about their clothing. For example, there was the joy a plus-size, divorced woman described when she got a whistle from her boyfriend while wearing her "foolproof (sexiest) outfit." According to one P&G account, "Day-to-day fabrics in women's lives hold meaning and touch them in many ways. Women like taking care of their clothes and fabrics because they are filled with emotions, stories, feelings, and memories. The fabrics in their lives (anything from jeans to sheets) allow them to express their personalities, their multidimensions as women, their attitudes." Such insights impacted everything the brand did moving forward. Tide, the marketers decided, can do more than solve women's laundry problems. It can make a difference in something they truly care about—the fabrics that touch their lives.

Based on these insights, P&G and Saatchi developed an award-winning advertising campaign built around the theme "Tide knows fabrics best." Rather than the unfeeling demonstrations and side-by-side comparisons of past Tide advertising, the new campaign employs rich visual imagery and meaningful emotional connections. For example, Toronto-based Saatchi & Saatchi Canada, which creates approximately 25 percent of Tide's advertising in North America, developed the campaign for the launch of 2x Ultra Tide featuring TV personality Kelly Ripa. This campaign has been among Tide's strongest and most unusual work in recent history, and Canadian consumers could relate to her and the values she personifies. The "Tide knows fabrics best" slogan says little about cleaning. Instead, the message is that Tide lets women focus on life's important things. "One of our rallying cries was to get out of the laundry basket and into [your] life," says a Tide marketer.

The "Tide knows fabrics best" ads have just the right mix of emotional connections and soft sell. In one TV commercial, a pregnant woman dribbles ice cream on the one last shirt that still fits. It's Tide with Bleach to the rescue, so that "your clothes can outlast your cravings." Another ad shows touching scenes of a woman first holding a baby and then cuddling romantically with her husband, all to the tune of "Be My Baby." Tide with Febreze, says the ad, can mean "the difference between smelling like a mom and smelling like a woman." In a third ad, a woman plays with her daughter at a park, still in her white slacks from the office, thanks to her confidence in Tide with Bleach: "Your work clothes. Your play clothes. Yup, they're the same clothes," the ad concludes. "Tide with bleach: For looking great, it's child's play." In all, the "Tide knows fabrics best" campaign shows women that Tide really does make a difference in fabrics that touch their lives.

So . . . back to that original question: Can you develop a relationship with a laundry detergent brand? Some critics wonder if P&G is taking this relationship thing too seriously. "Everybody wants to elevate their brand to this kind of more rarefied level," says one brand consultant, "but at the end of the day detergent is detergent." But it's hard to argue with success, and no brand is more successful than Tide. P&G's flagship brand captures an incredible 43 percent share of the cluttered and competitive laundry detergent market. That's right, 43 percent and growing—including a 7 percent increase in the year following the start of the "Tide knows fabrics best" campaign.

If you asked Jim Stengel, he'd say that this kind of success comes from deeply understanding consumers and connecting the company's brands to their lives. Stengel wants P&G to be more than a one-way communicator with customers. He wants it to be "a starter of conversations and a solver of consumers' problems." "It's not about telling and selling," he says. "It's about bringing a [customer] relationship mind-set to everything we do."[1]

Chapter Opening Discussion

Today's successful companies have one thing in common: Like Procter & Gamble, they are strongly customer-focused and heavily committed to marketing. These companies share a passion for understanding and satisfying customer needs in well-defined target markets. They motivate everyone in the organization to help build lasting customer relationships based on creating value. P&G's chief global marketer, Jim Stengel, puts it this way: "If we're going to make one big bet on our future—right here, right now—I'd say that the smart money is on building [customer] relationships."[2]

1 WHAT IS MARKETING?

Marketing, more than any other business function, deals with customers. Although we will soon explore more-detailed definitions of marketing, perhaps the simplest definition is this one: *Marketing is managing profitable customer relationships*. The twofold goal of marketing is to attract new customers by promising superior value and to keep and grow current customers by delivering satisfaction.

Walmart has become the world's largest retailer—and the world's largest company—by delivering on its promise, "Save money. Live Better." At Disney theme parks, "imagineers" work wonders in their quest to "make a dream come true today." Apple fulfills its motto to "Think Different" with dazzling, customer-driven innovation that captures customer imaginations and loyalty. Its wildly successful iPod grabs more than 70 percent of the music player market; its iTunes music store captures nearly 90 percent of the song download business.[3] Provigo, a supermarket chain owned by Loblaw that operates mainly in Quebec, now has 110 outlets and employs 5700 people. It has built its business by providing "quality, variety, and freshness throughout its stores," along with the promise to make the lives of its customers easier by offering quick, courteous service aligned with its customers' needs. The company also knows the importance of being involved in its customers' communities, and it focuses on providing financial assistance to the families of children who have physical or developmental challenges. These and other highly successful companies know that if they take care of their customers, market share and profits will follow.

Sound marketing is critical to the success of every organization. Canada's top five firms of 2008[4] (ranked according to profitability), RBC, Manulife Financial, Thomson Reuters, EnCana, and BCE, make extensive use of marketing. But so do not-for-profit organizations such as universities, hospitals, museums, symphony orchestras, and even churches.

You already know a lot about marketing—it's all around you. Marketing comes to you in traditional forms: You see it in the abundance of products at your nearby shopping mall and in the advertisements that fill your TV screen, spice up your magazines, or stuff your mailbox. But in recent years, marketers have assembled a host of new marketing approaches, everything from imaginative websites, Internet chat rooms, and social networks, to interactive TV and your cellphone. These new approaches aim to do more than just blast out messages to the masses. They aim to reach you directly and personally. Today's marketers want to become a part of your life and to enrich your experiences with their brands—to help you *live* their brands.

At home, at school, where you work, and where you play you see marketing in almost everything you do. Yet there is much more to marketing than meets the consumer's casual eye. Behind it all is a massive network of people and activities competing for your attention and purchases. This book will give you a complete introduction to the basic concepts and practices of today's marketing. In this chapter, we begin by defining marketing and the marketing process.

Marketing Defined

What is marketing? Many people think of marketing only as selling and advertising. And no wonder—every day we are bombarded with TV commercials, direct-mail offers, sales calls, and email pitches. However, selling and advertising are only the tip of the marketing iceberg.

Today, marketing must be understood not in the old sense of making a sale—"telling and selling"—but in the new sense of *satisfying customer needs* in a socially responsible and ethical manner. If the marketer understands consumer needs; develops products that provide superior customer value; and prices, distributes, and promotes them effectively and ethically, these products will sell easily. In fact, according to management guru Peter Drucker, "The aim of marketing is to make selling unnecessary."[5] Thus, selling and advertising are only part of a larger "marketing mix"—a set of marketing tools that work together to satisfy customer needs and build lasting customer relationships.

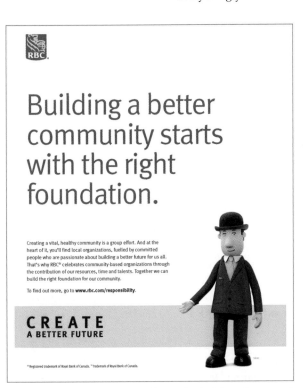

Business principles, moral principles, and principles of teamwork have helped make RBC Canada's most profitable company.

Figure 1.1 A simple model of the marketing process

Marketing
Marketing is the activity, set of institutions, and processes for creating, communicating, delivering, and exchanging offerings that have value for customers, clients, partners, and society at large.

Glossary Flashcards of Key Terms

In 2007, the American Marketing Association revised its definition of **marketing**: "Marketing is the activity, set of institutions, and processes for creating, communicating, delivering, and exchanging offerings that have value for customers, clients, partners, and society at large."[6] Thus, though the focus of marketing is on customers and profitability, marketers must also recognize the needs and rights of other groups affected by marketing decisions—the firm's stakeholders. Stakeholder groups include employees, unions, customers, members of the distribution channel, competitors, activists, government, and the press. Thus, broadly defined, marketing is a social and managerial process by which individuals and groups obtain what they need and want through creating and exchanging value with others. See how RBC, Canada's most profitable company in 2008, captures the essence of this definition in its statement on corporate social responsibility made by its president and CEO, Gordon M. Nixon:

> I believe that a company's actions speak louder than its words. At RBC, corporate responsibility can be seen in how we govern our business with integrity, have a positive economic impact, operate with integrity in the marketplace, provide a supportive workplace, support environmental sustainability, and contribute to communities.

The company's actions are indeed being recognized, since in 2009 RBC was named one of the world's top 100 sustainable companies for the fifth consecutive year.[7]

The Marketing Process

Figure 1.1 presents a simple five-step model of the marketing process. In the first four steps, companies work to understand consumers, create customer value, and build strong customer relationships. In the final step, companies reap the rewards of creating superior customer value. By creating value *for* consumers, companies capture value *from* consumers in return in the form of sales, profits, and long-term customer equity.

In this chapter and the next, we will examine the steps of this simple model of marketing. In this chapter, we will review each step but focus more on the customer relationship steps—understanding customers, building customer relationships, and capturing value from customers. In Chapter 2, we'll look more deeply into the second and third steps—designing marketing strategies and constructing marketing programs.

2 UNDERSTANDING THE MARKETPLACE AND CUSTOMER NEEDS

As a first step, marketers need to understand customer needs and wants and the marketplace within which they operate. We now examine five core customer and marketplace concepts: (1) *needs, wants, and demands;* (2) *market offerings (products, services, and experiences);* (3) *value and satisfaction;* (4) *exchanges and relationships;* and (5) *markets.*

Customer Needs, Wants, and Demands

Needs
States of felt deprivation.

The most basic concept underlying marketing is that of human needs. Human **needs** are states of felt deprivation. They include basic *physical* needs for food, clothing, warmth, and safety; *social* needs for belonging and affection; and *individual* needs for knowledge and self-expression. These needs were not created by marketers; they are a basic part of the human makeup.

Wants

The form human needs take as shaped by culture and individual personality.

Wants are the form human needs take as they are shaped by culture and individual personality. A Canadian *needs* food but *wants* a breakfast sandwich and a large double-double from Tim Hortons. Wants are shaped by one's society as well as by marketing programs. They are described in terms of objects that will satisfy needs. When backed by buying power, wants become **demands**. Given their wants and resources, people demand products with benefits that add up to the most value and satisfaction.

Demands

Human wants that are backed by buying power.

Outstanding marketing companies go to great lengths to learn about and understand their customers' needs, wants, and demands. They conduct consumer research and analyze mountains of customer data. Their people at all levels—including top management—stay close to customers. For example, at Southwest Airlines, all senior executives handle bags, check-in passengers, and serve as flight attendants once every quarter. At P&G, executives from the CEO down routinely spend time with consumers in their homes and other settings. "We all go out and really spend time with consumers," notes P&G's global marketing officer, Jim Stengel, "just to look at the differences in how they [think] about brands [and what's] important in their lives."[8]

Market offerings

Some combination of products, services, information, or experiences offered to a market to satisfy a need or want.

Market Offerings—Products, Services, and Experiences

Consumers' needs and wants are fulfilled through **market offerings**—some combination of products, services, information, or experiences offered to a market to satisfy a need or want. Market offerings are not limited to physical *products*. They also include *services*—activities or benefits offered for sale that are essentially intangible and do not result in the ownership of anything. Examples include banking, airline, hotel, tax preparation, and home repair services.

Marketing myopia

The mistake of paying more attention to the specific products a company offers than to the benefits and experiences produced by these products.

More broadly, market offerings also include other entities, such as *people, places, organizations, information,* and *ideas.* For example, EarthShare powerfully markets the idea that individuals and organizations can be involved in creating a healthy and sustainable environment.

Many sellers make the mistake of paying more attention to the specific products they offer than to the benefits and experiences produced by these products. These sellers suffer from **marketing myopia**. They are so taken with their products that they focus only on existing wants and lose sight of underlying customer needs.[9] They forget that a product is only a tool to solve a consumer problem. A manufacturer of quarter-inch drill bits may think that the customer needs a drill bit. But what the customer *really* needs is a quarter-inch hole. These sellers will have trouble if a new product comes along that serves the customer's need better or less expensively. The customer will have the same *need* but will *want* the new product.

Smart marketers look beyond the attributes of the products and services they sell. By orchestrating several services and products, they create *brand experiences* for consumers. For example, you don't just watch a NASCAR race, you immerse yourself in the exhilarating NASCAR experience. Similarly, Hewlett-Packard recognizes that a personal computer is much more than just a collection of wires and electrical components. It represents an intensely personal user experience. As noted in a recent HP ad, "There is hardly anything that you own that is *more* personal. Your personal computer is your backup brain. It's your life . . . It's your astonishing strategy, staggering proposal, dazzling calculation. It's your autobiography, written in a thousand daily words."[10]

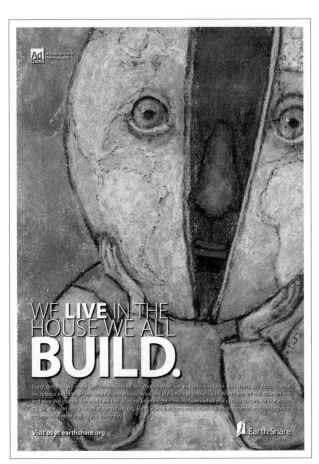

Market offerings are not limited to physical products. EarthShare powerfully markets the idea that individuals and organizations can be involved in creating a healthy and sustainable environment.

Customer Value and Satisfaction

Consumers usually face a broad array of products and services that might satisfy a given need. How do they choose among these many market offerings? Customers form expectations about the value and satisfaction that various market offerings will deliver and buy accordingly. Satisfied customers buy again and tell others about their good experiences. Dissatisfied customers often switch to competitors and disparage the product to others.

Marketers must be careful to set the right level of expectations. If they set expectations too low, they may satisfy those who buy but fail to attract enough buyers. If they raise expectations too high, buyers will be disappointed. Customer value and customer satisfaction are key building blocks for developing and managing customer relationships. We will revisit these core concepts later in the chapter.

Exchanges and Relationships

Exchange
The act of obtaining a desired object from someone by offering something in return.

Marketing occurs when people decide to satisfy needs and wants through exchange relationships. **Exchange** is the act of obtaining a desired object from someone by offering something in return. In the broadest sense, the marketer tries to bring about a response to some market offering. The response may be more than simply buying or trading products and services. A political candidate, for instance, wants votes, a church wants membership, an orchestra wants an audience, and a social action group wants idea acceptance.

Marketing consists of actions taken to build and maintain desirable exchange *relationships* with target audiences involving a product, service, idea, or other object. Beyond simply attracting new customers and creating transactions, the goal is to retain customers and grow their business with the company. Marketers want to build strong relationships by consistently delivering superior customer value. We will expand on the important concept of managing customer relationships later in the chapter.

Markets

Market
The set of all actual and potential buyers of a product or service.

The concepts of exchange and relationships lead to the concept of a market. A **market** is the set of actual and potential buyers of a product. These buyers share a particular need or want that can be satisfied through exchange relationships.

Marketing means managing markets to bring about profitable customer relationships. However, creating these relationships takes work. Sellers must search for buyers, identify their needs, design good market offerings, set prices for these offerings, promote them, and store and deliver them. Activities such as consumer research, product development, communication, distribution, pricing, and service are core marketing activities.

Although we normally think of marketing as being carried on by sellers, buyers also carry on marketing. Company purchasing agents do marketing when they track down sellers and bargain for good terms. Consumers do marketing when they search for products and interact with companies and obtain information and make their purchases. In fact, today's digital technologies, from websites and blogs to cellphones and other wireless devices, have empowered consumers and made marketing a truly interactive affair. Marketers are no longer asking only "How can we reach our customers?" but also "How should our customers reach us?" and even "How can our customers reach each other?"

Figure 1.2 shows the main elements in a marketing system. Marketing involves serving a market of final consumers in the face of competitors. The company and competitors research the market and interact with consumers to understand their needs. Then they create and send their market offerings and messages to consumers, either directly or through marketing intermediaries. All of the parties in the system are affected by major environmental forces (demographic, economic, physical, technological, political/legal, and social/cultural).

Each party in the system adds value for the next level. All of the arrows represent relationships that must be developed and managed. Thus, a company's success at building profitable relationships depends not only on its own actions but also on how well the entire system serves the needs of final consumers. Walmart cannot fulfill its promise of low prices

Figure 1.2 A modern marketing system

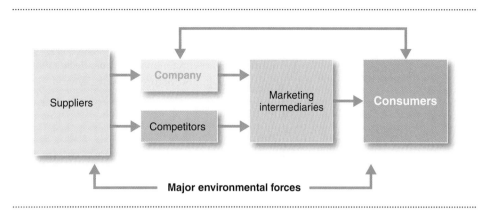

unless its suppliers provide merchandise at low costs. And Ford cannot deliver high quality to car buyers unless its dealers provide outstanding sales and service.

3 | DESIGNING A CUSTOMER-DRIVEN MARKETING STRATEGY

Marketing management
The art and science of choosing target markets and building profitable relationships with them.

Once it fully understands consumers and the marketplace, marketing management can design a customer-driven marketing strategy. We define **marketing management** as the art and science of choosing target markets and building profitable relationships with them. The marketing manager's aim is to find, attract, keep, and grow target customers by creating, delivering, and communicating superior customer value.

To design a winning marketing strategy, the marketing manager must answer two important questions: *What customers will we serve (what's our target market)?* and *How can we serve these customers best (what's our value proposition)?* We will discuss these marketing strategy concepts briefly here, and then look at them in more detail in the next chapter.

Selecting Customers to Serve

The company must first decide *who* it will serve. It does this by dividing the market into segments of customers (*market segmentation*) and selecting which segments it will go after (*target marketing*). Some people think of marketing management as finding as many customers as possible and increasing demand. But marketing managers know that they cannot serve all customers in every way. By trying to serve all customers, they may not serve any customers well. Instead, the company wants to select only customers that it can serve well and profitably. For example, Holt Renfrew and Harry Rosen stores profitably target affluent professionals; Dollarama stores profitably target families with more modest means.

Some marketers may even seek *fewer* customers and reduced demand. For example, many power companies have trouble meeting demand during peak usage periods. In these and other cases of excess demand, companies may practise *demarketing* to reduce the number of customers or to shift their demand temporarily or permanently. For instance, in March 2009 BC Hydro launched a campaign to get 210 000 British Columbians to reduce their power usage

Value propositions: Land Rover lets you "go beyond"—to "get a taste of adventure, whatever your tastes."

by 10 percent, with the goal of conserving the saved electricity to power the 2010 Olympic and Paralympic Winter Games. By joining "Team Power Smart," consumers can access tools to help track their conservation targets and have a chance to win Olympics tickets.[11]

Ultimately, marketing managers must decide which customers they want to target and on the level, timing, and nature of their demand. Simply put, marketing management is *customer management* and *demand management*.

Choosing a Value Proposition

The company must also decide how it will serve targeted customers—how it will *differentiate and position* itself in the marketplace. A company's *value proposition* is the set of benefits or values it promises to deliver to consumers to satisfy their needs. BMW promises "the ultimate driving machine," whereas Land Rover lets you "go beyond"—to "get a taste of adventure, whatever your tastes." And with cellphones, Nokia is "connecting people—anyone, anywhere," whereas with Apple's iPhone, "touching is believing."

Such value propositions differentiate one brand from another. They answer the customer's question "Why should I buy your brand rather than a competitor's?" Companies must design strong value propositions that give them the greatest advantage in their target markets.

Marketing Management Orientations

Marketing management wants to design strategies that will build profitable relationships with target consumers. But what *philosophy* should guide these marketing strategies? What weight should be given to the interests of customers, the organization, and society? Very often, these interests conflict.

There are five alternative concepts under which organizations design and carry out their marketing strategies: the *production, product, selling, marketing*, and *societal marketing concepts*.

The Production Concept

Production concept
The idea that consumers will favour products that are available and highly affordable and that the organization should therefore focus on improving production and distribution efficiency.

The **production concept** holds that consumers will favour products that are available and highly affordable. Therefore, management should focus on improving production and distribution efficiency. This concept is one of the oldest orientations that guides sellers.

The production concept is still a useful philosophy in some situations. For example, computer maker Lenovo dominates the highly competitive, price-sensitive Chinese PC market through low labour costs, high production efficiency, and mass distribution. However, although useful in some situations, the production concept can lead to marketing myopia. Companies adopting this orientation run a major risk of focusing too narrowly on their own operations and losing sight of the real objective—satisfying customer needs and building customer relationships.

The Product Concept

Product concept
The idea that consumers will favour products that offer the most quality, performance, and features and that the organization should therefore devote its energy to making continuous product improvements.

The **product concept** holds that consumers will favour products that offer the most in quality, performance, and innovative features. Under this concept, marketing strategy focuses on making continuous product improvements.

Product quality and improvement are important parts of most marketing strategies. However, focusing *only* on the company's products can also lead to marketing myopia. For example, some manufacturers believe that if they can "build a better mousetrap, the world will beat a path to their door." But they are often rudely shocked. Buyers may be looking for a better solution to a mouse problem, but not necessarily for a better mousetrap. The better solution might be a chemical spray, an exterminating service, or something else that works even better than a mousetrap. Furthermore, a better mousetrap will not sell unless the manufacturer designs, packages, and prices it attractively; places it in convenient distribution channels; brings it to the attention of people who need it; and convinces buyers that it is a better product.

The Selling Concept

Selling concept
The idea that consumers will not buy enough of the firm's products unless it undertakes a large-scale selling and promotion effort.

Many companies follow the **selling concept**, which holds that consumers will not buy enough of the firm's products unless it undertakes a large-scale selling and promotion effort. The selling concept is typically practised with unsought goods—those that buyers do not normally think of buying, like insurance, or things they don't normally think of doing, like giving blood. These industries must be good at tracking down prospects and selling them on product benefits.

Such aggressive selling, however, carries high risks. It focuses on creating sales transactions rather than on building long-term, profitable customer relationships. The aim often is to sell what the company makes rather than making what the market wants. It assumes that customers who are coaxed into buying the product will like it. Or, if they don't like it, they will possibly forget their disappointment and buy it again later. These are usually poor assumptions.

The Marketing Concept

Marketing concept
The marketing management philosophy that achieving organizational goals depends on knowing the needs and wants of target markets and delivering the desired satisfactions better than competitors do.

The **marketing concept** holds that achieving organizational goals depends on knowing the needs and wants of target markets and delivering the desired satisfactions better than competitors do. Under the marketing concept, customer focus and value are the paths to sales and profits. Instead of a product-centred "make and sell" philosophy, the marketing concept is a customer-centred "sense and respond" philosophy. The job is not to find the right customers for your product, but to find the right products for your customers.

Figure 1.3 contrasts the selling concept and the marketing concept. The selling concept takes an *inside-out* perspective. It starts with the factory, focuses on the company's existing products, and calls for heavy selling and promotion to obtain profitable sales. It focuses primarily on customer conquest—getting short-term sales with little concern about who buys or why. In contrast, the marketing concept takes an *outside-in* perspective. As Herb Kelleher, Southwest Airlines's colourful CEO, puts it, "We don't have a marketing department; we have a customer department." The marketing concept starts with a well-defined market, focuses on customer needs, and integrates all the marketing activities that affect customers. In turn, it yields profits by creating lasting relationships with the right customers based on customer value and satisfaction.

Implementing the marketing concept often means more than simply responding to customers' stated desires and obvious needs. *Customer-driven* companies research current customers deeply to learn about their desires, gather new product and service ideas, and test proposed product improvements. Such customer-driven marketing usually works well when a clear need exists and when customers know what they want.

In many cases, however, customers *don't* know what they want or even what is possible. For example, even 20 years ago, how many consumers would have thought to ask for now-commonplace products such as cellphones, notebook computers, iPods, digital

Figure 1.3 The selling and marketing concepts contrasted

The selling concept

The marketing concept

Customer-driving marketing: Even 20 years ago, how many consumers would have thought to ask for now-commonplace products such as cellphones, personal digital assistants, notebook computers, iPods, and digital cameras? Marketers must often understand customer needs even better than the customers themselves do.

cameras, 24-hour online buying, and satellite navigation systems in their cars? Such situations call for *customer-driving* marketing—understanding customer needs even better than customers themselves do and creating products and services that meet existing and latent needs, now and in the future. As an executive at 3M puts it, "Our goal is to lead customers where they want to go before *they* know where they want to go."

The Societal Marketing Concept

The **societal marketing concept** questions whether the pure marketing concept overlooks possible conflicts between consumer *short-run wants* and consumer *long-run welfare*.

Is a firm that satisfies the immediate needs and wants of target markets always doing what's best for consumers in the long run? The societal marketing concept holds that marketing strategy should deliver value to customers in a way that maintains or improves both the consumer's *and society's* well-being.

Societal marketing concept
The idea that a company's marketing decisions should consider consumers' wants, the company's requirements, consumers' long-run interests, and society's long-run interests.

Consider today's flourishing bottled water industry. You may view bottled water companies as offering a convenient, tasty, and healthy product. Its packaging suggests "green" images of pristine lakes and snow-capped mountains. Yet making, filling, and shipping billions of plastic bottles generates huge amounts of carbon dioxide emissions that contribute substantially to global warming. Further, the plastic bottles pose a substantial recycling and solid waste disposal problem. Thus, in satisfying short-term consumer wants, the highly successful bottled water industry may be causing environmental problems that run against society's long-run interests.[12]

As Figure 1.4 shows, companies should balance three considerations in setting their marketing strategies: company profits, consumer wants, *and* society's interests. Johnson & Johnson does this well. Its concern for societal interests is summarized in a company document called "Our Credo," which stresses honesty, integrity, and putting people before profits. Under this credo, Johnson & Johnson would rather take a big loss than ship a bad batch of one of its products. Consider the tragic tampering case of Tylenol bottles (a Johnson & Johnson brand) in 1982, in which eight people died from swallowing cyanide-laced capsules. Although Johnson & Johnson believed that the pills had been altered in only a few stores, not in the factory, it quickly recalled all of its product and launched an information

Figure 1.4 The considerations underlying the societal marketing concept

Our Credo

We believe our first responsibility is to the doctors, nurses and patients,
to mothers and fathers and all others who use our products and services.
In meeting their needs everything we do must be of high quality.
We must constantly strive to reduce our costs
in order to maintain reasonable prices.
Customers' orders must be serviced promptly and accurately.
Our suppliers and distributors must have an opportunity
to make a fair profit.

We are responsible to our employees,
the men and women who work with us throughout the world.
Everyone must be considered as an individual.
We must respect their dignity and recognize their merit.
They must have a sense of security in their jobs.
Compensation must be fair and adequate,
and working conditions clean, orderly and safe.
We must be mindful of ways to help our employees fulfill
their family responsibilities.
Employees must feel free to make suggestions and complaints.
There must be equal opportunity for employment, development
and advancement for those qualified.
We must provide competent management,
and their actions must be just and ethical.

We are responsible to the communities in which we live and work
and to the world community as well.
We must be good citizens — support good works and charities
and bear our fair share of taxes.
We must encourage civic improvements and better health and education.
We must maintain in good order
the property we are privileged to use,
protecting the environment and natural resources.

Our final responsibility is to our stockholders.
Business must make a sound profit.
We must experiment with new ideas.
Research must be carried on, innovative programs developed
and mistakes paid for.
New equipment must be purchased, new facilities provided
and new products launched.
Reserves must be created to provide for adverse times.
When we operate according to these principles,
the stockholders should realize a fair return.

Johnson & Johnson

The societal marketing concept: Johnson & Johnson's credo stresses putting people before profits.

campaign to instruct and reassure consumers. The recall cost the company $100 million in earnings. In the long run, however, the company's swift recall of Tylenol strengthened consumer confidence and loyalty, and today Tylenol remains one of the nation's leading brands of pain reliever.

Johnson & Johnson's management has learned that doing what's right benefits both consumers and the company. Says former CEO Ralph Larsen, "The credo should not be viewed as some kind of social welfare program . . . it's just plain good business. If we keep trying to do what's right, at the end of the day we believe the marketplace will reward us." And the company stands behind this credo with action. For example, as the founding corporate sponsor of Safe Kids Canada, Johnson & Johnson continues to show its dedication to being a world leader in childcare. Thus, over the years, Johnson & Johnson's dedication to consumers and community service has made it one of North America's most admired companies *and* one of the most profitable.[13]

PREPARING AN INTEGRATED MARKETING PLAN AND PROGRAM

The company's marketing strategy outlines which customers the company will serve and how it will create value for these customers. Next, the marketer develops an integrated marketing program that will actually deliver the intended value to target customers. The marketing program builds customer relationships by transforming the marketing strategy into action. It consists of the firm's *marketing mix*, the set of marketing tools the firm uses to implement its marketing strategy.

The major marketing mix tools are classified into four broad groups, called the *four Ps* of marketing: product, price, place, and promotion. To deliver on its value proposition, the firm must first create a need-satisfying market offering (product). It must decide how much it will charge for the offering (price) and how it will make the offering available to target consumers (place). Finally, it must communicate with target customers about the offering and persuade them of its merits (promotion). The firm must blend all of these marketing mix tools into a comprehensive *integrated marketing program* that communicates and delivers the intended value to chosen customers. We will explore marketing programs and the marketing mix in much more detail in later chapters.

4 BUILDING CUSTOMER RELATIONSHIPS

The first three steps in the marketing process—understanding the marketplace and customer needs, designing a customer-driven marketing strategy, and constructing marketing programs—all lead up to the fourth and most important step: building profitable customer relationships.

Customer Relationship Management

Customer relationship management is perhaps the most important concept of modern marketing. Some marketers define customer relationship management narrowly as a customer data management activity (a practice called *CRM*). By this definition, it involves managing detailed information about individual customers and carefully managing customer

Customer relationship management
The overall process of building and maintaining profitable customer relationships by delivering superior customer value and satisfaction.

"touchpoints" to maximize customer loyalty. We will discuss this narrower CRM activity in Chapter 5 when dealing with marketing information.

Most marketers, however, give the concept of customer relationship management a broader meaning. In this broader sense, **customer relationship management** is the overall process of building and maintaining profitable customer relationships by delivering superior customer value and satisfaction. It deals with all aspects of acquiring, keeping, and growing customers.

Relationship Building Blocks: Customer Value and Satisfaction

The key to building lasting customer relationships is to create superior customer value and satisfaction. Satisfied customers are more likely to be loyal customers and to give the company a larger share of their business.

Customer-perceived value
The customer's evaluation of the difference between all the benefits and all the costs of a market offering relative to those of competing offers.

Customer Value   Attracting and retaining customers can be a difficult task. Customers often face a bewildering array of products and services from which to choose. A customer buys from the firm that offers the highest **customer-perceived value**—the customer's evaluation of the difference between all the benefits and all the costs of a market offering relative to those of competing offers.

For example, consider the "premium denim" trend that has recently sent the price of jeans skyrocketing. A pair of Paige Premium Denim jeans, for instance, starts at $169. A woman who buys a pair of Paige jeans gains a number of benefits. Owner and designer Paige Adams-Geller uses the knowledge she learned as a jeans model to design jeans from the female perspective: "Most of us weren't blessed with perfect genes but we're bringing you the next best thing: perfect jeans." Her denim "will lift the derriere, lengthen your legs, and slenderize your hips and thighs—all with an uncompromising commitment to feminine detail and quality." In all, says Adams-Geller, her jeans are a real value—they will fit you better and last longer. When deciding whether to purchase a pair, customers will weigh these and other perceived values of owning Paige jeans against the money and psychological costs of acquiring them.

Customers often do not judge values and costs "accurately" or "objectively." They act on *perceived* value. For example, as compared to a pair of less expensive jeans that you'd pull off the shelf at Gap, do Paige jeans really provide superior quality and that perfect fit and look? If so, are they worth the much higher price? It's all a matter of personal value perceptions, but for many women the answer is yes. One woman notes that, for her, premium jeans always seem to fit just right, making the price irrelevant. "I work, so I have the money to buy them," she says. "I think they're worth it."[14]

Customer satisfaction
The extent to which a product's perceived performance matches a buyer's expectations.

Customer Satisfaction   **Customer satisfaction** depends on the product's perceived performance relative to a buyer's expectations. If the product's performance falls short of expectations, the customer is dissatisfied. If performance matches expectations, the customer is satisfied. If performance exceeds expectations, the customer is highly satisfied or delighted.

Outstanding marketing companies go out of their way to keep important customers satisfied. Most studies show that higher levels of customer satisfaction lead to greater customer loyalty, which in turn results in better company performance. Smart companies aim to delight customers by promising only what they can deliver, then delivering more than they promise. Delighted customers not only make repeat purchases, they become willing marketing partners and "customer evangelists" who spread the word about their good experiences to others (see Real Marketing 1.1).[15]

For companies interested in delighting customers, exceptional value and service are more than a set of policies or actions—they are a companywide attitude, an important part of the overall company culture. For example, year after year, Ritz-Carlton ranks at or near the top of the hospitality industry in terms of customer satisfaction. Its passion for satisfying customers is summed up in the company's credo, which promises that its luxury hotels will deliver a truly memorable experience—one that "enlivens

Real Marketing 1.1

iRobot's Roomba: The Power of Customer Delight

When you were a child, you probably didn't like it much when your mother made you vacuum. You probably still don't like vacuuming much—it's a thankless, seemingly never-ending task. But there's one group of people who don't mind vacuuming at all. In fact, they're absolutely delighted about it. They are the folks who own an iRobot Roomba, the cute little robotic vacuum that zips around rooms, avoiding furniture and other obstacles, tirelessly sniffing up dirt, dust, and pet hair.

People love their little Roombas. They name them, talk to them, and even buy a second Roomba so that the first one won't be lonely. Many Roomba owners spend more time watching their little petlike robots than they would spend vacuuming a room themselves. Recognizing the strong attachments that many Roomba owners have to these personable little machines, iRobot does all it can to involve its customers in everything from product development to technical support, turning them into an army of Roomba consumer evangelists and marketing partners.

iRobot began building devices for the U.S. military in the 1990s—small robots called PackBots now used to defuse improvised explosive devices (IEDs) in Iraq or explore caves in Afghanistan. Based on this advanced technology, the company introduced its first Roomba in 2002. Made up of more than 100 plastic parts, motors, controllers, sensors, brushes, and a dustbin, the 10-pound Roomba uses a sophisticated algorithm to scoot around a room, even going under tables, chairs, sofas, and beds. When it runs into obstacles, it figures out how to clean around them. And when its rechargeable battery begins to lose its charge, the Roomba finds its way to its home base unit, plugs itself in, and recharges automatically. Owners can even program more expensive models to clean at certain times of the day or days of the week, even when no one is home.

In the summer of 2002, iRobot negotiated distribution deals with Brookstone and Sharper Image and Roomba sales took off. Soon, the company began getting calls from major chains such as Target, Kohl's, and Linens 'n Things. The factory churned out 50 000 units just to meet that year's holiday demand.

Then the real fun began. As iRobot received Roombas back for servicing, customer service reps noted that many owners were customizing and humanizing their little robotic assistants. Rather than just selling a high-tech household appliance, it seems that iRobot had invented a new kind of family pet. Reps reported that owners were often painting their Roombas and referring to them by name and gender. The most popular name was Rosie, after the robotic maid on the classic animated TV series *The Jetsons*.

Before long, delighted Roomba owners became iRobot's best marketing partners. An independent website sprang up, myRoomBud.com, offering RoomBud costumes that transform a Roomba from "just a naked vacuum" into a lovable character such as "Roobit the Frog," "Mooba the Cow," or "RoomBette La French Maid." The site even lets Roomba enthusiasts print out official-looking birth certificates for their newly adopted robotic pets.

Delighting customers: People love their pet-like little Roombas. They name them, talk to them, and even buy a second Roomba so that the first one won't be lonely. Recognizing this, iRobot has turned customers into an army of Roomba consumer evangelists.

Smitten Roomba owners by the hundreds began posting video clips of their Roombas in action on YouTube. One mounted a camera on his Roomba to create a RoombaCam. Other Roomba customers created the Roomba Review website (www.roombareviews.com), which features news, chats, product reviews, and hacker information. Billed as the official Roomba lovers' forum, Roomba Review is loaded with posts and comments on everything from shared Roomba experiences and adventures to information on differences between models, tips on finding a Roomba at a good price, and tech support questions and answers—all supplied by customers. A disclaimer at the bottom notes that the website "is not affiliated with iRobot Corporation (We're just really big fans of the Roomba vacuum!)"

Noting all of this customer enthusiasm and delight, iRobot developed programs to strengthen and organize the growing sense of community among Roomba owners. For example, it opened its programmatic interface, encouraging owners, amateur robotics enthusiasts, and others to develop their own programs and uses for the Roomba. It also set up an iRobot Create webpage on its website (irobot.com), where customers could show off their latest inventions. These actions turned Roomba owners into a community of amateur tinkerers and hobbyists. Customers themselves began to develop improved features that iRobot would later adopt.

By monitoring interactions with and among enthusiastic Roomba customers, iRobot was able to discover product problems and additional customer needs. Complaints that animal hair often clogged the machines led the company to introduce the Roomba for Pets model, featuring easy-to-clean brushes that make removing pet hair easier. For customers who wanted a robotic "floor mopper," iRobot

introduced the Scooba floor washer, another personable little gizmo that preps, washes, scrubs, and squeegees tile, linoleum, and hardwood floors "so that you don't have to!" For customers who complained about cleaning gutters, iRobot developed the Looj Gutter Cleaning Robot. The Verro Pool Cleaning Robot "gets pools deep-down clean from floor to waterline—just drop it in and let it go!" Customers are now clamouring for a Roomba lawn mower!

Based on interactions with its customer community, iRobot has also continued to improve the original Roomba. Last year it introduced the 500 series—even smarter Roombas that can free themselves from almost any jam, including rug tassels and power cords, reducing the need to prep a room before unleashing the little sniffer. The new model also features a built-in voice tutorial for new users that explains the Roomba's features right out of the box.

Thus, iRobot has discovered the power of customer delight. More than that, it's working to harness that power by partnering with its satisfied-customer community to improve current products, develop new ones, and help spread the word to new customers. So far, iRobot has sold more than 2 million Roombas. Last year, the company's sales reached nearly US$250 million, up 75 percent in only the last two years. Profits surged 175 percent. With the help of its delighted customers, iRobot is filling the vacuum and really cleaning up.

Sources: Based on information found in Paul Gillin, "Cleaning Up with Customer Evangelists," *BtoB*, August 13, 2007, p. 10; Ben McConnell, "Roomba Robot Love," December 30, 2006, accessed at **www.churchofthecustomer.com**; Faith Arner, "How the Roomba Was Realized," *BusinessWeek*, October 6, 2003, p. 10; Joel Garreau, "Robots That Fill an Emotional Vacuum," *Washington Post*, December 29, 2006, p. C1; "iRobot Corporation," *Hoover's Company Records*, August 1, 2008, p. 132607; and **www.myroombud.com** and **www.roombareviews.com**, accessed November 2008.

the senses, instills well-being, and fulfills even the unexpressed wishes and needs of our guests."

Check into any Ritz-Carlton hotel around the world, and you'll be amazed by the company's fervent dedication to anticipating and meeting even your slightest need. Without ever asking, they seem to know that you want a king-size bed, a nonallergenic pillow, and breakfast with decaffeinated coffee in your room. Each day, hotel staffers—from those at the front desk to those in maintenance and housekeeping—discreetly observe and record even the smallest guest preferences. Then, every morning, each hotel reviews the files of all new arrivals who have stayed previously at a Ritz-Carlton and prepares a list of suggested extra touches that might delight each guest. And once they identify a special customer need, the Ritz-Carlton employees go to legendary extremes to meet it. For example, to serve the needs of a guest with food allergies, a Ritz-Carlton chef in Bali located special eggs and milk in a small grocery store in another country and had them delivered to the hotel. In another case, when the hotel's laundry service failed to remove a stain on a guest's suit before the guest departed, the hotel manager traveled to the guest's house and personally delivered a reimbursement check for the cost of the suit. As a result of such customer-service heroics, an amazing 95 percent of departing guests report that their stay has been a truly memorable experience. More than 90 percent of Ritz-Carlton's delighted customers return.[16]

THE RITZ-CARLTON®

CREDO

The Ritz-Carlton is a
place where the genuine care
and comfort of our guests is
our highest mission.

We pledge to provide the finest
personal service and facilities
for our guests who will always
enjoy a warm, relaxed, yet
refined ambience.

The Ritz-Carlton experience
enlivens the senses, instills
well-being, and fulfills even
the unexpressed wishes
and needs of our guests.

Customer satisfaction: Ritz-Carlton's passion for
satisfying customers is summed up in its credo,
which promises a truly memorable experience—
one that "enlivens the senses, instills well-being,
and fulfills even the unexpressed wishes and
needs of our guests."

However, although the customer-centred firm seeks to deliver high customer
satisfaction relative to competitors, it does not attempt to *maximize* customer satisfaction. A company can always increase customer satisfaction by lowering its
price or increasing its services. But this may result in lower profits. Thus, the purpose of marketing is to generate customer value profitably. This requires a very
delicate balance: The marketer must continue to generate more customer value
and satisfaction but not "give away the house."

Customer Relationship Levels and Tools

Companies can build customer relationships at many levels, depending on the nature of the target market. At one extreme, a company with many low-margin customers may seek to develop *basic relationships* with them. For example, Procter &
Gamble does not phone or call on all of its Tide consumers to get to know them personally. Instead, P&G creates relationships through brand-building advertising,
sales promotions, and its Tide Fabric Care Network website (www.tide.ca). At the
other extreme, in markets with few customers and high margins, sellers want to create *full partnerships* with key customers. For example, P&G customer teams work
closely with Walmart and other large retailers. In between these two extreme situations, other levels of customer relationships are appropriate.

Today, most leading companies are developing customer loyalty and retention programs. Beyond offering consistently high value and satisfaction, marketers
can use specific marketing tools to develop stronger bonds with consumers. For
example, many companies now offer *frequency marketing programs* that reward customers who buy frequently or in large amounts. Airlines offer frequent-flyer programs, hotels give room upgrades to their frequent guests, and supermarkets give
patronage discounts to "very important customers."

Other companies sponsor *club marketing programs* that offer members special
benefits and create member communities. For example, Harley-Davidson sponsors
the Harley Owners Group (H.O.G.), which gives Harley riders a way to share their common
passion of "making the Harley-Davidson dream a way of life." H.O.G. membership benefits
include two magazines (*Hog Tales* and *Enthusiast*), a H.O.G. Touring Handbook, a roadside assistance program, a specially designed insurance program, theft reward service, a travel centre, and a "Fly & Ride" program enabling members to rent Harleys while on vacation. The
worldwide club now numbers more than 1500 local chapters and more than 1 million members, and the Canadian market is expanding. In the first half of 2008, Harley-Davidson sold
10 870 bikes in Canada, an increase of over 13 percent from the previous year.[17]

Building customer relationships: Harley-Davidson sponsors the Harley Owners
Group (H.O.G.), which gives Harley owners "an organized way to share their passion and show their pride." The worldwide club now numbers more than 1500 local
chapters and 1 million members.

To build customer relationships, companies can
add structural ties as well as financial and social benefits. A business marketer might supply customers with
special equipment or online linkages that help them
manage their orders, payroll, or inventory. For example, McKesson Corporation, a leading pharmaceutical
wholesaler, has set up a supply management online
system that helps retail pharmacy customers manage
their inventories, order entry, and shelf space. The system also helps McKesson's medical-surgical supply
and equipment customers optimize their supply purchasing and materials management operations.

The Changing Nature of Customer Relationships

Significant changes are occurring in the ways
in which companies are relating to their customers.
Yesterday's big companies focused on mass marketing

Best Buy's "customer-centricity" strategy serves its best customers (angels) and exorcises less profitable ones (demons). Clerks steer high-income "Barrys" into the store's Magnolia Home Theater centre, a comfy store-within-a-store that mimics the media rooms popular with home-theatre fans.

to all customers at arm's length. Today's companies are building deeper, more direct, and more lasting relationships with more carefully selected customers. Here are some important trends in the way companies and customers are relating to one another.

Relating with More Carefully Selected Customers

Few firms today still practise true mass marketing—selling in a standardized way to any customer who comes along. Today, most marketers realize that they don't want relationships with every customer. Instead, they now are targeting fewer, more profitable customers. Called *selective relationship management*, many companies now use customer profitability analysis to weed out losing customers and to target winning ones for pampering. Once they identify profitable customers, firms can create attractive offers and special handling to capture these customers and earn their loyalty.

But what should the company do with unprofitable customers? If it can't turn them into profitable ones, it may even want to "fire" customers that are too unreasonable or that cost more to serve than they are worth. For example, consumer electronics retailer Best Buy recently rolled out a new "customer-centricity" strategy that distinguishes between its best customers (called *angels*) and less profitable ones (called *demons*). The aim is to embrace the angels while ditching the demons.[18]

The *angels* include the 20 percent of Best Buy customers who produce the bulk of its profits. They snap up high-definition televisions, portable electronics, and newly released DVDs without waiting for markdowns or rebates. In contrast, the demons form an "underground of bargain-hungry shoppers intent on wringing every nickel of savings out of the big retailer. They load up on loss leaders . . . then flip the goods at a profit on eBay. They slap down rock-bottom price quotes from websites and demand that Best Buy make good on its lowest-price pledge."

To attract the angels, Best Buy stores now stock more merchandise and offer better service to these good customers. For example, the stores set up digital photo centres and offer Geek Squad services, one-on-one in-store or at-home computer assistance, to high-value buyers. Best Buy also set up a Reward Zone loyalty program in which regular customers can earn points toward discounts on future purchases. To discourage the demons, Best Buy removed them from its marketing lists, reduced the promotions and other sales tactics that tended to attract them, and installed a 15 percent restocking fee.

However, Best Buy didn't stop there. Customer analysis revealed that its best customers fell into five groups: "Barrys," high-income men; "Jills," suburban moms; "Buzzes," male technology enthusiasts; "Rays," young family men on a budget; and small business owners. Each customer-centricity store now aligns its product and service mix to reflect the make-up of these customers in its market area. Best Buy then trains store clerks in the art of serving the angels and exorcising the demons. At stores targeting Barrys, for example, blue-shirted sales clerks steer promising candidates to the store's Magnolia Home Theater Center, a comfy store-within-a-store that mimics the media rooms popular with home-theatre fans. With sales up more than $10 billion in just the past three years, the customer-centric strategy appears to be a winner for Best Buy and its customers. As one store manager puts it, "The biggest thing now is to build better relationships with [our best] customers."

Relating More Deeply and Interactively

Beyond choosing customers more selectively, companies are now relating with chosen customers in deeper, more meaningful ways. Rather than relying only on one-way, mass-media messages, today's marketers are incorporating new, more interactive approaches that help build targeted, two-way customer relationships.

The deeper nature of today's customer relationships results in part from the rapidly changing communications environment. New technologies have profoundly changed the ways in which people relate to one another. For example, thanks to explosive advances in Internet and computer technology, people can now interact in direct and surprisingly personal ways with large groups of others, whether nearby or scattered around the world. New tools for relating include everything from email, blogs, websites, and video sharing to online communities and social networks such as MySpace, Facebook, YouTube, and Second Life.

This changing communications environment also affects how consumers relate to companies and products. Increasingly, marketers are using the new communications approaches to build closer customer relationships. The aim is to create deeper consumer involvement and a sense of community surrounding a brand—to make the brand a meaningful part of consumers' conversations and lives. "Becoming part of the conversation between consumers is infinitely more powerful than handing down information via traditional advertising," says one marketing expert. "It [makes] consumers . . . a part of the process, rather than being dumb recipients of the message from on high—and that is of huge potential value to brands."[19]

However, at the same time that the new communications tools create relationship-building opportunities for marketers, they also create challenges. They give consumers greater power and control. Today's consumers have more information about brands than ever before, and they have a wealth of platforms for airing and sharing their brand views with other consumers. And more than ever before, consumers can choose the brand conversations and exchanges in which they will participate. According to Mark Parker, chief executive of Nike, the new power of the consumer is "the most compelling change we've seen over the past four or five years. They are dictating what the dialogue is, how we're conducting it, and it's definitely a two-way conversation."[20]

Greater consumer control means that, in building customer relationships, companies can no longer rely on marketing by *intrusion*. They must practise marketing by *attraction*—creating market offerings and messages that involve consumers rather than interrupt them. Hence, most marketers now augment their mass-media marketing efforts with a rich mix of direct marketing approaches that promote brand–consumer interaction. For example, many are participating in the exploding world of *online social networks* or creating online communities of their own. Molson Canadian maintains an active Facebook page where almost 28 000 consumers of the brand share information with the company and other consumers. The company's 2010 Mural Project, designed to build the largest photo mosaic ever constructed in Canada in support of Canada's Olympic athletes, encourages consumers to submit their photos online and become part of Olympic history.

In another example, Toyota, the world's fifth-largest advertiser, spends $3.1 billion a year on media advertising. But it also sells Scions at Second Life and maintains a Scion presence on MySpace, Gaia Online, and other cyber-hangouts. And the company's Toyota.com/Hybrid

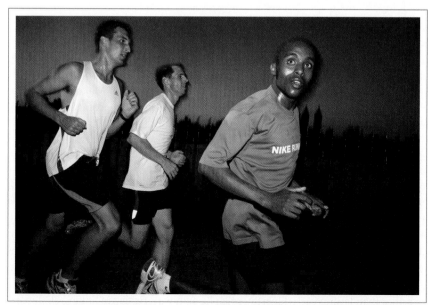

Creating community with customers: Nike's new, more interactive media include in-person events and other activities designed to build brand community and deeper customer relationships.

website creates a community in which more than 17 500 Prius, Camry, and Highlander hybrid "believers" meet to share their reasons for buying hybrid vehicles and videos and messages on their experiences, both good and bad. "There's value in being totally authentic and transparent [with your customers]," says a manager of consumer-generated media at Toyota, "as much as it hurts sometimes."[21]

Similarly, Nike has recently shifted a bigger chunk of its media budget toward new, more direct interactions with consumers. It now spends just 33 percent of its almost $700 million annual ad budget on television and other traditional media, down 55 percent from 10 years ago. Nike's new media include not only the Internet, but also in-person events and other activities designed to build brand community and deeper customer relationships.[22]

Twice a week, 30 or more people gather at a Nike store and go for an evening run. Afterward the members of the Niketown running club chat in the store over refreshments. Nike's staff keeps track of their performances and hails members who have logged more than 100 miles. The event is a classic example of up-close-and-personal relationship building with core customers. Nike augments such events with an online social network aimed at striking up meaningful long-term interactions with even more runners. Its Nike Plus running website lets customers with iPod-linked Nike shoes upload, track, and compare their performances. More than 200 000 runners are now using the Nike Plus site and more than half visit the site at least four times a week. Nike's goal is to have 15 percent of the world's 100 million runners using the system.

As part of the new customer control and dialogue, consumers themselves are now creating brand conversations and messages on their own. And increasingly, companies are even *inviting* consumers to play a more active role in shaping brand messages and ads. For example, Frito Lay, Southwest Airlines, and Heinz have run contests for consumer-generated commercials that have been aired on national television. Other companies, including marketing heavyweights such as Coca-Cola, McDonald's, and Apple, have snagged brand-related consumer videos from YouTube and other popular video-sharing sites and turned them into commercial messages.

Consumer-generated
marketing
Marketing messages, ads, and other brand exchanges created by consumers themselves—both invited and uninvited.

Consumer-generated marketing, whether invited by marketers or not, has become a significant marketing force. In fact, in 2006 *Advertising Age* magazine awarded its coveted Ad Agency of the Year designation to—you guessed it—the consumer. "The explosion of video, blogs, websites, [and consumer-generated ads] confirmed what we knew all along," says the magazine. When it comes to creative messages, "the consumer is king."[23] (See Real Marketing 1.2.)

Partner Relationship Management

When it comes to creating customer value and building strong customer relationships, today's marketers know that they can't go it alone. They must work closely with a variety of marketing partners. In addition to being good at *customer relationship management*, marketers must also be good at **partner relationship management**. Major changes are occurring in how marketers partner with others inside and outside the company to jointly bring more value to customers.

Partner relationship
management
Working closely with partners in other company departments and outside the company to jointly bring greater value to customers.

Partners Inside the Company

Traditionally, marketers have been charged with understanding customers and representing customer needs to different company departments. The old thinking was that marketing is done only by marketing, sales, and customer-support people. However, in today's more connected world every functional area can interact with customers, especially electronically. The new thinking is that every employee must be customer-focused. David Packard, late co-founder of Hewlett-Packard, wisely said, "Marketing is far too important to be left only to the marketing department."[24]

Today, rather than letting each department go its own way, firms are linking all departments in the cause of creating customer value. Rather than assigning only sales and marketing people to customers, they are forming cross-functional customer teams. For example,

Real Marketing 1.2

Consumer-Generated Marketing: Ad Agency of the Year? YOU!

Advertising Age, a must-read magazine for advertising professionals, recently awarded its prestigious Ad Agency of the Year award not to the usual big Madison Avenue agency, but to you, the consumer. Here's its explanation of why it picked consumer-generated advertising content over that prepared by seasoned advertising professionals.

Stop me if you've heard this one before. A pair of Maine theatre geeks decide to film an experiment in which a certain mint is dropped into a bottle of a certain no-calorie soft drink, unleashing a foamy geyser. Flavouring this bit of schoolyard chemistry lore with Vegas showmanship, they produce a cola version of the Bellagio fountain and put the clip on the Web, where it goes viral. Really viral. So viral, in fact, that millions watch it, hundreds of media outlets cover it, and the mint in question enjoys a 15 percent spike in sales.

It's a sign of our times: The most important piece of commercial content last year was created by a juggler named Fritz Grobe and a lawyer, Stephen Voltz. "The Diet Coke & Mentos Experiment" sensation raises a key question that gnaws at just about every company that wants to sell a product to consumers in the twenty-first century: Should I try to get my consumers to do something like this? Even if they haven't worked out exactly how to make that happen, many leading marketers have already answered with a resounding yes. Company after company, including the makers of blue-chip brands such as Pepsi, Jeep, Heinz, Sprint, and Converse, have given up at least some control and turned their brands over to consumers.

In truth, consumers have always had some measure of control, and a brand has only ever been as good as consumers' experiences with it. The difference today is that consumers have lots of ways of communicating those experiences, and they trust each other's views above marketers' overt sales pitches. Consequently, consumers are influencing marketing strategy as never before. And that's why last year's Advertising Age Ad Agency of the Year was (drum roll, please) . . . the consumer. A portfolio of consumer-generated commercial content over the past few years would easily beat out any single advertising agency's offering.

Today, as in our cola fountain story, not only do everyday people make the videos that earn that oh-so-coveted water-cooler buzz, they also reign supreme as distributors of content of all kinds. YouTube's explosion glopped a big new pile of distractions into an already cluttered communications world, which means that if you want anybody to see your ad, you'd better hope people are frenetically emailing links to it.

Here are just a few examples of consumer-generated marketing content. Two moonlighting comedians threw together video of themselves amateurishly rapping about Chicken McNuggets and slapped it on the Internet—McDonald's used the video in a popular New York-area commercial. Apple discovered an amateur video produced by a British teenager on YouTube. With the teen's permission, Apple recreated the ad for TV. MasterCard invited customers to help create a new "priceless" commercial, received 100 000 submissions, and showed the winning ad on regular TV. The credit card giant's Priceless.com website is now loaded with good consumer video.

And then there's the Super Bowl. Long a showcase for ad agencies' finest productions, the 2007 ad spectacular was invaded successfully by the unwashed masses. Frito Lay's Doritos solicited 30-second ads from consumers and ran the best two during the game. One of the ads, which showed a supermarket checkout girl getting frisky with a shopper, was judged in one poll as 67 percent more effective than the average Super Bowl ad in improving viewer opinion of the advertised product. The other Doritos ad, showing a young driver flirting with a pretty girl, cost only $12.79 to produce (the cost of four bags of chips) but was judged 45 percent more effective than other ads. The ads were extremely popular with viewers, both during and after the big game. "What this means is: You've got some kid with a video camera and he's playing on the same field as everyone else," says one ad agency veteran. Frito Lay followed up in 2008 by inviting consumers to submit original songs at SnackStrongProductions.com—its Second Life–inspired Doritos Web environment. Frito Lay then gave winner Kina Grannis the stage of a lifetime by airing a 60-second music video featuring her winning song during the Super Bowl.

Does the new wave of consumer-generated marketing mean the end of the big ad agency as we know it? Not likely. But the fact that an amateur could turn out a winning Doritos ad for $12.79, versus the $1 million or more that many large agencies spent crafting more spectacular but less effective ads, suggests that there are some lessons to be learned. As one ad agency creative executive suggests, "It's gonna keep professional idea makers on their toes." Marketers now "perk up when you talk about this stuff," he says.

The big question is how to harness consumer-generated creativity—so unpolished and unaccountable—and deploy it in the service of a brand. There's a big potential downside to putting your brand in the hands of consumers. For every Diet Coke & Mentos clip that's grown into a viral craze, there are several

▶

marketer-led disasters. For example, General Motors's Chevy Tahoe off-roaded into the consumer-content arena and, to its shock, found that some people aren't so crazy about the gas-guzzling SUV. At Chevy's invitation, consumers created some very creative ads, but many of the ads centred on the big vehicle's poor gas mileage and negative environmental impact.

Harnessing consumer-generated content can be time consuming and costly, and companies may find it difficult to glean even a little gold from all the garbage. H. J. Heinz recently invited consumers to submit homemade ads for its ketchup brand on its YouTube page, offering a $57 000 top prize

Harnessing consumer-generated marketing: When H. J. Heinz recently invited consumers to submit homemade ads for its ketchup brand on YouTube, it received more than 8000 entries—some very good but most only so-so or even downright dreadful.

and the promise of airing the winning ad on primetime TV. Heinz sifted through more than 8000 entries, of which nearly 4000 are posted on YouTube. Some of the amateur ads are very good—entertaining and potentially effective. Most, however, are so-so at best, and others are downright dreadful. In one ad, a contestant chugs ketchup straight from the bottle. In another, a teen contestant rubs ketchup over his face like acne cream, then puts pickles on his eyes. In still another, the would-be filmmaker brushes his teeth, washes his hair, and shaves his face with Heinz's product.

Heinz had to reject many of the submitted ads because they include copyrighted songs, displayed other brands, or "wouldn't be appropriate to show mom." But rejected submissions continue showing up on YouTube anyway. One of the most viewed Heinz videos, seen more than 12 800 times, ends with a close-up of a mouth with crooked, yellowed teeth—oops. Despite such problems, however, Heinz continues to invite consumers to submit their masterpieces. In all, the campaign has been very successful. Within only a few months, consumers had logged more than 2.3 million views of the spots on YouTube and spent more than 80 000 hours watching them. The YouTube exposure gives the venerable old brand lots of contemporary attention.

Today, more and more big marketers are loosening up and turning at least a piece of their brand marketing over to consumers. At a recent Association of National Advertisers meeting, P&G's CEO, A. G. Lafley, urged companies to invite more customer interaction and to "let go" of their brands. Coming from the normally tightly controlling P&G, such a provocative statement deeply impacted the advertiser audience. The same could be said of Lafley showing an animated Pringles commercial made by a U.K. teen to the audience full of advertisers. And you know what? The clip was pretty good.

Sources: Portions adapted from Matthew Creamer, "John Doe Edges Out Jeff Goodby," *Advertising Age*, January 8, 2007, pp. S4–S5; with information from Frank Ahrens, "$2 million Airtime, $13 Ad: In the YouTube Era, Even Super Bowl Advertisers Are Turning to Amateurs," *Washington Post*, January 31, 2007, accessed at **www.washingtonpost.com**; Elinor Mills, "Frito-Lay Turns to Netizens for Ad Creation," *CNET News*, March 21, 2007, accessed at **www.cnetnews.com**; Laura Petrecca, "Amateurs' Ad Ideas Come Up with Winners," *USA Today*, February 13, 2007, p. 2B; Gavin O'Malley, "Entries Pour in for Heinz Catsup Commercial Contest," August 13, 2007, accessed at **http://publications.mediapost.com**; and "Fans Vote 22-Year-Old Singer/Songwriter Kina Grannis Winner in Doritos Crash the Super Bowl Challenge," *PR* Newswire, February 3, 2008.

Procter & Gamble assigns "customer development teams" to each of its major retailer accounts. These teams—consisting of sales and marketing people, operations specialists, market and financial analysts, and others—coordinate the efforts of many P&G departments toward helping the retailer be more successful.

Marketing Partners Outside the Firm

Changes are also occurring in how marketers connect with their suppliers, channel partners, and even competitors. Most companies today are networked companies, relying heavily on partnerships with other firms.

Marketing channels consist of distributors, retailers, and others who connect the company to its buyers. The *supply chain* describes a longer channel, stretching from raw materials to components to final products that are carried to final buyers. For example, the supply chain for personal computers consists of suppliers of computer chips and other components, the computer manufacturer, and the distributors, retailers, and others who sell the computers.

Through *supply chain management*, many companies today are strengthening their connections with partners all along the supply chain. They know that their fortunes rest not just on how well they perform. Success at building customer relationships also rests on how well their entire supply chain performs against competitors' supply chains. These companies don't just treat suppliers as vendors and distributors as customers. They treat both as partners in delivering customer value. On the one hand, for example, Lexus works closely with carefully selected suppliers to improve quality and operations efficiency. On the other hand, it works with its franchise dealers to provide top-grade sales and service support that will bring customers in the door and keep them coming back.

CAPTURING VALUE FROM CUSTOMERS

The first four steps in the marketing process outlined in Figure 1.1 involve building customer relationships by creating and delivering superior customer value. The final step involves capturing value in return in the form of current and future sales, market share, and profits. By creating superior customer value, the firm creates highly satisfied customers who stay loyal and buy more. This, in turn, means greater long-run returns for the firm. Here, we discuss the outcomes of creating customer value: customer loyalty and retention, share of market and share of customer, and customer equity.

Creating Customer Loyalty and Retention

Good customer relationship management creates customer delight. In turn, delighted customers remain loyal and talk favourably to others about the company and its products. Studies show big differences in the loyalty of customers who are less satisfied, somewhat satisfied, and completely satisfied. Even a slight drop from complete satisfaction can create an enormous drop in loyalty. Thus, the aim of customer relationship management is to create not just customer satisfaction, but customer delight.[25]

Customer lifetime value
The value of the entire stream of purchases that a customer would make over a lifetime of patronage.

Companies are realizing that losing a customer means losing more than a single sale. It means losing the entire stream of purchases that the customer would make over a lifetime of patronage. For example, Stew Leonard, who operates a highly profitable four-store supermarket, offers a dramatic illustration of **customer lifetime value**. He believes that US$50 000 flies out of his store every time he sees a sulking customer. Why? Because his average customer spends about $100 a week, shops 50 weeks a year, and remains in the area for about 10 years. If this customer has an unhappy experience and switches to another supermarket, Stew Leonard's has lost US$50 000 in revenue. The loss can be much greater if the disappointed customer shares the bad experience with other customers and causes them to defect. To keep customers coming back, Stew Leonard's has created what the *New York Times* has dubbed the "Disneyland of Dairy Stores," complete with costumed characters,

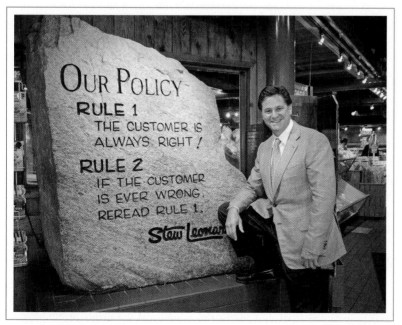

Customer lifetime value: To keep customers coming back, Stew Leonard's has created the "Disneyland of dairy stores." Rule #1: The customer is always right. Rule #2: If the customer is ever wrong, reread Rule #1.

scheduled entertainment, a petting zoo, and animatronics throughout the store. From its humble beginnings as a small dairy store in 1969, Stew Leonard's has grown at an amazing pace. It's built 29 additions onto the original store, which now serves more than 300 000 customers each week. This legion of loyal shoppers is largely a result of the store's passionate approach to customer service. Rule #1 at Stew Leonard's: The customer is always right. Rule #2: If the customer is ever wrong, reread rule #1![26]

Stew Leonard is not alone in assessing customer lifetime value. Lexus, for example, estimates that a single satisfied and loyal customer is worth more than US$600 000 in lifetime sales.[27] Thus, working to retain and grow customers makes good economic sense. In fact, a company can lose money on a specific transaction but still benefit greatly from a long-term relationship. This means that companies must aim high in building customer relationships. Customer delight creates an emotional relationship with a brand, not just a rational preference. And that relationship keeps customers coming back.

L.L.Bean, which regularly rates among the top five brands in the Brand Keys Customer Loyalty Engagement Index, was founded on a philosophy of customer satisfaction and long-term customer relationships. Founder L.L.Bean posted the following notice on the wall of his first store: "NOTICE: I do not consider a sale complete until goods are worn out and customer still satisfied." The company still preaches the following "golden rule": "Sell good merchandise, treat your customers like human beings, and they'll always come back for more."[28]

Growing Share of Customer

Share of customer
The portion of the customer's purchasing that a company gets in its product categories.

Beyond simply retaining good customers to capture customer lifetime value, good customer relationship management can help marketers to increase their **share of customer**— the share they get of the customer's purchasing in their product categories. Thus, banks want to increase "share of wallet." Supermarkets and restaurants want to get more "share of stomach." Car companies want to increase "share of garage," and airlines want greater "share of travel."

To increase share of customer, firms can offer greater variety to current customers. Or they can create programs to cross-sell and up-sell to market more products and services to existing customers. For example, Amazon.com is highly skilled at leveraging relationships with its 66 million customers to increase its share of each customer's purchases. Originally an online bookseller, Amazon.com now offers customers music, videos, gifts, toys, consumer electronics, office products, home improvement items, lawn and garden products, apparel and accessories, jewellery, tools, and even groceries. In addition, based on each customer's purchase history, the company recommends related products that might be of interest. This recommendation system may influence up to 30 percent of all sales.[29] In these ways, Amazon.com captures a greater share of each customer's spending budget.

Building Customer Equity

We can now see the importance of not just acquiring customers, but of keeping and growing them as well. One marketing consultant puts it this way: "The only value your company will ever create is the value that comes from customers—the ones you have now and the ones you will have in the future. Without customers, you don't have a business."[30] Customer relationship management takes a long-term view. Companies want not only to create profitable customers, but to "own" them for life, earn a greater share of their purchases, and capture their customer lifetime value.

What Is Customer Equity?

Customer equity
The total combined customer lifetime values of all of the company's customers.

The ultimate aim of customer relationship management is to produce high **customer equity**.[31] Customer equity is the total combined customer lifetime values of all of the company's current and potential customers. Clearly, the more loyal the firm's profitable customers, the higher the firm's customer equity. Customer equity may be a better measure of a firm's performance than current sales or market share. Whereas sales and market share reflect the past, customer equity suggests the future.

Consider the case of Cadillac and BMW. In the 1970s and 1980s, Cadillac had some of the most loyal customers in the industry. To an entire generation of car buyers, the name "Cadillac" defined luxury. Cadillac's share of the luxury car market reached a whopping 51 percent in 1976. Based on market share and sales, the brand's future looked rosy. However, measures of customer equity would have painted a bleaker picture. Cadillac customers were getting older (average age 60) and average customer lifetime value was falling. Many Cadillac buyers were on their last car. Thus, although Cadillac's market share was good, its customer equity was not. Compare this with BMW. Its more youthful and vigorous image didn't win BMW the early market share war. However, it did win BMW younger customers with higher customer lifetime values. The result: In the years that followed, BMW's market share and profits soared while Cadillac's fortunes eroded badly. Thus, market share is not the answer. We should care not just about current sales but also about future sales. Customer lifetime value and customer equity are the name of the game.

Recognizing this, in recent years Cadillac has attempted to make the Caddy cool again by targeting a younger generation of consumers with new high-performance models and more vibrant advertising. The average consumer aspiring to own a Cadillac is now about 36 years old.[32]

Building the Right Relationships with the Right Customers

Companies should manage customer equity carefully. They should view customers as assets that need to be managed and maximized. But not all customers, not even all loyal customers, are good investments. Surprisingly, some loyal customers can be unprofitable, and some disloyal customers can be profitable. Which customers should the company acquire and retain?

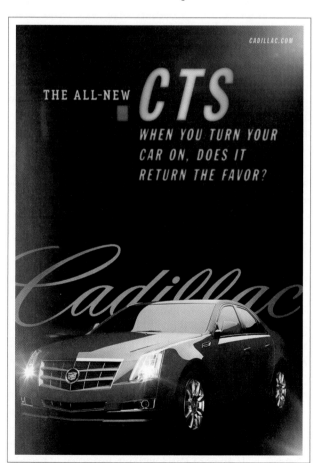

To increase customer lifetime value and customer equity, Cadillac is cool again. Its highly successful ad campaigns target a younger generation of consumers.

The company can classify customers according to their potential profitability and manage its relationships with them accordingly. Figure 1.5 classifies customers into one of four relationship groups, according to their profitability and projected loyalty.[33] Each group requires a different relationship management strategy. "Strangers" show low potential profitability and little projected loyalty; there is little fit between the company's offerings and their needs. The relationship management strategy for these customers is simple: Don't invest anything in them.

"Butterflies" are potentially profitable but not loyal. There is a good fit between the company's offerings and their needs. However, like real butterflies, we can enjoy them for only a short while and then they're gone. An example is stock market investors who trade shares often and in large amounts but who enjoy hunting out the best deals without building a regular relationship with any single brokerage company. Efforts to convert butterflies into loyal customers are rarely successful. Instead, the company should enjoy the butterflies for the moment. It should use promotional blitzes to attract them, create satisfying and profitable transactions with them, and then cease investing in them until the next time around.

"True friends" are both profitable and loyal. There is a strong fit between their needs and the company's offerings. The firm wants to make continuous relationship investments to delight these customers and nurture, retain, and grow them. It wants to turn true friends into "true believers," who come back regularly and tell others about their good experiences with the company.

"Barnacles" are highly loyal but not very profitable. There is a limited fit between their needs and the company's offerings.

Figure 1.5 Customer relationship groups

An example is smaller bank customers who bank regularly but do not generate enough returns to cover the costs of maintaining their accounts. Like barnacles on the hull of a ship, they create drag. Barnacles are perhaps the most problematic customers. The company might be able to improve their profitability by selling them more, raising their fees, or reducing service to them. However, if they cannot be made profitable, they should be "fired."

The point here is an important one: Different types of customers require different relationship management strategies. The goal is to build the *right relationships* with the *right customers*.

5 THE CHANGING MARKETING LANDSCAPE

Every day dramatic changes are occurring in the marketplace. Richard Love of Hewlett-Packard observes, "The pace of change is so rapid that the ability to change has now become a competitive advantage." Yogi Berra, the legendary New York Yankees catcher and manager, summed it up more simply when he said, "The future ain't what it used to be." As the marketplace changes, so must those who serve it.

In this section, we examine the major trends and forces that are changing the marketing landscape and challenging marketing strategy. We look at four major developments: the digital age, rapid globalization, the call for more ethics and social responsibility, and the growth of not-for-profit marketing.

The Digital Age

The recent technology boom has created a digital age. The explosive growth in computer, communications, information, and other digital technologies has had a major impact on the ways companies bring value to their customers. Now more than ever before we are all connected to each other and to information anywhere in the world. Where it once took days or weeks to receive news about important world events, we now learn about them as they are occurring through live satellite broadcasts and news websites. Where it once took weeks to correspond with others in distant places, they are now only moments away by cellphone, email, or webcam.

The digital age has provided marketers with exciting new ways to learn about and track customers and to create products and services tailored to individual customer needs. It's helping marketers communicate with customers in large groups or one-to-one. Through web videoconferencing, marketing researchers at a company's headquarters in Vancouver can look in on focus groups in Halifax or Paris without ever stepping onto a plane. With only a few clicks of a mouse button, a direct marketer can tap into online data services to learn anything from what car you drive to what you read to what flavour of ice cream you prefer. Or, using today's powerful computers, marketers can create their own detailed customer databases and use them to target individual customers with offers designed to meet their specific needs.

Digital technology has also brought a new wave of communication, advertising, and relationship building tools—ranging from online advertising, video sharing tools, cellphones, and video games to web widgets and online social networks. The digital shift means that marketers can no longer expect consumers to always seek them out. Nor can they always control conversations about their brands. The new digital world makes it easy for consumers to take marketing content that once lived only in advertising or on a brand website with them wherever they go and to share it with friends. More than just add-ons to traditional marketing channels, the new digital media must be fully integrated into the marketer's customer-relationship-building efforts. Says one marketer, "We're [now] building a network of experiences."[34]

Perhaps the most dramatic new digital technology is the Internet. The number of Internet users worldwide now stands at more than 1.2 billion and will reach an estimated 3.4 billion by 2015. Today's typical Internet users spend 47 percent of their time online—watching video, reading the news, or getting the lowdown on friends and celebrities on MySpace or Facebook. They spend another 33 percent of their online time communicating with each other, 15 percent shopping, and 5 percent googling or using other search engines. Computers and the Internet have become an indispensable part of our lives.[35]

What do we value most? Judging by how we spend our time, our computers. Most people spend more time with their computers than with their spouse or significant other. More than 80 percent report that they grow more dependent on their computer every year. Computers are also a growing source of stress. The average consumer experiences frustrating computer problems twice a month and wastes 12 hours a month due to computer problems. Eleven percent say they'd be willing to implant a device in their brains that would allow them to access the Internet. Twenty-four percent say the Internet can serve as a substitute for a significant other. Ten percent say the Web brings them closer to God.[36]

Internet usage surged in the 1990s with the development of the user-friendly World Wide Web. During the overheated Web frenzy of the late 1990s, dot-coms popped up everywhere. The frenzy cooled during the "dot-com meltdown" of 2000, when many poorly conceived etailers and other Web start-ups went out of business.

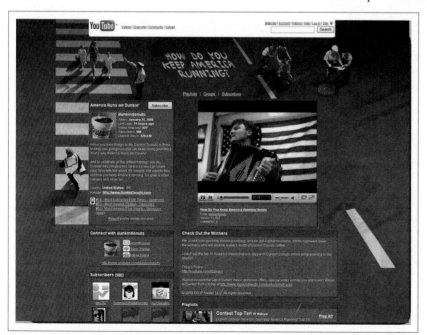

Today, a new version of the Internet has emerged—a "second coming" of the Web, often referred to as Web 2.0. Web 2.0 involves a more reasoned and balanced approach to marketing online. It also offers a fast-growing set of new Web technologies for connecting with customers, such as weblogs (blogs) and vlogs (video-based blogs), social networking sites, and video-sharing sites. The interactive, community-building nature of these new technologies makes them ideal for relating with consumers.[37]

Online marketing is now the fastest-growing form of marketing. These days it's hard to find a company that doesn't use the Web in a significant way. In addition to the "click-only" dot-coms, most traditional "brick-and-mortar" companies have now become "click-and-mortar" companies. They have ventured online to attract new customers and build stronger relationships with existing ones. Canada has the highest

Web 2.0—a "second coming" of the Internet—offers a fast-growing set of new Web technologies for connecting with customers. Here, Dunkin' Donuts offers a popular YouTube space where people can share their "that's why America runs on Dunkin'" stories and videos.

Internet penetration rate in the world: Roughly 85 percent of the population has Internet access and a large percentage of them are shopping online.[38] Business-to-business online commerce is also booming. It seems that almost every business has set up shop on the Web.

Thus, the technology boom is providing exciting new opportunities for marketers. We will explore the impact of the new digital marketing technologies in future chapters, especially Chapter 17.

Rapid Globalization

As they are redefining their relationships with customers and partners, marketers are also taking a fresh look at the ways in which they relate with the broader world around them. In an increasingly smaller world, many marketers are now connected *globally* with their customers and marketing partners.

Today, almost every company, large or small, is touched in some way by global competition. A neighbourhood florist buys its flowers from Mexican nurseries, and a large Canadian electronics manufacturer competes in its home markets with giant Japanese rivals. A fledgling Internet retailer finds itself receiving orders from all over the world at the same time that a Canadian consumer-goods producer introduces new products into emerging markets abroad.

North American firms have been challenged at home by the skilful marketing of European and Asian multinationals. Companies such as Toyota, Nokia, Nestlé, Sony, and Samsung have often outperformed their North American counterparts. Similarly, Canadian companies in a wide range of industries have developed truly global operations, making and selling their products worldwide.

Companies in a wide range of industries have developed truly global operations. The Waterloo-based company Research In Motion has truly evolved into a global company. With corporate offices in North America, Europe, and Asia, it now sells a wide variety of BlackBerry smartphones in countries around the globe.

The Waterloo-based company Research In Motion has truly evolved into a global company. With corporate offices in North America, Europe, and Asia, it now sells a wide variety of BlackBerry devices in countries around the globe. British Columbia–based lululemon, a yoga-inspired athletic apparel company, manufactures its products in seven countries and has over 100 retail locations in Canada, the United States, Australia, and Hong Kong.

Today, companies are not only trying to sell more of their locally produced goods in international markets, they are also buying more supplies and components abroad. For example, Alfred Sung, one of Canada's top fashion designers, may choose cloth woven from Australian wool with designs printed in Italy. He will design a dress and email the drawing to a Hong Kong agent, who will place the order with a Chinese factory. Finished dresses will be air-freighted to Toronto, where they will be redistributed to department and specialty stores around the country.

Thus, managers in countries around the world are increasingly taking a global, not just local, view of the company's industry, competitors, and opportunities. They are asking: What is global marketing? How does it differ from domestic marketing? How do global competitors and forces affect our business? To what extent should we "go global"? We will discuss the global marketplace in more detail in Chapter 18.

The Call for More Ethics and Social Responsibility

Marketers are re-examining their relationships with social values and responsibilities and with the very Earth that sustains us. As the worldwide consumerism and environmentalism movements mature, today's marketers are being called upon to take greater responsibility for the social and environmental impact of their actions. Corporate ethics and social responsibility have become hot topics for almost every business. And few companies can ignore the renewed and very demanding environmental movement. Every company action can affect customer relationships:

> There is an unwritten contract today between customers and the brands they buy. First, they expect companies to consistently deliver what they advertise. Second, they expect the companies they do business with to treat them with respect and to be honourable and forthright. . . . Everything a company does affects the brand in the eyes of the customer. For example, Celestial Seasonings incurred customers' wrath by ignoring its advertised corporate image of environmental stewardship when it poisoned prairie dogs on its property. By contrast, Google's decision to use solar energy for its server farms reinforces what Google stands for and strengthens the Google brand.[39]

The social responsibility and environmental movements will place even stricter demands on companies in the future. Some companies resist these movements, budging only when forced by legislation or organized consumer outcries. More forward-looking companies, however, readily accept their responsibilities to the world around them. They view socially responsible actions as an opportunity to do well by doing good. They seek ways to profit by serving the best long-run interests of their customers and communities.

Some companies—such as Patagonia, Ben & Jerry's, Timberland, EnCana, and others—are practising "caring capitalism," setting themselves apart by being civic-minded and responsible. They are building social responsibility and action into their company value and mission statements. For example, when it comes to environmental responsibility, outdoor gear marketer Patagonia is "committed to the core." "Those of us who work here share a strong commitment to protecting undomesticated lands and waters," says the company's website. "We believe in using business to inspire solutions to the environmental crisis." Patagonia backs these words with actions. Each year it pledges at least 1 percent of its sales or 10 percent of its profits, whichever is greater, to the protection of the natural environment.[40] We will revisit the topic of marketing and social responsibility in greater detail in Chapter 4.

The Growth of Not-for-Profit Marketing

As not-for-profit organizations like World Vision Canada increasingly use marketing techniques, marketing professionals like Caroline Riseboro are drawn to the sector.

In the past, marketing has been most widely applied in the for-profit business sector. In recent years, however, marketing has also become a major part of the strategies of many not-for-profit organizations, such as universities, hospitals, museums, zoos, symphony orchestras, and even churches. The nation's not-for-profits face stiff competition for support and membership. Sound marketing can help them to attract membership and support.[41] Organizations as diverse as the Sierra Club of Canada, the Heart and Stroke Foundation, and the Ivey School of Business at the University of Western Ontario are using marketing techniques to build better relationships with key stakeholders, such as donors, volunteers, and prospective students and alumni. They are hiring experienced marketers from the for-profit sector to help them accomplish their mission. Consider the experience of Caroline Riseboro. When she decided to leave one of Canada's largest advertising agencies to accept a job with World Vision Canada, many of her colleagues thought she was crazy. However, Riseboro wanted to use her marketing skills to give back to society. And she certainly had a chance to put them to work. Selling an intangible product to people with only a limited marketing budget is the first obvious challenge. The more subtle hurdle, however, is the fierce competition for a small share of consumers' discretionary income. As Riseboro noted,

"It's not easy to convince Canadians to forgo a daily latte to give a needy child overseas the opportunity for an education . . . try highlighting the benefits of self-sacrifice; it's not so sexy of a sell." Not-for-profit marketers also need impeccable ethics. Donors constantly look for assurance that their charitable dollars are not being wasted on needless marketing expenses. Thus, as Riseboro has learned, if you can successfully market charitable giving, you can market just about anything.[42]

Government agencies have also shown an increased interest in marketing. For example, both the Canadian military and the Royal Canadian Mounted Police have marketing plans to attract recruits to their different services, and various government agencies are now designing *social marketing campaigns* to encourage energy conservation and concern for the environment or to discourage smoking, excessive drinking, and drug use. According to *Strategy Magazine*, public sector advertising is annually among the top three categories of television advertising in English Canada.[43]

So, What is Marketing? Pulling It All Together

At the start of this chapter, Figure 1.1 presented a simple model of the marketing process. Now that we've discussed all of the steps in the process, Figure 1.6 presents an expanded model that will help you pull it all together. What is marketing? Simply put, marketing is the process of building profitable customer relationships by creating value for customers and capturing value in return.

The first four steps of the marketing process focus on creating value for customers. The company first gains a full understanding of the marketplace by researching customer needs and managing marketing information. It then designs a customer-driven marketing strategy based on the answers to two simple questions. The first question is "What consumers will we serve?" (market segmentation and targeting). Good marketing companies know that they cannot serve all customers in every way. Instead, they need to focus their resources on the customers they can serve best and most profitably. The second marketing strategy question is "How can we best serve targeted customers?" (differentiation and positioning). Here, the marketer outlines a value proposition that spells out what values the company will deliver to win target customers.

With its marketing strategy decided, the company now constructs an integrated marketing program—consisting of a blend of the four marketing mix elements, or the four Ps—that transforms the marketing strategy into real value for customers. The company develops product offers and creates strong brand identities for them. It prices these offers to create real customer value and distributes the offers to make them available to target consumers. Finally, the company designs promotion programs that communicate the value proposition to target consumers and persuade them to act on the market offering.

Perhaps the most important step in the marketing process involves building value-laden, profitable relationships with target customers. Throughout the process, marketers practise customer relationship management to create customer satisfaction and delight. In creating customer value and relationships, however, the company cannot go it alone. It must work closely with marketing partners both inside the company and throughout the marketing system. Thus, beyond practising good customer relationship management, firms must also practise good partner relationship management.

The first four steps in the marketing process create value *for* customers. In the final step, the company reaps the rewards of its strong customer relationships by capturing value *from* customers. Delivering superior customer value creates highly satisfied customers who will buy more and will buy again. This helps the company to capture customer lifetime value and greater share of customer. The result is increased long-term customer equity for the firm.

Finally, in the face of today's changing marketing landscape, companies must take into account three additional factors. In building customer and partner relationships, they must

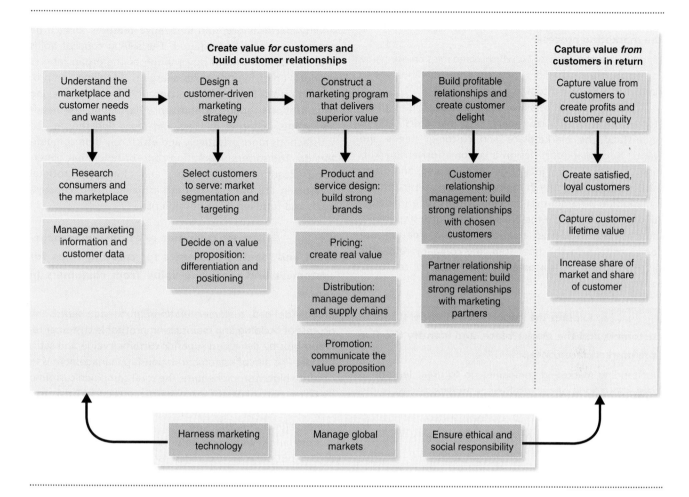

Figure 1.6 An expanded model of the marketing process

harness marketing technology, take advantage of global opportunities, and ensure that they act in an ethical and socially responsible way.

Figure 1.6 provides a good road map to future chapters of the text. Chapters 1 and 2 introduce the marketing process, with a focus on building customer relationships and capturing value from customers. Chapters 3 and 4 address the first steps of the marketing process—understanding the marketing environment, and understanding the impact marketing has on society and the ethical concerns associated with marketing practice. Chapter 5 focuses on managing marketing information. Chapters 6 and 7 are designed to help you understand consumer and business buying behaviour, respectively. In Chapter 8, we look more deeply into the two major marketing strategy decisions: selecting which customers to serve (segmentation and targeting) and deciding on a value proposition (differentiation and positioning). Chapters 9 through 17 discuss the marketing mix variables, one by one. Chapter 18 examines special marketing considerations related to global marketing.

REVIEWING OBJECTIVES AND KEY TERMS   mymarketinglab | Audio Chapter Summary

Today's successful companies—whether large or small, for-profit or not-for-profit, domestic or global—share a strong customer focus and a heavy commitment to marketing. The goal of marketing is to build and manage customer relationships. Marketing seeks to attract new customers by promising superior value and to keep and grow current customers by delivering satisfaction. To be successful, companies will have to be strongly market focused.

OBJECTIVE 1 **Define marketing and outline the steps in the marketing process.**

Marketing is the process by which companies create value for customers and build strong customer relationships to capture value from customers in return.

The marketing process involves five steps. The first four steps create value *for* customers. First, marketers need to understand the marketplace and customer needs and wants. Next, marketers design a customer-driven marketing strategy with the goal of getting, keeping, and growing target customers. In the third step, marketers construct a marketing program that actually delivers superior value. All of these steps form the basis for the fourth step, building profitable customer relationships and creating customer delight. In the final step, the company reaps the rewards of strong customer relationships by capturing value *from* customers.

OBJECTIVE 2 **Explain the importance of understanding customers and the marketplace, and identify the five core marketplace concepts.**

Outstanding marketing companies go to great lengths to learn about and understand their customers' needs, wants, and demands. This understanding helps them to design want-satisfying market offerings and build value-laden customer relationships by which they can capture customer lifetime value and greater share of customer. The result is increased long-term customer equity for the firm.

The core marketplace concepts are needs, wants, and demands; market offerings (products, services, and experiences); value and satisfaction; exchange and relationships; and markets. Wants are the form taken by human needs when shaped by culture and individual personality. When backed by buying power, wants become demands. Companies address needs by putting forth a value proposition, a set of benefits that they promise to consumers to satisfy their needs. The value proposition is fulfilled through a market offering, which delivers customer value and satisfaction, resulting in long-term exchange relationships with customers.

OBJECTIVE 3 **Identify the key elements of a customer-driven marketing strategy and discuss the marketing management orientations that guide marketing strategy.**

To design a winning marketing strategy, the company must first decide *who* it will serve. It does this by dividing the market into segments of customers (*market segmentation*) and selecting which segments it will cultivate (*target marketing*). Next, the company must decide *how* it will serve targeted customers (how it will *differentiate and position* itself in the marketplace).

Marketing management can adopt one of five competing market orientations. The *production concept* holds that management's task is to improve production efficiency and bring down prices. The *product concept* holds

that consumers favour products that offer the most in quality, performance, and innovative features; thus, little promotional effort is required. The *selling concept* holds that consumers will not buy enough of the organization's products unless it undertakes a large-scale selling and promotion effort. The *marketing concept* holds that achieving organizational goals depends on determining the needs and wants of target markets and delivering the desired satisfactions more effectively and efficiently than competitors do. The *societal marketing concept* holds that generating customer satisfaction *and* long-run societal well-being are the keys to both achieving the company's goals and fulfilling its responsibilities.

OBJECTIVE 4 **Discuss customer relationship management and identify strategies for creating value *for* customers and capturing value *from* customers in return.**

Broadly defined, *customer relationship management* is the process of building and maintaining profitable customer relationships by delivering superior customer value and satisfaction. The aim of customer relationship management is to produce high *customer equity*, the total combined customer lifetime values of all of the company's customers. The key to building lasting relationships is the creation of superior *customer value* and *satisfaction*.

Companies want not only to acquire profitable customers but also to build relationships that will keep them and grow "share of customer." Different types of customers require different customer relationship management strategies. The marketer's aim is to build the *right relationships* with the *right customers*. In return for creating value *for* targeted customers, the company captures value *from* customers in the form of profits and customer equity.

In building customer relationships, good marketers realize that they cannot go it alone. They must work closely with marketing partners inside and outside the company. In addition to being good at customer relationship management, they must also be good at *partner relationship management*.

OBJECTIVE 5 **Describe the major trends and forces that are changing the marketing landscape in this age of relationships.**

Dramatic changes are occurring in the marketing arena. The boom in computer, telecommunications, information, transportation, and other technologies has created exciting new ways to learn about and track customers, and to create products and services tailored to individual customer needs. It has also allowed new approaches by which marketers can target consumers more selectively and build closer two-way customer relationships.

In an increasingly smaller world, many marketers are now connected *globally* with their customers and marketing partners. Today, almost every company, large or small, is touched in some way by global competition. Today's marketers are also re-examining their ethical and societal responsibilities. Marketers are being called upon to take greater responsibility for the social and environmental impacts of their actions. Finally, in the past marketing has been most widely applied in the for-profit business sector. In recent years, however, marketing has also become a major part of the strategies of many not-for-profit organizations, such as universities, hospitals, museums, zoos, symphony orchestras, and even churches.

Pulling it all together, as discussed throughout the chapter, the major new developments in marketing can be summed up in a single word: *relationships*. Today, marketers of all kinds are taking advantage of new opportunities for building relationships with their customers, their marketing partners, and the world around them.

KEY TERMS

mymarketinglab | Glossary Flashcards

Objective 1
Marketing   6
Objective 2
Needs   6
Wants   7
Demands   7
Market offerings   7
Marketing myopia   7
Exchange   8
Market   8
Objective 3
Marketing management   9
Production concept   10

Product concept   10
Selling concept   11
Marketing concept   11
Societal marketing concept   12
Objective 4
Customer relationship management   14
Customer-perceived value   14
Customer satisfaction   14
Consumer-generated marketing   20
Partner relationship management   20
Customer lifetime value   23
Share of customer   24
Customer equity   24

DISCUSSING THE CONCEPTS

1. What is marketing and what is its primary goal?

2. Compare and contrast customer needs, wants, and demands. Describe the need versus the want for the following products: Gatorade, Nike shoes, and an iPod.

3. Explain how a company designs a customer-driven marketing strategy.

4. What are the five different marketing management orientations? Which orientation do you believe your school follows when marketing itself?

5. Explain the difference between share of customer and customer equity. Why are these concepts important to marketers?

6. How has the Internet changed consumers? Marketers?

APPLYING THE CONCEPTS

1. Ask five businesspeople from different industries (for example, food service, retailing, consumer-product manufacturing, industrial-product manufacturing, education, and so on) what they think marketing is. Evaluate their definitions and discuss whether or not they are consistent with the goal of creating customer value and managing profitable customer relationships.

2. In a small group, develop a marketing plan for a pet boarding service. Who is your target market? How will you enable customers to get the best value? Define what you mean by value and develop the value proposition of your offering for this target market.

3. Define the different relationship levels companies can build with customers. Pick a company and describe the types of relationships you have with it.

FOCUS ON TECHNOLOGY

Embracing the marketing concept is one thing; implementing it is another. How do marketers know what consumers' needs and wants are so that they can develop a marketing strategy and mix to satisfy those needs and wants? Research, of course. But that takes time and resources, so many companies are turning to the Internet to get continuous, timely, and innovative information from customers. For example, software maker SAP developed its Business Process Expert (BPX) community in which customers share feedback in forums, blogs, and articles. Procter & Gamble wants you to "Share Your Thoughts" at www.pg.com/getintouch. But

if you have a really good idea, perhaps you should look into licensing with P&G (see https://secure3.verticali.net/pg-connection-portal/ctx/noauth/PortalHome.do).

1. Explore the websites of other companies to learn how they get feedback from customers. Start by clicking on "Contact Us," then dig deeply to see if you can find a place where each company seeks or accepts feedback and ideas. Write a brief report of what you find.

2. Discuss other ways in which businesses can use the Internet to create greater customer value.

FOCUS ON ETHICS

Did you drive a car today? Use a laptop computer? Buy a product in a store? If so, you emitted carbon dioxide (CO_2) and created a carbon footprint. All of us do that every day. Many consumers feel badly about doing this; others expect companies to take action. What's the answer? Reducing carbon emissions is one solution, but another one is to offset your carbon emissions by purchasing carbon offsets and renewable energy certificates (RECs). Individual consumers do this, and companies are flocking to purchase carbon offsets for themselves or to offer to their customers, resulting in an estimated $100 million market. And experts predict exponential growth over the next few years. Airlines routinely offer flyers the option of paying a few extra dollars to offset their carbon emissions. For example, JetBlue Airways introduced its "Jetting to Green"

program, which allows flyers to make their flight "carbon-neutral" for as little as $2.00. Flyers' donations will then support reforestation, wind, and waste management projects.

1. Learn more about carbon offsets and discuss four examples of how businesses are using them. In your opinion, are these companies embracing the societal marketing concept?

2. One criticism of carbon offsetting is that companies are not really helping the environment by changing their behaviour; instead, they're merely buying "environmental pardons." Do you think carbon offsets are a responsible solution to environmental concerns? Write a brief essay debating this issue.

MARKETING BY THE NUMBERS

How much are you worth to a given company if you continue to purchase its brand for the rest of your life? Many marketers are grappling with that question, but it's not easy to determine how much a customer is worth to a company over his or her lifetime. Calculating customer lifetime value can be very complicated. Intuitively, however, it can be a fairly simple net present value calculation. To determine a basic customer lifetime value, each stream of profit is discounted back to its present value (PV) and then summed. The basic equation for calculating net present value (NPV) is as follows,

$$N P V = \sum_{t=0}^{N} \frac{C_t}{(1 + r)^t}$$

where,

t = time of the cash flow
N = total customer lifetime
r = discount rate
Ct = net cash flow (the profit) at time t (The initial cost of acquiring a customer would be a negative profit at time 0.)

NPV can be calculated easily on most financial calculators or by using one of the calculators available on the Internet, such as the one found at www.investopedia.com/calculator/NetPresentValue.aspx. For more discussion of the financial and quantitative implications of marketing decisions, see Appendix 3: Marketing by the Numbers.

1. Assume that a customer shops at a local grocery store spending an average of $150 a week and that the retailer earns a 5 percent margin. Calculate the customer lifetime value if this shopper remains loyal over a 10-year lifespan, assuming a 5 percent annual interest rate and no initial cost to acquire the customer. (AACSB Communication; Analytic Reasoning)

2. Discuss how a business can increase a customer's lifetime value. (AACSB: Communication; Reflective Thinking)

VIDEO CASE

 | Video Case Questions

Harley-Davidson

Few brands engender such intense loyalty as that found in the hearts of Harley-Davidson owners. Long ago, the folks at Harley-Davidson realized that the best way to create lasting relationships with customers was to understand them on their own terms. The company spends a great deal of time and money in pursuit of that goal. It wants to know who its customers are, how they think and feel, and why they buy a Harley. That customer-centric strategy has helped build Harley-Davidson into a multibillion-dollar company with the largest company-sponsored owner's group in the world.

Harley-Davidson has learned that it sells much more than motorcycles. The company sells a feeling of independence, individualism, and freedom. These strong emotional connections have made Harley-Davidson ownership much more of a lifestyle than merely a product consumption experience. To support that lifestyle, Harley-Davidson recognizes that its most important marketing tool is the network of individuals who ride Harleys. For this reason, Harley-Davidson engages its customer base through company-sponsored travel adventures, events, and other things, such as clothes and accessories both for riders and for those who simply like to associate with the brand.

After viewing the video featuring Harley-Davidson, answer the following questions about managing profitable customer relationships:

1. How does Harley-Davidson build long-term customer relationships?

2. What is Harley-Davidson's value proposition?

3. Relate the concept of customer equity to Harley-Davidson. How does Harley-Davidson's strategy focus on the right relationships with the right customers?

Visit MyMarketingLab at www.pearsoned.ca/mymarketinglab to view the video segment related to this case.

COMPANY CASE

Build-A-Bear: Build-A-Memory

In the late 1990s, it was all about the dot-com. While venture capital poured into the high-tech sector and the stock prices of dot-com start-ups rose rapidly, the performance of traditional companies paled in comparison. That era seemed like a bad time to start a chain of brick-and-mortar mall stores selling stuffed animals. Indeed, when Maxine Clark founded Build-A-Bear Workshop in 1996, many critics thought that she was making a poor business decision.

But with its first decade of doing business behind it, Build-A-Bear Workshop now has more cheerleaders than naysayers. In the last few years, it has won numerous awards, including being named one of the five hottest retailers by one retail consultancy. The company hit number 25 on *BusinessWeek*'s Hot Growth list of fast-expanding small companies. And founder and CEO Maxine Clark won *Fast Company*'s Customer-Centered Leader Award. How does a small start-up company achieve such accolades?

THE PRODUCT

On paper, it all looks simple. Maxine Clark opened the first company store in 1996. Since then, the company has opened more than 370 stores and has custom-made tens of millions of teddy bears and other stuffed animals. Annual revenues reached US$474 million in 2007 and are growing at a steady and predictable 15 percent annually. After going public in November 2004, the company's stock price soared 56 percent in just two years. Annual sales per square foot are $600, roughly double the average for U.S. mall stores. In fact, Build-A-Bear Workshop typically earns back almost all of its investment in a new store within the first year, a feat unheard of in retailing. On top of all this, the company's Internet sales are exploding.

But what all these numbers don't illustrate is how the company is achieving such success. That success comes not from the tangible object that children clutch as they leave a store. It comes from what Build-A-Bear is really selling: the experience of participating in the creation of personalized entertainment.

When children enter a Build-A-Bear store, they step into a cartoon land, a genuine fantasy world organized around a child-friendly assembly line composed of clearly labelled work stations. The process begins at the "Choose Me" station where customers select an unstuffed animal from a bin. At the "Stuff Me" station, the animal comes to life as the child operates a foot pedal that blows in the amount of "fluff" that she or he (25 percent of Build-A-Bear customers are boys) chooses. Other stations include "Hear Me" (where customers decide whether or not to include a "voice box"), "Stitch Me" (where the child stitches the animal shut), "Fluff Me" (where the child can give the animal a blow-dry spa treatment), "Dress Me" (filled with accessories galore), and "Name Me" (where a birth certificate is created with the child-selected name).

Unlike the experience at most retail stores, waiting in line behind other customers is not an unpleasant activity. In fact, because the process is much of the fun, waiting actually enhances the experience. By the time children leave the store, they have a product unlike any they've ever bought or received. They have a product that they have created. More than just a stuffed animal that they can have and hold, it's imbued with the memory created on their visit to the store. And because of the high price-to-delight ratio (bears start as low as $10 and average $25), parents love Build-A-Bear as much as the kids do.

WHY THE CONCEPT WORKS

The outside observer might assume that Build-A-Bear is competing with other toy companies or with other makers of stuffed animals, such as the Vermont Teddy Bear Company. Touting its product as the only bear made in America and guaranteed for life, Vermont Teddy Bear hand-makes all of its bears at a central factory in Vermont. Customers choose their bears through a catalogue or website, receiving their bear in the mail without the experience of having taken part in the creation of the bear. Quality is the key selling point (reinforced by its price of US$50–$100).

Although Vermont Teddy Bear has achieved great success since it sold its first bear in 1981, Maxine Clark does not consider it to be a serious Build-A-Bear competitor. "Our concept is based on customization," says Clark. "Most things today are high-tech and hard-touch. We are soft-touch. We don't think of ourselves as a toy store—we think of ourselves as an experience." It is widely recognized in many industries that the personalization feature builds fiercely loyal customers. As evidence, Clark points out that unlike the rest of the toy industry, Build-A-Bear sales do not peak during the holiday season, but are evenly distributed throughout the year.

Although not very common in the toy industry, Maxine Clark asserts that personalization is emerging because it lets customers be creative and express themselves. It provides far more value for the customer than they receive from mass-produced products. "It's empowerment—it lets the customer do something in their control," she adds. Build-A-Bear has capitalized on this concept by not just allowing for customization, but by making it a key driver of customer value. The extensive customer involvement in the personalization process is more of the "product" than the resulting item.

Although Build-A-Bear has performed impressively, some analysts question whether or not it is just another toy industry fad, comparing the brand to Beanie Babies and Cabbage Patch Kids. Although Maxine Clark has considered this, she is confident that the Build-A-Bear product and experience will evolve as quickly as the fickle tastes of children. Whereas some outfits and accessories might be trendy (the company added Spider-Man costumes to the bear-size clothing line at the peak of the movie's popularity), the assortment of available accessories changes 11 times each year.

KNOWING THE CUSTOMER

Maxine Clark has been viewed as the strategic visionary—and even the genius—who has made the Build-A-Bear concept work. But her success as CEO derives from more than just business skills relating to strategy development and implementation. Clark attributes her success to "never forgetting what it's like to be a customer." Given that Clark has no children of her own, this is an amazing feat indeed. Although understanding customers is certainly not a new concept, Clark has employed both low-tech and high-tech methods for making Build-A-Bear a truly customer-centric organization.

To put herself in the customer's shoes, Clark walks where they walk. Every week, she visits two or three of the more than 370 Build-A-Bear stores. She doesn't do this just to see how the stores are running operationally. She takes the opportunity to interact with her customer base by chatting with preteens and parents. She actually puts herself on the front line, assisting employees in serving customers. She even hands out business cards.

As a result, Clark receives thousands of emails each week, and she's been added to the buddy lists of preteens all over the world. Clark doesn't take this honour lightly and tries to respond to as many of those messages as possible via her BlackBerry. Also, to capitalize on these customer communications, she has created what she calls the "Virtual Cub Advisory Council," a panel of children on her email list. And what does Clark get in return from all this high-tech communication? "Ideas," she says. "I used to feel like I had to come up with all the ideas myself but it's so much easier relying on my customers for help."

From the location of stores to accessories that could be added to the Build-A-Bear line, Build-A-Bear actually puts customer ideas into practice. As the ideas come in, Clark polls the Cub Council to get real-time feedback from customers throughout the areas where the company does business. Mini-scooters, Hello Kitty bears, mascot bears at professional sports venues, and sequined purses are all ideas generated by customers that have become very successful additions.

Clark sees accessories as a tool for building the child/bear relationship. Build-A-Bear Workshops house in-store galleries of bear-sized furniture designed by kids for kids. An exclusive partnership with Skechers shoes makes Build-A-Bear Workshop the seller of more bear shoes, sandals, boots, and slippers than any other company worldwide. And with the sports licensing agreements that it has with the NBA, WNBA, MLB, NHL, NFL, and NASCAR, Build-A-Bear's offspring can become part of a child's affinity for a sports team. Clark's research efforts have also led to a media campaign focusing on the tween segment by playing up ideas of fashion and imagination.

As a means of further expanding the Build-A-Bear experience beyond the retail store, the company has created a website that connects real-world toys with the online world. Dubbed "BuildABearVille.com," the interactive site contains games and activities that feature the same themes as the brick-and-mortar stores. "The new virtual world was carefully created so that it reflects the core values of Build-A-Bear Workshop," Clark said. "It allows children to have fun as they grow their friendships and learn about being an active participant in the community." Although any child can register, the premium content is only accessible via a code that comes with the purchase of a bear from one of the chain's retail stores.

But growth for Build-A-Bear will come from more than just these improvements to same-store sales. Clark's expansion efforts include building a base of at least 350 stores in the United States and 120 stores in Europe, and franchising an additional 300 stores in other parts of the world. And Clark is taking action on the flood of "build-your-own" concepts that have come across her desk since the first Build-A-Bear Workshop opened. She will give much more attention to a new line of stores called "Friends 2B Made," a concept built around the personalization of dolls rather than stuffed animals. She's opened up the first Build-A-Dino stores. And Build-A-Bear has a 25 percent ownership stake in the start-up Ridemakerz, a make-and-outfit your own toy car shop.

Although Maxine Clark may communicate with only a fraction of her customers, she sees her efforts as the basis for a personal connection with all customers. "With each child that enters our store, we have an opportunity to build a lasting memory," she says. "Any business can think that way, whether you're selling a screw, a bar of soap, or a bear."

Questions for Discussion

1. Give examples of needs, wants, and demands that Build-A-Bear customers demonstrate, differentiating each of these three concepts. What are the implications of each on Build-A-Bear's actions?

2. In detail, describe all facets of Build-A-Bear's product. What is being exchanged in a Build-A-Bear transaction?

3. Which of the five marketing management concepts best describes Build-A-Bear Workshop?

4. Discuss in detail the value that Build-A-Bear creates for its customers.

5. Is Build-A-Bear likely to be successful in continuing to build customer relationships? Why or why not?

Sources: James Bickers, "Virtual Friends," *Retail Customer Experience*, April 2008, p. 20; Joanne Kaufman, "After Build-A-Bear, Build-A-Toy-Car," *New York Times*, May 29, 2007, p. C3; "Build-A-Bear Brings Out the Bulls," *BusinessWeek*, June 28, 2007, accessed at www.businessweek.com; Lucas Conley, "Customer-Centered Leader: Maxine Clark," *Fast Company*, October 2005, p. 54; Staff writer, "This Bear Doesn't Hibernate," *Business-Week*, June 6, 2005, accessed at www.businessweek.com; and Roger Crockett, "Build-A-Bear Workshop: Retailing Gets Interactive with Toys Designed by Tots," *BusinessWeek*, June 6, 2005, p. 77.

Visit **MyMarketingLab** at **www.pearsoned.ca/mymarketinglab** for access to online tutorials, interactive exercises, videos, and much more.

2

Company and Marketing Strategy
Partnering to Build Customer Relationships

**PREVIEWING
THE CONCEPTS**
In the first chapter we explored the marketing process by which companies create value for consumers to capture value from them in return. We will now dig deeper into steps two and three of the marketing process—designing customer-driven marketing strategies and constructing marketing programs. First, we look at the organization's overall strategic planning, which guides marketing strategy and planning. Next, we discuss how, guided by the strategic plan, marketers partner closely with others inside and outside the firm to create value for customers. We then examine marketing strategy and planning—how marketers choose target markets, position their market offerings, develop a marketing mix, and manage their marketing programs. Finally, we look at the important step of measuring and managing return on marketing investment.

To set the stage, let's first look at NASCAR Canada. The entity was born in June 2004, when the National Association of Stock Car Auto Racing (NASCAR) entered a partnership with TSN, Canada's leading sports broadcaster. Although NASCAR is broadcast to 150 countries in 23 languages, Canada has the largest NASCAR fan base outside of the United States. Despite its short history of operation, NASCAR Canada has already become a high-octane national marketing phenomenon. How? By creating value for its millions of fans. In return, NASCAR captures value from these fans, both for itself and for its many new Canadian sponsors. Read on and see how NASCAR does it.

When you first read about NASCAR just a few lines earlier, did you instantly think of tobacco-spitting American rednecks and run-down racetracks? Think again! Six million Canadians are NASCAR fans, and thanks to the fact that NASCAR is a great marketing organization, these numbers are bound to grow. For fans from around the world, NASCAR is a lot more than stock car races: It's a high-octane, totally involved experience.

As for the stereotypes, throw them away. NASCAR is the number-one televised motorsport in Canada. TSN's coverage of the 2006 Daytona 500 drew an audience of 568 000 viewers and was the most-watched motorsport race in TSN's history. As a result of its tremendous success, the partnership between NASCAR Canada and TSN has been extended into 2015. Canadian NASCAR fans come from all across the country. People living in Ontario make up the highest percentage of the audience at 39 percent, with Quebec taking second place with 24 percent. British Columbia makes up 12 percent of the market, with Alberta at 11 percent running close behind. In the United States, NASCAR is now the second-highest–rated regular season sport on TV—only the NFL draws more viewers. NASCAR fans are young, affluent, and decidedly family oriented. The combined North American fan base is more than 80 million strong—four of every ten people in Canada and the United States regularly watch or attend NASCAR events.

Most important, fans are passionate about NASCAR. As NASCAR Canada's website proclaims, its fans are the most brand conscious among all professional sports fans. An ardent NASCAR fan spends nearly $700 a year on NASCAR-related clothing, collectibles, and other items. So it's not surprising that firms as diverse as Procter & Gamble, Lilydale Incorporated (based in Edmonton, it boasts Canada's fastest-growing brand of fresh chicken), and the Canadian romance-novel giant Harlequin Enterprises Limited have signed licensing agreements with the ultra-popular auto-racing organization. Under the new agreement, Harlequin is publishing women's fiction titles with NASCAR plotlines and the NASCAR brand on the covers.

What's NASCAR's secret? Its incredible success results from a single-minded focus: creating lasting customer relationships. For fans, the NASCAR relationship develops through a careful blend of live racing events, abundant media coverage, and compelling websites.

Approximately 350 000 Canadian fans have travelled to a race in the United States to experience the adrenaline-charged, heart-stopping excitement of NASCAR racing first-hand. In August 2007, NASCAR Canada ran its first race on Canadian soil, the Busch race in Montreal, drawing over 130 000 fans. At these events, fans hold tailgate parties, camp and cook out, watch the cars roar around the track, meet the drivers, and swap stories with other NASCAR enthusiasts. Track facilities even include RV parks next to and right inside the racing oval. Marvels one sponsor, "[In] what other sport can you drive your beat-up RV or camper into the stadium and sit on it to watch the race?" NASCAR really cares about its customers and goes out of its way to show them a good time. For example, rather than fleecing fans with overpriced food and beer, NASCAR tracks encourage fans to bring their own. Such actions mean that NASCAR might lose a sale today, but it will keep the customer tomorrow.

To further the customer relationship, NASCAR makes the sport a wholesome family affair. The environment is safe for kids—uniformed security guards patrol the track to keep things in line. The family atmosphere extends to the drivers, too. Unlike the aloof and often distant athletes in other sports, NASCAR drivers seem like regular guys. They are friendly and readily available to mingle with fans and sign autographs.

Montreal proved to be a very receptive town for NASCAR events.

Can't make it to the track? No problem. Campaigns featuring NASCAR drivers and cars have proliferated across a broad range of media, from TV and multiple websites to cellphones, satellite radio, video game consoles, and mobile devices. "It's incredibly important to reach the fans in different ways as they engage with our sport in different ways," says NASCAR's chief marketing officer.

An average televised NASCAR event reaches 18 million TV viewers. Last year alone, through network partners like ABC, ESPN2, Fox Broadcasting, TSN, and Speed, NASCAR events captured more than 300 million viewers. NASCAR's most avid fans, roughly 30 million of them, consume eight hours a week of NASCAR media. Well-orchestrated coverage and in-car cameras put fans in the middle of the action, giving them vicarious thrills that keep them glued to the screen. "When the network gets it right, my surround-sound bothers my neighbours but makes my ears happy," says Angela Kotula, a 35-year-old human resources professional and avid NASCAR fan.

▶

OBJECTIVES

1. Explain companywide strategic planning and its four steps.

2. Discuss how to design business portfolios and develop growth strategies.

3. Explain marketing's role in strategic planning and how marketing works with its partners to create and deliver customer value.

4. Describe the elements of a customer-driven marketing strategy and mix and the forces that influence it.

5. List the marketing management functions, including the elements of a marketing plan, and discuss the importance of measuring and managing return on marketing investment.

NASCAR also delivers the NASCAR experience through its engaging websites. TSN's NASCAR site (www.tsn.ca/auto_racing/nascar) and NASCAR.com serve up a glut of information and entertainment—in-depth news, driver bios, background information, online games, community discussions, and merchandise. True die-hard fans can subscribe to TrackPass to get up-to-the-minute standings, race video, streaming audio from the cars, and access to a host of archived audio and video highlights. TrackPass with PitCommand even delivers a real-time data feed, complete with the GPS locations of cars and data from drivers' dashboards.

But a big part of the NASCAR experience is the feeling that the sport itself is personally accessible. Anyone who knows how to drive feels that he or she, too, could be a champion NASCAR driver. As 48-year-old police officer Ed Sweat puts it, "Genetics did not bless me with the height of a basketball player, nor was I born to have the bulk of a lineman in the NFL. But . . . on any given Sunday, with a rich sponsor, the right car, and some practice, I could be draftin' and passin,' zooming to the finish line, trading paint with Tony Stewart . . . Yup, despite my advancing age and waistline, taking Zocor, and driving by the gym, I could be Dale Jarrett!"

Ultimately, all of this fan enthusiasm translates into financial success for NASCAR and its sponsors. Television networks pay on average US$560 million per year for the rights to broadcast NASCAR events, and in turn charge advertisers nearly US$600 000 per 30-second advertising slot. With everything from NASCAR-branded bacon to its own series of Harlequin romance novels, the sport is third in licensed merchandise sales, behind only the NFL and the NCAA. NASCAR itself sells more than US$2 billion in merchandise a year.

Marketing studies show that NASCAR's fans are three times more loyal to the sport's sponsors than fans of any other sport. Seventy-two percent of NASCAR fans consciously purchase sponsors' products because of the NASCAR connection. Just ask dental hygienist Jenny German, an ardent fan of driver Jeff Gordon. According to one account, "She actively seeks out any product he endorses. She drinks Pepsi instead of Coke, eats Edy's ice cream for dessert, and owns a pair of Ray-Ban sunglasses. 'If they sold underwear with the number 24 on it, I'd have it on,' German says."

Because of such loyal fan relationships, NASCAR Canada and NASCAR have attracted more than 250 big-name sponsors, from Walmart and Home Depot to Canadian

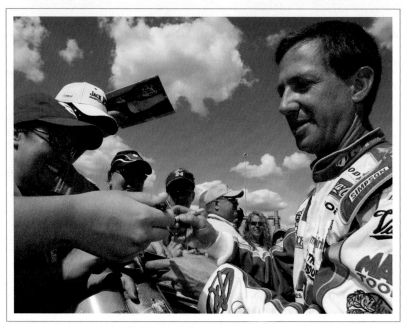

Because of its loyal fan relationships, NASCAR has attracted more than 250 big-name sponsors, who spend more than US$1 billion a year for NASCAR sponsorships and promotions.

Tire and Sun Media. In all, corporations spend more than US$1 billion a year for NASCAR sponsorships and promotions. Sprint Nextel is shelling out US$750 million over the next 10 years to be a NASCAR sponsor and to put its name on the NASCAR Sprint Cup series. "I could pay you US$1 million to try and not run into our name at a NASCAR race and you would lose," says a Sprint Nextel spokesperson.

Other sponsors eagerly pay on average US$18 million to US$20 million per year to sponsor a top car and to get their corporate colours and logos emblazoned on team uniforms and on the hoods or side panels of team cars. Or they spend big bucks to become the "official" (fill-in-the-blank) of NASCAR racing. For example, Molson Coors recently signed a US$25 million contract to have Coors Light be the official beer of NASCAR for five years. Is it worth the price? Office Depot certainly thinks so. It began sponsoring a car when its surveys showed that 44 percent of rival Staples' customers would switch office supply retailers if Office Depot hooked up with NASCAR.

So if you're still thinking of NASCAR as rednecks, pickup trucks, and moonshine, you'd better think again. NASCAR is a premier marketing organization that knows how to create customer value that translates into deep and lasting customer relationships. "Better than any other sport," says a leading sports marketing executive, "NASCAR listens to its fans and gives them what they want." In turn, fans reward NASCAR and its sponsors with deep loyalty and the promise of lasting profits.[1]

Like NASCAR Canada, outstanding marketing organizations employ strongly customer-driven marketing strategies and programs that create customer value and relationships. These marketing strategies and programs, however, are guided by broader companywide strategic plans, which must also be customer focused. Thus, to understand the role of marketing we must first understand the organization's overall strategic planning process.

COMPANYWIDE STRATEGIC PLANNING: DEFINING MARKETING'S ROLE

Each company must find the game plan for long-run survival and growth that makes the most sense given its specific situation, opportunities, objectives, and resources. This is the focus of **strategic planning**—the process of developing and maintaining a strategic fit between the organization's goals and capabilities and its changing marketing opportunities.

Strategic planning
The process of developing and maintaining a strategic fit between the organization's goals and capabilities and its changing marketing opportunities.

Strategic planning sets the stage for the rest of the planning in the firm. Companies usually prepare annual plans, long-range plans, and strategic plans. The annual and long-range plans deal with the company's current businesses and how to keep them going. In contrast, the strategic plan involves adapting the firm to take advantage of opportunities in its constantly changing environment.

At the corporate level, the company starts the strategic planning process by defining its overall purpose and mission (see Figure 2.1). This mission is then turned into detailed supporting objectives that guide the whole company. Next, headquarters decides what portfolio of businesses and products is best for the company and how much support to give each one. In turn, each business and product develops detailed marketing and other departmental plans that support the companywide plan. Thus, marketing planning occurs at the business-unit, product, and market levels. It supports company strategic planning with more detailed plans for specific marketing opportunities.

Defining a Market-Oriented Mission

An organization exists to accomplish something, and this purpose should be clearly stated. Forging a sound mission begins with the following questions: What is our business? Who is the customer? What do consumers value? What *should* our business be? These simple-sounding questions are among the most difficult the company will ever have to answer. Successful companies continuously raise these questions and answer them carefully and completely.

Many organizations develop formal mission statements that answer these questions. A **mission statement** is a statement of the organization's purpose—what it wants to accomplish in the larger environment. A clear mission statement acts as an "invisible hand" that guides people in the organization. Studies have shown that firms with well-crafted mission statements have better organizational and financial performance.[2]

Mission statement
A statement of the organization's purpose—what it wants to accomplish in the larger environment.

Some companies define their missions myopically in product or technology terms ("We make and sell furniture" or "We are a chemical-processing firm"). But mission statements should be *market oriented* and defined in terms of satisfying basic customer needs. Products and technologies eventually become outdated, but basic market needs may last forever.

Figure 2.1 Steps in strategic planning

About us

Canadian Tire Corporation, Limited is a growing, interrelated network of retail and financial services businesses offering goods and services that meet life's everyday needs. We are a proud Canadian family of over 57,000 people strengthened by one of the nation's longest-standing and most-trusted brands. Together, we strive to create customers for life and grow long-term shareholder value.

Canadian Tire's mission is "to offer products and services to meet the everyday needs of Canadian families—today and tomorrow."

For example, Canadian Tire's mission isn't simply to sell tools and home improvement items. Its mission is "to offer products and services to meet the everyday needs of Canadian families—today and tomorrow." Likewise, eBay's mission isn't simply to hold online auctions and trading. It aims "to provide a global trading platform where practically anyone can trade practically anything"—with eBay, "Shop victoriously!" It wants to be a unique Web community in which people can safely shop around, have fun, and get to know each other, for example, by chatting at the eBay Café.[3] Table 2.1 provides several other examples of product-oriented versus market-oriented business definitions.

Mission statements should be meaningful and specific yet motivating. They should emphasize the company's strengths in the marketplace. Too often, mission statements are written for public relations purposes and lack specific, workable guidelines. Says former GE super-CEO Jack Welch:

> Few leaders actually get the point of forging a mission with real grit and meaning. [Mission statements] have largely devolved into fat-headed jargon. Almost no one can figure out what they mean. [So companies] sort of ignore them or gussy up a vague package deal along the lines of: "our mission is to be the best fill-in-the-blank company in our industry." [Instead, CEOs should] make a choice about how your company will win. Don't mince words! Remember Nike's old mission, "Crush Reebok"? That's directionally correct. And Google's mission statement isn't something namby-pamby like "To be the world's best search engine." It's "To organize the world's information and make it universally accessible and useful." That's simultaneously inspirational, achievable, and completely graspable.[4]

Table 2.1 Market-Oriented Business Definitions

Company	Product-Oriented Definition	Market-Oriented Definition
M.A.C. Cosmetics	We make cosmetics.	We sell lifestyle and self-expression, tolerance of diversity, and a platform for the outrageous.
Amazon.ca	We sell books, videos, CDs, toys, consumer electronics, hardware, housewares, and other products online.	We make the Internet buying experience fast, easy, and enjoyable—we're the place where you can find and discover anything you want to buy online.
Zellers	We run discount stores.	We offer products and services that deliver superior style and value to Canadians.
Disney	We run theme parks.	We create fantasies—a place where dreams come true and America still works the way it's supposed to.
Google	We provide the world's best online search engine.	We help you organize the world's information and make it universally accessible and useful.
Home Depot	We sell tools and home repair and improvement items.	We empower consumers to achieve the homes of their dreams.
Nike	We sell athletic shoes and apparel.	We bring inspiration and innovation to every athlete* in the world. (*If you have a body, you are an athlete.)
Ritz-Carlton Hotels	We rent rooms.	We create the Ritz-Carlton experience—one that enlivens the senses, instills well-being, and fulfills even the unexpressed wishes and needs of our guests.

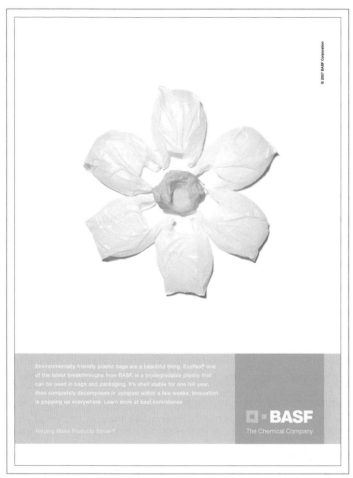

BASF's overall marketing objective is to work with commercial customers/partners to "help make products better." For example, it works with packaging firms to create biodegradable plastic bags and packaging that are "shelf stable for one full year, then completely decompose in compost within a few weeks."

Finally, a company's mission should not be stated as making more sales or profits—profits are only a reward for creating value for customers. A company's employees need to feel that their work is significant and that it contributes to people's lives. For example, Microsoft's aim is to help people to "realize their potential." "Your potential, our passion," says the company. Target tells customers to "Expect more. Pay less."

Setting Company Objectives and Goals

The company needs to turn its mission into detailed supporting objectives for each level of management. Each manager should have objectives and be responsible for reaching them. For example, giant chemical company BASF makes and markets a diverse product mix that includes everything from chemicals, plastics, and agricultural products to crude oil and natural gas. But BASF does more than just make chemicals. Its mission is to work with commercial customers in numerous industries to help them employ these chemicals to find innovative solutions and better products for their consumers.

This broad mission leads to a hierarchy of objectives, including business objectives and marketing objectives. BASF's overall objective is to build profitable customer relationships by developing better products. It does this by investing in research—nearly 10 percent of BASF's employees work in research and development. R&D is expensive and requires improved profits to plow back into research programs. So improving profits becomes another major BASF objective. Profits can be improved by increasing sales or reducing costs.

Sales can be increased by improving the company's share of domestic and international markets. These goals then become the company's current marketing objectives.[5]

Marketing strategies and programs must be developed to support these marketing objectives. To increase its market share, BASF might increase its products' availability and promotion in existing markets. To enter new global markets, the company can create new local partnerships within targeted countries. For example, BASF's Agricultural Products division has begun targeting China's farmers with a line of insecticides. To bring the right crop protection solutions to these farmers, BASF has formed working relationships with several Chinese agricultural research organizations, such as Nanjing Agricultural University.[6]

These are BASF's broad marketing strategies. Each broad marketing strategy must then be defined in greater detail. For example, increasing the product's promotion may require more salespeople, advertising, and public relations efforts; if so, both requirements will need to be spelled out. In this way, the firm's mission is translated into a set of objectives for the current period.

Designing the Business Portfolio

Business portfolio
The collection of businesses and products that make up the company.

Guided by the company's mission statement and objectives, management now must plan its **business portfolio**—the collection of businesses and products that make up the company. The best business portfolio is the one that best fits the company's strengths and weaknesses to opportunities in the environment. Business portfolio planning involves two steps. First, the company must analyze its current business portfolio and decide which businesses should receive more, less, or no investment. Second, it must shape the future portfolio by developing strategies for growth and downsizing.

Analyzing the Current Business Portfolio

Portfolio analysis
The process by which management evaluates the products and businesses that make up the company.

The major activity in strategic planning is business **portfolio analysis**, whereby management evaluates the products and businesses that make up the company. The company will want to put strong resources into its more profitable businesses and phase down or drop its weaker ones.

Management's first step is to identify the key businesses that make up the company, called *strategic business unit* (SBUs). An SBU can be a company division, a product line within a division, or sometimes a single product or brand. The company next assesses the attractiveness of its various SBUs and decides how much support each deserves. When designing a business portfolio, it's a good idea to add and support products and businesses that fit closely with the firm's core philosophy and competencies.

The purpose of strategic planning is to find ways in which the company can best use its strengths to take advantage of attractive opportunities in the environment. So most standard portfolio analysis methods evaluate SBUs on two important dimensions: the attractiveness of the SBU's market or industry and the strength of the SBU's position in that market or industry. The best-known portfolio-planning method was developed by the Boston Consulting Group, a leading management consulting firm.[7]

The Boston Consulting Group Approach Using the now-classic Boston Consulting Group (BCG) approach, a company classifies all its SBUs according to the **growth-share matrix** as shown in Figure 2.2. On the vertical axis, *market growth rate* provides a measure of market attractiveness. On the horizontal axis, *relative market share* serves as a measure of company strength in the market. The growth-share matrix defines four types of SBUs:

Growth-share matrix
A portfolio-planning method that evaluates a company's strategic business units in terms of its market growth rate and relative market share. SBUs are classified as stars, cash cows, question marks, or dogs.

- *Stars.* Stars are high-growth, high-share businesses or products. They often need heavy investments to finance their rapid growth. Eventually their growth will slow down, and they will turn into cash cows.

- *Cash cows.* Cash cows are low-growth, high-share businesses or products. These established and successful SBUs need less investment to hold their market share. Thus, they produce a lot of cash that the company uses to pay its bills and to support other SBUs that need investment.

- *Question marks.* Question marks are low-share business units in high-growth markets. They require a lot of cash to hold their share, let alone increase it. Management has to think hard about which question marks it should try to build into stars and which should be phased out.

- *Dogs.* Dogs are low-growth, low-share businesses and products. They may generate enough cash to maintain themselves but do not promise to be large sources of cash.

Figure 2.2 The BCG growth-share matrix

Managing the business portfolio: Most people think of Disney as theme parks and wholesome family entertainment, but over the past two decades it's become a sprawling collection of media and entertainment businesses that require big doses of the famed "Disney Magic" to manage.

The 10 circles in Figure 2.2 represent a company's 10 current SBUs. The company has two stars, two cash cows, three question marks, and three dogs. The areas of the circles are proportional to the SBUs' dollar sales. This company is in fair shape, although not in good shape. It wants to invest in the more promising question marks to make them stars and to maintain the stars so that they will become cash cows as their markets mature. Fortunately, it has two good-sized cash cows. Income from these cash cows will help finance the company's question marks, stars, and dogs. The company should take some decisive action concerning its dogs and its question marks.

Once it has classified its SBUs, the company must determine what role each will play in the future. One of four strategies can be pursued for each SBU. The company can invest more in the business unit to *build* its share. Or it can invest just enough to *hold* the SBU's share at the current level. It can *harvest* the SBU, milking its short-term cash flow regardless of the long-term effect. Finally, the company can *divest* the SBU by selling it or phasing it out and using the resources elsewhere.

As time passes, SBUs change their positions in the growth-share matrix. Many SBUs start out as question marks and move into the star category if they succeed. They later become cash cows as market growth falls, then finally die off or turn into dogs toward the end of their life cycle. The company needs to add new products and units continuously so that some of them will become stars and, eventually, cash cows that will help finance other SBUs.

Problems with Matrix Approaches The BCG and other formal methods revolutionized strategic planning. However, such centralized approaches have limitations: They can be difficult, time consuming, and costly to implement. Management may find it difficult to define SBUs and measure market share and growth. In addition, these approaches focus on classifying *current* businesses, but provide little advice for *future* planning.

Because of such problems, many companies have dropped formal matrix methods in favour of more customized approaches that better suit their specific situations. Moreover, unlike former strategic planning efforts that rested mostly in the hands of senior managers at company headquarters, today's strategic planning has been decentralized. Increasingly, companies are placing responsibility for strategic planning in the hands of cross-functional teams of divisional managers who are close to their markets.

For example, consider the Walt Disney Company. Most people think of Disney as theme parks and wholesome family entertainment. But in the mid-1980s Disney set up a powerful, centralized strategic planning group to guide the company's direction and growth. Over the next two decades, the strategic planning group turned the Walt Disney Company into a huge and diverse collection of media and entertainment businesses. The sprawling Disney grew to include everything from theme resorts and film studios (Walt Disney Pictures, Touchstone Pictures, Hollywood Pictures, and others) to media networks (ABC plus Disney Channel, ESPN, A&E, History Channel, and a half dozen others) to consumer products and a cruise line. The newly transformed company proved hard to manage and performed unevenly. Recently, Disney disbanded the centralized strategic planning unit, decentralizing its functions to Disney division managers.

Developing Strategies for Growth and Downsizing

Beyond evaluating current businesses, designing the business portfolio involves finding businesses and products the company should consider in the future. Companies need growth if they are to compete more effectively, satisfy their stakeholders, and attract top talent. "Growth is pure oxygen," states one executive. "It creates a vital, enthusiastic corporation where people see genuine opportunity." At the same time, a firm must be careful not to make growth itself an objective. The company's objective must be to manage "profitable growth."[8]

Marketing has the main responsibility for achieving profitable growth for the company. Marketing needs to identify, evaluate, and select market opportunities and lay down strategies for capturing them. One useful device for identifying growth opportunities is the **product/market expansion grid**, shown in Figure 2.3.[9] We apply it here to Tim Hortons (see Real Marketing 2.1).

Tim Hortons' strategy is deceptively simple and has long been founded on **market penetration**. It works to open a critical mass of outlets in a predefined geographic region and then it supports them with advertising. Increased awareness and the building of strong brand equity in turn builds requests for new franchises—which is how Tim Hortons plans to continue expansion in both Quebec and Western Canada. It also works to train people who come into Tim Hortons first thing in the morning for coffee and breakfast to return several times during the rest of the day. To that end, Tim Hortons routinely upgrades and refurbishes its outlets, adding double drive-throughs and establishing satellite outlets in settings such as hospitals and retail stores—bringing the restaurant to the consumer instead of the other way around. "Wherever you are," says one top manager, "there's a coffee and a doughnut waiting for you."

Second, the firm explores possibilities for **market development**—identifying and developing new markets for its current products. For instance, managers could review new *demographic markets*. Perhaps new groups—such as senior consumers or ethnic groups—could be encouraged to visit Tim Hortons coffee shops for the first time or to buy more from them. Tim Hortons has also practised market development *geographically*, and now operates 520 outlets in 11 different U.S. states.

Third, Tim Hortons' management focuses on **product development**—offering modified or new products to current markets. Tim Hortons introduced cappuccino, bagels, sandwiches, and soup to get consumers to see it as more than just a doughnut shop.

Fourth, Tim Hortons might consider **diversification**. It could start up or buy businesses outside of its current products and markets. For example, it might consider adding gas bars to complement its drive-through services. It could leverage its strong brand name onto products like sportswear that fit with its friendly, relaxed image. However, it must take care: Companies that diversify too broadly into unfamiliar products or industries can lose their market focus.

Companies must develop not only strategies for *growing* their business portfolios, but also strategies for **downsizing** them. There are many reasons that a firm might want to abandon products or markets. The market environment might change, making some of the company's products or markets less profitable. The firm may have grown too fast or entered areas where it lacks experience. This can occur when a firm enters too many international

Product/market expansion grid
A portfolio-planning tool for identifying company growth opportunities through market penetration, market development, product development, or diversification.

Market penetration
A strategy for company growth by increasing sales of current products to current market segments without changing the product.

Market development
A strategy for company growth by identifying and developing new market segments for current company products.

Product development
A strategy for company growth by offering modified or new products to current market segments.

Diversification
A strategy for company growth through starting up or acquiring businesses outside the company's current products and markets.

Downsizing
Reducing the business portfolio by eliminating products or business units that are not profitable or that no longer fit the company's overall strategy.

Figure 2.3 The product/market expansion grid

	Existing products	New products
Existing markets	Market penetration	Product development
New markets	Market development	Diversification

Real Marketing 2.1

Tim Hortons: Every Cup Tells a Story

Canadians, it appears, always have time for Tim Hortons. Founded in 1964, the firm recently celebrated its forty-fifth anniversary. Generations of competitors have come and gone, but none have managed to defeat Hortons, headquartered in Oakville, Ontario. In fact, it has become a Canadian icon. Throughout its history, Hortons' marketing savvy has turned this once simple doughnut shop into a giant with 3437 outlets that generated $2.4 billion in revenues in 2008. Today, Tim Hortons rivals McDonald's Canada for the number-one spot in terms of fast-food sales. The dominance of the chain can be seen in these facts: Tim Hortons is the fourth largest quick-service restaurant in North America and the largest in Canada, with approximately 42 percent of the sector traffic in Canadian stores. More than 40 percent of its customers visit four times or more each week, and Tim Hortons holds the largest market share of the breakfast market and the second largest share of the lunch market in Canada. Tim Hortons also employs over 100 000 people in Canada and the United States, making it one of Canada's largest employers.

Tim Hortons works relentlessly to build its brand, which has become an idealized image of the Canadian national character: friendly, neighbourly, unpretentious, gently playful, frugal, trustworthy, and yes, clean. It brings this brand image to life by featuring real people in its ads—both customers and employees. "Tim Hortons never fakes it," notes Philippe Garneau, a partner at Toronto's Garneau Würstlin Philp Brand Engineering. Tim Hortons communicates its brand image through its "true stories" television vignettes, which are based on the best of hundreds of suggestions the company receives from its customers every year. Each story exemplifies the emotional relationship the customer has with Tim Hortons and portrays how Hortons fits into customers' daily lives. The company's advertising is complemented by a unique social media site, EveryCup.ca, where consumers are encouraged to tell their stories and experiences about how Tim Hortons has enriched their lives.

The doughnut chain's long-running "Roll up the Rim to Win" promotion has become a beloved part of Canadian slang, and sketches set at Hortons are shown weekly on the comedy news show *Royal Canadian Air Farce*. Some of the approximately $9.5 million a year that Hortons spends on advertising is also focused on its new products—bagels, sandwiches, and soup—to get consumers to see Tim Hortons as more than just a doughnut shop and to build brand awareness in the U.S. market. New products have also increased revenues for both the corporation and its franchisees.

As impressive as these figures are, one has to wonder what else Tim Hortons has done to achieve this success—after all, it offers fairly standard products, such as coffee and baked goods. Hortons' strategy is deceptively simple. First, it has followed one consistent product and positioning strategy throughout its history. Its promise of "Always Fresh" is never broken, and it makes this promise concrete in many ways. For example, its interactive digital menus identify products just as they are being taken out of the oven. Next, it builds outlets in focal areas until there are enough outlets in the area to justify advertising. As Patti Jameson, director of corporate communications, notes, "Advertising is a lot more relevant to people when they actually see the stores on the street." Having the physical presence of a retail outlet makes brand messages more relevant and meaningful.

Given Tim Hortons' track record, it's hard to imagine how it could expand any further. There seems to be an outlet on the corner of every major intersection. Yet even an institution needs to be willing to change and grow. And change is exactly what Hortons has done in recent years. In a bid to broaden its appeal and attract more women and young people, the chain has branched out into new product lines, such as iced cappuccino. It also retooled its lunchtime offerings, serving up Tim's Own brand of soups and sandwiches.

The firm isn't about to stop there. Since Tim Hortons believes that the breakfast category is underdeveloped in the

Tim Hortons has formed a number of strategic alliances with U.S. firms to expand geographically, including co-branding stores with Cold Stone Creamery.

United States and that Americans are poorly served by current "morning destinations," it sees tremendous opportunity south of the border. Tim Hortons has formed a number of strategic alliances to build its U.S. market share, including opening 82 outlets in Tops supermarkets and a number of co-branded stores with premium ice cream chain Cold Stone Creamery. In 2008, it opened its 500th outlet in the United States. "In the U.S., they don't have high expectations for morning destinations . . . People will grab a coffee from a gas station in the morning, [but] we're promising that consistent experience. No one else is really doing everyday morning coffee and baked goods very well." Two television spots and a series of radio ads all portray Tim Hortons as the real reason morning people are so chipper. The tag line is: "Morning people. Where do they come from?" Despite exceeding growth expectations in terms of the number of outlets, a struggling U.S. economy and the dominance of Dunkin' Donuts led to some store closures in the United States and a fall in profits in the fourth quarter of 2008. Although success in the highly competitive U.S. market is far from guaranteed, if the history of professional hockey offers any indication, then Americans may also soon be claiming this Canadian institution as their own.

Sources: Tim Hortons' 2008 Annual Report, accessed at http://annualreport.timhortons.com, April 2009; "Cold Stone, Tim Hortons Expand Co-brand Test," *Nation's Restaurant News,* February 16, 2009, p. 6; "Tim Hortons to Open 82 Outlets in Tops Markets," *Nation's Restaurant News,* October 20, 2008, p. 8; "Tim Hortons' Profits Fall 8.6% in the Fourth Quarter," *Nation's Restaurant News,* March 2, 2009, p. 52; Emily Bryson York, "Hortons Stuggles for Growth in U.S.," *Advertising Age,* March 23, 2009, p. 6; Terry Poulton, Special Report: Top Clients 2002, "Long Live the Double Double," *Strategy,* July 29, 2002, p. 19; Natalie Bahadur, "Tim Hortons Plans Aggressive Roll-Out," *Strategy,* March 29, 1999, p. 7; Lesley Daw, "More Than Just a Doughnut Shop," *Marketing,* December 20/27, 1999, accessed at **www.marketingmag.ca**; Scott Gardiner, "In Praise of Saint Timmy," *Marketing,* August 21, 2000, accessed at **www.marketingmag.ca**; Laura Pratt, "Roll Up the Rim Major Player for Tim Hortons," *Strategy,* May 22, 2000, p. 22; Craig Saunders, "Tim Hortons Issues Wakeup Call," *Strategy,* February 14, 2000, p. 25; Sinclair Stewart, "Top Client, Retail–Restaurants: Tim Hortons Brews Up Fresh Ideas," *Strategy,* August 2, 1999, p. 7; and Sinclair Stewart, "Tim Hortons Brews New U.S. Campaign," *Strategy,* September 27, 1999, p. 3.

markets without the proper research, or when a company introduces new products that do not offer superior customer value. Finally, some products or business units simply age and die.

When a firm finds brands or business units that are unprofitable or that no longer fit its overall strategy, it must carefully prune, harvest, or divest them. Weak business units usually require a disproportionate amount of management attention. Managers should focus on promising growth opportunities, not fritter away energy trying to salvage fading ones.

3 PLANNING MARKETING: PARTNERING TO BUILD CUSTOMER RELATIONSHIPS

The company's strategic plan establishes what kinds of businesses the company will operate and its objectives for each. Then, within each business unit, more detailed planning takes place. The major functional departments in each unit—marketing, finance, accounting, purchasing, operations, information systems, human resources, and others—must work together to accomplish strategic objectives.

Marketing plays a key role in the company's strategic planning in several ways. First, marketing provides a guiding *philosophy*—the marketing concept—that suggests that company strategy should revolve around building profitable relationships with important consumer groups. Second, marketing provides *inputs* to strategic planners by helping to identify attractive market opportunities and by assessing the firm's potential to take advantage of them. Finally, within individual business units, marketing designs *strategies* for reaching the unit's objectives. Once the unit's objectives are set, marketing's task is to help carry them out profitably.

Customer value is the key ingredient in the marketer's formula for success. However, as we noted in Chapter 1, marketers alone cannot produce superior value for customers. Although marketing plays a leading role, it can be only a partner in attracting, keeping, and growing customers. In addition to *customer relationship management*, marketers must also practise *partner relationship management*. They must work closely with partners in other company departments to form an effective *value chain* that serves the customer. Moreover, they must partner effectively with other companies in the marketing system to form a competitively superior *value delivery network*. We now take a closer look at the concepts of a company value chain and a value delivery network.

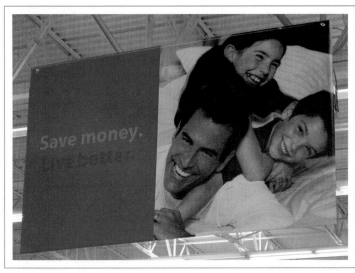

The value chain: Walmart's ability to help you "Save money. Live Better." by offering the right products at lower prices depends on the contributions of people in all of the company's departments.

Partnering with Other Company Departments

Each company department can be thought of as a link in the company's **value chain**.[10] That is, each department carries out value-creating activities to design, produce, market, deliver, and support the firm's products. The firm's success depends not only on how well each department performs its work, but also on how well the various departments coordinate their activities.

For example, Walmart's goal is to create customer value and satisfaction by providing shoppers with the products they want at the lowest possible prices. Marketers at Walmart play an important role. They learn what customers need and stock the store shelves with the desired products at unbeatable low prices. They prepare advertising and merchandising programs and assist shoppers with customer service. Through these and other activities, Walmart's marketers help deliver value to customers.

However, the marketing department needs help from the company's other departments. Walmart's ability to offer the right products at low prices depends on the purchasing department's skill in developing the needed suppliers and buying from them at low cost. Walmart's information technology department must provide fast and accurate information about which products are selling in each store. And its operations people must provide effective, low-cost merchandise handling.

A company's value chain is only as strong as its weakest link. Success depends on how well each department performs its work of adding customer value and on how well the activities of various departments are coordinated. At Walmart, if purchasing can't obtain the lowest prices from suppliers, or if operations can't distribute merchandise at the lowest costs, then marketing can't deliver on its promise of lowest prices.

Value chain
The series of departments that carry out value-creating activities to design, produce, market, deliver, and support a firm's products.

Ideally then, a company's different functions should work in harmony to produce value for consumers. But in practice, departmental relations are full of conflicts and misunderstandings. The marketing department takes the consumer's point of view. But when marketing tries to develop customer satisfaction, it can cause other departments to do a poorer job *in their terms*. Marketing department actions can increase purchasing costs, disrupt production schedules, increase inventories, and create budget headaches. Thus, the other departments may resist the marketing department's efforts.

Yet marketers must find ways to get all departments to "think consumer" and to develop a smoothly functioning value chain. The idea is to "maximize the customer experience across the organization and its various customer touch points," says one marketing consultant. Jack Welch, the highly regarded former GE CEO, told his employees, "Companies can't give job security. Only customers can!" He emphasized that all GE people, regardless of their department, have an impact on customer satisfaction and retention. His message: "If you are not thinking customer, you are not thinking."[11]

"If you are not thinking customer, you are not thinking." Jack Welch, former GE CEO

Partnering with Others in the Marketing System

In its quest to create customer value, the firm needs to look beyond its own value chain and into the value chains of its suppliers, its distributors and, ultimately, its customers. Consider McDonald's. McDonald's has nearly 30 000 restaurants in more than 100 countries that serve more than 52 million customers daily, capturing over 40 percent of the burger market.[12] People do not swarm to McDonald's only because they love the chain's hamburgers. In fact, consumers typically rank McDonald's behind Burger King and Wendy's in taste. Consumers flock to the McDonald's *system*, not just to its food products. Throughout

Toyota partners with its suppliers and helps them meet its very high expectations. Creating satisfied suppliers helps Toyota produce lower-cost, higher-quality cars, which in turn results in more satisfied customers.

Value delivery network
The network made up of the company, suppliers, distributors, and, ultimately, customers who "partner" with each other to improve the performance of the entire system.

the world, McDonald's uses a finely tuned system that delivers a high standard of what the company calls QSCV—quality, service, cleanliness, and value. McDonald's is effective only to the extent that it successfully partners with its franchisees, suppliers, and others to jointly deliver exceptionally high customer value.

More companies today are partnering with other members of their supply chain to improve the performance of the customer **value delivery network**. For example, Toyota knows the importance of building close relationships with its suppliers. In fact, it even includes the phrase "achieve supplier satisfaction" in its mission statement.

Achieving satisfying supplier relationships has been a cornerstone of Toyota's stunning success. In one recent survey of parts makers—which measured items such as degree of trust, open and honest communication, amount of help given to reduce costs, and the opportunity to make a profit—Toyota scored far higher than competitors. On a scale of 1 to 500, with an industry mean of 270, Toyota rated 415, whereas GM rated 174 and Ford rated just 162. U.S. competitors often alienate their suppliers through self-serving, heavy-handed dealings. "The [U.S. automakers] set annual cost-reduction targets [for the parts they buy]," says one supplier. "To realize those targets, they'll do anything. [They've unleashed] a reign of terror, and it gets worse every year." Says another, "[Ford] seems to send its people to 'hate school' so that they learn how to hate suppliers."

By contrast, rather than bullying suppliers Toyota partners with them and helps them to meet its very high expectations. Toyota learns about their businesses, conducts joint improvement activities, helps train supplier employees, gives daily performance feedback, and actively seeks out supplier concerns. It even recognizes top performers with annual performance awards. The high supplier satisfaction means that Toyota can rely on suppliers to help it improve its own quality, reduce costs, and develop new products quickly. For example, when Toyota recently launched a program to reduce prices by 30 percent on 170 parts that it would buy for its next generation of cars, suppliers didn't complain. Instead, they pitched in, trusting that Toyota would help them achieve the targeted reductions, in turn making them more competitive and profitable in the future. In all, creating satisfied suppliers helps Toyota to produce lower-cost, higher-quality cars, which in turn results in more satisfied customers.[13]

Increasingly in today's marketplace, competition no longer takes place between individual competitors. Rather, it takes place between the entire value delivery networks created by these competitors. Thus, Toyota's performance against Ford depends on the quality of Toyota's overall value delivery network versus Ford's. Even if Toyota makes the best cars, it might lose in the marketplace if Ford's dealer network provides more customer-satisfying sales and service.

4 | MARKETING STRATEGY AND THE MARKETING MIX

Marketing strategy
The marketing logic by which the business unit hopes to create customer value and achieve profitable customer relationships.

The strategic plan defines the company's overall mission and objectives. Marketing's role and activities are shown in Figure 2.4, which summarizes the major activities involved in managing a customer-driven marketing strategy and the marketing mix.

Consumers stand in the centre. The goal is to create value for customers and build profitable customer relationships. Next comes **marketing strategy**—the marketing logic by which the company hopes to create this customer value and achieve these profitable

Figure 2.4 Managing marketing strategies and the marketing mix

relationships. The company decides which customers it will serve (segmentation and targeting) and how it will serve them (differentiation and positioning). It identifies the total market, then divides it into smaller segments, selects the most promising segments, and focuses on serving and satisfying the customers in these segments.

Guided by marketing strategy, the company designs an integrated *marketing mix* made up of factors under its control—product, price, place, and promotion (the four Ps). To find the best marketing strategy and mix, the company engages in marketing analysis, planning, implementation, and control. Through these activities, the company watches and adapts to the actors and forces in the marketing environment. We will now look briefly at each activity. Then, in later chapters, we will discuss each one in more depth.

Customer-Driven Marketing Strategy

As we emphasized throughout Chapter 1, to succeed in today's competitive marketplace companies need to be customer centred. They must win customers from competitors, then keep and grow them by delivering greater value. But before it can satisfy consumers, a company must first understand their needs and wants. Thus, sound marketing requires a careful customer analysis.

Companies know that they cannot profitably serve all consumers in a given market—at least not all consumers in the same way. There are too many different kinds of consumers with too many different kinds of needs. And most companies are in a position to serve some segments better than others. Thus, each company must divide up the total market, choose the best segments, and design strategies for profitably serving chosen segments. This process involves *market segmentation, market targeting, differentiation*, and *positioning*.

Market Segmentation

Market segmentation
Dividing a market into distinct groups of buyers who have different needs, characteristics, or behaviours and who might require separate products or marketing programs.

The market consists of many types of customers, products, and needs. The marketer has to determine which segments offer the best opportunities. Consumers can be grouped and served in various ways based on geographic, demographic, psychographic, and behavioural factors. The process of dividing a market into distinct groups of buyers who have different needs, characteristics, or behaviours and who might require separate products or marketing programs is called **market segmentation**.

Market segment
A group of consumers who respond in a similar way to a given set of marketing efforts.

Every market has segments, but not all ways of segmenting a market are equally useful. For example, Tylenol would gain little by distinguishing between low-income and high-income pain reliever users if both respond the same way to marketing efforts. A **market segment** consists of consumers who respond in a similar way to a given set of marketing efforts. In the car market, for example, consumers who want the biggest, most comfortable car regardless of price make up one market segment. Consumers who care mainly about price and operating economy make up another segment. It would be difficult to make one car model that was the first choice of consumers in both segments. Companies are wise to focus their efforts on meeting the distinct needs of individual market segments.

Market Targeting

Market targeting
The process of evaluating each market segment's attractiveness and selecting one or more segments to enter.

After a company has defined market segments, it can enter one or many of these segments. **Market targeting** involves evaluating each market segment's attractiveness and selecting one or more segments to enter. A company should target segments in which it can profitably generate the greatest customer value and sustain it over time.

A company with limited resources might decide to serve only one or a few special segments or "market niches." Such "nichers" specialize in serving customer segments that major competitors overlook or ignore. For example, Ferrari sells only 1500 of its very high-performance cars in North America each year, but at very high prices—from an eye-opening US$190 000 for its Ferrari F430 model to an astonishing US$2 million for its FXX super sports car, which can be driven only on race tracks. Most nichers aren't quite so exotic. WhiteWave Foods, maker of Silk soymilk, has found its niche as the largest soymilk producer in North America. And Veterinary Pet Insurance is tiny compared with the insurance industry giants, but it captures a profitable 60 percent share of all health insurance policies for our furry—or feathery—friends (see Real Marketing 2.2).

Alternatively, a company might choose to serve several related segments—perhaps those with different kinds of customers but with the same basic wants. Abercrombie & Fitch, for example, targets university and college students, teens, and kids with the same upscale, casual clothes and accessories in three different outlets: the original Abercrombie & Fitch, Hollister, and Abercrombie. Or, a large company might decide to offer a complete range of products to serve all market segments.

Most companies enter a new market by serving a single segment, and if this proves successful they add more segments. Large companies eventually seek full market coverage. The leading company normally has different products designed to meet the special needs of each segment.

Sun-Rype Products Ltd., headquartered in Kelowna, British Columbia, evolved through its use of product-based and geographic segmentation. It began as a regional

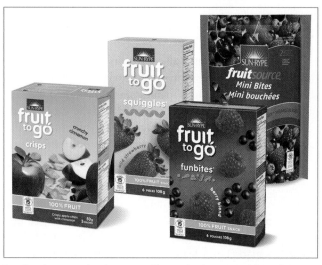

player, and thus it's not surprising that the Sun-Rype brand is the number-one player in Western Canada, holding a 55 percent share of the pure apple juice category in that region. Over the years, however, Sun-Rype has added other related products—more juice varieties and other fruit-based products, such as its Fruit to Go and Energy to Go products. Sun-Rype learned to stick to strategies based on its core competencies the hard way, however. In the mid-1990s, Sun-Rype strayed from its apple-and-fruit-based strengths and tried coffee-flavoured snack bars and granola-type bars. Because the products were outside of Sun-Rype's realm of expertise, these products' lives were short. "We're now focused on our core competencies of fruit-based juices and snacks," stressed marketing vice-president Cameron Johnston. "While diversifying from juices to fruit-based snacks was a wise fiscal and consumer move, over-diversifying to coffee and grain snacks was a mistake." With its product strategy now firmly entrenched, Sun-Rype is expanding its

Sun-Rype's strategy has been one of leveraging its core competencies to expand its product and geographic markets.

Real Marketing 2.2

Niching: Health Insurance for Our Furry—or Feathery—Friends

Health insurance for pets? Most large insurance companies haven't paid much attention to it. But that leaves plenty of room for more focused nichers, for whom pet health insurance has become a lucrative business. The largest of the small competitors is Veterinary Pet Insurance (VPI). VPI's mission is to "make the miracles of veterinary medicine affordable to all pet owners."

Pet insurance is a still-small but fast-growing segment of the insurance business. Insiders think the industry offers huge potential. Currently, 63 percent of all North American households own at least one pet. Collectively, North Americans own some 82 million dogs, 97 million cats, 156 million freshwater fish, 11 million saltwater fish, 17 million birds, 26 million small animals, 14 million reptiles, and 15 million horses. More than two-thirds have included their pets in holiday celebrations and one-third characterize their pet as a child. Some 42 percent of dogs now sleep in the same bed as their owners. North Americans spend a whopping US$45 billion a year on their pets, more than the gross domestic product of all but 64 countries in the world. They spend US$10.8 billion of that on pet health care.

Unlike in Britain and Sweden, where almost half of all pets owners carry pet health insurance, relatively few pet owners in North America currently carry such coverage. However, a recent study of pet owners found that nearly 75 percent are willing to go into debt to pay for veterinary care for their furry—or feathery—companions. And for many pet medical procedures, they'd have to! If not diagnosed quickly, even a mundane ear infection in a dog can result in $1000 worth of medical treatment. Ten days of dialysis treatment can reach $12 000 and cancer treatment as much as $40 000. All of this adds up to a lot of potential growth for pet health insurers.

VPI plans cover a multitude of pet medical problems and conditions. The insurance helps pay for office calls, prescriptions, treatments, lab fees, X-rays, surgery, and hospitalization. Like its handful of competitors, VPI issues health insurance policies for dogs and cats. Unlike its competitors, VPI covers a menagerie of exotic pets as well. Among other critters, the Avian and Exotic Pet Plan covers birds, rabbits, ferrets, rats, guinea pigs, snakes and other reptiles, iguanas, turtles, hedgehogs, and potbellied pigs. "There's such a vast array of pets," says a VPI executive, "and people love them. We have to respect that."

How's VPI doing in its niche? It's growing like a newborn puppy. VPI is by far the largest of the handful of companies that offer pet insurance, providing more than 60 percent of all U.S. pet insurance policies. Since its inception, VPI has issued more than 1 million policies, and it now serves more than 460 000 policyholders. Sales have grown rapidly, exceeding US$148 million in policy premiums last year. That might not amount to much for the likes of the big insurance corporations, which rack up tens of billions of dollars in yearly revenues. But it's profitable business for nichers like VPI. And there's room to grow. Only about 3 percent of pet owners currently buy pet insurance.

"Pet health insurance is no longer deemed so outlandish in a world where acupuncture for cats, hospice of dogs, and Prozac for ferrets are part of a veterinarian's routine," says one analyst. Such insurance is a real godsend for VPI's policyholders. Just ask Joe and Paula Sena, whose cocker spaniel, Elvis, is receiving radiation treatments for cancer. "He is not like our kids—he is our kid," says Paula. "He is a kid in a dog's body." VPI is making Elvis's treatment

Nichers: Market nicher VPI is growing faster than a newborn puppy. Its mission is to be the "trusted choice" of pet lovers.

possible by picking up the lion's share of the costs. As more people adopt the Senas' view toward their pets, it's hard to think the pet industry isn't just beginning to stretch its paws.

Sources: See Diane Brady and Christopher Palmeri, "The Pet Economy," *BusinessWeek*, August 6, 2007, pp. 45–54; Yilu Zhao, "Break a Leg, Fluffy, If You Have Insurance," *New York Times*, June 30, 2002, p. 9, 11; Damon Darlin, "Vet Bills and the Priceless Pet: What's a Practical Owner

to Do?" *New York Times*, May 13, 2006, p. C1; "New National Pet Owners Survey Details Two Decades of Evolving American Pet Ownership," American Pet Products Manufacturers Association, June 18, 2007, accessed at **www.appma.com**; "Multiple Pet Owners with VPI Pet Insurance Represent 17% of All Policyholders," *PR Newswire*, July 30, 2007, p. 1; "All in the Family," *Marketing Management*, January/February 2008, p. 7; and information accessed at **www.petinsurance.com**, September 2008.

Positioning
Arranging for a product to occupy a clear, distinctive, and desirable place relative to competing products in the minds of target consumers.

Differentiation
Actually differentiating the market offering to create superior customer value.

share of central and eastern Canadian marketplaces, and its Fruit to Go and Energy to Go bars command a 31 percent share of this broader market.[14]

Market Differentiation and Positioning

After a company has decided which market segments to enter, it must decide how it will differentiate its market offering for each targeted segment and what positions it wants to occupy in those segments. A product's *position* is the place the product occupies relative to competitors' products in consumers' minds. Marketers want to develop unique market positions for their products. If a product is perceived to be exactly like others on the market, consumers would have no reason to buy it.

Positioning is arranging for a product to occupy a clear, distinctive, and desirable place relative to competing products in the minds of target consumers. As one positioning expert puts it, positioning is "why a shopper will pay a little more for your brand."[15] Marketers plan positions that distinguish their products from competing brands and give them the greatest advantage in their target markets.

Thus, Walmart promises "Save Money. Live Better."; Target says "Expect More. Pay Less."; MasterCard gives you "priceless" experiences; and whether it's an everyday moment or the moment of a lifetime, "Life Takes VISA." Similarly, Epicurious.com is a site "for people who love to eat." Its ads tell you to "get closer to your food." Such deceptively simple statements form the backbone of a product's marketing strategy. For example, VISA has designed its entire integrated marketing campaign around the "Life Takes VISA" slogan.

In positioning its product, the company first identifies possible customer value differences that provide competitive advantages upon which to build the position. The company can offer greater customer value either by charging lower prices than competitors, or by offering more benefits to justify higher prices. But if the company *promises* greater value, it must then *deliver* that greater value. Thus, effective positioning begins with **differentiation**—actually *differentiating* the company's market offering so that it gives consumers more value. Once the company has chosen a desired position, it must take strong steps to deliver and communicate that position to target consumers. The company's entire marketing program should support the chosen positioning strategy.

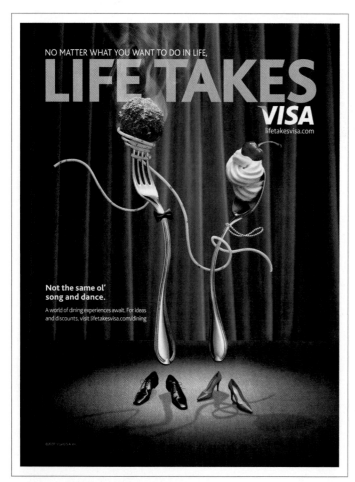

Positioning: VISA has designed its entire integrated marketing campaign around the deceptively simple "Life Takes VISA" slogan. Ads like this one take you to Life-TakesVisa.com microsites with articles, tips, and special offers tailored to specific interests and lifestyles—here the world of food and restaurants.

Developing an Integrated Marketing Mix

After deciding on its overall marketing strategy, the company is ready to begin planning the details of the marketing mix, one of the major concepts in modern marketing. The **marketing mix** is the set of controllable, tactical marketing tools that the firm blends to produce the response it wants in the target market. The marketing mix consists of everything the firm can do to influence the demand for its product. The many possibilities can be collected into four groups of variables known as "the four Ps": *product, price, place,* and *promotion*. Figure 2.5 shows the marketing tools under each P.

Product means the goods-and-services combination the company offers to the target market. Thus, a Ford Escape consists of nuts and bolts, spark plugs, pistons, headlights, and thousands of other parts. Ford offers several Escape models and dozens of optional features. The car comes fully serviced and with a comprehensive warranty that is as much a part of the product as the tailpipe.

Price is the amount of money customers must pay to obtain the product. Ford calculates suggested retail prices that its dealers might charge for each Escape. But Ford dealers rarely charge the full sticker price. Instead, they negotiate the price with each customer, offering discounts, trade-in allowances, and credit terms. These actions adjust prices for the current competitive situation and bring them into line with the buyer's perception of the car's value.

Place includes company activities that make the product available to target consumers. Ford partners with a large body of independently owned dealerships that sell the company's many different models. Ford selects its dealers carefully and supports them strongly. The dealers keep an inventory of Ford automobiles, demonstrate them to potential buyers, negotiate prices, close sales, and service the cars after the sale.

Promotion means activities that communicate the merits of the product and persuade target customers to buy it. Ford Motor Company spends more than US$2.5 billion each year on advertising to tell consumers about the company and its many products.[16] Dealership salespeople assist potential buyers and persuade them that Ford is the best car for them. Ford and its dealers offer special promotions—sales, cash rebates, low-financing rates—as added purchase incentives.

An effective marketing program blends all of the marketing mix elements into an integrated marketing program designed to achieve the company's marketing objectives by delivering value to consumers. The marketing mix constitutes the company's tactical tool kit for establishing strong positioning in target markets.

Marketing mix
The set of controllable, tactical marketing tools—product, price, place, and promotion—that the firm blends to produce the response it wants in the target market.

Figure 2.5 The four Ps of the marketing mix

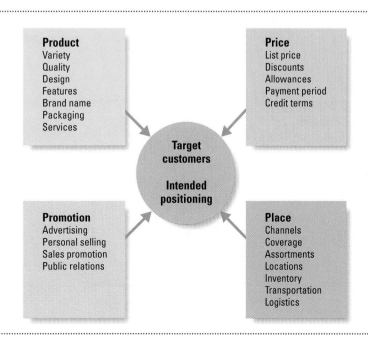

Some critics think that the four Ps may omit or underemphasize certain important activities. For example, they ask, "Where are services?" Just because they don't start with a P doesn't justify omitting them. The answer is that services, such as banking, airline, and retailing services, are products too. We might call them *service products*. "Where is packaging?" the critics might ask. Marketers would answer that they include packaging as just one of many product decisions. All said, as Figure 2.5 suggests, many marketing activities that might appear to be left out of the marketing mix are subsumed under one of the four Ps. The issue is not whether there should be four, six, or ten Ps so much as what framework is most helpful in designing integrated marketing programs.

There is another concern, however, that is valid. It holds that the four Ps concept takes the seller's view of the market, not the buyer's view. From the buyer's viewpoint, in this age of customer value and relationships, the four Ps might be better described as the four Cs:[17]

4Ps	4Cs
Product	Customer solution
Price	Customer cost
Place	Convenience
Promotion	Communication

Thus, whereas marketers see themselves as selling products, customers see themselves as buying value or solutions to their problems. And customers are interested in more than just the price; they are interested in the total costs of obtaining, using, and disposing of a product. Customers want the product and service to be as conveniently available as possible. Finally, they want two-way communication. Marketers would do well to think through the four Cs first and then build the four Ps on that platform.

5 | MANAGING THE MARKETING EFFORT

In addition to being good at the *marketing* in marketing management, companies also need to pay attention to the *management*. Managing the marketing process requires the four marketing management functions shown in Figure 2.6—*analysis, planning, implementation*, and *control*. The company first develops companywide strategic plans and then translates them into marketing and other plans for each division, product, and brand. Through implementation, the company turns the plans into actions. Control consists of measuring and evaluating the results of marketing activities and taking corrective action where needed. Finally, marketing analysis provides information and evaluations needed for all of the other marketing activities.

Figure 2.6 Managing marketing: Analysis, planning, implementation, and control

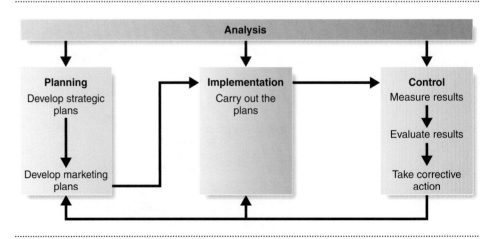

Marketing Analysis

Managing the marketing function begins with a complete analysis of the company's situation. The marketer should conduct a **SWOT analysis**, by which it evaluates the company's overall strengths (S), weaknesses (W), opportunities (O), and threats (T) (see Figure 2.7). Strengths include internal capabilities, resources, and positive situational factors that may help the company to serve its customers and achieve its objectives. Weaknesses include internal limitations and negative situational factors that may interfere with the company's performance. Opportunities are favourable factors or trends in the external environment that the company may be able to exploit to its advantage. And threats are unfavourable external factors or trends that may present challenges to performance.

The company should analyze its markets and marketing environment to find attractive opportunities and identify environmental threats. It should analyze company strengths and weaknesses as well as current and possible marketing actions to determine which opportunities it can best pursue. The goal is to match the company's strengths to attractive opportunities in the environment, while eliminating or overcoming the weaknesses and minimizing the threats. Marketing analysis provides inputs to each of the other marketing management functions. We discuss marketing analysis more fully in Chapter 3.

Marketing Planning

Through strategic planning, the company decides what it wants to do with each business unit. Marketing planning involves deciding on marketing strategies that will help the company attain its overall strategic objectives. A detailed marketing plan is needed for each business, product, or brand. What does a marketing plan look like? Our discussion focuses on product or brand marketing plans.

Table 2.2 outlines the major sections of a typical product or brand marketing plan. (See Appendix 2 for a sample marketing plan.) The plan begins with an executive summary that quickly reviews major assessments, goals, and recommendations. The main section of the plan presents a detailed SWOT analysis of the current marketing situation as well as potential threats and opportunities. The plan next states major objectives for the brand and outlines the specifics of a marketing strategy for achieving them.

A *marketing strategy* consists of specific strategies for target markets, positioning, the marketing mix, and marketing expenditure levels. It outlines how the company intends to create value for target customers to capture value in return. In this section, the planner explains how each strategy responds to the threats, opportunities, and critical issues spelled out earlier in the plan. Additional sections of the marketing plan lay out an action program for implementing the marketing strategy along with the details of a supporting *marketing budget*. The last section outlines the controls that will be used to monitor progress, measure return on marketing investment, and take corrective action.

Figure 2.7 SWOT analysis: Strengths (S), weaknesses (W), opportunities (O), and threats (T)

	Positive	**Negative**
Internal	**Strengths** Internal capabilities that may help a company reach its objectives	**Weaknesses** Internal limitations that may interfere with a company's ability to achieve its objectives
External	**Opportunities** External factors that the company may be able to exploit to its advantage	**Threats** Current and emerging external factors that may challenge the company's performance

Table 2.2 Contents of a Marketing Plan

Section	Purpose
Executive summary	Presents a brief summary of the main goals and recommendations of the plan for management review, helping top management find the plan's major points quickly. A table of contents should follow the executive summary.
Current marketing situation	Describes the target market and company's position in it, including information about the market, product performance, competition, and distribution. This section includes: • a market description that defines the market and major segments then reviews customer needs and factors in the marketing environment that may affect customer purchasing • a product review that shows sales, prices, and gross margins of the major products in the product line • a review of the competition that identifies major competitors and assesses their market positions and strategies for product quality, pricing, distribution, and promotion • a review of distribution that evaluates recent sales trends and other developments in major distribution channels
Threats and opportunities analysis	Assesses major threats and opportunities that the product might face, helping management anticipate important positive or negative developments that might have an impact on the firm and its strategies.
Objectives and issues	States the marketing objectives that the company would like to attain during the plan's term and discusses key issues that will affect their attainment. For example, if the goal is to achieve a 15 percent market share, this section looks at how this goal might be achieved.
Marketing strategy	Outlines the broad marketing logic by which the business unit hopes to create customer value and relationships and the specifics of target markets, positioning, and marketing expenditure levels. How will the company create value for customers to capture value from customers in return? This section also outlines specific strategies for each marketing mix element and explains how each responds to the threats, opportunities, and critical issues spelled out earlier in the plan.
Action programs	Spells out how marketing strategies will be turned into specific action programs that answer the following questions: What will be done? When will it be done? Who will do it? How much will it cost?
Budgets	Details a supporting marketing budget that is essentially a projected profit-and-loss statement. It shows expected revenues (forecasted number of units sold and the average net price) and expected costs of production, distribution, and marketing. The difference is the projected profit. Once approved by higher management, the budget becomes the basis for materials buying, production scheduling, personnel planning, and marketing operations.
Controls	Outlines the control that will be used to monitor progress and allow higher management to review implementation results and spot products that are not meeting their goals. It includes measures of return on marketing investment.

Marketing Implementation

Planning good strategies is only a start toward successful marketing. A brilliant marketing strategy counts for little if the company fails to implement it properly. **Marketing implementation** is the process that turns marketing *plans* into marketing *actions* to accomplish strategic marketing objectives. Whereas marketing planning addresses the *what* and *why* of marketing activities, implementation addresses the *who, where, when*, and *how*.

Many managers think that "doing things right" (implementation) is as important as, or even more important than, "doing the right things" (strategy). The fact is that both are critical to success, and companies can gain competitive advantages through effective implementation. One firm can have essentially the same strategy as another yet win in the marketplace through faster or better execution. Still, implementation is difficult—it is often easier to think up good marketing strategies than it is to carry them out.

In an increasingly connected world, people at all levels of the marketing system must work together to implement marketing strategies and plans. At Black & Decker, for example, marketing implementation for the company's power tools, outdoor equipment, and other products requires day-to-day decisions and actions by thousands of people both inside and outside the organization. Marketing managers make decisions about target

Marketing implementation
The process that turns marketing strategies and plans into marketing actions to accomplish strategic marketing objectives.

segments, branding, packaging, pricing, promoting, and distributing. They talk with engineering about product design, with manufacturing about production and inventory levels, and with finance about funding and cash flows. They also connect with outside people, such as advertising agencies to plan ad campaigns and the news media to obtain publicity support. The sales force urges Home Depot, RONA, Home Hardware, and other retailers to advertise Black & Decker products, provide ample shelf space, and use company displays.

To see this in action, check out the sample marketing plan in Appendix 2.

Marketing Department Organization

The company must design a marketing organization that can carry out marketing strategies and plans. If the company is very small, one person might do all of the research, selling, advertising, customer service, and other marketing work. As the company expands, a marketing department emerges to plan and carry out marketing activities. In large companies, this department contains many specialists. They have product and market managers, sales managers and salespeople, market researchers, advertising experts, and many other specialists.

To head up such large marketing organizations, many companies have now created a *chief marketing officer* (CMO) position. The CMO heads up the company's entire marketing operation and represents marketing on the company's top management team. The CMO position puts marketing on equal footing with other C-level executives, such as the chief executive officer (CEO) and the chief financial officer (CFO).[18]

Modern marketing departments can be arranged in several ways. The most common form of marketing organization is the *functional organization*. Under this organization, different marketing activities are headed by a functional specialist—a sales manager, advertising manager, marketing research manager, customer service manager, or new-product manager. A company that sells across the country or internationally often uses a *geographic organization*. Its sales and marketing people are assigned to specific countries, regions, or districts. Geographic organization allows salespeople to settle into a territory, get to know their customers, and work with a minimum of travel time and cost.

Companies with many very different products or brands often create a *product management organization*. Using this approach, a product manager develops and implements a complete strategy and marketing program for a specific product or brand. Product management first appeared at Procter & Gamble in 1929. A new company soap, Camay, was not doing well and a young P&G executive was assigned to give his exclusive attention to developing and promoting this product. He was successful, and the company soon added other product managers.[19] Since then, many firms, especially consumer-products companies, have set up product management organizations.

For companies that sell one product line to many different types of markets and customers that have different needs and preferences, a *market* or *customer management organization* might be best. A market management organization is similar to the product management organization. Market managers are responsible for developing marketing strategies and plans for their specific markets or customers. This system's main advantage is that the company is organized around the needs of specific customer segments. Many companies develop special organizations to manage their relationships with large customers. For example, companies such as Procter & Gamble and Black & Decker have large teams, or even whole divisions, set up to serve large customers such as Walmart, Zellers, Sobeys, or Home Depot.

Large companies that produce many different products flowing into many different geographic and customer markets usually employ some *combination* of the functional, geographic, product, and market organization forms. This ensures that each function, product, and market receives its share of management attention. However, it can also add costly layers of management and reduce organizational flexibility. Still, the benefits of organizational specialization usually outweigh the drawbacks.

Marketing organization has become an increasingly important issue in recent years. As we discussed in Chapter 1, today's marketing environment calls for less focus on products, brands, and territories and more focus on customer relationships. More and more, companies

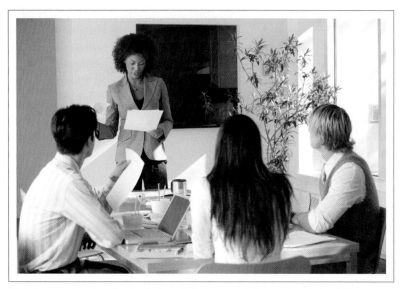

Marketers must continually plan their analysis, implementation, and control activities.

Marketing control
The process of measuring and evaluating the results of marketing strategies and plans and taking corrective action to ensure that objectives are achieved.

are shifting their brand management focus toward *customer management*—moving away from managing just product or brand profitability and toward managing profitability and customer equity. They think of themselves not as managing portfolios of brands, but as managing portfolios of customers.

Marketing Control

Because many surprises occur during the implementation of marketing plans, marketers must practise constant **marketing control**—evaluating the results of marketing strategies and plans and taking corrective action to ensure that objectives are attained. Marketing control involves four steps. Management first sets specific marketing goals. It then measures its performance in the marketplace and evaluates the causes of any differences between expected and actual performance. Finally, management takes corrective action to close the gaps between its goals and its performance. This may require changing the action programs or even changing the goals.

Operating control involves checking ongoing performance against the annual plan and taking corrective action when necessary. Its purpose is to ensure that the company achieves the sales, profits, and other goals set out in its annual plan. It also involves determining the profitability of different products, territories, markets, and channels. *Strategic control* involves looking at whether the company's basic strategies are well matched to its opportunities. Marketing strategies and programs can quickly become outdated, and each company should periodically reassess its overall approach to the marketplace.

The marketing audit covers *all* major marketing areas of a business, not just a few trouble spots. It assesses the marketing environment, marketing strategy, marketing organization, marketing systems, marketing mix, and marketing productivity and profitability. The audit is normally conducted by an objective and experienced outside party. The findings may come as a surprise—and sometimes as a shock—to management. Management then decides which actions make sense and how and when to implement them.

MEASURING AND MANAGING RETURN ON MARKETING INVESTMENT

Marketing managers must ensure that their marketing dollars are being well spent. In the past, many marketers spent freely on big, expensive marketing programs, often without thinking carefully about the financial returns on their spending. They believed that marketing produces intangible outcomes, which do not lend themselves readily to measures of productivity or return. But all that is changing:

> For years, corporate marketers have walked into budget meetings like neighbourhood junkies. They couldn't always justify how well they spent past handouts or what difference it all made. They just wanted more money—for flashy TV ads, for big-ticket events, for, you know, getting out the message and building up the brand. But those heady days of blind budget increases are fast being replaced with a new mantra: measurement and accountability. Armed with reams of data, increasingly sophisticated tools, and growing evidence that the old tricks simply don't work, there's hardly a marketing executive today who isn't demanding a more scientific approach to help defend marketing strategies in front of the chief financial officer. Marketers want to know the actual return on

investment (ROI) of each dollar. They want to know it often, not just annually. . . . Companies in every segment of business have become obsessed with honing the science of measuring marketing performance. "Marketers have been pretty unaccountable for many years," notes one expert. "Now they are under big pressure to estimate their impact."[20]

In response, marketers are developing better measures of *return on marketing investment.*

Return on marketing investment (or marketing ROI)
The net return from a marketing investment divided by the costs of the marketing investment.

Return on marketing investment (or *marketing ROI*) is the net return from a marketing investment divided by the costs of the marketing investment. It measures the profits generated by investments in marketing activities.

It's true that marketing returns can be difficult to measure. In measuring financial ROI, both the *R* and the *I* are uniformly measured in dollars. But there is as of yet no consistent definition of marketing ROI. "It's tough to measure, more so than for other business expenses," says one analyst. "You can imagine buying a piece of equipment . . . and then measuring the productivity gains that result from the purchase," he says. "But in marketing, benefits like advertising impact aren't easily put into dollar returns. It takes a leap of faith to come up with a number."[21]

One recent survey of CMOs from top marketing companies found that "make marketing accountable" emerged as a top strategic theme, second only to "put the consumer at the heart of marketing." However, another recent survey of top marketing executives found that although 58 percent of the companies surveyed have formal accountability programs, only 28 percent are satisfied with their ability to use marketing ROI measures to take action.[22]

A company can assess return on marketing in terms of standard marketing performance measures, such as brand awareness, sales, or market share. Many companies are assembling such measures into *marketing dashboards*—meaningful sets of marketing performance measures in a single display used to monitor strategic marketing performance. Just as automobile dashboards present drivers with details on how their cars are performing, the marketing dashboard gives marketers the detailed measures they need to assess and adjust their marketing strategies.[23]

Increasingly, however, beyond standard performance measures, marketers are using customer-centred measures of marketing impact, such as customer acquisition, customer retention, customer lifetime value, and customer equity. These measures capture not just current marketing performance but also future performance resulting from stronger customer relationships. Figure 2.8 views marketing expenditures as investments that produce returns in the form of more profitable customer relationships.[24] Marketing investments result in improved customer value and satisfaction, which in turn increases customer attraction and retention. This increases individual customer lifetime values and the firm's overall customer equity. Increased customer equity, in relation to the cost of the marketing investments, determines return on marketing investment.

Regardless of how it's defined or measured, the return on marketing investment concept is here to stay. "Marketing ROI is at the heart of every business," says an AT&T marketing executive. "[We've added another P to the marketing mix]—for *profit and loss* or *performance*. We absolutely have to . . . quantify the impact of marketing on the business. You can't improve what you can't measure."[25]

Many companies are assembling marketing dashboards—meaningful sets of marketing performance measures in a single display used to set and adjust their marketing strategies.

Figure 2.8 Return on marketing investment

Source: Adapted from Roland T. Rust, Katherine N. Lemon, and Valerie A. Zeithaml, "Return on Marketing: Using Consumer Equity to Focus Marketing Strategy," *Journal of Marketing*, January 2004, p. 112.

REVIEWING OBJECTIVES AND KEY TERMS

 | Audio Chapter Summary

In Chapter 1, we defined *marketing* and outlined the steps in the marketing process. In this chapter, we examined companywide strategic planning and marketing's role in the organization. Then, we looked more deeply into marketing strategy and the marketing mix and reviewed the major marketing management functions. So you've now had a pretty good overview of the fundamentals of modern marketing. In future chapters, we'll expand on these fundamentals.

OBJECTIVE 1   Explain companywide strategic planning and its four steps.

Strategic planning sets the stage for the rest of the company's planning. Marketing contributes to strategic planning, and the overall plan defines marketing's role in the company. Although formal planning offers a variety of benefits to companies, not all companies use it or use it well.

Strategic planning involves developing a strategy for long-run survival and growth. It consists of four steps: defining the company's mission, setting objectives and goals, designing a business portfolio, and developing functional plans. *Defining a clear company mission* is done by drafting a formal mission statement, which should be market oriented, realistic, specific, motivating, and consistent with the market environment. The mission is then transformed into detailed *supporting goals and objectives* to guide the entire company. Based on those goals and objectives, headquarters designs a *business portfolio*, deciding which businesses and products should receive more or fewer resources. In turn, each business and product unit must develop *detailed marketing plans* in line with the companywide plan.

OBJECTIVE 2   Discuss how to design business portfolios and develop growth strategies.

Guided by the company's mission statement and objectives, management plans its *business portfolio*, or the collection of businesses and products that make up the company. The firm wants to produce a business portfolio that best fits its strengths and weaknesses to opportunities in the environment. To do this, it must analyze and adjust its *current* business portfolio and develop growth and downsizing strategies for adjusting the *future* portfolio. The company might use a formal portfolio-planning method. But many companies are now designing more customized portfolio-planning approaches that better suit their unique situations. The *product/market expansion grid* suggests four possible growth paths: market penetration, market development, product development, and diversification.

OBJECTIVE 3   Explain marketing's role in strategic planning and how marketing works with its partners to create and deliver customer value.

Under the strategic plan, the major functional departments—marketing, finance, accounting, purchasing, operations, information systems, human resources, and others—must work together to accomplish strategic objectives. Marketing plays a key role in the company's strategic planning by providing a *marketing concept philosophy* and *inputs* regarding attractive market opportunities. Within individual business units, marketing designs strategies for reaching the unit's objectives and helps carry them out profitably.

Marketers alone cannot produce superior value for customers. A company's success depends on how well each department performs its customer value-adding activities and how well the departments work together to serve the customer. Thus, marketers must practise *partner relationship management*. They must work closely with partners in other departments to form an effective *value chain* that serves the customer. And they must partner effectively with other companies in the marketing system to form a competitively superior *value delivery network*.

OBJECTIVE 4 **Describe the elements of a customer-driven marketing strategy and mix and the forces that influence it.**

Consumer value and relationships are at the centre of marketing strategy and programs. Through market segmentation, targeting, differentiation, and positioning, the company divides the total market into smaller segments, selects segments it can best serve, and decides how it wants to bring value to target consumers. It then designs an *integrated marketing mix* to produce the response it wants in the target market. The marketing mix consists of product, price, place, and promotion decisions.

OBJECTIVE 5 **List the marketing management functions, including the elements of a marketing plan, and discuss the importance of measuring and managing return on marketing investment.**

To find the best strategy and mix and to put them into action, the company engages in marketing analysis, planning,

implementation, and control. The main components of a *marketing plan* are the executive summary, current marketing situation, threats and opportunities, objectives and issues, marketing strategies, action programs, budgets, and controls. To plan good strategies is often easier than to carry them out. To be successful, companies must also be effective at *implementation*—turning marketing strategies into marketing actions.

Much of the responsibility for implementation goes to the company's marketing department. Marketing departments can be organized in one or a combination of ways: *functional marketing organization, geographic organization, product management organization*, or *market management organization*. In this age of customer relationships, more and more companies are now changing their organizational focus from product or territory management to customer relationship management.

Marketing organizations carry out *marketing control*, both operating control and strategic control. They use *marketing audits* to determine marketing opportunities and problems and to recommend short-run and long-run actions to improve overall marketing performance.

Marketing managers must ensure that their marketing dollars are being well spent. Today's marketers face growing pressures to show that they are adding value in line with their costs. In response, marketers are developing better measures of *return on marketing investment*. Increasingly, they are using customer-centred measures of marketing impact as a key input into their strategic decision making.

KEY TERMS

mymarketinglab | Glossary Flashcards

DISCUSSING THE CONCEPTS

1. Define strategic planning and briefly describe the four steps that lead managers and the firm through the strategic planning process. Discuss the role marketing plays in this process.

2. Describe the Boston Consulting Group's approach to portfolio analysis. Briefly discuss why management may find it difficult to dispose of a "question mark."

3. Name and describe the four product/market expansion grid strategies. KFC is now rolling out a new Kentucky Grilled Chicken line to add to its traditional fried chicken lineup. Which growth strategy does this represent?

4. Discuss the differences between market segmentation, targeting, differentiation, and positioning. What two simple questions do they address?

5. Define each of the four Ps. Does the four Ps framework do an adequate job of describing marketer responsibilities in preparing and managing marketing programs? Why or why not? Do you see any issues with this framework in relation to service products?

6. What is return on marketing investment? Why is it difficult to measure?

APPLYING THE CONCEPTS

1. Explain what a SWOT analysis involves. Develop a SWOT analysis for a travel agency in your community.

2. In a small group, discuss whether the following statement from Burton Snowboards, manufacturers and marketers of a leading snowboard brand, meets the five criteria of a good mission statement: "Burton Snowboards is a rider-driven company solely dedicated to creating the best snowboarding equipment on the planet."

3. Explain the role of a chief marketing officer (CMO). Learn more about this C-level executive position and find an article that describes the importance of this position, the characteristics of an effective CMO, or any issues surrounding this position.

FOCUS ON TECHNOLOGY

Mobile marketing is touted as the next "big thing," offering the promise of connecting with consumers on the most personal medium—their cellphones. Technological advances are letting marketers send not only text messages to cellphones, but also video messages. In Japan, QR Codes (quick response codes), originally developed for manufacturing purposes, are now placed on outdoor, print, and other media advertisements so that consumers can snap pictures of them and be taken directly to mobile websites. Although not widely practised yet, some U.S. marketers are dabbling in mobile marketing. For example, Jaguar used a mobile campaign and sold over 1100 XFs in one month. Visa used mobile marketing in China to encourage consumers to pass video commercials on to their friends via mobile phones. Even textbook publishers are using mobile marketing to send updated information to students and teachers.

Although there are still technical roadblocks stifling rapid expansion of this marketing method, some experts claim that marketers had better jump on this bandwagon or risk being left behind.

1. Visit the Mobile Marketing Association's website at www.mmaglobal.com and click on "Resources," then choose "Case Studies" on the left. Discuss one case study and describe the factors you think made that application of mobile marketing a success.

2. Analysis is an important first step in the marketing management process. The rapid advance in mobile technology poses opportunities as well as threats for marketers. Discuss both the opportunities and threats for marketers.

FOCUS ON ETHICS

"Ever felt like everything happens at once? Well sometimes it does, the car breaks down, the kids are sick, the dog needs to go to the vet, and then to top it off the electric bill is past due again. Rather than letting the electric company cut off your lights and your kids suffer, simply stop by and get a payday loan."[26] Sounds easy, doesn't it? Well, for many Canadians payday loans have become a necessary alternative to traditional bank loans, and the trend is growing. Edmonton-based

Cash Store Financial, which has 415 stores across Canada, and Money Mart with over 350 have announced record profits in 2008 with plans for further market expansion in 2009. The Canadian Payday Loan Association, which represents 20 payday loan companies, maintains that its members provide a valuable service to cash-strapped consumers, but consumer advocate groups disagree, arguing that these firms prey on those who can least afford their services—low-income families who do not qualify for low-interest bank loans. In fact, according to Credit Canada, a not-for-profit credit counselling service, Canadians are now carrying in excess of $1 trillion in personal debt, and provincial governments across the nation are now enacting legislation to protect consumers from excessive interest rates charged by many of these payday loan companies.

1. What are the current and emerging external factors (that is, opportunities and threats) contributing to the growth of payday loan companies in Canada?

2. Visit www.apaydayloan.ca and answer the following questions: First, what are they offering consumers? Do you see any problems with the service they provide? Explain. Click on the online loan application link and calculate the cost of borrowing $500 for one month. Do the cost of borrowing and the annualized interest rate surprise you? What are the implications for consumer debt in Canada? In your opinion, are payday loan companies offering a legitimate service to consumers or are they merely loan sharks in disguise?

MARKETING BY THE NUMBERS

Appendix 3, Marketing by the Numbers, discusses other marketing profitability metrics beyond the return on marketing investment (marketing ROI) measure described in this chapter. The following is a profit-and-loss statement for a business. Review Appendix 3 and answer the following questions:

1. Calculate the net marketing contribution (NMC) for this company.

2. Calculate both marketing return on sales (or marketing ROS) and marketing return on investment (or marketing ROI) as described in Appendix 3. Is this company doing well?

Net sales		$800,000,000
Cost of goods sold		(375,000,000)
Gross margin		$425,000,000
Marketing Expenses		
Sales expenses	$70,000,000	
Promotion expenses	30,000,000	
		(100,000,000)
General and Administrative Expenses		
Marketing salaries and expenses	$10,000,000	
Indirect overhead	60,000,000	(70,000,000)
Net profit before income tax		$255,000,000

VIDEO CASE

mymarketinglab | Video Case Questions

Live Nation

Live Nation may not be a household name, but if you've been to a concert in the past few years, chances are you've purchased a Live Nation product. In fact, Live Nation has been the country's largest concert promoter for many years, promoting as many as 29 000 events annually. But through very savvy strategic planning, Live Nation is shaking up the structure of the music industry.

A recent $120 million deal with Madonna illustrates how this concert promoter is diving into other businesses as well. Under this deal, Live Nation will become Madonna's record label, concert promoter, ticket vendor, and merchan-

dise agent. Similar deals have been reached with other performers such as Jay-Z and U2.

But contracting with artists is only part of the picture. Live Nation is partnering with other corporations as well. A venture with Citi will expand its reach to potential customers through a leveraging of database technologies. And joining forces with ticket reseller powerhouses such as Stub-Hub will give Live Nation a position in the thriving business of secondary ticket sales.

After viewing the video featuring Live Nation, answer the following questions about the role of strategic planning:

1. What is Live Nation's mission?

2. Based on the product/market expansion grid, provide support for the strategy that Live Nation is pursuing.

3. How does Live Nation's strategy provide better value for customers?

Visit MyMarketingLab at www.pearsoned.ca/mymarketinglab to view the video segment related to this case.

COMPANY CASE

Trap-Ease America: The Big Cheese of Mousetraps

Conventional Wisdom

One April morning, Martha House, president of Trap-Ease America, entered her office in Costa Mesa, California. She paused for a moment to contemplate the Ralph Waldo Emerson quote that she had framed and hung near her desk:

> If a man [can] . . . make a better mousetrap than his neighbour . . . the world will make a beaten path to his door.

Perhaps, she mused, Emerson knew something that she didn't. She *had* the better mousetrap—Trap-Ease—but the world didn't seem all that excited about it.

The National Hardware Show

Martha had just returned from the National Hardware Show in Chicago. Standing in the trade show display booth for long hours and answering the same questions hundreds of times had been tiring. Yet all the hard work had paid off. Each year, National Hardware Show officials held a contest to select the best new product introduced at that year's show. The Trap-Ease had won the contest this year, beating out over 300 new products.

Such notoriety was not new for the Trap-Ease mousetrap, however. *People* magazine had run a feature article on the trap, and the trap had been the subject of numerous talk shows and articles in various popular press and trade publications.

Despite all of this attention, however, the expected demand for the trap had not materialized. Martha hoped that this award might stimulate increased interest and sales.

Background

A group of investors had formed Trap-Ease America in January after it had obtained worldwide rights to market the innovative mousetrap. In return for marketing rights, the group agreed to pay the inventor and patent holder, a retired rancher, a royalty fee for each trap sold. The group then hired Martha to serve as president and to develop and manage the Trap-Ease America organization.

Trap-Ease America contracted with a plastics-manufacturing firm to produce the traps. The trap consists of a square, plastic tube measuring about 6 inches long and 1-1/2 inches in diameter. The tube bends in the middle at a 30-degree angle, so that when the front part of the tube rests on a flat surface the other end is elevated. The elevated end holds a removable cap into which the user places bait (cheese, dog food, or some other aromatic tidbit). The front end of the tube has a hinged door. When the trap is "open," this door rests on two narrow "stilts" attached to the two bottom corners of the door (see Exhibit 1).

The simple trap works very efficiently. A mouse, smelling the bait, enters the tube through the open end. As it walks up the angled bottom toward the bait, its weight makes the elevated end of the trap drop downward. This action elevates the open end, allowing the hinged door to swing closed, trapping the mouse. Small teeth on the ends of the stilts catch in a groove on the bottom of the trap, locking the door closed. The user can then dispose of the mouse while it is still alive or leave it alone for a few hours to suffocate in the trap.

Martha believes the trap has many advantages for the consumer when compared with traditional spring-loaded traps or poisons. Consumers can use it safely and easily with no risk of catching their fingers while loading it. It poses no injury or poisoning threat to children or pets. Furthermore, with Trap-Ease, consumers avoided the unpleasant "mess" they often encounter with the violent spring-loaded traps. The Trap-Ease creates no "clean-up" problem. Finally, the user can reuse the trap or simply throw it away.

Martha's early research suggested that women were the best target market for the Trap-Ease. Men, it seemed, were more willing to buy and use the traditional spring-loaded trap. The targeted women, however, did not like the traditional trap. These women often stayed at home and took care of their children. Thus, they wanted a means of dealing with a mouse problem that avoided the unpleasantness and risks that the standard trap created in the home.

To reach this target market, Martha decided to distribute Trap-Ease through national grocery, hardware, and drugstore chains. She sold the trap directly to these large retailers, avoiding any wholesalers or other middlemen.

The traps sell in packages of two, with a suggested retail price of US$2.49. Although this price makes the Trap-Ease about five to ten times more expensive than smaller, standard traps, consumers appeared to offer little initial price resistance. The manufacturing cost for the Trap-Ease, including freight and packaging costs, is about 31 cents per unit. The company pays an additional 8.2 cents per unit in royalty fees. Martha priced the traps to retailers at 99 cents per unit (two units to a package) and estimated that, after sales and volume discounts, Trap-Ease would produce net revenue from retailers of 75 cents per unit.

To promote the product, Martha had budgeted approximately $60 000 for the first year. She planned to use $50 000 of this amount for travel costs to visit trade shows and to make sales calls on retailers. She planned to use the remaining $10 000 for advertising. So far, however, because the mousetrap had generated so much publicity, she had not felt that she needed to do much advertising. Still, she had placed ads in *Good Housekeeping* (after all, the trap had earned the *Good Housekeeping* Seal of Approval) and in other "home and shelter" magazines. Martha is the company's only salesperson, but she intends to hire more salespeople soon.

Martha had initially forecasted Trap-Ease's first-year sales at 5 million units. Through April, however, the company had only sold several hundred thousand units. Martha wondered if most new products got off to such a slow start or if she was doing something wrong. She had detected some problems, although none seemed overly serious. For one, there had not been enough repeat buying. For another, she had noted that many of the retailers upon whom she called kept their sample mousetraps on their desks as conversation pieces—she wanted the traps to be used and demonstrated. Martha wondered if consumers were also buying the traps as novelties rather than as solutions to their mouse problems.

Martha knew that the investor group believed that Trap-Ease America had a "once-in-a-lifetime chance" with its innovative mousetrap, and she sensed the group's impatience with the company's progress so far. She had budgeted approximately $250 000 in administrative and fixed costs for the first year (not including marketing costs). To keep the investors happy, the company needed to sell enough traps to cover those costs and make a reasonable profit.

Back to the Drawing Board

In these first few months, Martha had learned that marketing a new product was not an easy task. Some customers were

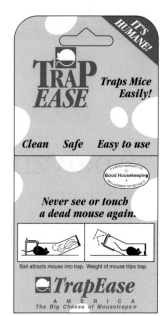

very demanding. For example, one national retailer had placed a large order with instructions that Trap-Ease America was to deliver the order to the loading dock at one of the retailer's warehouses between 1:00 and 3:00 p.m. on a specified day. When the truck delivering the order arrived after 3:00 p.m., the retailer had refused to accept the shipment. The retailer had told Martha it would be a year before she got another chance.

As Martha sat down at her desk, she realized she needed to rethink her marketing strategy. Perhaps she had missed something or made some mistake that was causing sales to be so slow. Glancing at the quotation again, she thought that perhaps she should send the picky retailer and other customers a copy of Emerson's famous quote.

Questions for Discussion

1. Martha and the Trap-Ease America investors believe they face a once-in-a-lifetime opportunity. What information do they need to evaluate this opportunity? How do you think the group would write its mission statement? How would you write it?

2. Has Martha identified the best target market for Trap-Ease? What other market segments might the firm target?

3. How has the company positioned the Trap-Ease for the chosen target market? Could it position the product in other ways?

4. Describe the current marketing mix for Trap-Ease. Do you see any problems with this mix?

5. Who is Trap-Ease America's competition?

6. How would you change Trap-Ease's marketing strategy? What kinds of control procedures would you establish for this strategy?

CHAPTER

3

Analyzing the Marketing Environment

PREVIEWING THE CONCEPTS
In Part 1 (Chapters 1 and 2), you learned about the basic concepts of marketing and the steps in the marketing process for building profitable relationships with targeted consumers. In Part 2, we'll look deeper into the first step of the marketing process—understanding the marketplace and customer needs and wants. In this chapter, you'll discover that marketing operates in a complex and changing environment. Other actors in this environment—suppliers, intermediaries, customers, competitors, publics, and others—may work with or against the company. Major environmental forces—demographic, economic, natural, technological, political, and cultural—shape marketing opportunities, pose threats, and affect the company's ability to build customer relationships. To develop effective marketing strategies, you must first understand the environment in which marketing operates.

Let's start with a look at Xerox. A half-century ago, this venerable old company harnessed changing technology to create a whole new industry—photocopying—and dominated that industry for decades. But did you know that barely a decade ago Xerox was on the verge of bankruptcy? Don't worry, the company is once again growing and profitable. But Xerox's harrowing experience provides a cautionary tale of what can happen when a company—even a dominant market leader—fails to adapt to its changing marketing environment.

Xerox introduced the first plain-paper office copier more than 50 years ago. In the decades that followed, the company that invented photocopying flat-out dominated the industry it had created. The name Xerox became almost generic for copying (as in "I'll Xerox this for you"). Through the years, Xerox fought off round after round of rivals to stay atop the fiercely competitive copier industry. Its Canadian operations were established in 1953 and the first of the revolutionary Xerox 914 copiers reached the Canadian market in 1960. By the early 1970s, Xerox Canada began manufacturing products domestically and opened its first research and development facility in Ontario. In 1998, Xerox's profits were growing at 20 percent a year and its stock price was soaring.

Then, things went terribly wrong for Xerox. The legendary company's stock and fortunes took a stomach-churning dive. In only 18 months, Xerox lost some US$38 billion in market value. By mid-2001, its stock price had plunged from almost US$70 in 1999 to under US$5. The once-dominant market leader found itself on the brink of bankruptcy. What happened? Blame it on change, or, rather, on Xerox's failure to adapt to its rapidly changing marketing environment. The world was quickly going digital but Xerox hadn't kept up.

In the new digital environment, Xerox customers no longer relied on the company's flagship products—stand-alone copiers—to share information and documents. Rather than pumping out and distributing stacks of black-and-white copies, they created digital documents and shared them electronically. Or they

Xerox's new brand logo better fits the changing digital environment, helping to complete the transformation of the company's image.

digital growth:
74%

Take a smart printer: Transcontinental Inc. Add relevant
data to a catalog run using Xerox digital technology and their
client, Reader's Digest Canada, has 74% more sales.
There's a new way to look at it.

Transcontinental Inc. thought a digital print solution could achieve a response breakthrough for Reader's Digest, one of the world's most successful direct marketers. A call to the digital experts from the Xerox 1:1 Lab more than proved them right. Using a Reader's Digest database and Xerox digital printing technology, personalized direct mail was created to test against a traditional direct mail campaign. The result? The 1-to-1 messaging outperformed the traditional by 74%. The more personalized messages simply had more pull. Could you benefit from our digital advantage? Just ask the pros at Reader's Digest and Transcontinental.

xerox.com/printing 1-800-ASK-XEROX

xerox

Xerox has rethought, redefined, and reinvented itself. The company now "connects closely with customers in a content-rich digital marketplace."

popped out copies on their nearby networked printer. On a broader level, while Xerox was busy perfecting copy machines, customers were looking for more sophisticated "document management solutions." They wanted systems that would let them scan documents in Frankfurt, weave them into colourful, customized showpieces in Calgary, and print them on demand in London—altering for British spelling.

As digital technology changed, so did Xerox's customers and competitors. Instead of selling copiers to equipment purchasing managers, Xerox found itself trying to develop and sell document management systems to high-level information technology managers. And instead of competing head-on with copy machine competitors such as Sharp, Canon, and Ricoh, Xerox was now squaring off against information technology companies such as HP and IBM.

Xerox's large and long-respected sales force—made up of those guys in the toner-stained shirts trained to sell and repair copy machines—simply wasn't equipped to deal effectively in the brave new world of digital document solutions. Xerox, the iconic "copier company," just wasn't cutting it in the new digital environment. Increasingly, Xerox found itself occupying the dusty and dying "copy machine" corner of the analogue office.

Since those dark days on the brink, however, Xerox has rethought, redefined, and reinvented itself. The company has undergone a remarkable transformation. Xerox no longer defines itself as a "copier company." In fact, it doesn't even make stand-alone copiers anymore. Instead, Xerox bills itself as "the world's leading document-management technology and services enterprise." Xerox's newly minted mission is to help companies and people "be smarter about their documents." Says the company in a recent annual report:

> Documenting any communication used to mean committing it to paper, getting it down in black and white. Now communication is generally scanned, sent, searched, archived, merged, and personalized—often in color. It can move back and forth, many times, from physical to digital. So when we say our mission is to help people be smarter about their documents, it really means giving them a range of tools and techniques to capture, organize, facilitate, and enhance how they communicate. In any form. To an audience of one or many millions.

The Xerox transformation started with a new focus on the customer. Before developing new products, Xerox researchers held seemingly endless customer focus groups. Xerox's Chief Technology Officer, Sophie Vandebroek, calls this "dreaming with the customer." The goal, she argues, is "involving experts who know the technology with customers who know the pain points. . . .

▶

OBJECTIVES

1. Describe the environmental forces that affect the company's ability to serve its customers.
2. Explain how changes in the demographic and economic environments affect marketing decisions.
3. Identify the major trends in the firm's natural and technological environments.
4. Explain the key changes in the political and cultural environments.
5. Discuss how companies can react to the marketing environment.

Ultimately innovation is about delighting the customer." Xerox even employed anthropologists, ethnographers, sociologists, and psychologists—what it calls "work-practice specialists"—to spend time with customers, understand their problems, and help develop customer-focused solutions. The new Xerox believes that understanding customers is just as important as understanding technology.

As a result, Xerox now offers a broad portfolio of customer-focused products, software, and services that help its customers manage documents and information. Xerox has introduced 100 innovative new products in the last three years. It now offers digital products and systems ranging from network printers and multifunction devices to colour printing and publishing systems, digital presses, and "book factories." It also offers an impressive array of consulting and outsourcing services that help businesses develop online document archives, operate in-house print shops or mailrooms, analyze how employees can most efficiently share documents and knowledge, and build web-based processes for personalizing direct mail, invoices, and brochures.

Now that Xerox has transformed its business, it's setting out to transform its image as well. Befitting its new identity, Xerox recently unveiled a new brand logo, retiring the staid red capital *X* and block-lettered XEROX that has dominated its logo for 40 years. In its place is "a brand identity that reflects the Xerox of today." The new brand logo consists of a bright red lowercase "xerox" that sits alongside a red sphere sketched with lines that link to form a stylized *X*. Xerox chose a ball to suggest forward movement and a holistic company, and to reflect the company's connection to customers, partners, industry, and innovation. The logo retains the good things that Xerox stands for (dependability and stability), jettisons the not-so-nice (formal, somewhat stodgy) and, most importantly, incorporates such attributes as modern, innovative, and flexible.

Like the new Xerox, the new brand logo better fits the changing digital environment. For example, the ball is designed to be animated easily for use in multimedia formats, particularly in messages that can be beamed to hand-held devices. Xerox settled on lowercase letters because they seemed friendlier and on a deeper red and a thicker font to stand out better on the Web and on high-definition television. Xerox thinks that the new logo and supporting marketing campaign will help to complete the transformation of the company's image.

Xerox CEO Anne Mulcahy sums things up this way: "We have transformed Xerox into a business that connects closely with customers in a content-rich digital marketplace. Our new brand reflects who we are, the markets we serve, and the innovation that differentiates us in our industry. We have expanded into new markets, created new businesses, acquired new capabilities, developed technologies that launched new industries—to ensure we make it easier, faster, and less costly for our customers to share information." A major Xerox customer agrees: "From the outside looking in, I've watched Xerox transition its business from a copier and printer company to a true partner in helping companies better manage information—whether it's digital, paper, or both. Changing the brand is the next logical step. Now the face of Xerox matches the tech savvy, innovative company Xerox is today."

Thus, Xerox isn't an old, fusty copier company anymore. And thanks to a truly remarkable turnaround, Xerox is once again growing and profitable. As of 2008, the company employed 3800 people and earned $1.2 billion in revenues in Canada. In 2009, Xerox Canada's CEO, Kevin Warren, was named one of the 100 most powerful executives in North America. Despite its turnaround, the message remains clear. Even the most dominant companies can be vulnerable to the often turbulent and changing marketing environment. Companies that understand and adapt well to their environments can thrive. Those that don't risk their very survival.[1]

Chapter Opening Discussion

Marketing environment
The actors and forces outside marketing that affect marketing management's ability to build and maintain successful relationships with target customers.

Microenvironment
The actors close to the company that affect its ability to serve its customers—the company, suppliers, marketing intermediaries, customer markets, competitors, and publics.

A company's **marketing environment** consists of the actors and forces outside marketing that affect marketing management's ability to build and maintain successful relationships with target customers. Like Xerox, companies constantly watch and adapt to the changing environment.

More than any other group in a company, marketers must be the environmental trend trackers and opportunity seekers. Although every manager in an organization needs to observe the outside environment, marketers have two special aptitudes. They have disciplined methods—marketing research and marketing intelligence—for collecting information about the marketing environment. They also spend more time in customer and competitor environments. By carefully studying the environment, marketers can adapt their strategies to meet new marketplace challenges and opportunities.

The marketing environment is made up of a *microenvironment* and a *macroenvironment*. The **microenvironment** consists of the actors close to the company that affect its ability to serve its customers—the company, suppliers, marketing intermediaries, customer

Macroenvironment
The larger societal forces that affect the microenvironment—demographic, economic, natural, technological, political, and cultural forces.

markets, competitors, and publics. The **macroenvironment** consists of the larger societal forces that affect the microenvironment—demographic, economic, natural, technological, political, and cultural forces. We look first at the company's microenvironment.

 1

Glossary Flashcards of Key Terms

The Company's Microenvironment

Marketing management's job is to build relationships with customers by creating customer value and satisfaction. However, marketing managers cannot do this alone. Figure 3.1 shows the major actors in the marketer's microenvironment. Marketing success will require building relationships with other company departments, suppliers, marketing intermediaries, customers, competitors, and various publics, which combine to make up the company's value delivery network.

The Company

In designing marketing plans, marketing management takes other company groups into account—groups such as top management, finance, research and development (R&D), purchasing, operations, and accounting. All of these interrelated groups form the internal environment. Top management sets the company's mission, objectives, broad strategies, and policies. Marketing managers make decisions within the strategies and plans made by top management. As we discussed in Chapter 2, marketing managers must work closely with other company departments. Other departments have an impact on the marketing department's plans and actions. And under the marketing concept, all of these functions must "think consumer." They should work in harmony to provide superior customer value and relationships.

Suppliers

Suppliers form an important link in the company's overall customer value delivery system. They provide the resources needed by the company to produce its goods and services. Supplier problems can seriously affect marketing. Marketing managers must watch supply availability and costs. Supply shortages or delays, labour strikes, and other events can cost sales in the short run and damage customer satisfaction in the long run. Rising supply costs may force price increases that can harm the company's sales volume.

Most marketers today treat their suppliers as partners in creating and delivering customer value. For example, Home Depot works closely with its army of almost 12 000 suppliers. Its Supplier Center website (https://suppliercenter.homedepot.com) provides valuable supplier information and assistance. Supplier scorecards give important feedback that helps suppliers improve their performance. The giant retailer also hosts regular international supplier workshops, held in the local language so that factory leaders can attend. In return,

Figure 3.1 Actors in the microenvironment

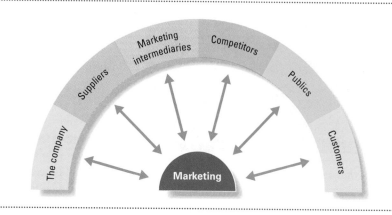

Home Depot's Supplier Council, consisting of its 15 most strategic suppliers, meets four times a year to provide supplier feedback. In these and other ways, Home Depot actively solicits the "voice of the supplier." It knows that good partner relationship management results in success for all—Home Depot, its suppliers and, ultimately, its customers.[2]

Marketing Intermediaries

Marketing intermediaries
Firms that help the company promote, sell, and distribute its goods to final buyers.

Marketing intermediaries help the company promote, sell, and distribute its products to final buyers. They include resellers, physical distribution firms, marketing services agencies, and financial intermediaries. *Resellers* are distribution channel firms that help the company find customers or make sales to them. These include wholesalers and retailers who buy and resell merchandise. Selecting and partnering with resellers is not easy. No longer do manufacturers have many small, independent resellers from which to choose. They now face large and growing reseller organizations such as Walmart, Winners, Home Depot, Costco, and Future Shop. These organizations frequently have enough power to dictate terms or even shut smaller manufacturers out of large markets.

Physical distribution firms help the company to stock and move goods from their points of origin to their destinations. *Marketing services agencies* are the marketing research firms, advertising agencies, media firms, and marketing consulting firms that help the company target and promote its products to the right markets. *Financial intermediaries* include banks, credit companies, insurance companies, and other businesses that help finance transactions or insure against the risks associated with the buying and selling of goods.

Like suppliers, marketing intermediaries form an important component of the company's overall value delivery system. In its quest to create satisfying customer relationships, the company must do more than just optimize its own performance. It must partner effectively with marketing intermediaries to optimize the performance of the entire system. Thus, today's marketers recognize the importance of working with their intermediaries as partners rather than simply as channels through which they sell their products.

For example, when Coca-Cola signs on as the exclusive beverage provider for a fast-food chain, such as McDonald's, Wendy's, or Subway, it provides much more than just soft drinks. It also pledges powerful marketing support. Coke assigns cross-functional teams dedicated to understanding the finer points of each retail partner's business. It conducts a staggering amount of research on beverage consumers and shares these insights with its partners. It analyzes the demographics of U.S. zip code areas and helps partners to determine which Coke brands are preferred in their areas. Coca-Cola has even studied the design of drive-through menu boards to better understand which layouts, fonts, letter sizes, colours, and visuals induce consumers to order more food and drink. Based on such insights, the Coca-Cola FoodService group develops marketing programs and merchandising tools that help its retail partners improve their beverage sales and profits. Coca-Cola FoodService's website, www.CokeSolutions.com, provides retailers with a wealth of information, business solutions, and merchandising tips. Such intense partnering efforts have made Coca-Cola a runaway leader in the fountain soft-drink market.[3]

Partnering with marketing intermediaries: Coca-Cola provides its retail partners with much more than just soft drinks. It also pledges powerful marketing support.

Competitors

The marketing concept states that, to be successful, a company must provide greater customer value and satisfaction than its competitors do. Thus, marketers must do more than simply adapt to the needs of target consumers. They also must gain strategic advantage by positioning their offerings strongly against competitors' offerings in the minds of consumers.

No single competitive marketing strategy is best for all companies. Each firm should consider its own size and industry position compared to those of its competitors. Large firms with dominant positions in an industry can use certain strategies that smaller firms cannot afford. But being large is not enough. There are winning strategies for large firms, but there are also losing ones. And small firms can develop strategies that give them better rates of return than large firms enjoy.

Publics

Public

Any group that has an actual or potential interest in or impact on an organization's ability to achieve its objectives.

The company's marketing environment also includes various publics. A **public** is any group that has an actual or potential interest in or impact on an organization's ability to achieve its objectives. We can identify seven types of publics:

- *Financial publics.* This group influences the company's ability to obtain funds. Banks, investment houses, and shareholders are the major financial publics.

- *Media publics.* This group carries news, features, and editorial opinion. It includes newspapers, magazines, and radio and television stations.

- *Government publics.* Management must take government developments into account. Marketers must often consult the company's lawyers on issues of product safety, truth in advertising, and other matters.

- *Citizen-action publics.* A company's marketing decisions may be questioned by consumer organizations, environmental groups, minority groups, and others. Its public relations department can help it stay in touch with consumer and citizen groups.

- *Local publics.* This group includes neighbourhood residents and community organizations. Large companies usually appoint a community relations officer to deal with the community, attend meetings, answer questions, and contribute to worthwhile causes. For example, Ronald McDonald House Charities recognize the importance of community publics.

- *General public.* A company needs to be concerned about the general public's attitude toward its products and activities. The public's image of the company affects buying habits.

- *Internal publics.* This group includes workers, managers, volunteers, and the board of directors. Large companies use newsletters and other means to inform and motivate their internal publics. When employees feel good about their company, this positive attitude spills over to external publics.

A company can prepare marketing plans for these major publics as well as for its customer markets. Suppose the company wants a specific response from a particular public, such as goodwill, favourable word of mouth, or donations of time or money. The company would have to design an offer to this public that is attractive enough to produce the desired response.

Publics: Ronald McDonald House Charities ® (RMHC®) recognizes the importance of community publics. The 12 Ronald McDonald Houses play a vital role in communities across Canada, providing a home-away-from-home for out of town families of children with serious illnesses being treated at a nearby children's hospital.

Customers

As we've emphasized throughout, customers are the most important actors in the company's microenvironment. The aim of the entire value delivery system is to serve target customers and create strong relationships with them. The company might target any or all of five types of customer markets. *Consumer markets* consist of individuals and households that buy goods and services for personal consumption. *Business markets* buy goods and services for further processing or for use in their production process, whereas *reseller markets* buy goods and services to resell at a profit. *Government markets* are made up of government agencies that buy goods and services to produce public services or transfer the goods and services to others who need them. Finally, *international markets* consist of these buyers in other countries, including consumers, producers, resellers, and governments. Each market type has special characteristics that call for careful study by the seller.

THE COMPANY'S MACROENVIRONMENT

The company and all of the other actors operate in a larger macroenvironment of forces that shape opportunities and pose threats to the company. Figure 3.2 shows the six major forces in the company's macroenvironment. In the remaining sections of this chapter, we examine these forces and show how they affect marketing plans.

2 Demographic Environment

Demography The study of human populations in terms of size, density, location, age, gender, race, occupation, and other statistics.

Demography is the study of human populations in terms of size, density, location, age, gender, race, occupation, and other statistics. The demographic environment is of major interest to marketers because it involves people, and people make up markets. The world population is growing at an explosive rate. It now exceeds 6.6 billion people and will grow to 8.1 billion by the year 2030.[4] The world's large and highly diverse population poses both opportunities and challenges.

Changes in the world demographic environment have major implications for business. For example, consider China. More than a quarter century ago, to curb its skyrocketing population, the Chinese government passed regulations limiting families to one child each. As a result, Chinese children—known as "little emperors and empresses"—have been showered with attention and luxuries under what's known as the "six-pocket syndrome." As many as six adults—two parents and four doting grandparents—may be indulging the whims of each only child.

The little emperors, now ranging in age from newborns to mid-20s, are affecting markets for everything from children's products to financial services, restaurants, and luxury goods. Parents with only one child at home now spend about 40 percent of their income on their cherished child, creating huge market opportunities for children's educational products. For example, Time Warner targeted the lucrative Chinese coddled-kiddies market with an interactive language course called English Time, a 200-lesson, 40-CD set that takes as long as four years for a child to complete. The course sells for US$3300, more than a year's salary for many Chinese parents.[5]

At the other end of the spectrum, Starbucks is targeting China's older little emperors, positioning itself as a new kind of informal but indulgent meeting place. China's one-child rule created a generation who have been pampered by parents and grandparents and have

Figure 3.2 Major forces in the company's macroenvironment

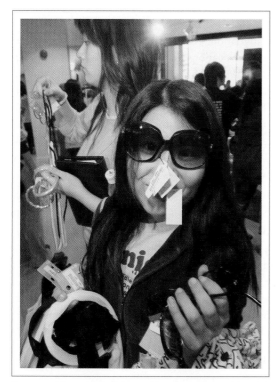

Demographics and business: Chinese regulations limiting families to one child have resulted in what's known as the "six-pocket syndrome." Chinese children and teens are being showered with attention and luxuries, creating opportunities for marketers.

Baby boomers

The 9.8 million Canadians born during the baby boom following World War II and lasting until the mid-1960s.

the means to make indulgent purchases. Instead of believing in traditional Chinese collective goals, these young people embrace individuality. "Their view of this world is very different," says the president of Starbucks Greater China. "They have never gone through the hardships of our generation." Starbucks is in sync with that, he says, given its customized drinks, personalized service, and original music compilations.[6]

Thus, marketers keep close track of demographic trends and developments in their markets, both at home and abroad. They track changing age and family structures, geographic population shifts, educational characteristics, and population diversity. Here, we discuss the most important demographic trends in Canada.

Changing Age Structure of the Population

The Canadian population exceeded 33 million in 2008 and is expected to exceed 39 million by 2031. The single most important demographic trend in Canada is the changing age structure of the population—the Canadian population is getting older. As of July 2008, the median age of Canada's population was 39.4 years. Almost one Canadian out of seven is aged 65 and over. However, these numbers vary considerably by geographic region. For example, the Atlantic region has the oldest populations, mainly as a result of lower fertility and migration outflows of young adults. Newfoundland and Labrador has the highest median age (42.5 years) in the country, while Nova Scotia has the highest proportion of seniors and is the first province or territory to have more seniors than youth. However, the population is younger in the three Prairie provinces as a result of higher fertility rates and strong migration inflows of young adults. Alberta has both the lowest median age (35.7 years) and the lowest proportion of seniors among provinces.[7] The Canadian population contains several generational groups. Here we discuss the three largest groups—the baby boomers, Generation X, and the Millennials—and their impact on today's marketing strategies.

The Baby Boomers The post–World War II baby boom, which began in 1947 and ran through 1966, produced 9.8 million **baby boomers** in Canada. Although there was a baby boom in both Canada and the United States, Canadian marketers have to recognize that our baby boom was unique. It started later than the American version (1947 versus 1946) and lasted longer (the American boom ended in 1964 while the Canadian boom continued until 1966). While the American baby boom resulted in 3.5 children per family, the Canadian boom produced an average of 4 children. Furthermore, the baby boom was not a worldwide phenomenon. Among other developed countries, only Australia and New Zealand experienced the same expansion in the birth rate. There was no baby boom in Europe, and in Japan the birth rate declined during our baby boom years, which explains why these countries have a higher proportion of older people in their societies.[8]

Over the years, the baby boomers have been one of the most powerful forces shaping the marketing environment. The baby boomers account for a third of Canada's population and control over 50 percent of the country's wealth. The youngest boomers are now in their mid-40s; the oldest are in their early 60s. The maturing boomers are rethinking the purpose and value of their work, responsibilities, and relationships. As they reach their peak earning and spending years, the boomers constitute a lucrative market for financial services, new housing and home remodelling, travel and entertainment, eating out, health and fitness products, and just about everything else.

It would be a mistake to think of the aging boomers as phasing out or slowing down. Today's boomers think young no matter how old they are. In fact, the boomers are spending US$30 billion a year on *anti*-aging products and services. And unlike previous generations, boomers are retiring later and working more after retirement. Rather than viewing themselves as phasing out, they see themselves as entering new life phases. According to one observer:

> The boomers thrive on change and reinvention. They did not grow up with the Internet, but they readily go online to plot out vacations and seek bargains. They grew up with television, but they have embraced TiVo and VCRs and other technologies that let them scoot past commercials. They may not like rap music, but they'll listen to their own music on the same types of iPods that their children use. For example, take Frank Zacherl and his wife Dixie. Frank is a Windows Vista guru. He loves to rip music, post videos on YouTube, and Skype his grandchildren. Frank is 65. His wife, Dixie, is an iPod fanatic and fellow Skype user. The older boomers get, it seems, the younger they seem to feel. . . . They see retirement not as an end but as just another stage in life.[9]

Toyota recognizes these changing boomer life phases. Ads for its Toyota Highlander show empty-nest boomers and declare "For your newfound freedom." Similarly, Curves fitness centres target older women, but not grandmas in rocking chairs. Curves' older regulars "want to be strong and fit," says an expert. "They just don't want to go into Gold's Gym and be surrounded by spandex-clad Barbie dolls."[10]

Similarly, cosmetics brands such as Dove, L'Oréal, CoverGirl, and Olay use 50- or 60-something spokesmodels such as Christie Brinkley and Diane Keaton to appeal to boomer women. And they use sensible, aspirational appeals aimed at confident older consumers who aren't trying to fight the aging process. "Boomers are saying 'I'm aging, but I'm going to do it in a way that's graceful and still about who I am'" says a marketer for Unilever's Dove Pro Age brand. Says another marketer, "I don't think boomers want to be young again—I don't think they feel old in the first place."[11]

Perhaps no one is targeting the baby boomers more fervently than the financial services industry. In coming years, the aging boomers in North America will transfer some $33 trillion in retirement nest eggs and other savings into new investments. They'll also be inheriting $9 trillion as their parents pass away. Thus, the boomers will be needing lots of money management help. An Ameriprise Financial marketer explains, "It's not just about the rational numbers. It's about how you are going to reinvent yourself for what could be 30 or 40 years of retirement." An Ameriprise ad promises retiring boomers that the company will "help you envision what exactly you want to do in the next phase of your life."[12] (See Real Marketing 3.1.)

Generation X The baby boom was followed by a "birth dearth," creating another generation of 7 million Canadians born between 1967 and 1976. Author Douglas Coupland calls them **Generation X** because they lie in the shadow of the boomers and lack obvious distinguishing characteristics.

Generation X
The 7 million Canadians born between 1967 and 1976 in the "birth dearth" following the baby boom.

The Generation Xers are defined as much by their shared experiences as by their age. Increasing parental divorce rates and higher employment for their mothers made them the first generation of latchkey kids. Having grown up during times of recession and corporate downsizing, they developed a more cautious economic outlook. Most Gen Xers are woefully behind in saving for retirement—and they worry about it. Still, nearly half of Gen Xers say they are so saddled with debt or live on such tight budgets that they can't even think about saving. They care about the environment and respond favourably to socially responsible companies. Although they seek success, they are less materialistic; they prize experience, not acquisition. For many of the Gen Xers that are parents, family comes first, career second.[13] From a marketing viewpoint, the Gen Xers are a more skeptical bunch. They tend to research products before they consider a purchase, and they tend to be less receptive to overt marketing pitches.

Once labelled as "the MTV generation" and viewed as body-piercing slackers who whined about "McJobs," the Gen Xers have grown up and are now taking over. The Gen Xers are displacing the lifestyles, culture, and materialistic values of the baby boomers. They represent close to $1.5 trillion in annual purchasing power in North America. With so much potential, many companies are focusing on Gen Xers as an important target segment. For example, Mountain Equipment Co-op (MEC), the largest retail cooperative in Canada, appeals to the Gen X consumers—those who value family, life experience, and environmen-

Real Marketing **3.1**

Ameriprise Financial: Still a Boomer Market

As the largest demographic bulge in North America's history, the baby boomers have always been a hot market to companies across a wide range of industries. These days, as the boomers reach their peak earning years and look ahead toward retirement, they've become downright irresistible to the financial services industry. In fact, Ameriprise Financial, a longstanding company (formerly American Express Financial Advisors) with a new brand name and a fresh new start, is pretty much staking its future on cultivating the baby boomers. Its entire positioning rests on a bedrock of helping the aging baby boomers realize their pre-retirement and retirement experiences through its Dream > Plan > Track approach to financial planning.

The baby boomers make up a huge and growing financial services market. Ameriprise Financial estimates that America's 41 million affluent and mass-affluent households hold more than $19 trillion in investable assets. More than half of these affluent households are headed by baby boomers. What's more, the first boomers, now in their 60s, will initiate a retirement gold rush that will continue for more than two decades. By the time that the last boomer turns 65, the boomers will control more than 40 percent of the nation's disposable income. During that time and beyond, the boomers will need a heap of financial planning help.

Consequently, whereas the eyes of marketers in some industries are now wandering toward the younger and fresher Millennials generation, the aging boomers comprise the bulk of revenues for Ameriprise Financial and other financial services firms. According to one expert, "If you are in the financial services industry, *this* is the baby-boomer decade."

But Ameriprise Financial knows that the boomers are very different from previous generations of pre-retirees and that connecting with them will require a deep understanding of what makes them tick. The image of the doddering old fool in mismatched flannel pouring lemonade for the grandkids simply doesn't resonate with today's boomer consumer. The boomers don't think of themselves as getting old. And they don't think of themselves as retiring—it's more like shifting gears and striking out in new directions. The boomers won't need help just managing their money, they'll need help planning for and realizing life's next phases. For Ameriprise Financial, says the company's CEO, "it all begins with understanding our clients' dreams." And "Dreams don't retire."

To better understand just what those retirement dreams entail, Ameriprise Financial linked up with baby boomer experts to conduct a large-scale "New Retirement Mindscape" study. It learned that retirement is characterized by five distinct stages, such as imagination (the six to 15 years preceding retirement when people envision the retirement

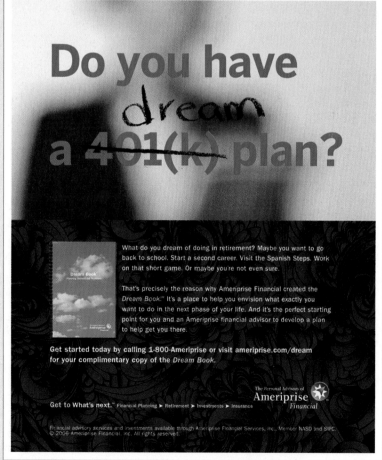

Targeting the baby boomers: The positioning of Ameriprise Financial rests on a bedrock of helping the boomers discover and realize their retirement dreams. And "Dreams don't retire."

they want) and liberation (the year following retirement when people begin reconnecting with their families, pursuing hobbies, travelling, and starting new businesses). Another key finding was that people want a financial advisor who understands them—this was rated just as important as return on their investments.

Based on these findings, Ameriprise Financial developed a *Dream Book* guide—a planning guide that helps boomers explore their retirement dreams and create a life strategy for retirement. It's "the best book on retirement—the one you'll write—that will help you get to a retirement defined by your dreams." The *Dream Book* guide becomes one of the first steps in the Dream > Plan > Track approach to financial planning through which more than 11 800 personal advisors from Ameriprise Financial form long-term relationships with clients. So far, the company has distributed more than 3 million of the popular planning guides.

Ameriprise Financial also used the New Retirement Mindscape study results to shape an innovative "Dreams don't retire" advertising campaign. The new campaign shuns the typical industry "Are *you* ready for retirement?" message of fear. Instead, it focuses on the positive, aspirational aspects of retirement—on what's next. The first phase of the ad campaign features 1960s icon Dennis Hopper, star of boomer-era counterculture classics such as *Easy Rider*. At 71 years old, Hopper himself is not a boomer. But boomers see him as an older brother type, one who has lived true to himself and done things his own way.

In the ads, Hopper talks plainly about what retirement means before the action shifts to boomers tackling ambitious retirement tasks, such as building a boat or designing an eco-friendly new home. One commercial, set in a field of yellow daisies, hits the old flower-power boomers right where they live. Speaking and looking directly into the lens, an impassioned Hopper says, "Some people say that dreams are like delicate little flowers. Wrong! Dreams are powerful. Dreams are what make you say 'When I'm 64, I'm going to start a new business. I want to make my own movie.' Flower power was then—your dreams are now."

In another commercial, Hopper stands on an expansive white, sandy beach reading from a dictionary. "To withdraw, to go away, to disappear—that's how the dictionary defines retirement," he intones. Tossing the dictionary aside, he continues, "Time to redefine! Your generation is definitely not headed for bingo night. In fact, you can write a book about how you're going to turn retirement upside down. I just don't see you playing shuffleboard—'ya know what I mean? The thing about dreams is—they don't retire." All of the ads employ a 1960s-style red chair as a visual icon. The chair symbolizes the launching pad for boomers' retirement dreams—it is an "anti-rocking chair."

The boomer-focused campaign has hit the right target with the right message. Although they scored low with the general audience, the ads hit it big with boomers. Half of the target group liked the ads a lot or somewhat, and 79 percent rated the ads as very effective or somewhat effective (both very good numbers, given that they're, well, ads). Perhaps more important, thanks to the campaign, the newly minted Ameriprise Financial brand achieved 56 percent awareness, up from just 24 percent two years ago. And the company experienced double-digit sales and profits growth in the year following the start of the campaign. Says the Ameriprise Financial chief marketing officer, "In just two years [of running the campaign], we've established a powerful and respected brand that has transformed financial services advertising and the way people look at financial planning."

According to an industry analyst, "Ameriprise Financial looks well on the way to securing a perch among the largest financial service providers serving baby boomers headed for retirement—it's a sleeping giant." But when it comes to catering to baby boomers, this giant isn't napping. It's working face to face with more than 2 million clients, "Putting millions of dreams on track. One dream at a time." As one ad promises: "What do you dream of doing in retirement? Maybe you want to go back to school. Start a second career. Visit the Spanish Steps. Work on that short game. Or maybe you're not even sure. . . . Ameriprise Financial [will help you] envision what exactly you want to do in the next phase of your life . . . and develop a plan to help get you there."

Sources: Quotes and other information from Laura Petrecca, "More Marketers Target Boomers' Eyes, Wallets," *USA Today*, February 26, 2007, p. 6B; "New Evolution of Ameriprise Financial Advertising Emphasizes That 'Dreams Don't Retire,'" September 7, 2006, accessed at **www.ameriprise.com**; Jack Willoughby, "Ameriprise Comes Alive," *Wall Street Journal*, August 27, 2006; Claudia H. Deutsch, "Not Getting Older, Just More Scrutinized," *New York Times*, October 11, 2006, accessed at **www.nyt.com**; Lisa Shidler, "Baby Boomers Are Tough Customers," *Investment News*, March 12, 2007, p. 28; "Online Strategy Plays a Primary Role in New Evolution of Ameriprise Financial Advertising," *Business Wire*, September 10, 2007; and annual reports and various pages at **www.ameriprise.com**, accessed December 2008.

tal sustainability. Founded in 1971, MEC has grown to service nearly 3 million members worldwide. With stores in 10 major Canadian cities and worldwide catalogue sales, the company has become Canada's leading supplier of quality outdoor gear, clothing, and camping equipment, surpassing $200 million in annual sales. It promotes itself as an ethical company through its commitment to green building, community grants, ethical purchasing, product sustainability, and promotion of Canada-wide parks and protected areas.[14]

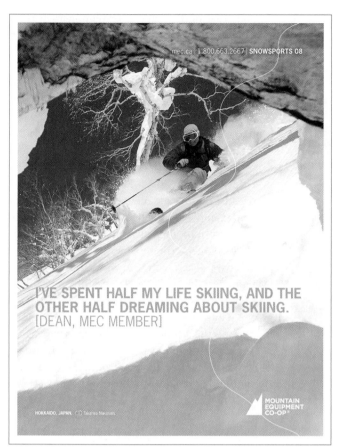

I'VE SPENT HALF MY LIFE SKIING, AND THE OTHER HALF DREAMING ABOUT SKIING.
[DEAN, MEC MEMBER]

HOKKAIDO, JAPAN. Takahiro Nakanishi

MOUNTAIN EQUIPMENT CO-OP®

mec.ca | 1.800.663.2667 | SNOWSPORTS 08

Targeting Gen Xers: MEC has been highly successful in serving a segment of Gen Xers who value family, life experiences, and environmental sustainability.

Millennials (or Generation Y)
The 10.4 million children of the Canadian baby boomers, born between 1977 and 2000.

Millennials Both the baby boomers and Gen Xers will one day be passing the reins to the **Millennials** (also called Generation Y or the echo boomers). Born between 1977 and 2000, these children of the baby boomers number 10.4 million, dwarfing the Gen Xers and larger even than the baby boomer segment. This group includes several age cohorts: *tweens* (aged 8–12), *teens* (13–18), and *young adults* (the 20-somethings). The younger Millennials are just beginning to wield their buying power. The older ones have now graduated from university and are moving up in their careers, significantly expanding both their earning and their spending. The Millennials are a diverse bunch. Whereas the baby boomers were 80 percent white, 45 percent of Millennials describe their race as something other than white.[15]

One thing that all of the Millennials have in common is their utter fluency and comfort with computer, digital, and Internet technology. "Whereas Gen X spent a lot of time in front of the TV," says one expert, the Millennials "are always 'on.' They're consumers of every imaginable means of communication: TV, radio, cell phone, Internet, video games—often simultaneously."[16] Here's a typical Millennial profile:

A.J. Sanjay can't start the day without first pulling out his laptop. Each morning, the 21-year-old, second year York University student downloads his schedule onto his Mac Powerbook, which—along with his iPod and cell phone—is always close at hand. Sanjay is a typical tech-savvy university student. He can access the social networking site Facebook from his cell phone. He uses e-mail and instant messaging anywhere on the wireless campus. He downloads music to his laptop and his iPod, and he uses a 4-gigabyte flash drive provided by the university to transfer files and songs and to access his digital portfolio. Technology is so second nature that it's just a part of life. Sanjay isn't a techno-geek. He's just a "digital native"—a term that has been used to describe Millennials, the first generation who grew up in a world filled with computers, cell phones, cable TV, and online social networks.[17]

Each Millennials segment constitutes a huge and attractive market. However, reaching these message-saturated segments effectively requires creative marketing approaches. For example, P&G's Tide, normally known for targeting women who are responsible for their household's laundry, has now set its marketing sights on the great, unwashed Millennial masses—university students:

Tide is experimenting with a new line of products, called Swash. Not only is Tide telling university students that it's okay to rewear their clothes between washes, it's *encouraging* them to do so. Swash offers students dewrinkling sprays, stain-removing pens, odour-removing sprays, clothes dryer sheets, and lint rollers that can help give their clothes the look and smell of having been washed without the trouble or expense of actual washing. In the process, the brand's helping eliminate the one domestic chore most university students do. The Swash products aren't actually new—they are old offerings cleverly repositioned to fit the lifestyle of multislackers— students who are juggling the demands of not doing their laundry, not finishing their homework, and not cleaning their rooms. Swash is here to tell them that it's okay, even environmentally heroic, to pick their wardrobes off the floor in the morning. A segment on SwashItOut.com, labelled "The Rewear Movement," touts reuse of unwashed clothes as "the effortless way to save water." Says the site, "Swash brings the experience

Targeting the Millennials: Tide's new Swash line targets the great unwashed—university students—telling them that it's not just okay to rewear their clothes between washes, but even environmentally heroic.

and trust of Tide into a revolutionary way to care for clothes, helping you rewear with confidence and conserve water between washes."[18]

Generational Marketing Do marketers need to create separate products and marketing programs for each generation? Some experts warn that marketers need to be careful about turning off one generation each time they craft a product or message that appeals effectively to another. Others caution that each generation spans decades of time and many socioeconomic levels. For example, marketers often split the baby boomers into three smaller groups—leading-edge boomers, core boomers, and trailing-edge boomers—each with its own beliefs and behaviours. Similarly, they split the Millennials into tweens, teens, and young adults.

Thus, marketers need to form more precise, age-specific segments within each group. More important, defining people by their birth date may be less effective than segmenting them by their lifestyle, life stage, or the common values they seek in the products they buy. We will discuss many other ways to segment markets in Chapter 8.

The Changing Canadian Household

When one uses the term *household*, a stereotype of a typical family living in the suburbs with two children may leap to mind. However, this stereotype is far from accurate. The 2006 census reveals some interesting trends. For example, there is a growing "crowded nest" syndrome. About 43.5 percent of young Canadians aged 20 to 29 now live with their parents. There are 8.9 million families in Canada, but fewer have children than in past years. In fact, the 2006 census marked the first time there were more census families without children than with children during the past 20 years. One-person households and couples without children grew more than twice as fast as the total population in private households, while households with children edged up only 0.4 percent. As a result, the average Canadian household shrank to 2.5 people in 2006. Two-thirds of Canada's children aged 14 and under lived with married parents in 2006, a decline from 81 percent in 1986. Lone-parent families headed by men increased almost 15 percent during the five years prior to 2006, more than twice the growth of lone-parent families headed by women.[19] Given these trends, marketers must increasingly consider the distinctive needs and buying habits of these nontraditional households, because they are now growing more rapidly than traditional ones.

Responsibility for household tasks and the care of children is also changing. There are now more dual-income families as more and more women enter the workforce. Today, women account for 48 percent of the Canadian workforce. The employment rate of women with children has grown particularly sharply in the past two decades, especially for those with preschool-aged children. More than 68 percent of women with children under six were employed, more than double the figure of 1976.[20]

The significant number of women in the workforce has spawned the child daycare business and increased consumption of career-oriented women's clothing, financial services, and convenience foods and services. An example is Épicerie Direct, an Internet grocer serving the greater Montreal area since 2007. Using www.epiceriedirect.com instead of trekking to the grocery store, battling traffic, and waiting in line, busy working moms and dads can simply buy their groceries online. Épicerie Direct offers a virtual selection of products from more than 20 categories and delivers customers' orders to their doorsteps, providing a "grocery cart at your fingertips."[21]

Geographic Shifts in Population

The population of Canada grew by approximately 4.3 percent between 2004 and 2008. As Table 3.1 shows, however, growth rates across all provinces and territories are not uniform. The population of Alberta reached double-digit increases while Newfoundland and Labrador, Nova Scotia, and New Brunswick saw slight declines during the 2004–2008 period. However, with the downturn in oil prices in 2008 and 2009, many people from the Atlantic provinces who moved to Alberta to work in the "oil patch" have returned home.

Canadians are a mobile people with itchy feet. For more than a century, Canadians have been moving from rural to urban areas. The urban areas have a faster pace of living, more commuting, higher incomes, and greater variety of goods and services than can be found in the small towns and rural areas that dot Canada. In 2007, more than 370 800 Canadian residents changed province, a record number since 1981. Alberta and British Columbia are now the top two choices when it comes to interprovincial moves. Since 2003, Ontario has seen the largest net loss of residents from interprovincial moves, but it maintains its growth in overall population through immigration from other countries. Recent research has shown that interprovincial moves and income are correlated. People who moved from one province to another tended to increase their earnings, especially if they moved away from a "have-not" province. The effects were especially strong for men and younger people.[22]

Canada's cities are changing as well. Canadian cities are often surrounded by large suburban areas. Statistics Canada calls these combinations of urban and suburban populations "census metropolitan areas" (CMAs). Over 50 percent of Canada's population lives in the top 10 CMAs. Marketers also track the relative growth of these markets to see which areas are expanding and which ones are contracting.

Population shifts interest marketers because people in different regions buy differently. For example, 46 percent of people classified as "serious technology users" reside in Ontario, compared with 18 percent who live in British Columbia and the 6 percent who live in Atlantic Canada.[23]

Table 3.1 Canada's Population

	2004 (thousands)	2008 (thousands)	Change (%)
Canada	31 940.7	33 311.4	4.3
Newfoundland and Labrador	517.4	507.9	−1.8
Prince Edward Island	137.7	139.8	1.5
Nova Scotia	939.4	938.3	−0.2
New Brunswick	749.4	747.3	−0.2
Quebec	7 535.9	7 750.5	2.8
Ontario	12 390.6	12 929.0	4.3
Manitoba	1 173.6	1 208.0	2.9
Saskatchewan	997.4	1 016.0	1.9
Alberta	3 239.5	3 585.1	10.6
British Columbia	4 155.2	4 381.6	5.4
Yukon	23.7	31.5	33.1
Northwest Territories	43.3	43.3	0
Nunavut	29.9	31.4	5

Source: Adapted from "Population by Year, by Province and Territory," accessed at www40.statcan.gc.ca/l01/cst01/demo02a-eng.htm, Statistics Canada, April 2009. Reproduced with the permission of the Minister of Public Works and Government Services Canada, 2010.

Cisco targets the growing telecommuter market with WebEx, which lets people meet and collaborate online, no matter what their work location.

The shift in where people live has also caused a shift in where they work. For example, the migration toward metropolitan and suburban areas has resulted in a rapid increase in the number of people who "telecommute"—work at home or in a remote office and conduct their business by phone, fax, modem, or the Internet.

This trend, in turn, has created a booming SOHO (small office/home office) market. Fifteen percent of Canadian households report that they have a home office. In addition to commuters, it is estimated that there were 618 000 home-based businesses in Canada. Typically, home-based business operators are male (60.3 percent) and between the ages of 25 and 54 (76.4 percent). Many (31 percent) are highly educated. The top five industries for home-based businesses are professional, scientific, and technical services (17.8 percent); agriculture (12.1 percent); trade (10.2 percent); health care and social assistance (9.2 percent); and construction (8.3 percent).[24]

Many marketers are actively courting the lucrative telecommuting market. For example, WebEx, the web-conferencing division of Cisco, helps overcome the isolation that often accompanies telecommuting. With WebEx, people can meet and collaborate online, no matter what their work location. "All you need to run effective online meetings is a browser and a phone," says the company. With WebEx, people working anywhere can interact with other individuals or small groups to make presentations, exchange documents, and share desktops, complete with audio and full-motion video. WebEx's MeetMeNow service can be launched from desktops, Microsoft Outlook and Office, and instant messaging clients such as Yahoo! Messenger and MSN Messenger. MeetMeNow automatically finds and configures users' webcams and lets meeting hosts switch among participants' video streams to form a virtual roundtable. More than 2.2 million people participate in WebEx sessions every day.[25]

A Better-Educated, More White-Collar, More Professional Population

The Canadian population is becoming better educated. As of 2004, 59.1 percent of the population had university degrees or postsecondary certificates. Eight percent have some postsecondary education. Those with a high school education equal 20.1 percent. However, 12.9 percent of the population has less than a high school education.[26] The rising number of educated people will increase the demand for quality products, books, magazines, travel, personal computers, and Internet services.

Increasing Diversity

Countries vary in their ethnic and racial makeup. At one extreme is Japan, where almost everyone is Japanese. At the other extreme are countries such as Canada and the United States, whose populations are "salad bowls" of mixed races. Anyone who has walked the streets of Vancouver, Montreal, Calgary, or Toronto will immediately understand that visible minorities in Canada are a force to be reckoned with. Over 5 million Canadians (16 percent) identified themselves as visible minorities in the 2006 census and over 200 ethnic origins were reported. Between 2001 and 2006, the visible minority population increased five times faster than the population as a whole, mainly due to immigration. According to Statistics Canada's population projections, members of visible minority groups could account for roughly one-fifth of the total population by 2017.[27]

The purchasing power of visible minorities is huge, so it is not surprising that Sharifa Khan of Balmoral Marketing, an ethnic ad agency in Toronto, has seen a dramatic increase in spending directed at these markets. Many clients allocate as much as 15 percent of their total communications budget to ethnic marketing, up from 2 percent just a few years ago. Khan points out that once her clients realized that visible minorities are "real people with real desires to own a home, a nice car, and all the goods and services that complemented those things they desired, it made the job of convincing [her clients] to embrace ethnic marketing a lot easier."[28] As the ethnic population continues to grow in Canada, large companies, from Sears, McDonald's, and Air Canada to Levi Strauss, Procter & Gamble, and General Mills, feature people from different backgrounds in their ads and can now target specially designed products and promotions to one or more of these groups. They can use a variety of media vehicles introduced to serve ethnic marketplaces. There are 18 television networks, 49 radio stations, and 190 newspapers and magazines available to reach various ethnic populations. Though there are approximately 200 different visible minorities living in Canada, only 12 groups are growing significantly and have well-developed media that target their communities: Chinese, Caribbean (predominantly Jamaican), South Asian (Indian, Pakistani, Tamil, Bangladeshi), Korean, Hispanic, Italian, Greek, Portuguese, Ukrainian, Polish, Filipino, and First Nations.[29] It must be remembered, however, that visible minorities often read the same media, such as daily newspapers, as other Canadians.

Targeting ethnic consumers involves far more than mere tokenism, as many ethnic marketing specialists warn. Merely placing a person from a visible minority in an advertisement is not sufficient evidence that one is an ethnic marketer. Communicating in the consumer's native language is often mandatory, but marketers must also face the challenge of not alienating sophisticated second-generation individuals. TD Bank demonstrated the power of providing information in potential customers' native language. The bank launched a Chinese Green Info Line to target potential Chinese investors. More than 300 callers per month take advantage of the service, which has generated considerable investments. Walmart now runs television spots targeting South Asian, Cantonese, Mandarin, Spanish, Portuguese, and Italian communities. Telus and Nokia use print advertising to target consumers from various ethnic backgrounds in Toronto and Vancouver. Professor Ashwin Joshi of the Schulich School of Business at York University in Toronto notes that IKEA is another marketer that is sensitive to the needs of consumers from different ethnic backgrounds. For example, through its extensive links with people of South Asian origins, it developed insights that it used to shape its marketing practices. IKEA learned that religion plays a key role for this community and that it is not uncommon for the different religious groups to have sacred places in their homes where they place their religious artifacts. This led IKEA to specifically design furniture to house these artifacts. IKEA also takes pride in participating in key festivals, such as Diwali and Idd el Fitr, by having the appropriate items (e.g., candle holders made of clay) on sale during the time of these events.[30]

The diversity in the Canadian marketplace isn't restricted to ethnic markets. The 2006 census enumerated 45 300 same-sex couples, up from 34 200 in 2001.[31] People's sexual orientation is another point of diversity, and there is growing tolerance of alternative lifestyles in Canada. For example, Toronto's Pride Week is the third largest outdoor festival in the world and attracts more than 1 million people each year. Since homosexual consumers tend to be cosmopolitan and professional with high incomes, they are desirable target markets for everything from technology products and health and beauty products to travel, fashion, entertainment, and financial services. It is not surprising, then, that the City of Toronto ran a campaign aimed at attracting more gay and lesbian tourists.

With hit TV shows such as Carson Kressley's (of *Queer Eye for the Straight Guy*) *How to Look Good Naked* and *The Ellen DeGeneres Show*, as well as Oscar-winning movies such as *Brokeback Mountain*, the LGBT (lesbian, gay, bisexual, and transgender) community has increasingly emerged into the public eye. A number of media now provide companies with

Firms such as Telus know the importance of cultural sensitivity and building meaningful connections with people of different ethnic backgrounds.

access to this market. For example, PlanetOut Inc. offers several successful magazines (*Out, Advocate, OutTraveler*) and websites (Gay.com and PlanetOut.com). Canada's only digital television channel specifically targeted at the LGBT community, OUTtv, was launched nationally in 2001. By 2008, it became Canada's fastest growing digital cable channel and had reached the half million mark in subscribers.

Companies in a wide range of industries are now targeting the LGBT community with gay-specific marketing efforts. For example, IBM fields a paid, full-time sales force dedicated to bringing LGBT decision makers in contact with the company. IBM also targets the gay small-business community with ads in *The Advocate*, *Out*, and 30 other gay-themed publications. American Airlines has a dedicated LGBT sales team, sponsors gay community events, and offers a special gay-oriented website (www.aa.com/rainbow) that features travel deals, an enewsletter, podcasts, and a gay events calendar. The airline's focus on gay consumers has earned it double-digit revenue growth from the LGBT community each year for more than a decade. And Levi's recently ran the same ad with different endings for gay and straight audiences:[32]

> A spot from the jeans maker features a young, attractive male in his second-floor apartment slipping on his Levi's. The motion of yanking up his pants inexplicably causes the street below his apartment to get pulled up as well, crashing through his floor and bringing with it an equally attractive female in a telephone booth. In the end, the guy gets the girl. But if you watch the ad on gay cable network LOGO, the same guy with the magic jeans is greeted by a fetching blond gentleman, and the two of them run off together in the same manner as their heterosexual counterparts.

Diversity goes beyond ethnicity or sexual preferences. For example, 14.3 percent of the Canadian population (4.4 million people) have some form of disability. This group has considerable spending power as well as great need for tailored products and services. Not only do they value services that make daily life easier, but they are also a growing market for travel, sports, and other leisure-oriented products. The Canadian Abilities Foundation provides a wealth of information ranging from products and services to housing and travel advice on its EnableLink website.

How are companies trying to reach consumers with disabilities? Many marketers now recognize that the worlds of people with disabilities and those without disabilities are one and the same. Says one marketer, "The 'us and them' paradigm is obsolete." Marketers such as McDonald's, Sears, and Honda have featured people with disabilities in their mainstream advertising.

Other companies use specially targeted media to reach this attractive segment. The new website Disaboom.com reaches people with disabilities through social networking features akin to Facebook combined with relevant information—everything from medical news to career advice, dating resources, and travel tips. Several large marketers, including Johnson & Johnson, Netflix, Avis, GM, and Ford, have already signed on as Disaboom.com marketing partners. Ford uses the site to highlight its Mobility Motoring Program. Among other things, the program provides $1000 allowances for new car

Ford highlights its Mobility Motoring Program in ads on the new website Disaboom.com, which reaches people with disabilities with relevant information on everything from medical news to career advice, dating resources, and travel tips.

buyers to defray the cost of adding adaptive equipment such as wheelchair or scooter lifts, pedal extensions, and steering wheel knobs. Marketing on Disaboom.com has "been a new concept for us and we are pleased with the performance so far," says Ford's mobility motoring manager.[33]

As the population in Canada grows more diverse, successful marketers will continue to diversify their marketing programs to take advantage of opportunities in fast-growing segments.

Economic Environment

Economic environment
Factors that affect consumer buying power and spending patterns.

Markets require buying power as well as people. The **economic environment** consists of factors that affect consumer purchasing power and spending patterns. Marketers must pay close attention to major trends and consumer spending patterns both across and within their world markets.

Nations vary greatly in their levels and distribution of income. Some countries have *industrial economies*, which constitute rich markets for many different kinds of goods. At the other extreme are *subsistence economies*—they consume most of their own agricultural and industrial output and offer few market opportunities. In between are *developing economies*, which can offer outstanding marketing opportunities for the right kinds of products.

Consider India, with its population of 1.1 billion people. In the past, only India's elite could afford to buy a car. In fact, only one in seven Indians now owns one. But recent dramatic changes in India's economy have produced a growing middle class and rapidly rising incomes. Now, to meet the new demand, European, North American, and Asian automakers are introducing smaller, more-affordable vehicles into India. But they'll have to find a way to compete with India's Tata Motors, which has unveiled the least expensive car ever in this market, the Tata Nano. Dubbed "the people's car," the Nano sells for only 100 000 rupees (about US$2500). It can seat four passengers, gets 50 miles per gallon, and travels at a top speed of 60 miles per hour. The car is designed to be India's Model T—the car that puts the developing nation on wheels. For starters, Tata hopes to sell one million of these vehicles a year.[34]

Changes in Income

In recent years, Canadian consumers fell into a consumption frenzy, fuelled by income growth, a boom in the stock market, rapid increases in housing values, and other economic good fortune. They bought and bought, seemingly without caution, amassing record levels of debt. However, the free spending and high expectations of those days were dashed by the recent economic downturn. Today's "tapped-out" consumers are now repaying debts acquired during earlier spending splurges, sweating out increased mortgage and household expenses, and saving ahead for children's university tuition payments and retirement.

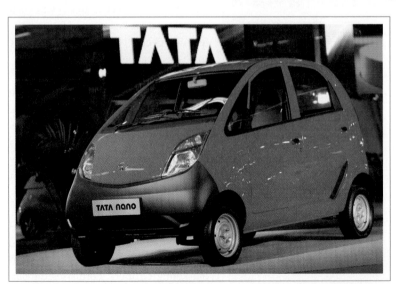

Economic environment: To capture India's growing middle class, Tata Motors introduced the small, affordable Tata Nano, designed to be India's Model T—the car that puts the developing nation on wheels.

These financially squeezed consumers are spending more carefully. *Value marketing* has become the watchword for many marketers. Rather than offering high quality at a high price, or lesser quality at very low prices, marketers are looking for ways to offer today's more financially cautious buyers greater value—just the right combination of product quality and good service at a fair price.

Changing economic conditions can have a big impact on even the most successful companies. For example, the recent economic downturn took a big bite out of Apple's sales growth and stock performance. Premium digital devices, such as the iPhone and iPod, account for more than 40 percent of Apple's sales. In a troubled economy, such products are often the hardest hit. When Apple issued lower-than-expected sales forecasts, its stock price hit an air pocket. "Apple sells premium products, and every [sign] we get on the economy is a negative one," said an analyst at the time. "[Not even] Apple's products are immune to that." Said Apple CEO Steve Jobs, "Our stock is being buffeted by factors a lot larger than ourselves."[35]

Marketers should pay attention to *income distribution* as well as income levels. Canadians in the top 5 percent of wage earners account for approximately 25 percent of the total income earned. According to the 2006 census, the median earnings among the top 20 percent of full-time workers increased over 16 percent, while the median earnings among those in the bottom one-fifth of the distribution fell by over 20 percent. In Canada, the rich are getting richer, the poor are getting poorer, and the earnings of the middle class are stagnating. Aboriginal workers also earn significantly less than the average Canadian. In 2005, the median income across all Canadians was $41 400 while the Aboriginal worker earned $25 600. Poverty is widespread among Aboriginal reserves, where education rates are low, unemployment is high, and individual incomes may be as low as $4000 per year. One observer noted, "Reserves, especially in Western Canada, are somewhere between Mexico and Somalia in terms of standard of living. The disparity between the reserves and the rest of Canada is immense. It should be a major embarrassment."[36]

This distribution of income has created a tiered market. Many companies, such as Holt Renfrew and La Maison Simons stores, aggressively target the affluent. Others, such as Buck or Two and Dollarama stores, target those with more modest means. In fact, such dollar stores are now the fastest-growing retailers in the nation. Still other companies tailor their marketing offers across a range of markets, from the affluent to the less affluent. For example, many high-end fashion designers whose designs sell at sky-high prices to those who can afford it now also sell merchandise at prices that the masses can manage. Isaac Mizrahi, a high-end fashion designer, pioneered the "fashion for the masses" trend by offering a line of clothing and accessories at Target. Now other designers, such as Nicole Miller and Stella McCartney, are offering less expensive lines at JCPenney and H&M, respectively. And Vera Wang, known for her $10 000 wedding gowns found in boutiques and high-end retailers such as Bergdorf Goodman, offers a line called "Simply Vera—Vera Wang" at Kohl's. In one fall collection, a Vera Wang gold brocade skirt that is nearly identical to a skirt that fetches US$890 at a high-end department store sells for US$68 at Kohl's.[37]

Changing Consumer Spending Patterns

Engel's laws
Differences noted over a century ago by Ernst Engel in how people shift their spending across food, housing, transportation, health care, and other goods and services categories as family income rises.

Food, housing, and transportation use up the most household income. However, consumers at different income levels have different spending patterns. Some of these differences were noted over a century ago by Ernst Engel, who studied how people shifted their spending as their income rose. He found that as family income rises, the percentage spent on food declines, the percentage spent on housing remains about constant (except for such utilities as gas, electricity, and public services, which decrease), and both the percentage spent on most other categories and that devoted to savings increase. **Engel's laws** generally have been supported by later studies.

Changes in major economic variables such as income, cost of living, interest rates, and savings and borrowing patterns have a large impact on the marketplace. Companies watch these variables by using economic forecasting. Businesses do not have to be wiped out by an economic downturn or caught short in a boom. With adequate warning, they can take advantage of changes in the economic environment.

3 Natural Environment

Natural environment
Natural resources that are needed as inputs by marketers or that are affected by marketing activities.

The **natural environment** involves the natural resources that are needed as inputs by marketers or that are affected by marketing activities. Environmental concerns have grown steadily during the past three decades. In many cities around the world, air and water pollution have reached dangerous levels. World concern continues to mount about the possibilities of global warming, and many environmentalists fear that we soon will be buried in our own trash.

Marketers should be aware of several trends in the natural environment. The first involves growing *shortages of raw materials*. Air and water may seem to be infinite resources, but some groups see long-run dangers. Air pollution chokes many of the world's large cities. Great Lakes water levels are low, causing problems in many Canadian interior port cities, and water shortages are already a big problem in some parts of the United States and the world. By 2030, more than one in three of the world's human beings will not have enough water to drink.[38] Renewable resources, such as forests and food, also have to be used wisely. Nonrenewable resources, such as oil, coal, and various minerals, pose a serious problem. Firms making products that require these scarce resources face large cost increases, even if the materials remain available.

A second environmental trend is *increased pollution*. Industry will almost always damage the quality of the natural environment. Consider the disposal of chemical and nuclear wastes; the dangerous mercury levels in the ocean; the quantity of chemical pollutants in the soil and food supply; and the littering of the environment with nonbiodegradable bottles, plastics, and other packaging materials.

A third trend is *increased government intervention* in natural resource management. The governments of different countries vary in their concern and efforts to promote a clean environment. Some, such as the German government, vigorously pursue environmental quality. Others, especially many poorer nations, do little about pollution, largely because they lack the needed funds or political will. Even the richer nations lack the vast funds and political accord needed to mount a worldwide environmental effort. The general hope is that companies around the world will accept more social responsibility, and that less expensive devices can be found to control and reduce pollution.

The Canadian government passed the *Environmental Protection Act* in 1989. This act established stringent pollution-control measures as well as the means for their enforcement, including fines as high as $1 million if regulations are violated. In the United States, the Environmental Protection Agency (EPA) was created in 1970 to set and enforce pollution standards and to conduct pollution research. Thus, companies doing business in Canada and the United States can expect strong controls from government and pressure groups. Instead of opposing regulation, marketers should help develop solutions to the material and energy problems facing the world.

Concern for the natural environment has spawned the so-called green movement. In 2008, the Canadian Standards Association published guidelines for the business community to ensure that environmental advertising and labelling were not false and misleading.[39] Today, enlightened companies go beyond what government regulations dictate. They are

Responding to the consumer demand for more environmentally responsible products, GE is using "ecomagination" to create products for a better world.

Environmental sustainability
Developing strategies and practices that create a world economy that the planet can support indefinitely.

developing strategies and practices that support **environmental sustainability**—an effort to create a world economy that the planet can support indefinitely. They are responding to consumer demands with more environmentally responsible products.

For example, General Electric is using its "ecomagination" to create products for a better world—cleaner aircraft engines, cleaner locomotives, cleaner fuel technologies. Taken together, for instance, all the GE Energy wind turbines in the world could produce enough power for 2.4 million homes. And in 2005, GE launched its Evolution series locomotives, diesel engines that cut fuel consumption by 5 percent and emissions by 40 percent compared to locomotives built just a year earlier. Up next is a triumph of sheer coolness: a GE hybrid diesel–electric locomotive that, just like a Toyota Prius, captures energy from braking and will improve mileage another 10 percent.[40]

Other companies are developing recyclable or biodegradable packaging, recycled materials and components, better pollution controls, and more energy-efficient operations. For example, Walmart Canada is expanding its private-label brand of environmentally preferable cleaning products. Created by two Canadian entrepreneurs with a deep commitment to making products greener and more effective, GreenLine was launched by Walmart Canada in April 2008. The products are certified by the Environmental Choice EcoLogo program, a leading North American environmental standard, to be better for the environment. Priced below many conventional cleaning products, GreenLine products' sales have steadily grown during the first year. "Walmart continues to take green mainstream as we launch an ever-increasing number of environmentally preferable products, not just in the cleaning aisle, but across the store," said Jim Thompson, senior vice-president of merchandising and operations for Walmart Canada. "Our aim remains bringing customers environmentally preferable products they can afford so they don't have to make financial trade-offs when adopting more sustainable lifestyles."[41]

Thus, companies today are looking to do more than just good deeds. More and more, they are recognizing the link between a healthy ecology and a healthy economy. They are learning that environmentally responsible actions can also be good business.

Technological Environment

Technological environment
Forces that create new technologies, creating new product and market opportunities.

The **technological environment** is perhaps the most dramatic force now shaping our destiny. Technology has released such wonders as antibiotics, robotic surgery, miniaturized electronics, laptop computers, and the Internet. It also has released such horrors as nuclear missiles, chemical weapons, and assault rifles, and such mixed blessings as the automobile, television, and credit cards.

Our attitude toward technology depends on whether we are more impressed with its wonders or its blunders. For example, what would you think about having tiny little transmitters implanted in all of the products you buy that would allow the tracking of products from their point of production through use and disposal? On the one hand, it would provide many advantages to both buyers and sellers. On the other hand, it could be a bit scary. Either way, it's already happening:

Envision a world in which every product contains a tiny transmitter, loaded with information. As you stroll through the supermarket aisles, shelf sensors detect your selections and beam ads to your shopping cart screen, offering special deals on related products. As your cart fills, scanners detect that you might be buying for a dinner party; the screen suggests a wine to go with the meal you've planned. When you leave the store, exit scanners total up your purchases and automatically charge them to your credit card. At home, readers track what goes into and out of your pantry,

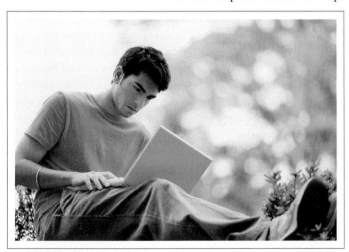

Technological environment: Technology is perhaps the most dramatic force shaping the marketing environment.

updating your shopping list when stocks run low. For Sunday dinner, you pop a Butterball turkey into your "smart oven," which follows instructions from an embedded chip and cooks the bird to perfection.[42]

Seem far-fetched? Not really. In fact, it might soon become a reality, thanks to tiny radio-frequency identification (RFID) transmitters—or "smart chips"—that can be embedded in the products you buy. Beyond benefits to consumers, the RFID chips also give producers and retailers an amazing new way to track their products electronically—anywhere in the world, anytime, automatically—from factories, to warehouses, to retail shelves, to recycling centres. Many large firms are adding fuel to the RFID fire. For example, Walmart requires all suppliers shipping products to its Sam's Club distribution centres to apply RFID tags to their pallets. If they don't, it charges $2 a pallet to do it for them. Sam's Club plans to use RFID tags on every pallet, case, and item by the fall of 2010. One study found that by using RFID, Walmart can improve its inventory accuracy by 13 percent, saving millions and millions of dollars a year.

The technological environment changes rapidly. Think of all of today's common products that were not available 100 years ago, or even 30 years ago. John A. Macdonald did not know about automobiles, airplanes, radios, or the electric light. William Lyon Mackenzie King did not know about xerography, synthetic detergents, tape recorders, birth control pills, jet engines, or earth satellites. John Diefenbaker did not know about personal computers, cellphones, the Internet, or googling.

New technologies create new markets and opportunities. However, every new technology replaces an older technology. Transistors hurt the vacuum-tube industry, xerography hurt the carbon-paper business, CDs hurt phonograph records, and digital photography hurt the film business. When old industries fought or ignored new technologies, their businesses declined. Thus, marketers should watch the technological environment closely. Companies that do not keep up will soon find their products outdated, and they will miss new product and market opportunities.

The United States leads the world in research and development spending. Total U.S. R&D spending reached an estimated US$367 billion in 2007.[43] Canada, in comparison, spends approximately $29 billion per year on R&D.[44] Canada ranks fifteenth in the world in research and development spending as a percentage of all products and services, but knowing the importance of R&D to economic growth, the Canadian government is aiming to be among the top five research-intensive countries in the world.[45] To accomplish this aim, Industry Canada and the National Research Council are funding new efforts to foster increased research. Other government-backed initiatives include the Canada Foundation for Innovation, which awards funds to help postsecondary educational institutions, research hospitals, and not-for-profit institutions modernize their research infrastructure and equip themselves for state-of-the-art research. Scientists today are researching a wide range of promising new products and services, ranging from practical solar energy, electric cars, paint-on computer and entertainment video displays, and powerful computers that you can wear or fold into your pocket to go-anywhere concentrators that produce drinkable water from the air.

Today's research is usually carried out by research teams rather than by lone inventors such as Thomas Edison or Alexander Graham Bell. Many companies are adding marketing people to R&D teams to try to obtain a stronger marketing orientation. Scientists also speculate on fantasy products, such as flying cars, three-dimensional televisions, and space colonies. The challenge in each case is not only technical but also commercial—to make *practical, affordable* versions of these products.

As products and technology become more complex, the public needs to know that these are safe. Canada has a complex web of departments and regulations devoted to issues associated with product safety. For example, Agriculture and Agri-Food Canada and the Canadian Food Inspection Agency monitor the safety of food products. The Department of Justice oversees the *Consumer Packaging and Labelling Act*, the *Food and Drug Act*, and the *Hazardous Products Act*. Health Canada also has a food safety and product safety division. Transport Canada governs vehicle recalls. Such regulations have resulted in much higher research costs and in longer times between new-product ideas and their introduction. Marketers should be aware of these regulations when applying new technologies and developing new products.

4 Political and Social Environment

Political environment
Laws, government agencies, and pressure groups that influence and limit various organizations and individuals in a given society.

Marketing decisions are strongly affected by developments in the political environment. The **political environment** consists of laws, government agencies, and pressure groups that influence or limit various organizations and individuals in a given society.

Legislation Regulating Business

Even the most liberal advocates of free-market economies agree that the system works best with at least some regulation. Well-conceived regulation can encourage competition and ensure fair markets for goods and services. Thus, to guide commerce, governments develop *public policy*—sets of laws and regulations that limit business for the good of society as a whole. Almost every marketing activity is subject to a wide range of laws and regulations.

Increasing Legislation Legislation affecting business around the world has increased steadily over the years. Canada has many laws covering issues such as competition, fair trade practices, environmental protection, product safety, truth in advertising, consumer privacy, packaging and labelling, pricing, and other important areas (see Table 3.2). The European Commission has been active in establishing a new framework of laws covering competitive behaviour, product standards, product liability, and commercial transactions for the nations of the European Union.

Understanding the public policy implications of a particular marketing activity is not a simple matter. For example, in Canada there are many laws created at the federal, provincial, and municipal levels, and these regulations often overlap. Moreover, regulations are constantly changing—what was allowed last year may now be prohibited, and what was

Table 3.2 Major Federal Legislation Affecting Marketing

The *Competition Act* is a major legislative act affecting the marketing activities of companies in Canada. Specific sections and the relevant areas are as follows:

- Section 34: Pricing—Forbids suppliers to charge different prices to competitors purchasing like quantities of goods (price discrimination). Forbids price-cutting that lessens competition (predatory pricing).

- Section 36: Pricing and Advertising—Forbids advertising prices that misrepresent the "usual" selling price (misleading price advertising).

- Section 38: Pricing—Forbids suppliers to require subsequent resellers to offer products at a stipulated price (resale price maintenance).

- Section 33: Mergers—Forbids mergers by which competition is, or is likely to be, lessened to the detriment of the interests of the public.

Other selected acts that have an impact on marketing activities include the following:

- *National Trade-mark and True Labelling Act*—Established the term Canada Standard, or CS, as a national trademark; requires certain commodities to be properly labelled or described in advertising for the purpose of indicating material content or quality.

- *Consumer Packaging and Labelling Act*—Provides a set of rules to ensure that full information is disclosed by the manufacturer, packer, or distributor. Requires that all prepackaged products bear the quantity in French and English in metric as well as traditional Canadian standard units of weight, volume, or measure.

- *Motor Vehicle Safety Act*—Establishes mandatory safety standards for motor vehicles.

- *Food and Drug Act*—Prohibits the advertisement and sale of adulterated or misbranded foods, cosmetics, and drugs.

- *Personal Information Protection and Electronic Documents Act*—Establishes rules to govern the collection, use, and disclosure of personal information and recognizes the right of privacy of individuals. The law recognizes the needs of organizations to collect, use, or disclose personal information for appropriate purposes. (For full details of the act, see http://laws.justice.gc.ca/en/P-8.6/258031.html.)

prohibited may now be allowed. Marketers must work hard to keep up with changes in regulations and their interpretations.

Business legislation has been enacted for a number of reasons. The first is to *protect companies* from each other. Although business executives may praise competition, they sometimes try to neutralize it when it threatens them. So laws are passed to define and prevent unfair competition.

The second purpose of government regulation is to *protect consumers* from unfair business practices. Some firms, if left alone, would make shoddy products, invade consumer privacy, tell lies in their advertising, and deceive consumers through their packaging and pricing. Unfair business practices have been defined and are enforced by various agencies.

The third purpose of government regulation is to *protect the interests of society* against unrestrained business behaviour. Profitable business activity does not always create a better quality of life. Regulation arises to ensure that firms take responsibility for the social costs of their production or products.

Changing Government Agency Enforcement International marketers will encounter dozens, or even hundreds, of agencies set up to enforce trade policies and regulations. In Canada, several federal agencies, such as Health Canada, the Canadian Food Inspection Agency, Industry Canada, and the Canadian Environmental Assessment Agency, have been established. Because such government agencies have some discretion in enforcing the laws, they can have a major impact on a company's marketing performance.

New laws and their enforcement will continue to increase. Business executives must watch these developments when planning their products and marketing programs. Marketers need to know about the major laws protecting competition, consumers, and society. They need to understand these laws at the local, provincial, national, and international levels.

Increased Emphasis on Ethics and Socially Responsible Actions

Written regulations cannot possibly cover all potential marketing abuses, and existing laws are often difficult to enforce. However, beyond written laws and regulations, business is also governed by social codes and rules of professional ethics.

Socially Responsible Behaviour Enlightened companies encourage their managers to look beyond what the regulatory system allows and simply "do the right thing." These socially responsible firms actively seek out ways to protect the long-run interests of their consumers and the environment.

The recent rash of business scandals and increased concerns about the environment have created fresh interest in the issues of ethics and social responsibility. Almost every aspect of marketing involves such issues. Unfortunately, because these issues usually involve conflicting interests, well-meaning people can honestly disagree about the right course of action in a given situation. Thus, many industrial and professional trade associations have codes of ethics. And more companies are now developing policies, guidelines, and other responses to complex social responsibility issues.

The boom in Internet marketing has created a new set of social and ethical issues. Critics worry most about online privacy issues. There has been an explosion in the amount of personal digital data available. Users themselves supply some of it. They voluntarily place highly private information on social networking sites such as Facebook or on genealogy sites, which are easily searched by anyone with a computer.

However, much of the information is systematically developed by businesses seeking to learn more about their customers, often without consumers realizing that they are under the microscope. Legitimate businesses plant cookies on consumers' computers and collect, analyze, and share digital data from every mouse click consumers make at their websites. Critics are concerned that companies may now know *too* much and that some companies might use digital data to take unfair advantage of consumers. Although most companies fully disclose their Internet privacy policies, and most work to use data to benefit their customers, abuses do occur. As a result, consumer advocates and policymakers are taking action to protect consumer privacy.

Throughout the text, we present "Real Marketing" exhibits that summarize the main public policy and social responsibility issues surrounding major marketing decisions. These exhibits discuss the legal issues that marketers should understand and the common ethical and societal concerns that marketers face. In Chapter 5, we discuss a broad range of societal marketing issues in greater depth.

Cause-Related Marketing To exercise their social responsibility and build more positive images, many companies are now linking themselves to worthwhile causes. These days, every product seems to be tied to some cause. Buy a pink mixer from KitchenAid and support breast cancer research. Purchase Ethos water from Starbucks and help bring clean water to children around the world. For every Staples Easy Button you buy, the office supplies retailer will donate a portion to Special Olympics Canada. Sign up for a monthly cellphone package with Virgin Mobile Canada and you can enroll in the Common Cents program. This program rounds up your monthly bill to the nearest dollar and, through its partnership with Virgin Unite (the Virgin Group's not-for-profit foundation), Virgin Mobile donates all proceeds to charitable initiatives such as RE*Generation Canada, which supports homeless youth.

Cause-related marketing has become a primary form of corporate giving. It lets companies "do well by doing good" by linking purchases of the company's products or services with fund-raising for worthwhile causes or charitable organizations. Companies now sponsor dozens of cause-related marketing campaigns each year. Many are backed by large budgets and a full complement of marketing activities. For example, consider P&G's "Pantene Beautiful Lengths" campaign, which last year received Cause Marketing Forum's Golden Halo Award for the best cause-related health campaign. The Pantene Beautiful Lengths campaign has involved a broad-based marketing effort, including a campaign website, public service TV and print ads, and promotional items and events. P&G kicked off the Pantene Beautiful Lengths with celebrity spokeswoman Diane Lane having her hair cut for donation on the *Today Show*. Since then the campaign has generated more than 700 million media impressions in major publications, TV shows, and websites. To date, the campaign has received more than 24 000 donated ponytails and more than 3000 free wigs have been distributed through the American Cancer Society's nationwide network of wig banks. Compare that to the 2000 wigs created over the past 10 years by charity Locks of Love. Pantene Beautiful Lengths has also contributed more than $1 million to the EIF Women's Cancer Research Fund, which raises funds and awareness for millions of women and their families affected by cancer. This year, two-time Oscar winner Hilary Swank cut her hair for Pantene and is partnering with the Beautiful Lengths campaign to raise an incredible 1 million additional inches of hair to make more free wigs.[46]

Cause-related marketing has stirred some controversy. Critics worry that cause-related marketing is more a strategy for selling than a strategy for giving—that "cause-related" marketing is really "cause-exploitative" marketing. Thus, companies using cause-related marketing might find themselves walking a fine line between increased sales and an improved image, and facing charges of exploitation.

However, if handled well, cause-related marketing can greatly benefit both the company and the cause. The company gains an effective marketing tool while building a more positive public image. The charitable organization or cause gains greater visibility and important new sources of funding and support. Spending on cause-related marketing in the United States skyrocketed from only $120 million in 1990 to more than $1.5 billion by 2008.[47]

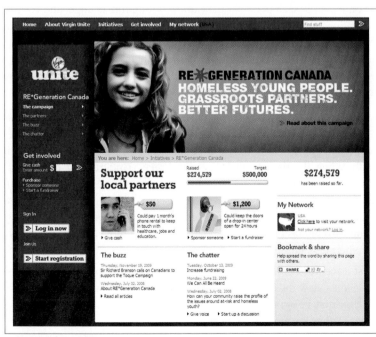

Cause-related marketing: Signing up for Virgin Mobile Canada's Common Cents program proves how a few cents can add up to enormous change for worthwhile charitable initiatives like RE*Generation Canada.

Cultural Environment

Cultural environment
Institutions and other forces that affect society's basic values, perceptions, preferences, and behaviours.

The **cultural environment** is made up of institutions and other forces that affect a society's basic values, perceptions, preferences, and behaviours. People grow up in a particular society that shapes their basic beliefs and values. They absorb a worldview that defines their relationships with others. The following cultural characteristics can affect marketing decision making.

Persistence of Cultural Values

People in a given society hold many beliefs and values. Their core beliefs and values have a high degree of persistence. For example, many Canadians believe in cultural diversity (versus assimilation), respect for human rights, democracy, gender equality, stability of government, the rule of law, sustainable development, social support for the underprivileged, universal health care, a love of nature, hard work, getting married, giving to charity, and being honest.[48] These beliefs shape more specific attitudes and behaviours found in everyday life.

Core beliefs and values are passed on from parents to children and are reinforced by schools, churches, business, and government. *Secondary* beliefs and values are more open to change. Believing in marriage is a core belief; believing that people should get married early in life is a secondary belief. Marketers have some chance of changing secondary values but little chance of changing core values. For example, family-planning marketers could argue more effectively that people should get married later than not get married at all.

Shifts in Secondary Cultural Values

Although core values are fairly persistent, cultural swings do take place. Consider the impact of popular music groups, movie personalities, and other celebrities on young people's hairstyling and clothing norms. Marketers want to predict cultural shifts to spot new opportunities or threats. Several firms offer "futures" forecasts in this connection. For example, the Yankelovich Monitor has tracked consumer value trends for years. Its annual "State of the Consumer" report analyzes and interprets the forces that shape consumers' lifestyles and their marketplace interactions. The major cultural values of a society are expressed in people's views of themselves and others, as well as in their views of organizations, society, nature, and the universe.

People's Views of Themselves People vary in their emphasis on serving themselves versus serving others. Some people seek personal pleasure, wanting fun, change, and escape. Others seek self-realization through religion, recreation, or the avid pursuit of careers or other life goals. People use products, brands, and services as a means of self-expression, and they buy products and services that match their views of themselves.

The Yankelovich Monitor identifies several consumer segments whose purchases are motivated by self-views. Here are two examples:

> *Do-It-Yourselfers—Recent Movers.* Embodying the whole do-it-yourself attitude, these active consumers not only tackle home improvement projects on their own, but they also view the experience as a form of self-expression. They view their homes as their havens, especially when it's time to kick back and relax. Undertaking decorating, remodelling, and auto maintenance projects to save money and have fun, Do-It-Yourselfers view their projects as personal victories over the high-priced marketplace. Mostly Gen X families with children at home, these consumers also enjoy playing board and card games and renting movies. As recent movers, they're actively spending to turn their new home into a castle.

> *Adventurers.* These adventuresome individuals rarely follow a single path or do the same thing twice. These folks view the experience as far more exciting than the entertainment value. Although they may be appreciative of the arts (including movies, museums, photography, and music), they are more likely to engage in activities most think are too dangerous, and they like to view themselves as doing things others wouldn't dare to do.[49]

Marketers can target their products and services based on such self-views. For example, MasterCard targets Adventurers who might want to use their credit cards to quickly set up the experience of a lifetime. It tells these consumers, "There are some things in life that money can't buy. For everything else, there's MasterCard."

People's Views of Others In past decades, observers have noted several shifts in people's attitudes toward others. Recently, for example, many trend trackers have seen a new wave of "cocooning," in which people are going out less with others and staying home more to enjoy the creature comforts of home and hearth—from the networked home office, to home entertainment centres, to just finding a quiet spot to plug into their iPods while they check their favourite web hangouts. "Call it Cocooning in the Digital Age," says one observer. "With DVD players in most homes, broadband connections proliferating, scores of new video game titles being released each year, and nearly 400 cable channels, consumers can be endlessly entertained right in their own living room or home theatre."[50]

This trend suggests less demand for theatre-going and greater demand for home improvement, home office, and home entertainment products. And "as the . . . 'nesting' or 'cocooning' trend continues, with people choosing to stay home and entertain more often, the trend of upgrading outdoor living spaces has [grown rapidly]," says a home industry analyst. People are adding bigger decks with fancy gas-ready barbeques, outdoor Jacuzzis, and other amenities that make the old house "home sweet home" for family and friends.[51]

People's Views of Organizations People vary in their attitudes toward corporations, government agencies, trade unions, universities, and other organizations. By and large, people are willing to work for major organizations and expect them, in turn, to carry out society's work.

The past two decades have seen a sharp decrease in loyalty toward and confidence in business and political organizations and institutions. In the workplace, there has been an overall decline in organizational loyalty. Waves of company downsizings bred cynicism and distrust. In just the last decade, corporate scandals at Enron, WorldCom, and Tyco, record-breaking profits for big oil companies during a time of all-time high prices at the pump, and other questionable activities have resulted in a further loss of confidence in big business. Many people today see work not as a source of satisfaction but as a required chore to earn money to enjoy their nonwork hours. This trend suggests that organizations need to find new ways to win consumer and employee confidence.

People's Views of Society People vary in their attitudes toward their society—nationalists defend it, reformers want to change it, malcontents want to leave it. People's orientation to their society influences their consumption patterns and attitudes toward the marketplace. For example, more and more Canadians have a sense of national pride. Some companies, such as Zellers, responded with "made-in-Canada" themes and promotions. Others, such as Petro-Canada, Clearly Canadian, Molson Canadian, and Upper Canada Brewing Company, made national identity a part of their branding strategy.

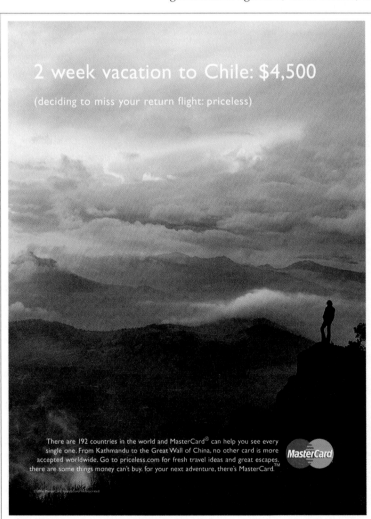

2 week vacation to Chile: $4,500

(deciding to miss your return flight: priceless)

There are 192 countries in the world and MasterCard® can help you see every single one. From Kathmandu to the Great Wall of China, no other card is more accepted worldwide. Go to priceless.com for fresh travel ideas and great escapes. there are some things money can't buy. for your next adventure, there's MasterCard.™

MasterCard

People's self-views: With its "priceless" campaign, MasterCard targets "Adventurers" who imagine themselves doing things others wouldn't dare do. MasterCard can help them quickly set up the experience of a lifetime—"Deciding to miss your return flight: priceless."

People's Views of Nature　People vary in their attitudes toward the natural world—some feel ruled by it, others feel in harmony with it, and still others seek to master it. A long-term trend has been people's growing mastery over nature through technology and the belief that nature is bountiful. More recently, however, people have recognized that nature is finite and fragile and that it can be destroyed or spoiled by human activities.

This renewed love of the natural world has created a sizable "lifestyles of health and sustainability" (LOHAS) market—consumers who seek out everything from natural, organic, and nutritional products to fuel-efficient cars and alternative medicine. This segment spends nearly US$215 billion annually on such products. In the words of one such consumer:

> I am not an early adopter, a fast follower, or a mass-market stampeder. But I am a gas-conscious driver. So that's why I was standing in a Toyota dealership . . . this week, the latest person to check out a hybrid car. Who needs $40 fill-ups? After tooling around in three different hybrid car brands—Toyota, Honda and a Ford—I thought, How cool could this be? Saving gas money and doing well by the environment. Turns out there's a whole trend-watchers' classification for people who think like that: LOHAS. Lifestyles of Health and Sustainability. Buy a hybrid. Shop at places like Planet Organic Market. No skin off our noses. Conscientious shopping with no sacrifice or hippie stigma.[52]

Many marketers are now tracking and responding to such cultural trends. For example, Walmart recently developed a Live Better Index by which it tracks the attitudes of its 180 million annual shoppers. The first Live Better Index tracked consumers' decisions regarding eco-friendly products such as compact fluorescent lightbulbs, organic milk, and concentrated liquid laundry detergents in reduced packaging. The index shows that 11 percent of North Americans now consider themselves to be converts to more sustainable living and that 43 percent say they will be "extremely green" within the next five years.[53]

Food producers have also found fast-growing markets for natural and organic products. Consider Earthbound Farm, a company that grows and sells organic produce. It started in 1984 as a 2.5-acre raspberry farm in California's Carmel Valley. Founders Drew and Myra Goodman wanted to do the right thing by farming the land organically and producing food they'd feel good about serving to their family, friends, and neighbours. Today, Earthbound Farm has grown to become the world's largest producer of organic vegetables, with 40 000 acres under plow, annual sales of US$480 million, and products available in 75 percent of North America's supermarkets.[54]

In total, the North American organic-food market generated US$19.5 billion in sales last year, a more than 20 percent increase over the year before. Niche marketers, such as Planet Organic Market, have sprung up to serve this market, and traditional food chains such as Loblaw's Superstore and Safeway have added separate natural and organic food sections. Even pet owners are joining the movement as they become more aware of what goes into Fido's food. Almost every major pet food brand now offers several types of natural foods.[55]

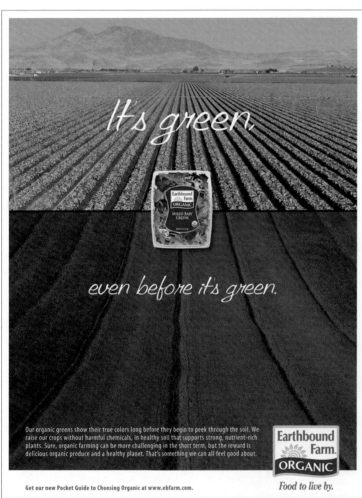

Riding the trend of all things natural, Earthbound Farm has grown to become the world's largest producer of organic salads, fruits, and vegetables, with products in 75 percent of North America's supermarkets.

People's Views of the Universe　Finally, people vary in their beliefs about the origin of the universe and their place in it. Although many Canadians have religious beliefs, attendance at religious services has been dropping off gradually over the years. A recent Statistics Canada survey shows Canadians' continuing slide out the doors of the country's churches, temples, and synagogues. In 1946, 67 percent of adult Canadians regularly attended religious services, but by 2001, the figure had dropped to 20 percent. Yann Martel, Canadian author of the acclaimed *Life of Pi,* noted in an interview that Canadians and Americans are going in opposite directions with regard to religion. "America is a very religious, almost puritanical country. In Canada, secularism is triumphant, and to talk noncynically, nonironically about religion is strange," he says. Only 30 percent of Canadians report that religion is very important to them, compared with 59 percent of Americans. The statistics would be even more skewed if it were not for the growing number of devout Muslim, Sikh, and Hindu immigrants now living in Canada. Canadian marketers have to use caution when picking up lifestyle ads from the United States. While showing people in religious settings may draw attention from American consumers, they may strike Canadians as inappropriate.[56]

5 RESPONDING TO THE MARKETING ENVIRONMENT

Someone once observed, "There are three kinds of companies: those who make things happen, those who watch things happen, and those who wonder what's happened."[57] Many companies view the marketing environment as an uncontrollable element to which they must react and adapt. They passively accept the marketing environment and do not try to change it. They analyze the environmental forces and design strategies that will help the company avoid the threats and take advantage of the opportunities the environment provides.

Other companies take a *proactive* stance toward the marketing environment. Rather than simply watching and reacting, these firms take aggressive actions to affect the publics and forces in their marketing environment. Such companies hire lobbyists to influence legislation affecting their industries and stage media events to gain favourable press coverage. They run advertorials (ads expressing editorial points of view) to shape public opinion. They press lawsuits and file complaints with regulators to keep competitors in line, and they form contractual agreements to better control their distribution channels.

By taking action, companies can often overcome seemingly uncontrollable environmental events. For example, whereas some companies view the seemingly ceaseless online rumour mill as something over which they have no control, others work proactively to prevent or counter negative word of mouth. Tim Hortons had to deal with a persistent and potentially damaging rumour when it started to spread by email:

> We've all heard the rumour—Tim Hortons coffee is so addictive it must contain nicotine (or MSG). This rumour began circulating via word of mouth several years ago, but it erupted in email form in 2006. The bogus email alleged that a man from Arkansas came to Canada and suffered cardiac arrest. He was allergic to nicotine. After asking Tim Hortons what was in their coffee and threatening legal action when they refused to divulge, the company supposedly admitted to adding nicotine to the coffee. The email also alleged that a girl on a nicotine patch was diagnosed with nicotine overload because, even though she had quit smoking, she had not given up her daily coffee from Tim Hortons. The company was quick to respond to this false allegation and even addresses the question on the FAQ page of their corporate website, stating "Tim Hortons would like to clearly state that there is absolutely NO nicotine or MSG in our coffee. Tim Hortons coffee has NO ADDITIVES whatsoever." In fact, all their products must pass independent testing by the Canadian Food Inspection Agency, so additives of any kind in their coffee would just not be possible. Still, the rumour persists and Tim Hortons must continue to proactively manage this type of negative word of mouth.[58]

Marketing management cannot always control environmental forces. In many cases, it must settle for simply watching and reacting to the environment. For example, a company would have little success trying to influence geographic population shifts, the economic environment, or major cultural values. But whenever possible, smart marketing managers will take a *proactive* rather than *reactive* approach to the marketing environment (see Real Marketing 3.2).

Real Marketing **3.2**

YourCompanySucks.com

The Internet has been hailed by marketers as the great new relational medium. Companies use the Web to engage customers, gain insights into their needs, and create customer community. In turn, web-empowered consumers share their brand experiences with companies and with each other. All of this back-and-forth helps both the company and its customers. But sometimes the dialogue can get nasty. Consider the following examples:

MSN Money columnist Scott Burns accuses Home Depot of being a "consistent abuser" of customers' time. Within hours, MSN's servers are caving under the weight of 14 000 blistering emails and posts from angry Home Depot customers who storm the MSN comment room, taking the company to task for pretty much everything. It is the biggest response in MSN Money's history.

Blogger Jeff Jarvis posts a series of irate messages to his BuzzMachine blog about the many failings of his Dell computer and his struggles with Dell's customer support. The post quickly draws national attention, and an open letter posted by Jarvis to Dell founder Michael Dell becomes the third most linked-to post on the blogosphere the day after it appears. Jarvis's headline—Dell Hell—becomes shorthand for the ability of a lone blogger to deliver a body blow to an unsuspecting business.

Systems engineer Michael Whitford wakes up one morning to find that his favourite-ever laptop, an Apple MacBook, still under warranty, has "decided not to work." Whitford takes the machine to his local Apple store, where the counter person obligingly sends it off for repairs. However, Whitford later gets a call from an AppleCare representative, who claims that the laptop has "spill damage" not covered by the warranty and says that repairs will cost him $774. "I did not spill anything on my laptop," declares Whitford. "Too bad," says the Apple rep, and the MacBook is returned unrepaired. But that's not the end of the story—far from it. A short time later, Whitford posts a video on YouTube (www. youtube.com/watch?v= hHbrQqrgVgg). In the video, a seemingly rational Whitford calmly selects among a golf club, an axe, and a sword before finally deciding on a sledgehammer as his weapon of choice for bashing his nonfunctioning MacBook to smithereens. More than 490 000 people have viewed the smash-up on YouTube and the video has been passed along on countless blogs and other websites.

Extreme events? Not anymore. "Web 2.0" has turned the traditional power relationship between businesses and consumers upside-down. In the good old days, disgruntled consumers could do little more than bellow at a company service rep or shout out their complaints from a street corner. Now, armed with only a PC and a broadband connection, they can take it public, airing their gripes to millions on blogs, chats, online communities, or even hate sites devoted exclusively to their least favourite corporations.

"I hate" and "sucks" sites are becoming almost commonplace. These sites target some highly respected companies with some highly disrespectful labels: PayPalSucks.com (a.k.a. NoPayPal); Walmart-Blows.com; MicrosoftSucks.org; AmexSux.com (American Express); IHateStarbucks.com; DeltaREALLYsucks.com; and UnitedPackageSmashers.com (UPS), to name only a few.

Some of these sites and other web attacks air legitimate complaints that should be addressed. Others, however, are little more than anonymous, vindictive slurs that unfairly ransack brands and corporate reputations. Some of the attacks are only a passing nuisance; others can draw serious attention and create real headaches.

How should companies react to web attacks? The real quandary for targeted companies is figuring out how far they can go to protect their images without fuelling the already raging fire. One point upon which all experts seem to agree: Don't try to retaliate in kind. "It's rarely a good idea to lob bombs at the fire starters," says one analyst. "Preemption, engagement, and diplomacy are saner tools."

Some companies have tried to silence the critics through lawsuits, but few have succeeded. The courts have tended to regard such criticism as opinion and therefore as protected speech. As it turns out, a company has legal recourse only when the unauthorized use of its trademarks, brand names, or other intellectual property is apt to be confusing to the public. And no reasonable person is likely to be confused that Walmart maintains and supports a site tagged Walmart-Blows.com. Beyond the finer legal points, companies also fear that a lawsuit will only draw more attention to the consumer hate site.

Given the difficulties of trying to sue consumer online criticisms out of existence, some companies have tried other strategies. For example, most big companies now routinely buy up web addresses for their firm names preceded by the words "IHate" or followed by "sucks.com." For example, Procter & Gamble has registered IHateProcterAndGamble .com and, interestingly, FebrezeKillsPets.com. But this approach is easily thwarted, as Walmart learned when it registered IHateWalmart.com, only to find that someone else then registered IReallyHateWalmart.com.

Today, armed only with a PC and a broadband connection, the little guy can take it public against corporate America. By listening and proactively responding to such seemingly uncontrollable environmental events, companies can prevent the negatives from spiralling out of control or even turn them into positives.

In general, attempts to block, counterattack, or shut down consumer attacks may be shortsighted. Such criticisms are often based on real consumer concerns and unresolved anger. Hence, the best strategy might be to proactively monitor these sites and respond to the concerns they express. "The most obvious thing to do is talk to the customer and try to deal with the problem, instead of putting your fingers in your ears," advises one consultant. For example, Home Depot CEO Francis Blake drew praise when he heeded the criticisms expressed in the MSN Money onslaught and responded positively. Blake posted a heartfelt letter in which he thanked critic Scott Burns, apologized to angry customers, and promised to make things better. He also created a new company site and a "dedicated taskforce" to deal specifically with Home Depot service problems. And within a month of the YouTube video, Apple fessed up to its misdeeds and replaced Michael Whitford's laptop. "I'm very happy now," says Whitford. "Apple has regained my loyalty. I guess I finally got their attention."

Many companies have now set up teams of specialists that monitor web conversations and engage disgruntled consumers. Others hire firms such as BuzzLogic, which creates "conversation maps" tracking not just who's talking about a company's product but also which opinions matter most. BuzzLogic recently helped computer maker Lenovo head off its own Dell Hell moment. When tech-oriented blogger Rick Klau posted his frustrations over his Lenovo ThinkPad's faulty hard drive, BuzzLogic quickly picked up the post and alerted Lenovo. Within only a few hours, Klau received a phone call from David Churbuck, Lenovo's VP of global web marketing. Churbuck offered to fix the problem, turning Klau's rants into raves. The good news was picked up by other bloggers before the bad news could catch fire.

Thus, by listening and proactively responding to seemingly uncontrollable events in the environment, companies can prevent the negatives from spiralling out of control or even turn them into positives. Who knows? With the right responses, Walmart-Blows.com might even become Walmart-Rules.com. Then again, probably not.

Sources: Quotes, excerpts, and other information from Michelle Conlin, "Web Attack," *BusinessWeek*, April 16, 2007, pp. 54–56; Oliver Ryan, "The Buzz Around Buzz," *Fortune*, March 19, 2007, p. 46; Gemma Charles, "Complaints Are There to Be Heard," *Marketing*, January 10, 2007, p. 15; "Top 10 Service Complaint Sites," *Time Out New York*, March 8, 2007, accessed at www.timeout.com; "Corporate Hate Sites," New Media Institute, accessed at www.newmedia.org/categories/Hot-Topics-&-Issues/Corporate-Hate-Sites/, February 2008; "Consumer Vigilantes," *BusinessWeek*, March 3, 2008, p. 38; and Christopher L. Marting and Nathan Bennett, "Corporate Reputation; What to Do About Online Attacks," *Wall Street Journal*, March 10, 2008, p. R6.

REVIEWING OBJECTIVES AND KEY TERMS   mymarketinglab | Audio Chapter Summary

In this chapter and the next two chapters, you'll examine the environments of marketing and how companies analyze these environments to better understand the marketplace and consumers. Companies must constantly watch and manage the *marketing environment* to seek opportunities and ward off threats. The marketing environment consists of all the actors and forces influencing the company's ability to transact business effectively with its target market.

OBJECTIVE 1   **Describe the environmental forces that affect the company's ability to serve its customers.**

The company's *microenvironment* consists of other actors close to the company that combine to form the company's value delivery network or that affect its ability to serve its customers. It includes the company's *internal environment*—its several departments and management levels—as it influences marketing decision making. *Marketing channel firms*—suppliers and marketing intermediaries, including resellers, physical distribution firms, marketing services agencies, and financial intermediaries—cooperate to create customer value. Five types of customer *markets* include consumer, business, reseller, government, and international markets. *Competitors* vie with the company in an effort to serve customers better. Finally, various *publics* have an actual or potential interest in or impact on the company's ability to meet its objectives.

The *macroenvironment* consists of larger societal forces that affect the entire microenvironment. The six forces making up the company's macroenvironment include demographic, economic, natural, technological, political, and cultural forces. These forces shape opportunities and pose threats to the company.

OBJECTIVE 2   **Explain how changes in the demographic and economic environments affect marketing decisions.**

Demography is the study of the characteristics of human populations. Today's *demographic environment* shows a changing age structure, shifting family profiles, geographic population shifts, a better-educated and more white-collar population, and increasing diversity. The *economic environment* consists of factors that affect buying power and patterns. The economic environment is characterized by more consumer concern for value and shifting consumer spending patterns. Today's squeezed consumers are seeking greater value—just the right combination of good quality and service at a fair price. The distribution of income is also shifting. The rich have grown richer, the middle class has shrunk, and the poor have remained poor, leading to a two-tiered market. Many companies now tailor their marketing offers to two different markets—the affluent and the less affluent.

OBJECTIVE 3   **Identify the major trends in the firm's natural and technological environments.**

The *natural environment* shows three major trends: shortages of certain raw materials, higher pollution levels, and more government intervention in natural resource management. Environmental concerns create marketing opportunities for alert companies. The *technological environment* creates both opportunities and challenges. Companies that fail to keep up with technological change will miss out on new product and marketing opportunities.

OBJECTIVE 4   **Explain the key changes in the political and cultural environments.**

The *political environment* consists of laws, agencies, and groups that influence or limit marketing actions. The political environment has undergone three changes that affect marketing worldwide: increasing legislation regulating business, strong government agency enforcement, and greater emphasis on ethics and socially responsible actions. The *cultural environment* is made up of institutions and forces that affect a society's values, perceptions, preferences, and behaviours. The environment shows trends toward digital "cocooning," a lessening trust of institutions, greater appreciation for nature, a new spiritualism, and the search for more meaningful and enduring values.

OBJECTIVE 5   **Discuss how companies can react to the marketing environment.**

Companies can passively accept the marketing environment as an uncontrollable element to which they must adapt, avoiding threats and taking advantage of opportunities as they arise. Or they can take a *proactive* stance, working to change the environment rather than simply reacting to it. Whenever possible, companies should try to be proactive rather than reactive.

KEY TERMS

mymarketinglab | Glossary Flashcards

DISCUSSING THE CONCEPTS

1. Name and describe the elements of a company's microenvironment and give an example illustrating why each is important.

2. List some of the demographic trends of interest to marketers in Canada and discuss whether these trends pose opportunities or threats for marketers.

3. Discuss current trends in the economic environment of which marketers must be aware and provide examples of companies' responses to each trend.

4. Discuss the primary reasons why a company would hire a lobbyist in Ottawa. Would it make sense for the same company to also hire lobbyists at the provincial level? Why?

5. Compare and contrast core beliefs/values and secondary beliefs/values. Provide an example of each and discuss the potential impact marketers have on each.

6. How should marketers respond to the changing marketing environment?

APPLYING THE CONCEPTS

1. Much of Canadian culture is influenced by products from Hollywood, including movies and television programs. In a small group, select a current television program and explain how it might affect the cultural environment in Canada.

2. In April 2009, the Canadian government introduced anti-spam legislation, the *Electronic Commerce Protection Act* (ECPA). Visit www.ic.gc.ca/eic/site/ic1.nsf/eng/04595.html and read about this new act. Discuss the implications for electronic commerce in Canada.

3. Cause-related marketing has grown considerably over the past 10 years. Visit www.causemarketingforum.com and learn about companies winning Halo Awards for outstanding cause-related marketing programs. Present two award-winning case studies to your class.

FOCUS ON TECHNOLOGY

Have you ever gone phishing? Probably not, but the Internet enables unscrupulous individuals to "phish" for your personal information. This and other types of attacks aimed at stealing your identity or your money are called "social engineering." Social engineering is a remake of an old-fashioned con game that tricks people into giving information and then uses it to rob them. You might receive an email, supposedly from PayPal, Amazon.ca, or your bank, asking you to update your personal information. To make it easier for you, says the message, just click on the link in the email to input your information. Don't do it! The click will take you to a site that looks legitimate but is really a skilfully designed fake, often located in another country. Even if you don't enter any personal information, just clicking on the link might put software on your computer that can track your keystrokes, revealing login and password information to the crooks.

1. Discuss two recommendations for how consumers might protect themselves from such Internet scams.

2. Phishing scams also victimize businesses. Visit the U.S. Federal Trade Commission's (www.ftc.gov) and Industry Canada's (www.ic.gc.ca) websites to learn how businesses can deal with this problem and discuss recommendations for marketers who face this threat.

FOCUS ON ETHICS

Since the mid-1990s, companies such as Northfield Laboratories and Biopure have been testing blood substitutes in hopes of attaining approval by the U.S. Food and Drug Administration (FDA). Blood substitutes are oxygen-carrying products designed to replace donated human blood. Unlike human donor blood, these products can be stored without refrigeration for long periods and don't have to be cross-matched with a patient's blood. These characteristics offer significant advantages in battlefield and trauma applications. However, clinical trials indicate that using blood substitutes results in a 30 percent increase in the risk of death and nearly as high a risk of having a heart attack, leading some to criticize the FDA for allowing continued clinical trials. A recent study published in the *Journal of the American Medical Association* faulted the FDA for not conducting prompt analysis of previous studies and claimed that the risks of using blood substitutes were evident as early as 2000. The FDA claimed it was aware of these risks but deemed some products worthy of further research. Some critics are pushing for more stringent legislation governing product testing, particularly if there are potentially significant health risks.

1. Discuss the environmental forces acting on these companies. What are Northfield's and Biopure's responsibilities and possible reactions to these environmental forces?

2. Is it ethical for these companies to continue clinical trials in this case?

MARKETING BY THE NUMBERS

China and India are emerging markets that will have a significant impact on the world in coming years. With China's population at over 1.3 billion and India's at 1 billion, they are the two most populous countries, comprising almost 40 percent of the world's population. The economies of both countries are growing at phenomenal rates as well. The term "Chindia" is used to describe the growing power of these two countries, and predictions are that these two will overtake the United States as the largest economies in the world within just a few decades.

1. Discuss a demographic and an economic trend related to Chindia's power and its impact on marketers in North America. Support your discussion of these trends with statistics.

2. Using the chain ratio method described in Appendix 3: Marketing by the Numbers, discuss factors to consider when estimating total market demand for automobiles in China or India.

VIDEO CASE

TOMS Shoes

 | Video Case Questions

"Get involved: Changing a life begins with a single step." This sounds like a mandate from a not-for-profit volunteer organization. But in fact, this is the motto of a for-profit shoe company located in Santa Monica, California. In 2006, Tom Mycoskie founded TOMS Shoes because he wanted to do something different. He wanted to run a company that would make a profit while at the same time helping those in need around the world.

Specifically, for every pair of shoes that TOMS sells, it gives a pair of shoes to a needy child somewhere in the world. So far, the company has given away tens of thousands of pairs of shoes and is on track to give away hundreds of thousands more. Can TOMS succeed and thrive based on this idealistic concept? That all depends on how TOMS executes its strategy within the constantly changing marketing environment.

After viewing the video featuring TOMS Shoes, answer the following questions about the marketing environment:

1. What trends in the marketing environment have contributed to the success of TOMS Shoes?

2. Did TOMS Shoes first scan the marketing environment in creating its strategy, or did it create its strategy and fit the strategy to the environment? Does this matter?

3. Is TOMS's strategy more about serving needy children or about creating value for customers? Explain.

Visit MyMarketingLab at www.pearsoned.ca/mymarketinglab to view the video segment related to this case.

COMPANY CASE

Prius: Leading a Wave of Hybrids

North Americans love their cars. In a place where SUVs have dominated the roads for more than a decade and the biggest sport is stockcar racing, it seems unlikely that a small, sluggish, hybrid vehicle would become such a hit. But against all odds, the Toyota Prius has become one of the top 10 selling vehicles in North America. Introducing a fuel sipper in a market where vehicle size and horsepower have reigned led one Toyota executive to profess, "Frankly, it was one of the biggest crapshoots I've ever been involved in." Considering these issues, it is nothing short of amazing that only five years later, the president of Toyota Motor Sales U.S.A., Jim Press, dubbed the Prius "the hottest car we've ever had."

THE NUTS AND BOLTS OF THE PRIUS

Like other hybrids currently available or in development, the Prius combines a gas engine with an electric motor. Different hybrid vehicles employ this combination of power sources in different ways to boost both fuel efficiency and power. The Prius runs on only the electric motor when starting up and under initial acceleration. At roughly 25 kph, the gas engine kicks in. This means that the auto gets power from only the battery at low speeds, and from both the gas engine and electric motor during heavy acceleration.

Once up to speed, the gas engine sends power directly to the wheels and, through the generator, to the electric motor or battery. When braking, energy from the slowing wheels—energy that is wasted in a conventional car—is sent back through the electric motor to charge the battery. At a stop, the gas engine shuts off, saving fuel. When starting up and operating at low speeds, the auto makes no noise, which seems eerie to some drivers and to pedestrians who don't hear it coming!

The Prius first sold in the United States in the 2001 model year. It was a small, cramped, slow compact car with a dull design. Three years later, the second-generation Prius benefited from a modest power increase. But it was still anything but a muscle car. However, there were countless other improvements. The sleek, Asian-inspired design was much better looking than the first generation Prius and came in seven colours. The interior was roomy and practical, with plenty of rear leg room and gobs of storage space.

The Gen II Prius also provided expensive touches typically found only in luxury vehicles. A single push button brought the car to life. A seven-inch energy monitor touch screen displayed fuel consumption, outside temperature, and battery charge level. It also indicated when the car was running on gas, electricity, regenerated energy, or a combination of these. Multiple screens within the monitor also provided controls for air conditioning, audio, and a satellite navigation system. And whereas the first Prius averaged an astounding 42 miles per gallon, its successor did even better at 48.

A RUNAWAY SUCCESS

Apparently, consumers liked the improvements. In its inaugural year, the Prius saw moderate sales of just over 15 000 units—not bad considering that Toyota put minimal promotional effort behind the new vehicle. But sales for the carbon fuel miser have increased exponentially ever since. In 2007, Toyota sold 181 000 Priuses in the United States alone, a 70 percent increase over 2006 sales. That makes the Prius Toyota's third-best-selling passenger car following the Camry and Corolla. Perhaps more significantly, in May of 2008 Toyota announced that it had sold a total of 1 028 000 Prius cars worldwide since the vehicle first went on sale in Japan in 1997.

The rapid increase in demand for the Prius created a rare automotive phenomenon. During a period when most automotive companies had to offer substantial incentives to move vehicles, many Toyota dealers had no problem getting price premiums of up to $5000 over sticker price for the Prius. Waiting lists for the Prius stretched up to six months. At one point, spots on dealers' waiting lists were being auctioned on eBay for $500. By 2006, the Prius had become the "hottest" car in the United States, based on industry metrics of time spent on dealer lots, sales incentives, and average sale price relative to sticker price. In fact, according to Kelley Blue Book, demand for new Priuses became so strong that, even after one year and more than 32 000 kilometres, a Prius could fetch thousands more than its original sticker price.

There are many reasons for the success of the Prius. For starters, Toyota's targeting strategy has been spot-on from the beginning. It focused first on early adopters, techies who were attracted by the car's advanced technology. Such buyers not only bought the car but found ways to modify it by hacking into the Prius's computer system. Soon, owners were sharing their hacking secrets through chat rooms such as PriusEnvy.com, boasting such modifications as using the dashboard display screen to play video games, show files from a laptop, watch TV, and look at images taken by a rear-view camera. One savvy owner found a way to plug the Prius into a wall socket and boost fuel efficiency to as much as 100 miles per gallon.

In addition to Toyota's effective targeting tactics, various external incentives helped to spur Prius sales. For example, some states in the U.S. issued permits for hybrids to drive in HOV (high occupancy vehicle) lanes, even if they only had one occupant. Some cities provide free parking. But the biggest incentives were monetary. The federal government gave huge tax breaks amounting to thousands of dollars. On top of all that, some eco-friendly companies such as Timberland and Google also joined in the incentive game, giving employees as much as $5000 toward the purchase of hybrids.

But after some time, the early adopter market had been skimmed. However, Toyota was already well into a $40 million campaign targeting a different set of consumers, the environmentally conscious and those desiring greater fuel efficiency. With the accuracy of a fortune teller, Toyota hit the nail right on the head. Gas prices skyrocketed, first to 90 cents per litre, then past $1. By the spring of 2008, Prius hysteria had reached an all-time high. Just as demand for full-sized SUVs began to tank, waiting lists and dealer mark-ups over sticker for the Prius once again became the norm.

"I'm selling every one I can get my hands on," said Kenny Burns, a general sales manager at a California Toyota dealer. With a 30-day waiting list for a new Prius, "The day the car comes in is the day the car goes out."

FUELLING THE HYBRID CRAZE

The overall category of gas–electric vehicles in North America is hotter than ever. Although hybrids accounted for only about 3 percent of total U.S. car sales in 2007, their share is growing rapidly. For the first quarter of 2008, hybrid sales were up 25 percent over the previous year. In April of that year, sales jumped a whopping 58 percent. The Prius alone

commands more than 50 percent of the market and is largely responsible for category growth.

While various hybrid models have hit the market in recent years, it appears that consumers like their green cars very green. Sales of the ultra-high-mileage Prius and Civic have grown significantly each year since their introductions. But less efficient (and more expensive) hybrid models such as the Honda Accord (now discontinued), the Ford Escape, and the Mercury Mariner have not fared nearly as well. Some analysts believe it is because consumers are doing the math and realizing that even with better fuel efficiency, they may not save money with a hybrid. In fact, a widely publicized 2006 report by Consumer Reports revealed that of six hybrid models studied, the Prius and the Civic were the only two to recover the price premium and save consumers money after five years and 120 000 kilometres. But as the price of gas rises, the break-even period for the price of a hybrid gets shorter and shorter. That may just mean greater demand for all hybrid models as consumers perceive that even the less efficient hybrids make financial sense.

Almost every automotive nameplate now wants a piece of the growing pie. In 2008, there were 15 hybrid models available in the United States from 9 different brand nameplates. General Motors offers both the only full-sized SUV hybrid in the Tahoe and the lowest priced hybrid option at US$2000 for the Saturn Vue and Aura. GM plans to extend the Saturn hybrid line to almost every vehicle in the lineup while continuing to introduce hybrids in other divisions. Ford plans to produce 250 000 hybrids a year by 2012. And while Subaru, Hyundai, and Honda are all promoting upcoming hybrid models, Audi, BMW, and numerous others are busy developing hybrid vehicles of their own.

Even with all the activity from these automotive brands, Toyota is currently the clear leader in hybrid sales and likely will be for some time to come. It makes six of the current 15 U.S. hybrid models (including three Lexus models). And with market conditions changing, Toyota is also showing its ability to adapt. In addition to the increased level of competition, the Prius faces more internal competition from new Toyota models like the Camry. Toyota faces a greater challenge in ramping up production to meet demand than from external competition.

All indications show that Toyota plans to maintain its hybrid momentum, doubling its line to 12 models and increasing its worldwide hybrid sales to 1 million vehicles per year by the early 2010s. At that time, it plans to unleash an entirely new lineup of hybrids based on next-generation lithium-ion batteries, which pack more power than the current nickel-metal-hydride batteries. If the past is any indication, Toyota's future looks very green.

Questions for Discussion

1. What microenvironmental factors affected both the first generation and second generation models of the Toyota Prius? How well has Toyota dealt with these factors?

2. Outline the major macroenvironmental factors—demographic, economic, natural, technological, political, and cultural—that have affected Prius sales. How well has Toyota dealt with each of these factors?

3. Evaluate Toyota's marketing strategy so far. What has Toyota done well? How might it improve its strategy?

4. GM's marketing director for new ventures, Ken Stewart, says "If you want to get a lot of hybrids on the road, you put them in vehicles that people are buying now." This seems to summarize the U.S. automakers' approach to hybrids. Would you agree with Mr. Stewart? Why or why not?

Sources: Martin Zimmerman, "Hybrid Car Sales Are Zoomin," *Los Angeles Times*, May 23, 2008, p. A1; David Welch, "Prius: Over 1 million Sold," *BusinessWeek*, May 15, 2008, accessed at www.businessweek.com; Peter Valdes-Dapena, "Prius Still King as Hybrid Auto Sales Rise," CNNMoney.com, August 2, 2007; Valdes-Dapena, "Mad Market for Used Fuel-Sippers," CNNMoney.com, May 18, 2006; David Kiley and David Welch, "Invasion of the Hybrids," *BusinessWeek*, January 10, 2006; and Brian Twomey, "The Prius Is the World's Best Selling Hybrid," *Mirror*, May 23, 2008, p. 44.

Visit **MyMarketingLab** at **www.pearsoned.ca/mymarketinglab** for access to online tutorials, interactive exercises, videos, and much more.

4

Social Responsibility and Ethics
Sustainable Marketing

PREVIEWING
THE CONCEPTS

In this chapter, we'll examine the concepts of sustainable marketing, meeting the needs of consumers, businesses, and society—now and in the future—through socially and environmentally responsible marketing actions. We'll start by defining sustainable marketing and then look at some common criticisms of marketing as it impacts individual consumers and other businesses. Next, we'll examine consumerism, environmentalism, and other actions that promote sustainable marketing. Finally, we'll see how companies themselves can benefit from proactively pursuing sustainable marketing practices that bring value not just to individual customers but to society as a whole. You'll see that sustainable marketing actions are more than just the right thing to do; they're also good for business.

First, let's look at several examples of sustainable marketing in action. When it comes to socially and environmentally responsible practices, few companies meet the standard set by Bullfrog Power.

You switch on a light or leave your computer up and running without a thought of the negative environmental impact such use of electricity may have. Bullfrog Power wants to change this by providing consumers and businesses with an affordable way to reduce their impact on the environment. It has successfully overcome a huge marketing challenge in the process: It had to convince potential customers to pay a 20–40 percent premium for something they can't see or touch. Despite the fact that it uses relatively low-key marketing focused on building strong customer relationships, Bullfrog was named *Marketing Magazine's* Marketer of the Year in 2008. It seems to have taken a page out of marketing guru Seth Godin's book: "In a field of black and white Holsteins, a purple cow gets all the attention!"

Bullfrog Power is Canada's 100 percent green electricity provider. The Toronto-based company was founded in Toronto in 2005. Today it stands out as the only company providing 100 percent renewable electricity to Prince Edward Island, Nova Scotia, New Brunswick, Ontario, Alberta, and British Columbia residents. "Bullfrog buys power in bulk and re-sells it, with the energy going into the grid, not directly to customers' homes. But unlike other resellers, all its electricity comes from wind-powered or small hydro generating stations."

Bullfrog is working hard to build its customer base of both end consumers and businesses. Its business and organizational clients include such firms as Walmart, BMO Financial Group, Toronto's City Hall, and Mountain Equipment Co-op, to name a few.

Bullfrog has excelled by living by strong brand values. Its mission is to provide practical energy choices that enable people to create a sustainable world for future generations. It works to help its business partners be part of the solution to environmental problems. As its website notes, "At Bullfrog Power, we believe businesses can serve a vital function as community leaders in promoting and fostering responsible environmental action. We are a "double bottom line" company that maintains a dual focus on environmental responsibility and profitability." The company has pledged to donate 10 percent of profits to organizations that support sustainability. Bullfrog not only delivers "green" power to its customers, it empowers them to be change agents in the world. Bullfrog and its clients hope to demonstrate that change can come through collective action. The more people who sign up with Bullfrog, the more demand grows for renewable power generation.

Bullfrog's brand values have resonated with many Canadians. Thus, it has been able to rely on grassroots marketing, word-of-mouth endorsements, and the Web to spread its message. "Word of mouth is an extremely powerful form of communication," says Tom Heintzman, Bullfrog's president. "To a large measure, we divest ourselves of the brand and put it in the hands of our customers." All of Bullfrog's communications are done in-house to ensure that it remains true to its brand.

It's not surprising that Bullfrog is a strong believer in relationship marketing. "Interpersonal contact is a really important part of our brand," says Heintzman, who communicates frequently with clients via the Bullfrog e-buzz newsletter. Bullfrog also works hard to add extra value for its business clients. Its website features a Green Directory—an easy-to-search source of companies that use 100 percent green electricity as part of their operations.

Bullfrog's website, BullfrogPower.com, has proven to be a powerful tool. First, it makes it easy for consumers and businesses alike to sign up for its energy services. People just fill in a simple-to-complete online form in a few minutes. Bullfrog also provides a toll-free number on the screen if people need help with the process.

Bullfrog uses social media to strengthen its relationships. You can see Bullfrog featured in a number of video clips on YouTube, and it maintains an up-to-date page on Facebook where it talks about its activities. Bullfrog also uses more traditional tools to market its service, including national newspapers like the *Globe and Mail*, but it has put a distinctive Bullfrog stamp on this use of traditional media by using information-rich content to explain its service and how customers can make changes.

Public relations are also a big part of Bullfrog's communication mix. Its people do a lot of public speaking to help bring

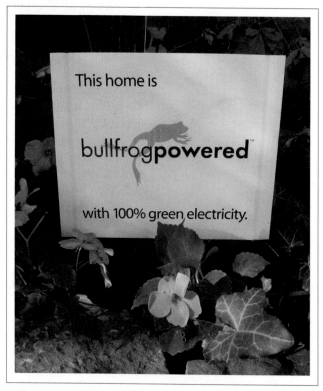

Bullfrog Power builds powerful relationships with its clients, demonstrating that change can be accomplished through collective action.

home their message. The Bullfrog team can also be seen at many events linked to environmental initiatives—it is involved in over 700 different events a year. For example, a recent event, the Bullfrog Bash, featured supporter Gord Downie of The Tragically Hip. Finally, Bullfrog uses a lot of outdoor signage. Its simple yet powerful signs featuring a leaping frog and the phrase "bullfrogpowered" seem to be everywhere, from front lawns to ATMs to beer cases and the websites and newsletters of countless customers and partners. As the Bullfrog story illustrates, a focus on sustainability and strong marketing can go hand-in-hand to build value for multiple stakeholders.[1]

OBJECTIVES

1. Define *sustainable marketing* and discuss its importance.

2. Identify the major social criticisms of marketing.

3. Define *consumerism* and *environmentalism* and explain how they affect marketing strategies.

4. Describe the principles of sustainable marketing.

5. Explain the role of ethics in marketing.

Responsible marketers like Bullfrog Power discover what consumers want and respond with responsible and sustainable offerings that create value for buyers to capture value in return. The *marketing concept* is a philosophy of customer value and mutual gain. Not all marketers follow the marketing concept, however. In fact, some companies use questionable marketing practices that serve their own rather than consumers' or society's interests. Responsible marketers must consider whether their actions are *sustainable* in the longer run.

Consider the sale of sport-utility vehicles (SUVs). These large vehicles meet the immediate needs of many drivers in terms of capacity, power, and utility. However, SUV sales involve larger questions of consumer safety and environmental responsibility. For example, SUVs are more likely to kill both their occupants and the occupants of other vehicles when involved in an accident. Research shows that SUV occupants are three times more likely to die from their vehicle rolling over than are occupants of sedans.[2] Moreover, gas-guzzling SUVs use more than their fair share of the world's energy and other resources and contribute disproportionately to pollution and congestion problems, creating costs that must be borne by both current and future generations.[3]

This chapter examines *sustainable* marketing and the social and environmental effects of private marketing practices. First we address the question: What is sustainable marketing and why is it important?

SUSTAINABLE MARKETING

Sustainable marketing
Marketing that meets the present needs of consumers and businesses while also preserving or enhancing the ability of future generations to meet their needs.

Sustainable marketing calls for meeting the present needs of consumers and businesses while also preserving or enhancing the ability of future generations to meet their needs. Figure 4.1 compares the sustainable marketing concept with other marketing concepts we studied in earlier chapters.[4]

The *marketing concept* recognizes that organizations thrive from day to day by determining the current needs and wants of target-group customers and fulfilling those needs and wants more effectively and efficiently than the competition. It focuses on meeting the company's short-term sales, growth, and profit needs by giving customers what they want now. However, satisfying consumers' immediate needs and desires doesn't always serve the future best interests of either customers or the business.

For example, McDonald's early decisions to market tasty but fat- and salt-laden fast foods created immediate satisfaction for customers and sales and profits for the company. However, critics assert that McDonald's and other fast-food chains contributed to a longer-term national obesity epidemic, damaging consumer health and burdening the national health care system. In turn, many consumers began looking for healthier eating options, causing a slump in the fast-food industry. Beyond issues of ethical behaviour and social welfare, McDonald's was also criticized for the sizable environmental footprint of its vast global operations—everything from wasteful packaging and solid waste creation to inefficient energy use in its stores. Thus, McDonald's strategy was not sustainable in terms of either consumer or company benefit.

Whereas the *societal marketing concept* identified in Figure 4.1 considers the future welfare of consumers and the *strategic planning concept* considers future company needs, the *sustainable marketing concept* considers both. Sustainable marketing calls for socially and environmentally

Figure 4.1 Sustainable marketing

BE OPEN TO NEW POSSIBILITIES.

NEW ASIAN SALAD   i'm lovin' it®

Sustainable marketing: McDonald's Canada has created value for its customers and communities while ensuring itself a profitable future.

responsible actions that meet both the immediate and future needs of customers and the company.

For example, in recent years McDonald's has responded with a more sustainable strategy of diversifying into salads, toasted deli sandwiches, fruits, grilled chicken, low-fat milk, and other healthy fare. Also, after a seven-year search for healthier cooking oil, McDonald's phased out traditional artery-clogging trans fat without compromising the taste of its french fries. As part of its Balanced, Active Lifestyles initiative, McDonald's Canada works to educate consumers about nutrition and it donates thousands of dollars to research organizations like the Canadian Foundation for Dietetic Research. Consumers can go to McDonald's Canada's website and use its nutrition calculator to verify the number of calories they consume in eating various McDonald's products. They can also find nutrition information on posters in-store and on the backs of tray liners. McDonald's Canada also issues an annual corporate social responsibility report that features McDonald's role in the balanced, healthy lifestyle of Canadians. It notes, "We believe in the principles of balance, variety, and moderation and that eating at McDonald's fits into any balanced lifestyle. Our varied menu and range of serving sizes make it easy for Canadians to create meal combinations that meet their dietary needs."

In addition, McDonald's Canada supports many social activities in the communities in which it operates, including the sponsorship of many sports teams. The cornerstone of its community commitment is its 12 Ronald McDonald Houses, which provide a home-away-from-home for families of children with serious illnesses.

McDonald's also addresses environmental issues. For example, it calls for food-supply sustainability, reduced and environmentally sustainable packaging, reuse and recycling, and more responsible store designs. McDonald's has even developed an environmental scorecard that rates its suppliers' performance in areas such as water use, energy use, and solid waste management.

McDonald's more sustainable strategy is benefiting the company as well as its customers. Profits and sales have increased steadily and the company is now included in the Dow Jones Sustainability Index, recognizing its commitment to sustainable economic, environmental, and social performance. Thus, McDonald's is well positioned for a sustainably profitable future.[5]

Truly sustainable marketing requires a smoothly functioning marketing system in which consumers, companies, public policymakers, and others work together to ensure socially responsible and ethical marketing actions. Unfortunately, however, the marketing system doesn't always work smoothly. The following sections examine several sustainability questions: What are the most frequent social criticisms of marketing? What steps have private citizens taken to curb marketing ills? What steps have legislators and government agencies taken to promote sustainable marketing? What steps have enlightened companies taken to carry out socially responsible and ethical marketing that creates sustainable value for both individual customers and society as a whole?

2   SOCIAL CRITICISMS OF MARKETING

Marketing receives much criticism. Some of this criticism is justified; much is not. Social critics claim that certain marketing practices hurt individual consumers, society as a whole, and other business firms.

Marketing's Impact on Individual Consumers

Consumers have many concerns about how well the marketing system serves their interests. Surveys usually show that consumers hold mixed or even slightly unfavourable attitudes toward marketing practices. Consumer advocates, government agencies, and other critics have accused marketing of harming consumers through high prices, deceptive practices, high-pressure selling, shoddy or unsafe products, planned obsolescence, and poor service to disadvantaged consumers. Such questionable marketing practices are not sustainable in terms of long-term consumer or business welfare.

High Prices

Many critics charge that the marketing system causes prices to be higher than they would be under more "sensible" systems. They point to three factors—*high costs of distribution, high advertising and promotion costs*, and *excessive markups*.

High Costs of Distribution   A long-standing charge is that greedy channel intermediaries mark up prices beyond the value of their services. Critics charge that there are too many intermediaries, that intermediaries are inefficient, or that they provide unnecessary or duplicate services. As a result, distribution costs too much, and consumers pay for these excessive costs in the form of higher prices.

How do resellers answer these charges? They argue that intermediaries do work that would otherwise have to be done by manufacturers or consumers. Markups reflect services that consumers themselves want—more convenience, larger stores and assortment of products, more service, longer store hours, return privileges, and others. In fact, they argue, retail competition is so intense that margins are actually quite low. For example, after taxes, supermarket chains are typically left with barely 1 percent profit on their sales. If some resellers try to charge too much relative to the value they add, other resellers will step in with lower prices. Low-price stores such as Walmart, Costco, and other discounters pressure their competitors to operate efficiently and keep their prices down.

High Advertising and Promotion Costs   Modern marketing is also accused of pushing up prices to finance heavy advertising and sales promotion. For example, a few dozen tablets of a heavily promoted brand of pain reliever sell for the same price as 100 tablets of less-promoted brands. Differentiated products—cosmetics, detergents, toiletries—include promotion and packaging costs that can amount to 40 percent or more of the manufacturer's price to the retailer. Critics charge that much of the packaging and promotion adds only psychological value to the product rather than functional value.

A heavily promoted brand, Aspirin sells for much more than a virtually identical nonbranded or store-branded product. Critics charge that promotion only adds psychological value to the product rather than functional value.

Marketers respond that advertising does add to product costs. But it also adds value by informing potential buyers of the availability and merits of a brand. Brand name products may cost more, but branding gives buyers assurances of consistent quality. Moreover, consumers can usually buy functional versions of products at lower prices. However, they *want* and are willing to pay more for products that also provide psychological benefits—that make them feel wealthy, attractive, or special. Also, heavy advertising and promotion may be necessary for a firm to match competitors' efforts—the business would lose "share of mind" if it did not match competitive spending. At the same time, companies are cost conscious about promotion and try to spend their money wisely.

Excessive Markups   Critics also charge that some companies mark up goods excessively. They point to the drug industry, where a pill costing five cents to make may cost the consumer $2 to buy. They point to the pricing tactics of funeral homes that prey on the confused emotions of bereaved relatives and to the high charges for auto repair and other services.

Marketers respond that most businesses try to deal fairly with consumers because they want to build customer relationships and repeat business. Most consumer abuses are unintentional. When shady marketers do take advantage of consumers, they should be reported to the Competition Bureau, the Canadian Marketing Association, Advertising Standards Canada, or the consumer's provincial Consumer Affairs office. Consumers can also go to the Canadian Consumer Information Gateway where they can find a wealth of information on federal and provincial departments and agencies as well as help in making an effective complaint.

Marketers sometimes respond that consumers don't understand the reasons for high markups. For example, pharmaceutical markups must cover the costs of purchasing, promoting, and distributing existing medicines plus the high research and development costs of formulating and testing new medicines. As pharmaceuticals company GlaxoSmithKline states in its ads, "Today's medicines finance tomorrow's miracles."

Deceptive Practices

Marketers are sometimes accused of deceptive practices that lead consumers to believe they will get more value than they actually do. Deceptive practices fall into three groups: pricing, promotion, and packaging. *Deceptive pricing* includes practices such as falsely advertising "factory" or "wholesale" prices or a large price reduction from a phony high retail list price. *Deceptive promotion* includes practices such as misrepresenting the product's features or performance or luring the customers to the store for a bargain that is out of stock. For example, Vancouver-based lululemon athletica withdrew its Vitasea shirts made from seaweed fibres when research conducted by a newspaper revealed that claims that the shirts released marine amino acids and minerals were false; the Vitasea shirts were no different than ordinary cotton T-shirts. *Deceptive packaging* includes exaggerating package contents through subtle design, using misleading labelling, or describing size in misleading terms.

The Competition Bureau acts as a watchdog to prevent such practices. In 2009, for example, it brought criminal charges against individuals and companies who formed a cartel and conspired to fix gas prices in Victoriaville, Quebec. It charged The Brick with misleading advertising related to a mail-in rebate promotion. The company subsequently cancelled the campaign in response to these concerns. It also took action against Edmonton-based Bio Energy Wellness and its director after unsubstantiated claims were made online regarding products used to treat or prevent cancer.

Deceptive practices have led to legislation and other consumer protection actions, but such regulations don't solve all the problems. Consider the glut of "environmental responsibility" claims marketers are now making:

Deceptive practices: Despite plenty of regulation, some critics argue that deceptive claims are still the norm. Consider all of those "green marketing" claims.

Are you a victim of "greenwashing"? Biodegradable, eco-friendly, recycled, green, carbon neutral, carbon offsets, made from sustainable resources—such phrases are popping up more and more on products worldwide, leading many to question their validity. In 2008, in an attempt to ensure greater accuracy of such claims, the Competition Bureau in collaboration with the Canadian Standards Association issued guidelines to provide the business community with tools to ensure that green marketing claims are not misleading. Examples of best practices were also provided. "Environmental Claims: A Guide for Industry and Advertisers" can be found online at www.competitionbureau.gc.ca/eic/site/cb-bc.nsf/eng/02701.html.[6]

The toughest problem is defining what is "deceptive." For instance, an advertiser's claim that its powerful laundry detergent "makes your washing machine 10 feet tall," showing a surprised homemaker watching her appliance burst through her laundry room ceiling, isn't intended to be taken literally. Instead, the advertiser might claim, it is "puffery"—innocent exaggeration for effect. One noted marketing thinker, Theodore Levitt, once claimed that advertising puffery and alluring imagery are bound to occur— and that they may even be desirable: "There is hardly a company that would not go down in ruin if it refused to provide fluff, because nobody will buy pure functionality. . . . Worse, it denies . . . people's honest needs and values. Without distortion, embellishment, and elaboration, life would be drab, dull, anguished, and at its existential worst."[7]

However, others claim that puffery and alluring imagery can harm consumers in subtle ways. Think about the popular and long-running MasterCard "priceless" commercials that paint pictures of consumers fulfilling their priceless dreams despite the costs. Similarly, Visa invites consumers to "Enjoy life's opportunities." Both suggest that your credit card can make it happen. But critics charge that such imagery by credit card companies encourages a spend-now-pay-later attitude that causes many consumers to *over*use their cards. Canadians love their plastic and 23 companies issue credit cards in Canada. Canadians possess more than 50 million Visa and MasterCards alone. While 60 percent of Canadians traditionally pay off their balance each month, others keep large balances on their cards. With the downturn in the economy, more people are creating credit card debt just to cover day-to-day living expenses. In early 2009, it was reported that Canadian household debt had risen to $1.3 trillion. Those using credit cards with overdue balances will eventually have to pay off this debt at rates ranging from 17.5 to 24 percent.[8]

Marketers argue that most companies avoid deceptive practices. Because such practices harm their business in the long run, they simply aren't sustainable. Profitable customer relationships are built upon a foundation of value and trust. If consumers do not get what they expect, they will switch to more reliable products. In addition, consumers usually protect themselves from deception. Most consumers recognize a marketer's selling intent and are careful when they buy, sometimes to the point of not believing completely true product claims.

High-Pressure Selling

Salespeople are sometimes accused of high-pressure selling that persuades people to buy goods they had no intention of buying. It is often said that insurance, real estate, and used cars are *sold*, not *bought*. Salespeople are trained to deliver smooth, canned talks to entice purchase. They sell hard because sales contests promise big prizes to those who sell the most.

But in most cases, marketers have little to gain from high-pressure selling. Such tactics may work in one-time selling situations for short-term gain. However, most selling involves building long-term relationships with valued customers. High-pressure or deceptive selling can do serious damage to such relationships. For example, imagine a Procter & Gamble account manager trying to pressure a Walmart buyer, or an IBM salesperson trying to browbeat a General Electric information technology manager. It simply wouldn't work.

Shoddy, Harmful, or Unsafe Products

Another criticism concerns poor product quality or function. One complaint is that too often products are not made well and services are not performed well. A second complaint is that many products deliver little benefit or that they might even be harmful. Consider what happened to Leslie Alexander, a Vancouver-based folk singer. Being afraid that prescription sleeping pills were addictive, she began taking the "all-natural" product Sleepees. While the product helped her sleep "beautifully," she developed a rash around her eyes and other symptoms indicating an allergic reaction. She ignored these ailments since she soon found herself unable to sleep without the herbal medication, and when she finally forced herself off the product she fell into a deep depression. She and her lawyer brought a class action lawsuit against the Canadian distributor of Sleepees, alleging that "hundreds of Canadians may have been harmed by the product and that some may not even be aware of the source of their health problems." These charges have yet to be proven, however.[9]

As suggested above, product safety is a major concern. Sometimes the processes used to produce products may make them unsafe, as was the case in 2008 when Maple Leaf Foods accidentally introduced deadly listeriosis into prepared meat products through its slicing machines. The company worked hard to rebuild its image and trust among consumers with an extensive PR campaign following the outbreak. Its open and honest communication accompanied by its extensive advertising campaign helped build purchase intent from 64 percent up to over 90 percent.[10]

Product safety has been a problem for several reasons, including company indifference, increased product complexity, and poor quality control. For years, Consumers Union—the not-for-profit testing and information organization that publishes the *Consumer Reports* magazine and website—has reported various hazards in tested products: electrical dangers in appliances, carbon monoxide poisoning from room heaters, injury risks from lawn mowers, and faulty automobile design, among many others. The organization's testing and other activities have helped consumers make better buying decisions and encouraged businesses to eliminate product flaws.

However, most manufacturers *want* to produce quality goods. The way a company deals with product quality and safety problems can damage or help its reputation. Companies selling poor-quality or unsafe products risk damaging conflicts with consumer groups and regulators. Unsafe products can result in product liability suits and large awards for damages. More fundamentally, consumers who are unhappy with a firm's products may avoid future purchases and talk other consumers into doing the same. Thus, quality missteps can have severe consequences and are not consistent with sustainable marketing. Today's marketers know that good quality results in customer value and satisfaction, which in turn creates sustainable customer relationships.

Planned Obsolescence

Critics have also charged that some companies practise planned obsolescence, causing their products to become obsolete before they actually should need replacement. They accuse some producers of using materials and components that will break, wear, rust, or rot sooner than they should. One writer put it this way: "The marvels of modern technology include the development of a soda can which, when discarded, will last forever—and a . . . car, which, when properly cared for, will rust out in two or three years."[11]

Others are charged with continually changing consumer concepts of acceptable styles to encourage more and earlier buying. An obvious example is constantly changing clothing fashions. Still others are accused of introducing planned streams of new products that make older models obsolete. Critics claim that this occurs in the consumer electronics and computer industries. For example, consider this writer's tale about an aging cellphone:

> Today, most people, myself included, are all agog at the wondrous outpouring of new technology, from cell phones to iPods, iPhones, laptops, BlackBerries, and on and on. Even though I am techno-incompetent and like to think I shun these new devices, I actually have a drawer filled with the detritus of yesterday's hottest product, now reduced to the status of fossils. I have video cameras that use tapes no longer available, laptops with programs incompatible with anything on today's market, portable CD players I no longer use, and more. But what really upsets me is how quickly some still-useful gadgets become obsolete, at least in the eyes of their makers.
>
> I recently embarked on an epic search for a cord to plug into my wife's cell phone to recharge it. We were traveling and the poor phone kept bleating that it was

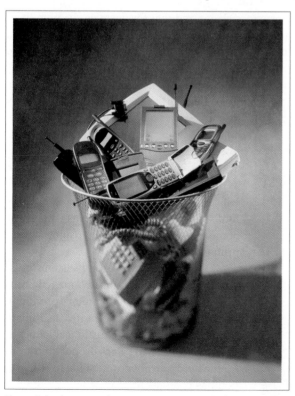

Planned obsolescence: Almost everyone, it seems, has a drawer filled with the detritus of yesterday's hottest products, now reduced to the status of fossils.

running low and the battery needed recharging. So, we began a search—from big-box technology superstores to smaller suppliers and the cell phone companies themselves—all to no avail. Finally, a salesperson told my wife, "That's an old model, so we don't stock the charger any longer." "But I only bought it last year," she sputtered. "Yeah, like I said, that's an old model," he replied without a hint of irony or sympathy. So, in the world of insanely rapid obsolescence, each successive model is incompatible with the previous one it replaces. The proliferation and sheer waste of this type of practice is mind-boggling.[12]

Marketers respond that consumers *like* style changes; they get tired of the old goods and want a new look in fashion. Or they *want* the latest high-tech innovations, even if older models still work. No one has to buy the new product, and if too few people like it, it will simply fail. Finally, most companies do not design their products to break down earlier, because they do not want to lose customers to other brands. Instead, they seek constant improvement to ensure that products will consistently meet or exceed customer expectations. Much of the so-called planned obsolescence is the working of the competitive and technological forces in a free society—forces that lead to ever-improving goods and services.

Poor Service to Disadvantaged Consumers

Finally, the marketing system has been accused of serving disadvantaged consumers poorly. For example, critics claim that the urban poor often have to shop in smaller stores that carry inferior goods and charge higher prices. The presence of large national chain stores in low-income neighbourhoods would help to keep prices down. However, the critics accuse major chain retailers of "redlining," drawing a red line around disadvantaged neighbourhoods and avoiding placing stores there.

Similar redlining charges have been levelled at the insurance, consumer lending, banking, and health care industries. Home and auto insurers have been accused of assigning higher premiums to people with poor credit ratings. The insurers claim that individuals with bad credit tend to make more insurance claims and that this justifies charging them higher premiums. However, critics and consumer advocates have accused the insurers of a new form of redlining. Says one writer, "This is a new excuse for denying coverage to the poor, elderly, and minorities."[13]

More recently, consumer advocates have charged that American mortgage companies have been taking advantage of the working poor by offering them subprime mortgages rather than fixed-rate mortgages to purchase homes. Subprime mortgages, also known as adjustable rate mortgages, have attractive low initial interest rates, but the rates fluctuate after a set time, usually upward. Recently, as the interest rates climbed and home values fell, many owners who could no longer afford their mortgage payments saw their homes go into foreclosure, creating a subprime mortgage crisis.[14]

Clearly, better marketing systems must be built to service disadvantaged consumers. In fact, many marketers profitably target such consumers with legitimate goods and services that create real value. In cases in which marketers do not step in to fill the void, the government likely will. Action has been taken against sellers who advertise false values, wrongfully deny services, or charge disadvantaged customers too much.

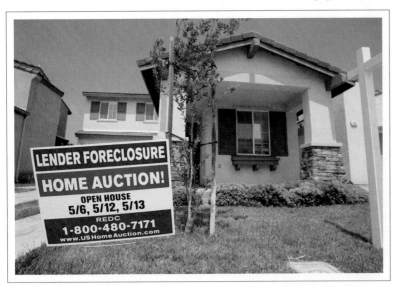

Critics have accused mortgage lenders of "reverse redlining," targeting disadvantaged consumers with subprime mortgages that they couldn't afford.

Marketing's Impact on Society as a Whole

The marketing system has been accused of adding to several "evils" in society at large. Advertising has been a special target.

False Wants and Too Much Materialism

Critics, led by professor emeritus Rick Pollay of the University of British Columbia and organizations like Adbusters Media Foundation, have charged that the marketing system urges too much interest in material possessions and that North Americans' love affair with worldly possessions is not sustainable. People are judged by what they *own* rather than by who they *are*. This drive for wealth and possessions hit new highs in the 1980s and 1990s, when phrases such as "greed is good" and "shop till you drop" seemed to characterize the times.

In the current decade, many social scientists have noted a reaction against the opulence and waste of the previous decades and a return to more basic values and social commitment. However, our infatuation with material things continues:

If you made a graph of North American life since the end of World War II, every line concerning money and the things that money can buy would soar upward, a statistical monument to materialism. Inflation-adjusted individual income has almost tripled. The size of the typical new house has more than doubled. A two-car garage was once a goal; now three-car garages seem to be the norm. Designer everything, personal electronics, and other items that didn't even exist a half-century ago are now affordable. Although our time spent shopping has dropped in recent years to just three hours a week, an increasing number of households spend more than they earn. Some consumers will let nothing stand between them and their acquisitions. Recently, in a Florida Walmart, post-Thanksgiving shoppers rushing to buy DVD players (on sale for $29) knocked down a woman, trampled her, and left her unconscious.[15]

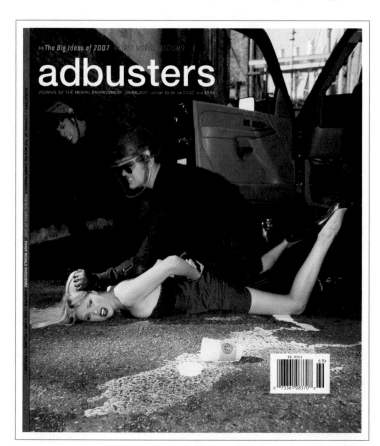

Adbusters magazine is a major critic of marketing's negative influence on our physical and cultural environments. Based in Vancouver, British Columbia, it has audiences around the world.

The critics do not view this interest in material things as a natural state of mind but rather as a matter of false wants created by marketing. Businesses hire advertisers to stimulate people's desires for goods, and advertisers use the mass media to create materialistic models of the good life. People work harder to earn the necessary money. Their purchases increase the output of industry, and industry in turn uses the services of advertisers to stimulate more desire for the industrial output.

Thus, marketing is seen as creating false wants that benefit industry more than they benefit consumers. "In the world of consumerism, marketing is there to promote consumption," says one marketing critic. It is "inevitable that marketing will promote overconsumption, and from this, a psychologically, as well as ecologically, unsustainable world." Events like Buy Nothing Day, started in Vancouver in 1992 by cartoonist Ted Dave, now span the globe. Buy Nothing Day's purpose is to draw attention to the harmful effects of over-consumption and not only asks consumers to stop shopping for 24 hours, it also asks them to think about issues like where their products originate from, why they are purchased, and what they do with them after purchase. Usually held the Friday after American Thanksgiving, the day has been praised for drawing attention to issues such as how many resources consumers use in developed versus developing countries. However, with the economy in a tailspin and layoffs taking place daily, the day has recently drawn criticism. Criticisms that marketing causes materialism overstate the power of business to create needs. People have strong defences against advertising and other marketing tools. Marketers are most effective when they appeal to existing wants rather than when they attempt to create new ones. Furthermore, people seek information when making important purchases and often do not rely on a single source. Even minor purchases that may be affected by advertising messages lead to repeat purchases only if the product delivers the promised customer value. Finally, the high failure rate of new products shows that companies are not able to control demand.[16]

On a deeper level, our wants and values are influenced not only by marketers but also by family, peer groups, religion, cultural background, and education. If North Americans are highly materialistic, these values arose out of basic socialization processes that go much deeper than business and mass media could produce alone.

Too Few Social Goods

Business has been accused of overselling private goods at the expense of public goods. As private goods increase, they require more public services that are usually not forthcoming. For example, an increase in automobile ownership (private good) requires more highways, traffic control, parking spaces, and police services (public goods). The overselling of private goods results in "social costs." For cars, some of the social costs include traffic congestion, gasoline shortages, and air pollution. Millions of litres of fuel and hours of time are wasted in traffic jams.[17]

A way must be found to restore a balance between private and public goods. One option is to make producers bear the full social costs of their operations. The government could require automobile manufacturers to build cars with more efficient engines and better pollution-control systems. Automakers would then raise their prices to cover the extra costs. If buyers found the price of some cars too high, however, the producers of these cars would disappear. Demand would then move to those producers that could support the sum of the private and social costs.

A second option is to make consumers pay the social costs. For example, many cities around the world are starting to charge "congestion tolls" in an effort to reduce traffic congestion. To unclog its streets, the City of London now levies a congestion charge of £8 per day (approximately $14) per car to drive in an eight-square-mile area downtown. The charge has not only reduced traffic congestion within the zone by 21 percent and increased cycling by 12 percent, but it also raises money to shore up London's public transportation system.[18]

Cultural Pollution

Critics charge the marketing system with creating *cultural pollution*. Our senses are constantly being assaulted by marketing and advertising. Commercials interrupt serious programs; pages of ads obscure magazines; billboards mar beautiful scenery; spam fills our inboxes. These interruptions continually pollute people's minds with messages of materialism, sex, power, or status. A recent study found that more than half of North Americans feel constantly bombarded with too many marketing messages, and some critics call for sweeping changes.[19]

Balancing private and public goods: In response to lane-clogging traffic congestion like that shown here, London now levies a congestion charge. The charge has reduced congestion by 21 percent and raised money to shore up the city's public transportation system.

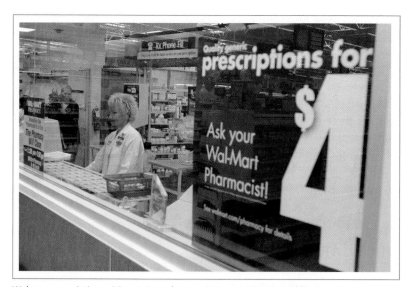

Walmart prescription pricing: Is it predatory pricing or is it just good business?

Marketers answer the charges of "commercial noise" with these arguments: First, they hope that their ads reach primarily the target audience. But because of mass-communication channels, some ads are bound to reach people who have no interest in the product and are therefore bored or annoyed. People who buy magazines addressed to their interests—such as *Vogue* or *Canadian Business*—rarely complain about the ads because the magazines advertise products of interest.

Second, ads make much of television and radio free to users and keep down the costs of magazines and newspapers. Many people think commercials are a small price to pay for these benefits. Consumers find many television commercials entertaining and seek them out—for example, ad viewership during the Super Bowl usually equals game viewership. Finally, today's consumers have alternatives. For example, they can zip or zap TV commercials on recorded programs or avoid them altogether on many paid cable or satellite channels. Thus, to hold consumer attention, advertisers are making their ads more entertaining and informative.

Marketing's Impact on Other Businesses

Critics also charge that a company's marketing practices can harm other companies and reduce competition. Three problems are involved: acquisitions of competitors, marketing practices that create barriers to entry, and unfair competitive marketing practices.

Critics claim that firms are harmed and competition reduced when companies expand by acquiring competitors rather than by developing their own new products. The large number of acquisitions and the rapid pace of industry consolidation over the past several decades have caused concern that vigorous young competitors will be absorbed and that competition will be reduced. In virtually every major industry—retailing, entertainment, financial services, utilities, transportation, automobiles, telecommunications—the number of major competitors is shrinking.

Acquisition is a complex subject. Acquisitions can sometimes be good for society. The acquiring company may gain economies of scale that lead to lower costs and lower prices. A well-managed company may take over a poorly managed company and improve its efficiency. An industry that was not very competitive might become more competitive after the acquisition. But acquisitions can also be harmful and, therefore, are closely regulated by the government.

Critics have also charged that marketing practices bar new companies from entering an industry. Large marketing companies can use patents and heavy promotion spending or tie up suppliers or dealers to keep out or drive out competitors. Those concerned with antitrust regulation recognize that some barriers are the natural result of the economic advantages of doing business on a large scale. Other barriers could be challenged by existing and new laws. For example, some critics have proposed a progressive tax on advertising spending to reduce the role of selling costs as a major barrier to entry.

Finally, some firms have, in fact, used unfair competitive marketing practices with the intention of hurting or destroying other firms. They may set their prices below costs, threaten to cut off business with suppliers, or discourage the buying of a competitor's products. Various laws work to prevent such predatory competition. It is difficult, however, to prove that the intent or action was really predatory.

In recent years, Walmart has been accused of using predatory pricing and poor labour practices. Some believe the giant drives smaller mom-and-pop retailers out of business. For instance, when Walmart recently began a program to sell generic drugs at $4 a prescription, local pharmacists complained of predatory pricing. They charged that at those low prices, Walmart must be selling under cost to drive them out of business. But Walmart claimed that, given its substantial buying power and efficient operations, it could make a profit at those prices. The $4 pricing program was not aimed at putting competitors out of business. Rather, it was simply a good competitive move that served customers better and brought more of them in the door.[20] Nonetheless, Walmart has become a lightning rod for protests by citizens and unions like the Canadian Labour Congress (CLC) in dozens of cities and towns across the country. CLC president Ken Georgetti noted, "We are upset at the way Walmart does business and its lack of respect for Canadian laws and people's rights. We want to make Walmart a better place to work. We want it to be a place Canadians can feel good about shopping [at] because it treats its workers fairly, respects the law and supports human rights."[21]

3   CONSUMER ACTIONS TO PROMOTE SUSTAINABLE MARKETING

Sustainable marketing calls for more responsible actions by both businesses and consumers. Because some people view business as the cause of many economic and social ills, grassroots movements have arisen from time to time to keep business in line. The two major movements have been *consumerism* and *environmentalism*.

Consumerism

North American business firms have been the target of organized consumer movements on three occasions. The first consumer movement took place in the early 1900s. It was fuelled by rising prices, Upton Sinclair's writings on conditions in the meat industry, and scandals in the drug industry. The second consumer movement, in the mid-1930s, was sparked by an upturn in consumer prices during the Great Depression and another drug scandal.

The third movement began in the 1960s. Consumers had become better educated, products had become more complex and potentially hazardous, and people were unhappy with rising prices. Ralph Nader appeared on the scene to force many issues, and other well-known writers accused big business of wasteful and unethical practices. President John F. Kennedy declared that consumers had the right to safety, to be informed, to choose, and to be heard. Since then, many consumer groups have been organized and several consumer laws have been passed. The consumer movement has spread internationally and has become very strong in Europe.

But what is the consumer movement? **Consumerism** is an organized movement of citizens and government agencies to improve the rights and power of buyers in relation to sellers. Traditional *sellers' rights* include the following:

Consumerism
An organized movement of citizens and government agencies to improve the rights and power of buyers in relation to sellers.

- The right to introduce any product in any size and style, provided it is not hazardous to personal health or safety; or, if it is, to include proper warnings and controls

- The right to charge any price for the product, provided no discrimination exists among similar kinds of buyers

- The right to spend any amount to promote the product, provided it is not defined as unfair competition

- The right to use any product message, provided it is not misleading or dishonest in content or execution

- The right to use any buying incentive programs, provided they are not unfair or misleading

  Traditional *buyers' rights* include:

- The right not to buy a product that is offered for sale

- The right to expect the product to be safe

- The right to expect the product to perform as claimed

Comparing these rights, many believe that the balance of power lies on the seller's side. True, the buyer can refuse to buy. But critics feel that the buyer has too little information, education, and protection to make wise decisions when facing sophisticated sellers. Consumer advocates call for the following additional consumer rights:

- The right to be well informed about important aspects of the product

- The right to be protected against questionable products and marketing practices

- The right to influence products and marketing practices in ways that will improve the "quality of life"

- The right to consume now in a way that will preserve the world for future generations of consumers

Each proposed right has led to more specific proposals by consumerists. The right to be informed includes the right to know the true interest on a loan (truth in lending), the true cost per unit of a brand (unit pricing), the ingredients in a product (ingredient labelling), the nutritional value of foods (nutritional labelling), product freshness (open dating), and the true benefits of a product (truth in advertising). Proposals related to consumer protection include strengthening consumer rights in cases of business fraud, requiring greater product safety, ensuring information privacy, and giving more power to government agencies. Proposals relating to quality of life include controlling the ingredients that go into certain products and packaging and reducing the level of advertising "noise." Proposals for preserving the world for future consumption include promoting the use of sustainable ingredients, recycling and reducing solid wastes, and managing energy consumption.

Sustainable marketing is up to consumers as well as businesses and governments. Consumers have not only the *right* but also the *responsibility* to protect themselves instead of leaving this function to someone else. Consumers who believe they got a bad deal have several remedies available, including contacting the company or the media; contacting federal, provincial, or local agencies; and going to small claims courts. Consumers should also make good consumption choices, rewarding companies that act responsibly while punishing those that don't.

Environmentalism

Whereas consumerists consider whether the marketing system is efficiently serving consumer wants, environmentalists are concerned with marketing's effects on the environment and with the environmental costs of serving consumer needs and wants. **Environmentalism** is an organized movement of concerned citizens, businesses, and government agencies to protect and improve people's current and future living environment.

Environmentalism
An organized movement of concerned citizens, businesses, and government agencies to protect and improve people's current and future living environment.

Environmentalists are not against marketing and consumption; they simply want people and organizations to operate with more care for the environment. The marketing system's goal, they assert, should not be to maximize consumption, consumer choice, or consumer satisfaction, but rather to maximize life quality. And "life quality" means not only the quantity and quality of consumer goods and services, but also the quality of the environment. Environmentalists want current and future environmental costs included in both producer and consumer decision making.

The first wave of modern environmentalism in North America was driven by environmental groups and concerned consumers in the 1960s and 1970s. They were concerned with damage to the ecosystem caused by strip mining, forest depletion, acid rain, global warming, toxic and solid wastes, and litter. They were also concerned with the loss of recreational areas and with the increase in health problems caused by bad air, polluted water, and chemically treated food.

The second environmentalism wave was driven by government, which passed laws and regulations during the 1970s and 1980s governing industrial practices impacting the environment. This wave hit some industries hard. Steel companies and utilities had to invest billions of dollars in pollution-control equipment and more costly fuels. The auto

Pollution prevention: UPS is developing a "green fleet" of alternative-fuel vehicles that provide 45 percent better fuel economy and a dramatic decrease in vehicle emissions.

Environmental sustainability
A management approach that involves developing strategies that both sustain the environment and produce profits for the company.

industry had to introduce expensive emission controls in cars. The packaging industry had to find ways to improve recyclability and reduce solid wastes. These industries and others have often resented and resisted environmental regulations, especially when they have been imposed too rapidly to allow companies to make proper adjustments. Many of these companies claim they have had to absorb large costs that have made them less competitive.

The first two environmentalism waves have now merged into a third and stronger wave in which companies are accepting more responsibility for doing no harm to the environment. They are shifting from protest to prevention and from regulation to responsibility. More and more companies are adopting policies of **environmental sustainability**. Simply put, environmental sustainability is about generating profits while helping to save the planet. Environmental sustainability is a crucial but difficult societal goal.

Some companies have responded to consumer environmental concerns by doing only what is required to avert new regulations or to keep environmentalists quiet. Enlightened companies, however, are taking action not because someone is forcing them to or to reap short-run profits, but because it is the right thing to do—for both the company and for the planet's environmental future. Air Canada, for example, recently partnered with Toronto-based Zero-footprint on a program that encourages passengers to contribute to an environmentally friendly project to cancel out their share of carbon dioxide generated by their flight.[22]

Figure 4.2 shows a grid that companies can use to gauge their progress toward environmental sustainability. It includes both internal and external "greening" activities that will pay off for the firm and environment in the short run and "beyond greening" activities that will pay off in the longer term. At the most basic level, a company can practise *pollution prevention*. This involves more than pollution control—cleaning up waste after it has been created. Pollution prevention means eliminating or minimizing waste before it is created. Companies emphasizing prevention have responded with internal "green marketing" programs—designing and developing ecologically safer products, recyclable and biodegradable packaging, better pollution controls, and more energy-efficient operations.

For example, Nike produces PVC-free shoes, recycles old sneakers, and educates young people about conservation, reuse, and recycling. Fairmont Hotels encourages recycling, grows products used in its restaurants in roof gardens, and educates guests about the harm caused by excess water and towel usage. Loblaw has stopped providing plastic bags in some stores and has encouraged consumers to bring reusable bags made from recycled fibre. General Mills shaved 20 percent off the paperboard packaging for Hamburger Helper, resulting in 500 fewer distribution trucks on the road each year. Sun Microsystems created its "open work" program which gives employees the option to

Figure 4.2 The environmental sustainability portfolio

Source: Stuart L. Hart, "Innovation, Creative Destruction, and Sustainability," *Research Technology Management*, September–October 2005, pp. 21–27.

	Today: Greening	**Tomorrow:** Beyond Greening
Internal	**Pollution prevention** Eliminating or reducing waste before it is created	**New clean technology** Developing new sets of environmental skills and capabilities
External	**Product stewardship** Minimizing environmental impact throughout the entire product life cycle	**Sustainability vision** Creating a strategic framework for future sustainability

work from home, preventing nearly 29 000 tons of CO_2 emissions while at the same time saving $67.8 million in real-estate costs and increasing worker productivity by 34 percent. And UPS continues to develop a "green fleet" of alternative-fuel vehicles to replace its old fleet of diesel delivery trucks. In 2009 it deployed 200 new next-generation hybrid electric delivery vehicles to join the roughly 2000 low-carbon, hybrid, and compressed natural gas vehicles already in use. The hybrid vehicles provide 45 percent better fuel economy and a dramatic decrease in vehicle emissions.[23]

At the next level, companies can practise *product stewardship*—minimizing not just pollution from production and product design but all environmental impacts throughout the full product life cycle, all the while reducing costs. Many companies are adopting *design for environment (DFE)* and *cradle-to-cradle* practices. This involves thinking ahead to design products that are easier to recover, reuse, recycle, or safely return to nature after usage, becoming part of the ecological cycle. DFE and cradle-to-cradle practices not only help to sustain the environment, they can also be highly profitable for the company.

An example is Xerox Corporation's equipment remanufacture and parts reuse program, which converts end-of-life office equipment into new products and parts. Equipment returned to Xerox can be remanufactured, reusing 70 to 90 percent by weight of old machine components while still meeting performance standards for equipment made with all new parts. The program creates benefits for both the environment and for the company. So far, it has diverted nearly 2 billion pounds of waste from landfills. And it reduces the amount of raw material and energy needed to produce new parts. Energy savings from parts reuse total an estimated 320 000 megawatt hours annually—enough energy to light more than 250 000 homes for a year.[24]

Today's "greening" activities focus on improving what companies already do to protect the environment. The "beyond greening" activities identified in Figure 4.2 look to the future. First, internally, companies can plan for *new clean technology*. Many organizations that have made good sustainability headway are still limited by existing technologies. To create fully sustainable strategies, they will need to develop innovative new technologies. For example, Coca-Cola is investing heavily in research addressing many sustainability issues:

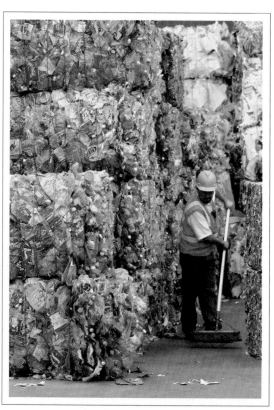

New clean technologies: Coca-Cola is investing heavily to build a state-of-the-art plastic-bottle-to-bottle recycling plant. It's also researching new alternatives such as bottles made from corn or bioplastics.

> From a sustainability viewpoint for Coca-Cola, an aluminum can is an ideal package. Aluminum can be recycled indefinitely. Put a Coke can in a recycling bin, and the aluminum finds its way back to a store shelf in about six weeks. The trouble is, people prefer clear plastic bottles with screw-on tops. Plastic bottles account for nearly 50 percent of Coke's global volume, three times more than aluminum cans. And they are not currently sustainable. They're made from oil, a finite resource. Most wind up in landfills or, worse, as roadside trash. They can't be recycled indefinitely because the plastic discolors. To attack this waste problem, Coca-Cola will invest about US$44 million to build the world's largest state-of-the-art plastic-bottle-to-bottle recycling plant. As a more permanent solution, the company is researching new ideas like bottles made from corn or bioplastics.
>
> Coke is also investing in new clean technologies to solve other environmental issues. For example, about 10 million vending machines and refrigerated coolers use potent greenhouse gases called HFCs to keep Cokes cold. To eliminate them, the company invested US$40 million in research and formed a refrigeration alliance with McDonald's and even competitor PepsiCo. Coca-Cola has also promised to become "water neutral" by researching ways to help its bottlers waste less water and ways to protect or replenish watersheds around the world.[25]

Finally, companies can develop a *sustainability vision*, which serves as a guide to the future. It shows how the company's products and services, processes, and policies must evolve and what new technologies must be developed to get there. This vision of sustainability provides a framework for pollution control, product stewardship, and new environmental technology for the company and others to follow.

Most companies today focus on the upper-left quadrant of the grid in Figure 4.2, investing most heavily in pollution prevention. Some forward-looking companies practise product stewardship and are developing new environmental technologies. Few companies have well-defined sustainability visions. However, emphasizing only one or a few quadrants in the environmental sustainability grid can be shortsighted. Investing only in the left half of the grid puts a company in a good position today but leaves it vulnerable in the future. In contrast, a heavy emphasis on the right half suggests that a company has good environmental vision but lacks the skills needed to implement it. Thus, companies should work at developing all four dimensions of environmental sustainability.

Walmart, for example, is doing just that. Through its own environmental sustainability actions and its impact on the actions of suppliers, Walmart has emerged in recent years as the world's super "eco-nanny" (see Real Marketing 4.1). Alcoa, the world's leading producer of aluminum, is also setting a high sustainability standard. For four years running it has been named one of the most sustainable corporations in the annual Global 100 Most Sustainable Corporations in the World ranking:

> Alcoa has distinguished itself as a leader through its sophisticated approach to identifying and managing the material sustainability risks that it faces as a company. From pollution prevention via greenhouse gas emissions reduction programs to engaging stakeholders over new environmental technology, such as controversial hydropower projects, Alcoa has the sustainability strategies in place needed to meld its profitability objectives with society's larger environmental protection goals. . . . Importantly, Alcoa's approach to sustainability is firmly rooted in the idea that sustainability programs can indeed add financial value. Perhaps the best evidence is the company's efforts to promote the use of aluminum in transportation, where aluminum—with its excellent strength-to-weight ratio—is making inroads as a material of choice that allows automakers to build low-weight, fuel-efficient vehicles that produce fewer tailpipe emissions. This kind of forward-thinking strategy of supplying the market with the products that will help solve pressing global environmental problems shows a company that sees the future, has plotted a course, and is aligning its business accordingly. Says CEO Alain Belda, "Our values require us to think and act not only on the present challenges, but also with the legacy in mind that we leave for those who will come after us . . . as well as the commitments made by those that came before us."[26]

Environmentalism creates some special challenges for global marketers. As international trade barriers come down and global markets expand, environmental issues are having an ever-greater impact on international trade. Countries in North America, Western Europe, and other developed regions are generating strict environmental standards. A side accord to the North American Free Trade Agreement (NAFTA) set up the Commission for Environmental Cooperation for resolving environmental matters. The European Union has passed "end-of-life" regulations affecting automobiles and consumer electronics products. And the EU's Eco-Management and Audit Scheme (EMAS) provides guidelines for environmental self-regulation.[27]

However, environmental policies still vary widely from country to country. Countries such as Denmark, Germany, Japan, and Canada have fully developed environmental policies and high public expectations. But major countries such as China, India, Brazil, and Russia are in only the early stages of developing such policies. Moreover, environmental factors that motivate consumers in one country may have no impact on consumers in another. For example, PVC soft-drink bottles cannot be used in Switzerland or Germany. However, they are preferred in France, which has an extensive recycling process for them. Thus, international companies have found it difficult to develop standard environmental practices that work around the world. Instead, they are creating general policies and then translating these policies into tailored programs that meet local regulations and expectations.

Real Marketing 4.1

Walmart: The World's Super Eco-Nanny

When you think of the corporate "good guys"—companies that are helping to save the world through sustainable actions—you probably think of names like Patagonia, Timberland, Ben & Jerry's, Honest Tea, Whole Foods Market, or Stonyfield Farm. But hold on to your seat. When it comes to sustainability, perhaps no company in the world is doing more good these days than Walmart. That's right—big, bad, Walmart.

Critics have long bashed Walmart for a broad range of alleged social misdeeds, from unfair labour practices to destroying small communities. So many consumers are surprised to learn that the world's largest company, whose Canadian headquarters are in Mississauga, Ontario, is also the world's biggest crusader for the cause of saving the Earth for future generations. When it comes to sustainability, Walmart is rapidly emerging as the world's super "eco-nanny." In 2008, it was featured on the cover of *Strategy* magazine as Canada's top "green" company. In the long run, Walmart's stated environmental goals are to use 100 percent renewable energy, to create zero waste, and to sell only products that sustain the world's resources and environment. Toward that goal, not only is Walmart greening up its own operations, it's also urging its vast network of suppliers to do the same.

Walmart operates more than 7350 stores around the world. Walmart Canada operates a growing network of 318 stores across Canada and employs more than 77 000 Canadians. Its huge stores are gluttons for energy and other resources. So even small steps toward making stores more efficient can add up to huge environmental savings. But Walmart isn't settling for small steps—it's moving in large leaps to develop new eco-technologies. It's testing a 143-foot-tall wind turbine outside its Supercenter in Aurora, Colorado. Incongruous as it might seem, it is clearly a sign that something about this particular store is different. On the outside, the store's facade features row upon row of windows to allow in as much natural light as possible. The landscaping uses native, drought-tolerant plants well adapted to the hot, dry Colorado summers, cutting down on watering, mowing, and the amount of fertilizer and other chemicals needed. Inside the store, an efficient high-output linear fluorescent lighting system saves enough electricity annually from this store alone to supply the needs of 52 single-family homes. The store's heating system burns recovered cooking oil from the deli's fryers.

In the chain's Tire & Lube Express centres in Canada, it recovers used oil and oil filters, car batteries, antifreeze, and automotive tires. These are collected by recycling companies that will use the waste materials in the manufacturing of new products. For example, cardboard from bulk product packaging is recovered, baled, and sold to the manufacturer to make new boxes. As well, store offices recycle waste paper, cardboard, and beverage containers.

At the same time that Walmart presses forward with its own sustainability initiatives, it's laying down the law to suppliers. To demonstrate Walmart's environmental leadership and determination, CEO Lee Scott recently called a meeting of 250 other CEOs. At the meeting, Scott outlined Walmart's plans for holding its 61 000 suppliers accountable for reducing their "carbon footprints" and for eliminating excessive packaging. And in a show of force few governments could pull off, the company also "urged" another 600 supplier executives to attend a Walmart-sponsored seminar on sustainability. When imposing its environmental demands on suppliers, Walmart "has morphed into . . . a sort of privatized Environmental Protection Agency, only with a lot more clout," says an industry observer. "The EPA can levy [only] a seven-figure fine; Walmart can wipe out more than a quarter of a business in one fell swoop."

With its immense buying power, Walmart can humble even the mightiest supplier. Take, for example, the super-concentrated liquid laundry detergent market. Procter & Gamble and other detergent makers have long had the capability to formulate concentrated detergents. But it wasn't until Walmart declared that it would sell nothing but super-concentrated detergents that P&G decided to invest US$100 million to make them, even in the face of uncertain financial returns. Walmart's decision resulted in smaller plastic detergent containers, conserving raw materials and eliminating millions of tons of solid waste each year.

Because of Walmart's size, even small supplier product and packaging changes have a substantial environmental impact. For example, to meet Walmart's requests, P&G developed a mega-roll technology for its Charmin brand, which combines the sheets of four regular toilet paper rolls into one small roll. The seemingly minor change saves 89.5 million cardboard rolls and 360 000 pounds of plastic packaging wrap a year. It also allows Walmart to ship 42 percent more units on its trucks, saving about 54 000 gallons of fuel a year. Walmart also pressured General Mills to straighten the once curly noodles in boxes of Hamburger Helper. This small change eliminated thousands of pounds of packaging.

Walmart is working with the Carbon Disclosure Project, an independent not-for-profit environmental organization, to measure the amount of energy consumed in creating products throughout its supply chain. About 3400 suppliers of more than 13 000 products are participating in the project. Accordingly, Walmart has developed a packaging scorecard that rates the vendors and will soon be used to guide Walmart purchasing

▶

decisions. Walmart has also established more than a dozen "sustainable value networks." These networks connect Walmart people with suppliers, advocacy groups, academics, and independent experts who work together on "hot-button" environmental issues in various product categories, such as greenhouse gases, logistics, packaging, and alternative fuels.

So there you have it—Walmart the eco-nanny. Walmart's sustainability efforts have earned praise from even its harshest critics. As one skeptic begrudgingly admits, "Walmart has more green clout than anyone." But for Walmart, leading the eco-charge is about more than just doing the right thing. Above all, it also makes good business sense. More efficient operations and less wasteful products are not only good for the environment, they save Walmart money. Lower costs, in turn, let Walmart do more of what it has always done best—save customers money.

Says one Walmart executive, "We've laid the foundation for a long-term effort that will transform our business by driving out hidden costs, conserving our natural resources for future generations, and providing sustainable and affordable products for our customers so they can save money and live better."

Sources: Quotes and other information from Walmart Canada website http://www.walmart.ca/wps-portal/storelocator/Canada-About_Walmart.jsp?content=ourenviro, accessed June 2009; Jack Neff, "Why Walmart Has More Green Clout Than Anyone," *Advertising Age*, October 15, 2007, p. 1; "Walmart Says Latest High-Efficiency Store Cuts Energy Use 45%," *Environmental Leader*, March 18, 2008, accessed at www.environmentalleader.com; Danielle Sacks, "Working with the Enemy," *Fast* Company, September 2007, pp. 74–81; Joseph Tarnowski, "Green Monster," *Progressive Grocer*, April 1, 2006, pp. 20–26; Ylan Q. Mui, "Walmart Green Chief to Shift Jobs," *Washington Post*, October 20, 2007, p. D2; Ylan Q. Mui, "At Walmart, 'Green' Has Various Shades," *Washington Post*, November 16, 2007, p. D1; and "Sustainable Value Networks," accessed at http://walmartstores.com/Sustainability/7672.aspx, November 2008.

For Walmart, sustainability is about more than just doing the right thing. Above all, it makes good business sense—"driving out hidden costs, conserving our natural resources for future generations, and providing sustainable and affordable products for our customers so they can save money and live better."

Public Actions to Regulate Marketing

Citizen concerns about marketing practices will usually lead to public attention and legislative proposals. New bills will be debated—many will be defeated, others will be modified, and a few will become workable laws.

Many of the laws that affect marketing are listed in Chapter 3. The task is to translate these laws into a language that marketing executives understand as they make decisions about competitive relations, products, price, promotion, and channels of distribution. Figure 4.3 illustrates the major legal issues facing marketing management.

4   BUSINESS ACTIONS TOWARD SUSTAINABLE MARKETING

At first, many companies opposed consumerism, environmentalism, and other elements of sustainable marketing. They thought the criticisms were either unfair or unimportant. But by now most companies have grown to embrace the new consumer rights, at least in principle. They might oppose certain pieces of legislation as inappropriate ways to solve specific consumer problems, but they recognize the consumer's right to information and protection. Many of these companies have responded positively to sustainable marketing as a way to create greater immediate and future customer value and to strengthen customer relationships.

Figure 4.3 Major marketing decision areas that may be called into question under the law

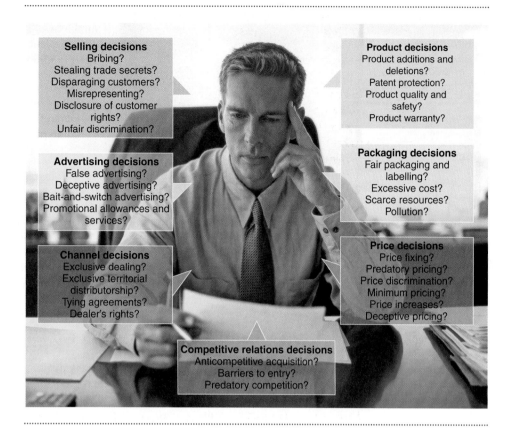

Selling decisions
Bribing?
Stealing trade secrets?
Disparaging customers?
Misrepresenting?
Disclosure of customer rights?
Unfair discrimination?

Product decisions
Product additions and deletions?
Patent protection?
Product quality and safety?
Product warranty?

Advertising decisions
False advertising?
Deceptive advertising?
Bait-and-switch advertising?
Promotional allowances and services?

Packaging decisions
Fair packaging and labelling?
Excessive cost?
Scarce resources?
Pollution?

Channel decisions
Exclusive dealing?
Exclusive territorial distributorship?
Tying agreements?
Dealer's rights?

Price decisions
Price fixing?
Predatory pricing?
Price discrimination?
Minimum pricing?
Price increases?
Deceptive pricing?

Competitive relations decisions
Anticompetitive acquisition?
Barriers to entry?
Predatory competition?

Sustainable Marketing Principles

Under the sustainable marketing concept, a company's marketing should support the best long-run performance of the marketing system. It should be guided by five sustainable marketing principles: *consumer-oriented marketing, customer-value marketing, innovative marketing, sense-of-mission marketing,* and *societal marketing.*

Consumer-Oriented Marketing

Consumer-oriented marketing
The philosophy of sustainable marketing that holds that the company should view and organize its marketing activities from the consumer's point of view.

Consumer-oriented marketing means that the company should view and organize its marketing activities from the consumer's point of view. It should work hard to sense, serve, and satisfy the needs of a defined group of customers, both now and in the future. All of the good marketing companies that we've discussed in this text have had this in common—an all-consuming passion for delivering superior value to carefully chosen customers. Only by seeing the world through its customers' eyes can the company build lasting and profitable customer relationships.

Customer-Value Marketing

Customer-value marketing
A principle of sustainable marketing that holds that a company should put most of its resources into customer-value–building marketing investments.

According to the principle of **customer-value marketing**, the company should put most of its resources into customer-value–building marketing investments. Many things marketers do—one-shot sales promotions, cosmetic packaging changes, direct-response advertising—may raise sales in the short run but add less *value* than would actual improvements in the product's quality, features, or convenience. Enlightened marketing calls for building long-run consumer loyalty and relationships by continually improving the value consumers receive from the firm's market offering. By creating value *for* consumers, the company can capture value *from* consumers in return.

Innovative Marketing

Innovative marketing
A principle of sustainable marketing that requires that a company seek real product and marketing improvements.

The principle of **innovative marketing** requires that the company continuously seek real product and marketing improvements. The company that overlooks new and better ways

Innovative marketing: Nintendo's customer-focused innovation not only attracted new gamers and bruised competitors Sony and Microsoft, "it has opened doors of creativity throughout the video-game business."

to do things will eventually lose customers to another company that has found a better way. An excellent example of an innovative marketer is Nintendo:

> After Sony and Microsoft kicked the Mario out of Nintendo's GameCube in the Video Game War of 2001, the smallest of the three game platform makers needed a new plan. "Nintendo took a step back from the technology arms race and chose to focus on [customers and] the fun of playing, rather than cold tech specs," says the president of Nintendo of America. The resulting Wii system, with its intuitive motion-sensitive controller and interactive games, appealed not only to teen boys typically targeted by the game industry but also to their sisters, moms, dads, and even grandparents. The result: the perpetually sold-out Wii system quickly outsold both the PlayStation 3 and Xbox 360. But get this: Unlike its competitors—which lose money on each console and earn it back on software—Nintendo actually turns a profit on its consoles, makes more selling games, then takes in still more in licensing fees. "Not to sound too obvious," says the Nintendo executive, "but it makes good business sense to make a profit on the products you sell." Wall Street thinks so too. The company's stock has more than doubled over the past year. Nintendo's upset is doing more than attracting new gamers and bruising Sony and Microsoft. Says the president of Sega of America, "It has opened doors of creativity throughout the video-game business."[28]

Sense-of-Mission Marketing

Sense-of-mission marketing
A principle of sustainable marketing that holds that a company should define its mission in broad social terms rather than narrow product terms.

Sense-of-mission marketing means that the company should define its mission in broad *social* terms rather than narrow *product* terms. When a company defines a social mission, employees feel better about their work and have a clearer sense of direction. Brands linked with broader missions can serve the best long-run interests of both the brand and consumers. For example, Dove wants to do more than just sell its beauty care products. It's on a mission to discover "real beauty" and to help women be happy just the way they are:

> It all started with a Unilever study that examined the impact on women of images seen in entertainment, in advertising, and on fashion runways. The startling result: Only 2 percent of 3300 women and girls surveyed in 10 countries around the world considered themselves beautiful. Unilever's conclusion: It's time to redefine beauty. So in 2004, Unilever launched the global Dove Campaign for Real Beauty, with ads that featured candid and confident images of real women of all types (not actresses or models) and headlines that made consumers ponder their perceptions of beauty. Among others, it featured full-bodied women ("Oversized or Outstanding?"), older women ("Gray or Gorgeous?") and a heavily freckled woman ("Flawed or Flawless?"). The following year, as the campaign's popularity skyrocketed, Dove introduced six new "real beauties" of various proportions, in sizes ranging from 6 to 14. These women appeared in ads wearing nothing but their underwear and big smiles, with headlines proclaiming, "New Dove Firming: As Tested on Real Curves." "In Dove ads," says one advertising expert, "normal is the new beautiful."
>
> The Dove Campaign for Real Beauty quickly went digital, with a CampaignForRealBeauty.com website and award-winning viral videos with names such as "Evolution" and "Onslaught" that attacked damaging beauty stereotypes. As the campaign has taken off, so have sales of Dove products. But the people behind the Dove brand

and the Campaign for Real Beauty have noble motives beyond sales and profits. According to a Unilever executive, Dove's bold and compelling mission to redefine beauty and reassure women ranks well above issues of dollars and cents. "You should see the faces of the people working on this brand now," he says. "There is a real love for the brand."[29]

Some companies define their overall corporate missions in broad societal terms. For example, defined in narrow product terms, the mission of Unilever's Ben & Jerry's unit might be "to sell ice cream." However, Ben & Jerry's states its mission more broadly, as one of "linked prosperity," including product, economic, and social missions. From its beginnings, Ben & Jerry's championed a host of social and environmental causes, and it donated a whopping 7.5 percent of pre-tax profits to support worthy causes. By the mid-1990s, Ben & Jerry's had become the nation's number-two superpremium ice cream brand.

However, having a "double bottom line" of values and profits is no easy proposition. Throughout the 1990s, as competitors not shackled by "principles before profits" missions invaded its markets, Ben & Jerry's growth and profits flattened. In 2000, after several years of less-than-stellar financial returns, Ben & Jerry's was acquired by giant food producer Unilever. Looking back, the company appears to have focused too much on social issues at the expense of sound business management. Ben Cohen once commented, "There came a time when I had to admit 'I'm a businessman.' And I had a hard time mouthing those words."[30]

Such experiences taught the socially responsible business movement some hard lessons. The result is a new generation of activist entrepreneurs—not social activists with big hearts who hate capitalism, but well-trained business managers and company builders with a passion for a cause. Founded by businesspeople who are proud of it, the new mission-driven companies are just as dedicated to building a viable, profitable business as to shaping the mission. They know that to "do good," they must first "do well" in terms of successful business operations.

Societal Marketing

Following the principle of **societal marketing**, a company makes marketing decisions by considering consumers' wants and interests, the company's requirements, and society's long-run interests. The company is aware that neglecting consumer and societal long-run interests is a disservice to consumers and society. Alert companies view societal problems as opportunities.

Sustainable marketing calls for products that are not only pleasing but also beneficial. The difference is shown in Figure 4.4. Products can be classified according to their degree of immediate consumer satisfaction and long-run consumer benefit. **Deficient products**, such as hard-to-swallow and ineffective medicine, have neither immediate appeal nor long-run benefits. **Pleasing products** give high immediate satisfaction but may hurt consumers in the long run. Examples include cigarettes and junk food.

Societal marketing
A principle of sustainable marketing that holds that a company should make marketing decisions by considering consumers' wants, the company's requirements, consumers' long-run interests, and society's long-run interests.

Deficient products
Products that have neither immediate appeal nor long-run benefits.

Pleasing products
Products that give high immediate satisfaction but may hurt consumers in the long run.

Figure 4.4 Societal classification of products

IMMEDIATE SATISFACTION

		Low	High
LONG-RUN CONSUMER BENEFIT	High	Salutary products	Desirable products
	Low	Deficient products	Pleasing products

Salutary products
Products that have low appeal but may benefit consumers in the long run.

Desirable products
Products that give both high immediate satisfaction and high long-run benefits.

Salutary products have low immediate appeal but may benefit consumers in the long run; for instance, bicycle helmets or some insurance products. **Desirable products** give both high immediate satisfaction and high long-run benefits, such as a tasty *and* nutritious breakfast food.

Examples of desirable products abound. GE's Energy Smart compact fluorescent lightbulb provides good lighting at the same time that it gives long life and energy savings. Toyota's hybrid Prius gives both a quiet ride and fuel efficiency. Maytag's front-loading Neptune washer provides superior cleaning along with water savings and energy efficiency.

Companies should try to turn all of their products into desirable products. The challenge posed by pleasing products is that they sell very well but may end up hurting the consumer. The product opportunity, therefore, is to add long-run benefits without reducing the product's pleasing qualities. The challenge posed by salutary products is to add some pleasing qualities so that they will become more desirable in consumers' minds.

5 MARKETING ETHICS

Good ethics is a cornerstone of sustainable marketing. In the long run, unethical marketing harms customers and society as a whole. Further, it eventually damages a company's reputation and effectiveness, jeopardizing the company's very survival. Thus, the sustainable marketing goals of long-term consumer and business welfare can be achieved only through ethical marketing conduct.

Conscientious marketers face many moral dilemmas. The best thing to do is often unclear. Because not all managers have fine moral sensitivity, companies need to develop *corporate marketing ethics policies*—broad guidelines that everyone in the organization must follow. These policies should cover distributor relations, advertising standards, customer service, pricing, product development, and general ethical standards.

The finest guidelines cannot resolve all the difficult ethical situations the marketer faces. Table 4.1 lists some ethical issues associated with marketing practices. Table 4.2 lists some difficult ethical issues marketers could face during their careers. If marketers choose immediate sales-producing actions in all these cases, their marketing behaviour might well be described as immoral or even amoral. If they refuse to go along with *any* of the actions, they might be ineffective as marketing managers and unhappy because of the constant moral tension. Managers need a set of principles that will help them figure out the moral importance of each situation and decide how far they can go in good conscience.

But *what* principle should guide companies and marketing managers on issues of ethics and social responsibility? One philosophy is that such issues are decided by the free market and legal system. Under this principle, companies and their managers are not responsible for making moral judgments. Companies can in good conscience do whatever the market and legal systems allow.

A second philosophy puts responsibility not on the system but in the hands of individual companies and managers. This more enlightened philosophy suggests that a company should have a "social conscience." Companies and managers should apply high standards of ethics and morality when making corporate decisions, regardless of "what the system allows." History provides an endless list of examples of company actions that were legal but highly irresponsible.

Each company and marketing manager must work out a philosophy of socially responsible and ethical behaviour. Under the societal marketing concept, each manager must look beyond what is legal and allowed and develop standards based on personal integrity, corporate conscience, and long-run consumer welfare.

As with environmentalism, the issue of ethics presents special challenges for international marketers. Business standards and practices vary a great deal from one country to the next. For example, whereas bribes and kickbacks are illegal for Canadian firms, they are standard business practice in many South American countries. One recent study found that companies from some nations were much more likely to use bribes when seeking contracts

Table 4.1 Ethical Issues Associated with Marketing Practice

Marketing Element	Examples of Ethical Issues
Marketing Research	Invalid and/or unreliable research studies (agencies conducting research studies using inappropriate methods or measures)
	Invasion of consumer's privacy
	Disguising sales as research
	Failure to ensure voluntary and informed participation (pressuring consumers to comply through high-pressure tactics or high-value incentives)
	Failure to respect the confidentiality of respondents (revealing respondents' individual identities)
	Competitive intelligence gathering using unethical tactics (hiring competitors' employees, dumpster diving, spying)
Segmentation and Target Marketing	Redlining: discriminating against poor or disadvantaged consumers
	Targeting inappropriate products to vulnerable audiences (diet pills to anorexic women, violent video games to children)
Positioning	Making socially undesirable products desirable (promoting the use of disposable cleaning devices that add to landfill crises versus reusable ones)
	Positioning on questionable benefits (the objectification of women in advertising and the suggestion that alcohol consumption makes males more sexually attractive, when alcohol may diminish sexual function and rape and physical abuse have been found to be associated with drinking)
Product	Failure to market products that are safe for the intended use (lead in children's toys)
	Product testing (animal testing, failure to test sufficiently to reveal safety concerns)
	Marketing socially controversial products (cigarettes, firearms)
Packaging and Labelling	Actual size vs. apparent size (using design elements to make packages look larger than they are)
	Inadequate efforts with regard to product recalls
	Nutritional information (is information displayed in a fashion that can and will be processed?)
	Unclear or misleading labelling (use of terms such as "lite," "healthy," etc., which are ambiguous and may imply benefits not actually associated with the product)
	Excessive or environmentally unfriendly packaging (use of double and triple packaging that does little to protect the product but adds to waste stream, use of harmful dyes, failure to use recycled materials)
Pricing	Price collusion: the illegal practice of forming price agreements with competitors
	Negative option billing: sending unrequested goods and billing consumers for them
	Prejudice in negotiated prices: research has demonstrated that women and racial minorities pay more in negotiated price situations, such as car buying
	Price discrimination: charging different segments different prices that are not based on cost (e.g., charging high prices in low-income neighbourhoods)
Advertising	Sex-role stereotyping in advertising (always showing women in domestic roles, not using women's voices in voice-overs in advertising)
	Dehumanizing images and portraying people as products: showing body parts versus the whole human being
	Bait-and-switch advertising: enticing consumers into retail establishments with offers of low-priced goods then switching them to higher-priced alternatives
Sales and Channel Management	High-pressure sales tactics
	Unfairly disparaging competitors' goods
	Channel loading: pressuring channel members to take unneeded inventory at the end of a sales period to make the firm's sales numbers look better for reporting purposes

Table 4.2 Some Morally Difficult Situations in Marketing

1. You work for a fast-food company and up until now have not been convinced that eating fast food leads to obesity for many people, especially children. However, recent public policy debates now leave no doubt in your mind about the link between overconsumption of these foods and health problems. What do you do?

2. Your R&D department has changed one of your products slightly. It is not really "improved," but you know that putting this statement on the package and in advertising will increase sales. What would you do?

3. You have been asked to add a stripped-down model to your line that could be advertised to pull customers into the store. The product won't be very good, but salespeople will be able to switch buyers up to higher-priced units. You are asked to give the green light for the stripped-down version. What would you do?

4. You are thinking of hiring a product manager who has just left a competitor's company. She would be more than happy to tell you all the competitor's plans for the coming year. What would you do?

5. One of your top dealers in an important territory recently has had family troubles and his sales have slipped. It looks like it will take him a while to straighten out his family trouble. Meanwhile you are losing many sales. Legally, on performance grounds, you can terminate the dealer's franchise and replace him. What would you do?

6. You have a chance to win a big account that will mean a lot to you and your company. The purchasing agent hints that a "gift" would influence the decision. Your assistant recommends sending a big-screen HDTV television to the buyer's home. What would you do?

7. You have heard that a competitor has a new product feature that will make a big difference in sales. The competitor will demonstrate the feature in a private dealer meeting at the annual trade show. You can easily send a snooper to this meeting to learn about the new feature. What would you do?

8. You have to choose between three ad campaigns outlined by your agency. The first (a) is a soft-sell, honest, straight-information campaign. The second (b) uses sex-loaded emotional appeals and exaggerates the product's benefits. The third (c) involves a noisy, somewhat irritating commercial that is sure to gain audience attention. Pretests show that the campaigns are effective in the following order: c, b, and a. What would you do?

9. You are interviewing a capable female applicant for a job as salesperson. She is better qualified than the men just interviewed. Nevertheless, you know that in your industry some important customers prefer dealing with men and you will lose some sales if you hire her. What would you do?

in emerging-market nations. The most flagrant bribe-paying firms were from India, Russia, and China. Other countries where corruption is common include Iraq, Myanmar, and Haiti. The least corrupt were companies from Iceland, Finland, New Zealand, and Denmark.[31]

The question arises as to whether a company must lower its ethical standards to compete effectively in countries with lower standards. The answer is no. Companies should make a commitment to a common set of shared standards worldwide. For example, John Hancock Mutual Life Insurance Company operates successfully in Southeast Asia, an area that by Western standards has widespread questionable business and government practices. Despite warnings from locals that Hancock would have to bend its rules to succeed, the company set out strict guidelines. "We told our people that we had the same ethical standards, same procedures, and same policies in these countries that we have in the United States, and we do," says Hancock chairman Stephen Brown. "We just felt that things like payoffs were wrong—and if we had to do business that way, we'd rather not do business." Hancock employees feel good about the consistent levels of ethics. "There may be countries where you have to do that kind of thing," says Brown. "We haven't found that country yet, and if we do, we won't do business there."[32]

Many industrial and professional associations have suggested codes of ethics, and many companies are now adopting their own codes. For example, the Canadian Marketing Association has a code to regulate practices of its members; excerpts are given in Table 4.3. Companies are also developing programs to teach managers about important ethics issues and help them find the proper responses. They hold ethics workshops and seminars and set up ethics committees. Furthermore, most major North American companies have appointed high-level ethics officers to champion ethics issues and to help resolve ethics problems and concerns facing employees.

PricewaterhouseCoopers (PwC) is a good example. In 2002, PwC established a global ethics office and comprehensive ethics program, headed by a high-level global ethics officer. The ethics program begins with a code of conduct, called "The Way We Do Business."

Table 4.3 Excerpts from the Canadian Marketing Association's Code of Ethics & Standards of Practice

A1. Purpose of Code of Ethics and Standards of Practice

Preamble: Marketers acknowledge that the establishment and maintenance of high standards of practice are a fundamental responsibility to the public, essential to winning and holding public confidence, and the foundation of a successful and independent information-based marketing industry in Canada.

A2. Application and Governing Legislation

A2.2 Members of the Canadian Marketing Association recognize an obligation—to the public, to the integrity of the discipline in which they operate and to each other—to practice to the highest standards of honesty, truth, accuracy and fairness.

A2.4 No marketer shall participate in any campaign involving the disparagement of any person or group on the grounds of race, colour, religion, national origin, gender, sexual orientation, marital status.

B. Accuracy of Representation

B1 Accuracy: Offers must be clear and truthful and shall not misrepresent a product, service, solicitation or program and shall not mislead by statement, or technique of demonstration or comparison.

B4 Identity: Every offer and shipment shall identify the marketer and provide the consumer with sufficient information to be able to contact the marketer.

B5 Disguise: No person shall make offers or solicitations in the guise of research or a survey when the real intent is to sell products, services, or to raise funds.

B6 Disparagement: No offer shall attack or discredit, or disparage products, services, advertisements or companies using inaccurate information.

B7 Representation: Photography, artwork or audio-visual representation must accurately and fairly illustrate the product offered.

C. Constituent Elements and Characteristics of the Offer

C1 Disclosure: The offer shall contain clear and conspicuous disclosure of the following terms:

- The exact nature of what is offered;
- The price;
- The terms of payment, including any additional charges, such as shipping and handling; and
- The consumer's commitment and any ongoing obligation in placing an order.

C2 Comparisons: Comparisons included in offers must be factual, verifiable and not misleading.

C10 Guarantees and Warranties: Where an offer includes a guarantee or warranty, the terms and conditions shall be set forth in full with the offer, or made available to the consumer upon request.

D. Fulfilment Practices

D1 Shipment: Goods offered shall be shipped within 30 days of the receipt of a properly completed order, or within the time limit stated in the original offer.

D2 Delay: The customer shall be advised within 30 days of the receipt of the order, or within the time limit stated in the original offer, if delivery will be late.

D4 Substitution: Any substitution of goods to those originally offered and ordered shall be disclosed to the consumer and shall be of the same or better quality, or be approved by the customer before shipment.

E. Media-Specific Standards of Practice

E1.2 Misrepresentation: Marketers shall not employ presentations likely to mislead reasonable consumers that the presentation is news, information, public service or entertainment programming.

E2.2 Printed Media—Description: All printed materials shall accurately and fairly describe the product or service offered. Type size, colour, contrast, style, placement or other treatment shall not be used to reduce the legibility or clarity of the offer, exceptions to the offer, or terms and conditions.

E3.3 Telephone—Identification: Marketers shall identify themselves and the business or organization represented promptly at the beginning of each outbound telemarketing call.

E3.3 Telephone—Privacy: No marketer shall knowingly call any person who has an unlisted or unpublished telephone number, except where the telephone number was furnished by the customer to that marketer. In addition:

- Marketers will promptly remove from their lists the telephone numbers of consumers who request them to do so, or non-customers who have registered with the CMA's Do Not Call Service.

E4.2 Internet and Other Electronic Media—Consent: Marketers shall not transmit marketing email without the consent of the recipient or unless the marketer has an existing relationship with the recipient.

E4.5 Internet and Other Electronic Media—Disclosure: When gathering data from individual consumers that could identify the consumer, and which will be linked with "clickstream" data, marketers shall advise consumers: a) what information is being collected; and b) how the information will be used. The marketer shall provide access to this advisory before consumers submit data that could identify them.

Marketers shall also provide a meaningful opportunity for consumers to decline to have information that identifies them collected, or transferred, for marketing purposes. In addition, access to this advisory shall be provided in every location, site or page from which the marketer is collecting such data.

F. Product Safety

F1 Introduction: Products offered by marketers shall be safe in normal use and, where applicable, shall conform to product safety regulations established by Health and Welfare Canada and by the Canadian Standards Association and/or other recognized Canadian authorities.

G. Special Considerations in Marketing to Children

G1 Age: For purposes of this Code of Ethics and Standards of Practice, the term child refers to someone who has not reached his or her 13th birthday.

In addition:

- Marketers are expected to use discretion and sensitivity in marketing to persons between 13 years and the age of majority, to address the age, knowledge, sophistication and maturity of this audience.

G2 Responsibility: Marketing to children imposes a special responsibility on marketers. Marketers shall recognize that children are not adults and that not all marketing techniques are appropriate for children.

G3 Consent: Except as provided below under G4 Contests, Games or Sweepstakes, all marketing interactions directed to children including collection, transfer and requests for personal information require the express consent of the child's parent or guardian.

H. Protection of the Environment

H1 Environmental Responsibility: Marketers recognize and acknowledge a continuing responsibility to manage their businesses to minimize environmental impact.

H2 Three Rs: Marketers shall incorporate the "Three Rs" of environmental responsibility in the operation of their businesses. More specifically, to:

- Reduce material use;
- Reuse materials; and,
- Recycle materials.

I. Protection of Personal Privacy

Privacy: All marketers shall recognize and abide by the six principles of personal privacy adopted by the Canadian Marketing Association:

Principle #1: Giving Consumers Control of How Information About Them Is Used

1.1 Consumers must be provided with a meaningful opportunity to decline to have their name or other information used for any further marketing purposes by a third party.

Principle #2: Providing Consumers with the Stage of Access to Information

2.1 The industry endorses the right of the consumer to know the source of his/her name used in any information-based marketing program. Marketers must make all reasonable efforts to provide this information to the consumer on request.

Principle #3: Enabling Consumers to Reduce the Amount of Mail They Receive

All CMA members must use the Do Not Mail/Do Not Call service of the Association when conducting a campaign in order to delete the name of any consumer, other than a current customer, who has requested that he or she be removed from mail and telemarketing lists. A "current customer" is defined as any consumer who has made a purchase from the marketer within the last six months or during a normal buying cycle.

Principle #4: Controlling the Use of Information by Third Parties

The purposes for which information is collected shall be identified by the organization at or before the time the information is collected.

Principle #5: Safely Storing Information About Consumers

All those involved in the transfer, rental, sale or exchange of mailing lists must be responsible for the protection of list data and should take appropriate measures to ensure against unauthorized access, alteration or dissemination of list data. Those who have access to such data should agree in advance to use data only in an authorized manner.

Principle #6: Respecting Confidential and Sensitive Information

All list owners and users must be protective of the consumer's right to privacy and sensitive to the information collected on lists and subsequently considered for use, transfer, rental or sale.

J. Enforcement Procedures for the Standards of Practice

J1 Upon receipt of information that would indicate a violation of the criminal laws of Canada, the Association will promptly forward such information to the appropriate authorities and the organization concerned.

J2 Upon receipt of a customer complaint regarding violation of this Code, whether regarding a member or a non-member, the Association will contact the company and use its mediation procedures to attempt to resolve the consumer complaint.

Source: Canadian Marketing Association, "Code of Ethics & Standards of Practice," www.the-cma.org/public.asp?WCE=C=47|K=225849 (accessed October 2009).

PwC employees learn about the code of conduct and about how to handle thorny ethics issues in comprehensive ethics training programs, which start when the employee joins the company and continue through the employee's career. The program also includes an ethics help line and regular communications at all levels. "It is obviously not enough to distribute a document," says PwC's CEO, Samuel DiPiazza. "Ethics is in everything we say and do."[33]

Still, written codes and ethics programs do not ensure ethical behaviour. Ethics and social responsibility require a total corporate commitment. They must be a component of the overall corporate culture. According to PwC's DiPiazza, "I see ethics as a mission-critical issue. . . deeply embedded in who we are and what we do. It's just as important as our product development cycle or our distribution system. . . . It's about creating a culture based on integrity and respect, not a culture based on dealing with the crisis of the day. . . . We ask ourselves every day, 'Are we doing the right things?'"[34]

THE SUSTAINABLE COMPANY

At the foundation of marketing is the belief that companies that fulfill the needs and wants of customers will thrive. Companies that fail to meet customer needs or that intentionally or unintentionally harm customers, others in society, or future generations will decline. Sustainable companies are those that create value for customers through socially, environmentally, and ethically responsible actions.

Sustainable marketing goes beyond caring for the needs and wants of today's customers. It means having concern for tomorrow's customers in assuring the survival and success of the business, shareholders, employees, and the broader world in which they all live. Sustainable marketing provides the context in which companies can build profitable customer relationships by creating value *for* customers to capture value *from* customers in return, now and in the future.

REVIEWING OBJECTIVES AND KEY TERMS

 | Audio Chapter Summary

In this chapter, we've discussed many important sustainable marketing concepts related to marketing's sweeping impact on individual consumers, other businesses, and society as a whole. You learned that sustainable marketing requires socially, environmentally, and ethically responsible actions that bring value not just to present-day consumers and businesses, but also to future generations and to society as a whole. Sustainable companies are those that act responsibly to create value for customers to capture value from customers in return, now and in the future.

OBJECTIVE 1 **Define *sustainable marketing* and discuss its importance.**

Sustainable marketing calls for meeting the present needs of consumers and businesses while still preserving or enhancing the ability of future generations to meet their needs. Whereas the marketing concept recognizes that companies thrive by fulfilling the day-to-day needs of

customers, sustainable marketing calls for socially and environmentally responsible actions that meet both the immediate and future needs of customers and the company. Truly sustainable marketing requires a smoothly functioning marketing system in which consumers, companies, public policymakers, and others work together to ensure responsible marketing actions.

Identify the major social criticisms of marketing.

Marketing's *impact on individual consumer welfare* has been criticized for its high prices, deceptive practices, high-pressure selling, shoddy or unsafe products, planned obsolescence, and poor service to disadvantaged consumers. Marketing's *impact on society* has been criticized for creating false wants and too much materialism, too few social goods, and cultural pollution. Critics have also criticized marketing's *impact on other businesses* for harming competitors and reducing competition through acquisitions, practices that create barriers to entry, and unfair competitive marketing practices. Some of these concerns are justified; some are not.

Define *consumerism* and *environmentalism* and explain how they affect marketing strategies.

Concerns about the marketing system have led to *citizen action movements*. *Consumerism* is an organized social movement intended to strengthen the rights and power of consumers relative to sellers. Alert marketers view it as an opportunity to serve consumers better by providing more consumer information, education, and protection. *Environmentalism* is an organized social movement seeking to minimize the harm done to the environment and quality of life by marketing practices. The first wave of modern environmentalism was driven by environmental groups and concerned consumers, whereas the second wave was driven by government, which passed laws and regulations governing industrial practices impacting the environment. The first two environmentalism waves are now merging into a third and stronger wave in which companies are accepting responsibility for doing no environmental harm. Companies are now adopting policies of *environmental sustainability*—developing strategies that both sustain the environment and produce profits for the company. Both consumerism and environmentalism are important components of sustainable marketing.

Describe the principles of sustainable marketing.

Many companies originally opposed these social movements and laws, but most of them now recognize a need for positive consumer information, education, and protection. Under the sustainable marketing concept, a company's marketing should support the best long-run performance of the marketing system. It should be guided by five sustainable marketing principles: *consumer-oriented marketing, customer-value marketing, innovative marketing, sense-of-mission marketing*, and *societal marketing*.

Explain the role of ethics in marketing.

Increasingly, companies are responding to the need to provide company policies and guidelines to help their managers deal with questions of *marketing ethics*. Of course even the best guidelines cannot resolve all the difficult ethical decisions that individuals and firms must make. But there are some principles among which marketers can choose. One principle states that such issues should be decided by the free market and legal system. A second and more enlightened principle puts responsibility not on the system but in the hands of individual companies and managers. Each firm and marketing manager must work out a philosophy of socially responsible and ethical behaviour. Under the sustainable marketing concept, managers must look beyond what is legal and allowable and develop standards based on personal integrity, corporate conscience, and long-term consumer welfare.

KEY TERMS

DISCUSSING THE CONCEPTS

1. What is sustainable marketing? Explain how the sustainable marketing concept differs from the marketing concept and the societal marketing concept.

2. Marketing's impact on individual consumers has been criticized. Discuss the issues relevant to this impact.

3. Discuss the types of harmful impact that marketing practices can have on competition and the associated problems.

4. Can an organization focus on both consumerism and environmentalism at the same time? Explain.

5. Describe the five sustainable marketing principles and explain how companies benefit from adhering to them.

6. Good ethics is the cornerstone of sustainable marketing. Explain what this means and discuss how companies practise good ethics.

APPLYING THE CONCEPTS

1. The Consumers' Association of Canada represents and informs consumers about issues affecting their quality of life. Visit www.consumer.ca to learn about this association. Select one of the issues or activities listed on their home page. Discuss how the information helped you become a more informed consumer.

2. In a small group, discuss each of the morally difficult situations in marketing presented in Table 4.2. Which philosophy is guiding your decision in each situation?

FOCUS ON TECHNOLOGY

A recent controversial report by the Conference Board of Canada, an independent not-for-profit applied research organization located in Ottawa, named Canada as one of the leaders in the world in terms of illegal computer file-swapping. Because of lax regulation and enforcement, Internet piracy is on the rise in Canada, the Conference Board believes. The board called for government action to address the situation. The board said it agreed with the Organisation for Economic Cooperation and Development's conclusion that Canada has the highest per capita incidence of unauthorized file-swapping in the world. The board said the estimated 1.3 billion illicit downloads in Canada outnumber the 20 million legal ones by 65 times.

1. File sharing may benefit consumers, but it hurts members of the entertainment industry. Discuss the ethical pros and cons of file sharing.

2. Should the Canadian government do more to regulate file sharing? Why or why not?

FOCUS ON ETHICS

R&B singer Chris Brown's "Forever" tune claimed the number-four spot on *Billboard* magazine's Hot 100 in July 2008. "Tonight is the night to join me in the middle of ecstasy /. . . Cause we only got one night / Double your pleasure / Double your fun." If that last part sounds familiar, it's because it comes from Wrigley's Doublemint gum's timeless jingle. "Forever" is an extended version of a new Doublemint jingle, but it was released months before the commercial without indication that it was also a commercial jingle. Actually, the song and the jingle not only share the "Double your pleasure / Double your fun" element, but the melody is the same. Brown was paid by Wrigley to write and perform the song and jingle.

1. Was Wrigley's sponsorship of the song and later release of the jingle deceptive?

2. Discuss other examples of product placement—that is, brands appearing in songs, movies, television programs, or video games. Are these different than Chris Brown's and Wrigley's "Forever"?

MARKETING BY THE NUMBERS

"High-low" pricing is popular with retailers but considered deceptive by some. Using this practice, retailers set initial prices very high for a short period and then discount the merchandise for the majority of the selling season. Critics complain that the supposed discounted price is in reality the regular price. For example, Canadian retailers like Suzy Shier and the Bay were accused of double tagging—placing sale tags on goods right in the factory, so that the sale price was in fact the regular price.

1. Refer to Appendix 3: Marketing by the Numbers, to answer the following questions. If the Bay's cost for a piece of jewellery is $50 and it was marked up five times the cost, what is the "high" retail price? What is the "low" sales price if the price is reduced 60 percent off the "regular" price? What is the Bay's markup percentage on cost at this price? What is its markup percentage on the "low" selling price?

2. Judgments of some cases of high-low pricing have ruled that the retailer did not violate any laws and that one retailer cannot be singled out because most jewellery competitors promote sales prices in a similar way. Is it ethical for retailers to use this pricing tactic?

VIDEO CASE

| Video Case Questions

Land Rover

The automotive industry has seen better days. Many auto companies are now facing declining revenues and negative profits. Additionally, because of its primary dependence on products that consume petroleum, the auto industry has a big environmental black eye, especially companies that primarily make gas-guzzling trucks and SUVs.

During the past few years, however, Land Rover has experienced tremendous growth in revenues and profits. It is currently selling more vehicles than ever worldwide. How is this possible for a company that sells only SUVs? One of the biggest reasons is Land Rover's strategic focus on social responsibility and environmentalism. Land Rover believes that it can meet consumer needs for luxury all-terrain vehicles while at the same time providing a vehicle that is kinder to the environment. As a corporation, it is also working feverishly to reduce its carbon emissions, waste, and water consumption and pollution. With actions like this, Land Rover is

successfully repositioning its brand away from the standard perceptions of SUVs as environmental enemies.

After viewing the video featuring Land Rover, answer the following questions about the company's efforts toward social responsibility:

1. Make a list of social criticisms of the automotive industry. Discuss all of the ways that Land Rover is combating those criticisms.

2. By the definition given in this chapter, does Land Rover practise "sustainable marketing"?

3. Do you believe that Land Rover is sincere in its efforts to be environmentally friendly? Is it even possible for a large SUV to be environmentally friendly? Present support for both sides of these arguments.

Visit MyMarketingLab at www.pearsoned.ca/mymarketinglab to view the video segment related to this case.

COMPANY CASE

Mountain Equipment Co-op

Over the past 25 years, companies such as Ben & Jerry's and The Body Shop have reflected their sensitivity to ethics and social responsibility by using pioneering ideas like "values-led business" or "caring capitalism"—putting "principles ahead of profits." But can a company dedicated to doing good still do well? Can it successfully serve a "triple bottom line"—simultaneously being economically, socially, and environmentally responsible? Canadian organizations like Mountain Equipment Co-op (MEC) have demonstrated that aligning these goals is not only possible, it is an inspirational business model.

Organizations that pioneered the concepts of "values-led business" and "caring capitalism" use business to make the world a better place. Ben & Jerry's, for example, bought only hormone-free milk and cream from local dairy farms and used only organic fruits and nuts to make its ice cream, which it sold in environmentally friendly containers. In a similar fashion, Anita Roddick, founder of The Body Shop, put "passion before profits." Her mission was to "dedicate our business to the pursuit of social and environmental change." The firm's natural-ingredient-based cosmetics are formulated without any animal testing, and supplies were often sourced from developing countries. The Body Shop, which now operates in 61 countries, donates a percentage of profits each year to animal-rights groups, women's causes, homeless shelters, Amnesty International, AIDS research, Save The Rainforest, and other social causes. In recent years these two companies have been acquired by multinationals, but they still operate relatively independently (Unilever owns Ben & Jerry's and L'Oréal owns The Body Shop).

Caring about the environment and social issues is not enough. Values-led companies must also be profitable, sustainable enterprises; therefore, they must have well-trained business managers and company builders with a passion for a cause. Mountain Equipment Co-op is one such organization. In its new Charter it clearly articulates the values that drive all its operations: quality, integrity, cooperation, creativity, leadership, sustainability, stewardship of wild places, humanity, and adventure.

MEC's logo has become a Canadian national icon despite the fact that the company has shunned traditional marketing tactics like mass-media advertising. MEC was born in Vancouver in 1971 to fill a set of unmet needs for quality outdoor equipment at affordable prices. But it was how MEC met these needs that shaped it into what it has become today. As the company's website notes, "We're driven by passion, not profit. We continue to look for ways to protect our wild spaces and reduce the ecological footprint of our business." MEC also knows that actions speak louder than words. It donates 1 percent of all its sales revenues to support Canadian environmental causes. In 2008, MEC took pride in reporting that it recycled, composted, or donated 92 percent of the waste generated in its stores and offices; only 8 percent ended up in landfills. MEC is also using more and more certified green energy for its operations. For its 2009 catalogues, it used 100 percent recycled paper.

MEC is a cooperative that exists to serve the needs of its members. Its affordable, quality products are built with "purpose, people, and the planet in mind." But the company goes far beyond products in thinking about its purpose. It has "a long-standing focus on social, environmental, and economic sustainability." In speaking about its sustainability agenda, the path it takes to accomplish its goals, MEC notes, "we decentralized accountability to make sustainability part of everyone's job."

As noted above, MEC is a member-owned cooperative and it is the largest retail cooperative in Canada. A "cooperative is a democratically owned business structure in which members pool their resources to obtain a benefit. At MEC, members use their shared purchasing power to obtain goods and services for outdoor activities." Lifetime membership is open to anyone for a low fee of $5. Membership allows people to purchase MEC products and use its services through its stores, website, or catalogues. Members can also vote on how MEC is governed.

Throughout its history, MEC has consistently offered a narrow set of products and has placed considerable attention on the quality of its products and services. While recognizing that it is a retailer that survives by promoting "consumption," it works to do so in an environmentally responsible and sustainable manner. For example, it has featured organic cotton clothing for more than five years. It is committed to green building, community grants, ethical purchasing, product sustainability, and promotion of Canada-wide parks and protected areas, trying to be "green" in all it does. MEC prides itself on building ecologically friendly stores: it reduces energy consumption, recoups onsite groundwater, uses recycled building materials whenever possible, and even cultivates small rooftop gardens designed to filter smoggy air and reduce the building's heating and cooling costs. Even when it replaces a store, as it did in Ottawa, MEC works to be sensitive to environmental issues. Thus, it worked hard so that 86 percent of the previous building that stood on MEC's Ottawa site was recycled, and most of it was used in the new building.

While MEC certainly focuses on customer needs, quality products, and high service, it has long realized that many stakeholder groups are critically connected to its long-term success. Just look at its second Accountability Report posted on its website to see its stakeholder focus. The report describes how it works with others throughout the process of selecting, designing, and manufacturing its products. It works with its upstream textile mills and equipment manufacturers to do things like reduce the amount of petrochemicals that go into many of its products. It partners with factories to ensure fair labour practices and working conditions. It looks downstream to users and helps them extend the lives of their products through its repair programs. MEC also reduces excess consumption through its gear swaps for people who no longer need their equipment or want to trade up or down. It has developed a "take-back" program

to recycle polyester clothing into new, useful items. Since the shipping of products to its stores results in more greenhouse gases than what is generated by its facilities, it works with transportation providers to help reduce MEC's carbon footprint. Where possible, MEC ships by rail rather than road. It also encourages its employees to use alternative transportation to get to their jobs (transit, walking, or biking).

MEC also knows that simply working to make a one-time sale to a customer isn't enough. Developing lifetime relationships with its members has been another touchstone of the cooperative. As part of its vision, MEC sets the goal of having its members purchase most of their needs for outdoor activities from MEC. It sends members catalogues twice yearly that are filled with high-quality information as well as products. It also sends out newsletters and is beginning to rely more and more on its website (see the Connect tab on www.mec.ca) and MECmail to maintain the link with its 2.9 million members. It's also using more social media sites like YouTube to enhance relationships with its members.

Such relationships are critical since MEC has no doubt that its best marketers are the members themselves. Member-generated word-of-mouth communication has long worked to help the company grow. And grow it has. In 2007, its sales were $239 million (a 15 percent increase since 2005). By 2009, MEC operated stores in Victoria, Vancouver (2), Calgary, Edmonton, Winnipeg, Burlington, Toronto, Ottawa, Montreal, Longueuil, Quebec City, and Halifax. But no matter what it does today or in the future, MEC tries to take the high road and be an exemplar of ethics, integrity, and environmental responsibility in its undertakings.

Questions for Discussion

1. Excess consumption of goods and services is put forth as a root cause of environmental degradation. Some critics blame consumers for this state of affairs. Others blame firms. How has MEC worked with consumers to reduce excess consumption? How have its marketing programs contributed to this agenda?

2. Describe MEC's key stakeholders. How has MEC's desire to create value for its stakeholders helped it become the successful organization it is today?

3. MEC is an exceptional organization. How has its behaviour changed consumer expectations for how retailers should behave with regard to social, economic, and environmental responsibilities?

4. Click on the Sustainability tab on MEC's website. List the three initiatives that you think best illustrate why MEC is considered a leader in sustainability.

Source: Information accessed at www.mec.ca, October 2009.

Visit **MyMarketingLab** at **www.pearsoned.ca/mymarketinglab** for access to online tutorials, interactive exercises, videos, and much more.

5

Managing Marketing Information to Gain Customer Insights

PREVIEWING THE CONCEPTS In Chapter 3, you learned about the complex and changing marketing environment. In Chapter 4, you were presented with issues relating to marketing's social responsibility and ethics that managers must deal with as they engage with the marketing environment. In this chapter, we continue our exploration of how marketers gain insights into consumers and the marketplace. We look at how companies develop and manage information about important marketplace elements—customers, competitors, products, and marketing programs. To succeed in today's marketplace, companies must know how to turn mountains of marketing information into fresh customer insights that will help them deliver greater value to customers.

We'll start this chapter with a story about what Unilever Canada did with Dove. Dove, the world's top cleansing brand, was born in 1957 as a beauty soap bar that was clinically proven to be milder than other leading soaps. It was especially suitable for dry, sensitive skin. Research revealed that 50 percent of women have dry skin, so the bar soon became popular. It wasn't long before it became the world's number-one cleansing brand. It is sold in more than 80 countries and generates annual sales revenues of more than $5 billion. In North America alone, more than 1 billion showers are taken with Dove products each year. Dove beauty soap still racks up double-digit growth, and it outsells all other skin care bars combined.

Why, you might wonder, would such a successful brand spend much on marketing research? The impetus for the project came from the need to extend the meaning of the Dove brand beyond bar soap. Over the years a number of extensions had been launched to take advantage of the powerful Dove brand name. In February 2003, for example, the Dove name was put onto a new line of hair care products. In July of the same year, a line of face care products was also launched bearing the Dove name.

The brand team at Unilever Canada quickly realized that consumers were confused about the brand, and the tried-and-true associations linking the name with bar soap were outdated. The positioning just wasn't sufficient to link all the products bearing the Dove name. As Erin Iles, the head of the Dove brand team, noted, "The brand was a bar of soap with a quarter of moisturizing cream. People trusted it and saw it as an honest brand, but they also saw it as a bit of a boring brand. That's fine when your product mix is a bar of soap. But as soon as your product mix includes moisturizers that sell for $16 and toners and shampoos, it can't be this boring brand that lives in your shower that you don't think about. We really needed to make it a beauty brand."

The Dove team needed solid research and a lot of insight before this repositioning task could be undertaken. While other companies were using thin, perfect, air-brushed models to peddle their lines of beauty products, this didn't seem right for Dove. For the Dove team, the first question to answer was "How is women's self-esteem affected by body image?" As part of its primary data-gathering initiative, a global survey was commissioned by Unilever. The company also undertook *ethnographic* research. The term comes from a branch of anthropology that deals with the scientific description of specific human cultures. Thus, to understand women's culture and how they thought about beauty, researchers would go shopping with women and spend time in their homes talking about the meaning of beauty and deciphering what they consider beautiful.

New Dove Firming Lotion. As tested on real curves.

Dove's research-driven campaign has helped make it a market-leading beauty brand.

The research uncovered that only 2 percent of women—only 1 percent in Canada—consider themselves beautiful. Despite this finding, women feel pressured to be beautiful. Sixty-three percent of women strongly agree that women today are expected to be more attractive than their mother's generation. Even more troubling was other secondary data (published research undertaken by others) that showed that girls as young as nine years old were dissatisfied with their body image, and girls as young as seven expressed the desire to be thinner.

Paradoxically, Dove's research also suggested that all women want to be beautiful in their own unique way, not in a way dictated by Hollywood movies or fashion magazines. In fact, 36 percent of Canadian women surveyed described themselves as "natural," but very few viewed themselves as "sexy," "stunning," or "gorgeous." Although many of the women's responses referred to physical aspects of beauty, they also rated kindness, happiness, confidence, dignity, and humour as powerful, inner components of beauty. As Dr. Susie Orbach, one of the chief researchers on the project, noted, "What's interesting is women explaining the notion of beauty in a much broader sense." If the research team hadn't designed the study to ask the right questions and if they hadn't really probed to get to the heart of what

makes women feel beautiful, they would have missed the insights that later made the Campaign for Real Beauty such a success.

The research initiative led the Dove marketers to the conclusion that it was time to change the definition of beauty. Although the research itself is fascinating, it is how Unilever used the insights that is really exceptional. From the beginning of the repositioning effort, the Dove team had women look at themselves and open a dialogue on what beauty is. This desire for dialogue could be seen in the marketing campaign that followed the research efforts. Take the most visible and striking example—the large billboards and print "tick-box" ads that featured images of everyday women along with two choices consumers could use to interpret their beauty (for example, "Fab? or Fat?," "Bald? or Beautiful?"). People could record their votes by phone or on the website. Another example was the Beyond Compare photo tour. Renowned photographers from around the world were asked to contribute pictures of women they considered beautiful. As the exhibit toured the country, Dove again asked women what they thought of the photographs and what they said about beauty. This again created an opportunity for the brand team to learn even more deeply about what women considered beauty to be.

OBJECTIVES ▶

1. Explain the importance of information in gaining insights about the marketplace and customers.

2. Define the marketing information system and discuss its parts.

3. Outline the steps in the marketing research process.

4. Explain how companies analyze and use marketing information.

5. Discuss the special issues some marketing researchers face, including public policy and ethics issues.

The research and resulting marketing campaign won Unilever Canada a number of awards, including the 2005 Media Innovation Award, a Cassie Award, a *Marketing Magazine* Gold Promo Award, and *Strategy Magazine's* 2004 Marketer of the Year. Even more important than the awards, however, is the fact that packaged goods giant Unilever and the Dove marketing and research teams imbued the brand with the kind of cultural relevance usually reserved for "lifestyle" brands like MINI or Apple. The campaign has been extended to young girls who are also concerned about their looks. It was this rendition of the campaign, developed by the Toronto office of Ogilvy & Mather, that viewers saw nestled in the U.S. broadcast of the 2006 Super Bowl. "There were questions about whether to put something like that on the Super Bowl. . ." said Janet Kestin, creative director of Ogilvy & Mather in Toronto. "But of course, there are tons of women who watch, too. According to *Advertising Age* magazine, the 2006 Super Bowl attracted an audience comprising 44 per cent women." In 2007, Ogilvy & Mather's viral film, *Evolution*, created in Canada for the Dove Self-Esteem Fund, won the prestigious Film Grand Prix at the Cannes Lions International Advertising Festival in France. This hugely popular look at how images in the media are altered to present what society knows as "beautiful" has been viewed over 10 million times on YouTube and has even spawned dozens of parody videos. This research-driven campaign has certainly been a touchdown with women of all ages![1]

Chapter Opening Discussion

As the Dove story highlights, good products and marketing programs begin with good customer information. Companies also need an abundance of information on competitors, resellers, and other actors and marketplace forces. But more than just gathering information, marketers must *use* the information to gain powerful *customer and market insights*.

1 MARKETING INFORMATION AND CUSTOMER INSIGHTS

To create value for customers and to build meaningful relationships with them, marketers must first gain fresh, deep insights into what customers need and want. Companies use such customer insights to develop competitive advantage. "In today's hypercompetitive world," states a marketing expert, "the race for competitive advantage is really a race for customer and market insights." Such insights come from good marketing information.[2]

Other Marketing Information Considerations

Consider Apple's phenomenally successful iPod. The iPod wasn't the first digital music player, but Apple was the first to get it right. Apple's research uncovered a key insight into how people want to consume digital music—they want to take all their music with them but they want personal music players to be unobtrusive. This insight led to two key design goals—make it as small as a deck of cards and build it to hold 1000 songs. Add a dash of Apple's design and usability magic to this insight and you have a recipe for a blockbuster. Apple's expanded iPod line now captures more than 75 percent market share.

However, although customer and market insights are important for building customer value and relationships, these insights can be very difficult to obtain. Customer needs and buying motives are often anything but obvious—consumers themselves usually can't tell you exactly what they need and why they buy. To gain good customer insights, marketers must effectively manage marketing information from a wide range of sources.

Today's marketers have ready access to plenty of marketing information. With the recent explosion of information technologies, companies can now generate information in great quantities. In fact, most marketing managers are overloaded with data and often overwhelmed by it. For example, Walmart refreshes

Key customer insights, plus a dash of Apple's design and usability magic, have made the iPod a blockbuster. It now captures more than 75 percent of market share.

sales data from checkout scanners hourly, adding a billion rows of data a day, equivalent to about 96 000 DVD movies. That's a *lot* of data to analyze.[3] Still, despite this data glut, marketers frequently complain that they lack enough information of the right kind. They don't need *more* information, they need *better* information. And they need to make better use of the information they already have. Says another marketing information expert, "transforming today's vast, ever-increasing volume of consumer information into actionable marketing insights . . . is the number-one challenge for digital-age marketers."[4]

Thus, a company's marketing research and information system must do more than simply generate lots of information. The real value of marketing research and marketing information lies in how it is used—in the **customer insights** that it provides. "The value of the market research department is not determined by the number of studies that it does," says one marketing expert, "but by the business value of the *insights* that it produces and the decisions that it influences." Says another expert, "Companies that gather, disseminate, and apply deep customer insights obtain powerful, profitable, sustainable competitive advantages for their brands."[5]

Based on such thinking, many companies are now restructuring and renaming their marketing research and information functions. They are creating "customer insights teams," headed by a vice-president of customer insights and made up of representatives from all of the firm's functional areas. For example, the head of marketing research at Kraft Foods is called the director of consumer insights and strategy.

Customer insight groups collect customer and market information from a wide variety of sources—ranging from traditional marketing research studies to mingling with and observing consumers to monitoring consumer online conversations about the company and its products. They then *use* the marketing information to develop important customer insights from which the company can create more value for its customers. For example, Unilever's customer insights group states its mission simply as "getting better at understanding our consumers and meeting their needs."

In gathering and using customer insights, however, companies must be careful not to go too far and become *customer controlled*. The idea is not to give customers everything they request. Rather, it's to understand customers to the core and give them what they need—to create value for customers as a means of capturing value for the firm in return.[6]

Thus, companies must design effective marketing information systems that give managers the right information, in the right form, at the right time and help them to use this information to create customer value and stronger customer relationships. A **marketing information system (MIS)** consists of people and procedures for assessing informational needs, developing the needed information, and helping decision makers to use the information to generate and validate actionable customer and market insights.

Figure 5.1 shows that the MIS begins and ends with information users—marketing managers, internal and external partners, and others who need marketing information. First it interacts with these information users to *assess information needs*. Next it interacts with the marketing environment to *develop needed information* through internal company databases, marketing intelligence activities, and marketing research. Finally the MIS helps users analyze and use the information to develop customer insights, make marketing decisions, and manage customer relationships.

ASSESSING MARKETING INFORMATION NEEDS

The marketing information system primarily serves the company's marketing and other managers. However, it may also provide information to external partners, such as suppliers, resellers, or marketing services agencies. For example, Walmart's Retail Link system gives key suppliers access to information on customer buying patterns and inventory levels. And Dell creates tailored Premium Pages for large customers, giving them access to

Customer insights
Fresh understandings of customers and the marketplace derived from marketing information that become the basis for creating customer value and relationships.

Glossary Flashcards of Key Terms

Marketing information system (MIS)
People and procedures for assessing information needs, developing the needed information, and helping decision makers to use the information to generate and validate actionable customer and market insights.

Figure 5.1 The marketing information system

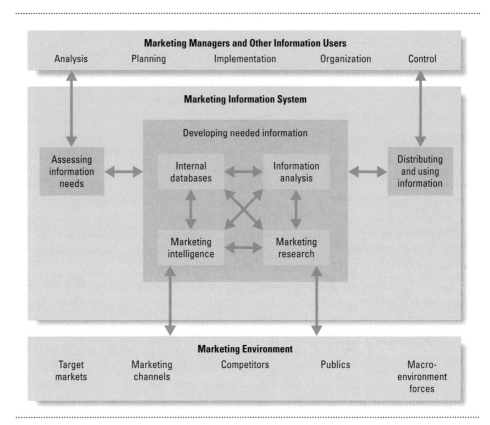

product design, order status, and product support and service information. In designing an information system, the company must consider the needs of all of these users.

A good marketing information system balances the information users would *like* to have against what they really *need* and what is *feasible* to offer. The company begins by interviewing managers to find out what information they would like. Some managers will ask for whatever information they can get without thinking carefully about what they really need. Too much information can be as harmful as too little. Other managers may omit things they ought to know, or they may not know to ask for some types of information they should have. For example, managers might need to know about surges in favourable or unfavourable consumer "word-of-web" discussions about their brands on blogs or online social networks. Because they do not know about these discussions, they do not think to ask about them. The MIS must monitor the marketing environment to provide decision makers with information they should have to better understand customers and make key marketing decisions.

Sometimes the company cannot provide the needed information, either because it is not available or because of MIS limitations. For example, a brand manager might want to know how competitors will change their advertising budgets next year and how these changes will affect industry market shares. The information on planned budgets probably is not available. Even if it is, the company's MIS may not be advanced enough to forecast resulting changes in market shares.

Finally, the costs of obtaining, analyzing, storing, and delivering information can mount quickly. The company must decide whether the value of insights gained from additional information is worth the costs of providing it, and both value and cost are often hard to assess. By itself, information has no worth; its value comes from its use. In many cases, additional information will do little to change or improve a manager's decision, or the costs of the information may exceed the returns from improved customer insights and decision making. Marketers should not assume that additional information will always be worth obtaining. Rather, they should weigh carefully the costs of getting more information against the benefits resulting from it.[7]

Developing Marketing Information

Marketers can obtain the needed information from *internal data, marketing intelligence,* and *marketing research.*

Internal Data

Internal databases
Electronic collections of consumer and market information obtained from data sources within the company's network.

Many companies build extensive **internal databases**, electronic collections of consumer and market information obtained from data sources within the company's network. Marketing managers can readily access and work with information in the database to identify marketing opportunities and problems, plan programs, and evaluate performance.

Information in the database can come from many sources. The marketing department furnishes information on customer transactions, demographics, psychographics, and buying behaviour. The customer service department keeps records of customer satisfaction or service problems. The accounting department prepares financial statements and keeps detailed records of sales, costs, and cash flows. Operations reports on production schedules, shipments, and inventories. The sales force reports on reseller reactions and competitor activities, and marketing channel partners provide data on point-of-sale transactions. Harnessing such information can provide powerful customer insights and competitive advantage.

Here is an example of how one company uses its internal database to make better marketing decisions:

> When the Hudson's Bay Co. and Zellers merged their loyalty programs, they created one of the most comprehensive and potentially far-reaching customer databases in Canada. The database contains information on more than 8.5 million members, according to the database managers. As one VP noted, "When someone's buying kids' clothing at either the Bay or at Zellers, we now have the data to tell us that." In fact, the data is so detailed that by matching the stock keeping unit number (the SKU number) with the purchase information, the database managers and the marketers who depend on it can determine not only what size the child is, but also make an informed guess about the sex and age of the purchasers' children. And the information goes far beyond kids' clothes. The stores carry a massive array of merchandise that is purchased by the 85 percent of the Canadian population who come through their doors every year.[8]

Internal databases usually can be accessed more quickly and cheaply than other information sources, but they also present some problems. Because internal information was often collected for other purposes, it may be incomplete or in the wrong form for making marketing decisions. For example, sales and cost data used by the accounting department for preparing financial statements must be adapted for use in evaluating the value of a specific customer segment, sales force, or channel performance. Data also ages quickly; keeping the database current requires a major effort. In addition, a large company produces mountains of information that must be well integrated and readily accessible so that managers can find it easily and use it effectively. Managing that much data requires highly sophisticated equipment and techniques.

Because of the costs of updating and maintaining internal databases, many companies are buying services from other organizations. Rogers Publishing, for example, is the first magazine publisher to tap Canada Post's vast database of 1.2 million people who register address changes to distribute a home décor magazine called *Chocolat.* Rogers knows that people who move are a prime market for new furniture or home decorations.[9]

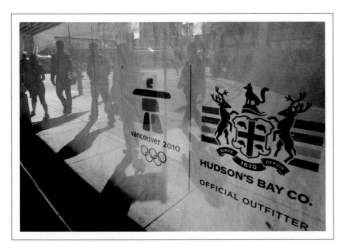

Internal databases: Hbc's database of over 8.5 million Canadian consumers is one of the most comprehensive customer databases in Canada.

Many companies routinely monitor consumers' online chatter with the help of monitoring services like Nielsen Online.

Marketing intelligence
The systematic collection and analysis of publicly available information about consumers, competitors, and developments in the marketing environment.

Marketing Intelligence

Marketing intelligence is the systematic collection and analysis of publicly available information about consumers, competitors, and developments in the marketplace. The goal of marketing intelligence is to improve strategic decision making by understanding the consumer environment, assessing and tracking competitors' actions, and providing early warnings of opportunities and threats.

Marketing intelligence gathering has grown dramatically as more and more companies are now busily eavesdropping on the marketplace and snooping on their competitors. Techniques range from monitoring Internet buzz or observing consumers firsthand to quizzing the company's own employees, benchmarking competitors' products, researching the Internet, lurking around industry trade shows, and even rooting through rivals' trash bins.

Good marketing intelligence can help marketers gain insights into how consumers talk about and connect with their brands. Many companies send out teams of trained observers to mix and mingle with customers as they use and talk about the company's products. Other companies routinely monitor consumers' online chatter with the help of online monitoring services such as Nielsen Online or BrandIntel. For example, Ford employs marketing intelligence firm BrandIntel to monitor blogs and other Internet sites. Ford wants to know what people are saying about its products, their performance, and their looks. It also wants to know about any important issues—positive or negative—that might have consumers buzzing online about specific Ford models. For example, if BrandIntel discovers unanswered product questions or service complaints, it forwards them to Ford's customer service staff. When appropriate, the service staff can respond online, identifying themselves and asking if they can join the online discussions.[10]

Companies also need to actively monitor competitors' activities. Firms use competitive intelligence to gain early warnings of competitor moves and strategies, new-product launches, new or changing markets, and potential competitive strengths and weaknesses. A recent analysis by consulting firm PricewaterhouseCoopers found that companies employing competitive intelligence as a critical element in their strategic thinking grow 20 percent faster than those that do not.[11]

Much competitor intelligence can be collected from people inside the company—executives, engineers and scientists, purchasing agents, and the sales force. The company can also obtain important intelligence information from suppliers, resellers, and key customers. Or it can get good information by observing competitors and monitoring their published information. It can buy and analyze competitors' products, monitor their sales, check for new patents, and examine various types of physical evidence. For example, one company regularly checks out competitors' parking lots—full lots might indicate plenty of work and prosperity; half-full lots might suggest hard times.

Some companies have even rifled their competitors' garbage, which is legally considered abandoned property once it leaves the premises. In one classic garbage-snatching incident, Procter & Gamble admitted to "dumpster diving" at rival Unilever's headquarters. Unilever's dumpsters yielded a wealth of information about strategies for Unilever's hair care brands. However, when news of the questionable tactics reached top P&G managers, they were shocked and immediately stopped the project. Although P&G claims it broke no laws, it noted that dumpster raids violated its business policies.

Competitors often reveal intelligence information through their annual reports, business publications, trade show exhibits, press releases, advertisements, and webpages. The Web has become an invaluable source of competitive intelligence. Using Internet search engines, marketers can search specific competitor names, events, or trends and see what

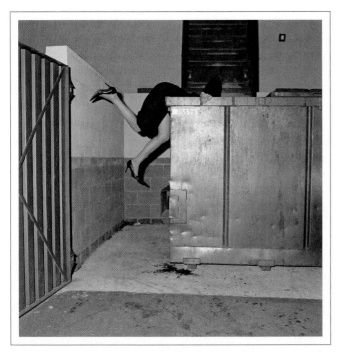

Marketing Intelligence: Procter & Gamble admitted to "dumpster diving" at rival Unilever's Helene Curtis headquarters. When P&G's top management learned of the questionable practice it stopped the project, voluntarily informed Unilever, and set up talks to right whatever competitive wrongs had been done.

turns up. Moreover, most companies now place volumes of information on their websites, providing details to attract customers, partners, suppliers, investors, or franchisees. This can provide a wealth of useful information about competitors' strategies, markets, new products, facilities, and other happenings.

Intelligence seekers can also pore through any of thousands of online databases. Some are free. For example, you can search the System for Electronic Document Analysis and Retrieval (SEDAR) database for the documents and information filed by public companies and investment funds with the Canadian Securities Administrators. The Howard Ross Library of Management at McGill University lists many resources for learning more about Canadian businesses, and Hoovers.com has a searchable website containing financial information on publicly traded Canadian and U.S. companies. And for a fee, companies can subscribe to any of more than 3000 online databases and information search services, such as Dialog, DataStar, LexisNexis, Dow Jones News/ Retrieval, UMI ProQuest, and Dun & Bradstreet's online access. Notes one marketing intelligence consultant, companies "are often surprised that there's so much out there to know. They're busy with their day-to-day operations and they don't realize how much information can be obtained with a few strategic keystrokes."[12]

The intelligence game goes both ways. Facing determined marketing intelligence efforts by competitors, most companies are now taking steps to protect their own information. For example, Unilever conducts widespread competitive intelligence training. Employees are taught not just how to collect intelligence information but also how to protect company information from competitors. According to a former Unilever staffer, "We were even warned that spies from competitors could be posing as drivers at the minicab company we used." Unilever even performs random checks on internal security. Says one former staffer, "At one [internal marketing] conference, we were set up when an actor was employed to infiltrate the group. The idea was to see who spoke to him, how much they told him, and how long it took to realize that no one knew him. He ended up being there for a long time."[13]

The growing use of marketing intelligence raises a number of ethical issues. Although most of the preceding techniques are legal, and some are considered to be shrewdly competitive, some may involve questionable ethics. Clearly, companies should take advantage of publicly available information. However, they should not stoop to snooping. With all the legitimate intelligence sources now available, a company does not need to break the law or accepted codes of ethics to get good intelligence.

MARKETING RESEARCH

In addition to marketing intelligence information about general consumer, competitor, and marketplace happenings, marketers often need formal studies that provide customer and market insights for specific marketing situations and decisions. For example, Budweiser wants to know what appeals will be most effective in its Super Bowl advertising. Google wants to know how web searchers will react to a proposed redesign of its site. Or Samsung wants to know how many and what kinds of people will buy its next-generation LCD televisions. In such situations, marketing intelligence will not provide the detailed information needed. Managers will need marketing research.

Marketing research is the systematic design, collection, analysis, and reporting of data relevant to a specific marketing situation facing an organization. Companies use

Marketing research
The systematic design, collection, analysis, and reporting of data relevant to a specific marketing situation facing an organization.

Figure 5.2 The marketing research process

marketing research in a wide variety of situations. For example, marketing research gives marketers insights into customer motivations, purchase behaviour, and satisfaction. It can help them assess market potential and market share or measure the effectiveness of pricing, product, distribution, and promotion activities.

Some large companies have their own research departments that work with marketing managers on marketing research projects. This is how Procter & Gamble, GE, and many other corporate giants handle marketing research. In addition, these companies—like their smaller counterparts—frequently hire outside research specialists to consult with management on specific marketing problems and conduct marketing research studies. Sometimes firms simply purchase data collected by outside firms to aid in their decision making.

The marketing research process has four steps (see Figure 5.2): defining the problem and research objectives, developing the research plan, implementing the research plan, and interpreting and reporting the findings.

Defining the Problem and Research Objectives

Marketing managers and researchers must work closely together to define the problem and agree on research objectives. The manager best understands the decision for which information is needed; the researcher best understands marketing research and how to obtain the information. Defining the problem and research objectives is often the hardest step in the research process. The manager may know that something is wrong without knowing the specific causes. For example, in the Dove case, Unilever began with a broad problem statement, "How do women themselves define beauty?" and then designed a series of more specific questions to tap into this broader issue.

After the problem has been defined carefully, the manager and researcher must set the research objectives. A marketing research project might have one of three types of objectives. The objective of **exploratory research** is to gather preliminary information that will help define the problem and suggest hypotheses. The objective of **descriptive research** is to describe things, such as the market potential for a product or the demographics and attitudes of consumers who buy the product. The objective of **causal research** is to test hypotheses about cause-and-effect relationships. For example, would a 10 percent decrease in tuition at a university result in an enrolment increase sufficient to offset the reduced tuition? Managers often start with exploratory research and later follow with descriptive or causal research.

The statement of the problem and research objectives guides the entire research process. The manager and researcher should put the statement in writing to be certain that they agree on the purpose and expected results of the research.

Developing the Research Plan

Once the research problems and objectives have been defined, researchers must determine the exact information needed, develop a plan for gathering it efficiently, and present the plan to management. The research plan outlines sources of existing data and spells out the specific research approaches, contact methods, sampling plans, and instruments that researchers will use to gather new data.

Research objectives must be translated into specific information needs. For example, suppose Unilever decides to conduct research on how consumers would react to a proposed new premium cologne line sold under its Axe brand. The Axe line of body sprays, shower gels, and deodorants has grown rapidly in recent years to become the world's top

Exploratory research
Marketing research to gather preliminary information that will help define problems and suggest hypotheses.

Descriptive research
Marketing research to better describe marketing problems, situations, or markets, such as the market potential for a product or the demographics and attitudes of consumers.

Causal research
Marketing research to test hypotheses about cause-and-effect relationships.

male grooming brand. Axe targets 18- to 24-year-old males with a coolly seductive, adventurous, and unconventional positioning that promises to give them "an edge in the dating game." However, research suggests that many younger consumers see themselves as outgrowing "inexpensive" body scents and switching to cologne.[14] Creating a line of cologne fragrances for the Axe brand would be expensive, but it might help to keep current customers as they mature. The proposed research might call for the following specific information:

- The demographic, economic, and lifestyle characteristics of current Axe users. (Maturing teen and young adult users might move readily to Axe cologne if it's priced right, carries a more mature scent, and is positioned to meet their changing lifestyles.)

- Characteristics and usage patterns of young male cologne users: What do they need and expect from their fragrances, where do they buy them, when and how do they use them, and what existing cologne brands and price points are most popular? (The new Axe cologne will need strong, relevant positioning in the crowded men's fragrance market.)

- Retailer reactions to the proposed new product line: Would they stock it? Where would they display it? (Failure to get retailer support would hurt sales of the premium cologne.)

- Forecasts of sales of both the new and current Axe products. (Will the new cologne line create new sales or simply take sales away from current Axe products? Will the cologne increase Unilever's overall profits?)

Axe brand managers will need these and many other types of information to decide whether and how to introduce the new cologne product.

The research plan should be presented in a *written proposal*. A written proposal is especially important when the research project is large and complex or when an outside firm carries it out. The proposal should cover the management problems addressed and the research objectives, the information to be obtained, and the way the results will help management decision making. The proposal should also include research costs.

Secondary data
Information that already exists somewhere, having been collected for another purpose.

Primary data
Information collected for the specific purpose at hand.

To meet the manager's information needs, the research plan can call for gathering secondary data, primary data, or both. **Secondary data** consist of information that already exists somewhere, having been collected for another purpose. **Primary data** consist of information collected for the specific purpose at hand.

The decision by the Axe brand to offer a new cologne line that would give maturing customers a new "edge in the dating game" might call for marketing research that provides lots of specific information.

Gathering Secondary Data

Researchers usually start by gathering secondary data. The company's internal database provides a good starting point. However, the company can also tap into a wide assortment of external information sources, including commercial data services and government sources (see Table 5.1).

Companies can buy secondary data reports from outside suppliers. For example, ACNielsen sells buyer data from a consumer panel of more than 260 000 households in 27 countries worldwide, with measures of trial and repeat purchasing, brand loyalty, and buyer demographics. Experian Simmons sells information on more than 8000 brands in 450 product categories, including detailed consumer profiles that assess everything from the products consumers buy and the brands they prefer to their lifestyles, attitudes, and media preferences. The Monitor service by Yankelovich sells information on important social and lifestyle

Table 5.1 Selected External Information Sources

For business data:

Scott's Directories (www.scottsinfo.com) lists, on an annual basis, manufacturers, their products, and their North American Industry Classification (NAICS) codes, alphabetically as well as by city and region. The directory also provides the names and telephone and fax numbers of chief executives, as well as corporate information like annual sales. Directories come in four volumes: Ontario, Quebec, Atlantic Canada, and Western Canada.

SEDAR (www.sedar.com) has an extensive database that includes the financial filing information, annual reports, and company profiles for Canadian public companies.

Canadian Trade Index (www.ctidirectory.com) and Fraser's Canadian Trade Directory (www.frasers.com) provide information on manufacturers of different product categories, manufacturing equipment, and supplies.

Nielsen Corporation (http://ca.nielsen.com) provides point-of-sale scanner data on sales, market share, and retail prices; data on household purchasing; and data on television audiences (a unit of VNU NV).

Experian Simmons (http://smrb.com) provides detailed analysis of consumer patterns in 400 product categories in selected markets.

Information Resources, Inc. (www.infores.com) provides supermarket scanner data for tracking grocery product movement and new product purchasing data.

IMS Health (www.imshealth.com) tracks drug sales, monitors performance of pharmaceutical sales representatives, and offers pharmaceutical market forecasts.

Arbitron (http://arbitron.com) provides local-market and Internet radio audience and advertising expenditure information, among other media and ad spending data.

J.D. Power and Associates (www.jdpower.com) provides information from independent consumer surveys of product and service quality, customer satisfaction, and buyer behaviour.

Dun & Bradstreet (www.dnb.com) maintains a database containing information on more than 50 million individual companies around the globe.

comScore Networks (http://comscore.com) provides consumer behaviour information and geodemographic analysis of Internet and digital media users around the world.

Dialog (www.dialog.com) offers access to more than 900 databases containing publications, reports, newsletters, and directories covering dozens of industries.

LexisNexis (www.lexisnexis.com) features articles from business, consumer, and marketing publications plus tracking of firms, industries, trends, and promotion techniques.

Dow Jones Factiva (http://factiva.com) specializes in in-depth financial, historical, and operational information on public and private companies.

Hoover's (http://hoovers.com) provides business descriptions, financial overviews, and news about major companies around the world.

Canoe (www.canoe.ca) bills itself as Canada's leading news and information site.

CNN (www.cnn.com) reports U.S. and global news and covers the markets and newsmaking companies in detail.

Advertising Age Whitepapers (http://adage.com/whitepapers) reports on demographic trends and their significance for businesses.

For government data:

Statistics Canada (www.statcan.gc.ca) provides summary data on demographic, economic, social, and other aspects of the Canadian economy and society.

Industry Canada's Strategis website (www.strategis.ic.gc.ca) provides resources for Canadian businesses.

Western Economic Diversification Canada (www.wd.gc.ca) provides information for people starting or operating a business in Western Canada.

Ontario Ministry for Economic Development and Trade (www.ontariocanada.com) and other provincial governments have sites that provide information for small business development.

Stat-USA (http://stat-usa.gov), a Department of Commerce site, highlights statistics on U.S. business and international trade.

U.S. Census Bureau (www.census.gov) provides detailed statistics and trends about the U.S. population.

For Internet data:

ClickZ (www.clickz.com) brings together a wealth of information about the Internet and its users, from consumers to ecommerce.

Interactive Advertising Bureau (www.iab.net) covers statistics about advertising on the Internet.

Forrester (www.forrester.com) monitors web traffic and ranks the most popular sites.

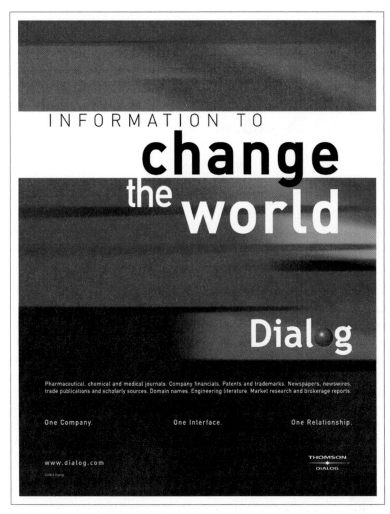

Online database services, such as Dialog, put an incredible wealth of information at the keyboards of marketing decision makers. Dialog puts "information to change the world, or your corner of it," at your fingertips.

Commercial online databases
Computerized collections of information available from online commercial sources or via the Internet.

trends. These and other firms supply high-quality data to suit a wide variety of marketing information needs.[15]

Using **commercial online databases**, marketing researchers can conduct their own searches of secondary data sources. General database services such as Dialog, ProQuest, and LexisNexis put an incredible wealth of information at the keyboards of marketing decision makers. Beyond commercial websites offering information for a fee, almost every industry association, government agency, business publication, and news medium offers free information to those tenacious enough to find their websites. There are so many websites offering data that finding the right ones can become an almost overwhelming task.

Web search engines can also be a big help in locating relevant secondary information sources. However, they can also be very frustrating and inefficient. For example, an Axe marketer googling "men's colognes" would come up with some 2 060 000 hits! Still, well-structured, well-designed web searches can be a good starting point to any marketing research project. For example, the fourth hit in the "men's colognes" Google search list would take the Axe marketer to a Shopping.Yahoo.com page containing consumer reviews and price comparisons of hundreds of men's cologne brands.

Secondary data can usually be obtained more quickly and at a lower cost than primary data. Also, secondary sources can sometimes provide data an individual company cannot collect on its own—information that either is not directly available or would be too expensive to collect. For example, it would be too expensive for Axe marketers to conduct a continuing retail store audit to find out about the market shares, prices, and displays of competitors' brands. But it can buy the InfoScan service from Information Resources, Inc., which provides this information from thousands of scanner-equipped supermarkets.[16]

Secondary data can also present problems. The needed information may not exist—researchers can rarely obtain all the data they need from secondary sources. For example, Unilever will not find existing information about consumer reactions to a new cologne line that it has not yet placed on the market. Even when data can be found, the information might not be very usable. The researcher must evaluate secondary information carefully to make certain it is relevant (fits research project needs), accurate (reliably collected and reported), current (up-to-date enough for current decisions), and impartial (objectively collected and reported).

Primary Data Collection

Secondary data provide a good starting point for research and often help to define research problems and objectives. In most cases, however, the company must also collect primary data. Just as researchers must carefully evaluate the quality of secondary information, they also must take great care when collecting primary data. They need to make sure that it will be relevant, accurate, current, and unbiased. Table 5.2 shows that designing a plan for primary data collection calls for a number of decisions on research approaches, contact methods, the sampling plan, and research instruments.

Table 5.2 Planning Primary Data Collection

Research Approaches	Contact Methods	Sampling Plan	Research Instruments
Observation	Mail	Sampling unit	Questionnaire
Survey	Telephone	Sample size	Mechanical instruments
Experiment	In person	Sampling procedure	
	Online		

Research Approaches

Research approaches for gathering primary data include observation, surveys, and experiments. We will discuss each one in turn.

Observational research
Gathering primary data by observing relevant people, actions, and situations.

Observational Research **Observational research** involves gathering primary data by observing relevant people, actions, and situations. For example, a bank might evaluate possible new branch locations by checking traffic patterns, neighbourhood conditions, and the location of competing branches.

Researchers often observe consumer behaviour to glean customer insights they can't obtain by simply asking customers questions. For instance, Fisher-Price has set up an observation lab in which it can observe the reactions of little tots to new toys. The Fisher-Price PlayLab is a sunny, toy-strewn space where lucky kids get to test Fisher-Price prototypes under the watchful eyes of designers who hope to learn what will get kids worked up into a new-toy frenzy. Others employ "Mindcams," which allow a company to observe through the consumers' eyes in their natural environments. For example, Kimberly-Clark used camera-equipped "glasses" to observe behaviour of consumers of their Huggies brand:

A few years back, Kimberly-Clark saw sales of its Huggies baby wipes slip just as the company was preparing to launch a line of Huggies baby lotions and bath products. When traditional research didn't yield any compelling customer insights, K-C's marketers decided they could get more useful feedback just from watching customers' daily lives. They came up with camera-equipped "glasses" to be worn by consumers at home, so that researchers could see what they saw. It didn't take long to spot the problems—and the opportunities. Although women in focus groups talked about changing babies at a diaper table, the truth was they changed them on beds, floors, and on top of washing machines in awkward positions. The researchers could see they were struggling with wipe containers and lotions requiring two hands. So the company redesigned the wipe package with a push-button one-handed dispenser and designed lotion and shampoo bottles that can be grabbed and dispensed easily with one hand.[17]

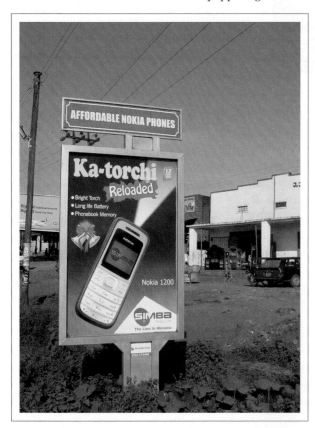

Ethnographic research: Teams of Nokia anthropologists "live with the locals" in emerging economies to glean subtle insights into each local culture. Such insights resulted in the robust Nokia 1200 phone, which makes shared use a top priority.

Observational research can obtain information that people are unwilling or unable to provide. In some cases, observation may be the only way to obtain the needed information. In contrast, some things simply cannot be observed, such as feelings, attitudes and motives, or private behaviour. Long-term or infrequent behaviour is also difficult to observe. Finally, observations can be very difficult to interpret. Because of these limitations, researchers often use observation along with other data collection methods.

Ethnographic research
A form of observational research that involves sending trained observers to watch and interact with consumers in their "natural habitat."

A wide range of companies now use **ethnographic research**. Ethnographic research involves sending trained observers to watch and interact with consumers in their "natural habitat." Consider this example:

Mobile phone maker Nokia wants to add two billion new customers by the end of the decade. To do so, it has invested heavily in ethnographic research, focusing especially on emerging economies. Nokia deploys teams of anthropologists to study deeply the behaviour of mobile-phone owners in vast markets such as China, Brazil, and India. By "living with the locals," from the shanty towns of Soweto to the bedrooms of Seoul's painfully tech-savvy teens, Nokia gleans subtle insights into nuances of each local culture. For example, it knows first-hand that 50 percent of the world's women keep their phones in their handbags (and miss 20 percent of their calls) and that most Asian early adopters who watch mobile TV ignore the mobile part and tune in from home.

One of the biggest discoveries came from researchers studying how people in poor rural areas overcome some of the barriers to communication they face in their daily lives. Surprisingly, although usually considered a one-owner item, mobile phones in these areas are often used by entire families or even villages because of the cost. Based on this finding, Nokia designed its 1200 and 1208 phones, which make shared use the top priority. The affordable phones offer many useful and durable features and are robust enough to accommodate many different people using them. For example, they contain a long-life battery and multiple phone books so each member of a family or village can keep his or her own contacts and numbers separately from others.[18]

Observational and ethnographic research often yield the kinds of details that just don't emerge from traditional research questionnaires or focus groups. Whereas traditional quantitative research approaches seek to test known hypotheses and obtain answers to well-defined product or strategy questions, observational research can generate fresh customer and market insights. "The beauty of ethnography," says a research expert, is that it "allows companies to zero in on their customers' unarticulated desires." Agrees another researcher, "Classic market research doesn't go far enough. It can't grasp what people can't imagine or articulate. Think of the Henry Ford quote: 'If I had asked people what they wanted, they would have said faster horses.'"[19]

Survey research
Gathering primary data by asking people questions about their knowledge, attitudes, preferences, and buying behaviour.

Survey Research **Survey research**, the most widely used method for primary data collection, is the approach best suited for gathering *descriptive* information. A company that wants to know about people's knowledge, attitudes, preferences, or buying behaviour can often find out by asking them directly.

The major advantage of survey research is its flexibility—it can be used to obtain many different kinds of information in many different situations. Surveys addressing almost any marketing question or decision can be conducted by phone or mail, in person, or on the Web. However, survey research also presents some problems. Sometimes people are unable to answer survey questions because they cannot remember or have never thought about what they do and why. People may be unwilling to respond to unknown interviewers or about things they consider private. Respondents may answer survey questions even when they do not know the answer to appear smarter or more informed. Or they may try to help the interviewer by giving pleasing answers. Finally, busy people may not take the time, or they might resent the intrusion into their privacy.

Experimental research
Gathering primary data by selecting matched groups of subjects, giving them different treatments, controlling other factors and checking for differences in group responses.

Experimental Research Whereas observation is best suited for exploratory research and surveys for descriptive research, **experimental research** is best suited for gathering causal information. Experiments involve selecting matched groups of subjects, giving them different treatments, controlling other factors, and checking for differences in group responses. Thus, experimental research tries to explain cause-and-effect relationships.

For example, before adding a new sandwich to its menu, McDonald's might use experiments to test the effects on sales of two different prices it might charge. It could introduce the new sandwich at one price in one city and at another price in another city. If the cities

Table 5.3 Strengths and Weaknesses of Contact Methods

	Mail	Telephone	In Person	Online
Flexibility	Poor	Good	Excellent	Good
Quantity of data that can be collected	Good	Fair	Excellent	Good
Control of interviewer effects	Excellent	Fair	Poor	Fair
Control of sample	Fair	Excellent	Good	Excellent
Speed of data collection	Poor	Excellent	Good	Excellent
Response rate	Poor	Poor	Good	Good
Cost	Good	Fair	Poor	Excellent

Source: Adapted with permission of the authors from Marketing Research: Measurement and Method, *7th ed., by Donald S. Tull and Del I. Hawkins. Copyright 1993 by Macmillan Publishing Company.*

are similar, and if all other marketing efforts for the sandwich are the same, then differences in sales in the two cities could be related to the price charged.

Contact Methods

Information can be collected by mail, telephone, personal interview, or online. Table 5.3 shows the strengths and weaknesses of each of these contact methods.

Mail, Telephone, and Personal Interviewing   *Mail questionnaires* can be used to collect large amounts of information at a low cost per respondent. Respondents may give more honest answers to more personal questions on a mail questionnaire than to an unknown interviewer in person or over the phone. Also, no interviewer is involved to bias the respondent's answers.

However, mail questionnaires are not very flexible—all respondents answer the same questions in a fixed order. Mail surveys usually take longer to complete, and the response rate—the number of people returning completed questionnaires—is often very low. Finally, the researcher often has little control over the mail questionnaire sample. Even with a good mailing list, it is hard to control *who* at the mailing address fills out the questionnaire.

Telephone interviewing is one of the best methods for gathering information quickly, and it provides greater flexibility than mail questionnaires. Interviewers can explain difficult questions and, depending on the answers they receive, skip some questions or probe on others. Response rates tend to be higher than with mail questionnaires, and interviewers can ask to speak to respondents with the desired characteristics or even by name.

However, the cost per respondent with telephone interviewing is higher than with mail questionnaires. Also, people may not want to discuss personal questions with an interviewer. The method introduces interviewer bias—the way interviewers talk, how they ask questions, and other differences may affect respondents' answers. Different interviewers may interpret and record responses differently, and under time pressures some interviewers might even cheat by recording answers without asking questions. Finally, in this age of do-not-call lists and promotion-harassed consumers, potential survey respondents are increasingly hanging up on telephone interviewers rather than talking with them. A recent poll revealed that 80 percent of Canadians who registered with Canada's National Do Not Call List, launched in September 2008 to cut down on unsolicited telemarketing, reported receiving fewer telemarketing calls and that awareness of and registration with this list continues to grow.[20] While market research firms and charitable organizations are exempt from Canada's new legislation, consumers often treat these calls no differently than those from unsolicited telemarketers.

Personal interviewing takes two forms—individual and group interviewing. *Individual interviewing* involves talking with people in their homes or offices, on the street, or in shopping malls. Such interviewing is flexible. Trained interviewers can guide interviews,

New focus group environments: To create a more congenial setting in which women could open up and share personal shaving and moisturizing stories, Schick Canada sponsored "Slow Sip" sessions in local cafés.

Focus group interviewing

Personal interviewing that involves inviting six to ten people to gather for a few hours with a trained interviewer to talk about a product, service, or organization. The interviewer "focuses" the group discussion on important issues.

explain difficult questions, and explore issues as the situation requires. They can show subjects actual products, advertisements, or packages and observe reactions and behaviour. However, individual personal interviews may cost three to four times as much as telephone interviews.

Group interviewing consists of inviting six to ten people to meet with a trained moderator to talk about a product, service, or organization. Participants normally are paid a small sum for attending. The moderator encourages free and easy discussion, hoping that group interactions will bring out actual feelings and thoughts. At the same time, the moderator "focuses" the discussion—hence the name **focus group interviewing**.

Researchers and marketers watch the focus group discussions from behind one-way glass and comments are recorded in writing or on video for later study. Today, focus group researchers can even use videoconferencing and Internet technology to connect marketers in distant locations with live focus group action. Using cameras and two-way sound systems, marketing executives in a far-off boardroom can look in and listen, using remote controls to zoom in on faces and pan the focus group at will.

Along with observational research, focus group interviewing has become one of the major qualitative marketing research tools for gaining fresh insights into consumer thoughts and feelings. However, focus group studies present some challenges. They usually employ small samples to keep time and costs down, and it may be hard to generalize from the results. Moreover, consumers in focus groups are not always open and honest about their real feelings, behaviour, and intentions in front of other people.

Thus, although focus groups are still widely used, many researchers are tinkering with focus group design. For example, Cammie Dunaway, chief marketing officer at Yahoo! prefers "immersion groups"—four or five people with whom Yahoo!'s product designers talk informally, without a focus group moderator present. That way, rather than just seeing videos of consumers reacting to a moderator, Yahoo! staffers can work directly with select customers to design new products and programs. "The outcome is richer if [consumers] feel included in our process, not just observed," says Dunaway.[21]

Other researchers are combining focus groups with hypnosis in an effort to get deeper, more vivid insights. Consider this example:

Volvo equals safety. In focus group after focus group, participants said the same thing. But to check these findings, Volvo called in a hypnotist. Members of Volvo focus groups were asked to test-drive a car. Immediately afterwards, they were hypnotized and asked their true feelings about the brand. It wasn't pretty: Many revealed that Volvo also equals being middle-aged. That idea "for some people was suffocating," says a Volvo researcher. "Hypnosis helped get past the clichés. We needed the conversation taken to a deeper, more emotional place."[22]

Still other researchers are changing the environments in which they conduct focus groups. To help consumers relax and to elicit more authentic responses, they use settings that are more comfortable and more relevant to the products being researched. For example, to get a better understanding of how women shave their legs, Schick Canada created the "Slow Sip" sessions designed to be like a simple get-together with girlfriends:

In these Slow Sip sessions, participants gathered round at a local café to sip coffee or tea and munch on snacks together. The structure was loose, and the congenial setting helped the women to open up and share personal shaving and moisturizing stories on a subject that might have been sensitive in a more formal setting. The Slow Sip sessions produced a number of new customer insights. For example, researchers discovered that the message for their Schick Quattro for Women razor—that Quattro has four-blade technology—was too technical. Women don't care about the engineering behind a razor, they care about shaving results. As a result, Schick Canada repositioned the Quattro as offering a smooth, long-lasting shave. As a side benefit, participants enjoyed the sessions so much that they wanted to stick around for more. They became a kind of ongoing advisory board for Schick's marketers and "brand ambassadors" for Schick's products.[23]

Online Marketing Research   The growth of the Internet has had a dramatic impact on how marketing research is conducted. Increasingly, researchers are collecting primary data through **online marketing research**—*Internet surveys, online panels, experiments,* and *online focus groups.* By one estimate, global online research spending reached an estimated US$4.4 billion in 2008, triple the amount spent in 2005. An estimated one-quarter to one-third of all research will be conducted online by 2010.[24]

Online marketing research
Collecting primary data online through Internet surveys, online focus groups, web-based experiments, or tracking consumers' online behaviour.

Online research can take many forms. A company can use the Web as a survey medium. It can include a questionnaire on its website and offer incentives for completing it. It can use email, weblinks, or pop-ups to invite people to answer questions and possibly win a prize. It can create online panels that provide regular feedback or conduct live discussions or online focus groups. Beyond surveys, researchers can conduct experiments on the Web. They can experiment with different prices, use different headlines, or offer different product features on different websites or at different times to learn the relative effectiveness of their offers. Or they can set up virtual shopping environments and use them to test new products and marketing programs. Finally, a company can learn about the behaviour of online customers by following their clickstreams as they visit the website and move to other sites.

The Internet is especially well suited to *quantitative* research—conducting marketing surveys and collecting data. Eighty-five percent of Canadians now have access to the Web, making it a fertile channel for reaching a broad cross-section of consumers. As response rates for traditional survey approaches decline and costs increase, the Web is quickly replacing mail and the telephone as the dominant data collection methodology. One industry analyst estimates that consumer packaged-goods firms may now invest as much as two-thirds of their total quantitative survey budgets online. And Internet surveys now command nearly 80 percent of all online research spending.[25]

Web-based survey research offers some real advantages over traditional phone and mail approaches. The most obvious advantages are speed and low costs. "Faster. Cheaper. It boils down to that," concludes one marketing research executive.[26] By going online, researchers can quickly and easily distribute Internet surveys to thousands of respondents simultaneously via email or by posting them on selected websites. Responses can be almost instantaneous, and because respondents themselves enter the information, researchers can tabulate, review, and share research data as they arrive.

Online research usually costs much less than research conducted through mail, phone, or personal interviews. Using the Internet eliminates most of the postage, phone, interviewer, and data-handling costs associated with the other approaches. As a result, Internet surveys typically cost 15 to 20 percent less than mail surveys and 30 percent less than phone surveys. Moreover, sample size has little impact on costs. Once the questionnaire is set up, there's little difference in cost between 10 and 10 000 respondents on the Web.

Beyond their speed and cost advantages, web-based surveys also tend to be more interactive and engaging, easier to complete, and less intrusive than traditional phone or mail surveys. As a result they usually garner higher response rates. The Internet is an excellent medium for reaching the hard-to-reach—the often-elusive teen, single, affluent, and well-educated audiences. It's also good for reaching working mothers and other people who lead busy lives. Such people are well represented online, and they can respond in their own space and at their own convenience.

Whereas marketing researchers have rushed to use the Internet for quantitative surveys and data collection, they are now also adopting *qualitative* web-based research approaches—such as online focus groups or depth interviews. Many marketers have learned that the Internet can provide a fast, low-cost way to gain qualitative customer insights. For example, Anheuser-Busch uses the Web—both formally and informally—as a research "test-lab" for advertising ideas.

> Anheuser-Busch is increasingly using the Web to spread and fine-tune its advertising. The Web allows it to test drive edgy material that, in years past, would never have seen the light of day for fear of causing offence on TV. Witness the strange life of "Swear Jar," a commercial that portrays an effort to clean up office language by fining staffers 25 cents per profanity. The twist: the cash goes toward buying Bud Light—and the wholesome plan backfires spectacularly. Although the language was too raw for TV, A-B tested it out on the Internet. Someone sent it to YouTube, where it got more than 2.5 million hits, despite never appearing on television. "The digital space. . . can be an incubator for ideas," says an Anheuser-Busch media executive. Using the Web to gauge fervour for offbeat ads promises broader and quicker insight than the traditional way—peeking through a one-way window as a test group watches new TV commercials. "The Web gives instant credibility or thumbs-down," says the executive.[27]

Online focus groups
Gathering a small group of people online with a trained moderator to chat about a product, service, or organization and gain qualitative insights about consumer attitudes and behaviour.

The primary qualitative web-based research approach is **online focus groups**. Such focus groups offer many advantages over traditional focus groups. Participants can log in from anywhere—all they need is a laptop and a web connection. Thus, the Internet works well for bringing together people from different parts of the country or world, especially those in higher-income groups who can't spare the time to travel to a central site. Also, researchers can conduct and monitor online focus groups from just about anywhere, eliminating travel, lodging, and facility costs. Finally, although online focus groups require some advance scheduling, results are almost immediate.

Online focus groups can take any of several formats. Most occur in real time, in the form of online chat room discussions in which participants and a moderator sit around a virtual table exchanging comments. Alternatively, researchers might set up an online message board on which respondents interact over the course of several days or a few weeks. Participants log in daily and comment on focus group topics. The focus group moderator monitors the online interactions and redirects the discussion as required to keep the group on track. This ongoing message board format gives participants a chance to reflect on their responses, talk to others, and check out products in the real world as the group progresses. It also gives researchers the opportunity to make ongoing adjustments as the discussion unfolds. As a result, this online approach can produce much more data and deeper insights than single-session, in-person focus groups.

Although low in cost and easy to administer, online focus groups can lack the real-world dynamics of more personal approaches. The online world is devoid of the eye contact, body language, and direct personal interactions found in traditional focus group research. And the Internet format—running, typed commentary and online "emoticons" (punctuation marks that express emotion, such as :-) to signify happiness)—greatly restricts respondent expressiveness. The impersonal nature of the Internet can prevent people from interacting with each other in a normal way and getting excited about a concept.

To overcome these shortcomings, some researchers are now adding real-time audio and video to their online focus groups. For example, online research firm Channel M2

Some researchers have now added real-time audio and video to their online focus groups. For example, Channel M2 "puts the human touch back into online research" by assembling focus group participants in people-friendly "virtual interview rooms."

"puts the human touch back into online research" by assembling focus group participants in people-friendly "virtual interview rooms."[28]

Participants are recruited using traditional methods and then sent a webcam so that both their verbal and nonverbal reactions can be recorded. Participants are then provided instructions via email, including a link to the Channel M2 online interviewing room and a toll-free teleconference number to call. At the appointed time, when they click on the link and phone in, participants sign on and see the Channel M2 interview room, complete with live video of the other participants, text chat, screen or slide sharing, and a whiteboard. Once the focus group is underway, questions and answers occur in "real time" in a remarkably lively setting. Participants comment spontaneously—verbally, via text messaging, or both. Researchers can "sit in" on the focus group from anywhere, seeing and hearing every respondent. Or they can review a recorded version at a later date.

Although the use of online marketing research is growing rapidly, both quantitative and qualitative web-based research does have drawbacks. For one, restricted Internet access can make it difficult to get a broad cross-section of respondents. However, with Internet penetration growing, this is less of a problem. Another major problem is controlling who's in the online sample. Without seeing respondents, it's difficult to know who they really are. Finally, online surveys can be dry and lacking in dynamics compared with other, more-personal approaches.

To overcome such sample and context problems, many online research firms use opt-in communities and respondent panels. For example, online research firm Greenfield Online provides access to 12 million opt-in panel members in more than 40 countries. Advances in technology—such as the integration of animation, streaming audio and video, and virtual environments—also help to overcome online research dynamics limitations. In another recent development, many companies are developing their own custom social networks and using them to gain customer inputs and insights (see Real Marketing 5.1).

Perhaps the most explosive issue facing online researchers concerns consumer privacy. Some fear that unethical researchers will use the email addresses and confidential responses gathered through surveys to sell products after the research is completed. They are concerned about the use of technologies that collect personal information online without the respondents' consent. Failure to address such privacy issues could result in angry, less-cooperative consumers and increased government intervention. For example, as outlined in Chapter 3, Canada's *Personal Information Protection and Electronic Documents Act* and the *Electronic Commerce Protection Act* are designed to protect consumer privacy and personal security. Despite these concerns, most industry insiders predict healthy growth for online marketing research.[29]

Sampling Plan

Sample
A segment of the population selected for marketing research to represent the population as a whole.

Marketing researchers usually draw conclusions about large groups of consumers by studying a small **sample** of the total consumer population. A sample is a segment of the population selected for marketing research to represent the population as a whole. Ideally, the sample should be representative so that the researcher can make accurate estimates of the thoughts and behaviours of the larger population.

Designing the sample requires three decisions. First, *who* is to be surveyed (what *sampling unit*)? The answer to this question is not always obvious. For example, to study the decision-making process for a family automobile purchase, should the researcher interview the husband, wife, other family members, dealership salespeople, or all of these people? The researcher must determine what information is needed and who is most likely to have it.

Second, *how many* people should be surveyed (what *sample size*)? Large samples give more reliable results than small samples. However, larger samples usually cost more, and it is not necessary to sample the entire target market or even a large portion to get reliable results. If well chosen, samples of less than 1 percent of a population can often give good reliability.

Real Marketing **5.1**

Custom Social Networks: Del Monte Unleashes Dog-Lover Insights

When Del Monte Foods—maker of such well-known dog food brands as Kibbles 'n Bits, Gravy Train, and Milk-Bone—was considering a new breakfast treat for dogs, it sent out a note to an online community of dog owners called "I Love My Dog," asking them what they most wanted to feed their pets in the morning. The consensus answer was something with a bacon-and-egg taste. The result: Del Monte introduced Snausages Breakfast Bites, born out of insights that a dedicated segment of dog owners love to share holiday events and mealtimes with their pets. The Snausages Breakfast Bites are flavoured like bacon and eggs and contain an extra dose of vitamins and minerals, which the dog owners said was also important to them.

The "I Love My Dog" online community isn't some random chat room or yet another website for dog enthusiasts—it's a custom social network created by Del Monte working with research firm Market-Tools, Inc. Its 400 members were hand-picked to join the private social network, which the company uses to help create products, test marketing campaigns, and stir up buzz. "The idea is to develop a relationship . . . create ad hoc surveys and get feedback," says Del Monte senior customer insights manager Gala Amoroso. "If one of the brand managers has a new product idea or a different positioning, instead of just internal brainstorming within the company and before putting real research dollars behind it, we'll float it with the [online] community."

Such online networks are now rapidly spreading to companies ranging from Coca-Cola and P&G to Walt Disney's ABC Studios. They are often cheaper and more effective than phone surveys or traditional focus groups because companies can draw on the participants in a much broader and deeper way than they could in an offline setting.

Del Monte found that traditional market research techniques simply weren't providing enough depth of customer understanding. Traditional qualitative methods (such as ethnographies and focus groups) were either too time-consuming or too shallow. Surveys and other quantitative methods,

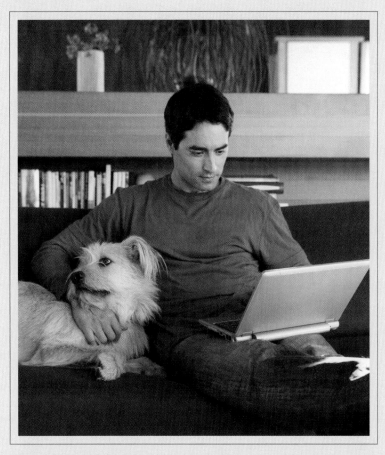

Del Monte's "I Love My Dog" custom social network lets the company continuously observe and interact with important customers to obtain authentic, in-depth insights.

although helpful in answering specific questions, did not allow for interactive exploration. In contrast, the custom dog-lover network lets Del Monte continuously observe and interact with important customers to obtain authentic, in-depth insights.

The "I Love My Dog" site and other custom networks bear a resemblance to other online social networking sites, where members create profile pages and post to discussion boards. Companies use them to administer polls, chat in real time with consumers, and even ask members to go to the store to try out specific products. The rapid back-and-forth between the company and the online community can help to substantially shorten the product-development cycle, a process that typically takes a year or more from the time a company comes up with a product idea until the item arrives in stores.

▶

For Snausages Breakfast Bites, that process took only six months. During that time, Del Monte contacted "I Love My Dog" members dozens of times, both as a group and individually. The company has also tapped network members for prelaunch insights into other products, including its Pup-Peroni treat that recently landed on store shelves. "It is not just a focus group that you see for three hours; you are developing a relationship with these pet parents," says Amoroso.

As with any social networking site, these private networks face the constant risk of member boredom and, ultimately, member dropout. There can be a fair amount of turnover on the private networks, and to keep members around, the companies that set them up have to constantly add games and other features, along with incentives such as coupons, giveaways, and sneak peeks at new products. Properly tended, however, networks such as "I Love My Dog" help remove some of the guesswork for marketers by letting brands know exactly to whom they are talking and giving them more control over the discussions.

Based on the success of the "I Love My Dog" network, Del Monte has now worked with MarketTools to create another custom network, this one consisting of 10 200 moms. It plans to tap this Mom's Insight Network for advice and collaboration on current brands as well as new-product launches. One key insight already gleaned from the moms network is that moms trust experts less than ever and are more interested in hearing from other moms in similar situations. This finding lends even greater importance to the Moms Insight Network, which not only seeks in-depth inputs from mothers but connects them with each other in the context of Del Monte brands.

Amoroso has high hopes for Del Monte's custom social networks. "The online community website gives us a wealth of information about our target consumers' pains and needs and provides a platform for us to explore and understand their attitudes and behaviours," she says. "It helps us anticipate and identify opportunities, and it enables us to collaborate with our target market to develop new solutions that truly meet their needs. It's different than receiving a report from a study. It's about taking the time to go to the community and listen."

Sources: Portions adapted from Emily Steel, "The New Focus Groups: Online Networks," *Wall Street Journal*, January 14, 2008, p. B6; with quotes and other information from Abbey Klaassen, "Del Monte to Take Its Cues from Moms," *Advertising Age*, July 2, 2007, accessed at http://adage.com/print?article_id=118908; and "Del Monte Foods Turns to Dog Owners to Unleash Innovation," MarketTools Case Study, May 2008, accessed at http://www.markettools.com/resources/files/CS_DelMonte.pdf.

Third, *how* should the people in the sample be chosen (what *sampling procedure*)? Table 5.4 describes different kinds of samples. Using *probability samples*, each population member has a known chance of being included in the sample, and researchers can calculate confidence limits for sampling error. But when probability sampling costs too much or takes too much time, marketing researchers often take *nonprobability samples*, even though their sampling error cannot be measured. These varied ways of drawing samples have different costs and time limitations as well as different accuracy and statistical properties. Which method is best depends on the needs of the research project.

Table 5.4 Types of Samples

Probability Sample	
Simple random sample	Every member of the population has a known and equal chance of selection.
Stratified random sample	The population is divided into mutually exclusive groups (such as age groups), and random samples are drawn from each group.
Cluster (area) sample	The population is divided into mutually exclusive groups (such as blocks), and the researcher draws a sample of the groups to interview.
Nonprobability Sample	
Convenience sample	The researcher selects the easiest population members from which to obtain information.
Judgment sample	The researcher uses his or her judgment to select population members who are good prospects for accurate information.
Quota sample	The researcher finds and interviews a prescribed number of people in each of several categories.

Research Instruments

In collecting primary data, marketing researchers have a choice of two main research instruments—the *questionnaire* and *mechanical devices*.

Questionnaires   The *questionnaire* is by far the most common survey instrument, whether administered in person, by phone, or online. Questionnaires are very flexible—there are many ways to ask questions. *Closed-end questions* include all the possible answers, and subjects make choices among them. Examples include multiple-choice questions and scale questions. *Open-end questions* allow respondents to answer in their own words. In a survey of airline users, for example, Air Canada might simply ask, "What is your opinion of Air Canada?" Or it might ask people to complete a sentence: "When I choose an airline, the most important consideration is. . ." These and other kinds of open-end questions often reveal more than closed-end questions because they do not limit respondents' answers.

Open-end questions are especially useful in exploratory research, when the researcher is trying to find out *what* people think but not measuring *how many* people think in a certain way. Closed-end questions, on the other hand, provide answers that are easier to interpret and tabulate.

Researchers should also use care in the *wording* and *ordering* of questions. They should use simple, direct, unbiased wording. Questions should be arranged in a logical order. The first question should create interest if possible, and difficult or personal questions should be asked last so that respondents do not become defensive. A carelessly prepared questionnaire usually contains many errors (see Table 5.5).

Mechanical Instruments   Although questionnaires are the most common research instrument, researchers also use *mechanical instruments* to monitor consumer behaviour. Nielsen Media Research attaches *people meters* to television sets in selected homes to record who watches which programs. Retailers use *checkout scanners* to record shoppers' purchases.

Other mechanical devices measure subjects' physical responses. For example, advertisers use eye cameras to study viewers' eye movements while watching ads—at what points their eyes focus first and how long they linger on any given ad component. IBM's BlueEyes technology interprets human facial reactions by tracking pupil, eyebrow, and mouth movements. BlueEyes offers a host of potential marketing uses, such as marketing machines that "know how you feel" and react accordingly. An elderly man squints at a bank's ATM screen and the font size doubles almost instantly. A woman at a shopping centre kiosk smiles at a travel ad, prompting the device to print out a travel discount coupon.[30]

Still other researchers are applying "neuromarketing," measuring brain activity to learn how consumers feel and respond. Marketing scientists using MRI scans have learned that "strong brands trigger activity in parts of the brain associated with self-identification, positive emotions, and rewards." According to one observer, it "turns out the Nike swoosh

Table 5.5 A "Questionable Questionnaire"

Suppose that a summer camp director has prepared the following questionnaire to use in interviewing the parents of prospective campers. How would you assess each question?

1. What is your income to the nearest hundred dollars? *People don't usually know their income to the nearest hundred dollars, nor do they want to reveal their income that closely. Moreover, a researcher should never open a questionnaire with such a personal question.*

2. Are you a strong or weak supporter of overnight summer camping for your children? *What do "strong" and "weak" mean?*

3. Do your children behave themselves well at a summer camp? Yes ( ) No ( ) *"Behave" is a relative term. Furthermore, are yes and no the best response options for this question? Besides, will people answer this honestly and objectively? Why ask the question in the first place?*

4. How many camps mailed or emailed information to you last year? This year? *Who can remember this?*

5. What are the most salient and determinant attributes in your evaluation of summer camps? *What are salient and determinant attributes? Don't use big words on me!*

6. Do you think it is right to deprive your child of the opportunity to grow into a mature person through the experience of summer camping? *A loaded question. Given the bias, how can any parent answer yes?*

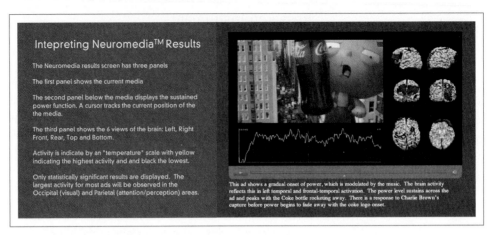

Neuromarketing: When researchers strapped electrode-loaded caps on the noggins of test subjects during the Super Bowl, they learned that brain activity soared for some ads but lagged for others.

is more than just a feel-good brand logo. It actually lights up your brain." Similarly, when researchers strapped electrode-loaded caps on the noggins of test subjects during last year's Super Bowl to measure advertising engagement, they learned that brain activity soared for some ads but lagged for others.[31] Here's an example of neuromarketing at work:

> Thirty-four bathroom-cleanser users recently went to a research lab to watch "Prison Visitor," the much-awarded TV spot for Unilever's Vim line of home cleaners, positioned as a product that "deals with the toughest dirt." The ad shows a young girl visiting her distraught mother, who appears to be behind a prison glass but is revealed to be scrubbing a grimy shower. Researchers wanted a "clean read" on the ad, so they tested consumers in places where the ad never aired and where the product wasn't yet available. Participants reacted strongly to a "hands on glass" sequence, particularly during a dramatic "I love you, Momma!" "I love you too, baby!" exchange. However, the scenes showing the product demonstration and brand message evoked a much weaker response. In all, the ad stirred up very strong, mostly negative emotions. Follow-up interviews showed that consumers actually hated the ad. How did researchers measure viewers' response to such emotionally charged advertising? Easy. Each participant in the study was asked how they felt about the ad. Oh, and even more telling, there were six electrodes attached to each person's head. Welcome to the world of neuromarketing, which peers into consumers' minds by measuring brain activity to discover how consumers respond to brands and marketing.[32]

Although neuromarketing techniques can measure consumer involvement and emotional responses minute by minute, such brain responses can be difficult to interpret. Thus, neuromarketing is usually used in combination with other research approaches to gain a more complete picture of what goes on inside consumers' heads.[33]

Implementing the Research Plan

The researcher next puts the marketing research plan into action. This involves collecting, processing, and analyzing the information. Data collection can be carried out by the company's marketing research staff or by outside firms. The data collection phase of the marketing research process is generally the most expensive and the most subject to error. Researchers should watch closely to make sure that the plan is implemented correctly. They must guard against problems with contacting respondents, with respondents who refuse to cooperate or who give biased answers, and with interviewers who make mistakes or take shortcuts.

Researchers must also process and analyze the collected data to isolate important information and findings. They need to check data for accuracy and completeness and code it for analysis. The researchers then tabulate the results and compute statistical measures.

Interpreting and Reporting the Findings

The market researcher must now interpret the findings, draw conclusions, and report them to management. The researcher should not try to overwhelm managers with numbers and fancy statistical techniques. Rather, the researcher should present important findings and insights that are useful in the major decisions faced by management.

However, interpretation should not be left only to the researchers. They are often experts in research design and statistics, but the marketing manager knows more about the problem and the decisions that must be made. The best research means little if the manager blindly accepts faulty interpretations from the researcher. Similarly, managers may be biased—they might tend to accept research results that show what they expected and to reject those that they did not expect or hope for. In many cases, findings can be interpreted in different ways, and discussions between researchers and managers will help point to the best interpretations. Thus, managers and researchers must work together closely when interpreting research results, and both must share responsibility for the research process and resulting decisions.

4 ANALYZING AND USING MARKETING INFORMATION

Information gathered in internal databases and through marketing intelligence and marketing research usually requires additional analysis. And managers may need help applying the information to gain customer and market insights that will improve their marketing decisions. This help may include advanced statistical analysis to learn more about the relationships within a set of data. Information analysis might also involve the application of analytical models that will help marketers make better decisions.

Once the information has been processed and analyzed, it must be made available to the right decision makers at the right time. In the following sections, we look deeper into analyzing and using marketing information.

Customer Relationship Management (CRM)

The question of how best to analyze and use individual customer data presents special problems. Most companies are awash in information about their customers. In fact, smart companies capture information at every possible customer *touchpoint*. These touchpoints include customer purchases, sales force contacts, service and support calls, website visits, satisfaction surveys, credit and payment interactions, market research studies—every contact between the customer and the company.

The trouble is that this information is usually scattered widely across the organization. It is buried deep in the separate databases and records of different company departments. To overcome such problems, many companies are now turning to **customer relationship management (CRM)** to manage detailed information about individual customers and carefully manage customer touchpoints to maximize customer loyalty.

Customer relationship management (CRM)
Managing detailed information about individual customers and carefully managing customer "touchpoints" to maximize customer loyalty.

CRM first burst onto the scene in the early 2000s. Many companies rushed in, implementing overly ambitious CRM programs that produced disappointing results and many failures. More recently, however, companies are moving ahead more cautiously and implementing CRM, spending US$7.3 billion on CRM systems from companies such as Oracle, Microsoft, Salesforce.com, and SAS.[34]

CRM consists of sophisticated software and analytical tools that integrate customer information from all sources, analyze it in depth, and apply the results to build stronger customer relationships. CRM integrates everything that a company's sales, service, and marketing teams know about individual customers to provide a 360-degree view of the customer relationship.

CRM analysts develop *data warehouses* and use sophisticated *data mining* techniques to unearth the riches hidden in customer data. A data warehouse is a companywide electronic database of finely detailed customer information that needs to be sifted through for gems. The purpose of a data warehouse is not just to gather information, but to pull it together into a central, accessible location. Then, once the data warehouse brings the data together, the

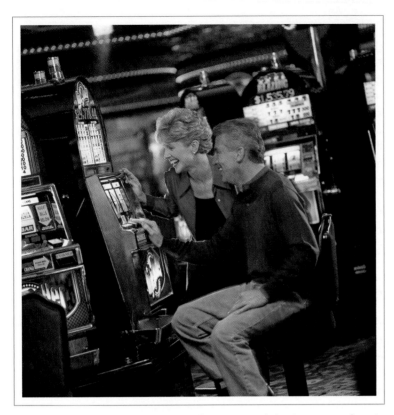

Customer relationship management: Harrah's CRM system helps the company focus its branding, marketing, and service development strategies on the needs of its most important customers. "We're trying to figure out which products sell, and we're trying to increase our customer loyalty."

company uses high-powered data mining techniques to sift through the mounds of data and dig out interesting findings about customers.

These findings often lead to marketing opportunities. For example, Bell Canada, the largest provider of telecommunications services in Canada, was recently recognized for excellence in CRM marketing optimization. Fielding tens of thousands of customer calls each year, the company's CRM system automatically analyzes historical, personal and contextual data to provide customized offers based on previous interactions, which helps the company improve the customer experience, increase revenue, and reduce customer turnover. It identifies when customers are most receptive to its marketing initiatives and enables the company to up-sell its services.[35]

By using CRM to understand customers better, companies can provide higher levels of customer service and develop deeper customer relationships. They can use CRM to pinpoint high-value customers, target them more effectively, cross-sell the company's products, and create offers tailored to specific customer requirements. For example, Harrah's Entertainment, the world's largest casino operator, uses CRM to manage day-to-day relationships with important customers at its Harrah's, Caesars, Horseshoe, Bally's, Flamingo, and Showboat casinos around the world. During the past decade, Harrah's Total Rewards Program has become the model for good CRM and customer-loyalty management.

More than 80 percent of Harrah's customers worldwide—40 million in all—use a Harrah's Total Rewards card. Information from every swipe of every card at each of Harrah's 40 casinos zips off to a central computer in Memphis, Tennessee, creating a vast customer database. Harrah's carefully mines this motherlode of information to gain insights into customer characteristics and behaviour. It then uses these insights to manage day-to-day customer relationships. In fact, Harrah's now processes customer information in real time, from the moment customers swipe their rewards cards, creating the ideal link between data and the customer experience.

Based on up-to-the-minute customer information, casino personnel know which customers should be rewarded with free show tickets, dinner vouchers, or room upgrades. Says Harrah's chief information officer, "A person might walk up to you while you're playing and offer you $5 to play more slots, or a free meal, or maybe just wish you a happy birthday." Compared with nonmembers, Total Rewards customers visit the company's casinos more frequently, stay longer, and spend a lot more of their dollars in Harrah's rather than in rival casinos. Through smart CRM, Harrah's has hit the customer-loyalty jackpot. In just the past five years the entertainment giant's sales have nearly tripled while profits have more than doubled.[36]

CRM benefits don't come without cost or risk, either in collecting the original customer data or in maintaining and mining it. The most common CRM mistake is to view CRM only as a technology and software solution. But technology alone cannot build profitable customer relationships. "CRM is not a technology solution—you can't achieve . . . improved customer relationships by simply slapping in some software," says a CRM expert. Instead, CRM is just one part of an effective overall *customer relationship management strategy*. "Focus on the *R*," advises the expert. "Remember, a relationship is what CRM is all about."[37]

When it works, the benefits of CRM can far outweigh the costs and risks. Based on a study by SAP, customers using its mySAP CRM software reported an average 10 percent increase in customer retention and a 30 percent increase in sales leads. Overall, 90 percent of the companies surveyed increased in value from use of the software and reported an attractive return on investment. The study's conclusion: "CRM pays off."[38]

Distributing and Using Marketing Information

Marketing information has no value until it is used to gain customer insights and make better marketing decisions. Thus, the marketing information system must make the information readily available to the managers and others who make marketing decisions or deal with customers. In some cases, this means providing managers with regular performance reports, intelligence updates, and reports on the results of research studies.

But marketing managers may also need nonroutine information for special situations and on-the-spot decisions. For example, a sales manager having trouble with a large customer may want a summary of the account's sales and profitability over the past year. Or a retail store manager who has run out of a best-selling product may want to know the current inventory levels in the chain's other stores. Increasingly, therefore, information distribution involves entering information into databases and making it available in a timely, user-friendly way.

Many firms use a company *intranet* to facilitate this process. The intranet provides ready access to research information, reports, shared work documents, contact information for employees and other stakeholders, and more. For example, iGo, a catalogue and web retailer, integrates incoming customer service calls with up-to-date database information about customers' web purchases and email inquiries. By accessing this information on the intranet while speaking with the customer, iGo's service representatives can get a well-rounded picture of each customer's purchasing history and previous contacts with the company.

In addition, companies are increasingly allowing key customers and value-network members to access account, product, and other data on demand through *extranets*. Suppliers, customers, resellers, and select other network members may access a company's extranet to update their accounts, arrange purchases, and check orders against inventories to improve customer service. For example, Walmart's Retail Link extranet system provides suppliers with a two-year history of every product's daily sales in every Walmart store worldwide, letting them track when and where their products are selling and current inventory levels. And Target's Partners Online extranet lets its supplier/partners review current sales, inventory, delivery, and forecasting data. Such information sharing helps Target, its suppliers, and its customers by elevating the performance of the supply chain.[39]

Thanks to modern technology, today's marketing managers can gain direct access to the information system at any time and from virtually any location. They can tap into the system while working at a home office, from a hotel room, or from the local Starbucks through a wireless network—anyplace where they can turn on a laptop and link up. Such systems allow managers to get the information they need directly and quickly and to tailor it to their own needs. From just about anywhere, they can obtain information from company or outside databases, analyze it using statistical software, prepare reports and presentations, and communicate directly with others in the network.

5 OTHER MARKETING INFORMATION CONSIDERATIONS

This section discusses marketing information in two special contexts: marketing research in small businesses and not-for-profit organizations and international marketing research. Finally, we look at public policy and ethics issues in marketing research.

Before opening Bibbentuckers dry cleaner, owner Robert Byerley conducted research to gain insights into what customers wanted. First on the list was quality.

Marketing Research in Small Businesses and Not-for-profit Organizations

Just like larger firms, small organizations need market information and the customer and market insights that it can provide. Start-up businesses need information about their potential customers, industries, competitors, unfilled needs, and reactions to new market offers. Existing small businesses must track changes in customer needs and wants, reactions to new products, and changes in the competitive environment.

Managers of small businesses and not-for-profit organizations often think that marketing research can be done only by experts in large companies with big research budgets. True, large-scale research studies are beyond the budgets of most small businesses. However, many of the marketing research techniques discussed in this chapter can also be used by smaller organizations in a less formal manner and at little or no expense. Consider how one small-business owner conducted market research on a shoestring before even opening his doors:

> After a string of bad experiences with his local dry cleaner, Robert Byerley decided to open his own dry-cleaning business. But before jumping in, he conducted plenty of market research. He needed a key customer insight: How would he make his cleaners stand out? To start, Byerley spent an entire week in the library and online, researching the dry-cleaning industry. To get input from potential customers, using a marketing firm, Byerley held focus groups on the store's name, look, and brochure. He also took clothes to the 15 best competing cleaners in town and had focus group members critique their work. Based on his research, he made a list of features for his new business. First on his list: quality. His business would stand behind everything it did. Not on the list: cheap prices. Creating the perfect dry-cleaning establishment simply didn't fit with a discount operation.
>
> With his research complete, Byerley opened Bibbentuckers, a high-end dry cleaner positioned on high-quality service and convenience. It featured a bank-like drive-through area with curbside delivery. A computerized bar code system read customer cleaning preferences and tracked clothes all the way through the cleaning process. Byerley added other differentiators, such as decorative awnings, refreshments, and TV screens. "I wanted a place . . . that paired five-star service and quality with an establishment that didn't look like a dry cleaner," he says. The market research yielded results. Today, Bibbentuckers is a thriving three-store operation.[40]

"Too [few] small-business owners have a . . . marketing mind-set," says a small-business consultant. "You have to think like Procter & Gamble. What would they do before launching a new product? They would find out who their customer is and who their competition is."[41]

Managers of small businesses and not-for-profit organizations can obtain good marketing insights simply by *observing* things around them and talking with their customers. They can conduct informal *surveys* using small convenience samples. Small organizations can also obtain most of the secondary data available to large businesses. And many associations, local media, chambers of commerce, and government agencies provide special help to small organizations. For example, the Conference Board of Canada and the Canadian Council for Small Business and Entrepreneurship offer dozens of free publications that give advice on topics ranging from preparing a business plan to ordering business signs. Other excellent web resources for small businesses include Statistics Canada (www.statcan.gc.ca) and Industry Canada (www.ic.gc.ca). Finally, small businesses can collect a considerable amount of information at very little cost on the Internet. They can scour competitor and customer websites and use Internet search engines to research specific companies and issues.

In summary, secondary data collection, observation, surveys, and experiments can all be used effectively by small organizations with small budgets. However, although these informal research methods are less complex and less costly, they still must be conducted with care. Managers must think carefully about the objectives of the research, formulate questions in advance, recognize the biases introduced by smaller samples and less skilled researchers, and conduct the research systematically.[42]

International Marketing Research

International marketing research has grown tremendously over the past decade. In 1995, the top 25 global marketing research organizations had total combined revenues of US$5.7 billion, with 45 percent of these revenues coming from outside companies' home countries. By 2006, total revenues for these organizations had grown to US$15.5 billion, and the out-of-home-country share had grown to more than 55 percent.[43]

International marketing researchers follow the same steps as domestic researchers, from defining the research problem and developing a research plan to interpreting and reporting the results. However, these researchers often face more and different problems. Whereas domestic researchers deal with fairly homogenous markets within a single country, international researchers deal with diverse markets in many different countries. These markets often vary greatly in their levels of economic development, cultures and customs, and buying patterns.

In many foreign markets, the international researcher may have a difficult time finding good secondary data. Whereas North American marketing researchers can obtain reliable secondary data from dozens of domestic research services, many countries have almost no

Some of the largest research services firms have large international organizations. Nielsen has offices in more than 100 countries, including Germany and Japan.

research services at all. Some of the largest international research services, however, do operate in many countries. For example, The Nielsen Company, the world's largest marketing research company, has offices in more than 100 countries, from Schaumburg, Illinois, to Hong Kong to Nicosia, Cyprus.[44] However, most research firms operate in only a relative handful of countries. Thus, even when secondary information is available, it usually must be obtained from many different sources on a country-by-country basis, making the information difficult to combine or compare.

Because of the scarcity of good secondary data, international researchers often must collect their own primary data. For example, they may find it difficult simply to develop good samples. North American researchers can use current telephone directories, email lists, census tract data, and any of several sources of socioeconomic data to construct samples. However, such information is largely lacking in many countries.

Once the sample is drawn, the North American researcher can usually reach most respondents easily by telephone, by mail, on the Internet, or in person. Reaching respondents is often not so easy in other parts of the world. Researchers in Mexico cannot rely on telephone, Internet, and mail data collection—most data collection is done door to door and concentrated in three or four of the largest cities. In some countries, few people have phones or personal computers. For example, whereas there are 605 main telephone lines, 680 cellphone subscribers, and 762 PCs per thousand people in Canada, there are only 189 phone lines, 460 cellphone subscribers, and 136 PCs per thousand in Mexico. In Kenya, the numbers drop to 8 phone lines, 135 cellphone subscribers, and 9 PCs per thousand people.

In some countries, the postal system is notoriously unreliable. In Brazil, for instance, an estimated 30 percent of the mail is never delivered. In many developing countries, poor roads and transportation systems make certain areas hard to reach, making personal interviews difficult and expensive.[45]

Cultural differences from country to country cause additional problems for international researchers. Language is the most obvious obstacle. For example, questionnaires must be prepared in one language and then translated into the languages of each country researched. Responses must then be translated back into the original language for analysis and interpretation. This adds to research costs and increases the risks of error.

Translating a questionnaire from one language to another is anything but easy. Many idioms, phrases, and statements mean different things in different cultures. For example, a Danish executive noted, "Check this out by having a different translator put back into English what you've translated from English. You'll get the shock of your life. I remember [an example in which] 'out of sight, out of mind' had become 'invisible things are insane.'"[46]

Consumers in different countries also vary in their attitudes toward marketing research. People in one country may be very willing to respond; in other countries, nonresponse can be a major problem. Customs in some countries may prohibit people from talking with strangers. In certain cultures, research questions are often considered too personal. For example, in many Latin American countries people may feel embarrassed to talk with researchers about their choices of shampoo, deodorant, or other personal care products. Similarly, in most Muslim countries mixed-gender focus groups are taboo, as is videotaping female-only focus groups. Even when respondents are *willing* to respond, they may not be *able* to because of high functional illiteracy rates.

Despite these problems, as global marketing grows, global companies have little choice but to conduct such international marketing research. Although the costs and problems associated with international research may be high, the costs of not doing it—in terms of missed opportunities and mistakes—might be even higher. Once recognized, many of the problems associated with international marketing research can be overcome or avoided.

Public Policy and Ethics in Marketing Research

Most marketing research benefits both the sponsoring company and its consumers. Through marketing research, companies learn more about consumers' needs, resulting in more satisfying products and services and stronger customer relationships. However, the misuse of marketing research can also harm or annoy consumers. Two major public policy and ethics issues in marketing research are intrusions on consumer privacy and the misuse of research findings.

Intrusions on Consumer Privacy

Many consumers have positive feelings about marketing research and believe that it serves a useful purpose. Some actually enjoy being interviewed and giving their opinions. However, others strongly resent or even mistrust marketing research. They worry that marketers are building huge databases full of personal information about customers. Or they fear that researchers might use sophisticated techniques to probe our deepest feelings, peek over our shoulders as we shop, or eavesdrop on our conversations and then use this knowledge to manipulate our buying.

There are no easy answers when it comes to marketing research and privacy. For example, is it a good or bad thing that marketers track and analyze consumers' web clicks and target ads to individuals based on their browsing behaviour? (See Real Marketing 5.2.) Should we applaud or resent the fact that ConAgra Foods, the giant food company known for its Butterball turkeys and Healthy Choice meals, listens in on consumer web discussions to learn all it can about diet trends and reactions to its brands? On the one hand, most online chatter is public information, and listening in helps ConAgra improve its products and bring more value to customers. On the other hand, although it tracks only public forums, the company does not inform consumers or obtain participants' formal consent. Many consumers would find it disconcerting to learn that ConAgra and other companies are tuning in to their online conversations.

Interestingly, however, many consumers don't seem to mind. Occasionally, the monitoring of discussion groups itself becomes a topic of online conversation. In one online car forum, a discussion of BuzzMetrics (a Nielsen company that specializes in tracking consumer-generated media, including online exchanges) and its research for General Motors produced no objections—just disbelief that the carmaker could listen to their conversations and still produce such unappealing products. Consumers often moan that companies do not listen to them. Perhaps the monitoring of discussion groups can provide an answer to that problem.[47]

Consumers may also have been taken in by previous "research surveys" that actually turned out to be attempts to sell them something. Still other consumers confuse legitimate marketing research studies with promotional efforts and say "no" before the interviewer can even begin. Most, however, simply resent the intrusion. They dislike mail, telephone, or web surveys that are too long or too personal or that interrupt them at inconvenient times.

Increasing consumer resentment has become a major problem for the marketing research industry, leading to lower survey response rates in recent years. Just as companies face the challenge of unearthing valuable but potentially sensitive consumer data while also maintaining consumer trust, consumers wrestle with the tradeoffs between personalization and privacy. Although many consumers willingly exchange personal information for free services, easy credit, discounts, upgrades, points, and all sorts of rewards, they also worry about the growth in online identity theft. One study found that 62 percent of consumers express concern over personal privacy when buying online, an increase of 47 percent over a year earlier. So it's no surprise that they are now less than willing to reveal personal information on websites.[48]

Banking is one industry where privacy has long been a concern, whether it is with regard to research or everyday transactions. RBC has been a leader in the area of privacy protection, believing that protecting confidentiality of personal and financial information is fundamental to the way it does business. RBC's commitment has not changed with the arrival of new technologies, such as the Internet and online services. Instead, it was extended to ensure that all clients' experiences with the bank were safe and secure. RBC was a strong supporter of industry privacy standards and related government regulation, playing an active role in the development of the Canadian Bankers Association's (CBA) Privacy Model Code and the Canadian Standards Association's (CSA) Model Code for the Protection of

Real Marketing **5.2**

Tracking Consumers on the Web: Smart Targeting or a Little Creepy?

On the Internet today, everybody knows who you are. In fact, legions of Internet companies also know your gender, your age, the neighbourhood you live in, that you like pickup trucks, and that you spent, say, three hours and 43 seconds on a website for pet lovers on a rainy day in January. All that data streams through myriad computer networks where it's sorted, catalogued, analyzed, and then used to deliver ads aimed squarely at you, potentially anywhere you travel on the Web. It's called *behavioural targeting*—tracking consumers' online browsing behaviour and using it to target ads to them.

Targeting ads on the Web is nothing new. Sites such as Google and Yahoo! routinely do "contextual targeting"—placing ads related to keyword searches alongside the search results. Most of Google's more than US$10 billion in revenues come from search-related advertising. But consider this revealing fact: Internet users spend a mere 5 percent of their time actually searching. The rest of the time, they're trolling the vast expanse of Internet space. To fill that space more effectively, online advertisers are now deploying a new breed of supersmart, supertargeted display ads geared to individual web-browsing behaviour.

What you do when you aren't searching—the other 95 percent of the time you spend online—is pure gold to advertisers. And companies such as Yahoo!, Microsoft's MSN, and AOL are busy mining that gold, helping advertisers to target ads based on just about everything you do on the Internet. Yahoo!, the Web's most-visited destination, has an estimated 131 million monthly unique visitors to its sites. By dropping "cookies" onto every web browser that calls up one of its sites, Yahoo! has amassed a staggering amount of data about its users.

Yahoo!'s head of research and data, Usama Fayyad, manages the 12 terabytes of user information that flow into Yahoo!'s servers every day. Fittingly, Fayyad is a former rocket

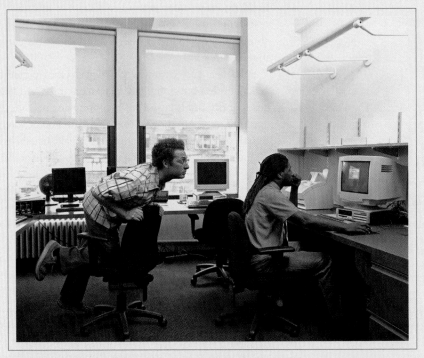

Behavioural targeting: Wherever you go on the Internet, marketers are looking over your shoulder, then targeting you with ads based on your web browsing behaviour. Is it smart marketing or just "a little bit creepy"?

scientist whose resumé includes a seven-year stint at NASA's Jet Propulsion Lab. He's an intense numbers guy who went on to found two data mining companies, one of which he sold to Yahoo!. Fayyad and his group crunch all that online user data, blend it with information about what people do on Yahoo!'s search engine, and feed it into models that predict consumer behaviour. This has led Fayyad to an important conclusion: What you do on the Web reveals far more about you than what you type into a search box.

Armed with this mass of data, Yahoo! often sells ad space based not on a site's content but on an individual consumer's online behaviour. Say you spent time at Yahoo! Autos sizing up cars based on fuel efficiency, then clicked over to Yahoo!'s Green Center to read about alternative fuels, then looked at cars on eBay (which has a partnership with Yahoo!). Fayyad can probably predict your next move. In fact, he says he can tell with 75 percent certainty which of the 300 000 monthly visitors to Yahoo! Autos will actually purchase a car within the next three months. And the next time you visit Yahoo! Sports or Finance, you'll likely see ads for hybrid cars.

Also moving quickly into online display advertising are a special breed of behavioural targeting advertising agencies, such as AudienceScience (www.audiencescience.com). To get an even broader view of what consumers are thinking and doing online, such agencies track consumer behaviour across multiple websites. These companies "are, in effect, taking the trail of crumbs people leave behind as they move around the Internet, and then analyzing them to anticipate people's next steps," says an analyst. This lets them merge audience data from one group of sites with ad placements on another. So if you surf home lawn and garden sites, don't be surprised to see ads for Scotts lawn products the next time you visit Weather.com. Or if you seek car-buying advice at sites such as Edmunds.com or nadaguides.com, expect to see some ads for the very types of cars you researched the next time you visit your favourite TSN site to catch up on the latest sports scores.

But what about consumer privacy? Yup. As you've no doubt already considered, that's the downside and the biggest danger to the rapidly expanding world of behavioural targeting. As the practice becomes more common, it faces growing consumer backlash. One observer calls it "the dark art of behavioural ad targeting"—eavesdropping on consumers without their knowledge or consent. "When you start to get into the details, it's scarier than you might suspect," says the director of a consumer privacy rights group. "We're recording preferences, hopes, worries, and fears." A coalition of privacy groups has already asked the U.S. Federal Trade Commission to consider a "Do Not Track" list (akin to telephone Do-Not-Call Lists) to let consumers opt out of behavioural ad targeting.

Some companies are addressing such privacy issues on their own. For example, AOL recently launched a campaign to educate consumers about online behavioural targeting and promises improved technology for opting out of personalized ads. "We want to make the opt-out process as simple and transparent as possible," says AOL's chief privacy officer. Google has pledged to make the data it collects anonymous after 18 months and to expire cookie files after two years.

Ask.com has gone even further, pledging to make web searches and cookies anonymous after 18 months and to give users the option of deleting their search histories using a tool called AskEraser.

Despite privacy concerns, proponents claim that behavioural targeting benefits consumers more than abuses them. "What we have here is person-centric marketing," says the CEO of one behavioural targeting ad agency. "That's been the holy grail of brand advertisers for a long, long time." Behavioural ad targeting takes information from users' web browsing behaviour and feeds back ads that are more relevant to their needs and interests.

Although the practice may seem sinister to some consumers, advertisers like what they see so far. According to one survey, more than half of marketers already use behavioural targeting and another third plan to start soon. Companies spent an estimated US$1.65 billion on behavioural targeting in 2009. According to one research firm, dollars spent on behavioural targeting yield a 37 percent return on investment.

Still, it won't be easy to maintain consumer trust while at the same time walking the fine line between personalization and privacy. And as more and more companies enter the behavioural targeting ad space, the chances of the tactic getting a bad name grow. "We have something new and powerful," says one CEO, "and there are likely to be people who abuse it." Abusive or beneficial, it'll be a hard sell to consumers. As one analyst observes, following consumers online and stalking them with ads just "feels a little creepy."

Sources: Based on information found in Paul Sloan, "The Quest for the Perfect Online Ad," *Business 2.0*, March 2007, pp. 88–92; Thomas Claburn, "Call Off the Wolves," *InformationWeek*, November 12, 2007; Brian Morissey, "Limits of Search Lead Some to Web Behavior," *Adweek*, March 27, 2006, p. 11; Sam Matthews, "Behavioral Targeting Still Not Appreciated," *New Age Media*, December 14, 2006, p. 2; Brian Morissey, "Aim High: Ad Targeting Moves to the Next Level," *Adweek*, January 14, 2008, pp. 49–50; Louise Story, "To Aim Ads, Web Is Keeping a Closer Eye on You," *New York Times*, March 10, 2008; and Jonathan Lemonnier, "Contextual Targeting Boost Loyal Following," *Advertising Age*, April 14, 2008, p. 7.

Personal Information. These models were the foundation upon which RBC tailored its own to meet the needs and expectations of its clients.[49]

Most major companies—including IBM, Citigroup, American Express, Eli Lilly, and Microsoft—have now appointed a "chief privacy officer (CPO)," whose job is to safeguard the privacy of consumers who do business with the company. IBM's CPO claims that her job requires "multidisciplinary thinking and attitude." She needs to get all company departments, from technology, legal, and accounting to marketing and communications, working together to safeguard customer privacy.[50]

American Express, which deals with a considerable volume of consumer information, has long taken privacy issues seriously. The company developed a set of formal privacy principles in 1991, and in 1998 it became one of the first companies to post privacy policies on its website. Its Internet privacy statement tells customers in clear terms what

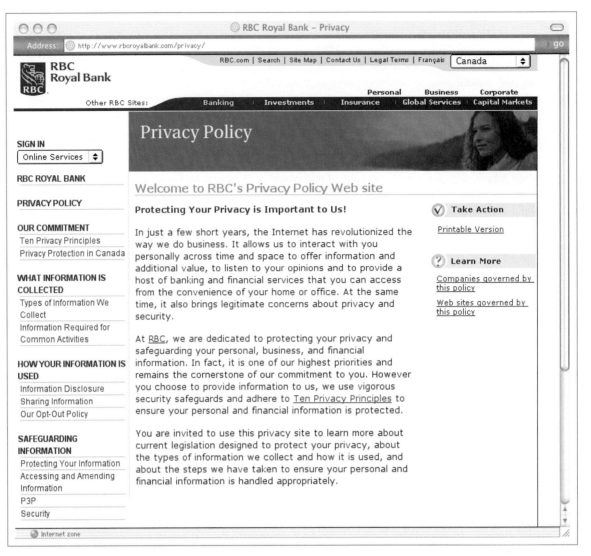

RBC has a long history of respecting privacy and protecting financial information, which it sees as fundamental to the way it does business, whether in person or online. It played an active role in developing Canadian privacy standards. Its website lists its Ten Privacy Principles, which were designed to meet the needs and expectations of its clients.

information American Express collects and how it uses it, how it safeguards the information, and how it uses the information to market to its customers (with instructions on how to opt out).[51]

In the end, if researchers provide value in exchange for information, customers will gladly provide it. For example, Amazon.ca's customers do not mind if the firm builds a database of products they buy to provide future product recommendations. This saves time and provides value. Similarly, BizRate users gladly complete surveys rating online seller sites because they can view the overall ratings of others when making purchase decisions. The best approach is for researchers to ask only for the information they need, to use it responsibly to provide customer value, and to avoid sharing information without the customer's permission.

Misuse of Research Findings

Research studies can be powerful persuasion tools; companies often use study results as claims in their advertising and promotion. Today, however, many research studies appear to be little more than vehicles for pitching the sponsor's products. In fact, in some cases, the research surveys appear to have been designed just to produce the intended effect. Few advertisers openly rig their research designs or blatantly misrepresent the findings; most abuses tend to be subtle "stretches."

For example, the choice of wording in a survey can greatly affect the conclusions reached. In one survey, Black Flag, a pest-control products company, asked: "A roach disk . . . poisons a roach slowly. The dying roach returns to the nest and after it dies is eaten by other roaches. In turn these roaches become poisoned and die. How effective do you think this type of product would be in killing roaches?" Not surprisingly, 79 percent said effective.[52]

Recognizing that surveys can be abused, several associations—including the Marketing Research and Intelligence Association, the Canadian Marketing Association, and the American Marketing Association—have developed codes of research ethics and standards of conduct. In the end, however, unethical or inappropriate actions cannot simply be regulated away. Each company must accept responsibility for policing the conduct and reporting of its own marketing research to protect consumers' best interests and its own.

REVIEWING OBJECTIVES AND KEY TERMS

 | Audio Chapter Summary

To create value for customers and to build meaningful relationships with them, marketers must first gain fresh, deep insights into what customers need and want. Such insights come from good marketing information. As a result of the recent explosion of marketing technology, companies can now obtain great quantities of information, sometimes even too much. The challenge is to transform today's vast volume of consumer information into actionable customer and market insights. A company's marketing research and information system must do more than simply generate lots of information. The real value of marketing research and marketing information lies in how it is used—in the customer insights that it provides.

OBJECTIVE 1 Explain the importance of information in gaining insights about the marketplace and customers.

The marketing process starts with a complete understanding of the marketplace and consumer needs and wants. Thus, the company needs sound information to produce superior value and satisfaction for customers. The company also requires information on competitors, resellers, and other actors and forces in the marketplace. Increasingly, marketers are viewing information not only as an input for making better decisions, but also as an important strategic asset and marketing tool.

OBJECTIVE 2 Define the marketing information system and discuss its parts.

The *marketing information system (MIS)* consists of people and procedures for assessing information needs, developing the needed information, and helping decision makers to use the information to generate and validate actionable customer and market insights. A well-designed information system begins and ends with users.

The MIS first *assesses information needs*. The marketing information system primarily serves the company's marketing and other managers, but it may also provide information to external partners. Then, the MIS *develops information* from internal databases, marketing intelligence activities, and marketing research. *Internal databases* provide information on the company's own operations and departments. Such data can be obtained quickly and cheaply but often needs to be adapted for marketing decisions. *Marketing intelligence* activities supply everyday information about developments in the external marketing environment. *Market research* consists of collecting information relevant to a specific marketing problem faced by the company. Lastly, the MIS helps users analyze and use the information to develop customer insights, make marketing decisions, and manage customer relationships.

OBJECTIVE 3 Outline the steps in the marketing research process.

The first step in the marketing research process involves *defining the problem and setting the research objectives,* which may be exploratory, descriptive, or causal research. The second step consists of *developing a research plan* for collecting data from primary and secondary sources. The third step calls for *implementing the marketing research plan* by gathering, processing, and analyzing the information. The fourth step consists of *interpreting and reporting the findings*. Additional information analysis helps marketing managers apply the information and provides them with sophisticated statistical procedures and models from which to develop more rigorous findings.

Both *internal* and *external* secondary data sources often provide information more quickly and at a lower cost than primary data sources, and they can sometimes yield information that a company cannot collect by itself. However, needed information might not exist in secondary sources. Researchers must also evaluate secondary information to ensure that it is *relevant, accurate, current*, and *impartial*. Primary research must also be evaluated for these features. Each primary data collection method—*observational, survey,* and *experimental*—has its own advantages and disadvantages. Similarly, each of the various research contact methods—mail, telephone, personal interview, and online—also has its own advantages and drawbacks.

OBJECTIVE 4   Explain how companies analyze and use marketing information.

Information gathered in internal databases and through marketing intelligence and marketing research usually requires more analysis. This may include advanced statistical analysis or the application of analytical models that will help marketers make better decisions. To analyze individual customer data, many companies have now acquired or developed special software and analysis techniques—called *customer relationship management (CRM)*—that integrate, analyze, and apply the mountains of individual customer data contained in their databases.

Marketing information has no value until it is used to make better marketing decisions. Thus, the marketing information system must make the information available to the managers and others who make marketing decisions or deal with customers. In some cases, this means providing regular reports and updates; in other cases it means making nonroutine information available for special situations and on-the-spot decisions. Many firms use company intranets and extranets to facilitate this process. Thanks to modern technology, today's marketing managers can gain direct access to the information system at any time from virtually any location.

OBJECTIVE 5   Discuss the special issues some marketing researchers face, including public policy and ethics issues.

Some marketers face special marketing research situations, such as those conducting research in small business, not-for-profit, or international situations. Marketing research can be conducted effectively by small businesses and not-for-profit organizations with limited budgets. International marketing researchers follow the same steps as domestic researchers but often face more and different problems. All organizations need to act responsibly regarding major public policy and ethical issues surrounding marketing research, including issues of intrusions on consumer privacy and misuse of research findings.

KEY TERMS

  | Glossary Flashcards

DISCUSSING THE CONCEPTS

1. Discuss the real value of marketing research and marketing information and how that value is attained.

2. Which information is more valuable to marketing managers: information from internal databases, from marketing intelligence, or from marketing research? How do these information sources differ?

3. Explain the differences between primary and secondary data. When is each appropriate and how are they collected?

4. What are the advantages of web-based survey research over traditional survey research?

5. How does customer relationship management (CRM) help companies develop customer insights and deliver superior customer value?

6. What are the similarities and differences when conducting research in another country versus the domestic market?

APPLYING THE CONCEPTS

1. Visit www.zoomerang.com or another free online web survey site. Using the tools at the site, design a five-question survey on the entertainment opportunities in your area. Send the survey to six friends and look at the results. What did you think of the online survey method?

2. Assume you are interested in opening a children's retail clothing store specializing in upscale children's fashions for newborns to 10-year-olds. You are unsure whether there is enough demand in your area to be profitable. In a small group, discuss what information you need before making this decision and decide on which secondary sources can provide that information. Furthermore, assume you plan to conduct a survey to better estimate demand for this product and describe the best primary data collection method for your needs.

3. One source of competitive marketing intelligence is a company's website. Visit Apple's website (www.apple.com) to search for information that might be useful to competitors. Write a brief report on what you found.

FOCUS ON TECHNOLOGY

If you've ever complained to friends about a bad product or service experience, the marketer probably never heard you. That is, until now. If you complain on a social networking site you just might get a response. That's what Moosehead, Canada's oldest independent and third-largest brewery, did. Moosehead learned of a customer who complained on a blog about purchasing spoiled beer that had not been stored properly at the retail level. The brewer's quick remedy resulted in the blogger posting a "glowing review" of the treatment he received. But how do companies monitor online communications among the millions of consumers worldwide using social media such as blogs, video sharing (YouTube), photo sharing (Flickr), and microblogging (Twitter) sites? The key is that users of social media leave clues, such as social bookmarks, friends, followers, comments, favourites, votes, and so on. Companies could monitor these clues themselves, but most hire experts specializing in social media monitoring to track how people are talking about their brands.

1. Search "social media monitoring" on a search engine to find companies specializing in monitoring social media. Many of these sites discuss examples of how businesses use their service. Discuss two examples in which businesses used social media monitoring successfully.

2. Monitoring "tagging" is hailed as the way to keep tabs on the Internet. Explain what is meant by a "tag" and explain why monitoring such tags is beneficial for marketers.

FOCUS ON ETHICS

You probably looked at a lot of information before selecting the college or university you are currently attending. Perhaps you even looked at *Maclean's* annual university ranking issue, which rates universities on a number of factors including average entering grades, class size, calibre of faculty, and breadth and currency of its libraries. One survey suggests that 80 percent of first-year students used *Maclean's* rankings when deciding what school to attend. Since its inception nearly 20 years ago, however, the ranking has been fraught with controversy over the methods used. For example, Alberta universities once accused the Ontario education system of inflating high school grades, thus resulting in higher rankings for Ontario universities whose student body is primarily from that province. In one year, *Maclean's* admitted to using data from a previous year's survey when some universities refused to provide current data.

Many universities have called the survey methodology "oversimplified and arbitrary" and have gone so far as to refuse to participate. Critics argue that since we do not have standardized high school testing in Canada, such as the SAT in the United States, it is very difficult to compare the quality of incoming students province to province. Others have voiced concerns with how *Maclean's* handles missing or outdated information when generating a ranking.

1. Find the latest *Maclean's* annual university survey. Does the article explain how data are collected and what the values mean? Describe how data are collected and critique the information for usefulness.

2. Do you agree with the critics' assessment that this ranking is "oversimplified and arbitrary"? Why or why not? Cite specific examples to support your argument.

MARKETING BY THE NUMBERS

"Company X has 34 percent market share," "Brand A is preferred by over 60 percent of consumers," "Prices are increasing at a rate of 44 percent," and "The average customer satisfaction rating is 4, satisfied, on a 1–5 scale." These are all conclusions based on statistics. Statistics lend credibility to conclusions and can be very persuasive. But are the conclusions legitimate? Many are survey-based claims, meaning survey research is used to substantiate claims such as those used in advertising. Claiming 60 percent of consumers prefer your brand is powerful but can be misleading if only five consumers were sampled and three preferred that brand (that is, 60 percent). Interpretation of data can vary by who's interpreting it. For example, saying that your average customer is satisfied may not be accurate, as an average rating of 4 could result from half of respondents indicating 5 (extremely satisfied) and the other half rating 3 (neither satisfied nor dissatisfied), which paints a different picture. Market share is the ratio of the company's sales to total market sales, and a 34 percent market share is nice. But how is

"market" defined? As you can see, numbers can say almost anything you want them to say. For more discussion of the financial and quantitative implications of marketing decisions, see Appendix 3: Marketing by the Numbers.

1. Using Statistics Canada data on education, training, and learning (available at www40.statcan.ca/l01/ind01/l2_1821-eng.htm?hili_none), develop statistics, such as percentages, to support the argument for tuition freezes for undergraduate education in Canada. Use any portion of the data you deem important to support your argument.

2. Using the same data on that website, develop different statistics to support the counterargument to the one above. That is, interpret the data and present it in a way that supports the universities' position for the need to increase tuition fees. Again, use any portion of the data you deem important to support your argument.

VIDEO CASE

 Video Case Questions

Ziba

How do companies design new products? Quite often, they get someone else to do it for them. That's where design firms such as Ziba come in. Ziba is one of a new breed of consultancies whose sole purpose is to help corporations

better understand customer needs and turn that understanding into groundbreaking new products.

The foundation for Ziba's product-development process is market research. That research seeks to understand the brand itself, the competition, and market trends. But most important, Ziba's research efforts centre on getting to know the customer. It has taken a novel approach to market research by using the likes of social anthropologists and cultural ethnographers to get to the heart of what makes consumers tick. Their efforts often include actually following customers around, observing them in their natural environment, and understanding their experiences.

The unique focus that Ziba takes has earned it contracts with major corporations, including P&G, KitchenAid, Logitech, Microsoft, and Intel, as well as various small start-up companies.

After viewing the video featuring Ziba, answer the following questions about new-product development:

1. Illustrate some ways in which Ziba engages in each phase of the marketing research process.

2. Discuss the various ways in which Ziba's research efforts are focused on customer relationships.

3. Identify evidence of how Ziba uses the information it acquires to make marketing decisions.

Visit MyMarketingLab at www.pearsoned.ca/mymarketinglab to view the video segment related to this case.

COMPANY CASE

Enterprise Rent-A-Car: Measuring Service Quality

Kevin Kirkman wheeled his shiny blue BMW coupe into his driveway, put the gearshift into park, set the parking brake, and got out to check his mailbox, as he did every day when he returned home. As he flipped through the deluge of catalogues and credit card offers, he noticed a letter from Enterprise Rent-A-Car. He wondered why Enterprise would be writing him.

THE WRECK

Then he remembered. Earlier that month, Kevin had been involved in a wreck. As he was driving to work one rainy morning, another car had been unable to stop on the slick pavement and had plowed into his car as he waited at a stoplight. Thankfully, neither he nor the other driver was hurt, but both cars had sustained considerable damage. In fact, he was not able to drive his car.

Kevin had used his cellphone to call the police, and while he was waiting for the officers to come he had called his auto insurance agent. The agent had assured Kevin that his policy included coverage to pay for a rental car while he was having his car repaired. He told Kevin to have the car towed to a nearby auto repair shop and gave him the telephone number for the Enterprise Rent-A-Car office that served his area. The agent noted that his company recommended using Enterprise for replacement rentals and that Kevin's policy would cover up to $20 per day of the rental fee.

Once Kevin had checked his car in at the body shop and made the necessary arrangements, he telephoned the Enterprise office. Within 10 minutes, an Enterprise employee had driven to the repair shop and picked him up. They drove back to the Enterprise office, where Kevin completed the paperwork and rented a Ford Taurus. He drove the rental car for 12 days before the repair shop completed work on his car.

"Don't know why Enterprise would be writing me," Kevin thought. "The insurance company paid the $20 per day, and I paid the extra because the Taurus cost more than that. Wonder what the problem could be?"

TRACKING SATISFACTION

Kevin tossed the mail onto the passenger's seat and drove up the driveway. Once inside his house, he opened the Enterprise letter to find that it was a survey to determine how satisfied he was with his rental. The survey itself was only one page long and consisted of 13 questions (see exhibit).

Enterprise's executives believed that the company had become the largest rent-a-car company in North America (in terms of number of cars, rental locations, and revenue) because of its laserlike focus on customer satisfaction and because of its concentration on serving the home-city replacement market. It aimed to serve customers like Kevin who were involved in wrecks and suddenly found themselves without a car. While the more well-known companies like Hertz and Avis battled for business in the cutthroat airport market, Enterprise quietly built its business by cultivating insurance agents and body-shop managers as referral agents so that when one of their clients or customers needed a replacement vehicle, they would recommend Enterprise. Although such replacement rentals accounted for about 80 percent of the company's business, it also served the discretionary market (leisure/vacation rentals), and the business market (renting cars to businesses for their short-term needs). It had also begun to provide onsite and offsite service at some airports.

Throughout its history, Enterprise had followed founder Jack Taylor's advice. Taylor believed that if the company took care of its customers and employees first, profits would follow. So the company was careful to track customer satisfaction.

About 1 in 20 randomly selected customers received a letter like Kevin's. An independent company mailed the letter and a postage-paid return envelope to the selected customers. Customers who completed the survey used the envelope to return it to the independent company. That company compiled the results and provided them to Enterprise.

CONTINUOUS IMPROVEMENT

Meanwhile, back at Enterprise's St. Louis, Missouri, headquarters, the company's top managers were interested in taking the next steps in their customer satisfaction program. Enterprise had used the percentage of customers who were completely satisfied to develop its Enterprise Service Quality index (ESQi). It used the survey results to calculate an overall average ESQi score for the company and a score for each individual branch. The company's branch managers believed in and supported the process.

However, top management believed that to really "walk the walk" on customer satisfaction, it needed to make the ESQi a key factor in the promotion process. The company wanted to take the ESQi for the branch or branches a manager supervised into consideration when it evaluated that manager for a promotion. Top management believed that such a process would ensure that its managers and all its employees would focus on satisfying Enterprise's customers.

But, the top managers realized they had two problems in taking the next step. First, they wanted a better survey response rate. Although the company got a 25 percent response rate, which was good for this type of survey, it was concerned that it might still be missing important information. Second, it could take up to two months to get results back, and Enterprise believed it needed a process that would get the customer satisfaction information more quickly, at least on a monthly basis, so its branch managers could identify and take action on customer service problems quickly and efficiently.

Enterprise's managers wondered how they could improve the customer-satisfaction-tracking process.

Questions for Discussion

1. Analyze Enterprise's Service Quality Survey. What information is it trying to gather? What are its research objectives?

2. What decisions has Enterprise made with regard to primary data collection—research approach, contact methods, sampling plan, and research instruments?

3. In addition to or instead of the mail survey, what other means could Enterprise use to gather customer satisfaction information?

4. What specific recommendations would you make to Enterprise to improve the response rate and the timeliness of feedback from the process?

Source: Officials at Enterprise Rent-A-Car contributed to and supported the development of this case.

 Visit **MyMarketingLab** at **www.pearsoned.ca/mymarketinglab** for access to online tutorials, interactive exercises, videos, and much more.

SERVICE QUALITY SURVEY

Please mark the box that best reflects your response to each question.

	Completely Satisfied	Somewhat Satisfied	Neither Satisfied Nor Dissatisfied	Somewhat Dissatisfied	Completely Dissatisfied
1. Overall, how satisfied were you with your recent car rental from Enterprise?	☐	☐	☐	☐	☐

2. What, if anything, could Enterprise have done better? *(Please be specific)* _____
_____
_____

3a. Did you experience any problems during the rental process?	Yes ☐ No ☐	3b. If you mentioned any problems to Enterprise, did they resolve them to your satisfaction? Yes ☐ No ☐ Did not mention ☐

	Excellent	Good	Fair	Poor	N/A
4. If you personally called Enterprise to reserve a vehicle, how would you rate the telephone reservation process?	☐	☐	☐	☐	☐

	Both at start and end of rental	Just at start of rental	Just at end of rental	Neither time	
5. Did you go to the Enterprise office	☐	☐	☐	☐	

	Both at start and end of rental	Just at start of rental	Just at end of rental	Neither time	
6. Did an Enterprise employee give you a ride to help with your transportation needs	☐	☐	☐	☐	

7. After you arrived at the Enterprise office, how long did it take you to:	Less than 5 minutes	5–10 minutes	11–15 minutes	16–20 minutes	21–30 minutes	More than 30 minutes	N/A
• pick up your rental car?	☐	☐	☐	☐	☐	☐	☐
• return your rental car?	☐	☐	☐	☐	☐	☐	☐

8. How would you rate the . . .	Excellent	Good	Fair	Poor	N/A
• timeliness with which you were either picked up at the start of the rental or dropped off afterwards?	☐	☐	☐	☐	☐
• timeliness with which the rental car was either brought to your location and left with you or picked up from your location afterwards?	☐	☐	☐	☐	☐
• Enterprise employee who handled your paperwork . . .					
at the START of the rental?	☐	☐	☐	☐	☐
at the END of the rental?	☐	☐	☐	☐	☐
• mechanical condition of the car?	☐	☐	☐	☐	☐
• cleanliness of the car interior/exterior?	☐	☐	☐	☐	☐

	Yes	No	N/A
9. If you asked for a specific type or size of vehicle, was Enterprise able to meet your needs?	☐	☐	☐

	Car repairs due to accident	All other car repairs/ maintenance	Car was stolen	Business	Leisure/ vacation	Some other reason
10. For what reason did you rent this car?	☐	☐	☐	☐	☐	☐

	Definitely will call	Probably will call	Might or might not call	Probably will not call	Definitely will not call
11. The next time you need to pick up a rental car in the city or area in which you live, how likely are you to call Enterprise?	☐	☐	☐	☐	☐

	Once—this was first time	2 times	3–5 times	6–10 times	11 or more times
12. Approximately how many times in total have you rented from Enterprise (including this rental)?	☐	☐	☐	☐	☐

	0 times	1 time	2 times	3–5 times	6–10 times	11 or more times
13. Considering *all rental companies,* approximately how many times *within the past year* have you rented a car in the city or area in which you live (including this rental)?	☐	☐	☐	☐	☐	☐

6

Consumer Markets and Consumer Buyer Behaviour

PREVIEWING
THE CONCEPTS

In the previous chapter, you studied how marketers obtain, analyze, and use information to understand the marketplace and to assess marketing programs. In this and the next chapter, we'll continue with a closer look at the most important element of the marketplace—customers. The aim of marketing is to affect how customers think and act. To affect the *whats*, *whens*, and *hows* of buying behaviour, marketers must first understand the *whys*. In this chapter, we look at final consumer buying influences and processes. In the next chapter, we'll study the buyer behaviour of *business customers*. You'll see that understanding buyer behaviour is an essential but very difficult task.

To get a better sense of the importance of understanding consumer behaviour, let's look first at Harley-Davidson, maker of North America's top-selling heavyweight motorcycles. Who rides these big Harley "Hogs"? What moves them to tattoo their bodies with the Harley-Davidson emblem, abandon home and hearth for the open road, and flock to Harley rallies by the hundreds of thousands? You might be surprised, but Harley-Davidson knows *very* well.

F ew brands engender such intense loyalty as that found in the hearts of Harley-Davidson owners. Harley buyers are granitelike in their devotion to the brand. "You don't see people tattooing Yamaha on their bodies," observes the publisher of *American Iron*, an industry publication. And according to another industry insider, "For a lot of people, it's not that they want a motorcycle; it's that they want a Harley—the brand is that strong."

Each year in early March more than 350 000 Harley bikers rumble through the streets of Daytona Beach, Florida, to attend the Daytona Bike Week celebration. Bikers from Canada and the United States lounge on their low-slung Harleys, swap biker tales, and sport T-shirts proclaiming "I'd rather push a Harley than drive a Honda."

Riding such intense emotions, Harley-Davidson has rumbled its way to the top of the heavyweight motorcycle market. Harley's "Hogs" capture nearly a quarter of all North American bike sales and almost 50 percent of the heavyweight segment. For several years running, sales have outstripped supply, with customer waiting lists of up to two years for popular models and street prices running well above suggested list prices. During the past 10 years, annual revenues and earnings have grown at better than 14 percent and 23 percent, respectively. By 2007, Harley-Davidson had experienced 21 straight years of record sales and income, and its stock was at a record high.

Although you may think of Harley as the quintessential American brand, it has a long history in Canada, too. Fred Deeley established the first Canadian dealership in 1917, making it the second-oldest Harley-Davidson dealership in the world. Today Deeley Harley-Davidson Canada acts as the sole distributor for all of Canada, and it is the only Harley distribution system not completely owned and controlled by the American parent. The firm's mission is to see the

Few brands engender such intense loyalty as that found in the hearts of Harley-Davidson owners. "You don't see people tattooing Yamaha on their bodies."

Harley-Davidson lifestyle as an increasing and permanent part of Canadian society. The firm has been recognized for its efforts and has been placed multiple times on the prestigious list of Canada's 50 Best-Managed Companies. Deeley Harley-Davidson Canada attributes its success to a continuous improvement culture, its commitment to innovation, and customer service excellence. It constantly works to forge new markets for its products. It also prides itself on its desire to stay close to the customer through efforts such as "The Ride Home From Canada" program, which celebrated Harley-Davidson's 100th Anniversary. The 8400 kilometre cross-country trek brought riders from across Canada. They rode together and raised funds for Muscular Dystrophy Canada.

Harley-Davidson's marketers spend a great deal of time thinking about customers and their buying behaviour. They want to know who their customers are, what they think and how they feel, and why they buy a Harley Fat Boy Softail rather than a Yamaha or a Kawasaki or a big Honda American Classic. What is it that makes Harley buyers so fiercely loyal? These are difficult questions; even Harley owners themselves don't know exactly what motivates their buying. But Harley management puts top priority on understanding customers and what makes them tick.

Who rides a Harley? You might be surprised. Motorcycles are attracting a new breed of riders—older, more affluent, and better educated. "While the outlaw bad-boy biker image is what we might typically associate with Harley riders," says an analyst, "they're just as likely to be CEOs and investment bankers." "You take off the leathers and the helmet and you'll never know who you'll find," says one hard-core Harley enthusiast. The average Harley customer is a 47-year-old male with a median income of $82 000. More than 12 percent of Harley purchases today are made by women.

Harley-Davidson makes good bikes, and to keep up with its shifting market the company has upgraded its showrooms and sales approaches. But Harley customers are buying a lot more than just a quality bike and a smooth sales pitch. To a Harley owner, whether it's the guy who sweeps the floors of the factory or the CEO at that factory, it's about something much deeper. To the hard-core Harley fan, it's all about independence, freedom, and power.

"It's much more than a machine," says the analyst. "It is part of their own self-expression and lifestyle." Another analyst suggests that owning a Harley makes you "the toughest, baddest guy on the block. Never mind that [you're] a dentist or an accountant. You [feel] wicked astride all that power." Your Harley renews your spirits and announces your independence.

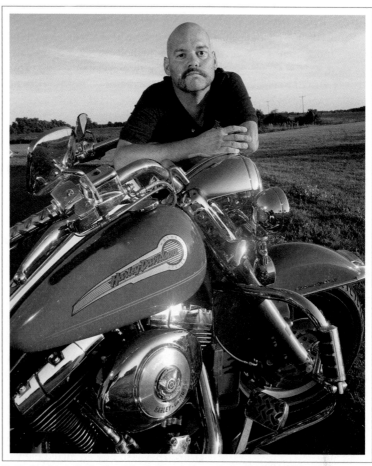

To the hard-core Harley fan, it's all about independence, freedom, and power. Says one Harley owner, "Four wheels move the body . . . two wheels move the soul."

OBJECTIVES

1. Define the consumer market and explain the process of consumer buyer behaviour.

2. Name the four major factors that influence consumer buyer behaviour.

3. List and define the major types of buying decision behaviour and the stages in the buyer decision process.

4. Describe the adoption and diffusion process for new products.

One Harley owner sums it up this way on the Harley Owners Group website: "I believe in the itch that can only be scratched on a motorcycle. I believe in riding alone, with my wife, with a group. I believe in high mountain passes, tunnels of trees, lonely two-lane roads. I believe in family, friends, and God. I believe my Harley-Davidson can get me to all these places." Adds another, "Four wheels move the body . . . two wheels move the soul." The classic look, the throaty sound, the very idea of a Harley all contribute to its mystique. Owning this "American legend" makes you a part of something bigger, a member of the Harley-Davidson family.

Such strong emotions and motivations are captured in a classic Harley-Davidson advertisement. The ad shows a close-up of an arm, the bicep adorned with a Harley-Davidson tattoo. The headline asks, "When was the last time you felt this strongly about anything?" The ad copy outlines the problem and suggests a solution: "Wake up in the morning and life picks up where it left off. . . . What once seemed exciting has now become part of the numbing routine. It all begins to feel the same. Except when you've got a Harley-Davidson. Something strikes a nerve. The heartfelt thunder rises up, refusing to become part of the background. Suddenly things are different. Clearer. More real. As they should have been all along. Riding a Harley changes you from within. The effect is permanent. Maybe it's time you started feeling this strongly. Things are different on a Harley."[1]

1 WHAT IS CONSUMER BEHAVIOUR?

Chapter Opening Discussion

Consumer buyer behaviour
The buying behaviour of final consumers—individuals and households that buy goods and services for personal consumption.

Consumer market
All the individuals and households who buy or acquire goods and services for personal consumption.

Glossary Flashcards of Key Terms

The Harley-Davidson example shows that many different factors affect consumer buying behaviour. Buying behaviour is never simple, yet understanding it is the essential task of marketing management. **Consumer buyer behaviour** refers to the buying behaviour of final consumers—individuals and households that buy goods and services for personal consumption. All of these final consumers combine to make up the **consumer market**. The North American consumer market consists of more than 333 million people (more than 33 million in Canada and 300 million in the United States) who consume trillions of dollars' worth of goods and services each year, making it one of the most attractive consumer markets in the world. The world consumer market consists of more than 6.6 billion people who annually consume an estimated US$65 trillion worth of goods and services.[2]

Consumers around the world vary tremendously in age, income, education level, and tastes. They also buy an incredible variety of goods and services. How these diverse consumers relate with each other and with other elements of the world around them impacts their choices among various products, services, and companies. Here we examine the fascinating array of factors that affect consumer behaviour.

Consumers make many purchase decisions, and some are more complex than others. For example, a consumer buying a cup of coffee would go through a very different decision-making process than one buying his or her first house. Most large companies research consumer buying decisions in great detail to answer questions about what consumers buy, where they buy, how and how much they buy, when they buy, and why they buy. Marketers can study actual consumer purchases to find out what they buy, where, and how much. But learning about the *whys* of consumer buying behaviour is not so easy—the answers are often locked deep within the consumer's mind.

Often, consumers themselves don't know exactly what influences their purchases. "The human mind doesn't work in a linear way," says one marketing expert. "The idea that the mind is a computer with storage compartments where brands or logos or recognizable packages are stored in clearly marked folders that can be accessed by cleverly written ads or commercials simply doesn't exist. Instead, the mind is a whirling, swirling, jumbled mass of neurons bouncing around, colliding and continuously creating new concepts and thoughts and relationships inside every single person's brain all over the world."[3]

The central question for marketers, then, is this: Given all the characteristics (cultural, social, personal, and psychological) affecting consumer behaviour, how do we best design our marketing efforts to reach our consumers most effectively? Thus, the study of consumer behaviour begins and ends with the individual. In the past, the field was often referred to as *buyer behaviour*, reflecting an emphasis on the actual exchange of goods for money. Marketers now recognize the study of consumer behaviour as an ongoing process that starts long before the consumer purchases a product or service and continues long after

Figure 6.1 Some issues that arise during stages in the consumption process

Source: Consumer Behaviour: Buying, Having, and Being, 4th Canadian Edition, by Michael R. Solomon, Judith L. Zaichkowsky, and Rosemary Polegato. Toronto: Pearson Education Canada, 2008.

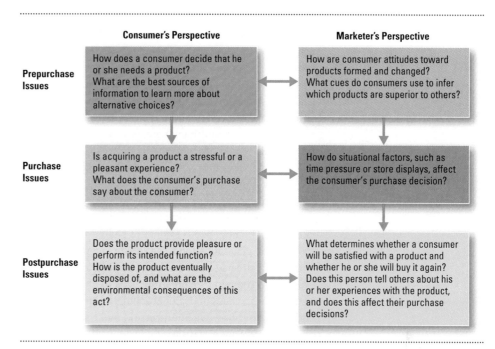

they consume it. This extended definition of consumer behaviour means that marketers must be aware of a number of issues before, during, and after purchase to build brand loyalty and lasting relationships with their customers. Figure 6.1 illustrates some issues that arise during each stage of the consumption process, but there are many more.

Consumers' responses, which can range from actual purchase to merely engaging in word-of-mouth communications about the product, is the ultimate test of whether or not a marketing strategy is successful. In the next section, we will examine each of the characteristics affecting consumer behaviour in more detail.

2 FACTORS AFFECTING CONSUMER BEHAVIOUR

Consumer purchases are influenced strongly by cultural, social, personal, and psychological factors, shown in Figure 6.2. For the most part, marketers cannot control such factors, but they must take them into account.

Cultural Factors

Cultural factors exert a broad and deep influence on consumer behaviour. The marketer needs to understand the role played by the consumer's *culture, subculture,* and *social class.*

Culture

Culture is the most basic cause of a person's wants and behaviour. Human behaviour is largely learned. Growing up in a society, a child learns basic values, perceptions, wants,

Culture
The set of basic values, perceptions, wants, and behaviours learned by a member of society from family and other important institutions.

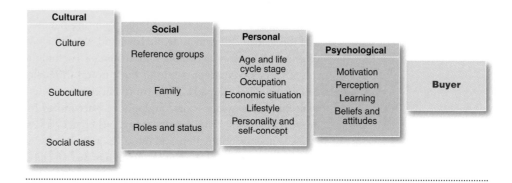

Figure 6.2 Factors influencing consumer behaviour

and behaviours from the family and other important institutions. A child in the United States normally learns or is exposed to the following values: achievement and success, activity and involvement, efficiency and practicality, progress, hard work, material comfort, individualism, freedom, humanitarianism, youthfulness, and fitness and health. In contrast, *Maclean's* magazine's annual poll of Canadian values suggests that the majority of Canadians treasure freedom; the beauty of our natural landscape; our beliefs in respect, equality, and fair treatment; our flag; our social safety net; our international role; and our multicultural and multiracial makeup. We see ourselves as unique and distinctly different from Americans. One commonality between our two cultures, however, for better or worse, is that we are a consumer culture, and marketing practices reinforce this as a way of life.[4]

Every group or society has a culture, and cultural influences on buying behaviour may vary greatly from country to country. Failure to adjust to these differences can result in ineffective marketing or embarrassing mistakes. It should not be assumed, however, that culture is a homogeneous system of shared meaning, way of life, or unifying values.[5] It is too broad a generalization to say that Canadians have one culture and the Japanese have another. In diverse societies like Canada, there is a multiplicity of overlapping cultural groupings. These in turn are influenced by the fact that we are part of a global marketplace. Marketing practices and global media influence our values and consumption behaviours and even affect how we interpret and make sense of the world around us.

Marketers are always trying to spot *cultural shifts* to discover new products that might be wanted. For example, the cultural shift toward greater concern about health and fitness has created a huge industry for health-and-fitness services, exercise equipment and clothing, organic foods, and a variety of diets. The shift toward informality has resulted in more demand for casual clothing and simpler home furnishings.

Subculture

Subculture

A group of people with shared value systems based on common life experiences and situations.

Each culture contains smaller **subcultures**, or groups of people with shared value systems based on common life experiences and situations. Subcultures include nationalities, religions, racial groups, and geographic regions. Many subcultures make up important market segments, and marketers often design products and marketing programs tailored to their needs. Examples of four such important subculture groups in Canada include regional subcultures, founding nations, ethnic subcultures, and mature consumers.

Regional Subcultures Canada is a regional country, so marketers may develop distinctive programs for the Atlantic provinces, Quebec, Central Canada, the Prairies, and British Columbia. The sheer size of the country and its varied geographic features and climate have certainly shaped regional character and personality. For example, Atlantic Canada is largely defined by its proximity to and historical relationship with the sea. Equally, the isolation imposed by the mountain barrier, along with the abundance and grandeur of British Columbia's natural environment, shaped the outlook of that region's residents. Immigration has also had a differential effect on the different regions within Canada. The economy of each region furthers these differences. The fate of regions linked to the rise and fall of commodities, such as fish, timber, wheat, minerals, or oil, has affected regional mindsets as well as economies. Perceived disparities in political power have also increased regionalism, especially in Quebec, Newfoundland and Labrador, and Alberta.[6]

Founding Nations Canada had three founding nations: Aboriginal peoples, the English, and the French (some include the Irish and Scottish as well, noting that the Canadian coat of arms reflects their founding nation status). The unique history and language of each of these nations has driven many of the cultural differences that result in different buying behaviours across Canada. The most recent census results (2006) reported that people noting their English language roots (anglophones) accounted for approximately 57 percent of the population, people whose mother tongue is French (francophones) made up approximately 22 percent of the population, and those reporting Aboriginal ancestry represented 3.7 percent of the total population. Because Canada has two official languages, Canadian law makes it mandatory that nutritional information on food labels be bilingual. (See Real Marketing 6.1

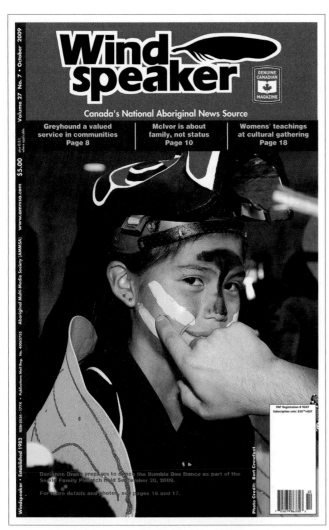

Windspeaker magazine is one tool promoted by the Aboriginal Multi-Media Society (AMMSA) to assist marketers who want to communicate with Canada's Aboriginal peoples effectively and efficiently.

for more insight on marketing to French-Canadian consumers.)

Aboriginal Canadians are making their voices heard both in the political arena and in the marketplace. There are more than 1.17 million Aboriginal Canadians, including Métis and Inuit. Among Canada's Aboriginal population, Cree is reported as the most common mother tongue. Not only do Aboriginal Canadians have distinct cultures that influence their values and purchasing behaviour, they also have profoundly influenced the rest of Canada through their art, love of nature, and concern for the environment.

Banks have been particularly responsive to the unique needs of Aboriginal Canadians.[7] Scotiabank, for example, has maintained its relationship with Aboriginal clients through its three on-reserve branches and 24 Aboriginal banking centres. It also uses a lot of grassroots marketing and public relations efforts, including its sponsorship of the Aboriginal Achievement Awards and 10 annual scholarships of $2500 for young Aboriginal entrepreneurs. Publications like *Windspeaker* magazine can be used as vehicles to effectively advertise to Canada's Aboriginal peoples.

Ethnic Consumers According to Statistics Canada, roughly one out of every five people in Canada could be a member of a visible minority by 2017, when Canada celebrates its 150th anniversary. Approximately 200 000 new immigrants come to Canada each year.[8] Thus, being sensitive to their cultural values is important because 70 percent of the visible minority population were born outside Canada. According to Balmoral Marketing, an ethnic ad agency in Toronto, many firms are now spending as much as 15 percent of their total communications budget on ethnic marketing.[9]

People with a Chinese background are still the largest group among visible minorities in Canada. According to a 2006 *Marketing Magazine* report, 3.74 percent of Canada's population is Chinese, with 40 percent of this group residing in Toronto and 31 percent living in Vancouver. The average Chinese household spends $63 500 each year, slightly higher than the Canadian average of $58 500. People of South Asian origin (currently 23 percent of visible minorities) may represent as large a marketplace as Chinese consumers by 2017. According to a recent survey, 50 percent of South Asians say their opinion of a company would improve if they saw the ads on South Asian TV, and 62 percent stated that they would look more positively on companies that sponsored community events. When asked for advice on how to communicate with ethnic markets, Chris Bhang from Allard Johnson Direct, speaking at the 2005 Canadian Marketing Association's Diversity Conference, said, "Be colloquial, be creative, but be relevant."

Canadian companies are realizing the importance of culturally relevant advertising that includes a multimedia approach to reach the Chinese Canadian market. A 2008 poll conducted by Solutions Research Group revealed that Internet use among Chinese Canadians exceeds time spent listening to radio and watching TV combined. Internet portals such as Toronto-based 51.ca or Ottawa-based ComeFromChina.com, which serve as free markets for information for Canada's Chinese community, have captured the attention of many Canadian advertisers. Chinese Canadians appreciate advertising delivered in their native tongue. "There's a certain emotional connection a person makes when somebody speaks their own language," said Solutions Research Group president Kaan Yigit. "It speaks to the issue of showing respect or feeling like you're being acknowledged."[10]

Toronto-based 51.ca serves as a free market for information for Canada's Chinese community and has captured the attention of many Canadian advertisers.

People who identified themselves as black in the 2006 census are Canada's third-largest visible minority.[11] While some members of this group trace their ancestry back to Africa, many others have more recently immigrated from the Caribbean.

In recent years, many companies have developed special products, appeals, and marketing programs for black consumers. For example, P&G's roots run deep in this market. Procter & Gamble currently spends six times more on media targeting black consumers than it did just five years ago. It has a long history of using black spokespeople in its ads, beginning in 1969 with entertainer Bill Cosby endorsing Crest. Today, you'll see Angela Bassett promoting the benefits of Olay body lotion for black skin, Tiger Woods discussing the virtues of Gillette razors, and Queen Latifah in commercials promoting a CoverGirl line for black women. "The new Queen Collection was inspired by me to celebrate the beauty of women of colour," says Latifah, "and it gives women the confidence they are looking for by accentuating our natural features."[12]

P&G has also tailored a number of its products to the special preferences of black consumers. For example, when market research showed that blacks prefer more scents and flavours, P&G added new scents to Gain detergent and flavours to Crest Whitening Expressions toothpaste. And the consumer products giant has created a line of Pantene Relaxed and Natural shampoos specially formulated for women of colour. Such moves have made P&G an acknowledged leader in serving this group of consumers. Says one industry watcher, "Without question, P&G has to be seen as one of the companies that other companies pattern their behaviour after."[13]

Canada is increasingly becoming a multilingual society. Statistics Canada reports that almost one out of every five Canadians reported having a mother tongue other than English or French—in fact, more than 100 languages were reported in the 2006 census. Some marketers who resist ethnic marketing claim they don't know enough about these markets, fear that they may make a mistake, or say there are just too many languages to deal with to effectively tailor their campaigns.[14] They are neglecting a sizable market. Allophones, people who report a mother tongue other than English or French, exceed 6.1 million (up from 5.3 million in the 2001 census). People who speak Mandarin or Cantonese form the third-most-common language group in Canada, followed by Italian, German, Punjabi, and Spanish.

Mature Consumers Though age is a demographic variable, some researchers also contend that different age cohorts have distinct cultures. As of July 2008, the median age in Canada was 39.4 years, which is higher than ever before (median age is defined as the point where exactly one-half of the population is older and the other half is younger). According to the 2001 census, the median age was 37.6. To see how rapidly the Canadian population has aged, it is interesting to note that the median age in Canada in 1966 (the year when the last of the baby boomers was born) was 25.4 years. Thus, Canada's working-age population today is dominated by older individuals, but there are regional variations. Newfoundland and Labrador has the oldest population, with a median age of 42.5. Alberta is the youngest, with a median age of 35.7. Because of high immigration rates, however, Canada's population is not aging as fast as the population of the United States.

As the Canadian population ages, *mature consumers* are becoming a very attractive market. By 2015, the entire baby boom generation, the largest and wealthiest demographic cohort in the country for more than half a century, will have moved into the 50-plus age bracket. They will control a larger proportion of wealth, income, and consumption than any other generation. Pharmaceuticals, travel, and financial services companies have long targeted older consumers. But as this group grows in numbers and buying power, companies

Real Marketing **6.1**

Marketing to Quebec and French-Canadian Consumers

Quebec has long prided itself on being a "distinct society." Marketers must be aware of Quebec's uniqueness if they are to be successful in the province. Quebec is characterized by unique laws, a different mix of indigenous and national businesses and industries, and distinct attitudes and values when compared with the rest of Canada. According to the most recent census data, almost 6 million of the 7 435 905 people who make up Quebec's population claim French as their mother tongue (this equates to 79 percent of the Quebec population). This is compared to almost 600 000 who claim English as their native language, or the 700 000 who note another language as their native tongue.

Known for their *joie de vivre*, the majority of Quebec's population (46 percent, or 3.4 million people) lived in the Montreal area in 2006. Montreal has a large number of high-tech industries. As well as being the second-largest metropolitan area in Canada (behind Toronto and leading Vancouver), Montreal is also the second-largest French-speaking city in the world. One must not assume that the population of the Montreal region is homogeneous and made up only of francophones, however. Bilingualism is very common, and like other large Canadian cities, the population is diverse as a result of immigration, though Montreal does not receive as many immigrants as Toronto or Vancouver.

To protect its French culture and affirm the province's French-speaking identity, successive Quebec governments have passed legislation to ensure the use of French in various areas of public life. Education in the province is also mostly in French, although it is also available in English.

Marketers who want to appeal to Quebec consumers need to do more than communicate in French using dictionary translations of words. Language and the meanings derived from it are very cultural and context-based. Take a successful campaign by the Bank of Montreal that used the tag line, "*Profitez.*" You wouldn't fully understand the campaign if you used only a dictionary-based interpretation of the word. Dictionaries say *profitez* means "profit from," "profit," "earn," or "something profitable." However, for Quebec consumers the meaning is more nuanced. They translate it as "make the most of it," "enjoy," or "take advantage," and it is strongly associated with the enjoyment of life, meanings that make the campaign more powerful and rich.

Research has revealed differences in the activities, interests, opinions, and consumption habits of French-Canadian versus English-Canadian consumers. Many French Canadians value their European roots, their rich and diverse cultural venues, gourmet food, and fine wines. As a result, Montreal is known as one of the trendiest cities in the world. Research also suggests that many French-Canadian women are more family oriented and fashion conscious than women in the rest of Canada.

A study undertaken by SC Johnson suggested that even attitudes toward cleaning vary between English and French Canada. Although many English Canadians just want to get the job done and see cleaning as a necessary evil, many people in Quebec get a sense of pride and accomplishment after they clean. Using this research, SC Johnson designed a highly successful campaign for its cleaning products that centred on the distinctly Québécois custom of July 1, Moving Day—the date on which people tend to move from one apartment to another because leases in Quebec traditionally expire on June 30.

Such differences are partly derived from culture; their Latin roots may make many French Canadians more emotional and impulsive. Demographic and socioeconomic differences also exist: education and income are both lower in Quebec than in Ontario. The legal environment is also different for marketers in Quebec. Besides strict language laws, there are stronger restrictions on advertising to children, for example. To be successful in French Canada, marketers must develop appeals that take these differences into account. For example, although many marketers are using national symbols to appeal to their customers, the separatist sentiments held by some Quebecers may make this an unwise choice for some marketers.

Quebec also has a distinct business and retail climate. Lavo Group, for example, is a packaged-goods manufacturer whose products rival those of Procter & Gamble and Colgate in the province. Many Québécois buy such Lavo products as La Parisienne laundry detergent and fabric softener instead of Tide and Downy, Hertel liquid cleanser instead of Mr. Clean, and Old Dutch powder cleanser instead of Comet. The financial services industry is also very different in Quebec than it is in the rest of Canada. Two players that are almost nonexistent in English Canada, the Mouvement Desjardins (the federation of Quebec credit unions) and the National Bank, account for more than 60 percent of the province's financial services marketplace. Both organizations use integrated and Quebec-specific communications campaigns.

Quebec-based hardware chains Réno-Dépôt and RONA have many loyal customers in the province. When Home Depot entered Quebec in 2000, it had to compete

▶

with these companies—a completely different set of competitors than it had confronted in the rest of Canada. To help Home Depot gain acceptance, Montreal-based Cossette Communications developed an advertising campaign that appealed to Quebecers' unique sense of humour. Rather than creating ads with rational appeals that proclaimed Home Depot's high-quality service, Cossette conducted qualitative research to uncover examples of realistic and believable bad shopping experiences of Quebec consumers. The campaign that resulted from this research features one commercial that shows a clerk literally running away from a client. In another commercial, a group of clerks chant, "It is not my department" despite customers' looks of dismay. The campaign not only created awareness of Home Depot, but it was also listed among Montrealers' favourite commercials in a recent survey.

For a long time, Quebec lagged the rest of Canada in terms of Internet adoption and usage. Today, however, more than 70 percent of Quebec adults are online. There are a growing number of French sites and online services, such as La Toile du Québec (www.toile.com) and Petit-Monde (www.petitmonde.com), as well as the French versions of popular portals like Sympatico, Yahoo!, and MSN. Marketers have been quick to leverage this new interconnectivity. Volkswagen, Avon, L'Oréal, and La Senza are some of the Quebec-based companies that have jumped on the bandwagon. Not only are they building French versions of their company websites, they have intensified their email marketing campaigns in the province. The race is on to build databases to further this effort. Sympatico.ca, for example, has an opt-in email database of 700 000 French Canadians, comprising adults aged 25 to 49, most with families.

If marketers respect Quebec's unique laws with regard to contests and sweepstakes, they can use these tools to help build their databases. Sympatico.ca experienced phenomenal results when it ran a contest to meet Bryan Adams in Scotland. People had to register online, and Sympatico amassed 20 000 new Quebec subscribers as a result of the campaign. As their marketing manager noted, "French-speaking people love to play. And because they love to play, they tend to give their personal information freely—and by that I mean their postal code, age, and gender." Marketers have to tread softly, however. Quebecers still like to be wooed, especially when it comes to developing a one-to-one relationship. People from Quebec prefer more face-to-face interactions and personal contact than do people from the rest of the country.

Marketers must also be aware that Quebec has its own icons and unique media personalities. For example, while Tide's successful campaign featuring Kelly Ripa aired in the rest of Canada, television personality Sonia Vachon was used in Quebec. Bell Canada's long-running Monsieur B campaign, which originated in 1992, is almost unknown in the rest of Canada. However, it has approached legendary status in the province, the way other advertising icons like the Green Giant, Aunt Jemima, and the lonely Maytag repairman have done in the rest of Canada. Jean-François Richard, vice-president of marketing communications at Bell in Montreal, notes, "I don't know of any creative platform (anywhere) that has lasted so long and generated such results for so long for any advertiser!"

Because of all of these differences, many marketers develop unique programs designed just for the Quebec marketplace. Take the case of Mountain Equipment Co-op. Even though it has a small annual budget of just $40 000 devoted to the markets of Montreal, Quebec City, and the French part of Ottawa, MEC tailors its campaigns to the unique perceptions of the French-speaking marketplace. For example, Louise Arbique, director of French marketing, had four staffers kayak down the St. Lawrence River with the new store's front door key for the grand opening of the Quebec City store. The event generated tremendous media coverage. She also developed "Le Petit MEC," a visual dictionary of more than 6000 words that translated all of the company's products into French. The glossary received a *Mérite du français* award from *L'Office québécois de la langue française,* garnering even more publicity. MEC, a western-based retailer, saw its membership jump from 75 000 to 200 000 in Quebec in just two years, and sales from the Quebec City and Montreal stores are projected to make up 17 percent of MEC's national sales. What were the secrets to success? According to Arbique, it's MEC's respect

LE PETIT
MEC

DICTIONNAIRE ILLUSTRÉ
DU MATÉRIEL D'ACTIVITÉS
DE GRANDE NATURE

MEC's respect for the Quebec culture, its long history of social and environmental values, and the major investment it made in "francization," helped this B.C.-based retailer win over French-Canadian consumers.

for the culture, its long history of social and environmental values, and the major investment it made in "francization." "Quebecers share MEC values," she says. "People really appreciate that they feel respected in their language and their culture, and we worked very hard to adapt MEC for the Quebecers."

Sources: Eve Lazarus, "Getting into Gear," *Marketing*, June 13, 2005; "Vive la difference: Does That Mean I Have to Have a Separate Campaign?" *Strategy*, October 15, 2004; Nicolette Flemming, "The True Meaning of 'Profitez'," *Marketing*, June 10, 2002, p. 31; "Quebec Success: Weather Network and Dairy Farmers of Canada Hit the Right Formula," *Strategy*, October 15, 2004, p. 32; Bernadette Johnson, "Email Marketing Begins to Flourish in La Belle Province," *Strategy*, May 20, 2002, p. D10; Helena Katz, "Johnson Sharpens Its Quebec Strategy," *Marketing*, October 12, 1998, p. 3; Danny Kucharsky, "Monsieur B's Family," *Marketing*, June 11, 2001; Nathalie Fortier, "Building Success: How Cossette Poked Fun at Bad Customer Service to Give Home Depot a Firm Foundation in Quebec," *Marketing*, September 24, 2001; Tracey Arial, "Taking Aim at the Giants," *Marketing*, June 11, 2001; and Matt Semansky, "Plus Ça Change," *Marketing*, October 27, 2008, p. 21.

in all industries—from groceries, beauty products, and clothing to furniture and consumer electronics—are devising new ways to lure aging big spenders.[15]

Contrary to popular belief, mature consumers are not "stuck in their ways." To the contrary, a recent study showed that older consumers for products such as stereos, computers, and mobile phones are more willing to shop around and switch brands than their younger Generation X counterparts. For example, notes one expert, "some 25 percent of Apple's recently released iPhones—the epitome of cool, cutting-edge product—have been bought by people over 50."[16]

The growing cadre of mature consumers creates an attractive market for convenient services. For example, Home Depot and Lowe's now target older consumers who are less enthusiastic about do-it-yourself chores than with "do-it-for-me" handyman services. And their desire to look as young as they feel also makes more-mature consumers good candidates for cosmetics and personal care products, health foods, fitness products, and other items that combat the effects of aging. The best strategy is to appeal to their active, multidimensional lives. For example, Dove's Pro Age hair and skin care product line claims that "Beauty has no age limit." Pro Age ads feature active and attractive real women who seem to be benefiting from the product's promise. Says one ad, "Embrace the best years of your life with Dove Pro Age, a new line of products for skin and hair created to let women in their best years realize the beautiful potential that lies within. This isn't anti-age, it's pro-age."

Social Class

Social class
Relatively permanent and ordered divisions in a society whose members share similar values, interests, and behaviours.

Almost every society has some form of social class structure. **Social classes** are society's relatively permanent and ordered divisions whose members share similar values, interests, and behaviours. Social class is not determined by a single factor, such as income, but is measured as a combination of occupation, income, education, wealth, and other variables. In some social systems, members of different classes are reared for certain roles and cannot change their social positions. In North America, however, the lines between social classes are not fixed and rigid; people can move to a higher social class or drop into a lower one.

Most Canadians see themselves as middle class, and we are less willing to think of ourselves in terms of social class than our neighbours south of the border. It is for this reason that the New Democratic Party no longer tries to appeal to "the working class" but to "ordinary Canadians." Marketers are interested in social class because people within a given social class tend to exhibit similar buying behaviour. Social classes show distinct product and brand preferences in areas such as clothing, home furnishings, leisure activity, and automobiles.

Social Factors

A consumer's behaviour is also influenced by social factors, such as the consumer's *small groups*, *family*, and *social roles* and *status*.

Groups and Social Networks

Broadly defined, *reference groups* are any external influence that serve as direct (face-to-face) or indirect points of comparison or reference in forming a person's attitudes or behaviour. Many small **groups** influence a person's behaviour directly. Groups that have a direct influence and to which a person belongs are called *membership groups*. Your family, friends, or organizations you belong to would fall into this category. People are also influenced by reference groups to which they do not belong. For example, an *aspirational group* is one to which the individual wishes to belong, as when a young hockey player hopes to someday emulate Sidney Crosby and play in the NHL.

Marketers try to identify the reference groups of their target markets. Reference groups expose a person to new behaviours and lifestyles, influence the person's attitudes and self-concept, and create pressures to conform that may affect the person's product and brand choices. The importance of group influence varies across products and brands. It tends to be strongest when the product is visible to others whom the buyer respects.

Word-of-Mouth Influence and Buzz Marketing Marketers of brands subjected to strong group influence must figure out how to reach **opinion leaders**—people within a reference group who, because of special skills, knowledge, personality, or other characteristics, exert social influence on others. Some experts call this 10 percent of consumers *the influentials* or *leading adopters*. One recent study found that these influencers are "four times more likely than average consumers to belong to five or more organizations, four times more likely to be considered experts, and twice as likely to recommend a product they like." And when influential friends talk, consumers listen. Another survey found that nearly 78 percent of respondents trusted "recommendations from consumers," 15 percentage points higher than the second most-credible source, newspapers.[17]

Marketers often try to identify opinion leaders for their products and direct marketing efforts toward them. They use *buzz marketing* by enlisting or even creating opinion leaders to serve as "brand ambassadors" who spread the word about their products. Many companies are now creating brand ambassador programs in an attempt to turn influential but everyday customers into brand evangelists.

P&G has created a huge word-of-mouth marketing arm—Vocalpoint—consisting of 350 000 moms. This army of natural-born buzzers leverages the power of peer-to-peer communication to spread the word about brands. Vocalpoint recruits "connectors"—people with vast networks of friends and a gift for gab. They create buzz not just for P&G brands but for those of other client companies as well.

> Procter & Gamble couldn't ask for a better salesperson than Vocalpointer Donna Wetherell. The gregarious mom works at a customer service call centre unaffiliated with P&G, where she knows some 300 co-workers by name. Lately, Wetherell has spent so much time at work talking about P&G products and handing out discount coupons that her colleagues have given her a nickname. "I am called the coupon lady," Wetherell says.[18]

> Except for educating Vocalpointers about products, the company doesn't coach the moms. The connectors themselves choose whether or not to pitch the product to friends and what to say. What's more, they do the work without pay. What's in it for them? For one thing, they receive a steady flow of coupons and samples. But more important, it makes them insiders, seeing cool new ideas before their friends have them. Second, it gives them a voice. "They're filled with great ideas, and they don't think anybody listens to them," says Vocalpoint's CEO.

Online Social Networks Over the past few years, a new type of social interaction has exploded onto the scene—online social networking. **Online social networks** are online communities where people socialize or exchange information and opinions. Social networking media range from blogs to social networking websites, such as MySpace and YouTube, to entire virtual worlds, such as Second Life. This new form of high-tech buzz has big implications for marketers.

Group
Two or more people who interact to accomplish individual or mutual goals.

Opinion leader
A person within a reference group who, because of special skills, knowledge, personality, or other characteristics, exerts social influence on others.

Online social networks
Online social communities—blogs, social networking websites, or even virtual worlds—where people socialize or exchange information and opinions.

Buzz marketing: The Vocalpoint marketing arm of Procter & Gamble has enlisted an army of buzzers to create word-of-mouth for brands. "We know that the most powerful form of marketing is a message from a trusted friend."

Personal connections—forged through words, pictures, video, and audio posted just for the [heck] of it—are the life of the new Web, bringing together the estimated 60 million bloggers, more than 110 million MySpace.com users (230 000 more sign up every day), and millions more on single-use social networks where people share one category of stuff, like Flickr (photos), Del.icio.us (links), Digg (news stories), Wikipedia (encyclopedia articles), and YouTube (video). . . . It's hard to overstate the coming impact of these new network technologies on business: They hatch trends and build immense waves of interest in specific products. They serve up giant, targeted audiences to advertisers. They edge out old media with the loving labour of amateurs. They effortlessly provide hyperdetailed data to marketers. The new social networking technologies provide an authentic, peer-to-peer channel of communication that is far more credible than any corporate flackery.[19]

Marketers are working to harness the power of these new social networks to promote their products and build closer customer relationships. Instead of throwing more one-way commercial messages at ad-weary consumers, they hope to use social networks to *interact* with consumers and become a part of their conversations and lives. For example, brands ranging from Victoria's Secret to the Canadian Opera Company and Walmart have set up MySpace pages and Facebook groups. The Facebook group of Victoria's Secret offers free downloads, contests, and printable coupons—the group has more than 300 000 "members." The Canadian Opera Company's Facebook page lists upcoming events, pictures, and links to relevant YouTube videos. And Walmart set up the "Roommate Style Match" Facebook group, aimed at jump-starting university student back-to-school sales. Members take a quiz to determine their decorating style and get a list of "recommended products" they can buy at Walmart to match their style with their roommate's.[20]

A rush of marketers—from Dell and Sears to BMW, Coca-Cola, Adidas, and even CNN—have now set up their brands and are even selling digital goods in Second Life, the Internet-based digital world that is "imagined, created, and owned" by its nearly 6 million residents. Adidas has sold 21 000 pairs of virtual shoes in Second Life, and the average avatar (your Second Life character) spends 20 minutes in its store. CNN opened a news-gathering outpost in Second Life staffed by "residents" by which visitors can get the latest news via kiosks throughout the virtual community.[21]

Other companies regularly post ads or custom videos on video-sharing sites like YouTube. Viewers watch more than 2.5 billion YouTube videos in a single month, making it an attractive marketing outlet. For example, American Eagle Outfitters posts short, entertaining movies on YouTube. Heinz runs the Top This TV Challenge, which invites amateurs to submit homemade Heinz Ketchup commercials with the chance to win a grand prize of US$57 000 and have their commercial aired on national television. And Jack in the Box posts specially made, highly irreverent ads on YouTube that draw tens of thousands of page views from its targeted young male audience. Such ads have turned the Jack in the Box character into a cultural icon.[22]

Following the success of large social networking sites such as MySpace and Facebook, thousands of niche sites have popped up that cater to more selective online communities:

There is at least one social networking site for every interest or hobby. Yub.com is for shopaholics; Fuzzster.com is for pet lovers; OnLoq.com is for hip-hop fans; Jango.com lets music fans find others with similar tastes; and PassportStamp.com is one of several sites

Using online social networks: Following the success of large social networking sites, thousands of niche sites have popped up that cater to more selective online communities. MakeItSeven.ca connects a community of Canadian NHL fans who want a seventh NHL team in Canada.

for avid travelers. Some sites cater to the obscure. Passions Network, with 600 000 members, has 106 groups for special interests, including "Star Trek" fans, truckers, atheists, and people who are shy. The most popular group is a dating site for the overweight. Membership on niche networking sites varies greatly, ranging from a few hundred to a few million. MakeItSeven.ca is a website for Canadian hockey fans wanting to bring another NHL team to Canada and attracted over 5000 members in its first day of operations! Flixster.com has 40 million members who rate movies and gossip about actors.[23]

These more selective sites often provide richer, more targeted marketing opportunities for brands. "The bigger sites have become so cluttered and overrun with advertisers that members are used to tuning stuff out, even personalized ads," says an analyst. "But on networking sites that have a self-selecting demographic, people tend to trust the content, including ads."[24]

But marketers must be careful when tapping into online social networks. Results are difficult to measure and control. Ultimately, the users control the content, so online network marketing attempts can easily backfire. For example, when Chevrolet launched a web contest inviting folks to create their own ads for its Chevy Tahoe, it quickly lost control. Says one observer, "the entries that got passed around, blogged about, and eventually covered in the mainstream media were all about the SUV's abysmal gas mileage and melting polar ice caps." One user-generated ad proclaimed, "Like this snowy wilderness? Better get your fill of it now. Then say hello to global warming." Another concluded, "$70 to fill up the tank, which will last less than 400 miles. Chevy Tahoe."[25] We will dig deeper into online social networks as a marketing tool in Chapter 17.

Family

Family members can strongly influence buyer behaviour. The family is the most important consumer buying organization in society, and it has been researched extensively. Marketers are interested in the roles and influence of the husband, wife, and children on the purchase of different products and services.

Husband–wife involvement varies widely by product category and by stage in the buying process. Buying roles change with evolving consumer lifestyles. In Canada and the United States, the wife traditionally has been the main purchasing agent for the family in the areas of food, household products, and clothing. But with 70 percent of women holding jobs outside the home and the willingness of husbands to do more of the family's purchasing, all this is changing. Men now account for about 40 percent of all food-shopping dollars. Women influence 65 percent of all new car purchases, 91 percent of new home purchases, and 92 percent of vacation purchases. In all, women now make almost 85 percent of all family purchases.[26]

Such changes suggest that marketers in industries that have sold their products only to men or only to women are now courting the opposite sex. For example, after realizing that women today account for 50 percent of all technology purchases, Dell has stepped up its efforts to woo female buyers. It now advertises regularly in female-focused magazines such as *O, The Oprah Magazine, Ladies' Home Journal, Real Simple,* and *CosmoGirl* and on woman-centric cable-TV channels such as Oxygen and Lifetime.

Children may also have a strong influence on family buying decisions. Research indicates that Canadian kids influence some $20 million in household spending each year and have memorized between 300 and 400 brand names by the age of 10.[27] One recent study found that kids significantly influence family decisions about where they take vacations and what cars and cellphones they buy. As a result, marketers of cars, full-service restaurants, cellphones, and travel destinations are now placing ads on networks such as YTV and Teletoon.

As part of its efforts to target families, Chrysler recently signed promotional sponsorship and advertising deals with Nickelodeon for its Town & Country minivans. It signed on as a sponsor for Nickelodeon's Slime Across America summer tour and runs ads in Nick's printed publications, websites, and TV programs. Nick's boy-genius inventor Jimmy Neutron has appeared prominently in the Chrysler Town & Country advertising.[28]

Roles and Status

A person belongs to many groups—family, clubs, organizations. The person's position in each group can be defined in terms of both role and status. A role consists of the activities people are expected to perform according to those around them. Each role carries a status reflecting the general esteem given to it by society.

People usually choose products appropriate to their roles and status. Consider the various roles a working mother plays. In her company, she plays the role of a brand manager; in her family, she plays the role of wife and mother; at her favourite sporting events, she plays the role of avid fan. As a brand manager, she will buy the kind of clothing that reflects her role and status in her company.

Personal Factors

A buyer's decisions also are influenced by personal characteristics such as the buyer's *age and life-cycle stage*, *occupation*, *economic situation*, *lifestyle*, and *personality and self-concept*.

Age and Life-Cycle Stage

People change the goods and services they buy over their lifetimes. Tastes in food, clothes, furniture, and recreation are often age related. Buying is also shaped by the stage of the family life cycle—the stages through which families might pass as they mature over time. Marketers often define their target markets in terms of life-cycle stage and develop appropriate products and marketing plans for each stage.

Traditional family life-cycle stages include young singles and married couples with children. Today, however, marketers are increasingly catering to a growing number of alternative, nontraditional stages such as unmarried couples, singles marrying later in life, childless couples, same-sex couples, single parents, extended parents (those with adult children returning home), and others.

RBC has identified five life-stage segments. The *Youth* segment includes customers younger than 18. *Getting Started* consists of customers aged 18 to 35 who are going through first experiences, such as their graduation, first credit card, first car, first loan, marriage, and first child. *Builders*, customers aged 35 to 50, are in their peak earning years. As they build careers and family, they tend to borrow more than they invest. *Accumulators*, aged 50 to 60, worry about saving for retirement and investing wisely. Finally, *Preservers*, customers over 60, want to maximize their retirement income to maintain a desired lifestyle. RBC markets different services to the different segments. For example, with *Builders*, who face many expenses, it emphasizes loans and debt-load management services.[29]

Family buying: Family buying roles are changing. For example, men now account for about 40 percent of all food-shopping dollars, while women influence 50 percent of all new technology purchases.

Occupation

A person's occupation affects the goods and services bought. Blue-collar workers tend to buy more rugged work clothes, whereas executives buy more business suits. Marketers try to identify the occupational groups that have an above-average interest in their products and services. A company can even specialize in making products needed by a given occupational group.

Long known for its rugged workwear, Mark's Work Wearhouse faced the challenge of changing its image in the marketplace:

> Michael Strachan is the first marketing VP in Calgary-based Mark's Work Wearhouse's 28-year history (the firm owns L'Équipeur stores in Quebec). The retail chain is now owned by Canadian Tire. The chain is on a growth spurt, expanding from 320 stores across Canada to more than 400. His aim is to turn the store into a "Canadian super brand." To accomplish this aim, he must reinvent its brand image in the minds of Canadian consumers so it can compete more successfully against powerhouse competitors such as Wal-Mart and Costco. Strachan, a firm believer in extensive consumer research, began the journey with qualitative research that included customer exit interviews. Members of his marketing team also "physically went out and sat in the closets of a number of Canadians to try and understand how they thought about clothes and what they wanted in clothes." Next, more than 1000 English- and French-speaking Canadians between 30 and 55 were invited to attend focus groups in Vancouver, Edmonton, Toronto, Calgary, Montreal, and Quebec City. Though 95 percent of those interviewed were aware of the Mark's Work Wearhouse name, 66 percent thought of Mark's as primarily a blue-collar, workwear store. Although workwear continues to make up a healthy 25 percent of sales, Mark's now carries a much larger selection of items and is focused on men's and women's casual clothing. Thus, Strachan's job was to convince consumers "that we aren't about blue-collar clothes, but about clothes that work." This has become its major brand proposition and a company mantra "that's on every single thing from the smallest indoor sign to the biggest billboard."[30]

Lifestyle
A person's pattern of living as expressed in his or her activities, interests, and opinions.

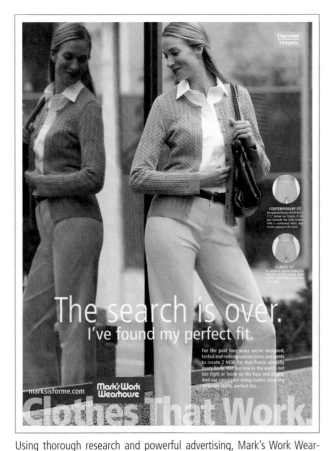

Using thorough research and powerful advertising, Mark's Work Wearhouse has transformed itself into a Canadian superbrand using the slogan "clothes that work."

Economic Situation

A person's economic situation will affect product choice. Marketers of income-sensitive goods watch trends in personal income, savings, and interest rates. If economic indicators point to a recession, marketers can take steps to redesign, reposition, and reprice their products closely. Some marketers target consumers who have lots of money and resources, charging prices to match. For example, Rolex positions its luxury watches as "a tribute to elegance, an object of passion, a symbol for all time." Other marketers target consumers with more modest means. Timex makes more affordable watches that "take a licking and keep on ticking."

Lifestyle

People coming from the same subculture, social class, and occupation may have quite different lifestyles. **Lifestyle** is a person's pattern of living as expressed in his or her *psychographics*. It involves measuring consumers' major AIO dimensions—activities (work, hobbies, shopping, sports, social events), interests (food, fashion, family, recreation), and opinions (about themselves, social issues, business, products). Lifestyle captures something more than the person's social class or personality. It profiles a person's whole pattern of acting and interacting in the world.

Lifestyle: Consumers don't just buy products, they buy the values and lifestyles those products represent. BMW doesn't just sell convertibles, it sells the convertible lifestyle.

When used carefully, the lifestyle concept can help marketers understand changing consumer values and how they affect buying behaviour. Consumers don't just buy products, they buy the values and lifestyles those products represent. For example, BMW doesn't just sell convertibles, it sells the convertible lifestyle: "Skies never bluer. Knuckles never whiter." Says one marketer, "People's product choices are becoming more and more like value choices. It's not, 'I like this water, the way it tastes.' It's 'I feel like this car, or this show is more reflective of who I am.'"

For example, Pottery Barn, with locations in Toronto, Calgary, and Vancouver, sells more than just home furnishings. It sells a lifestyle to which its customers aspire. Pottery Barn Kids offers idyllic scenes of the perfect childhood, whereas PB Teens offer a trendy fashion-forward self-expression. The flagship Pottery Barn stores serve an upscale yet casual, family- and friend-focused lifestyle—affluent but sensibly so:

> Shortly after Hadley MacLean got married, she and her husband, Doug, agreed that their old bed had to go. It was a mattress and box spring on a cheap metal frame, a relic of Doug's Harvard days. But Hadley never anticipated how tough it would be to find a new bed. "We couldn't find anything we liked, even though we were willing to spend the money," says Hadley, a 31-year-old marketing director. It turned out to be much more than just finding a piece of furniture at the right price. It was a matter of emotion: They needed a bed that meshed with their lifestyle—with who they are and where they are going. The couple finally ended up at a Pottery Barn, where Doug fell in love with a mahogany sleigh bed that Hadley had spotted in the store's catalogue. The couple was so pleased with how great it looked in their Dutch Colonial home that they hurried back to the store for a set of end tables. And then they bought a quilt. And a mirror for the living room. And some stools for the dining room. "We got kind of addicted," Hadley confesses.[31]

Personality and Self-Concept

Personality
The unique psychological characteristics that lead to relatively consistent and lasting responses to one's own environment.

Each person's distinct personality influences his or her buying behaviour. **Personality** refers to the unique psychological characteristics that lead to relatively consistent and lasting responses to one's own environment. Personality is usually described in terms of traits such as self-confidence, dominance, sociability, autonomy, defensiveness, adaptability, and aggressiveness. Personality can be useful in analyzing consumer behaviour for certain product or brand choices.

Brand personality
The specific mix of human traits that may be attributed to a particular brand.

The idea is that brands also have personalities, and that consumers are likely to choose brands with personalities that match their own. A **brand personality** is the specific mix of human traits that may be attributed to a particular brand. One researcher identified five brand personality traits:[32]

1. Sincerity (down-to-earth, honest, wholesome, and cheerful)
2. Excitement (daring, spirited, imaginative, and up-to-date)
3. Competence (reliable, intelligent, and successful)
4. Sophistication (upper class and charming)
5. Ruggedness (outdoorsy and tough)

Most well-known brands are strongly associated with one particular trait: Jeep with "ruggedness," Apple with "excitement," CNN with "competence," and Dove with "sincerity." Hence, these brands will attract people who are high on the same personality traits.

Many marketers use a concept related to personality—a person's *self-concept* (also called *self-image*). The basic self-concept premise is that people's possessions contribute to and reflect their identities—that is, "we are what we have." Thus, to understand consumer behaviour, the marketer must first understand the relationship between consumer self-concept and possessions.

Apple applies these concepts in a recent series of ads that characterize two people as computers—one guy plays the part of an Apple Mac and the other plays a PC. The two have very different personalities and self-concepts. "Hello, I'm a Mac," says the guy on the right, who's younger and dressed in jeans. "And I'm a PC," says the one on the left, who's wearing dweeby glasses and a jacket and tie. The two men discuss the relative advantages of Macs versus PCs, with the Mac coming out on top. The ads present the Mac brand personality as young, laid back, and hip. The PC is portrayed as buttoned down, corporate, and a bit dorky. The message? If you see yourself as young and with-it, you need a Mac.[33]

Psychological Factors

A person's buying choices are further influenced by four major psychological factors: *motivation*, *perception*, *learning*, and *beliefs and attitudes*.

Motivation

A person has many needs at any given time. Some are biological, arising from states of tension such as hunger, thirst, or discomfort. Others are psychological, arising from the need for recognition, esteem, or belonging. A need becomes a motive when it is aroused to a sufficient level of intensity. A **motive (or drive)** is a need that is sufficiently pressing to direct the person to seek satisfaction. Psychologists have developed theories of human motivation. Two of the most popular—the theories of Sigmund Freud and Abraham Maslow—have quite different meanings for consumer analysis and marketing.

Motive (drive)
A need that is sufficiently pressing to direct the person to seek satisfaction of the need.

Sigmund Freud assumed that people are largely unconscious about the real psychological forces shaping their behaviour. He saw the person as growing up and repressing many urges. These urges are never eliminated or under perfect control; they emerge in dreams, in slips of the tongue, in neurotic and obsessive behaviour, or ultimately in psychoses.

Freud's theory suggests that a person's buying decisions are affected by subconscious motives that even the buyer may not fully understand. Thus, an aging baby boomer who buys a sporty BMW 330Ci convertible might explain that he simply likes the feel of the wind in his thinning hair. At a deeper level, he may be trying to impress others with his success. At a still deeper level, he may be buying the car to feel young and independent again.

The term *motivation research* refers to qualitative research designed to probe consumers' hidden, subconscious motivations. Consumers often don't know or can't describe just why they act as they do. Thus, motivation researchers use a variety of probing techniques to uncover underlying emotions and attitudes toward brands and buying situations.

Many companies employ teams of psychologists, anthropologists, and other social scientists to carry out motivation research. One ad agency routinely conducts one-on-one, therapy-like interviews to delve into the inner workings of consumers. Another company asks consumers to describe their favourite brands as animals or cars (say, Cadillacs versus Chevrolets) to assess the prestige associated with various brands. Still others rely on hypnosis, dream therapy, or soft lights and mood music to plumb the murky depths of consumer psyches.

Such projective techniques seem pretty goofy, and some marketers dismiss such motivation research as mumbo jumbo. But many marketers use such touchy-feely approaches, now sometimes called *interpretive consumer research*, to dig deeper into consumer psyches and develop better marketing strategies.[34]

Abraham Maslow sought to explain why people are driven by particular needs at particular times. Why does one

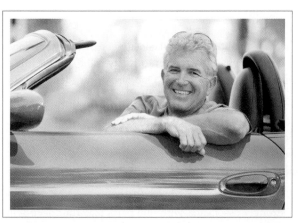

Motivation: An aging baby boomer who buys a sporty convertible might explain that he or she simply likes the feel of the wind in his or her thinning hair. At a deeper level, the person may be buying the car to feel young and independent again.

person spend a lot of time and energy on personal safety and another on gaining the esteem of others? Maslow's answer is that human needs are arranged in a hierarchy, as shown in Figure 6.3, from the most pressing at the bottom to the least pressing at the top.[35] They include *physiological* needs, *safety* needs, *social* needs, *esteem* needs, and *self-actualization* needs.

A person tries to satisfy the most important need first. When that need is satisfied, it will stop being a motivator and the person will then try to satisfy the next most important need. For example, starving people (physiological need) will not take an interest in the latest happenings in the art world (self-actualization need), nor in how they are seen or esteemed by others (social or esteem need), nor even in whether they are breathing clean air (safety need). But as each important need is satisfied, the next most important need will come into play.

Perception

Perception
The process by which people select, organize, and interpret information to form a meaningful picture of the world.

A motivated person is ready to act. How the person acts is influenced by his or her own perception of the situation. All of us learn by the flow of information through our five senses: sight, hearing, smell, touch, and taste. However, each of us receives, organizes, and interprets this sensory information in an individual way. **Perception** is the process by which people select, organize, and interpret information to form a meaningful picture of the world.

People can form different perceptions of the same stimulus because of three perceptual processes: selective attention, selective distortion, and selective retention. People are exposed to a great number of stimuli every day. For example, people are exposed to an estimated 3000 to 5000 ad messages every day.[36] It is impossible for a person to pay attention to all these stimuli. *Selective attention*—the tendency for people to screen out most of the information to which they are exposed—means that marketers must work especially hard to attract the consumer's attention.

Even noticed stimuli do not always come across in the intended way. Each person fits incoming information into an existing mindset. *Selective distortion* describes the tendency of people to interpret information in a way that will support what they already believe. For example, if you distrust a company, you might perceive even honest ads from the company as questionable. Selective distortion means that marketers must try to understand the mindsets of consumers and how these will affect interpretations of advertising and sales information.

People will also forget much of what they learn. They tend to retain information that supports their attitudes and beliefs. Because of *selective retention*, consumers are likely to

Figure 6.3 Maslow's hierarchy of needs

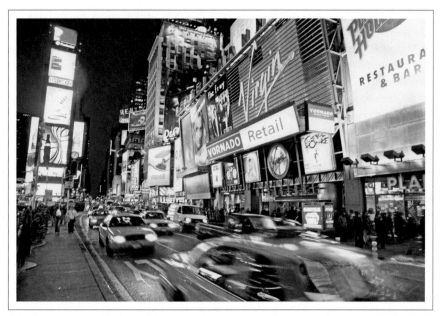

Selective perception: It's impossible for people to pay attention to the thousands of ads they're exposed to every day, so they screen most of them out.

remember good points made about a brand they favour and to forget good points made about competing brands. Because of selective attention, distortion, and retention, marketers must work hard to get their messages through. This fact explains why marketers use so much drama and repetition in sending messages to their market.

Interestingly, although most marketers worry about whether their offers will be perceived at all, some consumers worry that they will be affected by marketing messages without even knowing it—through *subliminal advertising*. In 1957, a researcher announced that he had flashed the phrases "Eat popcorn" and "Drink Coca-Cola" on a screen in a New Jersey movie theatre every five seconds for 1/300th of a second. He reported that although viewers did not consciously recognize these messages, they absorbed them subconsciously and bought 58 percent more popcorn and 18 percent more Coke. Suddenly, advertisers and consumer-protection groups became intensely interested in subliminal perception. People voiced fears of being brainwashed, and California and Canada declared the practice illegal. Although the researcher later admitted to making up the data, the issue has not died. Some consumers still fear that they are being manipulated by subliminal messages.

Numerous studies by psychologists and consumer researchers have found little or no link between subliminal messages and consumer behaviour. Recent brainwave studies have found that in certain circumstances our brains may register subliminal messages. However, it appears that subliminal advertising simply doesn't have the power attributed to it by its critics. Most advertisers scoff at the notion of an industry conspiracy to manipulate consumers through "invisible" messages. Says one industry insider, "[Some consumers believe we are] wizards who can manipulate them at will. Ha! Snort! Oh my sides! As we know, just between us, most of [us] have difficulty getting a 2 percent increase in sales with the help of $50 million in media and extremely *liminal* images of sex, money, power, and other [motivators] of human emotion. The very idea of [us] as puppeteers, cruelly pulling the strings of consumer marionettes, is almost too much to bear."[37]

Learning

Learning
Changes in an individual's behaviour arising from experience.

When people act, they learn. **Learning** describes changes in an individual's behaviour arising from experience. Learning theorists say that most human behaviour is learned. Learning occurs through the interplay of *drives*, *stimuli*, *cues*, *responses*, and *reinforcement*.

A *drive* is a strong internal stimulus that calls for action. A drive becomes a motive when it is directed toward a particular *stimulus object*. For example, a person's drive for self-actualization might motivate him or her to look into buying a camera. The consumer's response to the idea of buying a camera is conditioned by the surrounding cues. *Cues* are minor stimuli that determine when, where, and how the person responds. For example, the person might spot several camera brands in a shop window, hear of a special sale price, or discuss cameras with a friend. These are all cues that might influence a consumer's *response* to his or her interest in buying the product.

Suppose the consumer buys a Nikon camera. If the experience is rewarding, the consumer will probably use the camera more and more, and his or her response will be *reinforced*.

FUZE fits well with people's attitudes about health and well-being. Its "healthy infusion" beverages promise drinks that are "good-tasting but also good for you."

Belief
A descriptive thought that a person holds about something.

Attitude
A person's consistently favourable or unfavourable evaluations, feelings, and tendencies toward an object or idea.

Then, the next time the consumer shops for a camera, or for binoculars or some similar product, the probability is greater that he or she will buy a Nikon product. The practical significance of learning theory for marketers is that they can build up demand for a product by associating it with strong drives, using motivating cues, and providing positive reinforcement.

Beliefs and Attitudes

Through doing and learning, people acquire beliefs and attitudes. These, in turn, influence their buying behaviour. A **belief** is a descriptive thought that a person has about something. Beliefs may be based on real knowledge, opinion, or faith and may or may not carry an emotional charge. Marketers are interested in the beliefs that people formulate about specific products and services because these beliefs make up product and brand images that affect buying behaviour. If some of the beliefs are wrong and prevent purchase, the marketer will want to launch a campaign to correct them.

People have attitudes regarding religion, politics, clothes, music, food, and almost everything else. **Attitude** describes a person's relatively consistent evaluations, feelings, and tendencies toward an object or idea. Attitudes put people into a frame of mind of liking or disliking things, of moving toward or away from them. Our camera buyer may hold attitudes such as "Buy the best," "The Japanese make the best electronics products in the world," and "Creativity and self-expression are among the most important things in life." If so, the Nikon camera would fit well into the consumer's existing attitudes.

Attitudes are difficult to change. A person's attitudes fit into a pattern, and to change one attitude may require difficult adjustments in many others. Thus, a company should usually try to fit its products into existing attitudes rather than attempt to change attitudes.

For example, today's beverage marketers now cater to people's new attitudes about health and well-being with drinks that do a lot more than just taste good or quench your thirst. Coca-Cola's FUZE brand, for example, offers a line of "healthy infusion" beverages packed with vitamins, minerals, and antioxidants but without artificial preservatives, sweeteners, or colours. FUZE promises drinks that are good-tasting (with flavours like Blueberry Raspberry, Strawberry Melon, and Dragonfruit Lime) but also good for you—containing only natural ingredients that "help your metabolism work in your favour." By matching today's attitudes about life and healthful living, the FUZE brand has become a leader in the New Age beverage category. Its sales last year grew by more than 50 percent.

We can now appreciate the many forces acting on consumer behaviour. The consumer's choice results from the complex interplay of cultural, social, personal, and psychological factors.

3   TYPES OF BUYING DECISION BEHAVIOUR

Buying behaviour differs greatly for a tube of toothpaste, an iPod, financial services, or a new car. More complex decisions usually involve more buying participants and more buyer deliberation. Figure 6.4 shows types of consumer buying behaviour based on the degree of buyer involvement and the degree of differences among brands.

Complex buying behaviour
Consumer buying behaviour in situations characterized by high consumer involvement in a purchase and significant perceived differences among brands.

Complex Buying Behaviour

Consumers undertake **complex buying behaviour** when they are highly involved in a purchase and perceive significant differences among brands. Consumers may be highly involved when the product is expensive, risky, purchased infrequently, or highly self-

Figure 6.4 Four types of buying behaviour

Source: Adapted from Henry Assael, *Consumer Behaviour and Marketing Action* (Boston: Kent Publishing Company, 1987), p. 87. Copyright © 1987 by Wadsworth, Inc. Printed by permission of Kent Publishing Company, a division of Wadsworth, Inc.

	High involvement	Low involvement
Significant differences between brands	Complex buying behaviour	Variety-seeking buying behaviour
Few differences between brands	Dissonance-reducing buying behaviour	Habitual buying behaviour

expressive. Typically, the consumer has much to learn about the product category. For example, a PC buyer may not know what attributes to consider, because many product features carry no real meaning: take, for example, a "3.4 GHz Pentium processor," "WUXGA active matrix screen," or "4 GB dual-channel DDR2 DRAM memory."

This buyer will pass through a learning process, developing first beliefs about the product, then attitudes, and then making a thoughtful purchase choice. Marketers of high-involvement products must understand the information-gathering and evaluation behaviour of high-involvement consumers. They need to help buyers learn about product-class attributes and their relative importance. They need to differentiate their brand's features, perhaps by describing the brand's benefits using print media with long copy. They must motivate store salespeople and the buyer's acquaintances to influence the final brand choice.

Dissonance-Reducing Buying Behaviour

Dissonance-reducing buying behaviour
Consumer buying behaviour in situations characterized by high involvement but few perceived differences among brands.

Dissonance-reducing buying behaviour occurs when consumers are highly involved with an expensive, infrequent, or risky purchase, but see little difference among brands. For example, consumers buying carpeting may face a high-involvement decision because carpeting is expensive and self-expressive. Yet buyers may consider most carpet brands in a given price range to be the same. In this case, because perceived brand differences are not large, buyers may shop around to learn what is available but buy relatively quickly. They may respond primarily to a good price or to purchase convenience.

After the purchase, consumers might experience *postpurchase dissonance* (after-sale discomfort) when they notice certain disadvantages of the purchased carpet brand or hear favourable things about brands not purchased. To counter such dissonance, the marketer's after-sale communications should provide evidence and support to help consumers feel good about their brand choices.

Habitual Buying Behaviour

Habitual buying behaviour
Consumer buying behaviour in situations characterized by low consumer involvement and few significantly perceived brand differences.

Habitual buying behaviour occurs under conditions of low consumer involvement and little significant brand difference. Take salt, for example. Consumers have little involvement in this product category—they simply go to the store and reach for a brand. If they keep reaching for the same brand, it is out of habit rather than strong brand loyalty. Consumers appear to have low involvement with most low-cost, frequently purchased products.

In such cases, consumer behaviour does not pass through the usual belief-attitude-behaviour sequence. Consumers do not search extensively for information about the brands, evaluate brand characteristics, and make weighty decisions about which brands to buy. Instead, they passively receive information as they watch television or read magazines. Ad repetition creates *brand familiarity* rather than *brand conviction*. Consumers do not form strong attitudes toward a brand; they select the brand because it is familiar. Because they are not highly involved with the product, consumers may not evaluate the choice even after purchase. Thus, the buying process involves brand beliefs formed by passive learning, followed by purchase behaviour, which may or may not be followed by evaluation.

Because buyers are not highly committed to any brands, marketers of low-involvement products with few brand differences often use price and sales promotions to stimulate product trial. In advertising for a low-involvement product, ad copy should stress only a few key points. Visual symbols and imagery are important because they can be remembered easily and associated with the brand. Ad campaigns should include high repetition of short-duration messages. Television is usually more effective than print media because it is a low-involvement medium suitable for passive learning. Advertising planning should be based on classical conditioning theory, in which buyers learn to identify a certain product by a symbol repeatedly attached to it.

Variety-Seeking Buying Behaviour

Variety-seeking buying behaviour
Consumer buying behaviour in situations characterized by low consumer involvement but significant perceived brand differences.

Consumers undertake **variety-seeking buying behaviour** in situations characterized by low consumer involvement but significant perceived brand differences. In such cases, consumers often do a lot of brand switching. For example, when buying cookies a consumer may hold some beliefs, choose a cookie brand without much evaluation, and then evaluate that brand during consumption. But the next time, the consumer might pick another brand out of boredom or simply to try something different. Brand switching occurs for the sake of variety rather than because of dissatisfaction.

In such product categories, the marketing strategy may differ for the market leader and minor brands. The market leader will try to encourage habitual buying behaviour by dominating shelf space, keeping shelves fully stocked, and running frequent reminder advertising. Challenger firms will encourage variety seeking by offering lower prices, special deals, coupons, free samples, and advertising that presents reasons for trying something new.

THE BUYER DECISION PROCESS

Now that we have looked at the influences that affect buyers, we are ready to look at how consumers make buying decisions. Figure 6.5 shows that the buyer decision process consists of five stages: *need recognition, information search, evaluation of alternatives, purchase decision,* and *postpurchase behaviour.* Clearly, the buying process starts long before the actual purchase and continues long after. Marketers need to focus on the entire buying process rather than on just the purchase decision.

The figure suggests that consumers pass through all five stages with every purchase. But in more routine purchases, consumers often skip or reverse some of these stages. A woman buying her regular brand of toothpaste would recognize the need and go right to the purchase decision, skipping information search and evaluation. However, we use the model in Figure 6.5 because it shows all the considerations that arise when a consumer faces a new and complex purchase situation.

Need Recognition

Need recognition
The first stage of the buyer decision process, in which the consumer recognizes a problem or need.

The buying process starts with **need recognition**—the buyer recognizes a problem or need. The need can be triggered by *internal stimuli* when one of the person's normal needs—hunger, thirst, sex—rises to a level high enough to become a drive. A need can also be triggered by *external stimuli.* For example, an advertisement or a discussion with a friend might get you thinking about buying a new car. At this stage, the marketer should research consumers to find out what kinds of needs or problems arise, what brought them about, and how they led the consumer to this particular product.

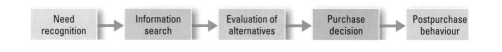

Figure 6.5 Buyer decision process

Information Search

Information search
The stage of the buyer decision process in which the consumer is aroused to search for more information; the consumer may simply have heightened attention or may go into an active information search.

An interested consumer may or may not search for more information. If the consumer's drive is strong and a satisfying product is near at hand, the consumer is likely to buy it then. If not, the consumer may store the need in memory or undertake an **information search** related to the need. For example, once you've decided you need a new car, at the least you will probably pay more attention to car ads, cars owned by friends, and car conversations. Or you may actively search the Web, talk with friends, and gather information in other ways. The amount of searching you do will depend on the strength of your drive, the amount of information you start with, the ease of obtaining more information, the value you place on additional information, and the satisfaction you get from searching.

Consumers can obtain information from any of several sources. These include *personal sources* (family, friends, neighbours, acquaintances), *commercial sources* (advertising, salespeople, dealer websites, packaging, displays), *public sources* (mass media, consumer rating organizations, Internet searches), and *experiential sources* (handling, examining, using the product). The relative influence of these information sources varies with the product and the buyer.

Generally, the consumer receives the most information about a product from commercial sources—those controlled by the marketer. The most effective sources, however, tend to be personal. Commercial sources normally *inform* the buyer, but personal sources *legitimize* or *evaluate* products for the buyer. A recent Nielsen survey found that 78 percent of consumers found recommendations from others to be the most credible form of endorsement. As one marketer states, "It's rare that an advertising campaign can be as effective as a neighbour leaning over the fence and saying, 'This is a wonderful product.'" Increasingly, that "fence" is a virtual one, as more and more customers pour through the online ratings and reviews of other buyers on sites like Amazon.ca before making a purchase.[38]

Alternative evaluation
The stage of the buyer decision process in which the consumer uses information to evaluate alternative brands in the choice set.

As more information is obtained, the consumer's awareness and knowledge of the available brands and features increase. In your car information search, you may learn about the several brands available. The information might also help you to drop certain brands from consideration. A company must design its marketing mix to make prospects aware of and knowledgeable about its brand. It should carefully identify consumers' sources of information and the importance of each source.

Evaluation of Alternatives

We have seen how the consumer uses information to arrive at a set of final brand choices. But how does the consumer choose among the alternative brands? The marketer needs to know about **alternative evaluation**—that is, how the consumer processes information to arrive at brand choices. Unfortunately, consumers do not use a simple and single evaluation process in all buying situations. Instead, several evaluation processes are at work.

The consumer arrives at attitudes toward different brands through some evaluation procedure. How consumers go about evaluating purchase alternatives depends on the individual consumer and the specific buying situation. In some cases, consumers use careful calculations and logical thinking. At other times, the same consumers do little or no evaluating;

Need recognition can be triggered by advertising. This innovative ad from Clorox reminds parents that "This is how babies see the world. Keep it clean."

instead they buy on impulse and rely on intuition. Sometimes consumers make buying decisions on their own; sometimes they turn to friends, consumer guides, or salespeople for buying advice.

Suppose you're buying a new car and you've narrowed your choices down to three brands. And suppose that you are primarily interested in four attributes—styling, operating economy, warranty, and price. By this time, you've probably formed beliefs about how each brand rates on each attribute. Clearly, if one car rated best on all the attributes, we could predict that you would choose it. However, the brands will no doubt vary in appeal. You might base your buying decision on only one attribute, and your choice would be easy to predict. If you wanted styling above everything else, you would buy the car that you think has the best styling. But most buyers consider several attributes, each with different importance. If we knew the importance that you assigned to each of the four attributes, we could predict your car choice more reliably.

Marketers should study buyers to find out how they actually evaluate brand alternatives. If they know what evaluative processes go on, marketers can take steps to influence the buyer's decision.

Purchase Decision

Purchase decision
The buyer's decision about which brand to purchase.

In the evaluation stage, the consumer ranks brands and forms purchase intentions. Generally, the consumer's **purchase decision** will be to buy the most preferred brand, but two factors can come between the purchase *intention* and the purchase *decision*. The first factor is the *attitudes of others*. If someone important to you thinks that you should buy the lowest-priced car, then the chances of you buying a more expensive car are reduced.

The second factor is *unexpected situational factors*. The consumer may form a purchase intention based on factors such as expected income, expected price, and expected product benefits. However, unexpected events may change the purchase intention. For example, the economy might take a turn for the worse, a close competitor might drop its price, or a friend might report being disappointed in your preferred car. Thus, preferences and even purchase intentions do not always result in actual purchase choice.

Postpurchase Behaviour

Postpurchase behaviour
The stage of the buyer decision process in which consumers take further action after purchase based on their satisfaction or dissatisfaction.

The marketer's job does not end when the product is bought. After purchasing the product, the consumer will be satisfied or dissatisfied and will engage in **postpurchase behaviour** of interest to the marketer. What determines whether the buyer is satisfied or dissatisfied with a purchase? The answer lies in the relationship between the *consumer's expectations* and the product's *perceived performance*. If the product falls short of expectations, the consumer is disappointed; if it meets expectations, the consumer is satisfied; if it exceeds expectations, the consumer is delighted. The larger the gap between expectations and performance, the greater the consumer's dissatisfaction. This suggests that sellers should promise only what their brands can deliver so that buyers are satisfied.

Cognitive dissonance
Buyer discomfort caused by postpurchase conflict.

Almost all major purchases, however, result in **cognitive dissonance**, or discomfort caused by postpurchase conflict. After the purchase, consumers are satisfied with the benefits of the chosen brand and are glad to avoid the drawbacks of the brands not bought. However, every purchase involves compromise. So consumers feel uneasy about acquiring the drawbacks of the chosen brand and about losing the benefits of the brands not purchased. Thus, consumers feel at least some postpurchase dissonance for every purchase.[39]

Why is it so important to satisfy the customer? Customer satisfaction is a key to building profitable relationships with consumers—to keeping and growing consumers and reaping their customer lifetime value. Satisfied customers buy a product again, talk favourably to others about the product, pay less attention to competing brands and advertising, and buy other products from the company. Many marketers go beyond merely *meeting* the expectations of customers—they aim to *delight* the customer (see Real Marketing 6.2).

Real Marketing **6.2**

Lexus: Delighting Customers After the Sale to Keep Them Coming Back

Close your eyes for a minute and picture a typical car dealership. Not impressed? Talk to a friend who owns a Lexus, and you'll no doubt get a very different picture. The typical Lexus dealership is . . . well, anything but typical. And some Lexus dealers will go to almost any extreme to take care of customers and keep them coming back.

For many people, a trip to the auto dealer means a mind-numbing hour or two in a plastic chair with some tattered magazines and stale coffee. But at Lexus dealerships across North America, this is not the case. Lexus customers waiting for their cars to be serviced may lounge on over-stuffed sofas, watch big-

THE LEXUS COVENANT

Lexus will enter the most competitive, prestigious automobile race in the world. Over 50 years of Toyota automotive experience has culminated in the creation of Lexus cars. They will be the finest cars ever built.

Lexus will win the race because Lexus will do it right from the start. Lexus will have the finest dealer network in the industry.

Lexus will treat each customer as we would a guest in our home.

If you think you can't, you won't... If you think you can, you will! We can, we will.

Lexus has revolutionized the luxury motoring experience through its passionate commitment to the finest products and the most satisfying automobile ownership experience. We vow to value the customer as an important individual; to do things right the first time; and to always exceed expectations. We brought together these principles in the Lexus Covenant, which inspires our dealers and associates to treat customers as they would treat guests and to go to any lengths to serve them better.

The Lexus Covenant is the basis for every decision we make, from cars that are designed with the driver in mind to dealers that make customer satisfaction their most important goal. This commitment to excellence not only makes a Lexus more enjoyable to drive, but also a joy to own.

To delight customers and keep them coming back, the Lexus Covenant promises that its dealers will "treat each customer as we would a guest in our home" and "go to any lengths to serve them better."

screen TVs, surf the Internet, or sip lattes in the beverage areas. One dealership features four massage chairs, in addition to its Starbucks coffee shop, two putting greens, two customer lounges, plus a library. At another gleaming glass-and-stone Lexus dealership, "guests," as Lexus calls its customers, leave their cars with a valet and are then guided by a concierge to a European-style coffee bar offering complimentary espresso, cappuccino, and a selection of pastries prepared by a chef trained in Rome. "We have customers checking into world-class hotels," says a dealership executive. "They shop on Fifth Avenue and they expect a certain kind of experience."

Lexus knows that good marketing doesn't stop with making the sale. Keeping customers happy after the sale is the key to building lasting relationships. Dealers across North America have a common goal: to delight customers and keep them coming back. Lexus believes that if you "delight the customer, and continue to delight the customer, you will have a customer for life." And Lexus understands just how valuable a customer can be—it estimates that the average lifetime value of a Lexus customer is US$600 000.

Despite the amenities, few Lexus customers spend much time hanging around the dealership. Lexus knows that the best dealership visit is the one that you don't have to

make at all. So it builds customer-pleasing cars to start with—high-quality cars that need little servicing. In its "Lexus Covenant," the company vows that it will make "the finest cars ever built." In survey after industry survey, Lexus rates at or near the top in quality. Lexus has topped the list in five of the last seven annual J.D. Power and Associates Initial Quality Study ratings.

Still, when a car does need to be serviced, Lexus goes out of its way to make it easy and painless. Most dealers will even pick up the car and then return it when the maintenance is finished. And the car comes back spotless, thanks to a complimentary cleaning to remove bugs and road grime from the exterior and smudges from the leather interior. You might even be surprised to find that they've touched up a door ding to help restore the car to its fresh-from-the-factory lustre. "My wife will never buy another car except a Lexus," says one satisfied Lexus owner. "They come to our house, pick up the car, do an oil change, [spiff it up,] and bring it back. She's sold for life."

And when a customer does bring a car in, Lexus repairs it right the first time, on time. Dealers know that their well-heeled customers have money, "but what they don't have is time." So dealers are testing a system that uses three technicians instead of one for 50 000 km service checkups. The new system will cut a customer's wait in half. "I'm not in the car business," says one dealer. "I'm in the service business."

According to its website, from the very start Lexus set out to "revolutionize the automotive experience with a passionate commitment to the finest products supported by dealers who create the most satisfying ownership experience the world has ever seen. We vow to value the customer as an important individual. To do things right the first time. And to always exceed expectations." Jordan Case of Park Place Lexus fully embraces this philosophy: "You've got to do it right, on time, and make people feel like they are the only one in the room." Proclaims the Lexus Covenant, "Lexus will treat each customer as we would a guest in our own home."

At Lexus, exceeding customer expectations sometimes means fulfilling even seemingly outrageous customer requests. Dave Wilson, owner of several Lexus dealerships in Southern California, tells of a letter he received from an angry Lexus owner who spent US$374 to repair her car at his dealership. She'd owned four prior Lexus vehicles without a single problem. She said in her letter that she resented paying to fix her current one. Turns out, she thought they were maintenance free—as in get in and drive . . . and drive and drive. "She didn't think she had to do anything to her Lexus," says Wilson. "She had 60 000 miles on it, and never had the oil changed." Wilson sent back her US$374.

By all accounts, Lexus has lived up to its ambitious customer-satisfaction promise. It has created what appear to be the world's most satisfied car owners. Lexus regularly tops not just the J.D. Power quality ratings, but also its customer-satisfaction ratings, and not just in the United States but worldwide. Lexus often ranks number one in the J.D. Power and Associates Sales Satisfaction Index, which measures customer satisfaction with the new-vehicle sales process. Customer satisfaction translates into sales and customer loyalty. Lexus is North America's number-one selling luxury car. And once a Lexus customer, always a Lexus customer—Lexus retains 84 percent of customers who've gone to the dealership for service.

Just ask a Lexus customer. "I'm telling you, this is class, buddy," says customer Barry Speak while reclining in a vibrating massage chair at the Palm Beach Lexus store. Owner of a late-model Lexus LS 4300 sedan, Speak says there is no doubt he will come to the Palm Beach store for a new vehicle in a year or two. "My wife and I are going to be fighting over who gets to take the car in now," he says over the chair's hum. "You're not kidding!" Jane Speak chimes in from the store's other massage chair.

Sources: The examples are adapted from Mac Gordon, "He Runs the Largest Lexus Store," *Ward's Dealer Business*, February 2008, p. 64; Neil E. Boudette, "Luxury Car Sellers Put on the Ritz," *Wall Street Journal*, December 18, 2007, p. B1; and Julia Chang, "At Your Service," *Sales & Marketing Management*, June 2006, pp. 42–43. Other information and quotes from Steve Finlay, "At Least She Put Fuel in It," *Ward's Dealer Business,* August 1, 2003; "J.D. Power and Associates Reports: Lexus Ranks Highest in Sales Satisfaction as Industry Achieved Record Highs Sales for a Second Consecutive Year," *PR Newswire*, November 14, 2007; "Toyota Reports 2007 and December Sales," *PR Newswire*, January 3, 2008; and "Lexus Covenant," accessed at www.lexus.com/about/corporate/covenant.html, December 2008.

A dissatisfied consumer responds differently. Bad word of mouth often travels farther and faster than good word of mouth. It can quickly damage consumer attitudes about a company and its products. But companies cannot simply rely on dissatisfied customers to volunteer their complaints when they are dissatisfied. Most unhappy customers never tell the company about their problem. Therefore, a company should measure customer satisfaction regularly. It should set up systems that *encourage* customers to complain. In this way, the company can learn how well it is doing and how it can improve.

By studying the overall buyer decision, marketers may be able to find ways to help consumers move through it. For example, if consumers are not buying a new product because they do not perceive a need for it, marketing might launch advertising messages that trigger the need and show how the product solves customers' problems. If customers know about the product but are not buying because they hold unfavourable attitudes toward it, the marketer must find ways either to change the product or change consumer perceptions.

4 | THE BUYER DECISION PROCESS FOR NEW PRODUCTS

We have looked at the stages buyers go through in trying to satisfy a need. Buyers may pass quickly or slowly through these stages, and some of the stages may even be reversed. Much depends on the nature of the buyer, the product, and the buying situation.

New product
A good, service, or idea that is perceived by some potential customers as new.

We now look at how buyers approach the purchase of new products. A **new product** is a good, service, or idea that is perceived by some potential customers as new. It may have been around for a while, but our interest is in how consumers learn about products for the

Adoption process
The mental process through which an individual passes from first hearing about an innovation to final adoption.

first time and make decisions on whether to adopt them. We define the **adoption process** as "the mental process through which an individual passes from first learning about an innovation to final adoption," and *adoption* as the decision by an individual to become a regular user of the product.[40]

Stages in the Adoption Process

Consumers go through five stages in the process of adopting a new product:

- *Awareness:* The consumer becomes aware of the new product but lacks information about it.

- *Interest:* The consumer seeks information about the new product.

- *Evaluation:* The consumer considers whether trying the new product makes sense.

- *Trial:* The consumer tries the new product on a small scale to improve his or her estimate of its value.

- *Adoption:* The consumer decides to make full and regular use of the new product.

This model suggests that the new-product marketer should think about how to help consumers move through these stages. For example, to encourage consumers to try its new Gillette Fusion razor, P&G featured coupons offering substantial savings. Similarly, a luxury car producer might find that many potential customers know about and are interested in its new model but aren't buying because of uncertainty about the model's benefits and the high price. The producer could launch a "take one home for the weekend" promotion to high-value prospects to move them into the trial process and lead them to purchase.

Individual Differences in Innovativeness

People differ greatly in their readiness to try new products. In each product area, there are "consumption pioneers" and early adopters. Other individuals adopt new products much later. People can be classified into the adopter categories shown in Figure 6.6. After a slow start, an increasing number of people adopt the new product. The number of adopters reaches a peak and then drops off as fewer nonadopters remain. Innovators are defined as the first 2.5 percent of the buyers to adopt a new idea (those beyond two standard deviations from mean adoption time); the early adopters are the next 13.5 percent (between one and two standard deviations); and so forth.

The five adopter groups have differing values. *Innovators* are venturesome—they try new ideas at some risk. *Early adopters* are guided by respect—they are opinion leaders in their communities and adopt new ideas early but carefully. The *early majority* are deliberate—although they are rarely leaders, they adopt new ideas before the average person. The *late majority* are skeptical—they adopt an innovation only after a majority of people have tried it. Finally, *laggards* are tradition bound—they are suspicious of changes and adopt the innovation only when it has become something of a tradition itself.

This adopter classification suggests that an innovating firm should research the characteristics of innovators and early adopters and should direct marketing efforts toward them. In general, innovators tend to be relatively younger, better educated, and higher in income than later adopters and nonadopters. They are more receptive to unfamiliar things, rely more on their own values and judgment, and are more willing to take risks. They are less brand loyal and more likely to take advantage of special promotions such as discounts, coupons, and samples.

Influencing the adoption process: This Gillette Fusion ad encourages trial of the Gillette Fusion Power Phantom by saving $4 on a Fusion razor.

Figure 6.6 Adopter categorization on the basis of relative time of adoption of innovations

Source: Reprinted with permission of the Free Press, a Division of Simon & Schuster, from *Diffusion of Innovations,* Fifth Edition, by Everett M. Rogers. Copyright © 2003 by the Free Press.

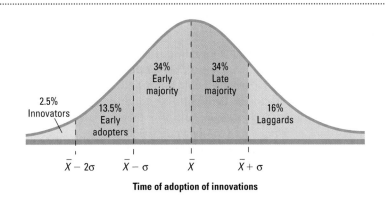

Influence of Product Characteristics on Rate of Adoption

The characteristics of the new product affect its rate of adoption. Some products catch on almost overnight—for example, the iPod flew off retailers' shelves at an astounding rate from the first day it was introduced. Others take a longer time to gain acceptance. For example, the first HDTVs were introduced in North America in the 1990s, but by 2007 only about 14 percent of TV households were what Nielsen describes as "HD capable"—equipped with HD televisions and HD tuners capable of receiving HDTV signals.[41]

Five characteristics are especially important in influencing an innovation's rate of adoption. For example, consider the characteristics of HDTV in relation to the rate of adoption:

- *Relative advantage*: the degree to which the innovation appears superior to existing products. HDTV offers substantially improved picture quality. This will speed its rate of adoption.

- *Compatibility*: the degree to which the innovation fits the values and experiences of potential consumers. HDTV, for example, is highly compatible with the lifestyles of the TV-watching public. However, many programs and channels have only recently become available in HD, which has slowed HDTV adoption.

- *Complexity*: the degree to which the innovation is difficult to understand or use. HDTVs are not very complex and, therefore, are taking less time to penetrate Canadian homes than more complex innovations.

- *Divisibility*: the degree to which the innovation may be tried on a limited basis. Early HDTVs and HD cable and satellite systems were very expensive, slowing the rate of adoption. As prices fall, adoption rates will increase.

- *Communicability*: the degree to which the results of using the innovation can be observed or described to others. Because HDTV lends itself to demonstration and description, its use will spread faster among consumers.

Other characteristics influence the rate of adoption, such as initial and ongoing costs, risk and uncertainty, and social approval. The new-product marketer must research all these factors when developing the new product and its marketing program.

REVIEWING OBJECTIVES AND KEY TERMS

 | Audio Chapter Summary

The North American consumer market consists of almost 333 million people who consume trillions of dollars' worth of goods and services each year, making it one of the most attractive consumer markets in the world. The world consumer market consists of more than 6.6 billion people. Consumers around the world vary greatly in age, income, education level, and tastes. Understanding how these differences affect *consumer buying behaviour* is one of the biggest challenges marketers face.

OBJECTIVE 1   Define the consumer market and explain the process of consumer buyer behaviour.

The *consumer market* consists of all the individuals and households who buy or acquire goods and services for personal consumption. Consumer behaviour should be viewed as an ongoing process that starts long before the consumer purchases a product or service and continues long after they consume it. This extended definition of consumer behaviour means that marketers must be aware of a number of issues before, during, and after purchase to build brand loyalty and lasting relationships with their customers.

OBJECTIVE 2   Name the four major factors that influence consumer buyer behaviour.

Consumer buyer behaviour is influenced by four key sets of buyer characteristics: cultural, social, personal, and psychological. Although many of these factors cannot be influenced by the marketer, they can be useful in identifying interested buyers and in shaping products and appeals to serve consumer needs better.

Culture is the most basic determinant of a person's wants and behaviours. It includes the basic values, perceptions, preferences, and behaviours that a person learns from family and other important institutions. *Subcultures* are "cultures within cultures" that have distinct values and lifestyles and can be based on anything from age to ethnicity. People with different cultural and subcultural characteristics have different product and brand preferences. As a result, marketers may want to focus their marketing programs on the special needs of certain groups.

Social factors also influence a buyer's behaviour. A person's *reference groups*—family, friends, social networks, professional associations—strongly affect product and brand choices. The buyer's age, life-cycle stage, occupation, economic circumstances, lifestyle, personality, and other *personal characteristics* influence his or her buying decisions. Consumer *lifestyles*—the whole pattern of acting and interacting in the world—are also an important influence on purchase decisions. Finally, consumer buying behaviour is influenced by four major *psychological factors*—motivation, perception, learning, and beliefs and attitudes. Each of these factors provides a different perspective for understanding the consumers' decision-making process.

OBJECTIVE 3   List and define the major types of buying decision behaviour and the stages in the buyer decision process.

Buying behaviour may vary greatly across different types of products and buying decisions. Consumers undertake *complex buying behaviour* when they are highly involved in a purchase and perceive significant differences among brands. *Dissonance-reducing behaviour* occurs when consumers are highly involved but see little difference among brands. *Habitual buying behaviour* occurs under conditions of low involvement and little significant brand difference. In situations characterized by low involvement but significant perceived brand differences, consumers engage in *variety-seeking buying behaviour.*

When making a purchase, the buyer goes through a decision process consisting of need recognition, information search, evaluation of alternatives, purchase decision, and postpurchase behaviour. The marketer's job is to understand the buyer's behaviour at each stage and the influences that are operating. During *need recognition*, the consumer recognizes a problem or need that could be satisfied by a product or service in the market. Once the need is recognized, the consumer is aroused to seek more information and moves into the *information search* stage. With information in hand, the consumer proceeds to *alternative evaluation,* during which the information is used to evaluate brands in the choice set. From there, the consumer makes a *purchase decision* and actually buys the product. In the final stage of the buyer decision process, *postpurchase behaviour,* the consumer takes action based on satisfaction or dissatisfaction.

OBJECTIVE 4   Describe the adoption and diffusion process for new products.

The product adoption process is composed of five stages: awareness, interest, evaluation, trial, and adoption. Initially, the consumer must become aware of the new product. *Awareness* leads to *interest,* and the consumer seeks information about the new product. Once information has been gathered, the consumer enters the *evaluation* stage and considers buying the new product. Next, in the *trial* stage, the consumer tries the product on a small scale to improve his or her estimate of its value. If the consumer is satisfied with the product, he or she enters the *adoption* stage, deciding to use the new product fully and regularly.

With regard to diffusion of new products, consumers respond at different rates, depending on the consumer's characteristics and the product's characteristics. Consumers may be innovators, early adopters, early majority, late majority, or laggards. *Innovators* are willing to try risky new ideas; *early adopters*—often community opinion leaders—accept new ideas early but carefully; the *early majority*—rarely leaders—decide deliberately to try new ideas, doing so before the average person does; the *late majority* try an innovation only after a majority of people have adopted it; whereas *laggards* adopt an innovation only after it has become a tradition itself. Manufacturers try to bring their new products to the attention of potential early adopters, especially those who are opinion leaders.

KEY TERMS

Objective 1
  Consumer buyer behaviour   180
  Consumer market   180
Objective 2
  Culture   181
  Subculture   182
  Social class   187
  Group   188
  Opinion leader   188
  Online social networks   188
  Lifestyle   192
  Personality   193
  Brand personality   193
  Motive (drive)   194
  Perception   195
  Learning   196

  Belief   197
  Attitude   197
Objective 3
  Complex buying behaviour   197
  Dissonance-reducing buying behaviour   198
  Habitual buying behaviour   198
  Variety-seeking buying behaviour   199
  Need recognition   199
  Information search   200
  Alternative evaluation   200
  Purchase decision   201
  Postpurchase behaviour   201
  Cognitive dissonance   201
Objective 4
  New product   203
  Adoption process   204

DISCUSSING THE CONCEPTS

1. How do consumers respond to various marketing efforts the company might use? List the buyer characteristics that affect buyer behaviour and discuss which one(s) influence you most when making a new-car purchase decision.

2. Name and describe the types of consumer buying behaviour. Which one would you most likely use if deciding on a laptop computer purchase and which for picking a restaurant for dinner?

3. Explain the stages of the consumer buyer decision process and describe how you or your family went through this process to make a recent purchase.

4. How might a marketer influence a consumer's information search through each of the four information sources discussed in the chapter?

5. What is a "new" product and how do consumers go about deciding whether to adopt a new product?

6. What product characteristics influence an innovation's rate of adoption? Discuss the characteristics of mobile navigation systems in relation to the rate of adoption.

APPLYING THE CONCEPTS

1. Marketers often target consumers before, during, or after a trigger event, an event in one's life that triggers change. For example, after having a child, new parents have an increased need for baby furniture, clothes, diapers, car seats, and lots of other baby-related goods. Consumers who never paid attention to marketing efforts for certain products may now be focused on ones related to their life change. In a small group, discuss other trigger events that may provide opportunities to target the right buyer at the right time.

2. You are the vice-president of marketing for a small software company that has developed new and novel spam-blocking software. You are charged with selecting the target market for the product launch. Discuss the adopter groups shown in Figure 6.6 and explain how this knowledge can help you with your targeting decision.

3. How did you decide on the college or university you are currently attending? Describe the factors that influenced your decision and the decision-making process you followed.

FOCUS ON TECHNOLOGY

With so many choices available, the decision process for consumers can be daunting, especially for high-risk purchases. Looking for a new digital camera, computer, sunscreen, or coffee maker? Product reviews abound that provide information on products in just about every category. Product reviews and rankings are available from *Consumer Reports* (considered the "gold standard"), *Good Housekeeping*, *Car & Driver*, *Backpacker Magazine* and websites providing consumer reviews. So finding information is not the problem—sorting it is. ConsumerSearch.com has just what consumers need—a service that reviews the reviews. This source is recognized for excellence by the likes of *USA Today*, the *Wall Street Journal*, and Yahoo! Internet Life. It not only reviews the product reviews with respect to credibility, it also consolidates the analyses in its Fast Answers and Full Reports. It also provides a Consensus Report showing the extent of agreement among reviewers regarding the best product.

1. Go to www.consumersearch.com, select a product category that interests you, and learn about the best products/brands in that category. Which review is rated the best? Which brand is rated best by the reviews? Based on this analysis, which brand would you select if actually purchasing this product? How useful is this source? Write a brief report with your answers to these questions.

2. Many websites provide consumer reviews, such as www.epinions.com. Usually there is a five-star rating, the number of reviews that rating is based on, and the actual written reviews. How influential are these types of reviews for you when deciding on a purchase?

FOCUS ON ETHICS

Apple's iPod revolutionized music listening, with over 100 million iPods sold worldwide. However, iPod and other brands of MP3 players have revolutionized the music industry as well, causing sales of prerecorded CDs to plummet and music file sharing from the Internet—both legal and illegal—to skyrocket. Pay-per-song sites, such as Apple's iTunes, let consumers purchase songs legally and inexpensively. While purchases of songs from these types of sites continue to increase, illegal music file sharing is increasing as well, with hundreds of millions of files downloaded illegally each year worldwide. The story is somewhat different here in Canada. While many countries have adopted laws to make Internet piracy illegal, Canada's copyright laws have not been changed since 1997, two years before Napster and four years before the first iPod. In fact, the United States recently placed Canada on an international watch list of the worst digital piracy havens and copyright offenders in the world! Not surprisingly, many university students hold favourable attitudes toward this activity and have little fear of prosecution.

1. What is your attitude toward music file downloading? Should Canadian laws be changed to make this an illegal activity?

2. Discuss how marketers can combat this problem.

MARKETING BY THE NUMBERS

One way that consumers can evaluate alternatives is to decide on important attributes and assess how the alternatives perform on those attributes. Each attribute, such as automobile gas mileage, is given a weight to reflect its level of importance to that consumer. Then, the consumer evaluates each alternative on each attribute. For example, in the table on the next page, gas mileage (weighted at 0.5) is the most important automobile purchase attribute for this consumer. The consumer believes that Brand C performs best on gas mileage, rating it 7 (higher ratings indicate higher performance), and Brand B rates worst on gas mileage (rating of 3). Styling and price are the consumer's next two most important attributes; warranty is least important.

A score for each brand can be calculated by multiplying the importance weight for each attribute by the brand's score on that attribute. These weighted scores are then summed to determine the score for that brand. For example, $Score_{Brand\ A} = (0.2 \times 4) + (0.5 \times 6) + (0.1 \times 5) + (0.2 \times 4) = 0.8 + 3.0 + 0.5 + 0.8 = 5.1$. This consumer will select the brand with the highest score. For more discussion of the financial and quantitative implications of marketing decisions, see Appendix 3: Marketing by the Numbers.

1. Determine the scores for Brands B and C. Which brand would this consumer likely choose?

2. Discuss some other "rules" consumers may use when evaluating alternatives to make a purchase decision.

		Alternative Brands		
Attributes	Importance Weight	A	B	C
Styling	0.2	4	6	2
Gas Mileage	0.5	6	3	7
Warranty	0.1	5	5	4
Price	0.2	4	6	7

VIDEO CASE

Wild Planet

 mymarketinglab | Video Case Questions

Of the many factors that affect consumer buyer behaviour, social responsibility is playing an increasing role. While there have always been companies that have integrated "doing good" with corporate strategy, a new generation of activist entrepreneurs has now taken up the reins. The ones most likely to succeed are those who recognize that beyond just doing good, social responsibility can provide a powerful means for connecting with consumers.

For example, Wild Planet markets high-quality, nonviolent toys that encourage kids to be imaginative and creative and to explore the world around them. Wild Planet sells more than just toys; it sells positive play experiences. To better understand those experiences, the company conducts a tremendous amount of consumer research through state-of-the-art methods to better understand consumer buyer behaviour. Wild Planet even created a Toy Opinion Panel to evaluate current products and develop new product ideas.

After viewing the video featuring Wild Planet, answer the following questions about consumer buyer behaviour:

1. Explain how each of the four sets of factors affecting consumer behaviour affects the consumer purchase process as it relates to toys from Wild Planet.

2. What demographic segment of consumers is Wild Planet targeting?

3. Visit the Wild Planet website at www.wildplanet.com to learn more about the company. How does the website help consumers through the buyer decision process?

Visit MyMarketingLab at www.pearsoned.ca/mymarketinglab to view the video segment related to this case.

COMPANY CASE

Victoria's Secret Pink: Keeping the Brand Hip

When most people think of Victoria's Secret, they think of lingerie. Indeed, the Limited Brands division has done a very good job of developing this association by placing images of supermodels donning its signature bras, panties, and "sleepwear" in everything from standard broadcast and print advertising to the controversial primetime television fashion shows that the company airs each year. Such promotional tactics have paid off for Victoria's Secret, a subsidiary of Limited Brands, which continues to achieve healthy sales and profit growth.

How does a successful company ensure that its hot sales don't cool off? One approach is to sell more to existing customers. Another is to find new customers. Victoria's Secret is doing plenty of both. One key component in its quest to find new customers is the launch and growth of its sub-brand, Pink.

Expanding the Target Market

Victoria's Secret launched its line of Pink products in 50 test markets in 2003. Based on very positive initial results, the company expanded the sub-brand quickly to a national level. With the Pink introduction, Victoria's Secret hoped to add a new segment to its base: young, hip, and fashionable customers. "Young" in this case means 18 to 30 years of age. More specifically, Pink is geared toward university co-eds. According to company spokesperson Anthony Hebron, "It's what you see around the dorm. It's the fun, playful stuff she needs, but is still fashionable."

The company classifies the Pink line as "loungewear," a very broad term that includes sweatpants, T-shirts, pajamas, bras and panties, pillows and bedding, and even dog accessories. In keeping with the "young and fun" image, the product line includes bright colours (Pink is not a misnomer) and often incorporates stripes and polka dots. The garments feature comfortable cuts and mostly soft cotton fabrics. To keep things fresh for the younger segment, stores introduce new Pink products every three or four weeks.

According to those at Victoria's Secret, in sharp contrast to the sexy nature of the core brand, Pink is positioned as cute and playful. "It's spirited and collegiate. It's not necessarily sexy—it's not sexy at all—but young, hip, and casual. It's fashion-forward and accessible," said Mary Beth Wood, a spokesperson for Victoria's Secret. The Pink line does include underwear that some might consider to be on par with standard Victoria's Secret items. But management is quick to point out that the designs, such as heart-covered thongs, are more cute than racy. Displays of Pink merchandise often incorporate stuffed animals, and many articles display Pink's trademark mascot, a pink dog.

Originally, Pink was considered to be a store-within-a-store concept. But Pink sales have surpassed expectations. To date, Victoria's Secret has opened six stand-alone Pink stores. In 2007, Pink revenues hit US$900 million, almost one-sixth of the company's US$5.6 billion take for the year. Because of this, the company is giving far more serious consideration to expanding the presence of Pink lifestyle shops in several markets.

A KEY DRIVER OF VICTORIA'S SECRET'S FUTURE GROWTH

Limited Brands has been experiencing good times, and executives have been quick to recognize that Victoria's Secret is a huge part of that success. In fact, the Victoria's Secret and Bath & Body Works divisions have accounted for roughly 70 percent of revenue (Victoria's Secret alone was good for more than 50 percent) and almost all the profit in recent years.

But Limited Brands CEO Les Wexner is not content to let the chain rest. "The Victoria brand is really the power of the business," he says. "We can double the Victoria's Secret business in the next five years." This would mean increasing the division's sales to more than US$10 billion. The umbrella strategy for achieving this growth is to continually broaden the customer base. This will include a focus on new and emerging lines, such as Ipex and Angels Secret Embrace (bras), Intimissimi (a line of Italian lingerie for women and men appealing to younger customers), and a new line of fitness apparel called VSX. Pink is a key component of this multibrand strategy.

The future of Victoria's Secret will also include a move toward bigger stores. Currently, the typical Victoria's Secret store is approximately 6000 square feet. More than 80 percent of Victoria's Secret stores will be remodelled over the next five years, nearly doubling its average store size to 11 000 square feet. Larger stores will allow the company to give more space and attention to the store-within-a-store brands, such as Pink.

BROADENING THE CUSTOMER BASE . . . TOO FAR?

While Victoria's Secret's introduction and expansion of Pink seems well founded, it has raised some eyebrows. As Pink's young and cute line has expanded rapidly, it has become apparent that the brand's appeal goes far beyond that of its intended target market. Some women much older than 30 have shown an interest (41-year-old Courteney Cox Arquette was photographed wearing Pink sweats). But stronger interest is being shown by girls younger than 18. Girls as young as 11 years old are visiting Victoria's Secret stores to buy Pink items, with and without their mothers.

Two such 11-year-olds, Lily Feingold and Brittany Garrison, were interviewed while shopping at a Victoria's Secret store with Lily's mother. As they browsed exclusively through the Pink merchandise, the two confessed that Victoria's Secret was one of their favourite stores. Passing up cotton lounge pants because each already had multiple pairs, both girls bought US$68 pairs of sweatpants with the "Pink" label emblazoned on the derriere. The girls denied buying the items because they wanted to seem more grown up, instead saying that they simply liked the clothes.

The executives at Victoria's Secret are quick to say that they are not targeting girls younger than 18. Perhaps that is due to the backlash that retailer Abercrombie & Fitch experienced not long ago for targeting teens and preteens with sexually charged promotional materials and merchandise. But regardless of Victoria's Secret's intentions, Pink is fast becoming popular among teens and "tweens." Most experts agree that by the time children reach 10, they are rejecting childlike images and aspiring to more mature things associated with being a teenager. Called "age compression," it explains the trend toward preteens leaving their childhoods earlier and giving up traditional toys for more mature interests, such as cellphones, consumer electronics, and fashion products.

Tweens are growing in number and purchasing power. While the 33 million teens (ages 12 to 19) in the United States spend more than US$179 billion annually (more than 60 percent have jobs), the 25 million tweens spend US$51 billion annually, a number that continues to increase. But perhaps even more telling than the money being spent directly by teens is the US$170 billion per year spent by parents and other family members directly for the younger consumers who may not have as much income as their older siblings. "Parents are giving them money or credit cards and children make most of the decisions about whatever purchases are made for them, whether it's toiletries, a bedspread or undergarments," said James McNeal, a former professor of marketing at Texas A&M University and author of *Kids as Customers: A Handbook of Marketing to Children.*

With this kind of purchasing power, as they find revenue for their older target markets levelling off, marketers everywhere are focusing on the teen and tween segments. "Right now, every retailer is looking for growth opportunities," said Marshall Cohen, an industry analyst. And more young women are wearing loungewear, not just at home, but to school and the mall. "Pajamas are streetwear. Slippers are shoes," Cohen continued. "It's amazing how casual we've gotten. This retail segment could get very competitive."

Although executives at Victoria's Secret deny targeting the youth of America, experts disagree. David Morrison, president of marketing research agency Twentysomething, says he is not surprised that Victoria's Secret denies marketing to teens and preteens: "If Victoria's Secret is blatantly catering to seventh and eighth graders, that might be considered exploitative." Morrison also acknowledges that the age group is drawn to the relative maturity and sophistication of the Pink label.

Natalie Weathers, assistant professor of fashion-industry management at Philadelphia University, says that Victoria's Secret is capitalizing on a trend known as co-shopping—mothers and tweens shopping together. "They are advising their daughters about their purchases, and their daughters are advising them," she said. This type of activity may have been strange 20 years ago, but according to Weathers, the preteens of today are more savvy and, therefore, more likely to be shopping partners for moms. "They are not little girls, and they aren't teenagers, but they have a lot of access to sophisticated information about what the media says is beautiful, what is pretty, what is hot and stylish and cool. They are very visually literate."

In general, introducing a brand to younger consumers is considered a sound strategy for growth and for creating long-term relationships. Marketers of everything from packaged foods to shampoo use this strategy. In most cases, it's not considered controversial to engender aspirational motives in young consumers through an entry-level product line. But many critics have questioned the aspirations that Pink engenders in tweens. Specifically, to what does it make them aspire? Based on years of experience working as a creative director for ad agencies in New York, Timothy Matz calls Pink "beginner-level lingerie." Matz does not question the practice of gateway marketing (getting customers to use the brand at an earlier age). But he admits that a "gateway" to a sexy lingerie shop may make parents nervous: "Being a 45-year-old dad, do I want my 10-year-old going to Victoria's Secret?"

Thus far, Victoria's Secret has avoided the negative reactions of the masses who opposed Abercrombie & Fitch's blatant marketing of thong underwear to preteens. Perhaps that's because it adamantly professes its exclusive focus on young adults. But it may also be because Victoria's Secret is not alone in its efforts to capitalize on the second-fastest growing apparel category (loosely defined as "lingerie") by focusing on the younger target market. An almost exhaustive list of retailers are expanding their lingerie lines. Companies that specifically target the same Pink segment include the Gap, Kohl's, Macy's, and JC Penney. But the biggest competition comes from fellow mall store American Eagle Outfitters, which has rolled out its own new Aerie line of "fun lingerie." And like Victoria's Secret Pink, the brand has opened stand-alone Aerie stores. In fact, results have been so good for American Eagle that it has opened a whopping 56 new Aerie stores in just a couple of years.

But Victoria's Secret was the first to market with lingerie for young adults and still has the greatest presence. And whether Pink's appeal to the pre-adult crowd is intentional or unintentional, many critics question the effort. Big tobacco companies have been under fire for years for using childlike imagery to draw the interest of youth to an adult product. Is Pink the Joe Camel of early adolescent sexuality? Are Pink's extreme low-rise string bikini panties the gateway drug to pushup teddies and Pleasure State Geisha thongs? These are questions that Victoria's Secret may have to address more directly at some point in the near future.

Questions for Discussion

1. Analyze the buyer decision process of a typical Pink customer.

2. Apply the concept of aspirational groups to Victoria Secret's Pink line. Should marketers have boundaries with regard to this concept?

3. Explain how both positive and negative consumer attitudes toward a brand like Pink develop. How might someone's attitude toward Pink change?

4. What role does Pink appear to be playing in the self-concept of tweens, teens, and young adults?

Sources: Suzanne Ryan, "Would Hannah Montana Wear It?" *Boston Globe,* January 10, 2008, p. D1; Heather Burke, "Victoria's Secret to Expand Its Stores," *International Herald Tribune,* August 13, 2007, p. F15; Ann Zimmerman, "Retailers' Panty Raid on Victoria's Secret New Lines Target Hot Fashion Lingerie," *Wall Street Journal,* June 20, 2007, p. B1; Fae Goodman, "Lingerie Is Luscious and Lovely—For Grown-Ups," *Chicago Sun Times,* February 19, 2006, p. B02; Vivian McInerny, "Pink Casual Loungewear Brand Nicely Colors Teen Girls' World," *Oregonian,* May 7, 2006, p. O13; and Jane M. Von Bergen, "Victoria's Secret? Kids," *Philadelphia Inquirer,* December 22, 2005.

Visit **MyMarketingLab** at **www.pearsoned.ca/mymarketinglab** for access to online tutorials, interactive exercises, videos, and much more.

7

Business Markets and Business Buyer Behaviour

PREVIEWING THE CONCEPTS In the previous chapter, you studied final consumer buying behaviour and factors that influence it. In this chapter, we'll do the same for business customers—those that buy goods and services for use in producing their own products and services or for resale to others. As when selling to final buyers, firms marketing to business customers must build profitable relationships by creating superior customer value.

To start, let's look at GE—one of the best-run, most-admired companies in the world. GE has operated in Canada for over 100 years and has major manufacturing facilities and sales and service locations across the country. Most of us grew up surrounded by GE consumer products in our homes. But did you know that most of GE's business comes not from consumer products sold to you and me but from a diverse portfolio of commercial and industrial products sold to large business customers? To succeed in its business-to-business markets, GE must do more than just design good products and make them available to customers. It must work closely and deeply with its business customers to become a strategic, problem-solving partner.

F ew brands are more familiar than GE. For years, we've packed our homes with GE products—from good ol' GE light-bulbs to refrigerators, ranges, clothes washers and dryers, microwave ovens, dishwashers, coffee makers, room air conditioners, and hundreds of other products bearing the familiar GE logo. The company's consumer finance unit—GE Money—helps finance these and other purchases through credit cards, loans, mortgages, and other financial services. GE even entertains us—its NBC Universal division serves up a diverse fare of net-work and cable television channels, movie entertainment, and even theme parks. In all, GE offers a huge assortment of consumer products and services.

But here's a fact that would startle most consumers: Did you know that GE's consumer products contribute less than one-third of the company's total US$173 billion in annual sales? To the surprise of many, most of GE's business comes not from final consumers but from commercial and industrial customers across a wide range of industries. Beyond lightbulbs and electronics, GE sells everything from medical imaging technologies, water processing systems, and security solutions to power generation equipment, aircraft engines, and diesel locomotives.

At a general level, marketing medical imaging technology or diesel locomotives to business customers is like selling refrigerators to final buyers. It requires a deep-down understanding of customer needs and customer-driven marketing strategies that create superior customer value. But that's about where the similarities end. In its business markets, rather than selling to large numbers of small buyers, GE sells to a few very large buyers. Whereas it might be disappointing when a refrigerator buyer

Most of GE's business comes not from consumer products sold to you and me, but from commercial and industrial products sold to large business customers.

chooses a competing brand, losing a single sale to a large business customer can mean the loss of hundreds of millions of dollars in business. Also, with GE's business customers, buying decisions are much more complex. An average consumer buying a refrigerator might do a little online research and then pop out to the local Best Buy to compare models before buying one. In contrast, buying a batch of jet engines involves a tortuously long buying process, dozens or even hundreds of decision makers from all levels of the buying organization, and layer upon layer of subtle and not-so-subtle buying influences.

To get an idea of the complexities involved in selling one of GE's industrial products, let's dig deeper into the company's GE Transportation division and one of its bread-and-butter products, diesel locomotives. GE locomotives might not seem glamorous to you, but they are beautiful brutes to those who buy and use them. It's not difficult to identify potential buyers for a 207 ton, 4400 horsepower GE locomotive with an average list price of US$2.2 million. The real challenge is to win buyers' business by building day-in, day-out, year-in, year-out partnerships with them based on superior products and close collaboration.

In the buying decision, locomotive performance plays an important role. In such big-ticket purchases, buyers carefully scrutinize factors such as cost, fuel efficiency, and reliability. By most measures, GE's locomotives outperform competing engines on most of these dimensions. The company's innovative Evolution Series locomotives, part of a broader GE "ecomagination" initiative to build environmentally friendly products, are now the most technically advanced, fuel-efficient, and eco-friendly diesel–electric locomotives in history. Compared with their predecessors, they produce full power but cut fuel consumption by 5 percent and reduce particulate pollution by 40 percent. "If every freight locomotive in North America were as clean as

GE locomotives might not seem glamorous to you, but they are beautiful brutes to those who buy and use them. In this market, GE's real challenge is to win buyers' business by building day-in, day-out, year-in, year-out partnerships with them.

GE's Evolution," notes one expert, "the annual reduction of emissions would compare to removing 48 million cars from the road each year." GE's next-generation Evolution Hybrid diesel–electric engines, scheduled for production in 2010, will reduce fuel consumption by another 15 percent and emissions by as much as 50 percent.

But locomotive performance is only part of the buying equation. GE wins contracts by partnering with business customers to help them translate that performance into moving their passengers and freight more efficiently and reliably. CSX Transportation (CSXT), one of GE Transportation's largest customers, has purchased more than 300 GE Evolution locomotives since they were launched in 2005. According to a CSXT purchasing executive, the company "evaluates many cost factors before awarding . . . a locomotive contract. Environmental impact, fuel consumption, reliability, serviceability [are] all key elements in this decision." But also important is "the value of our ongoing partnership with GE."

OBJECTIVES

1. Define the business market and explain how business markets differ from consumer markets.

2. Identify the major factors that influence business buyer behaviour.

3. List and define the steps in the business buying decision process.

4. Compare the institutional and government markets and explain how institutional and government buyers make their buying decisions.

A recent high-stakes international deal involving hundreds of GE locomotives demonstrates the potential importance, scope, and complexity of some business-to-business decisions:

> GE Transportation recently landed a huge US$650 million contract to supply 310 Evolution locomotives to the Kazakhstan National Railway (KTZ)—the largest-ever order for locomotives delivered outside North America. Befitting its importance to not just the companies, but to their countries as well, the deal was inked at the Kazakhstan embassy in Washington, DC. The signing was attended by high-level executives from both organizations, including the chief executive of GE Transportation and the president of KTZ.
>
> The buying decision was based on a host of factors. KTZ wanted the very best performance technology available, and GE's Evolution locomotives fit the bill nicely. But the deal also hinged on many factors that had little to do with the engine performance. For example, important matters of international economics and politics came into play as well. Whereas the first 10 locomotives were built at GE's U.S. plant, most of the remaining 300 locomotives will be assembled at a newly built, state-owned plant in Pavlodar, Kazakhstan.
>
> Finally, the current contract was anything but an impulsive, one-and-done deal. Rather, it represented the culmination of years of smaller steps between the two

> organizations—the latest episode in a long-running relationship between GE and KTZ that dates back to the mid-1990s. The relationship accelerated in 2003 when GE won the first of several contracts for modernization kits that updated older KTZ locomotives. "I am proud that KTZ and GE are extending our relationship," said the CEO of GE Transportation, "one that has proven to be very beneficial to both organizations over several years."

Thanks to stories like this one, GE Transportation dominates the worldwide rail locomotive industry, now capturing a phenomenal 80 percent market share. More broadly, people throughout the entire GE organization know that success in business-to-business markets involves more than just developing and selling superior products and technologies. Business customer buying decisions are made within the framework of a strategic, problem-solving partnership. "We love the challenge of a customer's problem," says the company on its GE Transportation website. "Why? It's an opportunity for a true collaborative partnership. We enjoy the exchange of ideas, whether we're developing a brand new technology or applying existing technologies in innovative new ways. [We] go to great lengths to help our customers succeed."

"Customer partnerships are at the center of GE and Ecomagination," confirms GE chairman and CEO Jeffrey Immelt in a recent letter to shareholders. "We are viewed as a technical partner by customers around the world."[1]

Business buyer behaviour
The buying behaviour of the organizations that buy goods and services for use in the production of other products and services or to resell or rent to others at a profit.

Business buying process
The decision process by which business buyers determine which products and services their organizations need to purchase, and then find, evaluate, and choose among alternative suppliers and brands.

Like GE, in one way or another most large companies sell to other organizations. Companies such as DuPont, Bombardier, IBM, Caterpillar, and countless other firms sell *most* of their products to other businesses. Even large consumer-products companies, which make products used by final consumers, must first sell their products to other businesses. For example, General Mills makes many familiar consumer brands—cereals (Cheerios, Wheaties, Trix, Chex), baking products (Pillsbury, Betty Crocker, Gold Medal flour), snacks (Nature Valley, Pop Secret, Chex Mix), Yoplait yogurt, Häagen-Dazs ice cream, and others. But to sell these products to consumers, General Mills must first sell them to its wholesale and retail customers, who in turn serve the consumer market.

Business buyer behaviour refers to the buying behaviour of the organizations that buy goods and services for use in the production of other products and services that are sold, rented, or supplied to others. It also includes the behaviour of retailing and wholesaling firms that acquire goods to resell or rent to others at a profit. In the **business buying process**, business buyers determine which products and services their organizations need to purchase and then find, evaluate, and choose among alternative suppliers and brands. *Business-to-business (B2B) marketers* must do their best to understand business markets and business buyer behaviour. Then, like businesses that sell to final buyers, they must build profitable relationships with business customers by creating superior customer value.

1 BUSINESS MARKETS

The business market is *huge*. In fact, business markets involve far more dollars and items than do consumer markets. For example, think about the large number of business transactions involved in the production and sale of a single set of Goodyear tires. Various suppliers sell Goodyear the rubber, steel, equipment, and other goods that it needs to produce tires. Goodyear then sells the finished tires to retailers, who in turn sell them to consumers.

Table 7.1 Characteristics of Business Markets

Market Structure and Demand
Business markets contain *fewer but larger buyers*.
Business buyer demand is *derived* from final consumer demand.
Demand in many business markets is *more inelastic*—not affected as much in the short run by price changes.
Demand in business markets *fluctuates more*, and more quickly.

Nature of the Buying Unit
Business purchases involve *more buyers*.
Business buying involves a *more professional purchasing effort*.

Types of Decisions and the Decision Process
Business buyers usually face *more complex buying decisions*.
The business buying process is *more formalized*.
In business buying, buyers and sellers work more closely together and build close, long-term *relationships*.

Thus, many sets of *business* purchases were made for only one set of *consumer* purchases. In addition, Goodyear sells tires as original equipment to manufacturers who install them on new vehicles, and as replacement tires to companies that maintain their own fleets of company cars, trucks, buses, or other vehicles.

Characteristics of Business Markets

Derived demand
Business demand that ultimately comes from (derives from) the demand for consumer goods.

In some ways, business markets are similar to consumer markets. Both involve people who assume buying roles and make purchase decisions to satisfy needs. However, business markets differ in many ways from consumer markets. The main differences, shown in Table 7.1, are in *market structure and demand*, the *nature of the buying unit*, and the *types of decisions and the decision process* involved.

Market Structure and Demand

The business marketer normally deals with *far fewer but far larger buyers* than the consumer marketer does. Even in large business markets, a few buyers often account for most of the purchasing. For example, when Goodyear sells replacement tires to final consumers, its potential market includes the owners of the millions of cars currently in use in North America and around the world. But Goodyear's fate in the business market depends on getting orders from one of only a handful of large automakers. Similarly, Black & Decker sells its power tools and outdoor equipment to tens of millions of consumers worldwide. However, it must sell these products through huge retail customers—Home Depot, Lowe's, RONA, and Walmart—which combined account for more than half its sales.

Further, business demand is **derived demand**—it ultimately derives from the demand for consumer goods. Hewlett-Packard and Dell buy Intel microprocessor chips because consumers buy personal computers. If consumer demand for PCs drops, so will the demand for computer chips. Therefore, B2B marketers sometimes promote their products directly to final consumers to increase business demand. For example, Intel advertises heavily to personal computer buyers, selling them on the virtues of Intel microprocessors. "Multiply your mobility," it tells consumers—"great computing starts with

Derived demand: Intel advertises heavily to personal computer buyers, selling them on the virtues of Intel microprocessors. Both Intel and its business partners benefit.

Intel inside." The increased demand for Intel chips boosts demand for the PCs containing them, and both Intel and its business partners win.

Many business markets have *inelastic demand*; that is, total demand for many business products is not affected much by price changes, especially in the short run. A drop in the price of leather will not cause shoe manufacturers to buy much more leather unless it results in lower shoe prices that, in turn, will increase consumer demand for shoes.

Finally, business markets have more *fluctuating demand*. The demand for many business goods and services tends to change more—and more quickly—than the demand for consumer goods and services does. A small percentage increase in consumer demand can cause large increases in business demand. Sometimes a rise of only 10 percent in consumer demand can cause as much as a 200 percent rise in business demand during the next period.

Nature of the Buying Unit

Compared with consumer purchases, a business purchase usually involves *more decision participants* and a *more professional purchasing effort*. Often, business buying is done by trained purchasing agents who spend their working lives learning how to buy better. The more complex the purchase, the more likely it is that several people will participate in the decision-making process. Buying committees made up of technical experts and top management are common in the buying of major goods. Beyond this, B2B marketers now face a new breed of higher-level, better-trained supply managers. Therefore, companies must have well-trained marketers and salespeople to deal with these well-trained buyers.

Supplier development
Systematic development of networks of supplier–partners to ensure an appropriate and dependable supply of products and materials for use in making products or reselling them to others.

Types of Decisions and the Decision Process

Business buyers usually face *more complex* buying decisions than do consumer buyers. Business purchases often involve large sums of money, complex technical and economic considerations, and interactions among many people at many levels of the buyer's organization. Because the purchases are more complex, business buyers may take longer to make their decisions. The business buying process also tends to be *more formalized* than the consumer buying process. Large business purchases usually call for detailed product specifications, written purchase orders, careful supplier searches, and formal approval.

Finally, in the business buying process, the buyer and seller are often much *more dependent* on each other. B2B marketers may roll up their sleeves and work closely with their customers during all stages of the buying process—from helping customers define problems, to finding solutions, to supporting after-sale operation. They often customize their offerings to individual customer needs. In the short run, sales go to suppliers who meet buyers' immediate product and service needs. In the long run, however, business-to-business marketers keep a customer's sales and create customer value by meeting current needs *and* by partnering with customers to help them solve their problems. For example, when UPS supplies a broad range of logistics services and resources to its business customers, it asks them "What can Brown do for you?" (See Real Marketing 7.1.)

In recent years, relationships between customers and suppliers have been changing from downright adversarial to close and chummy. In fact, many customer companies are now practising **supplier development**, systematically developing networks of supplier–partners to ensure an appropriate and dependable supply of products and materials that they will use in making their own products or resell to others. For example, Caterpillar no longer calls its buyers "purchasing agents"—they are managers of "purchasing and supplier development."

Giant Scandinavian furniture retailer IKEA doesn't just buy from its suppliers, it involves them deeply in the process of designing and making stylish but affordable furniture that keeps customers coming back.

Real Marketing 7.1

UPS Partners with Business Customers: What Can Brown Do for You?

Mention UPS and most people envision one of those familiar brown trucks with a friendly driver rumbling around their neighbourhood dropping off packages. That makes sense. The company's brown-clad drivers deliver more than 4 billion packages annually, an average of 15.8 million each day. For most of us, seeing a brown UPS truck evokes fond memories of past package deliveries. If you close your eyes and listen, you can probably imagine the sound of the UPS truck pulling up in front of your home.

Even the company's brown colour has come to mean something special to customers. UPS has been referred to for years as "Big Brown." "People love our drivers, they love our brown trucks, they love everything we do," says one UPS executive. Thus was born UPS's current "What Can Brown Do for You?" advertising theme.

For most residential customers, the answer to the question "What can Brown do for you?" is pretty simple: "Deliver my package as quickly as possible." But most of UPS's revenues don't come from the residential customers who receive the packages, but from the business customers who send them. And for these business customers, UPS does more than just get Grandma's holiday package there on time. Whereas residential consumers might look to "Brown" simply for fast, friendly, low-cost package delivery, business customers usually have much more complex needs. For these customers, UPS becomes an ally in finding solutions for a broad range of logistics issues.

For businesses, package delivery is just part of a much more complex logistics process that involves purchase orders, inventory, order status checks, invoices, payments, returned merchandise, and fleets of delivery vehicles. Beyond the physical package flow, companies must also handle the accompanying information and money flows. They need timely information about packages—what's in them, where they're currently located, to whom they are going, when they will get there, how much has been paid, and how much is owed. UPS knows that for many companies, all these daily logistical concerns can be a nightmare. Moreover, most companies don't see these activities as strategic competencies that provide competitive advantage.

That's where Big Brown comes in. These are exactly the things that UPS does best. Over the years, UPS has grown to become much more than a small neighbourhood package delivery service. It is now a US$50 billion corporate giant providing a broad range of logistics solutions. UPS handles the logistics, allowing customers to focus on what they do best.

For its business customers, UPS does more than just deliver packages from point A to point B. It becomes a strategic logistics partner, helping customers solve their complex distribution problems. "What Can Brown Do for You?"

It offers everything from ground and air package distribution, freight delivery (air, ocean, rail, and road), and mail services to inventory management, third-party logistics, international trade management, logistics management software and ecommerce solutions, and even financing. If it has to do with logistics, at home or abroad, UPS can probably do it better than anyone can. For example, UPS Canada's Supply Chain Solutions was awarded the Supply Chain Vendor award of the year in 2009 by Staples Canada. "This award reflects our mission to provide exceptional customer service at every level of the supply chain, to each and every one of our customers," says Scott Lane, director of operations.

UPS has the resources to handle the logistics needs of just about any size business. It employs 425 300 people and owns some 93 600 vehicles (package cars, vans, tractors, and motorcycles), 600 owned and chartered aircraft, and more than 1000 warehouse facilities in 200 countries. UPS now moves an astounding 6 percent of the gross domestic product in the United States, links 1.8 million sellers with 6.1 million buyers every day, and processes more than 460 million electronic transactions every week. It serves 90 percent of the world population and 99 percent of businesses in the *Fortune* 1000. UPS invests US$1 billion a year in information technology to support its highly synchronized, by-the-clock logistics services and to provide customers with information at every point in the process.

Beyond moving their packages around domestically, UPS can also help business customers navigate the complexities of international shipping, with some 700 international flights per day to or from 377 international destinations. For example, although most residential customers don't need

▶

next-day air service to or from China, many businesses do seek help shipping to and from the burgeoning Asian manufacturing zones. UPS helps ensure the timely flow of crucial business documents, prototypes, high-value goods (such as semiconductors), and emergency repair parts that wing their way across the Pacific every day.

UPS Canada employs more than 8750 people in 48 facilities across the country and provides service to every address in Canada, the United States, and over 200 countries worldwide. The company also plays a key role in the timely and accurate importation and clearance of packages through Canada customs for all modes of transportation, regardless of whether the shipment is carried by UPS or another carrier. In addition to shipping and receiving packages, UPS provides a wide range of financial services for its business customers. For example, its UPS Capital division will handle clients' accounts receivable—UPS shippers can choose to be reimbursed immediately and have UPS collect payment from the recipient. Other financial services include credit cards for small businesses and programs to fund inventory, equipment leasing, and asset financing. UPS even bought a bank to underpin UPS Capital's operations.

At a deeper level, UPS can provide the advice and technical resources needed to help business customers large and small improve their own logistics operations. UPS advises companies on redesigning logistics systems to align them better with business strategies. It helps customers synchronize the flow of goods, funds, and information up and down their supply chains. UPS Logistics Technologies supplies software that improves customers' distribution efficiency, including street-level route optimization, territory planning, mobile delivery execution, real-time wireless dispatch, and GPS tracking.

So what can Brown do for you? As it turns out, the answer depends on who you are. For its residential consumers, UPS uses those familiar chugging brown trucks to provide simple and efficient package pickup and delivery services. But in its business-to-business markets, it develops deeper and more-involved customer relationships. For their business customers, UPS employees around the world must do more than just deliver packages from point A to point B. They must roll up their sleeves and work hand in hand with customers to help solve their complex logistics problems. More than just providing shipping services, they must become strategic logistics allies.

Sources: Facts and information from various UPS websites, including - www.ups-scs.com; www.ups.ca; www.ups.com/content/us/en/about/facts/worldwide.html; www.upslogisticstech.com; and http://capital.ups.com/contact; accessed September 2008. UPS®, What Can Brown Do for You?®, and UPS Capital® are registered trademarks of United Parcel Service of America, Inc. Big Brown™ is a trademark of United Parcel Service of America, Inc.

Walmart doesn't have a "purchasing department," it has a "supplier development department." And giant Swedish furniture retailer IKEA doesn't just buy from its suppliers, it involves them deeply in the process of delivering a stylish and affordable lifestyle to IKEA's customers:

> IKEA, the world's largest furniture retailer, is the quintessential global cult brand. Customers from Beijing to Moscow to Edmonton flock to the Scandinavian retailer's more than 267 huge stores in 25 countries, drawn by IKEA's trendy but simple and practical furniture at affordable prices. But IKEA's biggest obstacle to growth isn't opening new stores and attracting customers. Rather, it's finding enough of the right kinds of *suppliers* to help design and produce the billions of dollars of affordable goods that those customers will carry out of its stores every year. IKEA currently relies on about 1220 suppliers in more than 55 countries to stock its shelves. IKEA doesn't just rely on spot suppliers who might be available when needed. Instead, it has systematically developed a robust network of supplier–partners that reliably provide the more than 10 000 items it stocks. IKEA's designers start with a basic customer value proposition. Then, they find and work closely with key suppliers to bring that proposition to market. And IKEA does more than just buy from suppliers; it also involves them deeply in the process of designing and making stylish but affordable products to keep IKEA's customers coming back.[2]

2   BUSINESS BUYER BEHAVIOUR

At the most basic level, marketers want to know how business buyers will respond to various marketing stimuli. Figure 7.1 shows a model of business buyer behaviour. In this model, marketing and other stimuli affect the buying organization and produce certain

Figure 7.1 The model of business buyer behaviour

The environment		The buying organization	Buyer responses
Marketing stimuli	**Other stimuli**	*The buying centre*	Product or service choice
Product	Economic		Supplier choice
Price	Technological	**Buying decision process**	Order quantities
Place	Political		Delivery terms and times
Promotion	Cultural	(Interpersonal and individual influences)	Service terms
	Competitive	(Organizational influences)	Payment

buyer responses. These stimuli enter the organization and are turned into buyer responses. In order to design good marketing strategies, the marketer must understand what happens within the organization to turn stimuli into purchase responses.

Within the organization, buying activity consists of two major parts: the buying centre, made up of all the people involved in the buying decision, and the buying decision process. The model shows that the buying centre and the buying decision process are influenced by internal organizational, interpersonal, and individual factors as well as by external environmental factors.

The model in Figure 7.1 suggests four questions about business buyer behaviour: What buying decisions do business buyers make? Who participates in the buying process? What are the major influences on buyers? How do business buyers make their buying decisions?

Major Types of Buying Situations

There are three major types of buying situations.[3] At one extreme is the *straight rebuy*, which is a fairly routine decision. At the other extreme is the *new task*, which may call for thorough research. In the middle is the *modified rebuy*, which requires some research.

In a **straight rebuy**, the buyer reorders something without any modifications. It is usually handled on a routine basis by the purchasing department. Based on past buying satisfaction, the buyer simply chooses from the various suppliers on its list. "In" suppliers try to maintain product and service quality. They often propose automatic reordering systems so that the purchasing agent will save reordering time. "Out" suppliers try to find new ways to add value or exploit dissatisfaction so that the buyer will consider them.

In a **modified rebuy**, the buyer wants to modify product specifications, prices, terms, or suppliers. The modified rebuy usually involves more decision participants than does the straight rebuy. The in suppliers may become nervous and feel pressured to put their best foot forward to protect an account. Out suppliers may see the modified rebuy situation as an opportunity to make a better offer and gain new business.

A company buying a product or service for the first time faces a **new task** situation. In such cases, the greater the cost or risk, the larger the number of decision participants and the greater their efforts to collect information. The new task situation is the marketer's greatest opportunity and challenge. The marketer not only tries to reach as many key buying influences as possible, but also provides help and information.

The buyer makes the fewest decisions in the straight rebuy and the most in the new task decision. In the new task situation, the buyer must decide on product specifications, suppliers, price limits, payment terms, order quantities, delivery times, and service terms. The order of these decisions varies with each situation, and different decision participants influence each choice.

Many business buyers prefer to buy a complete solution to a problem from a single seller instead of buying separate products and services from several suppliers and putting them together. The sale often goes to the firm that provides the most complete *system* for

Straight rebuy
A business buying situation in which the buyer routinely reorders something without any modifications.

Modified rebuy
A business buying situation in which the buyer wants to modify product specifications, prices, terms, or suppliers.

New task
A business buying situation in which the buyer purchases a product or service for the first time.

Systems selling (solutions selling)
Buying a packaged solution to a problem from a single seller, thus avoiding all the separate decisions involved in a complex buying situation.

meeting the customer's needs and solving its problems. Such **systems selling** (or **solutions selling**) is often a key business marketing strategy for winning and holding accounts. Thus, as we discovered in Real Marketing 7.1, transportation and logistics giant UPS does more than just ship packages for its business customers. It develops entire solutions to customers' transportation and logistics problems. For example, UPS bundles a complete system of services that support Nikon's consumer products supply chain—including logistics, transportation, freight, and customs brokerage services—into one smooth-running system:

> When Nikon entered the digital camera market it decided that it needed an entirely new distribution strategy as well. So it asked transportation and logistics giant UPS to design a complete system for moving its entire electronics product line from its Asian factories to retail stores throughout the United States, Canada, Latin America, and the Caribbean. Now, products leave Nikon's Asian manufacturing centres and arrive on retailers' shelves in as few as two days, with UPS handling everything in between. UPS first manages air and ocean freight and related customs brokerage to bring Nikon products from Korea, Japan, and Indonesia to its Louisville, Kentucky, operations centre. There, UPS can either "kit" the Nikon merchandise with accessories such as batteries and chargers or repackage it for in-store display. Finally, UPS distributes the products to thousands of retailers across the United States or exports them to Canadian, Latin American, or Caribbean retail outlets and distributors. Along the way, UPS tracks the goods and provides Nikon with a "snapshot" of the entire supply chain, letting Nikon keep retailers informed of delivery times and adjust them as needed.[4]

Participants in the Business Buying Process

Who does the buying of the trillions of dollars' worth of goods and services needed by business organizations? The decision-making unit of a buying organization is called its **buying centre**—all the individuals and units that play a role in the business purchase decision-making process. This group includes the actual users of the product or service, those who make the buying decision, those who influence the buying decision, those who do the actual buying, and those who control buying information.

Buying centre
All the individuals and units that play a role in the purchase decision-making process.

Users
Members of the buying organization who will actually use the purchased product or service.

Influencers
People in an organization's buying centre who affect the buying decision; they often help define specifications and also provide information for evaluating alternatives.

Buyers
People in the organization's buying centre who make an actual purchase.

Deciders
People in the organization's buying centre who have formal or informal power to select or approve the final suppliers.

Gatekeepers
People in the organization's buying centre who control the flow of information to others.

The buying centre includes all members of the organization who play any of five roles in the purchase decision process:[5]

- **Users** are members of the organization who will use the product or service. In many cases, users initiate the buying proposal and help define product specifications.

- **Influencers** often help define specifications and also provide information for evaluating alternatives. Technical personnel are particularly important influencers.

- **Buyers** have formal authority to select the supplier and arrange terms of purchase. Buyers may help shape product specifications, but their major role is in selecting vendors and negotiating. In more complex purchases, buyers might include high-level officers participating in the negotiations.

- **Deciders** have formal or informal power to select or approve the final suppliers. In routine buying, the buyers are often the deciders, or at least the approvers.

- **Gatekeepers** control the flow of information to others. For example, purchasing agents often have authority to prevent salespersons from seeing users or deciders. Other gatekeepers include technical personnel and even personal secretaries.

The buying centre is not a fixed and formally identified unit within the buying organization. It is a set of buying roles assumed by different people for different purchases. Within the organization, the size and makeup of the buying centre will vary for different products and for different buying situations. For some routine purchases, one person—say, a purchasing agent—may assume all the buying centre roles and serve as the only person involved in the buying decision. For more complex purchases, the buying centre may include 20 or 30 people from different levels and departments in the organization.

The buying centre concept presents a major marketing challenge. The business marketer must learn who participates in the decision-making proces, each participant's relative influence, and what evaluation criteria each decision participant uses. This can be difficult. Says one supplier of health care information technology solutions to large hospitals:

> You have to understand what [doors] to knock on. A lot of salespeople give up on working with hospitals because they don't understand how big the business is, and you have a lot of people you have to deal with. You also have to understand that you're selling to committees, which means 10 or 20 people have to make a decision. For them to make a decision they have to have lots of meetings, and sales can [take] anywhere from six months to two years."[6]

For instance, the medical products and services group of Cardinal Health sells disposable surgical gowns to hospitals. It identifies the hospital personnel involved in this buying decision as the vice-president of purchasing, the operating room administrator, and the surgeons. Each participant plays a different role. The vice-president of purchasing analyzes whether the hospital should buy disposable gowns or reusable gowns. If analysis favours disposable gowns, then the operating room administrator compares competing products and prices and makes a choice. This administrator considers the gowns' absorbency, antiseptic qualities, design, and cost and normally buys the brand that meets requirements at the lowest cost. Finally, surgeons affect the decision later by reporting on their satisfaction or dissatisfaction with the brand.

The buying centre usually includes some obvious participants who are involved formally in the buying decision. For example, the decision to buy a corporate jet will probably involve the company's CEO, chief pilot, a purchasing agent, some legal staff, a member of top management, and others formally charged with the buying decision. It may also involve less obvious, informal participants, some of whom may actually make or strongly affect the buying decision. Sometimes even the people in the buying centre are not aware of all the buying participants. For example, the decision about which corporate jet to buy may actually be made by a corporate board member who has an interest in flying and who knows a lot about airplanes. This board member may work behind the scenes to sway the decision. Many business buying decisions result from the complex interactions of ever-changing buying centre participants.

Major Influences on Business Buyers

Business buyers are subject to many influences when they make their buying decisions. Some marketers assume that the major influences are economic. They think buyers will

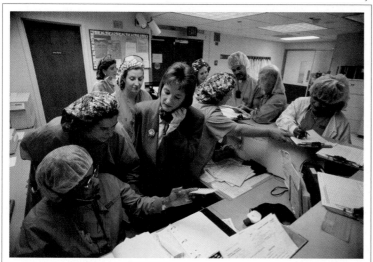

Buying centre: Cardinal Health deals with a wide range of buying influences, from purchasing executives and hospital administrators to the surgeons who actually use its products.

favour the supplier who offers the lowest price or the best product or the most service. They concentrate on offering strong economic benefits to buyers. However, business buyers actually respond to both economic and personal factors. Far from being cold, calculating, and impersonal, business buyers are human and social as well. They react to both reason and emotion.

Today, most B2B marketers recognize that emotion plays an important role in business buying decisions. For example, you might expect that an advertisement promoting large trucks to corporate fleet buyers or independent owner–operators would stress objective technical, performance, and economic factors. For instance, premium heavy-duty truck maker Peterbilt does stress performance—its dealers and website provide plenty of information about factors such as manoeuvrability, productivity, reliability, comfort,

Emotions play an important role in business buying. This Peterbilt ad stresses performance factors, such as fuel efficiency. But it also stresses more emotional factors, such as the raw beauty of Peterbilt trucks and the pride of owning and driving one. "Class Pays."

and fuel efficiency. But Peterbilt ads appeal to buyers' emotions as well. They show the raw beauty of the trucks, and the Peterbilt slogan—"Class Pays"—suggests that owning a Peterbilt truck is a matter of pride as well as superior performance. Says the company, "On highways, construction sites, city streets, logging roads—everywhere customers earn their living—Peterbilt's red oval is a familiar symbol of performance, reliability, and pride."

When suppliers' offers are very similar, business buyers have little basis for strictly rational choice. Because they can meet organizational goals with any supplier, buyers can allow personal factors to play a larger role in their decisions. However, when competing products differ greatly, business buyers are more accountable for their choices and tend to pay more attention to economic factors. Figure 7.2 lists various groups of influences on business buyers—environmental, organizational, interpersonal, and individual.[7]

Environmental Factors

Business buyers are heavily influenced by factors in the current and expected *economic environment*, such as the level of primary demand, the economic outlook, and the cost of money. Another environmental factor is *shortages* in key materials. Many companies now are more willing to buy and hold larger inventories of scarce materials to ensure adequate supply. Business buyers also are affected by technological, political, and competitive developments in the environment. Finally, *culture and customs* can strongly influence business buyer reactions to the marketer's behaviour and strategies, especially in the international marketing environment (see Real Marketing 7.2). The business buyer must watch these factors, determine how they will affect the buyer, and try to turn these challenges into opportunities.

Organizational Factors

Each buying organization has its own objectives, policies, procedures, structure, and systems, and the business marketer must understand these factors well. Questions such as these arise: How many people are involved in the buying decision? Who are they? What are their evaluative criteria? What are the company's policies and limits on its buyers?

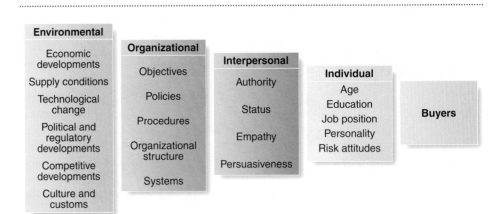

Figure 7.2 Major influences on business buyer behaviour

Environmental	Organizational	Interpersonal	Individual	
Economic developments	Objectives	Authority	Age	
Supply conditions	Policies	Status	Education	
Technological change	Procedures	Empathy	Job position	**Buyers**
Political and regulatory developments	Organizational structure	Persuasiveness	Personality	
Competitive developments	Systems		Risk attitudes	
Culture and customs				

Real Marketing 7.2

International Marketing Manners: When in Rome, Do as the Romans Do

Picture this: Consolidated Amalgamation, Inc. thinks it's time that the rest of the world enjoyed the same fine products it has offered Canadian consumers for two generations. It dispatches vice-president Harry E. Slicksmile to Europe, Africa, and Asia to explore the territory. Mr. Slicksmile stops first in London, where he makes short work of some bankers—he rings them up on the phone. He handles Parisians with similar ease: After securing a table at La Tour d'Argent, he greets his luncheon guest, the director of an industrial engineering firm, with the words, "Just call me Harry, Jacques."

In Germany, Mr. Slicksmile is a powerhouse. Whisking through a lavish, state-of-the-art multimedia marketing presentation on his Toshiba tablet laptop, he shows 'em that this Alberta boy knows how to make a buck. Heading on to Milan, Harry strikes up a conversation with the Japanese businessman sitting next to him on the plane. He flips his card onto the guy's tray and, when the two say goodbye, shakes hands warmly and clasps the man's right arm. Later, for his appointment with the owner of an Italian packaging design firm, our hero wears his comfy corduroy sport coat, khaki pants, and Topsiders. Everybody knows Italians are zany and laid back.

Mr. Slicksmile next swings through Saudi Arabia, where he coolly presents a potential client with a multimillion-dollar proposal in a classy pigskin binder. At his next stop in Beijing, he talks business over lunch with a group of Chinese executives. After completing the meal, he drops his chopsticks into his bowl of rice and presents each guest with an elegant Tiffany clock as a reminder of his visit. Then, at his final junket in Phuket, Thailand, Mr. Slicksmile wastes no time diving into his business proposal before treating his Thai clients to a first-class lunch.

A great tour, sure to generate a pile of orders, right? Wrong. Six months later, Consolidated Amalgamation has nothing to show for the trip but a stack of bills. Abroad, they weren't wild about Harry.

This hypothetical case has been exaggerated for emphasis. Canadians are seldom such dolts. We are used to dealing with ethnic diversity here at home. But experts say success in international business has a lot to do with knowing the territory and its people. By learning English and extending themselves in other ways, the world's business leaders have met North Americans more than halfway. In contrast, some businesspeople too often do little except assume that others will march to their music. They want things to be just the way they are at home when they travel. Fast. Convenient. Easy. So they may become rude and pushy by demanding that

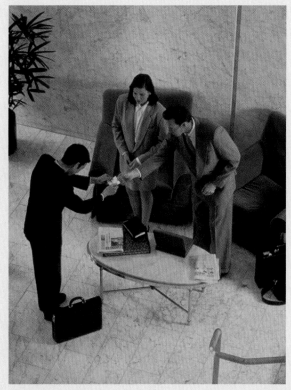

Canadian companies must help their managers understand international customers and customs. For example, Japanese people revere the business card as an extension of the self—they do not hand it out to people, they present it.

others change. Says one North American world trade expert, "I think more business would be done if we tried harder."

Poor Harry tried, all right, but in all the wrong ways. The British do not, as a rule, make deals over the phone as much as North Americans do. It's not so much a "cultural" difference as a difference in approach. A proper Frenchman neither likes instant familiarity—questions about family, church, or alma mater—nor refers to strangers by their first names. "That poor fellow, Jacques, probably wouldn't show anything, but he'd recoil. He'd not be pleased," explains an expert on French business practices. "It's considered poor taste," he continues. "Even after months of business dealings, I'd wait for him or her to make the invitation [to use first names]. . . . You are always right, in Europe, to say 'Mister.'"

Harry's flashy presentation would likely have been a flop with the Germans, who dislike overstatement and showiness. And when Harry grabbed his new Japanese acquaintance by the arm, the executive probably considered him disrespectful and presumptuous. Japan, like many Asian countries, is a "no-contact culture" in which even shaking

▶

hands is a strange experience. Harry made matters worse by tossing his business card. Japanese people revere the business card as an extension of the self and as an indicator of rank. They do not hand it to people, they present it—with both hands. In addition, the Japanese are sticklers about rank. Unlike North Americans, they don't heap praise on subordinates in a room; they will praise only the highest-ranking official present.

Hapless Harry also goofed when he assumed that Italians are like Hollywood's stereotypes of them. The flair for design and style that has characterized Italian culture for centuries is embodied in the businesspeople of Milan and Rome. They dress beautifully and admire flair, but they blanch at garishness or impropriety in others' attire.

To the Saudi Arabians, the pigskin binder would have been considered vile. An American salesperson who really did present such a binder was unceremoniously tossed out and his company was blacklisted from working with Saudi businesses. In China, Harry's casually dropping his chopsticks could have been misinterpreted as an act of aggression. Stabbing chopsticks into a bowl of rice and leaving them signifies death to the Chinese. The clocks Harry offered as gifts might have confirmed such dark intentions. To "give a clock" in Chinese sounds the same as "seeing someone off to his end." Finally, not surprisingly, Harry

flunked his Phuket junket—in Thailand, it's off limits to speak about business matters until after the meal is served and eaten.

Thus, to compete successfully in global markets, or even to deal effectively with international firms in their home markets, companies must help their managers understand the needs, customs, and cultures of international business buyers. "When doing business in a foreign country and a foreign culture—particularly a non-Western culture—assume nothing," advises an international business specialist. "Take nothing for granted. Turn every stone. Ask every question. Dig into every detail. Because cultures really are different, and those differences can have a major impact." So the old advice is still good advice: When in Rome, do as the Romans do.

Sources: Portions adapted from Susan Harte, "When in Rome, You Should Learn to Do What the Romans Do," *Atlanta Journal-Constitution*, January 22, 1990, pp. D1, D6. Additional information and examples from James K. Sebenius, "The Hidden Challenge of Cross-Border Negotiatons," *Harvard Business Review*, March 2002, pp. 76–85; Gary Stroller, "Doing Business Abroad? Simple Faux Pas Can Sink You," *USA Today*, August 24, 2007, p. 1B; Janette S. Martin and Lillian H. Chaney, *Global Business Etiquette: A Guide to International Communication and Customs* (Westport, CT: Greenwood Press, 2008); and information accessed at www.executiveplanet.com, December 2008.

Interpersonal Factors

The buying centre usually includes many participants who influence each other, so *interpersonal factors* also influence the business buying process. However, it is often difficult to assess such interpersonal factors and group dynamics. Buying centre participants do not wear tags that label them as "key decision maker" or "not influential." Nor do buying centre participants with the highest rank always have the most influence. Participants may influence the buying decision because they control rewards and punishments, are well liked, have special expertise, or have a special relationship with other important participants. Interpersonal factors are often very subtle. Whenever possible, business marketers must try to understand these factors and design strategies that take them into account.

Individual Factors

Each participant in the business buying decision process brings in personal motives, perceptions, and preferences. These individual factors are affected by personal characteristics such as age, income, education, professional identification, personality, and attitudes toward risk. Also, buyers have different buying styles. Some may be technical types who make in-depth analyses of competitive proposals before choosing a supplier. Other buyers may be intuitive negotiators who are adept at pitting the sellers against one another for the best deal.

3   The Business Buying Process

Figure 7.3 lists the eight stages of the business buying process.[8] Buyers who face a new task buying situation usually go through all stages of the buying process. Buyers making modified or straight rebuys may skip some of the stages. We will examine these steps for the typical new task buying situation.

Figure 7.3 Stages of the business buying process

Problem recognition
The first stage of the business buying process in which someone in the company recognizes a problem or need that can be met by acquiring a good or a service.

General need description
The stage in the business buying process in which the company describes the general characteristics and quantity of a needed item.

Product specification
The stage of the business buying process in which the buying organization decides on and specifies the best technical product characteristics for a needed item.

Problem Recognition

The buying process begins when someone in the company recognizes a problem or need that can be met by acquiring a specific product or service. **Problem recognition** can result from internal or external stimuli. Internally, the company may decide to launch a new product that requires new production equipment and materials. Or a machine may break down and need new parts. Perhaps a purchasing manager is unhappy with a current supplier's product quality, service, or prices. Externally, the buyer may get some new ideas at a trade show, see an ad, or receive a call from a salesperson who offers a better product or a lower price.

In fact, in their advertising, business marketers often alert customers to potential problems and then show how their products provide solutions. For example, a Sharp ad notes that a multifunction printer can present data security problems and asks "Is your MFP a portal for identity theft?" The solution? Sharp's data security kits "help prevent sensitive information from falling into the wrong hands."

Problem recognition: Sharp uses ads like this one to alert customers to potential problems and then provide solutions.

General Need Description

Having recognized a need, the buyer next prepares a **general need description** that describes the characteristics and quantity of the needed item. For standard items, this process presents few problems. For complex items, however, the buyer may need to work with others—engineers, users, consultants—to define the item. The team may want to rank the importance of reliability, durability, price, and other attributes desired in the item. In this phase, the alert business marketer can help the buyers define their needs and provide information about the value of different product characteristics.

Product Specification

The buying organization next develops the item's technical **product specifications**, often with the help of a value analysis engineering team. *Product value analysis* is an approach to cost reduction in which components are studied carefully to determine if they can be redesigned, standardized, or made by less costly methods of production. The team decides on the best product characteristics and specifies them accordingly. Sellers, too, can use value analysis as a tool to help secure a new account. By showing buyers a better way to make an object, outside sellers can turn straight rebuy situations into new task situations that give them a chance to obtain new business.

Supplier Search

Supplier search
The stage of the business buying process in which the buyer tries to find the best vendors.

The buyer now conducts a **supplier search** to find the best vendors. The buyer can compile a small list of qualified suppliers by reviewing trade directories, doing computer searches, or phoning other companies for recommendations. Today, more and more companies are turning to the Internet to find suppliers. For marketers, this has levelled the playing field— the Internet gives smaller suppliers many of the same advantages as larger competitors.

The newer the buying task and the more complex and costly the item, the greater the amount of time the buyer will spend searching for suppliers. The supplier's task is to get listed in major directories and build a good reputation in the marketplace. Salespeople should watch for companies in the process of searching for suppliers and make certain that their firm is considered.

Proposal Solicitation

Proposal solicitation
The stage of the business buying process in which the buyer invites qualified suppliers to submit proposals.

In the **proposal solicitation** stage of the business buying process, the buyer invites qualified suppliers to submit proposals. In response, some suppliers will send only a catalogue or a salesperson. However, when the item is complex or expensive, the buyer will usually require detailed written proposals or formal presentations from each potential supplier.

Business marketers must be skilled in researching, writing, and presenting proposals in response to buyer proposal solicitations. Proposals should be marketing documents, not just technical documents. Presentations should inspire confidence and should make the marketer's company stand out from the competition.

Supplier Selection

Supplier selection
The stage of the business buying process in which the buyer reviews proposals and selects a supplier or suppliers.

The members of the buying centre now review the proposals and select a supplier or suppliers. During **supplier selection**, the buying centre often will draw up a list of the desired supplier attributes and their relative importance. Such attributes include product and service quality, reputation, on-time delivery, ethical corporate behaviour, honest communication, and competitive prices. The members of the buying centre will rate suppliers against these attributes and identify the best suppliers.

Buyers may attempt to negotiate with preferred suppliers for better prices and terms before making the final selections. In the end, they may select a single supplier or a few suppliers. Many buyers prefer multiple sources of supplies to avoid being totally dependent on one supplier and to allow comparisons of prices and performance of several suppliers over time. Today's supplier development managers want to develop a full network of supplier–partners that can help the company bring more value to its customers.

Order-Routine Specification

Order-routine specification
The stage of the business buying process in which the buyer writes the final order with the chosen supplier(s), listing the technical specifications, quantity needed, expected time of delivery, return policies, and warranties.

The buyer now prepares an **order-routine specification**. It includes the final order with the chosen supplier or suppliers and lists items such as technical specifications, quantity needed, expected time of delivery, return policies, and warranties. In the case of maintenance, repair, and operating items, buyers may use blanket contracts rather than periodic purchase orders. A blanket contract creates a long-term relationship in which the supplier promises to resupply the buyer as needed at agreed-upon prices for a set time period.

Many large buyers now practise *vendor-managed inventory*, in which they turn over ordering and inventory responsibilities to their suppliers. Under such systems, buyers share sales and inventory information directly with key suppliers. The suppliers then monitor inventories and replenish stock automatically as needed. For example, most major suppliers to large retailers such as Walmart, Home Depot, and Lowe's assume vendor-managed inventory responsibilities.

Performance Review

Performance review
The stage of the business buying process in which the buyer assesses the performance of the supplier and decides to continue, modify, or drop the arrangement.

In this stage, the buyer reviews supplier performance. The buyer may contact users and ask them to rate their satisfaction. The **performance review** may lead the buyer to continue, modify, or drop the arrangement. The seller's job is to monitor the same factors used by the

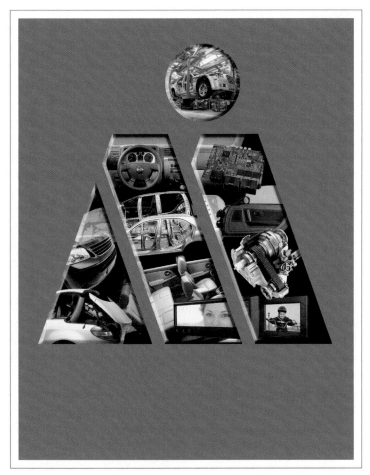

Magna is the most diversified automotive supplier in the world. Working closely with its customers throughout their buying process, it designs, develops, and manufactures automotive systems, assemblies, modules, and components, and it engineers and even assembles complete vehicles for manufacturers of cars and light trucks around the world.

buyer to make sure that the seller is giving the expected satisfaction.

This eight-stage buying-process model provides a simple view of business buying as it might occur in a new task buying situation. The actual process is usually much more complex. In a modified rebuy or straight rebuy situation, some of these stages would be compressed or bypassed. Each organization buys in its own way, and each buying situation has unique requirements.

Different buying centre participants may be involved at different stages of the process. Although certain buying-process steps usually do occur, buyers do not always follow them in the same order, and they may add other steps. Often, buyers will repeat certain stages of the process. Finally, a customer relationship might involve many different types of purchases ongoing at a given time, all in different stages of the buying process. The seller must manage the total customer relationship, not just individual purchases.

Aurora, Ontario–based Magna International, a leading global supplier of technologically advanced automotive systems, components, and complete modules, is well aware of the steps its customers go through when sourcing new parts or automotive systems. As of May 2009, Magna employed 82 000 people at 240 manufacturing divisions and 86 product-development and engineering centres located throughout North and South America, Europe, and Asia. As one of the most diversified automotive suppliers in the world, Magna doesn't sell to the public, but does provide automotive systems and components to almost every original equipment manufacturer (OEM) across the globe. Its top customer is DaimlerChrysler, but Magna also conducts business with almost every other automotive manufacturer firm in the world. Magna is recognized by these firms for its innovative technology, diverse capabilities, global presence, and unique culture. Magna delivers cost savings and competitive-edge technologies to all of its customers. When marketing, Magna cannot appeal to the needs of just one type of person. It reaches a vast array of decision makers and product users—everyone from automotive design engineers and professional purchasing managers to the end consumer. To understand its clients' needs and help them meet their challenges, Magna must continue to build strong relationships with its customer base. As one analyst notes when describing Magna, "building and keeping good relationships—it's what will separate a good company from a great one." Consider the story of how Magna came to the new Powerway technology, which it adopted as part of its ebusiness initiatives:

> Relationships are two-way streets that can benefit both partners, especially if they collaborate on a number of efforts. Magna learned of Powerway through DaimlerChrysler, which was nudging some of its suppliers to use the system for certain collaboration functions. Magna didn't resent this little push. Instead, the company saw it as a way to work better with DaimlerChrysler. Says Ted Wozniak, Magna's CIO, "We didn't come at this the way a lot of suppliers do. We came at it with a partnership process." Furthermore, by listening to the customer and quickly responding to DaimlerChrysler's needs and new way of doing business, Magna got a jump on its competitors. Not only did the Powerway technology save Magna both time and money, it helped the company consolidate a key relationship. Savings came through the elimination of a pile of paperwork and personal visits between Magna's plants and those of DaimlerChrysler.[9]

Eprocurement: Buying on the Internet

Eprocurement
Purchasing through electronic connections between buyers and sellers—usually online.

Advances in information technology have changed the face of the B2B marketing process. Electronic purchasing, often called **eprocurement**, has grown rapidly in recent years. Virtually unknown less than a decade ago, online purchasing is standard procedure for most companies today. Eprocurement gives buyers access to new suppliers, lowers purchasing costs, and hastens order processing and delivery. In turn, business marketers can connect with customers online to share marketing information, sell products and services, provide customer support services, and maintain ongoing customer relationships.

Companies can do eprocurement in any of several ways. They can conduct *reverse auctions*, in which they put their purchasing requests online and invite suppliers to bid for the business. Or they can engage in online *trading exchanges*, through which companies work collectively to facilitate the trading process. For example, Exostar is an online trading exchange that connects buyers and sellers in the aerospace and defence industry. Its goal is to improve trading efficiency and reduce costs among industry trading partners. Initially a collaboration among five leading aerospace and defence companies—Boeing, Lockheed Martin, Raytheon, BAE Systems, and Rolls-Royce—Exostar has now connected more than 300 procurement systems and 40 000 trading partners in 20 countries around the world.

Companies also can conduct eprocurement by setting up their own *company buying sites*. For example, General Electric operates a company trading site on which it posts its buying needs and invites bids, negotiates terms, and places orders. Or companies can create *extranet links* with key suppliers. For instance, they can create direct procurement accounts with suppliers such as Dell or Office Depot through which company buyers can purchase equipment, materials, and supplies directly.

B2B marketers can help customers who wish to purchase online by creating well-designed, easy-to-use websites. For example, *BtoB* magazine rated the site of Sun Microsystems—a market leader in network computing hardware, software, and services—as one of its "10 great B2B websites":

A few years ago, Sun Microsystems completely redesigned its website. It was most interested in finding a better way to present deep information on its thousands of complex server, storage, and software products and services while also giving the site a more humanistic view. Sun came up with a tab-driven menu design that puts an enormous amount of information within only a few clicks of customers' computers. Action-oriented menu labels—such as Evaluate, Get, Use, and Maintain—leave nothing to the imagination and make navigation a snap. Beyond product pictures and specifications, the site provides video walk-throughs of products, along with "success stories" of how other customers have benefited from doing business with Sun.

Customers can even create personalized MySun portals. "We provide you with a customized experience," says Sun's VP-Sun Web Experience. "Maybe you've downloaded software. Based on that download, you'll see a filtered blog, training classes that are available, and a link to unreleased code you can try out. It's integrated support tailored to the type of Sun products you use." Users who still need help can take advantage of the site's interactive features to request an immediate phone call, an email, or a live online chat in English, French, German, or Spanish with a Sun representative.[10]

Online buying: This Sun Microsystems site helps customers who want to purchase online by providing deep information on its thousands of complex products and services. Users who still need help can take advantage of the site's interactive features to request an immediate phone call, an email, or a live online chat with a Sun representative.

RBC Financial Group has created an eprocurement system that offers benefits to its current and potential vendors as well as to the firm.

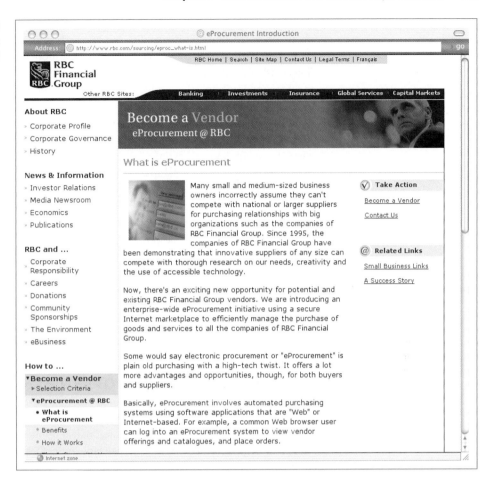

Service firms are also taking advantage of eprocurement. See what the RBC Financial Group has done:

> In 2005, the companies of RBC Financial Group announced a new opportunity for potential and existing RBC Financial Group vendors—an enterprise-wide eprocurement initiative using a secure Internet marketplace. RBC's eprocurement webpage notes, "Some would say electronic procurement or 'eProcurement' is plain old purchasing with a high-tech twist. It offers a lot more advantages and opportunities, though, for both buyers and suppliers." Vendors approved for RBC's eProcurement Initiative can upload a catalogue of goods and services. These catalogues can then be seen on the computer desktops of employees throughout all the companies of RBC Financial Group, creating an unrivalled selling opportunity for the vendor. The eProcurement network also provides fast transmission, order tracking and efficient processing of orders and payment of invoices, helping to eliminate delays or lost paper work.[11]

As the RBC example demonstrates, business-to-business eprocurement yields many benefits. First, it shaves transaction costs and results in more efficient purchasing for both buyers and suppliers. A web-powered purchasing program eliminates the paperwork associated with traditional requisition and ordering procedures and helps an organization keep better track of all purchases.

Eprocurement reduces the time between order and delivery. Time savings are particularly dramatic for companies with many overseas suppliers. Adaptec, a leading supplier of computer storage, used an extranet to tie all of its Taiwanese chip suppliers together in a kind of virtual family. Now messages from Adaptec flow in seconds from its headquarters to its Asian partners, and Adaptec has reduced the time between the order and delivery of its chips from as long as 16 weeks to just 55 days—the same turnaround time for companies that build their own chips.

Finally, beyond the cost and time savings, eprocurement frees purchasing people to focus on more-strategic issues. For many purchasing professionals, going online means reducing drudgery and paperwork and spending more time managing inventory and working creatively with suppliers. "That is the key," says an HP purchasing executive. "You can now focus people on value-added activities. Procurement professionals can now find different sources and work with suppliers to reduce costs and to develop new products."[12]

The rapidly expanding use of eprocurement, however, also presents some problems. For example, at the same time that the Web makes it possible for suppliers and customers to share business data and even collaborate on product design, it can also erode decades-old customer–supplier relationships. Many buyers now use the power of the Web to pit suppliers against one another and to search out better deals, products, and turnaround times on a purchase-by-purchase basis.

Eprocurement can also create potential security disasters. Although email and home banking transactions can be protected through basic encryption, the secure environment that businesses need to carry out confidential interactions is sometimes still lacking. Companies are spending millions of dollars on defensive strategies to keep hackers at bay. Cisco Systems, for example, specifies the types of routers, firewalls, and security procedures that its partners must use to safeguard extranet connections. In fact, the company goes even further—it sends its own security engineers to examine a partner's defences and holds the partner liable for any security breach that originates from its computers.

4 INSTITUTIONAL AND GOVERNMENT MARKETS

So far, our discussion of organizational buying has focused largely on the buying behaviour of business buyers. Much of this discussion also applies to the buying practices of institutional and government organizations. However, these two nonbusiness markets have additional characteristics and needs. In this final section, we address the special features of institutional and government markets.

Institutional Market

Institutional market
Schools, hospitals, nursing homes, prisons, and other institutions that provide goods and services to people in their care.

The **institutional market** consists of schools, hospitals, nursing homes, prisons, and other institutions that provide goods and services to people in their care. Institutions differ from one another in their sponsors and in their objectives. For example, a firm selling adjustable beds to the institutional market in Toronto would want to consider how the needs of the private Shouldice Hernia Centre would differ from those of Princess Margaret Hospital and various private nursing homes.

Many institutional markets are characterized by low budgets and captive patrons. For example, hospital patients have little choice but to eat whatever food the hospital supplies. A hospital purchasing agent has to decide on the quality of food to buy for patients. Because the food is provided as part of a total service package, the buying objective is not profit. Nor is strict cost minimization the goal—patients receiving poor-quality food will complain to others and damage the hospital's reputation. Thus, the hospital purchasing agent must search for institutional-food vendors whose quality meets or exceeds a certain minimum standard and whose prices are low.

Many marketers set up separate divisions to meet the special characteristics and needs of institutional buyers. For example, Kellogg's Food Away From Home business unit produces, packages, prices, and markets its broad assortment of cereals, cookies, snacks, and other products to better serve the specific food service requirements of hospitals, schools, the military, and other institutional markets.[13]

Government Market

Government market
Governmental units—federal, provincial or territorial, and municipal—that purchase or rent goods and services for carrying out the main functions of government.

The **government market** offers large opportunities for many companies, both big and small. In most countries, government organizations are major buyers of goods and services. The Government of Canada buys approximately $20 billion worth of goods and services every year from thousands of suppliers. There are more than 85 departments, agencies, Crown corporations, and special operating agencies. Public Works and Government Services Canada (PWGSC) is the government's largest purchasing organization, averaging 60 000 contracts totalling $10 billion annually. Provincial, territorial, and municipal governments also purchase a vast array of goods and services.[14] Government buying and business buying are similar in many ways, but there are also differences that must be understood by companies that wish to sell products and services to governments. To succeed in the government market, sellers must locate key decision makers, identify the factors that affect buyer behaviour, and understand the buying decision process.

Government organizations typically require suppliers to submit bids, and normally they award the contract to the lowest bidder. In some cases, the government unit will make allowances for the supplier's superior quality or reputation for completing contracts on time. Governments will also buy on a negotiated contract basis, primarily in the case of complex projects involving major R&D costs and risks, and in cases where there is little competition.

Government organizations tend to favour domestic suppliers over foreign suppliers. A major complaint of multinationals operating in Europe is that each country shows favouritism toward its nationals in spite of superior offers that are made by foreign firms. The European Economic Commission is gradually removing this bias.

Like consumer and business buyers, government buyers are affected by environmental, organizational, interpersonal, and individual factors. One unique thing about government buying is that it is carefully watched by outside publics, ranging from Parliament to a variety of private groups interested in how the government spends taxpayers' money. For example, when selling to the federal government, vendor bids and contracts must comply with Canada's trade obligations under the North American Free Trade Agreement (NAFTA), the World Trade Organization Agreement on Government Procurement (WTO-AGP), and the Agreement on Internal Trade (AIT). Because their spending decisions are subject to public review, government organizations require considerable paperwork from suppliers, who often complain about excessive paperwork, bureaucracy, regulations, decision-making delays, and frequent shifts in procurement personnel.

Despite these challenges, selling to the government has many advantages. Government represents one of the largest markets in Canada, and 80 percent of federal contracts are tendered outside of Ottawa. Furthermore, the government is a good credit risk, and when exporting it is a useful marketing tool to list the government as a customer. Finally, information about bidding opportunities in the federal government is widely available online through the electronic tendering system MERX. There are even sometimes extra benefits associated with supplying government departments. In an effort to improve the competitiveness of Canadian businesses, products purchased by the government are evaluated for the potential to be marketed worldwide. For example, rations developed for the military by Magic Pan are now marketed to global institutions.[15]

Most governments provide would-be suppliers with detailed guides describing how to sell to the government. For example, the Government of Canada website provides a lot of detailed information on how to sell to the government. Various trade magazines and associations provide information on how to reach schools, hospitals, highway departments, and other government agencies.

Noneconomic criteria also play a growing role in government buying. Government buyers are asked to favour depressed business firms and areas; small business firms; minority-owned firms; and business firms that avoid race, gender, or age discrimination. Sellers need to keep these factors in mind when deciding to seek government business.

Many companies that sell to the government have not been very marketing oriented for a number of reasons. Total government spending is determined by elected officials rather than by any marketing effort to develop this market. Government buying has emphasized price, making suppliers invest their effort in technology to bring costs down. When the product's characteristics are specified carefully, product differentiation is not a marketing factor. Nor do advertising or personal selling matter much in winning bids on an open-bid basis.

Several companies, however, have established separate government marketing departments, including General Electric, Bombardier, Kodak, and Goodyear. These companies anticipate government needs and projects, participate in the product specification phase, gather competitive intelligence, prepare bids carefully, and produce stronger communications to describe and enhance their companies' reputations.

Other companies have set up customized marketing programs for government buyers. For example, Dell has specific business units tailored to meet the needs of federal as well as provincial and municipal government buyers. Dell offers its customers tailor-made Premier.Dell.com webpages that include special pricing, online purchasing, and service and support.

REVIEWING OBJECTIVES AND KEY TERMS
mymarketinglab | Audio Chapter Summary

Business markets and consumer markets are alike in some key ways. For example, both include people in buying roles who make purchase decisions to satisfy needs. But business markets also differ in many ways from consumer markets. For one thing, the business market is *enormous,* far larger than the consumer market. Within Canada alone, the business market includes organizations that annually purchase billions of dollars' worth of goods and services.

OBJECTIVE 1 **Define the business market and explain how business markets differ from consumer markets.**

The *business market* comprises all organizations that buy goods and services for use in the production of other products and services or for the purpose of reselling or renting them to others at a profit. As compared to consumer markets, business markets usually have fewer, larger buyers. Business demand is derived demand, and the business buying decision usually involves more, and more professional, buyers.

OBJECTIVE 2 **Identify the major factors that influence business buyer behaviour.**

Business buyers make decisions that vary with the three types of *buying situations:* straight rebuys, modified rebuys, and new tasks. The decision-making unit of a buying organization—the *buying centre*—can consist of many different people playing many different roles. The business marketer needs to know the following: Who are the major buying centre participants? In what decisions do they exercise influence and to what degree? What evaluation criteria does each decision participant use? The business marketer also needs to understand the major environmental, organizational, interpersonal, and individual influences on the buying process.

OBJECTIVE 3 **List and define the steps in the business buying decision process.**

The *business buying decision process* itself can be quite involved, with eight basic stages: problem recognition, general need description, product specification, supplier search, proposal solicitation, supplier selection, order-routine specification, and performance review. Buyers who face a new task buying situation usually go through all stages of the buying process. Buyers making modified or straight rebuys may skip some of the stages. Companies must manage the overall customer relationship, which often includes many different buying decisions in various stages of the buying decision process.

Recent advances in information technology have given birth to *eprocurement*, by which business buyers are purchasing all kinds of products and services online. The Internet gives business buyers access to new suppliers, lowers purchasing costs, and hastens order processing and delivery. However, eprocurement can also erode customer–supplier relationships and create potential security problems. Still, business marketers are increasingly connecting with customers online to share marketing information, sell products and services, provide customer support services, and maintain ongoing customer relationships.

OBJECTIVE 4 **Compare the institutional and government markets and explain how institutional and government buyers make their buying decisions.**

The *institutional market* comprises schools, hospitals, prisons, and other institutions that provide goods and services to people in their care. These markets are characterized by low budgets and captive patrons. The *government market,* which is vast, consists of government units—federal, provincial or territorial, and municipal—that purchase or rent goods and services for carrying out the main functions of government.

Government buyers purchase products and services for defence, education, public welfare, and other public needs. Government buying practices are highly specialized and specified, with open bidding or negotiated contracts characterizing most of the buying. Government buyers operate under the watchful eye of Parliament and many private watchdog groups. Hence, they tend to require more forms and signatures, and to respond more slowly and deliberately when placing orders.

KEY TERMS

mymarketinglab | Glossary Flashcards

Objective 1
Business buyer behaviour   214
Business buying process   214
Derived demand   215
Supplier development   216

Objective 2
Straight rebuy   219
Modified rebuy   219
New task   219
Systems selling (solutions selling)   220
Buying centre   220
Users   220
Influencers   220
Buyers   220
Deciders   220
Gatekeepers   220

Objective 3
Problem recognition   225
General need description   225
Product specification   226
Supplier search   226
Proposal solicitation   226
Supplier selection   226
Order-routine specification   226
Performance review   226
Eprocurement   228

Objective 4
Institutional market   230
Government market   230

DISCUSSING THE CONCEPTS

1. Compare and contrast business and consumer markets.

2. Discuss several ways in which a straight rebuy differs from a new task situation.

3. In a buying centre purchasing process, which buying centre participant is most likely to make each of the following statements?

   • "This bonding agent better be good, because I have to put this product together."

   • "I specified this bonding agent on another job, and it worked for them."

   • "Without an appointment, no sales rep gets in to see Ms. Johnson."

   • "Okay, it's a deal—we'll buy it."

   • "I'll place the order first thing tomorrow."

4. List the major influences on business buyer behaviour. Why is it important for the business-to-business marketer to understand these major influences?

5. Name and briefly describe the stages of the business buying process.

6. How do the institutional and government markets differ from business markets?

APPLYING THE CONCEPTS

1. Business buying occurs worldwide, so marketers need to be aware of cultural factors influencing business customers. In a small group, select a country and develop a multimedia presentation on proper business etiquette and manners, including appropriate appearance, behaviour, and communication. Include a map showing the location of the country as well as a description of the country in terms of demographics, culture, and its economic history.

2. Interview a businessperson to learn how purchases are made in his or her organization. Ask this person to describe a straight rebuy, a modified rebuy, and a new task buying situation that took place recently or of which he or she is aware (define the terms if necessary).

Did the buying process differ based on the type of product or purchase situation? Ask the businessperson to explain the role he or she played in a recent purchase and to discuss the factors that influenced the decision. Write a brief report of your interview by applying the concepts you learned in this chapter regarding business buyer behaviour.

3. Form a small group and compare the similarities and differences between a buyer at the Halifax Regional School Board and a buyer at a for-profit school, such as Sacred Heart School of Halifax. Compare the buyers with reference to environmental, organizational, interpersonal, and individual factors.

FOCUS ON TECHNOLOGY

In today's competitive marketplace, many businesses strive to cut costs. One solution is for business buyers to drive down supplier prices. Online reverse auctions allow businesses to do this more efficiently and effectively. Reverse auctions, often called e-auctions, are conducted online with the buyer and seller roles reversed. Buyers announce auctions months in advance and vendors qualify to participate. During the live online auction, suppliers have a short time in which to bid down their prices anonymously. Such auctions started in the aerospace and automotive industries to reduce costs on commodity parts but have now spread to other industries. Buyers don't always go with the lowest bidder,

but the process puts pressure on suppliers to reduce prices and in turn reduce their own costs to maintain profitability. Although heralded as a "best practices" tool by some, reverse auctions are loathed by others. Some suppliers, bitten by the reverse auctions bug of their customers, turn around and reduce costs by requiring such auctions for their own suppliers.

1. Discuss at least three pros and three cons of reverse auctions for buyers. Do the same for suppliers.

2. How can a supplier succeed in reverse auctions? How can it avoid them altogether?

FOCUS ON ETHICS

China is an emerging economic giant with almost endless potential for business opportunities. *Guan xi*—meaning "connections" or "relationships"—is a Chinese way of doing business and is practically considered an art form there. It involves exchanging "favours" when you need something done. Many Chinese businesspeople see it as a way to solidify relationships, get things done, and cultivate well-being. To Westerners, however, it often looks more like graft in the form of bribery, nepotism, gift giving, and kickbacks. Transparency International, a German-based corruption watchdog, ranks China along with India, Russia, Taiwan, Turkey, Malaysia, and South Africa as the countries with the most

rampant corruption. However, China is cracking down by enacting stricter anticorruption laws and prosecuting violators. In 2007, China's former director of the State Food and Drug Administration was executed for taking bribes.

1. Is it right for Western civilizations to impose their ethical views and behaviour on other cultures, such as China?

2. What are the consequences for Canadian companies that refuse to engage in less-than-ethical practices that foreign businesses or governments expect or that competitors use in foreign markets?

MARKETING BY THE NUMBERS

The North American Industry Classification System (NAICS) code is very useful for marketers. It is a relatively new coding system that replaces the old product-based Standard Industrial Classification (SIC) system introduced in the 1930s. The NAICS system classifies businesses by production processes, better reflecting changes in the global economy, especially in the service and technology industries. It was developed jointly by the United States, Canada, and Mexico in 1997 in concert with the North American Free Trade Agreement (NAFTA), providing a common classification system for

the three countries and better compatibility with the International Standard Industrial Classification (ISIC) system. This six-digit number (in some cases, seven or ten digits) is very useful for understanding business markets.

1. What do the six digits of the NAICS code represent? What industry is represented by the NAICS code 721110? How many businesses does this code include?

2. How can marketers use NAICS codes to better deliver customer satisfaction and value?

VIDEO CASE | Video Case Questions

Eaton

With nearly 60 000 employees doing business in 125 countries and sales last year of more than US$11 billion, Eaton is one of the world's largest suppliers of diversified industrial goods. Eaton's products make cars more peppy, trial goods. Eaton's products make cars more peppy,

18-wheelers safer to drive, and airliners more fuel efficient. So why haven't you heard of the company? Because Eaton sells its products not to end consumers but to other businesses.

At Eaton, B2B marketing means working closely with customers to develop a better product. So the company partners with its sophisticated, knowledgeable clients to create total solutions that meet their needs. Along the way, Eaton maps the decision-making process to better understand the concerns and interests of decision makers. In the end, Eaton's success depends on its ability to provide high-quality, dependable customer service and product support. Through service and support, Eaton develops a clear understanding of consumer needs and builds stronger relationships with clients.

After viewing the video featuring Eaton, answer the following questions about business markets and business buyer behaviour:

1. What is Eaton's value proposition?

2. Who are Eaton's customers? Describe Eaton's customer relationships.

3. Discuss the different ways that Eaton provides value beyond that which companies can provide for themselves.

Visit MyMarketingLab at www.pearsoned.ca/mymarketingLab to view the video segment related to this case.

COMPANY CASE

Boeing: Selling a Dream(liner)

Think about the biggest purchase that you've ever made. Was it a car? A computer? A piece of furniture or an appliance? Think about the time you put into researching that decision, all the factors that you considered in making your choice, and how much the purchase ultimately cost.

Now imagine that you are part of a buying team for a major airline considering the purchase of multiple commercial jets, each costing over US$100 million. A slightly different situation? Such are the customers that Boeing deals with every day. Selling commercial and military aircraft involves some of the most complicated transactions in the world. At those prices, a single sale can add up to billions of dollars. And beyond initial prices, Boeing's clients must consider numerous factors that affect longer-term operating and maintenance costs. As a result, the airplane purchase process is nerve-wrackingly slow, often taking years from the first sales presentation to the day Boeing actually delivers an airplane.

For such purchases, Boeing knows that it takes more than fast talk and a firm handshake to sell expensive aircraft—it takes a lot of relationship building. So Boeing invests heavily in managing customer relationships. Individual salespeople head up an extensive team of company specialists—sales and service technicians, financial analysts, planners, engineers—all dedicated to finding ways to understand and satisfy airline customer needs. These teams work closely with clients through the lengthy buying process. Even after receiving an order, salespeople stay in almost constant contact to make certain the customer stays satisfied. The success of customer relationships depends on performance and trust. "When you buy an airplane, it is like getting married," quips Alan Mallaly, the head of Boeing's commercial airplane division. "It is a long-term relationship."

But even with this care in managing customer relationships, Boeing has experienced more than its share of challenges over the past decade. For starters, its only major rival, France-based Airbus, began to overtake Boeing in product innovation during the 1990s. In the wake of September 11, 2001, Boeing lost its industry lead in commercial airplane sales to Airbus. To make matters worse, Boeing soon found itself in the midst of a series of ethical scandals. In the early 2000s, the company faced two separate cases of cheating to win defence contracts with the U.S. Air Force. The scandals resulted in a Department of Justice investigation, the ousting of Boeing's CEO, prison terms for two other executives, and the loss of billions of dollars in business. To make matters even worse, in the face of a scandalous extramarital affair, the next CEO stepped down as well.

AN AIRLINE'S DREAM

With its reputation sullied and its financial situation suffering, Boeing got back to the business of serving its corporate clients. In April 2004, the giant airplane maker announced the program launch of its 787 Dreamliner, Boeing's first all-new aircraft since the 777, launched a decade earlier. The Dreamliner is not the world's biggest passenger jet—Airbus's A380 and even Boeing's own 747 are bigger. But with the 787, Boeing saw more potential in the midsized wide-body market. From the beginning, it set out to create a jet with groundbreaking innovations that would translate into true benefits for its customers—the types of benefits that really stand out to buyers and executives at major airlines.

Some 50 percent of the Dreamliner's fuselage is made from lightweight carbon-fibre materials. The plane is also made in one single piece, eliminating 40 000 to 50 000 fasteners and 1500 aluminum sheets and putting it in a design class with the B-2 stealth bomber. Combined with other weight-saving design features and advanced engine technologies, the 787 is the world's lightest and most fuel-efficient passenger jet, using 20 percent less fuel than comparably sized planes.

Another major benefit that the Boeing 787 Dreamliner brings to its category is flexibility. The 787 line is designed for multiple configurations that carry between 210 and 330 passengers. The plane also offers increased cargo capacity, a fuel range of up to 8500 nautical miles, and a maximum speed of Mach 0.85. Thus, the 787 brings big-jet speed, range, and capacity to the midsize market, rivalling the jumbo jets.

The cockpit of the 787 is also loaded with tech toys that will enhance safety and cut departure delays. The advances include a system that self-monitors the plane's vital functions and reports maintenance requirements to ground-based computer systems.

Whereas the airlines will certainly notice all of these improvements, airline passengers will also approve of many new 787 design features. The interior of the Dreamliner is designed to reduce long-haul flying misery and to better imitate life on the ground. The Dreamliner is 60 percent quieter than other planes in its class. It features more legroom, lighting that automatically adjusts to time zone shifts, and higher cabin pressure and humidity, making the flying experience more comfortable and reducing common flying symptoms like headaches, dry mouth, and fatigue. The Dreamliner also boasts the largest-ever overhead storage bins, 19-inch self-dimming windows, and a wireless Internet and entertainment system.

"We looked at every aspect of the flying experience," says Tom Cogan, chief project engineer for the 787. "It's not just an evolutionary step. From my perspective it almost borders on revolutionary." Opinions of industry insiders support Cogan's statement. Many analysts strongly believe that the 787 Dreamliner will one day be regarded as the plane that charted the next age of commercial aviation.

Boeing officially launched the 787 program in April of 2004. Even with the stratospheric list price of US$162 million and the fact that Boeing was not promising delivery for at least four years, companies scrambled to place orders. Japan's All Nippon Airways jumped in first with a record order for 50 Dreamliners. To date, 56 companies from six continents have lined up with orders for 892 of Boeing's newest aeronautic darling, including Air Canada, which is scheduled to take delivery of the first of its 37 ordered aircraft soon. That makes the Dreamliner the most successful new aircraft launch and the fastest selling plane in the history of the industry.

Combined with record sales for its 737 and freighter lines, Boeing's annual sales soared. In 2005, Boeing shattered its records with orders for 1002 commercial airplanes, edging within inches of Airbus's lead. That number is even more striking considering that Boeing and Airbus combined for a total of 622 orders in 2004. The sales spike was so dramatic that no one in the industry expected the numbers to repeat. But in 2006, Boeing reclaimed its title as the industry sales leader by surpassing Airbus with orders for 1044 more jets. Even more stunning, 2007 brought the third straight record-breaking year for Boeing with 1413 orders.

DREAM, OR NIGHTMARE?

As if massive revenue success weren't enough, Boeing was riding high for other reasons as well. In 2005, when Jim McNerney took over as CEO, he instituted a massive cost-cutting program that resulted in an 84 percent increase in company earnings on an 8 percent increase in revenue for 2007. Combined with the soaring orders, Boeing's stock price peaked at a record US$107 in July 2007. With over US$60 billion in revenue, Boeing once again reigned as the world's biggest aerospace company and the USA's largest exporter. But McNerney knew better than to revel in the glory of the then-current successes. Across the Atlantic, Airbus had committed severe production blunders resulting in its first jumbo A380s being delivered 22 months late, leading to a major shakeup in management at the French firm. Boeing had projected that it would deliver its first 787 to All Nippon in May 2008. With that date still more than a year away, McNerney knew that his biggest challenge would be to keep the Dreamliner on track.

McNerney had good reason for concern. The Dreamliner was not only an innovative design, it was being built by an innovative process that outsourced 70 percent of the work to dozens of partnering firms. Boeing's promises with respect to deadlines and delivery dates could only be met if all the pieces of the puzzle came together as planned. Even though it had so many orders secured, customers were counting on Boeing to make good. The last thing that it needed was for customer relationships to be rocked by delays or other problems.

But by mid-2007, the 787 production process was plagued with problems. Parts shortages and other bottlenecks led suppliers to ship incomplete sections of the first few planes to Boeing's final assembly line in Everett, Washington. By mid-2008, the date of the first 787 delivery had been pushed back three times. All Nippon would not take possession of its first plane until at least 15 months past the original deadline. To make matters worse, Boeing announced that it would only deliver 25 Dreamliners in the first year, rather than the previous estimate of 109.

Months later, Boeing Commercial Airplanes president Scott Carson announced that Boeing had made solid progress in overcoming start-up issues. He apologized and promised that the company would work closely with each customer to minimize the impact of the delays. Boeing also suggested that it would offer incentives and penalty payments as part of that process (some analysts estimate that Boeing could be liable for as much as US$4 billion in concessions and penalties). Still, understandably, Boeing's commercial customers quickly grew impatient. The delays began wreaking havoc with customer relationships. Boeing's biggest customer, All Nippon, stated, "We are extremely disappointed: This is the third delay in the delivery of the first aircraft and we still have no details about the full delivery schedule. We would urge Boeing to provide us with a 120 percent definitive schedule as soon as possible."

As Boeing's customers consider what is happening in the purchase process, it is easy to see how each might become seriously conflicted. On the one hand, they see the promise of a Dreamliner that they believe strongly will provide tremendous benefits, perhaps unlike any previous aircraft. On the other hand, every delay costs them dearly.

The delays upset plans to begin new routes and retire old aircraft, events that translate directly into revenue and profits. Customer options are limited—there's only one competitor, and its product in this class is substantially inferior to the Dreamliner. And even if customers switch, Airbus does not have planes sitting on the shelves waiting to be purchased. However, Boeing's customers still have the option of cancelling 787 orders and making do with what they have.

RIDING OUT THE STORM

Regardless of what its customers do, the way Boeing handles the 787 crisis will most certainly affect customer relations and future orders. Boeing has a lot on its side. The innovativeness of the current product line, Boeing's expertise in supply chain management, and the strength of its sales teams in managing customer relationships will all help to resolve the problems with the Dreamliner program. But Boeing had these things going for it before the crisis began. The question is, what will Boeing do differently in the future?

In a 2008 memo to employees, CEO McNerney said, "The simple reality is that it's time to get it done—and done right." McNerney has made it very clear that he expects more from everyone involved in the 787 Dreamliner program, from the top down. He has reached deeply into the company's executive roster, plucking a team from Boeing's defence unit to straighten out the Dreamliner process. He is pushing executives to act more aggressively. This includes sticking their noses into suppliers' operations, even stationing Boeing employees on the factory floors of every major supplier.

McNerney himself is more directly involved with the 787 program. He gets daily briefings on the plane's progress. He frequently makes his presence known on factory floors and even visits with assembly line workers. "We've got 240 programs in the company, and there's one that's got more of my attention right now than any one, and that's the 787," McNerney said. "I hope we are [eventually] defined by the 787. Just not right this instant."

McNerney took over as CEO well after the Dreamliner program was under way, so the current problems are not being attributed to him. But customers and others throughout the industry are watching him closely to see how he handles the situation. Says Charlie Smith, chief investment officer with Fort Pitt Capital Group, "No matter what other successes Jim McNerney has at Boeing, he will be judged on how he handles the 787. He's either going to win big or lose big," he said. And McNerney's outcome will be directly shared by the Boeing Company, including the teams that must deal day in and day out with anxious and frustrated customers.

Questions for Discussion

1. Discuss the nature of the market structure and demand for the Dreamliner. What are the implications of this for Boeing and its customers?

2. What examples of the major types of buying situations do you see in the case? Discuss the implications of each in terms of marketing strategy.

3. List the specific features of the Dreamliner. What customer benefits result from each?

4. Discuss the customer buying process for a Boeing airplane. In what major ways does this process differ from the buying process a passenger might go through in choosing an airline?

5. What marketing recommendations would you make to McNerney as he continues to try to resolve the problems with the 787 Dreamliner program?

Sources: Josh Dean, "Fast 50 2008: Boeing," *Fast Company*, February, 2008, p. 106; Laurence Zuckerman, "Selling Airplanes with a Smile," *New York Times*, February 17, 2002, p. 3.2; J. Lynn Lunsford, "Boeing CEO Fights Headwind," *Wall Street Journal*, April 25, 2008, p. B1; Michael V. Copeland, "Boeing's Big Dream," *Fortune*, April 24, 2008, accessed online at www.money.cnn.com; Marilyn Adams, "Boeing Bounces Back Against Odds," *USA Today*, January 11, 2007, p. 1B; and "Air Canada Increases Order for Boeing 787," CBC News, April 24, 2007, accessed at www.cbc.ca.

 Visit **MyMarketingLab** at **www.pearsoned.ca/mymarketinglab** for access to online tutorials, interactive exercises, videos, and much more.

Customer-Driven Marketing Strategy
Creating Value for Target Customers

PREVIEWING THE CONCEPTS So far, you've learned what marketing is and about the importance of understanding consumers and the marketplace environment. With that as background, you're now ready to delve deeper into marketing strategy and tactics. This chapter looks further into key customer-driven marketing strategy decisions—how to divide up markets into meaningful customer groups (segmentation), choose which customer groups to serve (targeting), create market offerings that best serve targeted customers (differentiation), and position the offerings in the minds of consumers (positioning). Then, the chapters that follow explore the tactical marketing tools—the Four Ps—by which marketers bring these strategies to life.

We've talked a lot about premier marketer Procter & Gamble, and we'll start this chapter with another P&G story. When it comes to targeting and positioning, perhaps no company does it better. Here, we'll look at how P&G discovered an important customer segment—university and college students—and skilfully positioned its fast-growing Febreze brand to meet the special needs of that niche.

One of Procter & Gamble's fastest-growing brands, odour fighter Febreze, is now targeting a new lifestyle segment: university and college students. How? By homing in on what stinks about university and college life—everything from armpits to boyfriends and ever-growing piles of laundry in the corner of a dorm room. The burgeoning $600 million Febreze brand recently kicked off "What Stinks," an online and viral campaign for its fabric-refresher spray aimed at this sometimes hard to reach, often fickle segment.

For most of the brand's existence, Febreze has targeted mostly working adults and soccer moms, positioning itself as a "Breath of Fresh Air" for people looking to remove odours from sweaty gym clothes, soiled furniture, and pet areas. However, P&G realized that this broader targeting and positioning leaves out an entire group of customers—the Millennials, which include university and college students. "There are 18 million college kids out there and we've never really targeted them," said Martin Hettich, North American marketing director for Febreze. However, despite the fact that Febreze has done little dedicated marketing toward the segment, pockets of students over the years have embraced the odour-fighting spray anyway.

P&G has launched a movement to help wash-day-reluctant students find ways to rewear unwashed clothes rather than doing laundry.

Why is Febreze a natural for university students? "Washing is not a convenient part of the lifestyle at college," says Hettich. And what better for wash-day-reluctant students than products that eliminate the need? So during the past few years P&G has launched a movement to help students find ways to rewear unwashed clothes rather than doing laundry. For example, it recently introduced a new Swash line of dewrinkling sprays, stain-removing pens, odour-removing sprays, clothes dryer sheets, and lint rollers designed to give students' clothes the look and smell of having been washed without the trouble or expense of actually washing

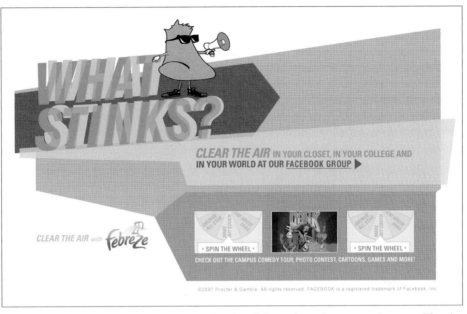

One of Procter & Gamble's fastest-growing brands, odour fighter Febreze, is now targeting a new lifestyle segment: university students

them. Extending the Febreze positioning toward the college and university student segment is a natural extension of this "rewash movement."

But targeting the potentially huge university student segment presents some problems. Febreze marketers recognized that university and college campuses are a far cry from where the brand has thrust its marketing efforts in the past. A mainstream marketing approach likely would fail to reach and persuade this student segment. "Our mainstream media buys are not effective for 18- to 22-year-olds," confirms a P&G advertising agency executive. "P&G had to figure out a clever marketing campaign aimed at these mysterious Millennials," says one analyst. "What better way than to rely on the media already used by this tech-savvy group?"

So Febreze opted for an online and viral approach, built around an interactive website, WhatStinks.com, linked directly through Facebook. Facebook is a real no-brainer

these days when it comes to youth marketing. In a recent brand survey of university and college students, Facebook beat out MySpace as the most popular social networking site for that group. It's no surprise, then, that WhatStinks.com is actually housed within Facebook, and that P&G plans to reach its university student target segment through media buys and banner ads on Facebook.

On the humorous "What Stinks?" Facebook site, Febreze swaps its broader "Breath of fresh air" positioning for the more university-oriented "Febreze . . . Because surprise! Your parents are visiting!" and "Febreze . . . Because the laundry room is sooooo far away!" It also adds a mascot in the form of a gigantic Converse-wearing nose.

Other features of the site include the "Dank Game," a video game where players aren't armed with machine guns, but bottles of Febreze to attack dirty socks and boxers, and a "What Stinks?" news feed that gathers news of smells all around the world. Recent posts include an AP wire report

▶

OBJECTIVES

1. Define the major steps in designing a customer-driven marketing strategy: market segmentation, targeting, differentiation, and positioning.

2. List and discuss the major bases for segmenting consumer and business markets.

3. Explain how companies identify attractive market segments and choose a market-targeting strategy.

4. Discuss how companies differentiate and position their products for maximum competitive advantage in the marketplace.

about a toilet-paper thief in Wisconsin. Spin the Wheel-O-Stink and get tips on everything from deodorizing the after-air of funky roomies to refreshing that old sweater that smells like grandma's attic. And a Clear the Air link takes visitors to a video of students telling Febreze "what stinks," such as fashion, boyfriends, the real world, and more. As part of the campaign, Febreze is also running a "What Stinks?" candid online photo contest with prizes that marry Febreze with another brand university students love—Apple and iTunes.

In step with its humorous tack, Febreze is also invading campuses across North America with a Febreze-branded comedy tour showcasing the improvisational troupe Upright Citizens Brigade. The tour features interactive performances in which the cast interviews students about what stinks in their lives. Related on-the-ground promotions feature giveaways of dorm-life staples such as marker boards and laundry bags (for fabric items beyond the help of Febreze).

The student-targeted Febreze "What Stinks?" campaign, along with P&G's other skilful targeting and positioning efforts for the brand, have helped make Febreze the world's leading fabric freshener and deodorizer. It's also one of P&G's fastest-growing brands. That really does make Febreze a breath of fresh air to both the company and its customers.[1]

Chapter Opening Discussion

| 1 |

Market segmentation
Dividing a market into smaller groups with distinct needs, characteristics, or behaviours that might require separate marketing strategies or mixes.

Market targeting (targeting)
The process of evaluating each market segment's attractiveness and selecting one or more segments to enter.

Differentiation
Actually differentiating the market offering to create superior customer value.

Positioning
Arranging for a market offering to occupy a clear, distinctive, and desirable place relative to competing products in the minds of target consumers.

Companies today recognize that they cannot appeal to all buyers in the marketplace, or at least not to all buyers in the same way. Buyers are too numerous, too widely scattered, and too varied in their needs and buying practices. Moreover, the companies themselves vary widely in their abilities to serve different segments of the market. Instead, like P&G, a company must identify the parts of the market that it can serve best and most profitably. It must design customer-driven marketing strategies that build the *right* relationships with the *right* customers.

Thus, most companies have moved away from mass marketing and toward *target marketing*—identifying market segments, selecting one or more of them, and developing products and marketing programs tailored to each. Instead of scattering their marketing efforts (the "shotgun" approach), firms are focusing on the buyers who have greater interest in the values they create best (the "rifle" approach).

Figure 8.1 shows the four major steps in designing a customer-driven marketing strategy. In the first two steps, the company selects the customers that it will serve. **Market segmentation** involves dividing a market into smaller groups of buyers with distinct needs, characteristics, or behaviours that might require separate marketing strategies or mixes. The company identifies different ways to segment the market and develops profiles of the resulting market segments. **Market targeting** (or **targeting**) consists of evaluating each market segment's attractiveness and selecting one or more market segments to enter.

In the final two steps, the company decides on a value proposition—how it will create value for target customers. **Differentiation** involves actually differentiating the firm's market offering to create superior customer value. **Positioning** consists of arranging for a market offering to occupy a clear, distinctive, and desirable place relative to competing products in the minds of target consumers. We discuss each of these steps in turn.

Figure 8.1 Designing a customer-driven marketing strategy

MARKET SEGMENTATION

Buyers in any market differ in their wants, resources, locations, buying attitudes, and buying practices. Through market segmentation, companies divide large, heterogeneous markets into smaller segments that can be reached more efficiently and effectively with products and services that match their unique needs. In this section, we discuss four important segmentation topics: segmenting consumer markets, segmenting business markets, segmenting international markets, and requirements for effective segmentation.

Segmenting Consumer Markets

There is no single way to segment a market. A marketer has to try different segmentation variables, alone and in combination, to find the best way to view the market structure. Table 8.1 outlines the major variables that might be used in segmenting consumer markets. Here we look at the major *geographic, demographic, psychographic,* and *behavioural* variables.

Geographic Segmentation

Geographic segmentation
Dividing a market into different geographical units such as nations, regions, provinces, counties, cities, or neighbourhoods.

Glossary Flashcards of Key Terms

Geographic segmentation calls for dividing the market into different geographical units such as nations, regions, provinces, counties, cities, or even neighbourhoods. A company may decide to operate in one or a few geographical areas, or to operate in all areas but pay attention to geographical differences in needs and wants.

Many companies today are localizing their products, advertising, promotion, and sales efforts to fit the needs of individual regions, cities, and even neighbourhoods. For example, one consumer-products company ships additional cases of its low-calorie snack foods to stores in neighbourhoods near Weight Watchers clinics. Baskin-Robbins practises what it calls "three-mile marketing," emphasizing local events and promotions close to its local store locations. On a global scale, video game companies create different versions of their games depending on the world region in which the game is sold. For example, Capcom sells its *Resident Evil* series as *Biohazard* in most other countries, such as Japan and France, where it is played in local languages.[2]

Other companies are seeking to cultivate as-yet-untapped geographic territory. For example, many large companies are fleeing the fiercely competitive major cities and suburbs to set up shop in small towns. Home Depot, for instance, is getting ready to unveil a junior version of its stores, roughly half the size of a regular store. These stores, geared toward small markets and vacation areas that can't support a full-size store, are designed to offer a more intimate neighbourhood hardware store setting. "We think there's a tremendous opportunity in smaller markets where it's harder to find land for a full-size store, and where they don't need a full-size store," says a Home Depot executive.[3]

Geographic segmentation is an important tool for Canadian marketers, especially when it comes to Quebec. See what Rogers Video is currently doing as it builds outlets throughout the province:

> Rogers sees Quebec as an attractive market because it knows that home video is a very large part of the Quebec lifestyle. Rogers's marketers, however, must not only be aware of the language differences in the province, they also have to deal with a unique set of competitors when serving this geographic segment. Quebecor Media's giant SuperClub Vidéotron chain is well entrenched, as is Blockbuster and other players like Club International. Rogers's outlets in Quebec will have a special section devoted to Quebec cinema and will stock far more foreign-language fare than in the rest of Canada. Rogers's research has shown Quebecers are bigger consumers of international cinema. Finally, Rogers's stores in the province will feature confectionery items exclusive to Quebec. To make its presence known, Rogers will use community-based marketing using tools like ads in community newspapers and on local radio.[4]

Table 8.1 Major Segmentation Variables for Consumer Markets

Geographic	
World region or country	North America, Western Europe, Middle East, Pacific Rim, China, Southeast Asia, Latin America
Country region	Maritimes, Quebec, Ontario, Prairies, British Columbia, Northern Territories
City or metro size	Under 5000; 5001–20 000; 20 001–50 000; 50 001–100 000; 100 001–250 000; 250 001–500 000; 500 001–1 000 000; 1 000 001–4 000 000; over 4 000 000
Density	Urban, suburban, rural
Climate	Northern, Southern, Maritime, Prairie, Mountain, West Coast
Demographic	
Age	Under 6, 6–11, 12–19, 20–34, 35–49, 50–64, 65+
Gender	Male, female
Family size	1–2, 3–4, 5+
Family life cycle	Young, single; young, married, no children; young, married with children; older, married with children; older, married, no children under 18; older, single; other
Income	Under $10 000; $10 000–$19 999; $20 000–$29 999; $30 000–$49 999; $50 000–$99 999; $100 000 and over
Occupation	Professional and technical; managers, officials, and proprietors; clerical; sales; craftspeople; supervisors; operatives; farmers; retired; students; homemakers; unemployed
Education	Grade school or less; some high school; high school graduate; some postsecondary, postsecondary graduate; graduate school
Religion	Catholic, Protestant, Jewish, Muslim, Hindu, etc.
Ethnic origin	Aboriginal, British, French, South Asian, Chinese, German, etc.
Generation	Baby boomer, Generation X, Generation Y
Psychographic	
Social class	Lower lowers, upper lowers, working class, middle class, upper middles, lower uppers, upper uppers
Lifestyle	Achievers, strivers, survivors
Personality	Compulsive, gregarious, authoritarian, ambitious
Behavioural	
Occasions	Regular occasion; special occasion
Benefits	Quality, service, economy, convenience, speed
User status	Nonuser, ex-user, potential user, first-time user, regular user
User rates	Light user, medium user, heavy user
Loyalty status	None, medium, strong, absolute
Readiness stage	Unaware, aware, informed, interested, desirous, intending to buy
Attitude toward product	Enthusiastic, positive, indifferent, negative, hostile

Demographic segmentation
Dividing the market into groups based on variables such as age, gender, family size, family life cycle, income, occupation, education, religion, race, generation, and nationality.

Demographic Segmentation

Demographic segmentation divides the market into groups based on variables such as age, gender, family size, family life cycle, income, occupation, education, religion, race, generation, and nationality. RBC, for example, recently targeted new Canadians with its

"Wicket Cricket" program as part of its commitment to serve multicultural communities. Says Mark Whitmell, director of cultural markets, "When somebody is new to Canada they're looking for things that are common, that are familiar, that even bring a sense of home.... Many immigrants love cricket and appreciate companies that can help them play the game in Canada."[5]

Demographic factors are the most popular bases for segmenting customer groups. One reason is that consumer needs, wants, and usage rates often vary closely with demographic variables. Another is that demographic variables are easier to measure than most other types of variables. Even when marketers first define segments using other bases, such as benefits sought or behaviour, they must know segment demographic characteristics to assess the size of the target market and to reach it efficiently.

Age and life-cycle segmentation

Dividing a market into different age and life-cycle groups.

Age and Life-Cycle Stage Consumer needs and wants change with age. Some companies use **age and life-cycle segmentation**, offering different products or using different marketing approaches for different age and life-cycle groups. For example, Oscar Mayer offers Lunchables for kids, full of fun, kid-appealing finger food. For older generations, it markets Deli Creations, everything they need to create a "hot and melty fresh-baked sandwich in a microwave minute." Not-for-profit organizations also use age and life-cycle segmentation to help them raise funds. For example, the Art Gallery of Ontario recently targeted the 30–40 age group since it was a relatively untapped market:

> Getting people 30 to 49 to support the AGO is not easy. Competition is stiff, and as one longtime fundraiser puts it, "Cultural institutions aren't on their radar. They want cars, houses, big jewellery. Private school for their children. If they're supporting art, they're putting it on their walls." Thus, the AGO had to create a distinct position for its program to attract these younger donors. It decided to name its marketing program the "New Founders" initiative, which immediately told potential patrons they won't be sitting in a room with their mother's friends. It created powerful new events, like its "Massive Party" that wasn't like the stuffy cocktail parties usually associated with cultural fundraisers. Organizers and waiters wore wigs of fuzzy pink clown hair. The goal of the New Founders initiative was to get 100 new philanthropists who would be willing to donate at least $50 000. In return for their support, they would be invited to small dinner parties and exclusive tours of exhibitions before they open to the public. The program has been considered a resounding success. As one consultant notes, "The institutions that have diversified their donor bases most are in the best shape now and will be in the future."[6]

Marketers must be careful to guard against stereotypes when using age and life-cycle segmentation. Although some 80-year-olds fit the doddering stereoypes, others play tennis. Similarly, whereas some 40-year-old couples are sending their children off to university, others are just beginning new families. Thus, age is often a poor predictor of a person's life cycle, health, work or family status, needs, and buying power. Companies marketing to mature consumers usually employ positive images and appeals. For example, take the cruise industry, which heavily targets baby boomers at all life stages. One Carnival Cruise Lines ad for its Fun Ships features an older boomer and child riding waterslides, stating "Fun has no age limit."

Gender segmentation

Dividing a market into different groups based on gender.

Gender **Gender segmentation** has long been used in clothing, cosmetics, toiletries, and magazines. For example, Procter & Gamble was among the first with Secret, an antiperspirant brand specially formulated for a woman's chemistry, packaged and advertised to reinforce the female image. More recently, Nestlé Canada launched a TV marketing campaign for its Aero chocolate bar that pokes fun at the differences between men and women, including attitudes toward chocolate. The company's research showed that women's appreciation of chocolate was deeper than men's—46 percent of women believed there were days where they "couldn't survive" without chocolate, whereas only 20 percent of men felt that way. "Women love chocolate and men don't seem to get that, partly because the word 'love' tends to be a bit scary for men," says Kate Beresford, marketing manager

Gender segmentation: Daisy Rock offers a complete line of smaller, lighter, professional-quality guitars with fun shapes and glossy finishes geared toward women.

for Aero. The survey also found that far more men would sooner give up chocolate than sex, while women rated the two equally.[7]

A neglected gender segment can offer new opportunities in markets ranging from motorcycles to guitars. For example, 10 years ago, 96 percent of guitars were purchased by and for men. But Daisy Rock Guitars, the Girl Guitar Company, is changing that statistic one guitar at a time. Starting with a daisy-shaped guitar with a leafy headstock, Daisy Rock now offers a complete line of smaller, lighter, professional-quality guitars with fun shapes and glossy finishes geared toward women. Guitars range from girly butterfly, heart, and daisy shapes for younger girls to glossy red, black, purple, and pink guitars for women. Daisy Rock's sales have doubled each year since the company was founded in 2000 and reached $2.4 million in 2006.[8]

Income   The marketers of products and services such as automobiles, clothing, cosmetics, financial services, and travel have long used **income segmentation**. Many companies target affluent consumers with luxury goods and convenience services. For example, for a price, luxury hotels provide amenities to attract specific groups of affluent travellers, such as families, expectant moms, and even pet owners:

Income segmentation
Dividing a market into different income groups.

> At the Four Seasons Hotel Chicago, guests can buy the Kids in the City package for $520 a night and, among other things, enjoy a visit in their room from the Ice Cream Man, who arrives with all the fixings to make any concoction they desire. At one spa in Scottsdale, Arizona, expectant parents can purchase the "Bundle of Joy" Babymoon package, which includes a 24-hour Cravings-Chef service, a couples massage, and breakfast in bed. The Benjamin Hotel in New York City provides dog beds in a variety of styles and doggie bathrobes, as well as canine room service and DVDs for dogs. And if that isn't decadent enough, how about dropping $100 000 for an extravagant weekend in Vegas? At The Ritz-Carlton, Lake Las Vegas, in Henderson, Nevada, the Love at Lake Las Vegas weekend package includes two nights in the 2400-square-foot presidential suite, helicopter and gondola rides, a champagne-tasting party on a yacht complete with rose petals strewn about and a string trio, use of a luxury car throughout the stay, in-room couples spa treatment, a $5000 casino line of credit, a $50 000 shopping spree at Neiman Marcus, 14 dozen roses, and a butler-drawn Cristal champagne bath.[9]

However, not all companies that use income segmentation target the affluent. For example, many retailers—such as the Dollar Store, Dollarama, and the Great Canadian Dollar Stores—successfully target low- and middle-income groups. The core market for such stores is families with incomes under $30 000. When real-estate experts scout locations for

Marketing to the affluent: For only $100 000, you can experience an extravagant Love at Lake Las Vegas weekend at The Ritz-Carlton, Lake Las Vegas, in Henderson, Nevada. It includes a $50 000 shopping spree at Neiman Marcus.

new stores for these chains, they look for lower-middle-class neighbourhoods where people wear less-expensive shoes and drive old cars that drip a lot of oil. With the downturn in the economy, the low-income strategies of dollar stores have helped make them the fastest-growing retailers in North America. Some experts predict that to meet the dollar store threat, Walmart will eventually buy one of these chains or start one of its own.[10]

Psychographic Segmentation

Psychographic segmentation divides buyers into different groups based on social class, lifestyle, or personality characteristics. People in the same demographic group can have very different psychographic makeups.

In Chapter 6, we discussed how the products people buy reflect their *lifestyles*. As a result, marketers often segment their markets by consumer lifestyles and base their marketing strategies on lifestyle appeals. For example, Rockport advertises that its shoes "are meant for a special occasion. It's called life. Live in Rockport." The ads feature people in everyday activities, conveying the wearable nature of Rockport shoes and how they fit into many lifestyles.

Psychographic segmentation
Dividing a market into different groups based on social class, lifestyle, or personality characteristics.

Marketers also use *personality* variables to segment markets. For example, cruise lines target adventure seekers. Royal Caribbean appeals to high-energy couples and families with hundreds of activities such as rockwall climbing and ice skating. Its commercials, set to Iggy Pop's "Lust for Life," tell them that "this is more than a cruise" and orders them to "get out there." By contrast, the Regent Seven Seas Cruise Line targets more serene and cerebral adventurers, mature couples seeking a more elegant ambiance and exotic destinations like the Orient. Regent invites them to come along as "luxury goes exploring."[11]

Behavioural Segmentation

Behavioural segmentation
Dividing a market into groups based on consumer knowledge, attitudes, uses, or responses to a product.

Behavioural segmentation divides buyers into groups based on their knowledge, attitudes, uses, or responses to a product. Many marketers believe that behaviour variables are the best starting point for building market segments.

Occasion segmentation
Dividing the market into groups according to occasions when buyers get the idea to buy, actually make their purchase, or use the purchased item.

Occasions Buyers can be grouped according to occasions when they get the idea to buy, actually make their purchase, or use the purchased item. **Occasion segmentation** can help firms build up product usage. For example, most consumers drink orange juice in the morning but orange growers have promoted drinking orange juice as a cool, healthful refresher at other times of the day. By contrast, Coca-Cola's "Good Morning" campaign attempts to increase Diet Coke consumption by promoting the soft drink as an early morning pick-me-up.

Some holidays, such as Mother's Day and Father's Day, were originally promoted partly to increase the sale of candy, flowers, cards, and other gifts. And many marketers prepare special offers and ads for holiday occasions. For example, Peeps creates different shaped sugar-and-fluffy-marshmallow treats for Easter, Valentine's Day, Halloween, and Christmas, when it captures most of its sales, but advertises that Peeps are "Always in Season" to increase the demand for nonholiday occasions.

Benefit segmentation
Dividing the market into groups according to the different benefits that consumers seek from the product.

Benefits Sought A powerful form of segmentation is to group buyers according to the different *benefits* that they seek from the product. **Benefit segmentation** requires finding the major benefits people look for in the product class, the kinds of people who look for each benefit, and the major brands that deliver each benefit. M&M Meat Shops, for example, target time-pressed working mothers with the promise that M&M can help

Occasion segmentation: Peeps creates different shaped marshmallow treats for special holidays when it captures most of its sales but advertises that Peeps are "Always in Season" to increase the demand for nonholiday occasions.

them serve a great meal no matter what their busy day throws at them.

Champion athletic wear segments its markets according to benefits that different consumers seek from their activewear. For example, "Fit and Polish" consumers seek a balance between function and style—they exercise for results but want to look good doing it. "Serious Sports Competitors" exercise heavily and live in and love their activewear—they seek performance and function. By contrast, "Value-Seeking Moms" have low sports interest and low activewear involvement—they buy for the family and seek durability and value. Thus, each segment seeks a different mix of benefits. Champion must target the benefit segment or segments that it can serve best and most profitably, using appeals that match each segment's benefit preferences.

User Status Markets can be segmented into nonusers, ex-users, potential users, first-time users, and regular users of a product. Marketers want to reinforce and retain regular users, attract targeted nonusers, and reinvigorate relationships with ex-users.

Included in the potential user group are consumers facing life-stage changes—such as newlyweds and new parents—who can be turned into heavy users. For example, upscale kitchen and cookware retailer Williams-Sonoma actively targets newly engaged couples. Eight-page ad inserts in bridal magazines show a young couple strolling through a park or talking intimately in the kitchen over a glass of wine. The bride-to-be asks, "Now that I've found love, what else do I need?" Pictures of Williams-Sonoma knife sets, toasters, glassware, and pots and pans provide some strong clues. The retailer also offers a bridal registry, of course. But it plans to take its registry a step further next year. Through a program called "The Store Is Yours," it will open its stores early, by appointment, exclusively for individual couples to visit and make their wish lists. This segment is very important to Williams-Sonoma. About half of the people who register are new to the brand—and they'll be buying a lot of kitchen items and cookware in the future.[12]

Usage Rate Markets can also be segmented into light, medium, and heavy product users. Heavy users are often a small percentage of the market but account for a high percentage of total consumption. For example, Burger King targets what it calls "Super Fans," young (age 18 to 34), Whopper-wolfing males who make up 18 percent of the chain's customers but account for almost half of all customer visits. They eat at Burger King an average of 16 times a month.[13] Burger King targets these Super Fans openly with ads that exalt monster burgers containing meat, cheese, and more meat and cheese that can turn "innies into outies."

Loyalty Status A market can also be segmented by consumer loyalty. Consumers can be loyal to brands (Tide), stores (Mountain Equipment Co-op), and companies (Toyota). Buyers can be divided into groups according to their degree of loyalty. Some consumers are completely loyal—they buy one brand all the time. For example, Apple has an almost cultlike following of loyal users:

> There are Mac *users*—folks who happen to own a Mac and use it for emailing, blogging, browsing, buying, and social networking. Then there are the Apple *diehards*—the Mac fanatics who buy Apple products and accessories that maximize their Mac lives. Some of these zealots buy two iPhones—one for themselves and the other just to take apart, to see what it looks like on the inside, and maybe, just to marvel at Apple's ingenious ability to cram so much into a tight little elegant package. These Mac fanatics (also called MacHeads or Macolytes) see Apple founder and CEO Steve Jobs as the Walt Disney of technology. Say the word "Apple" in front of Mac fans and they'll go into rhapsodies about the superiority of the brand. Put two MacHeads together and

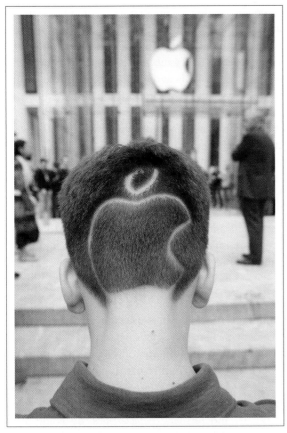

Consumer loyalty: "Mac fanatics"—fanatically loyal Apple users—helped keep Apple afloat during the lean years, and they are now at the forefront of Apple's burgeoning iPod and iTunes empire.

you'll never shut them up. "The Mac [comes] not just as a machine in a box, it [comes] with a whole community," notes one observer. Such fanatically loyal users helped keep Apple afloat during the lean years, and they are now at the forefront of Apple's burgeoning iPod and iTunes empire.[14]

Other consumers are somewhat loyal—they are loyal to two or three brands of a given product or favour one brand while sometimes buying others. Still other buyers show no loyalty to any brand. They either want something different each time they buy or they buy whatever's on sale.

A company can learn a lot by analyzing loyalty patterns in its market. It should start by studying its own loyal customers. For example, by studying Mac fanatics, Apple can better pinpoint its target market and develop marketing appeals. By studying its less-loyal buyers, the company can detect which brands are most competitive with its own. By looking at customers who are shifting away from its brand, the company can learn about its marketing weaknesses.

Using Multiple Segmentation Bases

Marketers rarely limit their segmentation analysis to only one or a few variables. Rather, they often use multiple segmentation bases in an effort to identify smaller, better-defined target groups. Thus, a bank may not only identify a group of wealthy retired adults but also, within that group, distinguish several segments based on their current income, assets, savings and risk preferences, housing, and lifestyles.

Several business information services—such as Claritas, Experian, Acxiom, and MapInfo—provide multivariable segmentation systems that merge geographic, demographic, lifestyle, and behavioural data to help companies segment their markets down to postal codes, neighbourhoods, and even households. One of the leading segmentation systems is the PRIZM NE (New Evolution) system by Claritas. PRIZM NE classifies every North American household based on a host of demographic factors—such as age, educational level, income, occupation, family composition, ethnicity, and housing—and behavioural and lifestyle factors—such as purchases, free-time activities, and media preferences.

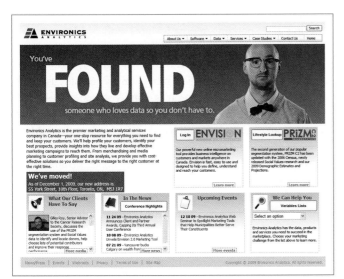

Using the PRIZM C2 segmentation system, Environics Analytics can help marketers paint a surprisingly precise picture of their target markets.

Environics Analytics, which describes itself as the premier marketing and analytical services company in Canada, uses the PRIZM C2 segmentation system. It uses updated data from Canada's 2006 census along with social values research. PRIZM C2 classifies Canadian households into 62 demographically and behaviourally distinct segments, organized into 7 different social groups. The segments carry such exotic names as "Fast-Track Families," "South Asian Society," "Continental Culture," "Les Québécois Sportifs," and "Gray Prider." The colourful names help to bring the clusters to life.[15]

PRIZM C2 and other such systems can help marketers segment people and locations into marketable groups of like-minded consumers. Each cluster has its own pattern of media use, likes, dislikes, lifestyles, and purchase behaviours. For example, the "Furs and Philanthropy" group, part of the "Urban Elite" social group, are educated, upscale people. Nearly half of them are adherents to the Jewish faith. They consist of larger families as well as

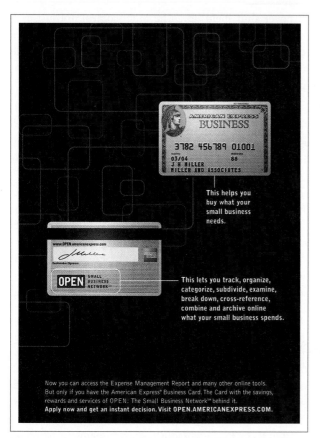

Segmenting business markets: For small buiness customers, American Express has created OPEN: The Small Business Network, "The one place that's all about small business."

empty nesters and widows who tend to live in a few big-city neighbourhoods like the Bathurst Street section of Toronto and Côtes-des-Neiges in Montreal. They tend to have late teens and older children, own elegant houses or condos, and work as white-collar professionals and corporate executives. Maintaining active social lives, they go to the ballet, frequent art galleries, attend health shows, and exercise at health clubs. These urban sophisticates are both well-travelled—they frequently fly to Israel, New York City, and the Caribbean—and are major philanthropists, donating to a wide range of medical, cultural, and religious groups, reinforcing the value they place in being members of a global community. Such segmentation provides a powerful tool for marketers of all kinds. It can help companies identify and better understand key customer segments, target them more efficiently, and tailor market offerings and messages to their specific needs.

Segmenting Business Markets

Consumer and business marketers use many of the same variables to segment their markets. Business buyers can be segmented geographically, demographically (industry, company size), or by benefits sought, user status, usage rate, and loyalty status. Yet business marketers also use some additional variables, such as *customer operating characteristics, purchasing approaches, situational factors,* and *personal characteristics.* By going after segments instead of the whole market, companies can deliver just the right value proposition to each segment served and capture more value in return.

Almost every company serves at least some business markets. For example, American Express targets businesses in three segments—merchants, corporations, and small businesses. It has developed distinct marketing programs for each segment. In the merchants segment, American Express focuses on convincing new merchants to accept the card and on managing relationships with those that already do. For larger corporate customers, the company offers a corporate card program, which includes extensive employee expense and travel management services. It also offers this segment a wide range of asset management, retirement planning, and financial education services. Finally, for small business customers, American Express has created OPEN: The Small Business Network, a system of small-business cards and financial services. It includes credit cards and lines of credit, special usage rewards, financial monitoring and spending report features, and 24/7 customized financial support services. "OPEN is how we serve small business," says American Express.[16]

Many companies set up separate systems for dealing with larger or multiple-location customers. For example, Steelcase, a major producer of office furniture, first segments customers into 10 industries, including banking, insurance, and electronics. Next, company salespeople work with independent Steelcase dealers to handle smaller, local, or regional Steelcase customers in each segment. But many national, multiple-location customers, such as ExxonMobil or IBM, have special needs that may reach beyond the scope of individual dealers. So Steelcase uses national account managers to help its dealer networks handle its national accounts.

Within a given target industry and customer size, the company can segment by purchase approaches and criteria. As in consumer segmentation, many marketers believe that *buying behaviour* and *benefits* provide the best basis for segmenting business markets.[17]

Segmenting International Markets

Few companies have either the resources or the will to operate in all or even most of the countries that dot the globe. Although some large companies, such as Coca-Cola or Sony, sell products in more than 200 countries, most international firms focus on a smaller set.

Operating in many countries presents new challenges. Different countries, even those that are close together, can vary greatly in their economic, cultural, and political makeup. Thus, just as they do within their domestic markets, international firms need to group their world markets into segments with distinct buying needs and behaviours.

Companies can segment international markets using one or a combination of several variables. They can segment by *geographic location*, grouping countries by regions such as Western Europe, the Pacific Rim, the Middle East, or Africa. Geographic segmentation assumes that nations close to one another will have many common traits and behaviours. Although this is often the case, there are many exceptions. For example, although the United States and Canada have much in common, both differ culturally and economically from Mexico. Even within a region, consumers can differ widely. For example, some U.S. marketers lump all Central and South American countries together. However, the Dominican Republic is no more like Brazil than Italy is like Sweden. Many Central and South Americans don't even speak Spanish, including 188 million Portuguese-speaking Brazilians. There are also millions of Aboriginal peoples in Central and South America who speak a variety of dialects.

World markets can also be segmented on the basis of *economic factors*. For example, countries might be grouped by population income levels or by their overall level of economic development. A country's economic structure shapes its population's product and service needs and, therefore, the marketing opportunities it offers. Countries can be segmented by *political and legal factors* such as the type and stability of government, receptivity to foreign firms, monetary regulations, and amount of bureaucracy. *Cultural factors* can also be used, grouping markets according to common languages, religions, values and attitudes, customs, and behavioural patterns.

Intermarket segmentation
Forming segments of consumers who have similar needs and buying behaviour even though they are located in different countries.

Segmenting international markets based on geographic, economic, political, cultural, and other factors assumes that segments should consist of clusters of countries. However, as new communications technologies, such as satellite TV and the Internet, connect consumers around the world, marketers can define and reach segments of like-minded consumers no matter where in the world they are. Using **intermarket segmentation** (also called *cross-market segmentation*), they form segments of consumers who have similar needs and buying behaviours even though they are located in different countries. For example, Lexus targets the world's well-to-do—the "global elite" segment—regardless of their country. Swedish furniture giant IKEA targets the aspiring global middle class—it sells good-quality furniture that ordinary people worldwide can afford. And Coca-Cola creates special programs to target teens, core consumers of its soft drinks the world over:

Coca-Cola wants to relate to the world's teens. To accomplish that, the global soft drink marketer needed to figure out what the majority of teens find appealing. The answer: music. So, throughout the world, Coca-Cola links itself with the local pop music scene. For example, in the United States, Coke is the official sponsor of *American Idol*, the country's number-one television show and a teen magnet. In the Middle East, Coca-Cola commercials feature Arab pop stars, such as Nancy Ajram—Coca-Cola even sponsors her world tour. In Europe, Coke has created the Coca-Cola Music Network, which features signed and unsigned musicians online at okeMusic.com, on stage, and in podcasts. And in Uganda, Coca-Cola sponsored the search for a new MTV VJ.[18]

Coke has taken a somewhat different approach in Canada, however. It couldn't pass up the rare opportunity that the 2010 Winter Olympics held in Vancouver presented. In early 2009, it launched its "Live Olympic" campaign with a national TV spot called "Stars." The ad

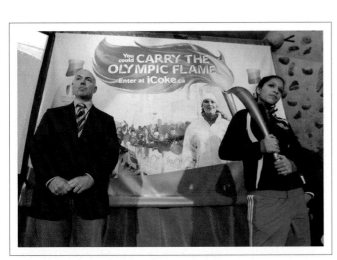

Coke is taking a different marketing focus in Canada to capture teen audiences using a powerful integrated campaign centred on the Olympics.

The "Leftie" segment can be hard to identify and measure. As a result, few companies tailor their offers to left-handers. However, some nichers, such as Anything Left Handed in the United Kingdom, target this segment.

directed people to iCoke.ca where they had a chance to enter a contest to be one of the 1000 Coke torchbearers. The campaign also spoke to two issues highly important to teens and other Canadians: environmental stewardship and active living. Says Dave Moran, director of communicatins for Coke, "All Coke products you can buy are made locally. The Coke you buy in Canada is made in Canada. We have a global mandate to promote sustainable communities based on the theory that a sustainable company can only survive within sustainable communities."[19]

Requirements for Effective Segmentation

Clearly, there are many ways to segment a market, but not all segmentations are effective. For example, buyers of table salt could be divided into blond and brunette customers. But hair colour obviously does not affect the purchase of salt. Furthermore, if all salt buyers bought the same amount of salt each month, believed that all salt is the same, and wanted to pay the same price, the company would not benefit from segmenting this market.

To be useful, market segments must be

- *Measurable:* The size, purchasing power, and profiles of the segments can be measured. Certain segmentation variables are difficult to measure. For example, there are 32.5 million left-handed people in the United States—almost equalling the entire population of Canada. Yet few products are targeted toward this left-handed segment. The major problem may be that the segment is hard to identify and measure. There are no data on the demographics of lefties, and the U.S. Census Bureau does not keep track of left-handedness in its surveys. Private data companies keep reams of statistics on other demographic segments, but not on left-handers.

- *Accessible:* The market segments can be effectively reached and served. Suppose a fragrance company finds that heavy users of its brand are single men and women who stay out late and socialize a lot. Unless this group lives or shops at certain places and is exposed to certain media, its members will be difficult to reach.

- *Substantial:* The market segments are large or profitable enough to serve. A segment should be the largest possible homogenous group worth pursuing with a tailored marketing program. It would not pay, for example, for an automobile manufacturer to develop cars especially for people whose height is greater than seven feet.

- *Differentiable:* The segments are conceptually distinguishable and respond differently to different marketing mix elements and programs. If married and unmarried women respond similarly to a sale on perfume, they do not constitute separate segments.

- *Actionable:* Effective programs can be designed for attracting and serving the segments. For example, although one small airline identified seven market segments, its staff was too small to develop separate marketing programs for each segment.

3   MARKET TARGETING

Market segmentation reveals the firm's market segment opportunities. The firm now has to evaluate the various segments and decide how many and which segments it can serve best. We now look at how companies evaluate and select target segments.

Evaluating Market Segments

In evaluating different market segments, a firm must look at three factors: segment size and growth, segment structural attractiveness, and company objectives and resources. The company must first collect and analyze data on current segment sales, growth rates, and expected profitability for various segments. It will be interested in segments that have the right size and growth characteristics.

But "right size and growth" is a relative matter. The largest, fastest-growing segments are not always the most attractive ones for every company. Smaller companies may lack the skills and resources needed to serve the larger segments. Or they may find these segments too competitive. Such companies may target segments that are smaller and less attractive, in an absolute sense, but that are potentially more profitable for them.

The company also needs to examine major structural factors that affect long-run segment attractiveness.[20] For example, a segment is less attractive if it already contains many strong and aggressive *competitors*. The existence of many actual or potential *substitute products* may limit prices and the profits that can be earned in a segment. The relative *power of buyers* also affects segment attractiveness. Buyers with strong bargaining power relative to sellers will try to force prices down, demand more services, and set competitors against one another—all at the expense of seller profitability. Finally, a segment may be less attractive if it contains *powerful suppliers* who can control prices or reduce the quality or quantity of ordered goods and services.

Even if a segment has the right size and growth and is structurally attractive, the company must consider its own objectives and resources. Some attractive segments can be dismissed quickly because they do not mesh with the company's long-run objectives. Or the company may lack the skills and resources needed to succeed in an attractive segment. For example, given current economic conditions the economy segment of the automobile market is large and growing. But given its objectives and resources, it would make little sense for luxury-performance carmaker BMW to enter this segment. A company should only enter segments in which it can create superior customer value and gain advantages over competitors.

Selecting Target Market Segments

Target market
A set of buyers sharing common needs or characteristics that the company decides to serve.

After evaluating different segments, the company must decide which and how many segments it will target. A **target market** consists of a set of buyers who share common needs or characteristics that the company decides to serve. Market targeting can be carried out at several different levels. Figure 8.2 shows that companies can target very broadly (undifferentiated marketing), very narrowly (micromarketing), or somewhere in between (differentiated or concentrated marketing).

Undifferentiated Marketing

Undifferentiated marketing (mass marketing)
A market coverage strategy in which a firm decides to ignore market segment differences and go after the whole market with one offer.

Using an **undifferentiated marketing** (or **mass marketing**) strategy, a firm might decide to ignore market segment differences and target the whole market with one offer. This mass marketing strategy focuses on what is *common* in the needs of consumers rather than on what is *different*. The company designs a product and a marketing program that will appeal to the largest number of buyers.

As noted earlier in the chapter, most modern marketers have strong doubts about this strategy. Difficulties arise in developing a product or brand that will satisfy all consumers. Moreover, mass marketers often have trouble competing with more-focused firms that do a better job of satisfying the needs of specific segments and niches.

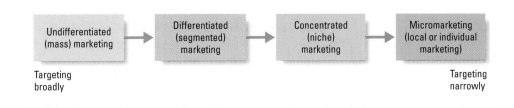

Figure 8.2 Marketing targeting strategies

Differentiated marketing: VF Corporation offers a closet full of over 30 premium lifestyle brands, each of which "taps into consumer aspirations to fashion, status, and well-being" in a well-defined segment.

Differentiated marketing (segmented marketing)
A market-coverage strategy in which a firm decides to target several market segments and designs separate offers for each.

Concentrated marketing (niche marketing)
A market coverage strategy in which a firm goes after a large share of one or a few segments or niches.

Differentiated Marketing

Using a **differentiated marketing** (or **segmented marketing**) strategy, a firm decides to target several market segments and designs separate offers for each. Procter & Gamble markets six different laundry detergent brands, which compete with each other on supermarket shelves. And VF Corporation offers a closet full of more than 30 premium lifestyle brands, each of which "taps into consumer aspirations to fashion, status, and well-being" in a well-defined segment:

> VF is North America's number-one jeans maker, with brands such as Lee, Riders, Rustler, and Wrangler. But jeans are not the only focus for VF. The company's brands are carefully separated into five major segments—Jeanswear, Imagewear (workwear), Outdoor, Sportswear, and Contemporary Brands. The North Face, part of the Outdoor unit, offers top-of-the-line gear and apparel for diehard outdoor enthusiasts, especially those who prefer cold weather activities. From the Sportswear unit, Nautica focuses on people who enjoy high-end casual apparel inspired by sailing and the sea. Vans began as a skate shoe maker, and Reef features surf-inspired footwear and apparel. In the Contemporary Brands unit, Lucy features upscale activewear, whereas 7 for All Mankind supplies premium denim and accessories sold in boutiques and high-end department stores. At the other end of the spectrum, Sentinel, part of the Imagewear unit, markets uniforms for security officers.[21]

By offering product and marketing variations to segments, companies hope for higher sales and a stronger position within each market segment. Developing a stronger position within several segments creates more total sales than undifferentiated marketing across all segments. VF Corporation's combined brands give it a much greater, more stable market share than any single brand could. The four Jeanswear brands alone account for a quarter of all jeans sold in North America. Similarly, Procter & Gamble's multiple detergent brands capture four times the market share of nearest rival Unilever (see Real Marketing 8.1).

But differentiated marketing also increases the costs of doing business. A firm usually finds it more expensive to develop and produce, say, 10 units of 10 different products than 100 units of one product. Developing separate marketing plans for the separate segments requires extra marketing research, forecasting, sales analysis, promotion planning, and channel management. And trying to reach different market segments with different advertising campaigns increases promotion costs. Thus, the company must weigh increased sales against increased costs when deciding on a differentiated marketing strategy.

Concentrated Marketing

Using a **concentrated marketing** (or **niche marketing**) strategy, instead of going after a small share of a large market, the firm goes after a large share of one or a few smaller segments or niches. For example, Whole Foods Market has only about 275 stores in the United States and 7 in Canada with approximately US$6.5 billion in sales, compared with goliaths such as Loblaw with over 1000 stores or Walmart with 7300 U.S. and 318 Canadian stores and sales of approximately US$400 billion.[22] Yet the smaller, upscale retailer is growing faster and more profitably than many of its giant rivals. Whole Foods thrives by catering to affluent customers whom the Walmarts of the world can't serve well, offering them "organic, natural, and gourmet foods, all swaddled in Earth Day politics." In fact, a typical Whole Foods customer is more likely to boycott the local Walmart than to shop at it.

Real Marketing 8.1

P&G: Competing with Itself—and Winning

Procter & Gamble is one of the world's premier consumer-goods companies. Some 99 percent of all North American households use at least one of P&G's 86 brands. Around the world, 156 P&G brands touch the lives of people some 3 billion times a day.

P&G sells four brands of laundry detergent in Canada (Tide, Cheer, Gain, and Ivory Snow), and six brands of laundry detergent in the United States (Tide, Cheer, Gain, Era, Dreft, and Ivory). In both countries, it also sells six brands of bath soap (Ivory, Safeguard, Camay, Olay, Zest, and Old Spice); five brands of shampoo (Pantene, Head & Shoulders, Aussie, Herbal Essences, and Infusium 23); four brands of dishwashing detergent (Dawn, Ivory, Joy, and Cascade); three brands each of tissues and towels (Charmin, Bounty, and Puffs) and skin care products (Olay, Gillette Complete Skincare, and Noxzema); and two brands each of deodorant (Secret and Old Spice), fabric softener (Downy and Bounce), and cosmetics (CoverGirl and Max Factor).

Moreover, P&G has many additional brands in each category for different international markets. For example, it sells 16 different laundry product brands in Latin America and 19 in Europe, the Middle East, and Africa. (See P&G's website at www.pg.ca for a full list of the company's impressive lineup of familiar brands.)

These P&G brands compete with one another on the same supermarket shelves. But why would P&G introduce several brands in one category instead of concentrating its resources on a single leading brand? The answer lies in the fact that different people want different *mixes of benefits* from the products they buy. Take laundry detergents as an example. People use laundry detergents to get their clothes clean. But they also want other things from their detergents—such as economy, strength or mildness, bleaching power, fabric softening, fresh smell, and lots of suds or only a few. We all want *some* of every one of these benefits from our detergent, but we may have different *priorities* for each benefit. To some people, cleaning and bleaching power are most important; to others, fabric softening matters most. Still others want a mild, fresh-scented detergent. Thus, each segment of laundry detergent buyers seeks a special combination of benefits.

Procter & Gamble has identified at least four important laundry detergent segments, along with numerous subsegments, and has developed a different brand designed to meet the special needs of each. The four brands are positioned for different segments as follows:

- *Tide* "knows fabrics best." It's the all-purpose family detergent that "gets to the bottom of dirt and stains to help keep your whites white and your colours bright."

- *Cheer* is the "colour expert." "Dirt goes. Colour stays." It helps protect against fading, colour transfer, and fabric wear, with or without bleach. *Cheer Free* is "dermatologist tested. . . contains no irritating perfume or dye."

- *Gain*, originally P&G's "enzyme" detergent, was repositioned as the detergent that gives you "excellent cleaning power and a smell that says clean."

- *Ivory* is "Ninety-nine and forty-four one-hundredths percent pure." It provides "mild cleansing benefits for a gentle, pure, and simple clean."

Within each segment, Procter & Gamble has identified even narrower niches. For example, you can buy regular Tide

Differentiated marketing: Procter & Gamble markets six different laundry detergents, including Tide—each with multiple forms and formulations—that compete with each other on store shelves. Yet together, these multiple brands capture four times the market share of nearest rival Unilever.

(in powder or liquid form) or any of more than 40 different formulations, including the following:

- *Tide Powder* helps keep everyday laundry clean and new. It comes in original and special scents such as *Tide Mountain Spring* ("the scent of crisp mountain air and fresh wildflowers"), *Tide Clean Breeze* (the fresh scent of laundry line-dried in a clean breeze), and *Tide Free* ("has no scent at all—leaves out the dyes or perfumes").

- *Tide Liquid* combines all the great stain-fighting qualities you've come to expect in Tide powder with the pretreating ease of a liquid detergent. Available in Original and Mountain Spring, Clean Breeze, Tropical Clean, and Free scents.

- *Tide with Bleach* helps to "clean even the dirtiest laundry without the damaging effects of chlorine bleach." Keeps "your family's whites white and colours bright." Available in Clean Breeze or Mountain Spring scents.

- *Tide with a Touch of Downy* provides "outstanding Tide clean with a touch of Downy softness and freshness." Available in April Fresh and Clean Breeze scents.

- *Tide Coldwater* is specially formulated to help reduce your energy bills by delivering outstanding cleaning, even on the toughest stains, in cold water. Available in

both liquid and powder formulas and in two new cool scents—Fresh Scent and Mountain Spring.

- *Tide HE* is specially formulated to unlock the cleaning potential of high-efficiency washers and provides excellent cleaning with the right level of sudsing. Available in Original, Free, and Clean Breeze scents.

- *2X Ultra Tide* is double-concentrated to provide the same cleaning power as regular Tide. One small capful gets your whole wash clean. P&G now offers 2X Ultra versions of all of its major liquid Tide sub-brands.

By segmenting the market and having several detergent brands, Procter & Gamble has an attractive offering for consumers in all important preference groups. As a result, P&G is really cleaning up in the North American laundry detergent market. Tide, by itself, captures a whopping 44 percent of the market and is growing. All P&G brands combined take an impressive 62 percent market share—forcing major competitors Unilever and Colgate to throw in the towel and sell off their laundry detergent brands.

Sources: See Ellen Byron, "How P&G Led Also-Ran to Sweet Smell of Success; By Focusing on Fragrance, Gain Detergent Developed a Billion-Dollar Following," *Wall Street Journal*, September 4, 2007, p. B2; Jack Neff, "Why Unilever Lost the Laundry War," *Advertising Age*, August 6, 2007, p.1; and information accessed at www.pg.com and www.tide.com/_en/CA, June 2009.

Through concentrated marketing, the firm achieves a strong market position because of its greater knowledge of consumer needs in the niches it serves and the special reputation it acquires. It can market more *effectively* by fine-tuning its products, prices, and programs to the needs of carefully defined segments. It can also market more *efficiently*, targeting its products or services, channels, and communications programs toward only consumers that it can serve best and most profitably.

Whereas segments are fairly large and normally attract several competitors, niches are smaller and may attract only one or a few competitors. Niching lets smaller companies focus their limited resources on serving niches that may be unimportant to or overlooked by larger competitors. Many companies start as nichers to get a foothold against larger, more-resourceful competitors and then grow into broader competitors. For example, WestJet began by serving no-frills commuters in Western Canada, but is now one of the country's largest airlines. And Enterprise Rent-A-Car began by building a network of neighbourhood offices rather than competing with Hertz and Avis in airport locations. Enterprise is now North America's largest car rental company.

In contrast, as markets change, some megamarketers develop niche markets to create sales growth. For example, in recent years Pepsi has introduced several niche products, such as Sierra Mist, Pepsi Twist, Mountain Dew Code Red, and Mountain Dew LiveWire. Initially, these brands combined accounted for barely 5 percent of Pepsi's overall soft-drink sales. However, Sierra Mist quickly blossomed and now is the number-two lemon-lime soft drink behind Sprite, and Code Red and LiveWire have revitalized the Mountain Dew brand. Says Pepsi-Cola North America's chief marketing officer, "The era of the mass brand has been over for a long time."[23]

Today, the low cost of setting up shop on the Internet makes it even more profitable to serve seemingly minuscule niches. Small businesses in particular are realizing riches from serving small niches on the Web. Consider Zappos:

Concentrated marketing: Web niching is paying off handsomely for Zappos and its CEO/founder Tony Hsieh.

Zappos began by selling shoes online—*only* shoes and *only* online. What gives this online nicher an edge? First, Zappos differentiates itself by its selection: Click to the Zappos site (Zappos ships to Canada for a flat rate of $10) and you can pick through some 3.2 million items representing 950 shoe brands—more inventory than any brick-and-mortar shoe peddler could dream of offering. Zappos also gives you convenience: The warehouse is open 24/7, so you can order as late as 11:00 p.m. and still get next-day delivery. Most important, Zappos has a near-fanatical devotion to pleasing its customers. "We offer the absolute best selection of shoes available anywhere," boasts the company, "but much more important to us is offering the absolute best service." Shipping and return shipping are free and you just can't beat the company's heartfelt returns policy: "If the shoe fits, wear it. If not, ship it back at our expense." All this adds up to a host of satisfied customers. "With Zappos, the shoe store comes to you," says one customer, Pamela Leo. "I can try the shoes on in the comfort of my own home. I can tell if the shoes I want will really work with a particular suit. It's fabulous." And if the shoes aren't just right, she can click on a Zappos-supplied link to print out a prepaid return shipping label. Web niching is paying off handsomely for Zappos. Although it captures only a small portion of the total shoe market, Zappos is now the Web's number-one shoe seller. Thanks to happy customers like Pamela, sales have soared from "almost nothing" in 1999 to an estimated US$1 billion this year. And based on its success in shoes, Zappos is now launching into clothing and other lines.[24]

Concentrated marketing can be highly profitable. At the same time, it involves higher-than-normal risks. Companies that rely on one or a few segments for all of their business will suffer greatly if the segment turns sour. Or larger competitors may decide to enter the same segment with greater resources. For these reasons, many companies prefer to diversify in several market segments.

Micromarketing

Micromarketing
The practice of tailoring products and marketing programs to the needs and wants of specific individuals and local customer groups—includes *local marketing* and *individual marketing*.

Local marketing
Tailoring brands and promotions to the needs and wants of local customer groups—cities, neighbourhoods, and even specific stores.

Differentiated and concentrated marketers tailor their offers and marketing programs to meet the needs of various market segments and niches. At the same time, however, they do not customize their offers to each individual customer. **Micromarketing** is the practice of tailoring products and marketing programs to suit the tastes of specific individuals and locations. Rather than seeing a customer in every individual, micromarketers see the individual in every customer. Micromarketing includes *local marketing* and *individual marketing*.

Local Marketing **Local marketing** involves tailoring brands and promotions to the needs and wants of local customer groups—cities, neighbourhoods, and even specific stores. For example, Walmart customizes its merchandise store by store to meet the needs of local shoppers. Walmart's store designers create each new store's format according to neighbourhood characteristics—stores near office parks, for instance, contain prominent islands featuring ready-made meals for busy workers. Then, using a wealth of customer data on daily sales in every store, Walmart tailors individual store merchandise with similar precision. For example, it uses more than 200 finely tuned planograms (shelf plans) to match soup assortments to each store's demand patterns.[25]

Advances in communications technology have given rise to a new high-tech version of location-based marketing. By coupling mobile phone services with GPS devices, many marketers are now targeting customers wherever they are with what they want:

Location. Location. Location. This is the mantra of the real-estate business. But it may not be long before marketers quote it, too. "Location-based technology allows [marketers] to reach people when they're mobile, near their stores, looking to make a decision," says one marketing expert. "When customers get information—even advertising information—linked to their location, research shows that's often perceived as value-added information, not as an advertisement." For example, Starbucks recently launched a store locator service for mobile devices, which allows people to use their phones and in-car GPS systems to search for the nearest Starbucks shop. A consumer sends a text message to "MYSBUX" (697289) including his or her zip code. Within 10 seconds, Starbucks replies with up to three nearby store locations. Starbucks plans to expand the service to include a wider range of text-messaging conversations with local customers that will "showcase Starbucks as a brand that truly listens." Such location-based marketing will grow astronomically as the sales of GPS devices skyrocket.[26]

Local marketing has some drawbacks. It can drive up manufacturing and marketing costs by reducing economies of scale. It can also create logistics problems as companies try to meet the varied requirements of different regional and local markets. Further, a brand's overall image might be diluted if the product and message vary too much in different localities.

Still, as companies face increasingly fragmented markets, and as new supporting technologies develop, the advantages of local marketing often outweigh the drawbacks. Local marketing helps a company market more effectively in the face of pronounced regional and local differences in demographics and lifestyles. It also meets the needs of the company's first-line customers—retailers—who prefer more finely tuned product assortments for their neighbourhoods.

Individual marketing

Tailoring products and marketing programs to the needs and preferences of individual customers—also labelled " one-to-one marketing," "mass customization," and "markets-of-one marketing."

Individual Marketing In the extreme, micromarketing becomes **individual marketing**—tailoring products and marketing programs to the needs and preferences of individual customers. Individual marketing has also been labelled *one-to-one marketing, mass customization,* and *markets-of-one marketing.*

The widespread use of mass marketing has obscured the fact that for centuries consumers were served as individuals: The tailor custom-made the suit, the cobbler designed shoes for the individual, the cabinetmaker made furniture to order. Today, however, new technologies are permitting many companies to return to customized marketing. More powerful computers, detailed databases, robotic production and flexible manufacturing, and interactive communication media such as cellphones and the Internet have all combined to foster "mass customization." *Mass customization* is the process through which firms interact one-to-one with masses of customers to design products and services tailor-made to individual needs.

Dell creates custom-configured computers. Hockey-stick maker Branches Hockey lets customers choose from more than two dozen options—including stick length, blade patterns, and blade curve—and turns out a customized stick in five days. Visitors to Nike's NikeID website can personalize their sneakers by choosing from hundreds of colours and putting an embroidered word or phrase on the tongue. At www.myMMs.com, you can upload your photo and order a batch of M&Ms with your face and a personal message printed on each little candy. Toyota even lets Scion owners design their own personal "coat of arms" online, "a piece of owner-generated art that is meant to reflect their own job,

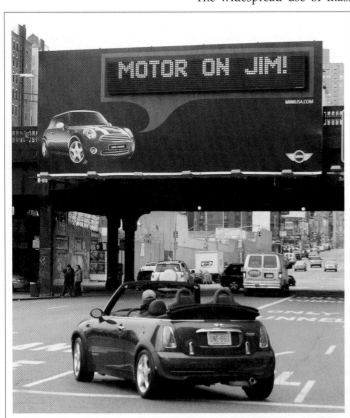

Individual marketing: MINI even uses personalized billboard messages to greet MINI drivers in selected major U.S. cities. The messages are triggered by personalized key fobs given to MINI owners.

hobbies, and—um, okay—Karma." Customers can download their designs and have them made into window decals or professionally airbrushed onto their cars.[27]

Marketers are also finding new ways to personalize promotional messages. For example, plasma screens placed in shopping malls around the country can now analyze shoppers' faces and place ads based on an individual shopper's gender, age, or ethnicity. Last year, MINI even began using personalized billboard messages to greet MINI drivers in four major U.S. cities. The messages are triggered by personalized key fobs given to new buyers. As the new MINI owner passes by, the fob contacts the billboard database, which then transmits a message such as "Motor on Jim!" or "Great day to be a lawyer in New York, Jim!"[28]

Business-to-business marketers are also finding new ways to customize their offerings. For example, John Deere manufactures seeding equipment that can be configured in more than 2 million versions to individual customer specifications. The seeders are produced one at a time, in any sequence, on a single production line. Mass customization provides a way to stand out against competitors.

Unlike mass production, which eliminates the need for human interaction, one-to-one marketing has made relationships with customers more important than ever. Just as mass production was the marketing principle of the past century, interactive marketing is becoming a marketing principle for the twenty-first century. The world appears to be coming full circle—from the good old days when customers were treated as individuals, to mass marketing when nobody knew your name, and back again.

The move toward individual marketing mirrors the trend in consumer *self-marketing*. Increasingly, individual customers are taking more responsibility for shaping both the products they buy and the buying experience. Consider two business buyers with two different purchasing styles. The first sees several salespeople, each trying to persuade him to buy his or her product. The second sees no salespeople but rather logs on to the Web. She searches for information on available products; interacts online with various suppliers, users, and product analysts; and then decides which offer is best. The second purchasing agent has taken more responsibility for the buying process, and the marketer has had less influence over the buying decision.

As the trend toward more interactive dialogue and less marketing monologue continues, marketers will need to influence the buying process in new ways. They will need to involve customers more in all phases of the product development and buying processes, increasing opportunities for buyers to practise self-marketing.

Choosing a Targeting Strategy

Companies need to consider many factors when choosing a market-targeting strategy. Which strategy is best depends on *company resources*. When the firm's resources are limited, concentrated marketing makes the most sense. The best strategy also depends on the degree of *product variability*. Undifferentiated marketing is more suited for uniform products such as grapefruit or steel. Products that can vary in design, such as cameras and automobiles, are more suited to differentiation or concentration. The *product's life-cycle stage* must also be considered. When a firm introduces a new product, it may be practical to launch only one version, and undifferentiated marketing or concentrated marketing may make the most sense. In the mature stage of the product life cycle, however, differentiated marketing begins to make more sense.

Another factor is *market variability*. If most buyers have the same tastes, buy the same amounts, and react the same way to marketing efforts, undifferentiated marketing is appropriate. Finally, *competitors' marketing strategies* are important. When competitors use differentiated or concentrated marketing, undifferentiated marketing can be suicidal. Conversely, when competitors use undifferentiated marketing, a firm can gain an advantage by using differentiated or concentrated marketing, focusing on the needs of buyers in specific segments.

Socially Responsible Target Marketing

Smart targeting helps companies be more efficient and effective by focusing on the segments that they can satisfy best and most profitably. Targeting also benefits consumers—

companies serve specific groups of consumers with offers carefully tailored to their needs. However, target marketing sometimes generates controversy and concern. The biggest issues usually involve the targeting of vulnerable or disadvantaged consumers with controversial or potentially harmful products.

For example, over the years, marketers in a wide range of industries—from cereal and toys to fast food and fashion—have been heavily criticized for their marketing efforts directed toward children and young teens. Critics worry that premium offers and high-powered advertising appeals presented through the mouths of lovable animated characters will overwhelm children's defences. The government of Nova Scotia took action against the distributor of Red Bull after it received reports that the high caffeine beverage had been handed out to high school students.

Other problems arise when the marketing of adult products spills over into the kid segment—intentionally or unintentionally. For example, Victoria's Secret targets its Pink line of young, hip, sexy clothing to young women 18 to 30 years old. However, critics charge that Pink is now all the rage among girls as young as 11. Responding to Victoria's Secret's designs and marketing messages, tweens are flocking into stores and buying Pink, with or without their mothers. More broadly, critics worry that marketers of everything from lingerie and cosmetics to Barbie dolls are directly or indirectly targeting young girls with provocative products, promoting a premature focus on sex and appearance:

> Ten-year-old girls can slide their low-cut jeans over "eye-candy" panties. French maid costumes, garter belt included, are available in preteen sizes. Barbie now comes in a "bling-bling" style, replete with halter top and go-go boots. And it's not unusual for girls under 12 to sing, "Don't-cha wish your girlfriend was hot like me?" North American girls, say experts, are increasingly being fed a cultural catnip of products and images that promote looking and acting sexy. "The message we're telling our girls is a simple one," laments one reporter about the Victoria's Secret Pink line. "You'll have a great life if people find you sexually attractive. Grown women struggle enough with this ridiculous standard. Do we really need to start worrying about it at 11?"[29]

Tobacco and beer companies have long been accused of targeting underage smokers and drinkers. For instance, a recent Adbowl poll found that in the most recent Super Bowl, Bud Light and Budweiser ads ranked first through fourth in popularity among viewers under age 17. Some critics have even called for a complete ban on advertising to children. Organizations such as Concerned Children's Advertisers and Advertising Standards Canada encourage responsible advertising to children and they partnered to publish a reference guide for advertisers. Fast-food marketers have also generated much controversy in recent years by their attempts to target children and other consumers. For example, as obesity rates in Canada increase, McDonald's and other chains have drawn criticism for pitching their high-fat, salt-laden fare. In early 2008, Toronto's medical officer, Dr. David McKeown, called for a federal and provincial ban on all commercial advertising of food and beverages to children under 13. McDonald's has responded to these criticisms by offering more healthy items on its menus and printing nutrition information on its tray liners. Sixteen leading Canadian food and beverage firms, including Campbell's, Kellogg, Kraft, and Weston Bakeries, recently began the Children's Food and Beverage Advertising Initiative to take action against the criticisms. The firms made a commitment to shift their advertising directed to children under 12 to the promotion of healthier dietary choices and healthy active living.[30]

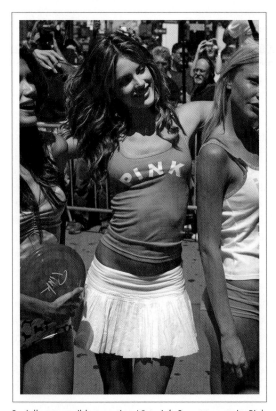

Socially responsible targeting: Victoria's Secret targets its Pink line of young, hip, sexy clothing to young women 18 to 30 years old. However, critics charge that Pink is now all the rage among girls as young as 11.

The growth of the Internet and other carefully targeted direct media has also raised fresh concerns about potential targeting abuses. The Internet allows increasing refinement of audiences and, in turn, more precise targeting. This might help makers of questionable products or deceptive advertisers more readily victimize the most vulnerable audiences. Unscrupulous marketers can now send tailor-made deceptive messages directly to the computers of millions of unsuspecting consumers.

Not all attempts to target children, minorities, or other special segments draw such criticism. In fact, most provide benefits to targeted consumers. For example, Pantene markets Relaxed and Natural hair products to women of colour. Samsung markets the Jitterbug phone directly to seniors who need a simpler cellphone that is bigger and has a louder speaker. And Colgate makes a large selection of toothbrush shapes and toothpaste flavours for children—from Colgate Shrek Bubble Fruit toothpaste to Colgate Bratz character toothbrushes. Such products help make tooth brushing more fun and get children to brush longer and more often.

Thus, in target marketing, the issue is not really *who* is targeted but rather *how* and for *what*. Controversies arise when marketers attempt to profit at the expense of targeted segments—when they unfairly target vulnerable segments or target them with questionable products or tactics. Socially responsible marketing calls for segmentation and targeting that serve not just the interests of the company but also the interests of those targeted.

4 DIFFERENTIATION AND POSITIONING

Beyond deciding which segments of the market it will target, the company must decide on a *value proposition*—on how it will create differentiated value for targeted segments and what positions it wants to occupy in those segments. **Product position** is the way the product is *defined by consumers* on important attributes—the place the product occupies in consumers' minds relative to competing products. "Products are created in the factory, but brands are created in the mind," says one positioning expert.[31]

Product position

The way the product is defined by consumers on important attributes—the place the product occupies in consumers' minds relative to competing products.

Tide is positioned as a powerful, all-purpose family detergent; Ivory is positioned as the gentle detergent for fine washables and baby clothes. At Subway restaurants, you "Eat Fresh"; whereas at Olive Garden, "When You're Here, You're Family." In the automobile market, the Nissan Versa and Honda Fit are positioned on economy, Mercedes and Cadillac on luxury, and Porsche and BMW on performance. Volvo positions powerfully on safety. And Toyota positions its fuel-efficient hybrid Prius as a high-tech solution to the energy shortage. "How far will you go to save the planet?" it asks.

Consumers are overloaded with information about products and services. They cannot re-evaluate products every time they make a buying decision. To simplify the buying process, consumers organize products, services, and companies into categories and "position" them in their minds. A product's position is the complex set of perceptions, impressions, and feelings that consumers have for the product compared with competing products.

Consumers position products with or without the help of marketers. But marketers do not want to leave their products' positions to chance. They must *plan* positions that will give their products the greatest advantage in selected target markets, and they must design marketing mixes to create these planned positions.

Positioning Maps

In planning their differentiation and positioning strategies, marketers often prepare *perceptual positioning maps*, which show consumer perceptions of their brands versus competing products on important buying dimensions. Figure 8.3 shows a positioning map for the large luxury sport-utility vehicle market.[32] The position of each circle on the map indicates the brand's perceived positioning on two dimensions—price and orientation (luxury versus performance). The size of each circle indicates the brand's relative market share.

Thus, customers view the original Hummer H1 (the little dot in the upper right corner) as a very high-performance SUV with a price tag to match. The market-leading Cadillac Escalade is positioned as a moderately priced large luxury SUV with a balance of luxury and performance. The Escalade is positioned on urban luxury, and in its case, "performance" probably means power and safety performance. You'll find no mention of off-road

Figure 8.3 Positioning
map: Large luxury SUVs

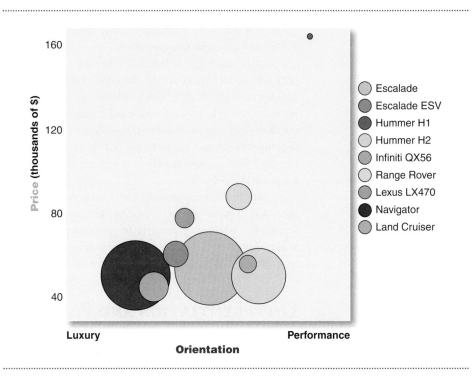

adventuring in an Escalade ad. In contrast, Range Rover and Land Cruiser are positioned on luxury with nuances of off-road performance.

For example, the Toyota Land Cruiser began in 1951 as a four-wheel drive, Jeep-like vehicle designed to conquer the world's most gruelling terrains and climates. In recent years, Land Cruiser has retained this adventure and performance positioning but with luxury added. Land Cruiser ads show the vehicle in adventurous settings, suggesting that it still has more trails to forge—"from the Dead Sea to the Himalayas," says the company's website. "Its husky VVT-i V8 will remind you of why Land Cruiser is a legend throughout the world." However, the company adds, "its available Bluetooth hands-free technology, DVD entertainment, and a sumptuous interior have softened its edges."

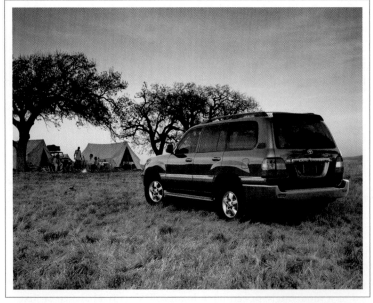

Toyota's Land Cruiser retains some of its adventure and performance positioning but with luxury added.

Choosing a Differentiation and Positioning Strategy

Some firms find it easy to choose a differentiation and positioning strategy. For example, a firm well known for quality in certain segments will go for this position in a new segment if there are enough buyers seeking quality. But in many cases, two or more firms will go after the same position. Then, each will have to find other ways to set itself apart. Each firm must differentiate its offer by building a unique bundle of benefits that appeals to a substantial group within the segment.

Above all else, a brand's positioning must serve the needs and preferences of well-defined target markets. For example, although both Tim Hortons and Starbucks are coffee shops, they offer very different product assortments and store atmospheres. Yet each succeeds because it creates just the right value proposition for its unique mix of customers.

And Air Canada and WestJet are both successful because each takes a completely different position when it comes to serving travellers.

The differentiation and positioning task consists of three steps: identifying a set of differentiating competitive advantages upon which to build a position, choosing the right competitive advantages, and selecting an overall positioning strategy. The company must then effectively communicate and deliver the chosen position to the market.

Identifying Possible Value Differences and Competitive Advantages

To build profitable relationships with target customers, marketers must understand customer needs better than competitors do and deliver more customer value. To the extent that a company can differentiate and position itself as providing superior customer value, it gains **competitive advantage**.

Competitive advantage
An advantage over competitors gained by offering greater customer value, either through lower prices or by providing more benefits that justify higher prices.

But solid positions cannot be built on empty promises. If a company positions its product as offering the best quality and service, it must actually differentiate the product so that it delivers the promised quality and service (see Real Marketing 8.2). Companies must do much more than simply shout out their positions in ad slogans and taglines. They must first live the slogan. For example, when Staples' research revealed that it should differentiate itself on the basis of "an easier shopping experience," the office supply retailer held back its "Staples: That was easy" marketing campaign for more than a year. First, it remade its stores to actually deliver the promised positioning.

Only a few years ago, things weren't so easy for Staples—or for its customers. The ratio of customer complaints to compliments was running an abysmal eight to one at Staples stores. Weeks of focus groups produced an answer: Customers wanted an easier shopping experience. That simple revelation has resulted in one of the most successful marketing campaigns in recent history, built around the now-familiar "Staples: That was easy" tagline. But Staples' positioning turnaround took a lot more than simply bombarding customers with a new slogan. Before it could promise customers a simplified shopping experience, Staples had to actually deliver one. First, it had to live the slogan.

So, for more than a year, Staples worked to revamp the customer experience. It remodelled its stores, streamlined its inventory, retrained employees, and even simplified customer communications. Only when all of the customer-experience pieces were in place did Staples begin communicating its new positioning to customers. The "Staples: That was easy" repositioning campaign has met with striking success, helping make Staples the runaway leader in office retail. And the campaign's "easy" button has become a pop culture icon. No doubt about it, clever marketing helped. But marketing promises count for little if not backed by the reality of the customer experience. "What has happened at the store has done more to drive the Staples brand than all the marketing in the world," says Staples' vice-president of marketing.[33]

To find points of differentiation, marketers must think through the customer's entire experience with the company's product or service. An alert company can find ways to differentiate itself at every customer contact point. In what specific ways can a company differentiate itself or its market offer? It can differentiate along the lines of *product, services, channels, people,* or *image.*

Through *product differentiation* brands can be differentiated on features, performance, or style and design. Thus, Bose positions its speakers on their striking design and sound characteristics. And Panasonic positions its Toughbook PCs, designed to stand up to rugged use on the road or in the field, as "durable, reliable, wireless—protect your work no matter where you work." The Toughbook website offers "Tough Stories," complete with pictures of battered and abused Toughbooks that are still functioning well.

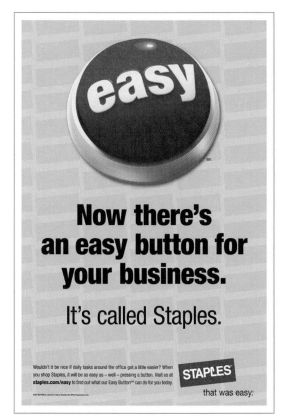

Now there's an easy button for your business.

It's called Staples.

Wouldn't it be nice if daily tasks around the office got a little easier? When you shop Staples, it will be as easy as – well – pressing a button. Visit us at staples.com/easy to find out what our Easy Button℠ can do for you today.

STAPLES

that was easy.

The "Staples: That was easy" marketing campaign has played a major role in repositioning Staples. But marketing promises count for little if not backed by the reality of the customer experience.

Real Marketing 8.2

WestJet's Proposition: "High Value for Less"

In an industry beset by hard times and rising fuel costs, WestJet soars above its competition. Today, it is Canada's second-largest airline and one of the most profitable airlines in North America. A 2009 study by research firm Leger Marketing revealed that it is Canada's most preferred airline. Forty-nine percent of Canadians chose WestJet as their airline of choice compared to 35 percent who selected Air Canada.

WestJet was founded in 1996 by Clive Beddoe, Mark Hill, Tim Morgan, and Donald Bell, four Calgary entrepreneurs who saw an opportunity to provide low-fare air travel across Western Canada. They carefully researched other successful North American airlines and concluded that Southwest Airlines and Morris Air were the firms to mimic. The airline started flight operations with 220 employees and three aircraft and flights to Vancouver, Kelowna, Calgary, Edmonton, and Winnipeg. It carved out a successful niche with these short-haul flights and its low prices combined with reliable service and an off-the-wall sense of humour.

To differentiate itself from other Canadian airlines, which it saw as look-alikes, it did not compete head on for the coveted business traveller market to ensure profitability. Rather, it began specializing in serving what it calls the VFR market (people visiting friends and relatives). It saw its main competitor as the family car and realized that if it could offer lower fares people would choose to fly rather than drive to visit friends and relatives.

WestJet transformed itself from a regional to a national to an international airline using a classic "more-value-for-less" proposition.

Over the years, the company continued to expand, first bringing more western cities into WestJet's world and then expanding nationally. To make noise in some of the new markets it was entering, it offered promotions that no other discount carrier had dared try, like the "Fly for a nickel" campaign it used when it began flying into Sudbury, Ontario. By 2009, WestJet employed 7500 people, over 83 percent of whom own shares in the company and therefore care about customers and the company's success. Through its employees, it works to realize its mission: "To enrich the lives of everyone in WestJet's world by providing safe, friendly and affordable air travel." In the wake of a global economic slump, most airlines have suffered huge losses in recent years or even declared bankruptcy. Yet even in bleak times, WestJet rarely went into the red. What's the secret? WestJet is one of the most strongly and clearly positioned airlines in the world. It offers a classic "more-value-for-less" proposition. Just look at its website and you'll see clear reasons why you should prefer WestJet: the best customer service in town, web check-in, new jets, and incredible on-time performance—all at reasonable prices.

To offer low prices, WestJet works to ensure its operating costs continue to be low. Authors of the book *Ikonica: A Field Guide to Canada's Brandscape* describe WestJet's model of success as follows:

> WestJet has a culture where its values are very clear. It's a very communitarian culture. If the CEO is flying on WestJet, he stays behind and cleans up the plane like everyone else. They don't have cleanup crews. The pilots, stewards and whoever else all clean up the plane together. [WestJet founder] Clive Beddoe says this creates a sense of "we're all in this together," and saves $12 million a year in not having separate cleaning crews. They get it done faster and are always in touch with the flying experience. Also, when they get a pay bonus for something, it's celebrated, not some anonymous sum on a paycheque. They have a big party. They give the same bonuses Air Canada does, but the perceived value of it is much higher because it's a personal interaction between the executives and the individual WestJetters.

> By 2009, WestJet offered 383 flights per day on only three types of planes, which also keeps maintenance costs in check. It offers only basic in-flight service and rapid turnaround at the gates to keep the planes in the air. The "more-value-for-less" philosophy is also

evident in various service choices. They offer a single class of service, without ticket offices at points other than airports. Nonetheless, in WestJet's case, "less service for less money" is defined as fewer amenities for a lower fare, not less customer service.

In 2008, WestJet booked its most profitable year generating more than $2.5 billion in revenue and $178 million in profits. As WestJet CEO Sean Durfy told analysts, "Keeping costs low throughout the year was a key component to our success and continues to be an important element in everything that we do." Despite its focus on cost, the airline also continues to be focused on growth. By 2016, it aims to be one of the five most successful international airlines in the world. It has already expanded its operations to many U.S. cities, including three Hawaiian destinations, as well as offering flights to the Caribbean and Mexico. In 2006 it began offering customized vacation packages.

Debi Andrus, a professor of marketing at the University of Calgary's Haskayne School of Business, for example, wonders "Why not take that fun, folksy Canadian airline image and make it work as a fun, folksy North American airline image?" Other analysts think these concerns are misplaced. Stuart Klaskin, a Miami-based strategic aviation consultant, believes WestJet's expansion strategy is bang on. He believes the low-cost market in the U.S. is stratified with some consumers still demanding the absolute lowest price, while others want an additional level of comfort such as leather seats and TV. Klaskin believes WestJet is on the leading edge of a new trend toward low-cost cross-border travel. WestJet may be on the verge of soaring even higher.

Sources: "WestJet is Canada's Preferred Airline," WestJet Press Release, June 9, 2009, accessed at http://micro.newswire.ca/release.cgi?rkey=1706094440&view=87295-2&Start=0, June 2009; WestJet website, http://c3dsp.westjet.com/guest/home.shtml, accessed June 2009; Jerony Lloyd, "Homegrown Ikons," *Marketing*, April 28, 2008; "WestJet Enjoys Most Profitable Year Ever," *Marketing*, February 13, 2008; Norma Ramage, "WestJet on the Fly," *Marketing*, June 20, 2005; WestJet Fact Sheet, accessed at www.westjet.com, April 2006; Peter Verburg, "Reach for the Bottom," *Canadian Business*, 2000; Helena Katz, "Peanuts and Pretzels Fly East," *Marketing*, March 6, 2000; Norma Ramage, "WestJet Fuels up Advertising Effort," *Marketing*, March 12, 2001.

Beyond differentiating its physical product, a firm can also differentiate the services that accompany the product. Some companies gain *services differentiation* through speedy, convenient, or careful delivery. For example, TD Bank has positioned itself as being the most convenient bank through advertising its longer operating hours and its willingness to take its services to customers rather than waiting for customers to come to them. Others differentiate their service based on high-quality customer care. Lexus makes fine cars but is perhaps even better known for the quality service that creates outstanding ownership experiences for Lexus owners.

Firms that practise *channel differentiation* gain competitive advantage through the way they design their channel's coverage, expertise, and performance. Amazon.ca and GEICO set themselves apart with their smooth-functioning direct channels. Companies can also gain a strong competitive advantage through *people differentiation*—hiring and training better people than their competitors do. Disney employees are known to be friendly and upbeat. And Singapore Airlines enjoys an excellent reputation largely because of the grace of its flight attendants. People differentiation requires that a company select its customer-contact people carefully and train them well. For example, Disney trains its theme park employees thoroughly to ensure that they are competent, courteous, and friendly—from the hotel check-in agents, to the monorail drivers, to the ride attendants, to the people who sweep Main Street, USA. Each employee is carefully trained to understand customers and to "make people happy."

Even when competing offers look the same, buyers may perceive a difference based on company or brand *image differentiation*. A company or brand image should convey the product's distinctive benefits and positioning. Developing a strong and distinctive image calls for creativity and hard work. A company cannot develop an image in the public's mind overnight using only a few advertisements. If Fairmont hotels mean quality, this image must be supported by everything the company says and does.

Symbols—such as the McDonald's golden arches, the Nike swoosh, or Google's colourful logo—can provide strong company or brand recognition and image differentiation. The company might build a brand around a famous person, as Nike did with its Air Jordan

Pledge Multi Surface is positioned on multiple benefits. The challenge is to convince customers that one brand can do it all.

basketball shoes and Tiger Woods golfing products. Some companies even become associated with colours, such as IBM (blue), UPS (brown), or the Bay (red, yellow and green stripes). The chosen symbols, characters, and other image elements must be communicated through advertising that conveys the company's or brand's personality.

Choosing the Right Competitive Advantages

Suppose a company is fortunate enough to discover several potential differentiations that provide competitive advantages. It now must choose the ones on which it will build its positioning strategy. It must decide *how many* differences to promote and *which ones*.

How Many Differences to Promote Many marketers think that companies should aggressively promote only one benefit to the target market. Ad man Rosser Reeves, for example, said a company should develop a *unique selling proposition* (USP) for each brand and stick to it. Each brand should pick an attribute and tout itself as "number one" on that attribute. Buyers tend to remember number one better, especially in this overcommunicated society. Thus, Walmart promotes its always low prices and Burger King promotes personal choice—"have it your way."

Other marketers think that companies should position themselves on more than one differentiator. This may be necessary if two or more firms are claiming to be best on the same attribute. Today, in a time when the mass market is fragmenting into many small segments, companies are trying to broaden their positioning strategies to appeal to more segments. For example, SC Johnson recently introduced a new Pledge multi-surface cleaner. Known mainly as a brand for cleaning and dusting wood furniture, the new Pledge is positioned as a cleaner that works on wood, electronics, glass, marble, stainless steel, and other surfaces. Says its website: "No need to keep switching products—this multi-surface cleaner is perfect for a quick and easy cleanup of the whole room!" Clearly, many buyers want these multiple benefits. The challenge was to convince them that one brand can do it all. However, as companies increase the number of claims for their brands, they risk disbelief and a loss of clear positioning.

Which Differences to Promote Not all brand differences are meaningful or worthwhile; not every difference makes a good differentiator. Each difference has the potential to create company costs as well as customer benefits. A difference is worth establishing to the extent that it satisfies the following criteria:

- *Important:* The difference delivers a highly valued benefit to target buyers.

- *Distinctive:* Competitors do not offer the difference, or the company can offer it in a more distinctive way.

- *Superior:* The difference is superior to other ways that customers might obtain the same benefit.

- *Communicable:* The difference is communicable and visible to buyers.

- *Preemptive:* Competitors cannot easily copy the difference.

- *Affordable:* Buyers can afford to pay for the difference.

- *Profitable:* The company can introduce the difference profitably.

Many companies have introduced differentiations that failed one or more of these tests. When the Westin Stamford Hotel in Singapore advertised that it is the world's tallest hotel, it was a distinction that was not important to most tourists—in fact, it turned many off. Polaroid's Polarvision, which produced instantly developed home movies, bombed too. Although Polarvision was distinctive and even preemptive, it was inferior to another way of capturing motion—camcorders. Thus, choosing competitive advantages upon which to position a product or service can be difficult, yet such choices may be crucial to success.

Selecting an Overall Positioning Strategy

Value proposition
The full positioning of a brand—the full mix of benefits upon which it is positioned.

The full positioning of a brand is called the brand's **value proposition**—the full mix of benefits upon which the brand is differentiated and positioned. It is the answer to the customer's question "Why should I buy your brand?" Volvo's value proposition hinges on safety but also includes reliability, roominess, and styling, all for a price that is higher than average but seems fair for this mix of benefits.

Figure 8.4 shows possible value propositions upon which a company might position its products. In the figure, the five blue cells represent winning value propositions—differentiation and positioning that gives the company competitive advantage. The brown cells, however, represent losing value propositions. The centre beige cell represents at best a marginal proposition. In the following sections, we discuss the five winning value propositions upon which companies can position their products: more for more, more for the same, the same for less, less for much less, and more for less.

More for More   "More-for-more" positioning involves providing the most upscale product or service and charging a higher price to cover the higher costs. The Ritz-Carlton Hotels, Montblanc writing instruments, Mercedes automobiles, Viking appliances—each claims superior quality, craftsmanship, durability, performance, or style and charges a price to match. Not only is the market offering high in quality, it also gives prestige to the buyer. It symbolizes status and a loftier lifestyle. Often, the price difference exceeds the actual increment in quality.

Sellers offering "only the best" can be found in every product and service category, from hotels, restaurants, food, and fashion to cars and household appliances. Consumers are sometimes surprised, even delighted, when a new competitor enters a category with an unusually high-priced brand. Starbucks coffee entered as a very expensive brand in a largely commodity category. When Apple premiered its iPhone, it offered higher-quality features than a traditional cellphone with a hefty price tag to match.

In general, companies should be on the lookout for opportunities to introduce a "more-for-more" brand in any underdeveloped product or service category. Yet "more-for-more" brands can be vulnerable. They often invite imitators who claim the same quality but at a lower price. Luxury goods that sell well during good times may be at risk during economic downturns when buyers become more cautious in their spending.

		Price		
		More	The same	Less
Benefits	More	More for more	More for the same	More for less
	The same			The same for less
	Less			Less for much less

Figure 8.4 Possible Value Propositions

More for the Same   Companies can attack a competitor's "more-for-more" positioning by introducing a brand offering comparable quality but at a lower price. For example, Toyota introduced its Lexus line with a "more-for-the-same" value proposition versus Mercedes and BMW. Its first ad headline read: "Perhaps the first time in history that trading a $72 000 car for a $36 000 car could be considered trading up." It communicated the high quality of its new Lexus through rave reviews in car magazines and through a widely distributed video-tape showing side-by-side comparisons of Lexus and Mercedes automobiles. It published surveys showing that Lexus dealers were providing customers with better sales and service experiences than were Mercedes dealerships. Many Mercedes owners switched to Lexus, and the Lexus repurchase rate has been 60 percent, twice the industry average.

The Same for Less   Offering "the same for less" can be a powerful value proposition—everyone likes a good deal. Discount stores such as Walmart and "category killers" such as Best Buy, Circuit City, and Sport Mart also use this positioning. They don't claim to offer different or better products. Instead, they offer many of the same brands as department stores and specialty stores but at deep discounts based on superior purchasing power and lower-cost operations. Other companies develop imitative but lower-priced brands in an effort to lure customers away from the market leader. For example, AMD makes less-expensive versions of Intel's market-leading microprocessor chips.

Less for Much Less   A market almost always exists for products that offer less and there-fore cost less. Few people need, want, or can afford "the very best" in everything they buy. In many cases, consumers will gladly settle for less-than-optimal performance or give up some of the bells and whistles in exchange for a lower price. For example, many travellers seeking lodgings prefer not to pay for what they consider unnecessary extras, such as a pool, attached restaurant, or mints on the pillow. Hotel chains such as Ramada suspend some of these amenities and charge less accordingly.

   "Less-for-much-less" positioning involves meeting consumers' lower performance or quality requirements at a much lower price. For example, Dollar Stores offer more afford-able goods at very low prices. Costco warehouse stores offer less merchandise selection and consistency and much lower levels of service; as a result, they charge rock-bottom prices. WestJet, one of the world's most consistently profitable air carriers, also practises "less-for-less" positioning.

More for Less   Of course, the winning value proposition would be to offer "more for less." Many companies claim to do this and, in the short run, some companies can actually achieve such lofty positions. For example, when it first opened for business, Home Depot had arguably the best product selection, the best service, *and* the lowest prices compared to local hardware stores and other home improvement chains.

   Yet in the long run, companies will find it very difficult to sustain such best-of-both positioning. Offering more usually costs more, making it difficult to deliver on the "for-less" promise. Companies that try to deliver both may lose out to more focused competitors. For example, facing determined competition from Lowe's stores, Home Depot must now decide whether it wants to compete primarily on superior service or on lower prices.

   All said, each brand must adopt a positioning strategy designed to serve the needs and wants of its target markets. "More for more" will draw one target market, "less for much less" will draw another, and so on. Thus, in any market, there is usually room for many dif-ferent companies, all successfully occupying different positions. The important thing is that each company must develop its own winning positioning strategy, one that makes it special to its target consumers.

Developing a Positioning Statement

Positioning statement
A statement that summarizes company or brand positioning— it takes this form: *To (target segment and need) our (brand) is (concept) that (point of difference).*

Company and brand positioning should be summed up in a **positioning statement**. The statement should follow the form: *To (target segment and need) our (brand) is (concept) that (point of difference).*[34] For example: *"To busy, mobile professionals who need to always be in the loop, BlackBerry is a wireless connectivity solution that gives you an easier, more reliable way to stay connected to data, people, and resources while on the go."*[35]

Note that the positioning first states the product's membership in a category (wireless connectivity solution) and then shows its point of difference from other members of the category (easier, more reliable connections to data, people, and resources). Placing a brand in a specific category suggests similarities that it might share with other products in the category. But the case for the brand's superiority is made on its points of difference.

Sometimes marketers put a brand in a surprisingly different category before indicating the points of difference. Delissio is a frozen pizza whose crust rises when the pizza is heated. But instead of putting it in the frozen pizza category, the marketers positioned it in the delivered pizza category. Delissio ads show delicious pizzas that look like anything but a frozen pizza, proclaiming "No calling. No tipping. No kidding. It's not delivery, its Delissio!" Another ad claims that Delissio "Makes mouths water. And delivery guys weep." Such positioning helps highlight Delissio's fresh quality and superior taste over the normal frozen pizza.

Communicating and Delivering the Chosen Position

Once it has chosen a position, the company must take strong steps to deliver and communicate the desired position to target consumers. All the company's marketing mix efforts must support the positioning strategy.

Positioning the company calls for concrete action, not just talk. If the company decides to build a position on better quality and service, it must first *deliver* that position. Designing the marketing mix—product, price, place, and promotion—involves working out the tactical details of the positioning strategy. Thus, a firm that seizes on a more-for-more position knows that it must produce high-quality products, charge a high price, distribute through high-quality dealers, and advertise in high-quality media. It must hire and train more service people, find retailers who have a good reputation for service, and develop sales and advertising messages that broadcast its superior service. This is the only way to build a consistent and believable more-for-more position.

Companies often find it easier to come up with a good positioning strategy than to implement it. Establishing a position or changing one usually takes a long time. In contrast, positions that have taken years to build can quickly be lost. Once a company has built the desired position, it must take care to maintain the position through consistent performance and communication. It must closely monitor and adapt the position over time to match changes in consumer needs and competitors' strategies. However, the company should avoid abrupt changes that might confuse consumers. Instead, a product's position should evolve gradually as it adapts to the ever-changing marketing environment.

REVIEWING OBJECTIVES AND KEY TERMS | Audio Chapter Summary

In this chapter, you've learned about the major elements of a customer-driven marketing strategy: segmentation, targeting, differentiation, and positioning. Marketers know that they cannot appeal to all buyers in their markets, or at least not to all buyers in the same way. Buyers are too numerous, too widely scattered, and too varied in their needs and buying practices. Therefore, most companies today practise *target marketing*—identifying market segments, selecting one or more of them, and developing products and marketing mixes tailored to each.

OBJECTIVE 1 **Define the major steps in designing a customer-driven marketing strategy: market segmentation, targeting, differentiation, and positioning.**

Customer-driven marketing strategy begins with selecting which customers to serve and deciding on a value proposition that best serves the targeted customers. It consists of

four steps. *Market segmentation* is the act of dividing a market into distinct groups of buyers with different needs, characteristics, or behaviours who might require separate products or marketing mixes. Once the groups have been identified, *market targeting* evaluates each market segment's attractiveness and selects one or more segments to serve. Market targeting consists of designing strategies to build the *right relationships* with the *right customers. Differentiation* involves actually differentiating the market offering to create superior customer value. *Positioning* consists of positioning the market offering in the minds of target customers.

OBJECTIVE 2   List and discuss the major bases for segmenting consumer and business markets.

There is no single way to segment a market. Therefore, the marketer tries different variables to see which give the best segmentation opportunities. For consumer marketing, the major segmentation variables are geographic, demographic, psychographic, and behavioural. In *geographic segmentation*, the market is divided into different geographical units such as nations, regions, provinces, counties, cities, or neighbourhoods. In *demographic segmentation*, the market is divided into groups based on demographic variables, including age, gender, family size, family life cycle, income, occupation, education, religion, race, generation, and nationality. In *psychographic segmentation*, the market is divided into different groups based on social class, lifestyle, or personality characteristics. In *behavioural segmentation*, the market is divided into groups based on consumers' knowledge, attitudes, uses, or responses to a product.

Business marketers use many of the same variables to segment their markets. But business markets can also be segmented by business consumer *demographics* (industry, company size), *operating characteristics, purchasing approaches, situational factors*, and *personal characteristics*. The effectiveness of segmentation analysis depends on finding segments that are *measurable, accessible, substantial, differentiable*, and *actionable*.

OBJECTIVE 3   Explain how companies identify attractive market segments and choose a market-targeting strategy.

To target the best market segments, the company first evaluates each segment's size and growth characteristics, struc-tural attractiveness, and compatibility with company objectives and resources. It then chooses one of four market-targeting strategies—ranging from very broad to very narrow targeting. The seller can ignore segment differences and target broadly using *undifferentiated (or mass) marketing*. This involves mass producing, mass distributing, and mass promoting the same product in about the same way to all consumers. Or the seller can adopt *differentiated marketing*—developing different market offers for several segments. *Concentrated marketing* (or *niche marketing*) involves focusing on only one or a few market segments. Finally, *micromarketing* is the practice of tailoring products and marketing programs to suit the tastes of specific individuals and locations. Micromarketing includes *local marketing* and *individual marketing*. Which targeting strategy is best depends on company resources, product variability, product life-cycle stage, market variability, and competitive marketing strategies.

OBJECTIVE 4   Discuss how companies differentiate and position their products for maximum competitive advantage in the marketplace.

Once a company has decided which segments to enter, it must decide on its *differentiation and positioning strategy*. The differentiation and positioning task consists of three steps: identifying a set of possible differentiations that create *competitive advantage*, choosing advantages upon which to build a position, and selecting an overall positioning strategy. The brand's full positioning is called its *value proposition*—the full mix of benefits upon which the brand is positioned. In general, companies can choose from one of five winning value propositions upon which to position their products: more for more, more for the same, the same for less, less for much less, or more for less. Company and brand positioning are summarized in *positioning statements* that state the target segment and need, positioning concept, and specific points of difference. The company must then effectively communicate and deliver the chosen position to the market.

KEY TERMS

mymarketinglab | Glossary Flashcards

DISCUSSING THE CONCEPTS

1. Briefly describe the four major steps in designing a customer-driven marketing strategy.

2. Name and describe the four major sets of variables that might be used in segmenting consumer markets. Which segmenting variable(s) do you think Starbucks is using?

3. Explain how marketers can segment international markets.

4. Compare and contrast undifferentiated, differentiated, concentrated, and micromarketing targeting strategies. Which strategy is best?

5. What is a product's "position" and how do marketers know what it is?

6. Name and define the five winning value propositions described in the chapter. Which value proposition describes Walmart? Explain your answer.

APPLYING THE CONCEPTS

1. The chapter described psychographics as one major variable used by marketers when segmenting consumer markets. SRI Consulting has developed a typology of consumers based on values and lifestyles. Go to Strategic Business Insights (www.strategicbusinessinsights.com), click on the VALS survey on the right side of the screen, and complete the VALS survey. How accurately do your primary and secondary VALS types describe you? How can marketers use this information? Write a brief report on your findings.

2. Assume you work at a university whose traditional target market, high school students within your region, is shrinking and projections are that this segment will decrease approximately 5 percent per year over the next 10 years. Recommend other potential market segments and discuss the criteria you should consider to ensure that the identified segments are effective.

3. Form a small group and create an idea for a new reality television show. Using the format provided in the chapter, develop a positioning statement for this television show. What competitive advantage does the show have over existing shows? How many and which differences would you promote?

FOCUS ON TECHNOLOGY

Have you noticed that ads on websites seem to reflect your interests? Do you ever wonder if someone is watching your Internet behaviour? Well, someone (that is, a computer) probably is watching and tracking you. Marketers use such tracking information to send targeted ads to consumers—it's called behavioural targeting. You've no doubt heard of "cookies," the files deposited on your computer when you visit a website. If you've ever given personally identifying information at a site, it remembers you when you return—it's all stored in the cookie file. But even if you don't give personally identifying information on a website, Internet protocol (IP) addresses can be tracked to follow where you go and where you've been on the Internet. This tracking lets marketers tailor webpages, information, offers, and prices to individuals based on their behavioural characteristics.

Behavioural targeting is coveted because it allows marketers to implement micromarketing strategies.

1. BV! Media is the only bilingual behavioural targeting ad network in Canada. Visit www.bvmedia.ca to learn more about this company. Explore its website to learn how it lets marketers send Internet ads to targeted consumers. Then write a brief report explaining behavioural targeting and how marketers are using it.

2. Many individuals are concerned that Internet behavioural tracking violates their privacy. Most websites have access to users' IP addresses. Are IP addresses alone "user identifiable" information? Learn more about this issue and write a brief report about it.

FOCUS ON ETHICS

KGOY stands for "kids getting older younger," and marketers are getting much of the blame. Kids today see all types of messages, especially on the Internet, that children would never have seen in the past. Whereas boys may give up G.I. Joe at an earlier age to play war games on their Xbox 360s, the greater controversy seems to surround claims of how girls have changed, or rather, how marketers have changed girls. Critics describe clothing designed for young girls aged 8–11 as "floozy" and sexual, with department stores selling youngsters thongs and T-shirts that say "Naughty Girl!" Although Barbie's sexuality has never been subtle, she was originally targeted to girls 9–12 years old. Now, Barbie dolls target primarily girls 3–7 years old! And Barbie's competitor, Bratz dolls, has an "in-your-face" attitude that has some parents complaining that they are too sexual.

1. Do you think marketers are to blame for kids getting older younger? Give some other examples.

2. Give an example of a company that is countering this trend by offering age-appropriate products for children.

MARKETING BY THE NUMBERS

North Americans love their pets. You may have one or more furry, feathery, or scaly friends yourself, so you know how much money you spend each year. Marketers need to know that information to estimate the size of a potential market segment. The American Pet Products Association (APPA) conducts a yearly survey of pet owners that provides useful information for estimating market size and potential.

1. Refer to Appendix 3: Marketing by the Numbers and use the information available from the APPA survey (go to - www.americanpetproducts.org) to develop an estimate of the market potential for dog food in the United States. Can you use this information to estimate the size of the potential market in Canada? Why or why not?

2. Using other information from the APPA's website, evaluate the usefulness of this market segment.

VIDEO CASE

Meredith

| Video Case Questions

The Meredith Corporation has developed an expertise in building customer relationships through segmentation, targeting, and positioning. Amazingly, however, it has done this by focusing on only half of the population—the female half. Meredith has developed the largest database of any U.S. media company and uses that database to meet the specific needs and desires of women.

Meredith is known for such leading titles as *Better Homes and Gardens, Family Circle*, and *Ladies' Home Journal*. But that list has grown to a portfolio of 14 magazines and more than 200 special interest publications. Through these magazines alone, Meredith regularly reaches about 30 million readers. By focusing on core categories of home, family, and personal development, Meredith has developed a product mix designed to meet various needs of women.

This creates multiple touch points as individual women engage with more than one magazine, as well as with specialty books and websites.

After viewing the video featuring Meredith, answer the following questions about segmenting, targeting, and positioning:

1. On what main variables has Meredith focused in segmenting its markets?

2. Which target marketing strategy best describes Meredith's efforts? Support your choice.

3. How does Meredith use its variety of products to build relationships with the right customers?

Visit MyMarketingLab at www.pearsoned.ca/mymarketinglab to view the video segment related to this case.

COMPANY CASE

Saturn: An Image Makeover

Things are changing at Saturn. The General Motors brand had only three iterations of the same compact car for the entire decade of the 1990s. But over the last couple of years, Saturn has introduced an all-new lineup of vehicles that includes a midsized sport sedan, an 8-passenger crossover vehicle, a 2-seat roadster, a new compact sport sedan, and a compact SUV. Having anticipated the brand's renaissance for years, Saturn executives, employees, and customers are beside themselves with joy.

But with all this change, industry observers wonder whether Saturn will be able to maintain the very characteristics that have distinguished the brand since its inception. Given that Saturn established itself based on a very narrow line of compact vehicles, many believe that the move from targeting one segment of customers to targeting multiple segments will be challenging. Will a newly positioned Saturn still meet the needs of one of the most loyal cadres of customers in the automotive world?

A NEW KIND OF CAR COMPANY

From its beginnings in 1985, Saturn set out to break through the GM bureaucracy and become "A different kind of car. A different kind of company." As the single-most defining characteristic of the new company, Saturn proclaimed that its sole focus would be people: customers, employees, and communities. The company's focus on employees included an unprecedented contract with the United Auto Workers (UAW) that focused on progressive work rules, benefits, work teams, and the concept of empowerment. It established a ground-breaking dealer network structure, reversing long-held customer perceptions of dealers as a nemesis. Saturn also received awards and recognition for socially responsible policies that were beneficial to employees, communities, and the environment.

But in addition to establishing an image as a people-oriented company, Saturn put significant resources into product development. The first Saturn cars were made "from scratch," without any allegiance to the GM parts bin or suppliers. The goal was to produce not only a high-quality vehicle, but one known for safety and innovative features that would "wow" the customer.

When the first Saturn vehicles rolled off the assembly line on July 30, 1990, the company offered a sedan, a coupe, and a wagon in two trim levels each, all based on a single compact vehicle platform. Despite this minimal approach, sales quickly exceeded expectations. By 1992, Saturn had sold 500 000 vehicles. That same year, the company achieved the highest new car sales per retail outlet, something that had not been done by a domestic car company for 15 years.

Indeed, customers were drawn to all the things that Saturn had hoped they would be. They loved the innovations, like dent-resistant body panels, the high-tech paint job designed to resist oxidization and chipping longer than any other car in the industry, and safety features like traction control, anti-lock brakes, and unparalleled body reinforcements. They were overwhelmed by the fresh sales approach that included no-haggle pricing, a 30-day return policy, and no hassle from the noncommissioned sales associates.

During Saturn's early years of operations, the accolades rolled in. The list included "Best Car" picks from numerous magazines and organizations, along with awards for quality, engineering, safety, and ease of maintenance. But the crowning achievement occurred in 1995 as the 1 000 000th Saturn took to the road. That year, Saturn ranked number one out of all automotive nameplates on the J.D. Power and Associates Sales Satisfaction Index Study, achieving the highest score ever given by the organization. It would be the only company ever to achieve the highest marks in all three categories ranked by the satisfaction index (salesperson performance, delivery activities, and initial product quality). Saturn earned that honour for an astounding four consecutive years, and it was the only nonluxury brand to be at or near the top of J.D. Power's scores for the better part of a decade.

THE HONEYMOON ENDS

Looking back, Saturn unquestionably defied the odds. To launch an all-new automotive company in such a fiercely competitive and barrier-entrenched industry is one thing. To achieve the level of sales, the customer base, and the list of awards that Saturn achieved in such a short period of time is truly remarkable. But despite all of Saturn's initial successes, one thing was always missing from the GM division. Profit. As the new millennium dawned, GM had yet to earn a nickel of return on billions of dollars invested in the brand. Saturn sales peaked early in 1994 at 286 000 and settled in at an average of about 250 000 units per year.

The lack of continued growth may have been partly due to the fact that Saturn released no new models in the 1990s. GM finally introduced the midsized L-series and compact SUV Vue for 2000 and 2002, respectively. It replaced the original S-series with the Ion in 2003. But while these new vehicles addressed the issue of a lack of model options, they brought with them a new concern: Saturn's history of high quality and its long-cherished J.D. Power ratings began to slide. In the early part of the new millennium, not only was

Saturn's J.D. Power initial-quality rating not near the top, it fell to below the industry average.

Even with the new models, Saturn's sales did not improve. In fact, they declined. This was partly due to an industrywide downturn in sales wrought by a recession. But Saturn's general manager, Jill Lajdziak, has conceded that for too long Saturn sold utilitarian vehicles. In 2005, Saturn sales fell to a record low of 213 000 units, only about 1 percent of the overall market. It seems that sales of the L-series and Vue were coming almost entirely from loyal Saturn customers who were trading up to something different, something bigger and, unfortunately, something not as good.

A NEW KIND OF SATURN

Given the troubles that Saturn was experiencing, it came as a surprise when GM executives announced in 2008 expectations that Saturn would be its growth brand in the ensuing years. GM hoped to perform a makeover similar to the one it achieved with Cadillac earlier in the decade, infusing another $3 billion into its import-fighter nameplate. Given that GM had just experienced a record loss of $38 billion, the world's biggest carmaker was clearly putting faith in one of its smallest brands to help turn the tide.

Jill Lajdziak said "Saturn's initial image as a smart innovation small-car company was blurred by bumps in quality and slow model turnover. We didn't grow the portfolio fast enough, and [now] we're growing it in a huge way." At the Vancouver International Auto Show in spring 2007, Lajdziak introduced one shiny new model after another: the 2007 Sky two-seat roadster, the 2007 Outlook crossover wagon, the completely redesigned 2008 Vue, the 2007 midsized Aura sedan, and the 2008 Astra. Not a single one of these models had been available in January 2006.

"By the end of this year, the oldest product in a Saturn showroom will be the Sky," said Lajdziak. Of GM's investment she remarked, "We've asked for beautifully designed products with a level of refinement, interiors, vehicle dynamics—we think we have it all. And we've got that married up with what consumers believe is the best industry experience in the marketplace." Commenting on the magnitude of the changes at Saturn, she said, "Nobody else has ever tried to grow the portfolio and turn it over as fast as we are, maintain industry-best customer satisfaction, and obviously deliver the [profit] results all at the same time."

At the heart of this makeover is something else all new to Saturn: taking advantage of the GM family of vehicles and parts bins to achieve efficiencies of scale and increase profit margins. In fact, the new Saturn models are largely rebranded Opels, GM's European division. In the future, new-product development will be carried out in a joint-venture fashion between the two divisions. For a company that in the past has been known as making the "car for people who hate cars," this is a 180-degree turnaround.

With a new lineup of European-engineered vehicles, Saturn is intent on repositioning its brand image with its "Rethink" campaign. The print and TV ads are designed to change consumers' perceptions of Saturn as a bland, functional, economy car. Saturn may have the advantage of youth in this undertaking. Some industry analysts suggest it can reposition itself more easily than other brands because it is such a young company.

As for the new positioning, GM makes it clear that with Saturn, it's not trying to make another Chevrolet. Chevrolet will remain the only GM brand positioned as "all things to all people." Along with the other GM brands, Saturn will play a niche role and target a specific market segment. In fact, GM says it's just trying to help Saturn do more of what it has been doing all along—reach the type of import-buying customer it can't reach with any of its other brands. Indeed, top executives at GM acknowledge that many Saturn owners already believe their car is an Asian brand, not a domestic one. "Saturn has always been the one brand in the GM lineup suitable for attracting import-intenders," commented one GM executive.

SWIMMING, OR SINKING?

GM set a lofty 2007 sales goal for Saturn of 400 000 vehicles, far more than the division had ever sold. However, it didn't even come close to that goal, selling only 240 000 vehicles. With so many new models, it is struggling to create brand awareness for each one. But although Saturn fell short of its goal, unit sales represented a 12 percent increase over the previous year. At a time when the entire industry was struggling, this was a notable achievement. Much more significant, however, was the fact that the average price of a Saturn transaction skyrocketed by a whopping US$7000. This translated into a huge 24 percent increase for dealer profitability.

"We're seeing more cross-shopping than ever," said Lajdziak. "Our retailers are seeing people they've never seen before in their showrooms, in terms of demographics and what they are trading in." And better yet, Saturn is not cannibalizing other GM brands. Saturn sales appear to be increasing at the expense of Honda, Nissan, and Toyota. In fact, not a single GM model ranks among the top-ten vehicles cross-shopped by potential Saturn buyers.

The new Saturn strategy is a big change: new positioning, new vehicles, even a new advertising agency. But despite all this change, Saturn is remaining focused on the core elements that have always made Saturn a different kind of car company: innovation, social responsibility, a focus on employees, and creating and maintaining strong customer relationships. This unique combination of change and consistency may just result in Saturn fulfilling GM's expectations of a growth brand.

Questions for Discussion

1. Using the full spectrum of segmentation variables, describe how GM has segmented the automobile market.

2. What segment(s) is Saturn now targeting? How is GM now positioning Saturn? How do these strategies differ from those employed with the original Saturn S-series?

3. Describe the role that social responsibility plays in Saturn's targeting strategy.

4. Do you think that GM will accomplish its goals with the "new Saturn"? Why or why not?

5. What segmentation, targeting, and positioning recommendations would you make to GM for future Saturn models?

Sources: Jamie LaReau, "Saturn Is Expected to Be GM's Growth Brand," *Automotive News*, February 18, 2008, p. 52; Frank Aukofer, "Resurgent Saturn Has Appealing Vue," *Washington Times*, April 18, 2008, p. G01; Gregory Solman, "Saturn Asks Americans to 'Rethink' Its Brand," *Adweek*, May 21, 2007, accessed at www.adweek.com; Jeremy Cato, "Saturn's Revival Shows What the 'New GM' Can Do," *Globe and Mail*, April 5, 2007, p. G10; Barbara Powell, "GM's Saturn Seeks to Shake Up Humdrum Image," *Ottawa Citizen*, April 12, 2006, p. F7; and "Our Story," accessed at www.saturn.com, November 2008.

Visit **MyMarketingLab** at **www.pearsoned.ca/mymarketinglab** for access to online tutorials, interactive exercises, videos, and much more.

9

Products, Services, and Brands
Building Customer Value

PREVIEWING **THE** CONCEPTS   Now that you've had a good look at customer-driven marketing strategy, we'll take a deeper look at the marketing mix—the tactical tools that marketers use to implement their strategies and deliver superior customer value. In this and the next chapter, we'll study how companies develop and manage products and brands. Then, in the chapters that follow, we'll look at pricing, distribution, and marketing communication tools. The product is usually the first and most basic marketing consideration. We'll start with a seemingly simple question: What is a product? As it turns out, however, the answer is not so simple.

Before starting the chapter, let's look at an interesting branding story. Brands may be the most important tools for creating customer value and profitable customer relationships. Marketing is all about building brands that connect deeply with customers. So, when you think of top brands, which ones pop up first? Here's a tale about one strong brand you may not have considered.

Suppose you've just joined a new gym and you're in the market for some new clothes to work out in. Where will you go? A mere five years ago, you likely would have driven to your local mall to the nearest Sportchek, Athletes World or Foot Locker. But chances are if you're a woman in your 20s (or a very hip "new age" kind of guy), your answer might be different. The lululemon name and unique logo, which has been described as a "flippy hairdo" (it's actually a stylized letter *A,* denoting the first letter of "Athletically Hip," one of the company's originally proposed names), have become famous in Canada. Lululemon stores are popping up everywhere both in Canada and around the globe, bringing their unique yoga-inspired clothing and philosophy to more and more satisfied customers.

Lululemon was founded in 1998 by Chip Wilson in Kitsilano, a trendy neighbourhood in Vancouver, British Columbia, in response to the growing number of women taking up sports, especially yoga. In 2008, a female CEO, Christine Day, took over the helm. Previously, sports had been largely male-dominated and, therefore, women were not a focus for the major athletic apparel companies. Thus, many women found themselves purchasing men's athletic clothes, which were both ill-fitting and masculine-looking. Lululemon started as a design studio surrounded by a retail store, which interestingly shared its space with a yoga studio. By putting "the guest experience" at the centre of its business strategy, lululemon continued to create clothing with its clientele's feedback in mind. It uses four pillars as the keys to success for creating this experience: the design and delivery of innovative athletic apparel, its culture and training of employees, cool stores that resonate with both its guests and the community, and strong, authentic community relations.

To a true lululemon convert, the gear isn't just clothing—it's a way of life; an experience. It's made to "exceed expectations" and "inspire health" and is "sexy and hot" with a "fit so good you want more." With every pair of "Groove Pants" it sells, lululemon creates a happy customer. And each happy customer can't wait to tell others about the experience. While lululemon's clothing was originally designed for athletes, Wilson notes that the clothing can be used by anyone for any activity. And therein, perhaps, lies its success—lululemon's clothes are functional, extremely comfortable and, most of all, trendy.

Lululemon is so focused on the experience it creates that the brand is largely defined through the store experience. In fact, the brand was built almost entirely via word of mouth. It is the positive shopping experience that turns customers into brand advocates who spread the word. A pretty amazing feat, especially when you consider lululemon's price point. Indeed, lululemon gear is not cheap—the average pair of pants costs $90, and a top will cost about $50. And yet people flock to its stores. Why? Lululemon's combination of superior-quality garments, enticing retail stores, and a community-based philosophy is a winning formula. Lululemon goes to great lengths to reinforce its philosophy in all that it does. From developing a store ambassador system with local yoga instructors or yoga enthusiasts who informally spread the good word about lululemon, to offering employees free yoga classes and making charitable contributions to its communities, lululemon reinforces its mission of "provid[ing] components for people to live longer, healthier, more fun lives." The result? Customers are passionate about the brand, and they share that passion with others.

The controversial but famous "Grin and Bare It" store opening illustrates just how much people love lululemon. Invited to attend the store opening in only their undies, many fans of the brand showed up to receive a free top and bottom for their efforts. It seems that people will go to great lengths to be a part of the lululemon franchise.

Thus, lululemon does much more than just sell athletic apparel. It creates an unparalleled experience for its customers. And these experiences have led to impressive business results. Between 2007 and 2008, lululemon's revenues

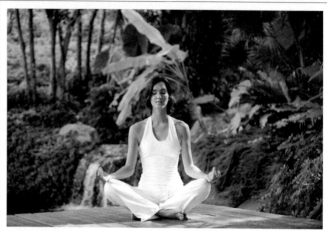

Comfortable, well-made clothing helps consumers live an active, healthy lifestyle.

increased by 30.9 percent. While it has stumbled occasionally (it entered Japan only to close its stores there), it has been growing rapidly since its inception. By 2009 it operated 114 stores in Canada and the United States and believes it has the potential to grow this number to over 300 stores. While expansion plans have slowed because of the downturn in the economy, lululemon stresses that it won't follow the path of price discounting that many of its rivals have taken. Instead, it plans to expand its lines of running wear and add a higher-priced line of clothing made from a new, high-performance organic cotton, and there are plans to develop a line of outerwear. It is also entering the world of online sales to expand its reach, using "shop nude" as one of the 10 reasons why its customers should shop online. However, lululemon is focused on growing only as quickly as it can find the right individuals to carry on its brand philosophy and ensure strong and consistent brand messaging. Thus, the future looks bright for lululemon and its many loyal customers.[1]

OBJECTIVES

1. Define *product* and the major classifications of products and services.

2. Describe the decisions companies make regarding their individual products and services, product lines, and product mixes.

3. Discuss branding strategy—the decisions companies make in building and managing their brands.

4. Identify the four characteristics that affect the marketing of a service and the additional marketing considerations that services require.

Chapter Opening Discussion

As the lululemon example shows, in their quest to create strong customer relationships and experiences, marketers must build and manage products and brands that connect with customers. This chapter begins with a deceptively simple question: *What is a product?* After addressing this question, we look at ways to classify products in consumer and business markets. Then we discuss the important decisions that marketers make regarding individual products, product lines, and product mixes. Next, we look into the critically important issue of how marketers build and manage brands. Finally, we examine the characteristics and marketing requirements of a special form of product—services.

1   WHAT IS A PRODUCT?

Product
Anything that can be offered to a market for attention, acquisition, use, or consumption that might satisfy a want or need.

We define a **product** as anything that can be offered to a market for attention, acquisition, use, or consumption that might satisfy a want or need. Products include more than just tangible objects, such as cars, computers, or cellphones. Broadly defined, "products" also include services, events, persons, places, organizations, ideas, or mixes of these. Throughout this text, we use the term *product* broadly to include any or all of these entities. Thus, an Apple iPod, a Toyota Camry, and a Caffè Mocha at Starbucks are products. But so are a trip to Banff, Scotia's iTRADE investing and trading services, and advice from your gardening centre.

Because of their importance in the world economy, we give special attention to services. **Services** are a form of product that consists of activities, benefits, or satisfactions offered for sale that are essentially intangible and do not result in the ownership of anything. Examples are banking, hotel, airline, retail, wireless communication, and home-repair services. We will look at services more closely later in this chapter.

Service
Any activity or benefit that one party can offer to another that is essentially intangible and does not result in the ownership of anything.

Products, Services, and Experiences

Product is a key element in the overall *market offering*. Marketing-mix planning begins with building an offering that brings value to target customers. This offering becomes the basis upon which the company builds profitable customer relationships.

Glossary Flashcards of Key Terms

A company's market offering often includes both tangible goods and services. At one extreme, the offer may consist of a *pure tangible good*, such as soap, toothpaste, or salt—no services accompany the product. At the other extreme are *pure services*, for which the offer consists primarily of a service. Examples include a doctor's exam or financial advice. Between these two extremes, however, many goods-and-services combinations are possible.

Today, as products and services become more commoditized, many companies are moving to a new level in creating value for their customers. To differentiate their offers beyond simply making products and delivering services, they are creating and managing customer *experiences* with their brands or company.

Experiences have always been an important part of marketing for some companies and organizations. Companies that market experiences realize that customers are really buying much more than just products and services. They are buying what those offers will *do* for them. Disney has long manufactured dreams and memories through its movies and theme parks. And Nike has long declared, "It's not so much the shoes but where they take you." Today, however, all kinds of firms are recasting their traditional goods and services to create experiences. For example, a visit to the Alberta Library involves a lot more than just borrowing a book:

> As part of Canadian library month, which occurs in October, the Alberta Library (a consortium of 290 libraries that work together to promote barrier-free access to information, ideas, and culture), launched a TV, radio, print and online campaign named "Books and beyond." It was designed to show people who had stopped using libraries the vast range of products and services libraries offer today. Tricia Bradshaw, the account manager at Rethink (the agency contracted to develop the campaign), noted, "A lot of people think that libraries are just stodgy old places that don't really have anything for them." If libraries are to continue to be vital institutions within their communities, this stereotype had to be destroyed. The campaign used an ironic,

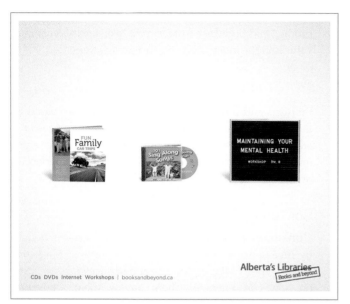

CDs DVDs Internet Workshops | booksandbeyond.ca

Alberta's Libraries
Books and beyond

The Alberta Library launched its award-winning campaign to convince people that libraries offer a vast range of services beyond just books.

humorous approach. One typical ad showed a man checking out a book called *Climbing Mount Everest*. A month later, with his arm in a cast, he returns to search the Web on left-handed living. The campaign generated both local and global buzz. It was featured as one of TBS's funniest ads. In 2009, the campaign was recognized as one of the best library marketing campaigns in the world by the International Federation of Library Associations.[2]

Levels of Product and Services

Product planners need to think about products and services on three levels (see Figure 9.1). Each level adds more customer value. The most basic level is the *core customer value*, which addresses the question, "What is the buyer really buying?" When designing products, marketers must first define the core, problem-solving benefits or services that consumers seek. A woman buying lipstick buys more than lip colour. Charles Revson of Revlon saw this early: "In the factory, we make cosmetics; in the store, we sell hope." And people who buy a BlackBerry smartphone (made by Waterloo, Ontario–based Research In Motion) are buying more than a cellphone, email device, or personal organizer. They are buying freedom and on-the-go connectivity to people and resources.

At the second level, product planners must turn the core benefit into an *actual product*. They need to develop product and service features, a design, a quality level, a brand name, and packaging. For example, the BlackBerry is an actual product. Its name, parts, styling, features, packaging, and other attributes have all been combined carefully to deliver the core customer value of staying connected.

Finally, product planners must build an *augmented product* around the core benefit and actual product by offering additional consumer services and benefits. The BlackBerry solution offers more than just a communications device. It provides consumers with a complete solution to mobile connectivity problems. Thus, when consumers buy a BlackBerry, the company and its dealers also might give buyers a warranty on parts and workmanship, instructions on how to use the device, quick repair services when needed, and a toll-free number and website to use if they have problems or questions.

Consumers see products as complex bundles of benefits that satisfy their needs. When developing products, marketers first must identify the *core customer value* that consumers

Figure 9.1 Three levels of product

Core, actual, and augmented product: People who buy a BlackBerry are buying more than a cellphone, email device, or organizer. They are buying freedom and on-the-go connectivity to people and resources.

Consumer product
A product bought by final consumers for personal consumption.

Convenience product
A consumer product that customers usually buy frequently, immediately, and with a minimum of comparison and buying effort.

Shopping product
A consumer product that the customer, in the process of selection and purchase, usually compares on such bases as suitability, quality, price, and style.

seek from the product. They must then design the *actual* product and find ways to *augment* it to create this customer value and the most satisfying customer experience.

Product and Service Classifications

Products and services fall into two broad classes based on the types of consumers that use them—*consumer products* and *industrial products*. Broadly defined, products also include other marketable entities such as experiences, organizations, persons, places, and ideas.

Consumer Products

Consumer products are products and services bought by final consumers for personal consumption. Marketers usually classify these products and services further based on how consumers go about buying them. Consumer products include conv*enience products, shopping products, specialty products,* and *unsought products*. These products differ in the ways consumers buy them and, therefore, in how they are marketed (see Table 9.1).

Convenience products are consumer products and services that customers usually buy frequently, immediately, and with a minimum of comparison and buying effort. Examples include laundry detergent, candy, magazines, and fast food. Convenience products are usually low priced and marketers place them in many locations to make them readily available when customers need them.

Shopping products are less frequently purchased consumer products and services that customers compare carefully on suitability, quality, price, and style. When buying shopping products and services, consumers spend much time and effort in gathering information and making comparisons. Examples include furniture, clothing, used cars, major appliances, and hotel and airline services. Shopping-products marketers usually distribute their products through fewer outlets but provide deeper sales support to help customers in their comparison efforts.

Specialty products are consumer products and services with unique characteristics or brand identification for which a significant group of buyers is willing to make a special

Table 9.1 Marketing Considerations for Consumer Products

Marketing Considerations	Type of Consumer Product			
	Convenience	Shopping	Specialty	Unsought
Customer buying behaviour	Frequent purchase, little planning, little comparison or shopping effort, low customer involvement	Less frequent purchase, much planning and shopping effort, comparison of brands on price, quality, style	Strong brand preference and loyalty, special purchase effort, little comparison of brands, low price sensitivity	Little product awareness or knowledge (or, if aware, little or even negative interest)
Price	Low price	Higher price	High price	Varies
Distribution	Widespread distribution, convenient locations	Selective distribution in fewer outlets	Exclusive distribution in only one or a few outlets per market area	Varies
Promotion	Mass promotion by the producer	Advertising and personal selling by both producer and resellers	More carefully targeted promotion by both producer and resellers	Aggressive advertising and personal selling by producer and resellers
Examples	Toothpaste, magazines, laundry detergent	Major appliances, televisions, furniture, clothing	Luxury goods, such as Rolex watches or fine crystal	Life insurance, blood donations

Specialty product

A consumer product with unique characteristics or brand identification for which a significant group of buyers is willing to make a special purchase effort.

Unsought product

A consumer product that the consumer either does not know about or knows about but does not normally think of buying.

Business product

A product bought by individuals and organizations for further processing or for use in conducting a business.

purchase effort. Examples include specific brands of cars, high-priced photographic equipment, designer clothes, and the services of financial or legal specialists. A Lamborghini automobile, for example, is a specialty product because buyers are usually willing to travel great distances to buy one. Buyers normally do not compare specialty products. They invest only the time needed to reach dealers carrying the wanted products.

Unsought products are consumer products that the consumer either does not know about or knows about but does not normally think of buying. Most major new innovations are unsought until the consumer becomes aware of them through advertising. Classic examples of known but unsought products and services are life insurance, preplanned funeral services, and blood donations. By their very nature, unsought products require a lot of advertising, personal selling, and other marketing efforts.

Business Products

Business products are those purchased for further processing or for use in conducting a business. Thus, the distinction between a consumer product and a business product is based on the *purpose* for which the product is bought. If a consumer buys a lawn mower for use around home, the lawn mower is a consumer product. If the same consumer buys the same lawn mower for use in a landscaping business, the lawn mower is a business product. The three groups of business products and services include materials and parts, capital items, and supplies and services.

Materials and parts include raw materials and manufactured materials and parts. Raw materials consist of farm products (wheat, cotton, livestock, fruits, vegetables) and natural products (fish, lumber, crude petroleum, iron ore). Manufactured materials and parts consist of component materials (iron, yarn, cement, wires) and component parts (small motors, tires, castings). Most manufactured materials and parts are sold directly to business users. Price and service are the major marketing factors; branding and advertising tend to be less important.

Capital items are business products that aid in the buyer's production or operations, including installations and accessory equipment. Installations consist of major purchases such as buildings (factories, offices) and fixed equipment (generators, drill presses, large computer systems, elevators). Accessory equipment includes portable factory equipment and tools (hand tools, lift trucks) and office equipment (computers, fax machines, desks). They have a shorter life than installations and simply aid in the production process.

The final group of business products is *supplies and services*. Supplies include operating supplies (lubricants, coal, paper, pencils) and repair and maintenance items (paint, nails, brooms). Supplies are the convenience products of the business field because they are usually purchased with a minimum of effort or comparison. Business services include maintenance and repair services (window cleaning, computer repair) and business advisory services (legal, management consulting, advertising). Such services are usually supplied under contract.

Organizations, Persons, Places, and Ideas

In addition to tangible products and services, marketers have broadened the concept of a product to include other market offerings—organizations, persons, places, and ideas.

Organizations often carry out activities to "sell" the organization itself. *Organization marketing* consists of activities undertaken to create, maintain, or change the attitudes and behaviour of target consumers toward an organization. Both profit and not-for-profit organizations practise organization marketing. Business firms sponsor public relations or *corporate image advertising* campaigns to market themselves and polish their images. For example, chemical giant BASF markets itself to the general public as a company whose "invisible contributions" result in "visible success." Its ads show how BASF works behind the scenes with its industrial customers to bring the world visible success in everything from water treatment and agricultural productivity to outdoor clothing, sun protection, and sports and leisure equipment. Similarly, not-for-profit organizations such as churches, universities, charities, museums, and performing arts groups market their organizations to raise funds and attract members or patrons.

Person marketing: Rachael Ray has become a one-woman marketing phenomenon.

People can also be thought of as products. *Person marketing* consists of activities undertaken to create, maintain, or change attitudes or behaviour toward particular people. People ranging from politicians, entertainers, and sports figures to professionals such as doctors, lawyers, and architects use person marketing to build their reputations. And businesses, charities, and other organizations use well-known personalities to help sell their products or causes. For example, Rachael Ray has built herself into a brand and whenever her names is featured on cookware, cookbooks, or TV shows, customers flock to them. She now has a media empire worth millions, led by four TV shows (including her original show, 30 Minute Meals) and she's published 16 cookbooks and a self-titled national magazine.[3]

The skilful use of marketing can turn a person's name into a powerhouse brand. Carefully managed and well-known names such as Canadians Don Cherry, Celine Dion, and Avril Lavigne or Americans Oprah Winfrey, Martha Stewart, and Donald Trump now adorn everything from sports apparel, housewares, and magazines to book clubs and casinos. Trump, who describes himself as "the hottest brand on the planet," has skilfully made his life a nonstop media event. Says a friend, "He's a skilful marketer, and what he markets is his name."[4]

Such well-known, well-marketed names hold substantial branding power. Consider Rachael Ray:

> Not unlike Oprah or Martha Stewart, Rachael Ray has become a one-woman marketing phenomenon. In less than a decade she's zipped from nobody to pop-culture icon. Beginning with her *30-Minute Meals* cookbooks, followed later by a Food Network TV show, Ray won her way into people's hearts by demystifying cooking and dishing out a ton of energy. Thanks to her perky personality, which has a sprinkling of catch phrases such as "yum-o" and "sammies," Rachael Ray has moved far beyond quick meals. Bearing her name are more than a dozen best-selling cookbooks (the latest is *Yum-o! The Family Cookbook*), a monthly lifestyle magazine, three Food Network shows, a syndicated daytime talk show, and assorted licensing deals that have stamped her name on kitchen essentials from knives to her own "E.V.O.O." (extra virgin olive oil, for those not familiar with Rayisms). There are even Ray-branded music CDs and ring tones. Ultimately, Ray's brand power derives from all that she has come to represent. Her brands "begin with food and move briskly on to the emotional, social, and cultural benefits that food gives us." Ray's persona—and hence her brand—is a "celebration of why food matters."[5]

Place marketing involves activities undertaken to create, maintain, or change attitudes or behaviour toward particular places. Cities, provinces, regions, and even entire nations compete to attract tourists, new residents, conventions, and company offices and factories. The Saskatchewan government used a $320 000 humorous advertising campaign based on quality of life to attract workers to the province using promises like the lack of a rush hour. Texas advertises that "It's like a whole other country" and California urges you to "Find yourself here." The China National Tourist Office (CNTO) invites travellers from around the world to "Discover China now!" The CNTO has 15 overseas tourist offices. Tourism in China has been booming as more and more travellers discover the treasures of China's ancient civilization alongside the towering skylines of modern cities such as Shanghai and Beijing (site of the 2008 Summer Olympics). On its website, the CNTO offers information about the country and its attractions, travel tips, lists of tour operators, and much more information that makes it easier to say "yes" to China travel.[6]

Ideas can also be marketed. In one sense, all marketing is the marketing of an idea, whether it is the general idea of brushing your teeth or the specific idea that Crest toothpastes

Social marketing
The use of commercial marketing concepts and tools in programs designed to influence individuals' behaviour to improve their well-being and that of society.

create "healthy, beautiful smiles for life." Here, however, we narrow our focus to the marketing of *social ideas*. This area has been called **social marketing**, defined by the Social Marketing Institute as the use of commercial marketing concepts and tools in programs designed to influence individuals' behaviour to improve their well-being and that of society.[7] Social marketing programs include public health campaigns to reduce smoking, alcoholism, drug abuse, and obesity. Other social marketing efforts include environmental campaigns to promote wilderness protection, clean air, and conservation. Still others address issues such as family planning, human rights, and racial equality.

But social marketing involves much more than just advertising—the Social Marketing Institute (SMI) encourages the use of a broad range of marketing tools. "Social marketing goes well beyond the promotional 'P' of the marketing mix to include every other element to achieve its social change objectives," says SMI's executive director. This advice was followed by the Canadian Medical Association in its recent campaign designed to build awareness among the general public and politicians about the growing shortage of doctors in Canada. It employed print, online, and direct-mail advertising as well as doctors' office displays, media relations, and special events. On the website, people could send their Member of Parliament a postcard simply by entering their postal code.[8]

2 PRODUCT AND SERVICE DECISIONS

Marketers make product and service decisions at three levels: individual product decisions, product line decisions, and product mix decisions. We discuss each in turn.

Individual Product and Service Decisions

Figure 9.2 shows the important decisions in the development and marketing of individual products and services. We will focus on decisions about *product attributes, branding, packaging, labelling,* and *product support services.*

Product and Service Attributes

Developing a product or service involves defining the benefits that it will offer. These benefits are communicated and delivered by product attributes such as *quality, features,* and *style and design.*

Product quality
The characteristics of a product or service that bear on its ability to satisfy stated or implied customer needs.

Product Quality **Product quality** is one of the marketer's major positioning tools. Quality has a direct impact on product or service performance; thus, it is closely linked to customer value and satisfaction. In the narrowest sense, quality can be defined as "freedom from defects." But most customer-centred companies go beyond this narrow definition. Instead, they define quality in terms of creating customer value and satisfaction. The American Society for Quality defines quality as the characteristics of a product or service that bear on its ability to satisfy stated or implied customer needs. Similarly, Siemens defines quality this way: "Quality is when our customers come back and our products don't."[9]

Total quality management (TQM) is an approach in which all the company's people are involved in constantly improving the quality of products, services, and business processes. For most top companies, customer-driven quality has become a way of doing business. Today, companies are taking a "return on quality" approach, viewing quality as an investment and holding quality efforts accountable for bottom-line results.

Product quality has two dimensions—level and consistency. In developing a product, the marketer must first choose a *quality level* that will support the product's positioning. Here, product quality means *performance quality*—the ability of a product to perform its functions. For example, a Rolls-Royce provides higher performance quality than a Chevrolet:

Figure 9.2 Individual product decisions

It has a smoother ride, provides more "creature comforts," and lasts longer. Companies rarely try to offer the highest possible performance quality level—few customers want or can afford the high levels of quality offered in products such as a Rolls-Royce automobile, a Viking range, or a Rolex watch. Instead, companies choose a quality level that matches target market needs and the quality levels of competing products.

Beyond quality level, high quality can also mean high levels of quality consistency. Here, product quality means *conformance quality*—freedom from defects and *consistency* in delivering a targeted level of performance. All companies should strive for high levels of conformance quality. In this sense, a Chevrolet can have just as much quality as a Rolls-Royce. Although a Chevy doesn't perform at the same level as a Rolls-Royce, it can deliver as consistently as a Rolls the quality that customers pay for and expect.

Product Features   A product can be offered with varying features. A stripped-down model, one without any extras, is the starting point. The company can create higher-level models by adding more features. Features are a competitive tool for differentiating the company's product from competitors' products. Being the first producer to introduce a valued new feature is one of the most effective ways to compete.

How can a company identify new features and decide which ones to add to its product? The company should periodically survey buyers who have used the product and ask these questions: How do you like the product? Which specific features of the product do you like most? Which features could we add to improve the product? The answers provide the company with a rich list of feature ideas. The company can then assess each feature's *value* to customers versus its *cost* to the company. Features that customers value highly in relation to costs should be added.

Product Style and Design   Another way to add customer value is through distinctive *product style and design*. Design is a larger concept than style. *Style* simply describes the appearance of a product. Styles can be eye-catching or yawn-producing. A sensational style may grab attention and produce pleasing aesthetics, but it does not necessarily make the product *perform* better. Unlike style, *design* is more than skin deep—it goes to the very heart of a product. Good design contributes to a product's usefulness as well as to its looks.

Design begins with a deep understanding of customer needs. More than simply creating product or service attributes, it involves shaping the customer's product-use experience. Consider OXO's outstanding design philosophy and process:

OXO's uniquely designed kitchen and gardening gadgets look pretty cool. But to OXO, good design means a lot more than good looks. It means that OXO tools work—*really* work—for anyone and everyone. For OXO, design means a salad spinner that can be used with one hand; tools with pressure-absorbing, nonslip handles that make them more efficient; or a watering can with a spout that rotates back toward the body, allowing for easier filling and storing. Ever since it came out with its supereffective Good Grips vegetable peeler in 1990, OXO has been known for its clever designs that make everyday living easier.

Much of OXO's design inspiration comes directly from users. "We . . . do a lot of talking to consumers and chefs . . . we do a lot of surveys, we talk to people we know . . . all over the country," says an OXO executive. OXO use-tests its product ideas exhaustively—in the OXO kitchen, in employees' homes, at a cooking school, or by

Product design: OXO focuses on the desired end-user experience and then translates its pie-cutter-in-the-sky notions into eminently usable gadgets.

just corralling casual shoppers outside its location near Manhattan's Chelsea Market. For example, after watching people struggle with the traditional Pyrex measuring cup, OXO discovered a critical flaw: You can't tell how full it is without lifting it up to eye level. The resulting OXO measuring cups have markings down the *inside* that can be read from above, big enough to read without glasses.

Interestingly, although OXO offers more than 500 really well-designed products, it doesn't actually do its own designs. Instead, OXOnians focus on the desired end-user experience and then work with design firms to translate their pie-cutter-in-the-sky notions into eminently usable gadgets.[10]

Thus, product designers should think less about product attributes and technical specifications and more about how customers will use and benefit from the product.

Branding

Brand

A name, term, sign, symbol, design, or a combination of these that identifies the products or services of one seller or group of sellers and differentiates them from those of competitors.

Packaging

The activities of designing and producing the container or wrapper for a product.

Perhaps the most distinctive skill of professional marketers is their ability to build and manage brands. A **brand** is a name, term, sign, symbol, design, or a combination of these, that identifies the maker or seller of a product or service. Consumers view a brand as an important part of a product and branding can add value to a product. Customers attach meanings to brands and develop brand relationships. For example, most consumers would perceive a bottle of White Linen Perfume as a high-quality, expensive product. But the same perfume in an unmarked bottle would likely be viewed as lower in quality, even if the fragrance was identical.

Branding has become so strong that today hardly anything goes unbranded. Salt is packaged in branded containers, common nuts and bolts are packaged with a distributor's label, and automobile parts—spark plugs, tires, filters—bear brand names that differ from those of the automakers. Even fruits, vegetables, dairy products, and poultry are branded—Sunkist oranges, Dole Classic iceberg salads, Horizon Organic milk, and Perdue chickens.

Branding helps buyers in many ways. Brand names help consumers identify products that might benefit them. Brands also say something about product quality and consistency—buyers who always buy the same brand know that they will get the same features, benefits, and quality each time they buy. Branding also gives the seller several advantages. The brand name becomes the basis on which a whole story can be built about a product's special qualities. The seller's brand name and trademark provide legal protection for unique product features that otherwise might be copied by competitors. And branding helps the seller to segment markets. For example, Toyota Motor Corporation can offer the major Lexus, Toyota, and Scion brands, each with numerous sub-brands—such as Camry, Prius, Matrix, Yaris, Tundra, Land Cruiser, and others—not just one general product for all consumers.

Building and managing brands are perhaps the marketer's most important tasks. We will discuss branding strategy in more detail later in the chapter.

Packaging

Packaging involves designing and producing the container or wrapper for a product. Traditionally, the primary function of the package was to hold and protect the product. In recent times, however, numerous factors have made packaging an important marketing tool as well. Increased competition and clutter on retail store shelves means that packages must now perform many sales tasks—from attracting attention, to describing the product, to making the sale.

Companies are realizing the power of good packaging to create immediate consumer recognition of a brand. For example, an average supermarket stocks 45 000 items; the average Walmart Supercenter carries 142 000 items. The typical shopper passes by some 300 items per minute, and more than 70 percent of all purchase decisions are made in stores. In this highly competitive environment, the package may be the seller's last and best chance to influence buyers. Thus, for many companies, the package itself has become an important promotional medium.[11]

Innovative packaging can give a company an advantage over competitors and boost sales. With Heinz's "fridge-door-fit" bottle, sales jumped 12 percent in the four months following its introduction.

Poorly designed packages can cause headaches for consumers and lost sales for the company. *Consumer Reports* even has an award for the most difficult to open packages, fittingly named the "Oyster Awards" (as in trying to pry open a tight-hinged oyster). One recent winner was packaging for the Bratz Sisterz dolls, which contained some 50 packaging restraints, from rubber bands to molded plastic covers. It took one test subject, a seven-year-old girl, eight minutes to free the dolls. Says one reporter, after wrestling with the packaging, the child was "noticeably agitated and breathing heavily," and the dolls "looked as if they'd just returned from a rough night on the town."[12]

In contrast, innovative packaging can give a company an advantage over competitors and boost sales. Sometimes even seemingly small packaging improvements can make a big difference. For example, Heinz revolutionized the 170-year-old condiments industry by inverting the good old ketchup bottle, letting customers quickly squeeze out even the last bit of ketchup. At the same time, it adopted a "fridge-door-fit" shape that not only slots into shelves more easily but also has a cap that is simpler for children to open. In the four months following the introduction of the new package, sales jumped 12 percent. What's more, the new package does double duty as a promotional tool. Says a packaging analyst, "When consumers see the Heinz logo on the fridge door every time they open it, it's taking marketing inside homes."[13]

In recent years, product safety has also become a major packaging concern. We have all learned to deal with hard-to-open "childproof" packaging. And after the rash of product tampering scares during the 1980s, most drug producers and food makers now put their products in tamper-resistant packages. In making packaging decisions, the company also must heed growing environmental concerns. Walmart, for example, has begun to put a lot of emphasis on sustainability. Packaging is so much a part of this agenda that it sponsored its third conference on sustainable packaging in Toronto in 2009. Arthur's Fresh Company, a firm that distributes real fruit juices across Canada through Walmart and other retailers, made a presentation about how it has worked to improve packaging and shipping procedures to make all its products more environmentally friendly.[14]

Labelling

Labels range from simple tags attached to products to complex graphics that are part of the package. They perform several functions. At the very least, the label *identifies* the product or brand, such as the name Sunkist stamped on oranges. The label might also *describe* several things about the product—who made it, where it was made, when it was made, its contents, how it is to be used, and how to use it safely. Finally, the label might help to *promote* the brand, support its positioning, and connect with customers. For many companies, labels have become an important element in broader marketing campaigns. For example, Pepsi recently recrafted the graphics on its soft drink cans as part of a broader effort to give the brand more meaning and social relevance to its youth audience.

In its quest for a refreshing, more relevant new look, Pepsi created no less than 35 new North American and international can designs. Beyond eye-catching artwork, each Pepsi design carried a unique web address that linked customers to a microsite created specifically for that design. The first microsites, aptly named "This Is the Beginning," allowed users from around the world to gather in real time to collectively design the next Pepsi billboard in Times Square. Additional experiences, such as the music-oriented "Move the Crowd," went live every few weeks in tandem with the can releases, all of which were catalogued at the "Pepsi Can Gallery" website. "What we did with the [can designs] and sites is create custom experiences

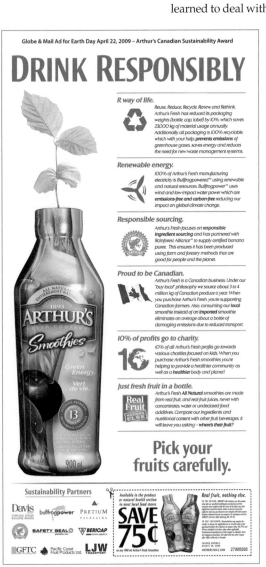

Arthur's Fresh Company has been highly innovative in changing its packaging and transportation processes to make its products more sustainable.

GROOVY

Labelling: Pepsi recently recrafted its soft drink cans as part of a broader effort to give the brand more meaning and social relevance to its youth audience.

that users discover on their own," said a Pepsi marketing executive. "Every time a consumer buys a Pepsi, they're getting a new experience."[15]

Along with the positives, labelling also raises concerns. There has been a long history of legal concerns about packaging and labels. Labels have the potential to mislead customers, fail to describe important ingredients, and fail to include needed safety warnings. Labelling regulations depend on the type of product being sold. Both federal and provincial legislation governs packaging and labelling in Canada. At the federal level the *Consumer Packaging and Labelling Act* and the *Food and Drugs Act* are designed to protect consumers from labelling or packaging that is false or misleading. The *Weights and Measures Act* deals with the units of measurement on labels. Provincial statutes cover things like the requirement for bilingual labelling in Quebec and things specific to certain product categories such as furniture or toys.

Labelling has been affected in recent times by *unit pricing* (stating the price per unit of standard measure), *open dating* (stating the expected shelf life of the product), and *nutritional labelling* (stating the nutritional values in the product). Nutrition labelling became mandatory in Canada for all prepackaged foods on December 12, 2007. The regulations stipulate that a consistent, easy to find and read Nutrition Facts table must appear on food labels. The table must provide information on calories and 13 nutrients: fat, saturated fat, trans fat, cholesterol, sodium, carbohydrate, fibre, sugars, protein, vitamin A, vitamin C, calcium, and iron.

Product Support Services

Customer service is another element of product strategy. A company's offer usually includes some support services, which can be a minor or a major part of the total offering. Later in the chapter, we will discuss services as products in themselves. Here, we discuss services that augment actual products.

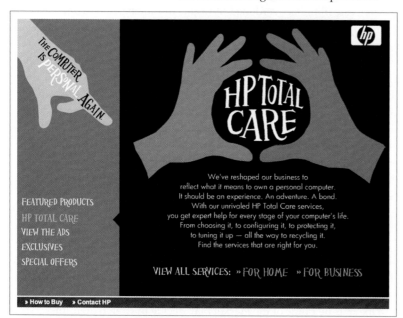

FEATURED PRODUCTS
HP TOTAL CARE
VIEW THE ADS
EXCLUSIVES
SPECIAL OFFERS

» How to Buy   » Contact HP

Product support services: HP promises "HP Total Care—expert help for every stage of your computer's life. From choosing it, to configuring it, to protecting it, to tuning it up—all the way to recycling it."

The first step is to survey customers periodically to assess the value of current services and to obtain ideas for new ones. For example, Cadillac holds regular focus group interviews with owners and carefully watches complaints that come into its dealerships. From this careful monitoring, Cadillac has learned that buyers are very upset by repairs that are not done correctly the first time. GM research indicates that customers who experience good service are five times more likely to repurchase the same brand than those who have had a bad service experience.

Once the company has assessed the quality of various support services to customers it can take steps to fix problems and add new services that will both delight customers and yield profits to the company. For instance, Cadillac tracks repair data to find out if certain dealerships or even individual technicians are frequently making the same repair mistakes. Then, to promote good first-time repairs, it informs dealers and rewards those that have high customer service ratings. And to keep customers happier after the sale, Cadillac also offers as a standard feature an early-warning system for mechanical problems, built into the onboard OnStar system.[16]

Many companies are now using a sophisticated mix of phone, email, fax, Internet, and interactive voice and data technologies to provide support services that were not possible before. For example, HP offers a complete set of sales and after-sale services. It promises "HP Total Care—expert help for every stage of your computer's life. From choosing it, to configuring it, to protecting it, to tuning it up—all the way to recycling it." Customers can click onto the HP Total Care service portal that offers online resources for HP products and 24/7 tech support, which can be accessed via email, instant online chat, and telephone.[17]

Product Line Decisions

Product line

A group of products that are closely related because they function in a similar manner, are sold to the same customer groups, are marketed through the same types of outlets, or fall within given price ranges.

Beyond decisions about individual products and services, product strategy also calls for building a product line. A **product line** is a group of products that are closely related because they function in a similar manner, are sold to the same customer groups, are marketed through the same types of outlets, or fall within given price ranges. For example, Nike produces several lines of athletic shoes and apparel, and Marriott offers several lines of hotels.

The major product line decision involves *product line length*—the number of items in the product line. The line is too short if the manager can increase profits by adding items; the line is too long if the manager can increase profits by dropping items. Managers need to analyze their product lines periodically to assess each product item's sales and profits and to understand how each item contributes to the line's overall performance.

Product line length is influenced by company objectives and resources. For example, one objective might be to allow for upselling. Thus, BMW wants to move customers up from its 3-series models to 5- and 7-series models. Another objective might be to allow cross-selling: Hewlett-Packard sells printers as well as cartridges. Still another objective might be to protect against economic swings: Gap runs several clothing-store chains (Gap, Old Navy, and Banana Republic) covering different price points.

A company can expand its product line in two ways: by *line filling* or by *line stretching*. *Product line filling* involves adding more items within the present range of the line. There are several reasons for product line filling: reaching for extra profits, satisfying dealers, using excess capacity, being the leading full-line company, and plugging holes to keep out competitors. However, line filling is overdone if it results in cannibalization and customer confusion. The company should ensure that new items are noticeably different from existing ones.

Product line stretching occurs when a company lengthens its product line beyond its current range. The company can stretch its line downward, upward, or both ways. Companies located at the upper end of the market can stretch their lines *downward*. A company may stretch downward to plug a market hole that otherwise would attract a new competitor or to respond to a competitor's attack on the upper end. Or it may add low-end products because it finds faster growth taking place in the low-end segments. Honda stretched downward for all of these reasons by adding its thrifty little Honda Fit to its line. The Fit, economical to drive and priced starting at $14 980, met increasing consumer demands for more frugal cars and preempted competitors in the new-generation minicar segment.

Companies can also stretch their product lines *upward*. Sometimes companies stretch upward to add prestige to their current products. Or they may be attracted by a faster growth rate or higher margins at the higher end. For example, some years ago each of the leading Japanese auto companies introduced an upmarket automobile: Honda launched Acura; Toyota launched Lexus; and Nissan launched Infiniti. They used entirely new names rather than their own names.

Companies in the middle range of the market may decide to stretch their lines in *both directions*. Marriott did this with its hotel product line. Along with regular Marriott hotels, it added eight new branded hotel lines to serve both the upper and lower ends of the market. For example, Renaissance Hotels & Resorts aims to attract and please top executives; Fairfield Inn by Marriott, vacationers and business travellers on a tight travel budget; and Courtyard by Marriott, salespeople and other "road warriors."[18] The major risk with this strategy is that some travellers will trade down after finding that the lower-price hotels in the Marriott chain give them pretty much everything they want. However, Marriott would rather capture its customers who move downward than lose them to competitors.

Product Mix Decisions

Product mix (product portfolio)
The set of all product lines and items that a particular seller offers for sale.

An organization with several product lines has a product mix. A **product mix** (or **product portfolio**) consists of all the product lines and items that a particular seller offers for sale. Some companies manage very complex product portfolios. For example, Sony's diverse portfolio consists of four primary product businesses worldwide: Sony Electronics, Sony Computer Entertainment (games), Sony Pictures Entertainment (movies, TV shows, music, DVDs), and Sony Financial Services (life insurance, banking, and other offerings).

Each major Sony business consists of several product lines. For example, Sony Electronics includes cameras and camcorders, computers, TV and home entertainment products, mobile electronics, and others. In turn, each of these lines contains many individual items. Sony's TV and home entertainment line includes TVs, DVD players, home audio components, digital home products, and more. Altogether, Sony's product mix includes a diverse collection of hundreds and hundreds of products.

A company's product mix has four important dimensions: width, length, depth, and consistency. Product mix *width* refers to the number of different product lines the company carries. Sony markets a wide range of consumer and industrial products around the world, from TVs and PlayStation consoles to semiconductors. Product mix *length* refers to the total number of items the company carries within its product lines. Sony typically carries many products within each line. The camera and camcorder line, for instance, includes digital cameras, camcorders, photo printers, memory media, and tons of accessories. Product mix *depth* refers to the number of versions offered of each product in the line. Sony has a very deep product mix. For example, it makes and markets about any kind of TV you'd ever want to buy—tube, flat panel, rear projection, front projection, HD, or low resolution—each in almost any imaginable size. Finally, the *consistency* of the product mix refers to how closely related the various product lines are in end use, in production requirements, in distribution channels, or in some other way. Within each major business, Sony's product lines are fairly consistent in that they perform similar functions for buyers and go through the same distribution channels. Companywide, however, Sony markets a very diverse mix of products. Managing such a broad and diverse product portfolio requires much skill.

These product mix dimensions provide the handles for defining the company's product strategy. The company can increase its business in four ways. It can add new product lines, widening its product mix. In this way, its new lines build on the company's reputation in its other lines. The company can lengthen its existing product lines to become a more full-line company. Or it can add more versions of each product and thus deepen its product mix. Finally, the company can pursue more product line consistency—or less—depending on whether it wants to have a strong reputation in a single field or in several fields.

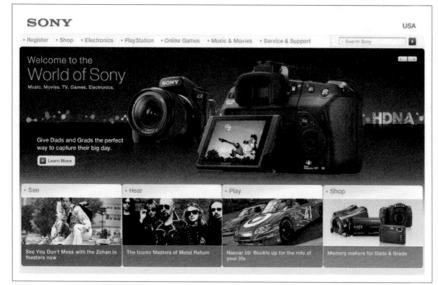

Product mix decisions: Sony has a large and diverse product portfolio, divided into four primary product businesses, each containing hundreds of products. "Welcome to the world of Sony."

Some analysts see brands as *the* major enduring asset of a company, outlasting the company's specific products and facilities. John Stewart, former CEO of Quaker Oats, once said, "If this business were split up, I would give you the land and bricks and mortar, and I would keep the brands and trademarks, and I would fare better than you." A former CEO of McDonald's declared, "If every asset we own, every building, and every piece of equipment were destroyed in a terrible natural disaster, we would be able to borrow all the money to replace it very quickly because of the value of our brand. . . . The brand is more valuable than the totality of all these assets."[19]

Thus, brands are powerful assets that must be carefully developed and managed. In this section, we examine the key strategies for building and managing brands.

Brand Equity

Brands are more than just names and symbols. They are a key element in the company's relationships with consumers. Brands represent consumers' perceptions and feelings about a product and its performance—everything that the product or service *means* to consumers. In the final analysis, brands exist in the heads of consumers. As one well-respected marketer once said, "Products are created in the factory, but brands are created in the mind."[20]

Brand equity
The differential effect that knowing the brand name has on customer response to the product or its marketing.

A powerful brand has high *brand equity*. **Brand equity** is the differential effect that knowing the brand name has on customer response to the product and its marketing. It's a measure of the brand's ability to capture consumer preference and loyalty. A brand has positive brand equity when consumers react more favourably to it than to a generic or unbranded version of the same product. It has negative brand equity if consumers react less favourably than to an unbranded version.

Brands vary in the amount of power and value they hold in the marketplace. Interbrand, in partnership with the *Globe and Mail*, publishes a ranking based on brand value for the top brands in the country. In 2008, the top 10 Canadian brands were BlackBerry, RBC, TD Canada Trust, Shoppers Drug Mart, Petro-Canada, Manulife, Bell, Scotiabank, Canadian Tire, and Tim Hortons.[21] Such brands become larger-than-life icons that maintain their power in the market for years, even generations. Other brands create fresh consumer excitement and loyalty, such as Google, YouTube, Apple, eBay, and Wikipedia. These brands win in the marketplace not simply because they deliver unique benefits or reliable service. Rather, they succeed because they forge deep connections with customers.

Ad agency Young & Rubicam's Brand Asset Valuator measures brand strength along four consumer perception dimensions: *differentiation* (what makes the brand stand out), *relevance* (how consumers feel it meets their needs), *knowledge* (how much consumers know about the brand), and *esteem* (how highly consumers regard and respect the brand). Brands with strong brand equity rate high on all of these dimensions. A brand must be distinct, or consumers will have no reason to choose it over other brands. But the fact that a brand is highly differentiated doesn't necessarily mean that consumers will buy it. The brand must stand out in ways that are relevant to consumers' needs. But even a differentiated, relevant brand is far from a shoo-in. Before consumers will respond to the brand, they must first know about and understand it. And that familiarity must lead to a strong, positive consumer–brand connection (see Real Marketing 9.1).[22]

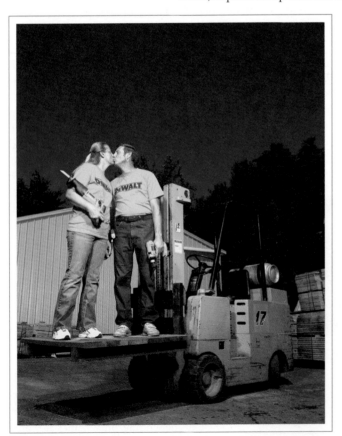

Consumers sometimes bond very closely with specific brands. Jokes the bride at this wedding: "He loves DeWalt nearly as much as he loves me."

Real Marketing 9.1

Breakaway Brands: Connecting with Customers

"Big blue-chip companies like General Electric and Microsoft do many things well," notes a brand analyst, "but showing up on lists of the hottest brands is typically not one of them. Yet these two lumbering giants both made their way onto brand consultancy Landor Associates' annual Breakaway Brands ranking—a comprehensive survey that measures consumer sizzle."

Each year, brand consultancy Landor Associates, an arm of ad agency Young & Rubicam, conducts a "Top Ten Breakaway Brands" survey in which it identifies the 10 brands with the greatest percentage gains in brand health and business value as a result of superb brand strategy and execution over a three-year period. The survey taps Young & Rubicam's Brand Asset Valuator, a database of responses from 9000 consumers evaluating 2500 brands measured across 56 metrics. Landor looks at brand factors such as differentiation, relevance, esteem, and knowledge. At the same time, another consultancy, BrandEconomics, assesses the financial performance of the brand ("Economic Value Added"). Combined, the Brand Asset Valuator and Economic Value Added models provide a brand valuation based on both consumer and financial measures.

Ideas about achieving brand strength, that elusive blend of awareness and trust, have changed in the past decade. "It's no longer, What can we blast out there about ourselves?" says another branding expert. "Brand theory now asks, How can we connect with the community in a really meaningful way?" It's a big question. Armed with information about price and quality, today's consumer is a tough challenge. But, says the expert, "if you're willing to talk directly and deeply to your audience, you can become a strong brand without a lot of fanfare."

The most recent Breakaway Brands list includes a strange agglomeration, from hot technology brands such as iPod and BlackBerry to blue chips such as GE and Microsoft to down-and-dirty discount retailers such as T.J. Maxx and Costco.

Breakaway Canadian brand BlackBerry has perfected a truly unique community-building tool. Today, it is becoming increasingly difficult within the business community to imagine life before BlackBerry.

older, so the youth-centric sensation doesn't show up yet). But Landor found that each brand that did make the list embraced one or more of three themes. "Today it's all about *trust, community,* and creating a *dialogue* with your customer that shares real knowledge," says Landor's chief marketing officer. That is, all of the brands really connect with customers.

So how are dinosaurs Microsoft and GE connecting with consumers? Microsoft's resurrection from its corporate-bad-guy status of past years results from several factors. More consumer-connecting products such as its Xbox game console now give Microsoft a cachet that even dominant office-related brands such as PowerPoint and Word never could. And the good works of the Bill & Melinda Gates Foundation have also helped boost consumer trust and community, helping to foster perceptions of a kinder, gentler Microsoft. Finally, as new corporate bogeymen like Google and MySpace owner News Corporation begin throwing their weight around, Microsoft now "comes off as an underdog even though it is a behemoth," says the brand expert.

General Electric's appearance on the Breakaway Brands list derives almost entirely from its "ecomagination" environmental

Top Ten Breakaway Brands	
1. T.J. Maxx	6. Costco
2. iPod	7. Propel
3. BlackBerry	8. Barnes & Noble
4. Stonyfield Farm	9. GE
5. Samsung	10. Microsoft

Missing are some brand titans such as Coca-Cola (big but not growing very quickly) and fresh-faced young brands like MySpace (the consumer panel consists of adults 18 and efforts. Between 2005 and 2010, the company aims to more than double its annual research budget for cleaner technologies—like energy-efficient refrigerators and wind turbines. Last year, GE's increasing connections with customer and community concerns about the environment generated US$12 billion in revenues from 45 ecomagination products and services. "They are trying to turn that entire ship into the ecovessel of the future," says Landor's chief marketing executive.

BlackBerry and iPod—now that's more like it! These are brands that you'd expect to see on a Breakaway Brands list. Among brands that foster customer community, the iPod is an obvious winner by virtue of its ability to create an online music ecosystem virtually overnight. With each new product introduction, iPod and Apple advance the causes of democratizing technology and approachable innovation. Similarly, BlackBerry maker Research In Motion (headquartered in Waterloo, Ontario) perfected a truly unique community-building tool: a user-friendly device that lets businesspeople stay connected to their jobs and to each other. Jokes about "CrackBerry addicts" and the appearance of BlackBerry smartphones in the hands of celebrities from Oprah to Madonna illustrate the brand's rapid rise. "Today, virtually the world over," says a Landor analyst, "it is becoming increasingly difficult among the business community to imagine life 'BB' (Before BlackBerry)."

If iPod and BlackBerry seem like naturals for a Breakaway Brands list, an unlikely pair of retailers—T.J. Maxx and Costco—just don't seem to fit. Yet in these difficult days of rising costs and spiralling economics, the two fast-growing discounters are creating treasure-hunt experiences that build strong emotional bonds with customers. T.J. Maxx—at number one, no less—fulfills the fantasy of luxury for less. At T.J. Maxx saving is no longer a priority reserved for lower- and middle-income consumers. Now even the most affluent shopper can experience the "thrill of the save" and the euphoria of a great "Maxx Moment." Similarly, Costco helps customers to save on everyday purchases while also experiencing great deals on high-end products. Says the Landor analyst, Costco has "perfected the art of understanding not only what customers need, but also what they fantasize about, and putting both at their fingertips."

As proves true each year, Landor's Breakaway Brands list includes some old standbys and a number of pleasant surprises. As the analyst concludes:

> In today's uncertain world it is no wonder that organizations have to work harder and harder to gain the trust of their [customers] in order to be successful. What's more, [with brands], as in life, trust must be earned, not bought, and it must be constantly validated. The . . . marketers at the helm of this year's Top Ten Breakaway Brands understand not only the need to connect with their customers and instill trust, they also understand that brand is one of the most powerful tools available for making those coveted relationships a reality.

Sources: Based on information from Matthew Boyle, "Microsoft and GE: Not Old and in the Way," *Fortune*, November 12, 2007, p. 28; Ellen McGirt, "Breakaway Brands," *Fortune*, September 18, 2006, p. 27; and Chelsea Greene, "Using Brands to Drive Business Results," Landor Brands, November 2008, accessed at www.wpp.com/WPP/Marketing/ReportsStudies/Usingbrandstodrivebusinessresults.htm.

Thus, positive brand equity derives from consumer feelings about and connections with a brand. Consumers sometimes bond *very* closely with specific brands. For example, one Michigan couple had such a passion for Black & Decker's DeWalt power tool brand that they designed their entire wedding around it. They wore trademark DeWalt black-and-yellow T-shirts, made their way to a wooden chapel that they'd built with their DeWalt gear, exchanged vows and power tools, and even cut cake with a power saw. Joked the wife about her husband (a carpenter by trade), "He loves DeWalt nearly as much as he loves me."[23]

A brand with high brand equity is a very valuable asset. *Brand valuation* is the process of estimating the total financial value of a brand. Measuring such value is difficult. However, according to the 2008 Best Canadian Brands survey, the total value of Canada's 25 top brands is $42.1 billion. The BlackBerry brand has a value of $5.6 billion, RBC a value of $4.1 billion, and TD Canada Trust has a value of $3.8 billion. As impressive as these numbers are, they pale in comparison to the value of Coca-Cola (US$65.3 billion), which is listed as the best global brand.[24]

High brand equity provides a company with many competitive advantages. A powerful brand enjoys a high level of consumer brand awareness and loyalty. Because consumers expect stores to carry the brand, the company has more leverage in bargaining with resellers. Because the brand name carries high credibility, the company can more easily launch line and brand extensions. A powerful brand offers the company some defence against fierce price competition.

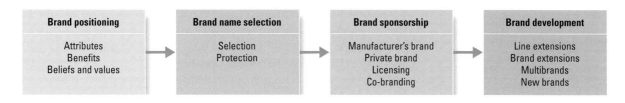

Figure 9.3 Major brand strategy decisions

Above all, however, a powerful brand forms the basis for building strong and profitable customer relationships. The fundamental asset underlying brand equity is *customer equity*—the value of the customer relationships that the brand creates. A powerful brand is important, but what it really represents is a profitable set of loyal customers. The proper focus of marketing is building customer equity, with brand management serving as a major marketing tool. Companies need to think of themselves not as portfolios of products, but as portfolios of customers.

Building Strong Brands

Branding poses challenging decisions to the marketer. Figure 9.3 shows that the major brand strategy decisions involve *brand positioning, brand-name selection, brand sponsorship,* and *brand development.*

Brand Positioning

Marketers need to position their brands clearly in target customers' minds. They can position brands at any of three levels.[25] At the lowest level, they can position the brand on *product attributes*. For example, P&G invented the disposable diaper category with its Pampers brand. Early Pampers marketing focused on attributes such as fluid absorption, fit, and disposability. In general, however, attributes are the least desirable level for brand positioning. Competitors can easily copy attributes. More importantly, customers are not interested in attributes as such; they are interested in what the attributes will do for them.

A brand can be better positioned by associating its name with a desirable *benefit*. Thus, Pampers can go beyond technical product attributes and talk about the resulting containment and skin-health benefits of dryness. "There are fewer wet bottoms in the world because of us," says Jim Stengel, P&G's global marketing officer. Some successful brands positioned on benefits are Volvo (safety), FedEx (guaranteed on-time delivery), Nike (performance), and Lexus (quality).

The strongest brands go beyond attribute or benefit positioning. They are positioned on strong *beliefs and values*. These brands pack an emotional wallop. Brands such as Godiva, Starbucks, Apple, and Victoria's Secret rely less on a product's tangible attributes and more on creating surprise, passion, and excitement surrounding a brand. Successful brands engage customers on a deep, emotional level. Thus, P&G knows that, to parents, Pampers mean much more than just containment and dryness. According to P&G's Stengel:

If you go back, we often thought of our brands in terms of functional benefits. But when we began listening very closely to customers, they told us Pampers meant much more to them—Pampers are more about parent–child

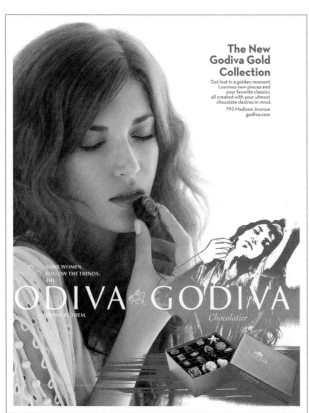

Brand positioning: The strongest brands go beyond attribute or benefit positioning. Godiva engages customers on a deeper level, touching universal emotions.

relationships and total baby care. So we started to say, "We want to be a brand experience; we want to be there to help support parents and babies as they grow and develop." In the initial days people thought we were nuts. How can a diaper help a baby's development? But babies wear diapers 24/7 for almost three years. It actually reorients R&D to ask a question like "How can we help babies sleep better?" Why are we concerned about babies sleeping better? Because sleep is important to brain development. It helps relationship skills. Thinking like that, we're able to help improve life for our consumers. The equity of great brands has to be something that a consumer finds inspirational and the organization finds inspirational. You know, our baby care business didn't start growing aggressively until we changed Pampers from being about dryness to being about helping mom with her baby's development.[26]

When positioning a brand, the marketer should establish a mission for the brand and a vision of what the brand must be and do. A brand is the company's promise to deliver a specific set of features, benefits, services, and experiences consistently to the buyers. The brand promise must be simple and honest. Moores, Canada's leading men's wear retailer, makes three simple promises with its brand: well made, well dressed, well priced. In contrast, Fairmont Hotels offer luxurious rooms and a truly memorable experience but do not promise low prices.

Brand-Name Selection

A good name can add greatly to a product's success. However, finding the best brand name is a difficult task. It begins with a careful review of the product and its benefits, the target market, and proposed marketing strategies. After that, naming a brand becomes part science, part art, and a measure of instinct. Desirable qualities for a brand name include the following:

1. It should suggest something about the product's benefits and qualities. Examples: Craftsman Tools (Sears), Mastercraft (Canadian Tire), Curves (women's fitness centres).

2. It should be easy to pronounce, recognize, and remember: Tide, Silk, iPod, WestJet.

3. The brand name should be distinctive: Lexus, Zappos.

4. It should be extendable: Chapters.ca began as an online bookseller but chose a name that would allow expansion into other categories.

5. The name should translate easily into foreign languages. Before changing its name to Exxon, Standard Oil of New Jersey rejected the name Enco, which it learned meant a stalled engine when pronounced in Japanese.

6. It should be capable of registration and legal protection. A brand name cannot be registered if it infringes on existing brand names.

Choosing a new brand name is hard work. After a decade of choosing quirky names (Yahoo!, Google) or trademark-proof made-up names (Novartis, Aventis, Lycos), today's style is to build brands around names that have real meaning. For example, names like Silk (soy milk), Method (home products), Smartwater (beverages), and Blackboard (school software) are simple and make intuitive sense. But with trademark applications soaring, *available* new names can be hard to find. Try it yourself. Pick a product and see if you can come up with a better name for it. How about Moonshot? Tickle? Vanilla? Treehugger? Simplicity? Google them and you'll find that they're already taken.

Once chosen, the brand name must be protected. Many firms try to build a brand name that will eventually become identified with the product category. Brand names such as Kleenex, Levi's, JELL-O, Band-Aid, Scotch Tape, Formica, and Ziploc have succeeded in this way. However, their very success may threaten the company's rights to the name. Many originally protected brand names—such as cellophane, aspirin, nylon, kerosene, linoleum, yo-yo, trampoline, escalator, thermos, and shredded wheat—are now generic names that any seller can use. To protect their brands, marketers present them carefully using the word "brand" and the registered trademark symbol, as in "Band-Aid®

Brand Adhesive Bandages." Even the long-standing "I am stuck on Band-Aid 'cause Band Aid's stuck on me" jingle has now become "I am stuck on Band-Aid *brand* 'cause Band-Aid's stuck on me."

Brand Sponsorship

A manufacturer has four sponsorship options. The product may be launched as a *national brand* (or *manufacturer's brand*), as when Sony and Kellogg sell their output under their own brand names (Sony Bravia HDTV or Kellogg's Frosted Flakes). Or the manufacturer may sell to resellers who give the product a *private brand* (also called a *store brand* or *distributor brand*). Although most manufacturers create their own brand names, others market *licensed brands*. Finally, two companies can join forces and *co-brand* a product.

Store brand (private brand)
A brand created and owned by a reseller of a product or service.

National Brands versus Store Brands   National brands (or manufacturers' brands) have long dominated the retail scene. In recent times, however, an increasing number of retailers and wholesalers have created their own **store brands** (or **private brands**). Store brand sales are soaring. In fact, they are growing much faster than national brands. A recent international survey found that 41 percent of shoppers now identify themselves as frequent buyers of store brands. In all, private brands now capture more than 20 percent of all North American supermarket sales, and sales of private-label foods, drinks, and personal care products will increase by 20 percent by 2010. Private-label apparel, such as Joe (Loblaw) and Cherokee and Carroll Reed (Zellers), have captured a growing share of the marketplace.[27]

Once known as "generic" or "no-name" brands, today's store brands are a far cry from the early no-frills generics. Store brands now offer much greater selection and higher quality. Rather than simply creating low-end generic brands that offer a low-price alternative to national brands, retailers are now moving toward higher-end private brands that boost both the store's revenues and its image. As store brand selection and quality have improved, so have consumer confidence and acceptance. It seems that almost every retailer now carries its own store brands. Walmart's private brands account for a whopping 40 percent of its sales: brands such as Sam's Choice beverages and food products; Equate pharmacy, health, and beauty products; and White Cloud brand toilet tissue, diapers, detergent, and fabric softener. Its private-label brands alone generate nearly twice the sales of all P&G brands.[28]

With the economy continuing in a downturn in 2009, more Canadians searched for cheaper alternatives. To meet this demand, Shoppers Drug Mart began introducing three to five new private-label items each day of its popular Life and other private-label products. As CEO Jürgen Schreiber noted, "There's so many more private-label (items) in the store . . . Chances are, you probably didn't notice most of them the last time you visited the stores because they were 'silently introduced' onto the shelves, selling under relatively covert names like Nativa Organics, Quo cosmetics, and Get office supplies."[29] And Costco, the world's largest warehouse club, offers a staggering array of goods and services under its Kirkland Signature brand. Costco customers can buy anything from Kirkland Signature rotisserie chickens to a $3439-per-person Kirkland Signature Tahitian cruise package. At the other end of the spectrum, upscale retailer Saks Fifth Avenue carries its own clothing line, which features $98 men's ties, $200 halter tops, and $250 cotton dress shirts.

In the so-called *battle of the brands* between national and private brands, retailers have many advantages. They control what products they stock, where they go on the shelf, what prices they charge, and which ones they will feature in local

Store brands: Costco offers a staggering array of goods and services under its Kirkland Signature brand—anything from Kirkland Signature rotisserie chickens to a $3439-per-person Kirkland Signature Tahitian cruise package.

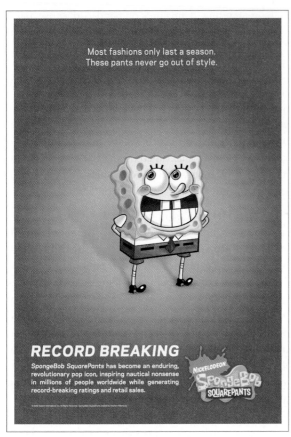

Most fashions only last a season.
These pants never go out of style.

RECORD BREAKING
SpongeBob SquarePants has become an enduring,
revolutionary pop icon, inspiring nautical nonsense
in millions of people worldwide while generating
record-breaking ratings and retail sales.

NICKELODEON
SpongeBob
SQUAREPANTS

Licensing: Nickelodeon has developed a stable of hugely popular characters—like SpongeBob SquarePants—that generate billions of dollars' worth of retail sales each year.

circulars. Retailers often price their store brands lower than comparable national brands, thereby appealing to the budget-conscious shopper in all of us. Although store brands can be hard to establish and costly to stock and promote, they also yield higher profit margins for the reseller. And they give resellers exclusive products that cannot be bought from competitors, resulting in greater store traffic and loyalty. To compete with store brands, leading brand marketers must invest in R&D to bring out new brands, new features, and continuous quality improvements. They must design strong advertising programs to maintain high awareness and preference. And they must find ways to "partner" with major distributors in a search for distribution economies and improved joint performance.

Licensing   Most manufacturers take years and spend millions to create their own brand names. However, some companies license names or symbols previously created by other manufacturers, names of well-known celebrities or characters from popular movies and books. For a fee, any of these can provide an instant and proven brand name.

Apparel and accessories sellers pay large royalties to adorn their products—from blouses to ties and linens to luggage—with the names or initials of well-known fashion innovators such as Calvin Klein, Tommy Hilfiger, Gucci, or Armani. Sellers of children's products attach an almost endless list of character names to clothing, toys, school supplies, linens, dolls, lunch boxes, cereals, and other items. Licensed character names range from classics such as *Sesame Street,* Disney, Peanuts, Winnie the Pooh, the Muppets, Scooby-Doo, and Dr. Seuss characters to the more recent *Dora the Explorer, Powerpuff Girls, Rugrats, Blue's Clues,* and Harry Potter characters. And currently, a number of top-selling retail toys are products based on television shows and movies, such as the Spider-Man 3 Deluxe Spinning Web Blaster and the Talking Friendship Adventures Dora.

Name and character licensing has grown rapidly in recent years. Annual retail sales of licensed products in the United States and Canada have grown from only US$4 billion in 1977 to US$55 billion in 1987 and more than US$187 billion today. Licensing can be a highly profitable business for many companies. For example, Nickelodeon has developed a stable of hugely popular characters, such as Dora the Explorer; Go, Diego, Go!; and SpongeBob SquarePants. Dora alone has generated more than US$5.3 billion in retail sales in under five years. "When it comes to licensing its brands for consumer products, Nickelodeon has proved that it has the Midas touch," states a brand licensing expert.[30]

Co-branding
The practice of using the established brand names of two different companies on the same product.

Co-branding   Although companies have been **co-branding** products for many years, there has been a recent resurgence in co-branding. Co-branding occurs when two established brand names of different companies are used on the same product or retail outlet. For example, financial services firms often partner with other companies to create co-branded credit cards, such as CIBC Visa. In 2009, Tim Hortons decided to experiment by co-branding 50 U.S. locations and six Ontario restaurants with ice cream chain Cold Stone Creamery. And Nike and Apple co-branded the Nike+iPod Sport Kit, which lets runners link their Nike shoes with their iPod nanos to track and enhance running performance in real time. "Thanks to a unique partnership between Nike and Apple, your iPod nano becomes your coach. Your personal trainer. Your favorite workout companion."[31]

In most co-branding situations, one company licenses another company's well-known brand to use in combination with its own. Co-branding offers many advantages. Because each brand dominates in a different category, the combined brands create broader consumer appeal and greater brand equity. Co-branding also allows a company to expand its existing brand into a category it might otherwise have difficulty entering alone, such as is

Figure 9.4 Brand development strategies

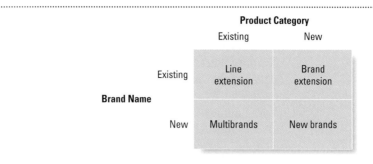

Product Category

		Existing	New
Brand Name	Existing	Line extension	Brand extension
	New	Multibrands	New brands

the case with Tim Hortons and Cold Stone Creamery, and Nike and iPod. Co-branding also has limitations. Such relationships usually involve complex legal contracts and licences. Co-branding partners must carefully coordinate their advertising, sales promotion, and other marketing efforts. Finally, when co-branding, each partner must trust that the other will take good care of its brand. Thus, as one manager puts it, "Giving away your brand is a lot like giving away your child—you want to make sure everything is perfect."[32]

Brand Development

Line extension
Extending an existing brand name to new forms, colours, sizes, ingredients, or flavours of an existing product category.

Brand extension
Extending an existing brand name to new product categories.

A company has four choices when it comes to developing brands (see Figure 9.4). It can introduce *line extensions, brand extensions, multibrands,* or *new brands.*

Line Extensions **Line extensions** occur when a company extends existing brand names to new forms, colours, sizes, ingredients, or flavours of an existing product category. To keep up with rapidly evolving competition and technology, BlackBerry has rapidly expanded its line to include BlackBerry Pearl (the first pocket-sized BlackBerry), the BlackBerry Curve (for those who wanted the added feature of a camera), and the BlackBerry Storm (a smartphone designed to compete directly with the iPhone). The vast majority of all new-product activity consists of line extensions.

A company might introduce line extensions as a low-cost, low-risk way to introduce new products. Or it might want to meet consumer desires for variety, to use excess capacity, or simply to command more shelf space from resellers. However, line extensions involve some risks. An overextended brand name might lose its specific meaning. For example, you can now pick from an array of seven different Jeep SUV models—Commander, Grand Cherokee, Compass, Patriot, Liberty, Wrangler, and Wrangler Unlimited. It's unlikely that many customers will fully appreciate the differences across the many similar models, and such "Jeep creep" can cause consumer confusion or even frustration.

Another risk is that sales of an extension may come at the expense of other items in the line. For example, the original Doritos tortilla chips have now morphed into a full line of 20 different types and flavours of chips, including such high-decibel flavours as Blazin' Buffalo Ranch, Black Pepper Jack, and Fiery Habanero. Although the line seems to be doing well, the original Doritos chips seem like just another flavour. A line extension works best when it takes sales away from competing brands, not when it "cannibalizes" the company's other items.

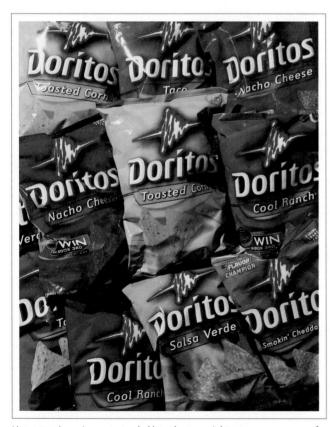

Line extensions: An overextended brand name might cause consumer confusion or frustration. The original Doritos tortilla chips have now morphed into a full line of 20 different types and flavours of chips, making the original Doritos seem like just another flavour.

Brand Extensions A **brand extension** extends a current brand name to new or modified products in a new category.

For example, Victorinox extended its venerable Swiss Army brand from multitool knives to products ranging from cutlery and ballpoint pens to watches, luggage, and apparel. And P&G has leveraged the strength of its Mr. Clean household cleaner brand to launch several new lines: cleaning pads (Magic Eraser), bathroom cleaning tools (Magic Reach), and home auto cleaning kits (Mr. Clean AutoDry). It's even launching Mr. Clean–branded car washes.

A brand extension gives a new product instant recognition and faster acceptance. It also saves the high advertising costs usually required to build a new brand name. At the same time, a brand extension strategy involves some risk. Brand extensions such as Bic pantyhose, Heinz pet food, Life Savers gum, and Roots Air met early deaths. The extension may confuse the image of the main brand. And if a brand extension fails, it may harm consumer attitudes toward the other products carrying the same brand name.

Furthermore, a brand name may not be appropriate to a particular new product, even if it is well made and satisfying—would you consider flying on Hooters Air or drinking Hooters energy drink? How about Donald Trump steaks or an Evian water-filled padded bra? All of these products failed. Companies that are tempted to transfer a brand name must research how well the brand's associations fit the new product.[33]

Multibrands   Companies often introduce additional brands in the same category. Thus, Procter & Gamble markets many different brands in each of its product categories. *Multibranding* offers a way to establish different features and appeal to different buying motives. It also allows a company to lock up more reseller shelf space.

A major drawback of multibranding is that each brand might obtain only a small market share, and none may be very profitable. The company may end up spreading its resources over many brands instead of building a few brands to a highly profitable level. These companies should reduce the number of brands they sell in a given category and set up tighter screening procedures for new brands.

New Brands   A company might believe that the power of its existing brand name is waning and a new brand name is needed. Or it may create a new brand name when it enters a new product category for which none of the company's current brand names are appropriate. For example, Toyota created the separate Scion brand, targeted toward Millennial consumers.

As with multibranding, offering too many new brands can result in a company spreading its resources too thin. And in some industries, such as consumer packaged goods, consumers and retailers have become concerned that there are already too many brands with too few differences between them. Thus, Procter & Gamble, Frito-Lay, Kraft, and other large consumer-product marketers are now pursuing *megabrand* strategies—weeding out weaker or slower-growing brands and focusing their marketing dollars only on brands that can achieve the number-one or number-two market share positions with good growth prospects in their categories.

Managing Brands

Companies must manage their brands carefully. First, the brand's positioning must be continuously communicated to consumers. Major brand marketers often spend huge amounts on advertising to create brand awareness and to build preference and loyalty. For example, Verizon spends more than US$2.8 billion annually to promote its brand. McDonald's spends more than US$1.7 billion.[34]

Such advertising campaigns can help to create name recognition, brand knowledge, and maybe even some brand preference. However, the fact is that brands are not maintained by advertising but by the *brand experience.*

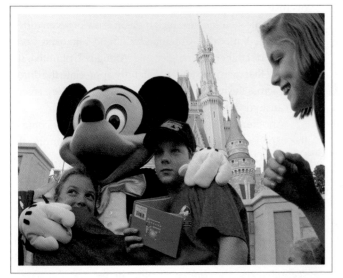

Managing brands requires managing "touchpoints." Says a former Disney executive: "A brand is a living entity, and it is enriched or undermined cumulatively over time, the product of a thousand small gestures."

Today, customers come to know a brand through a wide range of contacts and touchpoints. These include advertising, but also personal experience with the brand, word of mouth, company webpages, and many others. The company must put as much care into managing these touchpoints as it does into producing its ads. "Managing each customer's experience is perhaps the most important ingredient in building [brand] loyalty," states one branding expert. "Every memorable interaction . . . must be completed with excellence and . . . must reinforce your brand essence." A former Disney executive agrees: "A brand is a living entity, and it is enriched or undermined cumulatively over time, the product of a thousand small gestures."[35]

The brand's positioning will not take hold fully unless everyone in the company lives the brand. Therefore the company needs to train its people to be customer-centred. Even better, the company should carry on internal brand building to help employees understand and be enthusiastic about the brand promise. Many companies go even further by training and encouraging their distributors and dealers to serve their customers well.

Finally, companies need to periodically audit their brands' strengths and weaknesses.[36] They should ask: Does our brand excel at delivering benefits that consumers truly value? Is the brand properly positioned? Do all of our consumer touchpoints support the brand's positioning? Do the brand's managers understand what the brand means to consumers? Does the brand receive proper, sustained support? The brand audit may turn up brands that need more support, brands that need to be dropped, or brands that must be rebranded or repositioned because of changing customer preferences or new competitors.

4 | SERVICES MARKETING

Services have grown dramatically in recent years. Services now account for close to 69 percent of Canadian GDP, and are responsible for three of every four jobs. The trade subsector (made up of both wholesale and retail trade), makes up the largest proportion (approximately 35 percent) of the service sector in Canada, followed closely by the health care/social assistance sector (approximately 32 percent). Public administration is the next largest sector (19 percent), followed by educational services (18 percent), accommodation and food services (13 percent), and transportation and warehousing (10.5 percent). Professional, scientific, and technical services; information, culture and recreation; management and administration; and finance, insurance, and real estate each comprise approximately 8 percent of the entire sector.[37]

Service industries vary greatly. *Governments* offer services through courts, employment services, hospitals, military services, police and fire departments, postal services, and schools. *Private not-for-profit organizations* offer services through museums, charities, churches, colleges and universities, foundations, and hospitals. A large number of *business organizations* also offer services—airlines, banks, hotels, insurance companies, consulting firms, medical and legal practices, entertainment companies, real-estate firms, retailers, and others.

Nature and Characteristics of a Service

A company must consider four special service characteristics when designing marketing programs: *intangibility, inseparability, variability*, and *perishability* (see Figure 9.5).

Service intangibility A major characteristic of services—they cannot be seen, tasted, felt, heard, or smelled before they are bought.

Service intangibility means that services cannot be seen, tasted, felt, heard, or smelled before they are bought. For example, people undergoing cosmetic surgery cannot see the result before the purchase. Airline passengers have nothing but a ticket and the promise that they and their luggage will arrive safely at the intended destination, hopefully at the same time. To reduce uncertainty, buyers look for "signals" of service quality. They draw conclusions about quality from the place, people, price, equipment, and communications that they can see.

Therefore, the service provider's task is to make the service tangible in one or more ways and to send the right signals about quality. One analyst calls this *evidence management*, in which the service organization presents its customers with organized, honest evidence of

Figure 9.5 Four service characteristics

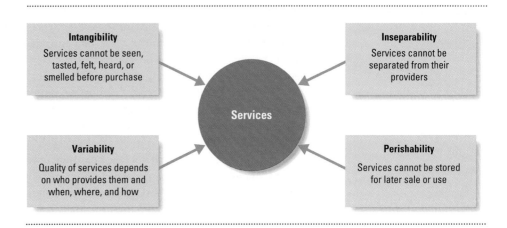

its capabilities. The famous Mayo Clinic located in the United States, practises good evidence management:

> When it comes to hospitals, it's hard for the average patient to judge the quality of the "product." You can't try it on, you can't return it if you don't like it, and you need an advanced degree to understand it. And so, when we're considering a medical facility, most of us unconsciously turn detective, looking for evidence of competence, caring, and integrity. The Mayo Clinic doesn't leave that evidence to chance. By carefully managing a set of visual and experiential clues, Mayo offers patients and their families concrete evidence of its strengths and values. For example, staff people at the clinic are trained to act in a way that clearly signals its patient-first focus. "My doctor calls me at home to check on how I am doing," marvels one patient. "She wants to work with what is best for my schedule." Mayo's physical facilities also send the right signals. They've been carefully designed to relieve stress, offer a place of refuge, create positive distractions, convey caring and respect, signal competence, accommodate families, and make it easy to find your way around. The result? Exceptionally positive word of mouth and abiding customer loyalty have allowed Mayo Clinic to build what is arguably the most powerful brand in health care with very little advertising. Ninety-five percent of Mayo Clinic patients report that they voluntarily praise the clinic to others.[38]

Physical goods are produced, then stored, later sold, and still later consumed. In contrast, services are first sold, then produced and consumed at the same time. In services marketing, the service provider is the product. **Service inseparability** means that services cannot be separated from their providers, whether the providers are people or machines. If a service employee provides the service, then the employee becomes a part of the service. Because the customer is also present as the service is produced, *provider–customer interaction* is a special feature of services marketing. Both the provider and the customer affect the service outcome.

Service variability means that the quality of services depends on who provides them as well as when, where, and how they are provided. For example, some hotels—say, Marriott—have reputations for providing better service than others. Still, within a given Marriott hotel, one registration-counter employee may be cheerful and efficient, whereas another standing just a few feet away may be unpleasant and slow. Even the quality of a single Marriott employee's service varies according to his or her energy and frame of mind at the time of each customer encounter.

Service perishability means that services cannot be stored for later sale or use. Some dentists charge patients for missed appointments because the service value existed only at that point and disappeared when the patient did not show up. The perishability of services is not a problem when demand is steady. However, when demand fluctuates, service firms often face difficult problems. For example, because of rush-hour demand, public transportation companies have to own much more equipment than they would if demand were even throughout the day. Thus, service firms often design strategies for

Service inseparability
A major characteristic of services—they are produced and consumed at the same time and cannot be separated from their providers.

Service variability
A major characteristic of services—their quality may vary greatly, depending on who provides them and when, where, and how.

Service perishability
A major characteristic of services—they cannot be stored for later sale or use.

producing a better match between demand and supply. Hotels and resorts charge lower prices in the off-season to attract more guests. And restaurants hire part-time employees to serve during peak periods.

Marketing Strategies for Service Firms

Just like manufacturing businesses, good service firms use marketing to position themselves strongly in chosen target markets. JetBlue promises "Happy Jetting"; Fairmont Hotels offers "authentic surroundings, genuine service, and lasting memories." And the Hospital for Sick Children in Toronto promises "Healthier children. A better world." These and other service organizations establish their positions through traditional marketing mix activities. However, because services differ from tangible products, they often require additional marketing approaches.

The Service–Profit Chain

Service–profit chain
The chain that links service firm profits with employee and customer satisfaction.

In a service business, the customer and front-line service employee *interact* to create the service. Effective interaction, in turn, depends on the skills of front-line service employees and on the support processes backing these employees. Thus, successful service companies focus their attention on *both* their customers and their employees. They understand the **service-profit chain**, which links service firm profits with employee and customer satisfaction. This chain consists of five links:[39]

- *Internal service quality:* superior employee selection and training, a quality work environment, and strong support for those dealing with customers, which results in . . .

- *Satisfied and productive service employees:* more satisfied, loyal, and hardworking employees, which results in . . .

- *Greater service value:* more effective and efficient customer-value creation and service delivery, which results in . . .

- *Satisfied and loyal customers:* satisfied customers who remain loyal, repeat purchase, and refer other customers, which results in . . .

- *Healthy service profits and growth:* superior service firm performance

Therefore, reaching service profits and growth goals begins with taking care of those who take care of customers. In fact, legendary founder and former CEO of Southwest Airlines Herb Kelleher always put employees first, not customers. His reasons? "If they're happy, satisfied, dedicated, and energetic, they'll take good care of customers," he says. "When the customers are happy, they come back, and that makes shareholders happy."[40] Consider Four Seasons Hotels and Resorts, a chain legendary for outstanding service:

At Four Seasons, every guest is a somebody. Other exclusive resorts pamper their guests, but Four Seasons offers a subtler brand of doting: helpful rather than subservient; instinctive rather than programmed. So it's easy to understand why Four Seasons has a cult-like clientele. As one Four Seasons Maui guest recently told a manager, "If there's a heaven, I hope it's run by Four Seasons." What makes the Four Seasons so special? It's the staff. The chain knows that happy, satisfied employees make for happy, satisfied customers. "Personal service is not something you can dictate as a policy," says the company's founder and CEO. "It comes from the culture. How you treat your employees is how you expect them to treat the customer."[41]

And Four Seasons treats its employees well. Compared with the competition, Four Seasons salaries are in the seventy-fifth to ninetieth percentile, with generous retirement and profit-sharing plans. All employees—seamstresses, valets, the ski concierge, the general manager—eat together regularly, free, in the hotel cafeteria. Another killer perk: free rooms. After six months, any staffer can stay three nights free per year at any Four Seasons hotel or resort. That number increases to six nights after a year and steadily thereafter. The room stays make employees feel as important and pampered as the guests. Says a Four Seasons

The service–profit chain: Happy employees make for happy customers. At Four Seasons, employees feel as important and pampered as the guests.

Internal marketing

Orienting and motivating customer-contact employees and supporting service people to work as a team to provide customer satisfaction.

Interactive marketing

Training service employees in the fine art of interacting with customers to satisfy their needs.

Maui pool attendant about his free stays, "You walk in and you say, 'Yeah, I'm somebody.'" Says another Maui employee, "You come back from those trips on fire. You want to do so much for the guest." As a result, the Four Seasons staff loves the hotel just as much as customers do. Although guests can check out anytime they like, employees never want to leave. The yearly turnover for full-time employees is around 18 percent, half the industry average. And that's the biggest secret to Four Seasons' success.

Thus, service marketing requires more than just traditional external marketing using the four Ps. Figure 9.6 shows that service marketing also requires *internal marketing* and *interactive marketing*. **Internal marketing** means that the service firm must orient and motivate its customer-contact employees and supporting service people to work as a *team* to provide customer satisfaction. Marketers must get everyone in the organization to be customer-centred. In fact, internal marketing must *precede* external marketing.

For example, Four Seasons hires the right people, orients them carefully, instills in them a sense of pride, and motivates them by recognizing and rewarding outstanding service deeds. Says one analysts, "Every job applicant, whether hoping to fold laundry or teach yoga, goes through at least four interviews. We look for people who say 'I'd be proud to be a doorman,'" says the CEO. Once hired, the training never stops. The most important guideline, contends the CEO, is "the golden rule: Do unto others. . . . That's not a gimmick," he says. "In the hiring process, we're looking for people who are very comfortable with this idea."[42] As a result, Four Seasons employees know what good service is and are highly motivated to give it.

Interactive marketing means that service quality depends heavily on the quality of the buyer–seller interaction during the service encounter. In product marketing, product quality often depends little on how the product is obtained. But in services marketing, service quality depends on both the service deliverer and the quality of the delivery. Service marketers, therefore, have to master interactive marketing skills. Thus, Four Seasons selects only people with an innate "passion to serve" and instructs them carefully in the fine art of interacting with customers to satisfy their every need. Employees learn quickly that guests paying $1000 a night "expect to have their [minds] read." All new hires complete a three-month training regimen that includes improvisation exercises to help them anticipate guest behaviour.

In today's marketplace, companies must know how to deliver interactions that are not only "high-touch" but also "high-tech." For example, TD Canada Trust customers can log onto its website and can "take a tour" to learn how to do transactions and invest online. Customers can change their address, lodge stop payment requests, set up new accounts, or order new cheques. They can manage their personal portfolio online, access the most recent financial news and timely articles of interest to investors, and get "action advice" about major companies. Customers seeking more personal interactions can contact service representatives by phone or visit a local TD branch (all locations are also easily found online). Thus, TD Canada Trust has mastered interactive marketing at all three levels—calls, clicks, *and* personal visits.

Today, as competition and costs increase and as productivity and quality decrease, more service marketing sophistication is needed. Service companies face three major marketing tasks: They want to increase their *service differentiation, service quality,* and *service productivity.*

Figure 9.6 Three types
of service marketing

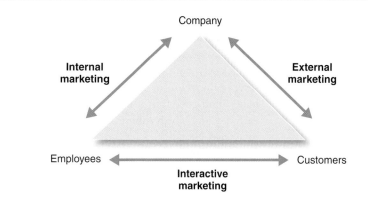

Managing Service Differentiation

In these days of intense price competition, service marketers often complain about the difficulty of differentiating their services from those of competitors. To the extent that customers view the services of different providers as similar, they care less about the provider than the price.

The solution to price competition is to develop a differentiated offer, delivery, and image. The *offer* can include innovative features that set one company's offer apart from competitors' offers. Some hotels offer car-rental, banking, and business-centre services in their lobbies and free high-speed Internet connections in their rooms. Airlines differentiate their offers though frequent-flyer reward programs and special services. For example, British Airways offers spa services at its Arrivals Lounge in Heathrow Airport and softer beds, plumper pillows, and cozier blankets in the air. Says one ad: "Our simple goal is to deliver the best service you could ask for, without you having to ask."

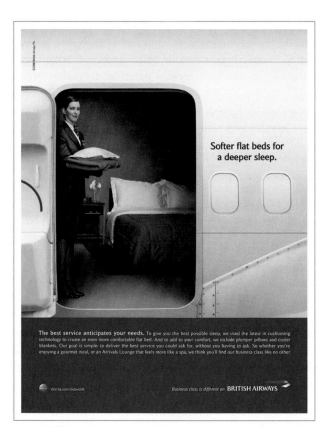

Service differentiation: At British Airways, says this ad, "Our goal is simple: to deliver the best service you can ask for, without you having to ask."

Service companies can differentiate their service *delivery* by having more able and reliable customer-contact people, by developing a superior physical environment in which the service product is delivered, or by designing a superior delivery process. For example, many grocery chains now offer online shopping and home delivery as a better way to shop than having to drive, park, wait in line, and tote groceries home.

Finally, service companies also can work on differentiating their *images* through symbols and branding. Aflac adopted the duck as its symbol in its advertising, and even as stuffed animals, golf club covers, and free ring tones and screensavers. The well-known Aflac duck, with the familiar voice of comedian Gilbert Gottfried, helped make the big but previously unknown insurance company memorable and approachable. Other well-known service symbols include RBC's lion, TD Canada Trust's big green armchair, Petro-Canada's maple leaf, Merrill Lynch's bull, McDonald's golden arches, and Allstate's "good hands."

Managing Service Quality

A service firm can differentiate itself by delivering consistently higher quality than its competitors provide. Like manufacturers before them, most service industries have now joined the customer-driven quality movement. And like product marketers, service providers need to identify what target customers expect in terms of service quality.

Unfortunately, service quality is harder to define and judge than product quality. For instance, it is harder to agree on the quality of a haircut than on the quality of a hair dryer. Customer retention is perhaps the best measure of quality—a service firm's ability to hang on to its customers depends on how consistently it delivers value to them.

Top service companies set high service-quality standards. They watch service performance closely, both their own and that of competitors. They do not settle for merely good service; they aim for 100 percent defect-free service. A 98 percent performance standard may sound good, but using this standard, UPS would lose or misdirect 316 000 packages each day and North American pharmacists would misfill close to 1.5 million prescriptions each week.[43]

Unlike product manufacturers who can adjust their machinery and inputs until everything is perfect, service quality will always vary, depending on the interactions between employees and customers. As hard as they try, even the best companies will have an occasional late delivery, burned steak, or grumpy employee. However, good *service recovery* can turn angry customers into loyal ones. In fact, good recovery can win more customer purchasing and loyalty than if things had gone well in the first place. Therefore, companies should take steps not only to provide good service every time but also to recover from service mistakes when they do occur (see Real Marketing 9.2).

The first step is to *empower* front-line service employees—to give them the authority, responsibility, and incentives they need to recognize, care about, and tend to customer needs. Restaurants known for their good service as well as their good food, for example, give employees the autonomy they need to create outstanding customer service experiences and offer free desserts or other items to make up for any service failures.

Managing Service Productivity

With their costs rising rapidly, service firms are under great pressure to increase service productivity. They can do so in several ways. They can train current employees better or hire new ones who will work harder or more skilfully. Or they can increase the quantity of their service by giving up some quality. The provider can "industrialize the service" by adding equipment and standardizing production, as in McDonald's assembly-line approach to fast-food retailing. Finally, the service provider can harness the power of technology. Although we often think of technology's power to save time and costs in manufacturing companies, it also has great—and often untapped—potential to make service workers more productive.

However, companies must avoid pushing productivity so hard that doing so reduces quality. Attempts to industrialize a service or to cut costs can make a service company more efficient in the short run. But they can also reduce its longer-run ability to innovate, maintain service quality, or respond to consumer needs and desires. Many airlines are learning this lesson the hard way as they attempt to streamline and economize in the face of rising costs:

> Over the past year, in the face of rising costs and fuel prices, Air Canada has cut some routes and reduced flight frequency on others. It has cut jobs, laying off many service providers, and has asked customers to do more and more of the work including self-check-in and tagging of bags. It stopped offering free magazines, pillows, blankets, and even minibags of pretzels on its domestic flights. Passengers can purchase in-flight snacks and meals, but at a cost of $2 to $10. It has stopped providing free earphones for its in-flight entertainment system. Passengers must pay $3 if they want to buy a pair of earphones. Such cuts have angered many customers. Just google "Air Canada sucks" and see how many hits you get. A services marketing expert agrees: "The upshot is that some companies, in their passion to drive down costs, have mangled their relationships with customers."[44]

Thus, in attempting to improve service productivity, companies must be mindful of how they create and deliver customer value. In short, they should be careful not to take the "service" out of service.

Real Marketing 9.2

Service Recovery: Doing Things Right When Service Goes Wrong

Good service is important for airline customers. But all service companies, even the great ones, make mistakes once in a while. Perhaps the truest test of good customer service is how well companies do when things go wrong. As airlines offer more and more extra services like hotel bookings and car rentals, they should also pay attention to the service their partners offer. Here is what one irate Air Canada frequent flyer wrote to the airline after a less than satisfactory service experience:

> I made car rental arrangements through your website when I booked my flight to Calgary. I was booked with Dollar. My reservation print out said they were "on terminal" with a pickup time of 18:00 (my flight was due to arrive at 18:25) but the flight was late. When I arrived in Calgary, I found that Dollar was not at the terminal. They had an "automatic" phone service (at the very end of the terminal—outside) with a broken computer voice tape. I was finally connected to someone in Oklahoma who had no information about pickup or my reservation. After about 20 minutes I was connected to someone in Calgary (I think) who was very rude and informed me that Dollar closed at 6:00, and that I would have to pay for the reservation anyway since I was late. Why would your web service book me with an offsite car company that closed before my flight was due to arrive? I had to get a car and was unable to negotiate a good rate (I was the only walk-in and the counters are all clustered together). Thus, I had to pay $335 (plus taxes) for a Budget car versus the $109 I was quoted for the Dollar car. I went to the Air Canada service desk to note the problem. People were sympathetic, but gave me a card for your Customer Solutions Centre that had no phone number on it (or email). While I understand that you are partnering with Destina, this type of service is unacceptable and it casts a very unfavourable light on Air Canada's brand and service.

Was Air Canada concerned about this message? Not exactly. Here is its reply:

> We were sorry to learn of the difficulties you encountered, as outlined in your email, and regret any inconvenience that you may have experienced. As this situation is beyond the control of Air Canada we are unable to fully address your concerns. Due to the nature of the airline industry, there are many outside variables which may impact on our operations. Since there is very little to add in way of an explanation, perhaps you may

wish to forward a copy of your letter directly to the parties concerned. Once again, thank you for contacting us.

> Sincerely,
> Michelle Sturge
> Customer Solutions

Compare the above story to one that took place at Jet-Blue Airways—a great service company. Since first taking off in 2000, JetBlue has amassed a soaring list of service honours, including Readers Choice Awards from discerning *Condé Nast Traveller* magazine for five years running and high rankings in every measured category in the airline satisfaction ratings by J.D. Power & Associates. As a result, Jet-Blue has been one of the very few consistently profitable air carriers in the otherwise troubled airline industry.

But consider the following tale, in which JetBlue committed a far more serious service blunder than the Air Canada example—but one it eventually dealt with through a change to its operations.

On February 14, 2007—Valentine's Day—a devastating ice storm struck JetBlue's main hub at New York's John F. Kennedy International Airport. The resulting disastrous mix of closed runways, aircraft congestion, and frozen equipment kept many JetBlue customers stranded for hours in grounded planes. A series of bad decisions resulted in chaos on the tarmac. In a fruitless attempt to eventually get planes off the ground, JetBlue waited too long to cancel flights and to bus enplaned passengers back to the terminal. Many passengers were trapped in planes for as long as 11 hours, as the tires of their planes literally froze to the runway. All the while, increasingly furious customers—both on the stranded planes and in the terminal—were kept pretty much in the dark about what was going to happen and why.

Even after passengers were returned to the terminal, the nightmare continued. The relatively new and rapidly growing JetBlue simply hadn't built the customer service and operational infrastructure needed to deal with such a crisis. JetBlue flight crews and terminal agents were befuddled and disorganized in helping passengers.

Over the next six days, JetBlue experienced major disruptions throughout its entire system, cancelling more than 1000 flights and leaving customers fuming over rough handling and lost vacations. During that critical week, JetBlue struggled just to get operations back to normal. The airline did little by way of responding to customers' seething emotions. It missed an opportunity for smooth and immediate service recovery, which could have created even stronger customer relationships. Instead JetBlue's meltdown created a serious crisis of customer trust.

▶

In the weeks following the six-day disaster, JetBlue went into long-term service recovery mode. JetBlue's chairman seemed to pop up everywhere—*The New York Times, The Late Show with David Letterman,* NPR, even YouTube—accepting responsibility, apologizing repeatedly, and promising refunds and credits to wronged customers. He quickly announced a new Customer Bill of Rights, a unique document that outlines policies for notifying customers about delays and cancellations, sets a limit before ground-delayed passengers must be deplaned, and provides for generous customer compensation for all types of service missteps.

But even more important than apologies, refunds, and guarantees, JetBlue later made sweeping systems changes that will prevent future customer service debacles. "We should have acted quicker. We should have had contingency plans that were better [tested] to be able to [unload] customers," says the chairman. "We've learned from this," he declares. "That's why it's never going to happen again."

How much damage did the Valentine's Day service disaster do to JetBlue's hard-earned customer service reputation? As it turns out, thanks to a ton of previously earned goodwill and a solid longer-term recovery effort, this single incident has not undone years of good customer relationships. Says one analyst, "[JetBlue's] customers largely accept that it cares, because it has demonstrated that it does, flight after flight." In fact, by mid-2007, for the third year running, JetBlue was awarded highest honours in customer satisfaction among low-cost airlines by J.D. Power and Associates. And in 2008, the airline was ranked number seven among *BusinessWeek's* Customer Service Champs across all industries.

But the message is clear. Even good service companies screw up from time to time. Good service recovery, however, can turn such screw-ups into opportunities to actually strengthen bonds with customers. Companies must think ahead and plan for good service recovery. In these two examples, both airlines had the opportunity to address service failures and win customer trust. As the industry becomes even more competitive, making the right moves when things go wrong to keep customer satisfaction high will become even more critical.

Sources: Portions from P. Cunningham's personal files, other portions adapted from Jena McGregor, "Customer Service Champs," *BusinessWeek,* March 5, 2007, pp. 52–64. Quotes and other information from Justin Bachman, "JetBlue's Fiasco Could Improve Flying," *BusinessWeek,* February 21, 2007, p. 10; Chuck Salter, "Lessons from the Tarmac," *Fast Company,* May 2007, pp. 31–32; Mel Duvall and Doug Bartholomew, "What Really Happened at JetBlue?" *Baseline,* April 2007, pp. 53–59; Melissa Waite, "Managing Under Crisis: The Source of Atonement at JetBlue Airways," *Business Review,* Cambridge, December 2007, pp. 187+; and Jena McGregor, "Customer Service Champs," *BusinessWeek,* March 3, 2008, p. 37.

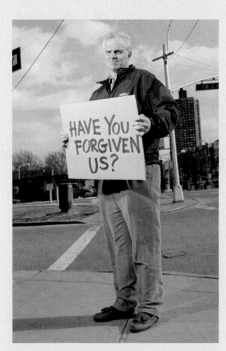

Service recovery: Following its Valentine's Day customer service meltdown, JetBlue announced a host of actions to repair its bond with customers. "We've learned from this," said JetBlue CEO David Needleman, shown here. "That's why it's never going to happen again."

REVIEWING OBJECTIVES AND KEY TERMS

A product is more than a simple set of tangible features. Each product or service offered to customers can be viewed on three levels. The *core customer value* consists of the core problem-solving benefits that consumers seek when they buy a product. The *actual product* exists around the core and includes the quality level, features, design, brand name, and packaging. The *augmented product* is the actual product plus the various services and benefits offered with it, such as a warranty, free delivery, installation, and maintenance.

OBJECTIVE 1 **Define *product* and the major classifications of products and services.**

Broadly defined, a *product* is anything that can be offered to a market for attention, acquisition, use, or consumption that might satisfy a want or need. Products include physical objects but also services, events, people, places, organizations, ideas, or mixes of these entities. *Services* are products that consist of activities, benefits, or satisfactions offered for sale that are essentially intangible, such as banking, hotel, tax preparation, and home-repair services.

Products and services fall into two broad classes based on the types of consumers that use them. *Consumer products*—those bought by final consumers—are usually classified according to consumer shopping habits (convenience products, shopping products, specialty products, and unsought products). *Business products*—purchased for further processing or for use in conducting a business—include materials and parts, capital items, and supplies and services. Other marketable entities—such as organizations, people, places, and ideas—can also be thought of as products.

OBJECTIVE 2 **Describe the decisions companies make regarding their individual products and services, product lines, and product mixes.**

Individual product decisions involve product attributes, branding, packaging, labelling, and product support services. *Product attribute* decisions involve product quality, features, and style and design. *Branding* decisions include selecting a brand name and developing a brand strategy. *Packaging* provides many key benefits, such as protection, economy, convenience, and promotion. Package decisions often include designing *labels*, which identify, describe, and possibly promote the product. Companies also develop *product support services* that enhance customer service and satisfaction and safeguard against competitors.

Most companies produce a product line rather than a single product. A *product line* is a group of products that are related in function, customer-purchase needs, or distribution channels. *Line stretching* involves extending a line downward, upward, or in both directions to occupy a gap that might otherwise be filled by a competitor. In contrast, *line filling* involves adding items within the present range of the line. All product lines and items offered to customers by a particular seller make up the *product mix*. The mix can be described by four dimensions: width, length, depth, and consistency. These dimensions are the tools for developing the company's product strategy.

OBJECTIVE 3 **Discuss branding strategy—the decisions companies make in building and managing their brands.**

Some analysts see brands as *the* major enduring asset of a company. Brands are more than just names and symbols—they embody everything that the product or service *means* to consumers. *Brand equity* is the positive differential effect that knowing the brand name has on customer response to the product or service. A brand with strong brand equity is a very valuable asset.

In building brands, companies need to make decisions about brand positioning, brand-name selection, brand sponsorship, and brand development. The most powerful *brand positioning* builds on strong consumer beliefs and values. *Brand-name selection* involves finding the best brand name based on a careful review of product benefits, the target market, and proposed marketing strategies. A manufacturer has four *brand sponsorship* options: it can launch a *manufacturer's brand* (or national brand), sell to resellers who use a *private brand*, market *licensed brands*, or join forces with another company to *co-brand* a product. A company also has four choices when it comes to developing brands. It can introduce *line extensions, brand extensions, multibrands,* or *new brands.*

Companies must build and manage their brands carefully. The brand's positioning must be continuously communicated to consumers. Advertising can help. However, brands are not maintained by advertising but by the *brand experience.* Customers come to know a brand through a wide range of contacts and interactions. The company must put as much care into managing these touchpoints as it does into producing its ads. Thus, managing a company's brand assets can no longer be left only to brand managers. Some companies are now setting up brand asset management teams to manage their major brands. Finally, companies must periodically audit their brands' strengths and weaknesses. In some cases, brands may need to be repositioned because of changing customer preferences or new competitors.

OBJECTIVE 4 **Identify the four characteristics that affect the marketing of a service and the additional marketing considerations that services require.**

Services are characterized by four key characteristics: they are *intangible, inseparable, variable,* and *perishable.* Each characteristic poses problems and marketing requirements. Marketers work to find ways to make the service more tangible, to increase the productivity of providers who are inseparable from their products, to standardize the quality of the service in the face of variability, and to improve demand movements and supply capacities in the face of service perishability.

Good service companies focus attention on *both* customers and employees. They understand the *service–profit chain,* which links service firm profits with employee and customer satisfaction. Services marketing strategy calls not only for external marketing but also for *internal marketing* to motivate employees and *interactive marketing* to create service delivery skills among service providers. To succeed, service marketers must create *competitive differentiation,* offer high *service quality,* and find ways to increase *service productivity.*

KEY TERMS

mymarketinglab | Glossary Flashcards

Objective 1
  Product   276
  Service   276
  Consumer product   278
  Convenience product   278
  Shopping product   278
  Specialty product   279
  Unsought product   279
  Business product   279
  Social marketing   281
Objective 2
  Product quality   281
  Brand   283
  Packaging   283
  Product line   286
  Product mix (product portfolio)   287

Objective 3
  Brand equity   288
  Store brand (private brand)   293
  Co-branding   294
  Line extension   295
  Brand extension   295
Objective 4
  Service intangibility   297
  Service inseparability   298
  Service variability   298
  Service perishability   298
  Service–profit chain   299
  Internal marketing   300
  Interactive marketing   300

DISCUSSING THE CONCEPTS

1. What is a product and how can product planners build customer value?

2. How does a business product differ from a consumer product? Discuss the types of business products and provide an example of each.

3. Discuss the product attributes through which benefits are communicated and delivered to customers.

4. Define brand equity. What competitive advantages does high brand equity provide to a company?

5. Discuss the brand development strategies marketers use to develop brands. Provide an example of each strategy.

6. Describe the four characteristics of services that marketers must consider when designing marketing programs. How do the services offered by a dentist differ from those offered by a drug store regarding these characteristics?

APPLYING THE CONCEPTS

1. What do Betty Crocker, Pillsbury, Cheerios, and Hamburger Helper have in common? They are all familiar brands that are part of the General Mills product mix. Visit the General Mills website (www.generalmills.com) and examine its list of brands. Name and define the four dimensions of a company's product mix and describe General Mills' product mix on these dimensions.

2. Using the six qualities that a good brand name should possess, create a brand name for a personal care product that has the following positioning statement: "Intended for X-Games sports participants and enthusiasts is a deodorant that combines effective odour protection with an enduring and seductive fragrance that will enhance your romantic fortunes."

3. List the names of the store brands found in the following stores: Loblaw, Shoppers Drug Mart, and the Bay. Identify the private-label brand(s) of another retailer of your choice.

FOCUS ON TECHNOLOGY

With the magazine industry's circulation and ad sales suffering, Time Inc. is offering a new Internet service called Maghound that allows customers the "convenience of subscriptions with the flexibility of newsstand sales." Instead of paying a fixed-term subscription fee for one magazine, customers pay a monthly fee for home delivery of a wanted publication plus the added benefit of being able to go online when desired and change to a different publication. The Maghound service is beginning with 300 consumer magazines, including Time's most popular titles, such as *People*, *Fortune*, and *Sports Illustrated*. Magazines from several other publishers are also available. Customers can get three magazines for about $5 a month, five magazines for $8, or seven magazines for $10, with each additional magazine

costing another $1. Maghound lets a reader who enjoys golfing or fishing to read about that in the summer and then switch to winter sports like skiing in the winter. Moreover, gone are the "renew now" nuisance offers and being locked into a subscription for a long time. The only drawback is that changes will not take effect immediately, so customers may not receive a specific issue of a magazine they're interested in.

1. Explain the core, actual, and augmented levels of this service.

2. Does this service have the potential to deliver customer value? Explain your answer.

FOCUS ON ETHICS

In 2008, a deadly listeriosis outbreak killed 20 people across Canada. The source of the outbreak was traced to a Maple Leaf Foods processing plant in Toronto. The firm quickly recalled all meat products that could have been affected and took measures to find and eliminate the problem in its plants.

Shortly after the outbreak was controlled, the president of Maple Leaf Foods, now CEO Michael McCain, hit television screens across Canada to make it clear that his company has an obsession with food safety and to outline the improvements made at the company's 24 packaged meat facilities. Said McCain, "We now dismantle our equipment, especially our slicing equipment, daily and weekly as part of enhanced cleaning and sanitization practices." The campaign was

launched when focus group research indicated that consumers still hadn't realized the recall had ended.

As the problem unfolded and the story was front page news across Canada, people's intent to purchase dropped to a very low 64 percent. However, Maple Leaf has long been a trusted brand, and its public apology, its efforts to address the problem quickly, and its massive PR campaign quickly restored consumer confidence. Purchase intent rose to a number in the low 90s.

1. Recalls are very common. You can find a list of many current recalls and consumer advisories by visiting the CBC News webpage www.cbc.ca/consumer/recalls. Health Canada is another organization that

posts information about recalls (see www.hc-sc.gc.ca/ahc-asc/media/advisories-avis/index-eng.php). Under what circumstances would you consider posting of recalls in this fashion to be an ethical and effective way to advise Canadians about faulty or dangerous products or services?

2. What obligations should a company have if it finds that it has inadvertently produced a faulty product or service? Were actions by Maple Leaf Foods a template for ethical or unethical behaviour? Explain your reasoning.

MARKETING BY THE NUMBERS

Mars, maker of the famous M&M's candy brand, recently introduced M&M Premiums. The new candies include flavours such as mint chocolate, mocha, chocolate almond, and raspberry-almond with white chocolate. They are wrapped in iridescent colours and sold in reclosable cartons. Mars also plans new offerings with its Snickers and Dove brands. Although the new M&M Premiums will garner a higher wholesale price for the company ($0.48 per ounce for the new product versus $0.30 per ounce for the original product), they also come with higher variable costs ($0.35 per ounce for the new product versus $0.15 per ounce for the original product).

1. What brand development strategy is Mars undertaking?

2. Assume the company expects to sell 300 million ounces of M&M Premiums within the first year after introduc-

tion but expects that half of those sales will come from buyers who would normally purchase M&M regular candies (that is, cannibalized sales). Assuming the sales of regular M&M candies are normally 1 billion ounces per year and that the company will incur an increase in fixed costs of $5 million during the first year of production for M&M Premiums, will the new product be profitable for the company? Refer to the discussion of cannibalization in Appendix 3: Marketing by the Numbers for an explanation regarding how to conduct this analysis.

VIDEO CASE

Swiss Army Brands

It seems appropriate that Swiss Army Brands, maker of multifunction knives, has become a multiproduct brand. Victorinox Swiss Army Inc. has made its famous knives for more than 100 years. Former product line extensions included different variations of the standard Swiss Army Knife for applications such as fishing, golf, and an accessory for women's purses.

But the popularity of the Swiss Army knife has enabled the company to expand into all manner of consumer goods, including watches, luggage, apparel, and other lines. These brand extensions have been based on consumer research to ensure that each fits within the concept that consumers hold for the brand. The success that Swiss Army Brands has achieved through expansion has even allowed it to open its own retail stores.

  Video Case Questions

After viewing the video featuring Swiss Army Brands, answer the following questions about product and branding strategies:

1. How might brand extensions affect Swiss Army Brands, in both positive and negative ways?

2. Why did Swiss Army Brands open retail stores? How do these stores help the company build its brand?

3. Do you think Swiss Army Brands could extend its brand to any type of product? What additional products and lines might Swiss Army Brands consider?

Visit MyMarketingLab at www.pearsoned.ca/mymarketinglab to view the video segment related to this case.

COMPANY CASE

ESPN: The Evolution of an Entertainment Brand

In the 2004 movie *Anchorman*, character Ron Burgundy (Will Ferrell) auditions for a position on *SportsCenter* with the very new and little known network ESPN (Entertainment and Sports Programming Network). The year was 1979. After pronouncing the name of the network "Espen," he then is shocked to find out that ESPN is a round-the-clock sports network. Through his laughter, he asserts that the concept is as ridiculous as a 24-hour cooking network or an all-music channel. "Seriously," he shouts. "This thing is going to be a financial and cultural disaster. *SportsCenter . . .* that's just dumb!"

While this comical sketch is fictitious, when a young college graduate named George Bodenheimer took a job in the mailroom at ESPN in 1981, it was for real. Today, Bodenheimer is president of the network that has become one of the biggest franchises in sports, not to mention one of the most successful and envied brands in the entertainment world. As a cable network, ESPN commands $2.91 from cable operators for each subscriber every month. Compare that to $1.67 for Fox Sports, 89 cents for TNT, and only 40 cents for CNN. The core ESPN channel alone is currently in more than 96 million homes. With that kind of premium power, it's no wonder that ESPN shocked the world in 2006 by becoming the first cable network to land the coveted TV contract for Monday Night Football, which went on to become the highest-rated cable series ever.

But even with its three sibling channels (ESPN2, ESPNews, and ESPN Classic), the ESPN cable network is only one piece of a bigger brand puzzle that has become Bodenheimer's $6 billion sports empire. Through very savvy strategic planning, Bodenheimer is realizing his vision of taking quality sports content across the widest possible collection of media assets to reach sports fans wherever they may be. Employing a hands-off management style, Bodenheimer has cultivated a brand that is brash, tech savvy, creative, and innovative. He tells employees that ESPN belongs to all of them. He gives them the freedom to come up with their own ideas and push them forward. His only rule is that every new idea must focus on fulfilling ESPN's mission of reaching sports fans and making them happy. In the process, ESPN has become as recognized and revered by its customers as other megabrands such as Tide, Nike, and Coca-Cola are to theirs.

Bodenheimer's career-spanning dedication has grown ESPN to well over 50 businesses. The all-sports network has become a truly multiplatform brand, a rarity for any TV network. This growth has given ESPN tremendous reach. ESPN.com alone reaches 22.4 million viewers a week. But even more stunning is the fact that during any seven-day period, 120 million people ages 12 to 64 interact with some ESPN medium. Here's a rundown of ESPN's portfolio of brands:

Television: ESPN has sprawled into six cable channels and other TV divisions that give it both a local (ESPN Regional Television) and global (ESPN International and ESPN Deportes) presence. It was one of the first networks to break new ground in HDTV with simulcast service for ESPN and ESPN2 and it still maintains the most HD programming content and highest level of HD viewership in sports. Cable operators and viewers alike consistently rank ESPN, ESPN2, and ESPN Classic above all other channels with respect to perceived value and programming quality.

But perhaps one of the most innovative moves in all of television sports occurred in 2003, when ESPN content was integrated into its sibling network ABC. ESPN on ABC is now the home for the NBA Finals, NASCAR, NCAA football, NCAA basketball, World Cup Soccer, the British Open, and the IndyCar Series.

Although ESPN has numerous cable channel brands, one program stands out as a brand in its own right. *SportsCenter* was ESPN's first program. And with as many as 93 million viewers each month, it remains the network's flagship studio show. *SportsCenter* is the only nightly, full-hour sports news program. And whereas in the past ESPN rebroadcast taped episodes of *SportsCenter* during the day, a new schedule incorporating nine straight hours of live *SportsCenter* every day from 6 a.m. to 3 p.m. began in the fall of 2008. Outside the United States, ESPN airs 14 local versions of *SportsCenter* that are broadcast in eight languages.

Radio: Whereas many radio formats are suffering, sports radio is thriving. And ESPN Radio is the nation's largest sports radio network with 750 U.S. affiliates and more than 335 full-time stations. In addition to college and major league sports events, the network broadcasts syndicated sports talk shows, providing more than 9000 hours of content annually.

Publishing: *ESPN The Magazine* launched in 1998 and immediately began carving out market share with its bold look, bright colours, and unconventional type, a combination consistent with its content. With the dominance of *Sports Illustrated*, many didn't give ESPN's magazine venture much of a chance. Within its first year, though, *ESPN The Magazine* was circulating 800 000 copies. Today, that number has ballooned two-and-a-half times to 2 million, whereas *Sports Illustrated* has remained at a stagnant 3.3 million.

At the same time, ESPN is making headway into one of the oldest of all media: books. Although ESPN Books is still waiting for a megaseller, because of the cross-marketing opportunities with the other arms of ESPN, this small division has considerable marketing clout in a struggling industry. "If they didn't have the TV stuff and everything else, they'd be as hard-pressed as other publishers to make these books into major events," said Rick Wolff, executive editor at Warner Books.

Internet: ESPN.com is the leading sports website, and ESPNRadio.com is the most listened-to online sports destination, boasting live streaming and 32 original podcasts each week. But the rising star in ESPN's online portfolio is ESPN360.com, a subscription-based broadband offering that delivers high-quality, customized, on-demand video content. Not only can fans access content carried on ESPN's other networks, but they also get exclusive content and sports video games. For the true sports fan, there's nothing like it—it allows viewers to watch up to six different events at the same time choosing from live events for all major professional and college sports. Since ESPN360.com began service in 2006, this broadband effort has doubled its distribution and now reaches 20 million homes.

Beyond working through its own websites, ESPN is exploring the limits of the Internet through an open distribution venture with AOL. By providing ESPN content via a branded ESPN video player in AOL's portal, viewers have more access to ESPN's content. But advertisers also benefit from a larger online audience than ever before.

Mobile: In 2005, ESPN ventured into one of its trickiest and riskiest brand extensions to date. Mobile ESPN was designed as ESPN's own cellphone network, putting content into sports fans' pockets 24/7. But after a year, the venture was far from breaking even and ESPN shut it down. However, even though Mobile ESPN is down, it's not out. ESPN has capitalized on the lessons learned and started over with a different strategy. Today, ESPN provides real-time scores, stats, news, highlights, and even programming through every major U.S. carrier, with premium content available through Verizon Wireless and Qualcomm. Mobile ESPN also reaches an international audience of mobile customers through more than 35 international carriers.

ESPN's mission with its mobile venture is to "serve the sports fan any time, anywhere, and from any device." In fall 2007, it reached a major milestone in that goal when more people sought NFL content from its mobile-phone website than from its PC website. "We're having extraordinary growth on ESPN.com's NFL pages, but we're also seeing extraordinary usage with mobile devices as well," said Ed Erhardt, president of ESPN Sports customer marketing and sales. Mr. Erhardt sees great potential in mobile, saying that it is "a big part of the future as it relates to how fans are going to consume sports."

Bodenheimer and his team see no limit to how far they can take the ESPN brand. In addition to the above ventures, ESPN extends its reach through event management (X Games, Winter X Games, ESPN Outdoors), consumer products (CDs, DVDs, ESPN video games, ESPN golf schools), and even a chain of ESPN Zone restaurants and SportsCenter Studio Stores. ESPN content is now reaching viewers through agencies that place it in airports and on planes, in health clubs, and even in gas stations. "Now you're not going to be bored when you fill up your tank. It gives new meaning to pulling into a full-service station," says Bodenheimer. "I've been on flights where people are watching our content and don't want to get off the flight."

A powerful media brand results not only in direct revenues from selling products but also in advertising revenues. Advertising accounts for about 40 percent of ESPN's overall revenues. With so many ways to reach the customer, ESPN offers very creative and flexible package deals for any marketer trying to reach the coveted and illusive 18–34-year-old male demographic. "Nobody attracts more men than we do," asserts Bodenheimer. "We've got a product and we know how to cater to advertisers' needs. The merchandising opportunities we provide, whether it's working with Home Depot, Walmart, or Dick's Sporting Goods, we want to partner if you want young men."

As amazing as the ESPN brand portfolio is, it is even more amazing when you consider that it is part of the mammoth ABC portfolio, which in turn is a part of The Walt Disney Company portfolio. However, it is no small piece of the Disney pie. ESPN revenues alone accounted for about 18 percent of Disney's total in 2007. Since obtaining ESPN as part of the 1995 ABC acquisition, Disney has allowed ESPN to do pretty much whatever it wants to do because ESPN has delivered on the numbers. Just a few years after the acquisition, Disney's then-CEO Michael Eisner told investors, "We bought ABC media network and ESPN for $19 billion in 1995. ESPN is worth substantially more than we paid for the entire acquisition." And Disney leverages that value every way that it can, from Mouse House advertising package deals to conditionally attaching its cable channels to the ESPN networks through cable operators.

Questions for Discussion

1. In a succinct manner, describe what the ESPN brand means to consumers.

2. What is ESPN selling? Discuss this in terms of the core benefit, actual product, and augmented product levels of ESPN.

3. Does ESPN have strong brand equity? How does its brand equity relate to its brand value?

4. Cite as many examples as you can of co-branding efforts involving the ESPN brand. For each of these cases, what are the benefits and possible risks to ESPN?

5. Analyze EPSN according to the brand development strategies from the text. What have they done in the past? What would you recommend to ESPN for future brand development?

Sources: Alice Cuneo, "More Football Fans Hit ESPN's Mobile Site Than Its PC Pages," *Advertising Age*, January 7, 2008, p. 17; Mike Shields, "ESPN, AOL Strike Web Video Deal," *Brandweek*, April 8, 2008, accessed at www.brandweek.com; Andrew Hampp, "ESPN Makes Jump to Major League," *Advertising Age*, May 14, 2007, p. 32; Ronald Grover, "Comcast's C-TV: Channeling Disney," *BusinessWeek.com*, December 1, 2006; Jeffrey Trachtenberg, "ESPN's Next Hurdle: Selling Its Audience on Books," *Wall Street Journal*, February 13, 2007; Jason Brown, "Out-of-Home TV Ads Finally Coming of Age," *Television Week*, January 28, 2008, p.12; see also www.espnmediazone.com.

Visit **MyMarketingLab** at **www.pearsoned.ca/mymarketinglab** for access to online tutorials, interactive exercises, videos, and much more.

10

New-Product Development and
Product Life-Cycle Strategies

PREVIEWING THE CONCEPTS   In the previous chapter, you learned how marketers manage and develop products and brands. In this chapter, we'll look into two additional product topics: developing new products and managing products through their life cycles. New products are the lifeblood of an organization. However, new-product development is risky, and many new products fail. So the first part of this chapter lays out a process for finding and growing successful new products. Once introduced, marketers want their products to enjoy long and happy lives. In the second part of the chapter, you'll see that every product passes through several life-cycle stages and that each stage poses new challenges requiring different marketing strategies and tactics. Finally, we'll wrap up our product discussion by looking at two additional considerations: social responsibility in product decisions and international product and services marketing.

For openers, consider Apple. More than two decades ago, as an early new-product innovator, Apple got off to a fast and impressive start. But only a decade later, as its creative fires cooled, Apple found itself on the brink of extinction. That set the stage for one of the most remarkable turnarounds in corporate history. Read on to see how Apple's co-founder, Steve Jobs, used lots of innovation and creative new products first to start the company and then to remake it 20 years later.

From the very start, the tale of Apple is a tale of dazzling creativity and customer-driven innovation. Under the leadership of its co-founder and creative genius, Steve Jobs, Apple's very first personal computers, introduced in the late 1970s, stood apart because of their user-friendly look and feel. The company's Macintosh computer, unveiled in 1984, and its LaserWriter printers blazed new trails in desktop computing and publishing, making Apple an early industry leader in both innovation and market share.

But then things took an ugly turn for Apple. In 1985, after tumultuous struggles with the new president he'd hired only a year earlier, Steve Jobs left Apple. With Jobs gone, Apple's creative fires cooled. By the late 1980s, the company's fortunes dwindled as a new wave of PC machines, sporting Intel chips and Microsoft software, swept the market. By the mid- to late-1990s, Apple's sales had plunged to US$5 billion, just 50 percent of previous highs. And its once-commanding share of the personal computer market had dropped to a tiny 2 percent. Even the most ardent Apple fans—the

"Apple is smoking, searing, blisteringly hot, not to mention hip, with a side order of funky—it's the keeper of all things cool."

"MacHeads"—wavered, and the company's days seemed numbered.

Yet Apple has engineered a remarkable turnaround. Last year's sales soared to a record US$24 billion, almost triple the sales just three years earlier. Profits rose a stunning 13-fold in that same three-year period. "To say Apple Computer is hot just doesn't do the company justice," said one analyst. "Apple is smoking, searing, blisteringly hot, not to mention hip, with a side order of funky. . . . Gadget geeks around the world have crowned Apple the keeper of all things cool."

What caused this breathtaking turnaround? Apple rediscovered the magic that had made the company so successful in the first place: customer-driven creativity and new-product innovation. The remarkable makeover began with the return of Steve Jobs in 1997. Since leaving Apple, Jobs had started a new computer company, NeXT. He'd then bought out Pixar Animation Studios, turning it into an entertainment-industry powerhouse. Jobs returned to Apple determined to breathe new creative life and customer focus into the company he'd co-founded 20 years earlier.

Jobs's first task was to revitalize Apple's computer business. For starters, in 1998 Apple launched the iMac personal computer, which featured a sleek, egg-shaped monitor and hard drive all in one unit, in a futuristic translucent turquoise casing. With its one-button Internet access, this machine was designed specifically for cruising the Internet (hence the "i" in "iMac"). The dramatic iMac won raves for design and lured buyers in droves. Within a year, it had sold more than a million units.

Jobs next unleashed Mac OS X, a ground-breaking new Apple operating system that one observer called "the equivalent of a cross between a Porsche and an Abram's tank." OS X served as the launching pad for a new generation of Apple computers and software products. Consider iLife, a bundle of lifestyle applications that comes with every new Mac. It includes applications such as iMovie (for video editing), iDVD (for recording movies, digital-photo slide shows, and music onto TV-playable DVDs), iPhoto (for managing and touching up digital pictures), GarageBand (for making and mixing your own music), iWeb (for creating websites and blogs and getting them online), and iWork (for making presentations and newsletters).

The iMac and Mac OS X put Apple back on the map in personal computing. But Jobs knew that Apple, still a nicher claiming just a 6 percent share of the North American market, would never catch up in computers with dominant competitors such as Dell and HP. Real growth and stardom would require even more creative thinking. And it just doesn't get much more creative than iPod and iTunes, innovations that would utterly change the way people acquire and listen to music.

A music buff himself, Jobs noticed that kids by the millions were using computers and CD writers to download digital songs from then-illegal online services such as Napster, and then burning their own music CDs. He moved quickly to make CD burners standard equipment on all Macs. Then, to help users download music and manage their music databases, Apple's programmers created state-of-the-art jukebox software called iTunes.

Even before iTunes hit the streets, according to Apple watcher Brent Schendler, Jobs "recognized that although storing and playing music on your computer was pretty cool, wouldn't it be even cooler if there was a portable, Walkman-type player that could hold all your digital music so that you could listen to it anywhere?" Less than nine months later, Apple introduced the sleek and sexy iPod. In another 18 months, the iTunes Music Store opened on the Web, enabling consumers to legally download CDs and individual songs.

The results, of course, have been astonishing. The iPod now ranks as one of the greatest consumer electronics hits of all time. By March 2008, Apple had sold more than 119 million iPods, and more than 4 billion songs had been downloaded from the iTunes Store. "We had hoped to sell a million songs in the first six months, but we did that in the first six days," notes an Apple spokesperson. The iPod captures more than 70 percent of the music player market; and Apple's iTunes Store is currently the number-two music store—online or offline—in the world (Walmart is number one).

OBJECTIVES

1. Explain how companies find and develop new-product ideas.

2. List and define the steps in the new-product development process and the major considerations in managing this process.

3. Describe the stages of the product life cycle and how marketing strategies change during the product life cycle.

4. Discuss two additional product issues: socially responsible product decisions and international product and services marketing.

Apple's success is attracting a horde of large, resourceful competitors. To stay ahead, the company must keep its eye on the consumer and continue to innovate. So Apple isn't standing still. Following the debut of its incredibly popular iPhone, Apple has introduced movie rentals via iTunes, which can be watched on an iPod, iPhone, PC, or via Apple TV; MacBook Air, the world's thinnest notebook computer; and Time Capsule, an appliance that automatically and wirelessly backs up everything on your Mac. Apple has also opened more than 200 chic and gleaming Apple Stores, now the world's fastest-growing retail chain. And observers see a host of new products just on or just over the horizon, such as iHome (a magical device that powers all your digital home entertainment devices) and an iPod on wheels (a digital hub that integrates your iPod with your car's entertainment system).

For the third straight year, Apple was named the world's most innovative company in Boston Consulting Group's "Most Innovative Company" survey of 2500 senior executives worldwide. Apple received an amazing 25 percent of the votes, twice the number of runner-up 3M and three times that of third-place Microsoft. The innovative company also topped the most recent *Fortune* magazine list of America's most admired companies.

Thus, almost overnight it seems, Steve Jobs has transformed Apple from a failing niche computer maker to a major force in consumer electronics, digital music and video,

Apple's co-founder, Steve Jobs, used lots of innovation and creative new products first to start the company and then to remake it 20 years later.

and who knows what else in the future. And he's done it through innovation—by helping those around him to "Think Different" (Apple's motto) in their quest to bring value to customers. *Fortune* sums it up this way: "Apple has demonstrated how to create real, breathtaking growth by dreaming up products so new and ingenious that they have upended one industry after another. Jobs's utter dedication to discovery and excellence has created a culture that has made Apple a symbol of innovation. There, innovation is a way of life."[1]

Chapter Opening Discussion

As the Apple story suggests, companies that excel at developing and managing new products reap big rewards. Every product seems to go through a life cycle—it is born, goes through several phases, and eventually dies as newer products come along that create greater value for customers. This product life cycle presents two major challenges. First, because all products eventually decline, a firm must be good at developing new products to replace aging ones (the challenge of *new-product development*). Second, the firm must be good at adapting its marketing strategies in the face of changing tastes, technologies, and competition as products pass through life-cycle stages (the challenge of *product life-cycle strategies*). We look first at the problem of finding and developing new products, and then at the problem of managing them successfully over their life cycles.

Glossary Flashcards of Key Terms

1 NEW-PRODUCT DEVELOPMENT STRATEGY

New-product development
The development of original products, product improvements, product modifications, and new brands through the firm's own product-development efforts.

A firm can obtain new products in two ways. One is through *acquisition*—by buying a whole company, a patent, or a licence to produce someone else's product. The other is through the firm's own **new-product development** efforts. By *new products* we mean original products, product improvements, product modifications, and new brands that the firm develops through its own research and development efforts. In this chapter, we concentrate on new-product development.

Visiting the NewProductWorks is like finding yourself in some nightmare version of a supermarket. Each product failure represents squandered dollars and hopes.

New-product development is the lifeblood of many firms, and Canadians have had a long history as inventors in this process. McIntosh apples, Pablum, frozen fish, and instant mashed potatoes are food products that all originated in Canada. Canadians are responsible for developing such sports and leisure activities as basketball, five-pin bowling, table hockey, Laser sailboats and Laser racing, and Trivial Pursuit. Many Canadian inventors spawned entire industries, such as is the case of Reginald Fessenden, born near Sherbrooke, Quebec, who invented amplitude modulation (AM) radio and transmitted his first broadcast in 1900. Charles Fenerty, with his ability to make paper from wood pulp, founded that industry. Modern air travel was made possible by another Canadian, Wallace Rupert Turnbull, who developed the variable-pitch propeller. Graeme Ferguson, Roman Kroitor, and Robert Kerr launched IMAX in 1968. James Gosling, currently a VP at Sun Microsystems, earned his B.Sc. in computer science at the University of Calgary in 1977 and did the original design of the Java programming language. Mike Lazaridis founded Research In Motion (RIM), best known for the BlackBerry, while he was a student in 1984. Dr. Frank Gunston of Brandon, Manitoba, may have been one of the most philanthropic inventors. After developing and building a total knee-joint replacement, he decided not to patent his invention. This made it freely available to manufacturers and allowed patients needing the joint to benefit quickly from the technology and walk without pain.

New products are important—to both customers and the marketers who serve them. For companies, new products are a key source of growth. For customers, they bring new solutions and variety to their lives. Yet innovation can be very expensive and very risky. New products face tough odds. According to one estimate, 90 percent of all new products fail. Each year, companies lose an estimated US$20 billion to $30 billion on failed food products alone.[2]

Why do so many new products fail? There are several reasons. Although an idea may be good, the company may overestimate market size. The actual product may be poorly designed, or it might be incorrectly positioned, launched at the wrong time, priced too high, or poorly advertised. A high-level executive might push a favourite idea despite poor marketing research findings. Sometimes the costs of product development are higher than expected, and sometimes competitors fight back harder than expected. However, the reasons behind some new-product failures seem pretty obvious. Try the following on for size:

Strolling the aisles at NewProductWorks is like finding yourself in some nightmare version of a supermarket. Most of the over 110 000 products on display were abject flops. Behind each of them are squandered dollars and hopes and the classic question, "What were they thinking?" Some products failed because they simply failed to bring value to customers—for example, Look of Buttermilk Shampoo, Cucumber antiperspirant spray, or Premier smokeless cigarettes. *Smokeless* cigarettes? What were they thinking? Other companies failed because they attached trusted brand names to something totally out of character. Can you imagine swallowing Bengay aspirin? Or how about Gerber Singles food for adults (perhaps the tasty pureed sweet-and-sour pork or chicken Madeira)? Other misbegotten attempts to stretch a good name include Cracker Jack cereal, Exxon fruit punch, Smucker's premium ketchup, Fruit of the Loom laundry detergent, and Harley-Davidson cake-decorating kits. Really, what were they thinking?[3]

Figure 10.1 Major stages in new-product development

2   THE NEW-PRODUCT DEVELOPMENT PROCESS

Companies face a problem—they must develop new products, but the odds weigh heavily against success. In all, to create successful new products a company must understand its consumers, markets, and competitors and develop products that deliver superior value to customers. It must carry out strong new-product planning and set up a systematic, customer-driven *new-product development process* for finding and growing new products. Figure 10.1 shows the eight major steps in this process.

Idea Generation

Idea generation

The systematic search for new-product ideas.

New-product development starts with **idea generation**—the systematic search for new-product ideas. A company typically generates hundreds of ideas, even thousands, to find a few good ones. For example, IBM recently held an "Innovation Jam"—a kind of online suggestion box—in which it invited IBM and customer employees worldwide to submit ideas for new products and services. The mammoth brainstorming session generated some 46 000 ideas from 150 000 people in more than 160 countries over three days. Since the jam fest, however, IBM has whittled down this surge of ideas to only 10 products, businesses, and services that it plans to develop.[4]

Major sources of new-product ideas include internal sources and external sources such as customers, competitors, distributors and suppliers, and others.

Internal Idea Sources

Using *internal sources*, the company can find new ideas through formal research and development. However, in one recent survey, 750 global CEOs reported that only 14 percent of their innovation ideas came from traditional R&D. Instead, 41 percent said the ideas come from employees, and 36 percent said customers.[5]

Thus, companies can pick the brains of employees—from executives to scientists, engineers, manufacturing staff, and salespeople. Using today's new Web 2.0 technology, many companies are making it everybody's business to come up with great ideas. For example, Cisco has set up an internal wiki called Idea Zone (or I-Zone for short) through which any Cisco employee can propose an idea for a new product or comment on or modify someone else's proposed idea. Since its inception, I-Zone has generated more than 400 business ideas, and another 10 000 people

Internal new-product idea sources: Samsung built a special Value Innovation Program Center in which company researchers, engineers, and designers co-mingle to come up with creative new-product ideas.

have added to those ideas. Cisco selects ideas that draw the most activity for further development. So far 12 I-Zone ideas have reached the project stage and four new Cisco business units have been formed.[6]

Some companies have developed successful "intrapreneurial" programs that encourage employees to think up and develop new-product ideas. For example, Samsung built a special Value Innovation Program (VIP) Center in Suwon, South Korea, to encourage and support internal new-product innovation:

> The VIP Center is the total opposite of Samsung's typical office facilities—which feature gray computers on gray desks inside gray walls—where workers adhere to strict Confucian traditions and would never dream of questioning a superior or making a wacky suggestion. Instead, the VIP Center features workrooms, dorm rooms, training rooms, a kitchen, and a basement filled with games, a gym, and a sauna. Grass sprouts from the ceilings, doors are covered with funhouse mirrors, and walls are covered with chalk drawings of ideas. Inside the center, Samsung researchers, engineers, and designers sport Viking and bumblebee hats, play with Elmo toys and inflatable dolphins, and throw around ideas without regard to rank. Recent ideas sprouting from the VIP Center include a 102-inch plasma HDTV and a process to reduce material costs on a multifunction printer by 30 percent. The center has helped Samsung, once known as the maker of cheap knock-off products, become one of the world's most innovative and profitable consumer electronics companies.[7]

External Idea Sources

Companies can also obtain good new-product ideas from any of a number of external sources. For example, *distributors and suppliers* can contribute ideas. Distributors are close to the market and can pass along information about consumer problems and new-product possibilities. Suppliers can tell the company about new concepts, techniques, and materials that can be used to develop new products. *Competitors* are another important source. Companies watch competitors' ads to get clues about their new products. They buy competing new products, take them apart to see how they work, analyze their sales, and decide whether they should bring out a new product of their own. Other idea sources include trade magazines, shows, and seminars; government agencies; advertising agencies; marketing research firms; university and commercial laboratories; and inventors. For example, Bioniche, a Canadian biotech company with operations in Belleville, Ontario, and Montreal, Quebec, sponsors research by university professors to help it generate ideas for new drugs and cancer treatments.

Some companies seek the help of outside new-product consultancies and design firms, such as Ziba, Frog Design, or IDEO, for new-product ideas and designs. For example, when Cranium needed innovative new ideas for extending its popular family board game, it turned to award-winning design firm IDEO. A team of IDEO and Cranium designers worked together to develop a suite of games focused on Cranium's four iconic characters: Word Worm, Creative Cat, Data Head, and Star Performer. The design team began with the core premise that the games should focus on laughter, togetherness, and creativity rather than competition. For inspiration, the team observed people who exemplified the Cranium characters and then tested prototypes in actual game-playing sessions with families. Based on customer insights gained from these observations and interactions, the IDEO–Cranium team developed four popular new character-based games: Tune Twister (Star Performer), Super Showdown (Data Head), Doodle Tales (Creative Cat), and Wacky Words (Word Worm).[8]

Many companies are also turning to online collaborative communities to help solve new-product problems. For example, collaborative network InnoCentive puts its corporate clients ("seekers") in touch with its global network of more than 100 000 scientists ("solvers"). The seeker companies post "challenges," and solvers can earn up to US$100 000 for providing solutions. For instance, P&G used InnoCentive to find a cost-effective way to print the trivia questions on Pringles Prints, snack chips with messages printed on them, dramatically reducing the time and expense of launching its new product.[9] Says P&G's CEO, "Someone outside your organization today knows how to answer your specific question, solve your specific problem, or take advantage of your current opportunity better than you do. You need to find them and find a way to work collaboratively and productively

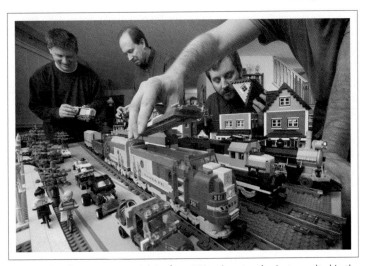

Product ideas from customers: Advice from 250 train-set enthusiasts resulted in the LEGO Santa Fe Super Chief set, a blockbuster new product that sold out in less than two weeks.

with them." It is estimated that 35 percent of P&G's new products today have elements that originated outside the company, up from 15 percent in 2000.[10]

Perhaps the most important source of new-product ideas is *customers* themselves. The company can analyze customer questions and complaints to find new products that better solve consumer problems. For example, Staples developed its Easy Rebate program in response to concerns expressed by small business customers that lost rebates were one of their biggest frustrations.[11]

Company engineers or salespeople can meet with and work alongside customers to get suggestions and ideas. LEGO did just that when it invited 250 LEGO train-set enthusiasts to visit its New York office to assess new designs. "We pooh-poohed them all," says one LEGO fan, an Intel engineer from Portland. But the group gave LEGO lots of new ideas, and the company put them to good use. The result was the Santa Fe Super Chief set. Thanks to word-of-mouth endorsements from the 250 enthusiasts, LEGO sold out the first 10 000 units in less than two weeks with no additional marketing.[12]

Other companies actively solicit ideas from customers and turn customers into co-creators. For example, Dell set up an interactive website forum called IdeaStorm that asks consumers for insights on how to improve its product offering. Users post suggestions, the community votes, and the most popular ideas rise to the top. Only two months after its launch, the site had received some 3850 ideas and 236 000 votes. Michael Dell sees such customer-driven innovation as a key to re-energizing Dell. "We are our best when we are hearing directly from customers," says Dell. "We listen, learn, and then improve and innovate based on what our customers want."[13]

Finally, customers often create new products and uses on their own, and companies can benefit by putting them on the market. For example, for years customers were spreading the word that Avon Skin-So-Soft bath oil and moisturizer was also a terrific bug repellant. Whereas some consumers were content simply to bathe in water scented with the fragrant oil, others carried it in their backpacks to mosquito-infested campsites or kept a bottle on the decks of their beach houses. Avon turned the idea into a complete line of Skin-So-Soft Bug Guard products, including Bug Guard Mosquito Repellant Moisturizing Towelettes and Bug Guard Plus, a combination moisturizer, insect repellant, and sunscreen.[14]

Although customer input on new products yields many benefits, companies must be careful not to rely *too* heavily on what customers say. For some products, especially highly technical ones, customers may not know what they need. "You can't ask people what they want if it's around the next corner," says Apple CEO Steve Jobs. And even when they think they know what they want, adds an innovation management consultant, "merely giving people what they want isn't always enough. People want to be surprised; they want something that's better than they imagined, something that stretches them in what they like."[15]

Idea Screening

Idea screening

Screening new-product ideas to spot good ideas and drop poor ones as soon as possible.

The purpose of idea generation is to create a large number of ideas. The purpose of the succeeding stages is to *reduce* that number. The first idea-reducing stage is **idea screening**, which helps spot good ideas and drop poor ones as soon as possible. Product-development costs rise greatly in later stages, so the company wants to go ahead only with the product ideas that will turn into profitable products.

Many companies require their executives to write up new-product ideas in a standard format that can be reviewed by a new-product committee. The write-up describes the product or service, the proposed customer value proposition, the target market, and the competition. It makes some rough estimates of market size, product price, development time and

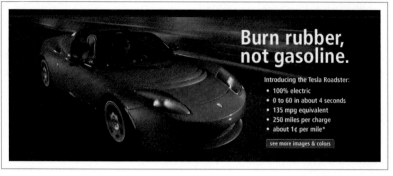

Concept development: The initial Tesla electric car goes from 0 to 90 kilometres per hour in 4 seconds, travels 400 kilometres on a single charge, and costs about a penny a kilometre to power.

costs, manufacturing costs, and rate of return. The committee then evaluates the idea against a set of general criteria.

One marketing expert proposes an R-W-W ("real, win, worth it") new-product screening framework that asks three questions. First, *Is it real?* Is there a real need and desire for the product and will customers buy it? Is there a clear product concept and will the product satisfy the market? Second, *Can we win?* Does the product offer a sustainable competitive advantage? Does the company have the resources to make the product a success? Finally, *Is it worth doing?* Does the product set the company's overall growth strategy? Does it offer sufficient profit potential? The company should be able to answer yes to all three R-W-W questions before developing the new-product idea further.[16]

Concept Development and Testing

Product concept
A detailed version of the new-product idea stated in meaningful consumer terms.

An attractive idea must be developed into a **product concept**. It is important to distinguish between a product idea, a product concept, and a product image. A *product idea* is an idea for a possible product that the company can see itself offering to the market. A *product concept* is a detailed version of the idea stated in meaningful consumer terms. A *product image* is the way consumers perceive an actual or potential product.

Concept Development

Suppose that a car manufacturer has developed a practical battery-powered all-electric car. Its initial prototype is a sleek, sporty convertible that sells for about US$100 000.[17] However, later this decade it plans to introduce more affordable mass-market models that will compete with today's hybrid-powered cars. This 100 percent electric car will accelerate from 0 to 90 kilometres per hour in 4 seconds, travel more than 400 kilometres on a single charge, recharge from a normal 120-volt electrical outlet, and cost about one penny per kilometre to power.

Looking ahead, the marketer's task is to develop this new product into alternative product concepts, find out how attractive each concept is to customers, and choose the best one. It might create the following product concepts for the electric car:

- *Concept 1* An affordably priced midsize car designed as a second family car to be used for running errands and visiting friends around town.

- *Concept 2* A midpriced sporty compact appealing to young singles and couples.

- *Concept 3* A "green" car appealing to environmentally conscious people who want practical, low-polluting transportation.

- *Concept 4* A high-end midsize utility vehicle appealing to those who love the space SUVs provide but lament the poor gas mileage.

Concept Testing

Concept testing
Testing new-product concepts with a group of target consumers to find out if the concepts have strong consumer appeal.

Concept testing calls for testing new-product concepts with groups of target consumers. The concepts may be presented to consumers symbolically or physically. Here, in words, is concept 3:

> An efficient, fun-to-drive, battery-powered compact car that seats four. This 100 percent electric wonder provides practical and reliable transportation with no pollution. It goes more than 400 kilometres on a single charge and costs pennies per kilometre to operate. It's a sensible, responsible alternative to today's pollution-producing gas-guzzlers. It's priced, fully equipped, at US$25 000.

Many firms routinely test new-product concepts with consumers before attempting to turn them into actual new products. For some concept tests, a word or picture description might be sufficient. However, a more concrete and physical presentation of the concept will increase the reliability of the concept test. After being exposed to the concept, consumers then may be asked to react to it by answering questions such as those in Table 10.1. The answers to such questions will help the company decide which concept has the strongest appeal. For example, the last question asks about the consumer's intention to buy. Suppose 2 percent of consumers say they "definitely" would buy, and another 5 percent say "probably." The company could project these figures to the full population in this target group to estimate sales volume. Even then, the estimate is uncertain because people do not always carry out their stated intentions.

Marketing Strategy Development

Suppose the car maker finds that concept 3 for the electric car tests best. The next step is **marketing strategy development**, designing an initial marketing strategy for introducing this car to the market.

The *marketing strategy statement* consists of three parts. The first part describes the target market; the planned value proposition; and the sales, market share, and profit goals for the first few years:

> The target market is younger, well-educated, moderate- to high-income individuals, couples, or small families seeking practical, environmentally responsible transportation. The car will be positioned as more fun to drive and less polluting than today's internal combustion engine or hybrid cars. The company will aim to sell 100 000 cars in the first year at a loss of not more than US$15 million. In the second year, the company will aim for sales of 120 000 cars and a profit of US$25 million.

The second part of the marketing strategy statement outlines the product's planned price, distribution, and marketing budget for the first year:

> The battery-powered electric car will be offered in three colours—red, white, and blue—and will have a full set of accessories as standard features. It will sell at a retail price of US$25 000—with 15 percent off the list price to dealers. Dealers who sell more than 10 cars per month will get an additional discount of 5 percent on each car sold that month. A marketing budget of US$50 million will be split 50–50 between a national media campaign and local event marketing. Advertising and website will emphasize the car's fun spirit and low emissions. During the first year, US$100 000 will be spent on marketing research to find out who is buying the car and their satisfaction levels.

Marketing strategy development
Designing an initial marketing strategy for a new product based on the product concept.

Table 10.1 Questions for Battery-Powered Electric Car Concept Test

1.   Do you understand the concept of a battery-powered electric car?

2.   Do you believe the claims about the car's performance?

3.   What are the major benefits of the battery-powered electric car compared with a conventional car?

4.   What are its advantages compared with a gas–electric hybrid car?

5.   What improvements in the car's features would you suggest?

6.   For what uses would you prefer a battery-powered electric car to a conventional car?

7.   What would be a reasonable price to charge for the car?

8.   Who would be involved in your decision to buy such a car? Who would drive it?

9.   Would you buy such a car (definitely, probably, probably not, definitely not)?

The third part of the marketing strategy statement describes the planned long-run sales, profit goals, and marketing mix strategy:

> We intend to capture a 3 percent long-run share of the total auto market and realize an after-tax return on investment of 15 percent. To achieve this, product quality will start high and be improved over time. Price will be raised in the second and third years if competition permits. The total marketing budget will be raised each year by about 10 percent. Marketing research will be reduced to US$60 000 per year after the first year.

Business Analysis

Business analysis
A review of the sales, costs, and profit projections for a new product to find out whether these factors satisfy the company's objectives.

Once management has decided on its product concept and marketing strategy, it can evaluate the business attractiveness of the proposal. **Business analysis** involves a review of the sales, costs, and profit projections for a new product to find out whether they satisfy the company's objectives. If they do, the product can move to the product development stage.

To estimate sales, the company might look at the sales history of similar products and conduct market surveys. It can then estimate minimum and maximum sales to assess the range of risk. After preparing the sales forecast, management can estimate the expected costs and profits for the product, including marketing, R&D, operations, accounting, and finance costs. The company then uses the sales and costs figures to analyze the new product's financial attractiveness.

Product Development

Product development
Developing the product concept into a physical product to ensure that the product idea can be turned into a workable market offering.

So far, for many new-product concepts, the product may have existed only as a word description, a drawing, or perhaps a crude mock-up. If the product concept passes the business test, it moves into **product development**. Here, R&D or engineering develops the product concept into a physical product. The product development step, however, now calls for a large jump in investment. It will show whether the product idea can be turned into a workable product.

The R&D department will develop and test one or more physical versions of the product concept. R&D hopes to design a prototype that will satisfy and excite consumers and that can be produced quickly and at budgeted costs. Developing a successful prototype can take days, weeks, months, or even years depending on the product and prototype methods.

Often, products undergo rigorous tests to make sure they perform safely and effectively, or that consumers will find value in them. Companies can do their own product testing or outsource testing to other firms that specialize in testing. Here are some examples of such product tests:[18]

> Thunk. Thunk. Thunk. Behind a locked door in the basement of Louis Vuitton's elegant Paris headquarters, a mechanical arm hoists a brown-and-tan handbag a half-meter off the floor—then drops it. The bag, loaded with an 8-pound weight, will be lifted and dropped, over and over again, for four days. This is Vuitton's test laboratory, a high-tech torture chamber for its fabled luxury goods. Another piece of lab equipment bombards handbags with ultraviolet rays to test resistance to fading. Still another tests zippers by tugging them open and shutting them 5000 times. There's even a mechanized mannequin hand, with a Vuitton charm bracelet around its wrist, being shaken vigorously to make sure none of the charms fall off.
>
> At Gillette, almost everyone gets involved in new-product testing. Every working day at Gillette, 200 volunteers from various departments come to work unshaven, troop to the second floor of the company's gritty South Boston plant, and enter small booths with a sink and mirror. There they take instructions from technicians on the other side of a small window as to which razor, shaving cream, or aftershave to use. The volunteers evaluate razors for sharpness of blade, smoothness of glide, and ease of handling. In a nearby shower room, women perform the same ritual on their legs, underarms, and what the company delicately refers to as the "bikini area." "We bleed so you'll get a good shave at home," says one Gillette employee.

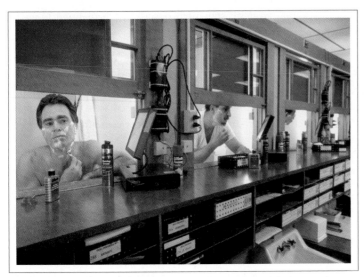

Product testing: Gillette uses employee-volunteers to test new shaving products—"We bleed so you'll get a good shave at home," says one Gillette employee.

Test marketing
The stage of new-product development in which the product and marketing program are tested in realistic market settings.

A new product must have the required functional features and also convey the intended psychological characteristics. The battery-powered electric car, for example, should strike consumers as being well built, comfortable, and safe. Management must learn what makes consumers decide that a car is well built. To some consumers, this means that the car has "solid-sounding" doors. To others, it means that the car is able to withstand heavy impact in crash tests. Consumer tests are conducted in which consumers test-drive the car and rate its attributes.

Test Marketing

If the product passes concept and product tests, the next step is **test marketing**, the stage at which the product and marketing program are introduced into realistic market settings. Test marketing gives the marketer experience with marketing the product before going to the great expense of full introduction. It lets the company test the product and its entire marketing program—targeting and positioning strategy, advertising, distribution, pricing, branding and packaging, and budget levels. Cadbury Beverages Canada, for example, uses Ontario as a test market for new Schweppes and Crush branded products that will eventually be rolled out to the entire North American market.

The amount of test marketing needed varies with each new product. Test marketing costs can be high, and it takes time that may allow competitors to gain advantages. When the costs of developing and introducing the product are low, or when management is already confident about the new product, the company may do little or no test marketing. In fact, test marketing by consumer-goods firms has been declining in recent years. Companies often do not test-market simple line extensions or copies of successful competitor products.

However, when introducing a new product requires a big investment, when the risks are high, or when management is not sure of the product or marketing program, a company may do a lot of test marketing. For instance, KFC has introduced a major new product—Kentucky Grilled Chicken. Although the fast-food chain built its legacy on serving crispy, seasoned fried chicken, it hopes that the new product will lure back health-conscious consumers who dropped fried chicken from their diets. "This is transformational for our brand," says KFC's chief food innovation officer. Given the importance of the decision, KFC conducted more than three years of product and market testing before rolling Kentucky Grilled Chicken out. Test marketing in Quebec and Ontario began in the summer of 2009, and the product rolled out across the country later that year. "You might say, 'what took you so long,'" says the chain's president. "I've asked that question a couple of times myself. The answer is we had to get it right."[19]

Although test marketing costs can be high, they are often small when compared with the costs of making a major mistake. Still, test marketing doesn't guarantee success. For example, Procter & Gamble tested its Fit produce rinse heavily for five years. Although market tests suggested the product would be successful, P&G pulled the plug on it shortly after its introduction.[20]

When using test marketing, consumer products companies usually choose one of three approaches—standard test markets, controlled test markets, or simulated test markets.

Standard Test Markets

Using standard test markets, the company finds a small number of representative test cities, conducts a full marketing campaign in those cities, and uses store audits, consumer and distributor surveys, and other measures to gauge product performance. The results are

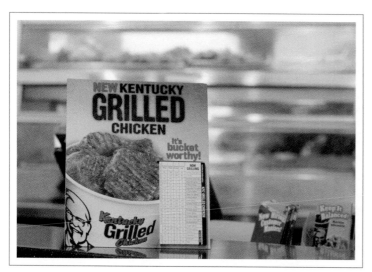

Test marketing: KFC test marketed its new Kentucky Grilled Chicken product for three years before rolling it out nationally. Says the chain's president, "We had to get it right."

used to forecast national sales and profits, discover potential product problems, and fine-tune the marketing program.

Standard test markets have some drawbacks. They can be very costly and they may take a long time. Moreover, competitors can monitor test market results or interfere with them by cutting their prices in test cities, by increasing their promotion, or even by buying up the product being tested. Finally, test markets give competitors a look at the company's new product well before it is introduced nationally. Thus, competitors may have time to develop defensive strategies, and may even beat the company's product to the market.

Despite these disadvantages, standard test markets are still the most widely used approach for major in-market testing. However, many companies today are shifting toward quicker and cheaper controlled and simulated test marketing methods.

Controlled Test Markets

Several research firms keep controlled panels of stores that have agreed to carry new products for a fee. Controlled test marketing systems such as ACNielsen's Scantrack and IRI's BehaviorScan track individual consumer behaviour for new products from the television set to the checkout counter.

In each BehaviorScan market, IRI maintains a panel of shoppers who report all of their purchases by showing an identification card at checkout in participating stores and by using a handheld scanner at home to record purchases at nonparticipating stores. Within test stores, IRI controls such factors as shelf placement, price, and in-store promotions for the product being tested. IRI also measures TV viewing in each panel household and sends special commercials to panel member television sets to test their effect on shopping decisions. Direct-mail promotions can also be tested.[21]

Detailed scanner information on each consumer's purchases is fed into a central computer where it is combined with the consumer's demographic and TV viewing information and reported daily. Thus, BehaviorScan can provide store-by-store, week-by-week reports on the sales of tested products. Such panel purchasing data enables in-depth diagnostics not possible with retail point-of-sale data alone, including repeat purchase analysis, buyer demographics, and earlier, more accurate sales forecasts after just 12 to 24 weeks in market. Most importantly, the system allows companies to evaluate their specific marketing efforts.

Controlled test markets, such as BehaviorScan, usually cost less than standard test markets. Also, because retail distribution is "forced" in the first week of the test, controlled test markets can be completed much more quickly than standard test markets. As in standard test markets, controlled test markets allow competitors to get a look at the company's new product. And some companies are concerned that the limited number of controlled test markets used by the research services may not be representative of their products' markets or target consumers. However, the research firms are experienced in projecting test market results to broader markets and can usually account for biases in the test markets used.

Simulated Test Markets

Companies can also test new products in a simulated shopping environment. The company or research firm shows ads and promotions for a variety of products, including the new product being tested, to a sample of consumers. It gives consumers a small amount of money and invites them to a real or laboratory store where they may keep the money or use it to buy items. The researchers note how many consumers buy the new product and competing brands.

New test marketing technologies: Frito Lay worked with research firm Decision Insight to create an online virtual convenience store in which to test new products and marketing ideas.

This simulation provides a measure of trial and the commercial's effectiveness against competing commercials. The researchers then ask consumers the reasons for their purchase or nonpurchase. Some weeks later, they interview the consumers by phone to determine product attitudes, usage, satisfaction, and repurchase intentions. Using sophisticated computer models, the researchers then project national sales from results of the simulated test market. Recently, some marketers have begun to use interesting new high-tech approaches, such as virtual reality and the Internet, to simulated-test-market research.

Simulated test markets overcome some of the disadvantages of standard and controlled test markets. They usually cost much less, can be run in eight weeks, and keep the new product out of competitors' view. Yet, because of their small samples and simulated shopping environments, many marketers do not think that simulated test markets are as accurate or reliable as larger, real-world tests. Still, simulated test markets are used widely, often as "pretest" markets. Because they are fast and inexpensive, they can be run in order to quickly assess a new product or its marketing program.

Many marketers are now using new simulated test marketing technologies to reduce the costs of test marketing and to speed up the process. For example, Frito Lay worked with research firm Decision Insight to create an online virtual convenience store in which to test new products and marketing ideas.

> Decision Insight's SimuShop online shopping environment lets Frito Lay's marketers test shopper reactions to different extensions, shelf placements, pricing, and packaging of its Lay's, Doritos, Cheetos, and Fritos brands in a variety of store setups without investing huge amounts of time and money on actual in-store research in different locations. Recruited shoppers visit the online store, browse realistic virtual shelves featuring Frito Lay's and competing products, click on individual products to view them in more detail, and select products to put in their carts. When the shopping is done, selected customers are questioned in one-on-one, on-screen interviews about why they chose the products they did. Watching the entire decision process unfold gives Frito Lay marketers reams of information about what would happen in the real world. With 200-some bags of Frito Lay products sitting on a typical store shelf, the company doesn't have the luxury of test marketing in actual market settings. "For us, that can only really be done virtually," says a Frito Lay marketer. The SimuShop tests produce a 90 percent or better correlation to real shopper behaviour when compared with later real-world data.[22]

Commercialization

Commercialization

Introducing a new product into the market.

Test marketing gives management the information needed to make a final decision about whether to launch the new product. If the company goes ahead with **commercialization**—introducing the new product into the market—it will face high costs. The company may need to build or rent a manufacturing facility. And, in the case of

Commercialization: Microsoft launched its new Windows Vista operating system in a swift global rollout. Its mammoth "Wow" advertising blitz hit more than 30 markets worldwide simultaneously, creating some 6.6 billion global impressions in just its first two months.

a major new consumer packaged good, it may spend hundreds of millions of dollars for advertising, sales promotion, and other marketing efforts in the first year. For example, when Unilever introduced its Sunsilk hair care line, it spent US$200 million in the United States alone, including US$30 million for nontraditional media such as MySpace ads and profiles, mall displays that used audio to catch the attention of passersby, 3-D ads in tavern bathrooms, and cinema ads.[23]

The company launching a new product must first decide on introduction *timing*. If the car maker's new battery-powered electric car will eat into the sales of the company's other cars, its introduction may be delayed. If the car can be improved further, or if the economy is down, the company may wait until the following year to launch it. However, if competitors are ready to introduce their own battery-powered models, the company may push to introduce its car sooner.

Next, the company must decide *where* to launch the new product—in a single location, a region, the national market, or the international market. Few companies have the confidence, capital, and capacity to launch new products into full national or international distribution right away. Instead, they develop a planned *market rollout* over time.

Some companies, however, may quickly introduce new models into the full national market. For example, in March 2009 Kraft Canada launched Kraft Dinner Crackers—macaroni-shaped crackers with the taste of the original KD—across the country. Targeting the 6–12-year-old lunchbox demographic, Kraft Canada launched a nationwide promotion with YTV that included prizes and online sponsorships. "We know the cheese cracker category is growing," says Chetan Dhole, KD brand manager, about the decision to launch the new product in March. "We're leveraging the great iconic brand that we have in Canada around KD. . . to be able to bring consumers that experience and occasion any time of the day." Kraft Canada also plans to target moms through *What's Cooking* magazine's million plus readers across Canada as well as in-store sampling and on-box promotions.[24]

Companies with international distribution systems may introduce new products through swift global rollouts. Microsoft recently did this with its Windows Vista operating system. Microsoft used a mammoth advertising blitz to launch Vista simultaneously in more than 30 markets worldwide. The campaign targeted 6.6 billion global impressions in just its first two months. "There won't be a PC sold anywhere in the world that doesn't have Vista within the next six months," said an industry analyst at the start of the campaign.[25]

MANAGING NEW-PRODUCT DEVELOPMENT

The new-product development process shown in Figure 10.1 highlights the important activities needed to find, develop, and introduce new products. However, new-product development involves more than just going through a set of steps. Companies must take a holistic approach to managing this process. Successful new-product development requires a customer-centred, team-based, and systematic effort.

Customer-Centred New-Product Development

Above all else, new-product development must be customer-centred. When looking for and developing new products, companies often rely too heavily on technical research in their R&D labs. But like everything else in marketing, successful new-product development begins with a thorough understanding of what consumers need and value. **Customer-centred new-product development** focuses on finding new ways to solve customer problems and create more customer-satisfying experiences.

Customer-centred new-product development
New-product development that focuses on finding new ways to solve customer problems and create more customer-satisfying experiences.

One recent study found that the most successful new products are ones that are differentiated, solve major customer problems, and offer a compelling customer value proposition. Another study showed that companies that directly engage their customers in the new-product innovation process had twice the return on assets and triple the growth in operating income of firms that don't.[26]

For products ranging from consumer packaged goods to power tools, today's innovative companies are getting out of the research lab and mingling with customers in the search for new customer value. Consider this example:

> Engineers and marketers from Black & Decker's DeWalt division—the division that makes power tools used by professional contractors—spend a great deal of time at job sites, generating ideas by talking to end users and observing how they work. Then, once prototypes of new products have been completed, those same people take them directly to the same job sites, leave the tools, and come back a week or so later to collect information on how they perform. Thanks to its strong customer focus, DeWalt now captures a more than 50 percent share of the North American professional power tool market.
>
> John Schiech, president of the DeWalt division, tells a valuable story about the importance of paying close attention to customers. "The best-selling miter saws on the market in the early 1990s cost about US$199, and they all had 10-inch blades. Our guys went out and did some research and found a lot of people building big colonial-style homes with big mouldings. Saw blades cut only half way through those big pieces of trim, so they had to pass a 16-foot piece of moulding out the window, flip it around, pass it back in, and make the rest of the cut. We realized that if we moved to a 12-inch blade, which required a completely different, much bigger saw, they could make these cuts in one pass. So we developed and launched a 12-inch miter saw, and charged US$399. It became the number-one-selling miter saw by a huge margin, and remains so to this day." When asked what makes his company so successful, Schiech summarized: "It's engineers and marketing product managers spending hours and hours on job sites talking to the guys who are trying to make their living with these tools."[27]

Thus, customer-centred new-product development begins and ends with solving customer problems (see Real Marketing 10.1 for a great example). As one expert asks: "What is innovation, after all, if not products and services that offer fresh thinking in a way that meets the needs of customers?"[28] Says another expert, "Getting consumer insights at the beginning of the process, using those insights consistently and respectfully throughout the process, and communicating them in a compelling form when you go to market is critical to a product's success in the market these days."[29]

Team-Based New-Product Development

Good new-product development also requires a total-company, cross-functional effort. Some companies organize their new-product development process into the orderly sequence of steps shown in Figure 10.1, starting with idea generation and ending with commercialization. Under this *sequential product development* approach, one company department works individually to complete its stage of the process before passing the new product along to the next department and stage. This orderly, step-by-step process can help bring control to complex and risky projects. But it also can be dangerously slow. In fast-changing, highly competitive markets, such slow-but-sure product development can result in product failures, lost sales and profits, and crumbling market positions.

Real Marketing 10.1

IDEO's Design Approach: Putting Customers First

IDEO, North America's hottest industrial design firm, has won countless awards for innovative product design. Its diverse roster of clients has included companies ranging from Apple, Microsoft, Marriott, Caterpillar, and Procter & Gamble to Boston Beer, Lufthansa, Mayo Clinic, and the Red Cross. IDEO's design teams came up with the first laptop computer; the first Apple mouse; the industry-changing, sleek and elegant Palm V PDA; and even Crest's first stand-up toothpaste tube.

But it's not so much IDEO's innovative designs that make it stand out. It's IDEO's design process. In designing new products, IDEO doesn't

Customer-centred new-product development: With the help of design firm IDEO, Shimano and bicycle makers like Trek learned that people didn't want better bikes, they wanted better biking experiences. The result: industry-changing "coasting" bikes that are simple, comfortable, and fun to use.

start with engineers working in design labs. It starts with customers. And it doesn't just design products, it designs customer product experiences. At the start of every design project, IDEO's "human factors" teams conduct "deep dives" into consumer behaviour. The design teams shadow customers, get to know them deeply, and analyze the intricacies of their product-use experiences. "Tech companies design from the inside out," says an IDEO executive. "We design from the outside in so that we can put customers first."

IDEO's work with bicycle components maker Shimano illustrates its customer-centred design approach. Shimano sells bike parts—gears, crank arms, derailleurs, and so on— to most of the world's major bicycle manufacturers. If you own a high-end bike, chances are good that it contains several Shimano parts. But in 2006, Shimano faced a problem. Bicycle manufacturers were selling fewer bikes, so Shimano was selling fewer parts.

U.S. bicycle sales had been flat for nearly a decade. Worse, the number of people riding bikes was actually declining. The proportion of North American bike riders over the age of seven who rode a bike at least six times per year plunged more than 17 percent in 2006 versus 2005, part of a more than 33 percent drop over the prior decade. About the only thing propping up the bicycle industry was the blip in sales of high-margin, top-of-the-line bikes following Lance

Armstrong's incredible string of seven Tour de France victories. The industry began to focus more heavily on developing the ever-more sophisticated—and ever-more expensive— bikes coveted by hard-core cycling enthusiasts. But Shimano knew that the surge in top-end sales couldn't last. The industry had to find a way to get more of North America's nonbikers back in the saddle.

So Shimano turned to IDEO for help. IDEO's challenge? Design a premium bike that would get North Americans— especially baby boomers and older Gen Xers—riding again. But IDEO didn't follow the usual industry design process— using computer models to turn out great-looking new high-tech marvels and then testing them out on bike riding enthusiasts. Instead, IDEO began by sending its design team into the homes of people who don't ride bikes.

IDEO's social scientists and designers, accompanied by Shimano's marketers and engineers, spent months observing and meeting with nonriders in Atlanta, Chicago, Phoenix, and San Francisco, talking in depth about their leisure activities and their thoughts about biking. These deep customer interactions yielded rich insights into why people have stopped riding bikes. According to one account:

> It wasn't so much that they were out of shape, or too busy or lazy. It was because cycling had become

intimidating, something for hard-core athletes who love all the technical minutiae. "Everything had changed in bicycling," says a senior Shimano marketing executive. "It had gone from fun to being a sport, and no one [in the industry] had noticed." For boomers, bikes changed from the 10-speed rides on steel frame bikes to 30-speed carbon fibre and titanium machines. Costs rose from a few hundred dollars to thousands. Handlebars, pedals, tires, even seats came in so many varieties that consumers got overwhelmed. Expensive helmets, special shoes, and tight-fitting spandex clothes simply didn't appeal to recreational riders. And bike shops, filled with workers who fawned over gear, had little time for customers interested in just plain bikes.

Still, IDEO concluded, there was hope for Shimano and the bicycle manufacturers. "Everyone we talked to, as soon as we talked about bikes, a [nostalgic] smile came to their face," says an IDEO researcher. That nostalgia gave IDEO and Shimano an opening. People didn't want better bikes. They wanted a better biking experience, one that took them back to their memories of riding a bike as a kid.

Based on these customer insights, IDEO and Shimano came up with the concept of a "coasting" bike—a bicycle with a classic look that is simple, comfortable, and fun to use. Shimano built a prototype and sold the concept to three top bike manufacturers—Giant, Raleigh, and Trek. Coasting bikes are designed to create the ideal casual biking experience. They feature a traditional heads-up riding position, wide and comfortable seats, a chain guard to keep grease off the cyclist's pants, and old-fashioned coaster brakes that stop when you pedal backwards. The coasting bikes are high-tech—for example, they come equipped with computer-controlled automatic gear shifting. But the technology remains hidden behind soft and familiar contours.

At first, it took some selling to convince the big bike makers to buy into the coasting concept:

The first Shimano prototype was unlike anything on the market, with rounded chrome hubs on the wheels, a swoopy curved frame, and handlebars with loops in them big enough to set a coffee cup inside. The cushy seat flipped up to reveal a mini-trunk to store a cellphone. "It was kind of like Audi meets Dr. Seuss," says a Raleigh executive. "Shimano thought this was the next big thing, and we were like, 'Is it?'"

However, Trek, Raleigh, and Giant soon embraced the idea and rolled out their first lines of coasting bikes in the spring of 2007, supported by a 15-city Shimano marketing campaign. The launch created more excitement than anything most industry insiders can remember. Surprised bicycle retailers soon found noncyclists making their way into their stores, and the three manufacturers quickly sold out of their 2007 inventories. By 2008, seven additional bicycle manufacturers had added the new old-fashioned coasting bikes to their lines.

The new designs appear to have hit the high-end casual biking market spot-on. "The automatic shifting [has really resonated] with customers," says one bicycle shop owner. "Shimano is onto something." Importantly, coasting bikes may help to reinvigorate the stagnant bicycle industry by pulling new types of buyers in the door—recreational buyers like Alice Wilkes:

This summer, cyclists in skintight shorts raced through the French countryside in the annual Tour de France. The winner rode to victory on a Trek Madone 6.9 Pro that would cost consumers US$8249.99. Alice Wilkes also bought a Trek bike this summer, but she had a very different experience. Wilkes bought a Trek Lime, which shifts automatically so riders don't have to fuss with gears, stops when cyclists pedal backwards (like in the old days), and has a big, comfy seat. It retails for US$589.99. With her new bike, the first one she has owned in 40 years, Wilkes hits the trails near her Lynchburg, Virginia, home. For Wilkes, it's not about speed and performance. "Tight cycling clothes—that's not my world," says the 55-year-old grandmother. "I like to feel free, with the wind flying up my sleeves."

Despite their initial success, it remains to be seen whether coasting bikes will be real industry-changers or just a passing fad. But whatever happens, IDEO's customer-driven design ideas are opening eyes in the traditionally myopic bicycle industry. IDEO knows that bike riding has never really been about the bikes themselves. In the end, it's about customer biking experiences. For the past decade, the Lance Armstrongs of the world have had theirs. And now, thanks to IDEO and Shimano, the Alice Wilkeses have theirs as well.

Sources: Extracts, quotes, and other information from Matt Wiebe, "Retailers Worry over Future Coasting Sales," *Bicycle Retailer and Industry News*, March 15, 2008, pp. 1, 2; Jay Green, "Return of the Easy Rider," *BusinessWeek*, September 17, 2007, p. 78; Philip Kotler and Kevin Lane Keller, *Marketing Management,* 13th edition (Upper Saddle River, NJ: Prentice Hall, 2008), p. 105; Jessi Hempel, "Bringing Design to Blue Chips," *Fortune*, November 12, 2007, p. 32; and www.coasting.com, October 2008.

To get their new products to market more quickly, many companies use a **team-based new-product development** approach. Under this approach, company departments work closely together in cross-functional teams, overlapping the steps in the product-development process to save time and increase effectiveness. Instead of passing the new product from department to department, the company assembles a team of people from various departments that stays with the new product from start to finish. Such teams

Team-based new-product development
An approach to developing new products in which various company departments work closely together, overlapping the steps in the product-development process to save time and increase effectiveness.

usually include people from the marketing, finance, design, manufacturing, and legal departments, and even supplier and customer companies. In the sequential process, a bottle-neck at one phase can seriously slow the entire project. In the team-based approach, if one area hits snags, it works to resolve them while the team moves on.

The team-based approach does have some limitations. For example, it sometimes creates more organizational tension and confusion than the more orderly sequential approach. However, in rapidly changing industries facing increasingly shorter product life cycles, the rewards of fast and flexible product development far exceed the risks. Companies that combine a customer-centred approach with team-based new-product development gain a big competitive edge by getting the right new products to market faster.

Systematic New-Product Development

Finally, the new-product development process should be holistic and systematic rather than compartmentalized and haphazard. Otherwise, few new ideas will surface, and many good ideas will sputter and die. To avoid these problems, a company can install an *innovation management system* to collect, review, evaluate, and manage new-product ideas.

The company can appoint a respected senior person to be the company's innovation manager. It can set up web-based idea management software and encourage all company stakeholders—employees, suppliers, distributors, dealers—to become involved in finding and developing new products. It can assign a cross-functional innovation management committee to evaluate proposed new-product ideas and help bring good ideas to market. It can create recognition programs to reward those who contribute the best ideas.

The innovation management system approach yields two favourable outcomes. First, it helps create an innovation-oriented company culture. It shows that top management supports, encourages, and rewards innovation. Second, it will yield a larger number of new-product ideas, among which will be some especially good ones. The good new ideas will be more systematically developed, producing more new-product successes. No longer will good ideas wither for the lack of a sounding board or a senior product advocate.

Thus, new-product success requires more than simply thinking up a few good ideas, turning them into products, and finding customers for them. It requires a holistic approach for finding new ways to create valued customer experiences, from generating and screening new-product ideas to creating and rolling out want-satisfying products to customers.

More than this, successful new-product development requires a whole-company commitment. At companies known for their new-product prowess—such as Google, Apple, IDEO, 3M, Procter & Gamble, and General Electric—the entire culture encourages, supports, and rewards innovation. Consider Google, which recently topped *Fast Company* magazine's list of the world's most innovative companies, and which regularly ranks among everyone else's top two or three innovators. Google is spectacularly successful. Despite formidable competition from giants such as Microsoft and Yahoo!, Google's share in its core business—online search—has climbed to a decisive 56 percent. Google is also wildly innovative. But at Google, innovation is more than a process—it's part of the company's DNA.

Google's famously chaotic innovation process has unleashed a flurry of diverse products, ranging from a blog search engine (Google Blog Search), an email service (Gmail), an online

Google is both spectacularly successful and wildly innovative. At Google, innovation is more than just a process—it's in the air, in the spirit of the place.

payment service (Google Checkout), and a news portal (Google News) to a universal platform for mobile-phone applications (Google Android) and projects for mapping and exploring the world (Google Maps and Google Earth). Talk to Googlers at various levels and departments and one powerful theme emerges: Whether they're designing search engines for the blind or preparing meals for their colleagues, these people feel that their work can change the world. The marvel of Google is its ability to continue to instill a sense of creative fearlessness and ambition in its employees. Prospective hires are often asked, "If you could change the world using Google's resources, what would you build?" But here, this isn't a goofy or even theoretical question: Google wants to know, because thinking—and building—on that scale is what Google does. This, after all, is the company that wants to make available online every page of every book ever published. Smaller-gauge ideas die of disinterest. When it comes to innovation, Google *is* different. But the difference isn't tangible. It's in the air, in the spirit of the place.[30]

3   PRODUCT LIFE-CYCLE STRATEGIES

After launching the new product, management wants the product to enjoy a long and happy life. Although it does not expect the product to sell forever, the company wants to earn a decent profit to cover all the effort and risk that went into launching it. Management is aware that each product will have a life cycle, although its exact shape and length are not known in advance.

Product life cycle
The course of a product's sales and profits over its lifetime. It involves five distinct stages: product development, introduction, growth, maturity, and decline.

Figure 10.2 shows a typical **product life cycle** (PLC), the course that a product's sales and profits take over its lifetime. The product life cycle has five distinct stages:

1. *Product development* begins when the company finds and develops a new-product idea. During product development, sales are zero and the company's investment costs mount.

2. *Introduction* is a period of slow sales growth as the product is introduced in the market. Profits are nonexistent in this stage because of the heavy expenses of product introduction.

3. *Growth* is a period of rapid market acceptance and increasing profits.

4. *Maturity* is a period of slowdown in sales growth because the product has achieved acceptance by most potential buyers. Profits level off or decline because of increased marketing outlays to defend the product against competition.

5. *Decline* is the period when sales fall off and profits drop.

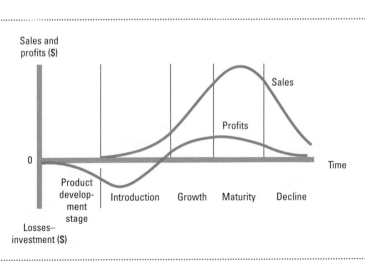

Figure 10.2 Sales and profits over the product's life from inception to decline

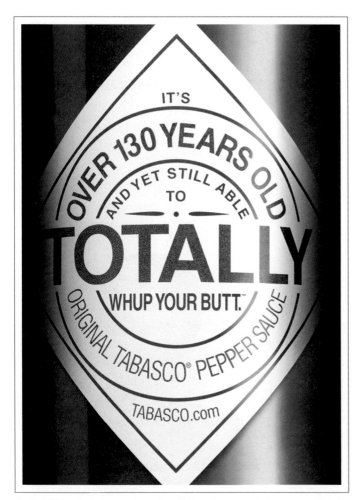

Product life cycle: Some products die quickly; others stay in the mature stage for a long, long time. TABASCO sauce is "over 130 years old and yet still able to totally whup your butt!"

Not all products follow this product life cycle. Some products are introduced and die quickly, as is the case for fads. For example, many of the carbohydrate-reduced products introduced when the Atkins diet was "hot" met an untimely demise. Other products stay in the mature stage for a long, long time. Companies and their products such as the Hudson's Bay Co. (founded in 1798), Waterford Crystal (1783), Levi's (1850), and Campbell's (1869) have stood the test of time and continue to hold a dominant place in their categories. Some products enter the decline stage and are then cycled back into the growth stage through strong promotion or repositioning. It seems that a well-managed brand could live forever.

The PLC concept can describe a *product class* (gasoline-powered automobiles), a *product form* (SUVs), or a *brand* (the Ford Escape). The PLC concept applies differently in each case. Product classes have the longest life cycles—the sales of many product classes stay in the mature stage for a long time. Product forms, in contrast, tend to have the standard PLC shape. Product forms such as "dial telephones" and "VHS tapes" passed through a regular history of introduction, rapid growth, maturity, and decline.

A specific brand's life cycle can change quickly because of changing competitive attacks and responses. For example, although laundry soaps (product class) and powdered detergents (product form) have enjoyed fairly long life cycles, the life cycles of specific brands have tended to be much shorter. Today's leading brands of powdered laundry soap are Tide and Cheer; the leading brands 75 years ago were Fels-Naptha, Octagon, and Kirkman.

The PLC concept can be applied by marketers as a useful framework for describing how products and markets work. And when used carefully, the PLC concept can help in developing good marketing strategies for different stages of the product life cycle. But using the PLC concept for forecasting product performance or for developing marketing strategies presents some practical problems. For example, in practice, it is difficult to forecast the sales level at each PLC stage, the length of each stage, and the shape of the PLC curve. Using the PLC concept to develop marketing strategy also can be difficult because strategy is both a cause and a result of the product's life cycle. The product's current PLC position suggests the best marketing strategies, and the resulting marketing strategies affect product performance in later life-cycle stages.

Moreover, marketers should not blindly push products through the traditional stages of the product life cycle. "As marketers instinctively embrace the old life-cycle paradigm, they needlessly consign their products to following the curve into maturity and decline," notes one marketing professor. Instead, marketers often defy the "rules" of the life cycle and position their products in unexpected ways. By doing this, "companies can rescue products foundering in the maturity phase of their life cycles and return them to the growth phase. And they can catapult new products forward into the growth phase, leapfrogging obstacles that could slow consumers' acceptance."[31]

The moral of the product life cycle is that companies must continually innovate or they risk extinction. No matter how successful its current product lineup, for future success a company must skilfully manage the life cycles of existing products. And to grow, it must develop a steady stream of new products that bring new value to customers (see Real Marketing 10.2).

Real Marketing 10.2

Kraft: Lots of Good Old Products; Too Few Good New Ones?

Kraft makes and markets an incredible portfolio of known and trusted brands, including half a dozen US$1 billion brands and another 50 that top US$100 million in sales. Beyond the Kraft label of cheeses, snacks, dips, and dressings, its megabrands include the likes of Oscar Mayer, Post cereals, Delissio Pizza, Maxwell House Coffee, JELL-O, Cool Whip, Kool-Aid, A1 steak sauce, Velveeta, Planters, Miracle Whip, Light 'n Lively, Grey Poupon, Capri Sun, and Nabisco (which includes Oreo, Chips Ahoy!, Triscuit, SnackWells, and a whole lot more). Search North America's pantries and you'll find at least one Kraft product in 199 of every 200 households.

KRAFT

Welcome to the new Kraft

Chairman and CEO
Irene Rosenfeld

Managing the product life cycle: Kraft CEO Irene Rosenfeld announces, "We are about to take this great portfolio of ours in a new direction that's more consistent with the reality of consumers' lives today. Welcome to the new Kraft."

However, despite its long list of familiar brands, Kraft hasn't done very well in recent years. Over the past six years, its sales and profits have stagnated and its stock price has flatlined. Investors would have made a better return on bank certificates of deposit than on their investments in Kraft stock. The problem? Until just recently, Kraft has done a poor job of managing the product life cycle. Although it's had a slew of good old products, it's had far too few good new products.

Many of Kraft's venerable old brands—such as Maxwell House, Velveeta, and JELL-O—have been showing their age. Other brands have been extended about as far as they can go—for instance, Kraft now markets more than 20 varieties of Oreos, from the original sandwich cookies, Oreo Double Stuf, Oreo Double Double Stuf, Chocolate-Covered Oreos, and Double Delight Chocolate Mint 'n Creme Oreos to Oreo Mini Bites, Oreo Snack Cakes, and even Oreo ice cream cones. How much pop would yet one more variety provide?

Over the years, competitors such as P&G have invested dollars and energy in their mature or declining brands, such as Mr. Clean and Old Spice, moving them back into the growth stage of the product life cycle. In contrast, Kraft has focused on cost-cutting, leaving its mature brands to wither. Whereas rival P&G has developed a constant stream of really new products—even inventing all new product categories, with products such as Swiffer and Febreze—Kraft has been slow to innovate. And while P&G has been intensely customer-focused, bringing innovative new solutions to its customers, Kraft has slowly lost touch with its customers.

In 2006, however, under pressure from investors, Kraft installed a brand-new leadership team, including a new CEO, a first-ever chief marketing officer, and a leader of consumer innovation and marketing services. Under the leadership of CEO Irene Rosenfeld, the new leadership team laid out an ambitious turnaround plan to restore Kraft's sales and profit growth.

For starters, the team announced that it would make heavy investments to reconnect with customers and to improve product quality. To better understand what customers think and want, "We're going to connect with the consumer wherever she is," said Rosenfeld. "On the quality side, [we need to] shift from 'good enough' to 'truly delicious,' turning brands that [our] consumers have lived with for years into brands they can't live without." Most importantly, pronounced Rosenfeld, Kraft would invest heavily in innovation and new-product development. Simply put, she said, "We need to rebuild our new-product pipeline."

Rosenfeld and her team began their new-product development efforts not in the test kitchens but by visiting consumer homes, viewing the world through customers' eyes rather than through a company's lens. "We are about to take this great portfolio of ours in a new direction that's more consistent with the reality of consumers' lives today," she declared. We need "customer-focused innovation!" The team discovered the simple truth that with the way customers live their lives today, they want high-quality but convenient and healthy foods. "Wouldn't it be a whole lot easier if you could have restaurant-quality food at home for a fraction of the cost?" asked Rosenfeld.

The team also realized that Kraft already had all the fixings it needed to complete this mission. It needed only to reframe its offerings in ways that fit customers' changing lifestyles. For example, Kraft developed the highly successful Deli Creations brand—a build-your-own premium sandwich kit that includes bread, Oscar Mayer meats, Kraft cheeses, and condiments such as A1 steak sauce and Grey Poupon mustard. Customers can quickly assemble the sandwiches, pop them into the microwave for one minute, and wrap their mouths around a hot, restaurant-style sandwich. In a similar fashion, Kraft rolled out Fresh Creations salads, complete with Oscar Mayer meat, Kraft cheese, Good Seasons salad dressing, and Planters nuts, a move that took its product portfolio into a whole new section of the grocery store, the produce section.

In addition to creating new brands and categories, Kraft quickly launched a pantry full of new products under the old familiar brand names. For example, it introduced Delissio Ultimate, its best-yet alternative to delivery pizza, featuring premium vine-ripened tomatoes, whole-milk mozzarella cheese, specialty meats, and julienne vegetables. Under previous management, this project had been black-balled because the premium ingredients were considered too hard to get and too expensive. With Rosenfeld's blessing, Delissio Ultimate was on the shelves in just 18 months.

Dozens of other new products ranged from higher-quality Oscar Mayer Deli Fresh cold cuts and an entirely rejuvenated line of Kraft salad dressings with no artificial preservatives to Kraft Bagel-fuls, handheld breakfast sandwiches, Cakesters snack cakes, healthy LiveActive products with probiotic cultures and prebiotic fibre, and Oscar Mayer Fast Franks, prepackaged microwavable stadium-style hotdogs.

Kraft even invested to reinvigorate some of its old brands. For example, it added four bold new flavours to the Grey Poupon brand, a name that had retained 70 percent consumer awareness even without much investment. The new flavours will be supported by a fresh version of the old and much-liked Grey Poupon "Pardon me" ad campaign. Kraft is also infusing new life into existing brands such as Knudsen and Breakstone by co-marketing them with the LiveActive health brand. And, to get the word out about all its new products, Kraft invested an additional US$400 million on a new marketing program designed to better tell the Kraft story. "We [are] telling the consumer that Kraft is back," said Rosenfeld.

And it appears that Kraft is back—or at least heading in the right direction. Although profits are still languishing, sales are now growing at a healthy clip. Rosenfeld and her team are optimistic. "Our brands are getting stronger every day," she says. "Our insights about consumers are deeper and richer than ever before. And our new product pipeline is flowing with exciting ideas that will accelerate our growth and improve our margins. I'm pleased to tell you, the new Kraft is taking shape."

Kraft has learned that a company can't just sit back basking in the glory of today's successful brands. Continued success requires skilful management of the product life cycle. But Rosenfeld knows that Kraft still has a long way to go in serving up a tastier investment to shareholders. "It's time to grow. Our investors have told us that, and I would agree with them," she says. "But this is not *Extreme Makeover: Home Edition* that'll get fixed in 60 minutes. We've [still] got some fundamental work to do."

Sources: Quotes and other information from Michael Arndt, "It Just Got Hotter in Kraft's Kitchen," *BusinessWeek*, February 12, 2007; "Kraft Highlights Growth Strategy, Reconfirms 2008 Guidelines and Unveils Product Innovations at CAGNY Conference," *Business Wire*, February 19, 2008; John Schmeltzer, "Foodmaker Whips Up Plan For a Comeback," *Chicago Tribune*, February 21, 2007, p. 1; and Kraft annual reports and other information from www.kraft.com, accessed September 2008.

We looked at the product-development stage of the product life cycle in the first part of this chapter. We now look at strategies for each of the other life-cycle stages.

Introduction Stage

Introduction stage
The product life-cycle stage in which the new product is first distributed and made available for purchase.

The **introduction stage** starts when the new product is first launched. Introduction takes time, and sales growth is apt to be slow. Well-known products such as instant coffee, frozen foods, and HDTVs lingered for many years before they entered a stage of more rapid growth.

In this stage, as compared to other stages, profits are negative or low because of the low sales and high distribution and promotion expenses. Much money is needed to attract distributors and build their inventories. Promotion spending is relatively high to inform consumers of the new product and get them to try it. Because the market is not generally ready for product refinements at this stage, the company and its few competitors produce basic versions of the product. These firms focus their selling on those buyers who are the most ready to buy.

A company, especially the *market pioneer*, must choose a launch strategy that is consistent with the intended product positioning. It should realize that the initial strategy is just the first step in a grander marketing plan for the product's entire life cycle. If the pioneer chooses its launch strategy to make a "killing," it may be sacrificing long-run revenue for the sake of short-term gain. As the pioneer moves through later stages of the life cycle, it must continuously formulate new pricing, promotion, and other marketing strategies. It has the best chance of building and retaining market leadership if it plays its cards correctly from the start.

Small and medium-sized enterprises form the majority of the businesses in Canada. Many of these firms were established when a market pioneer had a new product or service idea. The Running Room, for example, was launched by John Stanton, a man who developed a personal passion for running that he shared with other Canadians who valued outdoor sports and activities to form a highly successful business. Sometimes, founders of such firms translate hobbies into successful businesses. Take the case of Domaine Pinnacle, a Quebec company that was founded in 2000:

> Domaine Pinnacle (www.domainepinnacle.com) is a family-owned and -operated orchard and cidery located on a 175-hectare property on the slopes of Pinnacle Mountain near the historic village of Frelighsburg in the Eastern Townships of Quebec. Susan and Charles Crawford make "ice cider," which is similar to ice wine except that it is made with apples. To found their successful business with a distinct advantage, the pair focused on distinct locational competences in their region: cold climate, many varieties of apples, access to a cider maker from France who was living in Quebec, and their own marketing expertise. In the first few years of operations, they've been able to find markets worldwide for their high-quality products. Rapid penetration of the world market for alcoholic beverages was made possible through a strategic alliance with a distribution partner—Camus Cognac—the largest independent producer of cognac in the world. They've also won numerous prestigious awards for their products.

Growth Stage

Growth stage
The product life-cycle stage in which a product's sales start climbing quickly.

If the new product satisfies the market, it will enter a **growth stage**, in which sales will start climbing quickly. The early adopters will continue to buy, and later buyers will start following their lead, especially if they hear favourable word of mouth. Attracted by the opportunities for profit, new competitors will enter the market. They will introduce new product features, and the market will expand. The increase in competitors leads to an increase in the number of distribution outlets, and sales jump just to build reseller inventories. Prices remain where they are or fall only slightly. Companies keep their promotion spending at the same or a slightly higher level. Educating the market remains a goal, but now the company must also meet the competition.

Profits increase during the growth stage as promotion costs are spread over a large volume and as unit manufacturing costs fall. The firm uses several strategies to sustain rapid market growth as long as possible. It improves product quality and adds new product features and models. It enters new market segments and new distribution channels. It shifts some advertising from building product awareness to building product conviction and purchase, and it lowers prices at the right time to attract more buyers.

In the growth stage, the firm faces a trade-off between high market share and high current profit. By spending a lot of money on product improvement, promotion, and distribution, the company can capture a dominant position. In doing so, however, it gives up maximum current profit, which it hopes to make up in the next stage.

Maturity Stage

Maturity stage
The product life-cycle stage in which sales growth slows or levels off.

At some point, a product's sales growth will slow down, and the product will enter a **maturity stage**. The maturity stage normally lasts longer than the previous stages, and it poses strong challenges to marketing management. The slowdown in sales growth results in many producers with many products to sell. In turn, this overcapacity leads to greater competition. Competitors begin marking down prices, increasing their advertising and sales promotions, and upping their product development budgets to find better versions of the product. These steps lead to a drop in profit. Some of the weaker competitors start dropping out, and the industry eventually contains only well-established competitors.

Although many products in the mature stage appear to remain unchanged for long periods, most successful ones are actually evolving to meet changing consumer needs. Product managers should do more than simply ride along with or defend their mature products—after all, a good offence is the best defence. They should consider modifying the market, product, and marketing mix.

In *modifying the market*, the company tries to increase the consumption of the current product. It may look for new users and new market segments, as when John Deere targeted the retiring baby boomer market with the Gator, a vehicle traditionally used on a farm. For this new market, Deere has repositioned the Gator, promising that it can "take you from a do-it-yourselfer to a do-it-a-lot-easier." As one ad for the Gator XUV puts it, "When your plans include landscaping, gardening, or transporting people and materials on your property, the XUV provides a smooth, comfortable ride with heavy-duty performance."

The manager may also look for ways to increase usage among present customers. For example, Glad Products Company helps customers find new uses for its Press'n Seal wrap, the plastic wrap that creates a Tupperware-like seal. As more and more customers contacted the company about alternative uses for the product, Glad set up a special "1000s of Uses. What's Yours?" website (www.1000uses.com) where customers can swap usage tips. "We found out our heavy users use it for a lot more than just covering food," says a Glad brand manager. "And they all became heavy users when they had an 'aha' moment with Press'n Seal." Suggested uses for Press'n Seal range from protecting a computer keyboard from dirt and spills and keeping garden seeds fresh to soccer moms using them to sit on damp benches while watching their tykes play. "We just roll out the Glad Press'n Seal over the long benches," says the mom who shared the tip, "and everyone's bottom stays nice and dry."[32]

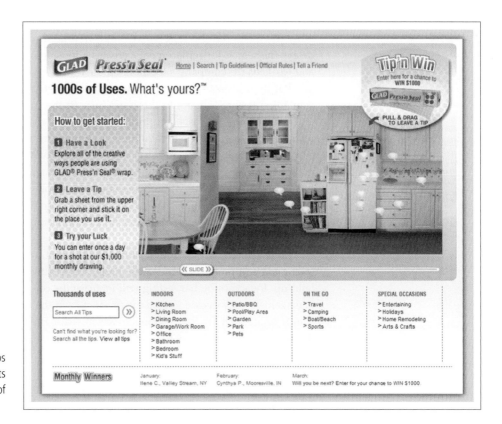

Modifying the market: Glad helps customers swap new uses for its Press'n Seal wrap on it's "1000s of Uses. What's Yours?" website.

The company might also try *modifying the product*—changing characteristics such as quality, features, style, or packaging to attract new users and to inspire more usage. It can improve the product's styling and attractiveness. It might improve the product's quality and performance—its durability, reliability, speed, and taste. Thus, makers of consumer food and household products introduce new flavours, colours, scents, ingredients, or packages to enhance performance and revitalize consumer buying. For example, TABASCO pepper sauce may have been around for more than 130 years, but to keep the brand young the company has added a full line of flavours (such as Garlic, Sweet & Spicy, and Chipotle) and a kitchen cabinet full of new products under the TABASCO name (such as steak sauces, spicy beans, a chili mix, jalapeno nacho slices, and even a TABASCO lollipop).

Finally, the company can try *modifying the marketing mix*—improving sales by changing one or more marketing mix elements. The company can offer new or improved services to buyers. It can cut prices to attract new users and competitors' customers. It can launch a better advertising campaign or use aggressive sales promotions—trade deals, cents-off, premiums, and contests. In addition to pricing and promotion, the company can also move into new marketing channels to help serve new users.

Decline Stage

The sales of most product forms and brands eventually dip. The decline may be slow, as in the case of oatmeal cereal, or rapid, as in the cases of cassette and VHS tapes. Sales may plunge to zero, or they may drop to a low level where they continue for many years. This is the **decline stage**.

Decline stage
The product life-cycle stage in which a product's sales decline.

Sales decline for many reasons, including technological advances, shifts in consumer tastes, and increased competition. As sales and profits decline, some firms withdraw from the market. Those remaining may prune their product offerings. They may drop smaller market segments and marginal trade channels, or they may cut the promotion budget and reduce their prices further.

Carrying a weak product can be very costly to a firm, and not just in terms of profit. There are many hidden costs. A weak product may take up too much of management's time. It often requires frequent price and inventory adjustments. It requires advertising and sales-force attention that might be better used to make "healthy" products more profitable. A product's failing reputation can cause customer concerns about the company and its other products. But the biggest cost may well lie in the future. Keeping weak products delays the search for replacements, creates a lopsided product mix, hurts current profits, and weakens the company's foothold on the future.

For these reasons, companies need to pay more attention to their aging products. A firm's first task is to identify those products in the decline stage by regularly reviewing sales, market shares, costs, and profit trends. Then, management must decide whether to maintain, harvest, or drop each of these declining products.

Management may decide to *maintain* its brand without change in the hope that competitors will leave the industry. For example, Procter & Gamble made good profits by remaining in the declining liquid soap business as others withdrew. Or management may decide to reposition or reinvigorate the brand in hopes of moving it back into the growth stage of the product life cycle. Procter & Gamble has done this with several brands, including Mr. Clean and Old Spice.

Management may decide to *harvest* the product, which means reducing various costs (plant and equipment, maintenance, R&D, advertising, sales force) and hoping that sales hold up. If successful, harvesting will increase the company's profits in the short run. Or management may decide to *drop* the product from the line. It can sell it to another firm or simply liquidate it at salvage value. In recent years, P&G has sold off a number of lesser or declining brands such as Crisco oil, Comet cleanser, Sure deodorant, Duncan Hines cake mixes, and Jif peanut butter. If the company plans to find a buyer, it will not want to run down the product through harvesting.

Table 10.2 summarizes the key characteristics of each stage of the product life cycle. The table also lists the marketing objectives and strategies for each stage.[33]

Table 10.2 Summary of Product Life-Cycle Characteristics, Objectives, and Strategies

Characteristics	Introduction	Growth	Maturity	Decline
Sales	Low sales	Rapidly rising sales	Peak sales	Declining sales
Costs	High cost per customer	Average cost per customer	Low cost per customer	Low cost per customer
Profits	Negative	Rising profits	High profits	Declining profits
Customers	Innovators	Early adopters	Middle majority	Laggards
Competitors	Few	Growing number	Stable number beginning to decline	Declining number
Marketing Objectives				
	Create product awareness and trial	Maximize market share	Maximize profit while defending market share	Reduce expenditure and milk the brand
Strategies				
Product	Offer a basic product	Offer product extensions, service, warranty	Diversify brand and models	Phase out weak items
Price	Use cost-plus	Price to penetrate market	Price to match or beat competitors	Cut price
Distribution	Build selective distribution	Build intensive distribution	Build more intensive distribution	Go selective: phase out unprofitable outlets
Advertising	Build product awareness among early adopters and dealers	Build awareness and interest in the mass market	Stress brand differences and benefits	Reduce to level needed to retain hard-core loyals
Sales Promotion	Use heavy sales promotion to entice trial	Reduce to take advantage of heavy consumer demand	Increase to encourage brand switching	Reduce to minimal level

Source: Philip Kotler and Kevin Lane Keller, Marketing Management, 13th ed. (Upper Saddle River, NJ: Prentice Hall, 2009), p. 288.

4 ADDITIONAL PRODUCT AND SERVICE CONSIDERATIONS

Here, we'll wrap up our discussion of products and services with two additional considerations: social responsibility in product decisions and issues of international product and service marketing.

Product Decisions and Social Responsibility

Product decisions have attracted much public attention. Marketers should carefully consider public policy issues and regulations regarding acquiring or dropping products, patent protection, product quality and safety, and product warranties.

Regarding new products, the government may prevent companies from adding products through acquisitions if the effect threatens to lessen competition. Companies dropping products must be aware that they have legal obligations, written or implied, to their suppliers, dealers, and customers who have a stake in the dropped product. Companies must also obey patent laws when developing new products. A company cannot make its product illegally similar to another company's established product.

Manufacturers must comply with specific laws regarding product quality and safety. Various acts provide for the inspection of sanitary conditions in the meat- and poultry-processing industries. Safety legislation has been passed to regulate fabrics, chemical substances, automobiles, toys, and drugs and poisons.

きっと、サクラサクよ。

Nestlé's Kit Kat chocolate bar in Japan benefits from the coincidental similarity between the bar's name and the Japanese phrase *kitto katsu*, which roughly translates to "You will surely win!" The brand's innovative "May cherries blossom" campaign has turned the Kit Kat bar and logo into national good luck charms.

If consumers have been injured by a product that has a defective design, they can sue manufacturers or dealers. A recent survey of manufacturing companies found that product liability was the second-largest litigation concern, behind only labour and employment matters. Product liability suits in the United States are now occurring in federal courts at the rate of almost 24 000 per year.

This litigation phenomenon has resulted in huge increases in product liability insurance premiums, causing big problems in some industries. Some companies pass these higher rates along to consumers by raising prices. Others are forced to discontinue high-risk product lines. Some companies are now appointing "product stewards," whose job is to protect consumers from harm and the company from liability by proactively ferreting out potential product problems. Many manufacturers also offer written product warranties to convince customers of their products' quality.

International Product and Services Marketing

International product and service marketers face special challenges. First, they must figure out what products and services to introduce and in which countries. Then they must decide how much to standardize or adapt their products and services for world markets.

On the one hand, companies would like to standardize their offerings. Standardization helps a company develop a consistent worldwide image. It also lowers the product design, manufacturing, and marketing costs of offering a large variety of products. On the other hand, markets and consumers around the world differ widely. Companies must usually respond to these differences by adapting their product offerings. For example, Nestlé sells a variety of very popular Kit Kat flavours in Japan that might make the average Western chocolate-lover's stomach turn, such as green tea, red bean, and red wine. Beyond taste, Kit Kat's strong following in Japan may also be the result of some unintended cultural factors:

> In recent years, Kit Kat—the world's number-two chocolate bar behind Snickers—has become very popular in Japan. Some of this popularity, no doubt, derives from the fact that the notoriously sweet-toothed Japanese love the bar's taste. But part of the bar's appeal may also be attributed to the coincidental similarity between its name and the Japanese phrase kitto katsu, which roughly translates in Japanese as "You will surely win!" Spotting this opportunity, marketers for Nestlé Japan developed an innovative Juken (college entrance exam) Kit Kat campaign. The multimedia campaign positions the Kit Kat bar and logo as good luck charms during the highly stressful university entrance exam season. Nestlé even developed a cherry-flavoured Kit Kat bar in packaging containing the message "May cherries blossom," wishing students luck in achieving their dreams. The campaign has been such a hit in Japan that it has led to a nationwide social movement to cheer up students for Juken. Kit Kat has also become an even broader national good luck charm. For example, a large flag featuring the Kit Kat logo and the phrase "Kitto Katsu!" has been used by fans of professional football team Jubilo Iwata, which is sponsored by Nestlé Japan. Since the Juken campaign began six years ago, Kit Kat sales in Japan have increased more than 250 percent.[34]

Packaging also presents new challenges for international marketers. Packaging issues can be subtle. For example, names, labels, and colours may not translate easily from one country to another. A firm using yellow flowers in its logo might fare well in the United States but meet with disaster in Mexico, where a yellow flower symbolizes death or disrespect. Similarly, although Nature's Gift might be an appealing name for gourmet mushrooms in America, it would be deadly in Germany, where *Gift* means "poison." Packaging may also need to be tailored to meet the physical characteristics of consumers in various parts of the world. For instance, soft drinks are sold in smaller cans in Japan to fit the smaller Japanese hand better. Thus, although product and package standardization can produce benefits, companies must usually adapt their offerings to the unique needs of specific international markets.

Service marketers also face special challenges when going global. Some service industries have a long history of international operations. For example, the commercial banking industry was one of the first to grow internationally. Banks had to provide global services to meet the foreign exchange and credit needs of their home country clients wanting to sell overseas. In recent years, many banks have become truly global. Germany's Deutsche Bank, for example, serves more than 13 million customers through 1868 branches in 73 countries. For its clients around the world who wish to grow globally, Deutsche Bank can raise money not only in Frankfurt but also in Zurich, London, Paris, Tokyo, and Moscow.[35]

Professional and business services industries such as accounting, management consulting, and advertising have also globalized. The international growth of these firms followed the globalization of the client companies they serve. For example, as more clients employ worldwide marketing and advertising strategies, advertising agencies have responded by globalizing their own operations. McCann Worldgroup, a large U.S.–based advertising and marketing services agency, operates in more than 130 countries. It serves international clients such as Coca-Cola, General Motors, ExxonMobil, Microsoft, Master-Card, Johnson & Johnson, and Unilever in markets ranging from the United States and Canada to Korea and Kazakhstan. Moreover, McCann Worldgroup is one company in the Interpublic Group of Companies, an immense worldwide network of advertising and marketing services companies.[36]

Retailers are among the latest service businesses to go global. As their home markets become saturated, American retailers such as Walmart, Office Depot, and Saks Fifth Avenue are expanding into faster-growing markets abroad. For example, since 1995, Walmart has entered 13 countries; its international division's sales grew nearly 18 percent last year, skyrocketing to more than $90.6 billion. Foreign retailers are making similar moves. Asian shoppers can now buy American products in French-owned Carrefour stores. Carrefour, the world's second-largest retailer behind Walmart, now operates more than 12 500 stores in more than 30 countries. It is the leading retailer in Europe, Brazil, and Argentina and the largest foreign retailer in China.[37]

The trend toward growth of global service companies will continue, especially in banking, airlines, telecommunications, and professional services. Today, service firms are no longer simply following their manufacturing customers. Instead, they are taking the lead in international expansion.

REVIEWING OBJECTIVES AND KEY TERMS

mymarketinglab | Audio Chapter Summary

A company's current products face limited lifespans and must be replaced by newer products. But new products can fail—the risks of innovation are as great as the rewards. The key to successful innovation lies in a total-company effort, strong planning, and a systematic *new-product development process*.

OBJECTIVE 1   **Explain how companies find and develop new-product ideas.**

Companies find and develop new-product ideas from a variety of sources. Many new-product ideas stem from *internal sources*. Companies conduct formal research and development, pick the brains of their employees, and brainstorm at executive meetings. Other ideas come from *external sources*. By conducting surveys and focus groups and analyzing *customer* questions and complaints, companies can generate new-product ideas that will meet specific consumer needs. Companies track *competitors'* offerings and inspect new products, dismantling them, analyzing their performance, and deciding whether to introduce a similar or improved product. *Distributors and suppliers* are close to the market and can pass along information about consumer problems and new-product possibilities.

OBJECTIVE 2   **List and define the steps in the new-product development process and the major considerations in managing this process.**

The new-product development process consists of eight sequential stages. The process starts with *idea generation*. Next comes *idea screening*, which reduces the number of ideas based on the company's own criteria. Ideas that pass the screening stage continue through *concept development and testing*, in which a detailed version of the new-product idea is stated in meaningful consumer terms and then the new-product concept is tested with a group of target consumers to determine whether it has strong consumer appeal. Strong concepts proceed to *marketing strategy development*, in which an initial marketing strategy for the new product is developed from the product concept. In the *business analysis* stage, a review of the sales, costs, and profit projections for a new product is conducted to determine whether the new product is likely to satisfy the company's objectives. With positive results here, the ideas become more concrete through *product development* and *test marketing* and finally are launched during *commercialization*.

New-product development involves more than just going through a set of steps. Companies must take a systematic, holistic approach to managing this process. Successful new-product development requires a customer-centred, team-based, systematic effort.

OBJECTIVE 3   **Describe the stages of the product life cycle and how marketing strategies change during the product life cycle.**

Each product has a *life cycle* marked by a changing set of problems and opportunities. The sales of the typical product follow an S-shaped curve made up of five stages. The cycle begins with the *product development stage* in which the company finds and develops a new-product idea. The *introduction stage* is marked by slow growth and low profits as the product is distributed to the market. If successful, the product enters a *growth stage*, which offers rapid sales growth and increasing profits. Next comes a *maturity stage* in which sales growth slows down and profits stabilize. Finally, the product enters a *decline stage* in which sales and profits dwindle. The company's task during this stage is to recognize the decline and to decide whether it should maintain, harvest, or drop the product.

In the *introduction stage*, the company must choose a launch strategy consistent with its intended product positioning. Much money is needed to attract distributors and build their inventories and to inform consumers of the new product and achieve trial. In the *growth stage*, companies continue to educate potential consumers and distributors. In addition, the company works to stay ahead of the competition and sustain rapid market growth by improving product quality, adding new product features and models, entering new market segments and distribution channels, shifting advertising from building product awareness to building product conviction and purchase, and lowering prices at the right time to attract new buyers.

In the *maturity stage*, companies continue to invest in maturing products and consider modifying the market, the product, and the marketing mix. When *modifying the market*, the company attempts to increase the consumption of the current product. When *modifying the product,* the company changes some of the product's characteristics—such as quality, features, or style—to attract new users or inspire more usage. When *modifying the marketing mix*, the company works to improve sales by changing one or more of the marketing mix elements. Once the company recognizes that a product has entered the *decline stage*, management must decide whether to *maintain* the brand without change, hoping that competitors will drop out of the market; *harvest* the product, reducing costs and trying to maintain sales; or *drop* the product, selling it to another firm or liquidating it at salvage value.

OBJECTIVE 4   **Discuss two additional product issues: socially responsible product decisions and international product and services marketing.**

Marketers must consider two additional product issues. The first is *social responsibility*. This includes public policy issues and regulations involving acquiring or dropping products, patent protection, product quality and safety, and product warranties. The second involves the special challenges facing international product and service marketers. International marketers must decide how much to standardize or adapt their offerings for world markets.

KEY TERMS

 | Glossary Flashcards

DISCUSSING THE CONCEPTS

1. Name and describe the major steps in the new-product development process.

2. Discuss the benefits and drawbacks of test marketing and explain why some companies do or do not use test marketing for new products. Name and describe the three approaches to test marketing.

3. Explain why successful new-product development requires a customer-centred, team-based, and systematic effort.

4. Name and describe the five stages of the product life cycle. Identify a product class, product form, or brand that is in each stage.

5. Discuss the special challenges facing international product and service marketers.

APPLYING THE CONCEPTS

1. Think of a problem that really bugs you or a need you have that is not satisfied by current market offerings. In a small group, brainstorm ideas for a new product or service that solves this problem or satisfies this need.

2. Coca-Cola has sustained success in the maturity stage of the product life cycle for many years. Visit Coca-Cola's website (www.thecoca-colacompany.com/heritage/ourheritage.html) and discuss how Coca-Cola has evolved over the years. Identify ways that Coca-Cola can continue to evolve to meet changing consumer needs and wants.

3. Write a marketing strategy statement for a new full-functioning but folding bicycle.

FOCUS ON TECHNOLOGY

If you think the flash-memory chip found in digital cameras and music players is small, wait until you see what's coming next. Researchers at Hewlett-Packard have developed a new kind of electronic circuit that could revolutionize computer data storage, making it smaller and more energy-efficient than current memory chip technology. The part is called a memory resistor, or "memristor," and it allows storage of information on memory chips for long periods of time without electrical current. The theory behind the circuit is not new—it dates back to an electrical engineering professor from the University of California at Berkley in 1971. Most consumers don't realize that flash chips lose data after a year or so. But with the memrister, the atomic structure is actually changed, allowing for permanent storage of data. This isn't the only revolutionary change on the horizon. In a joint venture called Numonyx, Intel Corporation and STMicroelectronics are betting on a new technology known as phase-change memory. One thing is for sure, big change is on the way for computers and handheld devices.

1. What stage of the product life cycle are these products currently in?

2. Discuss the factors HP and other tech companies should consider when conducting the business analysis for a product such as the "memristor." How will it add value for customers?

FOCUS ON ETHICS

Does your computer have a floppy disk drive or use the DOS operating system? Do you listen to music on a cassette deck? How about recording movies on a VCR tape? You probably answered no to all of these questions. In fact, you may not even be aware of these products. All are examples of obsolete or declining products. But did marketers plan it that way? Many companies have been accused of using planned obsolescence as a strategy to make more money. However, new products often provide greater value for customers, especially in fast-changing industries such as computers and electronics. But what happens to the old products? There is a growing concern over electronic waste, called ewaste. Although ewaste represents only 2 percent of the trash in our landfills, some analysts estimate that it accounts for 70 percent of overall toxic waste. The February 2009 digital programming mandate will generate a tidal wave of old TVs that will require disposal. Cathode ray tube (CRT) televisions

contain several pounds of lead as well as other toxic materials. Although recycling programs are increasing and are required by law in some places, the waste is often shipped for recycling or disposal to landfills in China, Kenya, India, and other developing countries, where concerns over worker and environmental welfare are more lax.

1. Who should be responsible for properly disposing of electronic products no longer needed—consumers or manufacturers? Is it appropriate to ship ewaste to developing countries? Discuss alternative solutions.

2. Visit several electronics manufacturers' websites to learn if they offer electronic recycling programs. Are manufacturers doing enough? Write a brief report on what you learned.

MARKETING BY THE NUMBERS

When introducing new products, some manufacturers set a high initial price and then reduce the price later. However, reducing price also reduces contribution margins, which in turn impacts profitability. To be profitable, the reduced price must sufficiently increase sales. For example, a company with a contribution margin of 30 percent on sales of $60 million realizes a total contribution to fixed costs and profits of $18 million ($60 million x 0.30 = $18 million). If this company decreases price, the contribution margin will also decrease. So to maintain or increase profitability, the price reduction must increase sales considerably.

1. Refer to Appendix 3: Marketing by the Numbers and calculate the new contribution margin for the company discussed here if it reduces price by 10 percent. Assume that unit variable costs are $70 and the original price was $100.

2. What level of total sales must a company capture at the new price to maintain the same level of total contribution as before the price reduction (that is, total contribution = $18 million)?

VIDEO CASE

Electrolux

 | Video Case Questions

Since the 1920s, the Swedish company Electrolux has been making and selling home appliances worldwide. Decade after decade, the company, originally known for its vacuum cleaners, has been turning out innovative products in a way that seems to magically predict what will work for consumers. The success of Electrolux's new-product development process results from more than just technological and design expertise. More importantly, it is rooted in what the company calls "consumer insight."

The concept of consumer insight is integrated into the Electrolux marketing strategy. It involves starting with the customer and working backward to design the product. Electrolux employs various methods to get deeply into the consumer's mind and to understand consumer needs. It then boils down that information to form concepts and, from concepts, it designs products. Because of its customer-centric approach, Electrolux refers to itself as the "thoughtful" design innovator and has for years stood behind the slogan "Thinking of you."

After viewing the video featuring Electrolux, answer the following questions about the company's new-product development process:

1. What is consumer insight? What are some ways in which Electrolux develops consumer insight?

2. Describe how Electrolux might go about developing products if it were focused solely on engineering and technology. What might be the result of this product-development process?

3. With household appliances in mind, identify some consumer trends from the video as well as any others that you can think of. Explain how new products could take advantage of each trend.

Visit MyMarketingLab at www.pearsoned.ca/mymarketinglab to view the video segment related to this case.

COMPANY CASE

Nintendo: Reviving a Company, Transforming a Market

In the world of video games, Nintendo has been a household name for nearly three decades. After all, it was one of the pioneers of home video game consoles with the Nintendo Entertainment System in the early 1980s. It continued as the market leader with its Super Nintendo and Nintendo 64 systems. But in the mid-1990s, all that began to change. Along came Sony with its Playstation and Playstation 2, and Microsoft introduced the Xbox. Before long, Nintendo was reduced to a fraction of its former glory, running a distant third in a highly competitive market.

What happened? In certain respects, Nintendo fell prey to the industry model that it had created. More advanced technology led to the creation of more powerful gaming consoles, which in turn paved the way for more sophisticated games with more realistic graphics. As each new generation of product hit the market, Nintendo found that it could not keep up with more technologically advanced rivals. While more than 120 million Sony PS2s became fixtures in homes, apartments, and dorm rooms around the world, Nintendo moved just slightly more than 20 million GameCubes. As the most recent generation of gaming platforms from the gaming industry's "big three" came to market, many industry insiders figured Nintendo was destined to continue its downward path. Sony's PS3 and Microsoft's Xbox 360 were so advanced that it looked like Nintendo was due for another drubbing.

Oh what a difference a couple of years make. For Nintendo, everything is now coming up Super Mario Bros. Last year, revenues and profits were up by 73 percent and 67 percent, respectively. In the last couple of years, during a time in which the Nikkei Stock Average fell nearly 25 percent, Nintendo's stock price tripled. In fact, Nintendo's stock price rose so high during 2007 that its market capitalization exceeded that of the Sony Corporation. On that measure alone, Nintendo became the second-largest corporation in Japan, trailing only Toyota Motor Company. How did this struggling number-three player go from product loser to product leader in such a short time?

FROM PRODUCT LOSER TO PRODUCT LEADER

Most people probably don't know that Nintendo was founded way back in 1889. Obviously, Nintendo did not make video games back then; it began as a playing card manufacturer. But it also found success in hotels, packaged foods, and toys. When it came time to revive itself as a veteran in the video game industry, Nintendo did something that it had done time and time again. It focused on customers to find true opportunities.

For the video game industry, "the customer" typically means one of two groups: the 18- to 35-year-old hard-core gamers and the children/teenagers. The industry earns most of its revenue and profits from these core consumers who spend a great deal of time and money enhancing their virtual skills. Over the years, as hardware became more sophisticated and games more realistic, these tech junkies were all the more pleased.

In the process, Nintendo watched its revenues slide and its rivals strengthen. It realized that it could not compete against technologically superior products. So when it set out to develop the Wii console, it didn't even try. Instead, it focused on something the others were ignoring. It set its sights on the masses. "Nintendo took a step back from the technology arms race and chose to focus on the fun of playing rather than cold tech specs," said Reggie Fils-Aimé, president and COO of Nintendo of America. "We took a more intuitive approach and developed something that could be fun for every member of the family."

For the Wii, this meant that Nintendo had to do more with less. The Wii boasts a humble combination of low-powered processors and a standard optical disc drive. Compared to the powerful, state-of-the-art chips and high-definition lasers contained in the PS3 and Xbox 360, the Wii's graphics are downright scrawny.

But at the core of the Wii's broad appeal lies a revolutionary motion-sensing wireless technology that forces the once sedentary gamer to get up off the couch and get into the game. The Wii controller resembles a television remote.

This feature was no accident, as Wii designers correctly speculated that the familiarity of a TV remote would be more inviting than the more typical and complex video game controllers. The Wii's basic software also allows users to custom design avatars from a seemingly infinite combination of characteristics. With this configuration, users play tennis, go bowling, and hit the links by swinging the controller like a racquet, ball, or golf club, all with characters resembling themselves.

The Wii met with immediate and drastic success. Entering the market *after* the release of the Xbox 360 and the PS3, Wii consoles flew off the shelves. Not only did the Wii contain an enticing combination of features, it also had a cost advantage. Microsoft and Sony had priced their offerings in the stratosphere. And even at US$599 for the top and most popular PS3 model, Sony was still losing hundreds of dollars on each unit that it sold! Nintendo's low-tech approach allowed it to earn a hefty profit *and* be the low-price leader at only US$250. With such a favourable benefit-to-cost ratio, the Wii easily won the launch phase, outselling each of the two competing consoles by nearly two-to-one in the first few months.

NOT JUST A FAD

Although the Wii was an instant smash hit, many analysts wondered whether its appeal would hold up. That speculation began to subside when retailers were still having trouble keeping the Wii in stock more than a year after it was introduced. In its first 18 months, Nintendo moved more than 24 million Wiis. Even though the Xbox 360 had been on the market a full year longer, it had sold only 19 million units. And Sony, once the undisputed industry champ, placed only 12 million PS3s.

Nintendo's willingness to reinvent what a video gaming system can mean continues to drive Wii sales. For example, the Wii can scan weather, news, and websites through a wireless Internet connection. Through the Wii Shop Channel, an iTunes-style store, customers can download classic Nintendo games as well as games from independent developers.

But in its pursuit to break gaming boundaries, Nintendo has also relentlessly pursued new applications for the basic motion-sensing technology. A plastic rifle contraption allows users to realistically play shooting gallery games. Snapping the Wii controller into a steering wheel has made driving games all the more electrifying. And tiny in-controller speakers add touches like the sound of an arrow being shot while the TV makes the "thwack" of that arrow hitting its target.

But perhaps one of the greatest strokes of creative genius in Nintendo's continuing stream of new applications is the Wii Fit, an add-on device targeted directly at women wanting to lose weight or keep in shape. The idea for the Wii Fit came to Takao Sawano, general manager of development for Nintendo, as he watched sumo wrestlers being weighed in for a television match. The tubby athletes were so heavy that they had to have each foot placed on a separate scale. The lightbulb went on as Sawano thought about the possibility of tracking a user's shifting weight on a game pad as he or she shimmied and twisted his or her way through virtual worlds.

That game pad is now called the Balance Board and lies at the heart (or rather the foot) of the Wii Fit's portfolio of exercise applications. Users can do aerobic, strength training, balancing, and yoga exercises all in realistic virtual settings. "It is now possible to go beyond the fingertip controls of past games and now use your whole body," Sawano told a crowd of game developers. The Wii Fit also facilitates exercise programs as it tracks and analyzes individual performance over time as well as keeps track of stats like weight and body mass index.

Perhaps the most promising part of the Wii Fit is not that it continues to broaden an ever-growing market segment. In addition, the Balance Board component has the potential to be integrated into a nearly limitless number of applications. Already, Nintendo has developed ski jump and slalom games. It's only a matter of time before Nintendo develops a Balance Board version for just about every sport imaginable.

Releasing hit after hit, Nintendo has vaulted to the top of the *Wall Street Journal's* Asia 200 survey. Placing first in the "Innovative in Responding to Customer Needs" category, the company placed second overall, trailing only Toyota. For a company that hadn't placed in the top 10 since 2002, the sudden turnaround is a telling demonstration of consumer confidence.

SECURING THE FUTURE

Although the success of the Wii has largely been attributed to attracting nontraditional gamers, hard-core gamers have hardly been absent. In fact, many of the industry faithful saw the Wii as a relatively cheap second gaming platform—as a nice diversion from more graphic-intensive games. The Wii also has the nostalgic advantage of appealing to the gaming elite with characters they grew up with, such as those from the Mario and Zelda franchises.

But developers and executives at Nintendo are not content to sit back and risk having hard-core gamers lose interest. Part of Nintendo's future strategy includes games focused on more serious gamers. CEO Satoru Iwata shocked the industry last year when he announced that Nintendo would soon add games from two Sony allies: Capcom's *Monster Hunter* series and Square Enix's *Final Fantasy Crystal Chronicles*. The release of these titles will do more than appeal to traditional gamers. It will elevate the Wii's image from that of a machine with little firepower to one that will run the industry's most advanced games. Said one game industry analyst at a tradeshow sneak preview, "It's symbolic. I didn't think the Wii could handle this type of game. Everyone in the room today saw that it can."

As Nintendo has successfully attracted an untapped audience of gamers over the past few years, it has done more than revive its business. It has transformed a market. The competitors that once trounced Nintendo now find that they must play catch-up. Both Sony and Microsoft are now developing easier-to-play games that depart from their usual fast-action fare. Game publishers, including power-houses like Electronic Arts, have started putting more resources into developing games for the Wii. And even small, independent shops are getting into the action as Nintendo's download channel reduces barriers to entry. All this is causing an already huge US$30 billion industry to swell.

Simon Jeffery, president and COO of Sega of America, summarizes why Nintendo has been successful and why the rest of the industry must keep up:

> The fundamental interface in games has always been a controller, and Nintendo is bringing opportunities to developers to think about how interactions use motion. That has opened doors of creativity throughout the video game business. Nintendo's success is about creative leadership and the willingness to do things differently.

As long as Nintendo can stay focused on these elements that have returned it to its throne, it will reign for a long time to come.

Questions for Discussion

1. Was Nintendo just lucky, or does the Wii's success have strategic merit?

2. Has Nintendo put the "fad" question to rest? State a case as to why the Wii is or is not here to stay.

3. In which stage of the product life cycle is the Wii? Based on that stage, is Nintendo employing good marketing mix strategies?

4. Develop a strategy for the Wii's next product life-cycle phase.

5. Discuss the potential threats to Nintendo's future success. What will help Nintendo avoid a premature decline for the Wii?

Sources: Robert Levine, "Fast 50 2008: Nintendo," *Fast Company*, February 19, 2008, accessed online at www.fastcompany.com; Yukari Iwatani Kane, "Nintendo Captures Top Spot in Japan for Innovation," *Wall Street Journal*, June 27, 2008, accessed online at www.wsj.com; Yukari Iwatani Kane, "Nintendo Is Ahead of the Game, But Sustaining May Be Hard," *Wall Street Journal*, April 15, 2008, p. C3; Yukari Iwatani Kane, "Wii Sales Help Nintendo Net Rise 48 percent," *Wall Street Journal*, April 25, 2008, p. B8; Kenji Hall, "Nintendo: Calling All Players," *BusinessWeek*, October 10, 2007, accessed online at www.businessweek.com; and Brian Caulfield, "Nintendo's Sumo-Inspired Hit," *Forbes*, February 21, 2008, accessed online at www.forbes.com.

Visit **MyMarketingLab** at **www.pearsoned.ca/mymarketinglab** for access to online tutorials, interactive exercises, videos, and much more.

11
Pricing

PREVIEWING THE CONCEPTS In this chapter, we look at a second major marketing mix tool—pricing. If effective product development, promotion, and distribution sow the seeds of business success, effective pricing is the harvest. Firms successful at creating customer value with the other marketing mix activities must still capture some of this value in the prices they earn. Yet, despite its importance, many firms do not handle pricing well. In this chapter, we focus on the process of setting prices. We define price, look at internal and external considerations that affect pricing decisions, and examine general pricing approaches. Then we'll look at pricing strategies available to marketers—new-product pricing strategies, product mix pricing strategies, price adjustment strategies, and strategies related to initiating or responding to price changes. Finally, we'll look at public policy and ethical issues related to pricing.

Let's start with a look at Kodak and its revolutionary new pricing strategy for inkjet printers. Are you tired of buying a reasonably priced printer, then paying scandalous prices for replacement ink cartridges? Kodak may have the answer. In a move that promises to turn the printer industry on its head, Kodak sells its EasyShare printers for more but charges you less for replacement ink.

H P, Epson, Canon, and Lexmark have long dominated the US$50 billion printer industry with a maddening "razor-and-blades" pricing strategy (as in give away the razor, then make your profits on the blades). They sell printers at little or no profit, but once you own the printer you're stuck buying their grossly overpriced, high-margin replacement ink cartridges. For example, depending on where you buy, you can pick up a nifty little HP multifunction Deskjet printer for only $39.99. But the HP inkjet cartridge (black) that goes with it costs $49.59. And a 100-count pack of HP 4-by-6-inch photo paper costs another $18.99. The price per ounce of inkjet printer ink can exceed the per-ounce price of an expensive perfume, premium champagne, or even caviar.

The big manufacturers seem content with this captive-product pricing strategy. In fact, they pull in four times more revenues from ink cartridges and paper than from the printers themselves. Customers don't like being held hostage and having to pay through the nose for ink and paper—some are outraged by it. But what can they do? Only HP cartridges work with HP printers. Buying another brand isn't the answer, either—all of the manufacturers pursue the same pricing strategy. Besides, it's difficult to compare long-term per-print prices across manufacturers. Few of us know or go to the trouble to figure out in advance how many cartridges we'll use or what future ink prices will be.

Enter Kodak with a unique solution. Kodak recently introduced its first line of printers—EasyShare All-in-One printers—with a revolutionary pricing strategy that threatens to turn the entire inkjet printer industry upside-down. In a twist on typical industry practice, Kodak sells its printers at premium

Kodak launched a "Think Ink" marketing campaign, built around the visual "think" image, with the first two letters in black and the last three in gold.

prices with no discounts, and then sells the ink cartridges for less. EasyShare printers sell for $157.00 to $249.95, depending on features, about $50 higher than comparable printers sold by competitors. However, EasyShare black and colour ink cartridges go for just $9.99 and $14.99, respectively, about half the prevailing competitor prices. It's a whole new concept in printer pricing and economics.

To make the strategy work, Kodak first had to create a new kind of inkjet printer. It developed an innovative technology that uses tiny nozzles to squirt pigment ink drops that are just a few atoms in size. EasyShare printers take about 55 seconds to produce a 4-by-6-inch print, longer than some competitive printers that do it in 32 seconds, but the resulting photos take up to 90 years to fade versus dye-based inks that can begin to fade in as little as a year.

Moreover, Kodak found a way to contain all of the printing electronics within the EasyShare printer itself, whereas rivals include some of the electronics in the cartridges. This lets Kodak charge less for the cartridges. As a result, according to one independent lab study, Kodak's new printers "whomped" rivals' printers in price per printout. The study showed that consumers using an EasyShare printer and buying specially priced packages of photo paper and an ink cartridge can print 4-by-6-inch photos for only 10 cents each, compared with about 29 cents each for typical home printers and 19 cents each at retail store photo services.

Thus, Kodak has the right printer and the right ink prices. Now all it has to do is re-educate consumers about printer pricing—about the benefits of paying more up front in order to reduce long-run printing costs. To do this, Kodak launched a "Think Ink" marketing campaign, built around the visual image "think," with the first two letters in black and the last three in gold. The campaign asks the pivotal question: "Is it smarter to save money on a printer or save money on ink? (Hint: You only buy the printer once.)"

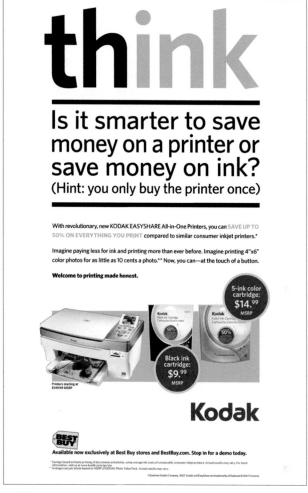

Kodak has the right printer and the right ink prices. Now all it has to do is re-educate consumers about the benefits of paying more up front to reduce long-term printing costs.

OBJECTIVES

1. Answer the question "What is a price?" and discuss the importance of pricing in today's fast-changing environment.

2. Identify and define the important factors affecting pricing decisions, including the impact of customer perceptions of value, the company and product costs, and other internal and external factors.

3. Describe the major strategies for pricing new products.

4. Explain how companies find a set of prices that maximizes the profits from the total product mix.

5. Discuss how companies adjust their prices to take into account different types of customers and situations.

6. Discuss the key issues related to initiating and responding to price changes.

The "think" campaign began with online viral efforts centred on a series of popular "Inkisit" videos featuring two dorky guys, Nathan and Max, who love to print photos but who don't like ink's high cost. In the videos, they ask enthusiastically, "Have you ever thought about what life would be like if ink was cheaper?" Kodak posted the videos on YouTube and MySpace and set up an entertaining and informative microsite.

Then came the bread-and-butter "think" media campaign, targeting budget-conscious consumers who want to print at home but have limited this activity because of high ink costs. Kodak's research showed that more than 70 percent of all families restrict their children's printing because of cost concerns. So the campaign targets "enterprising parents" who want to empower their kids' creativity and not have to worry about "silly economics."

The "think" campaign tackles the very difficult task of shifting consumer value perceptions away from initial printer prices and toward prices per print. "Our strategy," says a Kodak marketing executive, "is to crystallize for consumers that they're not only buying a printer today but also buying into three to four years of ink purchases." The campaign has sent shockwaves through the inkjet printer industry and its "razor-and-blades" pricing mentality. Says one analyst, Kodak is "plastering their costs per printed page all over the place. No one has ever done that before in this market. [The others] don't want to remind consumers how much it costs." Another analyst agrees:

> This is not your usual printer introduction. Kodak completely changes the game . . . and [these printers] will not be welcomed by competition. Competing openly on cost-per-print puts the profits of the printing industry in grave danger. To compete with Kodak, competitors will have to reveal their own printing costs and ultimately lower [their ink] prices. While this is great for consumers, it is bad for printer manufacturers' bottom lines. Kodak's [EasyShare printers] will take the market by storm.

It's still too soon to tell whether Kodak's revolutionary pricing strategy is working, but the early results are promising. The company sold 520 000 EasyShare printers in 2007, exceeding forecasts, and about 1.5 million in 2008. Competitors are now scrambling to introduce their own lower-priced cartridges and longer-lasting inks. But Kodak claims that EasyShare printers will still save customers up to 50 percent on everything they print.

As one observer concludes, Kodak "has its priorities straight: Great-looking photos that last a lifetime," with affordable per-print prices in the bargain. "It makes a world-rocking point about the razor-blades model that's lined the coffers of the inkjet industry for years. If you're mad as hell, you don't have to take it anymore."[1]

Chapter Opening Discussion

As the Kodak story illustrates, companies today face a fierce and fast-changing pricing environment, and pricing decisions are subject to a complex array of company, environmental, and competitive forces. Value-seeking customers have put increased pricing pressure on many companies. "Thank the Walmart phenomenon," says one analyst. "These days, we're all cheapskates in search of a spend-less strategy." In response, it seems that almost every company is looking for ways to slash prices.[2]

Yet cutting prices is often not the best answer. Reducing prices unnecessarily can lead to lost profits and damaging price wars. It can signal to customers that the price is more important than the customer value a brand delivers. Instead, companies should sell value, not price. With their innovative "Think Ink" campaign, Kodak hopes to promote the value of affordable per-print prices over the lower initial printer cost of competing brands.

Companies, like Kodak, should persuade customers that paying a higher price for the company's brand is justified by the greater value they gain. The challenge is to find the price that will let the company make a fair profit by getting paid for the customer value it creates. "Give people something of value," says Ronald Shaich, CEO of Panera Bread Company, "and they'll happily pay for it."[3]

Pricing: The challenge is to harvest the customer value the company creates. Says Panera Bread's CEO, Ronald Shaich, pictured here, "Give people something of value, and they'll happily pay for it."

Price
The amount of money charged for a product or service, or the sum of the values that customers exchange for the benefits of having or using the product or service.

Glossary Flashcards of Key Terms

1 WHAT IS A PRICE?

In the narrowest sense, **price** is the amount of money charged for a product or service. More broadly, price is the sum of all the values that customers give up to gain the benefits of having or using a product or service. Historically, price has been the major factor affecting buyer choice. In recent decades, nonprice factors have gained increasing importance. However, price still remains one of the most important elements determining a firm's market share and profitability.

Price is the only element in the marketing mix that produces revenue; all other elements represent costs. Price is also one of the most flexible marketing mix elements. Unlike product features and channel commitments, prices can be changed quickly. At the same time, pricing is the number-one problem facing many marketing executives, and many companies do not handle pricing well. One frequent problem is that companies are too quick to reduce prices to get a sale rather than convincing buyers that their product's greater value is worth a higher price. Other common mistakes include pricing that is too cost oriented rather than customer-value oriented, and pricing that does not take the rest of the marketing mix into account.

Some managers view pricing as a big headache, preferring instead to focus on the other marketing mix elements. However, smart managers treat pricing as a key strategic tool for creating and capturing customer value. Prices have a direct impact on a firm's bottom line. A small percentage improvement in price can generate a large percentage in profitability. More importantly, as a part of a company's overall value proposition, price plays a key role in creating customer value and building customer relationships. "Instead of running away from pricing," says an expert, "savvy marketers are embracing it."[4]

2 FACTORS TO CONSIDER WHEN SETTING PRICES

The price the company charges will fall somewhere between one that is too high to produce any demand and one that is too low to produce a profit. Figure 11.1 summarizes the major considerations in setting price. Customer perceptions of the product's value set the ceiling for prices. If customers perceive that the price is greater than the product's value, they will not buy the product. Product costs set the floor for prices. If the company prices the product below its costs, company profits will suffer. In setting its price between these two extremes, the company must consider a number of other internal and external factors, including its overall marketing strategy and mix, the nature of the market and demand, and competitors' strategies and prices.

Customer Perceptions of Value

In the end, the customer will decide whether a product's price is right. Pricing decisions, like other marketing mix decisions, must start with customer value. When customers buy a product, they exchange something of value (the price) to get something of value in return (the benefits of having or using the product). Effective, customer-oriented pricing involves understanding how much value consumers place on the benefits they receive from the product and setting a price that captures this value.

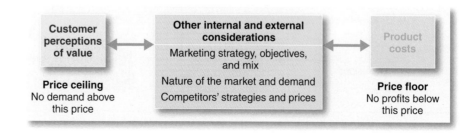

Figure 11.1
Considerations in setting price

Value-Based Pricing

Value-based pricing
Setting price based on buyers' perceptions of value rather than on the seller's cost.

Good pricing begins with a complete understanding of the value that a product or service creates for customers. **Value-based pricing** uses buyers' perceptions of value, not the seller's cost, as the key to pricing. Value-based pricing means that the marketer cannot design a product and marketing program and then set the price. Price is considered along with the other marketing mix variables *before* the marketing program is set.

Figure 11.2 compares value-based pricing with cost-based pricing. Cost-based pricing is product driven. The company designs what it considers to be a good product, adds up the costs of making the product, and sets a price that covers costs plus a target profit. Marketing must then convince buyers that the product's value at that price justifies its purchase. If the price turns out to be too high, the company must settle for lower markups or lower sales, both resulting in disappointing profits.

Value-based pricing reverses this process. The company first assesses customer needs and value perceptions. It then sets its target price based on customer perceptions of value. The targeted value and price then drive decisions about what costs can be incurred and the resulting product design. As a result, pricing begins with analyzing consumer needs and value perceptions, and price is set to match consumers' perceived value.

It's important to remember that "good value" is not the same as "low price." For example, some car buyers consider the luxurious Bentley Continental GT a real value, even at an eye-popping price of US$175 000:

> Stay with me here, because I'm about to [tell you why] a certain automobile costing US$175 000 is not actually expensive, but is in fact a tremendous value. Every Bentley GT is built by hand, an Old World bit of automaking requiring 160 hours per vehicle. Craftsmen spend 18 hours simply stitching the perfectly joined leather of the GT's steering wheel, almost as long as it takes to assemble an entire VW Golf. The results are impressive: Dash and doors are mirrored with walnut veneer, floor pedals are carved from aluminum, window and seat toggles are cut from actual metal rather than plastic, and every air vent is perfectly chromed. . . . The sum of all this is a fitted cabin that approximates that of a US$300 000 vehicle, matched to an engine the equal of a US$200 000 automobile, within a car that has brilliantly incorporated . . . technological sophistication. As I said, the GT is a bargain. [Just ask anyone on the lengthy waiting list.] The waiting time to bring home your very own GT is currently half a year.[5]

A company using value-based pricing must find out what value buyers assign to different competitive offers. However, companies often find it hard to measure the value customers will attach to a product. For example, calculating the cost of ingredients in a meal at a fancy restaurant is relatively easy. But assigning a value to other satisfactions such as taste, environment, relaxation, conversation, and status is very hard. And these values will vary both for different consumers and different situations.

Figure 11.2 Value-based pricing versus cost-based pricing

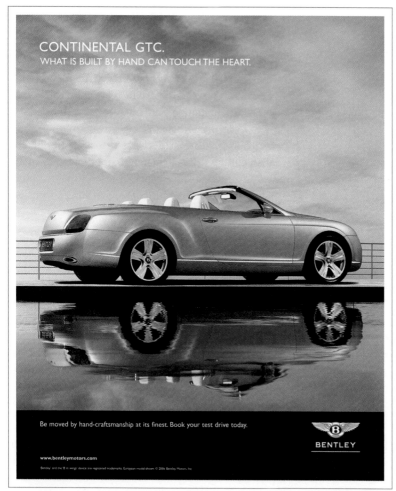

CONTINENTAL GTC.
WHAT IS BUILT BY HAND CAN TOUCH THE HEART.

Be moved by hand-craftsmanship at its finest. Book your test drive today.

BENTLEY

www.bentleymotors.com

Value-based pricing: "Good value" is not the same as "low price." Some car buyers consider the luxurious Bentley Continental GT automobile a real value, even at an eye-popping price of US$175 000.

Still, consumers will use these perceived values to evaluate a product's price, so the company must work to measure them. Sometimes, companies ask consumers how much they would pay for a basic product and for each benefit added to the offer. Or a company might conduct experiments to test the perceived value of different product offers. According to an old Russian proverb, there are two fools in every market—one who asks too much and one who asks too little. If the seller charges more than the buyers' perceived value, the company's sales will suffer. If the seller charges less, its products will sell very well, but they produce less revenue than they would if they were priced at the level of perceived value.

We now examine two types of value-based pricing: *good-value pricing* and *value-added pricing*.

Good-Value Pricing During the past decade, marketers have noted a fundamental shift in consumer attitudes toward price and quality. Many companies have changed their pricing approaches to bring them into line with changing economic conditions and consumer price perceptions. More and more, marketers have adopted good-value pricing strategies—offering just the right combination of quality and good service at a fair price.

In many cases, this has involved introducing less-expensive versions of established, brand-name products. To meet the tougher economic times and more frugal consumer spending habits, fast-food restaurants such as Taco Bell and McDonald's offer "value menus." Armani offers the less-expensive, more-casual Armani Exchange fashion line. Alberto Culver's TRESemmé hair care line promises "Curls you'll love. A price you'll adore." And Volkswagen recently reintroduced the Rabbit, an economical car with a base price under US$16 000, because "The people want an entry-level price and top-level features."[6]

In other cases, good-value pricing has involved redesigning existing brands to offer more quality for a given price or the same quality for less. Some companies even succeed by offering less value but at rock-bottom prices. For example, passengers flying low-cost European airline Ryanair won't get much in the way of free amenities, but they'll like the airline's unbelievably low prices.

An important type of good-value pricing at the retail level is *everyday low pricing (EDLP)*. EDLP involves charging a constant, everyday low price with few or no temporary price discounts. In contrast, *high–low pricing* involves charging higher prices on an everyday basis but running frequent promotions to lower prices temporarily on selected items. In recent years, high–low pricing has given way to EDLP in retail settings ranging from Saturn car dealerships to Costco warehouse clubs to furniture stores such as Leon's, with its Integrity Pricing guarantee. The king of EDLP is Walmart, which practically defined the concept. Except for a few sale items every month, Walmart promises everyday low prices on everything it sells.

Value-Added Pricing Value-based pricing doesn't mean simply charging what customers want to pay or setting low prices to meet the competition. In many marketing situations the

Good-value pricing
Offering just the right combination of quality and good service at a fair price.

Value-added pricing: Rather than dropping prices for its venerable Stag umbrella brand to match cheaper imports, Currims successfully launched umbrellas with funky designs, cool colours, and value-added features and sold them at even higher prices.

Value-added pricing

Attaching value-added features and services to differentiate a company's offers and charging higher prices.

challenge is to build the company's *pricing power*—its power to escape price competition and justify higher prices and profit margins. To increase pricing power, a firm must retain or build the value of its market offering. This is especially true for suppliers of commodity products, which are characterized by little differentiation and intense price competition.

To increase their pricing power, many companies adopt **value-added pricing** strategies. Rather than cutting prices to match competitors, they attach value-added features and services to differentiate their offers and thus support higher prices. Consider this example:

The monsoon season in Mumbai, India, is three months of near-nonstop rain. For 147 years, most Mumbaikars protected themselves with a Stag umbrella from venerable Ebrahim Currim & Sons. Like Ford's Model T, the basic Stag was sturdy, affordable, and of any colour, as long as it was black. By the end of the twentieth century, however, the Stag was threatened by cheaper imports from China. Stag responded by dropping prices and scrimping on quality. It was a bad move: For the first time since the 1940s, the brand began losing money. Finally, however, the company came to its senses. It abandoned the price war and vowed to improve quality. Surprisingly, even at higher prices, sales of the improved Stag umbrellas actually increased.

Then the company started innovating. Noting the new fashion consciousness of Indian men, it launched designer umbrellas in funky designs and cool colours. Teenagers and young adults lapped them up. Stag then launched umbrellas with a built-in high-power flashlight for those who walk unlit roads at night, and models with prerecorded tunes for music lovers. For women who walk secluded streets after dark, there's Stag's Bodyguard model, armed with glare lights, emergency blinkers, and an alarm. Customers willingly pay up to a 100 percent premium for the new products. Under the new value-added strategy, the Stag brand has now returned to profitability. Come the monsoon in June, the grand old black Stags still reappear on the streets of Mumbai—but now priced 15 percent higher than the imports.[7]

The Stag example illustrates once again that customers are motivated not by price, but by what they get for what they paid. "If consumers thought the best deal was simply a question of money saved, we'd all be shopping in one big discount store," says one pricing expert. "Customers want value and are willing to pay for it. Savvy marketers price their products accordingly."[8]

Company and Product Costs

Cost-based pricing

Setting prices based on the costs for producing, distributing, and selling the product plus a fair rate of return for effort and risk.

Whereas customer-value perceptions set the price ceiling, costs set the floor for the price that the company can charge. **Cost-based pricing** involves setting prices based on the costs for producing, distributing, and selling the product plus a fair rate of return for its effort and risk. A company's costs may be an important element in its pricing strategy.

Some companies, such as WestJet, Walmart, and Dell, work to become the "low-cost producers" in their industries. Companies with lower costs can set lower prices that result in smaller margins but greater sales and profits. Other companies, however, intentionally pay higher costs so that they can claim higher prices and margins. For example, it costs more to make a "built by hand" Bentley than a Toyota Camry. But the higher costs result in higher quality, justifying that US$175 000 price tag. The key is to manage the spread between costs and prices—how much the company makes for the customer value it delivers.

Types of Costs

Fixed costs (overhead)
Costs that do not vary with
production or sales level.

Variable costs
Costs that vary directly with the
level of production.

Total costs
The sum of the fixed and variable
costs for any given level of
production.

A company's costs take two forms: fixed and variable. **Fixed costs** (also known as **overhead**) are costs that do not vary with production or sales level. For example, a company must pay each month's bills for rent, heat, interest, and executive salaries, whatever the company's output. **Variable costs** vary directly with the level of production. Each PC produced by Hewlett-Packard involves a cost of computer chips, wires, plastic, packaging, and other inputs. These costs tend to be the same for each unit produced. They are called variable because their total varies with the number of units produced. **Total costs** are the sum of the fixed and variable costs for any given level of production. Management wants to charge a price that will at least cover the total production costs at a given level of production.

The company must watch its costs carefully. If it costs the company more than competitors to produce and sell its product, the company will need to charge a higher price or make less profit, putting it at a competitive disadvantage.

Costs at Different Levels of Production

To price wisely, management needs to know how its costs vary with different levels of production. For example, suppose Texas Instruments (TI) has built a plant to produce 1000 calculators per day. Figure 11.3A shows the typical short-run average cost curve (SRAC). It shows that the cost per calculator is high if TI's factory produces only a few per day. But as production moves up to 1000 calculators per day, average cost falls. This is because fixed costs are spread over more units, with each one bearing a smaller share of the fixed cost. TI can try to produce more than 1000 calculators per day, but average costs will increase because the plant becomes inefficient. Workers have to wait for machines, the machines break down more often, and workers get in each other's way.

If TI believed it could sell 2000 calculators a day, it should consider building a larger plant. The plant would use more efficient machinery and work arrangements. Also, the unit cost of producing 2000 calculators per day would be lower than the unit cost of producing 1000 calculators per day, as shown in the long-run average cost (LRAC) curve (Figure 11.3B). In fact, a 3000-capacity plant would be even more efficient, according to Figure 11.3B. But a 4000-daily production plant would be less efficient because of increasing diseconomies of scale—too many workers to manage, paperwork slowing things down, and so on. Figure 11.3B shows that a 3000-daily production plant is the best size to build if demand is strong enough to support this level of production.

Costs as a Function of Production Experience

Suppose TI runs a plant that produces 3000 calculators per day. As TI gains experience in producing calculators, it learns how to do it better. Workers learn shortcuts and become more familiar with their equipment. With practice, the work becomes better organized, and TI finds better equipment and production processes. With higher volume, TI becomes more

Figure 11.3 Cost Per Unit at Different Levels of Production Per Period

A. Cost behaviour in a fixed-size plant

B. Cost behaviour over different-size plants

Figure 11.4 Cost per unit as a function of accumulated production: the experience curve

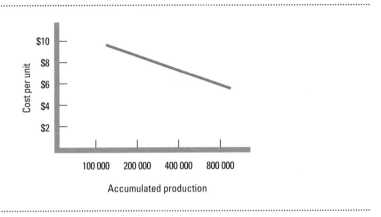

efficient and gains economies of scale. As a result, average cost tends to fall with accumulated production experience. This is shown in Figure 11.4.[9] Thus, the average cost of producing the first 100 000 calculators is $10 per calculator. When the company has produced the first 200 000 calculators, the average cost has fallen to $9. After its accumulated production experience doubles again to 400 000, the average cost is $7. This drop in the average cost with accumulated production experience is called the **experience curve** (or the **learning curve**).

Experience curve (learning curve)
The drop in the average per-unit production cost that comes with accumulated production experience.

If a downward-sloping experience curve exists, this is highly significant for the company. Not only will the company's unit production cost fall, but it will fall faster if the company makes and sells more during a given time period. But the market has to stand ready to buy the higher output. And to take advantage of the experience curve, TI must get a large market share early in the product's life cycle. This suggests the following pricing strategy: TI should price its calculators low; its sales will then increase, and its costs will decrease through gaining more experience, and then it can lower its prices further.

Some companies have built successful strategies around the experience curve. For example, Bausch & Lomb solidified its position in the soft contact lens market by using computerized lens design and steadily expanding its one SofLens plant. As a result, its market share climbed steadily to 65 percent.

However, a single-minded focus on reducing costs and exploiting the experience curve will not always work. Experience-curve pricing carries some major risks. The aggressive pricing might give the product a cheap image. The strategy also assumes that competitors are weak and not willing to fight it out by meeting the company's price cuts. Finally, while the company is building volume under one technology, a competitor may find a lower-cost technology that lets it start at prices lower than those of the market leader, who still operates on the old experience curve.

Cost-Plus Pricing

Cost-plus pricing
Adding a standard markup to the cost of the product.

The simplest pricing method is **cost-plus pricing**—adding a standard markup to the cost of the product. Construction companies, for example, submit job bids by estimating the total project cost and adding a standard markup for profit. Lawyers, accountants, and other professionals typically price by adding a standard markup to their costs. Some sellers tell their customers they will charge cost plus a specified markup; for example, aerospace companies price this way to the government.

To illustrate markup pricing, suppose a toaster manufacturer had the following costs and expected sales:

Variable cost	$10
Fixed costs	$300,000
Expected unit sales	50,000

Then the manufacturer's cost per toaster is given by the following:

$$\text{Unit Cost} = \text{Variable Cost} + \frac{\text{Fixed Costs}}{\text{Unit Sales}} = \$10 + \frac{\$300,000}{50,000} = \$16$$

Now suppose the manufacturer wants to earn a 20 percent markup on sales. The manufacturer's markup price is given by the following:[10]

$$\text{Markup Price} = \frac{\text{Unit Cost}}{(1 - \text{Desired Return on Sales})} = \frac{\$16}{1 - .2} = \$20$$

The manufacturer would charge dealers $20 per toaster and make a profit of $4 per unit. The dealers, in turn, will further mark up the toaster. If dealers want to earn 50 percent on the sales price, they will mark up the toaster to $40 ($20 + 50% of $40). This number is equivalent to a *markup on cost* of 100 percent ($20/$20).

Does using standard markups to set prices make sense? Generally, no. Any pricing method that ignores demand and competitor prices is not likely to lead to the best price. Still, markup pricing remains popular for many reasons. First, sellers are more certain about costs than about demand. By tying the price to cost, sellers simplify pricing—they do not need to make frequent adjustments as demand changes. Second, when all firms in the industry use this pricing method, prices tend to be similar and price competition is thus minimized. Third, many people feel that cost-plus pricing is fairer to both buyers and sellers. Sellers earn a fair return on their investment but do not take advantage of buyers when buyers' demand becomes great.

Break-Even Analysis and Target Profit Pricing

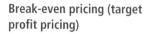

Break-even pricing (target profit pricing)
Setting price to break even on the costs of making and marketing a product, or setting price to make a target profit.

Another cost-oriented pricing approach is **break-even pricing** (or a variation called **target profit pricing**). The firm tries to determine the price at which it will break even or make the target profit it is seeking. Such pricing is used by General Motors, which prices its automobiles to achieve a 15 to 20 percent profit on its investment. This pricing method is also used by public utilities, which are constrained to make a fair return on their investment.

Target pricing uses the concept of a *break-even chart*, which shows the total cost and total revenue expected at different sales volume levels. Figure 11.5 shows a break-even chart for the toaster manufacturer discussed here. Fixed costs are $300 000 regardless of sales volume. Variable costs are added to fixed costs to form total costs, which rise with volume. The total revenue curve starts at zero and rises with each unit sold. The slope of the total revenue curve reflects the price of $20 per unit. The total revenue and total cost curves cross at 30 000 units. This is the *break-even volume*. At $20, the company must sell at least

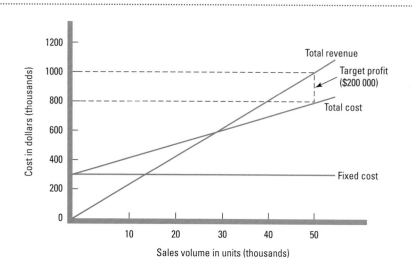

Figure 11.5 Break-even chart for determining target price

30 000 units to break even, that is, for total revenue to cover total cost. Break-even volume can be calculated using the following formula:

$$\text{Break-Even Volume} = \frac{\text{Fixed Cost}}{\text{Price} - \text{Variable Cost}} = \frac{\$300{,}000}{\$20 - \$10} = 30{,}000$$

If the company wants to make a target profit, it must sell more than 30 000 units at $20 each. Suppose the toaster manufacturer has invested $1 000 000 in the business and wants to set price to earn a 20 percent return, or $200 000. In that case, it must sell at least 50 000 units at $20 each. If the company charges a higher price, it will not need to sell as many toasters to achieve its target return. But the market may not buy even this lower volume at the higher price. Much depends on the price elasticity and competitors' prices.

The manufacturer should consider different prices and estimate break-even volumes, probable demand, and profits for each. This is done in Table 11.1. The table shows that as price increases, break-even volume drops (column 2). But as price increases, demand for the toasters also falls off (column 3). At the $14 price, because the manufacturer clears only $4 per toaster ($14 less $10 in variable costs), it must sell a very high volume to break even. Even though the low price attracts many buyers, demand still falls below the high break-even point, and the manufacturer loses money. At the other extreme, with a $22 price the manufacturer clears $12 per toaster and must sell only 25 000 units to break even. But at this high price, consumers buy too few toasters and profits are negative. The table shows that a price of $18 yields the highest profits. Note that none of the prices produce the manufacturer's target profit of $200 000. To achieve this target return, the manufacturer will have to search for ways to lower fixed or variable costs, thus lowering the break-even volume.

Other Internal and External Considerations Affecting Price Decisions

Customer perceptions of value set the upper limit for prices and costs set the lower limit. However, in setting prices within these limits, the company must consider a number of other internal and external factors. Internal factors affecting pricing include the company's overall marketing strategy, objectives, and marketing mix, as well as other organizational considerations. External factors include the nature of the market and demand, competitors' strategies and prices, and other environmental factors.

Overall Marketing Strategy, Objectives, and Mix

Price is only one element of the company's broader marketing strategy. Thus, before setting price the company must decide on its overall marketing strategy for the product or service. If the company has selected its target market and positioning carefully, then its marketing mix strategy, including price, will be fairly straightforward. For example, when Honda

Table 11.1 Break-Even Volume and Profits at Different Prices

(1) Price	(2) Unit Demand Needed to Break Even	(3) Expected Unit Demand at Given Price	(4) Total Revenue (1) × (3)	(5) Total Costs*	(6) Profit (4) – (5)
$14	75 000	71 000	$ 994 000	$1 010 000	$ −16 000
16	50 000	67 000	1 072 000	970 000	102 000
18	37 500	60 000	1 080 000	900 000	180 000
20	30 000	42 000	840 000	720 000	120 000
22	25 000	23 000	506 000	530 000	−24 000

Assumes fixed costs of $300 000 and constant unit variable costs of $10.

developed its Acura brand to compete with European luxury-performance cars in the higher-income segment, this required charging a high price. In contrast, when it introduced the Honda Fit model—billed as "a pint-sized fuel miser with feisty giddy up"—this positioning required charging a low price. Thus, pricing strategy is largely determined by decisions on market positioning.

Pricing may play an important role in helping to accomplish company objectives at many levels. A firm can set prices to attract new customers or to profitably retain existing ones. It can set prices low to prevent competition from entering the market or set prices at competitors' levels to stabilize the market. It can price to keep the loyalty and support of resellers or to avoid government intervention. Prices can be reduced temporarily to create excitement for a brand. Or one product may be priced to help the sales of other products in the company's line.

Price is only one of the marketing mix tools that a company uses to achieve its marketing objectives. Price decisions must be coordinated with product design, distribution, and promotion decisions to form a consistent and effective integrated marketing program. Decisions made for other marketing mix variables may affect pricing decisions. For example, a decision to position the product on high-performance quality will mean that the seller must charge a higher price to cover higher costs. And producers whose resellers are expected to support and promote their products may have to build larger reseller margins into their prices.

Companies often position their products on price and then tailor other marketing mix decisions to the prices they want to charge. Here, price is a crucial product-positioning factor that defines the product's market, competition, and design. Many firms support such price-positioning strategies with a technique called **target costing**, a potent strategic weapon. Target costing reverses the usual process of first designing a new product, determining its cost, and then asking, "Can we sell it for that?" Instead, it starts with an ideal selling price based on customer-value considerations and then targets costs that will ensure that the price is met. For example, when Honda set out to design the Fit, it began with a US$13 950 starting price point and 34 mpg (14.5 kilometres per litre) operating efficiency firmly in mind. It then designed a stylish, peppy little car with costs that allowed it to give target customers those values.

Other companies deemphasize price and use other marketing mix tools to create *non-price* positions. Often, the best strategy is not to charge the lowest price but rather to differentiate the marketing offer to make it worth a higher price. For example, Bang & Olufsen—known for its cutting-edge consumer electronics—builds more value into its products and charges sky-high prices. For example, a B&O 50-inch BeoVision 4 HDTV will cost you US$7500; a 65-inch model runs US$13 500. A complete B&O sound system? Well, you don't really want to know. But target customers recognize Bang & Olufsen's very high quality and are willing to pay more to get it.

Some marketers even position their products on *high* prices, featuring high prices as part of their product's allure (see Real Marketing 11.1). For example, Grand Marnier offers a US$225 bottle of Cuvée du Cent Cinquantenaire that's marketed with the tagline "Hard to find, impossible to pronounce, and prohibitively expensive." And Titus Cycles, a premium bicycle manufacturer, features its high prices and its advertising. One ad humorously shows a man giving his girlfriend a "cubic zirconia" engagement ring so that he can purchase a Titus Solera for himself. Suggested retail price: US$7750.

Thus, marketers must consider the total marketing strategy and mix when setting prices. If the product is positioned

Target costing
Pricing that starts with an ideal selling price, then targets costs that will ensure that the price is met.

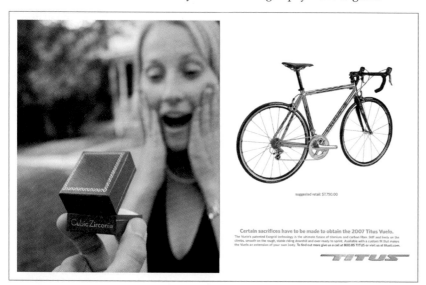

Positioning on high price: Titus features its lofty prices in its advertising—"suggested retail price: US$7750."

Real Marketing 11.1

Pricing High and Proud of It

Whereas some companies work to achieve irresistibly low prices that will pull in the masses, others take just the opposite position. They proudly pronounce higher prices on brands that appeal to a more select few. The higher prices actually add value, helping to position the brand—and the owner—as something special. Consider the following examples.

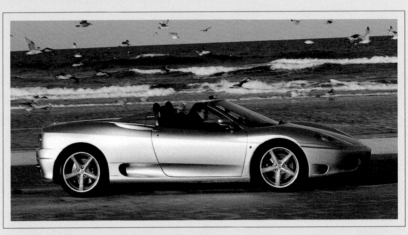

Ferraris are anything but cheap. But owners like this one will tell you that when it comes to a Ferrari, price is nothing. The Ferrari experience is everything.

Ferrari. Ferraris are anything but cheap. Prices run from a mere US$190 000 for the sleek Ferrari F430 to US$280 000 for the Ferrari 612. These prices don't include the lengthy list of expensive options or the typical markups over list price by dealers. And these are just the street models. For the real Ferrari fanatic, there's the ultralimited edition FXX that can be driven only on race tracks. It goes out the door for around US$2 million, give or take a few tens of thousands. And you don't need to worry too much about depreciation. At a recent auction, a 1959 Ferrari 250 GT LWB California Spyder sold for a show-stopping US$3.3 million.

How can any car be worth such high-octane prices? Part of it is the deeply rooted Ferrari racing heritage, which has established the brand as one of the world's fastest cars. "Racing is in our DNA," says a Ferrari spokesperson. Ferraris also feature some of the most beautiful automotive designs on the planet. These cars are thoroughbreds through and through. Still, there are plenty of other fast and stylish cars—Corvettes, Vipers, Porsches, Maseratis, Lotuses, and even some Mercedes and BMWs. These cars play in the same performance neighbourhood as Ferraris but can be had for a lot less money.

One pillar of Ferrari's special positioning is its exclusivity. People want what they can't get and it's not easy to get a Ferrari. Ferrari made just 5700 cars worldwide last year (Porsche made about 100 000). Each new Ferrari rolls off the assembly line presold, and the average buyer waits one year to take delivery. Buyers can wait as long as three years depending on the model, options, and location. "It's [part of] the value of the brand," says an investment banker who owns a Ferrari. "It's the cachet of being not easy to obtain."

But what really sets Ferrari apart from less-expensive rivals is what owners sum up as "the Ferrari experience." When you own a Ferrari, you become a part of something bigger, something special. Ferrari spends millions of dollars annually on managing relationships with its small, elite core of customers. "We have 20 000 owners in the United States and we need to know them by name," says Marco Mattiacci, vice-president of marketing in North America. The company knows that its millionaire, even billionaire, customers "are looking for more unique things with more adrenaline than a golf game on Sunday." So Ferrari sponsors several owner-only events that fuel owners' driving passions while at the same time making them feel very special.

For example, the Ferrari Quebec dealership hosted the Ferrari Fall Fun Run in 2008 where a few select consumers were invited to drive their Ferraris at the famed Circuit Mont-Tremblant race track. The automaker also sponsors the Ferrari Challenge, a series of six owners-only U.S. races, with the finals held in Italy. And for US$5925, owners can enter the Ferrari Challenge Rally, three-day touring trips on scenic back roads with stays at fine hotels. But the ultimate for owners and their spouses is the Ferrari Driving Experience. For an undisclosed amount, participants are coddled for two-and-a-half days at a five-star hotel. Ferrari loans each participant a sleek and powerful F430. Professional drivers school owners on the technical details of the car and how to get the best performance out of it. Then, Ferrari lets the owners loose on a Formula One race track to apply what they learned in the classroom.

Add it all up and it's not so surprising that Ferrari commands such high prices. Most owners will tell you that when it comes to a Ferrari, price is nothing—the Ferrari experience is everything.

Stella Artois. Positioning an exclusive, high-performance car on high price is one thing, but can such a strategy work for a more ordinary product—say, beer? Indeed it can. Consider

Stella Artois. As a premium lager, Stella Artois has long been positioned as a high-end brew, with a price to match. In its advertising and other promotions, Stella doesn't hide its higher price—it flaunts it. For more than two decades, Stella advertising has carried the tagline, "reassuringly expensive." Years of artful, critically acclaimed television ads featuring this tagline have become a Stella trademark, establishing the brand as something beyond the ordinary.

Stella Artois has even run an award-winning negative-savings coupon campaign featuring a series of authentic-looking Stella Artois coupons. Rather than offering discounts to coupon clippers, the coupons boast deals such as "$1.25 extra," "20% more," and "$4.00, regularly $2.75." The headline in each coupon affirms that Stella is "reassuringly expensive."

To further support the Stella Artois drinking experience, the brewer also promotes its well-known Nine-Step Pouring Ritual in ads and live pub appearances. Under the tutelage of a Stella Artois brewmaster, bar patrons learn important pouring steps, such as "The Purification" (cleansing and rinsing the trademark Stella Artois chalice), "The Liquid Alchemy" (the chalice glass is held at a 45-degree angle during filling), "The Beheading" (while the head is flowing over the edge of the glass, it is gently cut with a knife held at a 45-degree angle), and "The Judgment" (the foam is checked to insure two-finger thickness).

You can practise this ritual yourself in a classy, European style virtual bar—Le Cercle Bar et Brasserie—located at the Stella Artois website (www.stellaartois.com). There, you become the star in an interactive drama that begins when you order a Stella and ends when you've completed the nine-step ritual and proven yourself worthy of drinking such a perfect beer. "When you've spent over 600 years crafting the perfect beer," says the company, "you become very fastidious about the way it's served."

Premium pricing has worked well for Stella Artois. Over the years, the company has managed to convince a host of loyal beer drinkers around the globe that its high prices are a good thing, not a bad thing. Stella Artois is the number-one selling premium lager in most of the 80 countries in which it's distributed. The brand has been the number-one premium beer in the United Kingdom for years. In Canada, Labatt Breweries began distributing the beer in 2002 with solid sales growth, and other North American rivals are now adopting Stella-like strategies for their premium brands.

What is it that makes Stella Artois worth the premium price to so many beer drinkers? Like Ferrari buyers (okay, maybe with a little less conviction), Stella Artois loyalists will tell you this: It's not the price, it's the Stella experience. Or, maybe the higher price helps to create that experience.

Sources: Harry Hodge, "Stella Artois' 9-Step Ritual," *24 Hours*, April 18, 2007, p. 12; Mike Beirne, "Rivals Crib from Stella's Stellar Marketing Plan," *Brandweek*, January 2, 2007, accessed at www.brandweek.com; "Stella Artois: The Beater or the Beaten?" *Marketing Week*, February 7, 2008, p. 18; Michael Taylor, "'Red Mist—The Ferrari Mystique," *San Francisco Chronicle*, June 25, 2006, p. J1; Jean Halliday, "For $2M, They Throw in the Sheets," *Advertising Age*, February 6, 2006, p. 14; Gabriel Kahn, "How to Slow Down a Ferrari: Buy It," *Wall Street Journal*, May 8, 2007; "Gooding & Company Announces $21+ million Results from First-Ever Scottsdale Auction," *PR Newswire*, January 19, 2008; and information from www.stellaartois.com, accssed September 2008, and www.ferrariquebec.com, accessed May 2009.

on nonprice factors, then decisions about quality, promotion, and distribution will strongly affect price. If price is a crucial positioning factor, then price will strongly affect decisions made about the other marketing mix elements. But even when featuring price, marketers need to remember that customers rarely buy on price alone. Instead, they seek products that give them the best value in terms of benefits received for the price paid.

Organizational Considerations

Management must decide who within the organization should set prices. Companies handle pricing in a variety of ways. In small companies, prices are often set by top management rather than by the marketing or sales departments. In large companies, pricing is typically handled by divisional or product line managers. In industrial markets, salespeople may be allowed to negotiate with customers within certain price ranges. Even so, top management sets the pricing objectives and policies, and it often approves the prices proposed by lower-level management or salespeople.

In industries in which pricing is a key factor (airlines, aerospace, steel, railroads, oil companies), companies often have pricing departments to set the best prices or to help others in setting them. These departments report to the marketing department or top management. Others who have an influence on pricing include sales managers, production managers, finance managers, and accountants.

The Market and Demand

As noted earlier, good pricing starts with an understanding of how customers' perceptions of value affect the prices they are willing to pay. Both consumer and industrial buyers balance the price of a product or service against the benefits of owning it. Thus, before setting prices, the marketer must understand the relationship between price and demand for the company's product. In this section, we take a deeper look at the price–demand relationship and how it varies for different types of markets. We then discuss methods for analyzing the price–demand relationship.

Pricing in Different Types of Markets The seller's pricing freedom varies with different types of markets. Economists recognize four types of markets, each presenting a different pricing challenge.

Under *pure competition,* the market consists of many buyers and sellers trading in a uniform commodity such as wheat, copper, or financial securities. No single buyer or seller has much effect on the going market price. A seller cannot charge more than the going price, because buyers can obtain as much as they need at that price. Nor would sellers charge less than the market price, because they can sell all they want at this price. If price and profits rise, new sellers can easily enter the market. In a purely competitive market, marketing research, product development, pricing, advertising, and sales promotion play little or no role. Thus, sellers in these markets do not spend much time on marketing strategy.

Under *monopolistic competition,* the market consists of many buyers and sellers who trade over a range of prices rather than a single market price. A range of prices occurs because sellers can differentiate their offers to buyers. Either the physical product can be varied in quality, features, or style, or the accompanying services can be varied. Buyers see differences in sellers' products and will pay different prices for them. Sellers try to develop differentiated offers for different customer segments and, in addition to price, freely use branding, advertising, and personal selling to set their offers apart. Thus, Kohler differentiates itself from dozens of other kitchen and bath fixture brands through strong branding and advertising. Its ad campaign—"The Bold Look of Kohler"—emphasizes the brand's passion for design and craftsmanship, reducing the impact of price. Because there are many competitors in such markets, each firm is less affected by competitors' pricing strategies than in oligopolistic markets.

Under *oligopolistic competition,* the market consists of a few sellers who are highly sensitive to each other's pricing and marketing strategies. The product can be uniform (steel, aluminum) or nonuniform (cars, computers). There are few sellers because it is difficult for new sellers to enter the market. Each seller is alert to competitors' strategies and moves. If a steel company slashes its price by 10 percent, buyers will quickly switch to this supplier. The other steelmakers must respond by lowering their prices or increasing their services.

In a *pure monopoly,* the market consists of one seller. The seller may be a government monopoly (Canada Post), a private regulated monopoly (a power company), or a private nonregulated monopoly (DuPont when it introduced nylon). Pricing is handled differently in each case. In a regulated monopoly, the government permits the company to set rates that will yield a "fair return." Nonregulated monopolies are free to price at what the market will bear. However,

Monopolistic competition: Kohler sets its brand apart through strong branding and advertising, reducing the impact of price.

Figure 11.6 Demand curves

A. Inelastic demand   B. Elastic demand

they do not always charge the full price for a number of reasons: a desire not to attract competition, a desire to penetrate the market faster with a low price, or a fear of government regulation.

Analyzing the Price–Demand Relationship   Each price the company might charge will lead to a different level of demand. The relationship between the price charged and the resulting demand level is shown in the **demand curve** in Figure 11.6. The demand curve shows the number of units the market will buy in a given time period at different prices that might be charged. In the normal case, demand and price are inversely related; that is, the higher the price, the lower the demand. Thus, the company would sell less if it raised its price from P_1 to P_2. In short, consumers with limited budgets will probably buy less of something if its price is too high.

In the case of prestige goods, the demand curve sometimes slopes upward. Consumers think that higher prices mean more quality. For example, Gibson Guitar once toyed with the idea of lowering its prices to compete more effectively with Japanese rivals such as Yamaha and Ibanez. To its surprise, Gibson found that its instruments didn't sell as well at lower prices. "We had an inverse [price–demand relationship]," noted Gibson's chief executive. "The more we charged, the more product we sold." At a time when other guitar manufacturers have chosen to build their instruments more quickly, cheaply, and in greater numbers, Gibson still promises guitars that "are made one-at-a-time, by hand. No shortcuts. No substitutions." It turns out that low prices simply aren't consistent with "Gibson's century-old tradition of creating investment-quality instruments that represent the highest standards of imaginative design and masterful craftsmanship."[11]

Demand curve
A curve that shows the number of units the market will buy in a given time period, at different prices that might be charged.

Price elasticity
A measure of the sensitivity of demand to changes in price.

Most companies try to measure their demand curves by estimating demand at different prices. The type of market makes a difference. In a monopoly, the demand curve shows the total market demand resulting from different prices. If the company faces competition, its demand at different prices will depend on whether competitors' prices stay constant or change with the company's own prices.

Price Elasticity of Demand   Marketers also need to know **price elasticity**—how responsive demand will be to a change in price. Consider the two demand curves in Figure 11.6. In Figure 11.6A, a price increase from P_1 to P_2 leads to a relatively small drop in demand from Q_1 to Q_2. In Figure 11.6B, however, the same price increase leads to a large drop in demand from Q'_1 to Q'_2. If demand hardly changes with a small change in price, we say the demand is

The demand curve sometimes slopes upward: Gibson was surprised to learn that its high-quality instruments didn't sell as well at lower prices.

inelastic. If demand changes greatly, we say the demand is *elastic*. The price elasticity of demand is given by the following formula:

$$\text{Price Elasticity of Demand} = \frac{\% \text{ Change in Quantity Demanded}}{\% \text{ Change in Price}}$$

Suppose demand falls by 10 percent when a seller raises its price by 2 percent. Price elasticity of demand is therefore −5 (the minus sign confirms the inverse relation between price and demand) and demand is elastic. If demand falls by 2 percent with a 2 percent increase in price, then elasticity is −1. In this case, the seller's total revenue stays the same: The seller sells fewer items but at a higher price that preserves the same total revenue. If demand falls by 1 percent when price is increased by 2 percent, then elasticity is –1/2 and demand is inelastic. The less elastic the demand, the more it pays for the seller to raise the price.

What determines the price elasticity of demand? Buyers are less price sensitive when the product they are buying is unique or when it is high in quality, prestige, or exclusivity. They are also less price sensitive when substitute products are hard to find or when they cannot easily compare the quality of substitutes. Finally, buyers are less price sensitive when the total expenditure for a product is low relative to their income or when the cost is shared by another party.[12]

If demand is elastic rather than inelastic, sellers will consider lowering their prices. A lower price will produce more total revenue. This practice makes sense as long as the extra costs of producing and selling more do not exceed the extra revenue. At the same time, most firms want to avoid pricing that turns their products into commodities. In recent years, forces such as deregulation, dips in the economy, and the instant price comparisons afforded by the Internet and other technologies have increased consumer price sensitivity, turning products ranging from telephones and computers to new automobiles into commodities in some consumers' eyes.

Marketers need to work harder than ever to differentiate their offerings when a dozen competitors are selling virtually the same product at a comparable or lower price. More than ever, companies need to understand the price sensitivity of their customers and the trade-offs people are willing to make between price and product characteristics. In the words of marketing consultant Kevin Clancy, those who target only the price sensitive are "leaving money on the table."

Competitors' Strategies and Prices

In setting its prices, the company must also consider competitors' costs, prices, and market offerings. Consumers will base their judgments of a product's value on the prices that competitors charge for similar products. In some cases, firms have to consider not only what it costs to buy a product, but also what competitors may lease a product for. Remember the high cost of a Ferrari mentioned earlier? A new car club, the Private Collection, based in Toronto, positions itself as an alternative to ownership for exotic cars. By paying a $4995 initiation fee and just over $30 000 in annual dues, members can have access to cars like a Ferrari on a time-share basis.[13]

In addition, the company's pricing strategy may affect the nature of the competition it faces. If Canon follows a high-price, high-margin strategy, it may attract competition. A low-price, low-margin strategy, however, may stop competitors or drive them out of the market. Canon needs to benchmark its costs and value against competitors' costs and value. It can then use these benchmarks as a starting point for its own pricing.

In assessing competitors' pricing strategies, the company should ask several questions. First, how does the company's market offering compare with competitors' offerings in terms of customer value? If consumers perceive that the company's product or service provides greater value, the company can charge a higher price. If consumers perceive less value relative to competing products, the company must either charge a lower price or change customer perceptions to justify a higher price.

Next, how strong are current competitors and what are their current pricing strategies? If the company faces a host of smaller competitors charging high prices relative to the value they deliver, it might charge lower prices to drive weaker competitors out of the market. If the market is dominated by larger, low-price competitors, the company may decide to target unserved market niches with value-added products at higher prices. For example, Sleeman Breweries has adopted a two-pronged strategy for its premium and value-based brands as a result of its competitors' pricing strategies:

> Sleeman Breweries Ltd. of Guelph, Ontario, and its Quebec-based subsidiary, Unibroue, is Canada's third-largest brewery. It recently experienced declining sales and profits in the face of a continued price war in Ontario, Quebec, and Alberta, initiated by its rivals Labatt Breweries and Molson Coors. Dan Fox, Sleeman's managing director, outlines the company's response strategy when he says, "Our impetus and focus is on the premium side of business because that's where the big margins are, but the reality is you can't ignore the value segment, certainly in Ontario, given its growth in the last year or so." John Sleeman, chair and CEO of the company, echoes Fox's words, noting that "he recognizes consumers' expectations have been changed by low-priced 'value' brands. . . . Value pricing is here to stay." Thus Sleeman has worked hard to become a lower-cost producer while simultaneously introducing new premium brands under its John Sleeman Presents portfolio. The company still wants more than 50 percent of its sales to come from premium brands. To better market its products, the company has developed a tiered structure for its pricing while allocating more of its marketing budget to increase awareness of its less expensive brands.[14]

Finally, the company should ask, How does the competitive landscape influence customer price sensitivity?[15] For example, customers will be more price sensitive if they see few differences between competing products. They will buy whichever product costs the least. The more information customers have about competing products and prices before buying, the more price sensitive they will be. Easy product comparisons help customers assess the value of different options and decide what prices they are willing to pay. Finally, customers will be more price sensitive if they can switch easily from one product alternative to another.

What principle should guide decisions about what price to charge relative to those of competitors? The answer is simple in concept but often difficult in practice: No matter what price you charge—high, low, or in between—be certain to give customers superior value for that price.

Other External Factors

When setting prices, the company must also consider a number of other factors in its external environment. *Economic conditions* can have a strong impact on the firm's pricing strategies. Economic factors such as boom or recession, inflation, and interest rates affect pricing decisions because they affect both consumer perceptions of the product's price and value and the costs of producing a product.

The company must also consider what impact its prices will have on other parties in its environment. How will *resellers* react to various prices? The company should set prices that give resellers a fair profit, encourage their support, and help them sell the product effectively. The *government* is another important external influence on pricing decisions. Finally, *social concerns* may need to be taken into account. In setting prices, a company's short-term sales, market share, and profit goals may need to be tempered by broader societal considerations.

3   NEW-PRODUCT PRICING STRATEGIES

Pricing strategies usually change as the product passes through its life cycle. The introductory stage is especially challenging. Companies bringing out a new product face the challenge of setting prices for the first time. They can choose between two broad strategies: *market-skimming pricing* and *market-penetration pricing*.

Penetration pricing: To lure famously frugal Chinese customers, IKEA slashed its prices. The strategy worked. Weekend crowds at its cavernous Beijing store are so big that employees need to use megaphones to keep them in control.

Market-Skimming Pricing

Many companies that invent new products set high initial prices to "skim" revenues layer by layer from the market. Sony frequently uses this strategy, called **market-skimming pricing** (or price skimming). When Sony introduced the world's first high-definition television (HDTV) to the Japanese market in 1990, the high-tech sets cost US$43 000. These televisions were purchased only by customers who really wanted the new technology and could afford to pay a high price for it. Sony rapidly reduced the price over the next several years to attract new buyers. By 1993, a 28-inch HDTV cost a Japanese buyer just over US$6000. In 2001, a Japanese consumer could buy a 40-inch HDTV for about US$2000, a price that many more customers could afford. An entry-level HDTV set now sells for less than US$500 in North America, and prices con-

Market-skimming pricing
Setting a high price for a new product to skim maximum revenues layer by layer from the segments willing to pay the high price; the company makes fewer but more profitable sales.

tinue to fall. In this way, Sony skimmed the maximum amount of revenue from the various segments of the market.[16]

Market skimming makes sense only under certain conditions. First, the product's quality and image must support its higher price and enough buyers must want the product at that price. Second, the costs of producing a smaller volume cannot be so high that they cancel the advantage of charging more. Finally, competitors should not be able to enter the market easily and undercut the high price.

Market-Penetration Pricing

Rather than setting a high initial price to skim off small but profitable market segments, some companies use **market-penetration pricing**. They set a low initial price to *penetrate* the market quickly and deeply—to attract a large number of buyers quickly and win a large market share. The high sales volume results in falling costs, allowing the companies to cut their prices even further. For example, Dell used penetration pricing to enter the personal computer market, selling high-quality computer products through lower-cost direct channels. Its sales soared when HP, Apple, and other competitors selling through retail stores could not match its prices. And giant Swedish retailer IKEA used penetration pricing to boost its success in the Chinese market:

Market-penetration pricing
Setting a low price for a new product to attract a large number of buyers and a large market share.

> When IKEA first opened stores in China in 2002, people crowded in, but not to buy home furnishings. Instead, they came to take advantage of the freebies—air conditioning, clean toilets, and even decorating ideas. Chinese consumers are famously frugal. When it came time to actually buy, they shopped instead at local stores just down the street that offered knockoffs of IKEA's designs at a fraction of the price. So to lure the finicky Chinese customers, IKEA slashed its prices in China to the lowest in the world, the opposite approach of many Western retailers there. By increasingly stocking its Chinese stores with China-made products, the retailer pushed prices on some items as low as 70 percent below prices in IKEA's outlets outside China. The penetration pricing strategy worked. IKEA now captures a 43 percent market share of China's fast-growing home wares market alone, and the sales of its four mammoth Chinese stores surged 38 percent last year. The cavernous Beijing store draws nearly 6 million visitors annually. Weekend crowds are so big that employees need to use megaphones to keep them in control.[17]

Several conditions must be met for this low-price strategy to work. First, the market must be highly price sensitive so that a low price produces more market growth. Second, production and distribution costs must fall as sales volume increases. Finally, the low price must help keep out the competition, and the penetration pricer must maintain its low-price position—otherwise, the price advantage may be only temporary.

4 PRODUCT MIX PRICING STRATEGIES

The strategy for setting a product's price often has to be changed when the product is part of a product mix. In this case, the firm looks for a set of prices that maximizes the profits on the total product mix. Pricing is difficult because the various products have related demand and costs and face different degrees of competition. We now take a closer look at the five product mix pricing situations summarized in Table 11.2: *product line pricing, optional-product pricing, captive-product pricing, by-product pricing,* and *product bundle pricing.*

Product Line Pricing

Product line pricing
Setting the price steps between various products in a product line based on cost differences between the products, customer evaluations of different features, and competitors' prices.

Companies usually develop product lines rather than single products. For example, Samsonite offers some 20 different collections of bags of all shapes and sizes at prices that range from just over $20 for a duffle bag that you can buy through The Shopping Channel to more than $900 for a bag from its Black Label Vintage Collection, sold only through upscale stores like Taschen. In product line pricing, management must decide on the price steps to set between the various products in a line.

The price steps should take into account cost differences between the products in the line. More importantly, they should account for differences in customer perceptions of the value of different features. For example, Quicken offers an entire line of financial management software, including Cash Manager, Home & Business, and Suite versions priced at $39.99, $99.99, and $109.99, respectively. Although it costs Quicken no more to produce the CD containing the Suite version than the CD containing the Cash Manager version, many buyers happily pay more to obtain additional Suite features, such as tax preparation and investment monitoring tools. Quicken's task is to establish perceived value differences that support the price differences.

Optional-Product Pricing

Optional-product pricing
The pricing of optional or accessory products along with a main product.

Many companies use **optional-product pricing**—offering to sell optional or accessory products along with their main product. For example, a car buyer may choose to order a GPS navigation system and Bluetooth wireless communication. Refrigerators come with optional ice makers. And when you order a new PC, you can select from a bewildering array of hard drives, docking systems, software options, service plans, and carrying cases.

Pricing these options is a sticky problem. Automobile companies must decide which items to include in the base price and which to offer as options. Until recent years, General Motors' normal pricing strategy was to advertise a stripped-down model at a base price to pull people into showrooms and then to devote most of the showroom space to showing option-loaded cars at higher prices. The economy model was stripped of so many comforts and conveniences that most buyers rejected it. Then, GM and other North American automakers followed the examples of the Japanese and German companies and included in

Table 11.2 Product Mix Pricing Strategies

Strategy	Description
Product line pricing	Setting prices across an entire product line
Optional-product pricing	Pricing optional or accessory products sold with the main product
Captive-product pricing	Pricing products that must be used with the main product
By-product pricing	Pricing low-value by-products to get rid of them
Product bundle pricing	Pricing bundles of products sold together

Product line pricing: Quicken offers an entire line of financial management software, including Cash Manager, Home & Business, and Suite versions priced at $39.99, $99.99, and $109.99, respectively. Quicken's task is to establish perceived value differences that support the price differences.

the sticker price many useful items previously sold only as options. Thus, most advertised prices today represent well-equipped cars.

Captive-Product Pricing

Companies that make products that must be used along with a main product are using **captive-product pricing**. Examples of captive products are razor blade cartridges, video games, and printer cartridges. Producers of the main products (razors, video game consoles, and printers) often price them low and set high markups on the supplies. For example, Gillette sells low-priced razors but makes money on the replacement cartridges. You can buy a Gillette Fusion razor in Canada for $15. But once you've bought the razor, you're committed to buying replacement cartridges at $37.55 for a pack of eight. Companies that use captive-product pricing must be careful—consumers trapped into buying expensive supplies may come to resent the brand that ensnared them.

In the case of services, this captive-product pricing is called *two-part pricing*. The price of the service is broken into a *fixed fee* plus a *variable usage rate*. Thus, at Canada's Wonderland and other amusement parks, you pay a daily ticket or season pass charge plus additional fees for food and other in-park features. Theatres charge admission and then generate additional revenues from concessions. And cellphone companies charge a flat rate for a basic calling plan then charge for minutes over what the plan allows. The service firm must decide how much to charge for the basic service and how much for the variable usage. The fixed amount should be low enough to induce usage of the service; profit can be made on the variable fees.

By-Product Pricing

Producing products and services often generates by-products. If the by-products have no value and if getting rid of them is costly, this will affect the pricing of the main product. Using **by-product pricing**, the company seeks a market for these by-products to help offset the costs of disposing of them and to help make the price of the main product more competitive. The by-products themselves can even turn out to be profitable. For example, MacTara Limited, Nova Scotia's largest sawmill, is the only one in Canada that uses all of the wood by-products. It has even turned what was once considered waste into profit-making products.

MacTara's efforts began with the mission to make the family owned firm the most efficient lumber producer in Nova Scotia. It invested in computerized sawmill equipment that got the highest yield out of every log and reduced but could not eliminate by-products—wood chips, planer shavings, sawdust, and bark. But through insight and innovation, the firm found uses or markets for all of these. Wood chips are made into paper offsite, and planer shavings are used to heat the company's kilns, which are used to dry their lumber products. Bark, a traditionally low value

Captive-product pricing: At Six Flags, you pay a daily ticket or season charge plus additional fees for food and other in-park features.

Captive-product pricing
Setting a price for products that must be used along with a main product, such as blades for a razor and ink for a printer.

By-product pricing
Setting a price for by-products to make the main product's price more competitive.

Product bundle pricing
Combining several products and offering the bundle at a reduced price.

by-product, was the most challenging, but MacTara's research found a potential market in Sweden where wood pellets are burned in old coal furnaces. MacTara invested $17.5 million to build the largest pellet mill in North America, and its pellets now provide heat to a Swedish town whose population is 250 000. Sadly, with the downturn in the U.S. housing market reducing demand for lumber, a rising Canadian dollar, and a general downturn in the economy, MacTara faced bankruptcy in 2008 and found that its pellet mill was its most valuable asset. At the time this book was written, MacTara was in negotiations with a German renewable energy company for the sale of the firm.[18]

Product Bundle Pricing

Using **product bundle pricing**, sellers often combine several of their products and offer the bundle at a reduced price. For example, fast-food restaurants bundle a burger, fries, and a soft drink at a "combo" price. Resorts sell specially priced vacation packages that include airfare, accommodations, meals, and entertainment. And EastLink, Rogers Communications, and other cable companies bundle cable service, phone service, and high-speed Internet connections at a low combined price. Price bundling can promote the sales of products consumers might not otherwise buy, but the combined price must be low enough to get them to buy the bundle.[19]

5 PRICE ADJUSTMENT STRATEGIES

Companies usually adjust their basic prices to account for various customer differences and changing situations. Here we examine the seven price adjustment strategies summarized in Table 11.3: *discount and allowance pricing, segmented pricing, psychological pricing, promotional pricing, geographical pricing, dynamic pricing,* and *international pricing.*

Discount and Allowance Pricing

Most companies adjust their basic price to reward customers for certain responses, such as early payment of bills, volume purchases, and off-season buying. These price adjustments—called *discounts* and *allowances*—can take many forms.

Discount
A straight reduction in price on purchases during a stated period of time.

The many forms of **discounts** include a *cash discount*, a price reduction to buyers who pay their bills promptly. A typical example is "2/10, net 30," which means that although payment is due within 30 days, the buyer can deduct 2 percent if the bill is paid within 10 days. A *quantity discount* is a price reduction to buyers who buy large volumes. Such discounts provide an incentive to the customer to buy more from one given seller, rather than from many different sources. Under the provisions of the *Competition Act*, quantity discounts must be offered equally to all customers and must not exceed the seller's cost savings associated with selling large quantities.

Table 11.3 Price Adjustment Strategies

Strategy	Description
Discount and allowance pricing	Reducing prices to reward customer responses such as paying early or promoting the product
Segmented pricing	Adjusting prices to allow for differences in customers, products, or locations
Psychological pricing	Adjusting prices for psychological effect
Promotional pricing	Temporarily reducing prices to increase short-run sales
Geographical pricing	Adjusting prices to account for the geographic location of customers
Dynamic pricing	Adjusting prices continually to meet the characteristics and needs of individual customers and situations
International pricing	Adjusting prices for international markets

A *seasonal discount* is a price reduction to buyers who buy merchandise or services out of season. For example, lawn and garden equipment manufacturers offer seasonal discounts to retailers during the fall and winter months to encourage early ordering in anticipation of the heavy spring and summer selling seasons. Seasonal discounts allow the seller to keep production steady during an entire year.

Allowance
Promotional money paid by manufacturers to retailers in return for an agreement to feature the manufacturer's products in some way.

Allowances are another type of reduction from the list price. For example, *trade-in allowances* are price reductions given for turning in an old item when buying a new one. Trade-in allowances are most common in the automobile industry but are also given for other durable goods. *Promotional allowances* are payments or price reductions to reward dealers for participating in advertising and sales support programs.

Segmented Pricing

Segmented pricing
Selling a product or service at two or more prices, where the difference in prices is not based on differences in costs.

Companies will often adjust their basic prices to allow for differences in customers, products, and locations. In **segmented pricing**, the company sells a product or service at two or more prices, even though the difference in prices is not based on differences in costs.

Segmented pricing takes several forms. Under *customer-segment pricing*, different customers pay different prices for the same product or service. Museums, for example, may charge a lower admission for students and senior citizens. Under *product-form pricing*, different versions of the product are priced differently but not according to differences in their costs. For instance, a 1 litre bottle of Evian mineral water may cost $1.59 at your local supermarket. But a 150 mL aerosol can of Evian Brumisateur Mineral Water Spray sells for a suggested retail price of $11.39 at beauty boutiques and spas. The water is all from the same source in the French Alps and the aerosol packaging costs little more than the plastic bottles. Yet you pay $0.16 per 100 mL for one form and $7.59 per 100 mL for the other.

Using *location pricing*, a company charges different prices for different locations, even though the cost of offering in each location is the same. For instance, theatres vary their seat prices because of audience preferences for certain locations, and universities charge higher tuition to international students. Finally, using *time pricing*, a firm varies its price by the season, the month, the day, and even the hour. Some public utilities vary their prices to users by time of day and weekend versus weekday. Resorts give weekend and seasonal discounts.

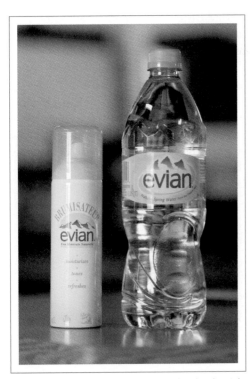

Product-form pricing: Evian water in a 1 litre bottle might cost you $0.16 per 100 mL at your local supermarket, whereas the same water might run $7.59 per 100 mL when sold in 150 mL aerosol cans as Evian Brumisateur Mineral Water Spray moisturizer.

Segmented pricing goes by many names. Robert Cross, a longtime consultant to the airlines, calls it *revenue management*. According to Cross, the practice ensures that "companies will sell the right product to the right consumer at the right time for the right price." Airlines, hotels, and restaurants call it *yield management* and practise it religiously.

The airlines, for example, routinely set prices hour-by-hour—even minute-by-minute—depending on seat availability, demand, and competitor price changes. Thus, the price you pay for a given seat on a given flight might vary greatly depending not just on class of service, but also on when and where you buy the ticket. Furthermore, the person sitting next to you might have paid half that price or twice as much. If these widely varying prices puzzle or infuriate you, imagine the pricing headaches they give an airline's revenue management team. Air Canada operates 340 aircraft that make multiple flights each day to its 170 destinations within Canada and around the world. There may be 10 or more prices for each flight. As a result, at any given moment, Air Canada may have thousands of prices in the market.[20]

For segmented pricing to be an effective strategy, certain conditions must exist. The market must be segmentable, and the segments must show different degrees of demand. The costs of segmenting and watching the market cannot exceed the extra revenue obtained from the price difference. Of course, the segmented pricing must also be legal.

Most importantly, segmented prices should reflect real differences in customers' perceived value. Consumers in higher price tiers must feel that they're getting their extra money's worth for the higher prices paid. By the same token, companies must be careful not to treat customers in lower price tiers as second-class citizens. Otherwise, in the long run, the practice will lead to customer resentment and ill will. For example, in recent years, the airlines have incurred the wrath of frustrated customers at both ends of the airplane. Passengers paying full fare for business or executive seats often feel that they are being gouged. At the same time, passengers in lower-priced economy seats feel that they're being ignored or abused. In all, the airlines today face many very difficult pricing issues (see Real Marketing 11.2).

Psychological Pricing

Price says something about the product. For example, many consumers use price to judge quality. A $100 bottle of perfume may contain only $3 worth of scent, but some people are willing to pay the $100 because this price indicates something special.

Psychological pricing
A pricing approach that considers the psychology of prices and not simply the economics; the price is used to say something about the product.

In using **psychological pricing**, sellers consider the psychology of prices and not simply the economics. For example, consumers usually perceive higher-priced products as having higher quality. When they can judge the quality of a product by examining it or by calling on past experience with it, they use price less to judge quality. But when they cannot judge quality because they lack the information or skill, price becomes an important quality signal. For example, some years ago Heublein produced Smirnoff, which was then North America's leading vodka brand. Smirnoff was attacked by another brand, Wolfschmidt, which claimed to have the same quality as Smirnoff but was priced at one dollar less per bottle. To hold on to market share, Heublein considered either lowering Smirnoff's price by one dollar or holding Smirnoff's price but increasing advertising and promotion expenditures. Either strategy would lead to lower profits, and it seemed that Heublein faced a no-win situation. At this point, however, Heublein's marketers thought of a third strategy. They raised the price of Smirnoff by one dollar! Heublein then introduced a new brand, Relska, to compete with Wolfschmidt. Moreover, it introduced yet another brand, Popov, priced even lower than Wolfschmidt. This clever strategy positioned Smirnoff as the elite brand and Wolfschmidt as an ordinary brand, producing a large increase in Heublein's overall profits. The irony is that Heublein's three brands were pretty much the same in taste and manufacturing costs. Heublein knew that a product's price signals its quality. Using price as a signal, Heublein sold roughly the same product at three different quality positions.

Reference prices
Prices that buyers carry in their minds and refer to when they look at a given product.

Another aspect of psychological pricing is **reference prices**—prices that buyers carry in their minds and refer to when looking at a given product. The reference price might be formed by noting current prices, remembering past prices, or assessing the buying situation. Sellers can influence or use these consumers' reference prices when setting price. For example, a company could display its product next to more expensive ones to imply that it belongs in the same class. Department stores often sell women's clothing in separate departments differentiated by price: Clothing found in the more expensive department is assumed to be of better quality.

For most purchases, consumers don't have all the skill or information they need to figure out whether they are paying a good price. They don't have the time, ability, or inclination to research different brands or stores, compare prices, and get the best deals. Instead, they may rely on certain cues that signal whether a price is high or low. Interestingly, such pricing cues are often provided by sellers:

It's Saturday morning and you stop by your local supermarket to pick up a few items for tonight's backyard barbeque. Cruising the aisles you're bombarded with prices. But are they good prices? If you're like most shoppers, you don't really know. So to help you out, retailers themselves give you a host of subtle and not-so-subtle signals telling you whether a given price is relatively high or low.

Psychological pricing: What do the prices marked on this tag suggest about the product and buying solution?

Real Marketing **11.2**

Airline Pricing: Balancing The Price–Value Equation

It's the same plane going to the same place at exactly the same time. But these days, not all airline passengers are equal. Nor do they all pay equally. No matter where they sit, however, it seems that all passengers have one thing in common: Very few travellers are happy with what they get for what they pay. At the front of the plane, business or executive class passengers—who might pay as much as three to six times the fare paid by economy class passengers at the back of the plane—are wondering whether it's worth it. At the same time, back in economy, tempers are flaring over rising air travel prices coupled with fewer amenities and less attentive customer service. Something is just not right with the airline price–value equation.

Flying in economy has become an increasingly miserable experience. Legroom is practically nonexistent. Passengers are more tightly packed together. Hot meals have been eliminated. Ditto pillows and blankets. And the next time that guy in front of you leans his seat back directly into your face, few of your fellow passengers are likely to blame you if you feel a brief, murderous urge to strike back.

Most of us have had experiences like those of Doug Fesler, an executive at a medical research group in Washington. He wasn't expecting much in the way of amenities on his American Airlines flight to Honolulu in September. In fact, knowing the airline no longer served free meals, he had packed his own lunch for the second leg of his flight from Dallas to Honolulu. But he said he was shocked at the lack of basic services and the overall condition of the cabin. On that flight, the audio for the movie was broken. The light that indicated when the bathroom was occupied was squirrelly, causing confusion and, in some cases, embarrassingly long waits for passengers in need of the lavatory. And though food was available for purchase, it ran out before the flight attendants could serve the entire cabin, leaving some fellow passengers looking longingly at the snack he had packed.

His return flight was just as disappointing. This time the audio for the movie worked—but only in Spanish—and his seat refused to stay in the upright position. "I was just appalled," said Fesler. "You pay $500 or $600 for a seat, and

The price–value equation: These days, when it comes to airline pricing, very few travellers are happy with what they get for what they pay. Back in economy, tempers are flaring over rising prices coupled with cattle-car service or fewer amenities.

you expect it to be functional." He said he has considered refusing to fly airlines with such poor service, but added that "if you did that with every airline that made you mad, you'd never get anywhere in this country."

The story is much different in the front of the plane—and it's not just things like the four-course meal (served on china, with real utensils, and with a choice of four wines) that American Airlines now serves its business class passengers on overseas flights and the fact that, yes, a pillow and a blanket still await you. Passengers flying executive class on Air Canada from Montreal to Geneva, for example, are now offered lie-flat bed suites with personal seatback entertainment units. American and other airlines are also upgrading their upper-class cabins on international flights with such features as in-flight entertainment and new food options.

What with all these privileges and the impeccable service that comes with them, you'd think that business class passengers would be delighted, but that's often not so. Premium passengers get more but, of course, they also pay a lot more—some think too much more. Many business class passengers complain that they're picking up an unfair share of the bill for those who fly cheaply in the back. And they may be right. United Airlines says just 8 percent of its customers—the ones paying a premium for first and business class—generate 36 percent of passenger revenue.

But it's the folks back in coach who are grumbling the most. Why, they ask, has the quality of their flying experience degraded so quickly, even as prices have risen? The fact is that airlines who flew so close to full capacity for many years began to think that they really didn't have to cater to economy passengers—most of whom are booking on price alone and who increasingly have no real airline loyalty. However, times have changed with a downturn in the economy, and some airlines are taking a different route. Porter Airlines, for example, a new entrant into the Canadian marketplace, promises and delivers much more. It offers convenient departure points, like the Island Airport in Toronto, which sits right next to the downtown business core. Porter offers upscale amenities like leather seats with more legroom than other airlines. It focuses on impeccable and innovative service that appeals to business and casual travellers alike. While other airlines believe pampering low-fare passengers would never be worth it in pure bottom-line terms, Porter is proving them wrong and is taking business away from its competitors.

Some of the major airlines are quickly discovering that hauling plane loads of increasingly grumpy passengers isn't good for the airline in the long run. With the industry once again headed into turbulent economic skies, it will need all the lift it can get from customer goodwill. Airlines like Porter, that get the price–value equation right, will surely reap the rewards.

More broadly, perhaps it's just a matter of adjusting passenger expectations. Some passengers seem to feel that the airlines should just acknowledge that the flying experience is no longer a glamorous or, at times, even tolerable one—especially back in economy—and that it's something passengers are going to have to accept. Low-cost carriers such as Southwest and WestJet have long managed to keep costs down while at the same time keeping customers delighted. "I actually have more respect for Southwest Airlines in this area," says one experienced traveller, referring to that historically no-frills airline. "They've never pretended to have more than they do."

Sources: Adapted from portions of Michelle Higgins, "Aboard Planes, Class Conflict," *New York Times*, November 25, 2007; with information from Jefferson George, "Want an Aisle Window? Get Ready to Pay for It," *McClatchy-Tribune Business News*, April 17, 2008; and Porter Airlines website, www.flyporter.com/en/experience.aspx, accessed July 2009.

For example, *sales signs* shout out "Sale!" "Reduced" "Price after rebate!" or "Now 2 for only...!" *Prices ending in 9* let you know that the product has to be a bargain. Another good clue is *signpost pricing* (also called *loss-leader pricing*)—low prices on products for which you have accurate price knowledge. You probably know a good price on a 12-pack of Coke when you see one, so a low price there suggests that the store's other prices must be low as well. A *price-matching guarantee* also suggests that one store's prices are lower than another's—how else could they make such a promise?[21]

Are such pricing signals really helpful hints, or are they just retailer ploys? These tactics certainly work for the retailer. For example, research shows that the word *sale* beside a price (even without actually varying the price) can increase demand by more than 50 percent. But do these signals really help customers? The answer, often, is yes—careful buyers really can take advantage of such cues to find good buys. And if used properly, retailers can use such tactics to provide useful price information to their customers, building more solid customer relationships. Used improperly, however, they can mislead consumers, tarnishing a brand and damaging customer relationships.

Even small differences in price can signal product differences. Consider a stereo receiver priced at $300 compared to one priced at $299.99. The actual price difference is only 1 cent, but the psychological difference can be much greater. For example, some consumers will see the $299.99 as a price in the $200 range rather than the $300 range. The $299.99 will more likely be seen as a bargain price, whereas the $300 price suggests more quality. Some psychologists argue that each digit has symbolic and visual qualities that should be considered in pricing. Thus, 8 is round and even and creates a soothing effect, whereas 7 is angular and creates a jarring effect.[22]

Promotional Pricing

Promotional pricing
Temporarily pricing products below the list price, and sometimes even below cost, to increase short-run sales.

With **promotional pricing**, companies will temporarily price their products below list price and sometimes even below cost to create buying excitement and urgency. Promotional pricing takes several forms. A seller may simply offer *discounts* from normal prices to increase sales and reduce inventories. Sellers also use *special-event pricing* in certain seasons to draw more customers. Thus, linens are promotionally priced every January to attract weary Christmas

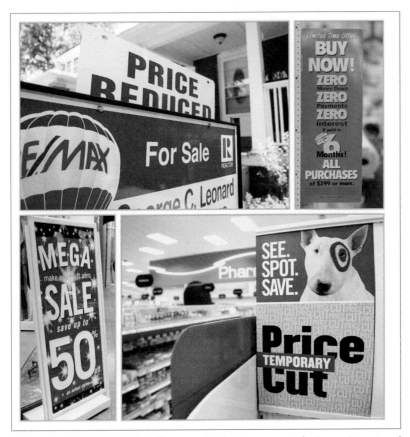

Promotional pricing: Companies offer promotional prices to create buying excitement and urgency.

shoppers back into stores. Manufacturers sometimes offer *cash rebates* to consumers who buy the product from dealers within a specified time; the manufacturer sends the rebate directly to the customer. Rebates have been popular with automakers and producers of durable goods and small appliances, but they are also used with consumer packaged goods. Some manufacturers offer *low-interest financing, longer warranties,* or *free maintenance* to reduce the consumer's "price." This practice has become another favourite of the auto industry.

Promotional pricing, however, can have adverse effects. Used too frequently and copied by competitors, price promotions can create "deal-prone" customers who wait until brands go on sale before buying them. Constantly reduced prices can also erode a brand's value in the eyes of customers. Marketers sometimes become addicted to promotional pricing, using price promotions as a quick fix instead of sweating through the difficult process of developing effective longer-term strategies for building their brands. The use of promotional pricing can also lead to industry price wars. Such price wars usually play into the hands of only one or a few competitors—those with the most efficient operations. For example, in the face of intense competition with Intel, computer chip maker Advanced Micro Devices (AMD) began to aggressively reduce its prices. Intel retaliated with even lower prices. In the resulting price war, AMD has seen its margins and profits skid against those of its larger rival.[23]

The point is that promotional pricing can be an effective means of generating sales for some companies in certain circumstances. But it can be damaging for other companies or if taken as a steady diet.

Geographical Pricing

A company also must decide how to price its products for customers located in different parts of the country or world. Should the company risk losing the business of more-distant customers by charging them higher prices to cover the higher shipping costs? Or should the company charge all customers the same prices regardless of location? We will look at three **geographical pricing** strategies for the following hypothetical situation:

> The Peerless Paper Company is located in northern British Columbia and sells paper products to customers all over Canada. The cost of freight is high and affects the companies from whom customers buy their paper. Peerless wants to establish a geographical pricing policy. It is trying to determine how to price a $10 000 order to three specific customers: Customer A (Vancouver), Customer B (Winnipeg), and Customer C (Halifax).

Geographical pricing
Setting prices for customers located in different parts of the country or world.

FOB-origin pricing
A geographical pricing strategy in which goods are placed free on board a carrier; the customer pays the freight from the factory to the destination.

One option is for Peerless to ask each customer to pay the shipping cost from the factory in northern B.C. to the customer's location. All three customers would pay the same factory price, with Customer A paying, say, $100 for shipping; Customer B $150; and Customer C $250. Called **FOB-origin pricing,** this practice means that the goods are placed *free on board* (hence, *FOB*) a carrier. At that point the title and responsibility pass to the customer, who pays the freight from the factory to the destination. Because each customer picks up its own cost, supporters of FOB pricing feel that this is the fairest way to assess freight charges. The disadvantage, however, is that Peerless will be a high-cost firm to distant customers.

Uniform-delivered pricing
A geographical pricing strategy in which the company charges the same price plus freight to all customers, regardless of their location.

Uniform-delivered pricing is the opposite of FOB pricing. Here, the company charges the same price plus freight to all customers, regardless of their location. The freight charge is set at the average freight cost. Suppose this is $150. Uniform-delivered pricing therefore results in a higher charge to the Vancouver customer (who pays $150 freight instead of $100) and a lower charge to the Halifax customer (who pays $150 instead of $250). Although the Vancouver customer would prefer to buy paper from another local paper company that uses FOB-origin pricing, Peerless has a better chance of winning over the Halifax customer. Other advantages of uniform-delivered pricing are that it is fairly easy to administer and it lets the firm advertise its price nationally.

Zone pricing
A geographical pricing strategy in which the company sets up two or more zones. All customers within a zone pay the same total price; the more distant the zone, the higher the price.

Zone pricing falls between FOB-origin pricing and uniform-delivered pricing. The company sets up two or more zones. All customers within a given zone pay a single total price; the more distant the zone, the higher the price. For example, Peerless might set up a West Zone and charge $100 freight to all customers in this zone, a Central Zone in which it charges $150, and an East Zone in which it charges $250. In this way, the customers within a given price zone receive no price advantage from the company. For example, customers in Halifax and St. John's pay the same total price to Peerless. The complaint, however, is that the Halifax customer is paying part of the St. John's customer's freight cost.

Dynamic Pricing

Throughout most of history, prices were set by negotiation between buyers and sellers. *Fixed price* policies—setting one price for all buyers—is a relatively modern idea that arose with the development of large-scale retailing at the end of the nineteenth century. Today, most prices are set this way. However, some companies are now reversing the fixed pricing trend. They are using **dynamic pricing**—adjusting prices continually to meet the characteristics and needs of individual customers and situations.

Dynamic pricing
Adjusting prices continually to meet the characteristics and needs of individual customers and situations.

For example, think about how the Internet has affected pricing. From the mostly fixed pricing practices of the past century, the Web seems now to be taking us back—into a new age of fluid pricing. The flexibility of the Internet allows web sellers to instantly and constantly adjust prices on a wide range of goods based on demand dynamics. In many cases, this involves regular changes in the prices that web sellers set for their goods. In others, such as eBay or Priceline, consumers negotiate the final prices they pay. Still other companies customize their offers based on the characteristics and behaviours of specific customers: Airlines are increasingly able to create unique prices and advertisements for people as they surf the Web.[24]

Dynamic pricing offers many advantages for marketers. For example, Internet sellers such as Amazon.ca can mine their databases to gauge a specific shopper's desires, measure his or her means, instantaneously tailor products to fit that shopper's behaviour, and price products accordingly. Catalogue retailers such as Tilley Endurables and Sears can change prices on the fly according to changes in demand or costs, changing prices for specific items on a day-by-day or even hour-by-hour basis.

Many direct marketers monitor inventories, costs, and demand at any given moment and adjust prices instantly. For example, Dell uses dynamic pricing to achieve real-time balancing of supply and demand for computer

Dynamic pricing: Alaska Airlines creates unique prices and advertisements for people as they surf the Web.

components. By raising prices on components in short supply and dropping prices for oversupplied items, Dell actually reshapes demand on the go to meet supply conditions.

Buyers also benefit from the Web and dynamic pricing. A wealth of price comparison sites—such as Shopbot.ca, PriceCanada.com, PriceGrabber.ca, and PriceNetwork.ca—offer instant product and price comparisons from thousands of vendors. Shopbot.ca, for instance, lets shoppers browse by category or search for specific products and brands in either English or French. It only lists products available from reliable Canadian retailers, allows users to compare prices from various sellers, and enables shoppers to order them right on the site.

Buyers can also negotiate prices at online auction sites and exchanges. Suddenly the centuries-old art of haggling is back in vogue. Want to sell that antique pickle jar that's been collecting dust for generations? Post it on eBay, the world's biggest online flea market. Want to name your own price for a hotel room or rental car? Visit Priceline.com or another reverse auction site. Want to bid on a ticket to a Coldplay show? Check out Ticketmaster.ca, which now offers an online auction service for concert tickets.

Dynamic pricing can also be controversial. Most customers would find it galling to learn that the person in the next seat on that flight from Calgary to Hamilton paid 10 percent less just because he or she happened to call at the right time or buy through the right sales channel. Amazon.com learned this some years ago when it experimented with lowering prices to new customers to woo their business. When regular customers learned through Internet chatter that they were paying generally higher prices than first-timers, they protested loudly. An embarrassed Amazon.com halted the experiments.

Dynamic pricing makes sense in many contexts—it adjusts prices according to market forces, and it often works to the benefit of the customer. But marketers need to be careful not to use dynamic pricing to take advantage of certain customer groups, damaging important customer relationships.

International Pricing

Companies that market their products internationally must decide what prices to charge in the different countries in which they operate. In some cases, a company can set a uniform worldwide price. For example, Bombardier sells its jetliners at about the same price everywhere, whether in Canada, Europe, or a developing country. However, most companies adjust their prices to reflect local market conditions and cost considerations.

The price that a company should charge in a specific country depends on many factors, including economic conditions, competitive situations, laws and regulations, and development of the wholesaling and retailing system. Consumer perceptions and preferences may also vary from country to country, calling for different prices. Or the company may have different marketing objectives in various world markets, which require changes in pricing strategy. For example, Samsung might introduce a new product into mature markets in highly developed countries with the goal of quickly gaining mass-market share—this would call for a penetration pricing strategy. In contrast, it might enter a less-developed market by targeting smaller, less price-sensitive segments; in this case, market-skimming pricing makes sense.

Costs play an important role in setting international prices. Travellers abroad are often surprised to find that goods that are relatively inexpensive at home may carry outrageously higher price tags in other countries. A pair of Levi's selling for $30 in North America might go for $63 in Tokyo and $88 in Paris. A McDonald's Big Mac selling for a modest $3.50 here might cost $7.50 in Reykjavik, Iceland, and an Oral-B toothbrush selling for $2.49 at home may cost $10 in China. Conversely, a Gucci handbag going for only $140 in Milan, Italy, might fetch $240 in North America. In some cases, such *price escalation* may result from differences in selling strategies or market conditions. In most instances, however, it is simply a result of the higher costs of selling in another

International pricing: Smart pricing plays a key role in Dell's marketing in China and other emerging markets.

country—the additional costs of product modifications, shipping and insurance, import tariffs and taxes, exchange-rate fluctuations, and physical distribution.

Price has become a key element in the international marketing strategies of companies attempting to enter emerging markets such as China, India, and Brazil. Consider Dell's current China strategy:

> It seems that every personal computer maker now wants a piece of China, where PC sales grew at a dazzling 21 percent rate last year, compared with just a 2.6 percent North American growth rate. By 2013, China will overtake North America as the world's largest PC market. To gain a stronger foothold in China, Dell is pursuing a penetration pricing strategy. It recently launched a new, low-priced computer designed especially for the still-developing, less-affluent Chinese market. The US$340 Dell EC280 uses only about a quarter of the power of a conventional desktop and has been simplified for first-time computer buyers. "We said to ourselves: 'Let's design something that doesn't have things that people don't use,'" says a Dell international marketing executive. "Those things cost money and add [unneeded] complexity." Smart pricing has helped Dell increase its share of the Chinese market by almost 30 percent in just the past four years. The PC maker is now adapting the low-cost China PC to Brazil, India, and other emerging markets.[25]

Thus, international pricing presents some special problems and complexities. We discuss international pricing issues in more detail in Chapter 18.

6   PRICE CHANGES

After developing their pricing structures and strategies, companies often face situations in which they must initiate price changes or respond to price changes by competitors.

Initiating Price Changes

In some cases, the company may find it desirable to initiate either a price cut or a price increase. In both cases, it must anticipate possible buyer and competitor reactions.

Initiating Price Cuts

Several situations may lead a firm to consider cutting its price. One such circumstance is excess capacity. Another is falling demand in the face of strong price competition. In such cases, the firm may aggressively cut prices to boost sales and share. But as the airline, fast-food, automobile, and other industries have learned in recent years, cutting prices in an industry loaded with excess capacity may lead to price wars as competitors try to hold on to market share.

A company may also cut prices in a drive to dominate the market through lower costs. Either the company starts with lower costs than its competitors, or it cuts prices in the hope of gaining market share that will further cut costs through larger volume. Bausch & Lomb used an aggressive low-cost, low-price strategy to become an early leader in the competitive soft contact lens market. Costco used this strategy to become the world's largest warehouse retailer.

Initiating Price Increases

A successful price increase can greatly improve profits. For example, if the company's profit margin is 3 percent of sales, a 1 percent price increase will boost profits by 33 percent if sales volume is unaffected. A major factor in price increases is cost inflation. Rising costs squeeze profit margins and lead companies to pass cost increases along to customers. Another factor leading to price increases is overdemand: When a company cannot supply all that its customers need, it may raise its prices, ration products to customers, or both.

Price changes: A brand's price and image are often closely linked and a change in price can adversely affect how consumers view the brand. Tiffany found this out when it attempted to broaden its appeal by offering a line of more affordable jewellery.

When raising prices, the company must avoid being perceived as a price gouger. For example, facing rapidly rising gasoline prices, angry customers are accusing the major oil companies of enriching themselves at the expense of consumers. Customers have long memories, and they will eventually turn away from companies or even whole industries that they perceive as charging excessive prices. In the extreme, claims of price gouging may even bring about increased government regulation.

There are some techniques for avoiding these problems. One is to maintain a sense of fairness surrounding any price increase. Price increases should be supported by company communications telling customers why prices are being raised. Making low-visibility price moves first is also a good technique: Some examples include dropping discounts, increasing minimum order sizes, and curtailing production of low-margin products. The company sales force should help business customers find ways to economize.

Wherever possible, the company should consider ways to meet higher costs or demand without raising prices. For example, Air Canada has worked to lower the weight of its planes through any and all possible means, from restricting its passenger luggage allowance to ditching glass wine bottles in favour of lightweight containers on its Montreal–Paris route, as it desperately struggles to save on fuel as oil prices soar.[26] Other tactics include considering more cost-effective ways to produce or distribute its products. A company can shrink the product or substitute less-expensive ingredients instead of raising the price, as chocolate bar manufacturers often do. Or it can "unbundle" its market offering, removing features, packaging, or services and separately pricing elements that were formerly part of the offer.

Buyer Reactions to Price Changes

Customers do not always interpret price changes in a straightforward way. A price *increase*, which would normally lower sales, may have some positive meanings for buyers. For example, what would you think if Rolex *raised* the price of its latest watch model? On the one hand, you might think that the watch is even more exclusive or better made. On the other hand, you might think that Rolex is simply being greedy by charging what the market will bear.

Similarly, consumers may view a price *cut* in several ways. For example, what would you think if Rolex were to suddenly cut its prices? You might think that you are getting a better deal on an exclusive product. More likely, however, you'd think that quality had been reduced, and the brand's luxury image might be tarnished.

A brand's price and image are often closely linked. A price change, especially a drop in price, can adversely affect how consumers view the brand. Tiffany found this out when it attempted to broaden its appeal by offering a line of more affordable jewelry:

> Tiffany is all about luxury and the cachet of its blue boxes. However, in the late 1990s, the high-end jeweller responded to the "affordable luxuries" craze with a new "Return to Tiffany" line of less expensive silver jewellery. The "Return to Tiffany" silver charm bracelet quickly became a must-have item, as teens jammed Tiffany's hushed stores clamouring for the US$110 silver bauble. Sales skyrocketed. But despite this early success, Tiffany's bosses grew worried that the bracelet fad could alienate the firm's older, wealthier, and more conservative clientele. Worse, it could forever damage Tiffany's reputation for luxury. So, in 2002, to chase away the teeny-boppers, the firm began hiking prices on the fast-growing, highly profitable line of cheaper silver jewellery. At the

same time, it introduced pricier jewellery collections, renovated its stores, and showed off its craftsmanship by highlighting spectacular gems like a US$2.5 million pink diamond ring. However, the jury is still out on whether Tiffany can fully regain its exclusivity. Although high-end jewellery has once again replaced silver as Tiffany's fastest growing business, the company's profit margins and stock price have suffered in recent years. Says one well-heeled customer: "You used to aspire to be able to buy something at Tiffany, but now it's not that special anymore."[27]

Competitor Reactions to Price Changes

A firm considering a price change must worry about the reactions of its competitors as well as those of its customers. Competitors are most likely to react when the number of firms involved is small, when the product is uniform, and when the buyers are well informed about products and prices.

How can the firm anticipate the likely reactions of its competitors? The problem is complex because, like the customer, the competitor can interpret a company price cut in many ways. It might think the company is trying to grab a larger market share or that it's doing poorly and trying to boost its sales. Or it might think that the company wants the whole industry to cut prices to increase total demand.

The company must guess each competitor's likely reaction. If all competitors behave alike, this amounts to analyzing only a typical competitor. In contrast, if the competitors do not behave alike—perhaps because of differences in size, market shares, or policies—then separate analyses are necessary. However, if some competitors will match the price change, there is good reason to expect that the rest will also match it.

Responding to Price Changes

Here we reverse the question and ask how a firm should respond to a price change by a competitor. The firm needs to consider several issues: Why did the competitor change the price? Is the price change temporary or permanent? What will happen to the company's market share and profits if it does not respond? Are other competitors going to respond? Besides these issues, the company must also consider its own situation and strategy and possible customer reactions to price changes.

Figure 11.7 shows the ways a company might assess and respond to a competitor's price cut. Suppose the company learns that a competitor has cut its price and decides that

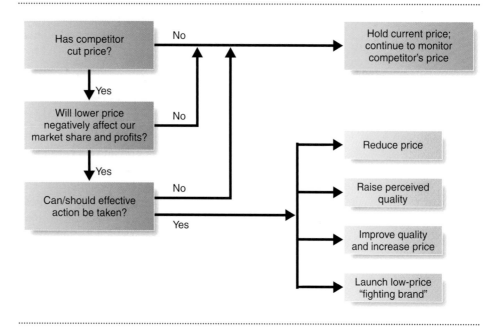

Figure 11.7 Assessing and responding to competitor price changes

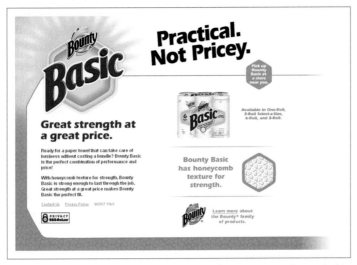

Fighting brands: P&G offers popular budget-priced Basic versions of several of its major brands. For example, Bounty Basic is "practical, not pricey."

this price cut is likely to harm company sales and profits. It might simply decide to hold its current price and profit margin. The company might believe that it will not lose too much market share, or that it would lose too much profit if it reduced its own price. Or it might decide that it should wait and respond when it has more information on the effects of the competitor's price change. However, waiting too long to act might let the competitor get stronger and more confident as its sales increase.

If the company decides that effective action can and should be taken, it might make any of four responses. First, it could *reduce its price* to match the competitor's price. It may decide that the market is price sensitive and that it would lose too much market share to the lower-priced competitor. Cutting the price will reduce the company's profits in the short run. Some companies might also reduce their product quality, services, and marketing communications to retain profit margins, but this will ultimately hurt long-run market share. The company should try to maintain its quality as it cuts prices.

Alternatively, the company might maintain its price but *raise the perceived value* of its offer. It could improve its communications, stressing the relative value of its product over that of the lower-priced competitor. The firm may find it cheaper to maintain price and spend money to improve its perceived value than to cut price and operate at a lower margin. Or the company might *improve quality and increase price*, moving its brand into a higher price–value position. The higher quality creates greater customer value, which justifies the higher price. In turn, the higher price preserves the company's higher margins.

Finally, the company might *launch a low-price "fighting brand"*— adding a lower-price item to the line or creating a separate lower-price brand. This is necessary if the particular market segment being lost is price sensitive and will not respond to arguments of higher quality. Thus, to counter store brands and other low-price entrants, Procter & Gamble turned a number of its brands into fighting brands. P&G offers popular budget-priced Basic versions of several of its major brands. For example, Charmin Basic is "the quality toilet tissue at a price you'll love." And Bounty Basic is "practical, not pricey." It offers "great strength at a great price—the paper towel that can take care of business without costing a bundle." In all, the Bounty brand claims an astounding 42.5 percent share of the paper towel market, and Bounty Basic has accounted for much of the brand's recent growth.[28]

PUBLIC POLICY AND PRICING

Price competition is a core element of our free-market economy. In setting prices, companies usually are not free to charge whatever prices they wish. Several laws restrict pricing practices and companies must also consider broader societal pricing concerns.

Legal issues surrounding pricing are outlined in Part VI: Offences in Relation to Competition and Part VII.1: Deceptive Marketing Practices of the *Competition Act*. Canadian pricing legislation was designed with two goals in mind: (1) to foster a competitive environment and (2) to protect consumers.[29] Although pricing decisions made by firms do not generally require regulatory approval, Canadian marketers should be aware of the major public policy issues in pricing outlined in Figure 11.8. These include potentially damaging pricing practices within a given level of the channel (price-fixing and predatory pricing) and across levels of the channel (retail price maintenance, discriminatory pricing, and deceptive pricing).[30]

Figure 11.8 Public policy issues in pricing

Pricing Within Channel Levels

Federal legislation on *price-fixing* states that sellers must set prices without talking to competitors. Otherwise, price collusion is suspected. Price-fixing is illegal per se—that is, the government does not accept any excuses for price-fixing. Under the *Competition Act*, the legal charge for offences of this nature is *conspiracy*. Companies found guilty of such practices can receive heavy fines. In fact, sweeping changes to the *Competition Act* passed in the 2009 budget increase potential fines by as much as $25 million and increase jail sentences to 14 years for breaching new conspiracy provisions.[31]

Recently, governments have been aggressively enforcing price-fixing regulations in industries ranging from gasoline, insurance, and concrete to credit cards, CDs, and computer chips. For example, the United States, Canada, and the European Union are investigating charges by major retailers that candy makers such as Hershey, Nestlé, Mars, Kraft, and Cadbury colluded with one another to raise candy prices higher than justified by recent increases in the price of raw materials. If the companies are found guilty, they could face fines of up to 10 percent of their annual profits.[32]

Another indictable offence pertaining to price-fixing is bid-rigging, which is listed in section 47 of the *Competition Act*. In bid-rigging, one party agrees, at the request of another party, not to submit a bid or tender in response to a call or agrees to withdraw a bid or tender submitted.

Under section 78 (Abuse of Dominant Position) of the *Competition Act*, sellers are prohibited from using *predatory pricing*—selling below cost with the intention of punishing a competitor or gaining higher long-run profits by putting competitors out of business. This protects small sellers from larger ones who might sell items below cost temporarily or in a specific locale to drive them out of business. The biggest problem is determining just what constitutes predatory pricing behaviour. Selling below cost to unload excess inventory is not considered predatory; selling below cost to drive out competitors is. Thus, the same action may or may not be predatory depending on intent, and intent can be very difficult to determine or prove.

In recent years, several large and powerful companies have been accused of predatory pricing. For example, Walmart has been sued by dozens of small competitors charging that it lowered prices in their specific geographic areas or on specific products—such as gasoline and generic drugs—to drive them out of business.

Pricing Across Channel Levels

The *Competition Act* seeks to prevent unfair *price discrimination* by ensuring that sellers offer the same price terms to customers at a given level of trade. For example, every retailer is entitled to the same price terms from a given manufacturer, whether the retailer is Sears or your local bicycle shop. However, price discrimination is allowed if the seller can prove that its costs are different when selling to different retailers—for example, that it costs less per unit to sell a large volume of bicycles to Sears than to sell a few bicycles to the local dealer. In other words, quantity or volume discounts are not prohibited. However, discriminatory promotional allowances (those not offered on proportional terms to all other competing customers) are illegal. Thus, large competitors cannot negotiate special discounts, rebates, and price concessions that are not made proportionally available to smaller competitors. For example, a small customer purchasing one-third as much as a larger competitor must receive a promotional allowance equal to one-third of what the large competitor was offered.

Although functional discounts (offering a larger discount to wholesalers than to retailers) are legal in the United States, they are illegal in Canada. In Canada, retailers and wholesalers are considered competing customers who must receive proportionally equal promotional allowances. Often, Canadian marketers who work for multinational firms must explain the differences in the law to their U.S. counterparts. Canadian marketers must also keep in mind that it is illegal for a buyer to knowingly benefit from any form of price discrimination. Price differentials may be used to "match competition" in "good faith," provided the firm is trying to meet competitors at its own level of competition and the price discrimination is temporary, localized, and defensive rather than offensive.

Canadian marketers are allowed to offer price breaks for one-shot deals, such as store-opening specials, anniversary specials, and stock clearance sales. However, regional price differentials that limit competition are illegal. Canadian firms cannot price products unreasonably low in one part of the country with the intent of driving out the competition.

Laws also prohibit *retail (or resale) price maintenance*—a manufacturer cannot require dealers to charge a specified retail price for its product. Although the seller can propose a manufacturer's *suggested* retail price to dealers, it cannot refuse to sell to a dealer who takes independent pricing action, nor can it punish the dealer by shipping late or denying advertising allowances.

Deceptive pricing occurs when a seller states prices or price savings that are not actually available to consumers and is outlined in section 74 of the *Competition Act.* For example, firms cannot advertise a product at a low price, carry very limited stock, and then tell consumers they are out of the product so that they can entice them to switch to a higher-priced item. This "bait and switch" advertising is illegal in Canada. Firms must offer their customers "rain cheques" to avoid legal sanctions if advertised items are not stocked in sufficient quantities to cover expected demand. Some deceptions are difficult for consumers to discern, such as when an airline advertises a low one-way fare that is available only with the purchase of a round-trip ticket, or when a retailer sets artificially high "regular" prices, then announces "sale" prices close to its previous everyday prices.

Other deceptive pricing issues include *scanner fraud* and price confusion. The widespread use of scanner-based computer checkouts has led to increasing complaints of retailers overcharging their customers. Most of these overcharges result from poor management—from a failure to enter current or sale prices into the system. Other cases, however, involve intentional overcharges. *Price confusion* results when firms employ pricing methods that make it difficult for consumers to understand just what price they are really paying. Canadian law requires firms to charge consumers the lesser price in cases where more than one price is supplied by the seller through its advertising, packaging, or in-store display.

Ethical Issues in Pricing

Compliance with the law is considered the minimum standard when judging whether pricing practices are ethical. For example, although charging inordinately high prices is not illegal, such a practice may lead to ethical concerns. Ethical criticisms have been levied when higher prices are charged for groceries in poor areas where consumers have limited access to transportation and have few choices in terms of retail outlets.

Other ethical questions centre on whether consumers can understand prices and realistically compare them. For example, consumer advocates have condemned many car-leasing contracts since the legal language used in the contracts prevents consumers from fully understanding the price they are paying for the car.

Ethical concerns about pricing also arise when consumers must negotiate prices. Often those who can least afford to pay a higher price (such as the poor, very young, elderly, or those with disabilities) have the least ability to negotiate prices. These concerns arise when prices are not fixed. This is the case when people purchase cars, houses, and professional services, or attend street markets. Many consumers are unaware that even when prices appear fixed, they may be subject to negotiation. For example, many consumers don't know that they can negotiate with their bank for more favourable terms on a consumer loan.[33]

REVIEWING OBJECTIVES AND KEY TERMS

Companies today face a fierce and fast-changing pricing environment. Firms successful at creating customer value with the other marketing mix activities must still capture some of this value in the prices they earn. Pricing decisions are subject to an incredibly complex array of environmental and competitive forces. A company sets not a single price, but rather a *pricing structure* that covers different items in its line. This pricing structure changes over time as products move through their life cycles. The company adjusts product prices to reflect changes in costs and demand and to account for variations in buyers and situations. As the competitive environment changes, the company considers when to initiate price changes and when to respond to them.

OBJECTIVE 1 **Answer the question "What is a price?" and discuss the importance of pricing in today's fast-changing environment.**

Price can be defined narrowly as the amount of money charged for a product or service. Or it can be defined more broadly as the sum of the values that consumers exchange for the benefits of having and using the product or service. The pricing challenge is to find the price that will let the company make a fair profit by getting paid for the customer value it creates.

Despite the increased role of nonprice factors in the modern marketing process, price remains an important element in the marketing mix. It is the only marketing mix element that produces revenue; all other elements represent costs. Price is also one of the most flexible elements of the marketing mix. Unlike product features and channel commitments, price can be raised or lowered quickly. Even so, many companies are not good at handling pricing—pricing decisions and price competition are major problems for many marketing executives. Pricing problems often arise because managers are too quick to reduce prices, prices are too cost oriented rather than customer-value oriented, or prices are not consistent with the rest of the marketing mix.

OBJECTIVE 2 **Identify and define the important factors affecting pricing decisions, including the impact of customer perceptions of value, the company and product costs, and other internal and external factors.**

Good pricing begins with a complete understanding of the value that a product or service creates for customers and setting a price that captures that value. Customer perceptions of the product's value set the ceiling for prices. If customers perceive that the price is greater than the product's value, they will not buy the product. *Value-based pricing* uses buyers' perceptions of value, not the seller's cost, as the key to pricing.

The price the company charges will fall somewhere between one that is too high to produce any demand and one that is too low to produce a profit. Whereas customer perceptions of value set the ceiling for prices, company and product costs set the floor. If the company prices the product below its costs, its profits will suffer. *Cost-based pricing* involves setting prices based on the costs for producing, distributing, and selling the product plus a fair rate of return for effort and risk.

The company must watch its costs carefully. If it costs the company more than it costs competitors to produce and sell its product, the company must charge a higher price or make less profit, putting it at a competitive disadvantage.

To price wisely, management also needs to know how its costs vary with different levels of production and accumulated production experience. Cost-based pricing approaches include *cost-plus pricing* and *break-even pricing* (or *target profit pricing*).

Other *internal* factors that influence pricing decisions include the company's overall marketing strategy, objectives, mix, and organization for pricing. Price is only one element of the company's broader marketing strategy. Some companies position their products on price and then tailor other marketing mix decisions to the prices they want to charge. Other companies de-emphasize price and use other marketing mix tools to create *nonprice* positions.

Other *external* pricing considerations include the nature of the market and demand, competitors' strategies and prices, and environmental factors such as the economy, reseller needs, and government actions. The seller's pricing freedom varies with different types of markets. Ultimately, the customer decides whether the company has set the right price. The customer weighs the price against the perceived values of using the product—if the price exceeds the sum of the values, consumers will not buy. So the company must understand concepts like demand curves (the price–demand relationship) and price elasticity (consumer sensitivity to prices). Consumers also compare a product's price to the prices of competitors' products. A company therefore must learn the customer value and prices of competitors' offers.

OBJECTIVE 3 Describe the major strategies for pricing new products.

Pricing is a dynamic process. Companies design a *pricing structure* that covers all their products. They change this structure over time and adjust it to account for different customers and situations. Pricing strategies usually change as a product passes through its life cycle. In pricing innovative new products, it can use *market-skimming pricing* by initially setting high prices to "skim" the maximum amount of revenue from various segments of the market. Or it can use *market-penetrating pricing* by setting a low initial price to penetrate the market deeply and win a large market share.

OBJECTIVE 4 Explain how companies find a set of prices that maximizes the profits from the total product mix.

When the product is part of a product mix, the firm searches for a set of prices that will maximize the profits from the total mix. In *product line pricing*, the company decides on price steps for the entire set of products it offers. In addition, the company must set prices for *optional products* (optional or accessory products included with the main product), *captive products* (products that are required for use of the main product), *by-products* (waste or residual products produced when making the main product), and *product bundles* (combinations of products at a reduced price).

OBJECTIVE 5 Discuss how companies adjust their prices to take into account different types of customers and situations.

Companies apply a variety of *price adjustment strategies* to account for differences in consumer segments and situations. One is *discount and allowance pricing*, whereby the company establishes cash, quantity, or seasonal discounts, or varying types of allowances. A second strategy is *segmented pricing*, where the company sells a product at two or more prices to accommodate different customers, product forms, locations, or times. Sometimes companies consider more than economics in their pricing decisions, using *psychological pricing* to better communicate a product's intended position. In *promotional pricing*, a company offers discounts or temporarily sells a product below list price as a special event, sometimes even selling below cost as a loss leader. Another approach is *geographical pricing*, whereby the company decides how to price to distant customers, choosing from such alternatives as FOB-origin pricing, uniform-delivered pricing, and zone pricing. Finally, *international pricing* means that the company adjusts its price to meet different conditions and expectations in different world markets.

OBJECTIVE 6 Discuss the key issues related to initiating and responding to price changes.

When a firm considers initiating a *price change*, it must consider customers' and competitors' reactions. There are different implications to *initiating price cuts* and *initiating price increases*. Buyer reactions to price changes are influenced by the meaning customers see in the price change. Competitors' reactions flow from a set reaction policy or a fresh analysis of each situation.

There are also many factors to consider in responding to a competitor's price changes. The company that faces a price change initiated by a competitor must try to understand the competitor's intent as well as the likely duration and impact of the change. If a swift reaction is desirable, the firm should preplan its reactions to different possible price actions by competitors. When facing a competitor's price change, the company might sit tight, reduce its own price, raise perceived quality, improve quality and raise price, or launch a fighting brand.

KEY TERMS

mymarketinglab | Glossary Flashcards

DISCUSSING THE CONCEPTS

1. Explain the differences between value-based pricing and cost-based pricing and describe the two types of value-based pricing methods.

2. Discuss other internal and external considerations besides cost and customer perceptions of value that affect pricing decisions.

3. Name and describe the four types of markets recognized by economists and discuss the pricing challenges posed by each.

4. Explain market-skimming and market-penetration pricing strategies. Why would a marketer of innovative high-tech products choose market-skimming pricing rather than market-penetration pricing when launching a new product?

5. Retailers often use psychological pricing as a price adjustment strategy. Explain this pricing strategy. How do reference prices affect psychological pricing decisions?

6. Compare and contrast the geographic pricing strategies companies use for customers located in different parts of the country or world. Which strategy is best?

APPLYING THE CONCEPTS

1. In a small group, discuss your perceptions of value and how much you are willing to pay for the following products: automobiles, frozen dinners, jeans, and athletic shoes. Are there differences among members of your group? Explain why those differences exist. Discuss some examples of brands of these products that are positioned to deliver different value to consumers.

2. Find estimates of price elasticity for a variety of consumer goods and services. Explain what price elasticities of 0.5 and 2.4 mean. (Note: these are absolute values, as price elasticity is usually negative.)

3. What does the following positioning statement suggest about the firm's marketing objectives, marketing mix strategy, and costs? "No one beats our prices. We crush the competition."

4. You are an owner of a small independent chain of coffee houses competing head-to-head with Starbucks. The retail price your customers pay for coffee is exactly the same as at Starbucks. The wholesale price you pay for roasted coffee beans has increased by 25 percent. You know that you cannot absorb this increase and that you must pass it on to your customers. However, you are concerned about the consequences of an open price increase. Discuss three alternative price-increase strategies that address these concerns.

FOCUS ON TECHNOLOGY

Most high-tech products are introduced at a high price, and consumers know that the price will come down eventually. However, Apple slashed $200 off the price of its 8 GB iPhone to $399 just two months after introducing the product in 2007. Apple's CEO Steve Jobs apologized to customers and said "this is life in the technology lane." To pacify customers who purchased the $599 iPhone, Apple gave them $100 in Apple store credit. Just one year later, the new iPhone 3G, priced at $199, was launched and was touted as twice as much for half the price.

1. Why did Apple reduce the price of the iPhone so soon? Was it a smart move?

2. Give examples of other recent high-tech products that have come down in price over a relatively short period of time.

FOCUS ON ETHICS

Businesses often charge different prices to different customers. For example, movie theatres charge less to students and senior citizens, and prices vary across times of the day. Women are charged more for dry cleaning and haircuts. Business flyers pay more than leisure travellers. And that person sitting next to you on the airplane may have paid more or less than you did—the same goes for hotel rooms. Consumers with arthritis pay more per milligram of pain relief when they buy the Tylenol Arthritis product than when they buy regular Tylenol, even though the active ingredient, acetaminophen, and dosage over an 8-hour period are identical. Technology offers marketers the ability to price-discriminate in various ways. For example, in 2000 Coca-Cola experimented with vending machines that raised prices at higher outdoor temperatures. Electronic shelf labels allow retailers to change prices based on supply and demand. Moreover, the Internet provides the capability for businesses to charge different prices on their websites to different customers of the same product.

1. Is it fair for businesses to charge different prices to different customers?

2. Go to www.answers.com/topic/price-discrimination?cat= biz-fin and research the "three degrees of price discrimination." Does this discussion impact your opinion stated in question 1 regarding the fairness of this practice? Explain.

MARKETING BY THE NUMBERS

One external factor manufacturers must consider when setting prices is reseller margins. Manufacturers do not have the final say concerning the price to consumers—retailers do. So manufacturers must start with their suggested retail prices and work backward, subtracting out the markups required by resellers that sell the product to consumers. Once that is considered, manufacturers know at what price to sell their products to resellers, and they can determine what volume they must sell to break even at that price and cost combination. To answer the following question, refer to Appendix 3: Marketing by the Numbers.

1. A consumer purchases a flat iron to straighten her hair for $150 from a salon at which she gets her hair cut. If the salon's markup is 40 percent and the wholesaler's markup is 15 percent, both based on their selling prices, for what price does the manufacturer sell the product to the wholesaler?

2. If the unit variable costs for each flat iron are $40 and the manufacturer has fixed costs totalling $200 000, how many flat irons must this manufacturer sell to break even? How many must it sell to realize a profit of $800 000?

VIDEO CASE

IKEA

 | Video Case Questions

Lots of companies have idealistic missions. But IKEA's vision, "To create a better everyday life for the many," seems somewhat implausible. How can a company that makes furniture improve everyday life for the masses? Interestingly, the most important part of that strategy is price. For every product that it designs, from leather sofas to plastic mugs, IKEA starts with a target price. The target price is one that's deemed affordable, making the product accessible to the masses.

Only then does IKEA begin the gruelling process of creating a high-quality, stylish, and innovative product that can be delivered to the customer for that target price. As IKEA points out, anyone can make high-quality goods for a high price or poor-quality goods for a low price. The real challenge is making high-quality products at a low price. To do so requires a relentless focus on costs combined with a thirst for innovation. That has been IKEA's quest for more than 65 years.

After viewing the video featuring IKEA, answer the following questions about the company's pricing strategy:

1. What is IKEA's promise of value?

2. Referring to the Klippan sofa, illustrate how IKEA delivers its promise of value to consumers.

3. Based on the concepts from the text, does IKEA employ a value-based pricing approach or a cost-based pricing approach? Support your answer.

COMPANY CASE

Payless ShoeSource: Paying Less for Fashion

When you think of New York's Fifth Avenue, what retailers come to mind? Tiffany? Gucci? Armani? One name that probably doesn't come to mind is Payless. But for the past few years, Payless ShoeSource has been operating one of its low-priced shoe stores on this avenue of luxury retailing. In fact, Payless is now well on its way to placing stores in more than 100 higher-end malls around North America.

Although the discount shoe peddler still focuses on selling inexpensive shoes to the masses, Payless is now moving upscale. It's on a mission to "democratize fashion"—to make truly fashionable products more accessible by applying its cost-effective model to a product portfolio infused with well-known brand labels and some of the hottest high-end designers in the business. Sound like a hare-brained scheme? Well, you might change your mind after hearing the whole story.

Founded in 1956 in Topeka, Kansas, Payless grew rapidly based on what was then a revolutionary idea: selling shoes in a self-service environment. Fifty years later, Payless had become the largest shoe retailer in the Western hemisphere, with over 4500 stores throughout the Americas. Targeting budget-minded families, Payless was serving up more than 150 million pairs of shoes each year, roughly 1 in every 10 pairs of shoes purchased in America.

However, although all seemed rosy for the choose-it-yourself shoe store, by 2005 Payless was losing market share and closing stores. The retail landscape had changed, and giant discount one-stop shops like Walmart, Target, and Kohl's had become the vendors of choice for budget-conscious shoppers buying shoes. Said one industry insider, "You can no longer produce the same boring shoes year after year and hope that price alone will get customers to your door." With thrift as its only positioning point, Payless had lost its edge.

NEW IMAGE, HIGHER PRICES

So in June 2005, Payless made its first move to turn things around. It hired a new CEO, Matt Rubel. Rubel knew that to regain its market leadership, Payless would have to design shoes that *Sex in the City's* Carrie Bradshaw would drool over but at prices that Roseanne could afford. It had to change its image from the dusty dungeon of cheap footwear into the fun, hip merchant of fashion. "We have the ability to make shoes at the most affordable prices anywhere in the world, and we want to marry that with the greatest creativity," Rubel said in a statement reflecting the company's new strategy.

Rubel wasted no time in making big changes. To reflect the new image and communicate change to consumers, Payless redesigned its logo for the first time in 20 years. It then launched new "Fashion Lab" and "Hot Zone" store formats. Both were a drastic improvement, making the stores more open, light, and airy, with a more satisfying consumer experience built around style and design rather than price. Of the new store atmosphere, Rubel said, "It makes the $12 shoe look like a $20 shoe." Rubel hopes not only that the new formats will attract more customers, but that customers will be willing to pay a little bit more than they have in the past. All new Payless stores now have one of the two new formats and old stores are being progressively remodelled.

A FASHION REVOLUTION

Beyond these changes in presentation, Rubel focused on the ultimate product. He implemented a "House of Brands" strategy, shifting the Payless product line from one comprising almost entirely store brands to one dominated by well-known national brands. Payless now sells shoes under numerous brand names that it either owns or licenses, including Airwalk, Champion, Spalding, Dexter, Shaquille O'Neal-endorsed Dunkman, and various Disney brands. Rubel also acquired the Stride Rite chain and all its associated brands. To organize the new corporate structure and keep track of all the brands, he created a holding company (Collective Brands) as an umbrella over Payless, Stride Rite, and all the licensing activities for the company's brands.

To develop products that would resonate better with consumers, Payless stepped up its emphasis on fashion. The Payless Design Team, an in-house design group, dedicated itself to developing original footwear and accessory designs to keep new styles on target with changing fashion trends. Top designers from Kenneth Cole and Michael Kors were hired as full-time employees to head the new team.

But in perhaps the biggest move to raise the cachet of the brand, Rubel started "Designer Collections." Aiming for the highest levels of haute couture, Payless has forged relationships with four top New York-based designers—Laura Poretzky, Lela Rose, Stacey Bendet, and Patricia Field. The four are designing everything from pumps to boots to handbags for Payless under the brands Abaeté, Lela Rose, alice + olivia, and Patricia Field.

To support this design effort and the new Fashion Lab store format, Payless has done something really out of character. After signing its first designer, Laura Poretzky, Payless took its designs to the runway of New York's Fashion Week, the invitation-only event where designers debut fall fashions for the industry. In another first, Payless began running full-page ads in *Elle, Vogue*, and *W* featuring the tagline, "Look Again."

Can Payless's luxury-meets-low-price strategy work? Or will this go down as a disaster of two drastically different worlds that collided, crashed, and burned? "There's nothing cool about shopping at Payless," says skeptic Marian Salzman, a trends forecaster at a major ad firm. "It gets the cash-strapped working girl." But Rubel refutes this view, quickly pointing out that Payless shoppers have median household incomes that are higher than those of both Walmart and Target. "All we've done is bring Payless into the twenty-first century. We're. . . speaking with greater clarity to who our customer already is."

Maxine Clark, former president of Payless and now CEO of Build-A-Bear Workshop, also recognizes the potential of the new strategy. "The customer who wants to buy Prada will not come to Payless. But this will energize the old customers who they lost and attract new ones." Mardi Larson, head of public relations for Payless, claims that the trendy new image is perfect for existing customers. "We target the 24-year-old demographic, because women in their 40s who shop for their family are nostalgic about that time in their lives, while [at the same time] teenagers aspire to that age group."

But what about that potential new customer? Does this risky venture into high fashion stand a chance of appealing to those who have never crossed the threshold of a Payless store? Rubel admits to going after new customers. The "cheap chic" approach is attempting to lure 20- to-30-year-old women who are looking for something trendy. Given that such fashion-conscious females buy 50 percent more shoes than most current Payless customers, going after new customers make sense.

Perhaps Lela Rose's experience in 2007 best illustrates why Payless might just succeed in attracting this previously out-of-reach customer:

> When actresses Sophia Bush (*One Tree Hill*) and Brittany Snow (*Hairspray*) landed backstage in Lela Rose's showroom at New York Fashion Week, they swooned over the designer's new shoe collection that was about to debut on the runway. Rose, best known for US$1500 frocks, happily handed pairs of navy peep-toe pumps and polka-dot round-toe pumps over to the young celebs, who would soon be flaunting them on the sidelines of the catwalk. "Did they know they were Payless shoes?" says Rose, who's now designing her fifth exclu-

sive line for the discounter. "Absolutely. They didn't care. They looked cute to them and that's all that mattered."

Additionally, Payless is not the first to try this new direction. In fact, co-branded designer lines for retailers date back decades. But in recent years, the trend is proliferating. Karl Lagerfeld has designed for Britain's H&M, Vera Wang has teamed up with Kohl's, Ralph Lauren has put store brands on JC Penney's shelves, and Todd Oldham has stepped out with Old Navy, to name just a few.

Although many ventures such as these have failed miserably, some have been wildly successful. Lela Rose claims that she would never have considered her arrangement with Payless if it hadn't been for the success of Target's alliance with Isaac Mizrahi. Mizrahi's couture career was pretty much on the rocks. Then he started designing preppy cashmere sweaters, cheerful jersey dresses, and trendy trench coats for Target, all priced at under US$40. With the low-rent strategy, Mizrahi became more popular and famous than ever. After that, he once again had high-end retailers knocking on his door. Since Mizrahi's successful entry to the mainstream in 2003, more than two dozen designers have co-branded with mass retailers.

PAYING LESS OR PAYING MORE?

There's more in it for Payless than just making the brand more attractive to both old and new customers. The company is looking to move its average price point up a notch or two. Whereas "higher price" is a relative term when most of a store's product line is priced below US$15, higher margins are higher margins. Rubel has suggested that in many cases, price increases may be as little as 50 cents per pair of shoes. But the expansion of its brand portfolio to include famous labels will certainly give Payless greater pricing flexibility. And the designer collections will allow for some of the highest priced products that have ever graced its shelves—think US$25 for pumps and up to US$45 for boots. Whereas that is a substantial price increase from Payless's average, it's a bargain for fashion-conscious consumers.

One industry insider declares, "Fashion isn't a luxury, it's a right." With Rubel's mission to democratize fashion, it seems that this right is becoming a reality in the shoe world. The benefits of such democracy are plentiful. The designers get tremendous exposure, a large customer base, and the power and budget of a mass retailer. Payless gets brand cachet that is almost certain to transform its outdated image. And consumers get runway styles they can afford. Payless is banking that making everyone happy will ring up the sales and profits it needs.

Questions for Discussion

1. Which of the different product mix pricing strategies discussed in the text applies best to Payless's new strategy? Discuss this in detail.

2. How do concepts such as psychological pricing and reference pricing apply to the Payless strategy? In what ways does Payless's strategy deviate from these concepts?

3. Discuss the benefits and risks of the new Payless strategy for both Payless and the designers. Which of these two stands to lose the most?

4. Consider the scale on which Payless operates. How much of a price increase does Payless need to achieve to make this venture worthwhile?

Sources: Danielle Sacks, "The Fast 50 Companies," *Fast Company*, March 2008, p. 112; Maria Puente, "Top Designers Go Down-Market," *USA Today*, September 26, 2007, p. 11B; Eric Wilson, "The Big Brand Theory," *New York Times Magazine*, September 9, 2007, p. 74; Bruce Horovitz, "Payless Is Determined to Put a Fashionably Shod Foot Forward," *USA Today*, July 28, 2006, p. 1B; Nicole Zerillo, "Payless Launches 'I Love Shoes.'" *PR Week*, March 10, 2008, p. 3; and www.paylessinfo.com, accessed September 2008.

 Visit **MyMarketingLab** at **www.pearsoned.ca/mymarketinglab** for access to online tutorials, interactive exercises, videos, and much more.

12

Marketing Channels Delivering
Customer Value

PREVIEWING
THE CONCEPTS

We now arrive at the third marketing mix tool—distribution. Firms rarely work alone in creating value for customers and building profitable customer relationships. Instead, most are only a single link in a larger supply chain and marketing channel. As such, an individual firm's success depends not only on how well *it* performs but also on how well its *entire marketing channel* competes with competitors' channels. To be good at customer relationship management, a company must also be good at partner relationship management. The first part of this chapter explores the nature of marketing channels and the marketer's channel design and management decisions. We then examine physical distribution—or logistics—an area that is growing dramatically in importance and sophistication. In the next chapter, we'll look more closely at two major channel intermediaries—retailers and wholesalers.

We'll start with a look at a company whose groundbreaking, customer-centred distribution strategy took it to the top of its industry.

Quick, which rental-car company is number one? Chances are good that you said Hertz. Okay, who's number two? That must be Avis, you say. After all, for years Avis advertising has said, "We're #2, so we try harder!" But if you said Hertz or Avis, you're about to be surprised. By any measure—most locations, revenues, profits, or number of cars—the number-one North American rental-car company is Enterprise Rent-A-Car. What's more, this is no recent development. Enterprise left number-two Hertz in its rear-view mirror in the late 1990s and has never looked back.

What may have fooled you is that for a long time, Hertz was number one in airport car rentals. However, with estimated revenues of US$9.5 billion and growing, Enterprise now has 30 percent more overall car rental sales than Hertz. What's more, analysts estimate that the privately owned Enterprise is twice as profitable as Hertz.

How did Enterprise become such a dominating industry leader? The company might argue that it was through better prices or better marketing. But what contributed most to Enterprise taking the lead was an industry-changing, customer-driven distribution strategy. While competitors such as Hertz and Avis focused on serving travellers at airports, Enterprise developed a new distribution doorway to a large and untapped segment. It opened off-airport, neighbourhood locations that provided short-term car-replacement rentals for people whose cars were wrecked, stolen, or being serviced, or for people who simply wanted a different car for a short trip or special occasion.

It all started more than half a century ago when Enterprise founder Jack Taylor discovered an unmet customer need. He was working at a St. Louis auto dealership, and customers often asked him where they could get a replacement car when theirs was in the shop for repairs or body work. To meet this need, Taylor opened a car-leasing business. But rather than competing head-on with

The tagline "Pick Enterprise. We'll Pick You Up" remains the company's main value proposition.

the likes of Hertz and Avis serving travellers at airports, Taylor located his rental offices in centre-city and neighbourhood areas, closer to his replacement-car target customers. These locations also gave Taylor a cost advantage—property rents were lower and he didn't have to pay airport taxes and fees.

Taylor's groundbreaking distribution strategy worked and the business grew quickly. As he opened multiple locations in St. Louis and other cities, he renamed his business Enterprise Rent-A-Car after the U.S. Navy aircraft carrier on which he had served as a naval aviator. Enterprise continued to focus steadfastly on what it called the "home-city" market, primarily serving customers who'd been in wrecks or whose cars were being serviced. Enterprise branch managers developed strong relationships with local auto insurance adjusters, dealership sales and service personnel, and body shops and service garages, making Enterprise their preferred neighbourhood rental-car provider.

Customers in the home-city market had special needs. Often, they were at the scene of a wreck or at a repair shop and had no way to get to an Enterprise office to pick up a rental car. So the company came up with another game-changing idea—picking customers up wherever they happen to be and bringing them back to the rental office. Hence the tagline: "Pick Enterprise. We'll Pick You Up," which remains the company's main value proposition to this day.

By the late 1980s, Enterprise had a large nationwide network of company-owned off-airport locations and a virtual lock on the home-city market. From this strong base, in the mid-1990s Enterprise began expanding its distribution system by directly challenging Hertz and Avis in the on-airport market. A decade later, it had operations in 230 airports in North America and Europe. Enterprise opened its first Canadian branch in 1993 in Windsor, Ontario, and since then has experienced double-digit growth in Canada. It now employs 2800 Canadians, and has over 35 000 vehicles and 400 locations, including 23 offices serving Canadian airports. In late 2007, Enterprise purchased the Vanguard Car Rental Group, which owned the National and Alamo brands. National focused on the corporate negotiated rental market while Alamo served primarily the leisure traveller airport market.

With the Vanguard acquisition, Enterprise now captures a 27.4 percent share of the airport market, putting it

While competitors Hertz and Avis focused on serving travellers at airports, Enterprise opened off-airport, neighbourhood locations that provided short-term car-replacement rentals for people whose cars had been wrecked, stolen, or were being serviced.

neck-and-neck with Hertz at 28.5 percent and jointly owned Avis/Budget at 30.1 percent. That, combined with its more than 55 percent share of the off-airport market, makes Enterprise the runaway leader in overall car rental sales. Enterprise owns a stunning one-half of all North American rental cars and is the world's largest automobile buyer. Last year, it purchased 800 000 cars to support its 7900 locations in the United States and four other countries.

However, rather than resting on its laurels, Enterprise continues to seek better ways to get its cars where customers want them. The enterprising company is now motoring into yet another innovative distribution venue—"car sharing" and hourly rentals. Car sharing was pioneered in the late 1990s by Zipcar, which operates on parking-starved university campuses and in congested urban areas, where it rents cars on an hourly or daily basis to people who want to run errands or make short trips. Zipcar does not currently serve the Canadian university market but does have branches serving the general public in Vancouver and Toronto.

Enterprise has now revved up its own car-sharing program, WeCar. This new operation will park automobiles at convenient locations in densely populated urban areas, where residents often don't own cars and where business

OBJECTIVES

1. Explain why companies use marketing channels and discuss the functions these channels perform.

2. Discuss how channel members interact and how they organize to perform the work of the channel.

3. Identify the major channel alternatives open to a company.

4. Explain how companies select, motivate, and evaluate channel members.

5. Discuss the nature and importance of marketing logistics and integrated supply chain management.

commuters would like to have occasional car access. Enterprise will also target businesses that want to have WeCar vehicles available in their parking lots for commuting employees to use. WeCar members pay a US$35 annual membership fee. They can then rent conveniently located, fuel-efficient cars (mostly Toyota Prius hybrids) for US$10 per hour or US$30 overnight—the rate includes gas and a 200-mile allotment. Renting a WeCar vehicle is a simple get-in-and-go operation. Just pass your member key fob over a sensor to unlock the car, then open the glove box and enter a PIN to release the car key. Although the car-sharing market now belongs to tiny Zipcar, a US$100 million company that has cars on more than 70 university campuses in several large metropolitan areas, look for giant Enterprise to perfect and expand the new distribution concept.

Thus, Enterprise continues to move ahead aggressively with its winning distribution strategy. Says Andy Taylor, founder Jack's son and now longtime Enterprise CEO, "We own the high ground in this business and we aren't going to give it up. As the dynamics of our industry continue to evolve, it's clear to us that the future belongs to the service providers who offer the broadest array of services for anyone who needs or wants to rent a car." The company intends to make cars available wherever, whenever, and however customers want them.[1]

As the Enterprise story shows, good distribution strategies can contribute strongly to customer value and create competitive advantage for both a firm and its channel partners. It demonstrates that firms cannot bring value to customers by themselves. Instead, they must work closely with other firms in a larger value delivery network.

1 SUPPLY CHAINS AND THE VALUE DELIVERY NETWORK

Value delivery network
The network made up of the company, suppliers, distributors, and ultimately customers who "partner" with each other to improve the performance of the entire system in delivering customer value.

Value delivery network: In making and marketing iPod touch products, Apple manages an entire network of people within Apple plus suppliers and resellers outside the company who work effectively together to give final customers "so much to touch."

Producing a product or service and making it available to buyers requires building relationships not just with customers, but also with key suppliers and resellers in the company's *supply chain*. This supply chain consists of "upstream" and "downstream" partners. Upstream from the company is the set of firms that supply the raw materials, components, parts, information, finances, and expertise needed to create a product or service. Marketers, however, have traditionally focused on the "downstream" side of the supply chain—on the *marketing channels* (or *distribution channels*) that look toward the customer. Downstream marketing channel partners, such as wholesalers and retailers, form a vital connection between the firm and its customers.

The term *supply chain* may be too limited—it takes a *make-and-sell* view of the business. It suggests that raw materials, productive inputs, and factory capacity should serve as the starting point for market planning. A better term would be *demand chain* because it suggests a *sense-and-respond* view of the market. Under this view, planning starts with the needs of target customers, to which the company responds by organizing a chain of resources and activities with the goal of creating customer value.

Even a demand chain view of a business may be too limited, because it takes a step-by-step, linear view of purchase–production–consumption activities. With the advent of the Internet and other technologies, however, companies are forming more numerous and complex relationships with other firms. For example, Ford manages numerous supply chains. It also sponsors or transacts on many B2B websites and online purchasing exchanges as needs arise. Like Ford, most large companies today are engaged in building and managing a continuously evolving *value delivery network*.

As defined in Chapter 2, a **value delivery network** is made up of the company, suppliers, distributors, and ultimately customers who "partner" with each other to improve the performance of the entire system. For example, in making and marketing its iPod touch products, Apple manages an entire network of people within Apple plus suppliers and resellers outside the company who work together effectively to give final customers "so much to touch."

This chapter focuses on marketing channels—on the downstream side of the value delivery network. We examine four major questions concerning marketing channels: What is the nature of marketing channels and why are they important? How do channel firms interact and organize to do the work of the channel? What problems do companies face in designing and managing their channels? What role do physical distribution and supply chain management play in attracting and satisfying customers? In Chapter 13, we will look at marketing channel issues from the viewpoint of retailers and wholesalers.

THE NATURE AND IMPORTANCE OF MARKETING CHANNELS

Marketing channel (distribution channel)
A set of interdependent organizations that help make a product or service available for use or consumption by the consumer or business user.

Glossary Flashcards of Key Terms

Few producers sell their goods directly to the final users. Instead, most use intermediaries to bring their products to market. They try to forge a **marketing channel** (or **distribution channel**)—a set of interdependent organizations that help make a product or service available for use or consumption by the consumer or business user.

A company's channel decisions directly affect every other marketing decision. Pricing depends on whether the company works with national discount chains, uses high-quality specialty stores, or sells directly to consumers via the Web. The firm's sales force and communications decisions depend on how much persuasion, training, motivation, and support its channel partners need. Whether a company develops or acquires certain new products may depend on how well those products fit the capabilities of its channel members. For example, Kodak initially sold its EasyShare printers only in Best Buy stores to take advantage of the retailer's on-the-floor sales staff and their ability to educate buyers on the economics of paying higher initial prices but lower long-term ink costs.

Companies often pay too little attention to their distribution channels, sometimes with damaging results. In contrast, many companies have used imaginative distribution systems to *gain* a competitive advantage. FedEx's creative and imposing distribution system made it a leader in express delivery. Enterprise revolutionized the car-rental business by setting up off-airport rental offices. And Amazon.com pioneered the sales of books and a wide range of other goods via the Internet.

Distribution channel decisions often involve long-term commitments to other firms. For example, companies such as Ford, HP, or McDonald's can easily change their advertising, pricing, or promotion programs. They can scrap old products and introduce new ones as market tastes demand. But when they set up distribution channels through contracts with franchisees, independent dealers, or large retailers, they cannot readily replace these channels with company-owned stores or websites if conditions change. Therefore, management must design its channels carefully, with an eye on tomorrow's likely selling environment as well as today's.

How Channel Members Add Value

Why do producers give some of the selling job to channel partners? After all, doing so means giving up some control over how and to whom they sell their products. Producers use intermediaries because they create greater efficiency in making goods available to target markets. Through their contacts, experience, specialization, and scale of operation, intermediaries usually offer the firm more than it can achieve on its own.

Figure 12.1 shows how using intermediaries can provide economies. Figure 12.1A shows three manufacturers, each using direct marketing to reach three customers. This system requires nine different contacts. Figure 12.1B shows the three manufacturers working through one distributor, which contacts the three customers. This system requires only six contacts. In this way, intermediaries reduce the amount of work that must be done by both producers and consumers.

From the economic system's point of view, the role of marketing intermediaries is to transform the assortment of products made by producers into the assortment wanted by consumers. Producers make narrow assortments of products in large quantities, but consumers want broad assortments of products in small quantities. Marketing channel members buy large quantities from many producers and break them down into the smaller quantities and broader assortments wanted by consumers.

A. Number of contacts without a distributor
M × C = 3 × 3 = 9

B. Number of contacts with a distributor
M + C = 3 + 3 = 6

Figure 12.1 How adding a distributor reduces the number of channel transactions

For example, Unilever makes millions of bars of Lever 2000 hand soap each day, but you want to buy only a few bars at a time. So big food, drug, and discount retailers, such as Superstore, Shoppers Drug Mart, and Walmart, buy Lever 2000 by the truckload and stock it on their store shelves. In turn, you can buy a single bar of Lever 2000, along with a shopping cart full of small quantities of toothpaste, shampoo, and other related products as you need them. Thus, intermediaries play an important role in matching supply and demand.

In making products and services available to consumers, channel members add value by bridging the major time, place, and possession gaps that separate goods and services from those who would use them. Members of the marketing channel perform many key functions. Some help to complete transactions:

- *Information:* Gathering and distributing marketing research and intelligence information about actors and forces in the marketing environment needed for planning and aiding exchange.

- *Promotion:* Developing and spreading persuasive communications about an offer.

- *Contact:* Finding and communicating with prospective buyers.

- *Matching:* Shaping and fitting the offer to the buyer's needs, including activities such as manufacturing, grading, assembling, and packaging.

- *Negotiation:* Reaching an agreement on price and other terms of the offer so that ownership or possession can be transferred.

Others help to fulfill the completed transactions:

- *Physical distribution:* Transporting and storing goods.

- *Financing:* Acquiring and using funds to cover the costs of the channel work.

- *Risk taking:* Assuming the risks of carrying out the channel work.

And a new item that has been added to the list of functions to be performed within the supply chain is *environmental sustainability.* Take the case of Toronto-based Grand & Toy:

In 2007, Grand & Toy, Canada's leading provider of business solutions, announced a new corporate strategy aimed at becoming a leader in environmental sustainability. Among its initiatives was a plan to significantly reduce its environmental footprint in supply chain carbon intensity, packaging, recycling of waste, and distribution centre management. In just a few short years, Grand & Toy has established itself as a leader in sustainable procurement practices. In 2009, for example, the company sponsored two free sustainable procurement showcases to help supply chain management professionals understand how sustainability is becoming a key driver for innovative procurement solutions, and how to adopt sustainable supply chain practices when working with suppliers and partners that maximize both profitability and corporate social responsibility.[2]

Grand & Toy's sustainability vision involves "powering the potential of Canadian businesses to lead the journey towards sustainability."

The question is not *whether* these functions need to be performed—they must be—but rather *who* will perform them. To the extent that the manufacturer performs these functions, its costs go up and its prices must be higher. When some of these functions are shifted to intermediaries, the producer's costs and prices may be lower, but the intermediaries must charge more to cover the costs of their work. In dividing the work of the channel, the various functions should be assigned to the channel members who can add the most value for the cost.

Number of Channel Levels

Companies can design their distribution channels to make products and services available to customers in different ways. Each layer of marketing intermediaries that perform some work in bringing the product and its ownership closer to the final buyer is a **channel level**. Because the producer and the final consumer both perform some work, they are part of every channel.

The *number of intermediary levels* indicates the *length* of a channel. Figure 12.2A shows several consumer distribution channels of different lengths. Channel 1, called a **direct marketing channel**, has no intermediary levels; the company sells directly to consumers. For example, Mary Kay and Amway sell their products door-to-door, through home and office sales parties, and on the Web; Veseys, located in York, Prince Edward Island, sells its plants and bulbs to gardeners across the country through mail catalogues, by telephone, and online. The remaining channels in Figure 12.2A are **indirect marketing channels**, containing one or more intermediaries.

Figure 12.2B shows some common business distribution channels. The business marketer can use its own sales force to sell directly to business customers. Or it can sell to various types of intermediaries, who in turn sell to these customers. Consumer and business marketing channels with even more levels can sometimes be found, but less often. From the producer's point of view, a greater number of levels means less control and greater channel complexity. Moreover, all of the institutions in the channel are connected by several types of *flows*. These include the *physical flow* of products, the *flow of ownership*, the *payment flow*, the *information flow*, and the *promotion flow*. These flows can make even channels with only one or a few levels very complex.

Channel level
A layer of intermediaries that perform some work in bringing the product and its ownership closer to the final buyer.

Direct marketing channel
A marketing channel that has no intermediary levels.

Indirect marketing channel
A marketing channel containing one or more intermediary levels.

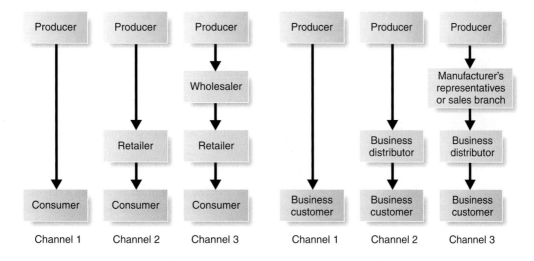

A. Consumer marketing channels   B. Business marketing channels

Figure 12.2 Consumer and business marketing channels

2 CHANNEL BEHAVIOUR AND ORGANIZATION

Distribution channels are more than simple collections of firms tied together by various flows. They are complex behavioural systems in which people and companies interact to accomplish individual, company, and channel goals. Some channel systems consist only of informal interactions among loosely organized firms. Others consist of formal interactions guided by strong organizational structures. Moreover, channel systems do not stand still—new types of intermediaries emerge and whole new channel systems evolve. Here we look at channel behaviour and at how members organize to do the work of the channel.

Channel Behaviour

A marketing channel consists of firms that have partnered for their common good. Each channel member depends on the others. For example, a Ford dealer depends on Ford to design cars that meet consumer needs. In turn, Ford depends on the dealer to attract consumers, persuade them to buy Ford cars, and service cars after the sale. Each Ford dealer also depends on other dealers to provide good sales and service that will uphold the brand's reputation. In fact, the success of individual Ford dealers depends on how well the entire Ford marketing channel competes with the channels of other auto manufacturers.

Each channel member plays a specialized role in the channel. For example, consumer electronics maker Samsung's role is to produce electronics products that consumers will like and to create demand through national advertising. Future Shop's role is to display these Samsung products in convenient locations, to answer buyers' questions, and to complete sales. The channel will be most effective when each member assumes the tasks it can do best.

Ideally, because the success of individual channel members depends on overall channel success, all channel firms should work together smoothly. They should understand and accept their roles, coordinate their activities, and cooperate to attain overall channel goals. However, individual channel members rarely take such a broad view. Cooperating to achieve overall channel goals sometimes means giving up individual company goals.

Channel conflict

Disagreements among marketing channel members on goals and roles—who should do what and for what rewards.

Although channel members depend on one another, they often act alone in their own short-run best interests. They often disagree about who should do what and for what rewards. Such disagreements over goals, roles, and rewards generate **channel conflict**.

Horizontal conflict occurs among firms at the same level of the channel. For instance, some Ford dealers in Vancouver might complain that the other dealers in the city steal sales from them by pricing too low or by advertising outside their assigned territories. Or Holiday Inn franchisees might complain about other Holiday Inn operators overcharging guests or giving poor service, hurting the overall Holiday Inn image.

Vertical conflict, conflicts between different levels of the same channel, is even more common. For example, Goodyear created hard feelings and conflict with its premier independent-dealer channel when it began selling through mass-merchant retailers:

> For more than 60 years Goodyear sold replacement tires exclusively through its premier network of independent Goodyear dealers. Then, in the 1990s, Goodyear shattered tradition and jolted its dealers by agreeing to sell its tires through mass merchants such as Sears and Walmart, placing dealers in direct competition with the nation's

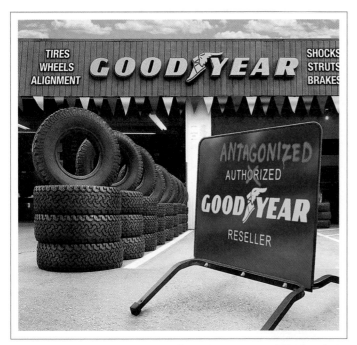

Channel conflict: Goodyear created conflict with its premier independent-dealer channel when it began selling through mass-merchant retailers. Fractured dealer relations weakened the Goodyear name and dropped the company into a more than decade-long profit funk.

most potent retailers. Goodyear claimed that value-minded tire buyers were increasingly buying from cheaper, multibrand discount outlets and department stores, and that it simply had to put its tires where many consumers were going to buy them.

Not surprisingly, Goodyear's aggressive moves into new channels set off a surge of channel conflict, and dealer relations deteriorated rapidly. Some of Goodyear's best dealers defected to competitors. Other angry dealers struck back by taking on competing brands of cheaper private-label tires. Such dealer actions weakened the Goodyear name, and the company's replacement tire sales—which make up 71 percent of its revenues—went flat, dropping the company into a more than decade-long profit funk. Although Goodyear has since actively set about repairing fractured dealer relations, it still has not fully recovered. "We lost sight of the fact that it's in our interest that our dealers succeed," admits a Goodyear executive.[3]

Some conflict in the channel takes the form of healthy competition. Such competition can be good for the channel—without it, the channel could become passive and non-innovative. But severe or prolonged conflict, as in the case of Goodyear, can disrupt channel effectiveness and cause lasting harm to channel relationships. Companies should manage channel conflict to keep it from getting out of hand.

Vertical Marketing Systems

Conventional distribution channel

A channel consisting of one or more independent producers, wholesalers, and retailers, each a separate business seeking to maximize its own profits, even at the expense of profits for the system as a whole.

Vertical marketing system (VMS)

A distribution channel structure in which producers, wholesalers, and retailers act as a unified system. One channel member owns the others, has contracts with them, or has so much power that they must all cooperate.

For the channel as a whole to perform well, each channel member's role must be specified and channel conflict must be managed. The channel will perform better if it includes a firm, agency, or mechanism that provides leadership and has the power to assign roles and manage conflict.

Historically, *conventional distribution channels* have lacked such leadership and power, often resulting in damaging conflict and poor performance. One of the biggest channel developments over the years has been the emergence of *vertical marketing systems* that provide channel leadership. Figure 12.3 contrasts the two types of channel arrangements.

A **conventional distribution channel** consists of one or more independent producers, wholesalers, and retailers. Each is a separate business seeking to maximize its own profits, perhaps even at the expense of the system as a whole. No channel member has much control over the other members, and no formal means exists for assigning roles and resolving channel conflict.

In contrast, a **vertical marketing system (VMS)** consists of producers, wholesalers, and retailers acting as a unified system. One channel member owns the others, has contracts with them, or wields so much power that they must all cooperate. The VMS can be dominated by the producer, wholesaler, or retailer. The Forzani Group, headquartered in Calgary, is an example of a retail-dominated VMS. It owns and operates a range of sporting

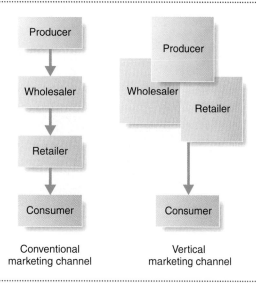

Figure 12.3 Comparison of a conventional distribution channel with a vertical marketing system

goods stores including Sport Chek, Coast Mountain Sports, Sport Mart, Athletes World, Hockey Experts, and National Sports.

We look now at three major types of VMSs: *corporate, contractual*, and *administered*. Each uses a different means for setting up leadership and power in the channel.

Corporate VMS

Corporate VMS

A vertical marketing system that combines successive stages of production and distribution under single ownership—channel leadership is established through common ownership.

A **corporate VMS** integrates successive stages of production and distribution under single ownership. Coordination and conflict management are attained through regular organizational channels. For example, U.S. grocery giant Kroger owns and operates 42 factories that crank out more than 8000 private-label items found on its store shelves. Similarly, to help supply products for its 1760 grocery stores, Safeway owns and operates nine milk plants, eight bakery plants, four ice cream plants, four soft drink bottling plants, and four fruit and vegetable processing plants. And little-known Italian eyewear maker Luxottica produces many famous eyewear brands—including its own Ray-Ban brand and licensed brands such as Polo Ralph Lauren, Dolce & Gabbana, Prada, Versace, and Bvlgari. It then sells these brands through two of the world's largest optical chains, LensCrafters and Sunglass Hut, which it also owns.[4]

Controlling the entire distribution chain has turned Spanish clothing chain Zara into the world's fastest-growing fashion retailer:

The secret to Zara's success is its control over almost every aspect of the supply chain, from design and production to its own worldwide distribution network. Zara makes 40 percent of its own fabrics and produces more than half of its own clothes, rather than relying on a hodgepodge of slow-moving suppliers. New designs feed into Zara manufacturing centres, which ship finished products directly to 1161 Zara stores in 68 countries, saving time, eliminating the need for warehouses, and keeping inventories low. Effective vertical integration makes Zara faster, more flexible, and more efficient than international competitors such as the Gap, Benetton, and H&M. And Zara's low costs let it offer midmarket chic at downmarket prices.

A couple of summers ago, Zara managed to latch onto one of the season's hottest trends in just four weeks (versus an industry average of nine months). The process started when trendspotters spread the word back to headquarters: White eyelet—cotton with tiny holes in it—was set to become white-hot. A quick telephone survey of Zara store managers confirmed that the fabric could be a winner, so in-house designers got down to work. They zapped patterns electronically to Zara's factory across the street, and the fabric was cut. Local subcontractors stitched white-eyelet V-neck belted dresses—think Jackie Kennedy, circa 1960—and finished them in less than a week. The US$129 dresses were inspected, tagged, and transported through a tunnel under the street to a distribution centre. From there, they were quickly dispatched to Zara stores from New York to Tokyo—where they were flying off the racks just two days later. In all, the company's stylish but affordable offerings have attracted a cult following. Zara store sales grew almost 40 percent last year to nearly US$9.8 billion.[5]

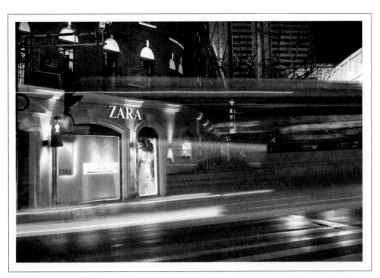

Corporate VMS: Effective vertical integration makes Zara more flexible and more efficient—a virtual blur compared with competitors. It can take a new line from design to production to worldwide distribution in its own stores in less than a month (versus an industry average of nine months).

Contractual VMS

A **contractual VMS** consists of independent firms at different levels of production and distribution who join together through contracts to obtain more economies or sales impact than each could achieve alone. Channel members coordinate their activities and manage conflict through contractual agreements.

Contractual VMS
A vertical marketing system in which independent firms at different levels of production and distribution join together through contracts to obtain more economies or sales impact than they could achieve alone.

Franchise organization
A contractual vertical marketing system in which a channel member, called a franchisor, links several stages in the production–distribution process.

The **franchise organization** is the most common type of contractual relationship—a channel member called a *franchisor* links several stages in the production–distribution process. Franchising has been the fastest-growing retailing form in Canada, growing more than 20 percent since 1993. It is estimated that Canada has four times more franchises per capita than the United States, with over 78 000 franchises across the country. Canadian franchising employs over 1 million people and represents over $100 billion in annual sales.[6] Almost every kind of business has been franchised—from motels and fast-food restaurants to dental centres and dating services, from wedding consultants and maid services to fitness centres and funeral homes.

There are three types of franchises. The first type is the *manufacturer-sponsored retailer franchise system*—for example, Ford and its network of independent franchised dealers. The second type is the *manufacturer-sponsored wholesaler franchise system*—Coca-Cola licenses bottlers (wholesalers) in various markets who buy Coca-Cola syrup concentrate and then bottle and sell the finished product to retailers in local markets. The third type is the *service-firm-sponsored retailer franchise system*—examples are found in the auto-rental business (Hertz, Avis), the fast-food service business (McDonald's, Burger King), the motel business (Holiday Inn, Ramada), and more recently in health care (Vancouver-based Nurse Next Door).

Let's face it: Canadians are getting older. And with the aging population comes a greater need for quality senior home health care. Enter Ken Sim and John DeHart, founders of Nurse Next Door Home Healthcare Services, who sought to "provide high quality services that could help improve the lives of those struggling with sick or aging family members." Established in 2001, the company began franchising in 2007. By 2009, Nurse Next Door had 30 franchises across Canada and continues to expand at a rate of two franchises per month across North America—a staggering 3400 percent growth rate since 2001! The company's success has largely been attributed to the way it supports its franchise operators. For example, client calls are handled through a centralized call centre in Vancouver, freeing franchisees from the time-consuming task of fielding urgent calls around the clock. Nurse Next Door is highly selective about which franchisee applicants it takes on, and those that are successful receive the highest level of support and training possible. The company has earned a number of awards, including being named the sixth best midsize franchise system in North America by *Franchise Business Review* in 2009. As it looks toward the future, Nurse Next Door's goal is to generate $1 billion in sales and have 500 franchisees worldwide by 2021. Given its explosive growth and the aging world population, this goal seems very achievable.[7]

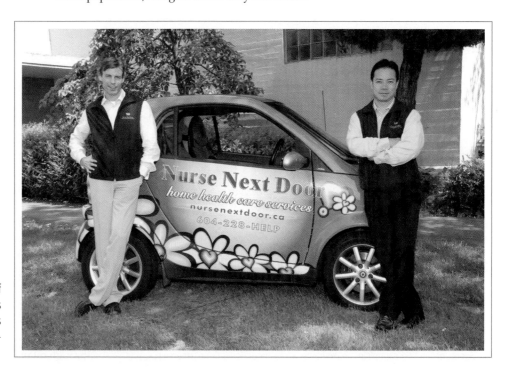

Nurse Next Door's strategy of "treating franchisees like customers it aims to retain for decades" has led to rapid growth for this Canadian company.

The fact that most consumers cannot tell the difference between contractual and corporate VMSs shows how successfully the contractual organizations compete with corporate chains. Chapter 13 presents a fuller discussion of the various contractual VMSs.

Administered VMS

Administered VMS

A vertical marketing system that coordinates successive stages of production and distribution, not through common ownership or contractual ties, but through the size and power of one of the parties.

In an **administered VMS**, leadership is assumed not through common ownership or contractual ties but through the size and power of one or a few dominant channel members. Manufacturers of a top brand can obtain strong trade cooperation and support from resellers. For example, General Electric, Procter & Gamble, and Kraft can command unusual cooperation from resellers regarding displays, shelf space, promotions, and price policies. Large retailers such as Walmart, Home Depot, and Chapters Indigo can exert strong influence on the manufacturers that supply the products they sell.

Horizontal Marketing Systems

Horizontal marketing system

A channel arrangement in which two or more companies at one level join together to follow a new marketing opportunity.

Another channel development is the **horizontal marketing system**, in which two or more companies at one level join together to follow a new marketing opportunity. By working together, companies can combine their financial, production, or marketing resources to accomplish more than any one company could alone.

Companies might join forces with competitors or noncompetitors. They might work with each other on a temporary or permanent basis, or they may create a separate company. For example, McDonald's now places "express" versions of its restaurants in Walmart stores. McDonald's benefits from Walmart's heavy store traffic, and Walmart keeps hungry shoppers from needing to go elsewhere to eat. In another example, once major competitors, Canada's two largest wineries, T.G. Bright & Co. and Cartier Inniskillin Vintners Inc., formed an alliance so that they could increase their economies of scale and resources. This was necessary because they wanted to export to the U.S. market, which is dominated by huge American vintners, such as E.&J. Gallo.

Multichannel distribution system

A distribution system in which a single firm sets up two or more marketing channels to reach one or more customer segments.

Such channel arrangements also work well globally. For example, McDonald's recently joined forces with Sinopec, China's largest gasoline retailer, to place drive-through restaurants at Sinopec's more than 31 000 gas stations. The move greatly speeds McDonald's expansion into China while at the same time pulling hungry motorists into Sinopec gas stations.[8]

Multichannel Distribution Systems

In the past, many companies used a single channel to sell to a single market or market segment. Today, with the proliferation of customer segments and channel possibilities, more and more companies have adopted **multichannel distribution systems**—often called *hybrid marketing channels*. Such multichannel marketing occurs when a single firm sets up two or more marketing channels to reach one or more customer segments. The use of multichannel systems has increased greatly in recent years.

Figure 12.4 shows a multichannel marketing system. In the figure, the producer sells directly to consumer segment 1 using direct-mail catalogues, telemarketing, and the Internet and reaches consumer segment 2 through retailers. It sells indirectly to business

Horizontal marketing systems: McDonald's recently joined forces with Sinopec, China's largest gasoline retailer, to place restaurants at its more than 31 000 gas stations. Here, the presidents of the two companies shake hands while announcing the partnership.

Figure 12.4 Multichannel distribution system

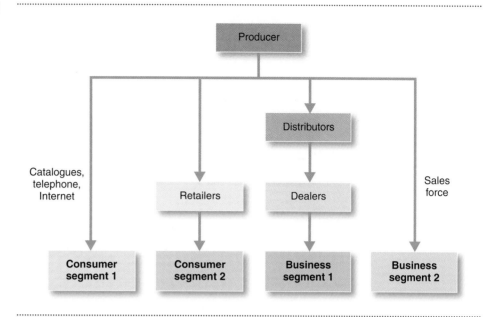

segment 1 through distributors and dealers and to business segment 2 through its own sales force.

These days, almost every large company and many small ones distribute through multiple channels. For example, John Deere sells its familiar green and yellow lawn and garden tractors, mowers, and outdoor power products to consumers and commercial users through several channels, including John Deere retailers, Home Depot stores, and online. It sells and services its tractors, combines, planters, and other agricultural equipment through its premium John Deere dealer network. And it sells large construction and forestry equipment through selected large, full-service dealers and their sales forces.

Multichannel distribution systems offer many advantages to companies facing large and complex markets. With each new channel, the company expands its sales and market coverage and gains opportunities to tailor its products and services to the specific needs of diverse customer segments. But such multichannel systems are harder to control, and they generate conflict as more channels compete for customers and sales. For example, when John Deere began selling selected consumer products through Home Depot, many of its dealers complained loudly. To avoid such conflicts in its Internet marketing channels, the company routes all of its website sales to John Deere dealers.

Changing Channel Organization

Changes in technology and the explosive growth of direct and online marketing are having a profound impact on the nature and design of marketing channels. One major trend is toward **disintermediation**—a big term with a clear message and important consequences. Disintermediation occurs when product or service producers cut out intermediaries and go directly to final buyers, or when radically new types of channel intermediaries displace traditional ones.

Thus, in many industries traditional intermediaries are dropping by the wayside. For example, Air Canada is selling directly to final buyers, cutting travel agents from its marketing channels altogether. In other cases, new forms of resellers are displacing traditional intermediaries. For example, online marketing is growing rapidly, taking business from traditional brick-and-mortar retailers to the Internet. Consumers can buy airline tickets and hotel rooms from Expedia.ca and Travelzoo.com; electronics from SonyStyle.com; clothes and accessories from Bluefly.com; and books, videos, toys, jewellery, sports, consumer electronics, home and garden items, and almost anything else from Amazon.ca—all without ever stepping into a traditional retail store. Online music download services such as iTunes and Yahoo! Music are threatening the very existence of traditional music-store retailers.

Disintermediation
The cutting out of marketing channel intermediaries by product or service producers, or the displacement of traditional resellers by radical new types of intermediaries.

Avoiding disintermediation problems: Black & Decker's website provides detailed information, but you can't buy any of the company's products there. Instead, Black & Decker refers you to resellers' websites and stores.

In fact, once-dominant music retailer Tower Records declared bankruptcy and closed its doors for good.

Disintermediation presents both opportunities and problems for producers and resellers. Channel innovators who find new ways to add value in the channel can sweep aside traditional resellers and reap the rewards. In turn, traditional intermediaries must continue to innovate to avoid being swept aside. For example, when Netflix pioneered online video rentals, it sent traditional brick-and-mortar video-rental stores such as Blockbuster reeling. To meet the threat, Blockbuster developed its own online DVD-rental service. Now, both Netflix and Blockbuster face disintermediation threats from an even hotter channel—digital video distribution (see Real Marketing 12.1).

Similarly, to remain competitive, product and service producers must develop new channel opportunities such as the Internet and other direct channels. However, developing these new channels often brings them into direct competition with their established channels, resulting in conflict. To ease this problem, companies often look for ways to make going direct a plus for the entire channel. For example, Black & Decker knows that many customers would prefer to buy its power tools and outdoor power equipment online. But selling directly through its website would create conflicts with important and powerful retail partners such as Home Depot, Lowe's, Walmart, and Amazon.ca. So, although Black & Decker's website provides detailed information about the company's products, you can't buy a new Black & Decker cordless drill, laser level, or leaf blower there. Instead, the Black & Decker website refers you to resellers' websites and stores. Thus, Black & Decker's direct marketing helps both the company and its channel partners.

3   CHANNEL DESIGN DECISIONS

We now look at several channel decisions manufacturers face. In designing marketing channels, manufacturers struggle between what is ideal and what is practical. A new firm with limited capital usually starts by selling in a limited market area. Deciding on the best channels might not be a problem: The problem might simply be how to convince one or a few good intermediaries to handle the line.

If successful, the new firm can branch out to new markets through the existing intermediaries. In smaller markets, the firm might sell directly to retailers; in larger markets, it might sell through distributors. In one part of the country, it might grant exclusive franchises; in another, it might sell through all available outlets. Then, it might add a web store that sells directly to hard-to-reach customers. In this way, channel systems often evolve to meet market opportunities and conditions.

Real Marketing **12.1**

Netflix: Disintermediator or Disintermediated?

Baseball great Yogi Berra, known more for his mangled phrasing than for his baseball prowess, once said, "The future ain't what it used to be." For Netflix, the world's largest online movie-rental service, no matter how you say it, figuring out the future is challenging and a bit scary. Netflix faces dramatic changes in how movies and other entertainment content will be distributed. The question is, will Netflix be among the disintermediat*ors* or among the disintermediat*ed*?

Less than a decade ago, if you wanted to watch a movie in the comfort of your own home, your only choice was to roust yourself out of that easy chair and trot down to the local Blockbuster or another neighbourhood movie-rental store. In fact, that's how most people still do it. Blockbuster has grown to become the world's largest store-rental chain, with more than 7800 outlets worldwide and more than US\$5.5 billion in annual sales.

But now, thanks to Netflix, that distribution model is changing quickly. In the late 1990s, Netflix pioneered a new way to rent movies—via the Web and direct mail. With Netflix, you pay a monthly subscription fee and create a movie wish list online. Netflix mails you a set number of DVDs from your list at a given time, which you can keep for as long as you like. As you return the DVDs in prepaid return envelopes, Netflix automatically sends you new ones from your list. While Netflix is not available in Canada, Zip.ca offers a very similar service, offering Canadians over 72 000 titles to choose from.

Netflix offers lots of advantages over the traditional Blockbuster brick-and-mortar system. With store video rentals, you have to make a special trip whenever you want a movie, and if you don't plan ahead, you'll probably find the latest hot releases out of stock. As for finding copies of oldies but goodies, or an old documentary or independent film, forget it—stores can hold only a limited selection of DVDs. Finally, many consumers are frustrated by short due dates and those dreaded late return fees. In contrast, Netflix isn't bound by store-space limitations. It offers a huge selection of more than 90 000 titles and 40 million DVDs. The Netflix system eliminates store trips—you always have a stack of DVDs on hand. And there are no per-movie charges, no due dates, and no late fees.

Netflix faces dramatic changes in how movies and other entertainment content will be distributed. Instead of simply watching the developments, Netflix intends to lead them.

Since first opening its virtual doors, Netflix has continued to add innovative features. Its "dynamic queue" lets customers select as many movie titles as they wish and rank them by preference. Netflix has also developed an online recommendation system, called Cinematch, to help customers find movies they'll love based on their own past ratings, member and critic reviews, and top-rented lists.

As a result, more and more customers are signing up with Netflix. Membership has grown to more than 7.5 million subscribers, and in just the past two years, sales and profits have surged 77 percent and 60 percent, respectively. Meanwhile, Netflix's success has sent Blockbuster and other video-rental stores reeling. As Netflix sales and profits have soared, Blockbuster's sales have lagged and losses have mounted. The video rental giant has lost money in 10 of the last 11 years. Although the traditional brick-and-mortar video-rental market is still alive and kicking, it's stagnating as the red-hot online channel gains momentum.

To meet the disintermediation threat, Blockbuster introduced its own online video-rental service. In fact, Blockbuster Total Access takes the new distribution model one step further. Total Access customers can order videos online and then return or exchange them either through the mail or at their local Blockbuster store. Blockbuster's online business quickly grew to over 2 million subscribers before levelling off.

▶

However, for the most part, Blockbuster is still struggling to find the right formula.

And so the video-rental channels battle continues. Blockbuster claims the advantages of a click-and-mortar model that offers both online and store services. In contrast, Netflix sees physical stores as an unnecessary and costly limitation. Says Netflix founder and CEO Reed Hastings, "For people who'd love never to go into a Blockbuster store ever again, we offer better selection, better tools for choosing movies, and more consistent overnight delivery." Either way, there's no going back to the past—the two competitors are rapidly disintermediating store-only video-rental outfits.

But just as the present isn't what it used to be, neither is the future. At the same time that Netflix is displacing traditional store channels, it faces its own disintermediation threat from a potentially even hotter channel—digital video distribution in the form of digital downloads and video on demand (VOD). Digital distribution is a fact of life in the music industry, where music download services are quickly making traditional CD retailers obsolete. Most experts agree that it's only a matter of time before digital video distribution displaces DVD video sales and rentals.

In fact, it's already begun. These days, you can download all kinds of video entertainment—from movies and TV shows to ads and amateur videos—to your computer, iPod, or even your cellphone. Satellite and cable TV companies are promising VOD services that will let you view movies and other video entertainment on television whenever and wherever you wish. And video-rental download services such as CinemaNow are already offering a growing list of downloadable titles via the Web.

Digital video downloads and video on demand create obvious cost, distribution, and customer convenience advantages over physically producing and distributing DVDs. For sure, the digital video distribution industry still faces problems. Downloading videos can take a lot of time and yields less-than-DVD quality. Perhaps the biggest barrier so far—Hollywood has been cautious about granting video distribution rights, severely limiting the number of available titles. In time, however, all these limitations will likely dissipate. When

that happens, it could be lights out for the DVD sales and rental industry.

Netflix CEO Hastings understands the future challenges. "We're sure that we're going to be buying cars in 25 years, whereas renting DVDs through the mail in 25 years—for sure that's not going to exist," he says. The solution? Keep innovating. Instead of simply watching digital video distribution developments, Netflix intends to lead them. Netflix has already added a "watch instantly" feature to its website that allows subscribers to instantly stream near-DVD-quality video for a limited but growing list of movie titles and TV programs. "Our intention," says Hastings, "is to get [our watch instantly] service to every Internet-connected screen, from cellphones to laptops to WiFi-enabled plasma screens." In this way, Netflix plans to disintermediate its own distribution model before others can do it. Compared to the United States, the online DVD market in Canada is still in its infancy. Thus, it is anticipated that Canadian firms like Zip.ca will experience more modest growth, primarily because of the lack of content rights in this country as compared to those in the Unites States.

To Hastings, the key to the future is all in how Netflix defines itself. "If [you] think of Netflix as a DVD rental business, [you're] right to be scared," he says. But "if [you] think of Netflix as an online movie service with multiple different delivery models, then [you're] a lot less scared. We're only now starting to deliver [on] that second vision." When asked what Netflix will be like in five years, Hasting responds, "We hope to be much larger, have more subscribers, and be successfully expanding into online video."

Sources: Quotes and other information from Matthew Boyle, "Reed Hastings," *Fortune*, May 28, 2007, p. 30; Nick Wingfield, "Netflix vs. Naysayers," *Wall Street Journal*, March 27, 2007, p. B1; Yuval Rosenberg, "What's Next for Netflix?" *Fortune*, November 29, 2006, p. 172; Paul R. La Monica, "DVD or Download?" *CNNMoney.com*, June 26, 2006; Nancy Macdonald, "Blockbuster Proves It's Not Dead Yet," *Maclean's*, March 17, 2008, p. 36; Michael V. Copeland, "Netflix Lives!" *Fortune*, April 28, 2008, p. 40; "Netflix, Inc.," *Hoover's Company Records*, April 15, 2008, p.100752; "Online DVD Rental Firms Find Big Profits in Tough Times," *CBC News*, January 27, 2009; and information from www.netflix.com and www.blockbuster.com, accessed November 2008.

Marketing channel design
Designing effective marketing channels by analyzing consumer needs, setting channel objectives, identifying major channel alternatives, and evaluating them.

For maximum effectiveness, however, channel analysis and decision making should be more purposeful. **Marketing channel design** calls for analyzing consumer needs, setting channel objectives, identifying major channel alternatives, and evaluating them.

Analyzing Consumer Needs

As noted previously, marketing channels are part of the overall *customer-value delivery network*. Each channel member and level adds value for the customer. Thus, designing the marketing channel starts with finding out what target consumers want from the channel. Do consumers want to buy from nearby locations or are they willing to travel to more distant centralized locations? Would they rather buy in person, by phone, or online? Do they value breadth of assortment or do they prefer specialization? Do consumers want many add-on services (delivery, repairs, installation), or will they obtain these elsewhere? The faster the delivery, the greater the assortment provided, and the more add-on services supplied, the greater the channel's service level.

Providing the fastest delivery, greatest assortment, and most services may not be possible or practical. The company and its channel members may not have the resources or skills needed to provide all the desired services. Also, providing higher levels of service results in higher costs for the channel and higher prices for consumers. The company must balance consumer needs not only against the feasibility and costs of meeting these needs but also against customer price preferences. The success of discount retailing shows that consumers will often accept lower service levels in exchange for lower prices.

Setting Channel Objectives

Companies should state their marketing channel objectives in terms of targeted levels of customer service. Usually, a company can identify several segments wanting different levels of service. The company should decide which segments to serve and the best channels to use in each case. In each segment, the company wants to minimize the total channel cost of meeting customer service requirements.

The company's channel objectives are also influenced by the nature of the company, its products, its marketing intermediaries, its competitors, and the environment. For example, the company's size and financial situation determine which marketing functions it can handle itself and which it must give to intermediaries. Companies selling perishable products may require more direct marketing to avoid delays and too much handling.

In some cases, a company may want to compete in or near the same outlets that carry competitors' products. In other cases, companies may avoid the channels used by competitors. Mary Kay, for example, sells direct to consumers through its network of more than 1 million independent beauty consultants in 34 markets worldwide rather than going head-to-head with other cosmetics makers for scarce positions in retail stores. And GEICO primarily markets automobile and homeowner's insurance directly to consumers via the telephone and Internet rather than through agents.

Finally, environmental factors such as economic conditions and legal constraints may affect channel objectives and design. For example, in a depressed economy producers want to distribute their goods in the most economical way, using shorter channels and dropping unneeded services that add to the final price of the goods.

Identifying Major Alternatives

When the company has defined its channel objectives, it should next identify its major channel alternatives in terms of *types* of intermediaries, the *number* of intermediaries, and the *responsibilities* of each channel member.

Types of Intermediaries

A firm should identify the types of channel members available to carry out its channel work. Most companies face many channel member choices. For example, until recently, Dell sold directly to final consumers and business buyers only through its sophisticated phone and Internet marketing channel. It also sold directly to large corporate, institutional, and government buyers using its direct sales force. However, to reach more consumers and to match competitors such as HP, Dell now sells indirectly through retailers such as Best Buy and Walmart. It also sells indirectly through "value-added resellers," independent distributors and dealers who develop computer systems and applications tailored to the special needs of small and medium-sized business customers.

Using many types of resellers in a channel provides both benefits and drawbacks. For example, by selling through retailers and value-added resellers in addition to its own direct channels, Dell can reach more and different kinds of buyers. However, the new channels will be more difficult to manage and control. And the direct and indirect channels will compete with each other for many of the same customers, causing potential conflict. In fact, Dell is already finding itself "stuck in the middle," with its direct sales reps complaining about new competition from retail stores, while at the same time value-added resellers complain that the direct sales reps are undercutting their business.[9]

Number of Marketing Intermediaries

Intensive distribution
Stocking the product in as many outlets as possible.

Companies must also determine the number of channel members to use at each level. Three strategies are available: intensive distribution, exclusive distribution, and selective distribution. Producers of convenience products and common raw materials typically seek **intensive distribution**—a strategy in which they stock their products in as many outlets as possible. These products must be available where and when consumers want them. For example, toothpaste, candy, and other similar items are sold in millions of outlets to provide maximum brand exposure and consumer convenience. Kraft, Coca-Cola, Kimberly-Clark, and other consumer goods companies distribute their products in this way.

Exclusive distribution
Giving a limited number of dealers the exclusive right to distribute the company's products in their territories.

In contrast, some producers purposely limit the number of intermediaries handling their products. The extreme form of this practice is **exclusive distribution**, in which the producer gives only a limited number of dealers the exclusive right to distribute its products in their territories. Exclusive distribution is often found in the distribution of luxury automobiles and prestige women's clothing. For example, exclusive Rolex watches are typically sold by only a handful of authorized dealers in any given market area. By granting exclusive distribution, Rolex gains stronger dealer selling support and more control over dealer prices, promotion, and services. Exclusive distribution also enhances the brand's image and allows for higher markups.

Selective distribution
The use of more than one but fewer than all of the intermediaries who are willing to carry the company's products.

Between intensive and exclusive distribution lies **selective distribution**—the use of more than one but fewer than all of the intermediaries who are willing to carry a company's products. Most television, furniture, and home appliance brands are distributed in this manner. For example, Whirlpool and General Electric sell their major appliances through dealer networks and selected large retailers. By using selective distribution, they can develop good working relationships with selected channel members and expect a better-than-average selling effort. Selective distribution gives producers good market coverage with more control and less cost than with intensive distribution.

Exclusive distribution: Rolex sells its watches exclusively through only a handful of authorized dealers in any given market. Such limited distribution enhances the brand's image and generates stronger retailer support.

Responsibilities of Channel Members

The producer and intermediaries need to agree on the terms and responsibilities of each channel member. They should agree on price policies, conditions of sale, territorial rights, and specific services to be performed by each party. The producer should establish a list price and a fair set of discounts for intermediaries. It must define each channel member's territory, and it should be careful about where it places new resellers.

Mutual services and duties need to be spelled out carefully, especially in franchise and exclusive distribution channels. For example, McDonald's provides franchisees with promotional support, a record-keeping system, training at Hamburger University, and general management assistance. In turn, franchisees must meet company standards for physical facilities and food quality, cooperate with new promotion programs, provide requested information, and buy specified food products.

Evaluating the Major Alternatives

Suppose a company has identified several channel alternatives and wants to select the one that will best satisfy its long-run objectives. Each alternative should be evaluated against economic, control, and adaptive criteria.

Using *economic criteria*, a company compares the likely sales, costs, and profitability of different channel alternatives. What will

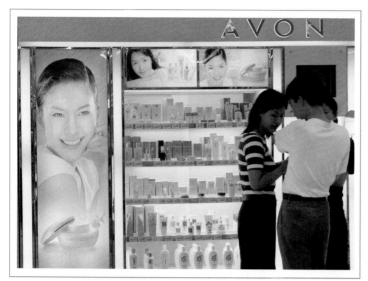

International channel complexities: When the Chinese government banned door-to-door selling, Avon had to abandon its traditional direct-marketing approach and sell through retail shops.

be the investment required by each channel alternative, and what returns will result? The company must also consider *control issues*. Using intermediaries usually means giving them some control over the marketing of the product, and some intermediaries take more control than others. Other things being equal, the company prefers to keep as much control as possible. Finally, the company must apply *adaptive criteria*. Channels often involve long-term commitments, yet the company wants to keep the channel flexible so that it can adapt to environmental changes. Thus, to be considered, a channel involving long-term commitments should be greatly superior on economic and control grounds.

Designing International Distribution Channels

International marketers face many additional complexities in designing their channels. Each country has its own unique distribution system that has evolved over time and changes very slowly. These channel systems can vary widely from country to country. Thus, global marketers must usually adapt their channel strategies to the existing structures within each country.

In some markets, the distribution system is complex and hard to penetrate, consisting of many layers and large numbers of intermediaries. At the other extreme, distribution systems in developing countries may be scattered, inefficient, or altogether lacking. For example, China and India are huge markets, each with a population of well over 1 billion people. However, because of inadequate distribution systems, most companies can profitably access only a small portion of the population located in each country's most affluent cities. "China is a very decentralized market," notes one China trade expert. "[It's] made up of two dozen distinct markets sprawling across 2000 cities. Each has its own culture.. . . It's like operating in an asteroid belt." China's distribution system is so fragmented that logistics costs amount to 15 percent of the nation's GDP, far higher than in most other countries. After years of effort, even Walmart executives admit that they have been unable to assemble an efficient supply chain in China.[10]

Sometimes government regulation can greatly restrict how a company distributes products in global markets. For example, it wasn't an inefficient distribution structure that caused problems for Avon in China—it was restrictive government regulations. Fearing the growth of multilevel marketing schemes, the Chinese government banned door-to-door selling altogether in 1998, forcing Avon to abandon its traditional direct-marketing approach and sell through retail shops. The Chinese government recently gave Avon and other direct sellers permission to sell door-to-door again, but that permission is tangled in a web of restrictions. Fortunately for Avon, its earlier focus on store sales is helping it weather the restrictions better than most other direct sellers.[11]

International marketers face a wide range of channel alternatives. Designing efficient and effective channel systems between and within various national markets poses a difficult challenge. We discuss international distribution decisions further in Chapter 18.

Marketing channel management
Selecting, managing, and motivating individual channel members and evaluating their performance over time.

CHANNEL MANAGEMENT DECISIONS

Once the company has reviewed its channel alternatives and decided on the best channel design, it must implement and manage the chosen channel. **Marketing channel management** calls for selecting, managing, and motivating individual channel members and evaluating their performance over time.

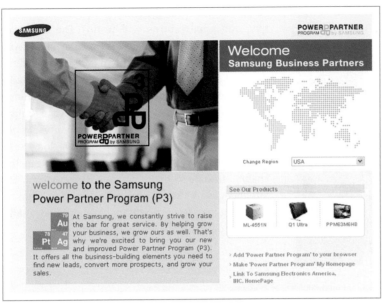

Partnering with marketing channel members: The Samsung Power Partner Program turns important resellers into strong, motivated marketing partners by helping them be more effective and profitable at selling Samsung.

Selecting Channel Members

Producers vary in their ability to attract qualified marketing intermediaries. Some producers have no trouble signing up channel members. For example, when Toyota first introduced its Lexus line in North America, it had no trouble attracting new dealers. In fact, it had to turn down many would-be resellers.

At the other extreme are producers who have to work hard to line up enough qualified intermediaries. For example, in 1986 when distributors were approached about an unknown new game called Nintendo, many refused to carry the product: They had recently been burned by the failure of Atari. But two Canadian distributors, Larry Wasser and Morey Chaplick, owners of Beamscope, accepted the product. Not a bad move considering that within one year after that decision their sales went from next to nothing to $24 million![12] Similarly, when Timex first tried to sell its inexpensive watches through regular jewellery stores, most jewellery stores refused to carry them. The company then managed to get its watches into mass-merchandise outlets. This turned out to be a wise decision because of the rapid growth of mass merchandising.

When selecting intermediaries, the company should determine what characteristics distinguish the better ones. It will want to evaluate each channel member's years in business, other lines carried, growth and profit record, cooperativeness, and reputation. If the intermediaries are sales agents, the company will want to evaluate the number and character of other lines carried and the size and quality of the sales force. If the intermediary is a retail store that wants exclusive or selective distribution, the company will want to evaluate the store's customers, location, and future growth potential.

Managing and Motivating Channel Members

Once selected, channel members must be continuously managed and motivated to do their best. The company must sell not only *through* the intermediaries but *to* and *with* them. Most companies see their intermediaries as first-line customers and partners. They practise strong *partner relationship management (PRM)* to forge long-term partnerships with channel members. This creates a value delivery system that meets the needs of both the company *and* its marketing partners. For example, heavy-equipment manufacturer Caterpillar and its worldwide network of independent dealers work in close harmony to find better ways to bring value to customers. Dealers play a vital role in almost every aspect of Caterpillar's operations (see Real Marketing 12.2).

In managing its channels, a company must convince distributors that they can succeed better by working together as a part of a cohesive value delivery system. For example, Samsung's information technology division works closely with value-added resellers through the industry-leading Samsung Power Partner Program (P3):

> The Samsung P3 program creates close partnerships with important value-added resellers (VARs)—channel firms that assemble IT solutions for their own customers using products from Samsung and other manufacturers. Through the Power Partner Program, Samsung provides extensive presale, selling, and postsale tools and support to some 17 255 registered North American VAR partners at one of three levels—silver, gold, or platinum. For example, platinum-level partners—those selling US$500 000 or more of Samsung IT products per year—receive access to a searchable online product and

Real Marketing 12.2

With the Help of Its Dealer Network, the Big Cat Is Purring

For more than eight decades Caterpillar has dominated the world's markets for heavy construction, mining, and logging equipment. Its familiar yellow tractors, crawlers, loaders, bulldozers, and trucks are a common sight at any construction area around the world. Caterpillar sells more than 300 products in nearly 200 countries, with sales of more than US$45 billion annually. Over the past four years, sales have nearly doubled and profits have more than tripled. The big Cat captures some 40 percent of the worldwide heavy-equipment business, twice that of number-two Komatsu. The waiting line for some of Caterpillar's biggest equipment is three years long. In Canada, Caterpillar distributes its products through independent dealerships, such as Finning (Canada), located in Edmonton, Alberta. Finning is one of Caterpillar's largest dealerships and aims to be Caterpillar's best global business partner, providing unrivalled services that earn customer loyalty.

Caterpillar works closely with its worldwide network of independent dealers to find better ways to bring value to customers. When a big piece of Cat equipment breaks down, customers know they can count on Caterpillar and its outstanding dealer network for support.

Many factors contribute to Caterpillar's enduring success—high-quality products, flexible and efficient manufacturing, and a steady stream of innovative new products. Yet these are not the most important reasons for Caterpillar's dominance. Instead, Caterpillar credits its focus on customers and its distribution network of 181 outstanding independent dealers worldwide, who work with Caterpillar to do a superb job of taking care of every customer need. According to a former Caterpillar CEO:

> After the product leaves our door, the dealers take over. They are the ones on the front line. They're the ones who live with the product for its lifetime. They're the ones customers see. . . . They're out there making sure that when a machine is delivered, it's in the condition it's supposed to be in. They're out there training a customer's operators. They service a product frequently throughout its life, carefully monitoring a machine's health and scheduling repairs to prevent costly downtime. The customer . . . knows that there is a [$45-bil-

lion-plus] company called Caterpillar. But the dealers create the image of a company that doesn't stand just behind its products but with its products, anywhere in the world. Our dealers are the reason that our motto—Buy the Iron, Get the Company—is not an empty slogan.

"Buy the Iron, Get the Company"—that's a powerful value proposition. It means that when you buy Cat equipment, you become a member of the Caterpillar family. Caterpillar and its dealers work in close harmony to find better ways to bring value to customers. Dealers play a vital role in almost every aspect of Caterpillar's operations, from product design and delivery, to product service and support, to market intelligence and customer feedback.

In the heavy-equipment industry, in which equipment downtime can mean big losses, Caterpillar's exceptional service gives it a huge advantage in winning and keeping customers. Consider BHP Billiton, a Caterpillar customer that operates the huge Antamina mine in Peru:

> More than a mile in length, the Antamina mine sits 14 100 oxygen-deprived feet above sea level in the Peruvian Andes. From the rim of the vast open pit, huge mechanized beasts of burden below look like scuttling yellow insects. Descend the dirt ramps to the floor of

the pit, however, and those bugs are transformed into Caterpillars. The industrial ballet goes on every hour of every day here, as Cat machines—giant trucks, mechanical shovels, scrapers, and other brutes—carve out massive amounts of copper and zinc from the earth. Forty-nine of those yellow bugs are mammoth 200- to 250-ton Caterpillar 793C and 793D trucks, 43-foot-high machines, costing millions of dollars each, which are powered by a diesel engine with more oomph than a tank. Made in Decatur, Illinois, each truck is shipped in pieces to Lima, hauled to the job site in nine tractor-trailers, and then assembled. Like sharks pursued by pilot fish, the big trucks are surrounded by a bevy of smaller Caterpillar equipment—wheel loaders to fill them, motor graders to keep the roads cleared, and bulldozers to clean up the spills. All told, BHP uses more than US$200 million worth of Caterpillar machinery at Antamina—and it will spend another US$200 million servicing them over their working life.

When equipment breaks down, BHP loses money fast. It gladly pays a premium price for machines and service it can count on. In fact, Caterpillar's reputation for gold-standard quality and service allows it to charge 10 percent to 20 percent more than its competitors. Customers know that they can count on Caterpillar and its outstanding dealer network for superb support.

The close working relationship between Caterpillar and its dealers comes down to more than just formal contracts and business agreements. Caterpillar really knows its dealers and cares about their success. It closely monitors each dealership's sales, market position, service capability, financial situation, and other performance measures. When it sees a problem, it jumps in to help. As a result, Caterpillar dealerships, many of which are longstanding family businesses, tend to be stable and profitable.

Caterpillar believes that it should "share the gain as well as the pain." When times are good, Caterpillar shares the bounty with its dealers rather than trying to grab all the riches for itself. When times are bad, Caterpillar protects its dealers. In the mid-1980s, facing a depressed global construction-equipment market and cutthroat competition, Caterpillar sheltered its dealers by absorbing much of the economic damage. It lost almost US$1 billion in just three years but didn't lose a single dealer. In contrast, competitors'

dealers struggled and many failed. As a result, Caterpillar emerged with its distribution partnerships intact and its competitive position stronger than ever.

Caterpillar provides extraordinary dealer support. Nowhere is this support more apparent than in the company's parts delivery system, the fastest and most reliable in the industry. Caterpillar maintains 23 distribution centres and 1500 service facilities around the world, which stock more than 150 000 different parts and ship 84 000 items per day, every day of the year. In turn, dealers have made huge investments in inventory, warehouses, fleets of trucks, service bays, diagnostic and service equipment, and information technology. Together, Caterpillar and its dealers guarantee parts delivery within 48 hours anywhere in the world, from the Alaskan tundra to the deserts of Timbuktu. The company ships 80 percent of parts orders immediately and 99 percent on the same day the order is received. In contrast, it's not unusual for competitors' customers to wait four or five costly days for a part.

Finally, in addition to more formal business ties, Cat forms close personal ties with its dealers in a kind of family relationship. One Caterpillar executive relates the following example: "When I see Chappy Chapman, a retired executive vice-president . . . out on the golf course, he always asks about particular dealers or about their children, who may be running the business now. And every time I see those dealers, they inquire, 'How's Chappy?' That's the sort of relationship we have. . . . I consider the majority of dealers personal friends."

Thus, Caterpillar's superb integrated distribution system serves as a major source of competitive advantage, for both the company and its independent dealers. The system is built on a firm base of mutual trust and shared dreams. Caterpillar and its dealers feel a deep pride in what they are accomplishing together. As a former CEO puts it, "There's a camaraderie among our dealers around the world that really makes it more than just a financial arrangement. They feel that what they're doing is good for the world because they are part of an organization that makes, sells, and tends to the machines that make the world work."

Sources: Quotes, examples, and other information from Alex Taylor III, "Caterpillar," *Fortune,* August 20, 2007, pp. 48–54; Donald V. Fites, "Make Your Dealers Your Partners," *Harvard Business Review,* March–April 1996, pp. 84–95; Tony Reid, "Caterpillar Predicts Record Sales, Profits," *McClatchy Tribune Business News,* March 19, 2008; and information accessed at www.caterpillar.com, November 2008.

pricing database and downloadable marketing materials. They can tap into partner-only Samsung training programs, special seminars, and conferences. A dedicated Samsung P3 team helps partners find good sales prospects and initiate sales. Then, a dedicated Samsung field sales rep works with each partner to close deals, and inside sales reps provide the partner with information and technical support. Platinum partners even participate in Samsung's Reseller Council. Finally, the P3 program rewards high-performing reseller–partners with rebates, discount promotions, bonuses, and sales awards. In all, the Power Partner Program turns important resellers into strong, motivated marketing partners by helping them be more effective and profitable at selling Samsung.[13]

Many companies are now installing integrated high-tech partner relationship management (PRM) systems to coordinate their whole-channel marketing efforts. Just as they use customer relationship management (CRM) software systems to help manage relationships with important customers, companies can now use PRM and supply chain management (SCM) software to help recruit, train, organize, manage, motivate, and evaluate relationships with channel partners.

Evaluating Channel Members

The producer must regularly check channel member performance against standards such as sales quotas, average inventory levels, customer delivery time, treatment of damaged and lost goods, cooperation in company promotion and training programs, and services to the customer. The company should recognize and reward intermediaries who are performing well and adding good value for consumers. Those who are performing poorly should be assisted or, as a last resort, replaced.

Finally, manufacturers need to be sensitive to their dealers. Those who treat their dealers poorly risk not only losing dealer support but also causing some legal problems. The next section describes various rights and duties pertaining to manufacturers and their channel members.

PUBLIC POLICY AND DISTRIBUTION DECISIONS

Supply chain management, logistics, and distribution present managers with countless ethical dilemmas—everything from what types of suppliers a company should use to the types of influence strategies that are appropriate to ensure channel members comply with channel policies. Under the heading "Fulfilment Practices," the Canadian Marketing Association's Code of Ethics covers some ethical issues with regard to distribution. For example, it stipulates that goods should be shipped within 30 days of the receipt of a properly completed order (or within the time limit stated in the original offer), and notes that customers have the right to cancel orders without penalty if this time frame is not respected. The American Marketing Association's (AMA) Code of Ethics (under which Canadian marketers also operate) focuses on issues of market power in the section dealing with distribution. Ethical marketers are advised not to manipulate product availability for purposes of exploitation and not to use coercion in the marketing channel. The AMA code puts into question practices around these issues:[14]

1. *Exclusive dealing.* Many producers and wholesalers like to develop exclusive channels for their products. When the seller allows only certain outlets to carry its products, this strategy is called *exclusive distribution*. When the seller requires that these dealers not handle competitors' products, its strategy is called *exclusive dealing*. Both parties benefit from exclusive arrangements: The seller obtains more loyal and dependable outlets, and the dealers obtain a steady source of supply and stronger seller support. But exclusive arrangements exclude other producers from selling to these dealers. They are legal as long as they do not substantially lessen competition or tend to create a monopoly and as long as both parties enter into the agreement voluntarily.

2. *Exclusive territories.* Exclusive dealing often includes exclusive territorial agreements. The producer may agree not to sell to other dealers in a given area, or the buyer may agree to sell only in its own territory. The first practice is normal under franchise systems as a way to increase dealer enthusiasm and commitment. It is also perfectly legal—a seller has no legal obligation to sell through more outlets than it wishes. The second practice, whereby the producer tries to keep a dealer from selling outside its territory, has become a major legal issue.

3. *Tying agreements.* Producers of a strong brand sometimes sell it to dealers only if the dealers will take some or all of the rest of the line—*full-line forcing*. Even though the practice isn't illegal, it causes considerable channel conflict.

4. *Dealers' rights.* Producers are free to select their dealers, but their right to terminate dealers is somewhat restricted. In general, sellers can drop dealers "for cause." But they cannot drop dealers if, for example, the dealers refuse to cooperate in a questionable legal arrangement, such as exclusive dealing or tying agreements.

5. *Sources of supply.* As price competition increases in many industries, many firms look to overseas suppliers who can provide them with low-cost inputs. A number of ethical concerns have arisen as a result of this practice, including the loss of jobs in Canada's manufacturing sector and the use of overseas suppliers that follow questionable practices. For example, in the sporting goods market, firms have been criticized for using suppliers that pay low wages (wages far below what they pay celebrities to endorse their products) to suppliers that are reported to produce goods in *sweatshops* that use child or prison labour. Few Canadians want to think that the high-fashion apparel they wear or the sports equipment they use is made by children forced into labour instead of going to school.

5 MARKETING LOGISTICS AND SUPPLY CHAIN MANAGEMENT

In today's global marketplace, selling a product is sometimes easier than getting it to customers. Companies must decide on the best way to store, handle, and move their products and services so that they are available to customers in the right assortments, at the right time, and in the right place. Logistics effectiveness has a major impact on both customer satisfaction and company costs. Here we consider the nature and importance of logistics management in the supply chain, goals of the logistics system, major logistics functions, and the need for integrated supply chain management.

Nature and Importance of Marketing Logistics

Marketing logistics (physical distribution)
Planning, implementing, and controlling the physical flow of materials, final goods, and related information from points of origin to points of consumption to meet customer requirements at a profit.

To some managers, marketing logistics means only trucks and warehouses. But modern logistics is much more than this. **Marketing logistics**—also called **physical distribution**—involves planning, implementing, and controlling the physical flow of goods, services, and related information from points of origin to points of consumption to meet customer requirements at a profit. In short, it involves getting the right product to the right customer in the right place at the right time.

In the past, physical distribution planners typically started with products at the plant and then tried to find low-cost solutions to get them to customers. However, today's marketers prefer *customer-centred* logistics thinking, which starts with the marketplace and works backward to the factory, or even to sources of supply. Marketing logistics involves not only *outbound distribution* (moving products from the factory to resellers and ultimately to customers) but also *inbound distribution* (moving products and materials from suppliers to the factory) and *reverse distribution* (moving broken, unwanted, or excess products returned by consumers or resellers). That is, it involves entire **supply chain management**—managing upstream and downstream value-added flows of materials, final goods, and related information among suppliers, the company, resellers, and final consumers, as shown in Figure 12.5.

Supply chain management
Managing upstream and downstream value-added flows of materials, final goods, and related information among suppliers, the company, resellers, and final consumers.

The logistics manager's task is to coordinate activities of suppliers, purchasing agents, marketers, channel members, and customers. These activities include forecasting, information systems, purchasing, production planning, order processing, inventory, warehousing, and transportation planning.

Companies today are placing greater emphasis on logistics for several reasons. First, companies can gain a powerful competitive advantage by using improved logistics to give customers better service or lower prices.

Second, improved logistics can yield tremendous cost savings to both the company and its customers. As much as 20 percent of an average product's price is accounted for by shipping and transport alone. This far exceeds the cost of advertising and many other

Figure 12.5 Supply chain management

marketing costs. North American companies spent over US$1.3 trillion last year to wrap, bundle, load, unload, sort, reload, and transport goods. That's more than the national GDPs of all but 12 countries worldwide. What's more, these costs have risen more than 50 percent over the past decade. By itself, Ford has more than 500 million tons of finished vehicles, production parts, and aftermarket parts in transit at any given time, running up an annual logistics bill of around US$4 billion.[15] Shaving off even a small fraction of these costs can mean substantial savings.

Third, the explosion in product variety has created a need for improved logistics management. For example, in 1911 the typical A&P grocery store carried only 270 items. The store manager could keep track of this inventory on about 10 pages of notebook paper stuffed in a shirt pocket. Today, the average A&P (which now goes by the name Metro) carries a bewildering stock of more than 25 000 items. A Walmart Supercentre store carries more than 100 000 products, 30 000 of which are grocery products.[16] Ordering, shipping, stocking, and controlling such a variety of products presents a sizable logistics challenge.

Improvements in information technology have also created opportunities for major gains in distribution efficiency. Today's companies are using sophisticated supply chain management software, web-based logistics systems, point-of-sale scanners, uniform product codes, satellite tracking, and electronic transfer of order and payment data. Such technology lets them quickly and efficiently manage the flow of goods, information, and finances through the supply chain.

Finally, more than almost any other marketing function, logistics affects the environment and a firm's environmental sustainability efforts. Transportation, warehousing, packaging, and other logistics functions are typically the biggest supply chain contributors to the company's environmental footprint. At the same time, they also provide one of the most fertile areas for cost savings. So developing a *green supply chain* is not only environmentally responsible, it can also be profitable. "Your CO_2 footprint of transportation and your cost of fuel are permanently linked," says one logistics manager. "The good news is if you can reduce logistics costs you can write an environmental story about it."[17]

Goals of the Logistics System

Some companies state their logistics objective as providing maximum customer service at the least cost. Unfortunately, no logistics system can *both* maximize customer service *and* minimize distribution costs. Maximum customer service implies rapid delivery, large inventories, flexible assortments, liberal return policies, and other services—all of which raise distribution costs. In contrast, minimum distribution costs imply slower delivery, smaller inventories, and larger shipping lots—which represent a lower level of overall customer service.

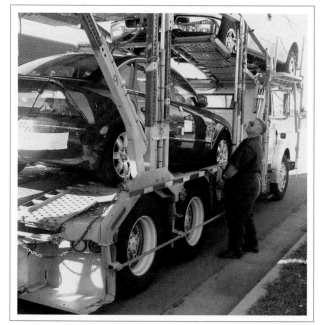

The importance of logistics: At any given time, Ford has more than 500 million tons of finished vehicles, production parts, and after-market parts in transit, running up an annual logistics bill of around US$4 billion.

High-tech distribution centres: Staples employs a team of super-retrievers—in day-glo orange—to keep its warehouse humming.

The goal of marketing logistics should be to provide a *targeted* level of customer service at the least cost. A company must first research the importance of various distribution services to customers and then set desired service levels for each segment. The objective is to maximize *profits*, not sales. Therefore, the company must weigh the benefits of providing higher levels of service against the costs. Some companies offer less service than their competitors and charge a lower price. Other companies offer more service and charge higher prices to cover higher costs.

Major Logistics Functions

Given a set of logistics objectives, the company is ready to design a logistics system that will minimize the cost of attaining these objectives. The major logistics functions include *warehousing, inventory management, transportation*, and *logistics information management*.

Warehousing

Production and consumption cycles rarely match. So most companies must store their goods while they wait to be sold. For example, Snapper, Toro, and other lawn mower manufacturers run their factories all year long and store up products for the heavy spring and summer buying seasons. The storage function overcomes differences in needed quantities and timing, ensuring that products are available when customers are ready to buy them.

A company must decide on *how many* and *what types* of warehouses it needs and *where* they will be located. The company might use either *storage warehouses* or *distribution centres*. Storage warehouses store goods for moderate to long periods. **Distribution centres** are designed to move goods rather than just store them. They are large and highly automated warehouses designed to receive goods from various plants and suppliers, take orders, fill them efficiently, and deliver goods to customers as quickly as possible.

For example, Walmart Canada operates a network of seven huge Canadian distribution centres, with plans to open another $115 million, 400 000 square-foot refrigerated hub north of Calgary in 2010. At a typical centre, laser scanners route as many as 190 000 cases of goods per day along several kilometres of conveyor belts, and a centre's workers load or unload some 500 trucks daily. The newest sustainable distribution facility in Balzac, Alberta, will also use only renewable energy and an array of other green systems, furthering Walmart's commitment to long-term environmental sustainability.[18]

Like almost everything else these days, warehousing has seen dramatic changes in technology in recent years. Outdated materials-handling methods are steadily being replaced by newer, computer-controlled systems requiring few employees. Computers and scanners read orders and direct lift trucks, electric hoists, or robots to gather goods, move them to loading docks, and issue invoices. For example, office supplies retailer Staples now employs "a team of super-retrievers—in day-glo orange—that keep its warehouse humming":

> Imagine a team of employees that works 16 hours a day, seven days a week. They never call in sick or show up late, because they never leave the building. They demand no benefits, require no health insurance, and receive no pay cheques. And they never complain. Sounds like a bunch of robots, huh? They are, in fact, robots—and they're dramatically changing the way Staples delivers notepads, pens, and paper clips to its customers. Every day, Staples' huge Chambersburg, Pennsylvania, distribution centre receives thousands of customer orders, each containing a wide range of office supply items. Having people run around a warehouse looking for those items is expensive, especially when the company has promised to delight customers by delivering orders the next day.

Distribution centre

A large, highly automated warehouse designed to receive goods from various plants and suppliers, take orders, fill them efficiently, and deliver goods to customers as quickly as possible.

Enter the robots. On the distribution centre floor, the 150 robots most resemble a well-trained breed of working dogs, say, golden retrievers. When orders come in, a centralized computer tells the robots where to find racks with the appropriate items. The robots retrieve the racks and carry them to picking stations, then wait patiently as humans pull the correct products and place them in boxes. When orders are filled, the robots neatly park the racks back among the rest. The robots pretty much take care of themselves. When they run low on power, they head to battery-charging terminals or, as warehouse personnel say, "They get themselves a drink of water." The robots now run 50 percent of the Chambersburg facility, where average daily output is up 60 percent since they arrived on the scene.[19]

Inventory Management

Inventory management also affects customer satisfaction. Here, managers must maintain the delicate balance between carrying too little inventory and carrying too much. With too little stock, the firm risks not having products when customers want to buy. To remedy this, the firm may need costly emergency shipments or production. Carrying too much inventory results in higher-than-necessary inventory-carrying costs and stock obsolescence. Thus, in managing inventory, firms must balance the costs of carrying larger inventories against resulting sales and profits.

Many companies have greatly reduced their inventories and related costs through *just-in-time* logistics systems. With such systems, producers and retailers carry only small inventories of parts or merchandise, often only enough for a few days of operations. New stock arrives exactly when needed, rather than being stored in inventory until being used. Just-in-time systems require accurate forecasting along with fast, frequent, and flexible delivery so that new supplies will be available when needed. However, these systems result in substantial savings in inventory-carrying and handling costs.

Marketers are always looking for new ways to make inventory management more efficient. In the not-too-distant future, handling inventory might even become fully automated. For example, in Chapter 3 we discussed RFID or "smart tag" technology, by which small transmitter chips are embedded in or placed on products and packaging on everything from flowers and razors to tires. "Smart" products could make the entire supply chain—which accounts for nearly 75 percent of a product's cost—intelligent and automated.

Companies using RFID would know, at any time, exactly where a product is located physically within the supply chain. "Smart shelves" would not only tell them when it's time to reorder, but would also place the order automatically with their suppliers. Such exciting new information technology applications will revolutionize distribution as we know it. Many large and resourceful marketing companies, such as Walmart, Procter & Gamble, Kraft, IBM, HP, and Best Buy, are investing heavily to make the full use of RFID technology a reality.[20]

Transportation

The choice of transportation carriers affects the pricing of products, delivery performance, and condition of the goods when they arrive—all of which will affect customer satisfaction. In shipping goods to its warehouses, dealers, and customers, the company can choose among five main transportation modes: truck, rail, water, pipeline, and air, along with an alternative mode for digital products—the Internet. Rather than choosing a single carrier, **intermodal transportation** (combining two or more modes of transportation) is increasingly being used. For example, products manufactured in Alberta may be shipped first by rail in containers that are then loaded onto trucks for delivery in the Toronto area or loaded onto ships in Montreal for transportation overseas.

Intermodal transportation
Combining two or more modes of transportation.

Logistics Information Management

Companies manage their supply chains through information. Channel partners often link up to share information and to make better joint logistics decisions. From a logistics perspective, information flows such as customer transactions, billing, shipment and inventory levels, and even customer data are closely linked to channel performance. The company wants to design a simple, accessible, fast, and accurate process for capturing, processing, and sharing channel information.

Information can be shared and managed in many ways but most sharing takes place through traditional or Internet-based *electronic data interchange (EDI)*, the computerized exchange of data between organizations. Walmart, for example, maintains EDI links with almost all of its 91 000 suppliers.[21]

In some cases, suppliers might actually be asked to generate orders and arrange deliveries for their customers. Many large retailers—such as Walmart and Home Depot—work closely with major suppliers such as Procter & Gamble or Black & Decker to set up *vendor-managed inventory* (VMI) systems or *continuous inventory replenishment* systems. Using VMI, the customer shares real-time data on sales and current inventory levels with the supplier. The supplier then takes full responsibility for managing inventories and deliveries. Some retailers even go so far as to shift inventory and delivery costs to the supplier. Such systems require close cooperation between the buyer and seller.

Cross-Functional Teamwork Inside the Company

Most companies assign responsibility for various logistics activities to many different departments—marketing, sales, finance, operations, and purchasing. Too often, each function tries to optimize its own logistics performance without regard for the activities of the other functions. However, transportation, inventory, warehousing, and information management activities interact, often in an inverse way. Lower inventory levels reduce inventory-carrying costs. But they may also reduce customer service and increase costs from stock-outs, back orders, special production runs, and costly fast-freight shipments. Because distribution activities involve strong trade-offs, decisions by different functions must be coordinated to achieve better overall logistics performance.

The goal of integrated supply chain management is to harmonize all of the company's logistics decisions. Close working relationships among departments can be achieved in several ways. Some companies have created permanent logistics committees made up of managers responsible for different physical distribution activities. Companies can also create supply chain manager positions that link the logistics activities of functional areas. For example, Procter & Gamble has created supply managers who manage all of the supply chain activities for each of its product categories. Many companies have a vice-president of logistics with cross-functional authority.

Finally, companies can employ sophisticated, systemwide supply chain management software, now available from a wide range of software enterprises large and small, from SAP and Oracle to Infor and Logility. The worldwide market for supply chain management software topped an estimated US$6.5 billion in 2006 and will reach an estimated US$11.6 billion by 2013.[22] The important thing is that the company must coordinate its logistics and marketing activities to create high market satisfaction at a reasonable cost.

REVIEWING OBJECTIVES AND KEY TERMS

 mymarketinglab | Audio Chapter Summary

Marketing channel decisions are among the most important decisions that management faces. A company's channel decisions directly affect every other marketing decision. Management must make channel decisions carefully, incorporating today's needs with tomorrow's likely selling environment. Some companies pay too little attention to their distribution channels, but others have used imaginative distribution systems to gain competitive advantage.

OBJECTIVE 1 **Explain why companies use marketing channels and discuss the functions these channels perform.**

Most producers use intermediaries to bring their products to market. They try to forge a *marketing channel* (or *distribution channel*)—a set of interdependent organizations involved in the process of making a product or service available for use or consumption by the consumer or business user. Through their contacts, experience, specialization, and scale of operation, intermediaries usually offer the firm more than it can achieve on its own.

Marketing channels perform many key functions. Some help *complete* transactions by gathering and distributing *information* needed for planning and aiding exchange, by developing and spreading persuasive *communications* about an offer, by performing *contact* work (finding and communicating with prospective buyers), by *matching* (shaping and fitting the offer to the buyer's needs), and by entering into *negotiation* to reach an agreement on price and other terms of the offer so that ownership can be transferred. Other functions help to *fulfill* the completed transactions by offering *physical distribution* (transporting and storing goods), *financing* (acquiring and using funds to cover the costs of the channel work), and *risk taking* (assuming the risks of carrying out the channel work).

OBJECTIVE 2 **Discuss how channel members interact and how they organize to perform the work of the channel.**

The channel will be most effective when each member is assigned the tasks it can do best. Ideally, because the success of individual channel members depends on overall channel success, all channel firms should work together smoothly. They should understand and accept their roles, coordinate their goals and activities, and cooperate to attain overall channel goals. By cooperating, they can more effectively sense, serve, and satisfy the target market.

In a large company, the formal organization structure assigns roles and provides needed leadership. But in a distribution channel made up of independent firms, leadership and power are not formally set. Traditionally, distribution channels have lacked the leadership needed to assign roles and manage conflict. In recent years, however, new types of channel organizations have appeared that provide stronger leadership and improved performance.

OBJECTIVE 3 **Identify the major channel alternatives open to a company.**

Each firm identifies alternative ways to reach its market. Available means vary from direct selling to using one, two, three, or more intermediary *channel levels*. Marketing channels face continuous and sometimes dramatic change. Three of the most important trends are the growth of *vertical, horizontal*, and *multichannel marketing systems*. These trends affect channel cooperation, conflict, and competition.

Channel design begins with assessing customer channel service needs and company channel objectives and constraints. The company then identifies the major channel alternatives in terms of the *types* of intermediaries, the *number* of intermediaries, and the *channel responsibilities* of each. Each channel alternative must be evaluated according to economic, control, and adaptive criteria. *Channel management* calls for selecting qualified intermediaries and motivating them. Individual channel members must be evaluated regularly.

OBJECTIVE 4 **Explain how companies select, motivate, and evaluate channel members.**

Producers vary in their ability to attract qualified marketing intermediaries. Some producers have no trouble signing up channel members. Others have to work hard to line up enough qualified intermediaries. When selecting intermediaries, the company should evaluate each channel member's qualifications and select those who best fit its channel objectives.

Once selected, channel members must be continuously motivated to do their best. The company must sell not only *through* the intermediaries but *with* them. It should work to forge strong partnerships with channel members to create a marketing system that meets the needs of both the manufacturer *and* the partners. The company must also regularly check channel member performance against established performance standards, rewarding intermediaries who are performing well and assisting or replacing weaker ones.

OBJECTIVE 5 **Discuss the nature and importance of marketing logistics and integrated supply chain management.**

Just as firms are giving the marketing concept increased recognition, more business firms are paying attention to *marketing logistics* (or *physical distribution*). Logistics is an area of potentially high cost savings and improved customer satisfaction. Marketing logistics addresses not only *outbound distribution* but also *inbound distribution* and *reverse distribution*. That is, it involves entire *supply chain management*—managing value-added flows between suppliers, the company, resellers, and final users. No logistics system can both maximize customer service and minimize distribution costs. Instead, the goal of logistics management is to provide a *targeted* level of service at the least cost. The major logistics functions include *warehousing, inventory management, transportation*, and *logistics information management*.

The *integrated supply chain management concept* recognizes that improved logistics requires teamwork in the form of close working relationships across functional areas inside the company and across various organizations in the supply chain.

KEY TERMS

Objective 1
Value delivery network   390
Marketing channel (distribution channel)   391
Channel level   393
Direct marketing channel   393
Indirect marketing channel   393

Objective 2
Channel conflict   394
Conventional distribution channel   395
Vertical marketing system (VMS)   395
Corporate VMS   396
Contractual VMS   397
Franchise organization   397
Administered VMS   398
Horizontal marketing system   398

Multichannel distribution system   398
Disintermediation   399

Objective 3
Marketing channel design   402
Intensive distribution   404
Exclusive distribution   404
Selective distribution   404

Objective 4
Marketing channel management   405

Objective 5
Marketing logistics (physical distribution)   410
Supply chain management   410
Distribution centre   412
Intermodal transportation   413

DISCUSSING THE CONCEPTS

1. Explain how channel members add value for manufacturers and consumers.

2. Discuss the various types of conflict that may arise in the channel of distribution. Is all channel conflict bad?

3. What factors should a cosmetics company consider when designing its marketing channel for a new low-priced line of cosmetics?

4. Describe the major types of vertical marketing systems and provide an example of each.

5. Discuss the complexities international marketers face when designing channels in other countries.

6. List and briefly describe the major logistics functions. Provide an example of a decision a logistics manager would make for each major function.

APPLYING THE CONCEPTS

1. ExerWise, a new company marketing a high-end ab-toner exercise machine, is considering direct marketing versus selling through Strongs, a national sporting goods retailer. As the buyer for Strongs, explain the functions your retail chain can offer to ExerWise.

2. Ward's Berry Farm specializes in fresh strawberries, which it sells to a variety of retailers through a produce wholesale distributor. Form a small group and have each member assume one of the following roles: berry farmer, wholesaler, and grocery retailer. In your role, discuss three things that might have recently angered you about the other channel members. Take turns voicing your gripes and attempting to resolve the conflict.

3. Visit http://electronics.howstuffworks.com/rfid.htm# and watch the video "How UPS Smart Labels Work." You can also learn more about RFID technology from this site. What impact will RFID tags have on each of the major logistical functions? What are the biggest current obstacles to adopting this technology?

FOCUS ON TECHNOLOGY

If you're eager to get the latest movie released on DVD, you don't have to go any farther than your iTunes account on your computer. In the past, these movies weren't available from Apple's iTunes until several weeks after they were released, but major movie studios are allowing Apple to sell movies the day they are released on DVD. Consumers have been able to get movies on the same day as the DVD release from services such as CinemaNow and Movielink for a few years, but those etailers don't have the same clout as iTunes, which is now the biggest retailer of music in North America.

Although movie studios get less revenue than selling through traditional retail channels, their profits will be bigger because of lower costs.

1. What costs are movie studios reducing by using this alternative channel of distribution?

2. Is this an example of disintermediation? Will electronic distribution displace traditional distribution channels for movies?

FOCUS ON ETHICS

Parallel imports, gray products, and *price diversion* all represent the same activity—diverting imported products meant for one market at lower prices and reselling them at higher profits in other markets. This happens in many industries, including pharmaceuticals, apparel, high-tech electronics, auto parts, luxury goods, cosmetics, and tobacco. The textbook you're using now might be a gray product if it was intended for an international market but you purchased it from Amazon.ca for much less than what you'd pay at your bookstore or the publisher's website. And the designer sweater you bought at Winners most likely got into those stores through gray market trading. Although North American laws prohibit importing prescription drugs from abroad, the same is not true in other countries. For example, gray traders purchase pharmaceutical drugs in poorer countries, such as Greece and Spain, and resell them in the United Kingdom or Sweden, where higher prices garner profits for the traders. In fact, parallel importing of most products is legal, and some experts claim that it's just the free market at work. In some cases, though, counterfeit goods are mixed in with the legitimate brands.

1. Learn more about this phenomenon. Who receives value in such transactions? Who loses value?

2. How are manufacturers dealing with this problem?

MARKETING BY THE NUMBERS

Lightco, Inc. is a manufacturer of decorative lighting fixtures sold primarily in Eastern Canada. Lightco wants to expand to Central and Western Canada and intends to hire 10 new sales representatives to secure distribution for its products. Sales reps will acquire new retail accounts and manage those accounts after acquisition. Each sales rep earns a salary of $50 000 plus 2 percent commission. Each retailer generates an average $50 000 in revenue for Lightco. Refer to Appendix 3: Marketing by the Numbers, to answer the following questions:

1. If Lightco's contribution margin is 40 percent, what increase in sales will it need to break even on the increase in fixed costs to hire the new sales reps?

2. How many new retail accounts must the company acquire to break even on this tactic? What average number of accounts must each new rep acquire?

VIDEO CASE

Progressive

 | Video Case Questions

Progressive has attained top-tier status in the insurance industry by focusing on innovation. Progressive was the first company to offer drive-in claims services, instalment payment of premiums, and 24/7 customer service. But some of Progressive's most innovative moves involve its channels of distribution. Whereas most insurance companies distribute their products to consumers via intermediary agents or direct-to-consumer methods, Progressive was one of the first companies to recognize the value in doing both. In the late 1980s, it augmented its agency distribution with a direct 800-number channel.

In 1995, Progressive moved into the future by becoming the first major insurer in the world to launch a website. In 1997, customers could buy auto insurance policies online in real time. Today at Progressive's website, customers can do everything from managing their own account information to reporting claims directly. Progressive even offers one-stop concierge claim service.

After viewing the Progressive video, answer the following questions about marketing channels:

1. Apply the concept of the supply chain to Progressive.

2. Using the model of consumer and business channels found in the chapter, sketch out as many channels for Progressive as you can. How does each of these channels meet distinct customer needs?

3. Discuss the various ways in which Progressive has had an impact on the insurance industry.

Visit MyMarketingLab at www.pearsoned.ca/mymarketinglab to view the video segment related to this case.

COMPANY CASE

Zara: The Technology Giant of the Fashion World

One global retailer is expanding at a dizzying pace. It's on track for what appears to be world domination of its industry. Having built its own state-of-the art distribution network, the company is leaving the competition in the dust in terms of sales and profits, not to mention speed of inventory management and turnover. Walmart, you might think? Dell, possibly? Although these two retail giants definitely fit the description, we're talking here about Zara, the flagship specialty chain of Spain-based clothing conglomerate, Inditex.

This dynamic retailer is known for selling stylish designs that resemble those of big-name fashion houses, but at moderate prices. "We sell the latest trends at low prices, but our clients value our design, quality, and constant innovation," a company spokesperson said. "That gives us the advantage even in highly competitive, developed markets, including Britain." More interesting is the way that Zara achieves its mission.

Fast-Fashion—The Newest Wave

A handful of European specialty clothing retailers are taking the fashion world by storm with a business model that has come to be known as "fast-fashion." In short, these companies can recognize and respond to fashion trends very quickly, create products that mirror the trends, and get those products onto shelves much faster and more frequently than the industry norm. Fast-fashion retailers include Sweden's Hennes & Mauritz (H&M), Britain's Topshop, Spain's Mango, and the Netherland's Mexx. Although all of these companies are successfully employing the fast-fashion concept, Zara leads the pack on virtually every level.

For example, "fast" at Zara means that it can take a product from concept through design, manufacturing, and store-shelf placement in as little as two weeks, much quicker than any of its fast-fashion competitors. For more mainstream clothing chains, such as the Gap or Abercrombie & Fitch, the process takes months.

This gives Zara the advantage of virtually copying fashions from the pages of *Vogue* and having them on the streets in dozens of countries before the next issue of the magazine even hits the newsstands! When Spain's Crown Prince Felipe and Letizia Ortiz Rocasolano announced their engagement, the bride-to-be wore a stylish white trouser suit. This raised some eyebrows, given that it violated royal protocol. But European women loved it and within a few weeks, hundreds of them were wearing a nearly identical outfit they had purchased from Zara.

But Zara is more than just fast. It's also prolific. In a typical year, Zara launches about 11 000 new items. Compare that to the 2000 to 4000 items introduced by both H&M and the Gap. In the fashion world, this difference is huge. Zara stores receive new merchandise two to three times each week, whereas most clothing retailers get large shipments on a seasonal basis, four to six times per year.

As part of its strategy to introduce more new items with greater frequency, Zara also produces items in smaller batches. Thus, it assumes less risk if an item doesn't sell well. But smaller batches also mean exclusivity, a unique benefit from a mass-market retailer that draws young fashionistas through Zara's doors like a magnet. When items sell out, they are not restocked with another shipment. Instead, the next Zara shipment contains something new, something different. Popular items can appear and disappear within a week. Consumers know that if they like something, they have to buy it or miss out. Customers are enticed to check out store stock more often, leading to very high levels of repeat patronage. But it also means that Zara doesn't have to follow the industry pattern of marking products down as the season progresses. Thus, Zara reaps the benefit of prices that average much closer to the list price.

The Vertical Secret to Zara's Success

Just how does Zara achieve such mind-blowing responsiveness? The answer lies in its distribution system. In 1975, Amancio Ortega opened the first Zara store in Spain's remote northwest town of La Coruña, home to Zara's headquarters. Having already worked in the textile industry for two decades, his experience led him to design a system in which he could control every aspect of the supply chain, from design and production to distribution and retailing. He knew, for example, that in the textile business, the biggest markups were made by wholesalers and retailers. He was determined to maintain control over these activities.

Ortega's original philosophy forms the heart of Zara's unique, rapid-fire supply chain today. But it's Zara's high-tech information system that has taken vertical integration in the company to an unprecedented level. According to CEO Pablo Isla, "Our information system is absolutely avant-garde. It's what links the shop to our designers and our distribution system."

Zara's vertically integrated system makes the starting point of a product concept hard to nail down. At Zara's headquarters, creative teams of more than 300 professionals carry out the design process. But they act on information fed to them from the stores. This goes far beyond typical point-of-sale data. Store managers act as trend spotters. Every day they report hot fads to headquarters, enabling popular lines to be tweaked and slow movers to be whisked away within hours. If customers are asking for a rounded neck on a vest rather than a V neck, such an item can be in stores in seven to ten days. This process would take traditional retailers months.

Managers also consult a personal digital assistant every evening to check what new designs are available and place their orders according to what they think will sell best in their area. Thus, store managers help shape designs by ensuring that the creative teams have real-time information based on the observed tastes of actual consumers. Ortega refers to this as the "democratization of fashion."

When it comes to sourcing, Zara's supply chain is unique as well. Current conventional wisdom calls for manufacturers in all industries to outsource their goods globally to the cheapest provider. Thus, most of Zara's competitors contract manufacturing out to low-wage countries, mostly in Asia. But Zara makes 40 percent of its own fabrics and produces more than half of its own clothes rather than relying on a hodgepodge of slow-moving suppliers. Even things that are farmed out are done locally to maximize time efficiency. Nearly all Zara clothes for its stores worldwide are produced in a remote northeast corner of Spain.

As it completes designs, Zara cuts fabric in-house. It then sends the designs to one of several hundred local cooperatives for sewing, minimizing the time for raw material distribution. When items return to Zara's facilities, they are ironed by an assembly line of workers who specialize in a specific task (lapels, shoulders, and so on). Clothing items are wrapped in plastic and transported on conveyor belts to a group of giant warehouses.

Zara's warehouses are a vision of modern automation, as swift and efficient as any automotive or consumer electronics plant. Human labour is a rare sight in these cavernous buildings. Customized machines patterned after the equipment used by overnight parcel services process up to 80 000 items an hour. The computerized system sorts, packs, labels, and allocates clothing items to every one of Zara's 1495 stores. For stores within a 24-hour drive, Zara delivers goods by truck, whereas it ships merchandise via cargo jet to stores farther away.

Domestic Manufacturing Pays Off

The same philosophy that has produced such good results for Zara has led parent company Inditex to diversify. Its other chains now include underwear retailer Oysho, teen-oriented Bershka and Stradivarius, children's Kiddy's Class, men's Massimo Dutti, and casual and sportswear chain Pull & Bear. Recently, Inditex opened its first nonclothing chain, Zara Home. Each chain operates under the same style of vertical integration perfected at Zara.

Making speed the main goal of its supply chain has really paid off for Inditex. In only three years, its sales and profits more than doubled. Last year, revenues increased over 15 percent over the previous year to US$14.5 billion. Not bad considering retail revenue growth worldwide averages single digits, and many major retailers were feeling the effects of slowing economies. Perhaps more importantly, Inditex's total profits grew by 25 percent last year to US$1.8 billion. Most of this performance was driven by Zara, now ranked number 64 on Interbrand's list of top 100 most valuable worldwide brands.

Although Inditex has grown rapidly, it wants more. Last year it opened 560 new stores worldwide (most of those were Zara stores) and plans to do the same this year. It's even considering an entry into the fast-growing Indian market. Global retailers are pushing into India in droves in response to India's thirst for premium brands. Zara can really capitalize on this trend. With more than one ribbon-cutting ceremony per day, Inditex could increase its number of stores from the current 3890 to more than 5000 stores in more than 70 countries by the end of this decade.

European fast-fashion retailers have thus far expanded cautiously in the United States (Zara has only 32 stores stateside). But the threat has U.S. clothing retailers rethinking the models they have relied on for years. According to one analyst, the industry may soon experience a reversal from outsourcing to China to "Made in the USA".

U.S. retailers are finally looking at lost sales as lost revenue. They know that to capture maximum sales they need to turn their inventory much more quickly. The disadvantage of importing from China is that it requires a longer lead time of between three and six months from the time an order is placed to when the inventory is stocked in stores. By then the trends may have changed and you're stuck with all the unsold inventory. If retailers want to refresh their merchandise more quickly, they will have to consider sourcing at least some of the merchandise locally.

So being the fastest of the fast-fashion retailers has not only paid off for Zara, but the model has reconfigured the fashion landscape everywhere. Zara has blazed a trail for cheaper and cheaper fashion-led mass-retailers, has put the squeeze on mid-priced fashion, and has forced luxury brands to scramble to find ways to set themselves apart from Zara's look-alike designs. Leadership certainly has its perks.

Questions for Discussion

1. As completely as possible, sketch the supply chain for Zara from raw materials to consumer purchase.

2. Discuss the concepts of horizontal and vertical conflict as they relate to Zara.

3. Which type of vertical marketing system does Zara employ? List all the benefits that Zara receives by having adopted this system.

4. Does Zara experience disadvantages from its "fast-fashion" distribution system? Are these disadvantages offset by the advantages?

5. How does Zara add value for the customer through major logistics functions?

Sources: James Hall, "Zara Helps Fashion Profit for Inditex," *Daily Telegraph*, April 1, 2008, p. 12; Christopher Bjork, "New Stores Boost Inditex's Results," *Wall Street Journal*, June 12, 2008, p. B4; "The Future of Fast-Fashion," *The Economist*, June 18, 2005, accessed online at www.economist.com; John Tagliabue, "A Rival to Gap that Operates Like Dell," *New York Times*, May 30, 2003, p. W1; Elizabeth Nash, "Dressed For Success," *Independent*, March 31, 2006, p. 22; Sarah Mower, "The Zara Phenomenon," *Evening Standard*, January 13, 2006, p. 30; also see www.inditex.com, accessed November 2008.

13

Retailing and
Wholesaling

PREVIEWING
THE CONCEPTS

In the previous chapter, you learned the basics of delivering customer value through good distribution channel design and management. Now we'll look more deeply into the two major intermediary channel functions: retailing and wholesaling. You already know something about retailing—you're served every day by retailers of all shapes and sizes. However, you probably know much less about the horde of wholesalers that work behind the scenes. In this chapter, we'll examine the characteristics of different kinds of retailers and wholesalers, the marketing decisions they make, and trends for the future.

When it comes to retailers, everyone always talks about Walmart, the US$379 billion behemoth whose "always low prices" strategy has made it the world's largest company. But we'll start the chapter with a story about one of its competitors, Costco. Surprisingly, although it captures only about one-sixth the sales of Walmart, in warehouse retailing Costco is trouncing Walmart at its own low-price game.

G iant Walmart is used to beating up on competitors. It outsells Toys "R" Us in the toy market, gives Blockbuster headaches in DVD sales, and puts a big dent in Best Buy's consumer electronics business. With a growing presence in the grocery market, it is now challenging Loblaw and Sobeys. Almost every retailer, no matter what the category, has its hands full devising strategies by which it can compete with Walmart and survive.

But this isn't a story about Walmart. It's about Costco, the red-hot warehouse retailer that competes head-on with Walmart. When it comes to warehouse retailing, it's Costco that's the boss, not the other way around.

Costco Wholesale Corporation (Costco) is an in-store retailer operating a chain of 77 membership warehouses in every Canadian province. It is the fourth-largest retailer in North America and one of Canada's most respected retailers with annual sales exceeding $9 billion. In recognition of its prowess, the Retail Council of Canada (RCC) named Louise Wendling, senior vice-president and country manager for Costco Wholesale Canada, as the 2009 Distinguished Canadian Retailer of the Year. In addition to its physical outlets, Costco offers its products online. In both Canada and the United States, it competes head-on with Sam's Club but outsells it by 50 percent. This may have led to Walmart's 2009 decision to close its six

In many ways, retailing boils down to the unglamorous art of getting the right product in the right place at the right time at the right price. But, says Costco founder and CEO Jim Sinegal, "Do that without being boring. That's the trick."

Sam's Club stores in Southern Ontario and concentrate instead on its Supercentre format in Canada. Supercentres include a full-service supermarket, pharmacy, optical and photo centres, as well as shops such as hair and nail salons, bank branches, and fast-food outlets. Unlike Walmart and Sam's Club, however, Costco is growing at a torrid pace. How is Costco beating U.S. and Canadian discounters at their own low-price game? The answer is simple: Despite its warehouse format, Costco adds a certain merchandising magic that its rivals just can't match.

Costco is a warehouse retailer. It offers a limited selection of nationally branded and private-label products in a wide range of categories at very low prices to shoppers who pay an annual membership fee. It stocks between 2000 and 4000 items, often only in jumbo sizes (a typical supermarket stocks 40 000 to 60 000 items; a Walmart Supercentre about 150 000 items). And to keep costs and prices low, it operates out of big, drafty, bare-bones stores and uses its substantial buying power to wring low prices from suppliers.

Price is an important part of the equation, and Costco seems addicted to selling every item at the lowest possible price, regardless of competitors' prices. It refuses to mark up any item more than 14 percent above costs. According to Costco founder and CEO Jim Sinegal, "Many retailers look at an item and say, 'I'm selling this for 10 bucks. How can I sell it for 11?' We look at it and say, 'How can we get it to 9 bucks?' And then, 'How can we get it to 8?' It is contrary to the thinking of [most retailers]. But once you start doing that, it's like heroin." Costco's operating profit margins average just 2.8 percent; lower than other discounters'.

Given that other retailers like Zellers also focus on low-cost operations and low prices, what is it, then, that sets Costco apart? It has to do with Costco's differentiated value proposition—with the products it carries and the sense of urgency that it builds into the Costco shopper's store experience. Alongside the gallon jars of peanut butter and 2250-count packs of Q-tips that make other warehouse clubs popular, Costco offers an ever-changing assortment of high-quality products—even luxuries—all at tantalizingly low margins. Costco Canada is also growing its gourmet-food section, presenting such brands as Martha Stewart hams and Quebec specialty cheeses. Here is what one Montreal shopper found on a recent visit to her local Costco:

> In a display case of luxury goods including Fendi bags and Royal Doulton figurines were Riedel wine glasses selling for 10 percent off retail and a block containing a nine-piece set of Global knives coming in at a cool $600. (Expect to pay upwards of $300 for the stand alone in kitchenware stores.) One aisle over I admired a pro-strength KitchenAid mixer for $400, a Breville juicer at $115, and a set of nine Henckels knives for $199—all cheaper than retail, yes, but not quite enough to justify an impulse buy.

Costco brings flair to an otherwise dreary setting. It has managed to make discount shopping fashionable, even for affluent North Americans. It's the place where high-end products meet deep-discount prices. In just one year, Costco sold 63 million hot dog and soda combinations (still priced at only $1.50). At the same time, it sold more than 96 000 carats of diamonds at up to US$100 000 per item. It's North America's biggest baster of poultry (77 000 rotisserie chickens a day) but also the country's biggest seller of fine wines (including the likes of a Château Cheval Blanc Premier Grand Cru Classé at US$1750 a bottle). It once even offered a Pablo Picasso drawing at Costco.com for only US$129 999.99!

Mixed in with its regular stock of staples, Costco features a glittering, constantly shifting array of one-time specials such as discounted Prada bags, Callaway golf clubs, or Kenneth Cole bags—deals you just won't find elsewhere. In fact, of the 2000 to 4000 items Costco carries, 1000 are designated as "treasure items" (Costco's words). The changing assortment and great prices keep people coming back, wallets in hand. Says Sinegal, "a customer knows they'd better buy because it will not be there next time, like Waterford crystal. We try to get that sense of urgency in our customers."

There was a time when only the great unwashed masses shopped at off-price retailers. But Costco has changed all that. Even people who don't have to pinch pennies shop there. Not by accident, Costco's stores tend to be located in more affluent locations than other discounters.

▶

OBJECTIVES

1. Explain the role of retailers in the distribution channel and describe the major types of retailers.
2. Describe the major retailer marketing decisions.
3. Discuss the future of retailing.
4. Explain the major types of wholesalers and their marketing decisions.

One-third of Costco's members have household incomes over $75 000; one-fourth over $100 000.

> [Costco] attracts a breed of urban sophisticates attuned to what one retail consultant calls the "new luxury." These shoppers shun Seiko watches for TAG Heuer; Jack Nicklaus golf clubs for Callaway; Maxwell House coffee (it goes without saying) for Starbucks. They "trade up," eagerly spending more for items that make their hearts pound and for which they don't have to pay full price. Then they "trade down" to private labels for things like paper towels, detergent, and vitamins. Catering to this fast-growing segment, Costco has exploded. "It's the ultimate concept in trading up and trading down," says one consultant. "It's a brilliant innovation for the new luxury."

Costco's flair even extends to its store brand—Kirkland Signature. Costco puts the Kirkland Signature brand on a wide range of goods—330 items accounting for 15 percent of its sales. Customers seek out Kirkland Signature products not just for price but also for quality. Costco customers can buy anything from a $20 bottle of Kirkland Signature Tierra de Chile Chilean red wine to a $1299 Kirkland Signature stainless steel outdoor grill to a $6330-per-person, 10-day package vacation to South Africa promising "luxury" accommodations.

So, it's Costco, not Walmart, that's beating up on competitors. In fact, a mighty but frustrated Walmart is even considering selling off its perennial runner-up Sam's Club division not only in Canada, but also in the United States.

Whereas Walmart stands for low prices, Costco is a retail treasure hunt, where one's shopping cart could contain a $50 000 diamond ring resting on top of a vat of mayonnaise.

Costco is more than a big box store that "stacks 'em high and sells 'em cheap"—more than just a place to load up on large sizes of consumer staples. Each Costco store is a theatre of retail that creates buying urgency and excitement for customers. In many ways, retailing boils down to the unglamorous art of getting the right product in the right place at the right time at the right price. But there's a lot more than that to Costco's value proposition. Says Sinegal: "Do that without being boring. That's the trick."[1]

Chapter Opening Discussion

The Costco story sets the stage for examining the fast-changing world of today's resellers. This chapter looks at *retailing* and *wholesaling*. In the first section, we look at the nature and importance of retailing, major types of store and nonstore retailers, the decisions retailers make, and the future of retailing. In the second section, we discuss these same topics as they relate to wholesalers.

1 RETAILING

Glossary Flashcards of Key Terms

Retailing
All activities involved in selling goods or services directly to final consumers for their personal, nonbusiness use.

Retailer
A business whose sales come *primarily* from retailing.

What is retailing? We all know that Costco, Home Depot, Reitmans, and Canadian Tire are retailers, but so are Avon representatives, Amazon.ca, the local Holiday Inn, and a physiotherapist seeing patients. **Retailing** includes all the activities involved in selling products or services directly to final consumers for their personal, nonbusiness use. Many institutions—manufacturers, wholesalers, and retailers—do retailing. But most retailing is done by **retailers**: businesses whose sales come *primarily* from retailing.

Retailing plays a very important role in most marketing channels. Each year, retailers account for more than US$4.5 trillion of sales to final consumers. They connect brands to consumers in what marketing agency OgilvyAction calls "the last mile"—the final stop in the consumer's path to purchase. It's the "distance a consumer travels between an attitude and an action," explains OgilvyAction's CEO. "Nearly 70 percent of purchase decisions are made near or in the store." Thus, retailers "reach consumers at key moments of truth, ultimately [influencing] their actions at the point of purchase."[2]

In fact, many marketers are now embracing the concept of *shopper marketing*, the idea that the retail store itself is an important marketing medium. Shopper marketing involves focusing the entire marketing process—from product and brand development to logistics, promotion, and merchandising—toward turning shoppers into buyers at the point of sale. Of course, every well-designed marketing effort focuses on customer buying behaviour. But the concept of shopper marketing suggests that these efforts should be coordinated around the shopping process itself. Shopper marketing emphasizes the importance of the retail environment on customer buying.[3]

Although most retailing is done in retail stores, in recent years *nonstore retailing* has been growing much faster than has store retailing. Nonstore retailing includes selling to final consumers through the Internet, direct mail, catalogues, the telephone, and other direct-selling approaches. We discuss such direct-marketing approaches in detail in Chapter 17. In this chapter, we focus on store retailing.

Types of Retailers

Retail stores come in all shapes and sizes—from your local hairstyling salon or family-owned restaurant to national specialty chain retailers such as Addition Elle or Williams-Sonoma to megadiscounters such as Costco or Walmart. The most important types of retail stores are described in Table 13.1 and discussed in the following sections. They can be classified in terms of several characteristics, including the *amount of service* they offer, the breadth and depth of their *product lines*, the *relative prices* they charge, and how they are *organized*.

Table 13.1 Major Store Retailer Types

Type	Description	Examples
Specialty stores	Carry a narrow product line with a deep assortment, such as apparel stores, sporting goods stores, furniture stores, florists, and bookstores. A clothing store would be a *single-line store*, a men's clothing store would be a *limited-line store*, and a men's custom-shirt store would be a *superspecialty store*.	The Body Shop, Birks, Mountain Equipment Co-op, Running Room, Chapters Indigo
Department Stores	Carry several product lines—typically clothing, home furnishings, and household goods—with each line operated as a separate department managed by specialist buyers or merchandisers.	Sears, the Bay
Supermarkets	A relatively large, low-cost, low-margin, high-volume, self-service operation designed to serve the consumer's total needs for grocery and household products.	Safeway Foods, Sobeys, Loblaw, Metro, Food Basics, Provigo
Convenience stores	Relatively small stores located near residential areas, open long hours seven days a week, and carrying a limited line of high-turnover convenience products at slightly higher prices.	7-Eleven, Mac's, Couche-Tard, Husky Market
Discount stores	Carry standard merchandise sold at lower prices with lower margins and higher volumes.	Zellers, Walmart (general); Sport Mart, The Brick, Best Buy (specialty)
Off-price retailers	Sell merchandise bought at less-than-regular wholesale prices and sold at less than retail, often leftover goods, overruns, and irregulars obtained at reduced prices from manufacturers or other retailers. These include *factory outlets* owned and operated by manufacturers; *independent off-price retailers* owned and run by entrepreneurs or by divisions of larger retail corporations; and *warehouse (or wholesale) clubs* selling a limited selection of brand-name groceries, appliances, clothing, and other goods at deep discounts to consumers who pay membership fees.	Liz Claiborne (factory outlet); Winners (independent off-price retailer); Costco (warehouse club)
Superstores	Very large stores traditionally aimed at meeting consumers' total needs for routinely purchased food and nonfood items. Includes *supercentres*, combined supermarket and discount stores, and *category killers*, which carry a deep assortment in a particular category and have a knowledgeable staff.	Walmart Supercentre, Loblaw Superstores (discount stores); Best Buy, PetSmart, Staples, (category killers)

Amount of Service

Different types of customers and products require different amounts of service. To meet these varying service needs, retailers may offer one of three service levels—self-service, limited service, and full service.

Self-service retailers serve customers who are willing to perform their own "locate–compare–select" process to save time or money. Self-service is the basis of all discount operations and is typically used by retailers selling convenience goods (such as supermarkets) and nationally branded, fast-moving shopping goods (such as Zellers). *Limited-service retailers*, such as the Bay or La Maison Simons in Quebec, provide more sales assistance because they carry more shopping goods about which customers need information. Their increased operating costs result in higher prices.

In *full-service retailers*, such as high-end specialty stores (for example, Birks or Williams-Sonoma) and first-class department stores (such as Holt Renfrew), salespeople assist customers in every phase of the shopping process. Full-service stores usually carry more specialty goods for which customers need or want assistance or advice. They provide more services resulting in much higher operating costs, which are passed along to customers as higher prices.

Product Line

Retailers can also be classified by the length and breadth of their product assortments. Some retailers, such as **specialty stores**, carry narrow product lines with deep assortments within those lines. Today, specialty stores are flourishing. The increasing use of market segmentation, market targeting, and product specialization has resulted in a greater need for stores that focus on specific products and segments.

In contrast, **department stores** carry a wide variety of product lines. In recent years, department stores have been squeezed between more focused and flexible specialty stores on the one hand, and more efficient, lower-priced discounters on the other. In response, many have added promotional pricing to meet the discount threat. Others are trying catalogue, telephone, and web selling. Service remains the key differentiating factor. High-end retailers like Holt Renfrew are doing well by emphasizing exclusive merchandise and high-quality service. Another strategy some have adopted is the use of store brands and single-brand "designer shops" to compete with specialty stores. This is what the Bay has done recently:

> In the middle of the 2009 recession, the Bay (which operates 94 stores across the country), cut 1000 jobs and seemed to be in serious trouble. But don't count Canada's oldest department store down and out. It has a new president and CEO, Bonnie Brooks, a dynamic woman who has certainly earned her stripes in the fashion industry. She's bounded from one success to the next at Fairweather, Holt Renfrew, and as the editor at *Flare*. Most recently she served as the head of Asia's Lane Crawford Joyce Group. As counterintuitive as it seems, Brooks wants to move the Bay chain more upscale, capturing a new breed of shopper—the pragmatist. The pragmatist spends an average of $1900 a year on clothing, and she covets timeless, classic pieces. Thus, Brooks is focusing more than ever on fashion and is doubling the Bay's stock of higher-end lines while, more importantly, expanding the mid-priced labels. She's also ditching half the store's 1200 brands—worth more than $1 billion in annual retail sales—in favour of more contemporary labels. She's building on the successful formula she used as part of her Asian experience. While in Asia, Brooks and her team transformed a handful of strategically located Lane Crawford stores into modern retail showpieces that

Specialty store
A retail store that carries a narrow product line with a deep assortment within that line.

Department store
A retail organization that carries a wide variety of product lines—each line is operated as a separate department managed by specialist buyers or merchandisers.

The Bay, Canada's oldest retailer, is working to re-vitalize itself through savvy marketing.

Facing increased competition, many supermarkets are moving upscale. For example, Safeway is converting to "lifestyle" stores, supported by a big-budget "Ingredients for Life" marketing campaign.

introduced upwardly mobile Asian consumers to sought-after Western brands, from Yves Saint Laurent to Hugo Boss. Brooks is moving the Bay in the same direction, starting with a major remodelling of the St. Regis Room, its store-within-a-store for high-end fashion. She hopes to rebuild the venerable brand into a fashion mecca.[4]

Supermarket

A large, low-cost, low-margin, high-volume, self-service store that carries a wide variety of grocery and household products.

Supermarkets are the most frequently shopped type of retail store. Today, however, they are facing slow sales growth because of slower population growth and an increase in competition from discount supercentres (Walmart) on the one hand and upscale specialty food stores (Whole Foods) on the other. Supermarkets also have been hit hard by the rapid growth of out-of-home eating. In fact, supermarkets' share of the groceries and consumables market plunged from 89 percent in 1989 to less than 50 percent in 2008.[5] Thus, many traditional supermarkets are facing hard times.

In the battle for "share of stomachs," some supermarkets are cutting costs, establishing more-efficient operations, lowering prices, and attempting to compete more effectively with food discounters. However, they are finding it difficult to profitably match the low prices of super-low-cost operators such as Costco and Walmart. In contrast, many other large supermarkets have moved upscale, providing improved store environments and higher-quality food offerings, such as from-scratch bakeries, gourmet deli counters, natural foods, and fresh seafood departments.

For example, consider Safeway's "lifestyle store" strategy:

To raise itself above the cutthroat low-price food frenzy, during the past four years Safeway has built more than 50 new "lifestyle" stores and remodelled nearly two-thirds of its existing stores under the lifestyle store concept. The lifestyle stores feature upscale touches, such as soft lighting and hardwood floors, along with higher-quality fare, including gourmet and organic foods and premium brands. The restyled stores are supported by a $100 million "Ingredients for Life" marketing campaign, which assures customers that Safeway's food offerings are designed for the way people live today. The strategy has resulted in increased customer loyalty and significant growth in earnings. The strategy has been so successful that Safeway plans to remodel all of its stores under the lifestyle concept.[6]

Loblaw Companies Limited, Canada's largest food distributor, in contrast, is using a two-pronged strategy. In a campaign dubbed "back to the best," it added staff and product specialists so that it can offer better service. Simultaneously, it is also refreshing its line of Club Pack items, and adding high-value fashion goods under its private Joe Fresh Style brand to appeal to the 30 percent of Canadian consumers who seek value brands. "Customers don't need to waste their time stocking up anywhere else when they can get large format products and a great selection of their favourite national brands without paying a membership fee," comments Inge van den Berg, vice-president of public affairs and investor relations.[7]

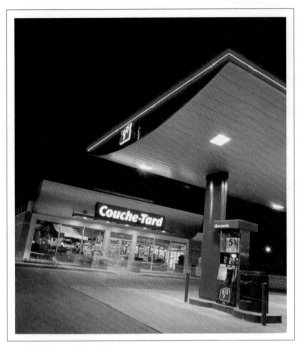

Alimentation Couche-Tard Inc. is the largest operator of highly successful convenience stores in Canada and the largest independent convience store operator (whether integratd with a petroleum company or not) in North America.

Convenience store
A small store, located near a residential area, that is open long hours seven days a week and carries a limited line of high-turnover convenience goods.

Superstore
A store much larger than a regular supermarket that offers a large assortment of routinely purchased food products, nonfood items, and services.

Category killer
A giant specialty store that carries a very deep assortment of a particular line and is staffed by knowledgeable employees.

Service retailer
A retailer whose product line is actually a service, including hotels, airlines, banks, universities, and many others.

Discount store
A retail operation that sells standard merchandise at lower prices by accepting lower margins and selling at higher volume.

Convenience stores are small stores that carry a limited line of high-turnover convenience goods. They are an important part of the Canadian economy. According to a 2009 study by HEC, the country boasts 23 500 convenience stores and 10.4 million Canadians shop at such a store every day. Convenience stores employ 165 000 Canadians and generate $32.1 billion in annual sales. The sector is highly competitive, and it is facing many rapid changes. Convenience store chains have expanded beyond their traditional market of young, blue-collar men, redesigning their stores to attract more female shoppers. One of the most successful chains is Quebec-based Alimentation Couche-Tard Inc. (the name translates into "Night Owl"), which is the largest convenience store operator in Canada. It operates a vast network of 5906 stores in both Canada and the United States under such banners as Mac's, Daisy Marts, and Circle K. The chain offers a full range of convenience products such as "Grab & Go" food like coffee, pastries, and sandwiches. Small independent stores are increasingly threatened by the major petroleum and convenience store chains who have spent millions of dollars upgrading their facilities, making them modern and attractive. The decline in tobacco sales and the sale of illegal tobacco products has also reduced sales, profits, and store traffic. Supermarkets are battling them for market share and are offering a larger range of "convenient" products for their grocery customers. They are also staying open longer. Given such a competitive climate, only the strongest convenience chains and stores will continue to thrive.[8]

Superstores are much larger than regular supermarkets and offer a large assortment of routinely purchased food products, nonfood items, and services. Loblaw, Walmart, and Costco offer *supercentres*, very large combination food and discount stores. Whereas a traditional grocery store brings in about $270 000 a week in sales, a supercentre brings in about $1.5 million a week. Walmart, which opened its first supercentre in 1988, now has more than 2200 supercentres worldwide and is opening new ones at a rate of 170 per year.[9]

Recent years have also seen the explosive growth of superstores that are actually giant specialty stores, the so-called **category killers**. They feature stores the size of airplane hangars that carry a very deep assortment of a particular line with a knowledgeable staff. Category killers are prevalent in a wide range of categories, including books, baby gear, toys, electronics, home-improvement products, linens and towels, party goods, sporting goods, and even pet supplies.

Finally, for many retailers, the product line is actually a service. **Service retailers** include hotels and motels, banks, airlines, universities, hospitals, movie theatres, tennis clubs, bowling alleys, restaurants, repair services, hair salons, and dry cleaners. Service retailers in North America are growing faster than product retailers.

Relative Prices

Retailers can also be classified according to the prices they charge (see Table 13.1). Most retailers charge regular prices and offer normal-quality goods and customer service. Others offer higher-quality goods and service at higher prices. The retailers that feature low prices are discount stores and "off-price" retailers.

Discount Stores A **discount store** sells standard merchandise at lower prices by accepting lower margins and selling higher volume. The early discount stores cut expenses by offering few services and operating in warehouse-like facilities in low-rent, heavily travelled districts. Today's discounters have improved their store environments and increased their services while at the same time keeping prices low through lean, efficient operations. Leading discounters now dominate the retail scene, and world-leading retailer Walmart—what one financial guru calls "the retailing machine of all time"—dominates the discounters (see Real Marketing 13.1).[10]

Off-price retailer

A retailer that buys at less-than-regular wholesale prices and sells at less than retail. Examples are factory outlets, independents, and warehouse clubs.

Independent off-price retailer

An off-price retailer that is either independently owned and run or is a division of a larger retail corporation.

Factory outlet

An off-price retailing operation that is owned and operated by a manufacturer and that normally carries the manufacturer's surplus, discontinued, or irregular goods.

Off-Price Retailers As the major discount stores traded up, a new wave of **off-price retailers** moved in to fill the ultralow-price, high-volume gap. Ordinary discounters buy at regular wholesale prices and accept lower margins to keep prices down. In contrast, off-price retailers buy at less-than-regular wholesale prices and charge consumers less than retail. Off-price retailers can be found in all areas, from food, clothing, and electronics to no-frills banking and discount brokerages.

The three main types of off-price retailers are *independents*, *factory outlets*, and *warehouse clubs*. **Independent off-price retailers** are either independently owned and run or are divisions of larger retail corporations. Although many off-price operations are run by smaller independents, most large off-price retailer operations are owned by bigger retail chains. Examples include store retailers such as Winners and HomeSense, which were founded in Toronto but were acquired by TJX Companies, the world's leading off-price retailer of home and fashion products. An exceptionally successful example of an independent off-price retailer is H&M:

> H&M's mission is to bring fashion and quality to its customers at the very best price. This has led the Swedish company to become wildly successful in 34 European and Asian countries where its storefronts dominate most main streets. But H&M Canada has a problem—Canada's national obsession with malls. "I'm still amazed that I meet a lot of people who have no clue what H&M is," laments Lucy van der Wal, president of H&M Canada. "Brand awareness and brand building is still a very big challenge across Canada. . . . We have to work a little harder to get our name out." H&M is using multimedia campaigns to change this state of affairs. In 2009, it had 48 stores in Canada and plans to expand this number rapidly. The recession may be helping its growth. With $25 being the average price of a garment at H&M, the company's success has been driven by its ability to reproduce runway fashions in Asian and European factories and ship them to stores within four months—slicing the industry's average in half—and replenishing the shelves daily with 20 to 50 items. To keep prices down, it uses few middlemen, buys large volumes, and has unparalleled expertise in design, fashion, and textiles.[11]

Factory outlets—manufacturer-owned and operated stores by firms such as Liz Claiborne, Levi Strauss, and others—sometimes group together in *factory outlet malls* and *value-retail centres* (sometimes called *power centres*), where dozens of outlet stores offer prices as low as 50 percent below retail on a wide range of mostly surplus, discontinued, or irregular goods. Whereas outlet malls consist primarily of manufacturers' outlets, value-retail centres combine manufacturers' outlets with off-price retail stores and department store clearance outlets, such as Sears, Mexx, or Laura. Factory outlet malls have become one of the hottest growth areas in retailing.

The malls now are moving upscale—and even dropping "factory" from their descriptions—narrowing the gap between factory outlet and more traditional forms of retailers. As the gap narrows, the discounts offered by outlets are getting smaller. However, a growing number of outlet malls now feature brands such as Coach, Polo Ralph Lauren, Dolce & Gabbana, Giorgio Armani, Gucci, and Versace, causing department stores to protest to the manufacturers of these brands. Given their higher costs, the department stores must charge more than the off-price outlets. Manufacturers counter that they send last year's merchandise and seconds to the factory outlet malls, not the new merchandise that they supply to the department stores. Still, the department stores are concerned about the growing

Sweden's Hennes & Mauritz AB (H&M) is one of the world's most successful off-price fashion retailers.

Real Marketing 13.1

Walmart: Almost Unimaginably Big

Walmart is almost unimaginably big. It's the world's largest retailer—in fact, it's the world's largest *company*. In 2008, it rang up an incredible US$401 billion in sales, far surpassing any of its competitors.

Walmart is the number-one seller in several categories of consumer products, including groceries, clothing, toys, CDs, and pet care products. It sells more groceries, clothing, and shoes than traditional retailers who specialize in these items. Incredibly, Walmart sells 30 percent of the disposable diapers purchased in North America, 30 percent of the hair care products, 30 percent of all health and beauty products, 26 percent of the toothpaste, and 20 percent of the pet food. On average, more than 180 million people around the globe visit Walmart stores each week.

It's also hard to fathom Walmart's impact on the economy. It entered the country in 1994 and today is one of Canada's largest employers, giving jobs to 77 000 Canadians. It has revolutionized the retail landscape, forcing some small independent retailers out of business and causing big changes in productivity, service, and the merchandise mix at others. In 2009, the *Globe and Mail* recognized it as a leader in corporate social responsibility. As noted by a Walmart Canada spokesperson, "It is also about leading our industry in employment opportunity, diversity, global sourcing, community involvement and environmental sustainability." Walmart Canada has also raised and donated more than $50 million to Canadian charitable and community organizations such as the Breakfast Clubs of Canada and the Children's Miracle Network.

Walmart's international sales annually exceed the GDPs of 26 countries. What's behind this spectacular success? First and foremost, Walmart is passionately dedicated to its longtime low-price value proposition and what its low prices mean to customers: "Save money. Live better." Its mission is to "lower the world's cost of living." To accomplish this mission, Walmart offers a broad selection of carefully selected goods at unbeatable prices. No other retailer has come nearly so close to mastering the concepts of everyday low prices and one-stop shopping. As one analyst puts it, "The company gospel . . . is relatively simple: Be an agent for customers—find out what they want, and sell it to them for

Walmart, the world's largest retailer, is passionately dedicated to its longtime low-price value proposition and what its low prices mean to customers—"Save money. Live better."

the lowest possible price." Says Walmart's president and CEO, "We're obsessed with delivering value to customers."

How does Walmart make money with such low prices? Walmart is a lean, mean distribution machine—it has the lowest cost structure in the industry. Low costs let the giant retailer charge lower prices but still reap higher profits. For example, grocery prices drop an average of 10 to 15 percent in markets Walmart has entered, and Walmart's food prices average 20 percent less than its grocery store rivals. Lower prices attract more shoppers, producing more sales, making the company more efficient, and enabling it to lower prices even more.

Walmart's low costs result in part from superior management and more sophisticated technology. Its Bentonville, Arkansas, and Mississauga, Ontario, headquarters contain a computer communications system that any firm would envy, giving managers around the country instant access to sales and operating information. And its huge, fully automated distribution centres, such as the one located in Cornwall, Ontario, employ the latest technology to supply stores efficiently.

Walmart also keeps costs down through good old "tough buying." The company is known for the calculated way it wrings low prices from suppliers. "Don't expect a greeter and don't expect friendly," says one supplier's sales executive after a visit to Walmart's buying offices. "Once you are ushered into one of the spartan little buyers' rooms, expect a steely eye across the table and be prepared to cut your price. They are very, very focused people, and they use their buying power more forcefully than anyone else."

Some critics argue that Walmart squeezes its suppliers too hard, driving some of them out of business. Walmart proponents counter, however, that it is simply acting in its customers' interests by forcing suppliers to be more efficient. "Walmart is tough, but totally honest and straightforward in its dealings with vendors," says an industry consultant. "Walmart has forced manufacturers to get their acts together."

Walmart also prides itself on being responsive to customers. In 2009, it started a new program where customers will be calling more of the shots when it comes to the products the company stocks. Walmart's Asda unit in the United Kingdom will begin emailing its panel of 18 000 customers images and details of products from buyers in Asia, asking whether Walmart should be putting these products in their stores. This program is one of the first of its type in the world. The Asda communications director, Dominic Burch, notes, "We're very keen on using the digital channel to enhance what we do and allow our customers into the business." As with many of its past innovations, this one may revolutionize the way retailing is performed.

Despite its incredible success over the past four decades, some analysts are noting chinks in the once seemingly invincible Walmart armour. True, Walmart's sales are huge, and through new-store and international expansion Walmart has kept its sales growing at a respectable 9 to 11 percent annually. However, Walmart seems now to be facing a midlife crisis. Profit growth has slowed and Walmart's stock has slumped a bit over the past few years.

Having grown so big, the maturing giant is having difficulty maintaining the speedy growth rates of its youth. "The glory days [of exploding sales and profits] are over," says an analyst. To reignite growth, the megaretailer is pushing into new, faster-growing product and service lines, including organic foods, in-store health clinics, and consumer financial services.

Walmart has also had to grapple with an aging image. To many mid-to-high-income consumers, Walmart seems downright dowdy compared with the younger, hipper Target. "Many of its upscale customers . . . come into the store for vegetables, cereal, detergent, and the like—but turn up their noses at higher-margin items like apparel and electronics," says an analyst. So, in an attempt to capture a larger share of wallet from higher-income consumers, Walmart has recently been giving itself a modest image facelift.

For example, it's sprucing up its stores and adding new, higher-quality merchandise. Many urban Walmarts now carry a slew of higher-end consumer electronics products, from Sony plasma televisions to Dell and Toshiba laptops to Apple iPods. The retailer has also dressed up its apparel racks with more stylish fashion lines under brand names such as Metro 7, George by designer Mark Eisen, and a new lifestyle brand by designer Norma Kamali. Finally, Walmart's new "Save money. Live better." slogan and supporting advertising have a softer, more refined feel than the old "Always low prices. *Always.*" pitch.

Even with its slightly more upscale image, in no way will Walmart ever give up its core low-price value proposition. After all, Walmart is and always will be a discount store. "I don't think Walmart's . . . ever going to be edgy," says one Walmart executive. "I don't think that fits our brand. Our brand is about saving people money" so that they can live better.

Sources: Quotes and other information from Karen Talley, "Retailer Asks Customers 'What Should We Be Selling?'" *Globe and Mail,* July 7, 2009, B6; information from www.walmart.ca/home.jsp, accessed July 2009; "David Cheesewright on Social Responsibility," *Globe and Mail*, March 31, 2009; Anthony Bianco, "Walmart's Midlife Crisis," *BusinessWeek*, April 30, 2007, p. 46; "The Fortune 500," *Fortune*, May 5, 2008, pp. F1–F3; Michael Barbaro and Stuart Elliot, "Clinging to Its Roots, Walmart Steps Back from an Edgy, New Image," *International Herald Tribune*, December 10, 2006, accessed at www.iht.com/articles/2006/12/10/business/walmart.php; Elizabeth Woyke, "Buffett, the Walmart Shopper," *BusinessWeek*, May 14, 2007, pp. 66–67; David Kiley, "Walmart Is Out to Change Its Story with New Ads," *BusinessWeek*, September 13, 2007, accessed at www.businessweek.com; Ann Zimmerman and Cheryl Lu-Lien Tan, "After Misstep, Walmart Revisits Fashion," *Wall Street Journal*, April 24, 2008, p. B1; and various fact sheets found at www.walmartstores.com, accessed November 2008.

number of shoppers willing to make weekend trips to stock up on branded merchandise at substantial savings.

Warehouse club

An off-price retailer that sells a limited selection of brand name grocery items, appliances, clothing, and a hodgepodge of other goods at deep discounts to members who pay annual membership fees.

Warehouse clubs (or wholesale clubs or membership warehouses), like Costco, operate in huge, drafty, warehouse-like facilities and offer few frills. Customers themselves must wrestle furniture, heavy appliances, and other large items to the checkout line. Such clubs make no home deliveries and often accept no credit cards. However, they do offer ultralow prices and surprise deals on selected branded merchandise. As we learned in the opening Costco story, these retailers appeal not just to low-income consumers seeking bargains on bare-bones products; they appeal to all kinds of customers shopping for a wide range of goods, from necessities to extravagances.

Table 13.2 Major Types of Retail Organizations

Type	Description	Examples
Corporate chain store	Two or more outlets that are commonly owned and controlled. Corporate chains appear in all types of retailing, but they are strongest in department stores, food stores, drug stores, shoe stores, and women's clothing stores.	Sears, Loblaw (grocery stores), Shoppers Drug Mart (drug stores), Williams-Sonoma (cookware and housewares)
Voluntary chain	Wholesaler-sponsored group of independent retailers engaged in group buying and merchandising.	Independent Grocers Alliance (IGA), Western Auto, True Value Hardware
Retailer cooperative	Group of independent retailers who set up a central buying organization and conduct joint promotion efforts.	True Value Hardware, credit unions (banking)
Franchise organization	Contractual association between a franchisor (a manufacturer, wholesaler, or service organization) and franchisees (independent businesspeople who buy the right to own and operate one or more units in the franchise system). Franchise organizations are normally based on some unique product or service, on a method of doing business, or on a trade name, goodwill, or patent that the franchisor has developed.	McDonald's, Subway, Pizza Hut, Jiffy Lube, 7-Eleven
Merchandising conglomerate	A free-form corporation that combines several diversified retailing lines and forms under central ownership, along with some integration of their distribution and management functions.	Limited Brands

Organizational Approach

Although many retail stores are independently owned, others band together under some form of corporate or contractual organization. The major types of retail organizations—*corporate chains, voluntary chains* and *retailer cooperatives, franchise organizations*, and *merchandising conglomerates*—are described in Table 13.2.

Chain stores
Two or more outlets that are commonly owned and controlled.

Chain stores are two or more outlets that are commonly owned and controlled. They have many advantages over independents. Their size allows them to buy in large quantities at lower prices and gain promotional economies. They can hire specialists to deal with areas such as pricing, promotion, merchandising, inventory control, and sales forecasting. Forty percent of Canadian retailers belong to some type of chain, making retailing more concentrated in Canada than it is in the United States, where only 20 percent of retailers are chain members. Many U.S.-based chain stores have invaded Canada, and more are on the way. For example, Abercrombie & Fitch, American Eagle Outfitters, and Skechers (a trendy California-based shoe store) have recently entered the Canadian market.

The great success of corporate chains caused many independents to band together in one of two forms of contractual associations. One is the *voluntary chain*—a wholesaler-sponsored group of independent retailers that engage in group buying and common merchandising—which we discussed in Chapter 12. Examples include Independent Grocers Alliance (IGA) and Western Auto. The other type of contractual association is the *retailer cooperative*—a group of independent retailers that band together to set up a jointly owned, central wholesale operation and conduct joint merchandising and promotion efforts. Examples are True Value Hardware and various credit unions. These organizations give independents the buying and promotion economies they need to meet the prices of corporate chains.

Franchise
A contractual association between a manufacturer, wholesaler, or service organization (a franchisor) and independent businesspeople (franchisees) who buy the right to own and operate one or more units in the franchise system.

Another form of contractual retail organization is a **franchise**. The main difference between franchise organizations and other contractual systems (voluntary chains and retail cooperatives) is that franchise systems are normally based on some unique product or service; on a method of doing business; or on the trade name, goodwill, or patent that the franchisor has developed. Franchising has been prominent in fast food and restaurants, motels, health

Franchising: These days, it's nearly impossible to stroll down a city block or drive on a suburban street without seeing a McDonald's, Jiffy Lube, Subway, or Holiday Inn.

and fitness centres, auto sales and service, and real estate.

But franchising covers a lot more than just burger joints and fitness centres. Franchises have sprung up to meet just about any need. For example, take the range of services offered by the 2009 winners of the Canadian Franchise awards. One winner was PropertyGuys.com, whose promise is "Sell Your House. Pay Yourself." Another was PostNet Canada, a firm that provides services to small businesses and home offices. A third was Sangster's Health Centres, which are becoming leaders in vitamin and herbal sales across Canada. Once considered upstarts among independent businesses, franchises now command 40 percent of all retail sales in Canada and account for more than $100 billion a year in sales. These days, it's nearly impossible to stroll down a city block or drive on a suburban street without seeing a McDonald's, Jiffy Lube, Subway, or Holiday Inn. One of the best-known and most successful franchisers, McDonald's, now has nearly 31 000 stores in 118 countries. It serves nearly 52 million customers a day and racks up nearly US$47 billion in annual systemwide sales. More than 78 percent of McDonald's restaurants worldwide are owned and operated by franchisees. Gaining fast is Subway, one of the fastest-growing franchises, with more than 29 000 shops in 86 countries.[12]

Finally, *merchandising conglomerates* are corporations that combine several different retailing forms under central ownership. An example is Limited Brands, which operates The Limited (fashion-forward women's clothing), Victoria's Secret (glamorous lingerie and beauty products), and Bath & Body Works (natural but luxurious beauty and body care products). Such diversified retailing, similar to a multibranding strategy, provides superior management systems and economies that benefit all the separate retail operations.

2 Retailer Marketing Decisions

Retailers are always searching for new marketing strategies to attract and hold customers. In the past, retailers attracted customers with unique product assortments and more or better services. Today, retail assortments and services are looking more and more alike. Many national-brand manufacturers, in their drive for volume, have placed their brands almost everywhere. You can find most consumer brands not only in department stores but also in mass-merchandise discount stores, off-price discount stores, and on the Web. Thus, it's now more difficult for any one retailer to offer exclusive merchandise.

Service differentiation among retailers has also eroded. Many department stores have trimmed their services, whereas discounters have increased theirs. Customers have become smarter and more price sensitive. They see no reason to pay more for identical brands, especially when service differences are shrinking. For all these reasons, many retailers today are rethinking their marketing strategies.

As shown in Figure 13.1, retailers face major marketing decisions about *segmentation and targeting, store differentiation and positioning,* and the *retail marketing mix*.

Segmentation, Targeting, Differentiation, and Positioning Decisions

Retailers must first segment and define their target markets and then decide how they will differentiate and position themselves in these markets. Should the store focus on upscale, midscale, or downscale shoppers? Do target shoppers want variety, depth of assortment, convenience, or low prices? Until they define and profile their markets, retailers cannot make consistent decisions about product assortment, services, pricing, advertising, store décor, or any of the other decisions that must support their positions.

Figure 13.1 Retailer
marketing strategy

Too many retailers, even big ones, fail to define their target markets and positions clearly. They try to have "something for everyone" and end up satisfying no market well. For example, what market does Sears target? What is its value proposition? For years now, the venerable retailer has struggled unsuccessfully to answer these questions well, resulting in customer apathy and stagnant sales and profits. "We have a lot of lapsed customers," says Sears's new chief marketing officer. "Sears is a great brand in people's minds. We've become just a little less top of mind." The answer? "We have to make sure that the overall customer experience—merchandise, in-store [environment], service, and marketing—are the best that they can be and working together to create a differentiated proposition that makes someone come to Sears versus going somewhere else."[13]

In contrast, successful retailers define their target markets well and position themselves strongly. For example, Walmart positions itself strongly on low prices. For decades, it consistently promised "Always low prices. *Always*." Recently, it successfully extended this positioning to include what those always low prices mean to its customers. It now promises that customers will "Save money. Live better."

If Walmart and Costco own the low-price position, how can other discounters hope to compete? Again, the answer is good targeting and positioning. For example, rather than facing Walmart head-on, the Bay, as noted earlier, is starting to revive sales by aiming at a seemingly oxymoronic "upscale discount" niche that it calls "pragmatic fashionistas." Similarly, Whole Foods Market has only 275 stores (only six of which are in Canada) and less than US$7 billion in sales versus Walmart's more than 6800 stores worldwide and sales of US$379 billion. How does this small grocery chain complete with giant Walmart? It doesn't— at least not directly. Whole Foods Market thrives by carefully positioning itself *away* from Walmart. It targets a select group of upscale customers and offers them "organic, natural, and gourmet foods, all swaddled in Earth Day politics." In fact, a devoted Whole Foods customer is more likely to boycott the local Walmart than to shop at it. One analyst sums up the Whole Foods shopping experience this way:

> Counters groan with creamy hunks of artisanal cheese. Medjool dates beckon amid rows of exotic fruit. Savory breads rest near fruit-drenched pastries, and prepared dishes like sesame-encrusted tuna rival what's sold in fine restaurants. In keeping with the company's positioning, most of the store's goods carry labels proclaiming "organic," "100% natural," and "contains no additives." Staff people smile, happy to suggest wines that go with a particular cheese, or pause to debate the virtues of peanut butter maltballs. And it's all done against a backdrop of eye-pleasing earth-toned hues and soft lighting. This is grocery shopping? Well, not as most people know it. Whole Foods Market has cultivated

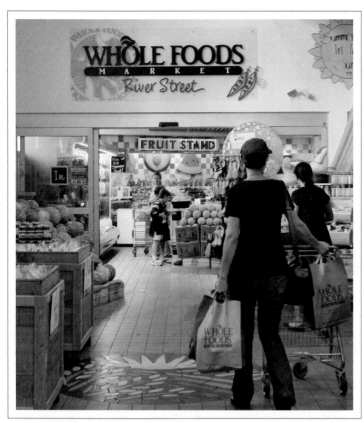

Retail targeting and positioning: By positioning itself strongly away from Walmart and other discounters, Whole Foods Market has made itself one of the nation's fastest-growing and most profitable food retailers.

its mystique with shoppers . . . by being anything but a regular supermarket chain. Whole Foods is, well, special.[14]

Whole Foods can't match Walmart's massive economies of scale, incredible volume purchasing power, ultraefficient logistics, wide selection, and hard-to-beat prices. But then again, it doesn't even try. By positioning itself strongly away from Walmart and other discounters, Whole Foods Market has made itself one of the nation's fastest-growing and most profitable food retailers.

Product Assortment and Services Decision

Retailers must decide on three major product variables: *product assortment, services mix,* and *store atmosphere.*

The retailer's *product assortment* should differentiate the retailer while matching target shoppers' expectations. One strategy is to offer merchandise that no other competitor carries, such as store brands or national brands on which it holds exclusives. Shoppers Drug Mart's Life brand and Loblaw's President's Choice and Joe Fresh brands are leading examples of how retailers use this tactic. Store brands or private-label brands account for a major proportion of retail sales. In the grocery industry, for example, they account for 22 percent of sales in Canada, 12 percent of sales in the United States, 37 percent in the United Kingdom, and a whopping 45 percent of sales in Switzerland.[15]

Another strategy is to feature blockbuster merchandising events. Bloomingdale's, an upscale U.S. chain of department stores, is known for running spectacular shows featuring goods from a certain country, such as India or China. Or the retailer can offer surprise merchandise, as when Costco offers surprise assortments of seconds, overstocks, and closeouts. Finally, the retailer can differentiate itself by offering a highly targeted product assortment—Addition Elle carries plus-size clothing, and Golf Town offers a broad assortment of clubs and clothing tailored to every golfer's needs.

The *services mix* can also help set one retailer apart from another. For example, some retailers invite customers to ask questions or consult service representatives in person or via phone or the Internet. Home Depot offers a diverse mix of services to do-it-yourselfers, from "how-to" classes to a proprietary credit card. Nordstrom promises to "take care of the customer, no matter what it takes."

The *store's atmosphere* is another important element in the reseller's product arsenal. The retailer wants to create a unique store experience, one that suits the target market and moves customers to buy. For example, Apple's retail stores are very seductive places. The store design is clean, simple, and just oozing with style—much like an Apple iPod or iPhone. The stores invite shoppers to stay a while, use the equipment, and soak up all of the exciting new technology:

> Not only has the company made many of its stores feel like gathering places, but the bright lights and equally bright acoustics create a buzz that makes customers feel more like they are at an event than in a retail store. Apple stores encourage a lot of purchasing, to be sure. But they also encourage lingering, with dozens of fully functioning computers, iPods, and iPhones for visitors to try—for hours on end. The policy has given some stores, especially those in urban neighbourhoods, the feel of a community centre. "Whenever we ask consumers to cite a great retail experience, the Apple store is the first store they mention," says

Store atmosphere: Apple's retail stores are very seductive places—real consumer meccas. The bright lights and equally bright acoustics create a buzz that makes customers feel more like they are at an event than in a retail store.

a retail research consultant. "Basically, everything about it works."[16]

It's not suprising that Apple stores are going gangbusters, averaging an incredible $4000 in sales per square foot a year. Today's successful retailers carefully orchestrate virtually every aspect of the consumer store experience, down to the music, lighting, and even the smells (see Real Marketing 13.2). Such "experiential retailing" confirms that retail stores are much more than simply assortments of goods. They are environments to be experienced by the people who shop in them. Store atmospheres offer a powerful tool by which retailers can differentiate their stores from those of competitors.

Price Decision

A retailer's price policy must fit its target market and positioning, product and service assortment, and competition. All retailers would like to charge high markups and achieve high volume, but the two seldom go together. Most retailers seek *either* high markups on lower volume (most specialty stores) *or* low markups on higher volume (mass merchandisers and discount stores).

Harry Rosen, for example, has grown from a single 500-square-foot Toronto tailor shop to a national upscale men's wear chain. Its flagship location in Toronto offers more than 50 000 square feet of apparel from around the world, featuring brands such as Hugo Boss, Ermenegildo Zegna, and Canali. Its growth has been supported by sophisticated customer relationship management (CRM) software to allow individual salespeople to maintain personal relationships with their customers. CRM has also enabled the company to use database analysis to identify key customers and develop targeted customer service, marketing, and sales efforts. Even within its upscale lines of clothing, it offers a range of prices. For example, men's dress shirts run from $175 to $295, jeans from $145 to $245, and ties from $70 to $195.[17] While the volume sales of the more upscale items may be low, there is a healthy margin on this type of sale. At the other extreme, Winners sells brand-name clothing at discount prices, settling for a lower margin on each sale but selling at a much higher volume.

Retailers must also decide on the extent to which they will use sales and other price promotions. Some retailers use no price promotions at all, competing instead on product and service quality rather than on price. Other retailers practise *"high–low"* pricing—charging higher prices on an everyday basis coupled with frequent sales and other price promotions to increase store traffic, create a low-price image, or attract customers who will buy other goods at full prices. Still others—such as Walmart, Costco, Dollar Store, and other mass retailers—practise *everyday low pricing (EDLP)*, charging constant, everyday low prices with few sales or discounts. Which strategy is best depends on the retailer's marketing strategy and the pricing approaches of competitors.

Promotion Decision

Retailers use any or all of the promotion tools—advertising, personal selling, sales promotion, public relations, and direct marketing—to reach consumers. They advertise in newspapers and magazines, on radio and television, and on the Internet. Advertising may be supported by newspaper inserts, catalogues, and direct mail. Personal selling requires careful training of salespeople in how to greet customers, meet their needs, and handle their complaints. Sales promotions may include in-store demonstrations, displays, contests, and visiting celebrities. Public relations activities, such as press conferences and speeches, store openings, special events, newsletters, magazines, and public service activities, are always available to

Real Marketing **13.2**

Orchestrating the Retail Experience

The next time that you step into a retail store—whether it sells consumer electronics, hardware, or high fashion—stop and carefully consider your surroundings. Think about the store's layout and displays. Listen to the background sounds. Smell the scents. Chances are good that everything in the store, from the layout and lighting to the music and even the smells, has been carefully orchestrated to help shape your shopping experience—and to open your wallet. In most cases, you're probably being affected in ways so subtle that you don't even realize what's happening to you.

It all starts at the store entrance. According to one reporter, "what's in the entrance is the spring on the trap"—it pulls you in and puts you in the mood to buy. "The entrance is important because it hints at what's inside that you must have."

One American chain, JC Penney, uses a "decompression area" at the front of the store that lets shoppers get acclimated and calm down from the noise in the mall or on the street. Dressed mannequins offer a taste of the season's hot trends and set up a line of sight to the shopping ahead. "We're trying to give [shoppers] ideas right as [they're] walking into the store," says JC Penney's vice-president of store design. In other department stores, the key items that draw women—the high-volume, high-profit goods—are right up front: handbags, cosmetics, jewellery, and sometimes intimate apparel.

At new Home Depot stores, the entranceway lures shoppers in with an open floor plan so they get a better "vista" of the store. Floor-to-ceiling racks of goods, long the signature of the warehouse store, are now farther back. Lower-down displays of expensive goods—riding lawn mowers, upscale porch furniture, a home design centre for redecorating your kitchen and bath, and flooring—are clustered so they're visible from the front door. All are ways to engage you in the store and draw you in.

Once inside a store, "how you as a shopper move in and around a store is not, really, up to you," continues the reporter. In a department store, you're funnelled from the entrance past the store's most expensive goods through a maze of aisles and into departments that are set up as stores-within-a-store. Then you find yourself on "the racetrack," an oval aisle that carries you around the entire building to get a look at everything. Mini-displays called "trend stations" are parked in the middle of aisles to stop shoppers' progress and entice them to look and buy.

Meanwhile, everything in a well-designed store is carefully constructed to create just the right moods and actions. At a Sony Style store, for instance, it's all designed to encourage touch, from the silk wallpaper to the smooth maple wood cabinets to the etched-glass countertops. Products are displayed like museum pieces and set up for you to touch and try. Once you touch something, Sony figures, you'll buy it. Sony Style even has mini-living rooms set up to showcase what its 40-inch flat-panel TV would look like over a fireplace. "We've had customers bring in their architect and say, 'Re-create this in my house. I want the whole setup,'" says a Sony retail executive.

A store's lighting can affect anything from your moods to the pace at which you move and shop. Bright lighting can create excitement, whereas softer lighting can create a mellow mood. Many retailers adjust lighting to regulate shoppers' "blink rates"—the slower you blink, they reason, the more likely you are to browse, pause, and eventually buy.

Sound is another important element of the retail experience. "Music has been used by retailers for decades as a way to identify their stores and affect a shopper's mood, to make you feel happy, nostalgic, or relaxed so that you linger," notes the reporter. "Think of '50s cocktail bar music in a Pottery Barn. But retailers are becoming more sophisticated in how they use music." They now hire "audio architects" to develop music and sounds that fit their unique positioning.

Next time you shop, stop, look, and listen. Successful retailers like Sony Style orchestrate every aspect of the shopper store experience, down to the music, lighting, and even the smells (a subtle fragrance of vanilla and mandarin orange).

"What does your business sound like?" asks background music provider Muzak. "A bikini and coconut oil or an oil change and a new set of tires? Muzak can create the ultimate music experience designed specifically for your business."

Perhaps the hottest store environment frontier these days is scent—that's right, the way the store smells:

Anyone who's walked into a mall has been enticed by the smell of cinnamon buns or chocolate chip cookies. Now, most large retailers are developing "signature scents" that you smell only in their stores. Luxury shirt-maker Thomas Pink pipes the smell of clean, pressed shirts into its stores—its signature "line-dried linen" scent. The essence of lavender wafts out of L'Occitane skin care stores. Bloomingdale's uses different essences in different departments: baby powder in the baby store; suntan lotion in the bathing suit area; lilacs in lingerie; cinnamon and pine scent during the holiday season. Last year, it pumped a sugar cookie scent into its Christmas shop. At a Sony Style store, the subtle fragrance of vanilla and mandarin orange—designed exclusively for Sony—wafts down on shoppers, relaxing them and helping them believe that this is a very nice place to be. Sony decided to create its own store scent

as one way to make the consumer electronics it sells less intimidating, particularly to women. At one Sony store, the scent is even pumped onto the street. "From research, we found that scent is closest to the brain and will evoke the most emotion, even faster than the eye," says a Sony retail executive. "Our scent helps us create an environment like no other." A scent expert agrees: "Scent is so closely aligned with your emotions, it's so primitive."

Thus, in their quest to orchestrate the optimal shopper experience, today's successful retailers leave no store environment stone unturned. The next time you visit a store, stop, look, and listen. See if you can spot the subtle and not-so-subtle things that retailers do to affect what you feel, think, and buy in their stores. "Most people know they are being influenced subliminally when they shop," says a retail consumer behaviour expert. "They just may not realize how much."

Sources: Extracts, quotes, and other information are from or adapted from Mindy Fetterman and Jayne O'Donnall, "Just Browsing at the Mall? That's What You Think," *USA Today*, September 1, 2006, accessed at www.usatoday.com; Ylan Q. Mui, "Dollars and Scents," *Washington Post*, December 19, 2006, p. D01, and Denise Power, "Something Is in the Air: Panel Says Scent Sells," *WWD*, March 25, 2008, p. 14.

retailers. Most retailers have also set up websites, offering customers information and other features and often selling merchandise directly.

Place Decision

Retailers often point to three critical factors in retailing success: *location, location,* and *location*! Loblaw struggled to win market share when it entered Quebec in the late 1990s because other chains owned the best locations. However, when it purchased Provigo this problem was solved. It's very important that retailers select locations that are accessible to the target market in areas that are consistent with the retailer's positioning. For example, Apple locates its stores in high-end malls and trendy shopping districts—not low-rent strip malls on the edge of town. Small retailers may have to settle for whatever locations they can find or afford. Large retailers, however, usually employ specialists who select locations using advanced methods.

Most stores today cluster together to increase their customer pulling power and to give consumers the convenience of one-stop shopping. *Central business districts* were the main form of retail cluster until the 1950s. Every large city and town had a central business district with department stores, specialty stores, banks, and movie theatres. When people began to move to the suburbs, however, these central business districts, with their traffic, parking, and crime problems, began to lose business. Downtown merchants opened branches in suburban shopping centres and the decline of the central business districts continued. In recent years, many cities have joined with merchants to try to revive downtown shopping areas by building malls and providing underground parking.

Shopping centre
A group of retail businesses planned, developed, owned, and managed as a unit.

A **shopping centre** is a group of retail businesses planned, developed, owned, and managed as a unit. A *regional shopping centre*, or *regional shopping mall*, the largest and most dramatic shopping centre, contains from 40 to over 200 stores, including two or more full-line department stores. West Edmonton Mall is North America's largest shopping and entertainment centre and the number-one tourist attraction in Alberta. It features over 800 stores, 100 eating establishments, 13 theatres, an NHL-sized ice arena,

West Edmonton Mall is the largest mall in North America and Alberta's largest tourist attraction. Like many other malls, it is working to create places to "be" rather than places to "buy."

an aquarium, the world's largest indoor wave pool, and many other attractions. It covers the equivalent of 48 city blocks and attracts customers from around the world. Thus, it also offers two unique hotels and presents 500 high-profile events annually. You can even purchase a special West Edmonton Mall prepaid MasterCard—the perfect gift for any shopaholic. A *community shopping centre* contains between 15 and 40 retail stores. It normally contains a branch of a department store or variety store, a supermarket, specialty stores, professional offices, and sometimes a bank. Most shopping centres are *neighbourhood shopping centres* or *strip malls* that generally contain between 5 and 15 stores. They are close and convenient for consumers. They usually contain a supermarket, perhaps a discount store, and several service stores—dry cleaner, drugstore, video-rental store, barber or beauty shop, hardware store, local restaurant, or other stores.[18]

Shopping malls seem to be everywhere. Toronto alone boasts almost 70 malls. Malls attract a majority of shoppers, but some malls are getting tired and have recently been receiving major makeovers. The most recent trend is to make the mall more "green" by using recycled materials in renovations and incorporating features such as the use of more natural light. Research conducted by Calgary's Sunridge Mall found that 61 percent of shoppers were "somewhat" to "highly likely" to shop at stores and centres that are more environmentally conscious. Claire Salaysay, Sunridge's marketing director, commented, "They have indicated in our research that they are more aware of the environment and are more likely to support businesses that are sharing their values . . . having the environmental initiatives in the mall is a point of differentiation for us."[19]

Another current trend is toward the so-called *power centres*, huge unenclosed shopping centres consisting of a long strip of retail stores, including large, freestanding anchors. Take the Bayers Lake Park in Halifax. It has such major stores as Walmart, Atlantic Superstore, Home Depot, Costco, Chapters Indigo, Bowring, Value Village, Staples, and Sears. Each store has its own entrance with parking directly in front for shoppers who wish to visit only one store. Power centres have increased rapidly during the past few years to challenge traditional indoor malls.

In contrast, *lifestyle centres* are smaller malls with upscale stores, convenient locations, and nonretail activities such as dining and a movie theatre. They are usually located near affluent residential neighbourhoods and cater to the retail needs of consumers in their areas. The original power centre and lifestyle centre concepts are now morphing into hybrid lifestyle–power centres. "The idea is to combine the hominess and community of an old-time village square with the cachet of fashionable urban stores; the smell and feel of a neighbourhood park with the brute convenience of a strip centre." In all, today's centres are more about "creating places to be rather than just places to buy."[20]

3   The Future of Retailing

Retailers operate in a harsh and fast-changing environment, which offers threats as well as opportunities. For example, the industry suffers from chronic overcapacity resulting in fierce competition for customer dollars, especially in tough economic times. Consumer demographics, lifestyles, and shopping patterns are changing rapidly, as are retailing technologies. A recent survey conducted by Deloitte reported that Canadian shoppers are far more complex for retailers to serve than U.S. shoppers. This is due to demographic factors, such as high levels of cultural diversity and changing family dynamics. Canadians also have higher expectations with regard to service and the quality received for the price paid.

Furthermore, the "Canadian consumer is older, time pressured, connected to the Internet, discerning, and focused on his or her well-being." And Canadians want clean, energy-efficient products, and they will respond positively to companies that are good stewards of the environment.[21] To be successful, then, retailers will need to choose target segments carefully and position themselves strongly. They will need to take the retailing developments discussed over the next few pages into account as they plan and execute their competitive strategies.

New Retail Forms and Shortening Retail Life Cycles

New retail forms continue to emerge to meet new situations and consumer needs, but the life cycle of new retail forms is getting shorter. Department stores took about 100 years to reach the mature stage of the life cycle; more recent forms, such as warehouse stores, reached maturity in about 10 years. In such an environment, seemingly solid retail positions can crumble quickly. The mantra of Canadian retailing today may have been best expressed by George Heller, who was the chief executive officer of Hudson's Bay Co. (Hbc): "Get good or get lost," he exclaimed in a recent speech.[22] The ground is shifting under retailers and many of Canada's most familiar names—Eaton"s, Simpsons, Woodward's, Robinson's, Bretton's, Kmart, Woolco—have disappeared over the past decade. Retailers that were unable to adapt to the fierce competition from powerhouses such as Walmart, Costco, and Home Depot are gone.

Wheel-of-retailing concept
A concept that states that new types of retailers usually begin as low-margin, low-price, low-status operations but later evolve into higher-priced, higher-service operations, eventually becoming like the conventional retailers they replaced.

Many retailing innovations are partially explained by the **wheel-of-retailing concept**. According to this concept, many new types of retailing forms begin as low-margin, low-price, low-status operations. They challenge established retailers that have become "fat" by letting their costs and margins increase. The new retailers' success leads them to upgrade their facilities and offer more services. In turn, their costs increase, forcing them to increase their prices. Eventually, the new retailers become like the conventional retailers they replaced. The cycle begins again when still newer types of retailers evolve with lower costs and prices. The wheel-of-retailing concept seems to explain the initial success and later troubles of department stores, supermarkets, and discount stores and the recent success of off-price retailers.

Growth of Nonstore Retailing

Most of us still make most of our purchases the old-fashioned way: We go to the store, find what we want, wait patiently in line to plunk down our cash or credit card, and bring home the goods. However, consumers now have a broad array of alternatives, including mail-order, television, phone, and online shopping. Many people are increasingly avoiding the hassles and crowds at malls by doing more of their shopping by phone or computer. As we'll discuss in Chapter 17, direct and online marketing are now the fastest-growing forms of marketing.

Only a few years ago, prospects for online retailing were soaring. As more and more consumers flocked to the Web, some experts even saw a day when consumers would bypass stodgy "old economy" store retailers and do almost all of their shopping via the Internet. However, the dot-com meltdown of 2000 dashed these overblown expectations. Many once-brash web sellers crashed and burned and expectations reversed almost overnight. The experts began to predict that online retailing was destined to be little more than a tag-on to in-store retailing.

However, today's online retailing is alive and thriving. With easier-to-use and more-enticing websites, improved online service, and the increasing sophistication of search technologies, online business is booming. Online shopping in Canada grew by a remarkable 61 percent between 2005 and 2007. Canadians spent $12.8 billion online for travel services, books and magazines, entertainment products like concert tickets, clothing, and jewellery and accessories, which are the most common types of goods purchased.[23] In Canada, online shopping serves as a complement to rather than a substitute for traditional retailing. According to Statistics Canada, 43 percent of Canadians do online research before purchasing, or just use the Internet to "window shop." Canadian Tire, for example, stopped selling goods online but kept its site just so consumers could browse for products before jumping into the car. The downturn in the economy caused even more consumers to compare prices online before buying and seek out online coupons. Here are some more surprising North American statistics: 69 percent of shoppers research products online before going to a store to make a purchase; 62 percent have looked at least once at online peer reviews before making a purchase; and 39 percent have compared a product's features and price across retail outlets online before buying.[24] So it's no longer a matter of customers deciding to shop in the store *or* to shop online. Increasingly, customers are merging store and online outlets into a single shopping process.

All types of retailers now employ direct and online channels. The online sales of traditional retailers such as lululemon, Harry Rosen, Home Depot, Sears, Staples, Walmart, and Best Buy are increasing rapidly. Several large online-only retailers—Amazon.ca, online auction site eBay, online travel companies such as Travelocity.ca and Expedia.ca, and others—are now making it big on the Web. At the other extreme, hordes of niche marketers are using the Web to reach new markets and expand their sales. Today's more-sophisticated search engines (Google, Yahoo!) and comparison-shopping sites (Shopping.com, Buy.com, Shopzilla.com, and others) put almost any online retailer a mouse click or two away from millions of customers.

Still, much of the anticipated growth in online sales will go to multichannel retailers— the marketers who can successfully merge the virtual and physical worlds. In a recent ranking of the top 500 online retail sites, 55 percent were multichannel retailers.[25]

Retail Convergence

Today's retailers are increasingly selling the same products at the same prices to the same consumers in competition with a wider variety of other retailers. For example, you can buy books at outlets ranging from independent local bookstores to warehouse clubs such as Costco, superstores such as Chapters, or websites such as Amazon.ca. As *Strategy Magazine* recently noted, "Mac's Milk now carries M&M Meats. Canadian Tire has Mark's Work Wearhouse and Budget Rent-A-Car. Canada Post sells gifts and Loblaw sells everything— just like Walmart." John Torella, a retail consultant at Toronto-based J.C. Williams Group, puts it this way: "Everybody is in everybody else's business and nobody is protected." Take the case of London Drugs, for example:

> London Drugs, based in Richmond, British Columbia, has 69 retail stores situated across British Columbia, Alberta, Saskatchewan, and Manitoba. But if there isn't a London Drugs store in your area, don't be dismayed. You can order many of its products online. As its name suggests, London Drugs offers a full-service pharmacy, but it is also one of the largest distributors of cameras and computers in Western Canada. It entered the computer age early, starting to sell its own computer brand in 1984. It started to offer high-end electronics in 1992 and introduced its own brand of insurance services in 1995. London Drugs also carries a wide range of beauty products as well as many grocery items and ethnic foods. If offers its customers home décor items, books, automotive accessories, and appliances as varied as air conditioners to espresso machines. It is currently test marketing its own London Spa in its newest drugstore in New Westminster, B.C. The spa is designed to fit into 350 square feet between the makeup department and the cashiers, and it offers most typical spa services like manicures, facials, and massages. As London Drugs president Wynne Powell notes, "London Drugs is a maverick retailer. . . . We get ahead of customer needs and wants, and this is just another example of us being ahead of the crowd."[26]

This merging of consumers, products, prices, and retailers is called *retail convergence*. Such convergence means greater competition for retailers and greater difficulty in differentiating offerings. The competition between chain superstores and smaller, independently owned stores has become particularly heated. Because of their bulk-buying power and high sales volume, chains can buy at lower costs and thrive on smaller margins. The arrival of a superstore can quickly force nearby independents out of business. For example, the decision by electronics superstore Best Buy to sell CDs as loss leaders at rock-bottom prices pushed a number of specialty record-store chains into bankruptcy. And with its everyday low prices, Walmart has been accused of destroying independents in countless small towns around the country who sell the same merchandise.

Yet the news is not all bad for smaller companies. Many small, independent retailers are thriving. They are finding that sheer size and marketing muscle are often no match for the personal touch small stores can provide or the specialty merchandise niches that small stores fill for a devoted customer base.

The Rise of Megaretailers

The rise of huge mass merchandisers and specialty superstores, the formation of vertical marketing systems, and a rash of retail mergers and acquisitions have created a core of superpower megaretailers. Canadian retailers are reflecting this trend. Three Canadian firms were recently recognized among the top 10 fastest-growing retailers in the world—Alimentation Couche-Tard Inc. (convenience stores), Jean Coutu Group (PJC) Inc. (drug stores), and Katz Group Inc. (mail-order pharmacy/drug stores).[27] Through their superior information systems and buying power, these giant retailers can offer better merchandise selection, good service, and strong price savings to consumers. As a result, they grow even larger by squeezing out their smaller, weaker competitors.

The megaretailers have shifted the balance of power between retailers and producers. A relative handful of retailers now control access to enormous numbers of consumers, giving them the upper hand in their dealings with manufacturers. For example, in North America Home Depot's sales are close to 13 times those of major supplier Black & Decker, and Home Depot generates well over 20 percent of Black & Decker's revenues. Home Depot can and often does use this power to wring concessions from Black & Decker and other suppliers.[28]

Growing Importance of Retail Technology

Retail technologies have become critically important as competitive tools. Progressive retailers are using advanced information technology and software systems to produce better forecasts, control inventory costs, interact electronically with suppliers, send information between stores, and even sell to customers within stores. They have adopted sophisticated systems for checkout scanning, RFID inventory tracking, merchandise handling, information sharing, and interacting with customers. While Canadian retailers are expanding their IT budgets to meet these needs, their budgets are still relatively low compared to other global retailers. Canadian retailing is structurally different from retailing in other countries. Because retailing is concentrated in 10 major centres, Canadian retailers cannot achieve the economies of scale needed to support larger IT investments.[29]

Perhaps the most startling advances in retailing technology concern the ways in which retailers are connecting with consumers. Today's customers have gotten used to the speed and convenience of buying online and to the control that the Internet gives them over the buying process. "The Web provides shopping when you like it, where you like it, with access to gobs of research—from a product's attributes to where it's cheapest," says one retail technology expert. "No real-world store can replicate all that."

But increasingly, retailers are attempting to meet these new consumer expectations by bringing web-style technologies into their stores. Many retailers

Improvements in technology have enabled consumers to serve themselves quickly and efficiently.

now routinely use technologies ranging from touch-screen kiosks, handheld shopping assistants, customer-loyalty cards, and self-scanning checkout systems to in-store access to store inventory databases. Consider the following examples. Today's customer doesn't always have the patience for traipsing around for the perfect cashmere scarf or obscure French novel. So Chapters, Canadian Tire, and other retailers are installing in-store kiosks that allow people to search inventory, locate merchandise, and order out-of-stock items. To enable customers to serve themselves, Loblaw has installed self-checkout systems, and Air Canada uses automated systems for passenger check-in. For impatient online customers who don't want to wait for the UPS truck, many retailers now offer in-store pickup. Importantly, getting people to show up at stores gives the retailer the opportunity to sell them more stuff.

Global Expansion of Major Retailers

Retailers with unique formats and strong brand positioning are increasingly moving into other countries. Many are expanding internationally to escape mature and saturated home markets. Over the years, some giant North American retailers, such as McDonald's, have become globally prominent as a result of their marketing prowess. Others, such as Walmart, are rapidly establishing a global presence.

However, most North American retailers are still significantly behind Europe and Asia when it comes to global expansion. Among foreign retailers that have gone global are France's Carrefour and Auchan chains, Germany's Metro and Aldi chains, and Britain's Tesco.[30]

French discount retailer Carrefour, the world's second-largest retailer after Walmart, has embarked on an aggressive mission to extend its role as a leading international retailer:

> The Carrefour Group has an interest in approximately 15 000 stores in over 30 countries in Europe, Asia, and the Americas, including 1108 hypermarkets (supercentres). It leads Europe in supermarkets and the world in hypermarkets. Carrefour is outpacing Walmart in several emerging markets, including South America, China, and the Pacific Rim. It's the leading retailer in Brazil and Argentina, where it operates more than 900 stores, compared to Walmart's 336 units in those two countries. Carrefour is the largest foreign retailer in China, where it operates more than 350 stores versus Walmart's 203. In short, although Walmart has more than three times Carrefour's overall sales, Carrefour is forging ahead of Walmart in most markets outside North America. The only question: Can the French retailer hold its lead? Although no one retailer can safely claim to be in the same league with Walmart as an overall retail presence, Carrefour stands a better chance than most to hold its own in global retailing.[31]

Retail Stores as "Communities" or "Hangouts"

With the rise in the number of people living alone, working at home, or living in isolated and sprawling suburbs, there has been a resurgence of establishments that, regardless of the product or service they offer, also provide a place for people to get together. These places include coffee shops and cafés, shopping malls, bookstores, children's play spaces, superstores, and urban greenmarkets. For example, today's bookstores have become part bookstore, part library, part living room, and part coffeehouse. On an early evening at your local Chapters, you'll likely find backpack-toting high school students doing homework with friends in the coffee bar. Nearby, retirees sit in cushy chairs thumbing through travel or gardening books, while parents read aloud to their children. Chapters sells more than just books; it sells comfort, relaxation, and community.

Retailers don't create communities only in their brick-and-mortar stores. Many also build virtual communities on the Internet. Take the case of the Virtual Museum of Canada:

> The idea for a virtual museum was born in 1999 with the goal of making collections in Canadian museums more accessible. It was formed as a partnership between Canada's museum community and the Department of Canadian Heritage. It has come a long way since its inception, and the site was totally redesigned in 2009. The

The Virtual Museum of Canada has created vibrant online communities, giving people access to the collections of Canada's 2500+ museums.

site receives millions of visits annually from people living in over 200 countries. It features over 680 000 images, and visitors can create their own collections. They can find announcements about special events at their local museum, or they can search a museum to better plan their next visit. Teachers are among its many users. They can interact to exchange ideas as well as find lesson plans and educational activities. The Virtual Museum of Canada certainly proves that museums are not the stuffy places of yesterday.[32]

4   WHOLESALING

Wholesaling
All activities involved in selling goods and services to those buying for resale or business use.

Wholesaler
A firm engaged *primarily* in wholesaling activities.

Wholesaling includes all activities involved in selling goods and services to those buying for resale or business use. We call **wholesalers** those firms engaged *primarily* in wholesaling activities.

Wholesalers buy mostly from producers and sell mostly to retailers, industrial consumers, and other wholesalers. As a result, many of the nation's largest and most important wholesalers are largely unknown to final consumers. For example, you may have never heard of Grainger, even though it's very well known and much valued by its more than 1.8 million business and institutional customers across North America:

> Grainger may be the biggest market leader you've never heard of. Its Canadian subsidiary, Acklands-Grainger Inc., was founded in 1889 in Winnipeg. Today, it has 155 branches and is Canada's largest supplier of industrial fleet and safety products. It's a US$6.4 billion North American business that offers more than 800 000 maintenance, repair, and operating (MRO) products to more than 1.8 million customers. Through its branch network, service centres, sales reps, catalogue, and website, Grainger links customers with the supplies they need to keep their facilities running

Wholesaling: Many of Canada's largest and most important wholesalers—like Acklands-Grainger—are largely unknown to final consumers. But they are very well known and much valued by the business customers they serve.

smoothly—everything from light bulbs, cleaners, and display cases to nuts and bolts, motors, valves, power tools, and test equipment. Grainger's 606 North American branches, 18 strategically located distribution centres, more than 17 000 employees, and innovative website handle more than 115 000 transactions a day. Its customers include organizations ranging from factories, garages, and grocers to schools and military bases. Most North American businesses are located within 20 minutes of a Grainger branch. Customers include such notables as Abbott Laboratories, General Motors, Campbell Soup, Chrysler, and the 2010 Vancouver Winter Olympics.[33]

Grainger operates on a simple value proposition: to make it easier and less costly for customers to find and buy MRO supplies. It starts by acting as a one-stop shop for products needed to maintain facilities. On a broader level, it builds lasting relationships with customers by helping them find *solutions* to their overall MRO problems. Acting as consultants, Grainger sales reps help buyers with everything from improving their supply chain management to reducing inventories and streamlining warehousing operations. So how come you've never heard of Grainger? Maybe it's because the company operates in the not-so-glamorous world of MRO supplies, which are important to every business but not so important to consumers. More likely, it's because Grainger is a wholesaler. And like most wholesalers, it operates behind the scenes, selling only to other businesses.

Why are wholesalers important to sellers? For example, why would a producer use wholesalers rather than selling directly to retailers or consumers? Simply put, wholesalers add value by performing one or more of the following channel functions:

- *Selling and promoting:* Wholesalers' sales forces help manufacturers reach many small customers at a low cost. The wholesaler has more contacts and is often more trusted by the buyer than the distant manufacturer.

- *Buying and assortment building:* Wholesalers can select items and build assortments needed by their customers, thereby saving the consumers much work.

- *Bulk breaking:* Wholesalers save their customers money by buying in carload lots and breaking bulk (breaking large lots into small quantities).

- *Warehousing:* Wholesalers hold inventories, thereby reducing the inventory costs and risks of suppliers and customers.

- *Transportation:* Wholesalers can provide quicker delivery to buyers because they are closer than the producers.

- *Financing:* Wholesalers finance their customers by giving credit, and they finance their suppliers by ordering early and paying bills on time.

- *Risk bearing:* Wholesalers absorb risk by taking title and bearing the cost of theft, damage, spoilage, and obsolescence.

- *Market information:* Wholesalers give information to suppliers and customers about competitors, new products, and price developments.

- *Management services and advice:* Wholesalers often help retailers train their sales clerks, improve store layouts and displays, and set up accounting and inventory control systems.

Types of Wholesalers

Merchant wholesaler
An independently owned business that takes title to the merchandise it handles.

Broker
A wholesaler who does not take title to goods and whose function is to bring buyers and sellers together and assist in negotiation.

Agent
A wholesaler who represents buyers or sellers on a relatively permanent basis, performs only a few functions, and does not take title to goods.

Wholesalers fall into three major groups (see Table 13.3): *merchant wholesalers, agents and brokers,* and *manufacturers' sales branches and offices.* **Merchant wholesalers** are the largest single group of wholesalers, accounting for roughly 50 percent of all wholesaling. Merchant wholesalers include two broad types: full-service wholesalers and limited-service wholesalers. *Full-service wholesalers* provide a full set of services, whereas the various *limited-service wholesalers* offer fewer services to their suppliers and customers. The several different types of limited-service wholesalers perform varied specialized functions in the distribution channel.

Brokers and *agents* differ from merchant wholesalers in two ways: They do not take title to goods, and they perform only a few functions. Like merchant wholesalers, they generally specialize by product line or customer type. A **broker** brings buyers and sellers together and assists in negotiation. **Agents** represent buyers or sellers on a more permanent basis. *Manufacturers' agents* (also called manufacturers' representatives) are the most common type of agent wholesaler. The third major type of wholesaling is that done in **manufacturers' sales branches and offices** by sellers or buyers themselves rather than through independent wholesalers.

Table 13.3 Major Types of Wholesalers

Type	Description
Merchant wholesalers	Independently owned businesses that take title to the merchandise they handle. In different trades they are called *jobbers, distributors,* or *mill supply houses.* They include *full-service wholesalers* and *limited-service wholesalers.*
Full-service wholesalers	Provide a full line of services: carrying stock, maintaining a sales force, offering credit, making deliveries, and providing management assistance. There are two types:
Wholesale merchants	Sell primarily to retailers and provide a full range of services. *General merchandise wholesalers* carry several merchandise lines, whereas *general line wholesalers* carry one or two lines in great depth. *Specialty wholesalers* specialize in carrying only part of a line. Examples: health food wholesalers, seafood wholesalers.
Industrial distributors	Sell to manufacturers rather than to retailers. Provide several services, such as carrying stock, offering credit, and providing delivery. May carry a broad range of merchandise, a general line, or a specialty line.
Limited-service wholesalers	Offer fewer services than full-service wholesalers. Limited-service wholesalers are of several types:
Cash-and-carry wholesalers	Carry a limited line of fast-moving goods and sell to small retailers for cash. Normally do not deliver. Example: A small fish store retailer may drive to a cash-and-carry fish wholesaler, buy fish for cash, and bring the merchandise back to the store.
Truck wholesalers (or truck jobbers)	Perform primarily a selling and delivery function. Carry a limited line of semi-perishable merchandise (such as milk, bread, snack foods), which they sell for cash as they make their rounds to supermarkets, small groceries, hospitals, restaurants, factory cafeterias, and hotels.
Drop shippers	Do not carry inventory or handle the product. On receiving an order, they select a manufacturer who ships the merchandise directly to the customer. The drop shipper assumes title and risk from the time the order is accepted to its delivery to the customer. They operate in bulk industries, such as coal, lumber, and heavy equipment.
Rack jobbers	Serve grocery and drug retailers, mostly in nonfood items. They send delivery trucks to stores where the delivery people set up toys, paperbacks, hardware items, health and beauty aids, or other items. They price the goods, keep them fresh, set up point-of-purchase displays, and keep inventory records. Rack jobbers retain title to the goods and bill the retailers only for the goods sold to consumers.
Producers' cooperatives	Are owned by farmer members and assemble farm produce to sell in local markets. The co-op's profits are distributed to members at the end of the year. They often attempt to improve product quality and promote a co-op brand name, such as Sun-Maid raisins, Sunkist oranges, or Diamond walnuts.
Mail-order wholesalers	Send catalogues to retail, industrial, and institutional customers featuring jewellery, cosmetics, specialty foods, and other small items. Maintain no outside sales force. Main customers are businesses in small outlying areas. Orders are filled and sent by mail, truck, or other transportation.

(Continued)

Table 13.3 Major Types of Wholesalers

Type	Description
Brokers and agents	Do not take title to goods. Main function is to facilitate buying and selling, for which they earn a commission on the selling price. Generally specialize by product line or customer type.
Brokers	Chief function is bringing buyers and sellers together and assisting in negotiation. They are paid by the party who hired them and do not carry inventory, get involved in financing, or assume risk. Examples: food brokers, real-estate brokers, insurance brokers, and security brokers.
Agents	Represent either buyers or sellers on a more permanent basis than brokers do. There are several types:
Manufacturers' agents	Represent two or more manufacturers of complementary lines. A formal written agreement with each manufacturer covers pricing, territories, order handling, delivery service and warranties, and commission rates. Often used in such lines as apparel, furniture, and electrical goods. Most manufacturers' agents are small businesses with only a few skilled salespeople as employees. They are hired by small manufacturers who cannot afford their own field sales forces and by large manufacturers who use agents to open new territories or to cover territories that cannot support full-time salespeople.
Selling agents	Have contractual authority to sell a manufacturer's entire output. The manufacturer either is not interested in the selling function or feels unqualified. The selling agent serves as a sales department and has significant influence over prices, terms, and conditions of sale. Found in product areas such as textiles, industrial machinery and equipment, coal and coke, chemicals, and metals.
Purchasing agents	Generally have a long-term relationship with buyers and make purchases for them, often receiving, inspecting, warehousing, and shipping the merchandise to the buyers. They provide helpful market information to clients and help them obtain the best goods and prices available.
Commission merchants	Take physical possession of products and negotiate sales. Normally they are not employed on a long-term basis. Used most often in agricultural marketing by farmers who do not want to sell their own output and do not belong to producers' cooperatives. The commission merchant takes a truckload of commodities to a central market, sells it for the best price, deducts a commission and expenses, and remits the balance to the producers.
Manufacturers' and retailers' branches and offices	Wholesaling operations conducted by sellers or buyers themselves rather than through independent wholesalers. Separate branches and offices can be dedicated to either sales or purchasing.
Sales branches and offices	Set up by manufacturers to improve inventory control, selling, and promotion. *Sales branches* carry inventory and are found in industries such as lumber and automotive equipment and parts. *Sales offices* do not carry inventory and are most prominent in dry-goods and notions industries.
Purchasing officers	Perform a role similar to that of brokers or agents but are part of the buyer's organization. Many retailers set up purchasing offices in major market centres such as Toronto and Calgary.

Manufacturers' sales branches and offices Wholesaling by sellers or buyers themselves rather than through independent wholesalers.

Wholesaler Marketing Decisions

Wholesalers now face growing competitive pressures, more-demanding customers, new technologies, and more direct-buying programs on the part of large industrial, institutional, and retail buyers. As a result, they have taken a fresh look at their marketing strategies. As with retailers, their marketing decisions include choices of segmentation and targeting, differentiation and positioning, and the marketing mix—product and service assortments, price, promotion, and distribution (see Figure 13.2).

Segmentation, Targeting, Differentiation, and Positioning Decisions

Like retailers, wholesalers must segment and define their target markets and differentiate and position themselves effectively—they cannot serve everyone. They can choose a target group by size of customer (only large retailers), type of customer (convenience stores only), need for service (customers who need credit), or other factors. Within the target group, they can identify the more profitable customers, design stronger offers, and build better relationships with them. They can propose automatic reordering systems, set up management-training and advising systems, or even sponsor a voluntary chain. They can discourage less-profitable customers by requiring larger orders or adding service charges to smaller ones.

Figure 13.2 Wholesaler marketing strategy

Marketing Mix Decisions

Like retailers, wholesalers must decide on product and service assortments, prices, promotion, and place. Wholesalers add customer value though the *products and services* they offer. They are often under great pressure to carry a full line and to stock enough for immediate delivery. But this practice can damage profits. Wholesalers today are cutting down on the number of lines they carry, choosing to carry only the more-profitable ones. They are also rethinking which services count most in building strong customer relationships and which should be dropped or paid for by the customer. The key is to find the mix of services most valued by their target customers.

Price is also an important wholesaler decision. Wholesalers usually mark up the cost of goods by a standard percentage—say, 20 percent. Expenses may run 17 percent of the gross margin, leaving a profit margin of 3 percent. In grocery wholesaling, the average profit margin is often less than 2 percent. Wholesalers are trying new pricing approaches. They may cut their margin on some lines to win important new customers. They may ask suppliers for special price breaks when they can turn those price breaks into an increase in the supplier's sales.

Although *promotion* can be critical to wholesaler success, most wholesalers are not promotion minded. They use largely scattered and unplanned trade advertising, sales promotion, personal selling, and public relations. Many are behind the times in personal selling—they still see selling as a single salesperson talking to a single customer instead of as a team effort to sell, build, and service major accounts. Wholesalers also need to adopt some of the nonpersonal promotion techniques used by retailers. They need to develop an overall promotion strategy and to make greater use of supplier promotion materials and programs.

Finally, *distribution* (location) is important—wholesalers must choose their locations, facilities, and web locations carefully. There was a time when wholesalers could locate in low-rent, low-tax areas and invest little money in their buildings, equipment, and systems. Today, however, as technology zooms forward, such behaviour results in outdated materials-handling, order-processing, and delivery systems.

Instead, today's large and progressive wholesalers have reacted to rising costs by investing in automated warehouses and information technology systems. Orders are fed from the retailer's information system directly into the wholesaler's, and the items are picked up by mechanical devices and automatically taken to a shipping platform where they are assembled. Most large wholesalers are using technology to carry out accounting, billing, inventory control, and forecasting. Modern wholesalers are adapting their services to the needs of target customers and finding cost-reducing methods of doing business.

Trends in Wholesaling

Today's wholesalers face considerable challenges. The industry remains vulnerable to one of the most enduring trends of the last decade—fierce resistance to price increases and the sifting out of suppliers who are not adding value based on cost and quality. Progressive wholesalers constantly watch for better ways to meet the changing needs of their suppliers and target customers. They recognize that, in the long run, their only reason for existence comes from adding value by increasing the efficiency and effectiveness of the entire marketing channel. As with other types of marketers, the goal is to build value-adding customer relationships. For example, Grainger (and its Canadian subsidiary Acklands-Grainger) succeeds by making life easier and more efficient for the commercial and institutional buyers and sellers it serves:

> Beyond making it easier for customers to find the products they need, Grainger also helps them streamline their acquisition processes. For most companies, acquiring MRO supplies is a very costly process. In fact, 40 percent of the cost of MRO supplies stems from the purchase process, including finding a supplier, negotiating the best deal, placing the order, receiving the order, and paying the invoice. Grainger constantly seeks ways to reduce the costs associated with MRO supplies acquisition, both internally and externally. One company found that working with Grainger cut MRO requisition time by more than 60 percent; lead times went from days to hours. Its supply chain dropped from 12 000 suppliers to 560—significantly reducing expenses. Similarly, a large timber and paper-products company has come to appreciate Grainger's selection and streamlined ordering process. It orders two-thirds of its supplies from Grainger's website at an annual acquisition cost of only $300 000. By comparison, for the remainder of its needs, this company deals with more than 1300 small distributors at an acquisition cost of $2.4 million each year—eight times the cost of dealing with Grainger for half of the volume. The company is now looking for ways to buy all of its MRO supplies from Grainger. As one Grainger branch manager puts it, "If we don't save [customers] time and money every time they come [to us], they won't come back."[34]

McKesson, North America's leading wholesaler of pharmaceuticals, health and beauty care products, home health care, and medical supply and equipment products, provides another example of progressive, value-adding wholesaling. To survive, McKesson has to remain more cost effective than manufacturers' sales branches. Thus, the company has built efficient automated warehouses, established direct computer links with drug manufacturers, and set up extensive online supply management and accounts receivable systems for customers. It offers retail pharmacists a wide range of online resources, including supply management assistance, catalogue searches, real-time order tracking, and an account management system. It has also created solutions such as automated pharmaceutical-dispensing machines that assist pharmacists by reducing costs and improving accuracy. Retailers can even use the McKesson system to maintain medical profiles on their customers.

McKesson's medical–surgical supply and equipment customers receive a rich assortment of online solutions and supply management tools, including an online order management system and real-time information on products and pricing, inventory availability, and order status. According to McKesson, it adds value in the channel by providing "supply, information, and health care management products and services designed to reduce costs and improve quality across healthcare."[35]

The distinction between large retailers and large wholesalers continues to blur. Many retailers now operate formats such as wholesale clubs and supercentres that perform many wholesale functions. In return, many large wholesalers are setting up their own retailing

Pharmaceuticals wholesaler McKesson helps its retail pharmacist customers be more efficient by offering a wide range of online resources. Retail pharmacists can even use the McKesson system to maintain medical profiles on their customers.

operations. For example, until recently, SuperValu was classified as a food wholesaler, with a majority of its business derived from supplying grocery products to independent grocery retailers. However, over the past decade SuperValu has started or acquired several retail food chains of its own—including Albertsons, Jewel-Osco, Save-A-Lot, Cub Foods, Acme Markets, and others—to become the third-largest food retailer in the United States. Thus, even though it remains America's largest food wholesaler, SuperValu is now classified as a retailer because 75 percent of its US$37 billion in sales come from retailing.[36]

Wholesalers will continue to increase the services they provide to retailers—retail pricing, cooperative advertising, marketing and management information reports, accounting services, online transactions, and others. Rising costs on the one hand and the demand for increased services on the other will put the squeeze on wholesaler profits. Wholesalers who do not find efficient ways to deliver value to their customers will soon drop by the wayside. However, the increased use of computerized, automated, and web-based systems will help wholesalers contain the costs of ordering, shipping, and inventory holding, boosting their productivity.

Finally, facing slow growth in their domestic markets and such developments as the North American Free Trade Agreement, many large wholesalers are now going global. For example, McKesson now derives more than 7 percent of its revenues from Canadian and other international operations, up 28 percent in just the past two years. Its Information Solutions group operates widely throughout North America, the United Kingdom, and other European countries.[37]

REVIEWING OBJECTIVES AND KEY TERMS | Audio Chapter Summary

Retailing and wholesaling consist of many organizations bringing goods and services from the point of production to the point of use. In this chapter, we first looked at the nature and importance of retailing, major types of retailers, the decisions retailers make, and the future of retailing. We then examined these same topics for wholesalers.

OBJECTIVE 1 **Explain the role of retailers in the distribution channel and describe the major types of retailers.**

Retailing includes all activities involved in selling goods or services directly to final consumers for their personal, non-business use. Retail stores come in all shapes and sizes, and new retail types keep emerging. Store retailers can be classified by the *amount of service* they provide (self-service, limited service, or full service), *product line sold* (specialty stores, department stores, supermarkets, convenience stores, superstores, and service businesses), and *relative prices* (discount stores and off-price retailers). Today many retailers are banding together in corporate and contractual *retail organizations* (corporate chains, voluntary chains and retailer cooperatives, franchise organizations, and merchandising conglomerates).

OBJECTIVE 2 **Describe the major retailer marketing decisions.**

Retailers are always searching for new marketing strategies to attract and hold customers. They face major marketing decisions about segmentation and targeting, store differentiation and positioning, and the retail marketing mix.

Retailers must first segment and define their target markets and then decide how they will differentiate and position themselves in these markets. Those that try to offer "something for everyone" end up satisfying no market well. In contrast, successful retailers define their target markets well and position themselves strongly.

Guided by strong targeting and positioning, retailers must decide on a retail marketing mix—product and services assortment, price, promotion, and place. Retail stores are much more than simply an assortment of goods—beyond the products and services they offer, today's successful retailers carefully orchestrate virtually every aspect of the consumer store experience. A retailer's price policy must fit its target market and positioning, products and services assortment, and competition. Retailers use any or all of the promotion tools—advertising, personal selling, sales promotion, public relations, and direct marketing—to reach consumers. Finally, it's very important that retailers select locations that are accessible to the target market in areas that are consistent with the retailer's positioning.

OBJECTIVE 3 **Discuss the future of retailing.**

Retailers operate in a harsh and fast-changing environment, which offers threats as well as opportunities. New retail forms continue to emerge to meet new situations and consumer needs, but the life cycle of new retail forms is getting shorter—retailers must pay attention to the *wheel-of-retailing concept*. Other trends in retailing include the rapid growth of nonstore retailing, retail convergence (the merging of consumers, products, prices, and retailers), the rise of megaretailers, the growing importance of retail technology, the global expansion of major retailers, and the resurgence of retail stores as consumer "communities" or "hangouts."

OBJECTIVE 4 **Explain the major types of wholesalers and their marketing decisions.**

Wholesaling includes all the activities involved in selling goods or services to those who are buying for the purpose of resale or for business use. Wholesalers fall into three groups. First, *merchant wholesalers* take possession of the goods. They include *full-service wholesalers* (wholesale merchants, industrial distributors) and *limited-service wholesalers* (cash-and-carry wholesalers, truck wholesalers, drop shippers, rack jobbers, producers' cooperatives, and mail-order wholesalers). Second, *brokers* and *agents* do not take possession of the goods but are paid a commission for aiding buying and selling. Finally, *manufacturers' sales branches and offices* are wholesaling operations conducted by nonwholesalers to bypass the wholesalers.

Like retailers, wholesalers must target carefully and position themselves strongly. And, like retailers, wholesalers must decide on product and service assortments, prices, promotion, and place. Progressive wholesalers constantly watch for better ways to meet the changing needs of their suppliers and target customers. They recognize that, in the long run, their only reason for existence comes from adding value by increasing the efficiency and effectiveness of the entire marketing channel. As with other types of marketers, the goal is to build value-adding customer relationships.

KEY TERMS

mymarketinglab | Glossary Flashcards

Objective 1

DISCUSSING THE CONCEPTS

1. Discuss how retailers and wholesalers add value to the marketing system. Explain why marketers are embracing the concept of *shopper marketing*.

2. Different types of customers and products require different amounts of service. Discuss the different levels of retailer service and give one example of each.

3. Discuss the different organizational approaches for retailers and provide an example of each.

4. What is the wheel-of-retailing concept? Does it apply to online retailing?

5. What is retail convergence? Has it helped or harmed small retailers?

6. Explain how wholesalers add value in the channel of distribution.

APPLYING THE CONCEPTS

1. Choose three retailers that you buy from often. Classify these retailers in terms of the characteristics presented in the chapter. Next, use Table 13.1 to categorize each retailer.

2. Deciding on a target market and positioning for a retail store are very important marketing decisions. In a small group, develop the concept for a new retail store. Who is the target market for your store? How is your store positioned? What retail atmospherics will enhance this positioning effectively to attract and satisfy your target market?

3. Suppose that you are a manufacturer's agent for three lines of complementary women's apparel. Discuss what types of marketing mix decisions you will be making.

FOCUS ON TECHNOLOGY

Thanks to today's shaky economy, many luxury goods are going unsold and are piling up in storerooms. However, this creates an opportunity for a whole new breed of online sellers, such as Gilt.com, Ideeli.com, and HauteLook.com. Within six months of launch, HauteLook.com had more than 100 000 members and was growing 10 percent per week. These members-only sites announce limited-time "flash sales" of designer goods discounted up to 70 percent. You can get $250 Rag & Bone jeans for $118, or Nina Ricci sunglasses for a fraction of the retail price. But you have to act fast because sales typically last only a few days, with digital clocks ticking down the time. Gilt.com reports unloading 600 dresses within six minutes and members buying within 45 seconds of logging on! Some sites offer free membership, whereas others are by invitation only. For $100, Ideeli.com offers members cellphone invitations to private sales.

1. Visit www.hautelook.com to learn more about this online retailer. In what ways does it provide value for manufacturers and consumers?

2. Do sites like these create conflicts between manufacturers and retailers within the traditional channel of distribution?

FOCUS ON ETHICS

Vancouver coffee roaster Roy Hardy wanted to get his fair-trade coffee widely distributed in local supermarkets, but gave up in frustration when he found he could not afford payments called "slotting fees" demanded by big retailers. "One supermarket was willing to take two SKUs (stock keeping units) of 20 units each," said Hardy, "but wanted the first one free 'on spec.' That would mean giving away 40 pounds (of coffee) per store. That was really beyond us." Hardy and other small business people believe slotting fees are unjust. "The big guys like Van Houtte, Sara Lee, and Procter & Gamble control the space and don't want us in there. There is so much money involved and the big guys control it." Slotting fees, also called slotting allowances, are fees that retailers charge manufacturers to get onto retail shelves. They also determine if the product is stocked at eye level or in end-of-aisle displays. Slotting fees range from $25 000 to $3 million per supermarket chain. Big consumer goods makers report total slotting fees in the $1 million to $2 million range per new brand. Retailers argue that slotting fees compensate them for the costs associated with entering new products into their inventory systems and the risks they bear since most new products fail. Critics argue that they are anticompetitive, prevent new products from small manufacturers from making it to market, and erode consumer choice. Mike Murphy, an officer at the Competition Bureau, notes, "A lot of people who have to pay these fees don't like it but don't want to complain. Manufacturers are reluctant to blow the whistle on slotting fees, fearing retribution from chain retailers and dominant manufacturers."[38]

1. Is it fair for retailers to charge manufacturers to get onto store shelves? Discuss both points of view on this issue.

2. Go to www.competitionbureau.gc.ca/eic/site/cb-bc.nsf/eng/01642.html#elements9 and read section 5.2.1(b), Slotting Allowances and Other Listing Fees. What did you learn from this report and what is the Competition Bureau's position on slotting fees?

MARKETING BY THE NUMBERS

Retailers need merchandise to make sales. In fact, a retailer's inventory is its biggest asset. Not stocking enough merchandise can result in lost sales, but carrying too much inventory increases costs and lowers margins. Both circumstances reduce profits. One measure of a reseller's inventory management effectiveness is its *stockturn* rate (also called *inventory turnover rate* for manufacturers). The key to success in retailing is realizing a large volume of sales on as little inventory as possible while maintaining enough stock to meet customer demands.

1. Refer to Appendix 3: Marketing by the Numbers, and determine the stockturn rate of a retailer carrying an average inventory at cost of $350 000 with a cost of goods sold of $800 000.

2. If this company's stockturn rate was 3.5 last year, is the stockturn rate calculated above better or worse? Explain.

VIDEO CASE

Wellbeing

 | Video Case Questions

In 2003, Dan Wales and Matt Lennox opened their first Wellbeing restaurant. As a retail concept, the team identified a gap in the market and developed a strong point of differentiation. "There are few truly healthy fast-food chains," says Wales. "People have been desperate for healthy options." With this perspective on the market, their goal was to offer consumers a healthy alternative to typical fast-food options. Working with fresh ingredients, bright and open stores, and a well-crafted, healthy menu, the new chain clearly offered something new. So it came as no surprise that customers responded with enthusiasm to Wellbeing's new choices as they gobbled up sandwiches, salads, soups, juices, smoothies, and fruit salads. In only a few years, the chain has

expanded to 18 stores. Within the next two years, it expects to nearly double that number.

After viewing the video featuring Wellbeing, answer the following questions about retailing:

1. Categorize Wellbeing according to the four characteristics of retailers discussed in the chapter.

2. How is Wellbeing positioned in the marketplace? Which consumers does the chain target? Are its product assortment, pricing, promotion, and place decisions consistent with this targeting and positioning?

3. Which trend affecting the future of retailing do you think will most impact Wellbeing in the coming years?

Visit MyMarketingLab at www.pearsoned.ca/mymarketinglab to view the video segment related to this case.

COMPANY CASE

Whole Foods: A Whole-istic Strategy

It's tough to compete in the grocery business these days. What was once a landscape littered with hundreds of local and regional players has now become an industry dominated by the mega-chains. Walmart, Sobeys, and Loblaw have each taken their own approach to expanding as far and wide as possible with one goal: sell massive amounts of

groceries to mainstream consumers at the lowest possible prices. Sure, there are still some small, regional grocers. But they exist mostly because some segment of customers wants to support local businesses. It's getting harder and harder for such grocers to stay alive or avoid getting gobbled up by the big dogs on the block.

So how does a smaller chain not only survive but thrive in such a dog-eat-dog environment? Perhaps the worst strategy is trying to out-Walmart Walmart. Instead of competing head-to-head, smart competitors choose their turf carefully. Rather than competing directly with the volume and price leaders, some have succeeded by reducing emphasis on price and focusing instead on providing something that the low-price, high-volume competitors simply can't supply.

The grocer that's doing the best job of this is Whole Foods Market. Growing from a single store in 1980, Whole Foods has gone far beyond the status of "regional player." It now operates more than 270 stores in 36 states, Canada, and the United Kingdom. Although that's tiny compared to Sobeys' 1300 stores or Walmart's 7300, Whole Foods is thriving and expanding.

How does Whole Foods do it? Through careful positioning—specifically, by positioning *away* from the industry giants. Rather than pursuing mass-market sales volume and razor-thin margins, Whole Foods targets a select group of upscale customers and offers them "organic, natural, and gourmet foods, all swaddled in Earth Day politics." As one analyst puts it, "While other grocers are looking over their shoulder, watching and worrying about Walmart, Whole Foods is going about business as usual. The tofu is still selling; the organic eggs are fresh in the back dairy cooler; and meats are still hormone free." The value package that Whole Foods offers to its unique customers is best summed up in its motto: "Whole Foods, Whole People, Whole Planet."

WHOLE FOODS

Customers that enter Whole Foods' doors are looking for the highest quality, least processed, most flavourful, and naturally preserved foods. Whole Foods claims that "Food in its purest state is the best tasting and most nutritious food available."

The Whole Foods website reinforces the company's positioning. The site offers up recipes for healthy and gourmet eating, such as "Sweet Potato Pancakes with Creamy Dill Sauce," "Baked Basmati & Currant Stuffed Trout," and "Beginner's Tips for Tofu, Tempeh, and Other Soy Foods."

One aspect of Whole Foods' strategy that allows it to deliver products that foodies love might seem like a step back in time in the supply chain–driven grocery industry. The bigger chains are centralized, sourcing their products from all over the world in identical batches through various distribution centres. But Whole Foods uses a more local approach. Each geographic division, headed by its own president, handles its own store network. Thus, in addition to gathering some foods globally, Whole Foods obtains a significant portion of its goods locally, often from small, uniquely dedicated food artisans. The company backs its talk with action on this issue. Its Local Producer Loan Program doles out US$10 million annually in long-term, low-interest loans to local suppliers.

WHOLE PEOPLE

Whole Foods' customers appreciate the fact that the store's quality commitment reaches far beyond what's on its shelves. In its "Declaration of Interdependence," the company recognizes that living up to its "Whole Foods, Whole People, Whole Planet" motto means doing more than simply selling food. It means caring about the well-being and quality of life of everyone associated with the business, from customers and employees to suppliers to the broader communities in which it operates.

Nowhere is this more evident than in the way that Whole Foods treats its employees. For 11 consecutive years, Whole Foods has been listed among *Fortune* magazine's "Top 100 Companies to Work for in America." Ranked as high as fifth, it is one of only 14 companies ranked every year since the list's inception. Said Whole Foods CEO and cofounder, John Mackey:

> To be among only 14 companies in the nation to be named as one of the Best Companies to Work for since the listing began is an amazing achievement and a validation that we are honoring our core value of "Supporting Team Member Excellence and Happiness" by creating an empowering work environment.

"Empowering work environment," "self-directed teams," and "self-responsibility" all sound like corporate catch phrases that get tossed around by management without permeating the culture. But at Whole Foods, employees believe in these pillars of the company's mission. In fact, two-thirds of *Fortune's* ranking is based on survey responses from randomly selected employees. Just ask Shateema Dillard, who after two years as an employee is a supervisor and proud owner of two stock option grants. Even though these grants are worth less than $200, Dillard feels "well-paid and confident that opportunities for growth are phenomenal."

Whole Foods is one of a shrinking number of companies that still pay 100 percent of their employees' health care premiums. It also ranks very high on the diversity of its employee team. Out of a sense of teamwork and fairness, it caps the salaries of its highest-paid team members at 19 times the average total compensation of all full-time team members in the company.

WHOLE PLANET

"We believe companies, like individuals, must assume their share of responsibility as tenants of Planet Earth," professes the company's value statement. While this might seem simple, the extensiveness of Whole Foods' environmental program illustrates just how complex a genuine "Earth first" philosophy can be.

For starters, Whole Foods actively supports organic farming on a global basis. This, it believes, is the best way to promote sustainable agriculture and protect both the environment and farm workers. This policy supports Whole Foods' core product offering, but it's just the tip of the company's sustainability iceberg.

In January 2006, Whole Foods became the first *Fortune* 500 company to offset 100 percent of its electricity use with the purchase of wind energy credits. The credits cover its stores, bakehouses, distribution centres, offices, and every other facility. Beyond energy conservation, Whole Foods has committed to completely eliminating disposable plastic grocery bags, not only conserving resources but also reducing nonbiodegradable wastes. No other U.S. grocer has made this commitment.

Such efforts represent a tremendous corporatewide commitment to environmental protection. However, the Whole Planet culture reaches right down to the store level. Each and every store has a Green Mission Team, a task force composed of team members who meet often to improve environmental actions for their stores. This has led many Whole Foods stores to serve as collection points for plastic bag recycling. Most stores also participate in composting programs for food waste and compostable paper goods. One store in Berkeley, California, even gets most of its electrical power from roof-top solar panels.

Under the Whole Planet mantra, Whole Foods also supports the local communities in which it operates. It believes that local efforts will create healthier and more productive societies at the micro-level, resulting in less need to ship products and waste long distances. This, in turn, lowers pollution and carbon emissions. Whole Foods supports food banks, sponsors neighbourhood events, and even provides financial support for employees doing voluntary community service. Perhaps most telling of Whole Foods' community commitment: It donates 5 percent of its after-tax profits to not-for-profit organizations.

A WHOLE LOT OF CUSTOMERS

Each element of the three-part philosophy underlying the Whole Foods strategy just happens to appeal strongly to a carefully targeted segment of consumers. Whole Foods is not for everyone—intentionally. Whole Foods' customers are affluent, liberal, educated people living in university towns such as Austin, Texas, Boulder, Colorado, and Ann Arbor, Michigan. Their median annual household income exceeds the U.S. average by almost US$8000. Whole Foods' customers live a health-conscious lifestyle, care about the food they eat, and worry about the environment. They tend to be social do-gooders who abhor soulless corporate greed. Whole Foods doesn't really need to compete with mass merchandisers such as Walmart for these customers. In fact, a Whole Foods customer is more likely to boycott the local Walmart than to shop at it.

But something beyond great food, environmental conscience, and human rights draws these people to Whole Foods. A store visit is more than just a shopping trip—it's an experience. And the experience is anything but what you'd find at Walmart. "We create store environments that are inviting, fun, unique, informal, comfortable, attractive, nurturing, and educational," the company claims. "We want our stores to become community meeting places where our customers come to join their friends and to make new ones." Whole Foods' concern for customers runs deep. "We go to extraordinary lengths to satisfy and delight our customers," says a company spokesperson. "We want to meet or exceed their expectations on every shopping trip."

Such commitment, along with strong targeting and positioning, have made Whole Foods one of the nation's fastest-growing and most profitable food retailers. After acquiring nearly 100 stores in its 2007 merger with Wild Oats, a growing chain with a similar positioning strategy, Whole Foods is now the world's number-one natural food chain. Its upscale stores ring up an average of $689 in sales per square foot, almost twice that of a traditional grocer. And the chain reaps 35 percent gross margins, which are much larger than those of its traditional competitors. Whereas other grocers have faced limited sales and profit growth or even declines in the face of the withering Walmart assault, Whole Foods' sales and profits have more than doubled over the past four years.

So, Whole Foods can't compete directly with the Walmarts of the world. It can't match Walmart's massive economies of scale, incredible volume purchasing power, ultra-efficient logistics, wide selection, and hard-to-beat prices. But then again, it doesn't even try. Instead, it targets customers that Walmart can't serve, offering them value that Walmart can't deliver. And while Whole Foods' future is not without challenges, it has found its own very profitable place in the world by positioning away from the grocery behemoths. Says Whole Foods' chief executive, "Not everyone is concerned with getting mediocre food at the lowest price."

Questions for Discussion

1. Define Whole Foods' "product." How does it deliver value to customers?

2. Organic foods are becoming very popular. Many chains, including Walmart, have begun offering and expanding their selection of organics. Does this pose a competitive threat to Whole Foods?

3. With respect to Whole Foods' targeting and positioning strategies, what challenges will the company face in the future as it continues to grow and expand?

4. In some places, Whole Foods is commonly known as "Whole Paycheque." While the firm has clearly positioned itself away from pricing issues, can it avoid this element of the marketing mix forever? Why or why not?

5. What other trends in the future of retailing do you think will have an impact on Whole Foods?

Sources: David Kesmodel, "Whole Foods Net Falls," *Wall Street Journal*, May 14, 2008, p. B5; "The Fast 50 Companies," *Fast Company*, March 2008, p. 111; Diane Brady, "Eating Too Fast at Whole Foods," *BusinessWeek*, October 24, 2005, p. 82; Samantha Thompson Smith, "Grocer's Success Seems Entirely Natural," *News & Observer*, May 21, 2004, p. D1; Marianne Wilson, "Retail as Theater, Naturally," *Chain Store Age*, May 25, 2005, p. 182; Carl Gutierrez, "Court Frees Whole Foods to Swallow Wild Oats," *Forbes*, August 23, 2007, accessed at www.forbes.com; and information from www.wholefoodsmarket.com.

Visit **MyMarketingLab** at **www.pearsoned.ca/mymarketinglab** for access to online tutorials, interactive exercises, videos, and much more.

Integrated Marketing
Communications Strategy

PREVIEWING THE CONCEPTS In this and the next three chapters, we'll examine the last of the marketing mix tools—promotion. Companies must do more than just create customer value. They must also use promotion to clearly and persuasively communicate that value. Promotion is not a single tool but, rather, a mix of several tools. Under the concept of *integrated marketing communications*, the company must carefully coordinate these promotion elements to deliver a clear, consistent, and compelling message about the organization and its brands. We'll begin by introducing you to the various promotion mix tools. Next, we'll examine the rapidly changing communications environment and the need for integrated marketing communications. Finally, we'll discuss the steps in developing marketing communications and the promotion budgeting process. In the next three chapters, we'll visit the specific marketing communications tools.

To start this chapter, let's look at one of the world's biggest marketers—Unilever—and at one of today's biggest marketing communications issues—the impact of the digital revolution on how marketers communicate with customers. More than most other companies, Unilever has mastered the digital marketing space. However, Unilever's marketers will tell you that they don't really do "digital campaigns" as such. Instead, they do integrated marketing communications campaigns.

These days, most advertisers are scrambling to make sense of the Web and other digital media, everything from websites and online social networks to webisodes and viral video. The digital revolution has created a kind of "media divide," pitting traditional media such as television and magazines against the new-age digital media. Consumer goods giant Unilever, however, appears to have mastered the new digital space. In fact, Unilever was recently anointed Digital Marketer of the Year by *Advertising Age*.

But here's the funny thing about Unilever being Digital Marketer of the Year: The company doesn't really do "digital campaigns" as such. For Unilever, it's not an either–or proposition—either traditional media or digital media. Instead, Unilever has made online and digital tactics just another important part of its mainstream marketing, seamlessly blending the old and the new into fully integrated communications campaigns.

Suave's "In the Motherhood" webisodes are only a small part of a much larger integrated communications campaign for the brand.

Sure, Unilever does plenty of stand-out digital. It creates innovative websites for its bevy of familiar brands, ranging from Dove, Suave, Axe, Lever 2000, and Vaseline to Hellmann's, Knorr, Lipton, Ragú, and Slim-Fast to Breyers, Bertolli, and Ben & Jerry's. And Unilever has made headlines for numerous web and viral video successes. For example, its Dove brand won a cyber Grand Prix award at Cannes last year for its spectacularly successful "Evolution" viral video, which was created by Ogilvy & Mather in Toronto. And Suave developed a series of "In the Motherhood" webisodes—the Web's version of TV soap operas—that drew more than 5.5 million viewers.

It seems that every Unilever brand has something big going digitally. At one extreme, Axe holds an online "World's Dirtiest Film" competition, which asks young male customers to create films so dirty that you'll beg for a shower when it's done—with Axe Shower Gel, of course. At the other extreme, comparatively stodgy Hellmann's produces an online "Real Food Summer School" program, which features recipes and cooking demos by celebrity chefs such as the Food Network's Bobby Flay. During its first season, about a million unique visitors visited the Real Food site, and more than 5000 visitors signed up to be a part of the Real Food online community. After Hellmann's aired the show, web searches for "Hellmann's" and related words jumped 50 percent on Yahoo!.

Although these and other Unilever digital efforts were highly successful in their own right, none was a purely digital campaign. Instead, each digital effort was carefully integrated with other media and marketing tactics, such as TV and print ads and broader PR initiatives. "Digital is [not] done in isolation," says Rob Master, Unilever's North American media director. "It's part of a broader campaign. In many cases now it's the centerpiece of a broader campaign. I think that's become a real integral part of how we use the Web, moving beyond just promoting web addresses in TV spots or print ads to really making them a critical part of the storytelling for the brands."

Unilever certainly has not abandoned traditional media in favour of digital—anything but. The world's number-two advertiser (behind only Procter & Gamble) still devotes a sizable majority of its huge US$7.8 billion global advertising and promotion spending to television and print media. But whereas its television budget increased by only 3 percent last year, its overall promotion budget soared 11 percent, with most of those extra dollars pouring into online and digital media. The real secret behind Unilever's digital success is its skilful blending of new media with old to build and extend customer involvement and the brand experience. "What I push for is to understand the space," says Master, "so when you're doing your [broader] campaigns, you make [digital] a part of it."

For example, Suave's "In the Motherhood" webisodes are only a small part of a much larger integrated communications campaign for the brand. It starts with television spots featuring real mothers sharing their experiences, including beauty experiences. "Is motherhood messing with your hair?" the commercials ask. "Say yes to beautiful without paying the price."

The TV ads pull customers onto two related websites. Suave.com confirms that "Motherhood Isn't Always Pretty" and lets visitors dig more deeply into the lives and trials of mothers featured in the TV ads. The other site, InTheMotherhood.com, presents entertaining and engaging webisodes created "For Moms. By Moms. About Moms" based on true-life experiences of motherhood. Each site is loaded with links to other Suave-related content.

Public relations has also played a role in the Suave campaign. When "In the Motherhood" was just starting, clips or even whole five-minute episodes aired on *The Ellen DeGeneres Show*, whose host called on moms to submit their real-life stories and to vote on the best entries. Thus, the entire Suave campaign—television, digital, and public relations—is all wonderfully integrated to create a "sisterhood" of moms and to deliver the brand's "Say yes to beautiful" positioning.

▶

OBJECTIVES

1   Define the five promotion mix tools for communicating customer value.

2   Discuss the changing communications landscape and the need for integrated marketing communications.

3   Outline the communication process and the steps in developing effective marketing communications.

4   Explain the methods for setting the promotion budget and factors that affect the design of the promotion mix.

The degree to which digital is integrated into the mainstream of Unilever's marketing is clear in how the efforts are managed. "We don't have a digital-media person in the media organization," Master says. "But all of us are very fluent in digital." Unlike many other advertisers today, Unilever doesn't hand its online promotional efforts off to digital shops. Instead, online efforts are handled by Unilever's mainstream advertising agencies, further helping to integrate digital with more traditional promotional tactics.

One powerful result of integrating digital with traditional media is what Master calls "superdistribution," the idea of getting web programs, most often video, picked up by other media—most often for free. One of the best examples is Dove's "Evolution" video created as part of its "Real Beauty" campaign. "Evolution" shows an ordinary young woman being transformed into a beautiful poster model with a lot of help from a make-up artist and photo-editing software. The end line: "It's no wonder our perception of beauty is distorted." "Evolution" has racked up an impressive 20 million views on YouTube and other video sites. But throw in viewership via everything from TV news and talk shows to classrooms and general word-of-web, and global viewership has exceeded 400 million. To put that in perspective, that level of distribution equates with some $150 million worth of free media coverage.

"Really, for us, superdistribution means [asking], 'Is the core of what you're doing big enough that it's going to be picked up in other channels such as PR, television, print, [and] radio . . . and be repurposed and replayed in those

Suave's TV and other ads pull customers onto two nicely integrated websites that create a "sisterhood" of moms and deliver the brand's "Say yes to beautiful" positioning in more detail.

other channels?'" Master says. "We used to repurpose things from television for the Internet. Now the ideas we have are so rich and creative . . . we're able to feed that into all these other channels from digital." Again, we're talking about *integrated* marketing communications.

In all, Unilever—Digital Marketer of the Year and all—understands that the growing shift to digital doesn't really change the fundamentals much. If anything, says Master, it means brand managers have to be more firmly grounded in what their brands are about to clearly and consistently define the brands across an exploding array of old and new media. But "almost inherent in what we do, I think, is the importance of storytelling for our brands," he says. "A 30-second ad is a story we pull together for consumers on TV. Digital is an extension of that storytelling in a typically longer format." The richness of the story and the resulting brand experience depend on everything communicating well together.[1]

Chapter Opening Discussion

Building good customer relationships calls for more than just developing a good product, pricing it attractively, and making it available to target customers. Companies must also *communicate* their value propositions to customers, and what they communicate should not be left to chance. All of their communications must be planned and blended into carefully integrated marketing communications programs. Good communication is a crucial element in a company's efforts to build profitable customer relationships.

1 THE PROMOTION MIX

Promotion mix (marketing communications mix)
The specific blend of promotion tools that the company uses to persuasively communicate customer value and build customer relationships.

A company's total **promotion mix**—also called its **marketing communications mix**—consists of the specific blend of advertising, public relations, personal selling, sales promotion, and direct-marketing tools that the company uses to persuasively communicate customer value and build customer relationships. Definitions of the five major promotion tools follow:[2]

- **Advertising:** Any paid form of nonpersonal presentation and promotion of ideas, goods, or services by an identified sponsor.

Advertising

Any paid form of nonpersonal presentation and promotion of ideas, goods, or services by an identified sponsor.

Sales promotion

Short-term incentives to encourage the purchase or sale of a product or service.

Personal selling

Personal presentation by the firm's sales force for the purpose of making sales and building customer relationships.

Public relations

Building good relations with the company's various publics by obtaining favourable publicity, building up a good corporate image, and handling or heading off unfavourable rumours, stories, and events.

Direct marketing

Direct connections with carefully targeted individual consumers to both obtain an immediate response and cultivate lasting customer relationships.

∙∙∙∙∙∙∙∙∙∙∙∙∙∙∙∙∙∙∙∙∙∙∙∙∙∙∙∙∙∙∙∙ 2

mymarketinglab

Glossary Flashcards of Key Terms

- **Sales promotion:** Short-term incentives to encourage the purchase or sale of a product or service.

- **Personal selling:** Personal presentation by the firm's sales force for the purpose of making sales and building customer relationships.

- **Public relations:** Building good relations with the company's various publics by obtaining favourable publicity, building up a good corporate image, and handling or heading off unfavourable rumours, stories, and events.

- **Direct marketing:** Direct connections with carefully targeted individual consumers to both obtain an immediate response and cultivate lasting customer relationships—the use of direct mail, the telephone, direct-response television, email, the Internet, and other tools to communicate directly with specific consumers.

Each category involves specific promotional tools used to communicate with consumers. For example, advertising includes broadcast, print, Internet, outdoor, and other forms. Sales promotion includes discounts, coupons, displays, and demonstrations. Personal selling includes sales presentations, trade shows, and incentive programs. Public relations includes press releases, sponsorships, special events, and webpages. And direct marketing includes catalogues, telephone marketing, kiosks, the Internet, mobile, and more.

At the same time, marketing communications goes beyond these specific promotion tools. The product's design, its price, the shape and colour of its package, and the stores that sell it *all* communicate something to buyers. Thus, although the promotion mix is the company's primary communications activity, the entire marketing mix—promotion *and* product, price, and place—must be coordinated for greatest communication impact.

INTEGRATED MARKETING COMMUNICATIONS

In past decades, marketers perfected the art of mass marketing—selling highly standardized products to masses of customers. In the process, they developed effective mass-media communications techniques to support these strategies. Large companies now routinely invest millions or even billions of dollars in television, magazine, or other mass-media advertising, reaching tens of millions of customers with a single ad. Today, however, marketing managers face some new marketing communications realities. Perhaps no other area of marketing is changing so profoundly as marketing communications, creating both exciting and scary times for marketing communicators.

The New Marketing Communications Landscape

Several major factors are changing the face of today's marketing communications. First, consumers are changing. In this digital, wireless age, they are better informed and more communications empowered. Rather than relying on marketer-supplied information, they can use the Internet and other technologies to seek out information on their own. More than that, they can more easily connect with other consumers to exchange brand-related information or even to create their own marketing messages.

The new marketing communications landscape: The digital age has spawned a host of new information and communication tools—from cellphones and iPods to the Internet and satellite and cable television systems.

Second, marketing strategies are changing. As mass markets have fragmented, marketers are shifting away from mass marketing. More and more, they are developing focused marketing programs designed to build closer relationships with customers in more narrowly defined micromarkets. Vast improvements in information technology are speeding the movement toward segmented marketing. Today's marketers can amass detailed customer information, keep closer track of customer needs, and tailor their offerings to narrowly target groups.

Finally, sweeping changes in communications technology are causing remarkable changes in the ways in which companies and customers communicate with each other. The digital age has spawned a host of new information and communication tools—from cellphones and iPods to satellite and cable television systems to the many faces of the Internet (email, social networks, brand websites, and so much more). The new communications technologies give companies exciting new media for interacting with targeted consumers. At the same time, they give consumers more control over the nature and timing of messages they choose to send and receive.

The Shifting Marketing Communications Model

The explosive developments in communications technology and changes in marketer and customer communication strategies have had a dramatic impact on marketing communications. Just as mass marketing once gave rise to a new generation of mass-media communications, the new digital media have given birth to a new marketing communications model.

Although television, magazines, and other mass media remain important, their dominance is declining. Advertisers are now adding a broad selection of more-specialized and highly targeted media to reach smaller customer segments with more-personalized, interactive messages. The new media range from specialty magazines, cable television channels, and video on demand (VOD) to Internet catalogues, email, podcasts, cellphones, and online social networks. In all, companies are doing less *broadcasting* and more *narrowcasting*.

Some advertising industry experts even predict a doom-and-gloom "chaos scenario," in which the old mass-media communications model will collapse entirely. They believe that marketers will increasingly abandon traditional mass media in favour of new digital technologies. These new technologies will let marketers "reach—and have a conversation with—small clusters of consumers who are consuming not what is force-fed to them, but exactly what they want."

> Maybe you'd better lean forward. . . . Consider something barely imaginable: a post-apocalyptic media world substantially devoid of brand advertising as we have long known it. It's a world in which . . . consumer engagement occurs without consumer interruption, in which listening trumps dictating. Perhaps you believe that the TV commercial and magazine spread—and radio spot and newspaper classified—are forever and immutable, like the planets orbiting the sun. Good for you. [But] the pillars of old media [will] soon be tumbling down. [Instead, imagine] a digital landscape in which marketing achieves hitherto unimaginable effectiveness, but in which traditional advertising's main goal will be to quickly, straightforwardly, and informatively draw you into a broader brand experience. Welcome to the chaos scenario.[3]

For example, just think about what's happening to television viewing these days. "Adjust your set," says one reporter, "television is changing as quickly as the channels. It's on cell phones. It's on digital music players. It's on almost anything with a screen. Shows can be seen at their regular times or when you want [with or without the commercials]. Some 'TV' programs aren't even on cable or network or satellite; they're being created just for Internet viewing."[4]

As mass-media costs rise, audiences shrink, ad clutter increases, and viewers use video on demand and TiVo-like systems to skip past disruptive television commercials; many skeptics even predict the demise of the old mass-media mainstays—30-second television commercials and glossy magazine advertisements. It will be a world, says a major "chaos scenario" proponent, "in which marketing—and even branding—are conducted without much reliance on [those traditional media] because nobody is much interested in seeing them and because soon they will be largely unnecessary."[5]

Thus, many large advertisers are shifting their advertising budgets away from network television in favour of more targeted, cost-effective, interactive, and engaging media. "The ad industry's plotline used to be a lot simpler: Audiences are splintering off in dozens of new directions, watching TV shows on iPods, watching movies on video game players, and listening to radio on the Internet," observes one analyst. So marketers must "start planning how to reach consumers in new and unexpected ways." Says the CEO and creative director of one large ad agency, "There's no medium we don't perform in."[6]

Rather than a "chaos scenario," however, other industry insiders see a more gradual shift to the new marketing communications model. They note that broadcast television and other mass media still capture the lion's share of the promotion budgets of most major marketing firms, a fact that isn't likely to change quickly. Although some may question the future of the 30-second spot, it's still very much in use today. Last year, more than 43 percent of advertising dollars were spent on national and local television commercials versus 7.6 percent on Internet advertising. "So if you think that TV is an aging dinosaur," says one media expert, "maybe you should think again." Another expert agrees: "Does TV work? Of course it does. It's just not the only game in town anymore."[7]

Thus, it seems likely that the new marketing communications model will consist of a shifting mix of both traditional mass media and a wide array of exciting, new, more-targeted, more-personalized media. The challenge for traditional advertisers is to bridge the "media divide" that too often separates traditional creative and media approaches from new interactive and digital ones. Many established Madison Avenue advertising agencies are struggling with this transition (see Real Marketing 14.1). Says one analyst, "advertisers need to look at old media and new media as just plain media. The real world demands that advertisers use a new cocktail of . . . media tools." Says another "The whole landscape has changed. . . . Marketers have to be savvy enough [to understand] what to do with all this stuff."[8]

The Need for *Integrated* Marketing Communications

The shift toward a richer mix of media and communication approaches poses a problem for marketers. Consumers today are bombarded by commercial messages from a broad range of sources. But consumers don't distinguish between message sources the way marketers do. In the consumer's mind, messages from different media and promotional approaches all become part of a single message about the company. Conflicting messages from these different sources can result in confused company images, brand positions, and customer relationships.

All too often, companies fail to integrate their various communications channels. The result is a hodgepodge of communications to consumers. Mass-media advertisements say one thing, while a price promotion sends a different signal, and a product label creates still another message. Company sales literature says something altogether different and the company's website seems out of sync with everything else.

The problem is that these communications often come from different parts of the company. Advertising messages are planned and implemented by the advertising department or an advertising agency. Personal selling communications are developed by sales management. Other company specialists are responsible for public relations, sales promotion events, Internet marketing, and other forms of marketing communications. However, whereas these companies have separated their communications tools, customers won't. Mixed communications from these sources will result in blurred consumer brand perceptions.

Integrated marketing communications (IMC)
Carefully integrating and coordinating the company's many communications channels to deliver a clear, consistent, and compelling message about the organization and its products.

Today, more companies are adopting the concept of **integrated marketing communications (IMC)**. Under this concept, as illustrated in Figure 14.1, the company carefully integrates its many communications channels to deliver a clear, consistent, and compelling message about the organization and its brands.

IMC calls for recognizing all touchpoints where the customer may encounter the company and its brands. Each *brand contact* will deliver a message, whether good, bad, or indifferent. Says one advertising executive, "the world has evolved to a place where

Real Marketing 14.1

Staying Relevant in a Shifting Advertising Universe: The Old Versus the New

In today's splintering advertising universe, advertising agency Saatchi & Saatchi is scrambling to stay relevant. As of now, the old-line Madison Avenue agency is one of the ad industry's brightest stars. It's still signing up blue-chip clients at an impressive rate and scooping up awards for its creative work. Yet Saatchi CEO Kevin Roberts worries that at a time when there are more new places than ever to stick ads—online, on cellphones, in all places digital and interactive—Saatchi may not be ready for this new universe.

Saatchi & Saatchi is a traditional Madison Avenue creative agency. It cut its teeth on developing creative ads for big-budget, mostly television and magazine campaigns. For example, its Canadian office was hired by Leon's to create a new campaign for the store's 100th anniversary in 2009. But the ad landscape is now shifting. Here is the universe as CEO Roberts sees it:

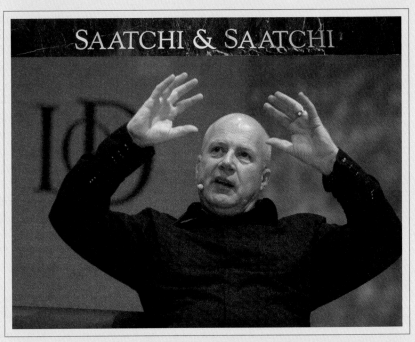

In today's splintered advertising universe, Saatchi & Saatchi's CEO Kevin Roberts is scrambling to keep his advertising agency relevant. To become a web-era player, "'We've got to reinvent and transform the way we work."

> TV viewers are using DVRs to blast through the very commercials that are Saatchi's bread and butter. Marketers are stampeding online, where Saatchi lacks the tools and talent to compete. Digital boutiques are proliferating, staffed with tech vets and Gen Y video artists dedicated to making ads for video sharing and social networking sites and whatever comes after them.

These days, Saatchi often finds itself outmanoeuvred by nimbler new-age rivals. Traditional agencies like Saatchi still have a long way to go to match the new-media prowess of today's digital, interactive, and media agencies. The traditional agencies didn't predict how dramatically the industry would go digital, and they must now struggle to catch up.

For most of the twentieth century the so-called creatives ruled the industry. They didn't worry about where or how an ad ran. They were about Big Ideas that would connect a brand emotionally with millions of consumers. Today, you might say, the Small Idea is ascendant. Ads are targeted at individuals or communities of consumers rather than at the masses. The media universe is now so fragmented—into blogs, social networks, television, magazines, and so on—that finding the right medium is fast becoming more important than the creative message itself. And the people best equipped to deal with this new world are not the big creative agencies. Instead, it is the direct marketers who are perfect for the Web—the folks who've always interacted directly with individual consumers. And as the media fragment and reform, media buyers—once consigned by the creative agencies to back-office obscurity—are playing a much bigger role in helping clients figure out where they should spend their advertising budgets. More and more, these media buyers are steering advertisers into new digital and direct media, a powerful threat to the venerable 30-second TV spot that has always been at the heart and soul of traditional creative agencies like Saatchi.

Saatchi's CEO still believes in the power of creative—the emotional connection to the customer. But the truth is that creative and media feed off of one another, and media is shifting into a new realm that Saatchi has yet to master. Most

►

clients still believe in creating an emotional bond with consumers. But in today's fragmented media universe, advertisers are looking for agencies that can help them create an integrated customer experience across multiple media, including both the traditional mass media that Saatchi knows so well and the new digital and direct media that remain a bit beyond Saatchi's comfort zone.

To fill the widening gap between traditional and digital, Saatchi is now hiring its own corps of web ad makers, direct marketers, and digital media specialists. In fact, a while back, Saatchi tried to buy an existing digital agency, Blast Radius, known for building websites and creating passionate online communities for with-it companies such as Nike and game maker Electronic Arts. However, in a deeply troubling development, Blast Radius declined Saatchi's proposal. Instead, it merged with Wunderman, one of the world's largest direct-marketing agencies. Said Blast Radius's CEO at the time, "As an interactive agency . . . we saw a big chasm between us . . . versus the more traditional agencies. The traditional agencies were still very much about [messages and creativity]."

Interestingly, Publicis Groupe, the mammoth holding company that owns Saatchi & Saatchi along with dozens of other communications agencies, appears not to be counting on Saatchi and its other traditional agencies to lead the digital transformation. Instead, Publicis invested heavily to purchase an existing interactive agency, Digitas, and to bankroll the creation of another, Droga5. Publicis's CEO sees these interactive agencies as defining the very future of both his company and the entire advertising industry. His goal is to make Publicis the industry's premier digital-marketing outfit—to create a blueprint of the agency of the future. "It's not about cosmetic changes," he says, "it's about profound and unsettling changes."

Such actions and thinking have created an undercurrent of near-panic at some traditional creative agencies, including large and successful ones like Saatchi & Saatchi. The question is clear: With digital and direct agencies muscling onto Saatchi's turf, is it "too late for an old-school creative shop to transform itself into a web-era player"? Kevin Roberts doesn't think so. But it won't be an easy transition for Saatchi and the other traditional agencies. "We've got to reinvent and transform the way we work," he says.

Sources: Excerpts and quotes adapted from Burt Helm, "Struggles of a Mad Man," *BusinessWeek*, December 3, 2007, pp. 44–49; and Linda Tischler, "A Mad Man Gets His Head Together," *Fast Company*, January 2008, pp. 90–97.

brands that need to speak to their audience have to understand that everything they do is media."[9] The company wants to deliver a consistent and positive message with each contact. IMC leads to a total marketing communications strategy aimed at building strong customer relationships by showing how the company and its products can help customers solve their problems.

IMC ties together all of the company's messages and images. The company's television and print advertisements have the same message, look, and feel as its email and personal

Figure 14.1 Integrated Marketing Communications

selling communications. And its public relations materials project the same image as its website or social network presence. Often, different media play unique roles in attracting, informing, and persuading consumers, and these roles must be carefully coordinated under the overall marketing communications plan.

For example, Nikon used a carefully coordinated mix of media in a recent campaign designed to demonstrate that even ordinary people can take amazing digital pictures with its Nikon D40 camera. To prove the point, Nikon gave 200 of the cameras to people in Georgetown, South Carolina, and then featured the people and their photos in TV and print ads. The ads delivered the brand message and referred consumers to a specially constructed supporting website where they could explore the stories and people behind the pictures, learn more about the Nikon D40 camera, and find out where to buy one. The ads, the website, the supporting PR, and even the event itself were carefully integrated to deliver a unified message.

In the past, no one person or department was responsible for thinking through the communications roles of the various promotion tools and coordinating the promotion mix. To help implement integrated marketing communications, some companies appoint a marketing communications director who has overall responsibility for the company's communications efforts. This helps to produce better communications consistency and greater sales impact. It places the responsibility in someone's hands—where none existed before—to unify the company's image as it is shaped by thousands of company activities.

3 | A VIEW OF THE COMMUNICATION PROCESS

Integrated marketing communications involve identifying the target audience and shaping a well-coordinated promotional program to obtain the desired audience response. Too often, marketing communications focus on immediate awareness, image, or preference goals in the target market. But this approach to communication is too shortsighted. Today, marketers are moving toward viewing communications as *managing the customer relationship over time.*

Because customers differ, communications programs need to be developed for specific segments, niches, and even individuals. And, given the new interactive communications technologies, companies must ask not only, "How can we reach our customers?" but also, "How can we find ways to let our customers reach us?"

Thus, the communications process should start with an audit of all the potential touchpoints that target customers may have with the company and its brands. For example, someone purchasing a new kitchen appliance may talk to others, see television ads, read articles and ads in newspapers and magazines, visit various websites for prices and reviews, and check out appliances in one or more stores. The marketer needs to assess what influence each of these communications experiences will have at different stages of the buying process. This understanding will help marketers allocate their communications dollars more efficiently and effectively.

To communicate effectively, marketers need to understand how communication works. Communication involves the nine elements shown in Figure 14.2. Two of these elements are the major parties in a communication—the *sender* and the *receiver.* Another two are the major communication tools—the *message* and the *media.* Four more are major communication functions—*encoding, decoding, response,* and *feedback.* The last element is *noise* in the system. Definitions of these elements follow and are applied to a McDonald's "I'm lovin' it" television commercial.

- Sender: The *party sending the message* to another party—here, McDonald's.

- Encoding: The process of *putting thought into symbolic form*—McDonald's advertising agency assembles words, sounds, and illustrations into an advertisement that will convey the intended message.

- Message: The *set of symbols* that the sender transmits—the actual McDonald's ad.

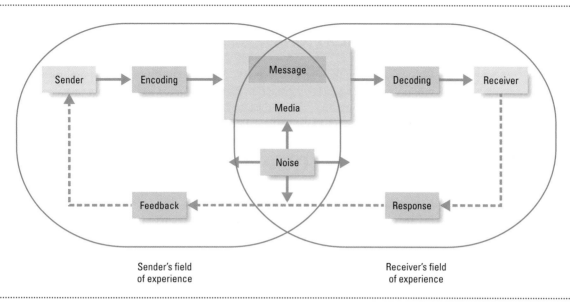

Figure 14.2 Elements in the communication process

- Media: The *communications channels* through which the message moves from sender to receiver—in this case, television and the specific television programs that McDonald's selects.

- Decoding: The process by which the receiver *assigns meaning to the symbols* encoded by the sender—a consumer watches the McDonald's ad and interprets the words and images it contains.

- Receiver: The *party receiving the message* sent by another party—the customer who watches the McDonald's ad.

- Response: The *reactions of the receiver* after being exposed to the message—any of hundreds of possible responses, such as the consumer likes McDonald's better, is more likely to eat at McDonald's next time, hums the "I'm lovin' it" jingle, or does nothing.

- Feedback: The part of the *receiver's response communicated back to the sender*—McDonald's research shows that consumers are struck by and remember the ad, or consumers write or call McDonald's praising or criticizing the ad or products.

- Noise: The *unplanned static or distortion* during the communication process, which results in the receiver getting a different message than the one the sender sent— the consumer is distracted while watching the commercial and misses its key points.

For a message to be effective, the sender's encoding process must mesh with the receiver's decoding process. The best messages consist of words and other symbols that are familiar to the receiver. The more the sender's field of experience overlaps with that of the receiver, the more effective the message is likely to be. Marketing communicators may not always *share* their consumer's field of experience. For example, an advertising copywriter from one socioeconomic stratum might create ads for consumers from another stratum— say, wealthy business owners. However, to communicate effectively, the marketing communicator must *understand* the consumer's field of experience.

This model points out several key factors in good communication. Senders need to know what audiences they wish to reach and what responses they want. They must be good at encoding messages that take into account how the target audience will decode them. They must send messages through media that reach target audiences, and they must develop feedback channels so that they can assess the audience's response to the message.

Steps in Developing Effective Marketing Communications

We now examine the steps in developing an effective integrated communications and promotion program. Marketers must do the following: *identify the target audience, determine the communication objectives, design a message, choose the media through which to send the message, select the message source,* and *collect feedback.*

Identifying the Target Audience

A marketing communicator starts with a clear target audience in mind. The audience may be current users or potential buyers, those who make the buying decision or those who influence it. The audience may be individuals, groups, special publics, or the general public. The target audience will heavily affect the communicator's decisions on *what* will be said, *how* it will be said, *when* it will be said, *where* it will be said, and *who* will say it.

Determining the Communication Objectives

Buyer-readiness stages
The stages consumers normally pass through on their way to purchase, including awareness, knowledge, liking, preference, conviction, and purchase.

Once the target audience has been defined, marketers must decide what response they seek. Of course, in many cases, they will seek a *purchase* response. But purchase may only be the result of a long consumer decision-making process. The marketing communicator needs to know where the target audience now stands and to what stage it needs to be moved. The target audience may be in any of six **buyer-readiness stages**, the stages consumers normally pass through on their way to making a purchase. These stages include *awareness, knowledge, liking, preference, conviction,* and *purchase* (see Figure 14.3).

The marketing communicator's target market may be totally unaware of the product, know only its name, or know only a few things about it. The communicator must first build *awareness* and *knowledge*. For example, when Apple launched the iPhone in mid-2007, it first ran a teaser ad during the Oscars to create initial awareness and curiosity. The Oscars teaser commercial featured clips of characters from famous movies and television shows answering the phone with "Hello" (to check it out, go to YouTube and search "iPhone Oscars Teaser"). At the end came a rotating image of the new iPhone with only the simple text "Hello" and "Coming in June."

Similarly, as in a business-to-business context, IBM used teaser ads to pique interest in its new BladeCenter server technology, which integrates servers, storage, and networking applications into one system, consolidating space and eliminating cables. BladeCenter print ads in IT magazines and videos released through YouTube made no mention at all of either IBM or BladeCenter. Instead, they showed a large, mysterious ball of cables and drove curious users to a website for answers.

Assuming that target consumers *know* about the product, how do they *feel* about it? Once potential buyers knew about the iPhone, Apple's marketers wanted to move them through successively stronger stages of feelings toward the innovative phone. These stages included *liking* (feeling favourable about the phone), *preference* (preferring the iPhone to other cellphone brands), and *conviction* (believing that the iPhone is the best cellphone for them). Apple marketers used a combination of the promotion mix tools to create positive

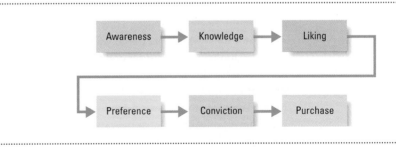

Figure 14.3 Buyer-readiness stages

Moving customers through the buyer-readiness stages: IBM used teaser ads to pique interest in its new BladeCenter server technology. The ads never mentioned IBM Blade-Center, instead driving curious users to a website for answers.

feelings and conviction. Advertising built an emotional brand connection and illustrated the iPhone's design and features. Press releases and other public relations activities helped build anticipation for the release of the iPhone. And a packed website informed potential buyers about technical specs, FAQs, software updates, and rate plans with partner AT&T.

Finally, some members of the target market might be convinced about the product but may not quite get around to making the *purchase*. Potential iPhone buyers might have decided to wait for more information or for the price to drop. The communicator must lead these consumers to take the final step. Actions might include offering special promotional prices, add-ons, rebates, or premiums. Apple might send out emails to customers of other Apple products urging them to add the eye-catching iPhone to their collection of Apple goodies.

Of course, marketing communications alone could not create positive feelings and purchases for the iPhone. The cellphone itself must provide superior value for the customer. In fact, outstanding marketing communications can actually speed the demise of a poor product. The more quickly potential buyers learn about the poor product, the more quickly they become aware of its faults. Thus, good marketing communication calls for "good deeds followed by good words."

Designing a Message

Having defined the desired audience response, the communicator turns to developing an effective message. Ideally, the message should get *attention*, hold *interest*, arouse *desire*, and obtain *action* (a framework known as the *AIDA model*). In practice, few messages take the consumer all the way from awareness to purchase, but the AIDA framework suggests the desirable qualities of a good message.

When putting the message together, the marketing communicator must decide what to say (*message content*) and how to say it (*message structure* and *format*).

Message Content

The marketer has to figure out an appeal or theme that will produce the desired response. There are three types of appeals: rational, emotional, and moral. *Rational appeals* relate to the audience's self-interest. They show that the product will produce the desired benefits. Examples are messages showing a product's quality, economy, value, or performance. Thus, in one ad, natural foods marketer Kashi proclaims "7 whole grains on a mission" and asks consumers "Why use fake flavours and additives when you can use lemongrass and coconut?" And a Weight Watchers ad states this simple fact: "The diet secret to end all diet secrets is that there is no diet secret."

Emotional appeals attempt to stir up either negative or positive emotions that can motivate purchase. Communicators may use emotional appeals ranging from love, joy, and humour to fear and guilt. Advocates of emotional messages claim that they attract more attention and create more belief in the sponsor and brand. "Brain science has proved [that] consumers feel before they think, and feelings happen fast," says one expert. "Real persuasion is emotional in nature."[10] Thus, Michelin sells tires using mildly fear-inducing appeals, showing families riding in cars and telling parents "Michelin: Because so much is riding on your tires." Or take the controversial TV ad created for Couche-Tard, a convenience store chain in the province of Quebec. The chain markets a frozen beverage similar to a slushie, called Sloche, primarily targeting youth. The brand has gained much publicity in the province due to its humorous and often controversial marketing campaigns. From the slogans on its cups to the drink names (which range from a traditional bubble gum flavour to the less than appetizing liposuction or dirty melted snow) to its bizarre website and offbeat TV ads, Sloche is celebrating its tenth anniversary with a bang: TV ads revealing that clowns actually bleed confetti and balloons! Check out the videos link at www.sloche.com to view the two TV ads. Offensive to some people? Sure. But wildly successful in attracting and entertaining its target demographic.

These days, it seems as though every company is using humour in its advertising. For example, 13 of the top 15 most popular ads in *USA Today's* Ad Meter consumer rankings of last year's Super Bowl advertisements used humour. Properly used, humour can capture attention, make people feel good, and give a brand personality.

Ad message content: United Way uses moral appeals—urging people to "Live United. Make a difference. Help create opportunities for everyone in your community."

However, advertisers must be careful when using humour. Used poorly, it can detract from comprehension, wear out its welcome fast, overshadow the product, or even irritate consumers.

Moral appeals are directed to the audience's sense of what is "right" and "proper." They are often used to urge people to support social causes such as a cleaner environment or aid to the disadvantaged. For example, the United Way's "Live United" campaign urges people to give back to their communities—to "Live United. Make a difference. Help create opportunities for everyone in your community." An EarthShare ad urges environmental involvement by reminding people that "Every decision we make has consequences. We choose the world we live in, so let's make the right choices. We live in the house we all build."

Message Structure

Marketers must also decide how to handle three message structure issues. The first is whether to draw a conclusion or leave it to the audience. Research suggests that in many cases the advertiser is better off asking questions and letting buyers come to their own conclusions. The second message structure issue is whether to present the strongest arguments first or last. Presenting them first gets strong attention but may lead to an anticlimactic ending.

The third message structure issue is whether to present a one-sided argument (mentioning only the product's strengths) or a two-sided argument (touting the product's strengths while also admitting its shortcomings). Usually, a one-sided argument is more effective in sales presentations—except when audiences are highly educated or likely to hear opposing claims, or when the communicator has a negative association to overcome.

Message format: To attract attention, advertisers can use novelty and contrast, eye-catching pictures and headlines, and distinctive formats, as in this Molson Canadian billboard ad.

In this spirit, Heinz ran the message "Heinz Ketchup is slow good" and Buckley's Mixture built its entire business around "It tastes awful. And it works." In such cases, two-sided messages can enhance the advertiser's credibility and make buyers more resistant to competitor attacks.

Message Format

The marketing communicator also needs a strong *format* for the message. In a print ad, the communicator has to decide on the headline, copy, illustration, and colour. To attract attention, advertisers can use novelty and contrast; eye-catching pictures and headlines; distinctive formats; message size and position; and colour, shape, and movement. If the message is to be carried over the radio, the communicator has to choose words, sounds, and voices. The "sound" of an ad promoting banking services should be different from one promoting an iPod.

If the message is to be carried on television or in person, then all these elements plus body language have to be planned. Presenters plan every detail—their facial expressions, gestures, dress, posture, and hairstyles. If the message is carried on the product or its package, the communicator has to watch texture, scent, colour, size, and shape. For example, one study revealed that people make subconscious judgments about an item within 90 seconds of initial viewing and that up to 90 percent of that assessment is based on colour. Another study suggests that colour increases brand recognition by up to 80 percent. Thus, in designing effective marketing communications, marketers must consider colour and other seemingly unimportant details carefully.[11]

Choosing Media

The communicator must now select *channels of communication*. There are two broad types of communication channels—*personal* and *nonpersonal*.

Personal Communication Channels

Personal communication channels

Channels through which two or more people communicate directly with each other, including face to face, on the phone, through mail or email, or even through an Internet "chat."

Word-of-mouth influence

Personal communication about a product between target buyers and neighbours, friends, family members, or associates.

In **personal communication channels**, two or more people communicate directly with each other. They might communicate face to face, on the phone, through mail or email, or even through an Internet "chat." Personal communication channels are effective because they allow for personal addressing and feedback.

Some personal communication channels are controlled directly by the company. For example, company salespeople contact target buyers. But other personal communications about the product may reach buyers through channels not directly controlled by the company. These channels might include independent experts—consumer advocates, online buying guides, and others—making statements to buyers. Or they might be neighbours, friends, family members, or associates talking to target buyers. This last channel, **word-of-mouth influence**, has considerable effect in many product areas.

Personal influence carries great weight for products that are expensive, risky, or highly visible. Consider the power of simple customer reviews on Amazon.com:

It doesn't matter how loud or often you tell consumers your "truth," few today are buying a big-ticket item before they know what existing users have to say about the product. This is a low-trust world. That's why "recommendation by a relative or friend" comes out on top in just about every survey of purchasing influences. A recent study found that more than 90 percent of customers trust "recommendations from consumers," whereas trust in ads runs from a high of about 40 percent to less than 10 percent. It's also a major reason for Amazon's success in growing sales per customer. Who hasn't made an Amazon purchase based on another customer's review or the "Customers who bought this also bought. . ." section? And it explains what a recent Shop.org survey found—that 96 percent of retailers find ratings and reviews to be an effective tactic in lifting online sales.[12]

Companies can take steps to put personal communication channels to work for them. For example, they can create *opinion leaders* for their brands—people whose opinions are sought by others—by supplying influencers with the product on attractive terms or by educating them so that they can inform others. **Buzz marketing** involves cultivating opinion leaders and getting them to spread information about a product or service to others in their communities. Consider BzzAgent, a Boston marketing firm that creates word-of-mouth campaigns for many of North America's best-known companies:

> BzzAgent has assembled a volunteer army of over 600 000 natural-born buzzers that channel their chatter toward products and services they deem authentically worth talking about. Last year, more than 34 million consumers were reached through 119 word-of-mouth programs. "Our goal is to find a way to capture honest word of mouth," says David Balter, BzzAgent's founder, "and to build a network that will turn passionate customers into brand evangelists." Once a client signs on, BzzAgent searches its database for "agents" matching the demographic and psychographic profile of target customers of the product or service. Selected volunteers receive a sample product and a training manual for buzz-creating strategies. These volunteers aren't just chatty teenagers on cellphones. Some 65 percent are over 25, 60 percent are women, and 40 percent are in managerial positions or above. The average campaign size uses about 10 000 agents, creating some 600 000 communications at an average cost of about US$300 000. BzzAgent has buzzed products as diverse as Estée Lauder facial masks, *TV Guide*, and Canadian Club whisky. The service's appeal is its authenticity. "What I like is that BzzAgents aren't scripted," says Steve Cook, vice-president of worldwide strategic marketing at Coca-Cola. "[The company tells its agents,] 'Here's the information; if you believe in it, say whatever you think.' It's . . . genuine."[13]

Buzz marketing
Cultivating opinion leaders and getting them to spread information about a product or service to others in their communities.

Nonpersonal communication channels
Media that carry messages without personal contact or feedback, including major media, atmospheres, and events.

Nonpersonal Communication Channels

Nonpersonal communication channels are media that carry messages without personal contact or feedback. They include major media, atmospheres, and events. *Major media* include print media (newspapers, magazines, direct mail), broadcast media (radio, television), display media (billboards, signs, posters), and online media (email, company websites, online social and sharing networks). *Atmospheres* are designed environments that create or reinforce the buyer's leanings toward buying a product. Thus, lawyers' offices and banks are designed to communicate confidence and other qualities that might be valued by clients. *Events* are staged occurrences that communicate messages to target audiences. For example, public relations departments arrange press conferences, grand openings, shows and exhibits, public tours, and other events.

Nonpersonal communication affects buyers directly. In addition, using mass media often affects buyers indirectly by causing more personal communication. Communications first flow from television, magazines, and other mass media to opinion leaders and then from these opinion leaders to others. Thus, opinion leaders step between the mass media and their audiences and carry messages to people who are less exposed to media. This suggests that mass communicators should aim their messages directly at opinion leaders, letting them carry the message to others. Interestingly,

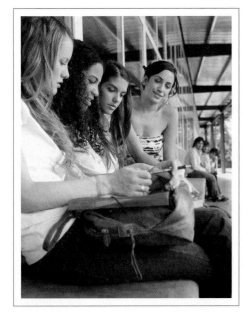

Personal communications channels: BzzAgent's army of 600 000 natural-born buzzers creates word-of-mouth chatter for many of the world's best-known brands.

Marketers hire celebrity endorsers to deliver their messages. Here, Sidney Crosby promotes Reebok's Rbk SC87 clothing line.

marketers often use nonpersonal communication channels to replace or stimulate personal communications by embedding consumer endorsements or word-of-mouth testimonials in their ads and other promotions.

Selecting the Message Source

In either personal or nonpersonal communication, the message's impact on the target audience is also affected by how the audience views the communicator. Messages delivered by highly credible sources are more persuasive. Thus, many food companies promote to doctors, dentists, and other health care providers to motivate these professionals to recommend their products to patients. And marketers hire celebrity endorsers—well-known athletes, actors, musicians, and even cartoon characters—to deliver their messages. Canadian-born NBA star Steve Nash only promotes products he deems socially responsible (such as Clearly Canadian bottled water, which funds self-sustainable pure water sources in developing countries) and he donates all endorsement earnings to the Steve Nash Foundation benefiting underprivileged kids. Mike Holmes, star of HGTV Canada's *Holmes on Homes*, signed a multi-year deal with Nestlé Canada to promote Nescafé instant coffee. And six-time Olympic speed-skating medallist Cindy Klassen signed a five-year, $1 million endorsement deal with MTS Allstream, Canada's oldest coast-to-coast provider of communications solutions.[14]

But companies must be careful when selecting celebrities to represent their brands. Picking the wrong spokesperson can result in embarrassment and a tarnished image. Nike, Coca-Cola, and Kraft faced embarrassment when NFL-quarterback Michael Vick was convicted in an illegal dog fighting case. And Alexander Keith's beer, made by Labatt Breweries, had to look for a new spokesperson after child pornography charges were filed against Robert Norman Smith, the actor who played the cantankerous, outlandish, kilt-clad Scotsman who sang the praises of a beer he called "the pride of Nova Scotia." Smith's character was the centrepiece for the beer's television advertising campaign for more than three years, and some say he had become a Canadian icon. The ads even made it to the Super Bowl and were credited with pushing Alexander Keith's into the number-one spot in the Canadian specialty beer market.[15] "Arranged marriages between brands and celebrities are inherently risky," notes an expert. "Today it's standard practice to sign a celeb only after an extensive background check. But accidents still happen."[16]

Collecting Feedback

After sending the message, the communicator must research its effect on the target audience. This involves asking the target audience members whether they remember the message, how many times they saw it, what points they recall, how they felt about the message, and their past and present attitudes toward the product and company. The communicator would also like to measure behaviour resulting from the message—how many people bought a product, talked to others about it, or visited the store.

Feedback on marketing communications may suggest changes in the promotion program or in the product offer itself. For example, Air Canada uses television and newspaper advertising to inform area consumers about the airline, its routes, and its fares. Suppose feedback research shows that 80 percent of all flyers in an area recall seeing the airline's ads and are aware of its flights and prices. Sixty percent of these aware flyers have flown

Air Canada, but only 20 percent of those who tried it were satisfied. These results suggest that although promotion is creating *awareness*, the airline isn't giving consumers the *satisfaction* they expect. Therefore, Air Canada needs to improve its service while staying with the successful communication program. In contrast, suppose the research shows that only 40 percent of area consumers are aware of the airline, only 30 percent of those who are aware have tried it, but 80 percent of those who have tried it return. In this case, Air Canada needs to strengthen its promotion program to take advantage of its power to create customer satisfaction.

4   SETTING THE TOTAL PROMOTION BUDGET AND MIX

We have looked at the steps in planning and sending communications to a target audience. But how does the company decide on the total *promotion budget* and its division among the major promotional tools to create the *promotion mix*? By what process does it blend the tools to create integrated marketing communications? We now look at these questions.

Setting the Total Promotion Budget

One of the hardest marketing decisions facing a company is how much to spend on promotion. John Wanamaker, the department store magnate, once said, "I know that half of my advertising is wasted, but I don't know which half. I spent $2 million for advertising, and I don't know if that is half enough or twice too much." Thus, it is not surprising that industries and companies vary widely in how much they spend on promotion. Promotion spending may be 10 to 12 percent of sales for consumer packaged goods, 14 percent for cosmetics, and only 1 percent for industrial machinery products. Within a given industry, both low and high spenders can be found.[17]

How does a company decide on its promotion budget? Here, we look at four common methods used to set the total budget for advertising: the affordable method, the *percentage-of-sales method*, the *competitive-parity method*, and the *objective-and-task method*.[18]

Affordable Method

Affordable method
Setting the promotion budget at the level management thinks the company can afford.

Some companies use the **affordable method**: They set the promotion budget at the level they think the company can afford. Small businesses often use this method, reasoning that the company cannot spend more on advertising than it has. They start with total revenues, deduct operating expenses and capital outlays, and then devote some portion of the remaining funds to advertising.

Unfortunately, this method of setting budgets completely ignores the effects of promotion on sales. It tends to place promotion last among spending priorities, even in situations in which advertising is critical to the firm's success. It leads to an uncertain annual promotion budget, which makes long-range market planning difficult. Although the affordable method can result in overspending on advertising, it more often results in underspending.

Percentage-of-Sales Method

Percentage-of-sales method
Setting the promotion budget at a certain percentage of current or forecasted sales or as a percentage of the unit sales price.

Other companies use the **percentage-of-sales method**, setting their promotion budget at a certain percentage of current or forecasted sales. Or they budget a percentage of the unit sales price. The percentage-of-sales method has advantages. It is simple to use and helps management think about the relationships between promotion spending, selling price, and profit per unit.

Despite these claimed advantages, however, the percentage-of-sales method has little to justify it. It wrongly views sales as the *cause* of promotion rather than as the *result*. Although studies have found a positive correlation between promotional spending and brand strength, this relationship often turns out to be effect and cause, not cause and effect. Stronger brands with higher sales can afford the biggest ad budgets.

Thus, the percentage-of-sales budget is based on availability of funds rather than on opportunities. It may prevent the increased spending sometimes needed to turn falling sales around. Because the budget varies with year-to-year sales, long-range planning is difficult. Finally, the method does not provide any basis for choosing a *specific* percentage, except what has been done in the past or what competitors are doing.

Competitive-Parity Method

Competitive-parity method
Setting the promotion budget to match competitors' outlays.

Still other companies use the **competitive-parity method**, setting their promotion budgets to match competitors' outlays. They monitor competitors' advertising or get industry promotion spending estimates from publications or trade associations, and then set their budgets based on the industry average.

Two arguments support this method. First, competitors' budgets represent the collective wisdom of the industry. Second, spending what competitors spend helps prevent promotion wars. Unfortunately, neither argument is valid. There are no grounds for believing that the competition has a better idea of what a company should be spending on promotion than does the company itself. Companies differ greatly, and each has its own special promotion needs. Finally, there is no evidence that budgets based on competitive parity prevent promotion wars.

Objective-and-Task Method

Objective-and-task method
Developing the promotion budget by (1) defining specific objectives, (2) determining the tasks that must be performed to achieve these objectives, and (3) estimating the costs of performing these tasks. The sum of these costs is the proposed promotion budget.

The most logical budget-setting method is the **objective-and-task method**, whereby the company sets its promotion budget based on what it wants to accomplish with promotion. This budgeting method entails (1) defining specific promotion objectives, (2) determining the tasks needed to achieve these objectives, and (3) estimating the costs of performing these tasks. The sum of these costs is the proposed promotion budget.

The advantage of the objective-and-task method is that it forces management to spell out its assumptions about the relationship between dollars spent and promotion results. But it is also the most difficult method to use. Often, it is hard to figure out which specific tasks will achieve stated objectives. For example, suppose Sony wants 95 percent awareness for its latest camcorder model during the six-month introductory period. What specific advertising messages and media schedules should Sony use to attain this objective? How much would these messages and media schedules cost? Sony management must consider such questions, even though they are hard to answer.

Shaping the Overall Promotion Mix

The concept of integrated marketing communications suggests that the company must blend the promotion tools carefully into a coordinated *promotion mix*. But how does the company determine what mix of promotion tools it will use? Companies within the same industry differ greatly in the design of their promotion mixes. For example, Mary Kay spends most of its promotion funds on personal selling and direct marketing, whereas competitor CoverGirl spends heavily on consumer advertising. We now look at factors that influence the marketer's choice of promotion tools.

The Nature of Each Promotion Tool

Each promotion tool has unique characteristics and costs. Marketers must understand these characteristics in shaping the promotion mix.

Advertising Advertising can reach masses of geographically dispersed buyers at a low cost per exposure, and it enables the seller to repeat a message many times. For example, television advertising can reach huge audiences. On an average day, 78 percent of Canadians view television at least once and the average weekly viewing time for Canadians is 23 hours and 11 minutes. An estimated 3.5 million Canadians and 8 million Americans tuned in to watch game seven of the 2009 Stanley Cup final, about 3 million Canadians watched the series finale of *Corner Gas*, and 28.8 million fans (including 2.6 million in Canada) tuned in to watch the season finale of the eighth season of *American Idol*. For companies that want to reach a mass audience, TV is the place to be.[19]

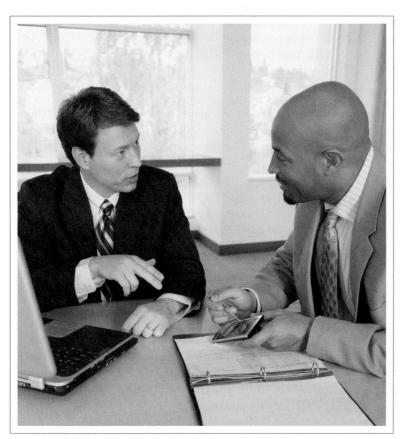

With personal selling, the customer feels a greater need to listen and respond, even if the response is a polite "No, thank you."

Beyond its reach, large-scale advertising says something positive about the seller's size, popularity, and success. Because of advertising's public nature, consumers tend to view advertised products as more legitimate. Advertising is also very expressive—it allows the company to dramatize its products through the artful use of visuals, print, sound, and colour. On the one hand, advertising can be used to build up a long-term image for a product (such as Coca-Cola ads). On the other hand, advertising can trigger quick sales (as when Shoppers Drug Mart advertises weekend specials).

Advertising also has some shortcomings. Although it reaches many people quickly, advertising is impersonal and cannot be as directly persuasive as can company salespeople. For the most part, advertising can carry on only a one-way communication with the audience, and the audience does not feel that it has to pay attention or respond. In addition, advertising can be very costly. Although some advertising forms, such as newspaper and radio advertising, can be done on smaller budgets, other forms, such as network TV advertising, require very large budgets.

Personal Selling   Personal selling is the most effective tool at certain stages of the buying process, particularly in building up buyers' preferences, convictions, and actions. It involves personal interaction between two or more people, so each person can observe the other's needs and characteristics and make quick adjustments. Personal selling also allows all kinds of customer relationships to spring up, ranging from matter-of-fact selling relationships to personal friendships. An effective salesperson keeps the customer's interests at heart to build a long-term relationship by solving customer problems. Finally, with personal selling, the buyer usually feels a greater need to listen and respond, even if the response is a polite "No, thank you."

These unique qualities come at a cost, however. A sales force requires a longer-term commitment than does advertising—advertising can be turned on and off, but sales force size is harder to change. Personal selling is also the company's most expensive promotion tool, costing companies $400 on average per sales call. In some industries, the average cost of a sales call reaches $550.[20] North American firms spend up to three times as much on personal selling as they do on advertising.

Sales Promotion   Sales promotion includes a wide assortment of tools—coupons, contests, cents-off deals, premiums, and others—all of which have many unique qualities. They attract consumer attention, offer strong incentives to purchase, and can be used to dramatize product offers and to boost sagging sales. Sales promotions invite and reward quick response—whereas advertising says, "Buy our product," sales promotion says, "Buy it now." Sales promotion effects are often short-lived, however, and often are not as effective as advertising or personal selling in building long-run brand preference and customer relationships.

Public Relations   Public relations is very believable—news stories, features, sponsorships, and events seem more real and believable to readers than ads do. Public relations can also reach many prospects who avoid salespeople and advertisements—the message gets to the buyers as "news" rather than as a sales-directed communication. And, as with advertising, public relations can dramatize a company or product. Marketers tend to underuse public relations or to use it as an afterthought. Yet a well-thought-out public relations campaign used with other promotion mix elements can be very effective and economical.

Direct Marketing Although there are many forms of direct marketing—direct mail and catalogues, telephone marketing, online marketing, and others—they all share four distinctive characteristics. Direct marketing is *less public*: The message is normally directed to a specific person. Direct marketing is *immediate* and *customized*: Messages can be prepared very quickly and can be tailored to appeal to specific consumers. Finally, direct marketing is *interactive*: It allows a dialogue between the marketing team and the consumer, and messages can be altered depending on the consumer's response. Thus, direct marketing is well suited to highly targeted marketing efforts and to building one-to-one customer relationships.

Promotion Mix Strategies

Push strategy

A promotion strategy that calls for using the sales force and trade promotion to push the product through channels. The producer promotes the product to channel members who in turn promote it to final consumers.

Pull strategy

A promotion strategy that calls for spending a lot on advertising and consumer promotion to induce final consumers to buy the product, creating a demand vacuum that "pulls" the product through the channel.

Marketers can choose from two basic promotion mix strategies—*push* promotion or *pull* promotion. Figure 14.4 contrasts the two strategies. The relative emphasis on the specific promotion tools differs for push and pull strategies. A **push strategy** involves "pushing" the product through marketing channels to final consumers. The producer directs its marketing activities (primarily personal selling and trade promotion) toward channel members to induce them to carry the product and promote it to final consumers.

Using a **pull strategy**, the producer directs its marketing activities (primarily advertising and consumer promotion) toward final consumers to induce them to buy the product. If the pull strategy is effective, consumers will then demand the product from channel members, who will in turn demand it from producers. Thus, under a pull strategy, consumer demand "pulls" the product through the channels.

Some industrial-goods companies use only push strategies; some direct-marketing companies use only pull strategies. However, most large companies use some combination of both. For example, Kraft uses mass-media advertising and consumer promotions to pull its products, and a large sales force and trade promotions to push its products through the channels. In recent years, consumer goods companies have been decreasing the pull portions of their mixes in favour of more push. This has caused concern that they may be driving short-run sales at the expense of long-term brand equity (see Real Marketing 14.2).

Companies consider many factors when designing their promotion mix strategies, including *type of product/market* and the *product life-cycle stage*. For example, the importance of different promotion tools varies between consumer and business markets.

Figure 14.4 Push versus pull promotion strategy

Real Marketing 14.2

Are Consumer Goods Companies Too Pushy?

Consumer packaged goods companies such as Procter & Gamble, Kraft Foods, Kellogg, and General Mills grew into giants by using mostly pull promotion strategies. They used massive doses of national advertising to differentiate their products, gain market share, and build brand equity and customer loyalty. But during the past few decades, such companies have gotten more "pushy," de-emphasizing national advertising and putting more of their marketing budgets into trade and consumer sales promotions.

General trade promotions (trade allowances, displays, cooperative advertising, slotting fees aimed at retailers) now account for 60 percent of total marketing spending by consumer product companies. That represents a seven-percentage-point increase in trade spending in just the past six years. Consumer promotions (coupons, discounts, premiums) account for another 14 percent of the typical marketing budget. That leaves less than 26 percent of total marketing spending for advertising, down from 42 percent 20 years ago.

Why have these companies shifted so heavily toward push strategies? One reason is that mass-media campaigns have become more expensive and less effective in recent years. Network television costs have risen sharply while audiences have fallen off, making national advertising less cost effective. Companies are also tailoring their marketing programs more narrowly, making national advertising less suitable than localized retailer promotions. And in these days of brand extensions and "me too" products, companies sometimes have trouble finding meaningful product differences to feature in advertising. So they have differentiated their products through price reductions, premium offers, coupons, and other push techniques.

Another factor speeding the shift from pull to push has been the growing strength of retailers. Retail giants such as Walmart, Loblaw, and Safeway now have the power to demand and get what they want—and what they want is more push. Whereas national advertising bypasses them on its way to the masses, push promotion benefits them directly. Thus, producers must often use push just to obtain good shelf space and other support from important retailers.

Too pushy? Some categories tend to self-destruct by always being on sale. For example, when automakers get promotion happy, the market just sits back and waits for a deal while the car companies lose money on profit-eating incentives.

However, many marketers are concerned that the reckless use of push will lead to fierce price competition and a never-ending spiral of price slashing and deal making. If used improperly, push promotion can mortgage a brand's future for short-term gains. Sales promotion buys short-run reseller support and consumer sales, but advertising builds long-run brand equity and consumer preference. By robbing the media advertising budget to pay for more sales promotion, companies might win the battle for short-run earnings but lose the war for long-run brand equity, consumer loyalty, and market share. "If brands are built over years, why are they managed over quarters?" laments one analyst.

Of special concern is the overuse of short-term price promotions. The regular use of price as a selling tool can destroy brand equity by encouraging consumers to seek value though price rather than through the benefits of the brand. In fact, some analysts blame the surge in promotions for a recent two-decade-long drop in the percentage of consumers who buy only well-known brands. And according to one source, consumers are now 50 percent more price sensitive than they were 25 years ago. In recent surveys, consumer goods managers pointed to pricing pressures and declining shopper loyalty as their primary concerns.

In cases where price is a key part of the brand's positioning, featuring price makes sense. But for brands where price does not underlie value, "price promotions are really desperate acts by brands that have their backs against the wall," says one marketing executive. "Generally speaking, it is better to stick to your guns with price and invest in advertising to drive sales."

Jack Trout, a well-known marketing consultant, cautions that some categories tend to self-destruct by always being on sale. Furniture, automobile tires, airline tickets, and many other categories of goods are rarely sold at anything near list price. And when automakers get rebate happy, the market just sits back and waits for a deal while the car companies lose money on profit-eating incentives. For example, General Motors has chopped US$1 billion out of its advertising budget over the past four years while doling out billions of dollars in sales incentives—discounted prices, rebates, low-cost financing, gas price guarantees—to move cars out of its showrooms. Such promotion tactics have done little to win profits or customer loyalty over the years. Over the past three years alone, GM has lost a staggering US$46 billion, and its domestic market share has dwindled to less than 25 percent, down from 44.5 percent in 1980. In 2009, the company filed for bankruptcy protection and was forced to sell off some of its product lines, including Saturn and Hummer.

Thus, many consumer companies are now rethinking their promotion strategies and reversing the trend by shifting their promotion budgets back toward advertising. They realize that it's not a question of sales promotion versus advertising, or of push versus pull. Success lies in finding the best mix of the two: consistent advertising to build long-run brand value and consumer preference, and sales promotion to create short-run trade support and consumer excitement. The company needs to blend both push and pull elements into an integrated marketing communications program that meets immediate consumer and retailer needs as well as long-run strategic needs.

Sources: Promotion spending statistics from *Shopper-Centric Trade: The Future of Trade Promotion* (Cannondale Associates: Wilton, CT, October 2007), p. 15. Other information and quotes from Jack Trout, "Prices: Simple Guidelines to Get Them Right," *Journal of Business Strategy*, November–December 1998, pp. 13–16; Jean Halliday, "GM Bleeds as Incentives Undermine Brand Value," *Advertising Age*, March 21, 2005, pp. 1, 37; Leonard M. Lodish and Carl F. Mela, "If Brands Are Built Over Years, Why Are They Managed Over Quarters?" *Harvard Business Review*, July–August 2007, pp. 107–112; John D. Stoll, "GM Is Still Facing Tricky Curves," *Wall Street Journal*, February 5, 2008, p. C3; and "General Motors Corporation," *Hoover's Company Records*, April 2008, p. 10640.

Business-to-consumer companies usually "pull" more, putting more of their funds into advertising, followed by sales promotion, personal selling, and then public relations. In contrast, business-to-business marketers tend to "push" more, putting more of their funds into personal selling, followed by sales promotion, advertising, and public relations. In general, personal selling is used more heavily with expensive and risky goods and in markets with fewer and larger sellers.

The effects of different promotion tools also vary with stages of the product life cycle. In the introduction stage, advertising and public relations are good for producing high awareness, and sales promotion is useful in promoting early trial. Personal selling must be used to get the trade to carry the product. In the growth stage, advertising and public relations continue to be powerful influences, whereas sales promotion can be reduced because fewer incentives are needed. In the mature stage, sales promotion again becomes important relative to advertising. Buyers know the brands, and advertising is needed only to remind them of the product. In the decline stage, advertising is kept at a reminder level, public relations is dropped, and salespeople give the product only a little attention. Sales promotion, however, might continue to be strong.

Integrating the Promotion Mix

Having set the promotion budget and mix, the company must now take steps to see that all of the promotion mix elements are smoothly integrated. Here is a checklist for integrating the firm's marketing communications:[21]

- *Start with customers.* Identify all customer touchpoints for the company and its brands. Work to ensure that communications at each touchpoint are consistent with the overall communications strategy and that communications efforts are occurring when, where, and how *customers* want them.

- *Analyze trends—internal and external—that can affect the company's ability to do business.* Look for areas where communications can help the most. Determine the strengths and weaknesses of each communications function. Develop a combination of promotional tactics based on these strengths and weaknesses.

- *Audit the pockets of communications spending throughout the organization.* Itemize the communications budgets and tasks and consolidate these into a single budgeting process. Reassess all communications expenditures by product, promotional tool, stage of the life cycle, and observed effect.

- *Team up in communications planning.* Engage all communications functions in joint planning. Include customers, suppliers, and other stakeholders at every stage of communications planning.

- *Create compatible themes, tones, and quality across all communications media.* Make sure each element carries the company's unique primary messages and selling points. This consistency achieves greater impact and prevents the unnecessary duplication of work across functions.

- *Create performance measures that are shared by all communications elements.* Develop systems to evaluate the combined impact of all communications activities.

- *Appoint a director responsible for the company's persuasive communications efforts.* This move encourages efficiency by centralizing planning and creating shared performance measures.

Socially Responsible Marketing Communications

In shaping its promotion mix, a company must be aware of the large body of legal and ethical issues surrounding marketing communications. Most marketers work hard to communicate openly and honestly with consumers and resellers. Still, abuses may occur, and public policymakers have developed a substantial body of laws and regulations to govern advertising, sales promotion, personal selling, and direct-marketing activities. In this section, we discuss issues regarding advertising, sales promotion, and personal selling. We discuss issues regarding direct marketing in Chapter 17.

Advertising and Sales Promotion

By law, companies must avoid false or deceptive advertising. Advertisers must not make false claims, such as suggesting that a product cures something when it does not. They must avoid ads that have the capacity to deceive, even though no one actually may be deceived. An automobile cannot be advertised as using seven litres of fuel per hundred kilometres unless it does so under typical conditions, and a diet bread cannot be advertised as having fewer calories simply because its slices are thinner.

Sellers must avoid bait-and-switch advertising that attracts buyers under false pretences. For example, a large retailer advertised a sewing machine for $179. However, when consumers tried to buy the advertised machine, the seller downplayed its features, placed faulty machines on showroom floors, understated the machine's performance, and took other actions in an attempt to switch buyers to a more expensive machine. Such actions are both unethical and illegal.

The advertising industry in Canada is controlled both by the Canadian Radio-television and Telecommunications Commission (CRTC) and by voluntary industry codes administered by Advertising Standards Canada. The CRTC (www.crtc.gc.ca), which independently governs broadcast licensing, is itself governed by the *Broadcasting Act* of 1991 and the *Telecommunications Act* of 1993. The primary objective of the *Broadcasting Act* is to ensure that all Canadians have access to a wide variety of high-quality Canadian programming. The main objective of the *Telecommunications Act* is to ensure that Canadians have access to reliable telephone and other telecommunications services at affordable prices.

Beyond simply avoiding legal pitfalls, such as deceptive or bait-and-switch advertising, companies can use advertising and other forms of promotion to encourage and promote socially responsible programs and actions. For example, Caterpillar is one of several companies

Many companies use promotion to encourage socially responsible actions. RONA created a unique ad to encourage consumers to recycle old paint responsibly.

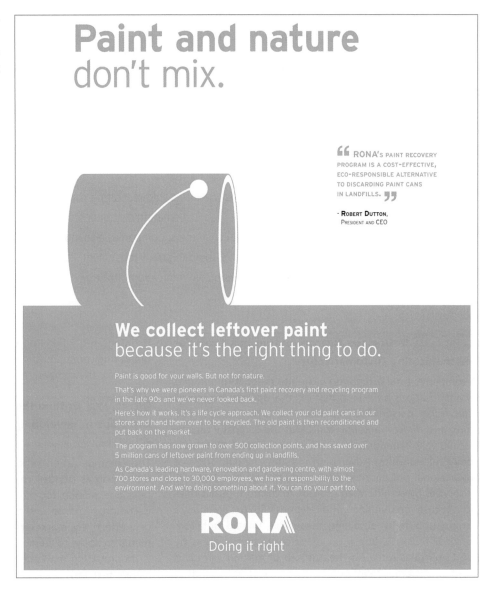

and environmental groups forming the Tropical Forest Foundation, which is working to save the great Amazon rainforest. Caterpillar promotes the cause through advertising and pages on its website.

Similarly, RONA created a unique billboard ad to promote its paint recovery program by piggybacking an existing ad for the Apple nano. The billboard, placed directly under the iPod ad, reads "We collect leftover paint" and was designed to encourage consumers to recycle old paint responsibly.

Personal Selling

A company's salespeople must follow the rules of "fair competition." For example, salespeople may not lie to consumers or mislead them about the advantages of buying a product. To avoid bait-and-switch practices, salespeople's statements must match advertising claims.

Different rules apply to consumers who are called on at home versus those who go to a store in search of a product. Because people called on at home may be taken by surprise and may be especially vulnerable to high-pressure selling techniques, most provincial governments have stipulated a *three-day cooling-off rule* to give special protection to customers who are not seeking products. Under this rule, customers who agree in their own homes to buy something have 72 hours in which to cancel a contract or return merchandise and get their money back, no questions asked.

Much personal selling involves business-to-business trade. In selling to businesses, salespeople may not offer bribes to purchasing agents or to others who can influence a sale. They may not obtain or use technical or trade secrets of competitors through bribery or industrial espionage. Finally, salespeople must not disparage competitors or competing products by suggesting things that are not true.[22]

REVIEWING OBJECTIVES AND KEY TERMS

In this chapter, you've learned how companies use integrated marketing communications (IMC) to communicate customer value. Modern marketing calls for more than just creating customer value by developing a good product, pricing it attractively, and making it available to target customers. Companies also must clearly and persuasively *communicate* that value to current and prospective customers. To do this, they must blend five promotion mix tools, guided by a well-designed and implemented integrated marketing communications strategy.

OBJECTIVE 1   **Define the five promotion mix tools for communicating customer value.**

A company's total *promotion mix*—also called its *marketing communications mix*—consists of the specific blend of *advertising, personal selling, sales promotion, public relations*, and *direct-marketing* tools that the company uses to persuasively communicate customer value and build customer relationships. Advertising includes any paid form of nonpersonal presentation and promotion of ideas, goods, or services by an identified sponsor. In contrast, public relations focuses on building good relations with the company's various publics by obtaining favourable unpaid publicity. Personal selling is any form of personal presentation by the firm's sales force for the purpose of making sales and building customer relationships. Firms use sales promotion to provide short-term incentives to encourage the purchase or sale of a product or service. Finally, firms seeking immediate response from targeted individual customers use non-personal direct-marketing tools to communicate with customers.

OBJECTIVE 2   **Discuss the changing communications landscape and the need for integrated marketing communications.**

Recent shifts toward targeted or one-to-one marketing, coupled with advances in information and communications technology, have had a dramatic impact on marketing communications. As marketing communicators adopt richer but more fragmented media and promotion mixes to reach their diverse markets, they risk creating a communications hodgepodge for consumers. To prevent this, more companies are adopting the concept of *integrated marketing communications (IMC)*. Guided by an overall IMC strategy, the company works out the roles that the various promotional tools will play and the extent to which each will be used. It carefully coordinates the promotional activities and when major campaigns will take place. Finally, to help implement

its integrated marketing strategy, the company appoints a marketing communications director who has overall responsibility for the company's communications efforts.

OBJECTIVE 3   **Outline the communications process and the steps in developing effective marketing communications.**

The communication process involves nine elements—two major parties (sender, receiver), two communication tools (message, media), four communication functions (encoding, decoding, response, and feedback), and noise. To communicate effectively, marketers must understand how these elements combine to communicate value to target customers.

In preparing marketing communications, the communicator's first task is to *identify the target audience* and its characteristics. Next, the communicator has to determine the *communication objectives* and define the response sought, whether it be *awareness, knowledge, liking, preference, conviction*, or *purchase*. Then a *message* should be constructed with an effective content and structure. *Media* must be selected, both for personal and nonpersonal communication. The communicator must find highly credible sources to deliver the messages. Finally, the communicator must collect *feedback* by watching how much of the market becomes aware of the product, tries the product, and is satisfied in the process.

OBJECTIVE 4   **Explain the methods for setting the promotion budget and factors that affect the design of the promotion mix.**

The company has to decide how much to spend for promotion. The most popular approaches are to spend what the company can afford, to use a percentage-of-sales method, to base promotion on competitors' spending, or to base it on an analysis and costing of the communication objectives and tasks. The company has to divide the *promotion budget* among the major tools to create the *promotion mix*. Companies can pursue a *push* or a *pull* promotional strategy, or a combination of the two. The best specific blend of promotion tools depends on the type of product/market, the buyer's readiness stage, and the product life-cycle stage. People at all levels of the organization must be aware of the many legal and ethical issues surrounding marketing communications. Companies must work hard and proactively at communicating openly, honestly, and agreeably with their customers and resellers.

KEY TERMS

mymarketinglab | Glossary Flashcards

DISCUSSING THE CONCEPTS

1. List and briefly describe the five major promotion mix tools.

2. Discuss the three major factors changing the face of today's marketing communications.

3. Name and briefly describe the nine elements of the communication process. Why do marketers need to understand these elements?

4. List the steps in developing effective marketing communications.

5. Name and describe the common methods for setting promotion budgets.

6. Compare and contrast push and pull promotion strategies. Which promotion tools are most effective in each?

APPLYING THE CONCEPTS

1. Describe the three types of appeals used in marketing communications messages and develop three different advertisements for the same brand of a product of your choice, each using a different appeal.

2. Energizer is introducing a new line of batteries that provide a longer life than its existing models. The brand manager for the new line believes most of the promotion budget should be spent on consumer and trade promotions, but the assistant brand manager thinks that the promotion mix should emphasize television advertising. Partner with another student. Play the roles of the brand manager and assistant brand manager and debate their opposing views on advertising versus promotion.

3. Montreal-based Gildan Activewear was named to the 2009 Jantzi-Macleans list of Canada's 50 Most Socially Responsible Corporations. Read the full article at www.macleans.ca, then visit Gildan's corporate website at www.gildan.com. What types of socially responsible programs or actions does the firm engage in?

FOCUS ON TECHNOLOGY

Businesses spend an estimated US$320 billion vying for consumers' attention to their advertising messages. And that's just in North America. Procter & Gamble alone spends US$8.5 billion worldwide on advertising. Add spending on other promotional elements to that and the figure grows much bigger. That's a lot of money! Marketers need to be accountable for these expenditures, so audience measurement is crucial. Technological solutions abound to help marketers assess how many people might see, read, or hear their marketing messages. For example, Nielsen Media Research, the goliath of television audience measurement, uses written diary and People Meter technology. But new upstarts are now entering the ring with other measurement tools that reflect the changing landscape of television viewing—live viewing, timeshift viewing, video on demand,

online viewing, and mobile viewing. The rapid shift to digital advertising leaves marketers with a dizzying array of measurement options but no industry standard, creating somewhat of a "wild west" phenomenon. Even once low-tech magazine audience measurement is getting a high-tech upgrade through radio frequency identification (RFID) tags embedded in individual magazines to measure each time they are opened or closed.

1. Research media audience measurement methods for electronic and print media and discuss how technology is changing the way media audiences are measured.

2. Are these audience measurement techniques adequate when accounting for return on promotional expenditures? Explain.

FOCUS ON ETHICS

Buying an automobile is a high-involvement purchase for consumers wanting to make a smart decision. That's why many car advertisements use rational appeals to relate to the audience's self-interest. The ads show that the product will produce the desired benefits in terms of quality, economy, value, or performance. Consumers pay attention to this information when deciding which automobile to purchase. For example, a recent television commercial for Mercury's Mariner SUV claimed that it could go "690 kilometres on a tank of gas . . . more than a Honda CR-V." Now, this is technically correct, because the CR-V's fuel tank capacity is smaller

(it can go 665 kilometres on a tank of gas). However, what the ad didn't say is that, in reality, the CR-V's gas mileage rating is slightly higher than the Mariner's.

1. Was Mercury guilty of deceptive advertising with its Mariner commercial?

2. Check the "Misleading Representations and Deceptive Marketing Practices" pamphlet " at the Competition Bureau's website (www.competitionbureau.gc.ca/eic/site/cb-bc.nsf/eng/01224.html). Has Mercury followed these guidelines?

MARKETING BY THE NUMBERS

Using the percentage-of-sales method, an advertiser sets its budget at a certain percentage of current or forecasted sales. However, determining what percentage to use is not always clear. Many marketers look at industry averages and competitor spending for comparisons. Trade publications, such as *Advertising Age*, publish data regarding industry averages as well as advertising-to-sales ratios for top advertisers.

1. Using information regarding industry and leading advertisers' advertising-to-sales ratios (see http://company.news-record.com/advertising/advertising/ratio.html and http://adage.com/datacenter/article?article_id=106575),

recommend percentages of sales that advertisers for the following businesses should use to set next year's advertising budget: beverage company, bicycle dealer, furniture store, jeweller, women's clothing store, and automobile manufacturer.

2. If a women's clothing store forecasted $100 million in sales next year, what amount would you recommend it spend on advertising? How useful are the percentages found above for this business? How might the percentage-of-sales figure be adjusted given this particular advertiser's situation?

VIDEO CASE

Crispin Porter + Bogusky

Crispin Porter + Bogusky (Crispin) may not be the oldest advertising agency in the world. It isn't the biggest either. But it has been working over time to prove that it is the most innovative firm at integrating marketing promotions. In fact, Crispin relies very little on the king of all advertising channels, broadcast TV. Instead, Crispin has worked miracles for companies such as Virgin Atlantic Airways, BMW's MINI Cooper, and Burger King by employing nontraditional campaigns on limited budgets.

Crispin attributes its success to the fact that it redefined what an advertisement is. Customer appropriate messages, Crispin discovered, could be delivered in many different ways. So its realm of "ad space" includes things as obscure as the side of a mailbox or an oversized phone booth in an

airport. By communicating a message in many different ways, Crispin has developed a reputation for truly integrating marketing communications.

After viewing the video featuring Crispin, answer the following questions about advertising and promotions:

1. Alex Bogusky once said, "Anything and everything is an ad." What does this mean? How is Crispin demonstrating this mantra?

2. In what ways has Crispin differentiated itself from other advertising agencies?

3. Give some examples of how Crispin balances strategy with creativity.

Visit MyMarketingLab at www.pearsoned.ca/mymarketinglab to view the video segment related to this case.

COMPANY CASE

Burger King: Promoting a Food Fight

CHALLENGING CONVENTIONAL WISDOM

Burger King Corporation is a large international chain of fast-food restaurants. It has operations in every Canadian province and it predominantly sells burgers, french fries, soft drinks, desserts, and various sandwiches. In early 2004, as Burger King's CEO Brad Blum reviewed the company's 2003 outcomes, he decided once again that he had to do something to spice up BK's bland performance. Industry leader McDonald's had just reported a 9 percent sales jump in 2003 to a total of US$22.1 billion while number-two BK's U.S. sales had *slipped* about 5 percent to US$7.9 billion. Further, number-three Wendy's sales had spiked 11 percent to US$7.4 billion, putting it in a position to overtake BK.

Blum surprised the fast-food industry by abruptly firing the firm's advertising agency, Young & Rubicam (Y&R), and awarding its global creative account to a small upstart firm Crispin Porter + Bogusky (Crispin). The switch marked the fifth time in four years that BK had moved its account! Ad agency Y&R had gotten the US$350 million BK account only 10 months earlier. To help revive BK's sales, it had developed a campaign with the theme "The Fire's Ready," which focused on BK's flame-broiled cooking method versus frying. However, observers found the message to be flat and uninspiring, and the declining sales sealed Y & R's fate.

With the move to Crispin, there was no shortage of speculation that the fickle Burger King would soon move

again. Many saw BK as a bad client, impossible to work for. Others predicted that the "win" of this account would ruin Crispin's quirky culture. But in announcing the Crispin selection, Blum indicated he had challenged the firm to develop "groundbreaking, next-level, results-oriented, and innovative advert-ising that strongly connects with our core customers." BK automatically became the small firm's largest client, but Crispin was not without an impressive track record. The creative shop was known for its offbeat, unorthodox, and even irreverent promotions. Because its clients often had little money for advertising, Crispin found inexpensive ways to gain attention, veering away from traditional mass media.

Crispin had produced award-winning, low-budget campaigns for BMW's MINI Cooper, IKEA furniture, Sunglass Hut, and Virgin Atlantic Airways, forging a reputation as an out-of-the-box, results-oriented agency. Along the way, Crispin developed some loose "rules." Among them were the following:

- Zero in on the product

- Kick the TV commercial habit

- Find the sweet spot (the overlap between product characteristics and customer needs)

- Surprise = buzz = exposure

- Don't be timid

- Think of advertising as a product rather than a service

HIT AFTER HIT FOR THE KING

It was these rules that guided Crispin's work for BK. Within a month of getting the burger giant's account, Crispin recommended going back to the firm's "Have It Your Way" tagline, developed by BK's second advertising agency, BBDO, way back in 1974. Crispin argued that it could take that old phrase and make it relevant to today's customers. Although Crispin's pitch may have initially seemed "same-old," it was anything but. Uncharacteristic of its past campaigns, Crispin kicked off the new BK campaign with TV commercials. In a series of offbeat ads that were a takeoff on the comedy series *The Office*, office workers competed and compared their "made my way" BK burgers, reinforcing the message that each customer could have a custom-made burger—no matter how unusual it might be. Crispin planned an entire package of promotions around the new–old theme, including everything from in-store signage to messages on cups.

Although *The Office* ads were unusual and catchy, they were also mainstream media. However, the TV campaign created an environment for the real Crispin approach to emerge. To promote BK's TenderCrisp chicken, Crispin launched a microsite, www.subservientchicken.com. Among other things, the site features a man dressed in a chicken suit who would respond by performing any commands that visitors typed into a text box. The only indication that the site is sponsored by Burger King is a small icon and a link marked "BK TenderCrisp." When Crispin launched the site, it told only 20 people—all of whom were friends of people who worked at the agency. Within the first 10 days, 20 million people visited the site, with the average visitor spending more than seven minutes.

As a follow-up to the "Subservient Chicken" promotion, Crispin created a campaign to launch a new BK product, chicken fries. The promotion was based on a faux heavy metal band called Coq Roq (the lead singer's name was Fowl Mouth). The whole idea was to create the charade of a real band, complete with songs, videos, cellphone ring tones, and promotional merchandise. Crispin targeted this campaign squarely at what it perceived to be the main BK target market—young men. Whatever those young men thought of Coq Roq, it led them to buy more than 100 million orders of chicken fries in the first four weeks of the new-product launch.

Crispin clearly demonstrated with both the "Subservient Chicken" and "Coq Roq" campaigns that it was a master at viral marketing—using unusual methods to get attention and to generate buzz and word of mouth. Despite the success of these campaigns in producing lots of website hits, many analysts wondered if they would turn BK's sliding market share around. There was also speculation as to whether or not Crispin could continue to produce ideas that would keep BK strong in the fast-food fight.

A VIRAL TURNAROUND

Largely because of years of poor performance, tension had been mounting between Burger King's franchisees and the corporation. Initially, the new direction of its ad campaigns didn't help. Franchisees hated the viral web campaigns, as they did an earlier Crispin campaign featuring an eerie bobblehead-looking King with a gargantuan ceramic head.

But at Burger King's 2006 annual franchisee convention, the feeling in the air was "long live the king." CEO Blum debuted a new Crispin ad entitled, "Manthem." A parody of the Helen Reddy song "I Am Woman," the spot was yet another example of BK's strategy to unapologetically embrace the young, male, fast-food "super fan." "Manthem's" lyrics spurned "chick food" and gleefully exalted the meat, cheese, and more meat and cheese combos that turn "innies into outies," all the while showing guys burning their briefs and pushing a minivan off a bridge.

After openly revolting at the convention the year before, BK's restaurant operators rose to their feet in a thunderous ovation, demanding an encore. They now embraced the kind of uncomfortably edgy advertising that they had rejected not so long before. Why this sudden change of heart?

Perhaps it was because Burger King was on the verge of a public offering. Or maybe it was because sales and profits go a long way in healing wounds. "I feel much better this year than I have in the last three, four, or five years," said Mahendra Nath, owner/operator of 90 stores in the United States. With sales up multiple years in a row, another franchisee, Alex Salgueiro, said, "I think our competitors are scared of the King . . . they should be. They say, 'What's with the King?' and my answer is 'It's better than clowns.'"

With BK's fortunes apparently changing, franchisees were much less likely to question the irreverent Crispin promotional tactics, whether they liked them or not. And why would they? With the young male demographic providing nearly half of all Burger King visits, Alex Salguiero said it best: "All opinions boil down to traffic and sales. Once that happens, everybody has to shut up with their opinion. We have a very old franchisee base at this point and some of us don't understand our customers. We have a lot of gray hair."

NO END IN SIGHT

The creative ads have continued to flow, including the humorous series to promote the Western Whopper. The spots, based on the tagline, "Bring out your inner cowboy," featured people from all walks of life developing huge handlebar moustaches after eating Burger King fare. The ads were accompanied by a link to www.petmoustache.com where people could register, upload a photo, and design a custom moustache. The moustache would then take on a life of its own. "It sends you emails that say, 'Hey, I miss you and why haven't you waxed me?' If you neglect it, it grows willy-nilly and wild," explained Rob Reilly, a creative director for Crispin.

But the most recent BK/Crispin promotional tactic took things to a whole new level. For the fiftieth anniversary of the Whopper, Crispin created the "Whopper Freakout" campaign. In doing so, Crispin did something it had never done before. Reilly explained the reasoning behind what can only be described as Whopper deprivation:

> If you really want to prove [that the Whopper is still North America's favourite burger] put your money where your mouth is and let's take it off the menu and film natural reactions from people. We knew technically we could pull it off, but this is really a social experiment, that's the new ground we're breaking, using a social experiment as marketing. There's no fake dialogue, no fake customers. We were really testing this: If you deprive people of a thing they love, even down to a hamburger, will they react with a thing that's visceral?

Visceral is truly what they got. The eight-minute film is taken from the perspective of hidden cameras in a real Burger King restaurant. After being told by employees that the Whopper had been discontinued, customers revolt in a way that only truly distraught brand-loyal fans could. In the movie, customers scoff, twitch, roll their heads, demand to speak to managers, and even yell. Some of the more wistful subjects give folksy anecdotes about family bonding and passage into manhood, all based on the Whopper.

Crispin plugged the film's website with 30-second spot ads and then let the viral marketing forces take over. The results were nothing short of astounding. The microsite received more than 1 million visits at an average logged time of eight minutes and 33 seconds. But what really stood out was that visitors watched the video in its entirety 4 million times, meaning that most visitors watched several times. Multiple parodies of the ad emerged on the Web, including one based on an animated Michael Jackson and an R-rated version called "Ghetto Freakout" (which racked up more than 3 million views on YouTube). The campaign won a 2008 *Creativity* magazine award and the 2009 Grand Effie Award, and IAG Research found recall of the campaign to be the highest of any it had seen in its six-year history.

But all these measures amount to very little if the overall objective is not achieved. On that score, Crispin has delivered in spades for the flame-broiler. Burger King is in its fourth consecutive year of same-store sales growth. Not only is it growing, but BK is currently delivering a solid thrashing to McDonald's and Wendy's, who are blaming the recession, housing crisis, and fuel prices for sluggish growth.

BK 2007 systemwide revenue reached US$13.2 billion, up nearly 60 percent since Crispin assumed the account. Burger King is also showing healthy profits, rising stock prices, and strong international growth.

Many analysts are giving Crispin's promotional efforts the lion's share of the credit for Burger King's success. "They're doing a super job on the advertising front," said UBS analyst David Palmer. "They're clearly connecting with the super fan that is the young, hungry male." Despite the previous speculation that Crispin would fail, the firm is now into its fifth year as Burger King's promotional agency, with no sign of being shown the door. As long as Crispin continues to hit home runs with its creative promotions, its franchisees, shareholders, and customers alike will continue to shout, "Long live the King!"

Questions for Discussion

1. What are Burger King's communication objectives for its target audience?

2. With its focus on the "super fan," does BK risk alienating other customers? What are the implications of this?

3. Why is viral or buzz marketing effective? Analyze the design of the "Subservient Chicken" website's message, including content, structure, and format. What can you conclude from this analysis?

4. Do the TV and viral elements of BK's campaigns work well together? What additional elements and media might Crispin add to the integrated marketing communications campaign?

5. What other recommendations would you make to BK and Crispin to help them improve the integration of Burger King's promotion mix?

Sources: "Burger King and Crispin Porter + Bogusky win Grand Effie Award for Whopper Freakout," *Reuters*, June 4, 2009, accessed at www.reuters.com; Emily Bryson York, "Economy, Rivals, No Match for BK's Marketing," *Advertising Age*, May 5, 2008, p.4; "Burger King: Whopper Freakout," *Creativity*, May 1, 2008, p. 76; Kevin, Kingsbury, "Burger King Swings to Net Profit," *Wall Street Journal*, August 24, 2007, accessed at www.wsj.com; Barbara Lippert, "King of All Media," *Adweek*, November 20, 2006, accessed at www.adweek.com; Kamau High, "BK Intros 'Inner Cowboy,'" *Adweek*, June 5, 2007, accessed at www.adweek.com; Kate Macarthur, "BK Rebels Fall in Love with King," *Advertising Age*, May 1, 2006, p. 1; Elaine Walker, "Franchisees, Burger King Work to Mend Rift," *Miami Herald*, March 27, 2006.

15

Advertising and
Public Relations

PREVIEWING
THE CONCEPTS

Now that we've looked at overall integrated marketing communications planning, let's dig more deeply into the specific marketing communications tools. In this chapter, we'll explore advertising and public relations. Advertising involves communicating the company's or brand's value proposition by using paid media to inform, persuade, and remind consumers. Public relations involves building good relations with various company publics—from consumers and the general public to the media, investor, donor, and government publics. As with all of the promotion mix tools, advertising and public relations must be blended into the overall integrated marketing communications program. In the two chapters that follow, we'll discuss the remaining promotion mix tools: personal selling, sales promotion, and direct marketing.

To start this chapter, let's look at the successful evolution of advertising for the United Way of Greater Toronto. In the fast-changing world of modern advertising, the organization managed to raise $107.5 million during its 2008 fundraising campaign, despite a depressed economy and numerous other charities competing for a share of the ever-shrinking donation pie.

In 2003, staff at the United Way knew their charity was in a heated battle for what they term "share of compassion." A downturn in the economy combined with recent government cutbacks in social services had created a difficult landscape for the many charitable organizations in Canada. Literally thousands of charities appeared to be fighting for the same small percentage of donors, as 5 percent of donors in Canada account for more than 50 percent of total donations. With charities aggressively marketing themselves in an already cluttered landscape, the United Way needed a campaign that would break through the clutter and, ultimately, entice potential donors to support its many charities.

With these objectives in mind, the Arnold Worldwide advertising agency went to work. First, informal focus groups with both donors and non-donors were conducted in an effort to uncover key consumer insights. As expected, participants reaffirmed the notion that many donors give to organizations that have personal meaning to them. Unexpectedly, however, the agency discovered that though people rationalized not giving to the poor by giving to other more "personal" causes, they felt an underlying guilt associated with this decision, just as most people feel a tinge of guilt when they walk past a homeless person. This sense of guilt is enhanced with feelings of conflict—what will the person do with the money if I give it to them? Do they really need it? This was a key insight for the creative team. Furthermore, the team found that there was a great deal of equity within the United Way's brand imagery. People viewed the United Way logo as a "helping hand to those in need."

Thus, a strategy was born: "Giving to the United Way is the simple way to take care of those most vulnerable in the city." By giving to the United Way of Greater Toronto, donors could be assured that they were helping those in need in the best possible way, and could thus assuage their feelings of guilt and conflict.

With a solid strategy in place, work began on executing it. The United Way relies entirely on donated media space, so compelling creative material was of paramount importance, as the amount of advertising space given is directly related to the media's perception of the campaign. As one analyst noted, "Good creative can often make or break pro bono work: If you're not paying for media space, your campaign had better be interesting, or it just won't get picked up."

The final campaign used the imagery of the hand as "an icon of protection." The lead execution, which ran in both print and outdoor transit, showed a homeless man being sheltered from the rain with a hand. The campaign also featured two TV spots, three print executions, three transit posters, zoom media (in bars and restaurants), and painted GO Transit trains in the Toronto area. In 2004, the campaign continued with superboards, online banner and skyscraper ads, as well as support from major websites, including GlobeandMail.com, TSN.ca, Toronto.com, and Chatelaine.com. As one advertising critic noted, "The hand, used properly, is a wonderful advertising device, because it evokes such warmth and unique humanity. Here, coupled with that dynamic yet quiet theme line, it is dramatic, and involving, and says precisely what the United Way wants it to say. I think I'm going to increase my gift this year, in tribute." The campaign ran for two years, and in 2004 alone it helped the United Way generate the equivalent of $10 million in donated editorial and promotional media. It also won two gold CASSIES (Canadian Advertising Success Stories) Awards.

Although the campaign was certainly a success from a media perspective, the question remains: What did it do for the United Way of Greater Toronto? First, donations increased in both 2003 and 2004 despite the competitive environment. Second, advertising awareness jumped by 10 percent in one year, with 58 percent of Torontonians recalling one or more executions of the 2003 campaign. Finally, brand image was positively affected, with almost 60 percent of those polled either agreeing or somewhat agreeing with the statement "United Way is the most effective way to deal with social issues in the community" and "United Way makes a positive and lasting difference in people's lives." In fact, the "Hands" campaign was so effective that it was picked up by other United Ways across Canada.

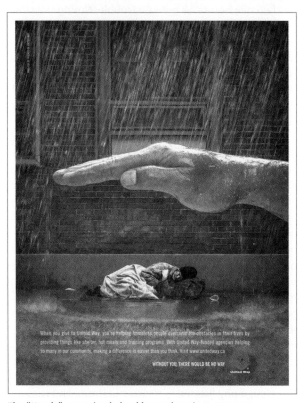

The "Hands" campaign helped boost donations, generate awareness, and enhance brand image for the United Way of Greater Toronto.

No matter how successful a campaign has been, however, time is not its friend. Viewers grow tired of the same message and imagery. Thus, in 2005 Arnold Worldwide and the United Way changed course. The next campaign built on the foundation of the previous campaign and its theme "Without you there would be no way." However, the 2005 campaign visually demonstrated exactly what donations can do and how individual donations can make a difference— from helping the homeless get off the streets to making sure the elderly aren't isolated. The 30-second TV spots used dramatic special effects to show what might happen if a person didn't receive help. In one spot, a boy plays baseball, but as he swings the bat, the screen goes dark and an image

▶

OBJECTIVES

1 Define the role of advertising in the promotion mix.

2 Describe the major decisions involved in developing an advertising program.

3 Define the role of public relations in the promotion mix.

4 Explain how companies use public relations to communicate with their publics.

emerges of him smashing a car window and running away. It then cuts back to the daylight shot, showing the same boy running bases, thanks to the fact that the United Way reached him before he got into trouble. Noting the strategy behind the two campaigns, Bill Newbery, Arnold Worldwide's co-creative director, says the "Hands" campaigns were part of the United Way's attempt to show how it helps with immediate needs. In contrast, the 2005 initiative was one where "we wanted to freshen it up, as well as address the strategy that the United Way wanted to get across, which was the long-term role it plays."

This new positive strategy was further developed in 2007 when the United Way announced a switch to a new ad agency, Toronto-based Publicis. "Arnold Worldwide had been extraordinarily generous to us and done exceptional work. However, we felt like they had served their time." said Lyn Whitham, vice-president of marketing and communications for the United Way of Greater Toronto. The pro bono work done by Publicis further developed the "Without you, there would be no way" theme, but focused even more on positive benefits of giving instead of the potential consequences of not giving. For example, the new ads targeted at youth depict a teenage boy struggling with pressure from a group of teens, one carrying a handgun. The boys turn to leave (likely to commit a crime), but one boy stays behind. He rubs his neck, obviously in conflict, and his outer skin starts to peel away. He sheds his "gang" layer, revealing a boy dressed in a soccer uniform, and runs in the other direction to join a game.

The United Way, like all charities, has a limited budget that it can devote to promotions. Thus, in addition to its advertising campaign, it must use other communications techniques to "speak" to donors and build relationships with them. It must be creative and innovative since its budget is small, and it must also ensure that all elements of its communication plan are integrated so that consumers hear a single message linked by a common theme.

It's not surprising, therefore, that the United Way also relies heavily on public relations and its own website as a means of maintaining relationships and keeping the United Way top of mind. For example, part of the Toronto United Way's website is devoted to true stories—tales of people who have been able to change their lives as a result of help from the United Way. Since the person's picture accompanies each story, a human face is provided for those interested in seeing concrete results from their donations. The stories are also used as a means of generating publicity for the United Way. Some of the stories currently featured on the United Way of Greater Toronto's website have also been featured in articles in the *Toronto Star*.

Another tool to generate publicity was employed in 2006. As part of its fiftieth anniversary, the United Way of Greater Toronto challenged the city's creative community to design a special logo to complement the familiar "hand" logo. This was a win–win idea as the winning agency would gain recognition for its creative work.

The United Way uses volunteers as its sales force. For its board of directors it recruits people who are well connected with others in the business community. When running its annual campaign, it relies on volunteers within firms, universities, and other organizations to head the campaign. These volunteers work tirelessly to convince their fellow workers to give generously to the United Way. The United Way, in turn, hosts a volunteer appreciation night at the end of the campaign. The United Way has also worked to build a community on several social networking sites. You can watch the TV ads on its YouTube channel, follow events on its Facebook page, view photo albums on Flickr, or get quick updates about the organization on Twitter.

As the United Way example illustrates, great advertising and a blend of other promotional tools are not only used for consumer products or services. Beginning with key consumer insights, the Arnold Worldwide team was able to create two arresting and compelling television campaigns that were nothing short of exceptional. The TV ads could be linked to other elements in the communications mix so that the United Way could have a unified voice when speaking to its key stakeholders.[1]

Chapter Opening Discussion

Glossary Flashcards of Key Terms

1

Advertising
Any paid form of nonpersonal presentation and promotion of ideas, goods, or services by an identified sponsor.

As we discussed in the previous chapter, companies must do more than simply create customer value. They must also clearly and persuasively communicate that value to target consumers. In this chapter, we'll take a closer look at two marketing communications tools: *advertising* and *public relations*.

ADVERTISING

Advertising can be traced back to the very beginning of recorded history. Archaeologists working in the countries around the Mediterranean Sea have dug up signs announcing various events and offers. The Romans painted walls to announce gladiator fights, and the Phoenicians painted pictures promoting their wares on large rocks along parade routes. During the golden age in Greece, town criers announced the sale of cattle, crafted items,

Figure 15.1 Major advertising decisions

and even cosmetics. An early "singing commercial" went as follows: "For eyes that are shining, for cheeks like the dawn / For beauty that lasts after girlhood is gone / For prices in reason, the woman who knows / Will buy her cosmetics from Aesclyptos."

Modern advertising, however, is a far cry from these early efforts. Canadian organizations spend more than $13 billion on advertising annually; worldwide ad spending exceeds an estimated US$604 billion. Procter & Gamble, the world's largest advertiser, last year spent US$8.5 billion worldwide.[2]

Although advertising is used mostly by business firms, a wide range of not-for-profit organizations, professionals, and social agencies also use advertising to promote their causes to various target publics. Advertising is a good way to inform and persuade, whether the purpose is to sell Coca-Cola worldwide or to get consumers in a developing nation to use birth control.

Marketing management must make four important decisions when developing an advertising program (see Figure 15.1): *setting advertising objectives*, *setting the advertising budget*, *developing advertising strategy* (*message decisions* and *media decisions*), and *evaluating advertising campaigns*.

2 SETTING ADVERTISING OBJECTIVES

The first step is to set *advertising objectives*. These objectives should be based on past decisions about the target market, positioning, and the marketing mix, which define the job that advertising must do in the total marketing program. The overall advertising objective is to help build customer relationships by communicating customer value. Here, we discuss specific advertising objectives.

Advertising objective
A specific communication *task* to be accomplished with a specific *target* audience during a specific period of *time*.

An **advertising objective** is a specific communication *task* to be accomplished with a specific *target* audience during a specific period of *time*. Advertising objectives can be classified by primary purpose—whether the aim is to *inform*, *persuade*, or *remind*. Table 15.1 lists examples of each of these specific objectives.

Informative advertising is used heavily when introducing a new product category. In this case, the objective is to build primary demand. Thus, early producers of DVD players first had to inform consumers of the image quality and convenience benefits of the new product. *Persuasive advertising* becomes more important as competition increases. Here, the company's objective is to build selective demand. For example, once DVD players became established, Sony began trying to persuade consumers that *its* brand offered the best quality for their money.

Table 15.1 Possible Advertising Objectives

Informative Advertising	
Communicating customer value	Suggesting new uses for a product
Building a brand and company image	Informing the market of a price change
Telling the market about a new product	Describing available services and support
Explaining how the product works	Correcting false impressions

Persuasive Advertising	
Building brand preference	Persuading customers to purchase now
Encouraging switching to your brand	Persuading customers to receive a sales call
Changing customers' perception of product value	Convincing customers to tell others about the brand

Reminder Advertising	
Maintaining customer relationships	Reminding consumers where to buy the product
Reminding consumers that the product may be needed in the near future	Keeping the brand in customers' minds during off-seasons

Some persuasive advertising has become *comparative advertising*, in which a company directly or indirectly compares its brand with one or more other brands. Comparative advertising has been used for products ranging from soft drinks, beer, and pain relievers to computers, batteries, car rentals, and credit cards. For example, in its classic comparative campaign, Avis positioned itself against market-leading Hertz by claiming, "We try harder." And Apple's familiar "I'm a Mac; I'm a PC" ads take jabs at rival Windows-based computers.

You see examples of comparative advertising in almost every product category. For example, Gatorade recently ran ads comparing the 25 calories in its Propel fitness beverage to the 125 calories found in Glacéau's Vitaminwater, asking "How Fit Is Your Water?" Advertisers should use comparative advertising with caution. All too often, such ads invite competitor responses, resulting in an advertising war that neither competitor can win.

Reminder advertising is important for mature products—it helps to maintain customer relationships and keep consumers thinking about the product. Expensive Coca-Cola television ads primarily build and maintain the Coca-Cola brand relationship rather than inform or persuade customers to buy in the short run.

Advertising's goal is to help move consumers through the buying process. Some advertising is designed to move people to immediate action. For example, a direct-response television ad by Sharper Image for its Ionic Breeze air purifier urges consumers to pick up the phone and order right away, and a Sears newspaper ad for a weekend sale encourages immediate store visits. However, many

Comparative advertising: Gatorade ran ads comparing the 25 calories in its Propel fitness beverage to the 125 calories in Glacéau's Vitaminwater, asking "How Fit Is Your Water?"

of the other ads focus on building or strengthening long-term customer relationships. For example, a Nike television ad in which well-known athletes work through extreme challenges in their Nike gear never directly asks for a sale. Instead, the goal is to somehow change the way the customers think or feel about the brand.

Setting the Advertising Budget

Advertising budget
The dollars and other resources allocated to a product or company advertising program.

After determining its advertising objectives, the company next sets its **advertising budget** for each product. Four commonly used methods for setting promotion budgets were discussed in Chapter 14. Here we discuss some specific factors that should be considered when setting the advertising budget.

A brand's advertising budget often depends on its *stage in the product life cycle*. For example, new products typically need large advertising budgets to build awareness and to gain consumer trial. In contrast, mature brands usually require lower budgets as a ratio to sales. *Market share* also affects the amount of advertising needed: Because building the market or taking market share from competitors requires larger advertising spending than does simply maintaining current share, low-share brands usually need more advertising spending as a percentage of sales. Also, brands in a market with many competitors and high advertising clutter must be advertised more heavily to be noticed above the noise in the market. Undifferentiated brands—those that closely resemble other brands in their product class (soft drinks, laundry detergents)—may require heavy advertising to set them apart. When the product differs greatly from competitors, advertising can be used to point out the differences to consumers.

No matter what method is used, setting the advertising budget is no easy task. How does a company know if it is spending the right amount? Some critics charge that large consumer packaged goods firms tend to spend too much on advertising and that business-to-business marketers generally underspend on advertising. They claim that, on the one hand, the large consumer companies use lots of image advertising without really knowing its effects. They overspend as a form of "insurance" against not spending enough. On the other hand, business advertisers tend to rely too heavily on their sales forces to bring in orders. They underestimate the power of company and product image in preselling business customers. Thus, they do not spend enough on advertising to build customer awareness and knowledge.

Companies such as Coca-Cola and Kraft have built sophisticated statistical models to determine the relationship between promotional spending and brand sales, and to help determine the "optimal investment" across various media. Still, because so many factors affect advertising effectiveness, some controllable and others not, measuring the results of advertising spending remains an inexact science. In most cases, managers must rely on large doses of judgment along with more quantitative analysis when setting advertising budgets.[3]

Developing Advertising Strategy

Advertising strategy
The strategy by which the company accomplishes its advertising objectives. It consists of two major elements: creating advertising messages and selecting advertising media.

Advertising strategy consists of two major elements: creating advertising *messages* and selecting advertising *media*. In the past, companies often viewed media planning as secondary to the message-creation process. The creative department first created good advertisements, and then the media department selected and purchased the best media for carrying these advertisements to desired target audiences. This often caused friction between creatives and media planners.

Today, however, soaring media costs, more-focused target marketing strategies, and the blizzard of new media have promoted the importance of the media-planning function. The decision about which media to use for an ad campaign—television, magazines, cellphones, a website, or email—is now sometimes more critical than the creative elements of the campaign. As a result, more and more advertisers are orchestrating a closer harmony between their messages and the media that deliver them.[4]

In fact, in a really good ad campaign, you often have to ask "Is that a media idea or a creative idea?" For example, BMW created a huge buzz for its quirky, anything-but-ordinary British-made MINI car with an anything-but-ordinary "Let's Motor" campaign:

> The "Let's Motor" campaign employed a rich mix of unconventional media, carefully integrated to create personality for the car and a tremendous buzz of excitement among consumers. To create buzz, the company put MINIs in all kinds of imaginative places. It mounted them atop Ford Excursion SUVs and drove them around 22 major cities, highlighting the car's sensible size. It set up "MINI Ride" displays outside department stores, featuring an actual MINI that looked like a children's ride. "Rides $16 850. Quarters only," the sign said. Displays in airport terminals featured oversized newspaper vending machines and pay phones next to billboards showing the undersized MINI and proclaiming, "Makes everything else seem a little too big." The car was also promoted on the Internet, in ads painted on city buildings, and on baseball-type cards handed out at auto shows. In addition, BMW created MINI games, MINI booklets, MINI suitcases, and MINI placements in movies. It worked closely with selected magazines to create memorable print ads. For example, ads in *Wired* magazine contained a cardboard fold-out of a MINI, suggesting that readers assemble it and drive it around their desks making "putt-putt" noises. The "Let's Motor" campaign has been a smashing success, creating an almost cult-like following for the personable little car. Building on this success, MINI Canada created instant buzz to promote its 2009 convertible in downtown Toronto. A team of drivers strapped imitation arms to themselves, raised high in the air to mimic the feeling one gets when riding a rollercoaster. The result: a creative, quirky, and very funny video now airing on MINI's YouTube channel (www.youtube.com/user/mini?blend=1&ob=4).[5] Were these clever media ideas or clever creative ideas? They were both—the product of a tight media–creative partnership.

Creating the Advertising Message

No matter how big the budget, advertising can succeed only if advertisements gain attention and communicate well. Good advertising messages are especially important in today's costly and cluttered advertising environment. In 1950, the average Canadian household received just two network television channels and a handful of major national magazines. Today, there are five networks and 143 commercial channels, plus numerous U.S. signals being picked up in Canada. Canadian media options also include 1238 radio stations, 126 daily newspapers, 1100 community newspapers, and more than 900 consumer magazines.[6] Add the continuous barrage of catalogues, direct mail, email and online ads, and out-of-home media, and consumers are being bombarded with ads at home, at work, and at all points in between. As a result, consumers are exposed to as many as 3000 to 5000 commercial messages every day.[7]

Breaking Through the Clutter If all this advertising clutter bothers some consumers, it also causes huge headaches for advertisers. Take the situation facing network television advertisers. They pay an average of US$381 000 to make a single 30-second commercial. Then, each time they show it, they regularly pay US$250 000 or more for 30 seconds of advertising time during a popular prime-time program. They pay even more if it's an especially popular program such as *Grey's Anatomy* (US$419 000), *The Simpsons* (US$315 000), *American Idol* (up to US$750 000 for one commercial spot; more than US$1.3 million for the season finale), or a mega-event such as the Super

Building on the success of its "Let's Motor" campaign, MINI Canada created instant buzz to promote its 2009 convertible in downtown Toronto with its "Always Open" test drive.

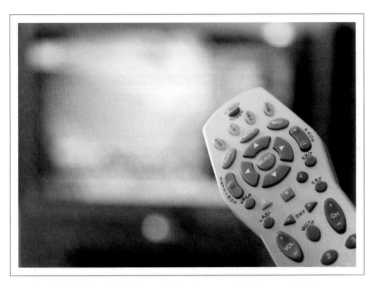

Advertising clutter: Today's consumers, armed with an arsenal of weapons, can choose what they watch and don't watch. Advertising messages must be better planned, more imaginative, more entertaining, and more rewarding to consumers.

Bowl (US$3 million per 30 seconds!).[8] In comparison, Canadian advertising is a bargain, but the reach is smaller. Thirty-second spots on national networks such as CBC and CTV are often less than $80 000, and ads on specialty channels, such as the Discovery Channel, may be as low as $5000.

Then, sponsors' ads are sandwiched in with a clutter of other commercials, announcements, and network promotions, totalling more than nearly 20 minutes of nonprogram material per prime-time hour with commercial breaks coming every 6 minutes on average. Such clutter in television and other ad media has created an increasingly hostile advertising environment. According to one recent study, 63 percent of people believe there are too many ads, and 47 percent say ads spoil their viewing enjoyment.[9]

Until recently, television viewers were pretty much a captive audience for advertisers. But today's digital wizardry has given consumers a rich new set of information and entertainment choices. With the growth in cable and satellite TV, the Internet, video on demand (VOD), video downloads, and DVD rentals, today's viewers have many more options. Digital technology has also armed consumers with an arsenal of weapons for choosing what they watch or don't watch. Increasingly, consumers are choosing *not* to watch ads. They "zap" commercials by fast-forwarding through recorded programs. With the remote control, they mute the sound during a commercial or "zip" around the channels to see what else is on. A recent study found that 40 percent of all television viewers now switch channels when the commercial break starts.[10]

Adding to the problem is the rapid growth of DVR (digital video recorder) systems. Almost 25 percent of North American homes now have DVR technology, and an estimated 39 percent will have it by 2011. Although DVRs increase total TV watching, research shows that 86 percent of DVR owners fast-forward through all or most commercials. As a result, according to one study, about 20 percent of brands experienced lower sales in ad-skipping households. One ad agency executive calls DVR systems "electronic weedwhackers." "In time, the number of people using them to obliterate commercials will totally erode faith in the 30-second commercial," he declares. Similarly, the number of VOD viewers is expected to quadruple during the next five years. These viewers will be able to watch programming on their own time, with or without commercials.[11]

Thus, advertisers can no longer force-feed the same old cookie-cutter ad messages to captive consumers through traditional media. Just to gain and hold attention, today's advertising messages must be better planned, more imaginative, more entertaining, and more rewarding to consumers. "Interruption or disruption as the fundamental premise of marketing" no longer works, says one advertising executive. Instead, "you have to create content that is interesting, useful, or entertaining enough to invite [consumers]." According to another, "Everything is about control. If an ad is interesting to you, you'll have a conversation with the brand. If it's not, it's a waste of time."[12]

In fact, many marketers are now subscribing to a new merging of advertising and entertainment, dubbed "**Madison & Vine**." You've probably heard of Madison Avenue. It's the New York City street that houses the headquarters of many of the nation's largest advertising agencies. You may also have heard of Hollywood & Vine, the intersection of Hollywood Avenue and Vine Street in Hollywood, California, long the symbolic heart of the U.S. entertainment industry. Now, Madison Avenue and Hollywood & Vine are coming together to form a new intersection—*Madison & Vine*—that represents the merging of advertising and entertainment in an effort to break through the clutter and create new avenues for reaching consumers with more engaging messages (see Real Marketing 15.1).

Madison & Vine
A term that has come to represent the merging of advertising and entertainment in an effort to break through the clutter and create new avenues for reaching consumers with more engaging messages.

Creative concept
The compelling "big idea" that will bring the advertising message strategy to life in a distinctive and memorable way.

Message strategy statements tend to be plain, straightforward outlines of benefits and positioning points that the advertiser wants to stress. The advertiser must next develop a compelling **creative concept**—or "big idea"—that will bring the message strategy to life in a distinctive and memorable way. At this stage, simple message ideas become great ad campaigns. Usually, a copywriter and art director will team up to generate many creative concepts, hoping that one of these concepts will turn out to be the big idea. The creative concept may emerge as a visualization, a phrase, or a combination of the two.

The creative concept will guide the choice of specific appeals to be used in an advertising campaign. Advertising appeals should have three characteristics. First, they should be meaningful, pointing out benefits that make the product more desirable or interesting to consumers. Second, appeals must be believable—consumers must believe that the product or service will deliver the promised benefits.

However, the most meaningful and believable benefits may not be the best ones to feature. Appeals should also be distinctive—they should tell how the product is better than the competing brands. For example, the most meaningful benefit of owning a wristwatch is that it keeps accurate time, yet few watch ads feature this benefit. Instead, based on the distinctive benefits they offer, watch advertisers might select any of a number of advertising themes. For years Timex has been the affordable watch that "Takes a lickin' and keeps on tickin'." In contrast, Fossil has featured style and fashion, whereas Rolex stresses luxury and status.

Message Execution The advertiser now has to turn the big idea into an actual ad execution that will capture the target market's attention and interest. The creative team must find the best approach, style, tone, words, and format for executing the message. Any message can be presented in different **execution styles**, such as the following:

Execution style
The approach, style, tone, words, and format used for executing an advertising message.

- *Slice of life:* This style shows one or more "typical" people using the product in a normal setting. For example, a Silk soymilk "Rise and Shine" ad shows a young professional starting the day with a healthier breakfast and high hopes.

- *Lifestyle:* This style shows how a product fits in with a particular lifestyle. For example, an ad for Liquidlogic kayaks shows kayakers challenging some serious white water and states, "Two-thirds of the earth is covered in playground—live wet."

- *Fantasy:* This style creates a fantasy around the product or its use. For example, one Travelers Insurance commercial features a gentleman carrying a giant red umbrella (the company's brand symbol). The man helps groups of people by using the umbrella to protect them from the rain, sail them across a flooded river, and fly home. The ad closes with "Travelers Insurance. There when you need it."

- *Mood or image:* This style builds a mood or image around the product or service, such as beauty, love, or serenity. Few claims are made about the product except through suggestion. For example, ads for Singapore Airlines feature soft lighting and refined flight attendants pampering relaxed and happy customers.

- *Musical:* This style shows people or cartoon characters singing about the product. For example, one of the most famous ads in history was a Coca-Cola ad built around the song "I'd Like to Teach the World to Sing." Similarly, Oscar Mayer has long run ads showing children singing its now-classic "I wish I were an Oscar Mayer wiener . . ." jingle. And is there anyone who doesn't know the Chili's advertising song, "I love my baby-back, baby-back, baby-back, . . . baby-back ribs"?

- *Personality symbol:* This style creates a character that represents the product. The character might be *animated* (Mr. Clean, Tony the Tiger, the Energizer Bunny) or *real* (Ol' Lonely, the Maytag repairman; the GEICO cavemen; or Hubert, the Whiskas "cat").

- *Technical expertise:* This style shows the company's expertise in making the product. Thus, Maxwell House shows one of its buyers carefully selecting coffee beans, and McAuslan Brewery in Montreal sells itself as "The Beer Professionals."

Chili's restaurant and orders his "awesome blossom, extra awesome"—in one episode, he even breaks into the restaurant's catchy "baby back ribs" jingle while entertaining a client there. In another, he sings the praises of Sandals resort in Jamaica—literally. "I've got two tickets to paradise. Pack your bags, we'll leave day after tomorrow," he croons.

These days you'd be hard-pressed to find any TV show that doesn't feature some kind of product placement. But the practice is particularly prevalent on reality TV. Last year, NBC's *The Biggest Loser* was responsible for almost 4000 different placements from companies ranging from Quaker Oats and Wrigley's chewing gum to Subway. Fox's *American Idol*, the nation's highest rated show, shoehorned in more than 3000 placements. Old Navy dressed the contestants while Clairol did their hair, and Ford supplied the winners with new cars.

Reality shows are big hits with advertisers because they top the charts in placement effectiveness as well as in ratings. Giving away products on a feel-good show like ABC's *Extreme Makeover: Home Edition* or having Donald Trump praise a brand on *The Apprentice* has a huge impact on product awareness. Just ask the folks at Tyson Foods, which topped IAG's list of products with the greatest number of TV viewers who recalled the brand from shows and thought better of it afterward. Tyson gave 20 000 pounds of meat to a community and a year's worth of food to a family featured on *Extreme Makeover: Home Edition*. The brand's appearance on the show—which included mentions by name plus a visual of a Tyson truck—was nearly four times more effective than the average TV show product placement. Matching the brand to the program is key. For example, Kraft got a good bump from being on Bravo's *Top Chef* and Propel fitness beverage got a boost from mentions on Bravo's *Work Out*. "On average, product placements are breaking through better in terms of recall than traditional commercials," says an industry executive.

Originally created with TV in mind, branded entertainment has spread quickly into other sectors of the entertainment industry. It's widely used in movies (remember all those GM vehicles in *Transformers* or the billboard of brands on Ricky Bobby's racing outfit in *Talladega Nights*?). If you look carefully, you'll also see subtle and not-so-subtle product placements in video games, comic books, Broadway musicals, and even pop music. A single mention of the new energy drink Fever in a music video by rapper Ludacris sent sales skyrocketing. One San Francisco firm even gauges brand equity by the number of mentions received in Billboard's top 100 (Nike, Mercedes, and Cadillac are typically at the top of that heap).

How much advertisers pay for a product placement depends on the magnitude of the placement, the size of the audience, and whether or not the deal is packaged with other stuff. More and more, the best placements are being sold with strings attached. "It's no longer, 'Here's $50 000, get my car in a background shot,'" says an analyst. "Now you negotiate a package of advertising, marketing, space on your website, and, in exchange, the product is in the picture." AT&T is rumoured to have paid US$50 million for an *American Idol* deal that mixes traditional ads with frequent product placements.

So Madison & Vine is *the* new meeting place for the advertising and entertainment industries. When done right, advertainment and branded entertainment can pay big dividends. However, experts caution that Madison & Vine can also be a dangerous crossing. They worry that making ads too entertaining might detract from the seller's brand message—consumers will remember the clever ad but forget the brand or advertiser. And they note that the intersection is getting pretty congested. With all these new ad formats and product placements, Madison & Vine threatens to create even more of the very clutter that it's designed to break through. At what point will consumers decide that the intersection of Madison & Vine is just too congested and take yet a different route?

But a spokesperson for *American Idol* says that show's having no such placement-overload problems. "We haven't heard [any complaints] from our focus groups, and the advertisers are pleased with the results. [In fact], we spend most of our time turning [advertisers] away." Ford's general marketing manager agrees. "If we didn't [re-sign, our slot] would be snapped up by a competitor in a heartbeat."

Sources: Quotes and information from Steve McClellan, "TiVo Helps Super Bowl Ad Ratings," *Adweek*, January 31, 2008, accessed online at www.adweek.com; Elizabeth Olson, "Practicing the Subtle Sell of Placing Products on Webisodes," *New York Times*, January 3, 2008, p. C3; Richard Huff, "Product Placement Outsells Ads," *Daily News*, December 27, 2007, p. 73; Phil Rosenthal, "'Office' Makes Pitch to Viewers: Watch and Buy," *Chicago Tribune*, December 10, 2007; Louise Story, "Viewers Fast-Forwarding Past Ads? Not Always," *New York Times*, February 16, 2007, p. 1; Ravi Somaiya, "Product Placement: 'Chloe, It's Jack. Who Does Our Phones?'" *The Guardian*, June 16, 2008, p. 3; Ken Bensinger, "Carmakers Stretch Mileage of Product Placement Deals," *Los Angeles Times*, June 14, 2008, p. C1; Ronald Grover, "*American Idol*'s Ads Infinitum," *BusinessWeek*, June 2, 2008, p. 38; and Alana Semuels, "Advertising's Matchmaker," *Los Angeles Times*, June 2, 2008, p. C1.

Message Strategy The first step in creating effective advertising messages is to plan a message strategy—to decide what general message will be communicated to consumers. The purpose of advertising is to get consumers to think about or react to the product or company in a certain way. People will react only if they believe that they will benefit from doing so. Thus, developing an effective message strategy begins with identifying customer benefits that can be used as advertising appeals. Ideally, advertising message strategy will follow directly from the company's broader positioning and customer value strategies.

Creative concept
The compelling "big idea" that will bring the advertising message strategy to life in a distinctive and memorable way.

Message strategy statements tend to be plain, straightforward outlines of benefits and positioning points that the advertiser wants to stress. The advertiser must next develop a compelling **creative concept**—or "big idea"—that will bring the message strategy to life in a distinctive and memorable way. At this stage, simple message ideas become great ad campaigns. Usually, a copywriter and art director will team up to generate many creative concepts, hoping that one of these concepts will turn out to be the big idea. The creative concept may emerge as a visualization, a phrase, or a combination of the two.

The creative concept will guide the choice of specific appeals to be used in an advertising campaign. Advertising appeals should have three characteristics. First, they should be meaningful, pointing out benefits that make the product more desirable or interesting to consumers. Second, appeals must be believable—consumers must believe that the product or service will deliver the promised benefits.

However, the most meaningful and believable benefits may not be the best ones to feature. Appeals should also be distinctive—they should tell how the product is better than the competing brands. For example, the most meaningful benefit of owning a wristwatch is that it keeps accurate time, yet few watch ads feature this benefit. Instead, based on the distinctive benefits they offer, watch advertisers might select any of a number of advertising themes. For years Timex has been the affordable watch that "Takes a lickin' and keeps on tickin'." In contrast, Fossil has featured style and fashion, whereas Rolex stresses luxury and status.

Message Execution The advertiser now has to turn the big idea into an actual ad execution that will capture the target market's attention and interest. The creative team must find the best approach, style, tone, words, and format for executing the message. Any message can be presented in different **execution styles**, such as the following:

Execution style
The approach, style, tone, words, and format used for executing an advertising message.

- *Slice of life:* This style shows one or more "typical" people using the product in a normal setting. For example, a Silk soymilk "Rise and Shine" ad shows a young professional starting the day with a healthier breakfast and high hopes.

- *Lifestyle:* This style shows how a product fits in with a particular lifestyle. For example, an ad for Liquidlogic kayaks shows kayakers challenging some serious white water and states, "Two-thirds of the earth is covered in playground—live wet."

- *Fantasy:* This style creates a fantasy around the product or its use. For example, one Travelers Insurance commercial features a gentleman carrying a giant red umbrella (the company's brand symbol). The man helps groups of people by using the umbrella to protect them from the rain, sail them across a flooded river, and fly home. The ad closes with "Travelers Insurance. There when you need it."

- *Mood or image:* This style builds a mood or image around the product or service, such as beauty, love, or serenity. Few claims are made about the product except through suggestion. For example, ads for Singapore Airlines feature soft lighting and refined flight attendants pampering relaxed and happy customers.

- *Musical:* This style shows people or cartoon characters singing about the product. For example, one of the most famous ads in history was a Coca-Cola ad built around the song "I'd Like to Teach the World to Sing." Similarly, Oscar Mayer has long run ads showing children singing its now-classic "I wish I were an Oscar Mayer wiener . . ." jingle. And is there anyone who doesn't know the Chili's advertising song, "I love my baby-back, baby-back, baby-back, . . . baby-back ribs"?

- *Personality symbol:* This style creates a character that represents the product. The character might be *animated* (Mr. Clean, Tony the Tiger, the Energizer Bunny) or *real* (Ol' Lonely, the Maytag repairman; the GEICO cavemen; or Hubert, the Whiskas "cat").

- *Technical expertise:* This style shows the company's expertise in making the product. Thus, Maxwell House shows one of its buyers carefully selecting coffee beans, and McAuslan Brewery in Montreal sells itself as "The Beer Professionals."

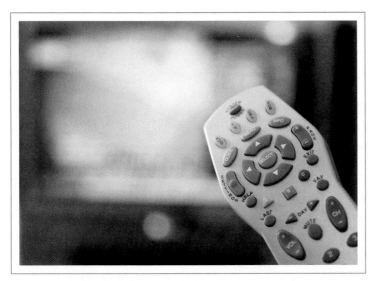

Advertising clutter: Today's consumers, armed with an arsenal of weapons, can choose what they watch and don't watch. Advertising messages must be better planned, more imaginative, more entertaining, and more rewarding to consumers.

Bowl (US$3 million per 30 seconds!).[8] In comparison, Canadian advertising is a bargain, but the reach is smaller. Thirty-second spots on national networks such as CBC and CTV are often less than $80 000, and ads on specialty channels, such as the Discovery Channel, may be as low as $5000.

Then, sponsors' ads are sandwiched in with a clutter of other commercials, announcements, and network promotions, totalling more than nearly 20 minutes of nonprogram material per prime-time hour with commercial breaks coming every 6 minutes on average. Such clutter in television and other ad media has created an increasingly hostile advertising environment. According to one recent study, 63 percent of people believe there are too many ads, and 47 percent say ads spoil their viewing enjoyment.[9]

Until recently, television viewers were pretty much a captive audience for advertisers. But today's digital wizardry has given consumers a rich new set of information and entertainment choices. With the growth in cable and satellite TV, the Internet, video on demand (VOD), video downloads, and DVD rentals, today's viewers have many more options. Digital technology has also armed consumers with an arsenal of weapons for choosing what they watch or don't watch. Increasingly, consumers are choosing *not* to watch ads. They "zap" commercials by fast-forwarding through recorded programs. With the remote control, they mute the sound during a commercial or "zip" around the channels to see what else is on. A recent study found that 40 percent of all television viewers now switch channels when the commercial break starts.[10]

Adding to the problem is the rapid growth of DVR (digital video recorder) systems. Almost 25 percent of North American homes now have DVR technology, and an estimated 39 percent will have it by 2011. Although DVRs increase total TV watching, research shows that 86 percent of DVR owners fast-forward through all or most commercials. As a result, according to one study, about 20 percent of brands experienced lower sales in ad-skipping households. One ad agency executive calls DVR systems "electronic weedwhackers." "In time, the number of people using them to obliterate commercials will totally erode faith in the 30-second commercial," he declares. Similarly, the number of VOD viewers is expected to quadruple during the next five years. These viewers will be able to watch programming on their own time, with or without commercials.[11]

Thus, advertisers can no longer force-feed the same old cookie-cutter ad messages to captive consumers through traditional media. Just to gain and hold attention, today's advertising messages must be better planned, more imaginative, more entertaining, and more rewarding to consumers. "Interruption or disruption as the fundamental premise of marketing" no longer works, says one advertising executive. Instead, "you have to create content that is interesting, useful, or entertaining enough to invite [consumers]." According to another, "Everything is about control. If an ad is interesting to you, you'll have a conversation with the brand. If it's not, it's a waste of time."[12]

Madison & Vine

A term that has come to represent the merging of advertising and entertainment in an effort to break through the clutter and create new avenues for reaching consumers with more engaging messages.

In fact, many marketers are now subscribing to a new merging of advertising and entertainment, dubbed "**Madison & Vine**." You've probably heard of Madison Avenue. It's the New York City street that houses the headquarters of many of the nation's largest advertising agencies. You may also have heard of Hollywood & Vine, the intersection of Hollywood Avenue and Vine Street in Hollywood, California, long the symbolic heart of the U.S. entertainment industry. Now, Madison Avenue and Hollywood & Vine are coming together to form a new intersection—*Madison & Vine*—that represents the merging of advertising and entertainment in an effort to break through the clutter and create new avenues for reaching consumers with more engaging messages (see Real Marketing 15.1).

Real Marketing 15.1

Madison & Vine: The New Intersection of Advertising and Entertainment

Welcome to the ever-busier intersection of Madison & Vine, where the advertising industry meets the entertainment industry. In today's cluttered advertising environment, Madison Avenue knows that it must find new ways to engage ad-weary consumers with more-compelling messages. The answer? Entertainment! And who knows more about entertainment than the folks at Hollywood & Vine? The term "Madison & Vine" has come to represent the merging of advertising and entertainment. It takes one of two primary forms: *advertainment* or *branded entertainment*.

The aim of *advertainment* is to make ads themselves so entertaining, or so useful, that people *want* to watch them. It's advertising by invitation rather than by intrusion. There's no chance that you'd watch ads on purpose, you say? Think again. For example, the Super Bowl has become an annual advertainment showcase. Tens of millions of people tune in to the Super Bowl each year, as much to watch the entertaining ads as to see the game.

In fact, rather than bemoaning TiVo and other DVR systems, many advertisers are now realizing that the devices can actually *improve* viewership of a really good ad. For example, one study showed that most Super Bowl ads last year were viewed more in DVR households than non-DVR households. Rather than zipping past the ads, many people were rewinding to watch them again and again.

Interestingly, this dynamic extends beyond Super Bowl ads. Although DVRs contribute to lower overall ad viewership, studies show that DVR users don't necessarily skip all the ads. According to one study, 55 percent of DVR users take their finger off the fast-forward button to watch a commercial that is entertaining or relevant, sometimes even watching it again. "If advertising is really entertaining [or informative], you don't zap it," notes an industry observer. "You might even go out of your way to see it."

Beyond making their regular ads more entertaining, advertisers are also creating new advertising forms that look less like ads and more like short films or shows. Online "webisode" spending is now growing faster (45 percent per year) than any other form of promotion. For example, American Eagle Outfitters has embraced the concept whole-heartedly. The clothing marketer has gone way beyond 30-second spots by introducing its own dedicated media channel, dubbed 77E, on its website. The channel's biggest hit thus far is the webisode series, "It's a Mall World." Featuring heartthrob Milo Ventimiglia from the NBC TV series *Heroes*, the 2- to 5-minute video shorts have racked up more than 150 million views. On nights when a new episode debuts, traffic on the main AEO site jumps 20 percent. More astounding, 75 percent of those who watch the episodes make a purchase.

Branded entertainment (or *brand integrations*) involves making the brand an inseparable part of some other form of entertainment. The most common form of branded entertainment is product placements—embedding brands as props within other programming. In all, U.S. advertisers shelled out an estimated $10 billion on product placements in 2007, more than the GDP of Paraguay. In only the first three months of 2008 alone, America's top 11 TV channels produced a massive 117 976 product placements.

The nature of these placements can vary widely. It might be a brief glimpse of a Motorola phone on the ABC hit show *Lost*, or *24's* Chloe clicking away at a Cisco terminal. Or it might involve actually scripting products into the theme of the program. For example, the boss of *The Office* frequents

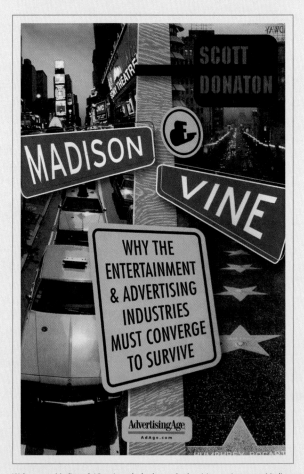

Welcome to Madison & Vine. In today's cluttered advertising environment, Madison Avenue must find new ways to engage ad-weary consumers with more compelling messages. The answer? Entertainment!

- *Scientific evidence:* This style presents survey or scientific evidence that the brand is better or better liked than one or more other brands. For years, Crest toothpaste has used scientific evidence to convince buyers that Crest is better than other brands at fighting cavities.
- *Testimonial evidence or endorsement:* This style features a highly believable or likable source endorsing the product. It could be ordinary people saying how much they like a given product. For example, Subway uses spokesman Jared, a customer who lost 245 pounds on a diet of Subway sandwiches. Or it might be a celebrity presenting the product, such as Jennifer Love Hewitt and Jessica Simpson speaking for Proactiv Solution.

The advertiser also must choose a *tone* for the ad. Procter & Gamble always uses a positive tone: Its ads say something very positive about its products. Other advertisers now use edgy humour to break through the commercial clutter. Bud Light commercials are famous for this.

The advertiser must use memorable and attention-getting *words* in the ad. For example, rather than claiming simply that "a BMW is a well-engineered automobile," BMW uses more creative and higher-impact phrasing: "The ultimate driving machine." Microsoft's Zune isn't just a "programmable digital media device." With Zune, "you make it you." The World Wildlife Fund doesn't say, "We need your money to help save nature." Instead, it says "We share the sky. We share the future. Together, we can be a force of nature."

Finally, *format* elements make a difference in an ad's impact as well as in its cost. A small change in ad design can make a big difference in its effect. In a print ad, the *illustration* is the first thing the reader notices—it must be strong enough to draw attention. Next, the *headline* must effectively entice the right people to read the copy. Finally, the *copy*—the main block of text in the ad—must be simple but strong and convincing. Moreover, these three elements must effectively work *together* to persuasively present customer value.

Consumer-Generated Messages   Taking advantage of today's interactive technologies, many companies are now tapping consumers for message ideas or actual ads. They are searching existing video sites, setting up their own sites, and sponsoring ad-creation contests and other promotions.

Sometimes, marketers capitalize on consumer videos that are already posted on sites such as YouTube, MySpace, Google, and Yahoo!. For example, one of the most viewed amateur videos on the Web last year showed Diet Coke mixed with Mentos candies to produce shooting fountains of soda. The video produced a windfall of free buzz for Coca-Cola. To gain even more mileage, Coca-Cola hired the amateur videographers—a professional juggler and a lawyer—to create another video and to star in a 30-second Coke ad.[13]

Other marketers hold contests or develop brand websites of their own that invite consumers to submit ad message ideas and videos. For example, PepsiCo's Doritos brand held a "Crash the Super Bowl Challenge" contest that invited consumers to create their own video ads about the tasty triangular corn chips. Doritos received 1080 user-generated videos and posted the top five on the contest website, where consumers could view the ads and vote for a winner. The five finalists received a US$10 000 prize and PepsiCo showed the winning ad during the Super Bowl. The campaign was a smashing success.

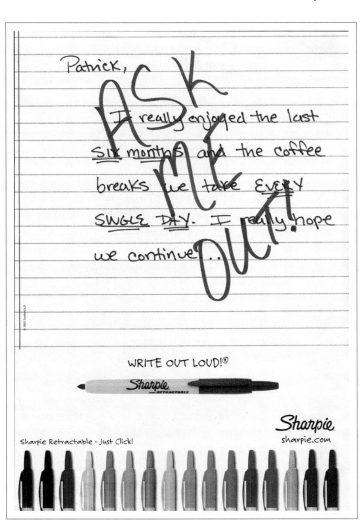

Ad format and design: In this ad, Sharpie uses humour along with an attention-getting layout to highlight the benefits of its colourful markers.

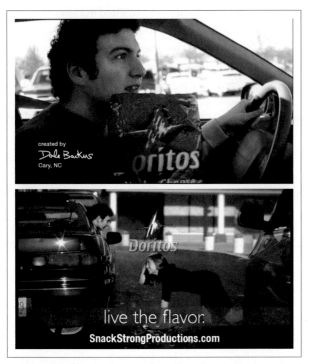

Consumer-generated messages: The Doritos "Crash the Super Bowl Challenge" contest invited consumers to create their own video ads. Frito Lay showed the winning ad during the Super Bowl.

The user-generated Doritos ad placed fifth in *USA Today's* Ad Meter of the most popular Super Bowl ads, and Doritos received a heap of pre- and post-Super Bowl buzz surrounding the contest and the finalist ads. The campaign was so successful that Frito Lay followed up in 2008 by inviting consumers to submit original songs at www.snackstrongproductions.com—its Second Life–inspired Doritos web environment. Frito Lay then gave winner Kina Grannis the stage of a lifetime by airing a 60-second music video featuring her winning song on the Super Bowl.[14]

Not all consumer-generated advertising efforts are so successful. In fact, it can be downright dangerous to give consumers too much creative freedom and control. For example, Quiznos recently invited the public to submit homemade commercials in a contest designed to attack rival Subway. The rules for its "Quiznos vs. Subway TV Ad Challenge" made it clear that the ads should depict Quiznos sandwiches as superior to Subway's. Subway promptly sued Quiznos, claiming that the submitted videos made false claims and portrayed Subway in a derogatory way.[15] In another case, when Chevrolet ran a promotion for its Tahoe SUV allowing consumers to write their own text for video clips of the vehicle, it got some unexpected negative results. Many of the user-created ads contained critical gibes about the big SUV's poor gas mileage, high operating costs, and harmful environmental impact. Thus, marketers should be cautious when inviting consumer creative inputs.[16]

If used carefully, however, consumer-generated advertising efforts can produce big benefits. First, for relatively little expense, companies can collect new creative ideas as well as fresh perspectives on the brand and what it actually means to consumers. "Companies have [their own] vision of what they want their brand to be," says the founder of AdCandy.com, a website that solicits consumer ideas for product and company taglines. "But if everyone is saying your brand is something else, it may be a battle. Powerful things come from the street, from the people who use the product."[17]

Second, consumer-generated message campaigns can boost consumer involvement and get consumers talking and thinking about a brand and its value to them. Not only do marketers get "a peek into the public's consciousness and what they are thinking . . . [but] by participating and interacting, [consumers] develop a vested interest in your brand," says the AdCandy.com founder. Adds another marketer, "Engage a satisfied customer in a dialogue about a product—and give them a forum to express their creative aspirations for that product—and you will have a brand advocate who speaks from the heart."[18]

Selecting Advertising Media

Advertising media
The vehicles through which advertising messages are delivered to their intended audiences.

The major steps in **advertising media** selection are (1) deciding on *reach, frequency,* and *impact*; (2) choosing among major *media types*; (3) selecting specific *media vehicles*; and (4) deciding on *media timing.*

Deciding on Reach, Frequency, and Impact To select media, the advertiser must decide on the reach and frequency needed to achieve advertising objectives. *Reach* is a measure of the *percentage* of people in the target market who are exposed to the ad campaign during a given period of time. For example, the advertiser might try to reach 70 percent of the target market during the first three months of the campaign. *Frequency* is a measure of how many *times* the average person in the target market is exposed to the message. For example, the advertiser might want an average exposure frequency of three.

But advertisers want to do more than just reach a given number of consumers a specific number of times. The advertiser must also decide on the desired *media impact*—the *qualitative value* of a message exposure through a given medium. For example, the same message in one magazine (say, *Maclean's*) may be more believable than in another (say, the *National Enquirer*). For products that need to be demonstrated, messages on television may have more impact than messages on radio because television uses sight *and* sound. Products for which consumers provide input on design or features might be better promoted at an interactive website than in a direct mailing.

More generally, the advertiser wants to choose media that will *engage* consumers rather than simply reach them. For example, for television advertising, "how relevant a program is for its audience and where the ads are inserted are likely to be much more important than whether the program was a Nielsen winner" numbers-wise, says one expert. "This is about 'lean to' TV rather than 'lean back.'"

Although Nielsen is beginning to measure levels of television *media engagement*, such measures are hard to come by for most media. "All the measurements we have now are media metrics: ratings, readership, listenership, click-through rates," says an executive of the Advertising Research Foundation, but engagement "happens inside the consumer, not inside the medium. What we need is a way to determine how the targeted prospect connected with, got engaged with, the brand idea. With engagement, you're on your way to a relationship. . . ."[19]

Choosing Among Major Media Types The media planner has to know the reach, frequency, and impact of each of the major media types. As summarized in Table 15.2, the major media types are television, the Internet, newspapers, direct mail, magazines, radio, and outdoor. Advertisers can also choose from a wide array of new digital media, such as cellphones and other digital devices, which reach consumers directly. Each medium has advantages and limitations. Media planners consider many factors when making their media choices. They want to choose media that will effectively and efficiently present the advertising message to target customers. Thus, they must consider each medium's impact, message effectiveness, and cost.

The mix of media must be re-examined regularly. For a long time, television and magazines dominated in the media mixes of national advertisers, with other media often being neglected. However, as discussed previously, the media mix appears to be shifting. As mass-media costs rise, audiences shrink, and exciting new digital media emerge, many advertisers are finding new ways to reach consumers. They are supplementing the traditional mass

Table 15.2 Profiles of Major Media Types

Medium	Advantages	Limitations
Television	Good mass-marketing coverage; low cost per exposure; combines sight, sound, and motion; appealing to the senses	High absolute costs; high clutter; fleeting exposure; less audience selectivity
Internet	High selectivity; low cost; immediacy; interactive capabilities	Relatively low impact; the audience controls exposure
Newspapers	Flexibility; timeliness; good local market coverage; broad acceptability; high believability	Short life; poor reproduction quality; small pass-along audience
Direct mail	High audience selectivity; flexibility; no ad competition within the same medium; allows personalization	Relatively high cost per exposure, "junk mail" image
Magazines	High geographic and demographic selectivity; credibility and prestige; high-quality reproduction; long life and good pass-along readership	Long ad purchase lead time; high cost; no guarantee of position
Radio	Good local acceptance; high geographic and demographic selectivity; low cost	Audio only, fleeting exposure; low attention ("the half-heard" medium); fragmented audiences
Outdoor	Flexibility; high repeat exposure; low cost; low message competition; good positional selectivity	Little audience selectivity; creative limitations

Marketers have discovered a dazzling array of "alternative media."

media with more-specialized and highly targeted media that cost less, target more effectively, and engage consumers more fully.

For example, cable television and satellite television systems are booming. Such systems allow narrow programming formats such as all sports, all news, nutrition, arts, home improvement and gardening, cooking, travel, history, finance, and others that target select groups. Advertisers can take advantage of such "narrowcasting" to "rifle in" on special market segments rather than use the "shotgun" approach offered by network broadcasting. Cable and satellite television media seem to make good sense. But, increasingly, ads are popping up in far-less-likely places. In their efforts to find less-costly and more highly targeted ways to reach consumers, advertisers have discovered a dazzling collection of "alternative media." These days, no matter where you go or what you do, you will probably run into some new form of advertising.

Tiny billboards attached to shopping carts, ads on shopping bags, and advertising decals on supermarket floors urge you to buy JELL-O Pudding or Pampers, while ads roll by on the store's checkout conveyor touting your local Volvo dealer. Even supermarket eggs are stamped with the names of CBS television shows. At the local laundromat, you load your laundry through a clever Pepto-Bismol ad plastered on the front of the washing machine. Step outside and there goes a city trash truck sporting an ad for Glad trash bags. You escape to the ballpark, only to find billboard-size video screens running Budweiser ads while a blimp with an electronic message board circles lazily overhead. How about a quiet trip in the country? Sorry—you find an enterprising farmer using his milk cows as four-legged billboards mounted with ads for Ben & Jerry's ice cream.

These days, you're likely to find ads—well, anywhere. Boats cruise along public beaches flashing advertising messages for Sundown Sunscreen as sunbathers spread their towels over ads for Snapple pressed into the sand. Taxi cabs sport electronic messaging signs tied to GPS location sensors that can pitch local stores and restaurants wherever they roam. Ad space is being sold on DVD cases, parking-lot tickets, subway turnstiles, golf scorecards, delivery trucks, pizza boxes, gas pumps, ATMs, municipal garbage cans, police cars, doctors' examining tables, and church bulletins. One agency even leases space on the foreheads of college students for temporary advertising tattoos. And the group meeting at the office water cooler has a new member—a "coolertising" ad sitting on top of the water cooler jug trying to start up a conversation about the latest episode of *American Idol*.[20]

Such alternative media seem a bit far-fetched, and they sometimes irritate consumers who resent it all as "ad nauseam." But for many marketers, these media can save money and provide a way to hit selected consumers where they live, shop, work, and play. Of course, all this may leave you wondering if there are any commercial-free havens remaining for ad-weary consumers. Public elevators, perhaps, or stalls in a public restroom? Forget it! Each has already been invaded by innovative marketers.

Another important trend affecting media selection is the rapid growth in the number of "media multitaskers," people who absorb more than one medium at a time:

It looks like people who aren't satisfied with "just watching TV" are in good company. According to a recent survey, three-fourths of TV viewers read the newspaper while they watch TV, and two-thirds of them go online during their TV time. Another study indicates that the tasks now carried out in a typical day would have taken 31 hours to do 10 years ago with more primitive systems. What's more, if today's kids are any indication, media multitasking is on the rise. North Americans aged 8 to 18 are managing to cram an average 8.5 hours of media consumption into 6.5 hours. What's more, 73 percent of multitasking kids are engaged in "active multitasking," with the content in one medium influencing concurrent behaviour in another. It's not uncommon to find a teenage boy chasing down photos of Keira Knightley on Google, IMing several friends at once, listening to a mix of music on iTunes, and talking on the cellphone to a friend—all while, in the midst of the multimedia chaos, trying to complete an essay he's got open in a Word file a few layers down on his desktop.[21]

Media planners need to take such media interactions into account when selecting the types of media they will use.

Selecting Specific Media Vehicles The media planner now must choose the best *media vehicles*—specific media within each general media type. For example, television vehicles include *This Hour Has 22 Minutes* and CBC's *The National*. Magazine vehicles include *Maclean's*, *Chatelaine*, and *LouLou*.

The media planner must also consider the costs of producing ads for different media. Whereas newspaper ads may cost very little to produce, flashy television ads can be very costly. For example, a typical television commercial might cost US$500 000 to US$1 million or more to produce. Guinness recently filmed a commercial titled "Tipping Point" in a tiny town of just 2000 people high in the mountains of northern Argentina, where you can't even get a pint of the stout. The cost to create the ad? An almost unimaginable US$20 million. Interestingly, the consumer-generated Doritos Super Bowl ad mentioned earlier cost just US$12.79, mostly spent on the bags of Doritos used in the ad.[22] There must be a lesson there somewhere for professional ad makers.

In selecting specific media vehicles, the media planner must balance media costs against several media effectiveness factors. First, the planner should evaluate the media vehicle's *audience quality*. For a Huggies disposable diaper advertisement, for example, *Today's Parent* magazine would have a high exposure value; *Maxim* would have a low exposure value. Second, the media planner should consider *audience engagement*. Readers of *Flare*, for example, typically pay more attention to ads than do readers of *The Economist*. Third, the planner should assess the vehicle's *editorial quality*—*Maclean's* and *Canadian Business* are more believable and prestigious than the *National Enquirer*.

Petro-Canada, a national partner of the Vancouver 2010 Olympic and Paralympic Winter Games, ran its "Dream Big" campaign extensively during the months leading up to the Beijing games.

Deciding on Media Timing The advertiser must also decide how to schedule the advertising over the course of a year. Suppose sales of a product peak in December and drop in March. The firm can vary its advertising to follow the seasonal pattern, to oppose the seasonal pattern, or to be the same all year. Most firms do some seasonal advertising. For example, Sears Portrait Studio advertises more heavily before major holidays such as Christmas, Easter, and Valentine's Day. And some marketers do only seasonal advertising. For instance, Hallmark advertises its greeting cards only before major holidays. Some firms advertise heavily around certain events rather than by seasons. For example, Petro-Canada, a national partner of the Vancouver 2010 Olympic and Paralympic Winter Games, ran its "Dream Big" campaign extensively during the months leading up to the Beijing games. The TV ads and supporting website, IWillDreamBig.ca, highlight Canadian athletes and their success stories.

Finally, the advertiser has to choose the pattern of the ads. *Continuity* means scheduling ads evenly within a given period. *Pulsing* means scheduling ads unevenly over a given time period. Thus, 52 ads could either be scheduled at one per week during the year or pulsed in several bursts. The idea behind pulsing is to advertise heavily for a short period to build awareness that carries over to the next advertising period. Those who favour pulsing feel that it can be used to achieve the same impact as a steady schedule but at a much lower cost. However, some media planners believe that although pulsing achieves minimal awareness, it sacrifices depth of advertising communications.

Evaluating Advertising Effectiveness and Return on Advertising Investment

Return on advertising investment
The net return on advertising investment divided by the costs of the advertising investment.

Advertising accountability and **return on advertising investment** have become hot issues for most companies. Two separate recent studies show that advertising effectiveness has fallen 40 percent over the past decade and that 37.3 percent of advertising budgets are wasted. This leaves top management and many companies asking their marketing managers, "How do we know that we're spending the right amount on advertising?" and "What return are we getting on our advertising investment?" According to a recent survey, measuring advertising's efficiency and effectiveness is the number-one issue in the minds of today's advertisers.[23]

Advertisers should regularly evaluate two types of advertising results: the communication effects and the sales and profit effects. Measuring the *communication effects* of an ad or ad campaign tells whether the ads and media are communicating the ad message well. Individual ads can be tested before or after they are run. Before an ad is placed, the advertiser can show it to consumers, ask how they like it, and measure message recall or attitude changes resulting from it. After an ad is run, the advertiser can measure how the ad affected consumer recall or product awareness, knowledge, and preference. Pre- and post-evaluations of communication effects can be made for entire advertising campaigns as well.

Advertisers have gotten pretty good at measuring the communication effects of their ads and ad campaigns. However, *sales and profit effects* of advertising are often much harder to measure. For example, what sales and profits are produced by an ad campaign that increases brand awareness by 20 percent and brand preference by 10 percent? Sales and profits are affected by many factors other than advertising—such as product features, price, and availability.

One way to measure the sales and profit effects of advertising is to compare past sales and profits with past advertising expenditures. Another way is through experiments. For example, to test the effects of different advertising spending levels, Coca-Cola could vary the amount it spends on advertising in different market areas and measure the differences in the resulting sales and profit levels. More complex experiments could be designed to include other variables, such as differences in the ads or media used.

However, because so many factors affect advertising effectiveness, some controllable and others not, measuring the results of advertising spending remains an inexact science. For example, dozens of advertisers spend lavishly on high-profile Super Bowl ads each year. Although they sense that the returns are worth the sizable investment, few could actually measure or prove it (see Real Marketing 15.2). A recent survey of marketing and advertising agency executives concluded that over 80 percent of marketers don't measure return on investment because it's just too difficult to measure.[24] The study cited earlier asked advertising managers if they would be able to "forecast the impact on sales" of a 10 percent cut in advertising spending—63 percent said no.

"Marketers are tracking all kinds of data and they still can't answer basic questions" about advertising accountability, says one marketing analyst, "because they don't have real models and metrics by which to make sense of it." Advertisers are measuring "everything they can, and that ranges from how many people respond to an ad to how many sales are closed and then trying to hook up those two end pieces," says another analyst. "The tough part is, my goodness, we've got so much data. How do we sift through it?"[25] Thus, although the situation is improving as marketers seek more answers, managers often must rely on large doses of judgment along with quantitative analysis when assessing advertising performance.

Real Marketing 15.2

The Super Bowl: The Mother of All Advertising Events—But Is It Worth It?

The Super Bowl is the mother of all advertising events. Each year, dozens of blue-chip advertisers showcase some of their best work to huge audiences around the world. But all this doesn't come cheap. In 2009, major advertisers plunked down an average of US$3 million per 30-second spot. Over the past two decades, they've spent over US$2 billion on just 11.5 hours of Super Bowl advertising time. But that's just for the air time. Throw in ad production costs—often US$1 million or more per showcase commercial—and running even a single Super Bowl ad becomes a super-expensive proposition. Anheuser-Busch ran *seven* spots in 2008.

So every year, as the Super Bowl season nears, up pops the BIG QUESTION: Is Super Bowl advertising worth all that money? Does it deliver a high advertising ROI? As it turns out, there's no easy answer to this question.

Advertiser and industry expert opinion varies widely. Super Bowl stalwarts such as Anheuser-Busch, FedEx, General Motors, CareerBuilder, and the Frito Lay, Gatorade, and Pepsi-Cola divisions of PepsiCo must think it's a good investment—they come back year after year. But what about savvy marketers such as Unilever, which opted out last year? In a survey of board members of the National Sports Marketing Network, 31 percent said they would recommend Super Bowl ads. But 41 percent said no—Super Bowl ads just aren't worth the money.

The naysayers make some pretty good arguments. Super Bowl advertising is outrageously expensive. Advertisers pay 85 percent more per viewer than they'd pay using prime-time network programming. And that US$3 million would buy a lot of alternative media—for example, 50 different product placements in movies, TV shows, and video games; or two massive billboards in New York's Times Square that would be seen by a million people each day for a year. Beyond the cost, the competition for attention during the Super Bowl is fierce. Every single ad represents the best efforts of a major marketer trying to design a knock-your-socks-off spectacular that will reap high ratings from both critics and consumers. Many advertisers feel they can get more for their advertising dollar in venues that aren't so crowded with larger-than-life commercials.

Then there's the question of strategic fit. Whereas the Super Bowl might be a perfect advertising event for big-budget companies selling beer, snacks, soft drinks, or sporting goods, it simply doesn't fit the pocketbooks or creative strategies of many other companies and their brands. One media executive likens a Super Bowl ad to a trophy wife: "It makes sense if you are an advertiser with a huge budget," he says. "But if you're an advertiser with a modest budget, that would not be the best use of your money."

Super Bowl ROI: The Super Bowl plays to a huge and receptive audience—90 million viewers who put away their DVR remotes and watch it live, glued to their screens, ads and all. But is the advertising worth the huge cost?

As for creative fit, consider Unilever's Dove. Three years ago, the company ran a sentimental 45-second commercial from the Dove "Campaign for Real Beauty." The ad was highly rated by consumers and it created considerable buzz—some 400 million impressions of the ad before and after its single appearance on the Super Bowl. But much of that buzz came from publicity surrounding the issue of girls' self-esteem rather than the product. And research showed that the ad produced low levels of involvement with the brand message.

Dove got almost equal exposure numbers and more engagement for a lot less money from an outdoor campaign that it ran that same year, and it got a much larger online response from its viral "Evolution" and "Onslaught" films, which incurred no media cost at all. "The Super Bowl really isn't the right environment for Dove," says a Unilever executive. The past two years, instead, Dove opted to run consumer-generated ads during the more-female-oriented Academy Awards, an event where beauty brands thrive.

Still, the Super Bowl has a lot to offer to the right advertisers. It's the most-watched TV event of the year. It plays to a huge and receptive audience—97.5 million viewers who put away their DVR remotes and watch it live, glued to their screens, ads and all. In fact, to many viewers, the Super Bowl ads are more important than what happens on the gridiron. Last year, the game itself drew an average 41.6 rating; the ads drew 41.22.

"There is no other platform quite like the Super Bowl," says the chief creative officer at Anheuser-Busch. "It's worth it. When you can touch that many households [with that kind of impact] in one sitting, it's actually efficient." In terms of dollars and cents, a study by one research firm found that consumer packaged goods firms get a return of $1.25 to $2.74 for every dollar invested in Super Bowl advertising, and one Super Bowl ad is as effective as 250 regular TV spots.

What's more, for most advertisers the Super Bowl ad itself is only the centrepiece of something much bigger. Long after the game is over, ad critics, media pundits, and consumers are still reviewing, rehashing, and rating the commercials. It's one of the few sports-related events where "it ain't over when it's over." Thus, measuring the effectiveness of Super Bowl advertising involves a lot more than just measuring eyeballs and reach. "Those 30 seconds of fame are only the tip of the iceberg," says the analyst, "with online views, water-cooler chatter, blog buzz, and *USA Today's* ratings all below the surface."

"The Super Bowl is the only media property where the advertising is as big a story as the content of the show," says Steven Schreibman, vice-president of advertising and brand management for Nationwide Financial, "so you want to see how much you can leverage it." Schreibman is still agog over the response to Nationwide's Super Bowl spot two years ago that featured the hunk Fabio demonstrating that "life comes at you fast." Months afterward, consumers were still visiting websites such as Spike.com to watch the commercial. "We got 1.8 million downloads on [just] that one site," says Schreibman. "Fabio himself keeps me apprised of that."

Advertisers don't usually sit back and just hope that consumers will talk about their ads. They build events that help to boost the buzz. For example, in 2007 at least three advertisers—Chevrolet, the NFL, and Doritos—held contests inviting consumers to create their own Super Bowl ads. As noted previously, Doritos' "Crash the Super Bowl Challenge" contest produced more than 1000 quality entries, considerable media attention, and a bunch of online consumer interest. The winning ad topped the IAG Top 10 Best-Liked Super Bowl Ads list and came in fourth in the *USA Today* Ad Meter rankings.

The Super Bowl's largest advertiser, Anheuser-Busch, extends the festivities far beyond game day. It follows up with a postgame email campaign to keep the fires burning. It also hosts a designated website where consumers can view all of the company's Super Bowl ads and vote for their favourites via the website or text messages.

So—back to the original question. Is Super Bowl advertising really worth the huge investment? It seems that there's no definitive answer—for some advertisers it's "yes"; for others, "no." The real trick is in trying to measure the returns. As the title of one recent article asserts, "Measuring Bowl Return? Good Luck!" The writer's conclusion: "For all the time, energy, and angst marketers spend crafting the perfect Super Bowl spot, [that's] a relative breeze compared to trying to prove its return on investment."

Sources: Quotes and other information from Claire Atkinson, "Measuring Bowl ROI? Good Luck," *Advertising Age*, January 29, 2007, p. 9; Lacey Rose, "Is a Super Bowl Ad a Super Deal?" *Forbes*, January 30, 2007, accessed at www.forbes.com; Jack Neff, "P&G, Unilever Sit Out the Super Bowl," *Advertising Age*, January 29, 2007, pp. 1, 36; Stuart Elliott, "Multiplying the Payoffs from a Super Bowl Spot," *New York Times*, January 26, 2007, p. C2; Stuart Elliott, "Tide to Make Its Super Bowl Debut," *New York Times*, January 11, 2008, p. 5; "20th Annual Super Bowl Ad Results," *USA Today*, February 4, 2008; Brian Steinberg, "Super Bowl Busts Ratings Record on 'the Greatest Day Ever' for Fox," *Advertising Age*, February 11, 2008, p. 21; and Brian Steinberg, "Super Bowl Spots Hit $3 Million," *Advertising Age*, May 12, 2008, p. 4.

Other Advertising Considerations

In developing advertising strategies and programs, the company must address two additional questions. First, how will the company organize its advertising function—who will perform which advertising tasks? Second, how will the company adapt its advertising strategies and programs to the complexities of international markets?

Organizing for Advertising

Different companies organize in different ways to handle advertising. In small companies, advertising might be handled by someone in the sales department. Large companies set up advertising departments whose job it is to set the advertising budget, work with the ad agency, and handle other advertising not done by the agency. Most large companies use outside advertising agencies because they offer several advantages.

Advertising agency
A marketing services firm that assists companies in planning, preparing, implementing, and evaluating all or portions of their advertising programs.

How does an **advertising agency** work? Advertising agencies were started in the mid- to late-1800s by salespeople and brokers who worked for the media and received a commission for selling advertising space to companies. As time passed, the salespeople began to help customers prepare their ads. Eventually, they formed agencies and grew closer to the advertisers than to the media.

Today's agencies employ specialists who can often perform advertising tasks better than the company's own staff can. Agencies also bring an outside point of view to solving the company's problems, along with lots of experience from working with different clients and situations. So even companies with strong advertising departments of their own use advertising agencies.

Some ad agencies are huge—the largest agency, BBDO Worldwide, has worldwide annual gross revenue of more than US$1.9 billion. In recent years, many agencies have grown by gobbling up other agencies, thus creating huge agency holding companies. The largest of these agency "megagroups," Omnicom Group, includes several large advertising, public relations, and promotion agencies with combined worldwide revenues of almost US$12.7 billion.[26] Most large advertising agencies have the staff and resources to handle all phases of an advertising campaign for their clients, from creating a marketing plan to developing ad campaigns and preparing, placing, and evaluating ads.

International Advertising Decisions

International advertisers face many complexities not encountered by domestic advertisers. The most basic issue concerns the degree to which global advertising should be adapted to the unique characteristics of various country markets. Some large advertisers have attempted to support their global brands with highly standardized worldwide advertising, with campaigns that work as well in Bangkok as they do in Battleford, Saskatchewan. For example, McDonald's now unifies its creative elements and brand presentation under the familiar "I'm lovin' it" theme in all of its 100-plus markets worldwide. Coca-Cola coordinates worldwide advertising for its flagship brand under the theme, "The Coke Side of Life." And the Mr. Clean you see in a French ad is the same guy you see in North American ads, but with the name translated to "Mr. Propre."

In recent years, the increased popularity of online social networks and video sharing has boosted the need for advertising standardization for global brands. Most big marketing and advertising campaigns include a large online presence. Connected consumers can now zip easily across borders via the Internet, making it difficult for advertisers to roll out adapted campaigns in a controlled, orderly fashion. As a result, at the very least, most global consumer brands coordinate their websites internationally. For example, check out the McDonald's websites from Germany to

Standardized worldwide advertising: The Mr. Clean you see in this French ad is the same guy you see in North American ads, but with the name translated to Mr. Propre. And in France, he'll get your floors clean enough that you can eat off of them.

Jordan to China and you'll find the golden arches logo, the "I'm lovin it" logo and jingle, a Big Mac equivalent, and maybe even Ronald McDonald himself.

Standardization produces many benefits—lower advertising costs, greater global advertising coordination, and a more consistent worldwide image. But it also has drawbacks. Most importantly, it ignores the fact that country markets differ greatly in their cultures, demographics, and economic conditions. Thus, most international advertisers "think globally but act locally." They develop global advertising *strategies* that make their worldwide advertising efforts more efficient and consistent. Then they adapt their advertising *programs* to make them more responsive to consumer needs and expectations within local markets.

For example, Apple uses "I'm a Mac; I'm a PC" commercials in many countries. In some markets, such as Spain, France, Germany, and Italy, it uses North American versions of the ads dubbed in the local language. However, it re-scripts and reshoots the ads to fit the Japanese culture:

> What's funny in one culture can seem ill-mannered in another. In the North American ads, a nerdy PC guy keeps getting trumped by his hip Mac counterpart, who uses pointed banter that demonstrates how Macs are better. But in Japanese culture, where direct-comparison ads have long been frowned upon, it's rude to brag about one's strengths. So Japanese versions of the ads include subtle changes to emphasize that Macs and PCs are not that different. Instead of clothes that cast PC clearly as a nerd and Mac as a hipster, PC wears plain office attire and Mac weekend fashion, highlighting the work/home divide between the devices more than personality differences. In the first ad of the series, Mac even gives PC a nickname: *waaku*—a playful Japanese version of the word "work." PC's body language is a big source of the humour in Japan: Mac looks embarrassed when PC touches his shoulder or hides behind Mac's legs to avoid viruses. "PC constantly makes friendship-level approaches that Mac rejects in a friendly, irritated way," says a Tokyo brand consultant. "The Western Mac ads would backfire in Japan, because the Mac would appear to lack class." In fact, the jury is still out on whether even the toned-down comparative ads will work there.[27]

Global advertisers face several special problems. For instance, advertising media costs and availability differ vastly from country to country. Countries also differ in the extent to which they regulate advertising practices. Many countries have extensive systems of laws restricting how much a company can spend on advertising, the media used, the nature of advertising claims, and other aspects of the advertising program. Such restrictions often require advertisers to adapt their campaigns from country to country.

For example, alcoholic products cannot be advertised in India or in Muslim countries. In many countries, such as Sweden, junk food ads are banned from kids' TV. To play it safe, McDonald's advertises itself as a family restaurant in Sweden. In the province of Quebec, no TV ads may be directed at children. Comparative ads, although acceptable and even common in the United States and Canada, are less commonly used in the United Kingdom and illegal in India and Brazil. China bans sending email for advertising purposes to people without their permission and all advertising email that is sent must be titled "advertisement."

China also has restrictive censorship rules for TV and radio advertising; for example, the words *the best* are banned, as are ads that "violate social customs" or present women in "improper ways." McDonald's once avoided government sanctions there by publicly apologizing for an ad that violated cultural norms by showing a customer begging for a discount. Similarly, Coca-Cola's Indian subsidiary was forced to end a promotion that offered prizes, such as a trip to Hollywood, because it violated India's established trade practices by encouraging customers to buy in order to "gamble."[28]

Thus, although advertisers may develop global strategies to guide their overall advertising efforts, specific advertising programs must usually be adapted to meet local cultures and customs, media characteristics, and advertising regulations.

PUBLIC RELATIONS

Public relations
Building good relations with the company's various publics by obtaining favourable publicity, building up a good corporate image, and handling or heading off unfavourable rumours, stories, and events.

Another major mass-promotion tool is **public relations**—building good relations with the company's various publics by obtaining favourable publicity, building up a good corporate image, and handling or heading off unfavourable rumours, stories, and events. Public relations departments may perform any or all of the following functions:[29]

- *Press relations or press agency:* Creating and placing newsworthy information in the news media to attract attention to a person, product, or service.

- *Product publicity:* Publicizing specific products.

- *Public affairs:* Building and maintaining national or local community relations.

- *Lobbying:* Building and maintaining relations with legislators and government officials to influence legislation and regulation.

- *Investor relations:* Maintaining relationships with shareholders and others in the financial community.

- *Development:* Public relations with donors or members of not-for-profit organizations to gain financial or volunteer support.

Public relations is used to promote products, people, places, ideas, activities, organizations, and even nations. Companies use public relations to build good relations with consumers, investors, the media, and their communities. Trade associations have used public relations to rebuild interest in declining commodities such as eggs, apples, potatoes, and milk. For example, the Prairie Milk Marketing Partnership launched a series of ads and an interactive website, NeverStopMilk.ca, targeting Canada's youth, with the tagline "Always grow. Grow all ways." Similarly, the U.S. milk industry's popular "Got Milk?" public relations campaign featuring celebrities with milk moustaches reversed a longstanding decline in milk consumption:

> By 1994, milk consumption had been in decline for 20 years. The general perception was that milk was unhealthy, outdated, just for kids, or good only with cookies and cake. To counter these notions, the National Fluid Milk Processor Education Program (MilkPEP) began a public relations campaign featuring milk be-moustached celebrities and the tagline "Got Milk?" The campaign has not only been wildly popular, it has been successful as well—not only did it stop the decline, milk consumption actually increased. The campaign is still running.
>
> Although initially targeted at women in their twenties, the campaign has been expanded to other target markets and has gained cult status with teens, much to their parents' delight. Starting with basic print ads featuring a musician (Kelly Clarkson), actor (Jessica Alba), or sports idol (Tracy McGrady), the campaign has naturally spread to the Internet. One website, WhyMilk.com, appeals to moms in a search for America's first "Chief Health Officer." Another, BodyByMilk.com, targets young people, who can bid on gear using saved milk UPCs, go behind the scenes of the latest "Got Milk?" photo shoot, or get facts on "everything you ever need to know about milk." There are milk moustache MySpace pages of celebrities such as David Beckham. The milk marketers even created the world's first branded emoticon—the milk moustache :-{).[30]

The Role and Impact of Public Relations

Public relations can have a strong impact on public awareness at a much lower cost than advertising can. The company does not pay for the space or time in the media. Rather, it pays for a staff to develop and circulate information and to manage events. If the company develops an interesting story or event, it could be picked up by several different media, having the same effect as advertising that would cost millions of dollars. And it would have more credibility than advertising.

Public relations results can sometimes be spectacular. Starting with preview events like this one, Nintendo's award-winning PR campaign for its new Wii game console produced non-stop stock-outs for more than two years.

Public relations results can sometimes be spectacular. Consider the launch of Nintendo's Wii game console:

> By 2006, once-dominant Nintendo had dropped to third place in the video game industry behind Sony and Microsoft. To get back on top, Nintendo's newest offering, the amazing Wii, needed to soar. The Wii's motion-sensitive controller makes it fun for almost anyone to play. This let Nintendo target the core gaming audience but also "dabblers," "lapsed gamers," and "nongamers," including girls, women, and seniors. But rather than investing millions in media advertising, Nintendo took advantage of the Wii's natural appeal to create a results-producing PR campaign. Prelaunch, Nintendo held preview events at which industry analysts and the media spent time with the amazing Wii. The company targeted consumers on MySpace, where the "How Wii Play" profile made more than 60 000 friends. Nintendo also launched an ambassador program that got the game into the hands of gamers, moms, and large intergenerational families, who spread information about the system through blogs and word of mouth.

On launch day, Nintendo midnight events held in New York and Los Angeles were attended by thousands of consumers, with coverage by media ranging from AP to MTV and *Good Morning America*. In the end, the Wii PR campaign earned a whopping 10 billion audience impressions over just three months, including 14 *Today Show* appearances and a stint on *South Park*. Despite early surveys showing that only 11 percent of consumers intended to buy it, Wii sales sizzled. Stores experienced two years of nonstop stock-outs and the Wii outsold the Xbox 360 by two to one and the newly introduced Playstation 3 by three to one. As a result, the Wii public relations effort was named *PRWeek's* 2008 Consumer Launch Campaign of the Year.[31]

Despite its potential strengths, public relations is sometimes described as a marketing stepchild because of its often limited and scattered use. The public relations department is often located at corporate headquarters or handled by a third-party agency. Its staff is so busy dealing with various publics—shareholders, employees, legislators, the press—that public relations programs to support product marketing objectives may be ignored. Moreover, marketing managers and public relations practitioners do not always speak the same language. Whereas many public relations practitioners see their jobs as simply communicating, marketing managers tend to be much more interested in how advertising and public relations affect brand building, sales and profits, and customer relationships.

This situation is changing, however. Although public relations still captures only a small portion of the overall marketing budgets of most firms, PR can be a powerful brand-building tool. Two well-known marketing consultants even go so far as to conclude that advertising doesn't build brands, PR does. In their book *The Fall of Advertising and the Rise of PR*, the consultants proclaim that the dominance of advertising is over and that public relations is quietly becoming the most powerful marketing communications tool:

> The birth of a brand is usually accomplished with [public relations], not advertising. Our general rule is [PR] first, advertising second. [Public relations] is the nail, advertising the hammer. [PR] creates the credentials that provide the credibility for advertising. . . . Anita Roddick built The Body Shop into a major brand with no advertising at all. Instead, she

traveled the world on a relentless quest for publicity. . . . Until recently Starbucks Coffee didn't spend a hill of beans on advertising, either. In 10 years, the company spent less than US$10 million on advertising, a trivial amount for a brand that delivers annual sales [in the billions]. Wal-Mart stores became the world's largest retailer . . . with very little advertising. . . . On the Internet, Amazon.com became a powerhouse brand with virtually no advertising.[32]

Although the book created much controversy, and most advertisers wouldn't agree about the "fall of advertising" part of the title, the point is a good one. Advertising and public relations should work hand in hand within an integrated marketing communications program to build brands and customer relationships.

4 MAJOR PUBLIC RELATIONS TOOLS

Public relations uses several tools. One of the major tools is *news*. PR professionals find or create favourable news about the company and its products or people. Sometimes news stories occur naturally, and sometimes the PR person can suggest events or activities that would create news. *Speeches* can also create product and company publicity. Increasingly, company executives must field questions from the media or give talks at trade associations or sales meetings, and these events can either build or hurt the company's image. Another common PR tool is *special events*, ranging from news conferences, press tours, grand openings, and fireworks displays to laser shows, hot air balloon releases, multimedia presentations, or educational programs designed to reach and interest target publics.

Public relations people also prepare *written materials* to reach and influence their target markets. These materials include annual reports, brochures, articles, and company newsletters and magazines. *Audiovisual materials*, such as slide-and-sound programs, DVDs, and online videos are being used increasingly as communications tools. *Corporate identity materials* can also help create a corporate identity that the public immediately recognizes. Logos, stationery, brochures, signs, business forms, business cards, buildings, uniforms, and company cars and trucks all become marketing tools when they are attractive, distinctive, and memorable. Finally, companies can improve public goodwill by contributing money and time to *public service activities*.

As we discussed in Chapter 6, many marketers are now also designing *buzz marketing* campaigns to generate excitement and favourable word of mouth for their brands. Buzz marketing takes advantage of *social networking* processes by getting consumers themselves to

Buzz marketing: Aveeno used social networking processes to get consumers to spread the word about its new product line. This YouTube video has captured over 1.5 million views.

spread information about a product or service to others in their communities. For example, Johnson & Johnson used buzz marketing to launch its Aveeno Positively Ageless product line:

> To build buzz for its new line, Johnson & Johnson employed talented street artist Julian Beever—the "Pavement Picasso"—to create a 3D "Fountain of Youth" chalk drawing on a sidewalk in the heart of New York City. Although the drawing captivated thousands of passersby, Aveeno turned "Fountain of Youth" into an online event via a four-minute time-lapse video of the artist at work posted on YouTube (www.youtube.com/watch?v=hfn8Dz_13Ms). In addition the brand distributed the video to more than 50 blogs, with 21 responding by promoting the YouTube posting. With a soft "Aveeno Presents" slate at the beginning of the video and a closeup of the Fountain of Youth artwork showing the Aveeno logo at the end, the spot was well branded but without appearing to be commercial. The video reverberated through video sites and the blogosphere via strong word of mouth. Within two weeks, on YouTube alone, the video was viewed more than 65 000 times and grew to reach 121 346 views within one month. As of October 2009, the YouTube video had been viewed over 1.5 million times.[33]

A company's website is another important public relations vehicle. Consumers and members of other publics often visit websites for information or entertainment. Such sites can be extremely popular. For example, Butterball's site (www.butterball.com), which features cooking and carving tips, once received 550 000 visitors in one day during Thanksgiving week. The website supplements the Butterball Turkey Talk-Line (1-800-BUTTERBALL)—called by some the "granddaddy of all help lines—staffed by 50 home economists and nutritionists who respond to more than 100 000 questions each November and December. Visitors to the site can even download a series of "Turkey Talk" podcasts containing tips on holiday food preparation.[34]

Websites can also be ideal for handling crisis situations. For example, when two Dominos employees posted a video showing them tampering with food on YouTube, the company responded within hours. They first contacted the consumer affairs blogger who initially alerted them to the store and employees responsible. They set up a Twitter account to respond to consumer concerns and posted a video on YouTube to apologize for the incident and to thank online customers for informing them of the situation. Some estimates put the number of views of the offensive video at over 1 million. However, almost 730 000 people viewed the response by Patrick Doyle, president of Dominos USA. However, it's still too soon to tell how the incident or the company's response will affect Dominos' brand image. In all, in this age where "it's easier to disseminate information through email marketing, blogs, and online chat," notes an analyst, "public relations is becoming a valuable part of doing business in a digital world."[35]

As with the other promotion tools, in considering when and how to use product public relations, management should set PR objectives, choose the PR messages and vehicles, implement the PR plan, and evaluate the results. The firm's public relations should be blended smoothly with other promotion activities within the company's overall integrated marketing communications effort.

REVIEWING OBJECTIVES AND KEY TERMS

 | Audio Chapter Summary

Companies must do more than make good products—they have to inform consumers about product benefits and carefully position products in consumers' minds. To do this, they must master *advertising* and *public relations*.

OBJECTIVE 1 **Define the role of advertising in the promotion mix.**

Advertising—the use of paid media by a seller to inform, persuade, and remind buyers about its products or organization—is an important promotion tool for communicating the value that marketers create for their customers. Canadian marketers spend more than $13 billion each year on advertising, and worldwide ad spending exceeds $600 billion. Advertising takes many forms and has many uses. Although advertising is used mostly by business firms, a wide range of not-for-profit organizations, professionals, and social agencies also use advertising to promote their causes to various target publics.

OBJECTIVE 2 **Describe the major decisions involved in developing an advertising program.**

Advertising decision making involves decisions about the advertising objectives, the budget, the message, the media, and finally the evaluation of results. Advertisers should set clear target, task, and timing *objectives*, whether the aim is to inform, persuade, or remind buyers. Advertising's goal is to move consumers through the buyer-readiness stages discussed in the previous chapter. Some advertising is designed to move people to immediate action. However, many of the ads you see today focus on building or strengthening long-term customer relationships. The advertising *budget* can be based on sales, on competitors' spending, or on the objectives and tasks of the advertising program. The size and allocation of the budget depends on many factors.

Advertising strategy consists of two major elements: creating advertising *messages* and selecting advertising *media*. The *message decision* calls for planning a message strategy and executing it effectively. Good advertising messages are especially important in today's costly and cluttered advertising environment. Just to gain and hold attention, today's advertising messages must be better planned, more imaginative, more entertaining, and more rewarding to consumers. In fact, many marketers are now subscribing to a new merging of advertising and entertainment, dubbed "Madison & Vine." The *media decision* involves defining reach, frequency, and impact goals; choosing major media types; selecting media vehicles; and deciding on media timing. Message and media decisions must be closely coordinated for maximum campaign effectiveness.

Finally, *evaluation* calls for evaluating the communication and sales effects of advertising before, during, and after the advertising is placed. Advertising accountability has become a hot issue for most companies. Increasingly, top management is asking: "What return are we getting on our advertising investment?" and "How do we know that we're spending the right amount?" Other important advertising issues involve *organizing* for advertising and dealing with the complexities of international advertising.

OBJECTIVE 3 **Define the role of public relations in the promotion mix.**

Public relations—gaining favourable publicity and creating a favourable company image—is the least used of the major promotion tools, although it has great potential for building consumer awareness and preference. Public relations is used to promote products, people, places, ideas, activities, organizations, and even nations. Companies use public relations to build good relations with consumers, investors, the media, and their communities. Public relations can have a strong impact on public awareness at a much lower cost than advertising can, and public relations results can sometimes be spectacular. Although public relations still captures only a small portion of the overall marketing budgets of most firms, PR is playing an increasingly important brand-building role.

OBJECTIVE 4 **Explain how companies use public relations to communicate with their publics.**

Companies use public relations to communicate with their publics by setting PR objectives, choosing PR messages and vehicles, implementing the PR plan, and evaluating PR results. To accomplish these goals, public relations professionals use several tools such as *news*, *speeches*, and *special events*. They also prepare *written*, *audiovisual*, and *corporate identity materials* and contribute money and time to *public service activities*. *Buzz marketing* is a form of public relations that gets consumers themselves to spread word-of-mouth information about the company and its brands. The Internet has also become a major public relations tool.

KEY TERMS

mymarketinglab | Glossary Flashcards

Objective 1
Advertising   486
Objective 2
Advertising objective   487
Advertising budget   489
Advertising strategy   489
Madison & Vine   491

Creative concept   494
Execution style   494
Advertising media   496
Return on advertising investment   500
Advertising agency   503
Objective 3
Public relations   505

DISCUSSING THE CONCEPTS

1. List and briefly describe the four important decisions marketing managers must make when developing an advertising program.

2. Why is it important that the advertising media and creative departments work closely together?

3. How do an advertisement's appeals differ from its execution style?

4. Define the terms *reach*, *frequency*, and *impact*.

5. What are the role and functions of public relations within an organization?

6. Discuss the tools used by public relations professionals.

APPLYING THE CONCEPTS

1. Any message can be presented using different execution styles. Select a brand and target audience and design two advertisements, each using a different execution style to deliver the same message to the target audience but in a different way. Identify the types of execution styles you are using and present your advertisements.

2. Recommend three advertising media for a campaign to introduce a new line of men's personal care products under a LeBron James label.

3. In a small group, discuss the major public relations tools and develop three public relations items for each of the following: a hospital, a restaurant, and any brand of your choice.

FOCUS ON TECHNOLOGY

Have you ever watched your favourite television program and wished you could immediately buy the clothes your favourite character was wearing or learn more about the car he or she was driving? Or how about ordering a pizza while watching an ad? Well, now you can—with interactive television. Marketers are increasingly using this vehicle to interact with consumers. For example, Unilever, one of the largest consumer packaged goods companies, is banking on consumers wanting more information and interactivity from their televisions and is planning several interactive TV-ad deals with DIRECTV and Comcast cable. Interactive TV works by providing links, known as triggers, that when clicked take viewers into a longer advertisement. These longer ads, called long-form or long-tail advertising, provide opportunities for deeper interaction.

1. Will interactive television catch on with consumers? What might be slowing the adoption of this innovative advertising technique?

2. Discuss the types of products or services that would benefit most from interactive television advertising.

FOCUS ON ETHICS

Word-of-mouth communications can be very persuasive. You're more likely to see a movie or buy a clothing brand when your friends recommend them. Marketers are harnessing the power of word of mouth with creative tactics. However, some tactics are criticized because consumers don't know they are being marketed to. For example, Sony Ericsson came under fire when it became known that it hired actors to pose as tourists asking strangers to take their picture with the cool T68i phone. Walmart was criticized for a blog about Laura and Jim RVing around North America, stopping at Walmarts across the country and writing glowing things about the retailer. Walmart never disclosed that it was sponsoring the trip. Procter & Gamble, while not paying moms to talk about its products, provides samples and coupons to these influential people recruited into its Vocalpoint network in the hopes that they say positive things about P&G products to others.

1. These types of activities are often called "stealth marketing" because they are not openly presented as promotional tactics. Learn more about this practice and decide if it is ethical.

2. Can some of the tools used in public relations be considered stealth marketing? How about product placement in movies or television shows? Others?

MARKETING BY THE NUMBERS

Reader's Digest has the second-largest magazine circulation worldwide. Although consumers aged 50+ are plugged in online like younger consumers, they still like print media, making this magazine a valuable media vehicle through which to reach seniors with advertising.

1. Using North American advertising rate information for this magazine (see www.rdtrustedbrands.com/rates), determine the cost per thousand readers for a full-page, four-colour advertisement in English and French Canada as well as English and Hispanic United States (use U.S. prices for the purposes of comparison). How

do the costs per thousand compare across the four versions?

2. Suppose a manufacturer of a diabetes testing monitor wants to advertise in *Reader's Digest*. Refer to Appendix 3: Marketing by the Numbers to determine by how much the manufacturer's sales must increase to break even on the purchase of 10 full-page, four-colour advertisements in *Reader's Digest*. Assume that the company has a 40 percent contribution margin. Should the advertiser purchase this advertising space?

VIDEO CASE

E*TRADE

 | Video Case Questions

Super Bowl XXXIV, the first of the new millennium, was known as the dot-com Super Bowl for the glut of Internet companies that plopped down an average of US$2.2 million per 30-second spot. Today, most of the companies that defined the dot-com glory days are gone. But one darling of the dot-com era, E*TRADE, remains one of the few survivors. Although E*TRADE has experienced challenges since the turn of the century, it has also turned profits.

Advertising on the big game hasn't worked out well for everyone. But for E*TRADE, Super Bowl ads have been part of a larger advertising effort that played a role in its survival. In this video, E*TRADE reports on its advertising

strategy as well as the advantages and disadvantages of Super Bowl advertising.

After viewing the video featuring E*TRADE, answer the following questions about advertising and promotions:

1. What makes E*TRADE different from now-defunct dot-coms?

2. What has been the role of advertising at E*TRADE?

3. Discuss the factors in E*TRADE's decision to advertise during the Super Bowl.

Visit MyMarketingLab at www.pearsoned.ca/mymarketinglab to view the video segment related to this case.

COMPANY CASE

Coca-Cola: Another Advertising Hit

When you think of Coca-Cola, what comes to mind? It wouldn't be surprising if you thought first of Coke ads. In the history of advertising, perhaps no other company has had such a strong and continuous impact on society through advertising. Not only have Coke's ads been successful at selling its soft drinks, but decade after decade Coca-Cola's ads and campaigns have influenced our very culture by making their way into the hearts and minds of consumers.

A BRIEF AD HISTORY

In the 1920s, Coca-Cola shifted its advertising strategy, focusing for the first time on creating brand loyalty. It began advertising the soft drink as fun and refreshing. Coke's 1929 campaign slogan was, "The Pause that

Refreshes." To this day, that slogan remains number two on *Advertising Age's* top 100 slogans of all time.

How about those famous Coca-Cola Santa Claus print ads? Most people probably have seen an example of such ads. What most people don't realize is that our modern-day vision of Santa as a jolly old man with a white beard in a red suit and hat is to some extent a result of those Coke ads that began emerging in popular magazines in 1931. Before that, the world's image of Santa was fragmented, with physical portrayals of the legendary holiday visitor ranging from a pixie to a leprechaun to even a frightening gnome! But Coca-Cola's long-running series of ads solidified what was becoming a common image, making our beloved Santa Claus recognizable around the world.

Those Coca-Cola campaigns were probably a little before your time. But what about Coca-Cola's 1971 "Hilltop" campaign? Perhaps you remember its lyrics: "I'd like to teach the world to sing, in perfect harmony. I'd like to buy the world a Coke, and keep it company." The song was sung by a choir of young people from all over the world, perched high on a hilltop, each holding an iconic hourglass-shaped bottle of Coke. Within months, Coca-Cola and its bottlers received more than 100 000 letters about the ad. The ad actually received requests at radio stations; so many, in fact, that a version of the song was released as a pop-music single. The jingle's tagline, "It's the real thing," served as the foundation for Coke ads for years.

Still too long ago for you? Maybe you've heard of Coke's ad showing a bruised and battered Mean Joe Greene tossing his shirt to a young fan after the boy shares his Coke with the pro football player. The ad appears consistently at the top of "Best Super Bowl Ads" lists. Or how about "Coke is it?" "Can't Beat the Feeling?" Certainly you would remember the jingle made famous in the 1990s, "Always Coca-Cola." And who doesn't make some association between the sweet, dark, bubbly beverage and polar bears? Innovative animation technology put those lovable creatures in only a handful of ads, but they are forever etched in the memories of consumers everywhere.

These are only some highlights of Coca-Cola's long advertising history, stretching back to the company's origin in 1886. With so many hits and such a huge impact on consumers, it's hard to imagine that the beverage giant ever gets into an advertising rut. But as the new millennium began to unfold, many thought that Coke had lost its advertising sizzle. The company was struggling to create ads that resonated with younger consumers while at the same time appealing to the older generation. And the company's ads were routinely out-pointed by those of rival Pepsi. Coca-Cola needed some new advertising fizz.

BACK TO THE BOWL

Where does a company turn when it wants to make a big ad splash? For Coca-Cola, its thoughts turned to the marquee of all advertising events—the Super Bowl. The company had certainly had success with the ad venue before. But scoring big with a Super Bowl ad isn't guaranteed. In fact, many cynics view the ad venue as a waste of money. One team of researchers found that average brand recall one week after the 2008 Super Bowl was an unimpressive 7 percent. Recall for specific commercials and the brand represented therein was even worse at only 4 percent. That doesn't speak very highly for a 30-second ad that cost US$2.7 million to air, and perhaps even more to produce. The Super Bowl has its share of critics who think it is far too costly for a single event, regardless of how many people tune in.

But for all the misses, there have been plenty of hits. In 1999, HotJobs.com blew half of its US$4 million advertising budget for the year on a single 30-second spot. The result? Traffic on its website immediately shot up 120 percent, choking its network and server system. Monster.com saw similar results that same year. And hundreds of advertisers throughout the Super Bowl's history have been very satisfied with the results of their ads.

For its 2008 campaign debut, Coca-Cola was confident that the Super Bowl was just right for its broad target market. It assigned Wieden+Kennedy the task of crafting a 60-second commercial. Hal Curtis, one of the top creative directors for the agency, took charge of the project. Two years before, Curtis had come up with an idea for an ad while working on a different campaign. He thought the idea was perfect for Coke.

By now, you've probably seen the ad. Titled "It's Mine," the spot is set at Macy's Thanksgiving Day Parade in New York City, a parade famous for its blimp-sized balloons marched through the Central Park area on long tethers. The Coke ad focuses on two particular characters, Stewie Griffin from Fox's *Family Guy* and the classic cartoon character Underdog. Both balloons sidle up to a huge Coke balloon. The two characters begin fighting over the Coke, bouncing around in a kind of slow-motion ballet against the New York skyline, bumping up against buildings. As the scuffle progresses above the streets, moving higher and higher, New Yorkers look on from hot dog stands, cabs, and even inside buildings. At the story's climactic moment, a giant Charlie Brown balloon emerges from nowhere, swooping in and claiming the giant Coke, leaving Stewie and Underdog empty-handed.

The spot cost Coca-Cola US$2.3 million to make and more than double that to air. It was also the most difficult ad that Curtis had ever produced. For starters, he encountered mounds of red tape in negotiating the rights to use the well-known cartoon characters in the ad. Choreographing and shooting footage of giant balloons in one of the world's biggest cities brought its own set of challenges. At one point, bad weather forced the project indoors and all the way across the country to Paramount Studios on the west coast. The post-shoot animation was considered yet a third shoot for the ad. It all added up to four months of production and postproduction time.

When asked about the challenge of simultaneously reaching consumers of all ages with an advertisement, Curtis responded, "A good story appeals to everyone. And a story that is well told appeals to young and old. Certainly, there are times where we want to skew a message younger, but for this spot that wasn't part of the thinking." Pio Schunker, Coca-Cola's head of creative excellence, added, "We are at our best when we speak to universal values that appeal to everyone rather than try and skew it to specific segments."

According to Schunker, the universal value referred to here was that "Good really wins in the end," a point that he thought was made strongly with the contrast of Charlie Brown over a character like Stewie Griffin. In fact, Curtis originally pitched the ad with an ending that had the Coke bottle getting punctured on a flagpole and neither balloon getting it. But Coca-Cola wanted something that was emotionally more positive, something that expressed optimism. "I felt it was such a downer of an ending to have these characters chase the Coke and not get it," stated

Schunker. It was Curtis's 12-year-old son, Will, who gave him the idea for what became the ending when he said, "Why can't another balloon get it?" For Hal Curtis, the next logical step was Charlie Brown.

Everyone was happy with the end result. Both Coca-Cola and Wieden Kennedy felt that the ad communicated the desired message perfectly while bringing out the kind of warm emotions that had emanated from Coca-Cola ads for decades.

The hunches of these ad veterans proved correct. The day after the game, Coke's balloon ad had 350 blog posts while Pepsi's ads had only 250. A week after that, the "It's Mine" ad was the most talked about ad online. SuperBowl-Ads.com had it rated as the top ad of the dozens that aired on the 2008 gridiron matchup. And later in the year, the spot won a Silver Lion at the Cannes Lions International Advertising Festival, the most prestigious award event in the industry.

There's no doubt that the "It's Mine" ad achieved more buzz and more sizzle than Coca-Cola's ads in recent history. But that's only a first step to advertising success. In the end, the only result that really matters is whether or not the ad has the intended effect on consumers. Although the impact of Coca-Cola's "It's Mine" ad or its history of other outstanding ads on actual beverage sales may never be known, one broader conclusion is clear. Every year, Interbrand publishes the premier ranking of global brands based on monetary value. And every year since Interbrand began publishing the

list in 2001, Coca-Cola has held the top spot. At US$65 billion, Coca-Cola is the world's most valuable brand. Thus, it's pretty easy to make the connection between Coca-Cola's brand value and more than 100 years of stellar advertising.

Questions for Discussion

1. Consider Coca-Cola's advertising throughout its history. Identify as many commonalities as possible for its various ads and campaigns. (For a list of Coca-Cola slogans over the years, check out http://en.wikipedia.org/wiki/Coca-Cola_slogans.)

2. Analyze the "It's Mine" ad based on the process of creating an advertising message as outlined in the text.

3. Discuss issues of selecting advertising media for the "It's Mine" ad. How might this process differ from that of other Coca-Cola campaigns? From other campaigns for other companies?

4. Based on the information in this case, how might Coca-Cola measure the effectiveness of the "It's Mine" ad? What else might Coca-Cola want to measure?

Sources: Lucinda Watrous, "The History of Coca-Cola's Advertising," *Associated Content*, January 14, 2008, accessed at www.associatedcontent.com; Suzanne Vranica, "Coca-Cola Ad Scores Big," *Wall Street Journal*, March 12, 2008, p. B3A; G. Michael Maddock and Raphael Louis Vitón, "Super Bowl Ads: A Big Fumble," *BusinessWeek*, March 27, 2008, accessed at www.businessweek.com; "Celebrating 75 Years of the Coca-Cola Santa," October 2006 press release, accessed at www.thecoca-colacompany.com.

Visit **MyMarketingLab** at **www.pearsoned.ca/mymarketinglab** for access to online tutorials, interactive exercises, videos, and much more.

Personal Selling and
Sales Promotion

PREVIEWING THE CONCEPTS In the previous chapter, you learned about communicating customer value through integrated marketing communications (IMC) and about two elements of the promotion mix—advertising and public relations. In this chapter, we'll look at two more IMC elements—personal selling and sales promotion. Personal selling is the interpersonal arm of marketing communications in which the sales force interacts with customers and prospects to build relationships and make sales. Sales promotion consists of short-term incentives to encourage purchase or sale of a product or service. As you read on, remember that although this chapter examines personal selling and sales promotion as separate tools, they must be carefully integrated with other elements of the promotion mix.

When someone says "salesperson," what image comes to mind? Perhaps you think about a stereotypical glad-hander who's out to lighten your wallet by selling you something you don't really need. Think again. Today, for most companies, personal selling plays an important role in building profitable customer relationships. Consider CDW Corporation, whose customer-focused sales strategy has helped it grow rapidly while competitors have faltered.

CDW Corporation, a leading provider of multibrand technology products and services, is thriving. In only 24 years since founder Michael Krasny started the business at his kitchen table, CDW has grown to become a high-tech heavyweight in its highly volatile and competitive industry. In just the past five years, CDW has increased its sales by 75 percent to US$8.1 billion annually. And CDW recently ranked first in the electronics wholesaler category on *Fortune's* 2008 list of America's Most Admired Companies and seventh on the list of Canada's Top 100 Solution Providers.

How has CDW managed to grow so profitably? The company owes its success to good old-fashioned high-touch personal selling that builds lasting one-to-one customer relationships. The strategy is fuelled by a genuine passion for solving customer problems. Under CDW's "Circle of Service" philosophy, "everything revolves around the customer."

CDW sells a complex assortment of more than 100 000 technology products and advanced technology services—computers, software, accessories, and networking products. Many of CDW's competitors chase after a relative handful of very large customers. However, although CDW serves customers of all sizes, one of the company's core customer segments is small and midsize businesses (SMBs). These

The major responsibility for managing customer relationships falls to CDW's energetic and passionately customer-focused account managers. "We want to become the trusted adviser for [customers]."

smaller customers often need lots of advice and support. "Many of our clients don't have IT departments," says one CDW executive, "so they look to us for expertise."

That's where CDW's sales force comes in. The major responsibility for building and managing customer relationships falls to CDW's sales force of over 2500 account managers. Each customer is assigned an account manager who helps the customer select the right products and technologies and keep them running smoothly. "The server room can be a cold and lonely place," notes one CDW advertisement. "We can definitely help with the lonely part. At CDW, we provide you with a personal account manager who knows your business and the IT challenges you face."

Account managers orchestrate the efforts of a team of CDW specialists who help customers select the best mix of products, services, and support. But they do more than just sell technology products and services. They work closely with customers to find solutions to their technology problems. "This is a big deal to us," says Jim Grass, CDW's senior director of state and local sales. "We want to go beyond fulfilling the order and become the trusted adviser for them. We [want to] talk . . . about what a customer is trying to accomplish and really add value to the sale, as opposed to just sending out a box."

To become trusted advisers and effective customer-relationship builders, CDW account managers really have to know their stuff. And CDW boasts some of the most knowledgeable salespeople in the industry. Before they make a single sales call, new account managers complete a six-week orientation and then a six-month training program. CDW University's College of Sales offers intensive schooling in the science behind the company's products and in the art of consultative selling. But that's just the beginning—the training never ends. Tenured

CDW's good old-fashioned high-touch personal selling strategy is fuelled by a genuine passion for solving customer problems.

account managers receive ongoing training to enhance their relationship-selling skills. Each year, CDW's sales force completes a whopping 339 000 hours of sales-specific training. John Edwardson, chairman and CEO of CDW and former head of United Airlines, likes to point out that CDW reps get more training than some pilots.

OBJECTIVES

1. Discuss the role of a company's salespeople in creating value for customers and building customer relationships.

2. Identify and explain the six major sales force management steps.

3. Discuss the personal selling process, distinguishing between transaction-oriented marketing and relationship marketing.

4. Explain how sales promotion campaigns are developed and implemented.

To further support salespeople's customer problem-solving efforts, the company's technology specialists help design customized solutions, while its advanced technology engineers help customers implement and manage those solutions. Account managers can draw on these teams to design customer-specific solutions in technology areas such as notebooks, desktops, printers, servers and storage, unified communications, security, wireless, power and cooling, networking, software licensing, and mobile wireless solutions.

Customers who want to access CDW's products and expertise without going through their account manager can do so easily at any of several CDW websites. Better yet, CDW will create a free personalized CDW@work extranet site that reflects a given customer's pricing, order status, account history, and special considerations. The extranet site serves as a 24-hour extension of the customer's account manager. But even here, the ever-present account managers are likely to add personal guidance. Account managers receive immediate notification of their customers' online activities. So if a bleary-eyed SMB manager makes a mistake on an emergency order placed in the middle of the night, chances are good that the account manager will find and correct the error first thing in the morning.

Beyond being knowledgeable and ever-present, CDW's account managers are energetic and passionately customer focused. Much of the energy has passed down from CDW founder and former CEO Michael Krasny. Selling has always been a top priority for Krasny, not surprising given that he began the company by selling used personal computers out of his home through classified ads. Krasny's most important legacy is the "Circle of Service" culture that he created—a culture that focuses on taking care of customers, and on the CDW employees who serve them.

So when someone says "salesperson," you may still think of the stereotypical "travelling salesman"—the fast-talking, ever-smiling peddler who travels his territory foisting his wares on reluctant customers. Such stereotypes, however, are out of date. Today, like CDW's account managers, most professional salespeople are well-educated, well-trained men and women who work to build valued customer relationships. They succeed not by taking customers in, but by helping them out—by assessing customer needs and solving customer problems.

CDW's sales force instills loyalty in what are traditionally very price-conscious SMB customers. The company wants to create customer satisfaction at every touchpoint. Says a former CDW marketing executive, "We're competitively priced, but what's most important is the service and the customers' relationships with their account managers. It's how we actually touch people that creates our most long-lasting [success]."[1]

Chapter Opening Discussion

In this chapter, we examine two more promotion mix tools—*personal selling* and *sales promotion*. Personal selling consists of interpersonal interactions with customers and prospects to make sales and maintain customer relationships. Sales promotion involves using short-term incentives to encourage customer purchasing, reseller support, and sales force efforts.

 # PERSONAL SELLING

Robert Louis Stevenson once noted that "everyone lives by selling something." Today, rather than focusing on *selling* to potential buyers, savvy marketers stress *building relationships* with potential buyers. Companies all around the world use sales forces to sell products and services to business customers and final consumers. But sales forces are also found in many other kinds of organizations. For example, universities use recruiters to attract new students and churches use membership committees to attract new members. Museums and fine arts organizations use fundraisers to contact donors and raise money. Even governments use sales forces. For example, Agriculture Canada sends specialists into the field to convince farmers to use new methods and products. In the first part of this chapter, we examine personal selling's role in the organization, sales force management decisions, and the personal selling process.

Glossary Flashcards of Key Terms

The Nature of Personal Selling

Personal selling
Personal presentation by the firm's sales force for the purpose of making sales and building customer relationships.

Personal selling is one of the oldest professions in the world. The people who do the selling go by many names: salespeople, sales representatives, district managers, account executives, sales consultants, sales engineers, agents, and account development reps, to name just a few.

People hold many stereotypes of salespeople—including some unfavourable ones. "Salesman" may bring to mind the image of Arthur Miller's pitiable Willy Loman in *Death of a Salesman*, or Meredith Willson's cigar-smoking, backslapping, joke-telling Harold Hill in *The Music Man*. These examples depict salespeople as loners, travelling their territories, trying to foist their wares on unsuspecting or unwilling buyers.

However, modern salespeople are a far cry from these unfortunate stereotypes. Today, most salespeople are well-educated, well-trained professionals who add value for customers and maintain long-term customer relationships. They listen to their customers, assess customer needs, and organize the company's efforts to solve customer problems:

> Sales is no longer the avenue of choice for washouts from other fields or for the glad-handers who anticipate doing business over steaks and a three-martini lunch. In today's hypercompetitive markets, "buying is not about transactions any more," says one sales expert. "Salespeople must know their customers' businesses better than customers do and align themselves with customers' strategies." That creates an entirely new role for salespeople. These days, "salespeople must have a wheelbarrow full of business savvy, combined with the credibility to sell to [empowered, well-informed buying] executives," says another expert. Today, sales is about building customer relationships through a "focus on differentiation and linking those differences to the customer's realization of value."[2]

Consider Boeing, the aerospace giant competing in the rough-and-tumble worldwide commercial aircraft market. It takes more than fast talk and a warm smile to sell expensive high-tech aircraft. A single big sale can easily run into the billions of dollars. Boeing salespeople head up an extensive team of company specialists—sales and service technicians, financial analysts, planners, engineers—all dedicated to finding ways to satisfy airline customer needs. The selling process is nerve-wrackingly slow—it can take two or three years from the first sales presentation to the day the sale is announced. After getting the order, salespeople then must stay in almost constant touch to make certain the customer stays satisfied. Success depends on building solid, long-term relationships with customers, based on performance and trust.

Salesperson
An individual representing a company to customers by performing one or more of the following activities: prospecting, communicating, selling, servicing, information gathering, or relationship building.

The term **salesperson** covers a wide range of positions. At one extreme, a salesperson might be largely an *order taker*, such as the department store salesperson standing behind the counter. At the other extreme are *order getters*, whose positions demand *creative selling* and *relationship building* for products and services ranging from appliances, industrial equipment, and airplanes to insurance and information technology services. Here, we focus on the more creative types of selling and on the process of building and managing an effective sales force.

Professional selling: It takes more than fast talk and a warm smile to sell high-tech aircraft, where a single big sale can easily run into the billions of dollars. Success depends on building solid, long-term relationships with customers.

The Role of the Sales Force

Personal selling is the interpersonal arm of the promotion mix. Advertising consists largely of nonpersonal communication with target consumer groups. In contrast, personal selling involves interpersonal interactions between salespeople and individual customers—whether face-to-face, by telephone, via email, through video or web conferences, or by other means. Personal selling can be more effective than advertising in more complex selling situations. Salespeople can probe customers to learn more about their problems and then adjust the marketing offer and presentation to fit the special needs of each customer.

The role of personal selling varies from company to company. Some firms have no salespeople at all—for example, companies that sell only

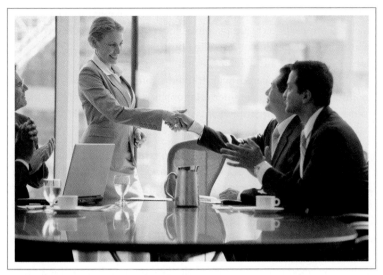

Salespeople link the company with its customers. To many customers, the salesperson *is* the company.

online or through catalogues, or companies that sell through manufacturer's reps, sales agents, or brokers. In most firms, however, the sales force plays a major role. In companies that sell business products and services, such as IBM or DuPont, the company's salespeople work directly with customers. In consumer product companies such as Procter & Gamble and Nike, the sales force plays an important behind-the-scenes role. It works with wholesalers and retailers to gain their support and to help them be more effective in selling the company's products.

Linking the Company with Its Customers

The sales force serves as a critical link between a company and its customers. In many cases, salespeople serve both masters—the seller and the buyer. First, they *represent the company to customers*. They find and develop new customers and communicate information about the company's products and services. They sell products by approaching customers, presenting their products, answering objections, negotiating prices and terms, and closing sales. In addition, salespeople provide customer service and carry out market research and intelligence work.

At the same time, salespeople *represent customers to the company*, acting inside the firm as "champions" of customers' interests and managing the buyer–seller relationship. Salespeople relay customer concerns about company products and actions back inside to those who can handle them. They learn about customer needs and work with other marketing and nonmarketing people in the company to develop greater customer value.

In fact, to many customers, the salesperson *is* the company—the only tangible manifestation of the company that they see. Hence, customers may become loyal to salespeople as well as to the companies and products they represent. This concept of "salesperson-owned loyalty" lends even more importance to the salesperson's customer relationship-building abilities. Strong relationships with the salesperson will result in strong relationships with the company and its products. Conversely, poor salesperson relationships will probably result in poor company and product relationships.[3]

Coordinating Marketing and Sales

Ideally, the sales force and the firm's other marketing functions should work together closely to jointly create value for both customers and the company. Unfortunately, however, some companies still treat "marketing" and "sales" as separate functions. When this happens, the separated marketing and sales functions often don't get along well. When things go wrong, the marketers (marketing planners, brand managers, and researchers) blame the sales force for its poor execution of an otherwise splendid strategy. In turn, the sales team blames the marketers for being out of touch with what's really going on with customers. The marketers sometimes feel that salespeople have their "feet stuck in the mud," whereas salespeople feel that the marketers have their "heads stuck in the clouds." Neither group fully values the other's contributions. If not repaired, such disconnects between marketing and sales can damage customer relationships and company performance.

A company can take several actions to help bring its marketing and sales functions closer together. At the most basic level, it can *increase communications* between the two groups by arranging joint meetings and by spelling out when and with whom each group should communicate. The company can also create *joint assignments:*

It's important to create opportunities for marketers and salespeople to work together. This will make them more familiar with each other's ways of thinking and acting. It's useful for marketers, particularly brand managers and researchers, to occasionally go along on sales calls. They should also sit in on important account-planning sessions. Salespeople, in turn, should help to develop marketing plans. They should sit in on product-planning reviews and share their deep knowledge about customers' purchasing habits. They should preview ad and sales promotion campaigns. Jointly, marketers and salespeople should generate a playbook for expanding business with the top 10 accounts in each market segment. They should also plan events and conferences together.[4]

A company can also create *joint objectives and reward systems* for sales and marketing or appoint *marketing–sales liaisons*—people from marketing who "live with the sales force" and help to coordinate marketing and sales force programs and efforts. Finally, the firm can appoint a *chief revenue officer* (or *chief customer officer*)—a high-level marketing executive who oversees both marketing and sales. Such a person can help infuse marketing and sales with the common goal of creating value for customers to capture value in return.

Managing the Sales Force

Sales force management
The analysis, planning, implementation, and control of sales force activities. It includes designing sales force strategy and structure, and recruiting, selecting, training, supervising, compensating, and evaluating the firm's salespeople.

We define **sales force management** as the analysis, planning, implementation, and control of sales force activities. It includes designing sales force strategy and structure, and recruiting, selecting, training, compensating, supervising, and evaluating the firm's salespeople. These major sales force management decisions are shown in Figure 16.1 and are discussed in the following sections.

Designing Sales Force Strategy and Structure

Marketing managers face several sales force strategy and design questions. How should salespeople and their tasks be structured? How big should the sales force be? Should salespeople sell alone or work in teams with other people in the company? Should they sell in the field or by telephone or on the Web? We address these issues next.

Sales Force Structure

A company can divide sales responsibilities along any of several lines. The decision is simple if the company sells only one product line to one industry with customers in many locations. In that case the company would use a *territorial sales force structure*. However, if the company sells many products to many types of customers, it might need either a *product sales force structure*, a *customer sales force structure*, or a combination of the two.

Territorial sales force structure
A sales force organization that assigns each salesperson to an exclusive geographic territory in which that salesperson sells the company's full line.

Territorial Sales Force Structure   In the **territorial sales force structure**, each salesperson is assigned to an exclusive geographic area and sells the company's full line of products or services to all customers in that territory. This organization clearly defines each salesperson's job and fixes accountability. It also increases the salesperson's desire to build local customer relationships that, in turn, improve selling effectiveness. Finally, because each salesperson travels within a limited geographic area, travel expenses are relatively small.

A territorial sales organization is often supported by many levels of sales management positions. For example, Campbell Soup Company uses a territorial structure in which each salesperson is responsible for selling all Campbell products. Starting at the bottom of the organization, sales merchandisers report to sales representatives, who report to *retail supervisors*, who report to *directors of retail sales operations*, who report to one

Figure 16.1 Major steps in sales force management

of 22 *regional sales managers*. Regional sales managers, in turn, report to one of four *general sales managers* (West, Central, South, and East), who report to a *vice-president and general sales manager*.

Product sales force structure
A sales force organization under which salespeople specialize in selling only a portion of the company's products or lines.

Product Sales Force Structure Salespeople must know their products—especially when the products are numerous and complex. This need, together with the growth of product management, has led many companies to adopt a **product sales force structure** in which the sales force sells along product lines. For example, GE employs different sales forces within different product and service divisions of its major businesses. Within GE Infrastructure, for instance, the company has separate sales forces for aviation, energy, transportation, and water processing products and technologies. Within GE Healthcare, it employs different sales forces for diagnostic imaging, life sciences, and integrated IT solutions products and services. In all, a company as large and complex as GE might have dozens of separate sales forces serving its diverse product and service portfolio.

The product structure can lead to problems, however, if a single large customer buys many different company products. For example, Cardinal Health, the large North American health care products and services company, has several product divisions, each with a separate sales force. Using a product sales force structure might mean that several Cardinal salespeople end up calling on the same hospital on the same day. This means that they travel over the same routes and wait to see the same customer's purchasing agents. These extra costs must be compared with the benefits of better product knowledge and attention to individual products.

Customer sales force structure
A sales force organization under which salespeople specialize in selling only to certain customers or industries.

Customer Sales Force Structure More and more companies are now using a **customer sales force structure**, in which they organize the sales force along customer or industry lines. Separate sales forces may be set up for different industries, for serving current customers versus finding new ones, and for major accounts versus regular accounts. Many companies even have special sales forces set up to handle the needs of individual large customers. For example, Black & Decker has a Home Depot sales organization and a Lowe's sales organization.

Organizing the sales force around customers can help a company build closer relationships with important customers. Consider Lear Corporation, one of the largest automotive suppliers in the world:

> Each year, Lear Corporation produces almost US$16 billion worth of automotive seating systems, electrical distribution systems, and related automotive electronics products. Its customers include all of the world's leading automotive companies, from Ford, General Motors, Chrysler, Toyota, and Volvo to BMW, Ferrari, Rolls-Royce, and more than a dozen others. Perhaps more than any other part of the organization, it's Lear's outstanding 145-person sales force that brings to life the company's credo, "Consumer driven. Customer focused." Lear salespeople work hard at relationship building and doing what's best for the customer. "Our salespeople don't really close deals," notes a senior marketing executive. "They consult and work with customers to learn exactly what's needed and when."
>
> Lear organizes its sales force around major customers. More than that, the company itself is broken up into separate divisions dedicated to specific customers. For example, there's a Ford division, a General Motors division, and a Fiat division. This organization lets Lear's sales teams get very close to their customers. In fact, Lear often locates its sales offices in customers' facilities. For instance, the team that handles GM's light truck division works at GM's truck operation campus. "We can't just be there to give quotes and ask for orders," says the marketing executive. "We need to be involved with customers every step of the way—from vehicle concept through launch."[5]

Complex Sales Force Structures When a company sells a wide variety of products to many types of customers over a broad geographic area, it often combines several types of sales force structures. Salespeople can be specialized by customer and territory, by

Some sales forces are huge. Therefore, salespeople constitute one of the company's most productive—and most expensive—assets.

product and territory, by product and customer, or by territory, product, and customer. No single structure is best for all companies and situations. Each company should select a sales force structure that best serves the needs of its customers and fits its overall marketing strategy.

A good sales structure can mean the difference between success and failure. Companies should periodically review their sales force organizations to be certain that they serve the needs of the company and its customers. Over time, sales force structures can grow complex, inefficient, and unresponsive to customers' needs. This happened recently to technology giant Hewlett-Packard. To correct the problem, the company's new CEO took dramatic steps to restructure HP's corporate sales force (see Real Marketing 16.1).

Sales Force Size

Once the company has set its structure, it is ready to consider *sales force size*. Sales forces may range in size from only a few salespeople to tens of thousands. Salespeople constitute one of the company's most productive—and most expensive—assets. Therefore, increasing their number will increase both sales and costs.

Many companies use some form of *workload approach* to set sales force size. Using this approach, a company first groups accounts into different classes according to size, account status, or other factors related to the amount of effort required to maintain them. It then determines the number of salespeople needed to call on each class of accounts the desired number of times.

The company might think as follows: Suppose we have 1000 Type-A accounts and 2000 Type-B accounts. Type-A accounts require 36 calls a year and Type-B accounts require 12 calls a year. In this case, the sales force's *workload*—the number of calls it must make per year—is 60 000 calls [(1000 × 36) + (2000 × 12) = 36 000 + 24 000 = 60 000]. Suppose our average salesperson can make 1000 calls a year. Thus, we need 60 salespeople (60 000 ÷ 1000).[6]

Other Sales Force Strategy and Structure Issues

Sales management must also decide who will be involved in the selling effort and how various sales and sales support people will work together.

Outside sales force (field sales force)
Outside salespeople who travel to call on customers in the field.

Inside sales force
Inside salespeople who conduct business from their offices via telephone, the Internet, or visits from prospective buyers.

Outside and Inside Sales Forces The company may have an **outside sales force** (or *field sales force*), an **inside sales force**, or both. Outside salespeople travel to call on customers in the field. Inside salespeople conduct business from their offices via telephone, the Internet, or visits from buyers.

Some inside salespeople provide support for the outside sales force, freeing them to spend more time selling to major accounts and finding new prospects. For example, *technical sales support people* provide technical information and answers to customers' questions. *Sales assistants* provide administrative backup for outside salespeople. They call ahead and confirm appointments, follow up on deliveries, and answer customers' questions when outside salespeople cannot be reached. Using such combinations of inside and outside salespeople can help to serve important customers better. As one sales manager notes, "You have the support and easy access to the inside rep and the face-to-face relationship building of the outside rep."[7]

Other inside salespeople do more than just provide support. Telemarketers and *web sellers* use the phone and Internet to find new leads and qualify prospects or to sell and service accounts directly. Telemarketing and web selling can be very effective, less costly ways to sell to smaller, harder-to-reach customers. Depending on the complexity of the product and customer, for example, a telemarketer can make from 20 to 33 decision-maker

Real Marketing 16.1

Hewlett-Packard Overhauls Its Vast Corporate Sales Force

Imagine this scenario: You need a new digital camera. You're not sure which one to buy or even what features you need. So you visit your nearest electronics superstore to talk with a salesperson. You walk through the camera section but can't find anyone to help you. When you finally find a salesperson, he yawns and tells you that he's responsible for selling all the products in the store, so he doesn't really know all that much about cameras—maybe you should talk to someone else. You finally find a camera-savvy salesperson. However, after answering a few questions, she disappears to handle some other task, handing you off to someone new. And the new salesperson seems to contradict what the first salesperson said, even quoting different prices on a couple of models you like.

As incredible as it seems, at least until recently, this is the kind of situation that many large business buyers faced when they attempted to buy from technology giant Hewlett-Packard. Before Mark Hurd took over as HP's new CEO in the spring of 2005, the company's revenues and profits had flattened and its stock price had plummeted. To find out why, Hurd first talked directly with 400 corporate customers. Mostly what he heard was gripes about HP's corporate sales force.

Customers complained that they had to deal with too many salespeople, and that HP's confusing management layers made it hard to figure out whom to call. They had trouble tracking down HP sales representatives, and once found, the reps often came across as apathetic, leaving the customer to take the initiative. HP reps were responsible for a broad range of complex products, so they sometimes lacked the needed depth of knowledge on any subset of them. Customers grumbled that they received varying price quotes from different sales reps, and that it often took weeks for reps to respond to seemingly simple requests. In all, HP's corporate customers were frustrated, not a happy circumstance for a company that gets more than 70 percent of its revenues from businesses.

But customers weren't the only ones frustrated by HP's unwieldy and unresponsive sales force structure. HP was organized into three main product divisions: the Personal Systems Group (PSG), the Technology Solutions Group (TSG), and the Image and Printing Group (IPG). However, these divisions had

One of CEO Mark Hurd's biggest challenges: overhauling HP's vast corporate sales force. The new HP sales force structure has reduced salesperson frustration and helped salespeople to create better value for customers.

little control over the sales process. Instead, HP's corporate sales force was housed in a fourth division, the Customer Sales Group (CSG). All salespeople reported directly to the CSG and were responsible for selling products from all three product divisions. To make matters worse, the CSG was bloated and underperforming. According to one reporter, "of the 17 000 people working in HP's corporate sales, only around 10 000 directly sold to customers. The rest were support staff or in management."

HP division executives were frustrated by the CSG structure. They complained that they had little or no direct control over the salespeople who sold their products. And multiple layers of management slowed sales force decision making and customer responsiveness. Finally, salespeople themselves were frustrated by the structure. They weren't being given the time and support they needed to serve their customers well. Burdened with administrative tasks and bureaucratic red tape, they were spending less than a third of their time with customers. And they had to work through multiple layers of bureaucracy to get price quotes and sample products for customers. "The customer focus was lacking," says an HP sales vice-president. "Trying to navigate inside HP was difficult. It was unacceptable."

As CEO Mark Hurd peeled back the layers, it became apparent that HP's organizational problems went deeper than the sales force. The entire company had become so centralized, with so many layers of management, that it was unresponsive and out of touch with customers. Thus began what one observer called "one of Hurd's biggest management challenges: overhauling HP's vast corporate sales force."

For starters, Hurd eliminated the CSG division, instead assigning salespeople directly to the three product divisions. He also did away with three layers of management and cut hundreds of unproductive sales workers. This move gave divisional marketing and sales executives direct control over a leaner, more efficient sales process, resulting in speedier sales decisions and quicker market response.

Hurd also took steps to reduce salesperson and customer frustrations. Eliminating the CSG meant that each salesperson was responsible for selling a smaller number of products and was able to develop expertise in a specific product area. Hurd urged sales managers to cut back on salesperson administrative requirements and to improve sales support so that salespeople could spend more quality time with customers. As a result, salespeople now spend more than 40 percent of their time with customers, up from just 30 percent last year. And HP salespeople are noticing big changes in the sales support they receive:

> Salesman Richard Ditucci began noticing some of the changes late last year. At the time, Ditucci was trying to sell computer servers to Staples. As part of the process, Staples had asked him to provide a sample server for the company to evaluate. In the past, such requests typically took two to three weeks to fulfill because of HP's bureaucracy. This time, Ditucci got the server he needed within three days. The quick turnaround helped him win the contract, valued at several million dollars.

To ensure that important customers are carefully tended, HP assigned each salesperson three or fewer accounts. The top 2000 accounts were assigned just one salesperson—"so they'll always know whom to contact."

Customers are noticing differences in the attention that they get from HP salespeople:

> James Farris, a senior technology executive at Staples, says HP has freed up its salesman to drop by Staples at least twice a month instead of about once a month as before. The extra face time has enabled the HP salesman to create more valuable interactions, such as recently arranging a workshop to explain HP's technology to Staples executives. As a result, Farris says he is planning to send more business HP's way. Similarly, Keith Morrow, chief information officer of convenience-store chain 7-Eleven, says his HP sales representative is now "here all the time," and has been more knowledgeable in pitching products tailored to his business. As a result, last October, 7-Eleven began deploying in its stores 10 000 HP pen pads—a mobile device that helps 7-Eleven workers on the sales floor.

So HP's sales force restructuring appears to be paying off. Since Hurd's arrival, HP has become a much leaner and more efficient sales organization. Last year, revenues rose 14 percent to US$104 billion and profits jumped 17 percent. More importantly, salespeople are happier and more productive, resulting in happier customers, suggesting that more good news is yet to come for the company. CEO Hurd knows that there's still much more work to be done. But step by step, through restructuring, HP is fixing its sales force to create better value for its business customers. Now, if your local electronics superstore would only do the same for you. . . .

Sources: Quotes and adapted examples from Pui-Wing Tam, "System Reboot: Hurd's Big Challenge at HP: Overhauling Corporate Sales," *Wall Street Journal*, April 3, 2006, p. A1. Other information from "HP Restructures, Putting More Assignments In Play," *Adweek*, March 27, 2006, accessed at www.adweek.com; Christopher Hosford, "Rebooting Hewlett-Packard," *Sales & Marketing Management*, July–August 2006, pp. 32–35; Mike McCue, "Solutions that Make a Difference," *Sales & Marketing Management*, October 2007, pp. 19–21; Louise Lee, "HP's Hurd Is About to Be Tested," *BusinessWeek*, February 28, 2008, p. 59; and information from www.hp.com, accessed November 2008.

contacts a day, compared to the average of four that an outside salesperson can make. And whereas an average business-to-business field sales call costs $329 or more, a routine industrial telemarketing call costs only about $5 and a complex call about $20.[8]

Although Canada's National Do Not Call List put a dent in telephone sales to consumers, telemarketing remains a vital tool for many business-to-business marketers. For some smaller companies, telephone and web selling may be the primary sales approaches. However, larger companies also use these tactics, either to sell directly to small and midsize customers or to help out with larger ones. For example, Avaya, a US$5 billion global telecommunications firm, formed a telemarketing sales force to service its smaller, more routine, less complex accounts. Not only did the telesales force do a better job of selling to these smaller accounts, it freed Avaya's outside salespeople to focus their attention on the company's highest-value customers and prospects. As a result, the company has experienced 40 percent higher sales in areas where the telesales model is being used.[9]

For many types of products and selling situations, phone or web selling can be as effective as a personal sales call. Notes a DuPont telemarketer: "I'm more effective on the phone.

[When you're in the field], if some guy's not in his office, you lose an hour. On the phone, you lose 15 seconds. . . . Through my phone calls, I'm in the field as much as the rep is." There are other advantages. "Customers can't throw things at you," quips the rep, "and you don't have to outrun dogs."[10] What's more, although they may seem impersonal, the phone and Internet can be surprisingly personal when it comes to building customer relationships.

Team selling
Using teams of people from sales, marketing, engineering, finance, technical support, and even upper management to service large, complex accounts.

Team Selling As products become more complex and as customers grow larger and more demanding, a single salesperson simply can't handle all of a large customer's needs. Instead, most companies now use **team selling** to service large, complex accounts. Sales teams can unearth problems, solutions, and sales opportunities that no individual salesperson could. Such teams might include experts from any area or level of the selling firm—sales, marketing, technical and support services, R&D, engineering, operations, finance, and others. In team selling situations, the salesperson shifts from "soloist" to "orchestrator."

In many cases, the move to team selling mirrors similar changes in customers' buying organizations. "Buyers implementing team-based purchasing decisions have necessitated the equal and opposite creation of team-based selling—a completely new way of doing business for many independent, self-motivated salespeople," says a sales force analyst. "Today, we're calling on teams of buying people, and that requires more firepower on our side," agrees one sales vice-president. "One salesperson just can't do it all—can't be an expert in everything we're bringing to the customer. We have strategic account teams, led by customer business managers, who basically are our quarterbacks."[11]

Some companies, such as IBM, Xerox, and Procter & Gamble, have used teams for a long time. P&G sales reps are organized into "customer business development (CBD) teams." Each CBD team is assigned to a major P&G customer, such as Walmart, Safeway, or Shoppers Drug Mart. Teams consist of a customer business development manager, several account executives (each responsible for a specific category of P&G products), and specialists in marketing strategy, operations, information systems, logistics, and finance. This organization places the focus on serving the complete needs of each important customer. It lets P&G "grow business by working as a 'strategic partner' with our accounts, not just as a supplier. Our goal: to grow their business, which also results in growing ours."[12]

Team selling does have some pitfalls. For example, salespeople are by nature competitive and have often been trained and rewarded for outstanding individual performance. Salespeople who are used to having customers all to themselves may have trouble learning to work with and trust others on a team. In addition, selling teams can confuse or overwhelm customers who are used to working with only one salesperson. Finally, difficulties in evaluating individual contributions to the team selling effort can create some sticky compensation issues.

Recruiting and Selecting Salespeople

At the heart of any successful sales force operation is the recruitment and selection of good salespeople. The performance difference between an average salesperson and a top salesperson can be substantial. In a typical sales force, the top 30 percent of the salespeople might bring in 60 percent of the sales. Thus, careful salesperson selection can greatly increase overall sales force performance. Beyond the differences in sales performance, poor selection results in costly turnover. When a salesperson quits, the costs of finding and training a new salesperson—plus the costs of lost sales—can be very high. Also, a sales force with many new people is less productive, and turnover disrupts important customer relationships.

What sets great salespeople apart from all the rest? In an effort to profile top sales performers, Gallup Management Consulting Group, a division of the well-known Gallup polling organization, has interviewed hundreds of thousands of salespeople. Its research suggests that the best salespeople possess four key talents: intrinsic motivation, disciplined work style, the ability to close a sale, and perhaps most important, the ability to build relationships with customers.[13]

Great salespeople: The best salespeople, such as Jennifer Hansen of 3M, possess intrinsic motivation, disciplined work style, the ability to close a sale, and perhaps most important, the ability to build relationships with customers.

Super salespeople are motivated from within—they have an unrelenting drive to excel. Some salespeople are driven by money, a desire for recognition, or the satisfaction of competing and winning. Others are driven by the desire to provide service and to build relationships. The best salespeople possess some of each of these motivations. They also have a disciplined work style. They lay out detailed, organized plans and then follow through in a timely way.

But motivation and discipline mean little unless they result in closing more sales and building better customer relationships. Super salespeople build the skills and knowledge they need to get the job done. Perhaps most important, top salespeople are excellent customer problem solvers and relationship builders. They understand their customers' needs. Talk to sales executives and they'll describe top performers in these terms: Empathetic. Patient. Caring. Responsive. Good listeners. Top performers can put themselves on the buyer's side of the desk and see the world through their customers' eyes. They don't want just to be liked; they want to add value for their customers.

When recruiting, a company should analyze the sales job itself and the characteristics of its most successful salespeople to identify the traits needed by a successful salesperson in their industry. Then it must recruit the right salespeople. The human resources department looks for applicants by getting names from current salespeople, using employment agencies, placing classified ads, searching the Web, and working through college and university placement services. Another source is to attract top salespeople from other companies. Proven salespeople need less training and can be productive immediately.

Recruiting will attract many applicants from whom the company must select the best. The selection procedure can vary from a single informal interview to lengthy testing and interviewing. Many companies give formal tests to sales applicants. Tests typically measure sales aptitude, analytical and organizational skills, personality traits, and other characteristics. But test scores provide only one piece of information in a set that includes personal characteristics, references, past employment history, and interviewer reactions.

Training Salespeople

New salespeople may spend anywhere from a few weeks or months to a year or more in training. And even after, most companies provide continuing sales training via seminars, sales meetings, and web e-learning throughout the salesperson's career. Although training can be expensive, it can also yield dramatic returns. For example, one recent study showed that sales training conducted by a major telecommunications firm paid for itself in 16 days and resulted in a six-month return on investment of 812 percent.[14] While some firms do their sales training in-house, others send their representatives to executive education programs, or turn to the Canadian Professional Sales Association (www.cpsa.com) for help.

Training programs have several goals. First, salespeople need to know about customers and how to build relationships with them. So the training program must teach them about different types of customers and their needs, buying motives, and buying habits. And it must teach them how to sell effectively and train them in the basics of the selling process. Salespeople also need to know and identify with the company, its products, and its competitors. So an effective training program teaches them about the company's objectives, organization, and chief products and markets, and about the strategies of major competitors.

Today, many companies are adding e-learning to their sales training programs. Most e-learning is web-based, but many companies now offer on-demand training for PDAs,

Training salespeople: International Rectifier created the online IR University to help keep its hundreds of global sales reps, internal sales staffers, and others trained on the constant stream of new products it introduces.

cellphones, and even video iPods. Online and other e-learning approaches cut training costs and make training more efficient. One recent study estimates that companies spend 40 cents of every sales training dollar on travel and lodging. Such costs can be greatly reduced through web-based training. As a result, in 2005 companies did 33 percent of their corporate training online, up from 24 percent two years earlier.[15]

Online training may range from simple text-based product information to Internet-based sales exercises that build sales skills to sophisticated simulations that re-create the dynamics of real-life sales calls. International Rectifier, a global manufacturer of power management semiconductors, has learned that using the Internet to train salespeople offers many advantages:

> To stay competitive in its complex, fast-changing industry, International Rectifier must continually retrain its sales and support people. For example, IR introduces an average of three or more major new products each month. For each new product, the company must coordinate and train hundreds of sales reps, internal sales staffers, field engineers, key executives, and independent inside sales reps across a variety of time zones in 17 locations around the world.
>
> The answer: International Rectifier's online IR University, which provides timely training in advance of new product launches, along with ongoing training on other company and industry developments. The e-learning centre provides enhanced presentations, complete with creative animation and streamlined text, to share knowledge accurately but in a way that excites and captures attention. The centre also allows for "real-time" visual and audio communications with the presenter via live chat and conference calls. Beyond learning about new products, salespeople can refresh their memories and sharpen their knowledge on almost any topic before meeting with customers. And evaluation diagnostics help sales managers identify the skill and knowledge levels of each individual salesperson for ongoing support and training.
>
> The sales force is thrilled about being able to "attend" training sessions at times convenient for them, without leaving their home offices. And online training results in significant cost savings. Approximately 500 IR sales and support people have completed more than 5500 online courses during the past nine months. The cost? Just an estimated $12 per trainee per course. Compared to the costs associated with onsite training, the online learning system has saved the company approximately $250 000 during the past year. In all, online training has reduced IR's training costs by 75 percent.[16]

Compensating Salespeople

To attract good salespeople, a company must have an appealing compensation plan. Compensation is made up of several elements—a fixed amount, a variable amount, expenses, and fringe benefits. The fixed amount, usually a salary, gives the salesperson some stable income. The variable amount, which might be commissions or bonuses based on sales performance, rewards the salesperson for greater effort and success.

Management must decide what *mix* of these compensation elements makes the most sense for each sales job. Different combinations of fixed and variable compensation give rise to four basic types of compensation plans—straight salary, straight commission, salary plus bonus, and salary plus commission. A recent study of sales force compensation showed that the average salesperson's pay consists of about 67 percent salary and 33 percent incentive pay.[17]

The sales force compensation plan can both motivate salespeople and direct their activities. Compensation should direct salespeople toward activities that are consistent with overall sales force and marketing objectives. For example, if the strategy is to acquire new business, grow rapidly, and gain market share, the compensation plan might include a larger commission component coupled with a new-account bonus to encourage high sales performance and new-account development. In contrast, if the goal is to maximize current account profitability, the compensation plan might contain a larger base-salary component with additional incentives for current account sales or customer satisfaction.

In fact, more and more companies are moving away from high commission plans that may drive salespeople to make short-term grabs for business. They worry that a salesperson who is pushing too hard to close a deal may ruin the customer relationship. Instead, companies are designing compensation plans that reward salespeople for building customer relationships and growing the long-run value of each customer.

Supervising and Motivating Salespeople

New salespeople need more than a territory, compensation, and training—they need supervision and motivation. The goal of *supervision* is to help salespeople "work smart" by doing the right things in the right ways. The goal of *motivation* is to encourage salespeople to "work hard" and energetically toward sales force goals. If salespeople work smart and work hard, they will realize their full potential, to their own and the company's benefit.

Supervising Salespeople

Companies vary in how closely they supervise their salespeople. Many help their salespeople identify target customers and set call norms. Some may also specify how much time the sales force should spend prospecting for new accounts and set other time management priorities. One tool is the weekly, monthly, or annual *call plan* that shows which customers and prospects to call on and which activities to carry out. Another tool is *time-and-duty analysis*. In addition to time spent selling, the salesperson spends time travelling, waiting, taking breaks, and doing administrative chores.

Figure 16.2 shows how salespeople spend their time. On average, active selling time accounts for only 10 percent of total working time! If selling time could be raised from 10 percent to 30 percent, this would triple the time spent selling.[18] Companies are always looking for ways to save time—simplifying administrative duties, developing better sales call and routing plans, supplying more and better customer information, and using phones, email, or videoconferencing instead of travelling. Consider the changes GE made to increase its sales force's face-to-face selling time:

> When Jeff Immelt became General Electric's new chairman, he was dismayed to find that members of the sales team were spending far more time on deskbound administrative chores than in face-to-face meetings with customers and prospects. "He said we needed to turn that around," recalls Venki Rao, an IT leader in global sales and marketing at GE Power Systems, a division focused on energy systems and products.

Figure 16.2 How salespeople spend their time

Source: Proudfoot Consulting. Data used with permission.

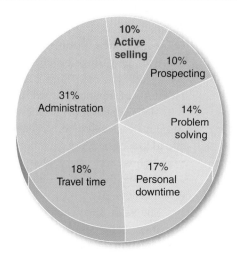

"[We need] to spend four days a week in front of the customer and one day for all the admin stuff." GE Power's salespeople spent much of their time at their desks because they had to go to many sources for the information needed to sell multimillion-dollar turbines, turbine parts, and services to energy companies worldwide. To fix the problem, GE created a new sales portal, a kind of "one-stop shop" for just about everything they need. The sales portal connects the vast array of existing GE databases, providing everything from sales tracking and customer data to parts pricing and information on planned outages. GE also added external data, such as news feeds. "Before, you were randomly searching for things," says Bill Snook, a GE sales manager. Now, he says, "I have the sales portal as my home page, and I use it as the gateway to all the applications that I have." The sales portal has freed Snook and 2500 other users around the globe from once time-consuming administrative tasks, greatly increasing their face time with customers.[19]

Many firms have adopted *sales force automation systems*—computerized, digitized sales force operations that let salespeople work more effectively anytime, anywhere. Companies now routinely equip their salespeople with technologies such as laptops, smart phones, wireless web connections, webcams for videoconferencing, and customer-contact and relationship management software. Armed with these technologies, salespeople can more effectively and efficiently profile customers and prospects, analyze and forecast sales, schedule sales calls, make presentations, prepare sales and expense reports, and manage account relationships. The result is better time management, improved customer service, lower sales costs, and higher sales performance.[20]

Selling and the Internet

Perhaps the fastest-growing technology tool is the Internet. The Internet offers explosive potential for conducting sales operations and for interacting with and serving customers. More and more companies are now using the Internet to support their personal selling efforts—not just for selling but for everything from training salespeople to conducting sales meetings and servicing accounts.

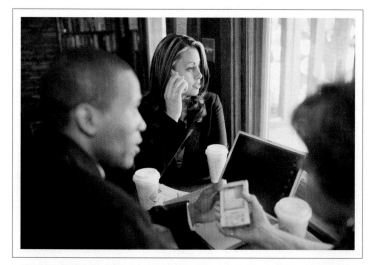

Sales force automation: Many sales forces have gone high tech, equipping salespeople with everything from smart phones, wireless web connections, and videoconferencing tools to customer-contact and relationship management software that helps them to be more effective and efficient.

Sales organizations around the world are now saving money and time by using a host of web approaches to train reps, hold sales meetings, and even conduct live sales presentations. The Web can be a good tool for selling to hard-to-reach customers. For example, consider the pharmaceuticals industry:

The big U.S. pharmaceutical companies currently employ some 87 000 sales reps (often called "detailers") to reach roughly 600 000 practising physicians. However, these reps are finding it harder than ever to get through to the busy doctors. "Doctors need immense amounts of medical information, but their patient loads limit their ability to see pharmaceutical reps or attend outside conferences," says an industry researcher. As a result, the average call lasts only 4.6 minutes and only 24 percent of sales calls on doctors result in quality, two-way discussions. The answer: Increasingly, it's the Web. The pharmaceutical companies now regularly use product websites, email marketing, and videoconferencing to help reps deliver useful information to physicians on their home or office PCs. One study found that last year more than 200 000 physicians participated in "e-detailing"—the process of receiving drug marketing information via the Web—a 400 percent jump in only three years. More than 20 percent have now substituted e-detailing for face-to-face meetings with reps entirely. Using direct-to-doctor web conferences, pharmaceutical reps can make live, interactive medical sales presentations to any physician with a PC and Internet access, saving both the customer's and the rep's time.[21]

Web-based technologies can produce big organizational benefits for sales forces. They help conserve salespeople's valuable time, save travel dollars, and give salespeople a new vehicle for selling and servicing accounts. But the technologies also have some drawbacks. For starters, they're not cheap. And such systems can intimidate low-tech salespeople or clients. What's more, web tools are susceptible to server crashes and other network difficulties, not a happy event when you're in the midst of an important sales meeting or presentation. Finally, there are some things you just can't do or teach via the Web, things that require personal interactions.

For these reasons, some high-tech experts recommend that sales executives use web technologies to supplement training, sales meetings, and preliminary client sales presentations, but resort to old-fashioned, face-to-face meetings when the time draws near to close the deal.

Motivating Salespeople

Beyond directing salespeople, sales managers must also motivate them. Some salespeople will do their best without any special urging from management. To them, selling may be the most fascinating job in the world. But selling can also be frustrating. Salespeople often work alone and they must sometimes travel away from home. They may face aggressive competing salespeople and difficult customers. Therefore, salespeople often need special encouragement to do their best.

Management can boost sales force morale and performance through its organizational climate, sales quotas, and positive incentives. *Organizational climate* describes the feeling that salespeople have about their opportunities, value, and rewards for good performance. Some companies treat salespeople as if they are not very important and performance suffers accordingly. Other companies treat their salespeople as valued contributors and allow virtually unlimited opportunity for income and promotion. Not surprisingly, these companies enjoy higher sales force performance and less turnover.

Sales quota
A standard that states the amount a salesperson should sell and how sales should be divided among the company's products.

Many companies motivate their salespeople by setting **sales quotas**—standards stating the amount they should sell and how sales should be divided among the company's products. Compensation is often related to how well salespeople meet their quotas. Companies also use various *positive incentives* to increase sales force effort. *Sales meetings* provide social occasions, breaks from routine, chances to meet and talk with "company brass," and opportunities to air feelings and to identify with a larger group. Companies also sponsor *sales contests* to spur the sales force to make a selling effort above what would normally be expected. Other incentives include honours, merchandise and cash awards, trips, and profit-sharing plans.

Evaluating Salespeople and Sales Force Performance

We have thus far described how management communicates what salespeople should be doing and how it motivates them to do it. This process requires good feedback. And good feedback means getting regular information about salespeople to evaluate their performance.

Management gets information about its salespeople in several ways. The most important source is *sales reports*, including weekly or monthly work plans and longer-term territory marketing plans. Salespeople also write up their completed activities on *call reports* and turn in *expense reports* for which they are partly or wholly repaid. The company can also monitor the sales and profit performance data in the salesperson's territory. Additional information comes from personal observation, customer surveys, and talks with other salespeople.

Using various sales force reports and other information, sales management evaluates members of the sales force. It evaluates salespeople on their ability to "plan their work and work their plan." Formal evaluation forces management to develop and communicate clear standards for judging performance. It also provides salespeople with constructive feedback and motivates them to perform well.

On a broader level, management should evaluate the performance of the sales force as a whole. Is the sales force accomplishing its customer relationship, sales, and profit objectives? Is it working well with other areas of the marketing and company organization? Are sales force costs in line with outcomes? As with other marketing activities, the company wants to measure its *return on sales investment*.

THE PERSONAL SELLING PROCESS

We now turn from designing and managing a sales force to the actual personal selling process. The **selling process** consists of several steps that the salesperson must master. These steps focus on the goal of getting new customers and obtaining orders from them. However, most salespeople spend much of their time maintaining existing accounts and building long-term customer *relationships*. We discuss the relationship aspect of the personal selling process in a later section.

Steps in the Selling Process

As shown in Figure 16.3, the selling process consists of seven steps: prospecting and qualifying, preapproach, approach, presentation and demonstration, handling objections, closing, and follow-up.

Prospecting and Qualifying

The first step in the selling process is **prospecting**—identifying qualified potential customers. Approaching the right potential customers is crucial to selling success. As one sales

---

Selling process
The steps that the salesperson follows when selling, which include prospecting and qualifying, preapproach, approach, presentation and demonstration, handling objections, closing, and follow-up.

Prospecting
The step in the selling process in which the salesperson or company identifies qualified potential customers.

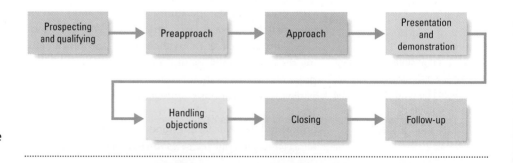

Figure 16.3 Steps in the selling process

expert puts it, "If the sales force starts chasing anyone who is breathing and seems to have a budget, you risk accumulating a roster of expensive-to-serve, hard-to-satisfy customers who never respond to whatever value proposition you have." He continues, "The solution to this isn't rocket science. [You must] train salespeople to actively scout the right prospects." Another expert concludes, "Increasing your prospecting effectiveness is the fastest single way to boost your sales."[22]

The salesperson must often approach many prospects to get just a few sales. Although the company supplies some leads, salespeople need skill in finding their own. The best source is referrals. Salespeople can ask current customers for referrals and cultivate other referral sources, such as suppliers, dealers, noncompeting salespeople, and bankers. They can also search for prospects in directories or on the Web and track down leads using the telephone and direct mail. Or they can drop in unannounced on various offices (a practice known as "cold calling").

Salespeople also need to know how to *qualify* leads—that is, how to identify the good ones and screen out the poor ones. Prospects can be qualified by looking at their financial ability, volume of business, special needs, location, and possibilities for growth.

Preapproach

Before calling on a prospect, the salesperson should learn as much as possible about the organization (what it needs, who is involved in the buying) and its buyers (their characteristics and buying styles). This step is known as the **preapproach**. "Revving up your sales starts with your preparation," says one sales consultant. "A successful sale begins long before you set foot in the prospect's office." Preapproach begins with good research. The salesperson can consult standard industry and online sources, acquaintances, and others to learn about the company. Then the salesperson must apply the research to develop a customer strategy. "Being able to recite the prospect's product line in your sleep isn't enough," says the consultant. "You need to translate the data into something useful for your client."[23]

The salesperson should set *call objectives*, which may be to qualify the prospect, to gather information, or to make an immediate sale. Another task is to decide on the best approach, which might be a personal visit, a phone call, or a letter or email. Timing should be considered carefully because many prospects are busiest at certain times. Finally, the salesperson should give thought to an overall sales strategy for the account.

Approach

During the **approach** step, the salesperson should know how to meet and greet the buyer and get the relationship off to a good start. This step involves the salesperson's appearance, opening lines, and the follow-up remarks. The opening lines should be positive in order to build goodwill from the beginning of the relationship. This opening might be followed by some key questions to learn more about the customer's needs or by showing a display or sample to attract the buyer's attention and curiosity. As in all stages of the selling process, listening to the customer is crucial.

Presentation and Demonstration

During the **presentation** step of the selling process, the salesperson tells the "value story" to the buyer, showing how the company's offer solves the customer's problems. The *customer-solution approach* fits better with today's relationship marketing focus than does a hard-sell or glad-handing approach. Buyers today want answers, not smiles; results, not razzle-dazzle. Moreover, they don't want just products—they want to know how those products will add value to their businesses. They want salespeople who listen to their concerns, understand their needs, and respond with the right products and services.

But before salespeople can *present* customer solutions, they must *develop* solutions to present. Many companies now train their salespeople to go beyond "product thinking."

Preapproach
The step in the selling process in which the salesperson learns as much as possible about a prospective customer before making a sales call.

Approach
The step in the selling process in which the salesperson meets the customer for the first time.

Presentation
The step in the selling process in which the salesperson tells the "value story" to the buyer, showing how the company's offer solves the customer's problems.

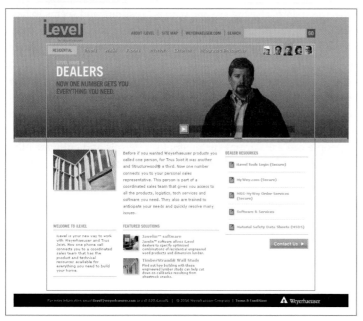

Weyerhaeuser created a customer-solutions-focused sales organization called iLevel. It promises customers "a coordinated sales team that gives you access to all the products, logistics, tech services, and software you need [to] quickly resolve issues."

Weyerhaeuser, the US$21 billion forestry products company, reorganized its entire sales force around customer-solutions selling:

> Weyerhaeuser, long a product-driven company, undertook an extreme makeover, creating a customer-solutions–focused sales organization called iLevel. Rather than selling wood products piecemeal, Weyerhaeuser wants to be considered the one-stop location for all of the innovation and products required to construct residential home frames—joists, beams, floors and all. The new iLevel organization assigns a single salesperson to each major builder or dealer. The sales rep leads a coordinated sales team that serves all of the customer's needs. To implement iLevel, Weyerhaeuser retrained its 250 salespeople to present customers with solutions, not products. "It is a consultative selling approach," says a Weyerhaeuser executive. Never again will salespeople merely sell orders of lumber. "What we want [our sales reps] to do is help our customers find solutions that make them [and us] money."[24]

The solutions approach calls for good listening and problem-solving skills. One study revealed that 74 percent of 200 purchasers surveyed at companies nationwide said they would be much more likely to buy from a salesperson if the seller would simply listen to them. Says one experienced salesperson, "That typecast chatty character may be the kind of person who's most often drawn to sales, but it's not often the one who's most successful at it. Unless you listen to what your customer is saying, you won't understand his deeper wants and needs. And you'll find that the more you listen to others, the more they'll listen to you. As the old saying goes, 'God gave us two ears and only one mouth, to use in that proportion.'"[25]

The qualities that buyers *dislike most* in salespeople include being pushy, late, deceitful, and unprepared or disorganized. The qualities they *value most* include good listening, empathy, honesty, dependability, thoroughness, and follow-through. Great salespeople know how to sell, but more importantly they know how to listen and to build strong customer relationships. Says one professional, "Salespeople must have the right answers, certainly, but they also have to learn how to ask those questions and listen."[26]

Finally, salespeople must also plan their presentation methods. Good interpersonal communication skills count when it comes to making effective sales presentations. However, today's media-rich and cluttered communications environment presents many new challenges for sales presenters:

> The goal of a sales presentation is to deliver a clear, concise, and consistent message to your prospects about your product and your brand, as well as why you are better than the competition. Doing that and keeping your audience's attention for longer than 30 minutes is the real challenge.

Presentation technology: Today's salespeople are employing advanced presentation technologies that allow for full multimedia presentations—in person, online, or both.

Today's information-overloaded prospects demand a richer presentation experience. And sales presenters must now overcome multiple distractions from cellphones, text messaging, and portable Internet viewers during a presentation. Sales presentations today take creativity, careful planning, and the application of the hottest technologies available. You can't fill your prospects' heads with unnecessary, useless information, and you have to capture their interest fast or risk losing them forever. So you must deliver your message in a more engaging and compelling way than your competition does, and you must deliver more information in less time.[27]

Thus, today's salespeople are employing advanced presentation technologies that allow for full multimedia presentations to only one or a few people. The venerable old flip chart has been replaced by CDs and DVDs, online presentation technologies, interactive white boards, and handheld and laptop computers with sophisticated presentation software.

Handling Objections

Handling objections
The step in the selling process in which the salesperson seeks out, clarifies, and overcomes customer objections to buying.

Customers almost always have objections during the presentation or when asked to place an order. The problem can be either logical or psychological, and objections are often unspoken. In **handling objections**, the salesperson should use a positive approach, seek out hidden objections, ask the buyer to clarify any objections, take objections as opportunities to provide more information, and turn the objections into reasons for buying. Every salesperson needs training in the skills of handling objections.

Closing

Closing
The step in the selling process in which the salesperson asks the customer for an order.

After handling the prospect's objections, the salesperson now tries to close the sale. Some salespeople do not get around to **closing** or do not handle it well. They may lack confidence, feel guilty about asking for the order, or fail to recognize the right moment to close the sale. Salespeople should know how to recognize closing signals from the buyer, including physical actions, comments, and questions. For example, the customer might sit forward and nod approvingly or ask about prices and credit terms.

Salespeople can use one of several closing techniques. They can ask for the order, review points of agreement, offer to help write up the order, ask whether the buyer wants this model or that one, or note that the buyer will lose out if the order is not placed now. The salesperson may offer the buyer special reasons to close, such as a lower price or an extra quantity at no charge.

Follow-Up

Follow-up
The last step in the selling process in which the salesperson follows up after the sale to ensure customer satisfaction and repeat business.

The last step in the selling process—**follow-up**—is necessary if the salesperson wants to ensure customer satisfaction and repeat business. Right after closing, the salesperson should complete any details on delivery time, purchase terms, and other matters. The salesperson then should schedule a follow-up call when the initial order is received to make sure there is proper installation, instruction, and servicing. This visit would reveal any problems, assure the buyer of the salesperson's interest, and reduce any buyer concerns that might have arisen since the sale.

Personal Selling and Managing Customer Relationships

The steps in the selling process as just described are *transaction oriented*—their aim is to help salespeople close a specific sale with a customer. But in most cases, the company is not simply seeking a sale: It has targeted a major customer that it would like to win and keep. The company would like to show that it has the capabilities to serve the customer over the long haul in a mutually profitable *relationship*. The sales force usually plays an important role in building and managing profitable customer relationships. Thus, as shown in Figure 16.3, the selling process must be understood in the context of building and maintaining profitable customer relationships.

Today's large customers favour suppliers who can sell and deliver a coordinated set of products and services to many locations, and who can work closely with customer teams to improve products and processes. For these customers, the first sale is only the beginning of the relationship. Unfortunately, some companies ignore these relationship realities. They sell their products through separate sales forces, each working independently to close sales. Their technical people may not be willing to lend time to educate a customer. Their engineering, design, and manufacturing people may have the attitude that "it's our job to make good products and the salesperson's to sell them to customers." Their salespeople focus on pushing products toward customers rather than listening to customers and providing solutions.

Other companies, however, recognize that winning and keeping accounts requires more than making good products and directing the sales force to close lots of sales. If the company wishes only to close sales and capture short-term business, it can do this by simply slashing its prices to meet or beat those of competitors. Instead, most companies want their salespeople to practise value selling—demonstrating and delivering superior customer value and capturing a return on that value that's fair for both the customer and the company (see Real Marketing 16.2). Value selling requires listening to customers, understanding their needs, and carefully coordinating the whole company's efforts to create lasting relationships based on customer value.

4 SALES PROMOTION

Sales promotion
Short-term incentives to encourage the purchase or sale of a product or service.

Personal selling and advertising often work closely with another promotion tool, sales promotion. **Sales promotion** consists of short-term incentives to encourage purchase or sales of a product or service. Whereas advertising offers reasons to buy a product or service, sales promotion offers reasons to buy *now*.

Examples of sales promotions are found everywhere. A freestanding insert in the Sunday newspaper contains a coupon offering $1 off Folgers coffee. An email from EddieBauer.ca offers free shipping on your next purchase over $100. The end-of-the-aisle display in the local supermarket tempts impulse buyers with a wall of Coke cases. An executive buys a new Sony laptop and gets a free carrying case, or a family buys a new Ford Escape and receives a factory rebate of $1000. A hardware store chain receives a 10 percent discount on selected Black & Decker portable power tools if it agrees to advertise them in local newspapers. Sales promotion includes a wide variety of promotion tools designed to stimulate earlier or stronger market response.

Rapid Growth of Sales Promotion

Sales promotion tools are used by most organizations, including manufacturers, distributors, retailers, and not-for-profit institutions. They can be targeted toward final buyers (*consumer promotions*), retailers and wholesalers (*trade promotions*), business customers (*business promotions*), and members of the sales force (*sales force promotions*). Today, in the average consumer packaged goods company, sales promotion accounts for 74 percent of all marketing expenditures.[28]

Several factors have contributed to the rapid growth of sales promotion, particularly in consumer markets. First, inside the company, product managers face greater pressures to increase their current sales, and promotion is viewed as an effective short-run

Sales promotions are found everywhere. For example, your Sunday newspaper is loaded with freestanding inserts that promote strong and immediate market response.

Real Marketing **16.2**

Value Selling: Value Merchants Versus Value Spendthrifts

It's the company's job to create a compelling value proposition for customers. Then, it's the salesperson's job to build profitable customer relationships based on that value proposition. Unfortunately, in the heat of closing sales, salespeople too often take the easy way out by cutting prices rather than selling value. It's usually much easier to win a sale by matching competitors' lower prices than by working to convince a customer that your product's greater value justifies its higher price.

In their book *Value Merchants: Demonstrating and Documenting Superior Value in Business Markets*, three marketing professors define two types of salespeople: *value spendthrifts* and *value merchants*. Value spendthrifts give value away, emphasizing low prices while getting little from customers in return. By contrast, value merchants emphasize customer value. They recognize the value that the company's offer gives the customer and work to obtain a return on that value that's fair for both the customer and company. Rather than simply dropping prices to get or keep short-term sales, value merchant salespeople document and demonstrate superior value to capture a customer's long-term business.

How can a company tell whether it has value spendthrift or value merchant salespeople? The following table compares the behaviours of the two salesperson types. For example, value spendthrifts prefer to give quick price concessions in order to close deals; value merchants "hang tough" in negotiations to capture profits in line with the value their market offering provides. Value spendthrifts complain to the company that its prices are too high, keeping them from winning a customer's business; value merchants explain that they need

more proof of superior customer value to win a customer's business. Value spendthrift salespeople give services away for free to close a deal, whereas value merchant salespeople employ services strategically to generate additional business.

The challenge for sales managers is to transform value spendthrifts into value merchants. Compensation plays an important role. To encourage salespeople to seek return on value rather than simply cutting price to gain or retain business, the sales compensation plan should reward value-selling behaviours and profitable outcomes rather than just short-term sales outcomes. Beyond compensation, management must install a value-selling process—one that starts with communicating the company's value proposition and ends with measures of actual value delivered. Finally, the company must equip salespeople with specific value-selling tools that they can use to forcefully demonstrate the value of the firm's offerings to target customers. These tools include value data,

Value-Merchant Versus Value-Spendthrift Salespeople

Value Spendthrifts	Value Merchants
Prefer to give quick price concessions to close deals and move on to other business	"Hang tough" in the negotiations to gain better profitability out of each deal based on customer value
Give price concessions without changes in the market offering	Only give price concessions in exchange for cost-saving reductions in the market offering
Routinely trade more business for lower prices	Routinely gain more business at the same price
Give services away for free to close a deal	Strategically employ services to generate additional business
Sell primarily on price comparisons with competitors	Sell primarily on cost of ownership comparisons versus competitors
Complain to the company that its prices are too high	Explain to the company that they need more proof of superior value
Believe management pursues a volume-driven strategy	Believe management pursues a value-driven strategy
Tell the company that customers are only interested in price	Provide customer insights to improve the value of the company's offerings
Make token, unsupported claims about superior value to customers	Demonstrate and document claims about superior value in monetary terms to customers
Focus on revenue and volume components of their compensation plan	Concentrate on gross margins and profitability components of their compensation plan

value calculators, and value case histories that provide evidence to customers about value gained versus competitors.

Here are examples of two companies that have applied value merchant thinking to transform their salespeople from customer advocates for price cuts into company advocates for value provided.

Applied Industrial Technologies. Bearings and industrial supplies reseller Applied Industrial Technologies has implemented a documented value added (DVA) program that requires salespeople to prepare formal DVA reports in which they record all of their efforts to provide value for individual customers. Importantly, customer managers must sign off on these reports, confirming that the value claimed has actually been delivered. Since its inception, the DVA program has documented more than US$1 billion in savings for Applied's customers.

Applied salespeople use DVA as an integral part of their everyday selling activities in a number of ways. They use DVA reports to build customer loyalty and gain future sales. DVA enables the salesperson to make compelling statements to a customer, such as "Last year the $200 000 worth of products you purchased from Applied gained you more than $85 000 in documented cost savings." Applied's salespeople report that such statements not only take the sting out of a 3 to 4 percent price increase, they also enable the reps to capture a sale even when competitors have undercut Applied's prices. The DVA program itself even adds value for customers. It provides customer purchasing managers with documentation that shows their managers how they have met their firm's cost reduction goals. Thus, the DVA program helps Applied's salespeople build profitable relationships with buyers based on mutual benefit.

Rockwell Automation. Facing considerable pressure from Walmart to lower its prices, a condiment producer hastily summoned several competing supplier representatives—including Rockwell Automation sales rep Jeff Policicchio—to participate in a "Continuous Improvement Conference" at one of its major plant sites. Policicchio and the competing sales reps were given full access to the plant for one day and asked to find ways to dramatically reduce the customer's operating costs. From discussions with plant personnel, Policicchio quickly learned that a major problem stemmed from lost production and downtime due to poorly performing pumps on 32 huge condiment tanks. Policicchio gathered relevant cost and usage data. Then he used a Rockwell Automation laptop value-assessment tool to analyze the data, find potential cost savings, and construct the best pump solution for the customer.

The next day, Policicchio and the competing reps presented their solutions to plant management. Policicchio offered this specific value proposition: "With this Rockwell Automation pump solution, through the elimination of downtime, reduced administrative costs associated with procurement, and lower spending on repair parts, your company will save at least $16 268 per pump—on up to 32 pumps—relative to our best competitor's solution." Soon after the presentations, Policicchio learned that he was the only rep to demonstrate tangible cost savings for his proposed solution. Everyone else made fuzzy promises about possible benefits, and many competing reps offered to save the customer money by simply shaving their prices.

The plant managers were so impressed with Policicchio's value proposition that—despite its higher initial price—they immediately purchased one Rockwell Automation pump solution for a trial. When they discovered that the actual savings were even better than predicted, they placed orders for the remaining pumps, which will be installed as the existing pumps wear out. Thus, Policicchio's value-selling approach not only landed the initial sale but also provided the basis for a profitable long-term relationship with the customer.

Sources: The examples and table are adapted from James C. Anderson, Nirmalya Kumar, and James A. Narus, "Be a Value Merchant," *Sales & Marketing Management*, May 6, 2008; and "Business Market Value Merchants," *Marketing Management*, March/April 2008, pp. 31+. They can also be found in Anderson, Kumar, and Narus, *Value Merchants: Demonstrating and Documenting Superior Value in Business Markets* (Boston: Harvard Business School Press, 2007).

---

sales tool. Second, externally, the company faces more competition and competing brands are less differentiated. Increasingly, competitors are using sales promotion to help differentiate their offers. Third, advertising efficiency has declined because of rising costs, media clutter, and legal restraints. Finally, consumers have become more deal oriented, and ever-larger retailers are demanding more deals from manufacturers.

The growing use of sales promotion has resulted in *promotion clutter*, similar to advertising clutter. Consumers are increasingly tuning out promotions, weakening their ability to trigger immediate purchase. Manufacturers are now searching for ways to rise above the clutter, such as offering larger coupon values, creating more dramatic point-of-purchase displays, or delivering promotions through new interactive media, such as the Internet or cellphones.

In developing a sales promotion program, a company must first set sales promotion objectives and then select the best tools for accomplishing these objectives.

Sales Promotion Objectives

Sales promotion objectives vary widely. Sellers may use *consumer promotions* to urge short-term customer buying or to enhance customer brand involvement. Objectives for *trade promotions* include getting retailers to carry new items and more inventory, buy ahead, or promote the company's products and give them more shelf space. For the *sales force*, objectives include getting more sales force support for current or new products or getting salespeople to sign up new accounts.

Sales promotions are usually used together with advertising, personal selling, direct marketing, or other promotion mix tools. Consumer promotions must usually be advertised and can add excitement and pulling power to ads. Trade and sales force promotions support the firm's personal selling process.

In general, rather than creating only short-term sales or temporary brand switching, sales promotions should help to reinforce the product's position and build long-term *customer relationships*. If properly designed, every sales promotion tool has the potential to build both short-term excitement and long-term consumer relationships. Increasingly, marketers are avoiding "quick fix," price-only promotions in favour of promotions designed to build brand equity.

Examples include all of the "frequency marketing programs" and loyalty clubs that have mushroomed in recent years. Most hotels, supermarkets, and airlines offer frequent-guest/buyer/flyer programs giving rewards to regular customers. Air Miles is one of the best-known programs, but many others flourish. For example, Shoppers Drug Mart offers the Optimum card, TD Canada Trust offers several Visa Travel Rewards options, and Petro-Canada rewards customers with Petro-Points.

Major Sales Promotion Tools

Many tools can be used to accomplish sales promotion objectives. Descriptions of the main consumer, trade, and business promotion tools follow.

Consumer Promotions

Consumer promotions
Sales promotion tools used to boost short-term customer buying and involvement or to enhance long-term customer relationships.

The **consumer promotions** include a wide range of tools—from samples, coupons, refunds, premiums, and point-of-purchase displays to contests, sweepstakes, and event sponsorships.

Samples are offers of a trial amount of a product. Sampling is the most effective—but most expensive—way to introduce a new product or to create new excitement for an existing one. Some samples are free; for others, the company charges a small amount to offset its cost. The sample might be delivered door-to-door, sent by mail, handed out in a store or kiosk, attached to another product, or featured in an ad. Sometimes samples are combined into sample packs, which can then be used to promote other products and services. Sampling can be a powerful promotional tool.

Coupons are certificates that give buyers a saving when they purchase specified products. Coupons can promote early trial of a new brand or stimulate sales of a mature brand. However, as a result of coupon clutter, redemption rates have been declining in recent years. Thus, most major consumer goods companies are issuing fewer coupons and targeting them more carefully.

Marketers are also cultivating new outlets for distributing coupons, such as supermarket shelf dispensers, electronic point-of-sale coupon printers, email and online media, or even mobile text-messaging systems. Mobile couponing is very popular in Europe, India, and Japan, and it's now gaining popularity in North America. For example, consider Cellfire, a mobile couponing company in California:

Cellfire (www.cellfire.com) distributes digital coupons to the cellphones of consumers nationwide who sign up for its free service. Cellfire's growing list of clients ranges from Domino's Pizza, T.G.I.Friday's, and Hardee's and Carl's Jr. restaurants to Kimberly-Clark, Supercuts, Hollywood Video, 1-800-FLOWERS.COM, and Enterprise Rent-A-Car. Cellfire sends an ever-changing assortment of digital coupons to users'

New forms of coupons: Cellfire distributes digital coupons to the cellphones of consumers who sign up for its free service.

cellphones. To use the coupons, users simply call up the stored coupon list, navigate to the coupon they want, press the "Use Now" button, and show the digital coupon to the store cashier. Domino's even permits consumers holding the mobile coupons to simply click on a link to have their cellphones dial the nearest Domino's store to place an order. To date, Cellfire users have redeemed more than US$28 million in coupon savings.

Coupons distributed through Cellfire offer distinct advantages to both consumers and marketers. Consumers don't have to find and clip paper coupons or print out web coupons and bring them along when they shop. They always have their cellphone coupons with them. For marketers, mobile coupons allow more careful targeting and eliminate the costs of printing and distributing paper coupons. "We don't pay for distribution of digital coupons," says one client. "We pay on redemptions." And the redemption rates can be dazzling. According to Cellfire's chief executive, "We're seeing redemption rates as high as 10 to 15 percent, while the industry average paper response is . . . less than 1 percent."[29]

Cash refunds (or *rebates*) are like coupons except that the price reduction occurs after the purchase rather than at the retail outlet. The consumer sends a "proof of purchase" to the manufacturer, who then refunds part of the purchase price by mail. For example, Toro ran a clever preseason promotion on some of its snowblower models, offering a rebate if the snowfall in the buyer's market area turned out to be below average. Competitors were not able to match this offer on such short notice, and the promotion was very successful.

Price packs (also called *cents-off deals*) offer consumers savings off the regular price of a product. The producer marks the reduced prices directly on the label or package. Price packs can be single packages sold at a reduced price (such as two for the price of one), or two related products banded together (such as a toothbrush and toothpaste). Price packs are very effective—even more so than coupons—in stimulating short-term sales.

Premiums are goods offered either free or at low cost as an incentive to buy a product, ranging from toys included with kids' products to phone cards and DVDs. A premium may come inside the package (in-pack), outside the package (on-pack), or through the mail. For example, over the years McDonald's has offered a variety of premiums in its Happy Meals—from Teenie Beanie Babies to Speed Racers. And for the past 18 years, McDonald's Canada has sold Upper Deck hockey cards at the low price of $0.99 per pack with the purchase of fries or a drink. Collectors and hockey fans alike visit the restaurant each fall to get their hands on these sets. In fact, a 2005–2006 autographed Martin Brodeur is listed on eBay for $600!

Advertising specialties, also called *promotional products*, are useful articles imprinted with an advertiser's name, logo, or message that are given as gifts to consumers. Typical items include T-shirts and other apparel, pens, coffee mugs, calendars, key rings, mouse pads, matches, tote bags, coolers, golf balls, and caps. Marketers spent almost US$19 billion on advertising specialties last year, but such items can be very effective. The "best of them stick around for months, subtly burning a brand name into a user's brain," notes one promotional products expert.[30]

Point-of-purchase (POP) promotions include displays and demonstrations that take place at the point of sale. Think of your last visit to the local Loblaw, Costco, or RONA. Chances are good that you were tripping over aisle displays, promotional signs, "shelf talkers," or demonstrators offering free tastes of featured food products. Unfortunately, many retailers do not like to handle the hundreds of displays, signs, and posters they receive from manufacturers each year. Manufacturers have responded by offering better POP materials, offering to set them up, and tying them in with television, print, or online messages.

Contests, sweepstakes, and games give consumers the chance to win something, such as cash, trips, or goods, by luck or through extra effort. A *contest* calls for consumers to submit an entry—a jingle, guess, suggestion—to be judged by a panel that will select the best entries. A *sweepstakes* calls for consumers to submit their names for a draw. A *game* presents consumers with something—bingo numbers, missing letters—every time they buy, which may or may not help them win a prize. Such promotions can create considerable brand attention and consumer involvement:

> Doritos recently ran a "Get It. Taste It. Name It" sweepstakes asking consumers to taste its newest flavour, initially labelled X-13D, and then suggest a name and write an ad for it. Those who submitted a name or ad were entered into the sweeps to become one of 100 Doritos Flavor Masters. Winners were selected through a random drawing. As Flavor Masters, the 100 grand-prize winners got the chance to take part in Doritos research and development, giving feedback on future flavour ideas. Each also got a year's supply of Doritos, 52 coupons good for one bag per week. The X-13D chips, packaged in a black bag with a label that looked like it's lifted from a science lab, built a lot of buzz. The promotion pulled in more than 100 000 entries within only a month of launch. And the promotion sparked considerable online chatter as bloggers wrote about stumbling upon the distinctive bag in convenience stores and tackled the question of what the flavour really was.[31]

Event marketing
Creating a brand-marketing event or serving as a sole or participating sponsor of events created by others.

Finally, marketers can promote their brands through **event marketing** (or *event sponsorships*). They can create their own brand-marketing events or serve as sole or participating sponsors of events created by others. The events might include anything from mobile brand tours to festivals, reunions, marathons, concerts, or other sponsored gatherings. Event marketing is huge, and it may be the fastest-growing area of promotion. Consumer event-marketing spending in the United States reached US$19 billion last year, up 12 percent from a year earlier.[32]

Most companies sponsor brand events. Harley-Davidson holds "HOG Rallies" and Harley biker reunions that draw hundreds of thousands of bikers each year. Sprint is paying US$700 million over 10 years to sponsor the NASCAR Sprint Cup Series. And Atlantic Superstore, Alexander Keith's, CTV, and others jointly sponsor the Tall Ships Nova Scotia Festival, one of the largest festivals in Atlantic Canada. Mentos Gum needed a unique event to stand out when it entered the highly competitive gum market:

Trade promotions
Sales promotion tools used to persuade resellers to carry a brand, give it shelf space, promote it in advertising, and push it to consumers.

> To engage consumers, Mentos Gum developed the "making art pop" campaign using packaging as part of the creative solution. Blister packs were placed side by side on a canvas and one by one, the round pieces of gum were removed from different areas on the canvas, transforming the images into pictures. For three days in high-traffic areas in Montreal, Toronto, and Vancouver, local artists created amazing, large scale pieces of art out of real Mentos Gum blister packs. Product samples were given out and consumers were driven to the MakeArtPop.ca microsite. The campaign was a huge success, with higher than anticipated brand awareness, market reach, and sales. It was also voted as the 2008 winner of the best brand-building campaign by the Marketing Agencies Association Worldwide.[33]

Event marketing: Mentos Gum created a buzz when it entered the market by holding artistic events in Montreal, Toronto, and Vancouver. Local artists created amazing, large-scale pieces of art out of real Mentos Gum blister packs.

Trade Promotions

Manufacturers direct more sales promotion dollars toward retailers and wholesalers (81 percent) than to final consumers (19 percent).[34] **Trade promotions** can persuade resellers to carry a brand, give it shelf space, promote it in advertising, and push it to consumers. Shelf space is so scarce these days that manufacturers often have to offer price-offs, allowances, buy-back guarantees, or free goods to retailers and wholesalers to get products on the shelf and, once there, to keep them on it.

Manufacturers use several trade promotion tools. Many of the tools used for consumer promotions—contests, premiums, displays—can also be used as trade promotions. Or the manufacturer may offer a straight *discount* off the list price on each case purchased during a stated period of time (also called a *price-off, off-invoice,* or *off-list*). Manufacturers may also offer an *allowance* (usually so much off per case) in return for the retailer's agreement to feature the manufacturer's products in some way. An advertising allowance compensates retailers for advertising the product. A display allowance compensates them for using special displays.

Manufacturers may offer *free goods,* which are extra cases of merchandise, to resellers who buy a certain quantity or who feature a certain flavour or size. They may offer *push money*—cash or gifts to dealers or their sales forces to "push" the manufacturer's goods. Manufacturers may give retailers free *specialty advertising items* that carry the company's name, such as pens, pencils, calendars, paperweights, matchbooks, memo pads, and yardsticks.

Business Promotions

Business promotions
Sales promotion tools used to generate business leads, stimulate purchases, reward customers, and motivate salespeople.

Companies spend billions of dollars each year on promotion to industrial customers. **Business promotions** are used to generate business leads, stimulate purchases, reward customers, and motivate salespeople. Business promotions include many of the same tools used for consumer or trade promotions. Here, we focus on two additional major business promotion tools—conventions and trade shows, and sales contests.

Many companies and trade associations organize *conventions and trade shows* to promote their products. Firms selling to the industry show their products at the trade show. Vendors receive many benefits, such as opportunities to find new sales leads, contact customers, introduce new products, meet new customers, sell more to present customers, and educate customers with publications and audiovisual materials. Trade shows also help companies reach many prospects not reached through their sales forces.

Some trade shows are huge. For example, the International Consumer Electronics Show has about 2700 exhibitors that attract more than 141 000 professional visitors. Even more impressive, at the BAUMA mining and construction equipment trade show in Munich, Germany, some 3000 exhibitors from 49 countries presented their latest product innovations to more than 500 000 attendees from 190 countries.[35] The success of trade shows is revealed in the bottom line of many Canadian companies. Recently, the 400 Canadian firms that displayed their wares at the 40 largest German trade fairs rang up more than $250 million in sales.

A *sales contest* is a contest for salespeople or dealers to motivate them to increase their sales performance over a given period. Sales contests motivate and recognize good company performers who may receive trips, cash prizes, or other gifts. Some companies award points for performance, which the receiver can turn in for any of a variety of prizes. Sales contests work best when they are tied to measurable and achievable sales objectives (such as finding new accounts, reviving old accounts, or increasing account profitability).

Developing the Sales Promotion Program

Beyond selecting the types of promotions to use, marketers must make several other decisions in designing the full sales promotion program. First, they must decide on the *size of the incentive*. A certain

Some trade shows are huge: The International Consumer Electronics Show has about 2700 exhibitors that attract more than 141 000 professional visitors.

minimum incentive is necessary if the promotion is to succeed; a larger incentive will produce more sales response. The marketer also must set *conditions for participation*. Incentives might be offered to everyone or only to select groups.

Marketers must decide how to *promote and distribute the promotion* program itself. A $2-off coupon could be given out in a package, at the store, via the Internet, or in an advertisement. Each distribution method involves a different level of reach and cost. Increasingly, marketers are blending several media into a total campaign concept. The *length of the promotion* is also important. If the sales promotion period is too short, many prospects (who may not be buying during that time) will miss it. If the promotion runs too long, the deal will lose some of its "act now" force.

Evaluation is also very important. Many companies fail to evaluate their sales promotion programs, and others evaluate them only superficially. Yet marketers should work to measure the returns on their sales promotion investments, just as they should seek to assess the returns on other marketing activities. The most common evaluation method is to compare sales before, during, and after a promotion. Marketers should ask, Did the promotion attract new customers or more purchasing from current customers? Can we hold onto these new customers and purchases? Will the long-run customer relationship and sales gains from the promotion justify its costs?

Clearly, sales promotion plays an important role in the total promotion mix. To use it well, the marketer must define the sales promotion objectives, select the best tools, design the sales promotion program, implement the program, and evaluate the results. Moreover, sales promotion must be coordinated carefully with other promotion mix elements within the overall integrated marketing communications program.

REVIEWING OBJECTIVES AND KEY TERMS

mymarketinglab | Audio Chapter Summary

This chapter is the second of three chapters covering the final marketing mix element—promotion. The previous chapter dealt with advertising and public relations. This one investigates personal selling and sales promotion. Personal selling is the interpersonal arm of the communications mix. Sales promotion consists of short-term incentives to encourage the purchase or sale of a product or service.

OBJECTIVE 1 Discuss the role of a company's salespeople in creating value for customers and building customer relationships.

Most companies use salespeople and many companies assign them an important role in the marketing mix. For companies selling business products, the firm's salespeople work directly with customers. Often, the sales force is the customer's only direct contact with the company and therefore may be viewed by customers as representing the company itself. In contrast, for consumer product companies that sell through intermediaries, consumers usually do not meet salespeople or even know about them. The sales force works behind the scenes, dealing with wholesalers and retailers to obtain their support and helping them become effective in selling the firm's products.

As an element of the promotion mix, the sales force is very effective in achieving certain marketing objectives and carrying out such activities as prospecting, communicating, selling, servicing, and information gathering. But with companies becoming more market oriented, a customer-focused sales force also works to produce both *customer satisfaction* and *company profit*. The sales force plays a key role in developing and managing profitable *customer relationships*.

OBJECTIVE 2 Identify and explain the six major sales force management steps.

High sales force costs necessitate an effective sales management process consisting of six steps: designing sales force strategy and structure, recruiting and selecting, training, compensating, supervising, and evaluating salespeople and sales force performance.

In *designing a sales force*, sales management must address strategy issues such as what type of sales force structure will work best (territorial, product, customer, or complex structure); how large the sales force should be; who will be involved in the selling effort; and how its various salespeople and sales-support people will work together (inside or outside sales forces and team selling).

To hold down the high costs of hiring the wrong people, salespeople must be recruited and selected carefully. In *recruiting* salespeople, a company may look to job duties and the characteristics of its most successful salespeople to suggest the traits it wants in its new salespeople. It must then look for applicants through recommendations of current salespeople, employment agencies, classified ads, the Internet, and contacting college and university students. In the *selection process*, the procedure can vary from a single informal interview to lengthy testing and interviewing. After the selection process is complete, *training* programs familiarize new salespeople not only with the art of selling but also with the company's history, its products and policies, and the characteristics of its market and competitors.

The sales force compensation system helps to reward, motivate, and direct salespeople. In *compensating* salespeople, companies try to have an appealing plan, usually close to the going rate for the type of sales job and needed skills. In addition to compensation, all salespeople need *supervision*, and many need continuous encouragement because they must make many decisions on their own and face many frustrations. Periodically, the company must *evaluate* their performance to help them do a better job. In evaluating salespeople, the company relies on getting regular information gathered through sales reports, personal observations, customers' letters and complaints, customer surveys, and conversations with other salespeople.

OBJECTIVE 3 **Discuss the personal selling process, distinguishing between transaction-oriented marketing and relationship marketing.**

The art of selling involves a seven-step selling process: prospecting and qualifying, preapproach, approach, presentation and demonstration, handling objections, closing, and follow-up. These steps help marketers close a specific sale and as such are transaction oriented. However, a seller's dealings with customers should be guided by the larger concept of relationship marketing. The company's sales force should help to orchestrate a whole-company effort to develop profitable long-term relationships with key customers based on superior customer value and satisfaction.

OBJECTIVE 4 **Explain how sales promotion campaigns are developed and implemented.**

Sales promotion campaigns call for setting sales promotions objectives (in general, sales promotions should be *consumer relationship building*); selecting tools; and developing and implementing the sales promotion program by using *consumer promotion tools* (from coupons, refunds, premiums, and point-of-purchase promotions to contests, sweepstakes, and events), *trade promotion tools* (discounts, allowances, free goods, push money) and *business promotion tools* (conventions, trade shows, sales contests), as well as deciding on such things as the size of the incentive, the conditions for participation, how to promote and distribute the promotion package, and the length of the promotion. After this process is complete, the company evaluates its sales promotion results.

KEY TERMS

mymarketinglab | Glossary Flashcards

DISCUSSING THE CONCEPTS

1. Discuss the role of personal selling in the promotion mix. In what situations is it more effective than advertising?

2. Briefly describe the activities involved in sales force management.

3. List and briefly describe the three sales force structures outlined in the chapter. What sales force structure does CDW, featured at the beginning of this chapter, employ?

4. Define sales promotion and discuss its objectives.

5. Name and describe the types of trade sales promotions.

APPLYING THE CONCEPTS

1. Work in pairs to describe the stages in the selling process for a small company in your community that sells cleaning services to owners of small businesses, such as hair salons, dentists' offices, and clothing stores. Role-play the actual selling process, from approach to close, with one team member acting as the salesperson. The other member of the team should act as a customer and raise at least three objections.

2. Suppose you are the marketing coordinator responsible for recommending the sales promotion plan for the market launch of a new brand of energy drink sold in supermarkets. What promotional tools would you consider for this task and what decisions must be made?

3. Find examples of five different types of consumer promotions and present them to your class.

FOCUS ON TECHNOLOGY

Consumers love saving money, especially during economic downturns. That makes coupons a very attractive promotional tool. And what better way to deliver coupons than via the Internet? After a slowdown following counterfeit Internet coupon problems between 2001 and 2003, manufacturers and retailers are now coming back to online printable coupons—and consumers are responding. Scarborough Research reports Internet coupon usage among North American households has increased 83 percent since 2005. Coupons, Inc. is the leading provider of printable coupons for more than 600 consumer packaged goods retailers and manufacturers, distributing coupons through 2000 websites. You can find coupons available just about everywhere on the Internet. Delta Airlines has even launched online boarding-pass ads containing coupons for discounts at flyers' destinations. However, Bud Miller, executive director of the Coupon Information Corporation, warns that counterfeit coupons are once again on the rise.

1. Find and print 10 coupons from the Internet for products you normally purchase. Use some of these coupons on your next purchase. Did all of the retailers accept your coupons? If not, explain why not.

2. How can consumers be certain that a coupon obtained from the Internet is legitimate? How can manufacturers and retailers ensure the coupons are not counterfeited? Go to the Coupon Information Corporation's website to learn more about this problem (www.cents-off.com).

FOCUS ON ETHICS

Free samples, gifts, educational conference sponsorships, dinners, and entertainment—these tools have been, and in some cases still are, widely used by pharmaceutical companies to influence doctors' prescribing behaviour, despite voluntary codes of conduct in both the Canadian and American pharmaceutical industries. Physicians control the majority of health care expenditures through their prescription writing authority. Since direct-to-consumer advertising is prohibited under Canada's *Food and Drug Act*, most pharmaceutical marketing dollars are directed at physicians. Pharmaceutical sales representatives vie for health care professionals' attention to pitch their drugs. Research has shown that pharmaceutical companies' marketing tactics do influence physicians, causing them to prescribe more expensive drugs over less expensive alternatives. Critics proclaim that these tactics are unethical. However, the pharmaceutical companies claim that their sales representatives help keep health care professionals well informed in this rapidly changing industry.

1. Is it ethical for pharmaceutical sales representatives to influence physicians' prescribing behaviour using free samples and promotional gifts?

2. National and international trade associations in the pharmaceuticals industry have codes of conduct regarding interactions with health care professionals. Visit the websites of Canada's Research-Based Pharmaceutical Companies (Rx&D) (www.canadapharma.org) and the International Federation of Pharmaceutical Manufacturers Association (IFPMA) (www.ifpma.org) and examine their codes of ethics regarding sales activities. Write a brief report on what you learn.

MARKETING BY THE NUMBERS

Salespeople do more than just sell products and services—they manage relationships with customers to deliver value to both the customer and their company. For many companies sales reps visit customers several times per year—often for hours at a time. Thus, sales managers must ensure that their companies have enough salespeople to adequately deliver value to customers.

1. Refer to Appendix 3: Marketing by the Numbers to determine the number of salespeople a company needs if it has 3000 customers who need to be called on 10 times per year. Each sales call lasts approximately 2 1/2 hours, and each sales rep has approximately 1250 hours per year to devote to customers.

2. If each sales representative earns a salary of $60 000 per year, what sales are necessary to break even on the sales force costs if the company has a contribution margin of 40 percent? What effect will adding each additional sales representative have on break-even sales?

VIDEO CASE

Principal Financial Group

Video Case Questions

Principal Financial Group delivered strong growth in its first six years as a public company. Operating earnings grew from US$577 million in 2001 to US$1.06 billion in 2007 alone. In that same year, total assets under management soared from US$98 billion to US$311 billion. Principal also achieved a 16.4 percent return on equity for 2007, compared to 8.9 percent for 2001. As a result, its stock price increased 236 percent from its opening price at the October 2001 initial public offering (IPO) through its closing price at year-end 2007.

One of the biggest reasons for this success is Principal Financial Group's strongly customer-centred sales force. The company's varied and complex product line (from retirement products to insurance) demands the one-on-one

attention of a salesperson who understands how to build customer relationships. The company's sales force has helped make Principal a global player in the financial services industry.

After viewing the video featuring Principal Financial Group, answer the following questions:

1. How is the sales force at Principal Financial Group structured?

2. Identify the selling process of the company. Give evidence of each step.

3. How does Principal build long-term customer relationships through its sales force?

Visit MyMarketingLab at www.pearsoned.ca/mymarketinglab to view the video segment related to this case.

COMPANY CASE

Procter & Gamble: Selling Through Customer Business Development

It seems that when it comes to personal selling, the term "win–win" gets thrown around so much that it has become a cliché. But at Procter & Gamble, the sales concept that the company benefits only as much as the customer benefits is a way of life. Since William Procter and James Gamble formed a family-operated soap and candle company in 1837, P&G has understood that if the customer doesn't do well, neither will the company.

That's why even though P&G boasts a massive sales force of more than 12 000 employees worldwide, P&G people rarely utter the term "sales." At P&G, it's called "customer business development," or CBD. The title alone pretty much says it all. Rather than just selling detergent or toothpaste, P&G's philosophy is to grow its own business by growing the business of its customers. In this case, customers are the thousands of retailers and wholesalers that distribute P&G's brands throughout the world. P&G isn't just a supplier, it's a strategic business partner with its customers. "We depend on them as much as they depend on us," says Jeff Weedman, a CBD manager.

THE CORE COMPETENCY OF CUSTOMER BUSINESS DEVELOPMENT

As the big-box retailers get bigger and bigger, they also grow more complex. Take companies such as Walmart or Loblaw. How can a vendor like P&G ever fully understand such a customer? These complex organizations have so many arms and legs that it becomes nearly impossible to get a full and firm grasp on their operations and needs.

To deal with such customer complexities, P&G organizes its sales representatives into customer business development teams. Rather than assigning reps to specific geographic regions or products, it assigns each CBD team to a P&G customer. For the company's biggest customer, Walmart (which tallies a massive 20 percent of all P&G sales), the CBD team consists of some 350 employees. For smaller customers, the CBD team may have as little as 30 employees. Regardless of the team's size, the strength of the CBD concept derives from the fact that each team, in and of itself, is a complete customer service unit, containing at least one support specialist for every important business function. In addition to a general CBD manager and several sales account executives (each responsible for a specific category of P&G products), each CBD team includes a marketing strategy, operations, information systems, logistics, finance, and human resources specialist. This "multifunctional" structure enables each team to meet the multiple and vast needs of its customer, whether the needs revolve around those of a chief finance officer or an entire IT department.

A real strength of the CBD teams is that team members function as a collaborative whole rather than as individuals performing their own tasks in isolation. Team members share information, organizational capabilities, and technologies. "I have all the resources I need right here," says Amy Fuschino, a health care and cosmetics account executive. "If I need to, I can go right down the hall and talk with someone in marketing about doing some kind of promotional deal. It's that simple."

But the multifunctional nature of the CBD team also means that collaboration extends far beyond internal interactions. Each time a CBD team member contacts the customer, he or she represents the entire team. For example, if during a customer call a CBD account executive receives a question about a promotional, logistical, or financial matter, the account executive acts as the liaison with the appropriate CBD specialist. So although each CBD member doesn't have specialized knowledge in every area, the CBD team as a unit does.

Competitors have attempted to implement some aspects of P&G's multifunctional approach. However, P&G pioneered the CBD structure. And it has built in some unique characteristics that have allowed it to leverage more power from its team structure than its rivals can.

THE TRUE ADVANTAGE

For starters, P&G's CBD structure is broader and more comprehensive, making it more multifunctional than similar team structures employed by other companies. But perhaps most important, P&G's structure is designed to accomplish four key objectives that are referred to internally as the "core work" of CBD:

- Align Strategy—to create opportunities for both P&G and the customer to benefit by collaborating in strategy development.

- Create Demand—to build profitable sales volume for P&G and the customer through consumer value and shopper satisfaction.

- Optimize Supply—to maximize the efficiency of the supply chain from P&G to the point of purchase to optimize cost and responsiveness.

- Enable the Organization—to develop capabilities to maximize business results by creating the capacity for frequent breakthrough.

More than just corporate catchphrases jotted down in an employee handbook, for CBD employees, these are words to live by. P&G trains sales employees in methods of achieving each objective and evaluates their effectiveness in meeting the objectives.

In fact, the CBD concept came about through the recognition that to develop true win–win relationships with each customer, P&G would need to accomplish the first objective. According to Bill Warren, a CBD senior account executive, "The true competitive advantage is achieved by taking a multifunctional approach from basic selling to strategic customer collaboration!"

Strategic collaboration starts with annual joint business planning. Both the P&G team and the customer come to the table focused on the most important thing: How can each best provide value for the final consumer? The team and customer give much attention during this planning phase to how products can best be presented and placed in the retail setting. This is because P&G and its customers know that the end consumer assesses value within the first three to seven seconds of seeing that product on the shelf. At P&G, this is known as "winning the first moment of truth." If customers quickly perceive that a product will meet their needs, they will likely purchase it.

CBD team members are very good at demonstrating to the retailer that the best way to win the first moment of truth is most often with a P&G product. But P&G is so committed to the principle of developing the *customer's* business as a means of developing its own, it is open to the possibility that the best way to serve the customer may be through a competitor's product. The CBD team's primary goal is to help the customer win in each product category. Sometimes, analysis shows that the best solution for the customer is "the other guy's product." For P&G, that's okay. P&G knows that creating the best situation for the retailer ultimately brings in more customer traffic, which in turn will likely result in increased sales for other P&G products in the same category. Because most of P&G's brands are market leaders, it stands to benefit more from the increased traffic than competitors. Again, it's a win–win situation. This type of honesty also helps build trust and strengthen the company–customer relationship.

The collaborative efforts between P&G and each of its customers do not only involve planning and the sharing of information. They may also involve cooperative efforts to share the costs of different activities. "We'll help customers run these commercials or do those merchandising events, but there has to be a return on investment," explains Amy Fuschino. "Maybe it's helping us with a new distribution or increasing space for fabric care. We're very willing if the effort creates value for us in addition to creating value for the customer and the consumer."

An example of such a joint effort is the recent rollout of PRISM. P&G partnered with Walmart to implement this system of infrared sensors that counts the number of times shoppers are exposed to product displays, banners, and video monitors. The goal with PRISM is to improve the effectiveness of in-store marketing, making consumers more aware of the value provided by P&G's products.

If the CBD team can effectively accomplish the first objective of aligning strategy and collaborating on strategic development, accomplishing the other three objectives will follow more easily. For example, if strategic planning leads to winning the first moment of truth, not only does the consumer benefit, but both the retailer and P&G achieve higher revenues and profits as well. Through proper strategic planning it is also more likely that both P&G and the customer will create greater efficiencies in the supply chain.

IT'S BETTER TO GIVE . . . THAN TO RECEIVE

As a result of collaborating with customers, P&G receives as much as or more than it gives. Among other things, P&G receives information that helps in achieving the fourth CBD objective, enabling the organization to achieve innovation. Where the research and development process is concerned, this means creating better products. This is one reason why, at the 2007 Product of the Year Awards held in London, P&G cleaned up, winning 10 of the 32 categories and taking home a special prize for "most innovative company." P&G's dominance in innovation is no one-time fluke. Gianni Ciserani, vice-president and managing director of P&G UK & Ireland, claims that some of P&G's strongest innovations are yet to come. "We have shared this portfolio with the key retailers and got strong collaboration on how we can drive these ideas forward."

In the five years leading up to 2008, P&G's profits doubled, revenues nearly doubled, and stock price increased by more than 50 percent. Not only is P&G the world's largest consumer products firm with US$76 billion in revenues, it ranks 23rd among all U.S. companies in the most recent *Fortune* 500 ranking. P&G manages a whopping 23 brands that each bring in over US$1 billion every year. Last year, Pampers sales exceeded US$7 billion, a figure that would have placed the leading diaper brand all by itself as number 350 on *Fortune's* prestigious list.

Many factors have contributed to P&G's growth and success. But the role that CBD plays can't be overestimated. And as P&G moves forward, Jeff Weedman's words that "We depend on them as much as they depend on us" ring ever truer. As P&G's megacustomers grow in size and power, developing P&G's business means first developing its customers' business. And the CBD sales organization lies at the heart of that effort.

Questions for Discussion

1. Which of the sales force structures discussed in the text best describes P&G's CBD structure?

2. From the perspective of team selling, discuss the positive as well as some possible negative aspects to the customer business development sales organization.

3. Visit www.mypgcareer.com and click on the Customer Business Development link at the bottom of the page to learn more about the P&G CBD organization. Based on information on this website and information in this case, discuss the importance of recruiting, training, and compensation in making the CBD structure more effective.

4. Discuss some ways that the CBD structure may be more effective than a single sales rep for each step in the personal selling process.

5. It seems that P&G has the most effective sales force structure of any company in its industry. Why have competitors not been able to match it?

Sources: Officials at Procter & Gamble contributed to and supported the development of this case; other information from www.pg.com, accessed July 2008. See also Craig Smith, "P&G Tops List for Innovation," *Marketing*, January 31, 2007, p. 6; and "Will She, Won't She?—Procter & Gamble," *Economist*, August 11, 2007, accessed at www.economist.com.

 Visit **MyMarketingLab** at **www.pearsoned.ca/mymarketinglab** for access to online tutorials, interactive exercises, videos, and much more.

17

Direct and Online
Marketing

PREVIEWING
THE CONCEPTS

In the previous three chapters, you learned about communicating customer value through integrated marketing communications (IMC) and about four specific elements of the marketing communications mix—advertising, public relations, personal selling, and sales promotion. In this chapter, we'll look at the final IMC element, direct marketing, and at its fastest-growing form, online marketing. Actually, direct marketing can be viewed as more than just a communications tool. In many ways it constitutes an overall marketing approach—a blend of communication and distribution channels all rolled into one. As you read on, remember that although this chapter examines direct marketing as a separate tool, it must be carefully integrated with other elements of the promotion mix.

For starters, let's look at Amazon.com and its Canadian subsidiary, Amazon.ca. Launched in 1995, Amazon.com has blossomed from an obscure dot-com upstart into one of the best-known names on the Internet. Today, Amazon has separate websites in Canada, the United Kingdom, Germany, France, China, and Japan. According to one estimate, 52 percent of people who recently shopped online started at Amazon.com. It is among the top 10 most visited sites in Canada, drawing more than 9 million unique visitors. Amazon is the largest web retailer in the world. It opened 12 new web stores in 2008 alone, including a microsite specializing in out-of-circulation and hard-to-find CDs. Sales outside the United States account for 46.6 percent of its total. How has Amazon.com become such an incredibly successful direct and online marketer in such a short time? It's all about creating a direct, personal, satisfying customer experience. Few direct marketers do that as well as Amazon. To support its relationship building efforts, it continues to invest 5 percent of its revenue (over US$1 billion) on technology and content.

When you think of shopping on the Web, chances are good that you think first of Amazon. Jeff Bezos, the company's CEO, founded the venture in his garage in suburban Seattle. The online pioneer still sells books—lots and lots of books—but it now also sells just about everything else, from music, videos, electronics, tools, housewares, apparel, groceries, and kids' products to loose diamonds and even lobsters. "We Have the Earth's Biggest Selection," declares the company's website.

In little more than a decade, Amazon has become one of the best-known names on the Web. In perfecting the art of online selling, it has also rewritten the rules of marketing. Many analysts view Amazon as the model for businesses in the digital age. They predict that it will one day become the Walmart of the Internet.

From the start, Amazon has grown explosively. Its annual sales have rocketed from a modest US$15 million in 1996 to more than US$19 billion in 2008. In the last quarter of 2008, sales jumped 18 percent in both Canada and the United States. More than 72 million active customers now spend an average of $184 a year at Amazon.com, and 50 percent of Amazon sales come from markets outside the United States, like Canada.

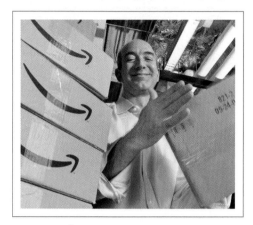

Says Amazon® founder and CEO Jeff Bezos, "We are not great advertisers. So we start with customers, figure out what they want, and figure out how to get it to them."

What has made Amazon one of the world's premier direct marketers? To its core, the company is relentlessly customer driven. "The thing that drives everything is creating genuine value for customers," says founder Jeff Bezos. "If you focus on what customers want and build a relationship, they will allow you to make money." In one promotion in Japan, for example, Bezos donned a delivery driver's uniform and went house to house with packages. His point: Everything at Amazon—from top to bottom—begins and ends with the customer.

Anyone at Amazon will tell you that the company wants to do much more than just sell books or DVDs or digital cameras. It wants to deliver a special experience to every customer. "The customer experience really matters," says Bezos. "We've focused on just having a better store, where it's easier to shop, where you can learn more about the products, where you have a bigger selection, and where you have the lowest prices. You combine all of that stuff together and people say, 'Hey, these guys really get it.'"

And customers do get it. Most Amazon.com regulars feel a surprisingly strong relationship with the company, especially unexpected given the almost complete lack of actual human interaction. Amazon obsesses over making each customer's experience uniquely personal. For example, the Amazon.ca website greets customers with their very own personalized home pages, and the site's "Recommended for You" feature prepares personalized product recommendations. Amazon was the first to use "collaborative filtering" technology, which sifts through each customer's past purchases and the purchasing patterns of customers with similar profiles to come up with personalized site content. "We want Amazon.com to be the right store for you as an individual," says Bezos. "If we have 72 million customers, we should have 72 million stores."

Visitors to Amazon.ca's website receive a unique blend of benefits: huge selection, good value, convenience, and what the company calls "discovery." In books alone, for example, Amazon.ca offers an easily searchable virtual selection of more than 3 million titles, 15 times more than in any physical bookstore. Good value comes in the form of reasonable prices, plus free delivery on orders over $39. And at Amazon.ca, it's irresistibly convenient to buy. You can log on, find anything and everything you want, and order with a single mouse click, all in less time than it takes to find a parking space at the local mall.

But it's the "discovery" factor that makes the Amazon marketing experience really special. Once on the website, you're compelled to stay for a while—looking, learning, and discovering. Amazon.ca has become a kind of online community in which customers can browse for products, research purchase alternatives, share opinions and reviews with other visitors, and chat online with authors and experts. In this way, Amazon does much more than just sell goods on the Web. It creates direct, personalized customer relationships and satisfying online experiences. Year after year, Amazon comes in number one or number two on the University of Michigan's American Customer Satisfaction Index, regardless of industry.

In fact, Amazon has become so good at managing online relationships that many traditional retailers are turning

▶

Objectives

1. Define direct marketing and discuss its benefits to customers and companies.
2. Identify and discuss the major forms of direct marketing.
3. Explain how companies have responded to the Internet and other powerful new technologies with online marketing strategies.
4. Discuss how companies go about conducting online marketing to profitably deliver more value to customers.
5. Overview the public policy and ethical issues presented by direct marketing.

to Amazon for help in improving traffic on their sites. For example, Amazon now partners with well-known retailers such as Target and bebe to help them run their web interfaces. And to create even greater selection and convenience for customers, Amazon allows competing retailers—from mom-and-pop operations to Marks & Spencer—to offer their products on its website, creating a virtual shopping mall of incredible proportions. It even encourages customers to sell used items on the site.

Amazon is constantly on the lookout for innovative new ways to use the power of the Web and direct marketing to create more shopping selection, value, convenience, and discovery for customers. For example, Amazon now offers music downloading, with music files that are not restricted by digital rights management software (DRM),

Amazon.ca obsesses over making each customer's experience uniquely personal. "If we have 72 million customers, we should have 72 million stores."

which means that (unlike with iTunes) you can freely and conveniently copy the songs. All four major music labels promptly signed on. The web merchant also launched Amazon Giver and Amazon Grapevine, applications for social networking website Facebook. These features allow Facebook users to see and purchase what their friends want via wish lists and to view recent public activity on the retail site.

Recently, Amazon took another bold customer-convenience and personalization step. It introduced the Kindle, a wireless reading device for downloading books, blogs, magazines, newspapers, and other matter. Lighter and thinner than a typical paperback book, the Kindle, priced at $259, holds more than 1500 titles and lets customers choose from among 230 000 titles. They can buy books for $9.99, a price much lower than traditional best-selling books, and

download them in 60 seconds. They can also download domestic or international newspapers and publications like the *Wall Street Journal* or *Time* magazine. The Kindle has a paper-like electronic-ink display that's easy to read even in bright daylight. In all, Amazon is betting that the Kindle will prove to be an ultimate direct-marketing device.

So what do you think? Will Amazon become the Walmart of the Web? That remains to be seen. But whatever its fate, the direct and online pioneer has forever changed the face of marketing. Most importantly, Amazon has set a very high bar for the online customer experience. "The reason I'm so obsessed with . . . the customer experience is that I believe [that our success] has been driven exclusively by that experience," says Jeff Bezos. "We are not great advertisers. So we start with customers, figure out what they want, and figure out how to get it to them."[1]

Chapter Opening Discussion

Many of the marketing and promotion tools that we've examined in previous chapters were developed in the context of *mass marketing*: targeting broad markets with standardized messages and offers distributed through intermediaries. Today, however, with the trend toward more narrowly targeted marketing, many companies are adopting *direct marketing*, either as a primary marketing approach, as in Amazon's case, or as a supplement to other approaches. In this section, we explore the exploding world of direct marketing.

Direct marketing

Connecting directly with carefully targeted individual consumers to both obtain an immediate response and cultivate lasting customer relationships.

Direct marketing consists of connecting directly with carefully targeted individual consumers to both obtain an immediate response and cultivate lasting customer relationships. Direct marketers communicate directly with customers, often on a one-to-one, interactive basis. Using detailed databases, they tailor their marketing offers and communications to the needs of narrowly defined segments or even individual buyers.

Beyond brand and relationship building, direct marketers usually seek a direct, immediate, and measurable consumer response. For example, as we learned in the chapter-opening story, Amazon interacts directly with customers on its websites to help them discover and buy almost anything and everything on the Internet, with only a few clicks of the mouse button. Similarly, Dell interacts directly with customers, by telephone or through its website, to design built-to-order systems that meet customers' individual needs. Buyers can order directly from Dell, and Dell quickly and efficiently delivers the new computers to their homes or offices.

Glossary Flashcards of Key Terms

THE NEW DIRECT MARKETING MODEL

Early direct marketers—catalogue companies, direct mailers, and telemarketers—gathered customer names and sold goods mainly by mail and telephone. Today, however, fired by rapid advances in database technologies and new marketing media—especially the Internet—direct marketing has undergone a dramatic transformation.

In previous chapters, we've discussed direct marketing as direct distribution—as marketing channels that contain no intermediaries. We also include direct marketing as one element of the promotion mix—as an approach for communicating directly with consumers. In actuality, direct marketing is both of these things and more.

Most companies still use direct marketing as a supplementary channel or medium. The *Globe and Mail*, for example, decided in early 2009 to shift from publishing its famous Books Section, which came out with the print version of the newspaper, to its website. The site includes a book club, enewsletters, and searchable archives. And not only does the site post reviews and commentary as it did in the print version, but customers are able to post their own opinions.[2] Similarly, most department stores, such as Sears or the Bay, sell the majority of their merchandise off their store shelves but also sell through direct mail and online catalogues.

However, for many companies today, direct marketing is more than just a supplementary channel or advertising medium. For these companies, direct marketing—especially in its most recent transformation, online marketing—constitutes a complete model for doing business. Rather than using direct marketing and the Internet only as supplemental approaches, firms employing this new *direct model* use it as the *only* approach. Companies such as Amazon, eBay, and GEICO have built their entire approach to the marketplace around direct marketing. The direct model is rapidly changing the way that companies think about building relationships with customers.

GROWTH AND BENEFITS OF DIRECT MARKETING

Direct marketing has become the fastest-growing form of marketing. According to the book *International Direct Marketing*, Canadian organizations spent US$9.669 billion on direct marketing in 2007, the eighth-largest amount in the world. Expenduture on direct marketing grew by 5.7 percent in Canada between 2003 and 2007.[3]

The new direct marketing model: Companies such as GEICO have built their entire approach to the marketplace around direct marketing. Just visit www.geico.com or call 1-800-947-AUTO.

Direct marketing continues to become more web-oriented, and Internet marketing is claiming a fast-growing share of direct-marketing spending and sales. According to a 2009 survey conducted by the Interactive Advertising Bureau of Canada (IAB), the Internet now stands third in Canada (just behind TV and radio) in terms of total weekly time spent by all adults with all media, and it reaches more adults each week than either magazines or newspapers. The Internet's share of media time has grown from 14 percent in 2001 to 23 percent in 2007. Even though Internet usage still lags in French Canada, among all Canadians aged 18–34, the Internet reaches more people than radio, and for those 18–24, it is tied for the number-one spot. The IAB predicts that by 2016, the Internet will be the number-one medium for most consumers, thus it is imperative that advertisers shift significant portions of their budgets from TV to the Internet.[4] Whether employed as a complete business model or as a supplement to a broader integrated marketing mix, direct marketing brings many benefits to both buyers and sellers.

Benefits to Buyers

For buyers, direct marketing is convenient, easy, and private. Direct marketers never close their doors, and customers don't have to battle traffic, find parking spaces, and trek through stores to find products. From the comfort of their homes or offices, they can browse catalogues or company websites at any time of the day or night. Business buyers can learn about products and services without tying up time with salespeople.

Direct marketing gives buyers ready access to a wealth of products. For example, unrestrained by physical boundaries, direct marketers can offer an almost unlimited selection to consumers almost anywhere in the world. Just compare the huge selections offered by many web merchants to the more meagre assortments of their brick-and-mortar counterparts. For instance, log onto Bulbs.com, "the Web's number-one light bulb superstore," and you'll have instant access to every imaginable kind of light bulb or lamp—incandescent bulbs, fluorescent bulbs, projection bulbs, surgical bulbs, automotive bulbs—you name it. Similarly, online shoes and accessories retailer Zappos.com stocks more than 3 million shoes, handbags, clothing items, and accessories from more than 1100 brands. No physical store could offer handy access to such vast selections.

Direct marketing channels also give buyers access to a wealth of comparative information about companies, products, and competitors. Good catalogues or websites often provide more information in more useful forms than even the most helpful retail salesperson can. For example, the Amazon.ca site offers more information than most of us can digest, ranging from top 10 product lists, extensive product descriptions, and expert and user product reviews to recommendations based on customers' previous purchases. And Sears catalogues offer a treasure trove of information about the store's merchandise and services. In fact, you probably wouldn't think it strange to see a Sears salesperson referring to a catalogue in the store for more detailed information while trying to advise a customer on a specific product or offer.

Finally, direct marketing is interactive and immediate—buyers can interact with sellers by phone or on the seller's website to create exactly the configuration of information, products, or services they desire, and then order them on the spot. Moreover, direct marketing gives consumers a greater measure of control. Consumers decide which catalogues they will browse and which websites they will visit.

Benefits to Sellers

For sellers, direct marketing is a powerful tool for building customer relationships. Using database marketing, today's marketers can target small groups or individual consumers and promote their offers through personalized communications. Because of the one-to-one nature of direct marketing, companies can interact with customers by phone or online, learn more about their needs, and tailor products and services to specific customer tastes. In turn, customers can ask questions and volunteer feedback.

Direct marketing also offers sellers a low-cost, efficient, speedy alternative for reaching their markets. Direct marketing has grown rapidly in business-to-business marketing,

Holt Renfrew is using a whole arsenal of high-tech tools to effectively engage current and potential customers.

partly in response to the ever-increasing costs of marketing through the sales force. When personal sales calls cost an average of more than $320 per contact, they should be made only when necessary and to high-potential customers and prospects.[5] Lower-cost-per-contact media—such as telemarketing, direct mail, and company websites—often prove more cost effective.

Similarly, online direct marketing results in lower costs, improved efficiencies, and speedier handling of channel and logistics functions, such as order processing, inventory handling, and delivery. Direct marketers such as Amazon.ca or Netflix also avoid the expense of maintaining a store and the related costs of rent, insurance, and utilities, passing the savings along to customers.

Direct marketing can also offer greater flexibility. It allows marketers like Air Canada or WestJet to make ongoing adjustments to prices and programs, or to make immediate, timely, and personal announcements and offers.

Holt Renfrew uses techie direct marketing tools—including infrared sensors that respond as pedestrians approach, touchscreens, blogs, and SMS interactivity—to inject itself directly into customers' everyday lives. It recently installed touchscreens at its Toronto Bloor Street location as part of its "Contemporary Correspondent Search" contest. The screen invites passersby to vote for their favourite fashion blogger. The Canadian Opera Company is using its website, podcasts, quizzes, blogs, and an online panel to better reach its audience and gather feedback. Research revealed that the average opera-goer is much more digitally inclined than the average person, and while only 20 percent of those interacting with the Canadian Opera Company transacted through its website, 40 percent of its audience fits into segments called "Loaded and Overloaded" (wealthy families who don't have much time but own every technology) and "City Clickers" (younger patrons who are urban, trendy, and technologically savvy). To engage these segments, the company designed an online experience as rich as visiting the opera house.[6]

Finally, direct marketing gives sellers access to buyers that they could not reach through other channels. Smaller firms can mail catalogues to customers outside their local markets and post 1-800 numbers to handle orders and inquiries. Internet marketing is a truly global medium that allows buyers and sellers to click from one country to another in seconds. A web user from Paris or Istanbul can access an online catalogue from PEI-based Vesey's Seeds as easily as someone living in Charlottetown. Even small marketers find that they have ready access to global markets.

CUSTOMER DATABASES AND DIRECT MARKETING

Customer database
An organized collection of comprehensive data about individual customers or prospects, including geographic, demographic, psychographic, and behavioural data.

Effective direct marketing begins with a good customer database. A **customer database** is an organized collection of comprehensive data about individual customers or prospects, including geographic, demographic, psychographic, and behavioural data. A good customer database can be a potent relationship-building tool. The database gives companies a 360-degree view of its customers and how they behave. A company is no better than what it knows about its customers.

In consumer marketing, the customer database might contain a customer's demographics (age, income, family members, birthdays), psychographics (activities, interests, and opinions), and buying behaviour (buying preferences and the recency, frequency, and

Direct marketing databases: The customer information database of casino operator Harrah's Entertainment contains roughly three times the number of printed characters found in the U.S. Library of Congress. It uses this data to create special customer experiences.

monetary value—RFM—of past purchases). Companies and not-for-profits alike often turn to specialist agencies for help managing databases and contact lists. The Cornerstone Group of Companies is Canada's largest manager of Canadian direct-mail and email lists. Each year it monitors, tracks trends, and assesses response activity on over 1200 lists. Its 2009 survey reported that fundraisers are now the dominant users of mailing lists in Canada, accounting for 30 percent of the total direct-mail volume. Cornerstone provides support to business clients as well as not-for-profits. In 2009, for example, it managed Yves Rocher Canada's package insert program designed to reach Canadian buyers of natural cosmetics that could be purchased from its direct-mail catalogue or online.[7]

In business-to-business marketing, the customer profile might contain the products and services the customer has bought, past volumes and prices, key contacts (and their ages, birthdays, hobbies, and favourite foods), competing suppliers, status of current contracts, estimated customer spending for the next few years, and assessments of competitive strengths and weaknesses in selling and servicing the account.

Some of these databases are huge. For example, casino operator Harrah's Entertainment has built a customer database containing 30 terabytes of customer information, roughly three times the number of printed characters in the U.S. Library of Congress. It uses this data to create special customer experiences. Similarly, Internet portal Yahoo! records every click made by every visitor, adding some 400 billion bytes of data per day to its database—the equivalent of 800 000 books! And Walmart captures data on every item, for every customer, for every store, every day. Its database contains more than 1 petabyte of data—that's a quadrillion bytes, far greater than the storage capacity of 250 000 four-gigabyte flash drives.[8]

Michelin is using its new microsite and powerful database to build even stronger relationships with Canadian travellers.

Companies use their databases in many ways. They use databases to locate good potential customers and to generate sales leads. They can mine their databases to learn about customers in detail, and then fine-tune their market offerings and communications to the special preferences and behaviours of target segments or individuals. In all, a company's database can be an important tool for building stronger long-term customer relationships. In the summer of 2009, for example, Michelin wanted to enhance its relationship with Canadian travellers, many of whom are fans of its Michelin Man mascot. Using its new MichelinOnTheRoad.ca microsite and its database of more than 10 000 Canadian members (built through its 2008 online Magic Moments photo contest), it provided a fuel calculator, fuel efficiency tips for summer road trips, and optimized map routes to consumers. Celine Messiha, Michelin's marketing communications manager, explains it this way: "What we're trying to do to help consumers, especially nowadays when gas [prices are] so high, is to share information in terms of fuel efficiency and how tires play such an important role when it comes to saving money." The site is promoted on the cover of Michelin's famous *Green Guides*.[9]

Like many other marketing tools, database marketing requires a special investment. Companies must invest in computer hardware, database software, analytical programs, communication links, and skilled personnel. The database system must be user-friendly and available to various marketing groups, including those in product and brand management, new-product development, advertising and promotion, direct mail, telemarketing, web marketing, field sales, order fulfillment, and customer service. However, a well-managed database should lead to sales and customer relationship gains that will more than cover its costs.

2 FORMS OF DIRECT MARKETING

The major forms of direct marketing—as shown in Figure 17.1—include direct-mail marketing, catalogue marketing, telephone marketing (telemarketing), direct-response television marketing, kiosk marketing, new digital direct marketing technologies, online marketing and personal (face-to-face) selling. We examined personal selling in depth in Chapter 16. Here, we examine the other direct-marketing forms.

Direct-Mail Marketing

Direct-mail marketing
Direct marketing by sending an offer, announcement, reminder, or other item to a person at a particular physical or virtual address.

Direct-mail marketing involves sending an offer, announcement, reminder, or other item to a person at a particular physical or virtual address. Using highly selective mailing lists, direct marketers send out millions of mail pieces each year—letters, catalogues, ads, brochures, samples, CDs and DVDs, and other "salespeople with wings." Direct mail is by far the largest direct-marketing medium.

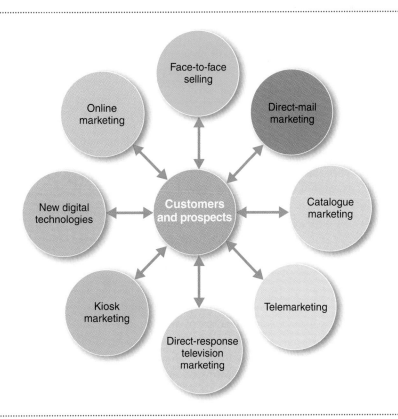

Figure 17.1 Forms of direct marketing

Direct mail is well suited to direct, one-to-one communication. It permits high target-market selectivity, can be personalized, is flexible, and allows easy measurement of results. Although direct mail costs more per thousand people reached than mass media such as television or magazines, the people it reaches are much better prospects. Direct mail has proven successful in promoting all kinds of products, from books, music, DVDs, and magazine subscriptions to insurance, gift items, clothing, gourmet foods, and industrial products. Charities also use direct mail heavily to raise billions of dollars each year.

The direct-mail industry constantly seeks new methods and approaches. For example, CDs and DVDs are now among the fastest-growing direct-mail media. One study showed that including a CD or DVD in a marketing offer generates responses between 50 and 1000 percent greater than traditional direct mail.[10] New forms of delivery have also become popular, such as *voice mail, text messaging,* and *email.* Voice mail is subject to the same do-not-call restrictions as telemarketing, so its use has been limited in recent years. However, permission-based mobile marketing (via cellphones) is growing rapidly and email is booming as a direct-marketing tool. Today's email messages have moved far beyond the drab text-only messages of old. The new breed of email ad uses animation, interactive links, streaming video, and personalized audio messages to reach out and grab attention.

Email, mobile, and other new forms deliver direct mail at incredible speeds compared to the post office's "snail mail" pace. Yet much like mail delivered through traditional channels, these messages may be resented as "junk mail" or spam if sent to people who have no interest in them. For this reason, smart marketers are targeting their direct mail carefully so as not to waste their money and recipients' time. They are designing permission-based programs, sending email and mobile ads only to those who want to receive them. We will discuss email and mobile marketing in more detail later in the chapter.

Although the new digital direct-mail forms are gaining popularity, the traditional form is still by far the most widely used. Despite the clutter, traditional direct mail can be highly effective, especially for reaching certain segments that don't get as much direct mail as the general population. For example, direct mail plays a big role in pitches by P&G's Tremor buzz-marketing unit to teens:

> You'd expect any marketing program for teens in the twenty-first century to be heavy on digital and light on most forms of old media. But P&G's Tremor found direct mail works particularly well with teens. "What we found was that teens don't get much mail," says a Tremor executive. "So they actually appreciate it when they get it." As a result, Tremor has made direct-mail product information, offers, and samples a cornerstone of its program, although the online component remains substantial as well.[11]

Catalogue Marketing

Catalogue marketing
Direct marketing through print, video, or digital catalogues that are mailed to select customers, made available in stores, or presented online.

Advances in technology, along with the move toward personalized, one-to-one marketing, have resulted in exciting changes in **catalogue marketing**. *Catalogue Age* magazine used to define a *catalogue* as "a printed, bound piece of at least eight pages, selling multiple products, and offering a direct ordering mechanism." Today, only a few years later, this definition is sadly out of date.

With the stampede to the Internet, more and more catalogues are going digital. A variety of web-only cataloguers have emerged, and most print cataloguers have added Web-based catalogues to their marketing mixes. For example, visit the Canadian Tire website (www.canadiantire.ca) and you can browse for products and weekly specials before you head for the store. Web-based catalogues eliminate production, printing, and mailing costs. And whereas print catalogue space is limited, online catalogues can offer an almost unlimited amount of merchandise. Finally, online catalogues allow real-time merchandising—products and features can be added or removed as needed and prices can be adjusted instantly to match demand.

However, despite the advantages of web-based catalogues, as your overstuffed mailbox may suggest, printed catalogues are still thriving. Why aren't companies ditching their old-fashioned paper catalogues in this new digital era? It turns out that printed catalogues are

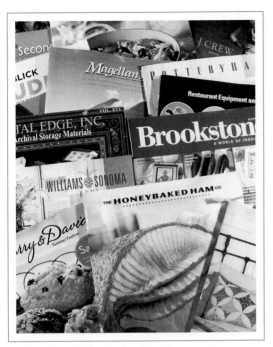

Catalogue marketing has grown explosively. Thousands of catalogues are sent to consumers every year.

one of the best ways to drive online sales. "Our catalogue is itself an advertising vehicle, and it is an effective way to drive traffic to our website," says an L.L. Bean marketer. While Sears terminated its catalogue in the United States several years ago, it is still a major marketing force in Canada. It is the largest mail-order catalogue in the country, and combined with its online catalogue it helps customers find products and services quickly and efficiently no matter what medium they choose.

In a recent study, 66 percent of retailers surveyed said that they measure a catalogue's success by its ability to boost web sales. Even online-only retailers, such as eBay and UncommonGoods, have started producing catalogues with the hopes of driving online sales. The retailers said that 13 percent of new online customers last year resulted from catalogue mailings, and about 43 percent of catalogue customers also buy online.[12]

In addition, paper catalogues can also create emotional connections with customers that web-based sales spaces simply can't (see Real Marketing 17.1). For example, Sears recently brought back its holiday Wish Book after a 14-year hiatus. According to Sears' chief marketing officer, many customers were nostalgic for the catalogue, reminiscing about the days when they would fold over pages and hope that Santa would notice.[13]

In all, catalogue marketing—printed and online—has grown explosively during the past 25 years. These days, Canadian consumers can buy just about anything from a catalogue, since there are 1500 or more catalogue and mail-order houses in Canada. Founded in London, Ontario, the Bradford Exchange features a vast range of collectibles ranging from dolls to specialty plates to coins to heirloom toys. If you've ever been involved in raising funds for your church, synagogue, or mosque, you are probably familiar with the Regal Gifts catalogue. Stuffed with giftware of every type, it has helped Canadians and Canadian organizations make money for over 80 years. You can search for horses using the Standardbred Canada catalogue, or high-quality gardening tools from Ottawa's Lee Valley Tools.

Telephone Marketing

Telephone marketing
Using the telephone to sell directly to customers.

Telephone marketing (or telemarketing) involves using the telephone to sell directly to consumers and business customers. Telephone marketing now accounts for nearly 20 percent of all direct marketing–driven sales. We're all familiar with telephone marketing directed toward consumers, but business-to-business marketers also use telephone marketing extensively, accounting for more than 55 percent of all telephone marketing sales.[14]

Marketers use *outbound* telephone marketing to sell directly to consumers and businesses. They use *inbound* toll-free numbers to receive orders from television and print ads, direct mail, or catalogues. The use of 1-800 numbers has taken off in recent years as more and more companies have begun using them, and as current users have added new features such as toll-free fax numbers. To accommodate this rapid growth, new toll-free area codes, such as 888, 877, and 866, have been added.

Properly designed and targeted telemarketing provides many benefits, including purchasing convenience and increased product and service information. However, the explosion in unsolicited outbound telephone marketing over the years annoyed many consumers, who objected to the almost daily "junk phone calls" that pulled them away from the dinner table or filled the answering machine.

In 2008, the CRTC established the "Unsolicited Telecommunications Rules," which encompass three sets of rules: telemarketing rules, the National Do Not Call List rules, and the Automatic Dialing and Announcing Device rules. Charities, political parties and riding associations, and newspapers are exempt from the rules. As of January 2009, 5.8 million consumers had registered their telephone numbers on the Do Not Call List, an indication of how many resented unsolicited calls. But the legislation has been "heavily criticized since its inception. University of Ottawa professor Michael Geist calls the legislation a disaster since it contains too many exceptions and provides little in the way of penalties. Consumers have complained that they received more calls after they had entered their names onto the list than before they had done so. Global News found it took less than 10 minutes on the CRTC's website to register as a telemarketer and download the list for a mere $50 fee. Apparently, many international marketers did the same thing and used the list for purposes opposite to those intended. Thus, unlike similar legislation in the United States, which "has been exceptionally successful," the Canadian version needs a major overhaul.[15]

Some believe that the do-not-call legislation has hurt the telemarketing industry, but not all that much. Two major forms of telemarketing—inbound consumer telemarketing and outbound business-to-business telemarketing—remain strong and growing. Telemarketing also remains a major fundraising tool for not-for-profit groups. However, many telemarketers are shifting to alternative methods for capturing new customers and sales, from direct mail, direct-response TV, and live-chat web technology to sweepstakes that prompt customers to call in.

For example, ServiceMaster's TruGreen lawn care service used to generate about 90 percent of its sales through telemarketing. It now uses more direct mail, as well as having employees go door-to-door in neighbourhoods where it already has customers. The new approach appears to be working even better than the old cold-calling one. The company's sales have grown under the new methods, and less than 50 percent of sales come from telemarketing. "We were nervous, but we are thrilled with what we've accomplished," says ServiceMaster's chief executive.[16]

In fact, the Do Not Call List appears to be helping most direct marketers more than it's hurting them. Many of these marketers are shifting their call centre activity from making cold calls on often resentful customers to managing existing customer relationships. They are developing "opt-in" calling systems in which they provide useful information and offers to customers who have invited the company to contact them by phone or email. These "sales tactics have [produced] results as good—or even better—than telemarketing," declares one analyst. "The opt-in model is proving [more] valuable for marketers [than] the old invasive one."[17]

Direct-Response Television Marketing

Direct-response television marketing Direct marketing via television, including direct-response television advertising (or infomercials) and home shopping channels.

Direct-response television marketing takes one of two major forms. The first is *direct-response television advertising* (DRTV). Direct marketers air television spots, often 60 or 120 seconds long, which persuasively describe a product and give customers a toll-free number or website for ordering. Television viewers also often encounter full 30-minute or longer advertising programs, or *infomercials*, for a single product.

Some successful direct-response ads run for years and become classics. For example, Dial Media's classic ads for Ginsu knives ran for seven years and sold almost 3 million sets of knives worth more than US$40 million in sales. Bowflex has grossed more than US$1.3 billion in infomercial sales. And little-known infomercial maker Guthy-Renker has helped propel Proactiv Solution acne treatment into a power brand that pulls in US$850 million in sales annually to 5 million active customers. Proactiv's incredible success derives from powerful, formulaic infomercials in which celebrities and average Joes gush about how Proactiv cleared their skin. "My skin is now clear and beautiful," says Serena Williams. "Yours can be too!"[18]

For years, infomercials have been associated with somewhat questionable pitches for juicers and other kitchen gadgets, get-rich-quick schemes, and nifty ways to stay in shape without working very hard at it. In recent years, however, a number of large companies—from Procter & Gamble, Dell, Sears, Disney, Bose, and Revlon to Apple, Land Rover, and Anheuser-Busch—have begun using infomercials to sell their wares, refer customers to retailers, send out product information, recruit members, or attract buyers to their websites. For example, P&G has used DRTV to market more than a dozen brands, including Dryel, Mr. Clean, CoverGirl, Iams pet food, and Old Spice. An estimated 20 percent of all new infomercials now come to you courtesy of *Fortune* 1000 companies.[19]

Home shopping offered by multichannel retailer The Shopping Channel provides an easy and convenient way to purchase for many time-pressed Canadian consumers.

Direct-response TV commercials are usually cheaper to make and the media purchase is less costly. Moreover, unlike most media campaigns, direct-response ads always include a 1-800 number or web address, making it easier for marketers to track the impact of their pitches. For these reasons, DRTV is growing more quickly than traditional broadcast and cable advertising. Some DRTV experts even predict that in 5 or 10 years, as marketers seek greater returns on their advertising investments, all television advertising will be some form of direct-response advertising. "In a business environment where marketers are obsessed with return on investment," notes one such expert, "direct response is tailor-made—[marketers can] track phone calls and website hits generated by the ads. [They can] use DRTV to build brand awareness while simultaneously generating leads and sales."[20]

Home shopping channels, another form of direct-response television marketing, are television programs or entire channels dedicated to selling goods and services. The Shopping Channel, a division of Rogers Media, is Canada's leader with hundreds of thousands of customers, mostly female. It closes only one day a year—Christmas. In addition to its 24/7 broadcasts, it issues a biannual catalogue and a website where customers will find over 20 000 items for sale (close to 35 percent of The Shopping Channel's sales come from the Web). Another offering is ShopTV Canada, which broadcasts to South-Central Ontario and Nova Scotia and reaches 1.7 million households. During both programs, hosts chat with viewers by phone and offer products ranging from jewellery, lamps, collectible dolls, and clothing to power tools and consumer electronics. Viewers call a toll-free number or go online to order goods. Despite their lowbrow images, home shopping channels have evolved into highly sophisticated, very successful marketing operations.[21]

Kiosk Marketing

As consumers become more and more comfortable with computer and digital technologies, many companies are placing information and ordering machines—called *kiosks* (in contrast to vending machines, which dispense actual products)—in stores, airports, and other locations. Kiosks are popping up everywhere these days, from self-service hotel and airline check-in devices to in-store ordering kiosks that let you order merchandise not carried in the store.

In-store Kodak, Fuji, and HP kiosks let customers transfer pictures from memory sticks, mobile phones, and other digital storage devices, edit them, and make high-quality colour prints. Toyota Canada used kiosks to target younger buyers. The Liquor Control Board of Ontario (LCBO) installed interactive kiosks to run advertisements for featured products and to enhance customer service. Kiosks in airports allow passengers to get their boarding passes and luggage tags, while those in Hilton hotel lobbies let guests view their reservations, get room keys, view prearrival messages, check in and out, and even change seat assignments and print boarding passes for flights on any of 18 airlines. Business marketers also use kiosks. For example, Dow Plastics places kiosks at trade shows to collect sales leads and to provide information on its 700 products. Trade and Investment Canada placed a kiosk at an Atlanta trade show to introduce Canadian telecommunication and computer products to international buyers. The kiosk system reads customer data from encoded registration badges and produces technical data sheets that can be printed at the kiosk or faxed or mailed to the customer. The system has resulted in a 400 percent increase in qualified sales leads.[22]

New Digital Direct-Marketing Technologies

Today, thanks to a wealth of new digital technologies, direct marketers can reach and interact with consumers just about anywhere, at any time, about almost anything. Here, we look

Mobile marketing: Mobile phones and wireless devices have quietly become the newest, hottest frontier for big-brand messages.

into several exciting new digital direct-marketing technologies: mobile phone marketing, podcasts and vodcasts, and interactive TV (ITV).

Mobile Phone Marketing

In 2009, about 65 percent of Canadians had a mobile phone, compared to 88 percent in the United States and 70 percent in Mexico. The Canadian market is dominated by three main players who control 95 percent of the market: Rogers, Bell, and Telus. Some claim that the big three have kept prices 45 percent higher than in the United States, thereby holding back wireless growth. A new entrant into the market may begin to change this situation, though. Public Mobile Holdings, a new Canadian wireless carrier, is in negotiations with Walmart and other retailers about selling phones with unlimited call plans to lure users away from the big players. An increasing number of cellphone users are using their phones to access the Web. Some 23 percent of cellphone users have seen advertising on their phones in the last 30 days and about half of them responded to the ads.[23]

A growing number of consumers—especially younger ones—are using their cellphones as a "third screen" for text messaging, surfing the Web, watching downloaded videos and shows, and checking email. According to one expert, "the cell phone, which makes on-the-go conversing so convenient, is morphing into a content device, a kind of digital Swiss Army knife with the capability of filling its owner's every spare minute with games, music, live and on-demand TV, Web browsing, and, oh yes, advertising." Cellphones allow "marketers to reach consumers anytime, anywhere, on a device they love."[24]

A recent study estimated that spending on mobile marketing will grow from US$1.8 billion in 2007 to as much as US$24 billion worldwide by 2013.[25]

> Mobile phones and wireless devices have quietly become the newest, hottest frontier for big brands, especially those itching to reach the coveted 18- to 34-year-old set. TV networks are prodding viewers to send text messages to vote for their favourite reality TV character. Wireless websites are lacing sports scores and news digests with banner ads for Lexus, Burger King, and Sheraton. A few companies are even customizing 10-second video ads for short, TV-style episodes that are edging their way onto mobile phones. For advertisers, the young audience is just one selling point. Wireless gadgets are always-on, ever-present accessories. The fact that a phone is tethered to an individual means that ads can be targeted. And users can respond instantly to time-sensitive offers. The mobile phone is very personal and it's always with you.

> Marketers of all kinds—from Pepsi and Nike to P&G, Burger King, Toyota, and McDonald's—are now integrating mobile phones into their direct marketing. Cellphone promotions include everything from ring-tone giveaways, mobile games, text-in contests, and ad-supported content to retailer announcements of discounts, special sales, and gift suggestions. For example, McDonald's recently put a promotion code on 20 million Big Mac packages in a joint sweepstakes contest with the House of Blues, urging participants to enter to win prizes and to text in from concerts. Some 40 percent of contest entries came via text messaging, resulting in a 3 percent sales gain for McDonald's. More important, 24 percent of those entering via cellphones opted in to receive future promotions and messages.[26]

As with other forms of direct marketing, however, companies must use mobile marketing responsibly or risk angering already ad-weary consumers. Most people are initially

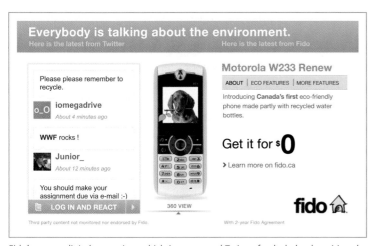

Fido's recent digital campaign, which incorporated Twitter feeds, helped position the company as a firm that cares about environmental issues.

skeptical about receiving cellphone ad messages. But they often change their minds if the ads deliver value in the form of lower cellphone bills, useful information, entertaining content, or discounted prices and coupons for their favourite products and services. A recent study found that 42 percent of cellphone users are open to mobile advertising if it's relevant.[27] When used properly, mobile marketing can greatly enrich the buyer's experience. BMW Canada added a mobile twist to its display of the Z4 Roadster that was set up outside the Royal York Hotel in Toronto. Potential customers could book a test drive by texting "drive" on their phones. Wireless provider Fido also used a relevant interactive digital campaign. It spoke to consumers' growing concerns about the environment:

Fido used expandable ads which incorporated Twitter feeds in French and English to promote the Motorola MOTO w233 Renew mobile phone, an eco-friendly product made largely from recycled water bottles. According to Sylvie Charette, vice-president of marketing and communications, the goal of the campaign was to promote Fido as a company that cares about green issues. "We were able to aggregate live tweet feeds about green issues from around the world in the online banners themselves, and associate the 'green phone' product with the user-generated tweets."[28]

Podcasts and Vodcasts

Podcasting and vodcasting are the latest on-the-go, on-demand technologies. The name *podcast* derives from Apple's now-everywhere iPod. With podcasting, consumers can download audio files (podcasts) or video files (vodcasts) via the Internet to an iPod or other handheld device and then listen to or view them whenever and wherever they wish. They can search for podcast topics through sites such as iTunes or through podcast networks such as Podtrac, Podbridge, or Mevio. These days, you can download podcasts or vodcasts on an exploding array of topics: everything from your favourite CBC Radio show, a recent sitcom episode, or current sports features to the latest music video or Molson Canadian commercial.

A 2008 survey of 12 000 Canadians by BBM Analytics found that podcast listening had doubled in English Canada since 2006. This growth is driven by the increase in sales of MP3 players and expanding consumer demand for more personal content. Twenty percent of Canadians listen to a podcast on a monthly basis.[29] Another recent study predicts that the North American podcast audience will exceed 65 million by 2012, up from just 6 million in 2005.[30] As a result, this new medium is drawing much attention from marketers. Many are now integrating podcasts and vodcasts into their direct-marketing programs in the form of ad-supported podcasts, downloadable ads and informational features, and other promotions.

For example, the Bank of Montreal launched a student-focused "Head of the Class" podcast on its website to help its young clients address finance-related questions that matter to students. Since its survey showed that 70 percent of students see paying off student debt as a top priority, it featured topics such as debt and money management. Volvo sponsors podcasts on Autoblog, and Hot Topic

With podcasting, consumers can download files via the Internet to an iPod or other handheld device and listen to or view them whenever and wherever they wish.

sponsors its own new music podcast featuring underground bands. Walt Disney World Resort offers weekly podcasts on a mix of topics, including behind-the-scenes tours, interviews, upcoming events, and news about new attractions. New podcasts automatically download to subscribers' computers, where they can transfer them to portable media players to enjoy and share. And Nestlé Purina publishes podcasts on animal training and behavioural issues. It invites customers to "Take these shows on the road—from serious discussions with veterinarians about pet health to wacky animal videos featuring dogs and cats, Purina has a podcast for you."[31]

Interactive TV (ITV)

Interactive TV (ITV) lets viewers interact with television programming and advertising using their remote controls. In the past, ITV has been slow to catch on. However, the technology now appears poised to take off as a direct-marketing medium. A recent poll indicated that 66 percent of viewers would be "very interested" in interacting with commercials that piqued their interest.[32] And satellite broadcasting systems such as DIRECTV, EchoStar, and Time Warner are now offering ITV capabilities.

Interactive TV gives marketers an opportunity to reach targeted audiences in an interactive, more involving way. For example, Procter & Gamble ran interactive ads for its Tide To Go brand. The 30-second TV spots contained remote control links giving interested consumers instant access to more information about the product as well as coupons and the opportunity to enter a sweepstakes to win a trip to an amusement park. Similarly, Nike's "Quick Is Deadly" campaign for its Zoom training-shoe line included more than 20 minutes of interactive content.

Mobile phone marketing, podcasts and vodcasts, and interactive TV offer exciting direct-marketing opportunities. But marketers must be careful to use these new direct-marketing approaches wisely. As with other direct-marketing forms, marketers who use them risk backlash from consumers who may resent such marketing as an invasion of their privacy. Marketers must target their direct-marketing offers carefully, bringing real value to customers rather than making unwanted intrusions into their lives.

3　ONLINE MARKETING

Online marketing
Company efforts to market products and services and build customer relationships over the Internet.

As noted earlier, **online marketing** is the fastest-growing form of direct marketing. Recent technological advances have created a digital age. Widespread use of the Internet is having a dramatic impact on both buyers and the marketers who serve them. In this section, we examine how marketing strategy and practice are changing to take advantage of today's Internet technologies.

Marketing and the Internet

Internet
A vast public web of computer networks that connects users of all types all around the world to each other and to an amazingly large information repository.

Much of the world's business today is carried out over digital networks that connect people and companies. The **Internet**, a vast public web of computer networks, connects users of all types all around the world to each other and to an amazingly large information repository. The Web has fundamentally changed customers' notions of convenience, speed, price, product information, and service. As a result, it has given marketers a whole new way to create value for customers and build relationships with them.

Internet usage and impact continues to grow steadily. Canada has the highest Internet penetration of any G8 country (with Atlantic Canada having the highest penetration rates). Canadians view the most content and spend the most time online. In 2008, 28 million Canadians, or 84.3 percent of the population, were Internet users. We are also good at multitasking—46 percent of Canadians browse the Web and watch TV at the same time at least once a day. Social networking is also a major trend in the country, with 90 percent of online users reporting that they belong to such networks. While Canada leads these trends, worldwide there are more than 540 million people who have Internet access.[33]

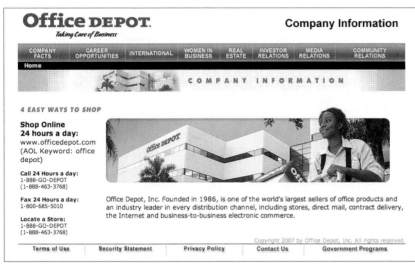

Click-and-mortar marketing: No click-only or brick-only seller can match the call, click, or visit convenience and support afforded by Office Depot's "4 easy ways to shop."

All kinds of companies now market online. **Online companies** operate only on the Internet. They include a wide array of firms, from *etailers*, such as Amazon.ca and Expedia.ca, that sell products and services directly to final buyers via the Internet to *search engines and portals* (such as Yahoo!, Google, and MSN), *transaction sites* (eBay), and *content sites* (Digg, a social-driven content site, and Canada.com, Canada's leading general news and information destination). After a frenzied and rocky start in the 1990s, many online firms are now prospering.

As the Internet grew, the success of online firms threatened existing manufacturers and retailers, forcing them to re-examine how they served their markets. Now almost all of these traditional companies have set up their own online sales and communications channels, becoming what some call **hybrid or click-and-mortar companies**. It's hard to find a company today that doesn't have a substantial web presence.

In fact, many hybrid companies are now having more online success than their online-only competitors. In a recent ranking of the top 10 online retail sites, only two were online-only retailers. All of the others were multichannel retailers.[34] For example, Office Depot's more than 1000 office-supply superstores rack up annual sales of US$15.5 billion in more than 42 countries. But you might be surprised to learn that Office Depot's fastest recent growth has come not from its traditional channels, but from the Internet:

> Office Depot's online sales have soared in recent years, now accounting for 31 percent of total sales. Selling on the Web lets Office Depot build deeper, more personalized relationships with customers large and small. For example, a large customer such as GE or P&G can create lists of approved office products at discount prices and then let company departments or even individuals do their own online purchasing. This reduces ordering costs, cuts through the red tape, and speeds up the ordering process for customers. At the same time, it encourages companies to use Office Depot as the sole source for office supplies. Even the smallest companies find 24-hour-a-day online ordering easier and more efficient. Importantly, Office Depot's web operations don't steal from store sales. Instead, the OfficeDepot.com site actually builds store traffic by helping customers find a local store and check stock. In return, the local store promotes the website through in-store kiosks. If customers don't find what they need on the shelves, they can quickly order it via the Web from the kiosk. Thus, Office Depot now offers a full range of contact points and delivery modes—online, by phone or fax, and in the store. No click-only or brick-only seller can match the call, click, or visit convenience and support afforded by Office Depot's click-and-mortar model.[35]

Online companies
The so-called dot-coms, which operate only online without any brick-and-mortar market presence.

Hybrid or click-and-mortar companies
Traditional companies that have added online marketing to their operations.

Online Marketing Domains

The four major online marketing domains are shown in Figure 17.2. They include B2C (business-to-consumer), B2B (business-to-business), C2C (consumer-to-consumer), and C2B (consumer-to-business).

Business-to-consumer (B2C) online marketing
Businesses selling goods and services online to final consumers.

Business-to-Consumer (B2C)

The popular press has paid the most attention to **business-to-consumer (B2C) online marketing**—businesses selling goods and services online to final consumers. Canadian firms have been pioneers in this arena. Canada Trust, for example, was one of the first

Figure 17.2 Online marketing domains

	Targeted to consumers	Targeted to businesses
Initiated by business	B2C (business to consumer)	B2B (business to business)
Initiated by consumer	C2C (consumer to consumer)	C2B (consumer to business)

banks in the world to allow its customers to conduct transactions online. Air Canada was another leader, launching its ecommerce site in 1998. Today's consumers can buy almost anything online—from clothing, kitchen gadgets, and airline tickets to computers and cars. Online consumer buying continues to grow at a healthy rate. In 2009, more than 30 percent of all Canadians 16 years of age and older purchase online, making almost $16 billion in purchases, a 21 percent increase since 2008. In a weak economy, it is one of the few sectors that are growing.[36]

Perhaps more importantly, the Internet now influences 57 percent of total retail sales—Canadians like to window shop online. Some purchase using this medium, but others then go to traditional retail stores to make the actual transaction.[37] Thus, smart marketers are employing integrated multichannel strategies that use the Web to drive sales to other marketing channels.

As more and more people find their way onto the Web, the population of online consumers is becoming more mainstream and diverse. The Web now offers marketers a palette of different kinds of consumers seeking different kinds of online experiences. However, Internet consumers still differ from traditional offline consumers in their approaches to buying and in their responses to marketing. In the Internet exchange process, customers initiate and control the contact. Traditional marketing targets a somewhat passive audience. In contrast, online marketing targets people who actively select which websites they will visit and what marketing information they will receive about which products and under what conditions. Thus, the new world of online marketing requires new marketing approaches.

People now go online to order a wide range of goods—clothing from Mountain Equipment Co-op or the Gap, books and a wide range of other products from Chapters or Amazon.ca, furniture from The Brick, food from Grocery Gateway, lobster from Clearwater Seafood Company, major appliances from Sears, flowers from Bloomex, or even home mortgages from all the major banks.

Business-to-Business (B2B)

Business-to-business (B2B) online marketing
Businesses using B2B websites, email, online catalogues, online trading networks, and other online resources to reach new business customers, serve current customers more effectively, and obtain buying efficiencies and better prices.

Although the popular press has given the most attention to B2C websites, **business-to-business (B2B) online marketing** is also flourishing. B2B marketers use B2B websites, email, online product catalogues, online trading networks, and other online resources to reach new business customers, serve current customers more effectively, and obtain buying efficiencies and better prices.

Most major business-to-business marketers now offer product information, customer purchasing, and customer-support services online. For example, corporate buyers can visit Sun Microsystems' website (www.sun.com), select detailed descriptions of Sun's products and solutions, request sales and service information, and interact with staff members. Some major companies conduct almost all of their business on the Web. Networking equipment and software maker Cisco Systems takes more than 80 percent of its orders over the Internet.

Beyond simply selling their products and services online, companies can use the Internet to build stronger relationships with important business customers. For example, Dell has set up customized websites for more than 113 000 business and institutional customers worldwide. These individualized Premier.Dell.com sites help business customers to more efficiently manage all phases of their Dell computer buying and ownership. Each customer's Premier.Dell.com website can include a customized online computer store, purchasing and asset management reports and tools, system-specific technical information, links to useful information throughout Dell's extensive website, and more. The site makes all the information a customer needs to do business with Dell available in one place, 24 hours a day, 7 days a week.[38]

Consumer-to-Consumer (C2C)

Consumer-to-consumer (C2C) online marketing

Online exchanges of goods and information between final consumers.

Much **consumer-to-consumer (C2C) online marketing** and communication occurs on the Web between interested parties over a wide range of products and subjects. In some cases, the Internet provides an excellent means by which consumers can buy or exchange goods or information directly with one another. For example, Kijiji (the Swahili word for *village*) allows consumers to post ads online for goods or services they want to sell to others in their community. In addition to its Canadian sites, it operates in France, Italy, China, India, Taiwan, and Japan and gets 45 million unique visitors per month worldwide. Craigslist is another popular market space for displaying and selling almost anything, from art and antiques, coins and stamps, and jewellery to computers and consumer electronics.

EBay's C2C online trading community of more than 275 million registered users worldwide (greater than the combined populations of France, Germany, Italy, and Britain!) transacted some US$60 billion in trades last year. At any given time, the company's website lists more than 115 million items up for auction in more than 50 000 categories. Interestingly, based on its huge success in the C2C market, eBay has now attracted more than 500 000 B2C sellers, ranging from small businesses peddling their regular wares to large businesses liquidating excess inventory at auction.[39]

In other cases, C2C involves interchanges of information through Internet forums that appeal to specific special interest groups. Such activities may be organized for commercial or noncommercial purposes. An example is web logs, or *blogs*, online journals where people post their thoughts, usually on a narrowly defined topic. Blogs can be about anything, from politics or baseball to haiku, car repair, or the latest television series. There are currently about 15 million active blogs read by 57 million people. Such numbers give blogs—especially those with large and devoted followings—substantial influence.[40]

Many marketers are now tapping into blogs as a medium for reaching carefully targeted consumers. One way is to advertise on an existing blog or to influence content there. Consider this example:

> When Nescafé launched its Dolce Gusto coffee maker in France in 2006, it turned to bloggers. It placed an ad on French website BlogBang.com, which has a community of more than 2000 bloggers. The site sent a message to its members telling them about the ad campaign, which came in the form of an interactive game. The bloggers were asked to put a link to the game on their sites. In return, Dolce Gusto's home page posted links to the blogs that joined up. "The advantage of using blogs is that the message gets around very quickly," says the Dolce Gusto brand manager, "and it focuses on our target audience" of 25- to 35-year-olds. "It really created a marketing buzz." Within three weeks of its launch, Dolce Gusto's ad was displayed on 500 blogs, and 320 000 people had played the online game.[41]

Other companies set up their own blogs. For example, GM maintains a blog called FastLane that helps it connect with its core consumers in a virtual grassroots kind of way. The log is penned by GM executives, including vice-chairman Bob Lutz, who some claim is the big reason for its popularity. The company says it wants all kinds of feedback—so the blog includes both positive and negative comments from readers. Says Lutz, "I'd say the biggest surprise is the passion in which people respond and comment on the blogs. You're getting the real deal there. There is so much passion that even the negative comments are palatable, and indeed, often helpful." The FastLane blog receives about 3000 visitors a day, helping GM build or rebuild relationships with customers. "If there is a gap between GM's excellence and people's perception of it, we believe blogs are a great opportunity to change those perceptions," says GM's digital marketing chief.[42]

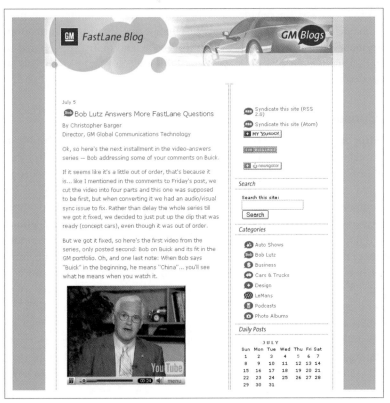

Many marketers are now tapping into consumer-to-consumer web communications by setting up their own blogs. GM's FastLane blog—penned primarily by vice-chairman Bob Lutz—helps GM connect with its core consumers in a virtual grassroots kind of way.

As a marketing tool, blogs offer some advantages. They can offer a fresh, original, personal, and cheap way to reach today's fragmented audiences. However, the blogosphere is cluttered and difficult to control. "Blogs may help companies bond with consumers in exciting new ways, but they won't help them control the relationship," says one blog expert. Such web journals remain largely a C2C medium. "That isn't to suggest companies can't influence the relationship or leverage blogs to engage in a meaningful relationship," says the expert, "but the consumer will remain in control."[43]

Whether or not they actively participate in the blogosphere, companies should show up, monitor them, and listen to them. For example, Starbucks sponsors its own blog (www.mystarbucksidea.com) but also closely follows consumer dialogue on the 30 or more other third-party sites devoted to the brand. It then uses the customer insights it gains from all of these proprietary and third-party blogs to adjust its marketing programs. For instance, it recently altered the remaining instalments of a four-part podcast based on the negative blog feedback it gleaned on the first one.[44]

In all, C2C means that online buyers don't just consume product information—increasingly, they create it. As a result, "word of web" is joining "word of mouth" as an important buying influence.

Consumer to Business (C2B)

Consumer-to-business (C2B) online marketing

Online exchanges in which consumers search out sellers, learn about their offers, and initiate purchases, sometimes even driving transaction terms.

The final online marketing domain is **consumer-to-business (C2B) online marketing**. Thanks to the Internet, today's consumers are finding it easier to communicate with companies. Most companies now invite prospects and customers to send in suggestions and questions via company websites. Beyond this, rather than waiting for an invitation, consumers can search out sellers on the Web, learn about their offers, initiate purchases, and give feedback. Using the Web, consumers can even drive transactions with businesses rather than the other way around. For example, using Priceline.com, would-be buyers can bid for airline tickets, hotel rooms, rental cars, cruises, and vacation packages, leaving the sellers to decide whether to accept their offers.

Consumers can also use websites such as GetSatisfaction.com to ask questions, offer suggestions, lodge complaints, or deliver compliments to companies. GetSatisfaction.com provides "people-powered customer service" by creating a user-driven customer service community. The site provides forums where customers discuss problems they're having with the products and services of 2500 companies—from Air Canada to Zappos.com— whether the company participates or not. GetSatisfaction.com also provides tools by which companies can adopt GetSatisfaction.com as an official customer service resource. Since launching in 2007, the site has drawn more than a million unique visitors.[45]

4   Setting Up an Online Marketing Presence

Clearly, all companies need to consider moving online. Companies can conduct online marketing in any of the four ways shown in Figure 17.3: creating a website, placing ads and promotions online, setting up or participating in online social networks, or using email.

Figure 17.3 Setting up for online marketing

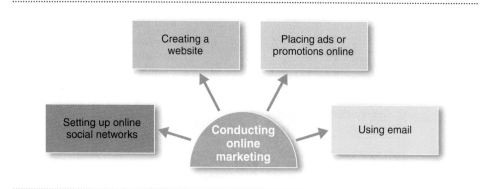

Creating a Website

For most companies, the first step in conducting online marketing is to create a website. However, beyond simply creating a website, marketers must design an attractive site and find ways to get consumers to visit the site, stay around, and come back often.

Types of Websites   Websites vary greatly in purpose and content. The most basic type is a **corporate (or brand) website**. These sites are designed to build customer goodwill, collect customer feedback, and supplement other sales channels rather than to sell the company's products directly. They typically offer a rich variety of information and other features in an effort to answer customer questions, build closer customer relationships, and generate excitement about the company or brand.

For example, you can't buy anything at P&G's Tide To Go brand site, but you can learn how to use the handy stain remover stick (including a video demo), watch recent ads, and share "Tide To Go saves the day!" stories with others. And Unilever's CampaignForReal-Beauty.com site doesn't sell Dove soaps and lotions. But it does provide a place for people interested in the cause of women's and girls' self-esteem to share their thoughts, view ads and viral videos such as "Evolution" or "Onslaught," and download self-esteem assessment tools and workbooks. They can even register for a free training guide to become a Dove Real Beauty Workshop for Girls facilitator. Such websites, once brushed aside as digital "brochureware," are now attracting consumers in numbers that vie with flashier consumer sites and even traditional mass media.[46]

Believe it or not, those boring corporate websites are pulling in more eyeballs—and more influencers—than flashy prime-time TV shows, print magazines, and general-interest sites. Packaged goods marketers such as P&G and Unilever don't sell many products directly online; their low-cost, low-involvement brands tend not to generate much search. Yet P&G and Unilever websites now reach over 6 million and 3 million unique visitors, respectively, each month, easily swamping the audiences of many magazines and cable and syndicated TV shows where the companies advertise. But more important than the volume may be who the visitors are. Corporate and brand website visitors are much more likely to influence others and to recommend brands to them. Of all options for influencing the online influencers, brand websites rank highest both in consumer acceptance and marketer control.

Other companies create a **marketing website**. These sites engage consumers in an interaction that will move them closer to a direct purchase or other marketing outcome. For example, visitors to HomeDepot.ca can search through dozens of categories of home improvement products, learn more about specific items, join auctions for select items, get advice that varies by season like how to stain a deck or maintain a weed-free garden, and read expert product reviews. They can check out the latest hot deals, place orders online, and pay by credit card, all with a few mouse clicks.

Designing Effective Websites   Creating a website is one thing; getting people to *visit* the site is another. To attract visitors, companies aggressively promote their websites in offline

---

Corporate (or brand) website
A website designed to build customer goodwill, collect customer feedback, and supplement other sales channels rather than to sell the company's products directly.

Marketing website
A website that engages consumers in interactions that will move them closer to a direct purchase or other marketing outcome.

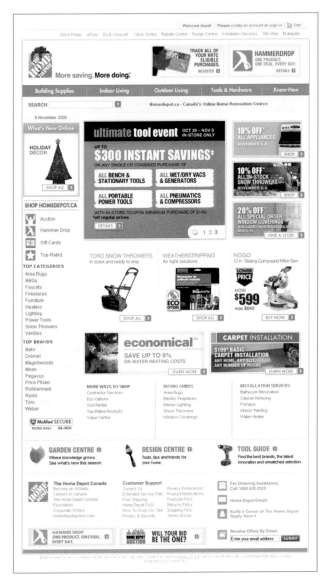

Home Depot operates a marketing site that helps consumers learn about products, find expert advice, and buy products, all with a few clicks of their mouse.

print and broadcast advertising and through ads and links on other sites. But today's web users are quick to abandon any website that doesn't measure up. The key is to create enough value and excitement to get consumers who come to the site to stick around and come back again. This means that companies must constantly update their sites to keep them current, fresh, and useful.

A key challenge is designing a website that is attractive on first view and interesting enough to encourage repeat visits. Many marketers create colourful, graphically sophisticated websites that combine text, sound, and animation to capture and hold attention (for examples, see www.looneytunes.com or www.nike.com). To attract new visitors and to encourage revisits, suggests one expert, online marketers should pay close attention to the seven Cs of effective website design:[47]

- *Context:* the site's layout and design

- *Content:* the text, pictures, sound, and video that the website contains

- *Community:* the ways in which the site enables user-to-user communication

- *Customization:* the site's ability to tailor itself to different users or to allow users to personalize the site

- *Communication:* the ways in which the site enables site-to-user, user-to-site, or two-way communication

- *Connection:* the degree to which the site is linked to other sites

- *Commerce:* the site's capability to enable commercial transactions

And to keep customers coming back to the site, companies need to embrace yet another C—constant change.

At the very least, a website should be easy to use, professional looking, and physically attractive. Ultimately, however, websites must also be *useful*. When it comes to web surfing and shopping, most people prefer substance over style and function over flash.

Thus, effective websites contain deep and useful information, interactive tools that help buyers find and evaluate products of interest, links to other related sites, changing promotional offers, and entertaining features that lend relevant excitement.

Placing Ads and Promotions Online

Online advertising

Advertising that appears while consumers are surfing the Web, including display ads, search-related ads, online classifieds, and other forms.

As consumers spend more and more time on the Internet, many companies are shifting more of their marketing dollars to **online advertising** to build their brands or to attract visitors to their websites. Online advertising is becoming a major medium. In 2008, it was estimated that Canadian companies spent $1.5 billion on online advertising, up an incredible 25 percent over the previous year. Interactive Advertising Bureau (IAB) Canada president Paula Gignac says the growth in online advertising in Canada speaks to "how important the medium has become to marketers in terms of its ability to reach, target, engage and dialogue with consumers."[48] The major forms of online advertising include display ads, search-related ads, and online classifieds. Online display ads might appear anywhere on an Internet user's screen. The most common form is *banners*, banner-shaped ads found at the top, bottom, left, right, or centre of a webpage. *Pop-ups* are online ads that

Effective websites: Check out the award-winning UPS website at http://whiteboard. ups.com/. How has it applied the seven *Cs* of effective website design?

appear suddenly in a new window in front of the window being viewed.

Many companies are developing exciting new *rich media* display ads, which incorporate animation, video, sound, and interactivity. Rich media ads attract and hold consumer attention better than traditional banner ads.

But many rich media ads do more than create a little bit of jumping animation—they also create interactivity. Many of today's rich media ads provide consumers with product information, a brand experience, and even local or online buying options without taking them away from the site they are viewing. Another hot growth area for online advertising is *search-related ads* (or *contextual advertising*), in which text-based ads and links appear alongside search engine results on sites such as Google and Yahoo!. Search ads can be an effective means of linking consumers to other forms of online promotion.

Other Forms of Online Promotion   Other forms of online promotions include content sponsorships, alliances and affiliate programs, and viral advertising.

Using *content sponsorships*, companies gain name exposure on the Internet by sponsoring special content on various websites, such as news or financial information or special-interest topics. For example, Dell and Intel place banner ads on the Weather Network's site. Sponsorships are best placed on carefully targeted sites where they can offer relevant information or service to the audience. Internet companies can also develop *alliances and affiliate programs* in which they work with other companies, online and offline, to "promote each other." For example, through its Amazon Associates Program, Amazon.com has more than 900 000 affiliates who post Amazon.com banners on their websites.

Viral marketing
The Internet version of word-of-mouth marketing—websites, videos, email messages, or other marketing events that are so infectious that customers will want to pass them along to friends.

Finally, online marketers use **viral marketing**, the Internet version of word-of-mouth marketing. Viral marketing involves creating a website, video, email message, or other marketing event that is so infectious that customers will want to pass it along to their friends. One observer describes viral marketing as "addictive, self-propagating advertisement that lives on websites, blogs, cellphones, message boards, and even in real-world stunts."[49] Because customers pass the message or promotion along to others, viral marketing can be very inexpensive. And when the information comes from a friend, the recipient is much more likely to open and read it.

Although marketers usually have little control over where their viral messages end up, a well-concocted viral campaign can gain vast exposure. Consider Hellmann's 2009 campaign that was built on Canadians' growing concerns about health and diet and challenged Canadians' assumptions about their food supply. Labelled "Eat Real, Eat Local," Hellmann's developed a viral video that uncovered some startling facts about the Canadian food system. It also used an online portal, EatRealEatLocal.ca. The video struck a chord, and it received over 60 000 hits by mid-July 2009 on YouTube. Online chatter is

Hellmann's used a viral video and this portal to inform Canadians about the vulnerability of our food supply. The campaign helped position the brand as one that is making a difference in Canadians' lives.

83 percent positive, and Hellmann's hopes the campaign will position the brand as one people recognize for trying to make a difference.[50]

Creating or Participating in Online Social Networks

Online social networks

Online social communities—blogs, social networking websites, or even virtual worlds—where people socialize or exchange information and opinions.

As we discussed in Chapter 6, the popularity of the Internet has resulted in a rash of **online social networks** or *web communities*. Countless independent and commercial websites have arisen that give consumers online places to congregate, socialize, and exchange views and information. These days, it seems, almost everyone is buddying up on MySpace or Facebook, tuning in to the day's hottest videos on YouTube, or even living a surprisingly real fantasy life through an avatar on Second Life. And, of course, wherever consumers congregate, marketers will surely follow. More and more marketers are now starting to ride the huge social networking wave.

Marketers can engage in online communities in two ways: They can participate in existing web communities or they can set up their own. Joining existing networks seems easiest. Thus, many major brands—from Burger King, Honda, and Motorola to Estée Lauder and Victoria's Secret—have set up MySpace pages and profiles. Burger King, for instance, has amassed more than 120 000 MySpace "friends," fellow users who have chosen to associate themselves with this profile. Similarly, the Apple Students group on Facebook, which offers information and deals on Apple products, has more than 500 000 members. And companies by the dozens are now hanging up virtual shingles in Second Life—from Nike and Coca-Cola to Dell, Toyota, IBM, 1-800-FLOWERS.COM, and H&R Block.

Although the large online social networks such as MySpace and Facebook have grabbed most of the headlines, a new breed of more focused niche networks has recently emerged. These more focused networks cater to the needs of smaller communities of like-minded people, making them ideal vehicles for marketers who want to target special interest groups (see Real Marketing 17.1).

But participating successfully in existing online social networks presents challenges. First, online social networks are new and results are hard to measure. Most companies are still experimenting with how to use them effectively. Second, such web communities are largely user controlled. The company's goal is to make the brand a part of consumers' conversations and their lives. However, marketers can't simply muscle their way into consumers' online interactions—they need to earn the right to be there. "You're talking about conversations between groups of friends," says one analyst. "And in those conversations a brand has no right to be there, unless the conversation is already about that brand." Says another expert, "Being force-fed irrelevant content, or feeling tricked into taking in a brand, is a major turn-off." Rather than intruding, marketers must learn to become a valued part of the online experience.[51]

When it comes to online networks, it's not enough just to be there. For example, when Toyota's Scion first opened a Second Life showroom last year, it quickly became a top destination. But only a few months later, Second Life residents had largely deserted the showroom. Toyota's mistake? It failed to understand that driving adds little value in a virtual world where Second Life avatars can walk underwater, fly, and "beam" themselves around. Instead, as in any other marketing endeavour, companies participating in web communities must learn how to add value for consumers to capture value in return.

To avoid the mysteries and challenges of building a presence on existing online social networks, many companies are now launching their own targeted web communities. For example, Coca-Cola has developed a Sprite Yard cellphone network—available to web-ready phones—where members can set up profiles, post pictures, and meet new friends. On the Nike Plus website, some 200 000 runners upload, track, and compare their performances. More than half visit the site at least four times a week, and Nike plans eventually to have 15 percent or more of the world's 100 million runners actively participating in the Nike Plus online community.

Real Marketing 17.1

Online Social Networks: Targeting Niches of Like-Minded People

Marketers who think bigger is better may want to reconsider, at least when it comes to online social networks. Although giant networks such as MySpace and Facebook get all the attention these days, social networks focused on topics as remote as knitting or bird watching can present marketers with strong targeting opportunities:

When jet-setters began flocking to an exclusive social networking website reserved for the rich, they got the attention of an online community's most valuable ally: advertisers. The invitation-only site, ASmallWorld.net, has 300 000 select members who have become a magnet for companies that make luxury goods and are trying to reach people who can afford them. The site's biggest advertisers include Burberry, Cartier, and Land Rover. Cognac maker Rémy Martin last month threw a tasting party for the site's elite members, at which its top-shelf, $1800-a-bottle liquor flowed freely.

Thousands of social networking sites have popped up to cater to specific interests, backgrounds, professions, and age groups. Nightclub frequenters can converge at DontStayIn.com. Wine connoisseurs have formed Snooth.com, and people going through divorce can commiserate at Divorce360.com.

More and more, marketers are taking a chance on smaller sites that could be more relevant to their products. AT&T, for example, recently promoted one of its global cellphones on WAYN.com (short for "Where are you now?"), a social network for international travellers. While AT&T advertises on the bigger sites like MySpace to reach a large audience quickly, the wireless carrier is also turning to niche networks, "where your ads are more meaningful—those are the real gems," says a social networking expert.

There's at least one social network for just about every interest or hobby. Fuzzster.com is for pet lovers, OnLoq.com is for hip-hop fans, Jango.com lets music fans find others with similar tastes, and Passport-Stamp.com is one of several sites for avid travellers. Some cater to the obscure. Passions Network, an online dating community with 600 000 members, has 106 groups for specific interests, including "Star Trek" fans, truckers, atheists, and people who are shy. The most popular group is a dating site for the overweight. Membership on niche networking sites varies greatly, ranging from a few hundred to a few million. Flixster.com has 40 million members who rate movies and gossip about actors.

According to a 2009 study from Ipsos Reid on social networking, 56 percent of Canadians have a profile on an online social network, up from 39 percent a year earlier. The author of the study, Mark Laver, notes, "Social networks get a lot of press and rightfully so; they are becoming the communications tool of the 21st century." Facebook continues to be the dominant site in Canada. While there has been a lot of hype about Twitter, only 26 percent of Canadians are aware of the service and only 6 percent use the tool. Social networks tend to be dominated by younger consumers, and women are slightly more likely to have a social network profile than men (59 percent compared to 52 percent). A running tally of emerging social networks, now upward of 7000 by one estimate, suggests an explosive market. That's both a golden opportunity and a colossal headache for brands trying to nail down the best new network for their campaigns.

Although the niche sites have fewer members than megasites such as MySpace (more than 110 million active profiles) and Facebook (59 million), they contain dedicated communities of like-minded people. And as on the bigger networks, members can build personalized pages and use them to share information, photos, and news with friends. That makes the niche sites ideal vehicles for marketers who want to target special interest groups.

The niche sites often provide a better marketing message environment. "Because members of niche social networks share common interests and experiences, they tend to spend more time on the site and contribute to the group by chatting and posting comments," notes an online consultant. On bigger sites, "members tend to be less involved . . . and are therefore less appealing to advertisers." Also, "the bigger sites have become so cluttered and overrun with advertisers that members are used to tuning stuff out, even personalized ads. . . . But on networking sites that have a self-selecting demographic, people tend to trust the content, including ads."

Not all niche networks welcome marketers. Sermo.com—a social networking site at which some 65 000 licensed physicians consult with colleagues specializing in areas ranging from dermatology to psychiatry—allows no marketing. However, for a fee, companies can gain access to Sermo.com data and member discussions. "They can monitor online discussions, with the doctors' names omitted, or see a tally of topics being discussed at the site to determine what's rising or falling in popularity," notes a health care industry analyst.

Still, most of the niche sites offer unique campaign opportunities to brands. Sites like imeem.com—a social

When it comes to marketing through online social networking sites, smaller might be better. Niche site imeem.com works with sponsors such as Burger King that target its younger and edgier membership community. "Relevance trumps size," says one expert.

thoughts on tour to imeem.com members through his T-Mobile sidekick.

The more-focused audiences offered by such niche networks are increasingly popular with brands because "relevance," says one consultant, "trumps size." But how brands execute social networking campaigns is as important as where they do it. Marketers must be careful not to become too commercial or too intrusive. Keeping sites hip and unencumbered by advertising is a balancing act for both the brands and the social networks. The best approach is not to market to network members but to interact with them on topics of mutual interest. Says one online marketer, "The real way of getting into social media is you don't advertise, you participate in the community."

Sources: Information on Canadians' usage of social networks from Martin Slofstra, "Social Networks Experiencing Surge in Popularity," *ExecDigital*, June 19, 2009, accessed at http://www.execdigital.ca/Social-networks-experiencing-surge-in-popularity_27260.aspx, July 2009. Other portions adapted from Betsey Cummings, "Why Marketers Love Small Social Networks," *Brandweek*, April 27, 2008, accessed at www.brandweek.com; with adapted extracts, quotes, and other information from Kim Hart, "Online Networking Goes Small, and Sponsors Follow," *Washington Post*, December 29, 2007; p. D1; and Jessica E. Vascellaro, "Social Networking Goes Professional," *Wall Street Journal*, August 28, 2007, p. D1. See also Heather Green, "Arts and Crafts Find New Life Online," *BusinessWeek*, January 14, 2008, pp. 60–61; and Paula Lehman, "Social Networks That Break a Sweat," *BusinessWeek*, February 4, 2008, p. 68.

network where "fans and artists discover new music, videos, and photos, and share their tastes with friends"—are carving out their niches and actively soliciting advertising dollars. "We tend to skew younger and edgier," with a demographic of 13–24, says imeem's chief marketer. An ever-growing niche of more than 100 million users interact with imeem, helping it to attract big-name sponsors such as Burger King, Scion, Nokia, and T-Mobile, which sponsor special features and events. For example, one promotion involved artist J. Holiday texting his

Using Email

Email is an important and growing online marketing tool. A recent study of ad, brand, and marketing managers found that nearly half of all the companies surveyed use email marketing to reach customers. To compete effectively in this ever-more-cluttered email environment, marketers are designing "enriched" email messages—animated, interactive, and personalized messages full of streaming audio and video. They then target these attention-grabbers more carefully to those who want them and will act upon them.

But there's a dark side to the growing use of email marketing. The explosion of **spam**—unsolicited, unwanted commercial email messages that clog up our inboxes—has produced consumer irritation and frustration. Last year, for the first time, the total number of spam emails sent worldwide surpassed the number of person-to-person emails. According to one research company, spam now accounts for between 80 and 95 percent of all email sent.[52] Email marketers walk a fine line between adding value for consumers and being intrusive.

To address these concerns, most legitimate marketers now practise *permission-based email marketing*, sending email pitches only to customers who "opt in." Financial services firms such as Charles Schwab use configurable email systems that let customers choose what they want to get. Others, such as Yahoo! or Amazon.ca, include long lists of opt-in boxes for different categories of marketing material. Amazon.ca targets opt-in customers with a limited number of helpful "we thought you'd like to know" messages based on their

Spam
Unsolicited, unwanted commercial email messages.

expressed preferences and previous purchases. Few customers object and many actually welcome such promotional messages.

When used properly, email can be the ultimate direct-marketing medium. Blue-chip marketers such as Amazon.ca, Mountain Equipment Co-op, Dell, Office Depot, Rbc, and others use it regularly and with great success. Email lets these marketers send highly targeted, tightly personalized, relationship-building messages to consumers who actually *want* to receive them. Consider Scotts:

> Scotts, the plant, lawn, and garden products company, designs its email marketing around the customer's preferences, season of the year, and the region of the recipient. When individuals sign up for the email program, Scotts asks them a series of questions about where they live and their particular plant and garden interests. It then uses this information to create content and offers that resonate with each recipient. For example, a city dweller, who may not even have a lawn, gets advice and tips on the care and feeding of houseplants and terrace shrubs, whereas a homeowner in the southwest receives information on maintaining a lawn or garden in a hot and arid climate. To deliver this level of customization, Scotts has developed an email template that allows it to incorporate appropriate, personal content into an otherwise mass emailing. Far from thinking of the Scotts online missives as irritating spam, recipients grow to rely on them as a valuable problem-solving tool.[53]

Given its targeting effectiveness and low costs, email can be an outstanding marketing investment. According to the Direct Marketing Association, email marketing produces a return on investment 40 to 50 percent higher than other forms of direct-marketing media.[54]

The Promise and Challenges of Online Marketing

Online marketing continues to offer both great promise and many challenges for the future. Its most ardent apostles still envision a time when the Internet and online marketing will replace magazines, newspapers, and even stores as sources for information and buying. Most marketers, however, hold a more realistic view. To be sure, online marketing will become a successful business model for some companies—Internet firms such as Amazon, eBay, and Google, and direct-marketing companies such as Dell. However, for most companies, online marketing will remain just one important approach to the marketplace that works alongside other approaches in a fully integrated marketing mix.

Despite the many challenges, companies large and small are quickly integrating online marketing into their marketing strategies and mixes. As it continues to grow, online marketing will prove to be a powerful direct marketing tool for improving sales, communicating company and product information, delivering products and services, and building deeper customer relationships.

5 PUBLIC POLICY ISSUES IN DIRECT MARKETING

Direct marketers and their customers usually enjoy mutually rewarding relationships. Occasionally, however, a darker side emerges. The aggressive and sometimes shady tactics of a few direct marketers can bother or harm consumers, giving the entire industry a black eye. Abuses range from simple excesses that irritate consumers to instances of unfair practices or even outright deception and fraud. The direct-marketing industry has also faced growing invasion-of-privacy concerns, and online marketers must deal with Internet security issues.

Irritation, Unfairness, Deception, and Fraud

Direct-marketing excesses sometimes annoy or offend consumers. Most of us dislike direct-response TV commercials that are too loud, too long, and too insistent. Our mailboxes fill up with unwanted junk mail, our inboxes bulge with unwanted spam, and our computer screens flash with unwanted banner or pop-up ads.

Beyond irritating consumers, some direct marketers have been accused of taking unfair advantage of impulsive or less-sophisticated buyers. TV shopping channels and program-long "infomercials" targeting television-addicted shoppers seem to be the worst culprits. They feature smooth-talking hosts, elaborately staged demonstrations, claims of drastic price reductions, "while they last" time limitations, and unequalled ease of purchase to inflame buyers who have low sales resistance.

Worse yet, so-called heat merchants design mailers and write copy intended to mislead buyers. Even well-known direct mailers have been accused of deceiving consumers. A few years back, sweepstakes promoter Publishers Clearing House paid US$52 million to settle accusations that its high-pressure mailings confused or misled consumers, especially the elderly, into believing that they had won prizes or would win if they bought the company's magazines. Even the venerable *Reader's Digest* has had to pay restitution to consumers for alleged deceptive marketing in its sweepstakes contests.[55]

Fraudulent schemes, such as investment scams or phony collections for charity, have also multiplied in recent years. Internet fraud, including identity theft and financial scams, has become a serious problem. The 2007 Internet Crime Complaint Report presented a troubling picture of Internet-based scams in Canada. The report grouped Canada alongside Nigeria and Romania as hotbeds of Internet crime, and Canada was cited as the place where online crimes affecting U.S. residents originated the most. The Edmonton Police Service claims that more than half of Canadians have lost money to online fraud, while PhoneBusters reported that victims lost $4.6 million to just one type of fraud in the month of January alone. Reasons for this problem include weak legislation and lax punishments for such crimes. Moreover, many of the rules that can be applied to the Internet were developed in the 1970s, and technology has far outstripped the ability of such rules to deter online crime.[56]

One common form of Internet fraud is *phishing*, a type of identity theft that uses deceptive emails and fraudulent websites to fool users into divulging their personal data. According to email security firm MessageLabs, one in 87 emails is now tagged as a phishing scam, compared with one in 500 a year ago. Although many consumers are now aware of such schemes, phishing can be extremely costly to those caught in the net. PhoneBusters, the Canadian antifraud call centre run by the RCMP, the Competition Bureau, and the Ontario Provincial Police, warns that recessions are "boom times for scammers." In these tough economic times, Canadians are falling for more scams than ever before, whether they are the famous Nigerian transfer payments letters or ploys offering jobs for a fee or lottery scams. Fraud also damages the brand identities of legitimate online marketers who have worked to build user confidence in web and email transactions.[57]

Many consumers also worry about online security. They fear that unscrupulous snoopers will eavesdrop on their online transactions, picking up personal information or intercepting credit and debit card numbers. A 2009 survey of more than 1000 Canadian youths aged 9 to 17 conducted by Microsoft Canada and Youthography found that more than three-quarters of them are very careful about the personal information they give out online. Parents are increasingly concerned about their children's online activities. The survey reported that 84 percent of the respondents said that they have had a discussion with their parents about the potential dangers of risky online behaviour.

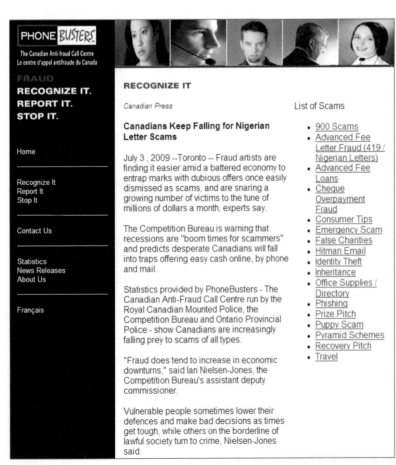

PhoneBusters provides a wealth of information to help Canadians avoid online scams and telephone fraud.

Eighty-six percent report that their parents have taken measures to ensure they are safe online, such as locating the computer in visible locations like the family room or kitchen. Nonetheless, the survey also found that while Canadian youth are aware of potential dangers, too many still engage in risky behaviours while online, such as posting too much personal information like pictures, home towns, and the name of their school or their email address on social networking sites. Almost a third have accepted a friend request from a stranger.[58]

In another survey, 68 percent of participants said they were concerned that their credit or debit card information will be stolen if they use their cards for online purchases. More than one-third also see the Internet as the medium most likely to result in identity theft.[59] Internet shoppers are also concerned about contracting annoying or harmful viruses, spyware, and other "malware" (malicious software). A recent Google study of 4.5 million websites found that 10 percent of them were downloading malware:[60]

> Spyware programs track where you go on the Internet and clutter your screen with annoying pop-up advertisements for everything from pornography to wireless phone plans. Spyware can get stuck in your computer's hard drive as you shop, chat, or download a song. It might arrive attached to that clever video you just nabbed at no charge. Web security company McAfee estimates that nearly three-quarters of all sites listed in response to Internet searches for popular phrases like "free screen savers" or "digital music" attempt to install some form of advertising software on visitors' computers. Once lodged there, spyware can sap a PC's processing power, slow its functioning, and even cause it to crash.

Invasion of Privacy

Invasion of privacy is perhaps the toughest public policy issue now confronting the direct marketing industry. Consumers often benefit from database marketing—they receive more offers that are closely matched to their interests. However, many critics worry that marketers may know *too* much about consumers' lives and that they may use this knowledge to take unfair advantage of consumers. At some point, they claim, the extensive use of databases intrudes on consumer privacy.

These days, it seems that almost every time consumers enter a sweepstakes, apply for a credit card, visit a website, or order products by mail, telephone, or the Internet, their names enter some company's already bulging database. Using sophisticated computer technologies, direct marketers can use these databases to "microtarget" their selling efforts. *Online privacy* causes special concerns. Most online marketers have become skilled at collecting and analyzing detailed consumer information. For example, behavioural tracking systems use data about consumers' web travels to deliver relevant ads to them. As web tracking technology grows in sophistication, digital privacy experts worry that unscrupulous marketers will use such information to take unfair advantage of unknowing customers.

A Need for Action

In response to these concerns, the Canadian government passed the *Personal Information Protection and Electronic Documents Act* (*PIPEDA*) in 2001. It came into full force in 2004. The act is based on four key principles:

- *Consumer knowledge and consent.* Consumers must know that information about them is being gathered and they must provide consent before firms can collect, use, or disclose consumers' personal information.

- *Limitations.* Firms can only collect and use information appropriate to the transaction being undertaken. For example, if a firm needs to mail you something, it can ask for your home address, but it may not request additional information unrelated to this task.

- *Accuracy.* Firms must be sure that the information they gather is recorded accurately. Firms must appoint a privacy officer to be responsible for this task. For example, to comply with this portion of the legislation, Peter Cullen was recently designated as the new corporate privacy officer at Rbc.

- *Right to access.* Finally, individuals have the right to know what information is being held about them. They can also demand that errors in their personal information be corrected, and they may request that their personal information be withdrawn from a firm's database.

In 2009, the Government of Canada announced that it is delivering on its commitment to protect consumers and businesses from the most dangerous and damaging forms of spam. It proposed the *Electronic Commerce Protection Act* (*ECPA*), legislation designed to boost confidence in online commerce by protecting privacy and addressing the personal security concerns that are associated with spam, counterfeit websites, and spyware. The proposed legislation also amends *PIPEDA*, which covers online privacy in detail and contains many provisions relevant to email marketing.[61]

Many companies have responded to consumer privacy and security concerns with actions of their own. Still others are taking an industrywide approach. For example, TRUSTe, a not-for-profit self-regulatory organization, works with many large corporate sponsors, including Microsoft, AT&T, and Intuit, to audit companies' privacy and security measures and help consumers navigate the Web safely. According to the company's website, "TRUSTe believes that an environment of mutual trust and openness will help make and keep the Internet a free, comfortable, and richly diverse community for everyone." To reassure consumers, the company lends its "trustmark" stamp of approval to websites that meet its privacy and security standards.[62]

The Canadian Marketing Association, which has 800 corporate members, also provides consumers with a wealth of information and smart shopping tips. It posts pages that help consumers know how to deal with online issues such as spam, identifying fraudlent offers, and protecting privacy. Ethical corporations are concerned with poor practices since they know that direct-marketing abuses will lead to increasingly negative consumer attitudes, lower response rates, and calls for more restrictive provincial and federal legislation. Most direct marketers want the same things that consumers want: honest and well-designed marketing offers targeted only toward consumers who will appreciate and respond to them. Direct marketing is just too expensive to waste on consumers who don't want it.

REVIEWING OBJECTIVES AND KEY TERMS

mymarketinglab | Audio Chapter Summary

This chapter is the last of four chapters covering the final marketing mix element—promotion. The previous chapters dealt with advertising, publicity, personal selling, and sales promotion. This one investigates the burgeoning field of direct and online marketing.

OBJECTIVE 1 **Define direct marketing and discuss its benefits to customers and companies.**

Direct marketing consists of direct connections with carefully targeted individual consumers to both obtain an immediate response and cultivate lasting customer relationships. Using detailed *customer databases*, direct marketers tailor their offers and communications to the needs of narrowly defined segments or even individual buyers.

For buyers, direct marketing is convenient, easy to use, and private. It gives buyers ready access to a wealth of products and information at home and around the globe. Direct marketing is also immediate and interactive, allowing buyers to create exactly the configuration of information, products, or services they desire, then order them on the spot. For sellers, direct marketing is a powerful tool for building customer relationships. Using database marketing, today's marketers can target small groups or individual consumers, tailor offers to individual needs, and promote these offers through personalized communications. It also offers them a low-cost, efficient alternative for reaching their markets. As a result of these advantages to both buyers and sellers, direct marketing has become the fastest-growing form of marketing.

OBJECTIVE 2 **Identify and discuss the major forms of direct marketing.**

The main forms of direct marketing include personal selling, direct-mail marketing, catalogue marketing, telephone marketing, direct-response television marketing, kiosk marketing, and online marketing. We discussed personal selling in the previous chapter.

Direct-mail marketing, the largest form of direct marketing, consists of the company sending an offer, announcement, reminder, or other item to a person at a specific address. Recently, new forms of "mail delivery" have become popular, such as email and text messages. Some marketers rely on *catalogue marketing*—selling through catalogues mailed to a select list of customers, made available in stores, or accessed on the Web. *Telephone marketing* consists of using the telephone to sell directly to consumers. *Direct-response television marketing* has two forms: *direct-response advertising* (or infomercials) and *home shopping channels*. *Kiosks* are information and ordering machines that direct marketers place in stores, airports, and other locations. In recent years, a number of new digital direct marketing technologies have emerged, including *mobile marketing*, *podcasts* and *vodcasts*, and *interactive TV*. *Online marketing* involves online channels that digitally link sellers with consumers.

OBJECTIVE 3 **Explain how companies have responded to the Internet and other powerful new technologies with online marketing strategies.**

Online marketing is the fastest-growing form of direct marketing. The *Internet* enables consumers and companies to access and share huge amounts of information with just a few mouse clicks. In turn, the Internet has given marketers a whole new way to create value for customers and build customer relationships. It's hard to find a company today that doesn't have a substantial web marketing presence.

Online consumer buying continues to grow at a healthy rate. Most North American online users now use the Internet to shop. Perhaps more importantly, the Internet influences offline shopping. Thus, smart marketers are employing integrated multichannel strategies that use the Web to drive sales to other marketing channels.

OBJECTIVE 4 **Discuss how companies go about conducting online marketing to profitably deliver more value to customers.**

Companies of all types are now engaged in online marketing. The Internet gave birth to the pure-play dot-coms, which operate only online. In addition, many traditional brick-and-mortar companies have now added online marketing operations, transforming themselves into *hybrid or click-and-mortar companies*. Many click-and-mortar companies are now having more online success than their click-only competitors.

Companies can conduct online marketing in four ways: creating a website, placing ads and promotions online, setting up or participating in web communities and online social networks, or using email. The first step typically is to set up a website. Beyond simply setting up a site, however, companies must make their sites engaging, easy to use, and useful to attract visitors, hold them, and bring them back again.

Online marketers can use various forms of online advertising and promotion to build their Internet brands or to attract visitors to their websites. Forms of online promotion include online display advertising, search-related advertising, content sponsorships, alliances and affiliate programs, and viral marketing, the Internet version of word-of-mouth marketing. Online marketers can also participate in online social networks and other web communities, which take advantage of the C2C properties of the Web. Finally, email marketing has become a fast-growing tool for both B2C and B2B marketers. Whatever direct-marketing tools they use, marketers must work hard to integrate them into a cohesive marketing effort.

OBJECTIVE 5 **Overview the public policy and ethical issues presented by direct marketing.**

Direct marketers and their customers usually enjoy mutually rewarding relationships. Sometimes, however, direct marketing presents a darker side. The aggressive and sometimes shady tactics of a few direct marketers can bother or harm consumers, giving the entire industry a black eye. Abuses range from simple excesses that irritate consumers to instances of unfair practices or even outright deception and fraud. New legislation will help address these concerns. Such concerns also call for strong action by marketers to curb direct-marketing abuses. In the end, most direct marketers want the same things that consumers want: honest and well-designed marketing offers targeted only toward consumers who will appreciate and respond to them.

KEY TERMS

Objective 1

Direct marketing   550

Customer database   553

Objective 2

Direct-mail marketing   555

Catalogue marketing   556

Telephone marketing   557

Direct-response television marketing   558

Objective 3

Online marketing   562

Internet   562

Online companies   563

Hybrid or click-and-mortar
companies   563

Business-to-consumer (B2C) online
marketing   563

Business-to-business (B2B) online
marketing   564

Consumer-to-consumer (C2C) online
marketing   565

Consumer-to-business (C2B) online
marketing   566

Objective 4

Corporate (or brand) website   567

Marketing website   567

Online advertising   568

Viral marketing   569

Online social networks   570

Spam   572

DISCUSSING THE CONCEPTS

1. Discuss the benefits of direct marketing to both buyers and sellers.

2. A local rug cleaning company has contacted you for advice on setting up its customer database. It needs this database for customer relationship management and for direct marketing of new products and services. Describe the qualities and features it must consider for an effective database and how it might go about creating one.

3. Name and describe the major forms of direct marketing.

4. Explain the ways in which companies can conduct online marketing.

5. Compare and contrast the different forms of online advertising. What factors should a company consider in deciding among these different forms?

6. What has been done to protect Canadians' privacy in the online environment?

APPLYING THE CONCEPTS

1. Visit your favourite retail website and evaluate the site according to the seven Cs of effective website design.

2. Visit Nike's website at http://nikeid.nike.com and design your own shoe. Print out your shoe design and bring it to class. Do you think the price is appropriate for the value received from being able to customize your shoe? Identify and describe two other websites that allow buyers to customize products.

3. Consumers can register with the National Do Not Call List to avoid unwanted phone solicitations from marketers. But what can consumers do to reduce unsolicited mail and email? Find out what options consumers have and report your findings.

FOCUS ON TECHNOLOGY

Electronic payment systems and databases are essential for today's competitive marketplace. Databases are essential for government and not-for-profit entities, too. But they can also create problems for organizations and individuals. Individuals ranging from military veterans to T.J. Maxx shoppers may suffer from identity theft following significant security breaches. Some data security breaches occur from sloppy security practices, ranging from laptops being stolen to high-tech electronic capture of information from companies' data systems. While you've no doubt seen headlines of large security breaches involving millions of personal and financial files, small businesses are just as vulnerable. A recent examination of 500 security breach cases concluded that more than half occurred in the retail and food-and-beverage industries. The same study concluded that in 90 percent of the cases, data breaches could have been prevented by using adequate security measures.

1. Find articles about two data security breaches in the news. How did the breaches occur and who is potentially affected by them?

2. What can organizations and businesses do to ensure adequate data security for their members and customers? What can consumers do to protect themselves if their personal information has been compromised?

FOCUS ON ETHICS

"Six books for 99¢," "12 CDs for $1.00," or "7 DVDs for FREE!" We've all seen these offers—but are they too good to be true? The Book-of-the-Month Club and Columbia House are just two well-known examples of the many buying clubs out there. These clubs can cause problems for consumers who do not always fully understand what they are getting themselves into. By accepting such offers, consumers may unwittingly join a "pre-notification negative option plan." Under these plans, if you don't tell the marketer that you don't want additional merchandise sent to you it is sent automatically and you are billed for it. Some clubs require a minimum number of purchases at regular prices before you can cancel membership. Critics claim that marketers offer enticing incentives to lure consumers in but are deceptive about the membership obligations.

1. Search the Internet for a book club, a music club, and a movie club that offer negative option plans. Describe the incentives offered to get consumers to join, the obligations of membership, and the mechanism by which members can deny future merchandise. Does that club give adequate information for consumers to understand their obligations or is some part of the offer deceiving?

2. In 1996, Parliament attempted to outlaw the practice of negative option billing after cable companies added new specialty services to their bundles of services. The federal law passed in 1999, and the Ontario government followed suit by outlawing negative option billing in July 2005. Despite this legislation, the *Toronto Star* reported in 2009 that these practices are alive and well.[63] Learn about these rules and discuss concerns the government and consumers have with this direct-marketing tactic.

MARKETING BY THE NUMBERS

Many companies are realizing the efficiency of telemarketing in the face of soaring sales force costs. Whereas an average cost of a business-to-business sales call by an outside salesperson costs more than $300, the cost of a telemarketing sales call can be as little as $5 to $20. And telemarketers can make 20 to 33 decision-maker contacts per day compared to a salesperson's four contacts per day. This has gotten the attention of many business-to-business marketers—where telemarketing can be very effective.

1. Refer to Appendix 3: Marketing by the Numbers to determine the marketing return on sales (marketing ROS) and return on marketing investment (marketing

ROI) for Company A and Company B in the chart below. Which company is performing better? Explain.

	Company A (sales force only)	Company B (telemarketing only)
Net sales	$1 000 000	$850 000
Cost of goods sold	500 000	425 000
Sales expenses	300 000	100 000

2. Should all companies consider reducing their sales forces in favour of telemarketing? Discuss the pros and cons of this action.

VIDEO CASE

Google

It's mind-boggling to think that only 20 years ago a company like Google was not within the realm of possibility. Yet when the World Wide Web went online, the foundation was set for Google's mission: to organize the world's information and make it universally accessible and useful.

Google was not the first search engine, but it has become the most successful. Its primary reason for success has been its customer-focused strategy. For Google, there are two basic types of customers. For the Internet search services customer, Google has been relentless in developing products that are both innovative and user-friendly. Google now offers dozens of services, including foreign language translation, stock quotes, maps, phone book listings, images, video, and news headlines. And the most amazing thing about these services? They're all free.

Google can offer all of its services free of charge because of its second customer, advertisers. Google has

turned Internet advertising upside down. Today, products such as AdWords (keyword search advertising) and AdSense (a method that generates only the most relevant ads for client websites) are breaking new ground because they result in ads that are actually useful and helpful to consumers.

After viewing the Google video, answer the following online marketing questions:

1. Brainstorm the many benefits that Google provides for consumers.

2. Brainstorm the many benefits that Google provides for online marketers.

3. Visit www.google.com. For each of the four major emarketing domains, discuss Google's presence.

Visit MyMarketingLab at www.pearsoned.ca/mymarketinglab to view the video segment related to this case.

COMPANY CASE

StubHub: Ticket Scalping, a Respectable Endeavour?

As the rock band KISS returned to the United States for the final performances of its "Alive/35" tour in the summer of 2008, Roger felt like reliving some old memories. Just because he was in his 50s didn't mean he was too old to rock. After all, he was an original KISS fan dating back to the 70s. It had been years since he had gone to a concert for any band. But on the day the KISS tickets went on sale, he grabbed a lawn chair and headed to his local Ticketmaster outlet to "camp out" in line. Roger knew that the terminal, located inside a large chain music store, wouldn't open until 10 a.m. when tickets went on sale. He got to the store at 6 a.m. to find only three people ahead of him. "Fantastic," Roger thought. With so few people in front of him, getting good seats would be a snap. Maybe he would even score something close to the stage.

By the time the three people in front of him had their tickets it was 10:13. As the clerk typed away on the Ticketmaster computer terminal, Roger couldn't believe what he heard. No tickets were available. The show at the Palms Resort in Las Vegas was sold out. Dejected, Roger turned to leave. As he made his way out the door, another customer said, "You can always try StubHub." As the fellow KISS fan

explained what StubHub was, it occurred to Roger that the world had become a very different place with respect to buying concert tickets.

Indeed, in this Internet age buying tickets for live events has changed dramatically since Roger's concert-going days. Originators such as Ticketmaster now sell tickets online for everything from Broadway shows to sporting events. Increasingly, however, event tickets are resold through websites such as eBay, RazorGator, TicketsNow, Craigslist, and StubHub, the fastest-growing company in the business. Various industry observers estimate that as many as 30 percent of all event tickets are resold. This secondary market for online sports and entertainment tickets has grown to billions of dollars in annual revenues.

And although prices are all over the map, tickets for sold-out hot events routinely sell for double or triple their face value. In some cases, the markup is astronomical. The nationwide average price for kids to see Miley Cyrus was $249, up from about $50 for the highest face value seat. A pair of tickets to see Bruce Springsteen at the Washington, D.C., Verizon Center set some back as much as $2000. Prices for a seat at Super Bowl XLII in Phoenix, one of the hottest ticket resale events of all time, were as high as $13 000. And one UK Led Zeppelin fan with obviously far too much money on his hands paid over $160 000 for a pair of Led Zeppelin tickets close enough to see a geriatric Robert Plant perspire. Extreme cases? Yes. But not uncommon.

When most people think of buying a ticket from a reseller, they probably envision a seedy scalper standing in the shadows near an event venue. But scalping is moving mainstream. While the Internet and other technologies have allowed professional ticket agents to purchase event tickets in larger numbers, anyone with a computer and broadband connection can instantly become a scalper. And regular folks, even fans, are routinely doing so. "Because we allowed people to buy four [tickets], if they only need two they put the other two up for sale," said Dave Holmes, manager for Coldplay. This dynamic, occurring for events across the board, has dramatically increased the number of ticket resellers.

STUBHUB ENTERS THE GAME

With the ticket resale market booming, StubHub started operations in 2000 as Liquid Seats. It all started with an idea by two first-year students at the Stanford Graduate School of Business. Eric Baker and Jeff Fluhr had been observing the hysteria on the ticket resale market. In their opinion, the market was highly fragmented and rampant with fraud and distorted pricing. Two buyers sitting side-by-side at the same event might find they'd paid wildly different prices for essentially the same product. Even with heavy hitter eBay as the biggest ticket reseller at the time, Baker and Fluhr saw an opportunity to create a system that would bring buyers and sellers together in a more efficient manner.

They entered their proposal in a new-business plan competition. Fluhr was utterly convinced the concept would work—so much so that he withdrew the proposal from the competition and dropped out of school to launch the business. At a time when dot-coms were dropping like flies, this might have seemed like a very poor decision. But Fluhr ultimately became CEO of StubHub, the leader and fastest-growing company of a $10 billion-a-year industry.

Home to over 300 employees, StubHub uses 20 000 square feet of prime office space in San Francisco's pricey financial district, seven satellite offices, and two call centres. Even more telling is the company's growth. In November of 2006, a little over six years after starting, StubHub sold its 5 millionth ticket. Just over one year later it sold its 10 millionth ticket. And six months after that, in June 2008, StubHub rewarded the buyer and seller of the 15 millionth ticket sold with a pair of $5000 gift certificates for its website. In its first few years of operations, StubHub posted a staggering growth rate of more than 3200 percent. According to comScore Networks, a firm that tracks web traffic, StubHub.com is the leading site among more than a dozen competitors in the ticket resale category.

THE DEVIL IS IN THE DETAILS

StubHub's model is showing that buying a ticket on the aftermarket doesn't have to mean paying a huge price premium. Sharing his own experience, a *New York Times* writer provides his own StubHub experience:

> To test the system I started with the New York Yankees. A series with the Seattle Mariners was coming up, just before the Yankees left town for a long road trip. Good tickets would be scarce. I went to StubHub. Lots of tickets there, many priced stratospherically. I settled on two Main Box seats in Section 313, Row G. They were in the right-field corner, just one section above field level. The price was $35 each, or face price for a season ticketholder. This was tremendous value for a sold-out game. I registered with StubHub, creating a user name and password, ordered the tickets, then sealed the deal by providing my credit card number. An email message arrived soon after, confirming the order and informing me that StubHub was contacting the seller to arrange for shipment. My card would not be charged until the seller had confirmed to StubHub the time and method of delivery. A second email message arrived a day later giving the delivery details. The tickets arrived on the Thursday before the game, and the seller was paid by StubHub on confirmation of delivery. On Saturday, under a clear, sunny sky, the Yankees were sending a steady stream of screaming line drives into the right-field corner.

From the beginning, Baker and Fluhr set out to provide better options for both buyers and sellers by making StubHub different. Like eBay, StubHub has no ticket inventory of its own, reducing its risk. It simply provides the venue that gives buyers and sellers the opportunity to come together. But it's the differences, perhaps, that have allowed StubHub to achieve such success in such a short period of time.

One of the first differences noticed by buyers and sellers is StubHub's ticket-listing procedure. Sellers can list tickets by auction or at a fixed price, a price that declines as the event gets closer. Whereas some sites charge fees just to list tickets, StubHub lists them for free. Thus, initially, the seller has no risk whatsoever. StubHub's system is simpler than most, splitting the fee burden between buyer and seller. It charges sellers a 15 percent commission and buyers a 10 percent fee.

StubHub's website structure also creates a marketplace that comes closer to pure competition than any other reseller's website. All sellers are equal on StubHub, as ticket listings are identical in appearance and seller identity is kept anonymous. StubHub even holds the shipping method constant, via FedEx. This makes the purchase process much more transparent for buyers. They can browse tickets by event, venue, and section. Comparison shopping is very easy as shoppers can simultaneously view different pairs of tickets in the same section, even in the same row.

Although prices still vary, this system makes tickets more of a commodity and allows market forces to narrow the gap considerably from one seller to another. In fact, while tickets often sell for high prices, this reselling model can also have the effect of pushing ticket prices down below face value. Many experts believe that the emergence of Internet resellers such as StubHub is having an equalizing effect, often resulting in fair prices determined by market forces.

Unlike eBay, StubHub provides around-the-clock customer service via a toll-free number. But perhaps the biggest and most important difference between StubHub and competitors is the company's 100 percent FanProtect guarantee. Initially, it might seem more risky buying from a seller whose identity is unknown. But StubHub puts the burden of responsibility on the seller, remaining involved after the purchase where competing sites bow out. Buyers aren't charged until they confirm receipt of the tickets. "If you open the package and it contains two squares of toilet paper instead of the tickets," Baker explains, "then we debit the seller's credit card for the amount of the purchase." StubHub will also revoke site privileges for fraudulent or unreliable sellers. In contrast, the eBay system is largely self-policing and does not monitor the shipment or verification of the purchased items.

WHAT THE FUTURE HOLDS

When StubHub was formed, it targeted professional ticket brokers and ordinary consumers. In examining individuals as sellers, Baker and Fluhr capitalized on the underexploited assets of sports team season ticketholders. "If you have season tickets to the Yankees, that's 81 games," Baker said. "Unless you're unemployed or especially passionate, there's no way you're going to attend every game." StubHub entered the equation, not only giving ticketholders a way to recoup some of their investment, but allowing them to have complete control over the process rather than selling to a ticket agent.

It quickly became apparent to StubHub's founders that the benefits of season ticketholders selling off unused tickets extended to the sports franchises as well. Being able to sell unwanted tickets encourages season ticketholders to buy again. It also puts customers in seats that would otherwise go empty—customers who buy hot dogs, souvenirs, and programs. Thus, StubHub began entering into signed agreements with professional sports teams. The company has signed agreements with numerous NFL, NBA, and NHL teams to be their official secondary marketplace for season ticketholders.

But most recently, StubHub scored a huge breakthrough deal by becoming the official online ticket reseller for Major League Baseball and its 30 teams. Given that an estimated US$10 billion worth of baseball tickets are resold each year, this single move will likely bring tremendous growth to StubHub. "This is the final vindication for the secondary ticketing market," StubHub spokesman Sean Pate said. "That really puts the final stamp of approval on StubHub."

Revenues from sporting events account for more than half of all StubHub sales. So it's not surprising that the company continues to pursue new partnerships with collegiate sports organizations and even media organizations, such as AOL, Sporting News, and CBS Sportsline. However, it has arranged similar contractual agreements with big-name performers such as Madonna, Coldplay, the Dixie Chicks, Justin Timberlake, Jessica Simpson, and country music's rising star, Bobby Pinson. Arrangements allow StubHub to offer exclusive event packages with a portion of the proceeds supporting charities designated by the performer.

The reselling of event tickets is here to stay. With the rise of safe and legal reseller websites and the repeal of long-standing antiscalping laws in many states, aftermarket ticket reselling continues to gain legitimacy. There are numerous hands in the fast-growing cookie jar that is the secondary ticket market. StubHub founder Eric Baker left the company and formed Viagogo, a European ticket reseller site that is entering the U.S. market. Even Ticketmaster—the longstanding dominant force in primary ticket sales—has jumped into the act. Not only has the ticket powerhouse turned to auctioning a certain portion of premium tickets to the highest bidders, but it has its own resale arm, TicketExchange.

Although there is more than one channel to buy or sell, StubHub's future looks bright. The company's model of entering into partnerships with event-producing organizations is establishing it as "the official" ticket reseller. In fact, in an "if you can't beat 'em, join 'em," move, rival reseller eBay bought StubHub last year for over US$300 million, allowing it to continue to function as its own entity. At this point, there is no end in sight to StubHub's growth curve. Who knows—at some point ticket-seeking consumers may even think of StubHub before thinking of Ticketmaster.

Questions for Discussion

1. Conduct a brief analysis of the marketing environment and the forces shaping the development of StubHub.

2. Discuss StubHub's business model. What general benefits does it afford to buyers and sellers? Which benefits are most important in terms of creating value for buyers and sellers?

3. Discuss StubHub as a new intermediary. What effects has this new type of intermediary had on the ticket industry?

4. Apply the text's emarketing domains framework to StubHub's business model. How has each domain played a role in the company's success?

5. What recommendations can you make for improving StubHub's future growth and success?

6. What are the legal or ethical issues, if any, for ticket reselling websites?

Sources: Ethan Smith, "StubHub Enlisted in Resale of Madonna Concert Tickets," *Wall Street Journal*, May 9, 2008, p. B6; Neil Best, "Want Super Bowl Tickets? Sell or Rent the House," *Newsday*, January 25, 2008, p. A70; Joe Nocera, "Internet Puts a Sugarcoat on Scalping," *New York Times*, January 19, 2008, p. C1; Amy Feldman, "Hot Tickets," *Fast Company*, September 1, 2007, p. 44; "Ticket Reseller StubHub Hits a Home Run," *Reuters*, August 2, 2007; William Grimes, "That Invisible Hand Guides the Game of Ticket Hunting," *New York Times*, June 18, 2004, p. E1; Steve Stecklow, "Can't Get No . . . Tickets?" *Wall Street Journal*, January 7, 2006, p. P1; Steve Stecklow, "StubHub's Ticket to Ride," *Wall Street Journal*, January 17, 2006, p. B1; and information from www.stubhub.com, accessed November 2008.

Visit **MyMarketingLab** at **www.pearsoned.ca/mymarketinglab** for access to online tutorials, interactive exercises, videos, and much more.

18

Creating
Competitive Advantage

PREVIEWING
THE CONCEPTS

In previous chapters, you explored the basics of marketing. You've learned that the aim of marketing is to create value for customers to capture value from consumers in return. Good marketing companies win, keep, and grow customers by understanding customer needs, designing customer-driven marketing strategies, constructing value-delivering marketing programs, and building customer and marketing partner relationships. In the final two chapters, we'll extend this concept to two special areas—creating competitive advantage and global marketing.

In this chapter, we pull all of the marketing basics together. Understanding customers is an important first step in developing profitable customer relationships, but it's not enough. To gain competitive advantage, companies must use this understanding to design market offerings that deliver more value than the offers of competitors seeking to win the same customers. In this chapter, we look first at competitor analysis, the process companies use to identify and analyze competitors. Then we examine competitive marketing strategies by which companies position themselves against competitors to gain the greatest possible competitive advantage.

Let's look first at Nike. During the past several decades, Nike has forever changed the rules of sports marketing strategy. In the process, it has built the Nike swoosh into one of the world's best-known brand symbols. But to stay on top in the intensely competitive sports apparel business, Nike will have to keep a keen eye on both customers and competitors, finding fresh ways to beat rivals at bringing value to its customers.

The Nike "swoosh"—it's everywhere! Just for fun, try counting the swooshes whenever you pick up the sports pages or watch a pickup basketball game or tune in to a televised golf match. Through innovative marketing, Nike has built the ever-present swoosh into one of the best-known brand symbols on the planet.

Some 45 years ago, when Phil Knight and college track coach Bill Bowerman co-founded the company, Nike was just a brash, young upstart in the athletic footwear industry. In 1964, the pair chipped in $500 apiece to start Blue Ribbon Sports. In 1970, Bowerman dreamed up a new sneaker tread by stuffing a piece of rubber into his wife's waffle iron. The Waffle Trainer quickly became the nation's best-selling training shoe. In 1972, the company became Nike, named after the Greek goddess of victory. The swoosh was designed by a graduate student for a fee of $35. By 1979, Nike had sprinted ahead of the competition, owning 50 percent of the North American running shoe market. It all seemed easy then. Running was in, sneakers were hot, and Nike had the right stuff.

Nike has built the swoosh into one of the world's best-known brand symbols, signifying the very close bond between customers and the Nike brand.

During the 1980s, under Phil Knight's leadership, Nike revolutionized sports marketing. To build its brand image and market share, Nike lavishly outspent its competitors on big-name endorsements, splashy promotional events, and in-your-face "Just Do It" ads. At Nike, however, good marketing meant more than just promotional hype and promises—it meant consistently building strong relationships with customers based on real value.

Nike's initial success resulted from the technical superiority of its running and basketball shoes. To this day, Nike leads the industry in research and development spending. But Nike gave customers much more than just good athletic gear. Customers didn't just wear their Nikes, they experienced them. As the company states on its website (www.nike.com), "Nike has always known the truth—it's not so much the shoes but where they take you." Beyond shoes, apparel, and equipment, Nike marketed a way of life, a sports culture, a just-do-it attitude. As Phil Knight said at the time, "Basically, our culture and our style is to be a rebel." The company was built on a genuine passion for sports, a maverick disregard for convention, and a belief in hard work and serious sports performance.

Throughout the 1980s and 1990s, still playing the role of the upstart underdog, Nike solidified its position as the dominant market leader. It leveraged its brand strength, moving aggressively into new product categories, sports, and regions of the world. The company slapped its familiar swoosh logo on everything from sunglasses and soccer balls to batting gloves and golf clubs. Nike invaded a dozen new sports, including baseball, golf, skateboarding, wall climbing, bicycling, and hiking. It seemed that things couldn't be going any better.

In the late 1990s, however, Nike stumbled as a new breed of competitor arose and the company's sales slipped. The whole industry suffered a setback, as a "brown shoe" craze for hiking and outdoor shoe styles ate into the athletic

Nike gives consumers more than just good athletic gear. It markets a way of life, a sports culture, and a just-do-it attitude.

sneaker business. Moreover, Nike's creative juices seemed to run dry. Ho-hum new sneaker designs collected dust on retailer shelves as buyers seeking a new look switched to competing brands.

But Nike's biggest obstacle may have been its own incredible success. The brand appeared to suffer from big-brand backlash, and the swoosh may have become too common to be cool. As sales moved past the US$10 billion mark, market leader Nike moved from maverick to mainstream. Rooting for Nike was like rooting for Microsoft. Instead of anti-establishment, Nike *was* the establishment. Once the brat of sports marketing, Nike now had to grow up and act its age.

And grow up it did. The company still spends hundreds of millions of dollars each year on very creative advertising, innovative brand-building promotions, and big-name endorsers. But behind the bright lights, Nike now focuses on the important marketing basics: customer relationships,

▶

OBJECTIVES

1. Discuss the need to understand competitors as well as customers through competitor analysis.

2. Explain the fundamentals of competitive marketing strategies based on creating value for customers.

3. Illustrate the need for balancing customer and competitor orientations in becoming a truly market-centred organization.

new-product innovation, and leaving competitors in its dust. When it comes to the competition, Nike is ruthless but a little paranoid. "As the industry gets bigger, as Nike gets bigger, it has to be even faster," says Knight. "That's an enormous challenge and always has been." Nike president and CEO Mark Parker agrees. "I don't fear any competitor, but I respect them all," he says. "Anybody who takes their competition for granted ends up watching them from behind."

With Nike's deep pockets, it can outspend most competitors on marketing by a wide margin. But where today's Nike really out-points its competitors is in its cutting-edge efforts to build a deep community with customers. Nike's mission is "to bring inspiration and innovation to every athlete* in the world (*if you have a body, you are an athlete.)" And whether customers come to know Nike through ads, its Niketown stores, a local Nike running club, or one of the company's many community websites—NikePlus.com, Joga.com, or another—the sports giant's customers build very close bonds with the Nike brand.

As a result, the modern-day Nike is once again achieving stunning results. In the past four years, as many competitors have struggled, Nike's sales have grown 53 percent to US$16.3 billion, and profits have more than tripled. Nike captures an eye-popping 45 percent of the North American athletic footwear market; next-biggest competitor Adidas captures less than half that figure. For four years running, Nike's return on invested capital has exceeded 20 percent. Nike is growing even faster abroad than at home, with international revenues now accounting for 57 percent of total Nike brand sales. Nike is now the fastest-growing running brand in Germany. In Russia, it has doubled its revenue in the last three years. Nike is the number-one athletic brand in China, a market that will be Nike's second-largest within three years.

To stay ahead of competitors, however, Nike will have to keep its marketing strategy fresh, finding new ways to deliver the kind of innovation and value that built the brand so powerfully in the past. Nike will have to act more like a fresh, young start-up than an aging market leader, constantly reassessing its competitive standing and rekindling its meaning to customers. Says Knight, "The spirit of entrepreneurship is key to our success. It certainly defined Nike when we started the company. And it's what keeps us nimble in this industry today."[1]

Chapter Opening Discussion

Competitive advantage
An advantage over competitors gained by offering consumers greater value than competitors do.

Competitor analysis
The process of identifying key competitors; assessing their objectives, strategies, strengths and weaknesses, and reaction patterns; and selecting which competitors to attack or avoid.

Competitive marketing strategies
Strategies that strongly position the company against competitors and give the company the strongest possible strategic advantage.

Glossary Flashcards of Key Terms

Today's companies face their toughest competition ever. In previous chapters, we argued that to succeed in today's fiercely competitive marketplace, companies will have to move from a product-and-selling philosophy to a customer-and-marketing philosophy. Guerrino De Luca, president and CEO of Logitech, puts it well: "It is now more critical than ever to keep the people who buy and use our products at the center of our focus—for all our customers to be delighted by their experience with our products."[2]

This chapter spells out in more detail how companies can go about outperforming competitors to win, keep, and grow customers. To win in today's marketplace, companies must become adept not just in *managing products*, but in *managing customer relationships* in the face of determined competition. Understanding customers is crucial, but it's not enough. Building profitable customer relationships and gaining **competitive advantage** requires delivering *more* value and satisfaction to target consumers than *competitors* do. Customers will see competitive advantages as *customer advantages*, giving the company an edge over its competitors.

In this chapter, we examine *competitive marketing strategies*—how companies analyze their competitors and develop successful, value-based strategies for building and maintaining profitable customer relationships. The first step is **competitor analysis**, the process of identifying, assessing, and selecting key competitors. The second step is developing **competitive marketing strategies** that strongly position the company against competitors and give it the greatest possible competitive advantage.

1   COMPETITOR ANALYSIS

To plan effective marketing strategies, the company needs to find out all it can about its competitors. It must constantly compare its marketing strategies, products, prices, channels, and promotions with those of close competitors. In this way the company can find areas of potential competitive advantage and disadvantage. As shown in Figure 18.1, competitor analysis involves first identifying and assessing competitors and then selecting which competitors to attack or avoid.

Figure 18.1 Steps in
analyzing competitors

Identifying Competitors

Normally, identifying competitors would seem a simple task. At the narrowest level, a company can define its competitors as other companies offering similar products and services to the same customers at similar prices. Thus, Banana Republic might see Gap as a major competitor, but not Sears or Zellers. The Ritz-Carlton might see Four Seasons Hotels as a major competitor, but not Holiday Inn, Hampton Inn, or any of the thousands of bed-and-breakfasts that dot the nation.

But companies actually face a much wider range of competitors. The company might define competitors as all firms making the same product or class of products. Thus, The Ritz-Carlton would see itself as competing against all other hotels. Even more broadly, competitors might include all companies making products that supply the same service. Here The Ritz-Carlton would see itself competing not only against other hotels but also against anyone who supplies rooms for weary travellers. Finally, and still more broadly, competitors might include all companies that compete for the same consumer dollars. Here The Ritz-Carlton would see itself competing with travel and leisure services, from cruises and summer homes to vacations abroad.

Companies must avoid "competitor myopia." A company is more likely to be "buried" by its latent competitors than its current ones. For example, Kodak's film business didn't suffer at the hands of direct competitor Fujifilm; it lost out to competitors that Kodak didn't see coming—Sony, Canon, and other digital camera makers, along with a host of digital image developers and online image-sharing services. Perhaps the classic example of competitor myopia is Encyclopaedia Britannica:

> For more than 200 years, Encyclopaedia Britannica saw itself as competing with other publishers of printed reference books and encyclopedia sets selling for as much as US$2200 per set. However, it learned a hard lesson when the world went digital in the 1990s. Microsoft introduced *Encarta*, a CD-ROM encyclopedia that sold for only $50. *Encarta* and other digital encyclopedias took the market by storm, followed quickly by web-based encyclopedias and reference sources. As a result, Britannica's sales plunged 50 percent during the next seven years. As it turns out, Britannica's real competitors weren't other print publishers, they were the computer, the Internet, and digital content. Britannica still publishes its flagship 32-volume *Encyclopedia Britannica* and several other printed reference sets. However, it also offers popular DVD and web versions of its information services. Britannica recognizes competitors ranging from World Book to Microsoft to free web upstarts such as Wikipedia, the bottom-up, dynamic, not-for-profit, Internet-based encyclopedia "that anyone can edit."[3]

Companies can identify their competitors from the *industry* point of view. They might see themselves as being in the oil industry, the pharmaceutical industry, or the beverage industry. A company must understand the competitive patterns in its industry if it hopes to be an effective "player" in that industry. Companies can also identify competitors from a *market* point of view. Here they define competitors as companies that are trying to satisfy the same customer need or build relationships with the same customer group.

From an industry point of view, Pepsi might see its competition as Coca-Cola, Dr Pepper, 7UP, and the makers of other soft drink brands. From a market point of view, however, the customer really wants "thirst quenching." This need can be satisfied by bottled water, energy drinks, fruit juice, iced tea, or many other fluids. Similarly, Hallmark's Binney & Smith, maker of Crayola crayons, might define its competitors as other makers of crayons and children's drawing supplies. But from a market point of view, it would include all firms making recreational and educational products for children. In general, the market concept of competition opens the company's eyes to a broader set of actual and potential competitors.

Assessing Competitors

Having identified the main competitors, marketing management now asks: What are competitors' objectives—what does each seek in the marketplace? What is each competitor's strategy? What are various competitors' strengths and weaknesses, and how will each react to actions the company might take?

Determining Competitors' Objectives

Each competitor has a mix of objectives. The company wants to know the relative importance that a competitor places on current profitability, market share growth, cash flow, technological leadership, service leadership, and other goals. Knowing a competitor's mix of objectives reveals whether the competitor is satisfied with its current situation and how it might react to different competitive actions. For example, a company that pursues low-cost leadership will react much more strongly to a competitor's cost-reducing manufacturing breakthrough than to the same competitor's advertising increase.

A company also must monitor its competitors' objectives for various segments. If the company finds that a competitor has discovered a new segment, this might be an opportunity. If it finds that competitors plan new moves into segments now served by the company, it will be forewarned and, hopefully, forearmed.

Strategic group
A group of firms in an industry following the same or a similar strategy in a given target market.

Identifying Competitors' Strategies

The more that one firm's strategy resembles another firm's strategy, the more the two firms compete. In most industries, the competitors can be sorted into groups that pursue different strategies. A **strategic group** is a group of firms in an industry following the same or a similar strategy in a given target market. For example, in the major appliance industry, GE and Whirlpool belong to the same strategic group. Each produces a full line of medium-price appliances supported by good service. In contrast, Sub-Zero and Viking belong to a different strategic group. They produce a narrower line of higher-quality appliances, offer a higher level of service, and charge a premium price.

Some important insights emerge from identifying strategic groups. For example, if a company enters one of the groups, the members of that group become its key competitors. Thus, if the company enters the first group, against GE and Whirlpool, it can succeed only if it develops strategic advantages over these competitors.

Although competition is most intense within a strategic group, there is also rivalry among groups. First, some of the strategic groups may appeal to overlapping customer segments. For example, no matter what their strategy, all major appliance manufacturers will go after the apartment and homebuilders segment. Second, the customers may not see much difference in the offers of different groups—they may see little difference in quality between GE and Whirlpool. Finally, members of one strategic group might expand into new strategy segments. Thus, GE's Monogram and Profile lines of appliances compete in the premium-quality, premium-price line with Viking and Sub-Zero.

IMAGINE YOUR LIFE IN A VIKING KITCHEN.

Strategic groups: Viking belongs to the appliance industry strategic group offering a narrow line of higher-quality appliances supported by good service.

The company needs to look at all of the dimensions that identify strategic groups within the industry. It must understand how each competitor delivers value to its customers. It needs to know each competitor's product quality, features, and mix; customer services; pricing policy; distribution coverage; sales force strategy; and advertising and sales promotion programs. And it must study the details of each competitor's R&D, manufacturing, purchasing, financial, and other strategies.

Assessing Competitors' Strengths and Weaknesses

Marketers need to assess each competitor's strengths and weaknesses carefully to answer a critical question: What *can* our competitors do? As a first step, companies can gather data on each competitor's goals, strategies, and performance over the past few years. Admittedly, some of this information will be hard to obtain. For example, business-to-business marketers find it hard to estimate competitors' market shares because they do not have the same syndicated data services that are available to consumer packaged goods companies.

Benchmarking
The process of comparing the company's products and processes to those of competitors or leading firms in other industries to identify "best practices" and find ways to improve quality and performance.

Companies normally learn about their competitors' strengths and weaknesses through secondary data, personal experience, and word of mouth. They can also conduct primary marketing research with customers, suppliers, and dealers. Or they can **benchmark** themselves against other firms, comparing the company's products and processes to those of competitors or leading firms in other industries to identify "best practices" and find ways to improve quality and performance. Benchmarking has become a powerful tool for increasing a company's competitiveness.

Estimating Competitors' Reactions

Next, the company wants to know: What *will* our competitors do? A competitor's objectives, strategies, and strengths and weaknesses go a long way toward explaining its likely actions. They also suggest its likely reactions to company moves such as price cuts, promotion increases, or new-product introductions. In addition, each competitor has a certain philosophy of doing business, a certain internal culture and specific guiding beliefs. Marketing managers need a deep understanding of a given competitor's mentality if they want to anticipate how the competitor will act or react.

Each competitor reacts differently. Some do not react quickly or strongly to a competitor's move. They may feel their customers are loyal, they may be slow in noticing the move, or they may lack the funds to react. Some competitors react only to certain types of moves and not to others. Other competitors react swiftly and strongly to any action. Thus, Procter & Gamble does not let a new detergent come easily into the market. Many firms avoid direct competition with P&G and look for easier prey, knowing that P&G will react fiercely if challenged.

In some industries, competitors live in relative harmony; in others, they fight constantly. Knowing how major competitors react gives the company clues on how best to attack competitors or how best to defend the company's current positions.

Selecting Competitors to Attack and Avoid

A company has already largely selected its major competitors through prior decisions on customer targets, distribution channels, and marketing mix strategy. Management now must decide which competitors to compete against most vigorously.

Strong or Weak Competitors

The company can focus on one of several classes of competitors. Most companies prefer to compete against *weak competitors*. This requires fewer resources and less time. But in the process, the firm may gain little. You could argue that the firm should also compete with *strong competitors* to sharpen its abilities. Moreover, even strong competitors have some weaknesses, and succeeding against them often provides greater returns.

Customer value analysis
Analysis conducted to determine what benefits target customers value and how they rate the relative value of various competitors' offerings.

A useful tool for assessing competitor strengths and weaknesses is **customer value analysis**. The aim of customer value analysis is to determine the benefits that target customers value and how customers rate the relative value of various competitors' offerings. In conducting a customer value analysis, the company first identifies the major attributes

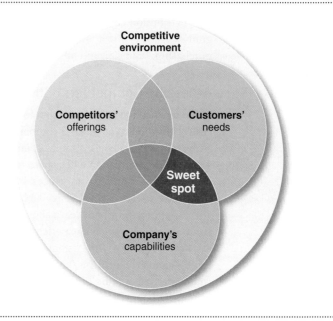

that customers value and the importance customers place on these attributes. Next, it assesses the company's and competitors' performance on the valued attributes.

The key to gaining competitive advantage is to take each customer segment and examine how the company's offer compares to that of its major competitors. As shown in Figure 18.2, the company wants to find the "strategic sweet spot"—the place where it meets customers' needs in a way that rivals can't. If the company's offering delivers greater value by exceeding the competitor's offering on important attributes, the company can charge a higher price and earn higher profits, or it can charge the same price and gain more market share. But if the company is seen as performing at a lower level than its major competitor on some important attributes, it must invest in strengthening those attributes or finding other important attributes where it can build a lead on the competitor.

Close or Distant Competitors

Most companies will compete with *close competitors*—those that resemble them most—rather than *distant competitors*. Thus, Nike competes more against Adidas than against Timberland or Keen. And Zellers competes against Walmart rather than Holt Renfrew or La Maison Ogilvy.

At the same time, the company may want to avoid trying to "destroy" a close competitor. For example, in the late 1970s, Bausch & Lomb moved aggressively against other soft lens manufacturers with great success. However, this forced weak competitors to sell out to larger firms such as Johnson & Johnson. As a result, Bausch & Lomb then faced much larger competitors—and it suffered the consequences. Johnson & Johnson acquired Vistakon, a small nicher with only US$20 million in annual sales. Backed by Johnson & Johnson's deep pockets, the small but nimble Vistakon developed and introduced its innovative Acuvue disposable lenses. With Vistakon leading the way, Johnson & Johnson is now the top North American contact lens maker, while Bausch & Lomb lags in fourth place. In this case, success in hurting a close rival brought in tougher competitors.

"Good" or "Bad" Competitors

A company needs and benefits from competitors. The existence of competitors results in several strategic benefits. Competitors may share the costs of market and product development and help to legitimize new technologies. They may serve less-attractive segments or lead to more product differentiation. Finally, competitors may help increase total demand. For example, you might think that an independent coffeehouse surrounded by Starbucks stores might have trouble staying in business. But that's often not the case:

After driving smaller competitors from the market, Bausch & Lomb faces larger, more resourceful ones, such as Johnson & Johnson's Vistakon division. With Vistakon's Acuvue lenses leading the way, J&J is now the top North American contact lens maker.

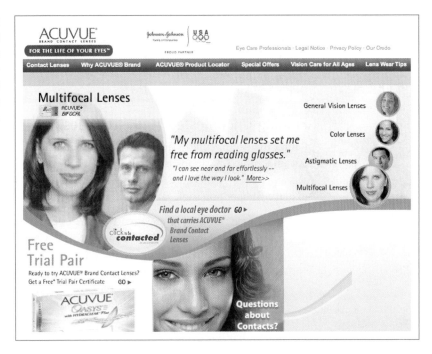

Coffee-shop owners have discovered that the corporate steamroller known as Starbucks is actually good for their business. It turns out that when a Starbucks comes to the neighbourhood, the result is new converts to the latte-drinking fold. When all those converts overrun the local Starbucks, the independents are there to catch the spillover. In fact, some independent storeowners now actually try to open their stores near a Starbucks if they can. That's certainly not how the coffee behemoth planned it. "Starbucks is actually *trying* to be ruthless," says the owner of a small coffeehouse chain. But "in its predatory store-placement strategy, Starbucks has been about as lethal a killer as a fluffy bunny rabbit."[4]

However, a company may not view all of its competitors as beneficial. An industry often contains *"good" competitors* and *"bad" competitors*.[5] Good competitors play by the rules of the industry. Bad competitors, in contrast, break the rules. They try to buy share rather than earn it, take large risks, and play by their own rules.

For example, Yahoo! Music Unlimited sees Napster, Rhapsody, AOL Music, Amazon.com, and most other digital music download services as good competitors. They share a common platform so that music bought from any of these competitors can be played on almost any playback device. However, it sees Apple's iTunes Music Store as a bad competitor, one that plays by its own rules at the expense of the industry as a whole:

> With the iPod, Apple initially created a closed system with mass appeal. In 2003, when the iPod was the only game in town, Apple cut deals with the four major music labels that locked up its device. The music companies wanted to sell songs on iTunes, but they were afraid of Internet piracy. So Apple promised to wrap their songs in its FairPlay digital rights management (DRM) technology—the only copy-protection encryption that is compatible with iPods and iPhones. Other digital music services such as Yahoo! Music Unlimited and Napster reached similar deals with the big music labels. When Apple refused to license FairPlay to them, those companies turned to Microsoft for DRM technology. But that meant that none of the songs sold by those services could be played on the wildly popular iPod and vice versa. The situation has been a disaster for Apple's competitors. Although some recording labels, notably EMI and Universal Music Group, are now forgoing DMR technology in an effort to weaken the bargaining power they gave to Apple by first insisting on it, iTunes still holds a commanding 80 percent of the digital music market. It recently sold its four billionth song.[6]

The implication is that "good" companies would like to shape an industry that consists of only well-behaved competitors. A company might be smart to support good competitors, aiming its attacks at bad competitors. Thus, Yahoo! Music Unlimited, Napster, and other digital music competitors will no doubt support one another in trying to break Apple's stranglehold on the market.

Finding Uncontested Market Spaces

Rather than competing head to head with established competitors, many companies seek out unoccupied positions in uncontested market spaces. They try to create products and services for which there are *no* direct competitors. Called a "blue ocean strategy," the goal is to make competition irrelevant:

> Companies have long engaged in head-to-head competition in search of profitable growth. They have flocked for competitive advantage, battled over market share, and struggled for differentiation. Yet in today's overcrowded industries, competing head-on results in nothing but a bloody "red ocean" of rivals fighting over a shrinking profit pool. In their book *Blue Ocean Strategy*, two marketing professors contend that although most companies compete within such red oceans, the strategy isn't likely to create profitable growth in the future. Tomorrow's leading companies will succeed not by battling competitors but by creating "blue oceans" of uncontested market space. Such strategic moves—termed "value innovation"—create powerful leaps in value for both the firm and its buyers, creating all-new demand and rendering rivals obsolete. By creating and capturing blue oceans, companies can largely take rivals out of the picture.[7]

An example of a company exhibiting blue ocean thinking is Quebec-based Cirque du Soleil, which reinvented the circus as a higher form of modern entertainment. At a time when the circus industry was declining, Cirque du Soleil innovated by eliminating high cost and controversial elements such as animal acts and instead focused on the theatrical experience. Cirque du Soleil did not compete with then market leaders Ringling Bros. and Barnum & Bailey—it was altogether different from anything that preceded it. Instead, it created an uncontested new market space that made existing competitors irrelevant. The results have been spectacular. Thanks to its blue ocean strategy, in only its first 20 years Cirque du Soleil achieved more revenues than Ringling Bros. and Barnum & Bailey achieved in their first 100 years.

"Blue ocean" strategies: Cirque du Soleil reinvented the circus, finding an uncontested new market space that created new demand and rendered rivals irrelevant.

Designing a Competitive Intelligence System

We have described the main types of information that companies need about their competitors. This information must be collected, interpreted, distributed, and used. The cost in money and time of gathering competitive intelligence is high, and the company must design its competitive intelligence system in a cost-effective way.

The competitive intelligence system first identifies the vital types of competitive information needed and the best sources of this information. Then the system continuously collects information from the field (sales force, channels, suppliers, market research firms, trade associations, websites) and from published data (government publications, speeches, articles). Next, the system checks the information for validity and reliability, interprets it, and organizes it in an appropriate way. Finally, it sends key information to relevant decision makers and responds to inquiries from managers about competitors.

With this system, company managers will receive timely intelligence information about competitors in the form of phone calls, emails, bulletins, newsletters, and reports. In addition, managers can connect with the system when they need an interpretation of a competitor's sudden move, or when they want to know a competitor's weaknesses and strengths, or when they need to know how a competitor will respond to a planned company move.

Smaller companies that cannot afford to set up formal competitive intelligence offices can assign specific executives to watch specific competitors. Thus, a manager who used to work for a competitor might follow that competitor closely; he or she would be the "in-house expert" on that competitor. Any manager needing to know the thinking of a given competitor could contact the assigned in-house expert.

2   COMPETITIVE STRATEGIES

Having identified and evaluated its major competitors, the company now must design broad competitive marketing strategies by which it can gain competitive advantage through superior customer value. But what broad marketing strategies might the company use? Which ones are best for a particular company, or for the company's different divisions and products?

Approaches to Marketing Strategy

No one strategy is best for all companies. Each company must determine what makes the most sense given its position in the industry and its objectives, opportunities, and resources. Even within a company different strategies may be required for different businesses or products. Johnson & Johnson uses one marketing strategy for its leading brands in stable consumer markets—such as Band-Aid, Tylenol, or Johnson's baby products—and a different marketing strategy for its high-tech health care businesses and products—such as Monocryl surgical sutures or NeuFlex finger joint implants.

Companies also differ in how they approach the strategy-planning process. Many large firms develop formal competitive marketing strategies and implement them religiously. However, other companies develop strategy in a less formal and orderly fashion. Some companies, such as Harley-Davidson, Virgin Atlantic Airlines, and BMW's MINI Cooper unit, succeed by breaking many of the "rules" of marketing strategy. Such companies don't operate large marketing departments, conduct expensive marketing research, spell out elaborate competitive strategies, and spend huge sums on advertising. Instead, they sketch out strategies on the fly, stretch their limited resources, live close to their customers, and create more satisfying solutions to customer needs. They form buyer's clubs, use buzz marketing, and focus on winning customer loyalty. It seems that not all marketing must follow in the footsteps of marketing giants such as IBM and Procter & Gamble.

In fact, approaches to marketing strategy and practice often pass through three stages: entrepreneurial marketing, formulated marketing, and intrepreneurial marketing.

Entrepreneurial marketing: Stonyfield Farm's idea of marketing strategy—"companies can do better with less advertising, less marketing research, more guerrilla marketing, and more acting from the gut."

- *Entrepreneurial marketing:* Most companies are started by individuals who live by their wits. They visualize an opportunity, construct flexible strategies on the backs of envelopes, and knock on every door to gain attention. Gary Hirshberg, who started the Stonyfield Farm yogurt company, will tell you that it's not about dumping millions of dollars into marketing and advertising. For Stonyfield, it's about company blogs, snappy packaging, environmental responsibility, and handing out free yogurt. And it's about telling the company story to the media. Hirshberg, known for wearing khakis and a vest, started making yogurt in Wilton, New Hampshire, with seven cows and a dream. His marketing strategy: build a strong connection with customers using guerrilla marketing. His idea is that "companies can do better with less advertising, less marketing research, more guerrilla marketing, and more acting from the gut." Using this strategy, Hirshberg has built Stonyfield Farm into a US$320 million company.[8]

- *Formulated marketing:* As small companies achieve success, they inevitably move toward more-formulated marketing. They develop formal marketing strategies and adhere to them closely. With 85 percent of the company now owned by Groupe Danone (which also makes Dannon yogurt), Stonyfield Farm has now developed a formal marketing department that carries out market research and plans strategy. Although Stonyfield may remain less formal in its strategy than the P&Gs of the marketing world, it employs many of the tools used in these more-developed marketing companies.

- *Intrepreneurial marketing:* Many large and mature companies get stuck in formulated marketing. They pore over the latest Nielsen numbers, scan market research reports, and try to fine-tune their competitive strategies and programs. These companies sometimes lose the marketing creativity and passion that they had at the start. They now need to re-establish within their companies the entrepreneurial spirit and actions that made them successful in the first place. They need to encourage more initiative and "intrepreneurship" at the local level. They need to refresh their marketing strategies and try new approaches. Their brand and product managers need to get out of the office, start living with their customers, and visualize new and creative ways to add value to their customers' lives.

The bottom line is that there are many approaches to developing effective competitive marketing strategy. There will be a constant tension between the formulated side of marketing and the creative side. It is easier to learn the formulated side of marketing, which has occupied most of our attention in this book. But we have also seen how marketing creativity and passion in the strategies of many of the companies we've studied—whether small or large, new or mature—have helped to build and maintain success in the marketplace. With this in mind, we now look at broad competitive marketing strategies companies can use.

Basic Competitive Strategies

Almost three decades ago, Michael Porter suggested four basic competitive positioning strategies that companies can follow—three winning strategies and one losing one.[9] The three winning strategies are as follows:

- *Overall cost leadership:* Here the company works hard to achieve the lowest production and distribution costs. Low costs let it price lower than its competitors and win a large market share. Texas Instruments, Dell, and Walmart are leading practitioners of this strategy.

- *Differentiation:* Here the company concentrates on creating a highly differentiated product line and marketing program so that it comes across as the class leader in the industry. Most customers would prefer to own this brand if its price is not too high. IBM and Caterpillar follow this strategy in information technology and services and heavy construction equipment, respectively.

- *Focus:* Here the company focuses its efforts on serving a few market segments well rather than going after the whole market. For example, The Ritz-Carlton focuses on the top 5 percent of corporate and leisure travellers. Tetra Food supplies 80 percent of pet tropical fish food. Similarly, Hohner owns a stunning 85 percent of the harmonica market.[10]

Companies that pursue a clear strategy—one of the above—will likely perform well. The firm that carries out that strategy best will make the most profits. But firms that do not pursue a clear strategy—*middle-of-the-roaders*—do the worst. Sears and Holiday Inn encountered difficult times because they did not stand out as the lowest in cost, highest in perceived value, or best in serving some market segment. Middle-of-the-roaders try to be good on all strategic counts, but end up being not very good at anything.

Two marketing consultants, Michael Treacy and Fred Wiersema, offer a more customer-centred classification of competitive marketing strategies.[11] They suggest that companies gain leadership positions by delivering superior value to their customers. Companies can pursue any of three strategies—called *value disciplines*—for delivering superior customer value:

- *Operational excellence:* The company provides superior value by leading its industry in price and convenience. It works to reduce costs and to create a lean and efficient value delivery system. It serves customers who want reliable, good-quality products or services, but who want them cheaply and easily. Examples include Walmart, WestJet, and Dell.

- *Customer intimacy:* The company provides superior value by precisely segmenting its markets and tailoring its products or services to exactly match the needs of targeted customers. It specializes in satisfying unique customer needs through a close relationship with and intimate knowledge of the customer. It builds detailed customer databases for segmenting and targeting, and empowers its marketing people to respond quickly to customer needs. Customer-intimate companies serve customers who are willing to pay a premium to get precisely what they want. They will do almost anything to build long-term customer loyalty and to capture customer lifetime value. Examples include Lexus, American Express, British Airways, and The Ritz-Carlton.

- *Product leadership:* The company provides superior value by offering a continuous stream of leading-edge products or services. It aims to make its own and competing products obsolete. Product leaders are open to new ideas, relentlessly pursue new solutions, and work to get new products to market quickly. They serve customers who want state-of-the-art products and services, regardless of the costs in terms of price or inconvenience. Examples include Nokia and Apple.

Some companies successfully pursue more than one value discipline at the same time. For example, FedEx excels at both operational excellence and customer intimacy. However, such companies are rare—few firms can be the best at more than one of these disciplines. By trying to be *good at all* of the value disciplines, a company usually ends up being *best at none*.

Treacy and Wiersema found that leading companies focus on and excel at a single value discipline while meeting industry standards on the other two. Such companies design their entire value delivery network to single-mindedly support the chosen discipline. For example, Walmart knows that customer intimacy and product leadership are important. Compared with other discounters, it offers very good customer service and an excellent product assortment. Still, it purposely offers less customer service and less product depth than do Nordstrom or Holt Renfrew, which pursue customer intimacy. Instead, Walmart focuses obsessively on operational excellence—on reducing costs and streamlining its order-to-delivery process to make it convenient for customers to buy just the right products at the lowest prices.

By the same token, The Ritz-Carlton wants to be efficient and to employ the latest technologies. But what really sets the luxury hotel chain apart is its customer intimacy. The Ritz-Carlton creates custom-designed experiences to coddle its customers (see Real Marketing 18.1).

Classifying competitive strategies as value disciplines is appealing. It defines marketing strategy in terms of the single-minded pursuit of delivering superior value to customers. Each value discipline defines a specific way to build lasting customer relationships.

Real Marketing **18.1**

The Ritz-Carlton: Creating Customer Intimacy

The Ritz-Carlton, a chain of luxury hotels renowned for outstanding service, caters to the top 5 percent of corporate and leisure travellers. The company's credo sets lofty customer service goals: "The Ritz-Carlton is a place where the genuine care and comfort of our guests is our highest mission. . . . The Ritz-Carlton experience enlivens the senses, instils well-being, and fulfills even the unexpressed wishes and needs of our guests."

The credo is more than just words on paper—The Ritz-Carlton delivers on its promises. In surveys of departing guests, some 95 percent report that they've had a truly memorable experience. In fact, at The Ritz-Carlton, exceptional service encounters have become almost commonplace. Take

When it comes to creating customer intimacy, The Ritz-Carlton sets the gold standard. "It's all about providing a unique, personal, memorable experience."

the experiences of Nancy and Harvey Heffner, who stayed at The Ritz-Carlton Naples in Florida (rated the best hotel in the United States and fourth best in the world, by *Travel + Leisure* magazine).

"The hotel is elegant and beautiful," Mrs. Heffner said, "but more important is the beauty expressed by the staff. They can't do enough to please you." When the couple's son became sick last year in Naples, the hotel staff brought him hot tea with honey at all hours of the night, she said. When Mr. Heffner had to fly home on business for a day and his return flight was delayed, a driver for the hotel waited in the lobby most of the night.

Such personal, high-quality service has also made The Ritz-Carlton a favourite among conventioneers. For seven of the last nine years, the luxury hotel came out on top in *Business Travel News*'s U.S. Hotel Chain Survey of business travel buyers. "They not only treat us like kings when we hold our top-level meetings in their hotels, but we just never get any complaints," comments one convention planner. Says another, who had recently held a meeting at The Ritz-Carlton Half Moon Bay in California, "The first-rate catering and convention services staff [and] The Ritz-Carlton's ambiance and beauty—the elegant, Grand Dame-style lodge, nestled on a bluff between two championship golf courses overlooking

the Pacific Ocean—makes a day's work there seem anything but."

Since its incorporation in 1983, The Ritz-Carlton has received virtually every major award that the hospitality industry bestows. In addition, it's the only hotel company ever to win the prestigious Malcolm Baldrige National Quality Award and one of only two companies from any industry to win the award twice. A recent *Consumer Reports* hotels issue ranked The Ritz-Carlton the number-one luxury hotel company in all areas, including value, service, upkeep, and problem resolution. More than 90 percent of customers return, and despite its hefty room rates, the chain enjoys a 70 percent occupancy rate, almost nine points above the industry average.

Most of the responsibility for keeping guests satisfied falls to The Ritz-Carlton's customer-contact employees. Thus, the hotel chain takes great care in finding just the right personnel—"people who care about people." Then The Ritz-Carlton goes to great lengths to rigorously—even fanatically—train employees in the art of coddling customers. New employees attend a two-day orientation in which top management drums into them the "12 Service Values." Service Value number one: "I build strong relationships and create Ritz-Carlton guests for life." The Ritz-Carlton trains every single employee worldwide every day, using a start-of-shift 15-minute meeting called "the lineup" to remind them of its service values.

Employees are taught to do everything they can to avoid never losing a guest. "There's no negotiating at Ritz-Carlton when it comes to solving customer problems," says a quality executive. Staff learn that *anyone* who receives a customer complaint *owns* that complaint until it's resolved (Service Value number six). They are trained to drop whatever they're doing to help a customer—no matter what they're doing or what their department. Ritz-Carlton employees are empowered to handle problems on the spot. Each employee can spend up to $2000 to redress a guest grievance without consulting higher-ups.

Beyond just fixing problems, Ritz-Carlton staff at all levels are "empowered to create unique, memorable, and personal experiences for our guests" (Service Value number three). The company expects employees to use their own good judgment rather than telling them what to do. "We are managing to outcomes, and the outcome is a happy guest," says the company's vice-president of global learning. "We don't care how you get there—as long as it's moral, legal, and ethical—but we want you to use your genuine talent, we want you to do what we call 'radar on, antenna up,' which means staying in the moment so you can read what a guest wants."

As a result, almost everyone who frequents The Ritz-Carlton has a "you won't believe this" story to tell about their experiences there. Employee heroics seem almost commonplace. For example, an administrative assistant at The Ritz-Carlton Philadelphia once overheard a guest lamenting that he'd forgotten to pack a pair of formal shoes and would have to wear hiking boots to an important meeting. Early the next morning, she delivered to the awestruck man a new pair of shoes in his size and favourite colour.

In another case, a business traveller arrived at The Ritz-Carlton Atlanta late on a cold, rainy December night, tired to the bone and suffering from a bad head cold. To her surprise and relief, hotel staff met her at the door, greeted her by name and, seeing her condition, escorted her directly to her room. When she arrived at her room, to her amazement, she found fresh flowers, two boxes of cough drops, and a personally addressed get-well card awaiting her. Such "Wow!" stories of service are read aloud every Monday to give Ritz-Carlton employees an understanding that they work among extraordinary people who do extraordinary things when the opportunity presents itself.

The Ritz-Carlton instils a sense of pride in its employees. "You serve," they are told, "but you are not servants." The company motto states, "We are ladies and gentlemen serving ladies and gentlemen." "When you invite guests to your house," it tells them, "you want everything to be perfect." As a result, Ritz-Carlton's employees appear to be just as satisfied as its customers. Employee turnover is less than 25 percent a year, compared to an 85 percent industry average.

Thus, when it comes to creating customer intimacy, The Ritz-Carlton sets the gold standard. The key is ensuring that guests don't feel like just another nameless face walking through the door. "It's all about personalization," says a Ritz-Carlton executive. "It's about providing a unique, personal, memorable experience, and what each person can do within your own environment to make that happen."

Sources: Quotes and other information from Julio Barker, "Power to the People," *Incentive*, February 2008, p. 34; "The World's Best Hotels 2007—Where Luxury Lives," *Institutional Investor*, November 2007, p. 1; Edwin McDowell, "Ritz-Carlton's Keys to Good Service," *New York Times*, March 31, 1993, p. D1; "The Ritz-Carlton, Half Moon Bay," *Successful Meetings*, November 2001, p. 40; Bruce Serlen, "Ritz-Carlton Retains Hold on Corporate Deluxe Buyers," *Business Travel News*, February 7, 2005, pp. 15–17; Michael B. Baker, "Four Seasons, Ritz-Carlton Tie as Deluxe Tier Leads Rate Growth," March 24, 2008, pp. 12–14; Margery Weinstein, "Service with a Smile," *Training*, March–April 2008, p. 40; and information from www.ritzcarlton.com, accessed October 2008.

Competitive Positions

Firms competing in a given target market, at any point in time, differ in their objectives and resources. Some firms are large, others small. Some have many resources, others are strapped for funds. Some are mature and established, others new and fresh. Some strive for rapid market share growth, others for long-term profits. And the firms occupy different competitive positions in the target market.

Market leader
The firm in an industry with the largest market share.

We now examine competitive strategies based on the roles firms play in the target market—leader, challenger, follower, or nicher. Suppose that an industry contains the firms shown in Figure 18.3. Forty percent of the market is in the hands of the **market leader**, the

Figure 18.3 Competitive market positions and roles

Table 18.1 Strategies for Market Leaders, Challengers, Followers, and Nichers

Market Leader Strategies	Market Challenger Strategies	Market Follower Strategies	Market Nicher Strategies
Expand total market	Full frontal attack	Follow closely	By customer, market, quality-price, service
Protect market share	Indirect attack	Follow at a distance	Multiple niching
Expand market share			

Market challenger
A runner-up firm that is fighting hard to increase its market share in an industry.

Market follower
A runner-up firm that wants to hold its market share in an industry without rocking the boat.

Market nicher
A firm that serves small segments that the other firms in an industry overlook or ignore.

firm with the largest market share. Another 30 percent is in the hands of **market challengers**, runner-up firms that are fighting hard to increase their market share. Another 20 percent is in the hands of **market followers**, other runner-up firms that want to hold their share without rocking the boat. The remaining 10 percent is in the hands of **market nichers**, firms that serve small segments not being pursued by other firms.

Table 18.1 shows specific marketing strategies that are available to market leaders, challengers, followers, and nichers.[12] Remember, however, that these classifications often do not apply to a whole company, but only to its position in a specific industry. Large companies such as GE, Microsoft, Procter & Gamble, or Disney might be leaders in some markets and nichers in others. For example, Procter & Gamble leads in many segments, such as laundry detergents and shampoo, but it challenges Unilever in hand soaps and Kimberly-Clark in facial tissues. Such companies often use different strategies for different business units or products, depending on the competitive situations of each.

Market Leader Strategies

Most industries contain an acknowledged market leader. The leader has the largest market share and usually leads the other firms in price changes, new-product introductions, distribution coverage, and promotion spending. The leader may or may not be admired or respected, but other firms concede its dominance. Competitors focus on the leader as a company to challenge, imitate, or avoid. Some of the best-known market leaders are Walmart (retailing), Microsoft (computer software), Caterpillar (earth-moving equipment), McDonald's (fast food), Nike (athletic footwear and apparel), and Google (Internet search services).

A leader's life is not easy. It must maintain a constant watch. Other firms keep challenging its strengths or trying to take advantage of its weaknesses. The market leader can easily miss a turn in the market and plunge into second or third place. A product innovation may come along and hurt the leader (as when Apple developed the iPod and took the market lead from Sony's Walkman portable audio devices). The leader might grow arrogant or complacent and misjudge the competition (as when Sears lost its lead to Walmart). Or the leader might look old-fashioned against new and peppier rivals (as when Levi's lost serious ground to more current or stylish brands like Gap, Tommy Hilfiger, DKNY, or GUESS).

To remain number one, leading firms can take any of three actions: (1) They can find ways to expand total demand; (2) they can protect their current market share through good defensive and offensive actions; or (3) they can try to expand their market share further, even if market size remains constant.

Expanding the Total Demand

The leading firm normally gains the most when the total market expands. If North Americans eat more fast food, McDonald's stands to gain the most because it holds more than three times the fast-food market share of nearest competitor Burger King. If McDonald's can convince more people that fast food is the best eating-out choice in these economic times, it will benefit more than its competitors.

Market leaders can expand the market by developing new users, new uses, and more usage of its products. They usually can find *new users* or untapped market segments in many places. For example, Nutrisystem has typically targeted its weight loss programs toward women. Recently, however, it stepped up its efforts to attract male customers:

> Prior to 2006, Nutrisystem featured only a few men in its customer testimonials. However, it now directly targets men with its Nutrisystem Advanced Men's Program. The weight-management company advertises regularly in male-skewing media such as ESPN TV and radio, *Sports Illustrated*, and *Men's Health*. Nutrisystem spends nearly one-third of its television advertising budget on male-oriented networks. The men's program offers pretty much the same types of meals offered to women. Ads feature sports legends such as Dan Marino (who lost 22 pounds on the Nutrisystem program) and Don Shula (who lost 32 pounds). They focus on what men want most: not having to think about losing weight, no group meetings, and prepackaged "man foods." In one commercial, Marino proclaims, "With Nutrisystem, I got to eat the foods I grew up with back in Pittsburgh—burgers, hot dogs, lasagna, pancakes, pot roast, meatballs—foods that guys love to eat. . . . Thanks to Nutrisystem, I ate like a man and still lost weight." The result? Since hiring the spokesmen and adding men's chat rooms to its website, the male share of Nutrisystem customers rose from 13 to 30 percent, fuelling substantial growth. Company sales increased 37 percent last year.[13]

Marketers can expand markets by discovering and promoting *new uses* for the product. For example, Arm & Hammer baking soda, whose sales had flattened after 125 years, discovered that consumers were using baking soda as a refrigerator deodorizer. It launched a heavy advertising and publicity campaign focusing on this use and persuaded consumers in half of North America's homes to place an open box of baking soda in their refrigerators and to replace it every few months. Today, its website (www.armandhammer.com) features new uses—"Solutions for my home, my family, my body"—ranging from removing residue left behind by hairstyling products and sweetening garbage disposals, laundry hampers, refrigerators, and trash cans to creating a home spa in your bathroom.

Finally, market leaders can encourage *more usage* by convincing people to use the product more often or to use more per occasion. For example, Campbell's urges people to eat soup and other Campbell's products more often by running ads containing new recipes. It also offers a toll-free hotline (1-888-MM-MM-GOOD), staffed by live "recipe representatives" who offer recipes to last-minute cooks at a loss for meal ideas. And the Campbell's Kitchen section of the company's website (www.campbellsoup.com) lets visitors search for or exchange recipes, set up their own personal recipe box, sign up for a daily or weekly Meal-Mail program, and even watch online video clips of guest chefs cooking any of 27 recipes on Campbell's Kitchen TV.

Creating more usage: Campbell's urges people to eat its soups and other products more often by running ads containing new recipes. It even offers online video clips of guest chefs cooking any of 27 recipes on Campbell's Kitchen TV.

Protecting Market Share

While trying to expand total market size, the leading firm also must protect its current business against competitors' attacks. Walmart must constantly guard against Zellers; Caterpillar against Komatsu; and McDonald's against Burger King.

What can the market leader do to protect its position? First, it must prevent or fix weaknesses that provide opportunities for competitors. It must always fulfill its value promise. Its prices must remain consistent with the value that customers see in the brand. It must work tirelessly to keep strong relationships with valued customers. The leader should "plug holes" so that competitors do not jump in.

But the best defence is a good offence, and the best response is *continuous innovation*. The leader

Protecting market share: In the face of market leader P&G's relentless assault in the laundry war, Unilever recently threw in the towel by putting its detergents business up for sale.

refuses to be content with the way things are and leads the industry in new products, customer services, distribution effectiveness, promotion, and cost cutting. It keeps increasing its competitive effectiveness and value to customers. And when attacked by challengers, the market leader reacts decisively. For example, in the laundry products category, market leader P&G has been relentless in its offence against challengers such as Unilever:

> In one of the most fabled marketing battles of the past century, P&G won the laundry war because it was bigger, better, more focused, and more aggressive than challenger Unilever. Last year alone, P&G outgunned Unilever on North American media spending for laundry brands by US$218 million to US$25 million. Entering this millennium, even though its laundry detergent market share was well over 50 percent, P&G kept raining blows on Unilever and all other comers with stepped-up product launches. Such products as Tide with Downy, Tide Coldwater, and the scent-focused Simple Pleasures lineup for Tide and Downy helped P&G steadily gain a share point or two per year in recent years, so that it now owns a 62.5 percent share of the US$3.6 billion laundry detergent market to Unilever's 12.9 percent (including Unilever's All and Wisk brands). It has an even bigger lead in fabric softeners—66 percent to Unilever's 8.4 percent (Unilever's Snuggle brand). Globally, P&G has gone from being the number-two laundry player in the early 1990s to dominant market leader today, with a global market share of 34 percent compared to Unilever's 17 percent. In the face of P&G's relentless assault, Unilever finally threw in the towel and recently put its detergents business up for sale.[14]

Expanding Market Share

Market leaders can also grow by increasing their market shares further. In many markets, small market share increases mean very large sales increases. For example, in the North American digital camera market, a 1 percent increase in market share is worth $99 million; in carbonated soft drinks the same percent increase is worth $792 million![15]

Studies have shown that, on average, profitability rises with increasing market share. Because of these findings, many companies have sought expanded market shares to improve profitability. GE, for example, declared that it wants to be at least number one or two in each of its markets or else get out. GE shed its computer, air-conditioning, small appliances, and television businesses because it could not achieve top-dog position in these industries.

However, some studies have found that many industries contain one or a few highly profitable large firms, several profitable and more focused firms, and a large number of medium-sized firms with poorer profit performance. It appears that profitability increases as a business gains share relative to competitors in its *served market*. For example, Lexus holds only a small share of the total car market, but it earns a high profit because it is the leading brand in the luxury performance car segment. And it has achieved this high share in its served market because it does other things right, such as producing high-quality products, creating good service experiences, and building close customer relationships.

Companies must not think, however, that gaining increased market share will automatically improve profitability. Much depends on their strategy for gaining increased share. There are many high-share companies with low profitability and many low-share companies with high profitability. The cost of buying higher market share may far exceed the returns. Higher shares tend to produce higher profits only when unit costs fall with increased market share, or when the company offers a superior-quality product and charges a premium price that more than covers the cost of offering higher quality.

Market Challenger Strategies

Firms that are second, third, or lower in an industry are sometimes quite large, such as Colgate, Ford, Lowe's, and Avis. These runner-up firms can adopt one of two competitive strategies: They can challenge the leader and other competitors in an aggressive bid for more market share (market challengers), or they can play along with competitors and not rock the boat (market followers).

A market challenger must first define which competitors to challenge and its strategic objective. The challenger can attack the market leader, a high-risk but potentially high-gain strategy. Its goal might be to take over market leadership. Or the challenger's objective may simply be to wrest more market share.

Although it might seem that the market leader has the most going for it, challengers often have what some strategists call a "second-mover advantage." The challenger observes what has made the leader successful and improves upon it. For example, Home Depot invented the home-improvement superstore. However, after observing Home Depot's success, number-two Lowe's, with its brighter stores, wider aisles, and arguably more helpful salespeople, has positioned itself as the friendly alternative to Big Bad Orange. For Lowe's, the advantage has been profitable. Although it still captures only 58 percent of Home Depot's revenues, over the past 10 years Lowe's has earned average annual returns of 14.7 percent compared with Home Depot's 4.1 percent.[16]

Alternatively, the challenger can avoid the leader and instead challenge firms its own size, or smaller local and regional firms. These smaller firms may be underfinanced and not serving their customers well. Several of the major beer companies grew to their present size not by challenging large competitors, but by gobbling up small local or regional competitors. If the company goes after a small local company, its objective may be to put that company out of business. The important point remains: The challenger must choose its opponents carefully and have a clearly defined and attainable objective.

How can the market challenger best attack the chosen competitor and achieve its strategic objectives? It may launch a *full frontal attack*, matching the competitor's product, advertising, price, and distribution efforts. It attacks the competitor's strengths rather than its weaknesses. The outcome depends on who has the greater strength and endurance.

If the market challenger has fewer resources than the competitor, however, a frontal attack makes little sense. Thus, many new market entrants avoid frontal attacks, knowing that the market leaders can head them off with ad blitzes, price wars, and other retaliations. Rather than challenging head-on, the challenger can make an *indirect attack* on the competitor's weaknesses or on gaps in the competitor's market coverage. It can carve out toeholds using tactics that the established leaders have trouble responding to or choose to ignore. For example, compare the vastly different strategies of two different European challengers—Virgin Drinks and Red Bull—when they entered the North American soft drink market in the late 1990s against market leaders Coca-Cola and PepsiCo:

> Virgin Drinks took on the leaders head-on, launching its own cola, advertising heavily, and trying to get into all the same retail outlets that stocked the leading brands. At Virgin Cola's launch, Virgin CEO Richard Branson even drove a tank through a wall of rivals' cans in New York's Times Square to symbolize the war he wished to wage on the big, established rivals. However, Coke's and Pepsi's viselike grip on shelf space proved impossible for Virgin Drinks to break. Although

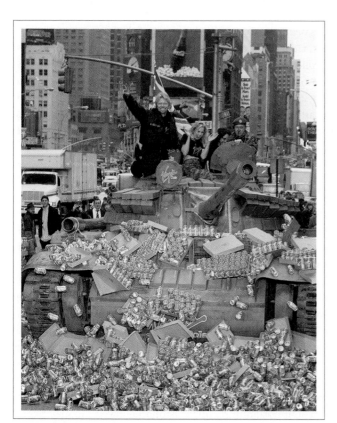

Market challenger strategies: Virgin Drinks mounted a full frontal attack on Coca-Cola and PepsiCo but couldn't break the leaders' viselike grip on shelf space.

Virgin Drinks is still around, it has never gained more than a 1 percent share of the North American cola market. Red Bull, by contrast, tackled the leaders indirectly. It entered the North American soft drink market with a niche product: a carbonated energy drink retailing at about twice what you would pay for a Coke or Pepsi. It started by selling Red Bull through unconventional outlets not dominated by the market leaders, such as bars and nightclubs, where twenty-somethings gulped down the caffeine-rich drink so they could dance all night. After gaining a loyal following, Red Bull used the pull of high margins to elbow its way into the corner store, where it now sits in refrigerated bins within arm's length of Coke and Pepsi. In North America, where Red Bull enjoys a 65 percent share of the energy drink market, its sales are growing at about 35 percent a year.[17]

Market Follower Strategies

Not all runner-up companies want to challenge the market leader. Challenges are never taken lightly by the leader. If the challenger's lure is lower prices, improved service, or additional product features, the leader can quickly match these to defuse the attack. The leader probably has more staying power in an all-out battle for customers. For example, a few years ago, when Zellers launched its everyday low prices policy with the slogan "Where the lowest price is the law. Everyday." directly challenging Walmart's everyday low prices, it started a price war that it couldn't win. Walmart had little trouble fending off Zellers' challenge, leaving Zellers worse off for the attempt. Thus, many firms prefer to follow rather than challenge the leader.

A follower can gain many advantages. The market leader often bears the huge expenses of developing new products and markets, expanding distribution, and educating the market. In contrast, as with challengers, the market follower can learn from the leader's experience. It can copy or improve on the leader's products and programs, usually with much less investment. Although the follower will probably not overtake the leader, it often can be as profitable.

Following is not the same as being passive or a carbon copy of the leader. A market follower must know how to hold current customers and win a fair share of new ones. It must find the right balance between following closely enough to win customers from the market leader but following at enough of a distance to avoid retaliation. Each follower tries to bring distinctive advantages to its target market—location, services, financing. The follower is often a major target of attack by challengers. Therefore, the market follower must keep its manufacturing costs and prices low or its product quality and services high. It must also enter new markets as they open up.

Market Nicher Strategies

Almost every industry includes firms that specialize in serving market niches. Instead of pursuing the whole market, or even large segments, these firms target subsegments. Nichers are often smaller firms with limited resources. But smaller divisions of larger firms also may pursue niching strategies. Firms with low shares of the total market can be highly successful and profitable through smart niching.

Why is niching profitable? The main reason is that the market nicher ends up knowing the target customer group so well that it meets their needs better than other firms that casually sell to that niche. As a result, the nicher can charge a substantial markup over costs because of the added value. Whereas the mass marketer achieves high volume, the nicher achieves high margins.

Nichers try to find one or more market niches that are safe and profitable. An ideal market niche is big enough to be profitable and has growth potential. It is one that the firm can serve effectively. Perhaps most importantly, the niche is of little interest to major competitors. And the firm can build the skills and customer goodwill to defend itself against a major competitor as the niche grows and becomes more attractive. For example, computer mouse and interface device maker Logitech is only a fraction the size of giant Microsoft.

Profitable niching: R.A.B. Food Group—with its Manischewitz and other brands—is North America's leading marketer of kosher foods. Although small, the company is growing faster and more profitably than Kraft and the other food giants.

Yet, through skilful niching, it dominates the PC mouse market, with Microsoft as its runner-up (see Real Marketing 18.2). Here's another example of a profitable nicher:

> R.A.B. Food Group is no Kraft. Then again, it doesn't aspire to be. Giant Kraft, with sales of more than US$37 billion, makes foods for all occasions, targeting broadly. In contrast, R.A.B. Food Group, with sales of little more than US$100 million, targets a narrow segment of consumers who want to cook kosher. R.A.B. is North America's leading marketer of kosher foods, fielding brands such as Manischewitz, Horowitz Margareten, Goodman's, and Rokeach. Kosher is a very attractive niche, and a profitable one. During the past five years, whereas Kraft has struggled for single-digit growth, R.A.B. Food Group's sales have grown nearly 50 percent. And the future looks bright for this profitable nicher. Fuelled by the boom in ethnic foods and an intensified interest in nutrition and food ingredient quality, kosher foods are now going mainstream. Research shows that consumers perceive kosher foods, made in accordance with centuries-old dietary laws, to be cleaner, purer, and higher in quality. Today, only one in five buyers of kosher foods is the traditional Jewish customer. In an effort to push its brands out of the smaller kosher sections of stores and into more heavily trafficked aisles, R.A.B. Food Group recently launched a "Simply Manischewitz" ad campaign (the Manischewitz brand accounts for about 54 percent of sales). Says the company's chief executive, "[Although] kosher foods are clearly our heritage and our anchor, we're reasserting our kosher credentials and positioning ourselves for broader growth."[18]

The key idea in niching is specialization. A market nicher can specialize along any of several market, customer, product, or marketing mix lines. For example, it can specialize in serving one type of *end user*, as when a law firm specializes in the criminal, civil, or business law markets. The nicher can specialize in serving a given *customer-size* group. Many nichers specialize in serving small and midsize customers who are neglected by the majors. Some nichers focus on one or a few *specific customers*, selling their entire output to a single company, such as Walmart or General Motors. Still other nichers specialize by *geographic market*, selling only in a certain locality, region, or area of the world. *Quality–price* nichers operate at the low or high end of the market. For example, HP specializes in the high-quality, high-price end of the hand-calculator market. Finally, *service nichers* offer services not available from other firms.

Niching carries some major risks. For example, the market niche may dry up, or it might grow to the point that it attracts larger competitors. That is why many companies practise *multiple niching*. By developing two or more niches, a company increases its chances for survival. Even some large firms prefer a multiple niche strategy to serving the total market. For example, Alberto Culver is a US$1.5 billion company that has used a multiple niching strategy to grow profitably without incurring the wrath of a market leader. The company, known mainly for its Alberto VO5 hair products, has focused its marketing muscle on acquiring a stable of smaller niche brands. It niches in hair, skin, and personal care products (Alberto VO5, St. Ives, Motions, Just for Me, Pro-Line, TRESemmé, and Consort men's hair products), seasonings and sweeteners (Molly McButter, Mrs. Dash, SugarTwin, Baker's Joy), and home products (static-cling fighter Static Guard). Most of its brands are number one in their niches. Alberto Culver's CEO explains the company's philosophy this way: "We know who we are and, perhaps more importantly, we know who we are not. We know that if we try to out-Procter Procter, we will fall flat on our face."[19]

Real Marketing 18.2

Nicher Logitech: The Little Mouse That Roars

Among the big tech companies, market leader Microsoft is the king of the jungle. When giant Microsoft looms, even large competitors quake. But when it comes to dominating specific market niches, overall size isn't always the most important thing. For example, in its own corner of the high-tech jungle, Logitech International is the little mouse that roars. In its niches, small but mighty Logitech is the undisputed market leader.

Logitech focuses on human interface devices—computer mice, keyboards, game controllers, remote controls, webcams, PC speakers, headsets, and other accessories. Logitech makes every variation of mouse imaginable. Over the years, it has flooded the world with more than 700 million computer mice of all varieties, mice for left- and right-handed people, wireless mice, travel mice, mini mice, 3-D mice, mice shaped like real mice for children, and even an "air mouse" that uses motion sensors to let you navigate your computer from a distance.

In the PC mouse market, Logitech competes head-on with Microsoft. At first glance it looks like an unfair contest. With more than US$51 billion in sales, Microsoft is nearly 25 times bigger than US$2.4 billion Logitech. But when it comes to mice, Logitech has a depth of focus and knowledge that no other company in the world—including Microsoft—can match. Whereas mice and other computer interface devices are pretty much a sideline for software maker Microsoft—almost a distraction—they are the main attraction for Logitech. As a result, each new-generation Logitech mouse is a true work of both art and science. Logitech's mice receive raves from designers, expert reviewers, and users alike.

A *BusinessWeek* analyst gives us a behind-the-scenes look at Logitech's deep design and development prowess:

One engineer, given the moniker "Teflon Tim" by amused colleagues, spent three months scouring the Far East to find just the right nonstick coatings and sound-deadening foam. Another spent hours taking apart wind-up toys. Others pored over the contours of luxury BMW motorcycles, searching for designs to crib. They were members of a most unusual team that spent thousands of hours during the past two years on a single goal: to build a better mouse. The result: Logitech's revolutionary MX Revolution, the next-generation mouse that hit consumer electronics shelves about two years ago. It represented the company's most ambitious attempt yet to refashion the lowly computer mouse into a

WANDERFUL

The world is your office. Anywhere you are, open your laptop and your cordless mouse is ready to go. The Logitech® VX Nano Cordless Laser Mouse for Notebooks. Its plug-and-forget nano receiver is the world's smallest USB receiver.® So small, it can stay plugged into your laptop. That means the ultra-slim mouse is ready to use in no time flat. Now, no layover is too short to get some work done. Sorry about that. To simplify your mobile life, go to Logitech.com

Logitech
Designed to move you®

Breeding mice has been so successful for nicher Logitech that it dominates the world mouse market, with giant Microsoft as its runner-up.

kind of control center for a host of PC applications. The sheer scope of the secret mission—which crammed 420 components, including a tiny motor, into a palm-sized device that usually holds about 20—brought together nearly three dozen engineers, designers, and marketers from around the globe.

Part of Logitech's product-development strategy is defensive. Once content to design mice and other peripherals for PC makers to slap their own names on, Logitech over the past half-decade has increasingly focused on selling its branded add-on equipment directly to consumers. Some 89 percent of Logitech's annual sales now come from retail. That forces Logitech to deliver regular improvements to entice new shoppers and purchases. "We think of mice as pretty simple," says one industry analyst, "but there's a pretty aggressive technology battle going on to prove what the mouse can do." Logitech's latest feat of cutting-edge wizardry is its MX Air, which promises to change the very definition of the computer mouse as we know it. More like an airborne remote control than a traditional mouse, you can surf the Web, play games, and control your home theatre PC from up to 30 feet away. There's also a "cool factor" at play. Wielding the MX Air is like holding a work of art.

Breeding mice has been very good for nicher Logitech. Thanks to its single-minded market focus and its dedication to creating the next best mouse, Logitech dominates the world mouse market, with giant Microsoft as its runner-up. Logitech mice have accompanied an estimated 55 percent of desktop PCs shipped out over the past two decades. And although Logitech isn't nearly as big as Microsoft, pound for pound and mouse for mouse it's even more profitable. In just the past five years, even as PC growth has slowed, Logitech's sales have more than doubled and profits have surged 225 percent.

"Our business is about the last inch between people and content and technology, and the mouse has always

been the icon of that last inch," explains Logitech CEO Guerrino De Luca. And nobody spans that last inch better than Logitech. The next time that you sit at your desktop PC, it's a pretty good bet that you'll have your hand on a Logitech mouse (regardless of the brand name on the outside). It's also a good bet that you'll really like the way it works and feels. "The goal [is] passing the 'ooooh' test," says a Logitech project leader, "creating a visceral experience that communicates both performance and luxury."

Sources: Quotes and other information from "Logitech Delivers Tenth Consecutive Record Year with Strongest Q4 Ever," Logitech press release, April 22, 2008, accessed at www.logitech.com; Cliff Edwards, "Here Comes Mighty Mouse," *BusinessWeek*, September 4, 2006, p. 76; Cliff Edwards, "The Mouse That Roars," *BusinessWeek*, August 20, 2007, p. 22; "Logitech International S.A.," *Hoover's Company Records*, May 15, 2008, p. 42459; and annual reports and other information from www.logitech.com, accessed October 2008.

3 BALANCING CUSTOMER AND COMPETITOR ORIENTATIONS

Whether a company is a market leader, challenger, follower, or nicher, it must watch its competitors closely and find the competitive marketing strategy that positions it most effectively. And it must continually adapt its strategies to the fast-changing competitive environment. So can the company spend *too* much time and energy tracking competitors, damaging its customer orientation? The answer is yes! A company can become so competitor centred that it loses its even more important focus on maintaining profitable customer relationships.

Competitor-centred company
A company whose moves are mainly based on competitors' actions and reactions.

A **competitor-centred company** is one that spends most of its time tracking competitors' moves and market shares and trying to find strategies to counter them. This approach has some pluses and minuses. On the positive side, the company develops a fighter orientation, watches for weaknesses in its own position, and searches out competitors' weaknesses. On the negative side, the company becomes too reactive. Rather than carrying out its own customer relationship strategy, it bases its own moves on competitors' moves. As a result, it may end up simply matching or extending industry practices rather than seeking innovative new ways to create more value for customers.

Customer-centred company
A company that focuses on customer developments in designing its marketing strategies and on delivering superior value to its target customers.

A **customer-centred company**, in contrast, focuses more on customer developments in designing its strategies. Clearly, the customer-centred company is in a better position to identify new opportunities and set long-run strategies that make sense. By watching customer needs evolve, it can decide what customer groups and what emerging needs are the most important to serve. Then it can concentrate its resources on delivering superior value to target customers. In practice, today's companies must be **market-centred companies**, watching both their customers and their competitors. But they must not let competitor watching blind them to customer focusing.

Market-centred company
A company that pays balanced attention to both customers and competitors in designing its marketing strategies.

Figure 18.4 shows that companies have moved through four orientations over the years. In the first stage, they were product oriented, paying little attention to either customers or competitors. In the second stage, they became customer oriented and started to pay attention to customers. In the third stage, when they started to pay attention to competitors, they became competitor oriented. Today, companies need to be market oriented, paying balanced attention to both customers and competitors. Rather than simply watching competitors and trying to beat them on current ways of doing business, they need to

Figure 18.4 Evolving
company orientations

watch customers and find innovative ways to build profitable customer relationships by delivering more customer value than competitors do. As noted previously, marketing begins with a good understanding of consumers and the marketplace.

REVIEWING OBJECTIVES AND KEY TERMS   mymarketinglab | Audio Chapter Summary

Today's companies face their toughest competition ever. Understanding customers is an important first step in developing strong customer relationships, but it's not enough. To gain competitive advantage, companies must use this understanding to design market offerings that deliver more value than the offerings of *competitors* seeking to win over the same customers. This chapter examined how firms analyze their competitors and design effective competitive marketing strategies.

OBJECTIVE 1   Discuss the need to understand competitors as well as customers through competitor analysis.

To prepare an effective marketing strategy, a company must consider its competitors as well as its customers. Building profitable customer relationships requires satisfying target consumer needs *better than competitors* do. A company must continuously analyze competitors and develop *competitive marketing strategies* that position it effectively against competitors and give it the strongest possible *competitive advantage*.

Competitor analysis first involves identifying the company's major competitors, using both an industry-based and a market-based analysis. The company then gathers information on competitors' objectives, strategies, strengths and weaknesses, and reaction patterns. With this information in hand, it can select competitors to attack or avoid. Competitive intelligence must be collected, interpreted, and distributed continuously. Company marketing managers should be able to obtain full and reliable information about any competitor affecting their decisions.

OBJECTIVE 2   Explain the fundamentals of competitive marketing strategies based on creating value for customers.

Which *competitive marketing strategy* makes the most sense depends on the company's industry and on whether it is a market leader, challenger, follower, or nicher. A *market*

leader has to mount strategies to expand the total market, protect market share, and expand market share. A *market challenger* is a firm that tries aggressively to expand its market share by attacking the leader, other runner-up companies, or smaller firms in the industry. The challenger can select from a variety of direct or indirect attack strategies.

A *market follower* is a runner-up firm that chooses not to rock the boat, usually from fear that it stands to lose more than it might gain. But the follower is not without a strategy and seeks to use its particular skills to gain market growth. Some followers enjoy a higher rate of return than the leaders in their industry. A *market nicher* is a smaller firm that is unlikely to attract the attention of larger firms. Market nichers often become specialists in some end use, customer size, specific customer, geographic area, or service.

OBJECTIVE 3   Illustrate the need for balancing customer and competitor orientations in becoming a truly market-centred organization.

A competitive orientation is important in today's markets, but companies should not overdo their focus on competitors. Companies are more likely to be hurt by emerging consumer needs and new competitors than by existing competitors. *Market-centred companies* that balance consumer and competitor considerations are practising a true market orientation.

KEY TERMS

mymarketinglab | Glossary Flashcards

DISCUSSING THE CONCEPTS

1. Which point of view is best for identifying competitors—industry or market?

2. Explain how having strong competitors can benefit a company.

3. What is the difference between entrepreneurial, intrepreneurial, and formulated marketing? What are the advantages and disadvantages of each?

4. Describe the three value disciplines for delivering superior customer value and explain why classifying competitive strategies in this way is appealing.

5. Discuss the strategies available to market leaders.

6. What are the advantages and disadvantages of a market nicher competitive strategy?

APPLYING THE CONCEPTS

1. Form a small group and conduct a customer value analysis for five local restaurants. Who are the strong and weak competitors? For the strong competitors, what are their vulnerabilities?

2. Research "blue ocean strategy" and discuss examples of companies that have succeeded in pursuing this strategy. Do companies succeeding in developing uncontested marketspaces necessarily have to be innovative upstarts?

3. Identify a company following a market niche strategy in each of the following industries: automobiles, restaurants, airlines, and golf equipment.

FOCUS ON TECHNOLOGY

Apple is the leader in MP3 players and wants to lead in the mobile smartphone segment, too. In 2008, only one in every 200 mobile phone users in North America owned an iPhone, but the recent introduction of the iPhone 3G is likely to change that. Unlike other phone applications, Apple opened up its heralded App Store where iPhone owners can find thousands of applications developed by third parties for their phones—everything from ring tones to games to accounting software and global positioning applications. Many of them are free because they display ads that produce revenues for developers. So far, Apple is not taking a cut of the ad revenues, and developers keep 70 percent of the money that they take in from paid-for consumer applications. This is a higher percentage than developers get from other applications markets in the cellphone industry. As a result, iPhone applications can be priced cheaper than similar applications for rivals BlackBerry and Windows Mobile smartphones. And these competitors offer fewer applications on their websites than Apple does. Within a month of the iPhone 3G's release, more than 500 applications were available from Apple's App Store. An estimated 20 million applications were downloaded by the end of 2008, followed by 110 million in 2009 and another projected 210 million in 2010.

1. What position does Apple hold in the smartphone industry? What competitive strategy is Apple using?

2. Why is Apple virtually giving away this platform to third-party applications developers? Wouldn't it be more profitable for Apple to generate more revenue from its App Store?

FOCUS ON ETHICS

After more than a year following the announcement of a potential merger between SIRIUS Satellite Radio and XM Satellite Radio, the United States Department of Justice and the Federal Communication Commission have now approved it. Since the January 2007 announcement, critics have voiced many concerns regarding programming redundancy and equipment compatibility, but the major issue was the effect the merger will have on competition. SIRIUS and XM are the only two providers of satellite radio, so a merger would create a monopoly with more than 17 million subscribers. The controversy was fuelled by fears of consumer price increases unabated by competitive pressures.

1. The U.S. Justice Department determined that the merger was not anticompetitive because forms of competition exist in the audio entertainment market. Discuss the competitors in this market.

2. Will this merger harm or benefit consumers?

MARKETING BY THE NUMBERS

Bottled water, consisting of still and sparkling unflavoured and flavoured waters, is a hot industry—sales grew by 8.8 percent between 2001 and 2006 and are expected to grow another 48.5 percent by 2011. The bottled water industry in North America totalled 31.4 billion litres valued at US$15.6 billion in 2006—that's an average of $0.50 in revenue per litre. Big players in this industry include Nestlé, PepsiCo, and Coca-Cola. Nestlé is the market leader, selling 9.58 billion litres, followed by PepsiCo's 4.33 billion litres and Coca-Cola's 3.74 billion litres.

1. Refer to Appendix 3: Marketing by the Numbers and calculate 2006 market shares by volume for Nestlé, PepsiCo, and Coca-Cola in the bottled water market.

2. How much revenue did one market share point represent in 2006? How much will it represent in 2011?

VIDEO CASE

mymarketinglab | Video Case Questions

Umpqua Bank

The U.S. retail banking industry has become very competitive. And with a few powerhouses dominating the market, how is a small bank to thrive? By differentiating itself through a competitive advantage that the big guys can't touch.

That's exactly what Umpqua has done. Step inside a branch of this Oregon-based community bank and you'll see immediately that this is not your typical Christmas club savings account/free toaster bank. Umpqua's business model has transformed banking from retail drudgery into a holistic experience. Umpqua has created an environment in which people just love to hang out. It not only has its own music download service featuring local artists, it even has its own blend of coffee.

But beneath all these bells and whistles lies the core of what makes Umpqua so different—a rigorous service culture where every branch and employee gets measured on how well they serve customers. That's why every customer feels like they get the help and attention they need from employees.

After viewing the video featuring Umpqua Bank, answer the following questions about creating competitive advantage:

1. With what companies does Umpqua compete?

2. What is Umpqua's competitive advantage?

3. Will Umpqua be able to maintain this advantage in the long run? Why or why not?

Visit MyMarketingLab at www.pearsoned.ca/mymarketinglab to view the video segment related to this case.

COMPANY CASE

Bose: Competing by Being Truly Different

Recently, Forrester Research announced the results of its semiannual survey ranking consumer electronics and personal computer companies on consumer trust. Based on a poll of more than 4700 customers as to their opinions of 22 of the best-known consumer technology brands, the company drew this conclusion: "North Americans' trust in consumer technology companies is eroding."

Why is consumer trust important? Forrester vice-president Ted Schadler answers that question this way: "Trust is a powerful way to measure a brand's value and its ability to command a premium price or drive consumers into a higher-profit direct channel. A decline in trust causes brand erosion and price-driven purchase decisions, which in turn correlates with low market growth."

But despite the decline in trust for most technology companies, Forrester made another surprising finding. Consumer trust in the Bose Corporation is riding high. In fact, Bose far outscored all other companies in Forrester's survey. That's not bad, considering that it was the first time the company had been included in the survey. Forrester points out that these results are no fluke, noting that Bose has 10 million regular users but more than 17 million consumers who aspire to use the brand (compared to 7 million for next highest company, Apple).

These high levels of consumer trust result from philosophies that have guided Bose for nearly 50 years. Most companies today focus heavily on building revenue, profits, and stock price. They try to outdo the competition by differentiating product lines with features and attributes that other companies do not have. While Bose doesn't exactly ignore such factors, its true competitive advantage is rooted in the company's unique corporate philosophy. Bose president Bob Maresca provides insights on that philosophy: "We are not in it strictly to make money," he says. Pointing to the company's focus on research and product innovation, he continues, "The business is almost a secondary consideration."

THE BOSE PHILOSOPHY

You can't understand Bose the company without taking a look at Bose the man. Amar Bose, the company's founder and still its CEO, has been in charge from the start. In the 1950s, Bose was working on his third degree at the Massachusetts Institute of Technology. He had a keen interest in research and studied various areas of electrical engineering. He also had a strong interest in music. When he purchased his first hi-fi system—a model that he believed had the best specifications—he was very disappointed in the system's ability to reproduce realistic sound. So he set out to find his own solution. Thus began a stream of research that would ultimately lead to the founding of the Bose Corporation in 1964.

From those early days, Amar Bose worked around certain core principles that have guided the philosophy of the company ever since. In conducting his first research on speakers and sound, he did something that has since been repeated time and time again at Bose: He ignored existing technologies and started entirely from scratch, something not very common in product-development strategies.

In another departure from typical corporate strategies, Bose plows all of the privately held company's profits back into research. This practice reflects his avid love of research and his belief that it will produce the highest quality products. But he also does this because he can. Bose has been quoted many times saying, "If I worked for another company, I would have been fired a long time ago," pointing to the fact that publicly held companies have long lists of constraints that don't apply to his privately held company. For this reason, Bose has always vowed that he will never take the company public. "Going public for me would have been the equivalent of losing the company. My real interest is research—that's the excitement—and I wouldn't have been able to do long-term projects with Wall Street breathing down my neck."

This commitment to research and development has led to the high level of trust that Bose customers have for the company. It also explains their almost cult-like loyalty. Customers know that the company cares more about their best interests—about making the best product—than about maximizing profits. But for a company not driven by the bottom line, Bose does just fine. According to market information firm NPD Group, Bose leads the market in home speakers with a 12.6 percent market share. And that market share translates into financial performance. Although figures are tightly held by the private corporation, the most recent known estimate of company revenue was US$1.8 billion for 2006. While that number doesn't come close to the US$88 billion that Sony reported last year, it does represent a 38 percent gain in just two years.

GROUNDBREAKING PRODUCTS

The company that started so humbly now has a breadth of product lines beyond its core home audio line. Additional lines target a variety of applications that have captured Amar Bose's creative attention over the years, including military, automotive, homebuilding/remodelling, aviation, and professional and commercial sound systems. It even has a division that markets testing equipment to research institutions, universities, medical device companies, and engineering companies worldwide. The following are just a few of the products that illustrate the innovative breakthroughs produced by the company.

Speakers. Bose's first product, introduced in 1965, was a speaker. Expecting to sell $1 million worth of speakers that first year, Bose made 60 but sold only 40. The original Bose speaker evolved into the 901 Direct/Reflecting speaker system launched in 1968. The speaker was so technologically advanced that the company still sells it today.

The system was designed around the concept that live sound reaches the human ear via direct as well as reflected channels (off walls, ceilings, and other objects). The configuration of the speakers was completely unorthodox. They were shaped like an eighth of a sphere and mounted facing into a room's corner. The speakers had no woofers or tweeters and were very small compared to the high-end speakers of the day. The design came much closer to the essence and emotional impact of live music than anything else on the market and won immediate industry acclaim.

However, Bose had a hard time convincing customers of the merits of these innovative speakers. At a time when woofers, tweeters, and size were everything, the 901 series initially flopped. In 1968, a retail salesman explained to Amar Bose why the speakers weren't selling:

> Look, I love your speaker but I cannot sell it because it makes me lose all my credibility as a salesman. I can't explain to anyone why the 901 doesn't have any woofers or tweeters. A man came in and saw the small size, and he started looking in the drawers for the speaker cabinets. I walked over to him, and he said, "Where are you hiding the woofer?" I said to him, "There is no woofer." So he said, "You're a liar," and he walked out.

Bose eventually worked through the challenges of communicating the virtues of the 901 series to customers through innovative display and demonstration tactics. The product became so successful that Amar Bose now credits the 901 series for building the company.

The list of major speaker innovations at Bose is a long one. In 1975, the company introduced concert-like sound in the bookshelf-size 301 Direct/Reflecting speaker system. Fourteen years of research led to the 1984 development of acoustic waveguide speaker technology, a technology today found in the award-winning Wave radio, Wave music system, and Acoustic Wave music system. In 1986, the company again changed conventional thinking about the relationship between speaker size and sound. The Acoustimass system enabled palm-size speakers to produce audio quality equivalent to that of high-end systems many times their size. And most recently, Bose has again introduced the state of the art with the MusicMonitor, a pair of compact computer speakers that rival the sound of three-piece subwoofer systems. It may sound simple, but at US$399, it's anything but.

Headphones. Bob Maresca recalls that "Bose invested tens of millions of dollars over 19 years developing headset technology before making a profit. Now, headsets are a major part of the business." Initially, Bose focused on noise reduction technologies to make headphones for pilots that would block out the high level of noise interference from planes. Bose headphones didn't just muffle noise, they electronically cancelled ambient noise so that pilots wearing them heard nothing but the sound coming through the phones. Bose quickly discovered that airline passengers could benefit as much as pilots from its headphone technology. Today, the Bose QuietComfort series, used in a variety of consumer applications, is the benchmark in noise cancelling headphones. One journalist considers this product to be so significant that it made his list of "101 gadgets that changed the world" (some of the other inventions on the list included aspirin, paper, and the light bulb).

Automotive suspensions. Another major innovation from Bose has yet to be introduced. The company has been conducting research since 1980 on a product outside of its known areas of expertise: automotive suspensions. Amar Bose's interest in suspensions dates back to the 1950s when he bought both a Citroën DS-19 C and a Pontiac Bonneville, each riding on unconventional air suspension systems. Since that time, he has been obsessed with the engineering challenge of achieving good cornering capabilities without sacrificing a smooth ride. "In cars today, there's always a compromise between softness over bumps and roll and pitch during maneuvering," Bose said in a recent interview. The Bose Corporation is now on the verge of introducing a suspension that it believes eliminates that compromise.

The basics of the system include an electromagnetic motor installed at each wheel. Based on inputs from road sensing monitors, the motor can retract and extend almost instantaneously. If there is a bump in the road, the suspension reacts by "jumping" over it. If there is a pothole, the suspension allows the wheel to extend downward, but then retracts it quickly enough that the pothole is not felt. In addition to these comfort-producing capabilities, the wheel motors are strong enough to keep a car completely level during an aggressive manoeuvre such as cornering or stopping. In a recent interview about this system, Bose said, "This system provides absolutely better handling than any sports car, and the most comfortable ride imaginable."

Thus far, Bose has invested more than US$100 million and 27 years in its groundbreaking suspension. And while it is ready to take the product to market, it is staying true to its philosophy by not rushing things. Bose plans first to partner with one automotive manufacturer in the near future. The cost of the system will put it in the class of higher-end luxury automobiles. But eventually, Bose anticipates that wider adoption and higher volume will bring the price down to the point where the suspension could be found in all but the least expensive cars.

At an age when most people have long since retired, 78-year-old Amar Bose still works every day, either at the company's headquarters in Framingham, Massachusetts, or at his home in nearby Wayland. "He's got more energy than an 18-year-old," says Maresca. "Every one of the naysayers only strengthens his resolve." This work ethic illustrates the passion of the man who has shaped one of today's most innovative and yet most trusted companies. His philosophies have produced Bose's long list of groundbreaking innovations. Even now, as the company prepares to enter the world of automotive suspensions, it continues to achieve success by following another one of Amar Bose's basic philosophies: "The potential size of the market? We really have no idea. We just know that we have a technology that's so different and so much better that many people will want it."

Questions for Discussion

1. Based on the business philosophies of Amar Bose, how do you think the Bose Corporation goes about analyzing its competition?

2. Which of the text's three approaches to marketing strategy best describes Bose's approach?

3. Using the Michael Porter and Treacy and Wiersema frameworks presented in the text, which basic competitive marketing strategies does Bose pursue?

4. What is Bose's competitive position in its industry? Do its marketing strategies match this position?

5. In your opinion, is Bose a customer-centric company?

6. What will happen when Amar Bose leaves the company?

Sources: Jeffrey Krasner, "Shocks and Awe," *Boston Globe*, December 3, 2007, p. E1; Simon Usborne, "101 Gadgets That Changed the World," *Belfast Telegraph*, November 5, 2007, accessed online at www.belfasttelegraph.co.uk; Brian Dumaine, "Amar Bose," *Fortune Small Business*, September 1, 2004, accessed online at www.money.cnn.com/magazines/fsb; Olga Kharif, "Selling Sound: Bose Knows," *Business-Week Online*, May 15, 2006, accessed at www.businessweek.com; Mark Jewell, "Bose Tries to Shake Up Auto Industry," *Associated Press*, November 27, 2005; "Bose Introduces New QuietComfort 3 Acoustic Noise Cancelling Headphones," *Business Wire*, June 8, 2006; "Forrester Research Reveals the Most Trusted Consumer Technology Brands," press release accessed at www.forrester.com; see also "About Bose," accessed at www.bose.com, June 2008.

Visit **MyMarketingLab** at **www.pearsoned.ca/mymarketinglab** for access to online tutorials, interactive exercises, videos, and much more.

19

The Global
Marketplace

PREVIEWING
THE CONCEPTS

You've now learned the fundamentals of how companies develop competitive marketing strategies to create customer value and build lasting customer relationships. In this chapter, we extend these fundamentals to global marketing. We've visited global topics in each previous chapter—it's difficult to find an area of marketing that doesn't contain at least some international issues. Here, however, we'll focus on special considerations that companies face when they market their brands globally. Advances in communication, transportation, and other technologies have made the world a much smaller place. Today, almost every firm, large or small, faces international marketing issues. In this chapter, we will examine six major decisions marketers make in going global. Let's begin by looking at a firm that has a long history of international success—McCain Foods Limited.

McCain Foods Limited was founded in 1957 by Harrison and Wallace McCain with support from their two brothers Andrew and Robert. Their first operation was a small factory located in Florenceville, New Brunswick, Canada. Today, it is a global leader among food processors and the most famous Canadian brand in the world. No matter where in the world you travel, chances are you will be tasting a McCain Foods french fry if you order this item off a menu or pick some up from a food stand. McCain Foods is the world's largest maker of frozen potato products and produces over one-third of the french fried potatoes produced internationally. McCain Foods' potato producing plants process more than 1 million pounds of potato products an hour.

McCain's product list goes far beyond frozen potatoes, however. It offers thousands of other foods including vegetables, desserts, pizzas, juices and other beverages, oven meals, entrees, and appetizers. McCain Foods takes considerable pride in being a socially responsible company that practises sustainable agriculture and implements energy efficiency projects at its processing plants around the world. In response to global concerns about diet, health, and obesity, McCain Foods created a line of *Better for You* products—products that may follow any of these criteria: trans fat free (under 0.5 grams); 30 percent or fewer total calories from fat, with less than 25 percent of this fat originating from saturated fats; controlled portions that follow local dietary intake guidance; or reduced salt. McCain Foods' mission is to create good food and a better life for its consumers, customers, and employees, and the communities in which it operates worldwide.

McCain Foods sells to both end consumers and to businesses like restaurants and institutions that have food operations (such as hospitals, schools, and restaurants). When selling to the food-service industry, McCain Foods must not only showcase its products' quality, but also be able to deliver this quality product at the right price and with the right level of service. McCain Foods has been highly successful and today is a supplier to huge customers such as McDonald's, KFC, and Burger King.

McCain Foods employs 20 000 people, generates over $6 billion in revenues, and operates 55 production facilities on six continents. It exports to 130 countries, including Argentina, Brazil, Denmark, Hungary, Mexico, Saudi Arabia,

South Africa, Taiwan, and Turkey. It has an especially strong presence in Europe and is a leader in almost all of its global markets with the exeption of the United States, where it is trounced by its rival ConAgra. But McCain Foods is gaining ground, growing quickly since its purchase of Ore-Ida Foods in 1997, the food-service business of H.J. Heinz Company. McCain is also breaking new ground in emerging markets like India and China. McCain's growth has been the result of the company's vision, unwavering devotion to product quality, careful operations management, advanced information technology, insightful marketing, sound acquisition strategy, innovative product development, and Canadian know-how.

In all of the markets it serves, McCain Foods' products are customized for local tastes and requirements. One of the company's core values is to "Drink the Local Wine." Such an attitude has led McCain Foods to great success. For example, ACNielson recently found that McCain Foods is one of only 23 food, beverage, and confectionery brands to qualify as a global megabrand.

When McCain Foods first enters a market, it often imports products from Canada and then gradually develops its own operations within the country. Take its recent entry into China. The shoestring fries that accompany a consumer's "Old Beijing" chicken and veggie wrap in a KFC restaurant first came from Coaldale, Alberta, the McCain Foods factory near Lethbridge that supplied much of the product sold in China.

However, McCain Foods understands that to really penetrate the market it requires in-country operations. McCain Foods strives to create its products from ingredients sourced locally. To that end, the company works closely with local farmers, sharing its agronomy knowledge and research and assisting local growers in advancing their technology and irrigation methods. According to the company's corporate social responsibility report, "providing a `hand up' rather than a 'hand out,' the concept that underlies our participation in our communities, . . .

Through product innovation, powerful marketing, and a strong sense of corporate responsibility, McCain Foods has grown to be a successful global giant.

has proven to enhance the wellbeing of ourselves, our customers, and our consumers in a long-term and sustainable manner." In China today, 95 percent of McCain Foods' products are grown locally.

Once the local agronomy is assured, the company then develops manufacturing facilities. After careful research and experimentation, McCain Foods began making french fries from locally grown potatoes in China in a new, state-of-the-art plant located near Harbin. Getting to this point took a lot of patience and investment. The new factory was the result of a decade of growing sales in China, six years of agricultural trials, endless lobbying to get New Brunswick , Canada, seed potatoes into China, and a $53 million investment in farms as well as the factory. In addition to french fries, the plant will also produce hash browns and vegetable products.

After building a plant, the next challenge was to sell that theme of local production and high quality to fast-food vendors. The dizzying pace of Chinese urbanization, industrialization, and rural depopulation is driving the proliferation of U.S.-style fast-food joints and major cultural shifts, including adding potatoes into a diet once dominated by rice.

OBJECTIVES

1. Discuss how the international trade system and the economic, political–legal, and cultural environments affect a company's international marketing decisions.

2. Describe three key approaches to entering international markets.

3. Explain how companies adapt their marketing mixes for international markets.

4. Identify the three major forms of international marketing organization.

McCain had to work closely with the Chinese government to accomplish its goals. In the beginning, McCain leased 600 hectares of land to grow its potatoes, mostly in 20- to 30-hectare fields, which are a far cry from the small plots common in Chinese agriculture. The company had to get government permission to allow it to lease huge tracts of land. McCain Foods won government officials over with its emphasis on value-added agriculture that will improve quality and yields, and technology transfer that teaches modern planting, irrigation, spraying, and harvesting methods to local farmers.

McCain Foods used similar tactics when it entered India. McCain Foods had been sending frozen potato products to India since 1998. However, as was the case in China, the company began planting test patches of potatoes around the country with an eye on in-country operations. The training and support McCain Foods has given to local farmers has been beneficial to both the farmers and the company. McCain has helped local producers reduce expenditures by 35 percent and increase income by 104 percent, and there are now more than 100 farmers in India cultivating 1500 acres of potatoes for McCain's use. McCain opened its first Indian plant in 2006. The new plant produces french fries as well as frozen versions of traditional Indian potato-based foods. Customizing products for the local market is crucial to foreign success in India, says Peter Nesbitt of Export Development Canada. "Canadian companies often think that because their product sells into the U.S. it will automatically work in India, too. That's not true."

Whether operating in India, China, or the United States, McCain Foods works to give the firm a local face and tailors its communications to local needs, attitudes, market

life-cycle stage, and consumers' media habits. For example, here at home McCain ran a campaign called "Tan Lines" for Crescendo Rising Crust Pizza. The ads showed people with a strip of tan across their eyes from watching their pizza cook in the oven. It was so popular that it crossed over into popular culture and was even parodied on *This Hour Has 22 Minutes*. McCain Foods got the last laugh, though, as sales leaped 34 percent and the campaign won a CASSIE, a Canadian advertising award.

In contrast, McCain took a very different approach in Great Britain. Research showed that Britons didn't understand how much fat should be in their diet or what foods contained fat. Of particular concern for McCain Foods was the fact that 52 percent of survey respondents felt guilty serving french fries to their family, believing they were high in fat. Because of these perceptions, McCain Foods took a significant hit to its sales in this region. In response the company developed an "It's All Good" business strategy, which included a full assessment and reformulation of its products with the goal of reducing fat and sodium and eliminating nonessential ingredients. In addition, an aggressive marketing campaign was launched that turned existing consumer perception on its head by showcasing the goodness of the potato. The results have been outstanding, with sales in 2008 growing twice as fast as the market for potato products. It even has some newspaper articles asking "Are chips the new health food?"

No matter where in the world McCain Foods operates, it follows its values of honesty, fairness, and integrity. So next time you are travelling and that urge for a french fry overwhelms you, rest assured that it may be a product from a world-leading Canadian company that you pop into your mouth.[1]

Chapter Opening Discussion

Canada has a long history of international trade. Our small domestic market forced companies to look beyond our borders for additional markets. Our diverse population has made us comfortable working in other countries with people from other cultures. Thus, Canada is well positioned to exploit opportunities in the global marketplace. Organizations of all kinds, from Canada Post to SNC-Lavalin to McCain Foods, have gone global.

1   GLOBAL MARKETING TODAY

The world is shrinking rapidly with the advent of faster communication, transportation, and financial flows. Products developed in one country—Gucci purses, McCain french fries, Sony electronics, Japanese sushi, German BMWs—have found enthusiastic acceptance in other countries. We would not be surprised to hear about a German businessman wearing an Italian suit meeting an English friend at a Japanese restaurant who later returns home to drink Russian vodka and watch *American Idol* on TV.

International trade is booming. Since 1990, the number of multinational corporations in the world has grown from 30 000 to more than 60 000. Some of these multinationals are true giants. In fact, of the largest 150 "economies" in the world, only 76 are countries. The remaining 74 are multinational corporations. Walmart, the world's largest company, has annual revenues greater than the gross domestic product of all but the world's 24 largest-GDP countries.[2]

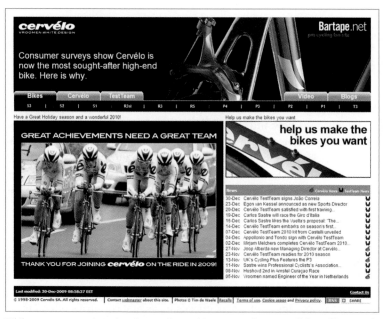

While many companies who play on the world stage are large, small firms like Cervélo Cycles can also be highly successful.

Between 2003 and 2006, total world trade grew at rates between 4.5 and 11 percent annually. However, buffeted by a deepening crisis in financial markets, global economic activity slowed to 3.2 percent in 2008, down from 5.2 percent in 2007.[3]

Many Canadian companies have long been successful at international marketing: Barrick Gold, Biovail, Bombardier, Bank of Nova Scotia, Cirque du Soleil, George Weston Ltd. (owner of Loblaw), Molson, Maple Leaf Foods, SNC-Lavalin, engineering services and dozens of other firms have made the world their market. While many global firms are large, others are minuscule, like world-leading firm Cervélo Cycles:

Cervélo Cycles is a small Toronto-based company that was founded by two McGill engineering students in 1995. From the beginning its mission was simple: to help its customers win bike races. Today it has become the world's most sought after high-end bike and sells more than 10 000 bikes a year (not bad when you consider that its bikes sell for between $2000 and $10 000). In 2003, it became the supplier to Team CSC, the fourteenth ranked bike team in the world. It was catapulted onto the world stage when a member of the team rode one of the firm's cycles to victory in one stage of the gruelling Tour de France bicycle race. The partnership between CSC and Cervélo lasted until 2008. In 2009, the company had its own team in the race, Cervélo TestTeam, becoming the first bike manufacturer to take on this challenge. Cyclists have also ridden Cervélo bikes to victory in Ironman triathlons, world time trial championships, and numerous road-racing World Cups. The company's bikes are sold to a tightly defined target market: cycling pros and committed weekend warriors. Today, Cervélo SA is the world's largest manufacturer of time trial and triathlon bikes. Its fame continues to grow. At the Beijing Olympics, Cervélo bikes were ridden by over 40 remarkable Olympic athletes, resulting in three gold, five silver, and two bronze medals. As one analyst notes, "They build good bikes . . . but they've been very good marketers. That's what has put them on the world stage."[4]

Many North American companies have made the world their market.

We've become so accustomed to international marketing that names of European and Asian firms such as Sony, Toyota, BP, IKEA, Nestlé, Nokia, and Prudential have become household words. Other products and services that appear to be North American are in fact produced or owned by foreign companies: Bantam books, Baskin-Robbins ice cream, GE and RCA televisions, Carnation milk, Inco, Universal Studios, and Motel 6, to name just a few. Michelin, the oh-so-French tire manufacturer, now does 32 percent of its business in North America; Johnson & Johnson, the maker of such products as Band-Aids and Johnson's Baby Shampoo, does 45 percent of its business abroad.[5]

Figure 19.1 Major international marketing decisions

Glossary Flashcards of Key Terms

Global firm

A firm that, by operating in more than one country, gains R&D, production, marketing, and financial advantages in its costs and reputation that are not available to purely domestic competitors.

But while global trade is growing, global competition is intensifying. Foreign firms are expanding aggressively into new international markets, and home markets are no longer as rich in opportunity as they used to be. Few industries are now safe from foreign competition. If companies delay taking steps toward internationalizing, they risk being shut out of growing markets in Western and Eastern Europe, China and the Pacific Rim, Russia, and elsewhere. Firms that stay at home to play it safe might not only lose their chances to enter other markets but also risk losing their home markets. Domestic companies that never thought about foreign competitors suddenly find these competitors in their own backyards.

Ironically, although the need for companies to go abroad is greater today than in the past, so is the risk in doing so. Companies that go global may face highly unstable governments and currencies, restrictive government policies and regulations, and high trade barriers. Corruption is also an increasing problem—officials in several countries often award business not to the best bidder but to the highest briber.

A **global firm** is one that, by operating in more than one country, gains marketing, production, R&D, and financial advantages that are not available to purely domestic competitors. The global company sees the world as one market. It minimizes the importance of national boundaries and develops "transnational" brands. It raises capital, obtains materials and components, and manufactures and markets its goods wherever it can do the best job. For example, Otis Elevator, the world's largest elevator maker, achieves four-fifths of its sales from outside North America. It gets its elevator door systems from France, small geared parts from Spain, electronics from Germany, and special motor drives from Japan. "Borders are so twentieth century," says one global marketing expert. "Transnationals take 'stateless' to the next level."[6]

This does not mean that small and medium-sized firms must operate in a dozen countries to succeed; these firms can practise global niching. But the world is becoming smaller, and every company operating in a global industry—whether large or small—must assess and establish its place in world markets.

The rapid move toward globalization means that all companies will have to answer some basic questions: What market position should we try to establish in our country, in our economic region, and globally? Who will our global competitors be and what are their strategies and resources? Where should we produce or source our products? What strategic alliances should we form with other firms around the world?

As shown in Figure 19.1, a company faces six major decisions in international marketing. We will discuss each decision in detail in this chapter.

LOOKING AT THE GLOBAL MARKETING ENVIRONMENT

Before deciding whether to operate internationally a company must understand the international marketing environment. That environment has changed a great deal in the past two decades, creating both new opportunities and new problems.

The International Trade System

Companies looking abroad must start by understanding the international *trade system*. When selling to another country, a firm may face restrictions on trade between nations. Foreign governments may charge *tariffs*, taxes on certain imported products designed to raise revenue or to protect domestic firms. For example, China slaps a 25 percent tariff on imported autos. Or they may set *quotas*, limits on the amount of foreign imports that they will accept in certain product categories. The purpose of a quota is to conserve on foreign exchange and to protect local industry and employment. North American firms may also face *exchange controls*, which limit the amount of foreign exchange and the exchange rate against other currencies.

The company also may face *nontariff trade barriers*, such as biases against North American company bids, restrictive product standards, or excessive regulations. For example, in 2009, Prime Minister Stephen Harper expressed "serious concern" about the "Buy American" provisions that were put in place in the United States to stimulate its economy.[7]

At the same time, certain forces *help* trade between nations. Examples include the General Agreement on Tariffs and Trade (GATT) and various regional free trade agreements.

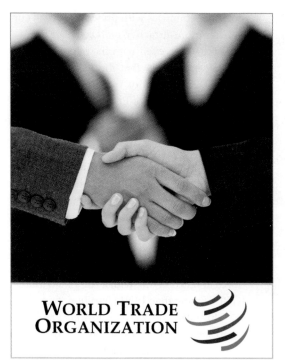

The WTO and GATT: The General Agreement on Tariffs and Trade (GATT) promotes world trade by reducing tariffs and other international trade barriers. The WTO oversees GATT, imposes trade sanctions, and mediates global disputes.

The World Trade Organization and GATT

The General Agreement on Tariffs and Trade (GATT) is a treaty designed to promote world trade by reducing tariffs and other international trade barriers. Since the treaty's inception in 1947, member nations (which numbered 153 in July 2008) have met in eight rounds of GATT negotiations to reassess trade barriers and set new rules for international trade. The first seven rounds of negotiations reduced the average worldwide tariffs on manufactured goods from 45 percent to just 5 percent.[8]

The second to last series of GATT negotiations, dubbed the Uruguay Round, dragged on for seven long years before concluding in 1994 but resulted in a reduction of trade barriers and the creation of more comprehensive and enforceable world trade rules. Beyond reducing trade barriers and setting global standards for trade, the Uruguay Round set up the World Trade Organization (WTO) to enforce GATT rules. In general, the WTO acts as an umbrella organization whose aim is to liberalize trade. Above all it is a negotiating forum, and it oversees legal ground rules for international trade, mediates global trade disputes, and imposes trade sanctions when necessary. The previous GATT organization never possessed such authority. The most recent round of GATT negotiations, the Doha Development Agenda, began in Doha, Qatar, in late 2001 and was set to conclude in 2005, but the discussions continued into 2008.[9]

Regional Free Trade Zones

Economic community
A group of nations organized to work toward common goals in the regulation of international trade.

Certain countries have formed *free trade zones* or **economic communities**. These are groups of nations organized to work toward common goals in the regulation of international trade. One such community is the *European Union (EU)*. Formed in 1957, the EU set out to create a single European market by reducing barriers to the free flow of products, services, finances, and labour among member countries and developing policies on trade with nonmember nations. Today, the EU represents one of the world's single largest markets. Currently, it has 27 member countries containing close to half a billion consumers and accounts for more than 20 percent of the world's exports.[10]

European unification offers tremendous trade opportunities. However, it also poses threats. As a result of increased unification, European companies have grown bigger and more competitive. Perhaps an even greater concern, however, is that lower barriers *inside* Europe will create only thicker *outside* walls. Some observers envision a "Fortress Europe" that heaps favours on firms from EU countries but hinders outsiders by imposing obstacles.

Progress toward European unification has been slow—many doubt that complete unification will ever be achieved. In recent years, 13 member nations have taken a significant step toward unification by adopting the euro as a common currency. Many other countries are expected to follow within the next few years. Widespread adoption of the euro will decrease much of the currency risk associated with doing business in Europe, making

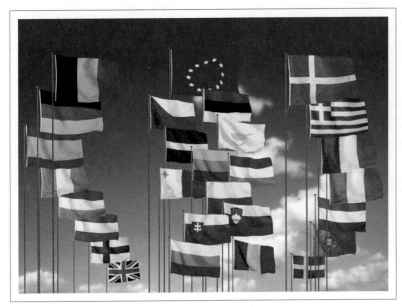

Economic communities: The European Union represents one of the world's single largest markets. Its current member countries contain more than half a billion consumers and account for 20 percent of the world's exports.

member countries with previously weak currencies more attractive markets.[11]

However, even with the adoption of the euro it is unlikely that the EU will ever go against 2000 years of tradition and become the "United States of Europe." A community with two dozen different languages and cultures will always have difficulty coming together and acting as a single entity. For example, efforts to forge a single European constitution appear to have failed following French and Dutch "no" votes in mid-2005. And economic disputes between member nations have stalled long-term budget negotiations. Still, although only partly successful so far, unification has made Europe a global force to reckon with, with a combined annual GDP of more than US$14.5 trillion.[12]

In 1994, the *North American Free Trade Agreement (NAFTA)* established a free trade zone among Canada, the United States, and Mexico. The agreement created a single market of 447 million people who produce and consume over US$16 trillion of goods and services annually. As it is implemented over a 15-year period, NAFTA will eliminate all trade barriers and investment restrictions among the three countries. Thus far, the agreement has allowed trade between the countries to flourish. In the dozen years following its establishment, trade among the NAFTA nations has risen 198 percent. The United States is Canada's largest trading partner. In 2008, Canada exported almost $490 billion of goods and services to the United States while it imported only $280 billion.[13]

Spurred on by NAFTA's success, Canada has been pursuing additional trade agreements. For example, 2009 was a busy year for trade negotiations. The Canada–EU Summit held in Prague began negotiations toward a comprehensive economic partnership agreement between Canada and the European Union. Another set of similar negotiations was undertaken with India. Also in 2009, Canada's free trade agreements with Peru, Colombia, and the European Free Trade Association (EFTA) came into effect. The latter agreement gives Canadian exporters free access to the markets of Iceland, Liechtenstein, Norway, and Switzerland—four countries who are not members of the EU. Canada also signed a new trade agreement with Jordan.[14]

Economic Environment

The international marketer must study each country's economy. Two economic factors reflect the country's attractiveness as a market: the country's industrial structure and its income distribution.

The country's *industrial structure* shapes its product and service needs, income levels, and employment levels. The four types of industrial structures are as follows:

- *Subsistence economies:* In a subsistence economy, the vast majority of people engage in simple agriculture. They consume most of their output and barter the rest for simple goods and services. They offer few market opportunities.

- *Raw material exporting economies:* These economies are rich in one or more natural resources but poor in other ways. Much of their revenue comes from exporting these resources. Examples are Chile (tin and copper), the Democratic Republic of the Congo (copper, cobalt, and coffee), and Saudi Arabia (oil). These countries are good markets for large equipment, tools and supplies, and trucks. If there are many foreign residents and a wealthy upper class, they are also a market for luxury goods.

- *Industrializing economies:* In an industrializing economy, manufacturing accounts for 10 to 20 percent of the country's economy. Examples include Egypt, India, and Brazil. As manufacturing increases, the country needs more imports of raw textile materials, steel, and heavy machinery and fewer imports of finished textiles, paper products, and automobiles. Industrialization typically creates a new rich class and a small but growing middle class, both demanding new types of imported goods.

- *Industrial economies:* Industrial economies, such as those found in Europe and North America, are major exporters of manufactured goods, services, and investment funds. They trade goods among themselves and also export them to other types of economies for raw materials and semifinished goods. The varied manufacturing activities of these industrial nations and their large middle class make them rich markets for all sorts of goods.

The second economic factor is the country's *income distribution*. Industrialized nations may have low-, medium-, and high-income households. In contrast, countries with subsistence economies may consist mostly of households with very low family incomes. Still other countries may have households with only either very low or very high incomes. However, even poor or developing economies may be attractive markets for all kinds of goods, including luxuries. For example, many luxury-brand marketers are rushing to take advantage of China's rapidly developing consumer markets:

> More than half of China's 1.3 billion consumers can barely afford rice, let alone luxuries. According to the World Bank, more than 400 million Chinese live on less than $2 a day. Yet posh brands—from Gucci and Cartier to Lexus and Bentley—are descending on China in force. How can purveyors of $2000 handbags, $20 000 watches, and $1 million limousines thrive in a developing economy? Easy, says a Cartier executive. "Remember, even medium-sized cities in China . . . have populations larger than Switzerland's. So it doesn't matter if the percentage of people in those cities who can afford our products is very small." Thus, even though China has only 0.2 millionaires per 1000 residents (compared with 8.4 per 1000 in the United States), it trails only the United States, Germany, and the United Kingdom in the total number of millionaires (Canada has approximately 900 000 millionaires). In 2005, China's luxury-goods consumption accounted for 12 percent of the world's total, slightly under half of that of America and Japan. By 2014, however, the figure is expected to jump to 23 percent, making China the world's largest consumer of luxury goods. Dazzled by the pace at which China's booming economy is minting millionaires and swelling the ranks of the middle class, luxury brands are rushing to stake out shop space and tout their wares. "The Chinese are a natural audience for luxury goods," notes one analyst. After decades of socialism and poverty, China's elite are suddenly "keen to show off their newfound wealth."[15]

Economic environment: Many luxury brand marketers are rushing to take advantage of China's rapidly developing consumer markets.

As a recent study by McKinsey & Company showed, there are other target markets in China that global marketers should be aware of. Caution must be taken, however, to carefully segment this marketplace. For example, buying behaviour for apparel differs widely across segments. While 40 percent of Chinese shoppers have undifferentiated wardrobes (i.e., they wear similar clothing at work, at celebrations and social events, and with family), other consumers buck this trend. In particular, China's urban young adults, aged 18 to 25 years old—a segment comprising about 15 million people—often favour international brands, seeing them as higher quality than local brands. Thirty-six percent of China's young adults say they often try on foreign products and brands, compared with an average of only 13 percent of other respondents. While it is not uncommon to differentiate young from older consumers, young consumers in China have far more pronounced differences. Young Chinese consumers also shop for apparel more frequently than do people in other age groups, spend larger sums of money on clothing, and are disposed to spend even more as their incomes rise.[16]

As global retailers contemplate entering China, they must recognize that they face more powerful local competitors for mass-marketed items than in the higher end of the market. Local players have cost advantages and are quick to learn from global retailers' store layouts and promotional campaigns. Zara, for example, uses an alternative approach. It identifies consumers willing to pay more for the latest fashions, then it creates low-cost yet trendy standalone outlets in upscale malls so it can appeal simultaneously to mass-market consumers with premium tastes and to higher-end customers prowling for bargains. As can be seen from this example, country, demographic, and regional economic environments will affect an international marketer's decisions about which global markets to enter and how to compete within them.

Political–Legal Environment

Nations differ greatly in their political–legal environments. In considering whether to do business in a given country, a company should consider factors such as the country's attitudes toward international buying, government bureaucracy, political stability, and monetary regulations.

Some nations are very receptive to foreign firms; others are less accommodating. For example, India has complicated the operations of some foreign businesses with import quotas, currency restrictions, and other limitations that make operating there a challenge. In contrast, neighbouring Asian countries such as Singapore and Thailand court foreign investors and shower them with incentives and favourable operating conditions. Canada wants to improve trade relationships with India, especially in the field of science and technology. Thus, in 2005, it signed a Joint Declaration on Science and Technology (S&T) Co-operation and began more comprehensive negotiations in 2009. As former international trade minister James Peterson noted, "India is a true economic giant that boasts the largest emerging consumer market in the world."[17]

Political and regulatory stability is another issue. For example, Venezuela's government is notoriously volatile because of economic factors such as inflation and steep public spending, increasing the risk of doing business there. Although most international marketers still find the Venezuelan market attractive, the unstable political and regulatory situation will affect how they handle business and financial matters.[18]

Companies must also consider a country's monetary regulations. Sellers want to take their profits in a currency of value to them. Ideally, the buyer can pay in the seller's currency or in other world currencies. Short of this, sellers might accept a blocked currency—one whose removal from the country is restricted by the buyer's government—if they can buy other goods in that country that they need themselves or can sell elsewhere for a needed currency. In addition to currency limits, a changing exchange rate also creates high risks for the seller.

Most international trade involves cash transactions. Yet many nations have too little hard currency to pay for their purchases from other countries. They may want to pay with other items instead of cash, which has led to a growing practice called **countertrade**. Countertrade takes several forms: *Barter* involves the direct exchange of goods or services, as when Azerbaijan imported wheat from Romania in exchange for crude oil, and Vietnam exchanged rice for Philippine fertilizer and coconuts. Another form is *compensation* (or *buyback*), whereby the seller sells a plant, equipment, or technology to another country and agrees to take payment in the resulting products. Thus, Japan's Fukusuke Corporation sold knitting machines and raw textile materials to Shanghai clothing manufacturer Chinatex in exchange for finished textiles produced on the machines. The most common form of countertrade is *counterpurchase*, in which the seller receives full payment in cash but agrees to spend some of the money in the other country. For example, Boeing sells aircraft to India and agrees to buy Indian coffee, rice, castor oil, and other goods and sell them elsewhere.[19]

Countertrade
International trade involving the direct or indirect exchange of goods for other goods instead of cash.

Countertrade deals can be very complex. For example, a few years back, Daimler-Chrysler agreed to sell 30 trucks to Romania in exchange for 150 Romanian jeeps, which it then sold to Ecuador for bananas, which were in turn sold to a German supermarket chain for German currency. Through this roundabout process, DaimlerChrysler finally obtained payment in German money.

Cultural Environment

Each country has its own folkways, norms, and taboos. When designing global marketing strategies, companies must understand how culture affects consumer reactions in each of its world markets. In turn, they must also understand how their strategies affect local cultures.

The Impact of Culture on Marketing Strategy

The seller must understand the ways in which consumers in different countries think about and use certain products before planning a marketing program. There are often surprises. For example, the average French man uses almost twice as many cosmetics and grooming aids as his wife. The Germans and the French eat more packaged, branded spaghetti than do Italians. Some 49 percent of Chinese eat on the way to work. Most North American women let down their hair and take off makeup at bedtime, whereas 15 percent of Chinese women style their hair at bedtime and 11 percent put *on* makeup.[20]

Companies that ignore cultural norms and differences can make some very expensive and embarrassing mistakes. Here are examples:

Nike inadvertently offended Chinese officials when it ran an advertisement featuring LeBron James crushing a number of culturally revered Chinese figures in a kung fu-themed TV spot. The Chinese government found that the ad violated regulations to uphold national dignity and respect of the "motherland's culture" and yanked the multimillion-dollar campaign. With egg on its face, Nike released a formal apology. Distiller Brown-Forman made a similar mistake when it created a window display in an Athens, Greece, bar showing Hindu Goddess Durga sitting on a tiger holding bottles of its Southern Comfort brand in all eight of her hands. Infuriated Hindus worldwide sent mail and email messages decrying the defamation of their goddess—consuming alcohol is a sin to Hindus. An embarrassed Brown-Forman quickly removed the display, stating "We didn't realize it was the image of a Hindu goddess. It was human error and a violation of our marketing code" (which prohibits the use of religious images in the promotion of the company's alcoholic beverages).[21]

Overlooking cultural differences can result in embarrassing mistakes. China imposed a nationwide ban on a "blasphemous" kung fu-themed TV spot featuring LeBron James crushing a number of culturally revered Chinese figures.

Business norms and behaviour also vary from country to country. For example, North American executives like to get right down to business and engage in fast and tough face-to-face bargaining. However, Japanese and other Asian businesspeople often find this behaviour offensive. They prefer to start with polite conversation, and they rarely say no in face-to-face conversations. As another example, South Americans like to sit or stand very close to each other when they talk business—in fact, almost nose-to-nose. The North American business executive tends to keep backing away as the South American executive moves closer. Both may end up being offended. North American business executives need to be briefed on these kinds of factors before conducting business in another country.[22]

By the same token, companies that understand cultural nuances can use them to their advantage when positioning products and preparing campaigns internationally. Consider LG Electronics, the US$60 billion South Korean electronics, telecommunications, and appliance powerhouse. LG now operates in more than 39 countries including Canada and captures 86 percent of its sales from markets outside its home country. LG's global success rests on understanding and catering to the unique characteristics of each local market through in-country research, manufacturing, and marketing.

If you've got kimchi in your fridge, it's hard to keep it a secret. Made from fermented cabbage seasoned with garlic and chili, kimchi is served with most meals in Korea. But when it's stored inside a normal refrigerator, its pungent odour taints nearby foods. That's why, two decades ago, LG introduced the kimchi refrigerator, featuring a dedicated compartment that isolates smelly kimchi from other foods. Kimchi refrigerators have now become a fixture in 65 percent of Korean homes, and LG is the country's top-selling manufacturer.

LG's mission is to make customers happy worldwide by creating products to change their lives, no matter where they live. In India, LG rolled out refrigerators with larger vegetable and water-storage compartments, surge-resistant power supplies, and brightly coloured finishes that reflect local preferences (red in the south, green in Kashmir). Some of LG's Indian microwaves have dark-coloured interiors to hide masala stains. In Iran, LG offers a microwave oven with a preset button for reheating shish kebabs—a favourite dish. In the Middle East, the company unveiled a gold-plated 71-inch flat-screen television that sells for US$80 000—a tribute to the region's famous affinity for gilded opulence. And in Russia, where many people entertain at home during the country's long winters, LG developed a karaoke phone that can be programmed with the top 100 Russian songs, whose lyrics scroll across the screen when they're played. The phone sold more than 220 000 handsets in the first year.[23]

LG is an incredibly successful international marketer because it deeply understands consumers in each market it serves. Its display at Yonge and Dundas, the busiest corner in Toronto, allows LG to target Canadians as they attend events, concerts, and sporting competitions.

LG also tailors its promotions so it can effectively communicate with people in a particular country market. In Canada, for example, it sponsors the popular show *Canada's Next Top Model* (a sponsorship that fits well with LG's TrueSteam laundry pair that helps people's clothes look their best). It also runs its own fashion week. Responding to Canadians' interest in independent film, it started its own film festival. It engaged Canadian consumers by asking them to come up with the "most popular, creative and stylish" name suggestions for the LGX120, a new computer. The most popular name submitted— LG Cyber Friend. "The 'Whatchamacallit' contest was a fun and unique way to engage Canadians with LG's brand," said Tim Barnes of LG Canada. "We were thrilled at the volume of entries we received, and were absolutely floored at the quality of the naming suggestions." Using the tag line "Enter the party of the summer," it also ran an online contest called the "Gourmet Gathering." Canadian entrants could win an LG French Door refrigerator stuffed with gourmet goodies. LG also built a huge outdoor display at the corner of Yonge and Dundas in Toronto. It picked a great spot to increase its visibility since the Yonge–Dundas Square is the city's number-one visitor destination.

Thus, understanding cultural traditions, preferences, and behaviours can help companies not only avoid embarrassing mistakes but also take advantage of cross-cultural opportunities.

The Impact of Marketing Strategy on Cultures

Whereas marketers worry about the impact of culture on their global marketing strategies, others may worry about the impact of marketing strategies on global cultures. For example, Canadian mining and power companies, like Talisman, Barrick Gold, and Acres International, have been accused of contributing to war efforts, degrading the environment, and supporting corruption. Social critics contend that large American multinationals such as McDonald's, Coca-Cola, Starbucks, Nike, Microsoft, Disney, and MTV aren't just "globalizing" their brands, they are "Americanizing" the world's cultures:

> Down in the mall, between the fast-food joint and the bagel shop, a group of young people huddle in a flurry of baggy combat pants, skateboards, and slang. They size up a woman teetering past wearing DKNY, carrying *Time* magazine in one hand and a latte in the other. She brushes past a guy in a Yankees baseball cap who is talking on his Motorola cellphone about the Martin Scorsese film he saw last night.
>
> It's a standard American scene—only this isn't America, it's Britain. U.S. culture is so pervasive, the scene could be played out in any one of dozens of cities. Budapest or Berlin, if not Bogota or Bordeaux. Even Manila or Moscow. As the unrivaled global superpower, America exports its culture on an unprecedented scale. . . . Sometimes, U.S. ideals get transmitted—such as individual rights, freedom of speech, and respect for women. At other times, materialism or worse becomes the message and local traditions get crushed. "Today, globalization often wears Mickey Mouse ears," says Thomas Friedman in his book *The Lexus and the Olive Tree*."[24]

Critics worry that American cultural imperialism is leading to the demise of individual cultures. Canada has long struggled to maintain an independent identity separate from that of the United States. Teens in India watch MTV and ask their parents for more westernized clothes and other symbols of American pop culture and values. Grandmothers in small European villages no longer spend each morning visiting local meat, bread, and produce markets to gather the ingredients for dinner. Instead, they now shop at Walmart Supercentres. Women in Saudi Arabia see North American films and question their societal roles. In China, most people never drank coffee before Starbucks entered the market. Now Chinese consumers rush to Starbucks stores "because it's a symbol of a new kind of lifestyle."

Such concerns have sometimes led to a backlash against North American–led globalization. Well-known North American brands have become the targets of boycotts and protests in some international markets. Companies such as Coca-Cola, McDonald's, Nike, and KFC have been singled out by anti-globalization protesters. Despite such problems, defenders of globalization argue that these concerns are overblown. People around the world increasingly value international brands. Research In Motion's BlackBerry, for example, is a highly successful global brand. Rbc, Canada's largest bank, operates successfully in 49 other countries. TD Canada Trust serves approximately 17 million customers around the world. Manulife Financial not only has major operations in Asia, but has also won a significant presence in the United States. Bombardier, Canada's leading transportation manufacturer, is also the world's third-largest civil aircraft maker.[25]

The success of Canadian companies rests on our ability as a country to brand ourselves. The stakes are huge according to Simon Anholt, author of the book *Competitive Identity*. Anholt says a country's brand is important to win a share of the world's "consumers, tourists, investors, students, entrepreneurs, and international sporting and cultural events. It is essential if we are to gain the attention of the international media, and respect of other governments, and the people of other countries." In commenting on Canada as a brand Paul Lavoie, founder of ad agency TAXI, notes, "We have not managed our brand carefully, or with a shared purpose, We've allowed our diversity to define us in broken fragments according to short-term tactics, not long-term goals." The Government of Canada has begun to respond to these concerns. Recent brand-building efforts have focused on projecting an accurate image of Canada to the world—one that reflects Canada as a modern, sophisticated, creative, diverse, tolerant, caring, and technologically advanced society.[26]

More fundamentally, most studies reveal that the cultural exchange goes both ways—North America gets as well as gives cultural influence:

> Hollywood dominates the global movie market—capturing 90 percent of audiences in some European markets. However, British TV is giving as much as it gets in serving up competition to U.S. and Canadian shows, spawning such hits as *The Office*, *Canadian Idol*, and *Dancing with the Stars*. Although West Indian sports fans are now watching more basketball and baseball, cricket is also becoming more popular in Canada. Young people in Asia are daubing the names of hockey, baseball, and basketball superstars on their jerseys, but soccer is also becoming increasing popular in many Canadian cities. Even childhood has increasingly been influenced by Asian and European cultural imports. Most kids know all about the Power Rangers, Tamagotchi and Pokémon, Sega and Nintendo. And J.K. Rowling's so-very-British Harry Potter books are shaping the thinking of a generation of North American youngsters, not to mention the millions of oldsters who've fallen under the spell as well. For the moment, English remains cyberspace's dominant language, and having web access often means that third-world youth have greater exposure to North American popular culture. Yet these same technologies enable Balkan students studying in Canada to hear webcast news and music from Serbia or Bosnia.[27]

North American companies have also learned that to succeed abroad they must adapt to local cultural values and traditions rather than trying to force their own. Disneyland Paris flopped at first because it failed to take local cultural values and behaviours into account. According to a Euro Disney executive, "When we first launched, there was the belief that it was enough to be Disney. Now we realize that our guests need to be welcomed on the basis of their own culture and travel habits."[28] That realization has made Disneyland Paris the number-one tourist attraction in Europe—with twice as many visitors each year as the Eiffel Tower. The movie-themed Walt Disney Studios Park now blends Disney entertainment and attractions with the history and culture of European film. A show celebrating the history of animation features Disney characters speaking six different languages. Rides are narrated by foreign-born stars speaking in their native tongues.

Thus, globalization is a two-way street. If globalization has Mickey Mouse ears, it is also wearing a French beret, talking on a Nokia cellphone, buying furniture at IKEA, driving a Toyota Camry, and watching a Sony big-screen plasma TV.

DECIDING WHETHER TO GO GLOBAL

Not all companies need to venture into international markets to survive. For example, most local businesses need to market well only in the local marketplace. Operating domestically is easier and safer. Managers don't need to learn another country's language and laws. They don't have to deal with unstable currencies, face political and legal uncertainties, or redesign their products to suit different customer expectations. However, companies that operate in global industries, where their strategic positions in specific markets are affected strongly by their overall global positions, must compete on a regional or worldwide basis to succeed.

Any of several factors might draw a company into the international arena. Global competitors might attack the company's home market by offering better products or lower prices. The company might want to counterattack these competitors in their home markets to tie up their resources. The company's customers might be expanding abroad and require international servicing. Or the company's home market might be stagnant or shrinking, and foreign markets may present additional sales and profit opportunities. For example, to offset declines in the North American soft drink market, Coca-Cola and Pepsi are rapidly expanding their presence in emerging markets such as Russia and China. And whereas Whirlpool's North American sales slipped by 1 percent last year, its European sales jumped 12 percent.[29]

Before going abroad, the company must weigh several risks and answer many questions about its ability to operate globally. Can the company learn to understand the preferences and buyer behaviour of consumers in other countries? Can it offer competitively attractive products? Will it be able to adapt to other countries' business cultures and deal effectively with foreign nationals? Do the company's managers have the necessary international experience? Has management considered the impact of regulations and the political environments of other countries?

Because of the difficulties of entering international markets, most companies do not act until some situation or event thrusts them into the global arena. Someone—a domestic exporter, a foreign importer, a foreign government—may ask the company to sell abroad. Or the company may be saddled with overcapacity and need to find additional markets for its goods.

DECIDING WHICH MARKETS TO ENTER

Before going abroad, the company should try to define its international mar*keting objectives and policies*. It should decide what *volume* of foreign sales it wants. Most companies start small when they go abroad. Some plan to stay small, seeing international sales as a small part of their business. Other companies have bigger plans, seeing international business as equal to or even more important than their domestic business.

The company also needs to choose in *how many* countries it wants to market. Companies must be careful not to spread themselves too thin or to expand beyond their capabilities by operating in too many countries too soon. Next, the company needs to decide on the *types* of countries to enter. A country's attractiveness depends on the product, geographical factors, income and population, political climate, and other factors. The seller may prefer certain country groups or parts of the world. In recent years, many major new markets have emerged, offering both substantial opportunities and daunting challenges.

After listing possible international markets, the company must carefully evaluate each one. It must consider many factors. For example, P&G's decision to enter the Chinese toothpaste market with its Crest brand is a no-brainer: China's huge population makes it the world's largest toothpaste market. And given that only 20 percent of China's rural dwellers now brush daily, this already huge market can grow even larger. Yet P&G must still question whether market size *alone* is reason enough for investing heavily in China.

P&G should ask some important questions: Can Crest compete effectively with dozens of local competitors, Colgate, and a state-owned brand managed by Unilever? Will the Chinese government remain stable and supportive? Does China provide the needed production and distribution technologies? Can the company master China's vastly different cultural and buying differences? Crest's current success in China suggests that it could answer yes to all of these questions.

"Just 10 years ago, Procter & Gamble's Crest brand was unknown to China's population, most of whom seldom—if ever—brushed their teeth," says one analyst. "Now P&G . . . sells more tubes of toothpaste there than it does in America, where Crest has been on store shelves for 52 years." P&G achieved this by sending researchers to get a feel for what urban and rural Chinese were willing to spend and what flavors they preferred. It discovered that urban Chinese are happy to pay more than $1 for tubes of Crest with exotic

P&G's decision to enter the Chinese toothpaste market with Crest is a no-brainer: China is the world's largest toothpaste market. But P&G must still question whether market size alone is reason enough for investing heavily in China.

Table 19.1 Indicators of Market Potential

Demographic characteristics	Sociocultural factors
Education	Consumer lifestyles, beliefs, and values
Population size and growth	Business norms and approaches
Population age composition	Cultural and social norms
Geographic characteristics	Languages
Climate	**Political and legal factors**
Country size	National priorities
Population density—urban, rural	Political stability
Transportation structure and market accessibility	Government attitudes toward global trade
	Government bureaucracy
Economic factors	Monetary and trade regulations
GDP size and growth	
Income distribution	
Industrial infrastructure	
Natural resources	
Financial and human resources	

flavours such as Icy Mountain Spring and Morning Lotus Fragrance. But Chinese living in the countryside prefer the 50-cent Crest Salt White, since many rural Chinese believe that salt whitens the teeth. Armed with such insights, Crest now leads all competitors in China with a 25 percent market share.[30]

Possible global markets should be ranked on several factors, including market size, market growth, cost of doing business, competitive advantage, and risk level. The goal is to determine the potential of each market using indicators such as those shown in Table 19.1. Then the marketer must decide which markets offer the greatest long-run return on investment.

Deciding How to Enter the Market

Once a company has decided to sell in a foreign country it must determine the best mode of entry. Its choices are *exporting, joint venturing*, and *direct investment*. Figure 19.2 shows three market entry strategies, along with the options each one offers. As the figure shows, each succeeding strategy involves more commitment and risk, but also more control and potential profits.

Figure 19.2 Market entry strategies

Exporting

Exporting
Entering a foreign market by selling goods produced in the company's home country, often with little modification.

The simplest way to enter a foreign market is through **exporting**. The company may passively export its surpluses from time to time, or it may make an active commitment to expand exports to a particular market. In either case, the company produces all of its goods in its home country. It may or may not modify them for the export market. Exporting involves the least change in the company's product lines, organization, investments, or mission.

Companies typically start with *indirect exporting*, working through independent international marketing intermediaries. Indirect exporting involves less investment because the firm does not require an overseas marketing organization or network. It also involves less risk. International marketing intermediaries bring know-how and services to the relationship, so the seller normally makes fewer mistakes.

Sellers may eventually move into *direct exporting*, whereby they handle their own exports. The investment and risk are somewhat greater in this strategy, but so is the potential return. A company can conduct direct exporting in several ways: It can set up a domestic export department that carries out export activities. It can set up an overseas sales branch that handles sales, distribution, and perhaps promotion. The sales branch gives the seller more presence and program control in the foreign market and often serves as a display centre and customer service centre. The company can also send home-based salespeople abroad at certain times to find business. Finally, the company can do its exporting either through foreign-based distributors who buy and own the goods or through foreign-based agents who sell the goods on behalf of the company.

Joint Venturing

Joint venturing
Entering foreign markets by joining with foreign companies to produce or market a product or service.

Licensing
A method of entering a foreign market in which the company enters into an agreement with a licensee in the foreign market.

A second method of entering a foreign market is **joint venturing**—joining with foreign companies to produce or market products or services. Joint venturing differs from exporting in that the company joins with a host-country partner to sell or market abroad. It differs from direct investment in that an association is formed with someone in the foreign country. There are four types of joint ventures: licensing, contract manufacturing, management contracting, and joint ownership.

Licensing

Licensing is a simple way for a manufacturer to enter international marketing. The company enters into an agreement with a licensee in the foreign market. For a fee or royalty, the licensee buys the right to use the company's manufacturing process, trademark, patent, trade secret, or other item of value. The company thus gains entry into the market at little risk; the licensee gains production expertise or a well-known product or name without having to start from scratch.

Coca-Cola markets internationally by licensing bottlers around the world and supplying them with the syrup needed to produce the product. In Japan, Budweiser beer flows from Kirin breweries and Marlboro cigarettes roll off production lines at Japan Tobacco, Inc. Tokyo Disney Resort is owned and operated by Oriental Land Company under licence from The Walt Disney Company.

Licensing has potential disadvantages, however. The firm has less control over the licensee than it would over its own operations. Furthermore, if the licensee is very successful, the firm has given up these profits, and if and when the contract ends it may find it has created a competitor.

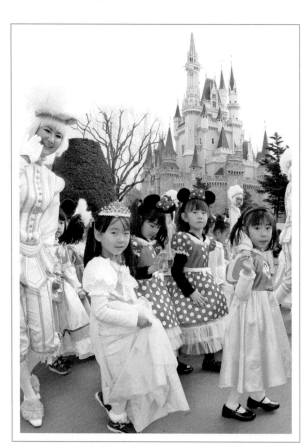

Licensing: Tokyo Disney Resort is owned and operated by the Oriental Land Company (a Japanese development company) under licence from The Walt Disney Company.

Contract Manufacturing

Contract manufacturing
A joint venture in which a company contracts with manufacturers in a foreign market to produce its product or provide its service.

Another option is **contract manufacturing**—the company contracts with manufacturers in the foreign market to produce its product or provide its service. Sears used this method in opening up department stores in Mexico and Spain where it found qualified local manufacturers to produce many of the products it sells. The drawbacks of contract manufacturing are decreased control over the manufacturing process and loss of potential profits on manufacturing. The benefits are the chance to start faster, with less risk, and the later opportunity either to form a partnership with or to buy out the local manufacturer.

Management Contracting

Management contracting
A joint venture in which the domestic firm supplies the management know-how to a foreign company that supplies the capital; the domestic firm exports management services rather than products.

Under **management contracting**, the domestic firm supplies management know-how to a foreign company that supplies the capital. The domestic firm exports management services rather than products. Hilton uses this arrangement in managing hotels around the world.

Management contracting is a low-risk method of getting into a foreign market, and it yields income from the beginning. The arrangement is even more attractive if the contracting firm has an option to buy some share in the managed company later on. The arrangement is not sensible, however, if the company can put its scarce management talent to better uses or if it can make greater profits by undertaking the whole venture. Management contracting also prevents the company from setting up its own operations for a period of time.

Joint Ownership

Joint ownership
A joint venture in which a company joins investors in a foreign market to create a local business in which the company shares joint ownership and control.

Joint ownership ventures consist of one company joining forces with foreign investors to create a local business in which they share joint ownership and control. A company may buy an interest in a local firm or the two parties may form a new business venture. Joint ownership may be needed for economic or political reasons. The firm may lack the financial, physical, or managerial resources to undertake the venture alone. Or a foreign government may require joint ownership as a condition for entry.

Hershey recently formed a joint venture with Indian-based Godrej Beverages and Foods to make and distribute its chocolates in that country. When it comes to selling chocolate in India, Hershey will need all the help it can get from its new local partner.

"Humans may have first cultivated a taste for chocolate 3000 years ago," comments one observer, "but India [has] just gotten around to it. Compared to the sweet-toothed Swiss and Cadbury-crunching Brits, both of whom devour about 24 pounds of chocolate per capita annually, Indians consume a paltry 5.8 ounces." Indian consumers currently favour a traditional candy known as mithai, and it will take a significant and culturally savvy marketing effort to persuade them to transfer their allegiance to chocolate. To make things even tougher, two global giants—Nestlé and Cadbury—already hold a 90 percent share of Indian chocolate between them. Still, given the sheer size of the Indian population, if consumers can be persuaded to acquire a taste for chocolate, the rewards for Hershey and Godrej could be substantial. Either company could have decided to go it alone, but both will likely benefit greatly from the joint venture. Godrej gains a highly respected global brand; Hershey reaps the benefits of a local partner that understands the intricacies of the Indian market.[31]

Hershey recently formed a joint venture with Indian-based Godrej Beverages and Foods to make and distribute its chocolates in that country.

Joint ownership has certain drawbacks. The partners may disagree over investment, marketing, or other policies. Whereas many North American firms like to reinvest earnings for growth, local firms often prefer to take out these earnings; and whereas North American firms emphasize the role of marketing, local investors may rely on selling.

Direct Investment

Direct investment
Entering a foreign market by developing foreign-based assembly or manufacturing facilities.

The biggest involvement in a foreign market comes through **direct investment**—the development of foreign-based assembly or manufacturing facilities. For example, HP has made direct investments in a number of major markets abroad, including India. It recently opened a second factory near Delhi to make PCs for the local market. Thanks to such commitments, HP has overtaken the favourite local brand, HCL, and now controls more than 21 percent of the market in India.[32]

If a company has gained experience in exporting and if the foreign market is large enough, foreign production facilities offer many advantages. The firm may have lower costs in the form of cheaper labour or raw materials, foreign government investment incentives, and freight savings. The firm may improve its image in the host country because it creates jobs. Generally, a firm develops a deeper relationship with government, customers, local suppliers, and distributors, allowing it to adapt its products to the local market better. Finally, the firm keeps full control over the investment and therefore can develop manufacturing and marketing policies that serve its long-term international objectives.

The main disadvantage of direct investment is that the firm faces many risks, such as restricted or devalued currencies, falling markets, or government changes. In some cases, a firm has no choice but to accept these risks if it wants to operate in the host country.

3   DECIDING ON THE GLOBAL MARKETING PROGRAM

Standardized global marketing
An international marketing strategy for using basically the same marketing strategy and mix in all the company's international markets.

Adapted global marketing
An international marketing strategy for adjusting the marketing strategy and mix elements to each international target market, bearing more costs but hoping for a larger market share and return.

Companies that operate in one or more foreign markets must decide how much, if at all, to adapt their marketing strategies and programs to local conditions. At one extreme are global companies that use **standardized global marketing**, using largely the same marketing strategy approaches and marketing mix worldwide. At the other extreme is **adapted global marketing**. In this case, the producer adjusts the marketing strategy and mix elements to each target market, bearing more costs but hoping for a larger market share and return.

The question of whether to adapt or standardize the marketing strategy and program has been much debated in recent years. On the one hand, some global marketers believe that technology is making the world a smaller place and that consumer needs around the world are becoming more similar. This paves the way for "global brands" and standardized global marketing. Global branding and standardization, in turn, result in greater brand power and reduced costs from economies of scale.

On the other hand, the marketing concept holds that marketing programs will be more effective if tailored to the unique needs of each targeted customer group. If this concept applies within a country, it should apply even more across international markets. Despite global convergence, consumers in different countries still have widely varied cultural backgrounds. They still differ significantly in their needs and wants, spending power, product preferences, and shopping patterns. Because these differences are hard to change, most marketers adapt their products, prices, channels, and promotions to fit consumer desires in each country.

However, global standardization is not an all-or-nothing proposition. It's a matter of degree. Most international marketers suggest that companies should "think globally but act locally"—that they should seek a balance between standardization and adaptation. The corporate level gives global strategic direction; regional or local units focus on individual consumer differences across global markets. Simon Clift, head of marketing for global consumer goods giant Unilever, puts it this way: "We're trying to strike a balance between being mindlessly global and hopelessly local."[33]

McDonald's operates this way. It uses the same basic fast-food look, layout, and operating model in its restaurants around the world but adapts its menu to local tastes. In Japan, it offers up Ebi Filet-O-Shrimp burgers and fancy Salad Macs salad plates. In Korea it sells the Bulgogi Burger, a grilled pork patty on a bun with a garlicky soy sauce. In India, where cows are considered sacred, McDonald's serves McChicken, Filet-O-Fish, McVeggie (a vegetable burger), Pizza McPuffs, McAloo Tikki (a spiced-potato burger), and the Maharaja Mac—two all-chicken patties, special sauce, lettuce, cheese, pickles, onions on a sesame-seed bun.

Similarly, to boost sales of Oreo cookies in China, Kraft Foods has tweaked its recipes and marketing programs to meet the tastes of Chinese consumers. It even developed a new Chinese version of the American classic (see Real Marketing 19.1).

Product

Five strategies allow for adapting product and marketing communication strategies to a global market (see Figure 19.3).[34] We first discuss the three product strategies and then turn to the two communication strategies.

Straight product extension means marketing a product in a foreign market without any change. Top management tells its marketing people, "Take the product as is and find customers for it." The first step, however, should be to find out whether foreign consumers use that product and what form they prefer.

Straight extension has been successful in some cases and disastrous in others. Kellogg cereals, Gillette razors, Heineken beer, and Black & Decker tools are all sold successfully in about the same form around the world. But General Foods introduced its standard powdered JELL-O in the British market only to find that British consumers prefer a solid wafer or cake form. Likewise, Philips began to make a profit in Japan only after it reduced the size of its coffeemakers to fit into smaller Japanese kitchens and its shavers to fit smaller Japanese hands. Straight extension is tempting because it involves no additional product development costs, manufacturing changes, or new promotion. But it can be costly in the long run if products fail to satisfy foreign consumers.

Product adaptation involves changing the product to meet local conditions or wants. For example, Finnish cellphone maker Nokia customizes its cellphones for every major market. Developers build in rudimentary voice recognition for Asia where keyboards are a problem and raise the ring volume so phones can be heard on crowded Asian streets. Nokia is also making a major push to create full-featured but rugged and low-cost phones that meet the needs of less-affluent consumers in large developing countries such as India, China, and Kenya:

> Looking for ways to make cellphones practical for people living in developing countries, Nokia has trekked to far corners of the globe, from the narrow alleys of Mumbai to the vast slums of Nairobi. The result is a slew of new features especially designed for places with harsh weather and harsher living conditions. One example: The company created dustproof keypads—crucial in dry, hot countries with many unpaved roads, as Nokia executives learned from visits to customers' homes in India. Low price is also important. On a recent visit to slums outside Nairobi, members of the emerging markets team discovered that many people form buying clubs, pooling their money to buy handsets one at a time until every member has one. Now Nokia is looking for ways to

Straight product extension
Marketing a product in a foreign market without any change.

Product adaptation
Adapting a product to meet local conditions or wants in foreign markets.

Figure 19.3 Five global product and communications strategies

Real Marketing 19.1

Oreos and Milk, Chinese Style

Unlike its iconic North American counterpart, the most popular Oreo in China is long, thin, four-layered, and coated in chocolate. Still, the two kinds of Oreos, sold half a world apart, have one important thing in common: Both are now bestsellers. But taking the dark chocolate treasure to China has been no easy journey for Kraft Foods. Although the Oreo has long been the top-selling cookie in the United States, to make Oreos sell well in the world's most populous nation Kraft has had to completely reinvent the popular cookie.

Oreos were first introduced in the United States in 1912, but it wasn't until 1996 that Kraft introduced Oreos to Chinese consumers. It began by selling the same Oreos in China that it markets in the United States—the ones that Americans love to twist apart to lick the creamy centres or dunk in milk until they're soggy. However, after nine years of trying mostly U.S. marketing themes and programs on Chinese consumers, Oreo sales remained flat. Albert Einstein's definition of insanity—doing the same thing repeatedly and expecting different results—"characterized what we were doing," says Kraft Foods International's vice-president of marketing. To make things happen, he concluded, it was time for a major Oreo makeover.

First up: Kraft changed the Oreo management team. Whereas previous decisions about Oreo marketing in China had been made at arm's length by people in Kraft's Northbrook, Illinois, headquarters, the company now handed the task of remaking the brand to an entrepreneurial team of local Chinese managers. The team began with in-depth research on Chinese consumers that yielded some interesting findings. First the team learned that the Chinese weren't big cookie eaters. Despite China's immense population, the Chinese biscuit and cookie market was one-third the size of the U.S. market. Second, Chinese consumers weren't much enamored with the Oreos that Americans have come to crave. Traditional Oreos were too sweet for Chinese tastes. Also, standard packages of 14 Oreos, priced at 72 cents, were too expensive for most Chinese food budgets.

So for starters the company developed 20 prototypes of reduced-sugar Oreos and tested them with Chinese consumers before arriving at a formula that tasted right. Kraft also introduced packages containing fewer Oreos for just 29 cents. However, some Chinese consumers still found even the reformulated Oreos too sweet. Said one 30-year-old consumer in the eastern part of Beijing, he liked the cookie but "many of my friends think I am a bit weird to stick to Oreo cookies—most think them too sweet to be accepted."

Kraft's research also revealed that Chinese consumers have a growing thirst for milk, which Kraft wasn't fully

To make Oreo cookies sell well in China, Kraft completely reinvented the popular all-American classic. Kraft has now begun selling the popular Chinese wafers elsewhere in Asia, as well as in Australia and Canada.

exploiting. So Kraft began a grassroots marketing campaign to educate Chinese consumers about the American tradition of pairing milk with cookies. The company created Oreo apprentice programs at 30 Chinese universities that drew 6000 student applications. Three hundred of the applicants were trained to become Oreo brand ambassadors. Some of the students rode around Beijing on bicycles, outfitted with wheel covers resembling Oreos, and handed out cookies to more than 300 000 consumers.

Other ambassadors held Oreo-themed basketball games to reinforce the idea of dunking cookies in milk. Television commercials showed kids twisting apart Oreo cookies, licking the cream centre, and dipping the chocolate cookie halves into glasses of milk. Kraft CEO Irene Rosenfeld calls the bicycle campaign "a stroke of genius that only could have come from local managers. [Letting] our local managers deal with local conditions will be a source of competitive advantage for us."

The product and marketing changes made a difference and Oreo sales in China improved. However, Kraft knew that if it was really serious about capturing a bigger share of the

Chinese biscuit market it needed to do more than just tweak its U.S. Oreo recipe and marketing. It needed to remake the Oreo itself.

So in 2006 Kraft introduced a second Oreo in China, one that looked almost nothing like the original. The new Chinese Oreo consisted of four layers of crispy wafer filled with vanilla and chocolate cream, coated in chocolate. The new Oreo was designed not only to satisfy the cravings of China's consumers, but also to stand up to the challenges of selling and distributing across China's vast landscape. Kraft even developed a proprietary handling process to ensure that the chocolate product could withstand the cold climate in the north and the hot, humid weather in the south, yet still be ready to melt in the customer's mouth.

Kraft's efforts to reshape the Oreo brand and its marketing have paid off. Within a year of introduction, Oreo Wafer Sticks became the best-selling biscuit in China, outpacing HaoChiDian, a biscuit brand made by the Chinese company Dali. The new Oreos are also outselling traditional round Oreos in China, and Kraft has begun selling the wafers elsewhere in Asia, as well as in Australia and Canada. Over the past two years, Kraft has doubled its Oreo revenues in China.

What's more, Kraft has learned, its "think globally, act locally" approach applies not just to Oreos and not just in China but to all of its products worldwide. For example, to take advantage of the European preference for dark chocolate, Kraft is introducing dark chocolate in Germany under its Milka brand. Research in Russia showed that consumers there like premium instant coffee, so Kraft is positioning its Carte Noire freeze-dried coffee as upscale by placing it at film festivals, fashion shows, and operas. And in the Philippines, where iced tea is popular, Kraft last year launched iced-tea–flavoured Tang. As a result of such moves, international business now represents 40 percent of Kraft's total sales. Kraft's profit in the European Union last year rose 48 percent, and profits in developing countries rose 57 percent, far outpacing U.S. profit growth.

Source: Adapted from portions of Julie Jargon, "Kraft Reformulated Oreo, Scores in China," *Wall Street Journal*, May 1, 2008, p. B1. Also see www.kraft.com, accessed October 2008.

---

encourage this form of self-financing. Communal finance is a far cry from manufacturing mobile phones, but Nokia knows it has to try all sorts of product and service ideas if it wants to capture its share of the industry's next 1 billion customers.[35]

Product invention

Creating new products or services for foreign markets.

Product invention consists of creating something new for a specific country market. This strategy can take two forms. It might mean maintaining or reintroducing earlier product forms that happen to be well adapted to the needs of a given country. Or a company might create a new product to meet a need in a given country. For example, Sony added the "U" model to its VAIO personal computer line to meet the unique needs of Japanese consumers. It found that Japanese commuters had difficulty using standard laptops on crowded rush-hour trains—standing commuters have no laps. So it created the U as a "standing computer." The U is lightweight and small: only seven inches wide with a five-inch diagonal screen. And it includes a touch screen and small keyboard that can be used while standing or on the move.[36]

Promotion

Companies can either adopt the same communications strategy they use in the home market or change it for each local market (as LG Electronics does). Consider advertising messages. Some global companies use a standardized advertising theme around the world. Of course, even in highly standardized communications campaigns, some adjustments might be required for language and cultural differences. For example, Guy Laroche uses virtually the same ads for its Drakkar Noir fragrances in Europe and Arab countries. However, it subtly tones down the Arab versions to meet cultural differences in attitudes toward sensuality. And although McDonald's uses its standardized "I'm lovin' it" theme worldwide, it varies its interpretations of the theme in different countries. In China, for instance, it presents the Quarter Pounder as a lot more than just a big North American-style burger:

Many Chinese hold the traditional view that eating beef boosts energy and heightens sex appeal. The word "beef" in Chinese has connotations of manliness, strength, and skill. That's the message McDonald's is sending Chinese consumers as it tries to seduce them into eating more hamburgers. One racy Quarter Pounder poster hanging in restaurants features a close-up of a woman's lips. "Flirt with your senses," the sign says. The burger chain's Quarter Pounder TV commercials are even steamier. In one, a man and a woman eat the burgers, and close-up shots of the woman's neck and mouth are interspersed with images of fireworks and spraying water. As the actors suck their fingers, the voice-over says: "You can feel it. Thicker. You can taste it. Juicier." A series of light-hearted print ads in trendy magazines lay out scenarios in which beef saves the day. In one, a young man frets about the five women he has met online who all want to go out on dates with him the next day. The ad offers some solutions: Hire four friends. Split up the meetings. Or "have enough beef tonight" to "be able to handle five princesses tomorrow."[37]

Colours are also changed sometimes to avoid taboos in other countries. Purple is associated with death in most of Latin America, white is a mourning colour in Japan, and green is associated with jungle sickness in Malaysia. Even names must sometimes be adjusted. The global name for Microsoft's operating system Vista turns out to be a disparaging term for a frumpy old woman in Latvia. And in the Americas, Mitsubishi changed the Japanese name of its Pajero SUV to Montero—it seems that *pajero* in Spanish is a slang term for sexual self-gratification. (See Real Marketing 19.2 for more on language blunders in international marketing.)

Communication adaptation
A global communication strategy of fully adapting advertising messages to local markets.

Other companies follow a strategy of **communication adaptation**, fully adapting their advertising messages to local markets. Kellogg ads in North America promote the taste and nutrition of Kellogg's cereals versus competitors' brands. In France, where consumers drink little milk and eat little for breakfast, Kellogg's ads must convince consumers that cereals are a tasty and healthful breakfast. In India, where many consumers eat heavy, fried breakfasts, Kellogg's advertising convinces buyers to switch to a lighter, more nutritious breakfast diet.

Similarly, Coca-Cola sells its low-calorie beverage as Diet Coke in North America, the United Kingdom, and the Middle and Far East, but as Coke Light elsewhere. According to Diet Coke's global brand manager, in Spanish-speaking countries Coke Light ads "position the soft drink as an object of desire, rather than as a way to feel good about yourself, as Diet Coke is positioned in the United States." This "desire positioning" plays off research showing that "Coca-Cola Light is seen in other parts of the world as a vibrant brand that exudes a sexy confidence."[38]

Media also need to be adapted internationally because media availability and regulations vary from country to country. TV advertising time is limited in Europe, for instance, ranging from four hours a day in France to none in Scandinavian countries. Advertisers must buy time months in advance, and they have little control over airtimes. However, cellphone ads are much more widely accepted in Europe and Asia than in North America. Magazines also vary in effectiveness. For example, magazines are a major medium in Italy but a minor one in Austria. Newspapers are national in the United Kingdom but are only local in Spain.[39]

Price

Companies also face many considerations in setting their international prices. For example, how might Black & Decker price its power tools globally? It could set a uniform price all around the world, but this amount would be too high a price in poor countries and not high enough in rich ones. It could charge what consumers in each country would bear, but this strategy ignores differences in the actual costs from country to country. Finally, the company could use a standard markup of its costs everywhere, but this approach might price Black & Decker out of the market in some countries where costs are high.

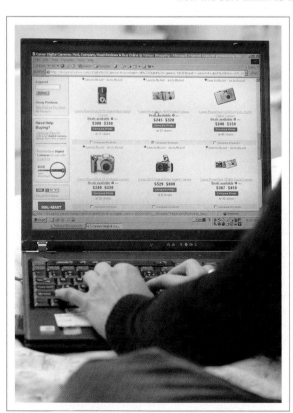

The Internet is making global price differences more obvious, forcing companies toward more standardized international pricing.

Real Marketing 19.2

Watch Your Language!

Many global companies have had difficulty crossing the language barrier, with results ranging from mild embarrassment to outright failure. Seemingly innocuous brand names and advertising phrases can take on unintended or hidden meanings when translated into other languages. Careless translations can make a marketer look downright foolish to consumers in another country. For example, companies marketing in Canada have to be careful that they don't use either formal or colloquial French incorrectly.

The classic language blunders involve standardized brand names that do not translate well. When Coca-Cola first marketed Coke in China in the 1920s, it developed a group of Chinese characters that, when pronounced, sounded like the product name. Unfortunately, the characters actually translated as "bite the wax tadpole." Now, the characters on Chinese Coke bottles translate as "happiness in the mouth."

Several modern-day marketers have had similar problems when their brand names crashed into the language barrier. When marketers for Hunt-Wesson introduced their Big John products into French Canada, they didn't understand why people smirked when they said the name—*gros jos* is the slang for "big breasts." Chevy's Nova translated into Spanish as *no va*—"it doesn't go." GM changed the name to Caribe (Spanish for "Caribbean") and sales increased. The name of Microsoft's operating system, Vista, turns out to be a disparaging term for a frumpy old woman in Latvia. Rolls-Royce avoided the name Silver Mist in German markets, where *mist* means "manure." Sunbeam, however, entered the German market with its Mist Stick hair-curling iron. As should have been expected, the Germans had little use for a "manure wand." Puffs tissues didn't do well, either—*puffs* means "brothel" in German. IKEA marketed a children's workbench named FARTFULL in North America (the word means "speedy" in Swedish)—it soon discontinued the product.

Interbrand of London, the firm that created household names such as Prozac and Acura, recently developed a brand-name "hall of shame" list, which contained these and other foreign brand names you're never likely to see inside the local Loblaw: Krapp toilet paper (Denmark), Crapsy Fruit cereal (France), Poo curry powder (Argentina), and Pschitt lemonade (France).

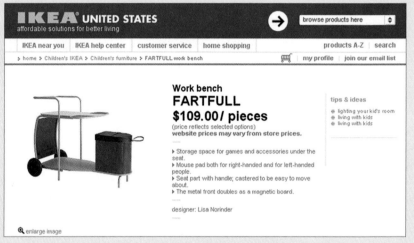

Global language barriers: Some standardized brand names do not translate well globally.

Travellers often encounter well-intentioned advice from service firms that takes on meanings very different from those intended. The menu in one Swiss restaurant proudly stated, "Our wines leave you nothing to hope for." Signs in a Japanese hotel pronounced, "You are invited to take advantage of the chambermaid." At a laundry in Rome, it was, "Ladies, leave your clothes here and spend the afternoon having a good time."

Advertising themes often lose—or gain—something in the translation. The Coors beer slogan "Get loose with Coors" in Spanish came out as "Get the runs with Coors." Coca-Cola's "Coke adds life" theme in Japanese translated into "Coke brings your ancestors back from the dead." The milk industry learned too late that its American advertising question "Got Milk?" translated in Mexico as a more provocative "Are you lactating?" In Chinese, the KFC slogan "Finger-lickin' good" came out as "Eat your fingers off." And Motorola's Hellomoto ring tone sounds like "Hello, Fatty" in India. Even when the language is the same, word usage may differ from country to country. Thus, the British ad line for Electrolux vacuum cleaners—"Nothing sucks like an Electrolux"—would capture few customers in North America.

So, crossing the language barrier involves much more than simply translating names and slogans into other languages. "You can't uproot a concept and just translate it and put it into another market," says one translation consultant. "It's not really about translating word for word, but actually adapting a certain meaning." Beyond just word meanings and nuances, international marketers must also consider things like phonetic appeal and even associations with historical figures, legends, and other factors. The consultant points to the Chinese adaptation of the name for eBay's online free classified ads service—Kijiji (which means "village" in Swahili)—as a localization success story. "In Chinese, the three characters used to phonetically represent the Kijiji name map almost exactly to the English pronunciation," she says. "Plus, they have the meaning of people pulling together to share things, which is totally descriptive of the business and brand."

Sources: Quotes from Randall Frost, "Lost in Translation," www.brandchannel.com, November 13, 2006. For the above and other examples, see Jason Drohn, "10 Product and Campaign Blunders to Learn From," *MarketingHackz*, accessed at **http://marketinghackz. com/10-product-and-campaign-blunders-to-learn-from**, July 2009; David A. Ricks, "Perspectives: Translation Blunders in International Business," *Journal of Language for International Business*, Vol. 7(2), 1996, pp. 50–55; Martin Croft, "Mind Your Language," *Marketing*, June 19, 2003, pp. 35–39; Mark Lasswell, "Lost in Translation," *Business 2.0*, August 2004, pp. 68–70; "Lost in Translation," *Hispanic*, May 2005, p. 12; Ross Thomson, "Lost in Translation," *Medical Marketing and Media*, March 2005, p. 82; and Eric Pfanner, "Marketers Take a Fresh Look at the Language Barrier," *International Herald Tribune*, July 22, 2007.

Regardless of how companies go about pricing their products, their foreign prices probably will be higher than their domestic prices for comparable products. A Gucci handbag may sell for $60 in Italy and $240 in North America. Why? Gucci faces a *price escalation* problem. It must add the cost of transportation, tariffs, importer margin, wholesaler margin, and retailer margin to its factory price. Depending on these added costs, the product may have to sell for two to five times as much in another country to make the same profit.

To overcome this problem when selling to less-affluent consumers in developing countries, many companies make simpler or smaller versions of their products that can be sold at lower prices. For example, in China and other emerging markets, Dell sells its simplified Dell EC280 model for US$340, and P&G sells everything from shampoo to toothpaste in less costly formulations and smaller packages at more affordable prices.

Another problem involves setting a price for goods that a company ships to its foreign subsidiaries. If the company charges a foreign subsidiary too much, it may end up paying higher tariff duties even while paying lower income taxes in that country. If the company charges its subsidiary too little, it can be accused of *dumping*. Dumping occurs when a company charges either less than its costs or less than it charges in its home market. For example, the U.S. lumber industry has claimed that the Canadian softwood lumber industry is unfairly subsidized by federal and provincial governments, allowing it to undercut American prices. This accusation has resulted in one of the most significant and enduring trade disputes between the two countries.[40] Various governments are always watching for dumping abuses, and they often force companies to set the price charged by other competitors for the same or similar products.

Recent economic and technological forces have had an impact on global pricing. For example, the Internet is making global price differences more obvious. When firms sell their wares over the Internet, customers can see how much products sell for in different countries. They can even order a given product directly from the company location or dealer offering the lowest price. This is forcing companies toward more standardized international pricing.

Distribution Channels

Whole-channel view
Designing international channels that take into account the entire global supply chain and marketing channel, forging an effective global value delivery network.

The international company must take a **whole-channel view** of the problem of distributing products to final consumers. Figure 19.4 shows the two major links between the seller and the final buyer. The first link, *channels between nations*, moves company products from points of production to the borders of countries within which they are sold. The second link, *channels within nations*, moves the products from their market entry points to the final consumers. The whole-channel view takes into account the entire global supply chain and marketing channel. It recognizes that to compete well internationally, the company must effectively design and manage an entire *global value delivery network*.

Channels of distribution within countries vary greatly from nation to nation. There are large differences in the numbers and types of intermediaries serving each country

Global value delivery network

Figure 19.4 Whole-channel concept for international marketing

market and in the transportation infrastructure serving these intermediaries. For example, whereas large-scale retail chains dominate the scene in North America, much retailing in other countries is done by many small, independent retailers. In India, millions of retailers operate tiny shops or sell in open markets. Thus, in its efforts to sell rugged, affordable phones to Indian consumers, Nokia has had to forge its own distribution structure:

Distribution channels vary greatly from nation to nation. In its efforts to sell rugged, affordable phones to Indian consumers, Nokia forged its own distribution structure, including a fleet of distinctive blue Nokia-branded vans that travel rutted country roads to visit remote villages.

In India, Nokia estimates there are 90 000 points-of-sale for its phones, ranging from modern stores to makeshift kiosks. That makes it difficult to control how products are displayed and pitched to consumers. "You have to understand where people live, what the shopping patterns are," says a Nokia executive. "You have to work with local means to reach people—even bicycles or rickshaws." To reach rural India, Nokia has outfitted its own fleet of distinctive blue Nokia-branded vans that prowl the rutted country roads. Staffers park these advertisements-on-wheels in villages, often on market or festival days. There, with crowds clustering around, Nokia reps explain the basics of how the phones work and how to buy them. Nokia has extended the concept to minivans, which can reach even more remote places.[41]

Similarly, Coca-Cola adapts its distribution methods to meet local challenges in global markets. For example, in rural China, an army of more than 10 000 Coca-Cola sales reps make regular visits to small retailers, often on foot or bicycle. To reach the most isolated spots, the company even relies on teams of delivery donkeys. In Montevideo, Uruguay, where larger vehicles are challenged by traffic, parking, and pollution difficulties, Coca-Cola recently purchased 30 small, efficient three-wheeled ZAP alternative transportation trucks. The little trucks average about one-fifth the fuel consumption and scoot around congested city streets with greater ease. If the model works well in Montevideo, Coca-Cola may adopt it in other congested urban areas that pose similar challenges.[42]

4 DECIDING ON THE GLOBAL MARKETING ORGANIZATION

Companies manage their international marketing activities in at least three different ways. Most companies first organize an export department, then create an international division, and finally become a global organization.

RIM is headquartered in Waterloo, Ontario, but views the entire world as its marketplace. In 2009, its BlackBerry App World storefront was launched in 10 new international markets.

A firm normally gets into international marketing by simply shipping out its goods. If its international sales expand, the company organizes an *export department* with a sales manager and a few assistants. As sales increase, the export department can expand to include various marketing services so that it can actively go after business. If the firm moves into joint ventures or direct investment, the export department will no longer be adequate.

Many companies get involved in several international markets and ventures. A company may export to one country, license to another, have a joint ownership venture in a third, and own a subsidiary in a fourth. Sooner or later it will create *international divisions* or subsidiaries to handle all of its international activity.

International divisions are organized in a variety of ways. An international division's corporate staff consists of marketing, manufacturing, research, finance, planning, and personnel specialists. It plans for and provides services to various operating units, which can be organized in one of three ways. They can be *geographical organizations*, with country managers who are responsible for salespeople, sales branches, distributors, and licensees in their respective countries. Or the operating units can be *world product groups*, each responsible for worldwide sales of different product groups. Finally, operating units can be *international subsidiaries*, each responsible for its own sales and profits. Many firms have passed beyond the international division stage and become truly *global organizations*. For example, Research In Motion (RIM), headquartered in Waterloo, Ontario, relies on international sales for much of its sales and profit.

Global organizations stop thinking of themselves as national marketers who sell abroad and start thinking of themselves as global marketers. The top corporate management and staff plan worldwide manufacturing facilities, marketing policies, financial flows, and logistical systems. The global operating units report directly to the chief executive or executive committee of the organization, not to the head of an international division. Executives are trained in worldwide operations, not just domestic *or* international operations. The company recruits management from many countries, buys components and supplies where they cost the least, and invests where the expected returns are greatest.

Today, major companies must become more global if they hope to compete. As foreign companies successfully invade their domestic markets, companies must move more aggressively into foreign markets. They will have to change from companies that treat their international operations as secondary to companies that view the entire world as a single borderless market.

REVIEWING OBJECTIVES AND KEY TERMS

mymarketinglab | Audio Chapter Summary

Companies today can no longer afford to pay attention only to their domestic market, regardless of its size. Many industries are global industries, and firms that operate globally achieve lower costs and higher brand awareness. At the same time, global marketing is risky because of variable exchange rates, unstable governments, protectionist tariffs and trade barriers, and several other factors. Given the potential gains and risks of international marketing, companies need a systematic way to make their global marketing decisions.

Discuss how the international trade system and the economic, political–legal, and cultural environments affect a company's international marketing decisions.

A company must understand the *global marketing environment*, especially the international trade system. It must assess each foreign market's *economic, political–legal*, and *cultural characteristics*. The company must then decide whether it wants to go abroad and consider the potential risks and benefits. It must decide on the volume of international sales it wants, how many countries it wants to market in, and which specific markets it wants to enter. This decision calls for weighing the probable rate of return on investment against the level of risk.

OBJECTIVE 2 **Describe three key approaches to entering international markets.**

The company must decide how to enter each chosen market—whether through *exporting, joint venturing,* or *direct investment*. Many companies start as exporters, move to joint ventures, and finally make a direct investment in foreign markets. In *exporting*, the company enters a foreign market by sending and selling products through international marketing intermediaries (indirect exporting) or the company's own department, branch, or sales representatives or agents (direct exporting). When establishing a *joint venture*, a company enters foreign markets by joining with foreign companies to produce or market a product or service. In *licensing*, the company enters a foreign market by contracting with a licensee in

the foreign market, offering the right to use a manufacturing process, trademark, patent, trade secret, or other item of value for a fee or royalty.

OBJECTIVE 3 **Explain how companies adapt their marketing mixes for international markets.**

Companies must also decide how much their products, promotion, price, and channels should be adapted for each foreign market. At one extreme, global companies use *standardized global marketing* worldwide. Others use *adapted global marketing*, in which they adjust the marketing strategy and mix to each target market, bearing more costs but hoping for a larger market share and return. However, global standardization is not an all-or-nothing proposition. It's a matter of degree. Most international marketers suggest that companies should "think globally but act locally"—that they should seek a balance between standardization and adaptation.

OBJECTIVE 4 **Identify the three major forms of international marketing organization.**

The company must develop an effective organization for international marketing. Most firms start with an *export department* and graduate to an *international division*. A few become *global organizations*, with worldwide marketing planned and managed by the top officers of the company. Global organizations view the entire world as a single, borderless market.

KEY TERMS

mymarketinglab | Glossary Flashcards

DISCUSSING THE CONCEPTS

1. Explain what is meant by the term *global firm* and list the six major decisions involved in international marketing.

2. Identify examples of economic communities and discuss their roles in international trade.

3. Name and define the four types of country industrial structures.

4. Discuss different forms of countertrade and explain why it is a growing practice.

5. Discuss the three ways to enter foreign markets. Which is the best?

6. Discuss the possible product strategies used for adapting to a global market.

APPLYING THE CONCEPTS

1. Visit the website of the Brazilian Embassy in Ottawa at www.brasembottawa.org/en/index.html. What can you learn about doing business in Brazil?

2. The United States restricts trade with Cuba. Visit the U.S. Department of the Treasury at www.ustreas.gov/offices/enforcement/ofac to learn more about economic and trade sanctions. Click on the "Cuba Sanctions" link to learn more about the trade restrictions on Cuba. Are these tariff, quota, or embargo restrictions? To what extent do these trade restrictions allow U.S. businesses to export their products to Cuba? What

opportunities do these restrictions present to Canadian businesses?

3. Visit the Department of Foreign Affairs and International Trade Canada (DFAIT) website at www.tradecommissioner.gc.ca/eng/market-reports-region.jsp?rid=12. Also visit the Export Development Canada (EDC) website at www.edc.ca/search/countryinformation_home.asp?sLang=e. Select a region and/or country and an industry sector. Summarize the information provided about that country and sector on these sites. How is this information useful to marketers?

FOCUS ON TECHNOLOGY

Most small to midsize businesses have small or nonexistent information technology departments, but to remain competitive, all need cutting-edge computing capabilities. The global market for these IT needs is estimated at US$500 billion, so IBM, a goliath company that does not yet serve this market, is developing a Global Applications Marketplace (also called Blue Business Platform) for small businesses. Through this platform, a small business can search and purchase software applications from independent software vendors around the world. However, local IBM partners will install and manage the applications for the business. When businesses enter information and receive recommendations through the Global Applications Marketplace, they receive product reviews along with access to an online IBM advisor.

IBM is setting up hundreds of local vendor partners—called "innovation centers"—around the world, several of them in emerging markets. The Global Applications Marketplace is designed much like Apple's iTunes—customers will need an IBM server to use the system. While IBM is making the world available to small businesses, IBM's local channel partners bring it to their doorstep.

1. Read more about this initiative at www-03.ibm.com/press/us/en/pressrelease/24111.wss. Explain how IBM is delivering value for small to midsize businesses. How is it delivering value to independent software vendors?

2. Who will be IBM's competitors in this market space? What advantage does IBM offer over these competitors?

FOCUS ON ETHICS

Advertising agency TBWA Worldwide came under fire in the months leading up to the 2008 Summer Olympics held in China for showing two sides of China in unrelated advertisements. On one side, ads developed for Adidas by TBWA's Beijing office showed athletes being lifted up by thousands of fans to depict Chinese pride. On the other side, ads developed by the agency's Paris office for

Amnesty International depicted China's dark human rights side by showing Chinese athletes being tortured by authorities with the copy, "After the Olympic Games, the fight for human rights must go on." This second side is the one that Chinese authorities do not want the world to see, and it's the one that marketers supporting the Games were tiptoeing around. Protests against China arose in cities around the world where the Olympic torch travelled, such as Paris, London, Vancouver, and San Francisco. China's Lenovo, the world's fourth-largest PC firm, spent more than $100 million on Olympic sponsorship and related marketing activities in hopes of boosting sales in major markets like North America. Other companies, such as Coca-Cola, McDonald's, and Samsung, were major sponsors of the Olympics, but fear of worldwide backlash for supporting China remains.

1. Was it right for businesses to sponsor the Olympic Games held in a country known for human rights violations?

2. Did sponsorship of the Beijing Olympic Games help or harm businesses supporting them?

MARKETING BY THE NUMBERS

Apple agreed to allow Hutchison Telecommunications International (also known as Hong Kong 3) to sell its iPhone in Hong Kong beginning in 2008. Consumers there can purchase an 8 GB iPhone for HK$2938 (that is, 2938 Hong Kong dollars) with a 24-month service contract of HK$188 per month or receive a free iPhone with a 24-month service contract of HK$498 per month. The first plan offers 5000 MB of voice and data, and the second provides 2200 minutes of airtime and unlimited data. For more discussion of the financial and quantitative implications of marketing decisions, see Appendix 3: Marketing by the Numbers.

1. Determine the total revenue generated by a customer over the life of each 24-month contract option. Which option generates more revenue for Hong Kong 3?

2. Using a currency conversion website such as www.xe.com/ucc, convert the revenue generated by both plans to Canadian dollars. Compare this with iPhone plans available in Canada. Do Canadian consumers pay more or less?

VIDEO CASE

 | Video Case Questions

Nivea

In 1911, the German company Nivea introduced the revolutionary Nivea Creme in a simple blue tin. Today that Creme is the centrepiece of a wide range of personal care products. The product line includes everything from soap, shampoo, and shaving products to baby care products, deodorant, and sunscreen. From small beginnings, the company's products are sold today in more than 150 countries worldwide.

But despite this global presence, most Nivea consumers believe that the products they buy are produced and marketed locally. Why? Although Nivea looks for commonalities between consumers around the globe, the company's marketers also recognize the differences between consumers in different markets. So Nivea adapts its marketing mix to reach local consumers while keeping its message consistent everywhere products are sold. This globally consistent, locally customized marketing strategy has sold more than 11 billion tins of the traditional Nivea Creme.

After viewing the video featuring Nivea, answer the following questions about the company and the global marketplace:

1. Which of the five strategies for adapting products and promotion for the global market does Nivea employ? How does it do so?

2. Visit Nivea's website, www.nivea.com, and tour the sites for several different countries. How does Nivea market its products differently in different countries? How does the company maintain the consistency of its brand?

3. How is Nivea's consistent brand message relevant to different target markets?

Visit MyMarketingLab at www.pearsoned.ca/mymarketinglab to view the video segment related to this case.

COMPANY CASE

Nokia: Envisioning a Connected World

What brand of cellphone do you have? If you're living in North America, chances are it isn't a Nokia. But if you're living anywhere else in the world, it probably is. While the Finnish electronics company grabs only a single-digit slice of the North American cellphone pie, it dominates the global cellphone market with close to a 40 percent share.

Few companies dominate their industries like Nokia does. Half of the world's population holds an active cellphone, and one in three of those phones is a Nokia. In 2007 alone, Nokia sold 437 million phones. That's 26 percent more phones than it sold the year before and almost as many phones as were sold by its four closest rivals—Samsung, Motorola, Sony-Ericsson, and LG—combined!

You might think that Nokia has accomplished this feat by being the product leader, always introducing the latest cutting-edge gadget. But Nokia has actually been slow to take advantage of design trends such as clamshell phones, "candy-bar" phones that slide open and closed, and ultra-thin, blingy, multifunction phones. Rather, Nokia has risen to global dominance based on a simple, age-old strategy: sell basic products at low prices. Although Nokia markets a huge variety of cellphone models, it is best known for its trademarked easy-to-use block handset. Nokia mass-produces this basic reliable hardware cheaply and ships it in huge volumes to all parts of the world.

FROM PAPER TO CELLPHONES

While Finland's largest company leads the world's most high-tech industry, it is not a new company. In fact, Nokia started humbly in 1865 as a wood-pulp mill. A few mergers and a hundred years or so later, the Nokia Corporation was making not only paper products, but bicycle and car tires, footwear, computers, televisions, and communications cables and equipment. Starting in the 1960s, one Nokia division made commercial and military mobile radios, a business unit that ultimately morphed into the cellphone giant that Nokia is today.

In 1984, Nokia marketed one of the world's first transportable phones, the Talkman. It weighed 11 pounds. Within three years, Nokia had slimmed the phone down to only 28 ounces. But that smaller model, the Cityman, cost a whopping $5000! Believe it or not, even at that price, Nokia could hardly keep up with demand.

But the 1990s brought on a mobile phone explosion that vastly exceeded even the most optimistic predictions. The growth was accompanied by many challenges. During that period, Nokia focused on logistics and scale, two competencies that now serve as Nokia's major competitive advantages.

GAINING STRENGTH AS THE VOLUME LEADER

Based in Finland, Nokia's single most profitable and revenue-generating region is Europe. But the company's global strategy has been likened to that of Honda decades ago. Honda started by focusing on developing markets with small motorbikes. As the economies of such countries emerged and people could afford cars, they were already loyal to Honda.

Nokia has followed that same model. It sells phones in more than 150 countries. In most of those countries it is the market leader. Nokia has a real knack for forging regional strategies based on the overall needs of consumers. But Nokia has filled its coffers by understanding the growth dynamics of specific emerging markets. Søren Petersen, Nokia's senior vice-president of mobile phones, understands that concept more than anyone. He spends a great deal of his time studying the needs of consumers in emerging markets. And for the most part, these consumers need cheap phones.

Recognizing the need to make less expensive cellphones, Petersen is on a crusade throughout his company. Although it has been a bit of a battle, Petersen has convinced others that Nokia can make as much profit as the competition without charging more than $72 retail per phone. As a result, Nokia has relentlessly pursued the goal of bringing down costs and making phones less expensive.

Petersen cites an example of one cost-cutting tactic that sparked a chain of events at Nokia. While on a visit to Kenya he stopped by an "excessively rural storefront," where he noticed that all products were displayed in plastic bags. When he asked the merchant where the boxes and manuals had gone, the man replied, "Make good fire."

Petersen quickly realized that packaging for many areas of the world barely needed to "last the journey." Packaging changes resulted in a savings of $147 million a year. "These numbers alone lit up a whole new drive within the business for these kinds of things," Petersen reported. Illustrating the magnitude of the large-scale manufacturer, Petersen explained that one cent in cost represents a million dollars for Nokia.

Among other notable discoveries for emerging markets, Petersen recognized that although many such customers spend a significant portion of their salary on one device, many of them will never know how to read or write. This led to an icon-based address book rather than the usual text-based version. Now millions of people around the world identify their contacts by simple pictures, such as a soccer ball or a flower. And once it realized that many people in less-developed countries share their phones with up to half a dozen other people, Nokia also added multiple phone books to its devices.

Because cellphone demand is growing so rapidly in emerging nations, Nokia will do well if it just holds its current market share in such countries. In India, for example, millions of people each month are buying their first cellphone. But Nokia isn't just holding on in such countries. In

China alone, Nokia sold more than 70 million phones in 2007, a 38 percent increase over the previous year and a 35 percent share of the Chinese market. China also represented one-sixth of Nokia's total unit sales.

Nokia shipped 150 million phones to emerging markets in 2007. For every five phones Nokia sells, one of them is an entry-level device, up from one in ten only two years ago. Most of those entry-level phones end up in developing countries. So whereas Europe accounts for 39 percent of Nokia's net sales, Asia, Latin America, Africa, and the Middle East account for 56 percent. The United States, with its market structure driven by the network carriers, produces only 5 percent of Nokia sales. With cellphone volume growing faster in developing regions, the gap will likely widen even more in coming years.

CAPITALIZING ON MARKET LEADERSHIP

Just as Honda used strength gained from selling motorbikes in emerging countries to establish itself as a manufacturer of virtually every kind of passenger vehicle, Nokia aims to do the same in the mobile phone industry. Although Nokia remains committed to the entry-level market and to emerging nations, it has developed a comprehensive global strategy. According to the company's own vision statement, that strategy has three facets: growing the number of people using Nokia devices, transforming the devices people use, and building new businesses.

For the first part of this plan, Nokia projects that global cellphone usage will almost double by 2015 to 5 billion users. Even if Nokia simply holds its current share of the market, that means that approximately 1.7 billion people will be holding Nokia phones, 67 percent more than today.

As for transforming the devices that people use, Nokia is becoming more than just an entry-level phone provider. Of its 112 000 employees, 30 000 of them work in research and development. Nokia hopes that as its customers in developing nations gain the resources, they will trade up and stay with Nokia. It's also aware of the changing needs and trends in Europe, North America, and the rest of the developed world.

To that end, Nokia was the first to launch a phone that was a serious contender to Apple's iPhone. Nokia's N95 is a smartphone with many of the same features as its rival.

Whereas Apple's iPhone sales of more than 4 million units in less than a year have more than met expectations, one Nokia vice-president was heard to say, "We've done that since we had dinner last Friday." But whereas Apple's sales represent a very small share of the total market, Nokia's answer to this product indicates a recognition that this niche may grow into something much more substantial.

Nokia has also been experimenting with nanotechnology and flexible materials. At the Museum of Modern Art in New York it recently unveiled a phone called the "Morph"

as part of a "Design and the Elastic Mind" exhibit. The phone literally flexes and twists—you can wrap it around your wrist like a watch. Although this exact phone may never reach the market, it suggests that future Nokia phones might become far thinner, more stretchable, more durable, and more energy efficient.

Nokia also recognizes that the biggest trends in mobile devices are music, navigation, and gaming. Focusing on these activities, it is collaborating with the best minds in the business to find ways to add value for the consumer. Nokia appears poised to take advantage of the convergence of the Internet, media, and the cellphone. In fact, at its 2008 shareholder meeting, Nokia announced a shift to the Internet business as a whole. It no longer wants to be seen as just a phone company. It wants to be a company that keeps people connected to everything important in their lives, whether that's other people, information, commerce, or entertainment.

This new emphasis creates a very logical transition to the third leg of Nokia's strategy, building new businesses. Last year Nokia sold more than 200 million camera phones (far more than Canon's camera sales) and 146 million music phones (Apple sold only 52 million iPods). Thus, through its mobile handsets, Nokia can claim to sell more computers, portable music players, and cameras than any other company. However, it has yet to find a way to secure a steady income stream from its devices once they are in place.

Nokia is spending a lot of money and resources on an ambitious plan that it calls "Ovi." The goal is to accomplish something that has eluded many mobile network operators—building a profitable business in mobile services. Nokia has acquired software companies like digital map maker Navteq because it hopes that satellite location services will be big in the future, charting a new path to sales and profits. Nokia has also lured executives from Yahoo!, Microsoft, eBay, and IBM to help build this business venture.

In expanding beyond the borders of its more traditional business, Nokia has a lot going for it. Beyond selling lots of phones, it is also one of the most trusted brands in the world. With a brand value of more than US$33 billion, Nokia is now the fifth most valuable brand in the world. "The trust is so high, it has less trouble than other brands getting a customer back who may have tried out a competing brand," says one branding expert. And Anssi Vanjoki, head of Nokia's multimedia business group, quickly points out that the company's push into new products and services is not a case of the brand stretching for acceptance in new segments, like Volkswagen trying to sell luxury cars. Rather, it is simply a natural extension of the company's product line to better meet the needs of its customers. "[We're] delivering on what our customers expected from us all along—there's a big difference in terms of managing your brand."

Questions for Discussion

1. Does Nokia have a truly global strategy, rather than just a series of regional strategies? Explain.

2. Consider the different global marketing environments discussed in the text. How do these environments differ in developing versus developed countries?

3. Discuss Nokia's global strategy in terms of the five global product and communications strategies.

4. Can competitors easily replicate Nokia's global strategy? Why or why not?

5. Will Nokia's planned expansion into other products and services work? Explain.

Sources: Lionel Laurent, "Nokia Still Looks Strong," *Forbes*, April 17, 2008, accessed at www.forbes.com; Matt Kapko, "Nokia World: Strategies for the U.S., Emerging Markets," *RCR Wireless News*, December 17, 2007, p. 16; James Ashton, "Emerging Markets Help Nokia to Win Race For Mobile Supremacy," *Sunday Times (London)*, January 27, 2008, p. 11; David Kiley, "Best Global Brands," *BusinessWeek*, August 6, 2007, p. 56; Lionel Laurent, "Nokia Intends to Take a Bite Out of Apple," *Forbes*, April 9, 2008, accessed at www.forbes.com; and information from www.nokia.com, accessed September 2008.

Visit **MyMarketingLab** at **www.pearsoned.ca/mymarketinglab** for access to online tutorials, interactive exercises, videos, and much more.

Zenn Motor Company Ltd.

Driving without guilt. This seems like an impossible dream in an era of climate change and global warming since for every litre of gas a traditional motor vehicle consumes, approximately 2.3 kilograms of carbon dioxide are emitted into the air. But with forward thinking, a vision of an alternative future, and true innovation, such problems can be overcome. Such thinking is what brought the ZENN Motor Company (ZMC) to life. The name of the company was based on its first product, the ZENN low-speed vehicle, which stands for Zero Emission No Noise.

Today the Toronto-based company is on an exciting path thanks to its partnership with Cedar Park, Texas–based EEStor, a secretive company that claims to be close to having a commercially viable ultra-capacitor, which it says will be longer lasting, lighter, more powerful, and more environmentally friendly than current battery technologies. Batteries have long been the Achilles heel of electric cars, limiting their range and speed. But if the technology's promise is realized, it will enable ZMC to develop a revolutionary all-electric drivetrain system for vehicles manufactured by large automakers from around the world.

ZMC was born as the brainchild of Canadian Ian Clifford. As is the case with any small entrepreneurial company, ZMC has had to change rapidly with evolving market conditions and changing consumer demand. Its story is compelling. In 1995, after sitting in traffic moving forward inches at a time, breathing in toxic fumes from the diesel-powered pickup truck in front of him, Ian Clifford asked, "Isn't there a better way?" His first solution was to look for an electric car that he could drive, but vehicles like Toyota's all-electric RAV4 were not available in Canada. He found a 50-year-old electric vehicle, but quickly realized it needed major repairs. That led him to his second "ah-ha" moment. He found a repair person working just around the corner at a forklift repair shop and suddenly realized that electric vehicles were everywhere when you looked at the world of manufacturing and industry.

It wasn't until 2000 that Ian had the capital to move forward with his dream. He sold his IT company and began his new business. The repair man he found a few years earlier, Probyn Gayle, became the chief technology officer in Ian's new company—Feel Good Cars, Inc. The next person Ian drafted was Marek Warunkiewicz, a marketing and branding expert. Together the three men set out to build a sustainable business that declared open war on climate change. They wanted to make the world a better place while giving drivers a quality urban transportation solution that would positively impact the environment *and* reduce vehicle operating costs.

The idea of "recycling" gave them their initial plan. They decided to convert the French economy car, the Renault Dauphine, from a gas car into an electric one. Millions of these old vehicles powered by internal combustion engines were still being driven, and the entrepreneurs believed it would be a fairly straightforward matter to restore the car bodies, remove the internal combustion components, and substitute a lead-acid battery system to power the car. The company called them Dauphine Electrics and their target selling price was $25 000.

In February 2001, the partners showcased their electric car at the Canadian International AutoShow held in Toronto. Anticipating only modest interest, they printed a mere 5000 brochures. To their surprise, the timing was right. Recent year-round smog alerts, rising gas prices, and extensive media coverage drove consumers to their booth. The company soon had 10 000 requests for additional information and 1000 requests for test drives. The partners soon sold 15 cars from the first 30 test drives! It was clear that the company's initial business model could not possibly meet demand. The partners needed a mass-production platform.

The company worked for two years developing the engineering necessary to create an efficient, safe, mass-produced electric vehicle. In June 2006, the first model produced in the company's manufacturing plant in Saint-Jérôme, Quebec, won the Michelin Challenge Bibendum in Paris for the Best Urban Vehicle, winning acclaim for excellent overall design, acceleration, braking, lowest power consumption, and lowest noise levels. Part of the partners' go-to-market strategy included a rebranding and overall name change. It was during this period that Feel Good Cars became ZENN Motor Company Ltd. The original plan was to have a company that would be both the manufacturer and the distributor of the cars.

Due to regulations that put restrictions on low-speed vehicles in Canada, the United States was the company's first target market. ZMC gathered lots of data on potential consumers, which suggested that self-contained communities (often called "gated communities") populated by wealthy people who wanted to make a difference through their consumption choices were ideal targets. In other words, such people demonstrated an element of altruism through their purchasing. Research also showed that some communities, like Lincoln, California, already had dedicated lanes for low-speed vehicles. Golf cart–type vehicles were already being used in such communities, but people seemed interested in having a second or third car that they could use for local errands or transportation. Others saw electric vehicles as environmentally friendly "toys" they could add to their personal fleets of four or five vehicles.

Research was also helpful in finalizing the car's design, since it revealed that golf cart–type vehicles had "social limitations." Drivers of these vehicles liked the open-air experience, and in gated communities drivers liked to see and be seen in them. But there were trade-offs. Golf cart–type vehicles offered little in comfort and no climate control or protection from the heat, cold, or rain. Some drivers preferred a car-like experience that overcame these shortcomings. Thus, the ZENN vehicle differentiated itself from other low-speed vehicles in the marketplace by offering a compelling alternative to a golf cart–type vehicle: a small, car-like vehicle that included comfort and air conditioning.

The ZENN car met with immediate consumer interest and sales began ramping up. The car often acts like its own billboard. No matter where it is driven, people stop and stare and want to know more about it. Al Gore's campaign to raise awareness of climate change helped to bring environmental technology and the concept of the electric car from the "socks-and-sandals fringe" to the mainstream. By mid-2007, 18 months after the company went public, cars were being delivered to a network of over 30 retailers in 20 states. By 2009, the company had built and sold about 500 of its all-electric two-seater vehicles across North America. The car sold for approximately $16 000. It plugs into a standard electrical outlet and take its owners distances of 50 to 80 kilometres on a single charge. While the launch of the ZENN was successful, the company knew that it would always be a vehicle that appealed only to a small niche market.

From Product Marketing to Corporate Branding

As the company and its strategy evolved, marketing also moved through distinct stages. The first stage was focused on tactics needed to build awareness of the product among potential consumers and retailers. It had to get people to understand the ZENN concept, what the car is, and what it can be used for. The next stage focused on building the corporate brand, getting the company name out into the marketplace, and establishing the company's credibility as a firm that really understands sustainable transportation. As Dennis Hancock notes, "The raw essence of the brand is people who know better, do better." In other words, if people are exposed to a means of making a difference—of choosing more environmentally friendly products—they will do so. People also won't buy a vehicle from a company they don't trust to be in business over the long run. They want to know that the company will be there to service their vehicle.

Developing a retail network was also critical if the new car manufacturer was to be a success. ZMC's first tactic was to approach automotive dealers through the National Automobile Dealers Association's Las Vegas trade show. It thought the small electric car might appeal to some retailers as a secondary franchise they could market in addition to their traditional cars and trucks. However, ZMC quickly realized these people were not their best target since they already had established businesses and weren't interested in providing the education and the service potential ZMC customers required. Thus, ZMC went with specialty retailers who viewed themselves as "environmental entrepreneurs"—those that carry a variety of electric vehicles. It was this type of retailer that could provide the true retail experience customers were looking for.

ZMC works closely with its retailers and never calls them "dealers." It does cooperative advertising with them, which helps both the retailer and ZMC since the costs are often split 50/50. ZMC closely controls the message and format, however. It does all its own design and layouts. It has put together a brochure entitled "Are you in the zone?" to demonstrate to potential owners how the ZENN fits into certain lifestyles (i.e., those of people who do most of their driving to places like the local grocery store or gym). The brochure also facilitates a dialogue between the retailer and the potential customer.

The company's website is also a critical element in the firm's communication mix. This low-cost tool has allowed ZMC to track visitors to the site. This enables the company to get an even better picture of the types of people who are interested in the car and the geographic region where they live. This allows the company to do regional promotions targeted to the specific region.

Product placement has also been a successful marketing strategy. Media producers and placement agencies, who are always on the lookout for innovative products, have started to seek out the company. For example, the ZENN car appeared in nine segments of the movie *G-Force* and was also shown in *Angels and Demons*. It has been featured on *The Ellen Degeneres* show, and it was given the spotlight in front of the renowned Bellagio hotel and casino in Las Vegas.

OIL change?

The 100% electric ZENN represents everything good about personal transportation. While it runs on electricity, the ZENN is fueled by optimism. It's stylish, comfortable, fun and socially responsible.

ZERO EMISSION   NO NOISE
ZENN

www.ZENNcars.com

The company enjoyed some initial success by executing its marketing plan. It began establishing a national retailer base in key American target markets and got legal approval for the car in 43 of 50 U.S. states as well as in Quebec. The main adopters of the car have been urban commuters and commercial fleets such as resorts, gated communities, airports, college and business campuses, municipalities, and parks.

Leveraging Viral Marketing

ZMC has created a customer following that is like no other in the automotive industry. The early adopters of the ZENN car quickly became evangelists for the product, and their passion for the vehicle and the company was unprecedented. Not everyone can say they are saving the world while driving to gym. When someone drives a ZENN car, they are constantly stopped and asked for information about the vehicle. The marketing team at ZMC quickly realized it had to respond to this opportunity. It also realized that the car actually created something of a liability for owners. One customer noted that although he was delighted with the car, he just didn't have the time to spend 20 minutes with people who stopped him to ask about the car each time he took it to the grocery store.

ZMC's response to this situation was the development of what it calls the Ambassador Program. ZMC has worked to engage such customers and has provided them with training and marketing materials. It even decided to compensate these customer advocates fairly in return for the marketing they do while they sing the praises of their cars.

OPPORTUNITY CAME KNOCKING: ESTABLISHING A NEW "GO FORWARD" STRATEGY

As ZMC evolved and began to make a name for itself, potential suppliers of parts and components began to send proposals to ZMC. One such suitor was a company called EEStor, a Texas-based firm that believed it was on-track to develop a revolutionary type of electrical energy storage unit (EESU). The new technology would be smaller and lighter than traditional battery technologies and would not be adversely affected by temperature extremes. The new ultra-capacitor would be made from new materials that have extremely high-energy and power-density characteristics. It represents a disruptive breakthrough in energy storage that could be applied to multiple sectors, including the automotive sector. The ultra-capacitor technology, once developed, would provide ZENN cars with numerous benefits: The unit would be quickly rechargeable, would outlast any vehicle it is installed in, and would exponentially increase the distance a vehicle can travel without being recharged. However, developing the technology would be expensive, so EEStor was looking for partners.

In 2001, EEStor approached the large automobile manufacturers, but their response was, "This sounds great, and when you get it up and running come and talk to us again." It was an era when gas was still relatively cheap, SUVs were dominating the marketplace, and interest in electric car technology was at an all time low. Thus, the big manufacturers just weren't interested in investing in upfront technology development in this area.

However, EEStor's approach to ZMC in 2002 resulted in a very different response. While Ian Clifford and ZMC knew that getting into technology development was like buying a low-cost lottery ticket, they quickly saw the potential of the new energy storage technology. Moreover, they also saw that batteries with limited life and a limited ability to hold a charge were a severe limitation on the type of vehicle ZMC could build and the appeal such cars would have in the marketplace.

There was another benefit to ZMC from partnering with EEStor. Ian Clifford and his team had been studying the automotive industry intensively as soon as they realized how small the niche market was for their electric cars. ZENN's analysis suggested that the one thing all alternatively powered vehicles had in common was drivetrain technology. A vehicle's drivetrain is *the* core component of any car. Clifford suddenly saw the possibility of appealing to a massive market. ZMC now had the opportunity to differentiate itself in the automotive industry by offering a drivetrain solution that would maximize the potential of EEStor's technology and enable the successful integration of such technology into any automotive platform. If ZMC could provide this major component to all car manufacturers, it would not only tap into a huge market—it would revolutionize the industry and transform it from one that was causing huge environmental damage and overreliance on oil and gas. Thus, ZMC took a gamble and entered into a partnership with EEStor in 2004.

The partnership has resulted in a big shift in strategy for ZMC (see Figure A1.1). The company sees itself moving through three distinct stages from where it is today as a manufacturer of low-speed vehicles, to a developer and manufacturer of cityZenn, a vehicle capable of competing with internal combustion engine (ICE) cars, to a company that develops, manufacturers, and markets drivetrain solutions to major car manufacturers around the world.

Rather than trying to compete with the large automotive firms, ZENN realized that it was better positioned to be a major supplier to them, using its expertise in electric cars and

Figure A1.1

Clear Technology Roadmap

▶ ZENN's technology roadmap positions the Company to continue to expand its market opportunity as demand for electric vehicles grows

Today

Tomorrow

ZENN LSV
- Built on proven automotive platform
- Designed for neighborhood and urban transportation – 25 mph regulated top speed
- 30-50 mile range
- 8 hour full charge time

cityZENN Development
- Highway speed capable
- 250 mile range
- Price competitive with ICE vehicles, with a fraction of the operating costs

ZENNergy Drive Systems
- Provide drivetrain solutions with EEStor's technology to vehicle OEMs
  - Maximum leverage
  - Speed-to-market
  - Low CapEx

what it has now called ZENNergy™ drive solutions. If it hadn't built considerable market recognition as a manufacturer of electric cars, the large car manufacturers—or original equipment manufacturers (OEMs)—like GM, Toyota, Volvo, Ford, and Daimler never would have given tiny ZMC a seat at the table. But ZMC's early work to build brand awareness and credibility paid off when it moved in this new direction.

Today, ZMC is organized into three lines of business as it evolves from a manufacturer of low-speed vehicles to becoming a tier-1 supplier to major automobile manufacturers. These three lines of business are illustrated in Figure A1.2. Each line of business is focused around ZENNergy as the company works to develop new passenger vehicles, convert existing internal combustion vehicles, and develop specialty vehicles such as airport utility vehicles and golf carts.

The opportunity to supply OEMs is a huge business. ZMC's licence with EEStor would give it the potential to sell its technology as a component in the 48 million new passenger vehicles sold annually around the world. The conversion market is also massive. There are over 800 million cars currently powered by internal combustion engines on the

Figure A1.2

ZENN MOTOR COMPANY LTD.

| ZENNergy™ drive solutions for New Passenger Vehicles (manufactured by OEMS—major automobile firms) | ZENNergy™ drive solutions for Internal Combustion Engine Conversions | ZENNergy™ drive solutions for Specialty Vehicles |

world's roads. Companies with huge fleets of vehicles are also prime targets. For example, if high-profile firms like FedEx or UPS were to convert their fleet of vehicles to the new drive system technology, their savings would be astronomical. Specialty low-speed vehicles are also a big market—golf carts alone represent a $1 billion market—and the technology can be applied to everything from airport vehicles to essential vehicles in warehousing operations.

Marketing to OEMs is very different than marketing to consumers, however. Here are some of the major challenges ZMC has encountered when marketing to OEMs:

1. The OEM market is very small in terms of the number of players, but the top 10 OEMs comprise 80 percent of the market.

2. As was the case when EEStor approached these large manufacturers, there is a lot of skepticism surrounding the electric storage unit technology. A typical response is, "We have 500 engineers working on battery technology; why should we believe you've developed something better?"

3. The technology being developed by ZMC and EEStor is a component. Few firms have been able to successfully brand a component. Intel with its long-lived "Intel Inside" campaign is one of the few exceptions. It is not surprising, therefore, that ZMC sensed it needed a compelling new brand name for the drive system technology, so a new brand was born—ZENNergy™.

4. Whereas ZMC had used a pull strategy to market to consumers, it needs to use a push strategy with OEMs. ZMC has to convince a number of sophisticated, highly knowledgeable people about the transformative power of its new technology. It has to get an audience with CEOs, CFOs, chief engineers, and company presidents who have the authority to make massive changes in manufacturing technology.

5. Timing is critical. Technologies can change quickly. ZMC has to make its big push to OEMs once it has a convincing story to tell, backed up with evidence of the new drive system's potential. However, it can't wait too long or another competitor may enter the game with a competing technology.

6. ZMC has to know which automotive firms are the prime targets. While almost all firms have begun some form of electric car development, many are experimenting with this alternative only as a public relations effort. Furthermore, given the current market downturn and low sales for many automotive brands, many manufacturers are very risk averse. In addition, some firms have already made huge investments in alternative technologies like lithium batteries.

Thus, marketing the new drive systems is a balancing act for ZMC. High-touch marketing that has high impact is the key to future success, in ZMC's view. Much of this is accomplished through personal visits and presentations. Before a visit is made, however, a lot of research has to be done so that the presentation team intimately understands the target's business.

To build credibility in advance of such visits, ZMC has been highly successful in getting what is known as *earned media*—articles in the public and trade presses. As a result of its marketing of the ZENN car, a cadre of journalists are following the company. Influential newspapers like the *New York Times* and the *Wall Street Journal* and high-profile magazines like the *Economist* are read by the type of senior managers that ZMC is targeting. Thus, ZMC works hard to "seed" stories so that they will be printed in these media. Canadian media outlets have also been highly supportive of the company, since it is a compelling business and technology story that can be told with pride to Canadian readers. ZMC has achieved huge media coverage relative to what it has spent. In fact, ZMC has been so masterful in terms of its public relations efforts that it must now filter its opportunities carefully since it has a small staff and a small budget. While ZMC knows that it must educate both consumers and OEMs about the benefits of the emerging technology, it can only accept so many speaking engagements or media interviews.

INTO THE FUTURE

ZMC's timing with regard to its change in strategy and its partnership with EEStor couldn't have been better. As the decade began to unfold, issues related to climate change became even more compelling and consumer demand for more environmentally friendly vehicles grew. At first this might have seemed like good news for the ZENN Motor Company, but growing consumer concern accompanied by a fall in demand for traditional cars due to the 2008–2009 economic crisis caused the major automakers to start paying attention to what had been only a small niche market up to this point in time. Says one auto industry analyst, "It's expected that [automakers will start] making every single effort in every single line to be green."

Thus, at automobile shows around the world many major car manufacturers including Ford, Honda, Volkswagen, Toyota, BMW, and Mercedes started showing prototypes of electric cars, hybrid vehicles, and fuel-cell cars. These companies didn't stop at just changing the technology they used to power their cars. They also incorporated more environmentally friendly materials into the cars' designs. For example, some had seats constructed with materials made from recycled plastic bottles and polyester waste. Others used soy-based materials for seat foam, and still others had car bodies built with recycled materials. "The whole issue around sustainability is not just about fuel economy," Mark Fields, Ford's president for the Americas, said at the North American International Auto Show. "It's not just about lowering CO_2 levels. It's being good stewards in the environment, and that means the materials that you use."

Thus, in a matter of months, ZMC's advantage as an environmentally friendly car manufacturer began to erode. It is fortunate that the company had a long-term vision that was based on ZENNergy™, its drivetrain solution, not on a single product, and the decision has been made to move from building low-speed vehicles (LSV's) to focus on developing, manufacturing, and marketing drivetrain solutions to automotive and specialty vehicle companies.

Furthermore, its credibility in the industry had been established, which has helped ZMC move rapidly in its new direction. It has a lot of work to do and a lot of decisions still to make. Timing will be critical. While the company is currently focusing on the big car manufacturers, it has to decide when to start talking to consumers so that they can help pull the new technology into the market. Continued development of the battery and drivetrain technology is also essential, so the partners have to promote themselves to potential investors. It is an exciting time for the small company and its partner, EEStor, Inc., as government, industry, and consumers are placing an increased focus on sustainable transportation.

QUESTIONS

Capstone Question

The ZENN Motor Company Ltd. case touches on many of the themes present in the book. By the time you have finished studying the various chapters in the book, you should be able to develop a detailed marketing plan (see Table 2.2 and Appendix 2) for one of the company's products (the two-seater ZENN car or the new cityZENN) or one of the company's three units—the ZENNergy™ drive solutions for **New Passenger Vehicles** (manufactured by OEMS—major automobile firms), ZENNergy™ drive solutions for Internal Combustion Engine **Conversions,** or ZENNergy™ drive solutions for **Specialty Vehicles.**

If you develop a plan for one of the products, use a one-year time period. Since timing is critical for the three lines of business, use a three- to five-year time horizon. No matter what the focus of your plan, be sure to clearly describe the company's target market(s) and how it should position and brand itself. Describe how it should build relationships with its OEM customers, retailers, and/or end consumers and how it should communicate with them. Be sure to think about what pricing changes it should make (if any), and the timing of these changes. If you are developing a plan for one of ZMC's vehicles, think about its different channels of distribution and where it should place most of its investment in management time and support dollars.

As you go through the different chapters of the book, work to apply the concepts presented in the chapters to the situation faced by ZMC. The questions which follow will help you apply what you are learning to this innovative company. Your answers to the questions will also be helpful to you when you develop your marketing plan.

Chapter 1

1. How has ZMC answered the question "What is marketing?" as it has evolved?
2. What relationships are most critical to ZMC as it moves forward?
3. Select one primary target group. What steps has ZMC taken to build relationships and value for this group?

Chapter 2

1. Describe ZMC's mission. The text notes that a clear mission statement acts as an "invisible hand" that guides people in the organization. Give reasons why you believe ZMC's mission is effective or ineffective in accomplishing this task.
2. Use Figure 2.2 (the BCG growth-share matrix) to describe ZMC's business units.
3. How can the concepts illustrated in Figure 2.3 (the product/market expansion grid) help ZMC formulate its plans as it moves its strategy forward?

Chapter 3

1. Describe the major marcoenvironmental forces (see Figure 3.2) have affected ZMC and its product offerings.

Chapter 4

1. Using the case and your own research about ZMC, provide examples of how the company is following the principles guiding socially responsible marketing.

Chapter 5

1. What sources of secondary data might be useful to ZMC as it gathers information in preparation for entry into the market as a supplier using its ZENNergy™ drive solutions system for specialty vehicles?
2. Using the steps described in Chapter 5, design a research study that ZMC could use to understand the factors that are important to consumers who might be interested in converting their internal combustion engine car into a vehicle that uses the ZENNergy™ drive solution.
3. In designing your study, what ethical issues would you want to be sensitive to?

Chapter 6

1. What type of decision process would a consumer follow if they were considering converting their current automobile to a more environmentally friendly version? Describe the steps they would go through.

2. What factors affecting consumer buying behaviour would ZENN need to consider?
3. Using Maslow's hierarchy of needs (see Figure 6.3), describe the needs that a vehicle converted to a more environmentally friendly drive train system would fulfill for a consumer.

Chapter 7

1. How will the buying process differ as ZMC moves forward and begins to market to buyers within large automotive manufacturers like Toyota, Ford, or Volkswagen?
2. Use Figure 7.2 and select five factors that you believe will influence buyers from the automotive companies. Describe how the factors may affect their decision to incorporate the ZENNergy™ drive solution into the new cars they are manufacturing.

Chapter 8

1. Describe a typical person from the ZENN car's target market.
2. What characteristics do you think will best describe a potential buyer of the new cityZENN?
3. How should the cityZENN be positioned? Draw a positioning map that captures how you believe the vehicle should be positioned. Be sure to include the vehicles you think will be the cityZENN's major competition.
4. Use Figure 8.4 to make a recommendation to ZMC about how the cityZENN should be priced.

Chapter 9

1. Use Table 9.1 to describe the type of product the ZENN car is and the type of marketing mix you might use for the car.
2. What tasks would ZMC have to undertake to make the ZENNergy™ drive solutions system a successful componenet brand? (Hint: Think about how Intel has accomplished this task.)
3. What brand values should be associated with the ZENNergy™ drive solutions system?
4. Retailers provide many services to the buyers of the ZENN car. What tactics can they use to help overcome the four key service characteristics as illustrated in Figure 9.5?

Chapter 10

1. Describe the steps a firm like ZMC would go through to develop and launch a new product. Where is the cityZENN in this process?
2. Examine the product life cycle. Where do the ZENN car, the cityZENN, and the ZENNergy™ drive solution system fall within the product life cycle?

Chapter 11

1. What factors should ZMC consider when setting the price for the cityZENN?
2. What pricing approach would you recommend to the management of ZMC for the cityZENN?

Chapter 12

1. Describe the current channel of distribution for the ZENN car.
2. How does each member of the ZENN car's distribution channel add value?

3. What criteria should ZMC use when selecting new retailers for the ZENN car?
4. What type of distribution strategy has ZMC been using for the ZENN car? Will it need to revise this strategy when it launches the cityZENN?

Chapter 13

1. What decisions do retailers who carry ZENN cars have to make?

Chapters 14 to 17

1. Describe the promotion mix that ZMC is currently using.
2. You have a budget of $1 million to help launch the cityZENN in the major city closest to where you live. Develop a communications plan for the launch of the vehicle in this city.

Chapter 18

1. What competitive advantages does ZMC have with regard to its marketing of the ZENN car or the cityZENN?
2. What competitive advantages does ZMC have when it comes to the marketing of the ZENNergy™ drive solution system?

Chapter 19

1. Select a country other than Canada or the United States that you think might have a viable target market for the cityZENN. How might consumers who live in this market differ from consumers in North America?
2. Describe three marketing tactics that you might want to change if ZMC were to enter the market you have selected?

Sources: ZENN Motor Company website, www.ZENNcars.com; "Finding ZENN on Canadian Roads," Driving.ca, http://autos.canada.com/news/story.html?id=61f65c9e-0994-400d-945f-3478ccc468b0 (accessed May 10, 2009); Duane R. Pendergast, "Nuclear Power and Carbon Dioxide Free Automobiles," Canadian Nuclear Society, www.computare.org/Support%20documents/Publications/CO2%20Free%20Cars.htm (accessed May 10, 2009); "Automakers Search for Green Solutions out of Slump at Frankfurt Show," Auto Industry, September 16, 2009, www.dw-world.de/dw/article/0,,4696500,00.html (accessed October 2009); "Automakers Push for Environmentally Friendly Cars," CTV News, January 22, 2008, www.ctv.ca/servlet/ArticleNews/story/CTVNews/20080122/auto_environment_080122/20080122?hub=SciTech (accessed October 2009); Steve Ladurantaye, "ZENN Motor Makes U-turn," Globe and Mail, September 28, 2009, www.theglobeandmail.com/report-on-business/ZENN-motor-makes-u-turn/article1303552 (accessed October 2009); "ZENN Motor Company Updates Business Strategy," ZENN Press Release, September 24, 2009, www.marketwire.com/press-release/ZENN-Motor-Company-TSX-VENTURE-ZNN-1050020.html (accessed October 2009).

THE MARKETING PLAN: AN INTRODUCTION

As a marketer, you'll need a good marketing plan to provide direction and focus for your brand, product, or company. With a detailed plan, any business will be better prepared to launch a new product or build sales for existing products. Not-for-profit organizations also use marketing plans to guide their fundraising and outreach efforts. Even government agencies put together marketing plans for initiatives such as building public awareness of proper nutrition and stimulating area tourism.

The Purpose and Content of a Marketing Plan

Unlike a business plan, which offers a broad overview of the entire organization's mission, objectives, strategy, and resource allocation, a marketing plan has a more limited scope. It serves to document how the organization's strategic objectives will be achieved through specific marketing strategies and tactics, with the customer as the starting point. It is also linked to the plans of other departments within the organization. Suppose that a marketing plan calls for selling 200 000 units annually. The production department must gear up to make that many units, the finance department must arrange funding to cover the expenses, the human resources department must be ready to hire and train staff, and so on. Without the appropriate level of organizational support and resources, no marketing plan can succeed.

Although the exact length and layout will vary from company to company, a marketing plan usually contains the sections described in Chapter 2. Smaller businesses may create shorter or less formal marketing plans, whereas corporations frequently require highly structured marketing plans. To guide implementation effectively, every part of the plan must be described in considerable detail. Sometimes a company will post its marketing plan on an internal website, which allows managers and employees in different locations to consult specific sections and collaborate on additions or changes.

The Role of Research

Marketing plans are not created in a vacuum. To develop successful strategies and action programs, marketers need up-to-date information about the environment, the competition, and the market segments to be served. Often, analysis of internal data is the starting point for assessing the current marketing situation, supplemented by marketing intelligence and research investigating the overall market, the competition, key issues, and threats and opportunities. As the plan is put into effect, marketers use a variety of research techniques to measure progress toward objectives and identify areas for improvement if results fall short of projections.

Finally, marketing research helps marketers learn more about their customers' requirements, expectations, perceptions, and satisfaction levels. This deeper understanding provides a foundation for building competitive advantage through well-informed segmentation, targeting, differentiation, and positioning decisions. Thus, the marketing plan should outline what marketing research will be conducted and how the findings will be applied.

The Role of Relationships

The marketing plan shows how the company will establish and maintain profitable customer relationships. In the process, however, it also shapes a number of internal and external relationships. First, it affects how marketing personnel work with each other and with other departments to deliver value and satisfy customers. Second, it affects how the company works with suppliers, distributors, and strategic alliance partners to achieve the objectives listed in the plan. Third, it influences the company's dealings with other stakeholders, including government regulators, the media, and the community at large. All of these relationships are important to the organization's success, so they should be considered when a marketing plan is being developed.

From Marketing Plan to Marketing Action

Companies generally create yearly marketing plans, although some plans cover a longer period. Marketers start planning well in advance of the implementation date to allow time for marketing research, thorough analysis, management review, and coordination between departments. Then, after each action program begins, marketers monitor ongoing results, compare them with projections, analyze any differences, and take corrective steps as needed. Some marketers also prepare contingency plans for implementation if certain conditions emerge. Because of inevitable and sometimes unpredictable environmental changes, marketers must be ready to update and adapt marketing plans at any time.

For effective implementation and control, the marketing plan should define how progress toward objectives will be measured. Managers typically use budgets, schedules, and performance standards for monitoring and evaluating results. With budgets, they can compare planned expenditures with actual expenditures for a given week, month, or other period. Schedules allow management to see when tasks were supposed to be completedóand when they were actually completed. Performance standards track the outcomes of marketing programs to see whether the company is moving toward its objectives. Some examples of performance standards are market share, sales volume, product profitability, and customer satisfaction.

SAMPLE MARKETING PLAN FOR SONIC

This section takes you inside the sample marketing plan for Sonic, a hypothetical start-up company. The company's first product is the Sonic 1000, a multimedia, cellular/Wi-Fi-enabled smartphone. Sonic will be competing with Apple, Nokia, Research In Motion, Motorola, and other well-established rivals in a crowded, fast-changing marketplace for smartphones that combine communication, entertainment, and storage functionality. The annotations explain more about what each section of the plan should contain and why.

Executive summary
This section summarizes the main goals, recommendations, and points as an overview for senior managers who will read and approve the marketing plan. A table of contents usually follows this section, for management convenience.

Executive Summary

Sonic is preparing to launch a new multimedia, dual-mode smartphone, the Sonic 1000, in a mature market. Our product offers a competitively unique combination of advanced features and functionality at a value-added price. We are targeting specific segments in the consumer and business markets, taking advantage of opportunities indicated by higher demand for easy-to-use smartphones with expanded communications, entertainment, and storage functionality.

The primary marketing objective is to achieve first-year sales of 500 000 units. The primary financial objectives are to achieve first-year sales revenues of $75 million, keep first-year losses to less than $8 million, and break even early in the second year.

Current marketing situation
In this section, marketing managers discuss the overall market, identify the market segments that they will target, and provide information about the company's current situation.

Current Marketing Situation

Sonic, founded 18 months ago by two entrepreneurs with experience in the PC market, is about to enter the maturing smartphone market. Multifunction cellphones, email devices, and wireless communication devices have become commonplace for both personal and professional use. Research shows that North America has 262 million wireless phone subscribers, and 85 percent of the population owns a cellphone.

Competition is therefore more intense even as demand flattens, industry consolidation continues, and pricing pressures squeeze profitability. Worldwide, Nokia is the smartphone leader, holding 45 percent of the global market. The runner-up is Research In Motion, maker of the BlackBerry, with 13 percent of the global market. In the North American market, BlackBerry is the market leader (with a 42 percent share) and Apple, maker of the iPhone, is the runner-up (with a 20 percent share). To gain market share in this dynamic environment, Sonic must carefully target specific segments with features that deliver benefits valued by each customer group.

Market description
Describing the targeted segments in detail provides context for the marketing strategies and detailed action programs discussed later in the plan.

Market Description

Sonic's market consists of consumers and business users who prefer to use a single device for communication, information storage and exchange, and entertainment on the go. Specific segments being targeted during the first year include professionals, corporations, students, entrepreneurs, and medical users. Table A2.1 shows how the Sonic 1000 addresses the needs of targeted consumer and business segments.

Benefits and product features
Table A2.1 clarifies the benefits that product features will deliver to satisfy the needs of customers in each targeted segment.

Buyers can choose between models based on several different operating systems, including systems from Microsoft, Symbian, and BlackBerry, plus Linux variations. Sonic licenses a Linux-based system because it is somewhat less vulnerable to attack by hackers and viruses. Hard drives and removable memory cards are popular smartphone options. Sonic is equipping its first entry with an ultra-fast 20-gigabyte removable memory card for information and entertainment storage. This will also allow users to transfer photos and other data from the smartphone to a home or office computer. Technology costs are decreasing even as capabilities are increasing, which makes value-priced models more appealing to consumers and to business users with older 0 who want to trade up to new, high-end multifunction units.

Table A2.1 Segment Needs and Corresponding Features/Benefits of Sonic

Targeted Segment	Customer Need	Corresponding Feature/Benefit
Professionals (consumer market)	• Stay in touch conveniently and securely while on the go • Perform many functions hands-free without carrying multiple gadgets	• Built-in cellphone and push-to-talk to communicate anywhere at any time; wireless email/web access from anywhere; Linux-based operating system less vulnerable to hackers • Voice-activated applications are convenient; GPS function, camera add value
Students (consumer market)	• Perform many functions hands-free without carrying multiple gadgets • Express style and individuality	• Compatible with numerous applications and peripherals for convenient, cost-effective communication and entertainment • Wardrobe of smartphone cases
Corporate users (business market)	• Security and adaptability for proprietary tasks • Obtain driving directions to business meetings	• Customizable to fit corporate tasks and networks; Linux-based operating system less vulnerable to hackers • Built-in GPS allows voice-activated access to directions and maps
Entrepreneurs (business market)	• Organize and access contacts, schedule details, business and financial files • Get in touch fast	• Hands-free, wireless access to calendar, address book, information files for checking appointments and data, connecting with contacts • Push-to-talk instant calling speeds up communications
Medical users (business market)	• Update, access, and exchange medical records • Photograph medical situations to maintain a visual record	• Removable memory card and hands-free, wireless information recording reduces paperwork and increases productivity • Built-in camera allows fast and easy photography, stores images for later retrieval

Product review
The product review summarizes the main features for all of the company's products, organized by product line, type of customer, market, or order of product introduction.

Product Review

Our first product, the Sonic 1000, offers the following standard features with a Linux OS:

- Built-in dual cellphone/Internet phone functionality and push-to-talk instant calling
- Digital music/video/television recording, wireless downloading, and playback
- Wireless web and email, text messaging, instant messaging
- Three-inch colour screen for easy viewing
- Organizational functions, including calendar, address book, synchronization
- Global positioning system for directions and maps
- Integrated 4-megapixel digital camera
- Ultra-fast 20-gigabyte removable memory card with upgrade potential
- Interchangeable case wardrobe of different colours and patterns
- Voice recognition functionality for hands-free operation

First-year sales revenues are projected to be $75 million, based on sales of 500 000 Sonic 1000 units at a wholesale price of $150 each. During the second year, we plan to introduce the Sonic 2000, also with Linux OS, as a higher-end smartphone product offering the following standard features:

- Global phone and messaging compatibility
- Translation capabilities to send English text as French text (other languages to be offered as add-on options)
- Integrated 8-megapixel camera with flash

Competitive review
The purpose of a competitive review is to identify key competitors, describe their market positions, and briefly discuss their strategies.

Competitive Review

The emergence of lower-priced smartphones, including the Apple iPhone, has increased competitive pressure. Competition from specialized devices for text and email messaging, such as BlackBerry devices, is also a major factor. Key competitors include the following:

- *Nokia:* The market leader in smartphones, Nokia offers a wide range of products for consumers and professionals. It recently purchased the maker of the Symbian operating system and made it into a separate foundation dedicated to improving and promoting this mobile software platform. Many of Nokia's smartphones offer full keyboards, similar to Research In Motion models, but stripped-down models are available for users who do not require the full keyboard and full multimedia capabilities.

- *Apple:* The stylish, popular iPhone 3G has a 3.5-inch colour screen and is well-equipped for music, video, and web access, as well as having communication, calendar, contact management, and file management functions. Its global positioning system technology can pinpoint a user's location. Also, users can erase data with a remote command if the smartphone is lost or stolen. The iPhone is priced at $199 and up, with a two-year service contract.

- *RIM:* Research In Motion makes the lightweight BlackBerry wireless multifunction products that are especially popular among corporate users. RIM's continuous innovation and solid customer service support clearly strengthen its competitive standing as it introduces smartphones with enhanced features and communication capabilities. RIM's newer smartphones come equipped with the BlackBerry OS.

- *Motorola:* Motorola, a global giant, has been losing market share to Apple and Research In Motion, in particular, because it has slowed the pace of new product introduction. One of its top smartphone models is the slender, lightweight quad-band Q, which incorporates email and text message functions, photo caller identification, a full keyboard, camera with flash, removable memory, updated multimedia audio/video/image capabilities, dual stereo speakers, and more. After rebate, the Q is priced at $149.99 with a two-year contract, although the retail price without a contract is considerably higher.

- *Samsung:* Value, style, function: Samsung is a strong competitor, offering a variety of smartphones for consumer and business segments. Some of its smartphones are available for specific telecommunications carriers and some are "unlocked," ready for any compatible telecommunications network. Its Instinct is a smartphone with features similar to the iPhone. After a mail-in rebate of $100, the Instinct's introductory price is $129.99 with a two-year contract.

Despite this strong competition, Sonic can carve out a definite image and gain recognition among the targeted segments. Our voice-recognition system for completely hands-off operation is a critical point of differentiation for competitive advantage. Also, offering GPS as a standard feature gives us a competitive edge compared with similarly priced smartphones. Moreover, our product is speedier than most and runs the Linux OS, which is an appealing alternative for customers concerned about security. Table A2.2 shows a sample of competitive products and prices.

Channels and logistics review
In this section, marketers list the most important channels, provide an overview of each channel arrangement, and identify developing issues in channels and logistics.

Channels and Logistics Review

Sonic-branded products will be distributed through a network of retailers in the top 50 North American markets. Among the most important channel partners being contacted are

- *Office supply superstores:* Office Depot and Staples will both carry Sonic products in stores, in catalogues, and online.
- *Computer stores:* Independent computer retailers in major cities will carry Sonic products.
- *Electronics specialty stores:* Circuit City, Future Shop, and Best Buy will feature Sonic products.
- *Online retailers:* Amazon.ca will carry Sonic products and, for a promotional fee, will give Sonic prominent placement on its home page during the introduction.

Initially, our channel strategy will focus on the United States and Canada; according to demand, we plan to expand into other markets, with appropriate logistical support.

Table A2.2   Sample of Competitive Products and Pricing

Competitor	Model	Features	Price
Nokia	E61i	Quad-band for worldwide phone, email, and Internet access, backlit keyboard, corporate and personal email integration, 2.8-inch screen, 2-megapixel camera, memory card, Symbian OS.	$355 without phone contract
Apple	iPhone 3G	Sleek styling, big screen, fast Internet functions, one-touch calling, GPS navigation, integrated personal and corporate email, open and edit Microsoft Office files, 2-megapixel camera, no keyboard, Apple Mac operating system.	$199 with phone contract
RIM	BlackBerry Curve	Phone, wireless email and Internet access, 2-megapixel camera, built-in maps and GPS, audio and video recording, expandable memory, keyboard, case colour options, BlackBerry OS.	$149.99 with rebate, phone contract
Motorola	Q	Extremely thin and light, with keyboard, quad-band functionality for worldwide use, integrated camera including flash, email and texting functions, Bluetooth connections, multimedia capabilities, voice-activated dialing, Windows OS.	$449.99 without phone contract
Samsung	Instinct	Phone plus email and speedy Internet access, voice-guided GPS, 3.1-inch touch-screen, expandable memory, 2-megapixel camera, live TV, video recording and transmission, FM radio, no keyboard, proprietary operating system.	$129.99 with rebate, phone contract

Strengths, Weaknesses, Opportunities, and Threats Analysis

Sonic has several powerful strengths on which to build, but our major weakness is lack of brand awareness and image. The major opportunity is demand for multimedia smartphones that deliver a number of valued benefits, eliminating the need for customers to carry more than one device. We also face the threat of ever-higher competition from consumer electronics manufacturers, as well as downward pricing pressure. Table A2.3 summarizes Sonic's main strengths, weaknesses, opportunities, and threats.

Strengths
Strengths are internal capabilities that can help the company reach its objectives.

Strengths

Sonic can build on three important strengths:

1. *Innovative product:* The Sonic 1000 offers a combination of features that would otherwise require customers to carry multiple devices: speedy, hands-free dual-mode cell/Wi-Fi telecommunications capabilities, GPS functions, and digital video/music/TV program storage/playback.

2. *Security:* Our smartphone uses a Linux-based operating system that is less vulnerable to hackers and other security threats that can result in stolen or corrupted data.

3. *Pricing:* Our product is priced lower than competing multifunction models—none of which offer the same bundle of features—which gives us an edge with price-conscious customers.

Weaknesses
Weaknesses are internal elements that may interfere with the company's ability to achieve its objectives.

Weaknesses

By waiting to enter the smartphone market until some consolidation of competitors has occurred, Sonic has learned from the successes and mistakes of others. Nonetheless, we have two main weaknesses:

1. *Lack of brand awareness:* Sonic has no established brand or image, whereas Apple and others have strong brand recognition. We will address this issue with aggressive promotion.

2. *Physical specifications:* The Sonic 1000 is slightly heavier and thicker than most competing models because it incorporates multiple features, offers sizable storage capacity, and is compatible with numerous peripheral devices. To counteract this weakness, we will emphasize our product's benefits and value-added pricing, two compelling competitive strengths.

Table A2.3 Sonic's Strengths, Weaknesses, Opportunities, and Threats

Strengths	Weaknesses
• Innovative combination of functions in one portable, voice-activated device • Security due to Linux-based operating system • Value pricing	• Lack of brand awareness and image • Heavier and thicker than most competing models
Opportunities	**Threats**
• Increased demand for multimedia, multifunction smartphones • Cost-efficient technology	• Intense competition • Downward pricing pressure • Compressed product life cycle

Opportunities
Opportunities are external
elements that the company may
be able to exploit to its advantage.

Opportunities

Sonic can take advantage of two major market opportunities:

1. *Increasing demand for multimedia smartphones with multiple functions:* The market for multimedia, multifunction devices is growing much faster than the market for single-use devices. Growth will accelerate as dual-mode capabilities become mainstream, giving customers the flexibility to make phone calls over cell or Internet connections. Smartphones are already commonplace in public, work, and educational settings, which is boosting primary demand. Also, customers who bought entry-level models are replacing older models with more advanced models.

2. *Cost-efficient technology:* Better technology is now available at a lower cost than ever before. Thus, Sonic can incorporate advanced features at a value-added price that allows for reasonable profits.

Threats
Threats are current or emerging
external elements that could
potentially challenge the
company's performance.

Threats

We face three main threats at the introduction of the Sonic 1000:

1. *Increased competition:* More companies are entering the North American market with smartphone models that offer some but not all of the features and benefits provided by Sonic's product. Therefore, Sonic's marketing communications must stress our clear differentiation and value-added pricing.

2. *Downward pressure on pricing:* Increased competition and market-share strategies are pushing smartphone prices down. Still, our objective of seeking a 10 percent profit on second-year sales of the original model is realistic, given the lower margins in this market.

3. *Compressed product life cycle:* Smartphones have reached the maturity stage of their life cycle more quickly than earlier technology products. We have contingency plans to keep sales growing by adding new features, targeting additional segments, and adjusting prices as needed.

Objectives and issues
The company's objectives should
be defined in specific terms so
management can measure
progress and plan corrective
action if needed to stay on track.
This section describes any major
issues that might affect the
company's marketing strategy and
implementation.

Objectives and Issues

We have set aggressive but achievable objectives for the first and second years of market entry.

First-Year Objectives

During the Sonic 1000's initial year on the market, we are aiming for unit sales volume of 500 000.

Second-Year Objectives

Our second-year objectives are to sell a combined total of 1 million units of our two models and to break even early in this period.

Issues

In relation to the product launch, our major issue is the ability to establish a well-regarded brand name linked to a meaningful positioning. We will have to invest heavily in marketing to create a memorable and distinctive brand image projecting innovation, quality, and value. We also must measure awareness and response so we can adjust our marketing efforts as necessary.

Marketing Strategy

Sonic's marketing strategy is based on a positioning of product differentiation. Our primary consumer target is middle- to upper-income professionals who need one portable device to coordinate their busy schedules, communicate with family and colleagues, get driving directions, and be entertained on the go. Our secondary consumer target is high school, postsecondary, and graduate students who want a multimedia, dual-mode device. This segment can be described demographically by age (16–30) and education status.

Our primary business target is mid- to large-sized corporations that want to help their managers and employees stay in touch and input or access critical data when out of the office. This segment consists of companies with more than $25 million in annual sales and more than 100 employees. We are also targeting entrepreneurs and small business owners as well as medical users who want to update or access patients' medical records while reducing paperwork.

Positioning
A positioning built on meaningful differentiation, supported by appropriate strategy and implementation, can help the company build competitive advantage.

Positioning

Using product differentiation, we are positioning the Sonic as the most versatile, convenient, value-added smartphone for personal and professional use. Our marketing will focus on the hands-free operation of multiple communication, entertainment, and information capabilities differentiating the Sonic 1000.

Product Strategy

The Sonic 1000, including all the features described in the earlier Product Review section, will be sold with a one-year warranty. We will introduce a more compact, powerful, high-end model (the Sonic 2000) during the following year. Building the Sonic brand is an integral part of our product strategy. The brand and logo (Sonic's distinctive yellow thunderbolt) will be displayed on the product and its packaging, and reinforced by its prominence in the introductory marketing campaign.

Marketing tools
These sections summarize the broad logic that will guide decisions made about the marketing tools to be used during the period covered by the plan.

Pricing Strategy

The Sonic 1000 will be introduced at $150 wholesale/$199 estimated retail price per unit. We expect to lower the price of this first model when we expand the product line by launching the Sonic 2000, to be priced at $175 wholesale per unit. These prices reflect a strategy of (1) attracting desirable channel partners and (2) taking share from Nokia, Research In Motion, and other established competitors.

Distribution Strategy

Our channel strategy is to use selective distribution, marketing Sonic smartphones through well-known stores and online retailers. During the first year, we will add channel partners until we have coverage in all major North American markets and the product is included in the major electronics catalogues and websites. We will also investigate distribution through cellphone outlets maintained by major carriers. In support of our channel partners, Sonic will provide demonstration products, detailed specification handouts, and full-colour photos and displays featuring the product. Finally, we plan to arrange special payment terms for retailers that place volume orders.

Marketing Communications Strategy

By integrating all messages in all media, we will reinforce the brand name and the main points of product differentiation. Research about media consumption patterns will help our advertising agency choose appropriate media and timing to reach prospects before and during product introduction. Thereafter, advertising will appear on a pulsing basis to maintain brand awareness and communicate various differentiation messages. The agency will also coordinate public relations efforts to build the Sonic brand and support the differentiation message. To create buzz, we will host a user-generated video contest on our website. To attract, retain, and motivate channel partners for a push strategy, we will use trade sales promotions and personal selling. Until the Sonic brand has been established, our communications will encourage purchases through channel partners rather than from our website.

Marketing research
This section shows how marketing research will be used to support development, implementation, and evaluation of strategies and action programs.

Marketing Research

Using research, we are identifying the specific features and benefits that our target market segments value. Feedback from market tests, surveys, and focus groups will help us develop the Sonic 2000. We are also measuring and analyzing customers' attitudes toward competing brands and products. Brand awareness research will help us determine the effectiveness and efficiency of our messages and media. Finally, we will use customer satisfaction studies to gauge market reaction.

Marketing organization
The marketing department may be organized by function, as in this sample, by geography, by product, or by customer (or some combination).

Marketing Organization

Sonic's chief marketing officer, Jane Melody, holds overall responsibility for all of the company's marketing activities. Figure A2.1 shows the structure of the eight-person marketing organization. Sonic has hired Worldwide Marketing to handle national sales campaigns, trade and consumer sales promotions, and public relations efforts.

Action programs
Action programs should be coordinated with the resources and activities of other departments, including production, finance, purchasing, and so on.

Action Programs

The Sonic 1000 will be introduced in February. Following are summaries of the action programs we will use during the first six months of next year to achieve our stated objectives:

January: We will launch a $200 000 trade sales promotion campaign and exhibit at the major industry trade shows to educate dealers and generate channel support for the product launch in February. Also, we will create buzz by providing samples to selected product reviewers, opinion leaders, influential bloggers, and celebrities. Our training staff will work with retail sales personnel at major chains to explain the Sonic 1000's features, benefits, and advantages.

February: We will start an integrated print/radio/Internet campaign targeting professionals and consumers. The campaign will show how many functions the Sonic smartphone can perform and emphasize the convenience of a single, powerful handheld device. This multimedia campaign will be supported by point-of-sale signage as well as online-only ads and video tours.

March: As the multimedia advertising campaign continues, we will add consumer sales promotions such as a contest in which consumers post videos to our website showing how they use the Sonic in creative and unusual ways. We will also distribute new point-of-purchase displays to support our retailers.

Figure A2.1 Sonic's Marketing Organization

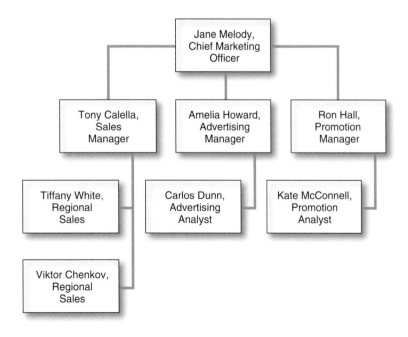

April: We will hold a trade sales contest offering prizes for the salesperson and retail organization that sells the most Sonic smartphones during the four-week period.

May: We plan to roll out a new advertising campaign this month. The radio ads will feature celebrity voices telling their Sonic smartphones to perform functions such as initiating a phone call, sending an email, playing a song or video, and so on. The stylized print and online ads will feature avatars of these celebrities holding their Sonic smartphones.

June: Our radio campaign will add a new voice-over tag line promoting the Sonic 1000 as a graduation gift. We will also exhibit at the semiannual electronics trade show and provide channel partners with new competitive comparison handouts as a sales aid. In addition, we will tally and analyze the results of customer satisfaction surveys for use in future promotions and to provide feedback for product and marketing activities.

Budgets

Managers use budgets to project profitability and plan for each marketing program's expenditures, scheduling, and operations.

Budgets

Total first-year sales revenue for the Sonic 1000 is projected at $75 million, with an average wholesale price of $150 per unit and variable cost of $100 per unit for a unit sales volume of 500 000. We anticipate a first-year loss of up to $8 million on the Sonic 1000 model. Break-even calculations indicate that the Sonic 1000 will become profitable after the sales volume exceeds 650 000, early in the product's second year. Our break-even analysis of Sonic's first smartphone product assumes per-unit wholesale revenue of $150 per unit, variable cost of $100 per unit, and estimated first-year fixed costs of $32 500 000. Based on these assumptions, the break-even calculation is

$$\frac{32\,500\,000}{\$150 - \$100} = 650\,000 \text{ units}$$

Controls

Controls help management assess results after the plan is implemented, identify any problems or performance variations, and initiate corrective action.

Controls

We are planning tight control measures to closely monitor quality and customer service satisfaction. This will enable us to react very quickly in correcting any problems that may occur. Other early warning signals that will be monitored for signs of deviation from the plan include monthly sales (by segment and channel) and monthly expenses. Given the market's volatility, we are developing contingency plans to address fast-moving environmental changes such as new technology and new competition.

Marketing Plan Tools

Pearson offers a package containing *The Marketing Plan: A Handbook* by Marian Burk Wood that explains the process of creating a marketing plan, complete with checklists, real-world examples, and a listing of marketing-related websites and *Marketing Plan Pro*, an award-winning software package that includes sample marketing plans, step-by-step guides, help wizards, and customizable charts for documenting a marketing plan.

Sources: Background information and market data adapted from Laura M. Holson, "Phone Giants Fight to Keep Subscribers," *New York Times,* July 23, 2008, p. C1; Olga Kharif and Roger O. Crockett, "Motorola's Market Share Mess," *BusinessWeek,* July 10, 2008, www.businessweek.com; "Follow the Leader," *Economist,* June 14, 2008, pp. 78–80; Chris Nutall et al., "Apple Set to Slash iPhone Prices to Lift Sales," *Financial Times,* June 10, 2008, p. 20; Walter S. Mossberg, "Samsung Instinct Doesn't Ring True as an iPhone Clone," *Wall Street Journal,* June 12, 2008, p. D1; "Smartphones Get Smarter, Thanks in Part to the iPhone," *InformationWeek,* July 21, 2007; "Hospital Uses PDA App for Patient Transport," *Health Data Management,* June 2007, p. 14.

Marketing managers are facing increased accountability for the financial implications of their actions. This appendix provides a basic introduction to measuring marketing financial performance. Such financial analysis guides marketers in making sound marketing decisions and in assessing the outcomes of those decisions.

The appendix is built around a hypothetical manufacturer of high-definition consumer electronics products—HDInhance. In the past, HDInhance has concentrated on making high-definition televisions for the consumer market. However, the company is now entering the accessories market. Specifically, HDInhance is introducing a new product—a Blu-ray high-definition optical disc player (DVD) that also plays videos streamed over the Internet. In this appendix, we will discuss and analyze the various decisions HDInhance's marketing managers must make before and after the new-product launch.

The appendix is organized into three sections. The *first section* introduces pricing, break-even, and margin analysis assessments that will guide the introduction of HDInhance's new product. The *second section* discusses demand estimates, the marketing budget, and marketing performance measures. It begins with a discussion of estimating market potential and company sales. It then introduces the marketing budget, as illustrated through a *pro forma* profit-and-loss statement followed by the actual profit-and-loss statement. Next we discuss marketing performance measures with a focus on helping marketing managers better defend their decisions from a financial perspective. In the *third section,* we analyze the financial implications of various marketing tactics, such as increasing advertising expenditures, adding sales representatives to increase distribution, lowering price, or extending the product line.

Each of the three sections ends with a set of quantitative exercises that provide you with an opportunity to apply the concepts you learned to situations beyond HDInhance.

Pricing, Break-Even, and Margin Analysis

Pricing Considerations

Determining price is one of the most important marketing mix decisions, and marketers have considerable leeway when setting prices. The limiting factors are demand and costs. Demand factors, such as buyer-perceived value, set the price ceiling. The company's costs set the price floor. In between these two factors, marketers must consider competitors' prices and other factors such as reseller requirements, government regulations, and company objectives.

Current competing high-definition DVD/Internet streaming products in this relatively new product category were introduced in 2007 and sell at retail prices between $500 and $1200. HDInhance plans to introduce its new product at a lower price to expand the market and to gain market share rapidly. We first consider HDInhance's pricing decision from a cost perspective. Then we consider consumer value, the competitive environment, and reseller requirements.

Determining Costs

Fixed costs
Costs that do not vary with production or sales level.

Recall from Chapter 11 that there are different types of costs. **Fixed costs** do not vary with production or sales level and include costs such as rent, interest, depreciation, and clerical and management salaries. Regardless of the level of output, the company must pay these costs. Whereas total fixed costs remain constant as output increases, the fixed cost per unit (or average fixed cost) will decrease as output increases because the total fixed costs are

Variable costs
Costs that vary directly with the level of production.

Total costs
The sum of the fixed and variable costs for any given level of production.

spread across more units of output. **Variable costs** vary directly with the level of production and include costs related to the direct production of the product (such as costs of goods sold—COGS) and many of the marketing costs associated with selling it. Although these costs tend to be uniform for each unit produced, they are called variable because their total varies with the number of units produced. **Total costs** are the sum of the fixed and variable costs for any given level of production.

HDInhance has invested $10 million in refurbishing an existing facility to manufacture the new product. Once production begins, the company estimates that it will incur fixed costs of $20 million per year. The variable cost to produce each device is estimated to be $250 and is expected to remain at that level for the output capacity of the facility.

Setting Price Based on Costs

Cost-plus pricing (or markup pricing)
A standard markup to the cost of the product.

HDInhance starts with the cost-based approach to pricing discussed in Chapter 11. Recall that the simplest method, **cost-plus pricing** (or **markup pricing**), simply adds a standard markup to the cost of the product. To use this method, however, HDInhance must specify expected unit sales so that total unit costs can be determined. Unit variable costs will remain constant regardless of the output, but *average unit fixed costs* will decrease as output increases.

To illustrate this method, suppose HDInhance has fixed costs of $20 million, variable costs of $250 per unit, and expects unit sales of 1 million units. Thus, the cost per unit is given by the following:

$$\text{Unit cost} = \text{variable cost} + \frac{\text{fixed costs}}{\text{unit sales}} = \$250 + \frac{\$20\,000\,000}{1\,000\,000} = \$270$$

Relevant costs
Costs that will occur in the future and that will vary across the alternatives being considered.

Note that we do *not* include the initial investment of $10 million in the total fixed cost figure. It is not considered a fixed cost because it is not a *relevant* cost. **Relevant costs** are those that will occur in the future and that will vary across the alternatives being considered. HDInhance's investment to refurbish the manufacturing facility was a one-time cost that will not reoccur in the future. Such past costs are *sunk costs* and should not be considered in future analyses.

Break-even price
The price at which total revenue equals total cost and profit is zero.

Also notice that if HDInhance sells its product for $270, the price is equal to the total cost per unit. This is the **break-even price**—the price at which unit revenue (price) equals unit cost and profit is zero.

Suppose HDInhance does not want to merely break even, but rather wants to earn a 25% markup on sales. HDInhance's markup price is as follows:[1]

$$\text{Markup price} = \frac{\text{unit cost}}{(1 - \text{desired return on sales})} = \frac{\$270}{1 - 0.25} = \$360$$

This is the price that HDInhance would sell the product to resellers such as wholesalers or retailers to earn a 25% profit on sales.

Return on investment (ROI) pricing (or target-return pricing)
A cost-based pricing method that determines price based on a specified rate of return on investment.

Another approach HDInhance could use is called **return on investment (ROI) pricing** (or **target-return pricing**). In this case, the company *would* consider the initial $10 million investment, but only to determine the dollar profit goal. Suppose the company wants a 30% return on its investment. The price necessary to satisfy this requirement can be determined by the following:[2]

$$\text{ROI price} = \text{unit cost} + \frac{\text{ROI} \times \text{investment}}{\text{unit sales}} = \$270 + \frac{0.3 \times \$10\,000\,000}{1\,000\,000} = \$273$$

That is, if HDInhance sells its product for $273, it will realize a 30% return on its initial investment of $10 million.

In these pricing calculations, unit cost is a function of the expected sales, which were estimated to be 1 million units. But what if actual sales were lower? Then the unit cost would be higher because the fixed costs would be spread over fewer units, and the realized percentage markup on sales or ROI would be lower. Alternatively, if sales are higher than the estimated 1 million units, unit cost would be lower than $270, so a lower price would produce the desired markup on sales or ROI. It's important to note that these cost-based pricing methods are *internally* focused and do not consider demand, competitors' prices, or reseller requirements. Because HDInhance will be selling this product to consumers through wholesalers and retailers offering competing brands, the company must consider markup pricing from this perspective.

Setting Price Based on External Factors

Whereas costs determine the price floor, HDInhance also must consider external factors when setting price. HDInhance does not have the final say concerning the final price to consumers—retailers do. So it must start with its suggested retail price and work back. In doing so, HDInhance must consider the markups required by resellers that sell the product to consumers.

Markup
The difference between a company's selling price for a product and its cost to manufacture or purchase it.

In general, a dollar **markup** is the difference between a company's selling price for a product and its cost to manufacture or purchase it. For a retailer, then, the markup is the difference between the price it charges consumers and the cost the retailer must pay for the product. Thus, for any level of reseller

$$\text{Dollar markup} = \text{selling price} - \text{cost}$$

Markups are usually expressed as a percentage, and there are two different ways to compute markups—on *cost* or on *selling price*:

$$\text{Markup percentage on cost} = \frac{\text{dollar markup}}{\text{cost}}$$

$$\text{Markup percentage on selling price} = \frac{\text{dollar markup}}{\text{selling price}}$$

To apply reseller margin analysis, HDInhance must first set the suggested retail price and then work back to the price at which it must sell the product to a wholesaler. Suppose retailers expect a 30% margin and wholesalers want a 20% margin based on their respective selling prices. And suppose that HDInhance sets a manufacturer's suggested retail price (MSRP) of $599.99 for its product.

Recall that HDInhance wants to expand the market by pricing low and generating market share quickly. HDInhance selected the $599.99 MSRP because it is lower than most competitors' prices, which can be as high as $1200. And the company's research shows that it is below the threshold at which more consumers are willing to purchase the product. By using buyers' perceptions of value and not the seller's cost to determine the MSRP, HDInhance is using **value-based pricing**. For simplicity, we will use an MSRP of $600 in further analyses.

Value-based pricing
Offering just the right combination of quality and good service at a fair price.

To determine the price HDInhance will charge wholesalers, we must first subtract the retailer's margin from the retail price to determine the retailer's cost ($600 − ($600 × 0.30) = $420). The retailer's cost is the wholesaler's price, so HDInhance next subtracts the wholesaler's margin ($420 − ($420 × 0.20) = $336). Thus, the **markup chain** representing the sequence of markups used by firms at each level in a channel for HDInhance's new product is as follows:

Markup chain
The sequence of markups used by firms at each level in a channel.

Suggested retail price:	$600
minus retail margin (30%):	−$180
Retailer's cost/wholesaler's price:	$420
minus wholesaler's margin (20%):	−$ 84
Wholesaler's cost/HDInhance's price:	$336

By deducting the markups for each level in the markup chain, HDInhance arrives at a price for the product to wholesalers of $336.

Break-Even and Margin Analysis

The previous analyses derived a value-based price of $336 for HDInhance's product. Although this price is higher than the break-even price of $270 and covers costs, that price assumed a demand of 1 million units. But how many units and what level of dollar sales must HDInhance achieve to break even at the $336 price? And what level of sales must be achieved to realize various profit goals? These questions can be answered through break-even and margin analysis.

Determining Break-Even Unit Volume and Dollar Sales

Break-even analysis

Analysis to determine the unit volume and dollar sales needed to be profitable given a particular price and cost structure.

Based on an understanding of costs, consumer value, the competitive environment, and reseller requirements, HDInhance has decided to set its price to wholesalers at $336. At that price, what sales level will be needed for HDInhance to break even or make a profit? **Break-even analysis** determines the unit volume and dollar sales needed to be profitable given a particular price and cost structure. At the break-even point, total revenue equals total costs and profit is zero. Above this point, the company will make a profit; below it, the company will lose money. HDInhance can calculate break-even volume using the following formula:[3]

$$\text{Break-even volume} = \frac{\text{fixed costs}}{\text{price} - \text{unit variable cost}}$$

Unit contribution

The amount that each unit contributes to covering fixed costs—the difference between price and variable costs.

The denominator (price − unit variable cost) is called **unit contribution** (sometimes called contribution margin). It represents the amount that each unit contributes to covering fixed costs. Break-even volume represents the level of output at which all (variable and fixed) costs are covered. In HDInhance's case, break-even unit volume is as follows:

$$\text{Break-even volume} = \frac{\text{fixed cost}}{\text{price} - \text{variable cost}} = \frac{\$20\,000\,000}{\$336 - \$250} = 232\,558.1 \text{ units}$$

Thus, at the given cost and pricing structure, HDInhance will break even at 232 559 units.

To determine the break-even dollar sales, simply multiply unit break-even volume by the selling price:

$$\text{BE}_{\text{sales}} = \text{BE}_{\text{vol}} \times \text{price} = 232\,559 \times \$336 = \$78\,139\,824$$

Contribution margin

The unit contribution divided by the selling price.

Another way to calculate dollar break-even sales is to use the percentage contribution margin (hereafter referred to as **contribution margin**), which is the unit contribution divided by the selling price:

$$\text{Contribution margin} = \frac{\text{price} - \text{variable cost}}{\text{price}} = \frac{\$336 - \$250}{\$336} = 0.256 \text{ or } 25.6\%$$

Then,

$$\text{Break-even sales} = \frac{\text{fixed costs}}{\text{contribution margin}} = \frac{\$20\,000\,000}{0.256} = \$78\,125\,000$$

Note that the difference between the two break-even sales calculations is due to rounding.

Such break-even analysis helps HDInhance by showing the unit volume needed to cover costs. If production capacity cannot attain this level of output, then the company should not launch this product. However, the unit break-even volume is well within HDInhance's capacity. Of course, the bigger question concerns whether HDInhance can sell this volume at the $336 price. We'll address that issue a little later.

Understanding contribution margin is useful in other types of analyses as well, particularly if unit prices and unit variable costs are unknown or if a company (say, a retailer) sells many products at different prices and knows the percentage of total sales variable costs represent. Whereas unit contribution is the difference between unit price and unit variable costs, total contribution is the difference between total sales and total variable costs. The overall contribution margin can be calculated as follows:

$$\text{Contribution margin} = \frac{\text{total sales} - \text{total variable costs}}{\text{total sales}}$$

Regardless of the actual level of sales, if the company knows what percentage of sales is represented by variable costs, it can calculate contribution margin. For example, HDInhance's unit variable cost is $250, or 74% of the selling price ($250 ÷ $336 = 0.74). That means for every $1 of sales revenue for HDInhance, $0.74 represents variable costs, and the difference ($0.26) represents contribution to fixed costs. But even if the company doesn't know its unit price and unit variable cost, it can calculate the contribution margin from total sales and total variable costs or from knowledge of the total cost structure. It can set total sales equal to 100% regardless of the actual absolute amount and determine the contribution margin:

$$\text{Contribution margin} = \frac{100\% - 74\%}{100\%} = \frac{1 - 0.74}{1} = 1 - 0.74 = 0.26 \text{ or } 26\%$$

Note that this matches the percentage calculated from the unit price and unit variable cost information. This alternative calculation will be very useful later when analyzing various marketing decisions.

Determining "Breakeven" for Profit Goals

Although it is useful to know the break-even point, most companies are more interested in making a profit. Assume HDInhance would like to realize a $5 million profit in the first year. How many units must it sell at the $336 price to cover fixed costs and produce this profit? To determine this, HDInhance can simply add the profit figure to fixed costs and again divide by the unit contribution to determine unit sales:[4]

$$\text{Unit volume} = \frac{\text{fixed cost} - \text{profit goal}}{\text{price} - \text{variable cost}} = \frac{\$20\,000\,000 + \$5\,000\,000}{\$336 - \$250} = 290\,697.7 \text{ units}$$

Thus, to earn a $5 million profit, HDInhance must sell 290 698 units. Multiply by price to determine dollar sales needed to achieve a $5 million profit:

$$\text{Dollar sales} = 290\,698 \text{ units} \times \$336 = \$97\,674\,528$$

Or use the contribution margin:

$$\text{Sales} = \frac{\text{fixed cost} + \text{profit goal}}{\text{contribution margin}} = \frac{\$20\,000\,000 + \$5\,000\,000}{0.256} = \$97\,656\,250$$

Again, note that the difference between the two break-even sales calculations is due to rounding.

As we saw previously, a profit goal can also be stated as a return on investment goal. For example, recall that HDInhance wants a 30% return on its $10 million investment. Thus, its absolute profit goal is $3 million ($10 000 000 × 0.30). This profit goal is treated the same way as in the previous example:[5]

$$\text{Unit volume} = \frac{\text{fixed cost} + \text{profit goal}}{\text{price} - \text{variable cost}} = \frac{\$20\,000\,000 + \$3\,000\,000}{\$336 - \$250} = 267\,442 \text{ units}$$

$$\text{Dollar sales} = 267\,442 \text{ units} \times \$336 = \$89\,860\,512$$

or

$$\text{Dollar sales} = \frac{\text{fixed cost} + \text{profit goal}}{\text{contribution margin}} = \frac{\$20\,000\,000 + \$3\,000\,000}{0.256} = \$89\,843\,750$$

Finally, HDInhance can express its profit goal as a percentage of sales, which we also saw in previous pricing analyses. Assume HDInhance desires a 25% return on sales. To determine the unit and sales volume necessary to achieve this goal, the calculation is a little different from the previous two examples. In this case, we incorporate the profit goal into the unit contribution as an additional variable cost. Look at it this way: If 25% of each sale must go toward profits, that leaves only 75% of the selling price to cover fixed costs. Thus, the equation becomes:[6]

$$\text{Unit volume} = \frac{\text{fixed cost}}{\text{price} - \text{variable cost} - (0.25 \times \text{price})} \text{ or } \frac{\text{fixed cost}}{(0.75 \times \text{price}) - \text{variable cost}}$$

So,

$$\text{Unit volume} = \frac{\$20\,000\,000}{(0.75 \times \$336) - \$250} = 10\,000\,000 \text{ units}$$

$$\text{Dollar sales necessary} = 10\,000\,000 \text{ units} \times \$336 = \$3\,360\,000\,000$$

Thus, HDInhance would need more than $3 billion in sales to realize a 25% return on sales given its current price and cost structure! Could it possibly achieve this level of sales? The major point is that although break-even analysis can be useful in determining the level of sales needed to cover costs or to achieve a stated profit goal, it does not tell the company whether it is *possible* to achieve that level of sales at the specified price. To address this issue, HDInhance needs to estimate demand for this product.

Before moving on, however, let's stop here and practise applying the concepts covered so far. Now that you have seen pricing and break-even concepts in action as they related to HDInhance's new product, here are several exercises for you to apply what you have learned in other contexts.

Marketing by the Numbers Exercise Set One

Now that you've studied pricing, break-even, and margin analysis as they relate to HDInhance's new-product launch, use the following exercises to apply these concepts in other contexts.

1.1 Sanborn, a manufacturer of electric roof vents, realizes a cost of $55 for every unit it produces. Its total fixed costs equal $2 million. If the company manufactures 500000 units, compute the following:
   a. Unit cost
   b. Markup price if the company desires a 10% return on sales
   c. ROI price if the company desires a 25% return on an investment of $1 million

1.2 An interior decorator purchases items to sell in her store. She purchases a lamp for $125 and sells it for $225. Determine the following:
   a. Dollar markup
   b. Markup percentage on cost
   c. Markup percentage on selling price

1.3 A consumer purchases a toaster from a retailer for $60. The retailer's markup is 20%, and the wholesaler's markup is 15%, both based on selling price. For what price does the manufacturer sell the product to the wholesaler?

1.4 A vacuum manufacturer has a unit cost of $50 and wishes to achieve a margin of 30% based on selling price. If the manufacturer sells directly to a retailer who then adds a set margin of 40% based on selling price, determine the retail price charged to consumers.

1.5 Advanced Electronics manufactures DVDs and sells them directly to retailers who typically sell them for $20. Retailers take a 40% margin based on the retail selling price. Advanced's cost information is as follows:

DVD package and disc	$2.50/DVD
Royalties	$2.25/DVD
Advertising and promotion	$ 500 000
Overhead	$ 200 000

Calculate the following:

a. Contribution per unit and contribution margin

b. Break-even volume in DVD units and dollars

c. Volume in DVD units and dollar sales necessary if Advanced's profit goal is 20% profit on sales

d. Net profit if 5 million DVDs are sold

DEMAND ESTIMATES, THE MARKETING BUDGET, AND MARKETING PERFORMANCE MEASURES

Market Potential and Sales Estimates

HDInhance has now calculated the sales needed to break even and to attain various profit goals on its new product. However, the company needs more information regarding demand to assess the feasibility of attaining the needed sales levels. This information is also needed for production and other decisions. For example, production schedules need to be developed and marketing tactics need to be planned.

Total market demand

The total volume that would be bought by a defined consumer group, in a defined geographic area, in a defined time period, in a defined marketing environment, under a defined level and mix of industry marketing effort.

Market potential

The upper limit of market demand.

The **total market demand** for a product or service is the total volume that would be bought by a defined consumer group, in a defined geographic area, in a defined time period, in a defined marketing environment, under a defined level and mix of industry marketing effort. Total market demand is not a fixed number but a function of the stated conditions. For example, next year's total market demand for high-definition DVD/ Internet streaming devices will depend on how much Samsung, Sony, LG, and other producers spend on marketing their brands. It also depends on many environmental factors, such as government regulations, economic conditions, and the level of consumer confidence in a given market. The upper limit of market demand is called **market potential**.

One general but practical method that HDInhance might incorporate for estimating total market demand uses three variables: (1) the number of prospective buyers, (2) the quantity purchased by an average buyer per year, and (3) the price of an average unit. Using these numbers, HDInhance can estimate total market demand as follows:

$$Q = n \times q \times p$$

where

Q = total market demand

n = number of buyers in the market

q = quantity purchased by an average buyer per year

p = price of an average unit

Chain ratio method

Estimating market demand by multiplying a base number by a chain of adjusting percentages.

A variation of this approach is the **chain ratio method**. This method involves multiplying a base number by a chain of adjusting percentages. For example, HDInhance's product is designed to play high-definition DVD movies on high-definition televisions as well as play videos streamed from the Internet. Thus, consumers who do not own a high-definition television will not likely purchase this player. Additionally, only households with broadband Internet access will be able to use the product. Finally, not all HDTV households will be willing and able to purchase the new product. HDInhance can estimate demand using a chain of calculations like the following:

Total number of households

× The percentage of households owning a high-definition television

× The percentage of households with broadband Internet access

× The percentage of these households willing and able to buy this device

Taking the United States as an example, ACNielsen, the television ratings company, estimates that there are almost 113 million TV households in the United States.[7] Experts estimate that 38% of TV households owned HDTVs at the end of 2008.[8] Research also indicates that 50% of U.S. households have broadband Internet access.[9] Finally, HDInhance's own research indicates that 87% of HDTV households possess the discretionary income needed and are willing to buy a device such as this. In the U.S. market, then, the total number of households willing and able to purchase this product is

$$113\,\text{million households} \times 0.38 \times 0.50 \times 0.87 = 18.7\,\text{million households}$$

Because HDTVs are relatively new and expensive products, most households have only one of these televisions, and it's usually the household's primary television.[10] Thus, consumers who buy a high-definition DVD player/Internet streaming device will likely buy only one per household. Assuming the average retail price across all brands is $750 for this product, the estimate of total market demand is as follows:

$$18.7\text{ million households} \times 1\text{ device per household} \times \$750 = \$14\text{ billion}$$

This simple chain of calculations gives HDInhance only a rough estimate of potential demand. However, more detailed chains involving additional segments and other qualifying factors would yield more accurate and refined estimates. Still, these are only *estimates* of market potential. They rely heavily on assumptions regarding adjusting percentages, average quantity, and average price. Thus, HDInhance must make certain that its assumptions are reasonable and defendable. As can be seen, the overall market potential in dollar sales can vary widely given the average price used. For this reason, HDInhance will use unit sales potential to determine its sales estimate for next year. Market potential in terms of units is 18.7 million (18.7 million households $\times$ 1 device per household).

Assuming that HDInhance wants to attain 2% market share (comparable to its share of the HDTV market) in the first year after launching this product, then it can forecast unit sales at 18.7 million units $\times$ 0.02 = 374 000 units. At a selling price of $336 per unit, this translates into sales of $125 664 000 (374 000 units $\times$ $336 per unit). For simplicity, further analyses will use forecasted sales of $125 million.

This unit volume estimate is well within HDInhance's production capacity and exceeds not only the break-even estimate (232 559 units) calculated earlier, but also the volume necessary to realize a $5 million profit (290 698 units) or a 30% return on investment (267 442 units). However, this forecast falls well short of the volume necessary to realize a 25% return on sales (10 million units!) and may require that HDInhance revise expectations.

To assess expected profits, we must now look at the budgeted expenses for launching this product. To do this, we will construct a pro forma profit-and-loss statement.

The Profit-and-Loss Statement and Marketing Budget

Pro forma (or projected) profit-and-loss statement (or income statement or operating statement)
A statement that shows projected revenues less budgeted expenses and estimates the projected net profit for an organization, product, or brand during a specific planning period, typically a year.

All marketing managers must account for the profit impact of their marketing strategies. A major tool for projecting such profit impact is a **pro forma** (or projected) **profit-and-loss statement** (also called an **income statement** or **operating statement**). A pro forma statement shows projected revenues less budgeted expenses and estimates the projected net profit for an organization, product, or brand during a specific planning period, typically a year. It includes direct product production costs, marketing expenses budgeted to attain a given sales forecast, and overhead expenses assigned to the organization or product. A profit-and-loss statement typically consists of several major components (see **Table A3.1**):

- *Net sales*—gross sales revenue minus returns and allowances (for example, trade, cash, quantity, and promotion allowances). HDInhance's net sales for 2011 are estimated to be $125 million, as determined in the previous analysis.

- *Cost of goods sold* (sometimes called *cost of sales*)—the actual cost of the merchandise sold by a manufacturer or reseller. It includes the cost of inventory, purchases, and other costs associated with making the goods. HDInhance's cost of goods sold is estimated to be 50% of net sales, or $62.5 million.

Table A3.1 Pro Forma Profit-and-Loss Statement for the 12-Month Period Ended December 31, 2011

			% of Sales
Net Sales		$125 000 000	100%
Cost of Goods Sold		62 500 000	50%
Gross Margin		$ 62 500 000	50%
Marketing Expenses			
Sales expenses	$17 500 000		
Promotion expenses	15 000 000		
Freight	12 500 000	45 000 000	36%
General and Administrative Expenses			
Managerial salaries and expenses	$ 2 000 000		
Indirect overhead	3 000 000	5 000 000	4%
Net Profit Before Income Tax		$ 12 500 000	10%

- *Gross margin (or gross profit)*—the difference between net sales and cost of goods sold. HDInhance's gross margin is estimated to be $62.5 million.

- *Operating expenses*—the expenses incurred while doing business. These include all other expenses beyond the cost of goods sold that are necessary to conduct business. Operating expenses can be presented in total or broken down in detail. Here, HDInhance's estimated operating expenses include *marketing expenses* and *general and administrative expenses*.

Marketing expenses include sales expenses, promotion expenses, and distribution expenses. The new product will be sold though HDInhance's sales force, so the company budgets $5 million for sales salaries. However, because sales representatives earn a 10% commission on sales, HDInhance must also add a variable component to sales expenses of $12.5 million (10% of $125 million net sales), for a total budgeted sales expense of $17.5 million. HDInhance sets its advertising and promotion to launch this product at $10 million. However, the company also budgets 4% of sales, or $5 million, for cooperative advertising allowances to retailers who promote HDInhance's new product in their advertising. Thus, the total budgeted advertising and promotion expenses are $15 million ($10 million for advertising plus $5 million in co-op allowances). Finally, HDInhance budgets 10% of net sales, or $12.5 million, for freight and delivery charges. In all, total marketing expenses are estimated to be $17.5 million + $15 million + $12.5 million = $45 million.

General and administrative expenses are estimated at $5 million, broken down into $2 million for managerial salaries and expenses for the marketing function and $3 million of indirect overhead allocated to this product by the corporate accountants (such as depreciation, interest, maintenance, and insurance). Total expenses for the year, then, are estimated to be $50 million ($45 million marketing expenses + $5 million in general and administrative expenses).

- *Net profit before taxes*—profit earned after all costs are deducted. HDInhance's estimated net profit before taxes is $12.5 million.

In all, as Table A3.1 shows, HDInhance expects to earn a profit on its new product of $12.5 million in 2011. Also note that the percentage of sales that each component of the profit-and-loss statement represents is given in the right-hand column. These percentages are determined by dividing the cost figure by net sales (that is, marketing expenses represent 36% of net sales determined by $45 million ÷ $125 million). As can be seen, HDInhance projects a net profit return on sales of 10% in the first year after launching this product.

MARKETING PERFORMANCE MEASURES

Profit-and-loss statement (or income statement or operating statement)
A statement that shows actual revenues less expenses and net profit for an organization, product, or brand during a specific planning period, typically a year.

Now let's fast-forward a year. HDInhance's product has been on the market for one year and management wants to assess its sales and profit performance. One way to assess this performance is to compute performance ratios derived from HDInhance's **profit-and-loss statement** (or **income statement** or **operating statement**).

Whereas the pro forma profit-and-loss statement shows *projected* financial performance, the statement given in **Table A3.2** shows HDInhance's *actual* financial performance based on actual sales, cost of goods sold, and expenses during the past year. By comparing the profit-and-loss statement from one period to the next, HDInhance can gauge performance against goals, spot favourable or unfavourable trends, and take appropriate corrective action.

The profit-and-loss statement shows that HDInhance lost $1 million rather than making the $12.5 million profit projected in the pro forma statement. Why? One obvious reason is that net sales fell $25 million short of estimated sales. Lower sales translated into lower variable costs associated with marketing the product. However, both fixed costs and the cost of goods sold as a percentage of sales exceeded expectations. Hence, the product's contribution margin was 21% rather than the estimated 26%. That is, variable costs represented 79% of sales (55% for cost of goods sold, 10% for sales commissions, 10% for freight, and 4% for co-op allowances). Recall that contribution margin can be calculated by subtracting that fraction from one ($1 - 0.79 = 0.21$). Total fixed costs were $22 million, $2 million more than estimated. Thus, the sales that HDInhance needed to break even given this cost structure can be calculated as follows:

$$\text{Break-even sales} = \frac{\text{fixed costs}}{\text{contribution margin}} = \frac{\$22\,000\,000}{0.21} = \$104\,761\,905$$

If HDInhance had achieved another $5 million in sales, it would have earned a profit.

Although HDInhance's sales fell short of the forecasted sales, so did overall industry sales for this product. Overall industry sales were only $2.5 billion. That means that HDInhance's **market share** was 4% ($100 million ÷ $2.5 billion = 0.04 = 4%), which was higher than forecasted. Thus, HDInhance attained a higher-than-expected market share but the overall market sales were not as high as estimated.

Market share
Company sales divided by market sales.

Analytic Ratios

Operating ratios
The ratios of selected operating statement items to net sales.

The profit-and-loss statement provides the figures needed to compute some crucial **operating ratios**—the ratios of selected operating statement items to net sales. These ratios let marketers compare the firm's performance in one year to that in previous years (or with industry

Table A3.2   Profit-and-Loss Statement for the 12-Month Period Ended December 31, 2011

			% of Sales
Net Sales		$100 000 000	100%
Cost of Goods Sold		55 000 000	55%
Gross Margin		$ 45 000 000	45%
Marketing Expenses			
Sales expenses	$15 500 000		
Promotion expenses	14 000 000		
Freight	10 000 000	39 000 000	39%
General and Administrative Expenses			
Managerial salaries and expenses	$ 2 000 000		
Indirect overhead	5 000 000	7 000 000	7%
Net Profit Before Income Tax		($ 1 000 000)	(1%)

standards and competitors' performance in that year). The most commonly used operating ratios are the *gross margin percentage,* the *net profit percentage,* and the *operating expense percentage.* The *inventory turnover rate* and *return on investment (ROI)* are often used to measure managerial effectiveness and efficiency.

Gross margin percentage
The percentage of net sales remaining after cost of goods sold—calculated by dividing gross margin by net sales.

The **gross margin percentage** indicates the percentage of net sales remaining after cost of goods sold that can contribute to operating expenses and net profit before taxes. The higher this ratio, the more a firm has left to cover expenses and generate profit. HDInhance's gross margin ratio was 45%:

$$\text{Gross margin percentage} = \frac{\text{gross margin}}{\text{net sales}} = \frac{\$45\,000\,000}{\$100\,000\,000} = 0.45 = 45\%$$

Note that this percentage is lower than estimated, and this ratio is seen easily in the percentage of sales column in Table A3.2. Stating items in the profit-and-loss statement as a percent of sales allows managers to quickly spot abnormal changes in costs over time. If there was previous history for this product and this ratio was declining, management should examine it more closely to determine why it has decreased (that is, because of a decrease in sales volume or price, an increase in costs, or a combination of these). In HDInhance's case, net sales were $25 million lower than estimated, and cost of goods sold was higher than estimated (55% rather than the estimated 50%).

Net profit percentage
The percentage of each sales dollar going to profit—calculated by dividing net profits by net sales.

The **net profit percentage** shows the percentage of each sales dollar going to profit. It is calculated by dividing net profits by net sales:

$$\text{Net profit percentage} = \frac{\text{net profit}}{\text{net sales}} = \frac{-\$1\,000\,000}{\$100\,000\,000} = -0.01 = -1.0\%$$

This ratio is easily seen in the percent of sales column. HDInhance's new product generated negative profits in the first year, not a good situation given that before the product launch, net profits before taxes were estimated at more than $12 million. Later in this appendix, we will discuss further analyses the marketing manager should conduct to defend the product.

Operating expense percentage
The portion of net sales going to operating expenses—calculated by dividing total expenses by net sales.

The **operating expense percentage** indicates the portion of net sales going to operating expenses. Operating expenses include marketing and other expenses not directly related to marketing the product, such as indirect overhead assigned to this product. It is calculated by

$$\text{Operating expense percentage} = \frac{\text{total expenses}}{\text{net sales}} = \frac{\$46\,000\,000}{\$100\,000\,000} = 0.46 = 46\%$$

This ratio can also be quickly determined from the percent of sales column in the profit-and-loss statement by adding the percentages for marketing expenses and general and administrative expenses (39% + 7%). Thus, 46 cents of every sales dollar went to operations. Although HDInhance wants this ratio to be as low as possible, and 46% is not an alarming amount, it is of concern if it is increasing over time or if a loss is realized.

Inventory turnover rate (or stockturn rate)
The number of times an inventory turns over or is sold during a specified time period (often one year)—calculated based on costs, selling price, or units.

Another useful ratio is the **inventory turnover rate** (also called **stockturn rate** for resellers). The inventory turnover rate is the number of times an inventory turns over or is sold during a specified time period (often one year). This rate tells how quickly a business is moving inventory through the organization. Higher rates indicate that lower investments in inventory are made, thus freeing up funds for other investments. It may be computed on a cost, selling price, or unit basis. The formula based on cost is as follows:

$$\text{Inventory turnover rate} = \frac{\text{cost of goods sold}}{\text{average inventory at cost}}$$

Assuming HDInhance's beginning and ending inventories were $30 million and $20 million, respectively, the inventory turnover rate is as follows:

$$\text{Inventory turnover rate} = \frac{\$55\,000\,000}{(\$30\,000\,000\,+\,\$20\,000\,000)/2} = \frac{\$55\,000\,000}{\$25\,000\,000} = 2.2$$

That is, HDInhance's inventory turned over 2.2 times in 2011. Normally, the higher the turnover rate, the higher the management efficiency and company profitability. However, this rate should be compared to industry averages, competitors' rates, and past performance to determine if HDInhance is doing well. A competitor with similar sales but a higher inventory turnover rate will have fewer resources tied up in inventory, allowing it to invest in other areas of the business.

Return on investment (ROI)
A measure of managerial effectiveness and efficiency—net profit before taxes divided by total investment.

Companies frequently use **return on investment (ROI)** to measure managerial effectiveness and efficiency. For HDInhance, ROI is the ratio of net profits to total investment required to manufacture the new product. This investment includes capital investments in land, buildings, and equipment (here, the initial $10 million to refurbish the manufacturing facility) plus inventory costs (HDInhance's average inventory totalled $25 million), for a total of $35 million. Thus, HDInhance's ROI for this product is as follows:

$$\text{Return on investment} = \frac{\text{net profit before taxes}}{\text{investment}} = \frac{-\$1\,000\,000}{\$35\,000\,000} = -.0286 = -2.86\%$$

ROI is often used to compare alternatives, and a positive ROI is desired. The alternative with the highest ROI is preferred to other alternatives. HDInhance needs to be concerned with the ROI realized. One obvious way HDInhance can increase ROI is to increase net profit by reducing expenses. Another way is to reduce its investment, perhaps by investing less in inventory and turning it over more frequently.

Marketing Profitability Metrics

Given the above financial results, you may be thinking that HDInhance should drop this new product. But what arguments can marketers make for keeping or dropping this product? The obvious arguments for dropping the product are that first-year sales were well below expected levels and the product lost money, resulting in a negative return on investment.

So what would happen if HDInhance did drop this product? Surprisingly, if the company drops the product, the profits for the total organization will decrease by $4 million! How can that be? Marketing managers need to look closely at the numbers in the profit-and-loss statement to determine the *net marketing contribution* for this product. In HDInhance's case, the net marketing contribution for the product is $4 million, and if the company drops this product, that contribution will disappear as well. Let's look more closely at this concept to illustrate how marketing managers can better assess and defend their marketing strategies and programs.

Net Marketing Contribution

Net marketing contribution (NMC)
A measure of marketing profitability that includes only components of profitability controlled by marketing.

Net marketing contribution (NMC), along with other marketing metrics derived from it, measures *marketing* profitability. It includes only components of profitability that are controlled by marketing. Whereas the previous calculation of net profit before taxes from the profit-and-loss statement includes operating expenses not under marketing's control, NMC does not. Referring back to HDInhance's profit-and-loss statement given in Table A3.2, we can calculate net marketing contribution for the product as follows:

NMC = net sales − cost of goods sold − marketing expenses

= $100 million − $55 million − $41 million = $4 million

The marketing expenses include sales expenses ($15 million), promotion expenses ($14 million), freight expenses ($10 million), and the managerial salaries and expenses of the marketing function ($2 million), which total $41 million.

Thus, the product actually contributed $4 million to HDInhance's profits. It was the $5 million of indirect overhead allocated to this product that caused the negative profit. Further, the amount allocated was $2 million more than estimated in the pro forma profit-and-loss statement. Indeed, if only the estimated amount had been allocated, the product would have earned a *profit* of $1 million rather than losing $1 million. If HDInhance drops the product, the $5 million in fixed overhead expenses will not disappear—it will simply have to be allocated elsewhere. However, the $4 million in net marketing contribution *will* disappear.

Marketing Return on Sales and Investment

To get an even deeper understanding of the profit impact of marketing strategy, we'll now examine two measures of marketing efficiency—*marketing return on sales* (marketing ROS) and *marketing return on investment* (marketing ROI).[11]

Marketing return on sales
(or **marketing ROS**)
The percent of net sales attributable to the net marketing contribution—calculated by dividing net marketing contribution by net sales.

Marketing return on sales (or **marketing ROS**) shows the percent of net sales attributable to the net marketing contribution. For our product, ROS is as follows:

$$\text{Marketing ROS} = \frac{\text{net marketing contribution}}{\text{net sales}} = \frac{\$4\,000\,000}{\$100\,000\,000} = 0.04 = 4\%$$

Thus, out of every $100 of sales, the product returns $4 to HDInhance's bottom line. A high marketing ROS is desirable. But to assess whether this is a good level of performance, HDInhance must compare this figure to previous marketing ROS levels for the product, the ROSs of other products in the company's portfolio, and the ROSs of competing products.

Marketing return on investment (or **marketing ROI**) measures the marketing productivity of a marketing investment. In HDInhance's case, the marketing investment is represented by $41 million of the total expenses. Thus, marketing ROI is as follows:

Marketing return on investment (or **marketing ROI**)
A measure of the marketing productivity of a marketing investment—calculated by dividing net marketing contribution by marketing expenses.

$$\text{Marketing ROI} = \frac{\text{net marketing contribution}}{\text{net marketing expenses}} = \frac{\$4\,000\,000}{\$41\,000\,000} = 0.0976 = 9.76\%$$

As with marketing ROS, a high value is desirable, but this figure should be compared with previous levels for the given product and with the marketing ROIs of competitors' products. Note from this equation that marketing ROI could be greater than 100%. This can be achieved by attaining a higher net marketing contribution and/or a lower total marketing expense.

In this section, we estimated market potential and sales, developed profit-and-loss statements, and examined financial measures of performance. In the next section, we discuss methods for analyzing the impact of various marketing tactics. However, before moving on to those analyses, here's another set of quantitative exercises to help you apply what you've learned to other situations.

Marketing by the Numbers Exercise Set Two

2.1 Determine the market potential for a product that has 50 million prospective buyers who purchase an average of 3 units per year and price averages $25. How many units must a company sell if it desires a 10% share of this market?

2.2 Develop a profit-and-loss statement for the Westgate division of North Industries. This division manufactures light fixtures sold to consumers through home improvement and hardware stores. Cost of goods sold represents 40% of net sales. Marketing expenses include selling expenses, promotion expenses, and freight. Selling expenses include sales salaries totalling $3 million per year and sales commissions (5% of sales). The company spent $3 million on advertising last year, and freight costs were 10% of sales. Other costs include $2 million for managerial salaries and expenses for the marketing function and another $3 million for indirect overhead allocated to the division.
   a. Develop the profit-and-loss statement if net sales were $20 million last year.
   b. Develop the profit-and-loss statement if net sales were $40 million last year.
   c. Calculate Westgate's break-even sales.

2.3 Using the profit-and-loss statement you developed in question 2.2b, and assuming that Westgate's beginning inventory was $11 million, ending inventory was $7 million, and total investment was $20 million (including inventory), determine the following:
   a. Gross margin percentage
   b. Net profit percentage
   c. Operating expense percentage
   d. Inventory turnover rate
   e. Return on investment (ROI)
   f. Net marketing contribution

g. Marketing return on sales (marketing ROS)

h. Marketing return on investment (marketing ROI)

i. Is the Westgate division doing well? Explain your answer.

FINANCIAL ANALYSIS OF MARKETING TACTICS

Although the first-year profit performance for HDInhance's new product was less than desired, management feels that this attractive market has excellent growth opportunities. Although the sales of HDInhance's product were lower than initially projected, they were not unreasonable given the size of the current market. Thus, HDInhance wants to explore new marketing tactics to help grow the market for this product and increase sales for the company.

For example, the company could increase advertising to promote more awareness of the new product and its category. It could add salespeople to secure greater product distribution. HDInhance could decrease prices so that more consumers could afford its product. Finally, to expand the market, HDInhance could introduce a lower-priced model in addition to the higher-priced original offering. Before pursuing any of these tactics, HDInhance must analyze the financial implications of each.

Increase Advertising Expenditures

Although most consumers understand DVD players, they may not be aware of high-definition DVD players that also stream video from the Internet. Thus, HDInhance is considering boosting its advertising to make more people aware of the benefits of this device in general and of its own brand in particular.

What if HDInhance's marketers recommend increasing national advertising by 50% to $15 million (assume no change in the variable cooperative component of promotional expenditures)? This represents an increase in fixed costs of $5 million. What increase in sales will be needed to break even on this $5 million increase in fixed costs?

A quick way to answer this question is to divide the increase in fixed cost by the contribution margin, which we found in a previous analysis to be 21%:

$$\text{Increase in sales} = \frac{\text{increase in fixed cost}}{\text{contribution margin}} = \frac{\$5\ 000\ 000}{0.21} = \$23\ 809\ 524$$

Thus, a 50% increase in advertising expenditures must produce a sales increase of almost $24 million to just break even. That $24 million sales increase translates into an almost 1 percentage point increase in market share (1% of the $2.5 billion overall market equals $25 million). That is, to break even on the increased advertising expenditure, HDInhance would have to increase its market share from 4% to 4.95% ($123 809 524 ÷ $2.5 billion = 0.0495% or 4.95% market share). All of this assumes that the total market will not grow, which might or might not be a reasonable assumption.

Increase Distribution Coverage

HDInhance also wants to consider hiring more salespeople to call on new retailer accounts and increase distribution through more outlets. Even though HDInhance sells directly to wholesalers, its sales representatives call on retail accounts to perform other functions in addition to selling, such as training retail salespeople. Currently, HDInhance employs 60 sales reps who earn an average of $50 000 in salary plus 10% commission on sales. The product is currently sold to consumers through 1875 retail outlets. Suppose HDInhance wants to increase that number of outlets to 2500, an increase of 625 retail outlets. How many additional salespeople will HDInhance need, and what sales will be necessary to break even on the increased cost?

Workload method
An approach to determining sales force size based on the workload required and the time available for selling.

One method for determining what size sales force HDInhance will need is the **workload method**. The workload method uses the following formula to determine the sales force size:

$$NS = \frac{NC \times FC \times LC}{TA}$$

where

NS = number of salespeople
NC = number of customers
FC = average frequency of customer calls per customer
LC = average length of customer call
TA = time an average salesperson has available for selling per year

HDInhance's sales reps typically call on accounts an average of 20 times per year for about 2 hours per call. Although each sales rep works 2000 hours per year (50 weeks per year × 40 hours per week), they spent about 15 hours per week on nonselling activities such as administrative duties and travel. Thus, the average annual available selling time per sales rep per year is 1250 hours (50 weeks × 25 hours per week). We can now calculate how many sales reps HDInhance will need to cover the anticipated 2500 retail outlets:

$$NS = \frac{2500 \times 20 \times 2}{1250} = 80 \text{ salespeople}$$

Therefore, HDInhance will need to hire 20 more salespeople. The cost to hire these reps will be $1 million (20 salespeople × $50 000 salary per salesperson).

What increase in sales will be required to break even on this increase in fixed costs? The 10% commission is already accounted for in the contribution margin, so the contribution margin remains unchanged at 21%. Thus, the increase in sales needed to cover this increase in fixed costs can be calculated by

$$\text{Increase in sales} = \frac{\text{increase in fixed cost}}{\text{contribution margin}} = \frac{\$1\ 000\ 000}{0.21} = \$4\ 761\ 905$$

That is, HDInhance's sales must increase almost $5 million to break even on this tactic. So how many new retail outlets will the company need to secure to achieve this sales increase? The average revenue generated per current outlet is $53 333 ($100 million in sales divided by 1875 outlets). To achieve the nearly $5 million sales increase needed to break even, HDInhance would need about 90 new outlets ($4 761 905 ÷ 53 333 = 89.3 outlets), or about 4.5 outlets per new rep. Given that current reps cover about 31 outlets apiece (1875 outlets ÷ 60 reps), this seems very reasonable.

Decrease Price

HDInhance is also considering lowering its price to increase sales revenue through increased volume. The company's research has shown that demand for most types of consumer electronics products is elastic—that is, the percentage increase in the quantity demanded is greater than the percentage decrease in price. It has also been found that when the price of HDTVs goes down, the quantity of accessory products like DVD players demanded increases because they are complementary products.

What increase in sales would be necessary to break even on a 10% decrease in price? That is, what increase in sales will be needed to maintain the total contribution that HDInhance realized at the higher price? The current total contribution can be determined by multiplying the contribution margin by total sales:[12]

$$\text{Current total contribution} = \text{contribution margin} \times \text{sales} = 0.21 \times \$100 \text{ million} = \$21 \text{ million}$$

Price changes result in changes in unit contribution and contribution margin. Recall that the contribution margin of 21% was based on variable costs representing 79% of sales. Therefore, unit variable costs can be determined by multiplying the original price by this percentage: $336 × 0.79 = $265.44 per unit. If price is decreased by 10%, the new price is $302.40. However, variable costs do not change just because price decreased, so the unit contribution and contribution margin decrease as follows:

	Old	New (reduced 10%)
Price	$336	$302.40
– Unit variable cost	$265.44	$265.44
= Unit contribution	$ 70.56	$ 36.96
Contribution margin	$ 70.56/$336 = 0.21 or 21%	$ 36.96/$302.40 = 0.12 or 12%

So a 10% reduction in price results in a decrease in the contribution margin from 21% to 12%.[13] To determine the sales level needed to break even on this price reduction, we calculate the level of sales that must be attained at the new contribution margin to achieve the original total contribution of $21 million:

New contribution margin × new sales level = original total contribution

So,

$$\text{New sales level} = \frac{\text{original contribution}}{\text{new contribution margin}} = \frac{\$21\ 000\ 000}{0.12} = \$175\ 000\ 000$$

Thus, sales must increase by $75 million ($175 million – $100 million) just to break even on a 10% price reduction. This means that HDInhance must increase market share to 7% ($175 million ÷ $2.5 billion) to achieve the current level of profits (assuming no increase in the total market sales). The marketing manager must assess whether or not this is a reasonable goal.

Extend the Product Line

As a final option, HDInhance is considering extending its product line by offering a lower-priced model. Of course, the new, lower-priced product would steal some sales from the higher-priced model. This is called **cannibalization**—the situation in which one product sold by a company takes a portion of its sales from other company products. If the new product has a lower contribution than the original product, the company's total contribution will decrease on the cannibalized sales. However, if the new product can generate enough new volume, it is worth considering.

To assess cannibalization, HDInhance must look at the incremental contribution gained by having both products available. Recall that in the previous analysis we determined that unit variable costs were $265.44 and unit contribution was just over $70. Assuming costs remain the same next year, HDInhance can expect to realize a contribution per unit of approximately $70 for every unit of the original product sold.

Assume that the first model offered by HDInhance is called HD1 and the new, lower-priced model is called HD2. HD2 will retail for $400, and resellers will take the same markup percentages on price as they do with the higher-priced model. Therefore, HD2's price to wholesalers will be $224, as follows:

Retail price:	$400
minus retail margin (30%):	–$120
Retailer's cost/wholesaler's price:	$280
minus wholesaler's margin (20%):	–$ 56
Wholesaler's cost/HDInhance's price	$224

Cannibalization

The situation in which one product sold by a company takes a portion of its sales from other company products.

If HD2's variable costs are estimated to be $174, then its contribution per unit will equal $50 ($224 − $174 = $50). That means for every unit that HD2 cannibalizes from HD1, HDInhance will *lose* $20 in contribution toward fixed costs and profit (that is, contribution$_{HD2}$ − contribution$_{HD1}$ = $50 − $70 = −$20). You might conclude that HDInhance should not pursue this tactic because it appears as though the company will be worse off if it introduces the lower-priced model. However, if HD2 captures enough *additional* sales, HDInhance will be better off even though some HD1 sales are cannibalized. The company must examine what will happen to *total* contribution, which requires estimates of unit volume for both products.

Originally, HDInhance estimated that next year's sales of HD1 would be 600 000 units. However, with the introduction of HD2, it now estimates that 200 000 of those sales will be cannibalized by the new model. If HDInhance sells only 200 000 units of the new HD2 model (all cannibalized from HD1), the company would lose $4 million in total contribution (200 000 units × −$20 per cannibalized unit = −$4 million)—not a good outcome. However, HDInhance estimates that HD2 will generate the 200 000 of cannibalized sales plus an *additional* 500 000 unit sales. Thus, the contribution on these additional HD2 units will be $25 million (i.e., 500 000 units × $50 per unit = $25 million). The net effect is that HDInhance will gain $21 million in total contribution by introducing HD2.

The following table compares HDInhance's total contribution with and without the introduction of HD2:

	HD1 only	HD1 and HD2
HD1 contribution	600 000 units × $70 = $42 000 000	400 000 units × $70 = $28 000 000
HD2 contribution	0	700 000 units × $50 = $35 000 000
Total contribution	$42 000 000	$63 000 000

The difference in the total contribution is a net gain of $21 million ($63 million − $42 million). Based on this analysis, HDInhance should introduce the HD2 model because it results in a positive incremental contribution. However, if fixed costs will increase by more than $21 million as a result of adding this model, then the net effect will be negative and HDInhance should not pursue this tactic.

Now that you have seen these marketing tactic analysis concepts in action as they related to HDInhance's new product, here are several exercises for you to apply what you have learned in this section in other contexts.

Marketing by the Numbers Exercise Set Three

3.1 Kingsford, Inc., sells small plumbing components to consumers through retail outlets. Total industry sales for Kingsford's relevant market last year were $80 million, with Kingsford's sales representing 10% of that total. Contribution margin is 25%. Kingsford's sales force calls on retail outlets and each sales rep earns $45 000 per year plus 1% commission on all sales. Retailers receive a 40% margin on selling price and generate average revenue of $10 000 per outlet for Kingsford.

a. The marketing manager has suggested increasing consumer advertising by $300 000. By how much would dollar sales need to increase to break even on this expenditure? What increase in overall market share does this represent?

b. Another suggestion is to hire three more sales representatives to gain new consumer retail accounts. How many new retail outlets would be necessary to break even on the increased cost of adding three sales reps?

    c. A final suggestion is to make a 20% across-the-board price reduction. By how much would dollar sales need to increase to maintain Kingsford's current contribution? (See endnote 13 to calculate the new contribution margin.)

    d. Which suggestion do you think Kingsford should implement? Explain your recommendation.

3.2 PepsiCo sells its soft drinks in approximately 400 000 retail establishments, such as supermarkets, discount stores, and convenience stores. Sales representatives call on each retail account weekly, which means each account is called on by a sales rep 52 times per year. The average length of a sales call is 75 minutes (or 1.25 hours). An average salesperson works 2000 hours per year (50 weeks per year × 40 hours per week), but each spends 10 hours a week on nonselling activities, such as administrative tasks and travel. How many salespeople does PepsiCo need?

3.3 Hair Zone manufactures a brand of hair-styling gel. It is considering adding a modified version of the product—a foam that provides stronger hold. Hair Zone's variable costs and prices to wholesalers are as follows:

	Current Hair Gel	New Foam Product
Unit selling price	2.00	2.25
Unit variable costs	0.85	1.25

Hair Zone expects to sell 1 million units of the new styling foam in the first year after introduction, but it expects that 60% of those sales will come from buyers who normally purchase Hair Zone's styling gel. Hair Zone estimates that it would sell 1.5 million units of the gel if it did not introduce the foam. If the fixed cost of launching the new foam will be $100 000 during the first year, should Hair Zone add the new product to its line? Why or why not?

Now that you have completed this marketing course you have a good idea of what the field entails. You may have decided you want to pursue a marketing career because it offers constant challenge, stimulating problems, the opportunity to work with people, and excellent advancement opportunities. But you still may not know which part of marketing best suits you—marketing is a very broad field offering a wide variety of career options.

This appendix helps you discover what types of marketing jobs best match your special skills and interests, shows you how to conduct the kind of job search that will get you the position you want in the company of your choice, describes the marketing career paths open to you, and suggests other information resources.

Marketing Careers Today

The marketing field is booming with nearly a third of all North Americans now employed in marketing-related positions. Marketing salaries may vary by company, position, and region, and salary figures change constantly. In general, entry-level marketing salaries usually are only slightly below those for engineering and chemistry but equal or exceed starting salaries in economics, finance, accounting, general business, and the liberal arts. Moreover, if you succeed in an entry-level marketing position, it's likely that you will be promoted quickly to higher levels of responsibility and salary. In addition, because of the consumer and product knowledge you will gain in these jobs, marketing positions provide excellent training for the highest levels in an organization.

Overall Marketing Facts and Trends

In conducting your job search, consider the following facts and trends that are changing the world of marketing.

Focus on customers: More and more companies are realizing that they win in the marketplace only by creating superior value for customers. To capture value from customers they must first find new and better ways to solve customer problems and improve customer brand experiences. This increasing focus on the customer puts marketers at the forefront in many of today's companies. As the primary customer-facing function, marketing's mission is to get all company departments to "think customer."

Technology: Technology is changing the way marketers work. For example, price coding allows instantaneous retail inventorying. Software for marketing training, forecasting, and other functions is changing the ways we market. And the Internet is creating new jobs and new recruiting rules. Consider the explosive growth in new media marketing. Whereas advertising firms have traditionally recruited "generalists" in account management, "generalist" has now taken on a whole new meaning—advertising account executives must now have both broad and specialized knowledge.

Diversity: The number of women and minorities in marketing continues to rise. They are also rising rapidly into marketing management. For example, women now outnumber men by nearly two to one as advertising account executives. As marketing becomes more global, the need for diversity in marketing positions will continue to increase, opening new opportunities.

Global: Companies such as Research In Motion (RIM), Bombardier, Coca-Cola, McDonald's, IBM, Walmart, and Procter & Gamble have become multinational, with manufacturing and marketing operations in hundreds of countries. Indeed, such companies often make more profit from sales outside North America than from within. And it's not just the big companies that are involved in international marketing. Organizations of all sizes have moved into the global arena. Many new marketing opportunities and careers will be directly linked to the expanding global marketplace.

The globalization of business also means that you will need more cultural, language, and people skills in the marketing world of the twenty-first century.

Not-for-profit organizations: Increasingly, colleges, arts organizations, libraries, hospitals, and other not-for-profit organizations are recognizing the need for effectively marketing their "products" and services to various publics. This awareness has led to new marketing positions—with these organizations hiring their own marketing directors and marketing vice-presidents or using outside marketing specialists.

Looking for a Job in Today's Marketing World

To choose and find the right job you will need to apply the marketing skills you've learned in this course, especially marketing analysis and planning. Follow these eight steps for marketing yourself: (1) Conduct a self-assessment and seek career counselling, (2) examine job descriptions, (3) explore the job market and assess opportunities, (4) develop search strategies, (5) prepare a résumé, (6) write a cover letter and assemble supporting documents, (7) interview for jobs, and (8) follow-up.

Conduct a Self-Assessment and Seek Career Counselling

If you're having difficulty deciding what kind of marketing position is the best fit for you, start by doing some self-testing or get some career counselling. Self-assessments require that you honestly and thoroughly evaluate your interests, strengths, and weaknesses. What do you do well (your best and favourite skills) and not so well? What are your favourite interests? What are your career goals? What makes you stand out from other job seekers?

The answers to such questions may suggest which marketing careers you should seek or avoid. For help in making an effective self-assessment, look for the following books in your local bookstore: Shoya Zichy, *Career Match: Connecting Who You Are with What You Love to Do* (AMACOM Books, 2007) and Richard Bolles, *What Color Is Your Parachute? 2008* (Ten Speed Press, 2007). Many websites also offer self-assessment tools, such as the Keirsey Temperament Sorter, a free but broad assessment available at Kiersey.com. For a more specific evaluation, CareerLeader.com offers a complete online business career self-assessment program designed by the directors of MBA career development at Harvard Business School. You can use this for a fee.

For help in finding a career counsellor to guide you in making a career assessment, Richard Bolles's *What Color Is Your Parachute? 2008* contains a useful sampling. CareerLeader.com also offers personal career counselling. (Some counsellors can help you in your actual job search, too.) You can also consult the career counselling, testing, and placement services at your college or university.

Examine Job Descriptions

After you have identified your skills, interests, and desires, you need to see which marketing positions are the best match for them. *Marketing* magazine (www.marketingmag.ca) and *Strategy* magazine (www.strategyonline.ca/careers) are valuable sources of information for anyone looking for a career in marketing. Job seekers can post résumés and search jobs using *Marketing* magazine's CareerZone link and access a wide variety of industry links using the website's Resources section. The Canadian Marketing Association is another rich source of job postings (www.marketing-jobs.ca).

Your initial career shopping list should be broad and flexible. Look for different ways to achieve your objectives. For example, if you want a career in marketing management, consider the public as well as the private sector and local and regional as well as national and international firms. Be open initially to exploring many options, then focus on specific industries and jobs, listing your basic goals as a way to guide your choices. Your list might include "a job in a start-up company, near Vancouver, doing new-product planning with a computer software firm."

Explore the Job Market and Assess Opportunities

At this stage, you need to look at the market and see what positions are actually available. You do not have to do this alone. Any of the following may assist you.

Career Development Centres

Your university's career development centre is an excellent place to start. For example, Management Career Services at Dalhousie University provides business students access to the Vault Online Career Library, which has a wide variety of information, including career guides and advice as well as industry and employer profiles. This is one example of the many tools that may be available from your university's career development centre.

In addition, find out everything you can about the companies that interest you by consulting business magazines, websites, annual reports, business reference books, faculty, career counsellors, and others. Try to analyze the industry's and the company's future growth and profit potential, advancement opportunities, salary levels, entry positions, travel time, and other factors of significance to you.

Job Fairs

Career development centres often work with corporate recruiters to organize on-campus job fairs. You might also use the Internet to check upcoming career fairs in your region. For example, the federal and Alberta governments sponsor the Canada Career Week Fair in Edmonton (www.canadacareerfairedmonton.com).

Networking and the Yellow Pages

Networking—asking for job leads from friends, family, people in your community, and career centres—is one of the best ways to find a marketing job. Studies estimate that 60 to 90 percent of jobs are found through networking. The idea is to spread your net wide, contacting anybody and everybody.

The phone book's yellow pages are another effective way to job search. Check out employers in your field of interest in whatever region you want to work, then call and ask if they are hiring for the position of your choice.

Cooperative Education and Internships

According to a recent survey, employers on average give full-time employment offers to about 61 percent of students who have had internships with their companies. Many company Internet sites have separate internship areas. For example, check out InternshipPrograms.com, MonsterCollege (www.college.monster.ca), CampusCareerCenter.com, InternJobs.com, and InternAbroad.com. If you know of a company that you wish to work for, go to that company's corporate website, enter the human resources area, and check for internships. If none are listed, try emailing the human resources department and ask if internships are offered.

The Internet

A constantly increasing number of sites on the Internet deal with job hunting. You can also use the Internet to make contacts with people who can help you gain information on companies that interest you. The Riley Guide offers a great introduction to what jobs are available (www.rileyguide.com). CareerBuilder.ca, Monster.ca, and Yahoo! HotJobs (http://hotjobs.yahoo.com) are good general sites for seeking job listings. Most companies have their own websites on which they post job listings. This may be helpful if you have a specific and fairly limited number of companies that you are keeping your eye on for job opportunities. But if this is not the case, remember that to find out what interesting marketing jobs the companies themselves are posting, you may have to visit hundreds of corporate sites.

Professional Networking Sites

Many companies have now begun to take advantage of social networking sites to find talented applicants. From Facebook to LinkedIn, social networking has become professional networking. For example, Ernst & Young has a career page on Facebook (www.facebook.com/ernstandyoungcareers) to find potential candidates for entry-level positions. For job seekers, online professional networking offers more efficient job targeting and reduces costs associated with traditional interaction methods such as travelling to job fairs and interviews, printing your résumé, and other expenses.

However, although the Internet offers a wealth of resources for searching for the perfect job, be aware that it constitutes a two-way street. Just as job seekers can search the Web to find job opportunities, employers can search for information on job candidates. A recent Execunet survey found that a growing number of job searches are being derailed by "digital dirt"—information mined from online social networking sites that reveals unintended or embarrassing anecdotes and photos. Web searches can also sometimes reveal inconsistencies and résumé inflation. According to the Execunet survey, 77 percent of recruiters interviewed use search engines to learn more about candidates. Some 35 percent said they've eliminated a candidate based on information that they uncovered.[1]

Develop Search Strategies

Once you've decided which companies you are interested in, you need to contact them. One of the best ways is through on-campus interviews. But not every company you are interested in will visit your school. In such instances, you can write, email, or phone the company directly or ask marketing professors or school alumni for contacts.

Prepare a Résumé

A résumé is a concise yet comprehensive written summary of your qualifications, including your academic, personal, and professional achievements, that showcases why you are the best candidate for the job. Since an employer will spend an average of 15 to 20 seconds reviewing your résumé, you want to be sure that you prepare a good one.

In preparing your résumé, remember that all information on it must be accurate and complete. Résumés typically begin with the applicant's full name, telephone and fax numbers, and mail and email addresses. A simple and direct statement of career objectives generally appears next, followed by work history and academic data (including awards and internships), and then personal activities and experiences applicable to the job sought.

The résumé sometimes ends with a list of references the employer may contact (at other times, references may be listed separately). If your work or internship experience is limited, nonexistent, or irrelevant, then it is a good idea to emphasize your academic and nonacademic achievements, showing skills related to those required for excellent job performance.

There are three types of résumés. *Reverse chronological* résumés, which emphasize career growth, are organized in reverse chronological order, starting with your most recent job. They focus on job titles within organizations, describing the responsibilities required for each job. *Functional* résumés focus less on job titles and work history and more on assets and achievements. This format works best if your job history is scanty or discontinuous. *Mixed,* or *combination,* résumés take from each of the other two formats. First, the skills used for a specific job are listed, then the job title is stated. This format works best for applicants whose past jobs are in other fields or are seemingly unrelated to the position.

Your local bookstore or library has many books that can assist you in developing your résumé. Popular guides are Brenda Greene, *Get the Interview Every Time: Fortune 500 Hiring Professionals' Tips for Writing Winning Résumés and Cover Letters* (Dearborn Trade, 2004) and Susan Britton Whitcomb's *Résumé Magic: Trade Secrets of a Professional Résumé Writer* (JIST Works, 2006). Computer software programs, such as *RésuméMaker* (www.resumemaker.com), provide hundreds of sample résumés and ready-to-use phrases while guiding you through the résumé preparation process. America's Career InfoNet offers a step-by-step résumé tutorial (www.acinet.org/acinet/resume/resume_intro.asp), and Monster offers résumé advice and writing services (http://content.monster.com/resume/home.aspx). Finally, you can even create your own personalized online résumé at sites such as OptimalResume.com.

Electronic Résumés

Use of the Internet as a tool in the job search process is increasing, so it's a good idea to have your résumé ready for the online environment. You can forward an electronic résumé to networking contacts or recruiting professionals through email. You can also post it in online databases with the hope that employers and recruiters will find it.

Successful electronic résumés require a different strategy than paper résumés. For instance, when companies search résumé banks, they search key words and industry buzz words that describe core work or a skill required for each job, so nouns are much more important than verbs. Two good resources for preparing electronic résumés are Susan Ireland's Electronic Résumé Guide (http://susanireland.com/eresumeguide) and The Riley Guide (www.rileyguide.com/eresume.html).

After you have written your electronic résumé, you need to post it. The following sites may be good locations to start: Monster.ca and Yahoo! HotJobs (http://hotjobs.yahoo.com). However, use caution when posting your résumé on various sites. In this era of identity theft, you need to select sites with care to protect your privacy. Limit access to your personal contact information and don't use sites that offer to "blast" your résumé into cyberspace.

Résumé Tips

- Communicate your worth to potential employers in a concrete manner, citing examples whenever possible.

- Be concise and direct.

- Use active verbs to show you are a doer.

- Do not skimp on quality or use gimmicks. Spare no expense in presenting a professional résumé.

- Have someone critique your work. A single typo can eliminate you from being considered.

- Customize your résumé for specific employers. Emphasize your strengths as they pertain to your targeted job.

- Keep your résumé compact, usually one page.

- Format the text to be attractive, professional, and readable. Times New Roman is often the font of choice. Avoid too much "design" or gimmicky flourishes.

Write Cover Letter, Follow Up, and Assemble Supporting Documents

Cover Letter

You should include a cover letter informing the employer that a résumé is enclosed. But a cover letter does more than this. It also serves to summarize in one or two paragraphs the contents of the résumé and explains why you think you are the right person for the position. The goal is to persuade the employer to look at the more detailed résumé. A typical cover letter is organized as follows: (1) the name and position of the person you are contacting; (2) a statement identifying the position you are applying for, how you heard of the vacancy, and the reasons for your interest; (3) a summary of your qualifications for the job; (4) a description of what follow-ups you intend to make, such as phoning in two weeks to see if the résumé has been received; (5) an expression of gratitude for the opportunity of being a candidate for the job. America's Career InfoNet offers a step-by-step tutorial on how to create a cover letter (www.acinet.org/acinet/resume/resume_intro.asp), and Susan Ireland's website contains more than 50 cover letter samples (http://susanireland.com/coverletterindex.htm).

Follow-Up

Once you send your cover letter and résumé to perspective employers via the method they prefer—email, their website, fax, or regular mail—it's often a good idea to follow up. In today's market, job seekers can't afford to wait for interviews to find them. A quality résumé and an attractive cover letter are crucial, but a proper follow-up may be the key to landing an interview. However, before you engage your potential employer, be sure to research the company. Knowing about the company and understanding its place in the industry will help you shine. When you place a call, send an email, or mail a letter to a company contact, be sure to restate your interest in the position, check on the status of your résumé, and ask the employer about any questions they may have.

Letters of Recommendation

Letters of recommendation are written references by professors, former and current employers, and others that testify to your character, skills, and abilities. Some companies may request letters of recommendation, to be submitted either with the résumé or at the interview. Even if letters of recommendation aren't requested it's a good idea to bring them with you to the interview. A good reference letter tells why you would be an excellent candidate for the position. In choosing someone to write a letter of recommendation, be confident that the person will give you a good reference. In addition, do not assume the person knows everything about you or the position you are seeking. Rather, provide the person with your résumé and other relevant data. As a courtesy, allow the reference writer at least a month to complete the letter and enclose a stamped, addressed envelope with your materials.

In the packet containing your résumé, cover letter, and letters of recommendation, you may also want to attach other relevant documents that support your candidacy, such as academic transcripts, graphics, portfolios, and samples of writing.

Interview for Jobs

As the old saying goes, "The résumé gets you the interview; the interview gets you the job." The job interview offers you an opportunity to gather more information about the organization, while at the same time allowing the organization to gather more information about you. You'll want to present your best self. The interview process consists of three parts: before the interview, the interview itself, and after the interview. If you pass through these stages successfully, you will be called back for the follow-up interview.

Before the Interview

In preparing for your interview, do the following:

1. Understand that interviewers have diverse styles, including the "chitchat," let's-get-to-know-each-other style; the interrogation style of question after question; and the tough-probing "why, why, why" style, among others. So be ready for anything.

2. With a friend, practise being interviewed and then ask for a critique. Or videotape yourself in a practice interview so that you can critique your own performance. Your university placement service may also offer "mock" interviews to help you.

3. Prepare at least five good questions whose answers are not easily found in the company literature, such as "What is the future direction of the firm?", "How does the firm differentiate itself from competitors?", or "Do you have a new-media division?"

4. Anticipate possible interview questions, such as "Why do you want to work for this company?" or "Why should we hire you?" Prepare solid answers before the interview. Have a clear idea of why you are interested in joining the company and the industry to which it belongs. (See Susan Ireland's website for additional interview questions: http://susanireland.com/interviewwork.html)

5. Avoid back-to-back interviews—they can be exhausting and it is unpredictable how long they will last.

6. Prepare relevant documents that support your candidacy, such as academic transcripts, letters of recommendation, graphics, portfolios, and samples of writing. Bring multiple copies to the interview.

7. Dress conservatively and professionally. Be neat and clean.

8. Arrive 10 minutes early to collect your thoughts and review the major points you intend to cover. Check your name on the interview schedule, noting the name of the interviewer and the room number. Be courteous and polite to office staff.

9. Approach the interview enthusiastically. Let your personality shine through.

During the Interview

During the interview, do the following:

1. Shake hands firmly in greeting the interviewer. Introduce yourself, using the same form of address that the interviewer uses. Focus on creating a good initial impression.

2. Keep your poise. Relax, smile when appropriate, and be upbeat throughout.

3. Maintain eye contact and good posture, and speak distinctly. Don't clasp your hands or fiddle with jewellery, hair, or clothing. Sit comfortably in your chair. Do not smoke, even if it's permitted.

4. Along with the copies of relevant documents that support your candidacy, carry extra copies of your résumé with you.

5. Have your story down pat. Present your selling points. Answer questions directly. Avoid either one-word or too-wordy answers.

6. Let the interviewer take the initiative but don't be passive. Find an opportunity to direct the conversation to things about yourself that you want the interviewer to hear.

7. To end on a high note, make your most important point or ask your most pertinent question during the last part of the interview.

8. Don't hesitate to "close." You might say, "I'm very interested in the position, and I have enjoyed this interview."

9. Obtain the interviewer's business card or address and phone number so that you can follow up later.

A tip for acing the interview: Before you open your mouth, find out *what it's like* to be a brand manager, sales representative, market researcher, advertising account executive, or other position for which you're interviewing. See if you can find a "mentor"—someone in a position similar to the one you're seeking, perhaps with another company. Talk with this mentor about the ins and outs of the job and industry.

After the Interview

After the interview, do the following:

1. After leaving the interview, record the key points that arose. Be sure to note who is to follow up and when a decision can be expected.

2. Analyze the interview objectively, including the questions asked, the answers to them, your overall interview presentation, and the interviewer's responses to specific points.

3. Immediately send a thank-you letter or email mentioning any additional items and your willingness to supply further information.

4. If you do not hear back within the specified time, write, email, or call the interviewer to determine your status.

Follow-Up Interview

If your first interview takes place offsite, such as at your university or at a job fair, and if you are successful with that initial interview, you will be invited to visit the organization. The in-company interview will probably run from several hours to an entire day. The organization will examine your interest, maturity, enthusiasm, assertiveness, logic, and company and functional knowledge. You should ask questions about issues of importance to you. Find out about the working environment, job role, responsibilities, opportunities for advancement, current industrial issues, and the company's personality. The company wants to discover if you are the right person for the job, whereas you want to find out if it is the right job for you. The key is to determine if the right *fit* exists between you and the company.

MARKETING JOBS

This section describes some of the key marketing positions.

Advertising

Advertising is one of today's hottest fields in marketing. In fact, *Money* magazine lists a position in advertising as among the 50 best jobs in North America.

Job Descriptions

Key advertising positions include copywriter, art director, production manager, account executive, and media planner/buyer.

- *Copywriters* write advertising copy and help find the concepts behind the written words and visual images of advertisements.

- *Art directors,* the other part of the creative team, help translate the copywriters' ideas into dramatic visuals called "layouts." Agency artists develop print layouts, package designs, television layouts (called "storyboards"), corporate logotypes, trademarks, and symbols. *Production managers* are responsible for physically creating ads in-house or by contracting through outside production houses.

- *Account development executives* research and understand clients' markets and customers and help develop marketing and advertising strategies to impact them.

- *Account executives* serve as liaisons between clients and agencies. They coordinate the planning, creation, production, and implementation of an advertising campaign for the account.

- *Account planners* serve as the voice of the consumer in the agency. They research consumers to understand their needs and motivations as a basis for developing effective ad campaigns.

- *Media planners (or buyers)* determine the best mix of television, radio, newspaper, magazine, digital, and other media for the advertising campaign.

Skills Needed, Career Paths, and Typical Salaries

Work in advertising requires strong people skills to interact closely with an often-difficult and demanding client base. In addition, advertising attracts people with strong skills in planning, problem solving, creativity, communication, initiative, leadership, and presentation. Advertising involves working under high levels of stress and pressure created by unrelenting deadlines. Advertisers frequently have to work long hours to meet deadlines for a presentation. But work achievements are very apparent, with the results of creative strategies observed by thousands or even millions of people.

Because they are so sought after, positions in advertising sometimes require an MBA. But there are many jobs open for business, graphics arts, and liberal arts undergraduates. Advertising positions often serve as gateways to higher-level management. Moreover, with large advertising agencies opening offices all over the world, there is the possibility of eventually working on global campaigns.

Starting advertising salaries are relatively low compared to some other marketing jobs because of strong competition for entry-level advertising jobs. You may even want to consider working for free to break in. Compensation will increase quickly as you move into account executive or other management positions. For more facts and figures, see the webpages of *Advertising Age*, a key ad industry publication (www.adage.com/talentworks), and the Institute of Communication Agencies (www.icacanada.ca).

Brand and Product Management

Brand and product managers plan, direct, and control business and marketing efforts for their products. They are involved with research and development, packaging, manufacturing, sales and distribution, advertising, promotion, market research, and business analysis and forecasting.

Job Descriptions

A company's brand management team consists of people in several positions.

- *Brand managers* guide the development of marketing strategies for a specific brand.
- *Assistant brand managers* are responsible for certain strategic components of the brand.
- *Product managers* oversee several brands within a product line or product group.
- *Product category managers* direct multiple product lines in the product category.
- *Market analysts* research the market and provide important strategic information to the project managers.
- *Project directors* are responsible for collecting market information on a marketing or product project.
- *Research directors* oversee the planning, gathering, and analyzing of all organizational research.

Skills Needed, Career Paths, and Typical Salaries

Brand and product management requires high problem-solving, analytical, presentation, communication, and leadership skills, as well as the ability to work well in a team. Product management requires long hours and involves the high pressure of running large projects. In consumer goods companies, the newcomer—often a marketing major with a bachelor of commerce degree—joins a brand team as an assistant and learns the ropes by doing numerical analyses and watching senior brand people. This person eventually heads the team and later moves on to manage a larger brand, then several brands.

Many industrial goods companies also have product managers. Product management is one of the best training grounds for future corporate officers. Product management also offers good opportunities to move into international marketing. Product managers command relatively high salaries. Because this job category encourages or requires a master's degree, starting pay tends to be higher than in other marketing categories such as advertising or retailing.

Sales and Sales Management

Sales and sales management opportunities exist in a wide range of profit and not-for-profit organizations and in product and service organizations, including financial, insurance, consulting, and government organizations.

Job Descriptions

Key jobs include consumer sales, industrial sales, national account manager, service support, sales trainer, sales management, and teleseller.

- *Consumer sales* involves selling consumer products and services through retailers.
- *Industrial sales* involves selling products and services to other businesses.
- *National account managers (NAMs)* oversee a few very large accounts.
- *Service support* personnel support salespeople during and after the sale of a product.
- *Sales trainers* train new hires and provide refresher training for all sales personnel.
- *Sales management* includes a sequence of positions ranging from district manager to vice-president of sales.
- *Teleseller* (not to be confused with the home consumer telemarketer) offer service and support to field salespeople.

Salespeople enjoy active professional lives, working outside the office, and interacting with others. They manage their own time and activities. And successful salespeople can be very well paid. Competition for top jobs can be intense. Every sales job is different, but some positions involve extensive travel, long workdays, and working under pressure. You can also expect to be transferred more than once between company headquarters and regional offices. However, most companies are now working to bring good work–life balance to their salespeople and sales managers.

Skills Needed, Career Paths, and Typical Salaries

Selling is a people profession in which you will work with people every day, all day long. In addition to people skills, sales professionals need sales and communication skills. Most sales positions also require strong problem-solving, analytical, presentation, and leadership abilities as well as creativity and initiative. Teamwork skills are increasingly important.

Career paths lead from salesperson to district, regional, and higher levels of sales management and, in many cases, to the top management of the firm. Today, most entry-level sales management positions require a college degree. Increasingly, people seeking selling jobs are acquiring sales experience in an internship capacity or from a part-time job before graduating. Sales positions are great springboards to leadership positions, with more CEOs starting in sales than in any other entry-level position. This possibly explains why competition for top sales jobs is intense.

Starting base salaries in sales may be moderate, but compensation is often supplemented by significant commission, bonus, or other incentive plans. In addition, many sales jobs include a company car or car allowance. Successful salespeople are among most companies' highest paid employees.

Other Marketing Jobs

Retailing

Retailing provides an early opportunity to assume marketing responsibilities. Key jobs include store manager, regional manager, buyer, department manager, and salesperson. *Store managers* direct the management and operation of an individual store. *Regional managers* manage groups of stores across several areas and report performance to head-quarters. *Buyers* select and buy the merchandise that the store carries. The *department manager* acts as store manager of a department, such as clothing. The *salesperson* sells merchandise to retail customers. Retailing can involve relocation, but generally there is little travel, unless you are a buyer. Retailing requires high people and sales skills because retailers are constantly in contact with customers. Enthusiasm, willingness, and communication skills are very helpful for retailers, too.

Retailers work long hours, but their daily activities are often more structured than some types of marketing positions. Starting salaries in retailing tend to be low, but pay increases as you move into management or some retailing specialty job.

Marketing Research

Marketing researchers interact with managers to define problems and identify the information needed to solve them. They design research projects, prepare questionnaires and samples, analyze data, prepare reports, and present their findings and recommendations to management. They must understand statistics, consumer behaviour, psychology, and sociology. A master's degree helps. Career opportunities exist with manufacturers, retailers, some wholesalers, trade and industry associations, marketing research firms, advertising agencies, and governmental and private not-for-profit agencies.

New-Product Planning

People interested in new-product planning can find opportunities in many types of organizations. They usually need a good background in marketing, marketing research, and sales forecasting; they need organizational skills to motivate and coordinate others; and they may need a technical background. Usually, these people work first in other marketing positions before joining the new-product department.

Marketing Logistics (Physical Distribution)

Marketing logistics, or physical distribution, is a large and dynamic field with many career opportunities. Major transportation carriers, manufacturers, wholesalers, and retailers all employ logistics specialists. Increasingly, marketing teams include logistics specialists and marketing managers' career paths include marketing logistics assignments. Coursework in quantitative methods, finance, accounting, and marketing will provide you with the necessary skills for entering the field.

Public Relations

Most organizations have a public relations staff to anticipate problems with various publics, handle complaints, deal with media, maintain relationships with governments and other key stakeholders, and build the corporate image. People interested in public relations should be able to speak and write clearly and persuasively, and they should have a background in journalism, communications, or the liberal arts. The challenges in this job are highly varied and very people-oriented.

Not-for-Profit Services

The key jobs in not-for-profits include marketing director, director of development, event coordinator, publication specialist, and intern/volunteer. The *marketing director* is in charge of all marketing activities for the organization. The *director of development* organizes, manages, and directs the fundraising campaigns that keep a not-for-profit in existence. An *event coordinator* directs all aspects of fundraising events, from initial planning through implementation. The *publication specialist* oversees publications designed to promote awareness of the organization.

Although typically an unpaid position, the *intern/volunteer* performs various marketing functions, and this work can be an important step to gaining a full-time position. The not-for-profit sector is typically not for someone who is money-driven. Rather, most not-for-profits look for people with a strong sense of community spirit and the desire to help others. Therefore, starting pay is usually lower than in other marketing fields. However, the bigger the not-for-profit, the better your chance of rapidly increasing your income when moving into upper management.

OTHER RESOURCES

Professional marketing associations and organizations are another source of information about careers. Marketers belong to many such societies. You may want to contact some of the following in your job search:

Advertising Standards Canada (www.adstandards.com)

Association of Canadian Advertisers (www.aca-online.com)

Association of Internet Marketing and Sales (www.aimscanada.com)

Canadian Advertising Research Foundation (www.carf.ca)

Canadian Professional Sales Association (www.cpsa.com)

The Canadian Public Relations Society (www.cprs.ca)

Marketing Research and Intelligence Association (www.mria-arim.ca)

Retail Council of Canada (www.retailcouncil.org)

Supply Chain and Logistics Association Canada (www.sclcanada.org)

Chapter 1

1. Quotes and other information from Jonah Bloom, "Stengel Exhorts 4As: It's Not about 'Telling and Selling,'" *Advertising Age*, March 1, 2007, accessed at http://adage.com/4asmedia07/article?article_id=115259; Robert Berner, "Detergent Can Be So Much More," *BusinessWeek*, May 1, 2006, pp. 66–67; Jack Neff, "New Tide Campaign Goes Beyond Stains," *Advertising Age*, February 13, 2006, p. 16; "For P&G, Success Lies in More Than Merely a Dryer Diaper," *Advertising Age*, October 15, 2007, p. 30; "Case Study: Tide Knows Fabrics Best," accessed at www.thearf.org/awards/ogilvy-current-winners.html, April 2008; "P&G: Our Purpose, Values, and Principles," accessed at www.pg.com/company/who_we_are/ppv.jhtml, November 2008; and Lucy Saddleton, "Tide Rolls On," *Strategy Magazine*, October 2008, accessed at http://www.strategymag.com/articles/magazine/20081001/tributetide.html?__s=yes&print=yes, May 2009.

2. Statement made in an address to the American Association of Advertising Agencies conference, accessed via Jonah Bloom, "Stengel Exhorts 4A's: It's Not About 'Telling and Selling,'" *Advertising Age*, March 1, 2007, accessed at http://adage.com/print?article_id=115259.

3. See "Markets: Since Launch of First Generation of iPod, Apple Inc. Has Sold More Than 88.7 Million Units Worldwide," *Associated Press Financial Wire*, March 14, 2007; Adam L. Penenberg, "All Eyes on Apple," *Fast Company*, December 2007–January 2008, pp. 83–91.

4. "Top 1000 Companies," *Globe and Mail*, accessed at http://business.theglobeandmail.com/v5/content/tp1000-2008/index.php, April 2009.

5. As quoted in Carolyn P. Neal, "From the Editor," *Marketing Management*, January–February 2006, p. 3.

6. The American Marketing Association offers the following definition: "Marketing is the activity, set of institutions, and processes for creating, communicating, delivering, and exchanging offerings that have value for customers, clients, partners, and society at large," accessed at http://www.marketingpower.com/AboutAMA/Pages/DefinitionofMarketing.aspx?sq=marketing+definition, April 2009; see also Lisa M. Keefe, "Marketing Defined," *Marketing News*, January 15, 2008, pp. 28–29.

7. "Corporate Responsibility," accessed at http://www.rbc.com/responsibility/index.html, April 2009; "RBC Named One of the World's Top 100 Sustainable Companies," *Forbes*, January 28, 2009, accessed at http://www.forbes.com/feeds/prnewswire/2009/01/28/prnewswire200901281245PR_NEWS_USPR_____TO317.html, April 2009.

8. Geoff Colvin, "Selling P&G," Fortune, September 17, 2007, pp. 163–169. For other examples, see Tim Laseter and Larry Laseter, "See for Yourself," *Strategy + Business*, Autumn 2007, pp. 20–24.

9. See Theodore Levitt's classic article, "Marketing Myopia," *Harvard Business Review*, July–August 1960, pp. 45–56. For more recent discussions, see Yves Doz, Jose Santos, and Peter J. Williamson, "Marketing Myopia Re-Visited: Why Every Company Needs to Learn from the World," *Ivey Business Journal*, January–February 2004, p. 1; "What Business Are You In?" *Harvard Business Review*, October 2006, pp. 127–137; and John D. Nicholson and Philip J. Kitchen, "The Development of Regional Marketing—Have Marketers Been Myopic?" *International Journal of Business Studies*, June 2007, pp. 107–125.

10. Information from a recent "The Computer Is Personal Again" advertisement and www.hp.com/personal, accessed August 2008.

11. "B.C. Residents Urged to Power the Games through Conservation," BC Hydro Press Release, March 30, 2009, accessed at www.bchydro.com/news/articles/press_releases/2009/bc_residents_urged_to_power_games_through_conservation.html, April 2009.

12. See Ben Elgin, "How 'Green' Is That Water?" *BusinessWeek*, August 13, 2007, p. 68.

13. See Larry Edwards et al., "75 Years of Ideas," *Advertising Age*, February 14, 2005, p. 14; "America's Most Admired Companies," *Fortune*, accessed at http://money.cnn.com/magazines/fortune/mostadmired/2007/index.html, August 2007; "The Top 10 PR Endeavors," PR News, October 30, 2006, p.1; and www.jnj.com/our_company/our_credo/index.htm, accessed December 2008.

14. Quotes and information from Blanca Torres, "Jeans' Genes Part of Price Tag Formula," *Knight Ridder Tribune Business News*, November 8, 2006, p. 1; "Paige Denim Week," *Toronto Fashion Monitor*, October 30, 2006, accessed at http://toronto.fashion-monitor.com/events.php/56, April 2009; Megan Kaplan, "Haute Mama," *Knight Ridder Tribune Business News*, March 22, 2007, p. 1; and www.paigepremiumdenim.com, accessed November 2008.

15. For more on how to measure customer satisfaction, see D. Randall Brandt, "For Good Measure," *Marketing Management*, January–February 2007, pp. 21–25.

16. Portions adapted from Julie Barker, "Power to the People," *Incentive*, February 2008, p. 34 and Carmine Gallo, "Employee Motivation the Ritz-Carlton Way," *BusinessWeek*, February 29, 2008, accessed at www.businessweek.com. Also see "The World's Best Hotels—Where Luxury Lives," *Institutional Investor*, November 2007, p. 1; and http://corporate.ritzcarlton.com/en/About/Awards.htm#Hotel, accessed November 2008.

17. Information about the Harley Owners Group accessed at www.hog.com, September 2008; Kate Lunau, "Harley's Big un-American Growth Bid," *Macleans*, October 2008, p. 52. For more on loyalty programs, see Yuping Liu, "The Long-Term Impact of Loyalty Programs on Consumer Purchase Behavior and Loyalty," *Journal of Marketing*, October 2007, p. 19; and "Reward Programs Pay for Customer Loyalty, but Fail to Engage, According to Allegiance, Inc.," *Business Wire*, February 28, 2008.

18. Quotes and other information from "Gunning for the Best Buy," *Knight Ridder Tribune Business News*, May 28, 2006, p. 1; Gary McWilliams, "Analyzing Customers, Best Buy Decides Not All Are Welcome," *Wall Street Journal*, November 8,

2004, p. A1; Shirley A. Lazo, "Let's Go Shopping," *Barron's*, June 26, 2006, p. 28; Matthew Boyle, "Best Buy's Giant Gamble," *Fortune*, April 3, 2006, pp. 69–75; Marc Millstein, "Best Buy Quest to Master Customer Centricity," *Chain Store Age*, December 2007, pp. 2A+; "Best Buy Co., Inc.," *Hoover's Company Records,* March 1, 2008, p. 10209; and www.bestbuy .com, accessed October 2008.

19. Andrew Walmsley, "The Year of Consumer Empowerment," *Marketing*, December 20, 2006, p. 9.

20. Walmsley, "The Year of Consumer Empowerment," p. 9; and "Who's in Control?" *Advertising Age*, January 28, 2008, p. C9.

21. Helen Coster, "Crowd Control," *Forbes*, November 26, 2007, pp. 38–39; and "Top 100 Global Marketers," *Advertising Age*, November 19, 2007, p. 4.

22. Adapted from information in Jonathan Birchall, "Just Do It, Marketers Say," *Los Angeles Times*, April 30, 2007, accessed at http://articles.latimes.com/2007/apr/30/business/ ft-brands30. Other facts and information from Louise Story, "New Advertising Outlet: Your Life," *New York Times*, October 14, 2007; Nicholas Casey, "Nike, New Coach Chase Serious Runners," *Wall Street Journal*, December 6, 2007, p. B7; and "Consumer Experiences: Nike," *Fast Company*, March 8, 2008, pp. 94–95.

23. Matthew Creamer, "John Doe Edges Out Jeff Goodby," *Advertising Age*, January 8, 2007, pp. S4–S5. See also Karen E. Klein, "Should Your Customers Make Your Ads?" *BusinessWeek*, January 2, 2008, accessed at www.businessweek.com.

24. Philip Kotler and Kevin Lane Keller, *Marketing Management*, 13th ed. (Upper Saddle River, NJ: Prentice Hall, 2009), p. 11.

25. For more on the relationship between customer satisfaction, loyalty, and company performance, see Fred Reichheld, *The Ultimate Question: Driving Good Profits and True Growth* (Boston: Harvard Business School Press, 2006); Bruce Cooil, et al., "A Longitudinal Analysis of Customer Satisfaction and Share of Wallet: Investigating the Moderating Effects of Customer Characteristics," *Journal of Marketing*, January 2007, pp. 67–83; Murali Chandrahsekaran, Kristin Rotte, Stephen S. Tax, and Rajdeep Grewal, "Satisfaction, Strength, and Customer Loyalty," *Journal of Marketing Research*, February 2007, pp. 153–163; and Leonard L. Berry and Lewis P. Carbone, "Build Loyalty Through Experience Management," *Quality Progress*, September 2007, pp. 26+.

26. "Stew Leonard's," *Hoover's Company Records*, July 15, 2007, pp. 104–226; and www.stewleonards.com/html/ about.cfm, accessed November 2007.

27. For interesting discussions on assessing and using customer lifetime value, see Rajkumar Venkatesan, V. Kumar, and Timothy Bohling, "Selecting Valuable Customers Using a Customer Lifetime Value Framework," Marketing Science Institute, Report No. 05–121, 2005; Sunil Gupta, et al., "Modeling Customer Lifetime Value," *Journal of Service Research*, November 2006, pp. 139–146; "Determining 'CLV' Can Lead to Making Magical Marketing Decisions," *BtoB*, May 7, 2007, p. 18; and Detlef Schoder, "The Flaw in Customer Lifetime Value," *Harvard Business Review*, December 2007, p. 26.

28. See www.brandkeys.com/awards/cli08.cfm, accessed April 2008; and www.llbean.com/customerService/ aboutLLBean/guarantee.html, accessed November 2008.

29. Erick Schonfeld, "Click Here for the Upsell," *Business 2.0*, July 11, 2007, accessed at http://cnnmoney.com; and

"Getting Shoppers to Crave More," *Fortune Small Business*, August 24, 2007, p. 85.

30. Don Peppers and Martha Rogers, "Customers Don't Grow on Trees," *Fast Company*, July 2005, p. 26.

31. See Roland T. Rust, Valerie A. Zeithaml, and Katherine A. Lemon, *Driving Customer Equity* (New York, NY: Free Press, 2000); Robert C. Blattberg, Gary Getz, and Jacquelyn S. Thomas, *Customer Equity* (Boston, MA: Harvard Business School Press, 2001); Rust, Lemon, and Zeithaml, "Return on Marketing: Using Customer Equity to Focus Marketing Strategy," *Journal of Marketing*, January 2004, pp. 109–127; Rust, Zeithaml, and Lemon, "Customer-Centered Brand Management," *Harvard Business Review*, September 2004, p. 110; Robert P. Leone et al., "Linking Brand Equity to Customer Equity," *Journal of Service Marketing*, November 2006, pp. 125–138; Julian Villanueva and Dominique Hanssens, *Customer Equity: Measurement, Management and Research Opportunities* (Hanover, MA: Now Publishers Inc., 2007); and Roland T. Rust, "Seeking Higher ROI? Base Strategy on Customer Equity," *Advertising Age*, September 10, 2007, pp. 26–27.

32. This example is adapted from information in Rust, Lemon, and Zeithaml, "Where Should the Next Marketing Dollar Go?" *Marketing Management*, September–October 2001, pp. 24–28. Also see David Welch and David Kiley, "Can Caddy's Driver Make GM Cool?" *BusinessWeek*, September 20, 2004, pp. 105–106; and Jean Halliday, "Comeback Kid Cadillac Stalls after Shop Swap," *Advertising Age*, September 24, 2007, p. 1.

33. Werner Reinartz and V. Kumar, "The Mismanagement of Customer Loyalty," *Harvard Business Review*, July 2002, pp. 86–94. For more on customer equity management, see Michael D. Johnson and Fred Selnes, "Customer Portfolio Management: Toward a Dynamic Theory of Exchange Relationships," *Journal of Marketing*, April 2004, pp. 1–17; Sunil Gupta and Donald R. Lehman, *Managing Customers as Investments* (Philadelphia, PA: Wharton School Publishing, 2005); Roland T. Rust, Katherine N. Lemon, and Das Narayandas, *Customer Equity Management* (Upper Saddle River, NJ: Prentice Hall, 2005); and Kathy Stevens, "Using Customer Equity Models to Improve Loyalty and Profits," *Journal of Consumer Marketing*, vol. 23, 2006, p. 379.

34. Brian Morrissey, "Is Social Media Killing the Campaign Micro-Site?" November 12, 2007, accessed at www.mediaweek.com.

35. Statistics from www.internetworldstats.com/stats.htm, accessed March 2008; "Internetic World in the Year 2015," February 7, 2007, accessed at www.weboma.com; and "Dawn of the Web Potato," *Fortune*, September 17, 2007, p. 52.

36. "The Way We Were in 2007," *The Week*, December 28, 2007–January 11, 2008, p. 26.

37. See Allison Enright, "Get Clued In: Mystery of Web 2.0 Resolved," *Marketing News*, January 15, 2007, pp. 20–22. See also Jessica Tsai, "Power to the People," *Customer Relationship Management*, December 2007, pp. 28+.

38. "Internet World Stats: Usage and Population Statistics," accessed at http://www.internetworldstats.com/am/ca. htm, April 2009.

39. Adapted from information in Don Frischmann, "Nothing Is Insignificant When It Comes to Brand Fulfillment," *Advertising Age*, January 21, 2008, p. 16.

40. Quotes and information accessed at www.patagonia.com/ web/us/contribution/patagonia.go?assetid=2329, August 2008.

41. For examples and for a good review of not-for-profit marketing, see Philip Kotler and Alan R. Andreasen, *Strategic Marketing for Nonprofit Organizations*, 6th ed. (Upper Saddle River, NJ: Prentice Hall, 2003); Philip Kotler and Karen Fox, *Strategic Marketing for Educational Institutions* (Upper Saddle River, NJ: Prentice Hall, 1995); Philip Kotler, John Bowen, and James Makens, *Marketing for Hospitality and Tourism*, 3rd ed. (Upper Saddle River, NJ: Prentice Hall, 2003); and Philip Kotler and Nancy Lee, *Marketing in the Public Sector: A Roadmap for Improved Performance* (Philadelphia, PA: Wharton School Publishing, 2007).

42. Caroline Riseboro, "The non-profit motive," *Marketing Magazine*, April 11, 2005.

43. "Media in Canada," *Strategy Magazine*, November 15, 2005. For other examples and for a good review of not-for-profit marketing, see Philip Kotler and Alan R. Andreasen, *Strategic Marketing for Nonprofit Organizations*, 6th ed. (Upper Saddle River, NJ: Prentice Hall, 2003).

Chapter 2

1. Quotes and other information from Stuart Elliott, "Marketers Are Putting NASCAR on Different Kinds of Circuits," *New York Times*, February 15, 2008; Lars Anderson, "O Canada: Montreal Busch Race More Exciting Than Cup Event," SI.com, August 7, 2007, accessed at http://sportsillustrated.cnn.com/2007/writers/lars_anderson/08/07/sixthings.0807/, April 2009; Paul Ferriss, "NASCAR, eh?," *Marketing*, February 12, 2007, p. 12; "Sold!," *Playback: Canada's Broadcast and Production Journal*, March 5, 2007, p.12; Paul Ferriss, "NASCAR Rides the Fast Track," *Marketing*, April 11, 2005, pp. 11–12; Mark Woods, "Readers Try to Explain Why Racin' Rocks," *Florida Times Union*, February 16, 2003, p. C1; Tony Kontzer, "Backseat Drivers—NASCAR Puts You in the Race," *InformationWeek*, March 25, 2002, p. 83; Jenny Kincaid, "NASCAR Beefs Up Its Brand Loyalty," *Knight Ridder Tribune Business News*, April 1, 2006, p. 1; Frank Litsky, "Bill France, Who Built NASCAR into Phenomenon, Dies," *International Herald Tribune*, June 6, 2007, p. 20; Barry Janoff, "NASCAR's 50th Daytona 500 Offers Golden Opportunities," *Brandweek*, February 4, 2008, p. 14; and www.NASCAR.com, accessed September 2008.

2. For more on mission statements, see Joseph Peyrefitte and Forest R. David, "A Content Analysis of Mission Statements of United States' Firms in Four Industries," *International Journal of Management*, June 2006, pp. 296–301; Jeffrey Abrahams, *101 Mission Statements from Top Companies* (Berkeley, CA: Ten Speed Press, 2007); and Jack and Suzy Welch, "State Your Business," *BusinessWeek*, January 14, 2008, p. 80.

3. Canadian Tire Corporation, 2008 Annual Report, accessed at http://corp.canadiantire.ca/EN/Investors/FinancialReports/Annual%20Reports%20Library/CTC_AR_2008.pdf, April 2009; and eBay, accessed at http://pages.ebay.com/aboutebay/the company/companyoverview.html, September 2008.

4. Jack and Suzy Welch, "State Your Business," *BusinessWeek*, January 14, 2008, p. 80.

5. See the BASF Innovations webpage, accessed at www.corporate.basf.com/en/innovationen/?id=Z_l-HA6M0bcp4PX, July 2008.

6. See "BASF Innovative Agricultural Products to Asian Growth Markets," February 28, 2007, accessed at www.corporate.basf.com/en/presse/mitteilungen/pm.htm?pmid=2586&id=Z_l-HA6M0bcp4PX, July 2008; and

"BASF in Greater China," accessed at www.greater-china.basf.com/apw/GChina/GChina/en_GB/portal, April 2008.

7. The following discussion is based in part on information found at www.bcg.com/publications/files/Experience_Curve_IV_Growth_Share_Matrix_1973.pdf, accessed December 2008.

8. For an interesting discussion on managing growth, see Matthew S. Olson, Derek van Bever, and Seth Verry, "When Growth Stalls," *Harvard Business Review*, March 2008, pp. 51–61.

9. H. Igor Ansoff, "Strategies for Diversification," *Harvard Business Review*, September–October 1957, pp. 113–124.

10. Michael E. Porter, *Competitive Advantage: Creating and Sustaining Superior Performance* (New York: Free Press, 1985); and Michael E. Porter, "What Is Strategy?" *Harvard Business Review*, November–December 1996, pp. 61–78. See also "The Value Chain," accessed at www.quickmba.com/strategy/value-chain, July 2008; and Philip Kotler and Kevin Lane Keller, *Marketing Management* (Upper Saddle River, NJ: Prentice Hall, 2009) pp. 35–36 and pp. 252–253.

11. Kotler, *Kotler on Marketing* (New York: The Free Press, 1999), pp. 20–22; and Marianne Seiler, "Transformation Trek," *Marketing Management*, January–February 2006, pp. 32–39.

12. "McDonald's Fetes 50th Birthday, Opens Anniversary Restaurant," *Knight Ridder Tribune Business News*, April 15, 2005, p. 1; and information from www.mcdonalds.com/corp.html, accessed September 2008.

13. Quotes and other information from Jeffery K. Liker and Thomas Y. Choi, "Building Deep Supplier Relationships," *Harvard Business Review*, 2004, pp. 104–113; Lindsay Chappell, "Toyota Aims to Satisfy Its Suppliers," *Automotive News*, February 21, 2005, p. 10; "Toyota Recognizes Top Suppliers for 2007," *PR Newswire*, March 4, 2008; and www.toyotasupplier.com, accessed November 2008.

14. Steve MacNaull, "When Life Hands You Apples, Make Juice," *Globe and Mail*, October 26, 2005, p. B9.

15. Jack Trout, "Branding Can't Exist Without Positioning," *Advertising Age*, March 14, 2005, p. 28.

16. "100 Leading National Advertisers," special issue of *Advertising Age*, June 23, 2008, p. 10.

17. The four Ps classification was first suggested by E. Jerome McCarthy, *Basic Marketing: A Managerial Approach* (Homewood, IL: Irwin, 1960). For the 4Cs, other proposed classifications, and more discussion, see Robert Lauterborn, "New Marketing Litany: 4P's Passé, C-Words Take Over," *Advertising Age*, October 1, 1990, p. 26; Don E. Schultz, "New Definition of Marketing Reinforces Idea of Integration," *Marketing News*, January 15, 2005, p. 8; and Phillip Kotler, "Alphabet Soup," *Marketing Management*, March–April 2006, p. 51.

18. For more discussion of the CMO position, see Pravin Nath and Vijay Mahajan, "Chief Marketing Officers: A Study of Their Presence in Firms' Top Management Teams," *Journal of Marketing*, January 2008, pp. 65–81; and Philip Kotler and Kevin Lane Keller, *Marketing Management* (Upper Saddle River: NJ: Prentice Hall, 2009), pp. 11–12.

19. For more on brand and product management, see Kevin Lane Keller, *Strategic Brand Management*, 3rd ed. (Upper Saddle River, NJ: Prentice Hall, 2008).

20. Adapted from Diane Brady, "Making Marketing Measure Up," *BusinessWeek*, December 13, 2004, pp. 112–113; with information from "Kotler Readies World for One-on-One," *Point*, June 2005, p. 3. See also Darryl E. Owens, "Champion ROI to Prove Worth," *Marketing News*, March 1, 2007, pp. 13, 22.

21. Mark McMaster, "ROI: More Vital Than Ever," *Sales & Marketing Management*, January 2002, pp. 51–52. See also Gordon A. Wyner, "Beyond ROI," *Marketing Management*, June 2006, pp. 8–9; James Lenskold, "Unlock Profit Potential," *Marketing Management*, May–June, 2007, pp. 26–31; Steven H. Seggie, Erin Cavusgil, and Steven Phelan, "Measurement of Return on Marketing Investment: A Conceptual Framework and the Future of Marketing Metrics," *Industrial Marketing Management*, August 2007, pp. 834–841.

22. See David Skinner and Doug Brooks, "Move from Metrics Overload to Actionable Insights," *Advertising Age*, May 28, 2007, pp. 14–15; and Gregor Harter, Edward Landry, and Andrew Tipping, "The New Complete Marketer," *Strategy + Business*, Autumn 2007, pp. 79–87.

23. For more discussion, see Bruce H. Clark, Andrew V. Abela, and Tim Ambler, "Behind the Wheel," *Marketing Management*, May–June 2006, pp. 19–23; Christopher Hosford, "Driving Business with Dashboards," *BtoB*, December 11, 2006, p. 18; and Allison Enwright, "Measure Up: Create a ROMI Dashboard That Shows Current and Future Value," *Marketing News*, August 15, 2007, pp. 12–13.

24. For a full discussion of this model and details on customer-centred measures of return on marketing investment, see Roland T. Rust, Katherine N. Lemon, and Valerie A. Zeithaml, "Return on Marketing: Using Customer Equity to Focus Marketing Strategy," *Journal of Marketing*, January 2004, pp. 109–127; Roland T. Rust, Katherine N. Lemon, and Das Narayandas, *Customer Equity Management* (Upper Saddle River, NJ: Prentice Hall, 2005); David Tiltman, "Everything You Know Is Wrong," *Marketing*, June 13, 2007, pp. 28–29; Roland T. Rust, "Seeking Higher ROI? Base Strategy on Customer Equity," *Advertising Age*, September 10, 2007, pp. 26–27; and Valerie P. Valente, "Redefining ROI," *Advertising Age*, January 28, 2008, p. C7.

25. Deborah L. Vence, "Return on Investment," *Marketing News*, October 15, 2005, pp. 13–14.

26. Quote taken directly from opening page of www.apaydayloan.ca.

Chapter 3

1. Quotes and other information from or adapted from Claudia Deutsch, "A Big Red X No Longer Marks the Spot," *New York Times*, January 8, 2008, p. C11; Nanette Byrnes, "Xerox's New Design Team: Customers," *BusinessWeek*, May 7, 2007, p. 72; "Xerox Unveils Biggest Change to Its Brand in Company History," January 7, 2008, Xerox news release, accessed at www.xerox.com; Paula Lehman, "The Issue: Putting the 'R' Back in R&D," *BusinessWeek*, March 18, 2008, accessed at www.businessweek.com/managing/content/mar2008/ca20080318_765446.htm; "About Xerox," accessed at www.xerox.com, October 2008; "Xerox Canada CEO named one of 100 Most Powerful Executives in North America," February 10, 2009, Xerox news release, accessed at www.xerox.com/index/enca.html; and "Xerox Canada History," accessed at www.xerox.com/index/enca.html, April 2009.

2. Robert J. Bowman, "Home Depot Turns Its Attention to Supplier Performance Management," SupplyChainBrain.com, accessed June 2006; and https://suppliercenter.homedepot.com, accessed April 2008.

3. Information from Robert J. Benes, Abbie Jarman, and Ashley Williams, "2007 NRA Sets Records," accessed at www.chefmagazine.com/nra.htm, September 2007; and www.cokesolutions.com, accessed November 2008.

4. World POPClock, U.S. Census Bureau, accessed at www.census.gov, September 2008. This website provides continuously updated projections of the U.S. and world populations.

5. See Frederik Balfour, "Educating the 'Little Emperors': There's a Big Market for Products That Help China's Coddled Kids Get Ahead," *BusinessWeek*, November 10, 2003, p. 22; Clay Chandler, "Little Emperors," *Fortune*, October 4, 2004, pp. 138–150; "Hothousing Little Tykes," *Beijing Review*, May 5, 2005, accessed at www.bjreview.cn/EN/En-2005/05-18-e/china-5.htm; and "China's 'Little Emperors,'" *Financial Times*, May 5, 2007, p. 1.

6. Adapted from information in Janet Adamy, "Different Brew: Eyeing a Billion Tea Drinkers, Starbucks Pours It On in China," *Wall Street Journal*, November 29, 2006, p. A1. See also "Where the Money Is," *Financial Times*, May 12, 2007, p. 8; and Loretta Chao, "Politics and Economics: China to Retain Its One-Child Policy," *Wall Street Journal*, March 11, 2008, p. A7.

7. Statistics Canada, "Population by Sex and Age Group, 2008," accessed at www40.statcan.gc.ca/l01/cst01/demo10a-eng.htm?sdi=age and www.statcan.gc.ca/daily-quotidien/090115/dq090115c-eng.htm; Statistics Canada, "Population Estimates and Projections," accessed at www40.statcan.gc.ca/l01/cst01/demo08c-eng.htm, April 2009; and U.S. Census Bureau, Projections and POPClock Projection, accessed at www.census.gov, September 2008.

8. Daniel Stoffman, "Completely Predictable People," *Report on Business*, November 1990, pp. 78–84; David Foot and Daniel Stoffman, *Boom, Bust and Echo* (Toronto: Macfarlane Walter & Ross, 1996), pp. 18–22; Louise Lee, "Love Those Boomers," *BusinessWeek*, October 24, 2005, pp. 94–102; Tom Ramstack, "The New Gray: Boomers Spark Retirement Revolution," *Washington Times*, December 29, 2005, p. A1; Ken Wheaton, "Marketers Would Be Foolish to Ignore Boomer Audience," *Advertising Age*, June 4, 2007, p. 26; and Abbey Klaassen, "Media Players to Go After Free-Spending Boomers," *Advertising Age*, September 3, 2007, pp. 3+.

9. Adapted from information in Claudia H. Deutsch, "Not Getting Older, Just More Scrutinized," *New York Times*, October 11, 2006, accessed at www.nyt.com; and Madhusmita Bora, "Gadgety Grandparents," *McClatchy-Tribune Business News*, February 24, 2008.

10. Dee Depass, "Designed with a Wink, Nod at Boomers," *Minneapolis-St. Paul Star Tribune*, April 1, 2006, p. 1. See also Victoria Knight, "Advisers Link Physical, Financial Health," *Wall Street Journal*, January 17, 2007, p. B3C.

11. Jack Neff, "Unilever Resuscitates the Demo Left for Dead," *Advertising Age*, May 28, 2007, pp. 1, 26; and Judann Pollack, "Boomers Don't Want Your Pity, but They Do Demand Your Respect," *Advertising Age*, October 8, 2007, p. 24.

12. Stuart Elliott, "Flower Power in Ad Land," *New York Times*, April 11, 2006. p. G2; and Jack Willoughby, "Good Morning, Ameriprise: A Financial-Services Giant Awakens," *Barron's*, August 21, 2006, pp. 15–16. See also Laura Petrecca, "More Marketers Target Boomers' Eyes, Wallets," *USA Today*, February 26, 2007, p. 6B; and Karla Freeman, "How to Attract the Baby Boomer Market," *Accounting Technology*, January 2008, p. 2.

13. Scott Schroder and Warren Zeller, "Get to Know Gen X and Its Segments," *Multichannel News*, March 21, 2005, p. 55; Jim Shelton, "When Children of Divorce Grow Up," *Knight*

Ridder Tribune Business News, March 4, 2007, p. 1; and James H. Barnett III and Ana Veciana-Suarez, "The Leaders of Today Are Diverse Group," *McClatchy-Tribune Business News*, January 21, 2008.

14. Information from www.mec.ca, accessed April 2009.

15. Julie Liesse, "Getting to Know the Millennials," *Advertising Age*, July 9, 2007, pp. A1–A6; and "The Millennials," *Time*, Spring 2008, p. 55.

16. John Jullens, "Marketers: Meet the Millennial Generation," *Strategy + Business*, Spring 2007, pp. 16–18. Also see "Generation Y Research: What Makes 'y' Tick," *Brand Strategy*, February 5, 2007, p. 38.

17. Sharon Jayson, "Totally Wireless on Campus," *USA Today*, October 2, 2006, accessed at www.usatoday.com/tech/news/2006-10-02-gennext-tech_x.htm. See also Barbara Rose, "Generation Y a Learning Experience for Firms," *Chicago Tribune*, March 4, 2007; and Carlos Grande, "Targeting the Millennial Mindset," *Financial Times*, February 19, 2008, p. 15.

18. Example adapted from Jack Neff, "Tide's 'Washday Miracle': Not Doing Laundry," *Advertising Age*, November 12, 2007, p. 12; with information from www.swashitout.com, accessed September 2008.

19. Statistics Canada, "2006 Census: Family portrait: Continuity and Change in Canadian Families and Households in 2006: Highlights," accessed at www12.statcan.ca/census-recensement/2006/as-sa/97-553/p1-eng.cfm, April 2009. See also "America's Families and Living Arrangements: 2006," U.S. Census Bureau, accessed at www.census.gov/population/www/socdemo/hh-fam.html, September 2007.

20. Statistics Canada, "The Canadian Labour Market at a Glance," accessed at www.statcan.gc.ca/pub/71-222-x/71-222-x2008001-eng.htm. See also Paul Nyhan, "Stay-Home Dads Connect with New Full-Time Job; Pay Stinks, but Benefits Are Great," *Seattle Post-Intelligencer*, April 25, 2006, p. A1; U.S. Census Bureau, "Single-Parent Households Showed Little Variation Since 1994, Census Bureau Reports," March 27, 2007, accessed at www.census.gov/Press-Release/www/releases/archives/families_households/009842.html; and U.S. Census Bureau, "Facts for Features," March 2008, accessed at www.census.gov/Press-Release/www/releases/archives/facts_for_features_special_editions/011179.html.

21. Information from www.epiceriedirect.com/index.php, accessed April 2009.

22. Statistics Canada, "Report on the Demographic Situation in Canada," accessed at www.statcan.gc.ca/bsolc/olc-cel/olc-cel?catno=91-209-x&lang=eng, April 2009; and Ross Finnie, "The Effects of Inter-Provincial Mobility on Individuals' Earnings: Panel Model Estimates for Canada," Analytical Studies Branch Research Paper Series, Report 163, Catalogue No. 11F0019MIE2001163, October 2001, accessed at http://collection.nlc-bnc.ca/100/200/301/statcan/research_paper_analytical_11f0019-e/no163/11F0019MIE01163.pdf.

23. Canadian Consumer Demographics, Industry Canada, Retail Interactive, accessed at http://strategis.ic.gc.ca/SSG/ri00140e.html May 2003. See also U.S. Census Bureau, www.census.gov/population/www/estimates/aboutmetro.html, accessed June 2008; Gordon F. Mulligan and Alexander C. Vias, "Growth and Change in Micropolitan Areas," *The Annals of Regional Science*, June 2006, p. 203; and Madeline Johnson, "Devilish Definitions as Urban Masses Evolve, New Terms and Labels Are Emerging to Try to Describe and Distinguish Them," *Financial Times*, December 29, 2007.

24. "Who Works from Home," *GDSourcing, The Business Researcher Newsletter Archives*, Vol. 5(3), March 22, 2002; Kate Lorenz, "What's the Advantage to Telecommuting," April 27, 2007, accessed at www.cnn.com. See also "Number of Worldwide Mobile Workers Increasing," *Workspan*, March 2008, p. 19; and Sue Shellenbarger, "Some Companies Rethink That Telecommuting Trend," *Wall Street Journal*, February 28, 2008, p. D1.

25. See Fahmida Y. Rashid and Mario Morejon, "Cisco WebEx MeetMeNow—Conferencing with Compatibility," *CRN*, November 19, 2007, p. 43; "WebEx Communications, Inc.," *Hoover's Company Records*, March 15, 2008, p. 99024; and "About WebEx," accessed at www.webex.com/companyinfo/company-overview.html, July 2008.

26. Adapted from "A Profile of Education in Canada," Canadian Council on Social Development, 2004, accessed at www.ccsd.ca/factsheets/education. See also "Educational Attainment," U.S. Census Bureau, January 2008, accessed at www.census.gov/population/www/socdemo/educattn.html.

27. Statistics Canada, "2006 Census: Ethnic Origin, Visible Minorities, Place of Work and Mode of Transportation," accessed at www.statcan.gc.ca/daily-quotidien/080402/dq080402a-eng.htm, May 2009. See also U.S. Bureau of Labor Statistics, "Labor Force, Employment, and Earnings," p. 416, accessed at http://landview.census.gov/prod/2001pubs/statab/sec13.pdf, June 2004; and U.S. Department of Labor, *Occupational Outlook Handbook, 2008–09 Edition*, accessed at www.bls.gov/oco/home.htm.

28. Hamlin Grange and Don Miller, "How to Leverage Diversity," *Marketing Magazine*, August 29, 2005. See also Mike Swift, "State's Diversity a Cue for U.S.," *McClatchy-Tribune Business News*, February 12, 2008.

29. Ibid.

30. Ashwin W. Joshi, "The Visible Majority," *Marketing Magazine*, August 29, 2005.

31. Statistics Canada, "2006 Census: Family portrait: Continuity and Change in Canadian Families and Households in 2006: Highlights," accessed at www12.statcan.ca/census-recensement/2006/as-sa/97-553/p1-eng.cfm, April 2009. For these and other statistics, see www.rivendellmedia.com/ngng/executive_summary/NGNG.PPT and www.gaymarket.com/ngng/ngng_reader.html, accessed April 2008; and www.planetoutinc.com/sales/market.html, accessed September 2008.

32. For these and other examples, see Edward Iwata, "More Marketing Aimed at Gay Consumers," *USA Today*, November 2, 2006, accessed at www.usatoday.com; Andrew Hampp, "An Ad in Which Boy Gets Girl . . . or Boy," *Advertising Age*, August 6, 2007, p. 4; and "Delta Airlines Sponsors City Navigaytour Gay and Lesbian Travel Guides," *Business Wire*, December 6, 2007.

33. Andrew Adam Newman, "Web Marketing to a Segment Too Big to Be a Niche," *New York Times*, October 30, 2007, p. 9; "Disaboom.com Unveils Expanded Content Platform and Marketing Campaign," *PR Newswire*, January 24, 2008; and information from Ford, July 2008.

34. Gavin Rabinowitz, "Carmaker in India Unveils $2,500 Car," *USA Today*, January 10, 2008, accessed at www.usatoday.com; Gavin Rabinowitz, "India's Tata Motors Unveils $2,500 Car, Bringing Car Ownership Within Reach of Millions," *Associated Press*, January 10, 2008; and Mark Phelan, "Automaker Tata's Presence Already Felt in Detroit Area," *McClatchy-Tribune Business News*, March 17, 2008.

35. See Arik Hesseldahl, "What's Eating Apple?" *BusinessWeek*, February 25, 2008, p. 36; and "Not-So-Big Spenders," *Marketing Management*, January/February 2008, p. 5.

36. Statistics Canada, "Study: High Income Canadians," September 2007, accessed at www.statcan.gc.ca/daily-quotidien/070924/dq070924a-eng.htm, April 2009; "2006 Census: Earnings, Income, and Shelter Costs," May 2008, accessed at www.statcan.gc.ca/daily-quotidien/080501/dq080501a-eng.htm, April 2009; and "Census Release Topics," accessed at www12.statcan.ca/census-recensement/2006/rt-td/index-eng.cfm, April 2009; Mark MacKinnon, "High-Income Neighbourhoods," *Globe and Mail*, March 1, 1999, p. B1; Mark MacKinnon, "The Lowest Incomes in Canada Are Found on Native Reserves," *Globe and Mail*, March 1, 1999, p. B2; and Mark Dolliver, "How the Rise of Inequality Fosters a New Culture of Antagonism," *Adweek*, December 17, 2007, pp. 30–31, 37.

37. Kelly Nolan, "Mass Movement of High Fashion," *Retailing Today*, January 8, 2007, pp. 4–6; Eric Wilson and Michael Barbaro, "Can You Be Too Fashionable?" *New York Times*, June 17, 2007, p. 1; Elizabeth Wellington, "Mirror, Mirror: Discounted to Distraction," *Philadelphia Inquirer*, November 4, 2007, p. M1; and Yelena Moroz, "Mass Fashion in Focus: Cheap Chic Fever Quickly Catching On," *Retailing Today*, February 11 2008, p. 1.

38. Andrew Zolli, "Business 3.0," *Fast Company*, March 2007, pp. 64–70.

39. Canadian Standards Association, "PLUS 14021—Environmental Claims: A Guide for Industry and Advertisers," June 2008, accessed at www.csa.ca/Default.asp?language=english, April 2009.

40. Steve Bronstein, "50 Ways to Green Your Business (and Boost Your Bottom Line)," *Fast Company*, November 2007, pp. 90–99.

41. CNW News Release, "Walmart Canada Expands Private-Label Green Cleaning Line," accessed at http://www.newswire.ca/en/releases/archive/April2009/29/c6265.html, April 2009.

42. See "RFID Market Nears $7B," *Journal of Commerce* Online Edition, July 9, 2007; Scott Denne, "After Being Overhyped, RFID Starts to Deliver," *Wall Street Journal*, November 7, 2007, p. 5F; "Wal-Mart Expands RFID Requirements," *McClatchy-Tribune Business News*, January 30, 2008; "Sam's Club Gets Serious about RFID," *Modern Materials Handling*, March 2008, p. 18; and information accessed online at www.autoidlabs.org, September 2008.

43. See "Slowing Economy Dampens 2008 R&D Spending," *R&D Magazine*, February 2008, pp. F3–F15.

44. Statistics Canada, "Domestic Spending on Research and Development (GERD)," accessed at www40.statcan.ca/l01/cst01/scte01a.htm, April 2009.

45. "OECD Countries Spend More on Research and Development, Face New Challenges," December 23, 2004, accessed at www.oecd.org/document/2/0,3343,en_2649_34487_34100162_1_1_1_1,00.html.

46. See Jack Neff, "Unilever, P&G War Over Which Is Most Ethical," *Advertising Age*, March 3, 2008, p. 1; "Hilary Swank Donates Her Hair to Pantene Beautiful Lengths," *PR Newswire*, November 2, 2007; and information from www.beautifullengths.com, accessed April 2008.

47. Wendy Meillo, "The Greed for Goodwill," *Adweek*, March 13, 2006, p. 14; and "The Growth of Cause Marketing," accessed at www.causemarketingforum.com/page.asp?ID=188, August 2008.

48. For one discussion of Canadian values, see "Projecting Canadian Values and Culture," Foreign Affairs Canada, February 17, 2003, accessed at www.dfait-maeci.gc.ca/foreign_policy/ cnd-world/chap5-en.asp.

49. Adapted from descriptions found at www.yankelovich.com/products/lists.aspx, accessed November 2006.

50. Ronald Grover, "Trading the Bleachers for the Couch," *BusinessWeek*, August 22, 2005, p. 32. See also "Examine the Impact Cocooning Is Having on Consumer Markets," *Business Wire*, February 22, 2007; and Paul Kagan, "Home Theatre 101," *Boxoffice*, January 2008, pp. 52–53.

51. "Decked Out," *Inside*, Spring 2006, pp. 76–77. Also see "Meet Me at the Oasis; From Saunas to Spas, People Are Turning Their Homes into a Personal Paradise," *Ottawa Citizen*, April 18, 2007, p. E8.

52. L. A. Chung, "New Greetings of Hybrid Fans: Aloha, LOHAS," *Mercury News*, April 29, 2005, accessed at www.mercurynews.com/mld/mercurynews/news/columnists/la_chung/11520890.htm; with information from www.lohas.com, accessed April 2008.

53. See "Wal-Mart Launches Live Better Index with First Focus on the Environment," April 17, 2007, accessed at www.walmartfacts.com/articles/4960.aspx; "Updated Wal-Mart Live Better Index Reveals More Americans Embrace Earth Friendly Products," *PR Newswire*, October 22, 2007; and www.livebetterindex.com/sustainability.html, accessed April 2008.

54. "Earthbound Farm Facts," accessed at www.earthboundfarm.com, September 2008.

55. See Joanne Friederick, "Evolution Leads to Niches," *Gourmet News*, September 2007, p. 22.

56. Michael Valpy, "Religious Observance Continues to Decline," *Globe and Mail*, March 19, 2003, p. A18; and Clifford Krauss, "In God We Trust . . . Canadians Aren't So Sure," *New York Times*, www.nytimes.com, March 26, 2003.Quotes from Myra Stark, "Celestial Season," *Brandweek*, November 16, 1998, pp. 25–26; and Becky Ebankamp, "The Young and Righteous," *Brandweek*, April 5, 2004, p. 18. See also "Where 'California' Bubbled Up; American Spirituality," *The Economist*, December 22, 2007, p. 75; and Suzanne Sataline, "The Changing Faiths of America; Study Shows Big Declines among Major Denominations," *Wall Street Journal*, February 26, 2008, p. D1.

57. See Philip Kotler, *Kotler on Marketing* (New York: Free Press, 1999), p. 3; and Kotler, *Marketing Insights from A to Z* (Hoboken, NJ: John Wiley & Sons, 2003), pp. 23–24.

58. Based on information found at http://urbanlegends.about.com/library/bl_tim_hortons_coffee.htm, www.snopes.com/food/ingredient/timhortons.asp, and www.timhortons.com/ca/en/about/faq.html, accessed May 2009.

Chapter 4

1. Information from Bullfrog Power website, www.bullfrogpower.com, accessed October 2009; Michelle Warren, "The Best of '08 Marketers: Bullfrog Power," *Marketing*, November 24, 2008; Peter Gorrie, "Tiny Bullfrog Power Making a Mark," thestar.com, www.thestar.com/article/429893, accessed October 2009.

2. For information on SUV safety, see www.citizen.org/autosafety/suvsafety, accessed December 2008.

3. For information on SUV safety and environmental performance, see www.citizen.org/autosafety/suvsafety, accessed July 2008.

4. The figure and the discussion in this section are adapted from Philip Kotler, Gary Armstrong, Veronica Wong, and John Saunders, *Principles of Marketing: European Edition*, 5th ed. (London, ON: Pearson Publishing, 2009), Chapter 2.

5. McDonald's financial information and other facts from www.mcdonalds.ca/pdfs/Health_Wellness.pdf, www.mcdonalds.ca/en/community/social.aspx, www.mcdonalds.com/corp/invest.html, and www.mcdonalds.com/corp/about/factsheets.html, accessed May 2009.

6. The actions described in this section and others undertaken each year by the Competition Bureau are outlined on its "Annoucements" webpage, www.cb-bc.gc.ca/eic/site/cbbc.nsf/eng/h_02705.html, accessed June 2009; Heather Green, "How Green Is That Gizmo?" *BusinessWeek*, December 31, 2007, p. 36; and Tom Wright, "False 'Green' Ads Draw Global Scrutiny," *Wall Street Journal*, January 30, 2008, p. B4. See also Louise Story, "FTC Asks if Carbon-Offset Money Is Winding Up True Green," *New York Times*, January 9, 2008, p. C1.

7. Theodore Levitt, "The Morality (?) of Advertising," *Harvard Business Review*, July–August 1970, pp. 84–92. For counterpoints, see Heckman, "Don't Shoot the Messenger," *Marketing News*, May 24, 1999, pp. 1, 9.

8. "Canadian Households $1.3 Trillion in Debt," The Canadian Press, May 26, 2009, accessed at http://cnews.canoe.ca/CNEWS/Canada/2009/05/26/9574516-cp.html; "Credit Card Debt Measures an 'Insult,'" TheStar.com, accessed at www.thestar.com/business/article/578881, January 2009; Tom McFeat, "Credit Cards—Convenience at a Price," CBC News Online, accessed at www.cbc.ca/news/background/personalfinance/creditcards.html, September 2004; "Elizabeth Warren on the Credit Card Industry," NPR's *Fresh Air*, March 27, 2007, accessed at www.npr.org/templates/story/story.php?storyId=9156929, June 2009; and Jennifer Levitz, "Hi, My Name Is Fred, and I'm Addicted to Credit Cards," *Wall Street Journal*, June 10, 2008, p. A1.

9. André Picard, "Losing Sleep Over 'Natural' Aids," *Globe and Mail*, August 14, 2007.

10. Canadian Press, "Maple Leaf Begins New PR Campaign for Christmas," *Marketing Magazine*, December 2008.

11. Cliff Edwards, "Where Have All the Edsels Gone?" *Greensboro News Record*, May 24, 1999, p. B6; Tim Cooper, "Inadequate Life? Evidence of Consumer Attitudes to Product Obsolescence," *Journal of Consumer Policy*, December 2004, pp. 421–448; David Hunter, "Planned Obsolescence Well Entrenched in Society," *Knoxville News-Sentinel*, August 15, 2005, p. B5; Atsuo Utaka, "Planned Obsolescence and Social Welfare," *Journal of Business*, January 2006, pp. 137–147; and Jessica Harbert and Caleb Pari Heeringga, "Camp Out for Days to Be First to Buy Apple iPhones," *Knight Ridder Tribune Business News*, June 30, 2007, p. 1.

12. Adapted from David Suzuki, "We All Pay for Technology," *Niagara Falls Review*, March 15, 2007, p. A4.

13. See Brian Grow and Pallavi Gogoi, "A New Way to Squeeze the Weak?" *BusinessWeek*, January 28, 2002, p. 92; Judith Burns, "Study Finds Links in Credit Scores, Insurance Claims," *Wall Street Journal*, February 28, 2005, p. D3; Erik Eckholm, "Black and Hispanic Home Buyers Pay Higher Interest on Mortgages, Study Finds," *New York Times*, June 1, 2006, p. A22; and Frank Phillips, "Battle Brewing on Auto Insurance," *Knight Ridder Tribune Business News*, July 1, 2007, p. 1.

14. Jeff Dickerson, "One Step Forward; Three Steps Back," *Atlanta Tribune: The Magazine*, May 2008, p. 68; Harry Alford, "Subprime Scandal—The Largest Hate Crime in History," *New York Beacon*, April 3–9, 2008, p. 12; Edward R. Culvert, "Sub-Prime Loans Should Be Treated as Bias Crimes," *Culvert Chronicles*, March 13–19, 2008, p. 1; "NAACP Mortgage Class Action Fast Tracked," *PR Newswire*, March 10, 2008.

15. Information from "Shop 'til They Drop?" *Christian Science Monitor*, December 1, 2003, p. 8; Gregg Easterbrook, "The Real Truth About Money," *Time*, January 17, 2005, pp. 32–35; and "Bankers Encourage 'Consumer Generation' to Save," *Texas Banking*, March 2006, pp. 25–26. For more on materialism as it relates to quality of life, see James A. Roberts and Aimee Clement, "Materialism and Satisfaction with Over-All Quality of Life Domains," *Social Indicators Research*, May 2007, pp. 72–92; and William Kilbourne and Gregory Pickett, "How Materialism Affects Environmental Beliefs, Concern, and Environmentally Responsible Behavior," *Journal of Business Research*, September 2008, pp. 885–893.

16. "Buy Nothing Day Spawns Debate," *Vancouver Courier*, November 28, 2008. The quote is from Oliver James, "It's More Than Enough to Make You Sick," *Marketing*, January 23, 2008, pp. 26–28.

17. See Michael Kanellos, "A Nationwide Map of Traffic Jams," CNET News.com, September 11, 2007, accessed at http://news.cnet.com/8301-10784_3-9776535-7.html.

18. See www.tfl.gov.uk/roadusers/congestioncharging/6710.aspx, accessed July 2008.

19. See Allison Linn, "Ads Inundate Public Places," MSNBC.com, January 22, 2007; and Bob Garfield, "The Chaos Scenario 2.0: The Post-Advertising Age," *Advertising Age*, March 26, 2007, pp. 1, 12–13.

20. For more discussion, see Martin Sipkoff, "Wal-Mart, Other Discounters Facing Predatory-Pricing Concerns," *Drug Topics*, April 2007, pp. S10–S11; Guy Bolton, "Legislator Targets Drug Prices: Bill Would Eliminate Minimal Markup Law," *McClatchy-Tribune Business News*, December 31, 2007; and "Wal-Mart Expands $4 Prescription List in Colorado," *PR Newswire*, June 5, 2008.

21. "Demonstrators Protest Wal-Mart's 'Always Low Standards,'" *National Union of Public and General Employees*, May 7, 2005, accessed at www.nupge.ca/news_2005/n07my05a.htm, June 2009.

22. "Air Canada Carbon Cutting Program Takes Off," *Marketing Daily*, May 29, 2007.

23. For these and other examples, see Mark Borden et al., "50 Ways to Green Your Business," *Fast Company*, November 2007, pp. 90–99; and "UPS Places Largest Order Ever for Hybrid Electric Trucks," UPS press release, May 13, 2008, accessed at www.pressroom.ups.com.

24. Information from "Because We Can't Remanufacture the Earth . . . ," March 2005, accessed at www.xerox.com/downloads/usa/en/e/ehs_remanufacture_2005.pdf; "Environmental Solutions That Work," April 2007, accessed at www.xerox.com/downloads/usa/en/e/Environmental_Overview.pdf; and "Nurturing a Greener World through Sustainable Innovation and Development," 2007 Report on Global Citizenship, accessed at www.xerox.com/Static_HTML/citizenshipreport/2007/nurturing-page9-2.html.

25. Based on information from Marc Gunther, "Coca-Cola's Green Crusader," *Fortune*, April 28, 2008, p. 150.

26. Adapted from "The Top 3 in 2005," Global 100, accessed at www.global100.org, July 2005. See also "Alcoa Again Named One of the World's Most Sustainable Companies at Davos," January 1, 2008, accessed at www.aloca.com; and information from www.global100.org, accessed August 2008. For further information on Alcoa's sustainability program, see Alcoa's Sustainability Report, found at www.alcoa.com.

27. See "EMAS: What's New?" accessed at http://europa.eu.int/comm/environment/emas, August 2008; "Special Report: Free Trade on Trial—Ten Years of NAFTA," *The Economist*, January 3, 2004, p. 13; Daniel J. Tschopp, "Corporate Social Responsibility: A Comparison Between the United States and Europe," *Corporate Social-Responsibility and Environmental Management*, March 2005, pp. 55–59; "Three Countries Working Together to Protect our Shared Environment," Commission for Environmental Cooperation, accessed at www.cec.org/who_we_are/index.cfm?varlan=english, August 2007.

28. Chuck Salter, "Fast 50 the World's Most Innovative Companies," *Fast Company*, March 2008, pp. 73+.

29. See Laurel Wentz, "'Evolution' Win Marks Dawn of New Cannes Era," *Advertising Age*, June 25, 2007, p. 1; Theresa Howard, "Ad Campaign Tells Women to Celebrate How They Are," *USA Today*, August 7, 2005, accessed at www.usatoday.com; "Beyond Stereotypes: Rebuilding the Foundation of Beauty Beliefs," February 2006, accessed at www.campaignforrealbeauty.com; "Cause: Conscience Marketing. You Stand for Something. Shouldn't Your Brand?" *Strategy*, June 2007, p. 22; Maeve Hosea, "Case Study—Dove: Beneath the Skin," Brand Strategy, May 8, 2008, p. 20; and information found at www.campaignforrealbeauty.com, accessed September 2008.

30. Information from Mike Hoffman, "Ben Cohen: Ben & Jerry's Homemade, Established in 1978," *Inc.*, April 30, 2001, p. 68; and the Ben & Jerry's website, www.benjerrys.com, accessed September 2008.

31. See Global Corruption Report 2008, Transparency International, accessed at www.transparency.org/publications/gcr/download_gcr#download.

32. John F. McGee and P. Tanganath Nayak, "Leaders' Perspectives on Business Ethics," *Prizm*, first quarter, 1994, pp. 71–72. See also Adrian Henriques, "Good Decision—Bad Business?" *International Journal of Management & Decision Making*, 2005, p. 273; and Marylyn Carrigan, Svetla Marinova, and Isabelle Szmigin, "Ethics and International Marketing: Research Background and Challenges," *International Marketing Review*, 2005, pp. 481–494.

33. See Samuel A. DiPiazza, "Ethics in Action," *Executive Excellence*, January 2002, pp. 15–16; Samuel A. DiPiazza, Jr., "It's All Down to Personal Values," accessed online at www.pwcglobal.com, August 2003; and "Code of Conduct: The Way We Do Business," accessed at www.pwc.com/ethics, December 2008. [PricewaterhouseCoopers (www.pwc.com) provides industry-focused assurance, tax, and advisory services to build public trust and enhance value for its clients and their stakeholders. More than 130 000 people in 148 countries across its network share their thinking, experience, and solutions to develop fresh perspectives and practical advice. "PricewaterhouseCoopers" refers to the network of member firms of PricewaterhouseCoopers International limited, each of which is a separate and independent legal entity.]

34. DiPiazza, "Ethics in Action," p. 15.

Chapter 5

1. "Campaign for Real Beauty" website, www.campaignforrealbeauty.com; Rebecca Harris, "Dove Celebrates 'Real Beauty,'" *Marketing Magazine*, September 30, 2004; Rebecca Harris, "Keeping It Real," *Marketing Magazine*, November 8, 2004; "Media Innovation Awards," *Marketing Magazine*, November 21, 2005; Samantha Yaffe, "Going Deep," *Strategy Magazine*, January 2005, p. 55; Lisa D'Innocenzo, "Braver Is Better," *Strategy Magazine*, November 2004; Keith McArthur, "Advertising to Women Gains Super Yardage," *Globe and Mail*, February 7, 2006, p. B3.

2. Unless otherwise noted, quotes in this section are from the excellent discussion of customer insights found in Mohanbir Sawhney, "Insights into Customer Insights," accessed at www.redmond.nl/hro/upload/Insights_into_Customer_Insights.pdf, March 2007. The Apple iPod example is also adapted from this article.

3. See Charles Babcock, "Data, Data, Everywhere," *InformationWeek*, January 9, 2006, pp. 49–53; Holly Wright, "Data Overload," *Marketing Direct*, June 2006, pp. 43–46; and Mary Hayes Weier, "HP Data Warehouse Lands in Wal-Mart's Shopping Cart," *InformationWeek*, August 6, 2007, pp. 31–32.

4. Michael Fassnacht, "Beyond Spreadsheets," *Advertising Age*, February 19, 2007, p. 15.

5. Quotes from Mohanbir Sawhney, "Insights into Customer Insights," p. 3; and Robert Schieffer and Eric Leininger, "Customers at the Core," *Marketing Management*, January/February 2008, pp. 31–37.

6. For more discussion, see Robert Schieffer and Eric Leininger, "Customers at the Core," *Marketing Management*, January/February 2008, pp. 31–37.

7. See Steve Wills and Sally Webb, "Measuring the Value of Insight—It Can and Must Be Done," *International Journal of Market Research*, vol. 49, no. 2, 2007, pp. 155–165.

8. Scott Gardiner, "A Truly Awesome Database," *Marketing Magazine*, April 29, 2002.

9. Grant Robertson, "You Can Move, but Can't Hide, from New Rogers Magazine," *Globe and Mail*, June 2, 2006.

10. See Jean Halliday, "Car Talk: Ford Listens in on Consumers' Online Chatter," *Advertising Age*, February 5, 2007, pp. 3, 34. See also Sean Hargrave, "Measuring Buzz: Ears to the Ground," *New Media Age*, January 17, 2008, p. 21.

11. See Richard L. Wilkins, "Competitive Intelligence: The New Supply Chain Edge," *Supply Chain Management Review*, January/February 2007, pp. 18–27.

12. Fred Vogelstein and Peter Lewis, "Search and Destroy," *Fortune*, May 2, 2005.

13. James Curtis, "Behind Enemy Lines," *Marketing*, May 21, 2001, pp. 28–29. See also Brian Caufield, "Know Your Enemy," *Business 2.0*, June 2004, p. 89; Michael Fielding, "Damage Control: Firms Must Plan for Counterintelligence," *Marketing News*, September 15, 2004, pp. 19–20; Bill DeGenaro, "A Case for Business Counterintelligence," *Competitive Intelligence Magazine*, September–October 2005, pp. 5+; and Jim Middlemiss, "Firms Look to Intelligence to Gain a Competitive Edge," *Law Times*, March 5, 2007, accessed at www.lawtimesnews.com.

14. See "What's Hot: Axe Extends its Aromatic Reach," *Drug Store News*, December 11, 2006, p. 67; David Colman, "Younger, and Faster to Pick Up the Scent," *New York Times*,

July 26, 2007, p. 5; and information from www.unilever.com/ourbrands/personalcare/Axe.asp, accessed July 2008.

15. For more on research firms that supply marketing information, see Jack Honomichl, "Honomichl Top 50," special section, *Marketing News*, June 15, 2008, pp. H1–H67. Other information from www.infores.com; www.smrb.com; www.acnielsen.com; and www.yankelovich.com/products/monitor.aspx, accessed August 2008.

16. See http://us.infores.com/page/solutions/market_content/infoscan, accessed April 5, 2008.

17. Example adapted from an example in David Kiley, "Shoot the Focus Group," *BusinessWeek*, November 14, 2005, pp. 120–121. See also Richard G. Starr and Karen V. Fernandez, "The Mindcam Methodology: Perceiving through the Native's Eye," *Quantitative Market Research*, Spring 2007, pp. 168+.

18. Example adapted from information in Rhys Blakely, "You Know When It Feels Like Somebody's Watching You . . . " *Times*, May 14, 2007, p. 46; and Nandini Lakshman, "Nokia: It Takes a Village to Design a Phone for Emerging Markets," *BusinessWeek*, September 10, 2007, p. 12.

19. Spencer E. Ante, "The Science of Desire," *BusinessWeek*, June 5, 2006, p. 100; and Rhys Blakely, "You Know When It Feels Like Somebody's Watching You..." *Times*, May 14, 2007, p. 46.

20. "National Do Not Call List Effective, but Challenges Remain, VoxPop Survey Finds," Marketing Research and Intelligence Association, press release, March 9, 2009, accessed at www.mria-arim.ca/DNCL/NEWS/PDF/VoxPopdnclv8Mar4_2009.pdf.

21. David Kiley, "Shoot the Focus Group," *BusinessWeek*, p. 120. See also Peter Noel Murray, "Focus Groups Are Valid When Done Right," *Marketing News*, September 1, 2006, pp. 21, 25.

22. Adapted from information in Kenneth Hein, "Hypnosis Brings Groups into Focus," *Brandweek*, May 23, 2008, p. 4.

23. Emily Spensieri, "A Slow, Soft Touch," *Marketing*, June 5, 2006, pp. 15–16.

24. Adam Woods, "Get to the Truth with Web 2.0," *Revolution*, December 2007, p. 39.

25. Gelb, "Online Options Change Biz a Little—and a Lot," *Marketing News*, November 1, 2006, p. 23.

26. Bradley Johnson, "Forget Phone and Mail: Online's the Best Place to Administer Surveys," *Advertising Age*, July 17, 2006, p. 23. See also Adam Woods, "Get to the Truth with Web 2.0," *Revolution*, December 4, 2007, p. 40.

27. Based on information found in Jeremiah McWilliams, "A-B Sees Web as Fertile Ground for Advertising Efforts," *St. Louis Post-Dispatch*, December 19, 2007.

28. Based on information found at www.channelm2.com/HowOnlineQualitativeResearch.html; accessed September 2008.

29. For more on Internet privacy, see Jessica E. Vascellaro "They've Got Your Number (and a Lot More), *Wall Street Journal*, March 13, 2007, pp. D1–D2; "Comment: Do Consumers Really Want Their Privacy?" *New Media Age*, December 13, 2007, p. 12; and Jim Puzzanghera, "Internet; Tough Cookies for Web Surfers Seeking Privacy," *Los Angeles Times*, April 19, 2008, p. C1.

30. See "Creating Computers That Know How You Feel," accessed at www.almaden.ibm.com/cs/BlueEyes/index.html, November 2008.

31. See Josh Goldstein, "Branding on the Brain," *News & Observer*, December 6, 2006, p. 9E; and Jack Neff, "This Is Your Brain on Super Bowl Spots," *Advertising Age*, February 11, 2008, pp. 1, 21.

32. This example is adapted from Rebecca Harris, "Brain Waves," *Marketing*, June 5, 2006, pp. 15–17. See also Douglas L. Fugate, "Neuromarketing: A Layman's Look at Neuroscience and Its Potential Application to Marketing Practice," *Journal of Consumer Marketing*, 2007, p. 385–394.

33. For more on neuromarketing, see Tameka Kee, "NeuroFocus Unveils 'Best Practices,' for Getting into Consumers' Brains," *MediaPost Publications*, April 23, 2008, accessed at http://publications.mediapost.com; Steve McClellan, "Mind Over Matter: New Tools Put Brands in Touch with Feelings," *Adweek*, February 18, 2008, accessed at www.adweek.com; and Stewart Elliott, "Is the Ad a Success? The Brain Waves Tell All," *New York Times*, March 31, 2008.

34. "Analysis: Customer Relationship Management Set to Grow," *Precision Marketing*, November 2, 2007, p. 12.

35. "Infor CRM Customer Bell Canada Wins Marketing Optimization Award," *Marketing Business Weekly*, Atlanta, October 5, 2008, p. 109.

36. Quotes and other information from Suzette Parmley, "Wooing with Loyalty," *Philadelphia Inquirer*, February 28, 2007; Sudhir H. Kale and Peter Klugsberger, "Reaping Rewards," *Marketing Management*, August 2007, pp. 14–17; and Harrah's annual reports and other information accessed at http://investor.harrahs.com/phoenix.zhtml?c=84772&p=irol-sec, August 2008.

37. Michael Krauss, "At Many Firms, Technology Obscures CRM," *Marketing News*, March 18, 2002, p. 5. See also William Boulding et al., "A Customer Relationship Management Roadmap: What Is Known, Potential Pitfalls, and Where to Go," *Journal of Marketing*, October 2005, pp. 155–166; Deborah L. Vence, "CRM: You Know What It Stands for, but Do You Know What It Means?" *Marketing News*, September 15, 2007, p. 12; and "Study: Marketers Stink When It Comes to CRM," *Brandweek*, April 14, 2008, p. 7.

38. See "Value Added with mySAP CRM: Benchmarking Study," accessed at www.sap.com/solutions/business-suite/crm/pdf/Misc_CRM_Study.pdf, June 2008.

39. See Darell K. Rigby and Vijay Vishwanath, "Localization: The Revolution in Consumer Markets," *Harvard Business Review*, April 2006, pp. 82–92; and information found at www.partnersonline.com, September 2008.

40. Adapted from information in Ann Zimmerman, "Small Business; Do the Research," *Wall Street Journal*, May 9, 2005, p. R3; with information from www.bibbentuckers.com, accessed July 2008.

41. Zimmerman, "Small Business; Do the Research," *Wall Street Journal*, p. R3.

42. For some good advice on conducting market research in a small business, see "Marketing Research . . . Basics 101," U.S. Small Business Administration, accessed at www.sba.gov/starting_business/marketing/research.html, August 2008; "Researching Your Market," U.S. Small Business Administration, accessed at www.sba.gov/idc/groups/public/documents/sba_homepage/pub_mt8.pdf, November 2008; and "Managing for Business Success," Industry Canada, accessed at www.ic.gc.ca/eic/site/mfbs-gprea.nsf/eng/h_lu00000.html.

43. See Jack Honomichl, "2006 Revenue Growth Remains Flat," *Marketing News*, August 15, 2007, p. H3.

44. See ACNielsen International Research website, accessed at www2.acnielsen.com/company/where.php, September 2008.

45. Phone, PC, and other country media stats are from http://devdata.worldbank.org/query/default.htm and www.nationmaster.com; accessed July 2008.

46. Subhash C. Jain, *International Marketing Management*, 3rd ed. (Boston: PWS-Kent, 1990), p. 338. For more discussion on international marketing research issues and solutions, see Michael Fielding, "Shift the Focus: Ethnography Proves Fruitful in Emerging Economies," *Marketing News*, September 1, 2006, pp. 18, 20; Robert B. Young and Rajshekhar G. Javalgi, "International Marketing Research: A Global Project Management Perspective," *Business Horizons*, March–April 2007, pp. 113–122; and Gordon A. Wyner, "The World Isn't Flat Yet," *Marketing Research*, Summer 2007, p. 6.

47. Portions of this example are adapted from "Listening to the Internet," *The Economist*, March 11, 2006, p. 8. Other information from Louise Story, "To Aim Ads, What Is Keeping a Closer Eye on You," *New York Times*, March 10, 2008; and www.nielsenbuzzmetrics.com, accessed August 2008.

48. Abbey Klaassen and Ira Teinowitz, "An Ad App You'll Love (and Privacy Groups Will Hate)," *Advertising Age*, November 5, 2007, pp. 3–4; Thomas Claburn, "Call Off the Wolves," *InformationWeek*, November 12, 2007, pp. 69+; and Anick Jesdanun, "Study: Online Privacy Concerns Increase," *Associated Press*, January 16, 2008.

49. Information from RBC's privacy policy website, www.rbcroyalbank.com/ privacy, accessed February 2006.

50. Jaikumar Vijayan, "Disclosure Laws Driving Data Privacy Efforts, Says IBM Exec," *Computerworld*, May 8, 2006, p. 26. See also Thornton A. May, "The What and Why of CPOs," *Computerworld*, November 27, 2006, p. 18.

51. Information accessed at www10.americanexpress.com/sif/cda/page/0,1641,14271,00.asp, July 2008.

52. Cynthia Crossen, "Studies Galore Support Products and Positions, but Are They Reliable?" *Wall Street Journal*, November 14, 1991, pp. A1, A9. See also Allan J. Kimmel, "Deception in Marketing Research and Practice: An Introduction," *Psychology and Marketing*, July 2001, pp. 657–661; Alvin C. Burns and Ronald F. Bush, *Marketing Research* (Upper Saddle River, NJ: Prentice Hall, 2005), pp. 63–75; and Jack Neff, "Who's No. 1? Depends on Who's Analyzing the Data," *Advertising Age*, June 12, 2006, p. 8.

Chapter 6

1. Quotes and other information from Elliott Ettenberg, "The Church of Harley-Davidson," *Marketing Magazine*, July 28, 2003; Vito J. Racanelli, "Bound for Hog Heaven," *Barron's*, November 26, 2007, p. 20–22; Greg Schneider, "Rebels with Disposable Income: Aging Baby Boomers Line Up to Buy High-End Versions of Youthful Indulgences," *Washington Post*, April 27, 2003, p. F1; Ted Bolton, "Tattooed Call Letters: The Ultimate Test of Brand Loyalty," accessed online at www.boltonresearch.com, April 2003; "Harley-Davidson Reports Fourth Quarter and Full Year Results for 2007," *PR Newswire*, January 25, 2008; and the Harley-Davidson website at www.Harley-Davidson.com, accessed October 2008.

2. GDP figures from *The World Fact Book*, February 7, 2008, accessed at www.cia.gov/cia/publications/factbook. Population figures from the World POPClock, U.S. Census Bureau, accessed at www.census.gov, September 2008. This website provides continuously updated projections of the U.S. and world populations.

3. Don E. Schultz, "Lines or Circles," *Marketing News*, November 5, 2007, p. 21.

4. Allan R. Gregg, "Strains Across the Border," *Maclean's*, December 30, 2002, accessed at www.macleans.ca; and "Maclean's Annual Poll," *Maclean's*, November 21, 2007, accessed at www.macleans.ca.

5. For a deeper discussion of consumer culture theory, see Eric J. Arnould and Craig J. Thompson, "Consumer Culture Theory (CCT): Twenty Years of Research," *Journal of Consumer Research*, 2005, Vol. 31 (4), pp. 868–883.

6. The Political Voice Of Canadian Regional Identities, The Centre for Canadian Studies, 2001, accessed at http://culturescope.ca/ev_en.php?ID=9417_201&ID2=DO_TOPIC, September 2006.

7. Sara Minogue, "Reaching New Canadians: Multicultural Experts Offer Their Best Practice Advice to Niche Marketers," *Strategy Magazine*, September 22, 2003, accessed at www.strategymag.com,July 2004; Caribana Festival website, www.caribana.com, accessed July 2004.

8. Statistics Canada, "Study: Canada's Visible Minority Population in 2017," *The Daily*, March 22, 2005.

9. Hamlin Grange and Don Miller, "How to Leverage Diversity," *Marketing Magazine*, August 29, 2005.

10. Huixia Sun, "Chinese Websites Beat Economic Blues," *Vancouver Sun*, May 15, 2009; Chris Powell, "New Chinese Canadians Prefer Internet to TV: Diversity Study," *Marketing Magazine*, April 2008.

11. Statistics Canada, "2006 Census Data Products," www12.statcan.ca/census-recensement/2006/dp-pd/index-eng.cfm, accessed May 15, 2009.

12. Quote from "Queen Latifah Turns CoverGirl," February 2, 2006, accessed at http://blogs.chron.com/shopgirl/archives/2006/02/queen_latifah_t.html. Facts from Cliff Peale, "P&G Showed the Way: Company's Ads Targeted to Blacks Paid Off," *Cincinnati Enquirer*, February 25, 2007, accessed at http://news.enquirer.com; and www.covergirl.com/products/collections/queen, accessed November 2008.

13. Cliff Peale, "Procter & Gamble Campaigns for Black Consumers Paying Off," *Cincinnati Inquirer*, March 6, 2007, accessed at www.clarionledger.com. See also Michael Bush, "P&G Unveils 'My Black Is Beautiful' Campaign," *PRWeek*, December 3, 2007, p. 5.

14. Hamlin Grange and Don Miller, "How to Leverage Diversity," *Marketing*, August 29, 2005.

15. Information accessed at www.census.gov, August 2008. See also Sherry L. Jarrell, "Picture of Retiree Spending Is Changing," *Marketing News*, September 15, 2006, p. 40; and "Mature Market in the U.S.," *M2 Presswire*, March 2, 2007.

16. "Boom Time of America's New Retirees Feel Entitled to Relax—and Intend to Spend," *Financial Times*, December 6, 2007, p. 9.

17. For a discussion of influencers, see Clive Thompson, "Is the Tipping Point Toast?" *Fast Company*, February 2008, pp. 75–105; Edward Keller and Jonathan Berry, *The Influentials* (New York: The Free Press, 2003); and Daniel B. Honigman, "Who's on First?" *Marketing News*, November 1, 2007, pp. 14–17. The study results and quotes are from Kenneth Hein, "Report Explores What Influences the Influencers," *Brandweek*, February 5, 2007, p. 13; Ryan McConnell, "Spread the News: Word-of-Mouth Worth $1 Billion," *Advertising Age*, November 15, 2007, p. 4; and Megan McIlroy, "Family, Friends Most Influential on Shoppers," *Advertising Age*, April 9, 2008, accessed at www.adage.com.

18. Extract adapted from Robert Berner, "I Sold It Through the Grapevine," *BusinessWeek*, May 29, 2006, pp. 32–34; and Melanie Wells, "Kid Nabbing," *Forbes*, February 2, 2004, p. 84. See also Jack Neff, "P&G, Unilever Are Ready to Clutter," *Advertising Age*, June 11, 2007, p. 4. Data on Vocalpoint from www.vocalpoint.com, accessed July 2008.

19. Adapted from Anya Kamenetz, "The Network Unbound," *Fast Company*, June 2006, pp. 69–73. Also see Brad Stone, "Social Networking's Next Phase," *New York Times*, March 3, 2007, accessed at www.nytimes.com; and Chuck Brymer, "The Birds and the Bees," *Adweek*, January 7, 2008, p. 16.

20. See Alana Semuels, "Small Business; This Advertising Shop Knows Jack," *Los Angeles Times*, February 7, 2008, p. C1; Jen Haberkorn, "Facebook, MySpace See Ads Invasion," *Washington Times*, August 17, 2007, p. C9; Nicole Maestri, "Wal-Mart Using Facebook to Win Back-to-School Sales," August 8, 2007, accessed at www.reuters.com.

21. Allison Enright, "How the Second Half Lives," *Marketing News*, February 15, 2007, pp. 12–14; Mike Shields, "CNN to Launch Bureau in Second Life Virtual World," Media Week.com, October 29, 2007, accessed at www.mediaweek.com; and http://secondlife.com, accessed July 2008.

22. Leslie Brooks Suzukamo, "Serious Joints Silly as Companies, Others See YouTube Marketing Promise," *McClatchy-Tribune Business News*, January 10, 2008; Stuart Elliott, "For Marketing, the MVP Might Be YouTube," *New York Times*, February 5, 2008, accessed at www.nytimes.com; Alana Semuels, "Small Business; This Advertising Shop Knows Jack," *Los Angeles Times*, February 7, 2008, p. C1; and Elizabeth A. Sullivan, "H.J. Heinz Company," *Marketing News*, February 1, 2008, p. 10.

23. Adapted from Kim Hart, "Online Networking Goes Small, and Sponsors Follow," *Washington Post*, December 29, 2007, p. D1.

24. Hart, "Online Networking Goes Small, and Sponsors Follow," p. D1.

25. Quote from Anya Kamenetz, "The Network Unbound," *Fast Company*, June 2006, p. 73. Also see Julie Bosman, "Chevy Tries a Write-Your-Own-Ad Approach," *New York Times*, April 4, 2006, p. C1.

26. See Scott Hidebrink, "Women and the Automotive Aftermarket," *Motor Age*, September 2007, pp. 60+; and "Finance and Economics: A Guide to Womenomics," *The Economist*, April 15, 2006, p. 80.

27. Chris Powell, "Under the Influence," *Marketing Magazine*, February 16, 2004, p. 9.

28. Jeff James, "Nickelodeon, Chrysler Announced a Deal to Promote '08 Minivans," June 27, 2007 accessed at www.about.com; and Anthony Crupi, "Nickelodeon, Chrysler Join Forces to Reach Families," *Brandweek*, June 26, 2007, accessed at www.brandweek.com.

29. Alice Dragoon, "How to Do Customer Segmentation Right," *CIO*, October 1, 2005, p. 1. For another example, see Teri Koenke, "Destroying Demographics: The New Art of Strategic Customer Communications." *U.S. Banker*, October 2006, pp. 22–23.

30. Norma Ramage, "Mark's Super Brand Ambition," *Marketing Magazine*, March 29, 2004.

31. Portions adapted from Linda Tischler, "How Pottery Barn Wins with Style," *Fast Company*, June 2003, pp. 106–113; and Carole Sloan, "Lifestyle Specialists Enjoy Strong Year," *Furniture Today*, August 28, 2006, p. 28; with information from www.potterybarn.com, www.potterybarnkids.com, and www.pbteen.com, October 2008.

32. Jennifer Aaker, "Dimensions of Measuring Brand Personality," *Journal of Marketing Research*, August 1997, pp. 347–356. See also Aaker, "The Malleable Self: The Role of Self-Expression in Persuasion," *Journal of Marketing Research*, May 1999, pp. 45–57; and Audrey Azoulay and Jean-Noel Kapferer, "Do Brand Personality Scales Really Measure Brand Personality?" *Journal of Brand Management*, November 2003, p. 143.

33. See "Apple Debuts New 'Get a Mac' Ads," *Apple Matters*, January 17, 2007; and "Apple 'Get a Mac' Ad Campaign Seen Taking Toll on Microsoft's Reputation," *MacDailyNews*, March 20, 2008, accessed at www.macdailynews.com.

34. See Mark Tadajewski, "Remembering Motivation Research: Toward an Alternative Genealogy of Interpretive Consumer Research," *Marketing Theory*, December 2006, pp. 429–466; and Leon G. Schiffman and Leslie L. Kanuk, *Consumer Behavior*, 9th ed. (Upper Saddle River, NJ: Prentice Hall, 2007), Chapter 4.

35. See Abraham. H. Maslow, "A Theory of Human Motivation," *Psychological Review*, 1943, Vol. 50, pp. 370–396. See also Maslow, *Motivation and Personality*, 3rd ed. (New York: HarperCollins Publishers, 1987); and Barbara Marx Hubbard, "Seeking Our Future Potentials," *Futurist*, May 1998, pp. 29–32.

36. Louise Story, "Anywhere the Eye Can See, It's Likely to See an Ad," *New York Times*, January 15, 2007, accessed at www.nytimes.com; and Matthew Creamer, "Caught in the Clutter Crossfire: Your Brand," *Advertising Age*, April 1, 2007, p. 35.

37. Bob Garfield, "'Subliminal' Seduction and Other Urban Myths," *Advertising Age*, September 18, 2000, pp. 4, 105; and Lewis Smith, "Subliminal Advertising May Work, but Only If You're Paying Attention," *Times*, March 9, 2007. For more on subliminal advertising, see Alastair Goode, "The Implicit and Explicit Role of Ad Memory in Ad Persuasion: Rethinking the Hidden Persuaders," *International Journal of Marketing Research*, vol. 49, no. 2, 2007, pp. 95–116; Don E. Shultz, "Subliminal Ad Notions Still Resonate Today," *Marketing News*, March 15, 2007, p. 5; Cynthia Crossen, "For a Time in the 50s, a Huckster Fanned Fears of an Ad 'Hypnosis,'" *Wall Street Journal*, November 5, 2007, p. B1; and Beth Snyder Bulik, "This Brand Makes You More Creative," *Advertising Age*, March 24, 2008, p. 4.

38. Quotes and information from "Ogilvy Public Relations Worldwide and BzzAgent Forge Strategic Alliance to Offer Clients More Word-of-Mouth Communications Solutions," *PR Newswire*, January 10, 2008; Duglas Pruden and Terry G. Vavra, "Controlling the Grapevine," *Marketing Management*, July–August 2004, pp. 25–30; and Yubo Chen and Jinhong Xie, "Online Consumer Review: Word-of-Mouth as a New Element of Marketing Communication Mix," *Management Science*, March 2008, pp. 477–491.

39. See Leon Festinger, *A Theory of Cognitive Dissonance* (Stanford, CA: Stanford University Press, 1957); Leon G. Schiffman and Leslie L. Kanuk, *Consumer Behavior*, 9th ed. (Upper Saddle River, NJ: Prentice Hall, 2007), pp. 219–220; "Cognitive Dissonance and the Stability of Service Quality Perceptions," *Journal of Services Marketing*, 2004, p. 433+; Cynthia Crossen, "'Cognitive Dissonance' Became a Milestone in the 1950s Psychology," *Wall Street Journal*, December 12, 2006, p. B1; and Mohammed N. Nadeem, "Post-Purchase Dissonance: The Wisdom of the Repeat Purchases," *Journal of Global Business Issues*, Summer 2007, pp. 183–194.

40. The following discussion draws from the work of Everett M. Rogers. See his *Diffusion of Innovations*, 5th ed. (New York: Free Press, 2003).

41. See Glen Dickson, "Nielsen Gives Fuzzy Picture of HDTV Penetration," *Broadcasting & Cable*, October 30, 2007, accessed at www.broadcastingandcable.com.

Chapter 7

1. Quotes and other information from "GE Transportation Endorses New Tier 3 and 4 Emission Regulations," *Business Wire*, March 14, 2008; "General Electric Signs Contract to Supply 310 Evolution Series Locomotives to Kazakhstan," *Business Wire*, September 28, 2006; Jim Martin, "GE to Seal $650 Million Deal," *Knight Ridder Tribune Business News*, September 28, 2006, p. 1; Rick Stouffer, "GE Locomotives: 100 Years and Still Chuggin'," *Knight Ridder Tribune Business News*, September 23, 2007; David Lustig, "GE Unveils Hybrid Loco," *Railway Gazette International*, July 2007, p. 1; "Collaborating with Partners," accessed at www.getransportation.com, May 2008; and various pages at www.ge.com, accessed October 2008.

2. See Kerry Capell, "How the Swedish Retailer Became a Global Cult Brand," *BusinessWeek*, November 14, 2005, p. 103; Greta Guest, "Inside IKEA's Formula for Global Success," *Detroit Free Press*, June 3, 2006; "IKEA," *Hoover's Company Records*, April 1, 2008, p, 42925; "IKEA Group Stores," accessed at www.ikea-group.ikea.com/?ID=11, April 2008; and "Our Vision: A Better Everyday Life," accessed at www.ikea.com, December 2008.

3. Patrick J. Robinson, Charles W. Faris, and Yoram Wind, *Industrial Buying Behavior and Creative Marketing* (Boston: Allyn & Bacon, 1967). See also James C. Anderson and James A. Narus, *Business Market Management*, 2nd ed. (Upper Saddle River, NJ: Prentice Hall, 2004), Chapter 3; James C. Anderson, James A. Narus, and Wouter van Rossum, "Customer Value Propositions in Business Markets," *Harvard Business Review*, March 2006, pp. 91–99; and Philip Kotler and Kevin Lane Keller, *Marketing Management*, 13th ed. (Upper Saddle River, NJ: Prentice Hall, 2009), Chapter 7.

4. Example adapted from information found in "Nikon Focuses on Supply Chain Innovation—and Makes New Product Distribution a Snap," UPS case study, accessed at www.ups-scs.com/solutions/case_studies/cs_nikon.pdf, July 2008. See also Roger Morton, "Keeping the Supply Chain in Focus," *Logistics Today*, July 2007, pp. 12+.

5. See Frederick E. Webster, Jr. and Yoram Wind, *Organizational Buying Behavior* (Upper Saddle River, NJ: Prentice Hall, 1972), pp. 78–80. See also James C. Anderson and James A. Narus, *Business Market Management: Understanding, Creating and Delivering Value* (Upper Saddle River NJ: Prentice Hall, 2004), Chapter 3; Jorg Brinkman and Markus Voeth, "An Analysis of Buying Center Decisions Through the Sales Force," *Industrial Marketing Management*, October 2007, p. 998; and Philip Kotler and Kevin Lane Keller, *Marketing Management*, 13th ed. (Upper Saddle River, NJ: Prentice Hall, 2009), pp. 188–191.

6. Jennifer Lawinski, "Good Checkup—Avent's HealthPath University Puts VARs in Touch with How Things Work at a Hospital," *CRN*, August 20, 2007, p. 57.

7. See Frederick E. Webster, Jr. and Yoram Wind, *Organizational Buying Behavior*, (Upper Saddle River, NJ: Prentice Hall, 1972), pp. 33–37.

8. Patrick J. Robinson, Charles W. Faris, and Yoram Wind, *Industrial Buying Behavior and Creative Marketing* (Boston: Allyn & Bacon, 1967), p. 14.

9. Magna International website, www.magnaint.com, accessed May 2009; Greg Keenan, "Auto Parts Maker Issues Brighter Earnings Picture for First-Quarter Results," *Globe and Mail*, February 25, 2003, accessed at www.globeandmail.com; John Buell, "The Year of Relationships" (editorial), *Constructech*, Vol. 5, No. 3, 2003, accessed at www.constructech.com/printresources/ viewarticle2.asp.

10. For this and other examples, see Kate Maddox, "10 Great Websites," *BtoB Online*, September 11, 2006; accessed at www.btobonline.com; and Karen J. Bannan, "10 Great Websites," September 10, 2007, accessed at www.btobonline.com. Other information from www.sun.com, accessed September 2008.

11. See RBC Financial Group's eprocurement pages at www.rbc.com/sourcing/eproc_what-is.html, accessed February 2006.

12. Michael A. Verespej, "E-Procurement Explosion," *Industry Week*, March 2002, pp. 25–28. For more information on eprocurement, see Amit Gupta, "E-Procurement Trials and Triumphs," *Contract Management*, January 2008, pp. 28–35; and Christian Tanner et al., "Current Trends and Challenges in Electronic Procurement: an Empirical Study," *Electronic Markets*, February 2008, pp. 6–18.

13. See "About Food Away From Home," accessed at www.fafh.com, April 2008.

14. Government of Canada, "The Basics of Selling to Government," November 3, 2004, accessed at http://contracts canada.gc.ca/en/how-e.htm, accessed February 2006; and "How the Government of Canada Buys Goods and Services," September 4, 2008, www.contractscanada.gc.ca/en/how-e.htm, accessed May 2009.

15. Western Economic Diversification Canada, "How to Sell (More) to Government," July 22, 2004, accessed at www.wd.gc.ca/tools/selgov/shoyour_e.asp, February 2006.

Chapter 8

1. Adapted from Ruple Parekh, "Febreze Sniffs Out New Target: Dorm Dwellers," *Advertising Age*, October 29, 2007, p. 12; with quotes and information from Leslie Benson, "Forget Laundry Day, Use Febreze," *GCI*, February 2008, p. 8; "Ten Years Marks Milestone for Procter & Gamble's Febreze Brand," *PR Newswire*, June 4, 2008; and www.whatstinks.com, accessed September 2008.

2. For these and other examples, see Jesse Harlin, "Speaking in Tongues—Localizing at Home and Abroad," *Game Developer*, November 2007, p. 40; and Philip Kotler and Kevin Lane Keller, *Marketing Management*, 13th ed. (Upper Saddle River, NJ: Prentice Hall, 2009), pp. 210–211.

3. Based on information from Patti Bond, "Home Depot to Test Superstores, Ministores," *Atlanta Journal-Constitution*, March 23, 2007.

4. Danny Kucharsky, "Rogers Video Plans Up to 60 Quebec Stores," *Marketing Daily*, March 5, 2004.

5. Kristin Laird, "Royal Bank Sponsors Cricket Program," *Marketing Daily*, February 29, 2008.

6. Gayle MacDonald and Val Ross, "Those Who Give—And Give Lots," *Globe and Mail*, April 15, 2006, p. E8; Sarah Hampson, "They're Young, Diverse and Brash. And They're

The Last Ones With Any Cash Left To Give. But They'll Only Do It Their Way," *Globe and Mail*, April 15, 2006, p. E6.

7. Matt Semansky, "Nestlé Aims Aero at Female Consumers," *Marketing Daily*, August 17, 2007.

8. Solvej Schou, "Sisters Doing It for Themselves," *Associated Press*, March 12, 2007; and www.daisyrock.com, accessed November 2008.

9. Adapted from information found in Laura Koss-Feder, "At Your Service," *Time*, June 11, 2007, p. 1.

10. Ibid.

11. Information from www.smartertravel.com, www.rssc.com, and www.royalcaribbean.com, accessed June 2008.

12. See Louise Story, "Finding Love and the Right Linens," *New York Times*, December 13, 2006, accessed at www.nytimes.com; and www.williams-sonoma.com/cust/storeevents/index.cfm, accessed September 2008.

13. Kate MacArthur, "BK Rebels Fall in Love with King," *Advertising Age*, May 1, 2006, pp. 1, 86; Kenneth Hein, "BK 'Lifestyle' Goods Aim for Young Males," *Adweek*, June 12, 2006, p. 8; and Janet Adamy, "Man Behind the Burger King Turnaround: Chidsey Says Identifying His Restaurant's Superfan Helped Beef Up Its Offerings," *Wall Street Journal*, April 2, 2008, p. B1.

14. See Manish Bhatt and Raghu Bhat, "Building a Brand, Creating a Cult," LiveMint.com, February 12, 2008, accessed at www.livemint.com/2008/02/12231611/Building-a-brand-creating-a-c.html; Chris Maxcer, "A Menagerie of Mac Fanatic Must-Haves," *MacNewsWorld*, November 19, 2007, www.macnewsworld.com/story/60367.html; and Asher Moses, "Doco Puts Macheads Under the Microscope," *Sydney Morning Herald*, February 19, 2008, accessed at www.smh.com.

15. See the "PRIZM NE Lifestyle Segmentation System" brochure and other cluster information, accessed at www.claritas.com/claritas/Default.jsp?ci=3&si=4&pn=prizmne, accessed July 2008; and Environics website, www.environicsanalytics.ca/prizmc2.aspx, accessed June 2009.

16. Information from https://home.americanexpress.com/home/open.shtml, accessed August 2008.

17. See Thomas L. Powers and Jay U. Stirling, "Segmenting Business-to-Business Markets: A Micro-Macro Linking Methodology," *Journal of Business & Industrial Marketing*, April 15, 2008, pp. 170–177.

18. Raed Rafei, "Cola Makers Target Mideast," *Los Angeles Times*, February 4, 2008, accessed at www.latimes.com; "Uganda: Carol Mgasha Is MTV VJ," *Africa News*, September 17, 2007; "Music on the Coke Side of Life," September 18, 2007, accessed at www.cokemusic.com.mt/subsites/news.htm; and Charles R. Taylor, "Lifestyle Matters Everywhere," *Advertising Age*, May 19, 2008, p. 24.

19. Jeromy Lloyd, "Coke Goes Live for the Olympics," *Marketing Magazine*, January 13, 2009.

20. See Michael Porter, *Competitive Advantage* (New York: Free Press, 1985), pp. 4–8, 234–236. For more recent discussions, see Stanley Slater and Eric Olson, "A Fresh Look at Industry and Market Analysis," *Business Horizons*, January–February 2002, p. 15–22; Kenneth Sawka and Bill Fiora, "The Four Analytical Techniques Every Analyst Must Know: 2. Porter's Five Forces Analysis," *Competitive Intelligence Magazine*, May–June 2003, p. 57; and Philip Kotler and Kevin Lane Keller, *Marketing Management*,

13th ed. (Upper Saddle River, NJ: Prentice Hall, 2009), pp. 342–343.

21. See Suzanne Kapner, "How Fashion's VF Supercharges Its Brands," *Fortune*, April 14, 2008, pp. 108–110; and www.vfc.com, accessed October 2008.

22. Store information found at www.walmartstores.com, www.walmart.ca, www.loblaw.ca, and www.wholefoodsmarket.com, accessed June 2009.

23. See Gerry Khermouch, "Call It the Pepsi Blue Generation," *BusinessWeek*, February 3, 2003, p. 96; Phyllis Furman, "Mist-Takes Made Again: New Ads for Sierra Mist," *Knight Ridder Tribune Business News*, April 10, 2006, p. 1; and Duane D. Stanford, "Coke, Pepsi-Cola Sales Down, Other Sodas Grow," *Cox News Service*, March 8, 2007.

24. Quotes and information from Sidra Durst, "Shoe In," *Business 2.0*, December 2006, p. 54; Kimberly Weisul, "A Shine on Their Shoes," *BusinessWeek*, December 12, 2006, p. 84; Connie Gentry, "Cultural Revolution," *Chain Store Age*, December 2007, pp. 32–33; Brian Morrissey, "Communal Branding," *Adweek*, May 12, 2008, pp. 8–9; and "About Zappos," accessed at www.zappos.com/about.zhtml, October 2008.

25. Examples from Darell K. Rigby and Vijay Vishwanath, "Localization: The Revolution in Consumer Markets," *Harvard Business Review*, April 2006, pp. 82–92. See also Jenny McTaggart, "Wal-Mart Unveils New Segmentation Scheme," *Progressive Grocer*, October 1, 2006, pp. 10–11.

26. See Arundhati Parmar, "On the Map," *Marketing News*, February 15, 2008, pp. 13–15; and information from http://mysbuxinteractive.com, accessed July 2008.

27. For these and other examples see Lynnley Browning, "Do-It-Yourself Logo for Proud Scion Owners," *New York Times*, March 24, 2008, accessed at www.nytimes.com; and Mike Beirne, "Mars Gives M&M's a Face," *Brandweek*, May 22, 2008, accessed at www.brandweek.com.

28. See Gigi Stone, "Advertisers Try New Way to Get into Your Head," December 16, 2006, accessed at http://abcnews.go.com/WNY/print?id=2731799; and Steve Miller, "Who Said That?" *Brandweek*, January 30, 2007, accessed at www.brandweek.com.

29. Adapted from portions of Fae Goodman, "Lingerie Is Luscious and Lovely—for Grown-Ups: But Is the Pink?" *Chicago Sun-Times*, February 19, 2006, p. B2; and Stacy Weiner, "Goodbye to Girlhood," *Washington Post*, February 20, 2007, p. HE01. See also Jayne O'Donnell, "As Kids Get Savvy, Marketers Move Down the Age Scale," *USA Today*, April 11, 2007, accessed at www.usatoday.com; and Maybeth Hicks, "No Secret: Victoria Pink Turns Mom's Cheeks Red," *Washington Times*, January 13, 2008, p. D1. Also view the CBC video "Buying Into Sexy," available at www.cbclearning.ca/CBCEDS/shopping/product.aspx?CatalogName=CBCEDSBase&CategoryName=business_and_economics_marketing&Product_ID=Y8M-04-04&Variant_ID=Y8M-04-04-020101.

30. Jeff Gray, "Medical Officer Calls for Ban of All Advertising of Food and Drink Aimed at Children," *Globe and Mail*, February 26, 2008; "Leading Food And Beverage Companies Release Commitments on Children's Advertising," Press release, Food and Consumer Products of Canada, February 6, 2008, accessed at www.fcpmc.com/issues/hal/splash/index.html, June 2009.

31. Jack Trout, "Branding Can't Exist Without Positioning," *Advertising Age*, March 14, 2005, p. 28.

32. Adapted from a positioning map prepared by students Brian May, Josh Payne, Meredith Schakel, and Bryana Sterns, University of North Carolina, April 2003. SUV sales data furnished by WardsAuto.com, accessed June 2008. Price data from www.edmunds.com, accessed June 2008.

33. Based on information found in Michael Myser, "Marketing Made Easy," *Business 2.0*, June 2006, pp. 43–44; Steve Smith, "Staples' Sales Rise While Office Depot's Drop," *Twice*, March 10, 2008, p. 62; and "Staples, Inc." *Hoover's Company Records*, June 1, 2008, p. 14790.

34. See Bobby J. Calder and Steven J. Reagan, "Brand Design," in Dawn Iacobucci, ed., *Kellogg on Marketing* (New York: John Wiley & Sons, 2001), p. 61. See also Philip Kotler and Kevin Lane Keller, *Marketing Management*, 13th ed. (Upper Saddle River, NJ: Prentice Hall, 2009), pp. 315–316.

35. For a fuller discussion, see Philip Kotler and Kevin Lane Keller, *Marketing Management*, 13th ed. (Upper Saddle River, NJ: Prentice Hall, 2009), Chapter 10.

Chapter 9

1. Quotes and other information from lululemon athletica corporate website, www.lululemon.ca, accessed June 2009; Shareholder Presentation, March 2009, accessed at http://files.shareholder.com/downloads/LULU/ 669145903x0x284185/73839a3a-cb29-40c6-b7a2- e907d17b39c4/TAG_Conference_Mar09_Final.pdf), June 2009; Hollie Shaw, "Price Cuts Not Part of lululemon's Strategy in Sales Slump," *Financial Post*, June 11, 2009; Kristen Vinakmens, "Lululemon: Building the Brand from the Ground—Yoga Mat—Up," *Strategy*, accessed at www.strategymag.com/articles/magazine,20040113/ lululemon,html?word=lululemon, March 2006.

2. Eve Lazarus, "Libraries Have More Than You Think, Shows New Ads," *Marketing Magazine*, October 23, 2008; The Alberta Library press release, "Alberta Campaign Gets International Recognition," May 4, 2009.

3. "Athletes Help Brands Win Big," *Marketing News*, March 15, 2008, p. 17.

4. See Diane Brady, "It's All Donald, All the Time," *BusinessWeek*, January 22, 2007, p. 51; and "Being Like a Celebrity Is Easier Than You Think," *PR Newswire*, June 3, 2008.

5. Based on information from Sonia Reyes, "Faster Than a Ray of Light," *Brandweek*, October 9, 2006, pp. M28–M31; Grant McCracken, "Rachael Ray: Branding Goddess?" *This Blog Sits at the Intersection of Anthropology and Economics*, October 17, 2006, accessed at www.cultureby.com/trilogy/2006/10/ rachael_ray_bra.html; Alec Foege, "The Rachael Way," *Adweek*, March 5, 2007, pp. SR22–SR24; "Food Network Orders More Helpings of Rachael Ray," *McClatchy-Tribune Business News*, December 17, 2007; and Rachael Ray, "10 Questions," *Time*, April 28, 2008, p. 6.

6. Information from www.cnto.org/aboutchina.asp, accessed April 2008; "Stuck in Traffic? Move to Saskatchewan, Ad Says," *Marketing Magazine*, April 21, 2007. See also www.TravelTex.com, and www.visitcalifornia.com, accessed October 2008.

7. Accessed at www.social-marketing.org/aboutus.html, accessed August 2008.

8. Kristin Laird, "Debate the Prescription for Doctor Shortage, CMA," *Marketing Daily*, February 27, 2008; Rob Gould and Karen Gutierrez, "Social Marketing Has a New Champion," *Marketing News*, February 7, 2000, p. 38. See also Alan R. Andreasen, *Social Marketing in the 21st Century* (Thousand Oaks, CA: Sage Publications, 2006); Philip Kotler and Nancy Lee, *Social Marketing: Improving the Quality of Life*, 3rd ed. (Thousand Oaks, CA: Sage Publications, 2008); and www.social-marketing.org, accessed November 2008.

9. Quotes and definitions from Philip Kotler, *Kotler on Marketing* (New York: Free Press, 1999), p. 17; and www.asq. org, accessed July 2008.

10. Quotes and other information from Regina Schrambling, "Tool Department: The Sharpest Knives in the Drawer," Los Angeles Times, March 8, 2006, p. F1; Arricca Elin SanSone, "OXO: Universal Design Innovator," *Cooking Light*, April 2007, p. 118; and www.oxo.com/OA_HTML/oxo/ about_what.htm, accessed July 2008.

11. See "Supermarket Facts," accessed at www.fmi.org/ facts_figs/?fuseaction=superfact, April 2008; and "Wal-Mart Facts," accessed at www.walmartfacts.com/StateByState/ ?id=2, April 2008.

12. "The Oyster Awards," *Consumer Reports*, March 2007, p. 12. See also Michael Antonucci, "Ouch! Why Do They Package Stuff Like That?" *McClatchy-Tribune Business News*, January 18, 2008; and Elsa Wenzel, "Killing the Oyster Pack," April 7, 2008, accessed at http://news.cnet.com/8301-11128_3- 9912173-54.html.

13. Sonja Reyes, "Ad Blitz, Bottle Design Fuel Debate over Heinz's Sales," *Brandweek*, February 12, 2007, accessed at www.brandweek.com/bw/news/recent_display. jsp?vnu_content_id=1003544497.

14. Travis Bell, "Drink Responsibly," Presentation at the Walmart Sustainable Packaging Conference III, May 6, 2009, accessed at www.pac.ca/ePromos/ Walmart_Conf_III_Travis_Bell.pdf, June 2009.

15. Example adapted from "Pepsi's New Set of Cans," *Creativity*, March 2007, p. 76; with quote from Martinne Geller, "PepsiCo Invites Designers to New Pepsi Challenge," *San Diego Union-Tribune*, April 4, 2007, accessed at www.SignOnSanDiego.com. See also www.pepsigallery. com; and "Pepsi Launches Creative Challenge with MyClick Application," *Telecomworldwire*, April 14, 2008.

16. See Jena McGregor, "Customer Service Champs," *BusinessWeek*, March 5, 2007, pp. 52–64; and David Welch, "Looser Rules, Happier Clients," *BusinessWeek*, March 5, 2007, p. 62.

17. See the HP Total Care website at http://h71036.www7.hp. com/hho/cache/309717-0-0-225-121.html, accessed December 2008.

18. Information accessed at www.marriott.com, August 2007.

19. See "McAtlas Shrugged," *Foreign Policy*, May–June 2001, pp. 26–37; and Philip Kotler and Kevin Lane Keller, *Marketing Management*, 13th ed. (Upper Saddle River, NJ: Prentice Hall, 2009), p. 254.

20. See Jack Trout, "'Branding' Simplified," *Forbes*, April 19, 2007, accessed at www.forbes.com.

21. "Competing in the Global Brand Economy: Best Canadian Brands 2008," *Interbrand and Report on Business, Globe and Mail*, accessed at www.ourfishbowl.com/images/surveys/ BestCanadianBrands2008.pdf, June 2009.

22. For more on Y&R's Brand Asset Valuator, see "Brand Asset Valuator," accessed at www.valuebasedmanagement.net/ methods_brand_asset_valuator.html, February 2008; W. Ronald Lane, Karen Whitehill King, and J. Thomas Russell,

Kleppner's Advertising Procedure, 17th ed. (Upper Saddle River, NJ: Prentice Hall, 2008), p. 105; and Chelsea Greene, "Using Brands to Drive Business Results," *Landor*, accessed at www.wpp.com/WPP/Marketing/ReportsStudies/Usingbrandstodrivebusinessresults.htm, March 2008.

23. Al Ehrbar, "Breakaway Brands," *Fortune*, October 31, 2005, pp. 153–170. See also "DeWalt Named Breakaway Brand," *Snips*, January 2006, p. 66.

24. "Competing in the Global Brand Economy: Best Canadian Brands 2008," *Interbrand and Report on Business, Globe and Mail*, accessed at www.ourfishbowl.com/images/surveys/BestCanadianBrands2008.pdf, June 2009. See also Millward Brown Optimor, "BrandZ Top 100 Most Powerful Brands 2008," accessed at www.brandz.com/output, July 2008.

25. See Scott Davis, *Brand Asset Management*, 2nd ed. (San Francisco: Jossey-Bass, 2002). For more on brand positioning, see Philip Kotler and Kevin Lane Keller, *Marketing Management*, 13th ed. (Upper Saddle River, NJ: Prentice Hall, 2009), Chapter 10.

26. Adapted from information found in Geoff Colvin, "Selling P&G," *Fortune*, September 17, 2007, pp. 163–169; and "For P&G, Success Lies in More Than Merely a Dryer Diaper," *Advertising Age*, October 15, 2007, p. 20.

27. See Nirmalya Kumar and Jan-Benedict E. M. Steenkamp, *Private Label Strategy* (Boston, MA: Harvard Business School Press, 2007), pp. 1–12; Vanessa L. Facenda, "A Swift Kick to the Privates," *Brandweek*, September 3, 2007, pp. 24+; and Janet Groeber, "Emphasizing Quality, Price and Value, Supermarkets Say Goodbye to Generics and Hello to Proprietary Programs," *Stores*, February 2008, accessed at www.stores.org/Current_Issue/2008/02/Edit1.asp.

28. Noreen O'Leary, "New and Improved Private Label Brands," *Adweek*, October 22, 2007, pp. 16+.

29. David Friend, "Shoppers Drug Mart Looks to Private Labels," *Canadian Press*, May 7, 2009, accessed at http://money.canoe.ca/News/Other/2009/05/07/9385741-cp.html, June 2009.

30. "Dora the Explorer Takes the Lead as Sales Growth Elevates Property to Megabrand Status as Number-One Toy License in 2006," *PR Newswire*, February 8, 2007; Clint Cantwell, "$187 Billion Global Licensing Industry Comes to Life at Licensing International Expo 2008," *Business Wire*, June 6, 2008; and "Nickelodeon Expands Product Offerings and Debuts New Properties for Kids and Teens at Licensing 2008 International Show," June 10, 2008, accessed at http://biz.yahoo.com/prnews/080610/nytu056.html?.v=101.

31. Quote from www.apple.com/ipod/nike, accessed August 2008. See also "Tim Hortons to Test Cold Stone Co-Branding in Canada," *Marketing Magazine*, June 12, 2009.

32. Gabrielle Solomon, "Cobranding Alliances: Arranged Marriages Made by Marketers," *Fortune*, October 12, 1998, p. 188.

33. For more examples of good and bad brand extensions, see Kenneth Hein, "Line Extensions to Cross the Line and '07," *Brandweek*, December 10, 2007, p. 4. For more discussion on the use of line and brand extensions and consumer attitudes toward them, see Philip Kotler and Kevin Lane Keller, *Marketing Management* (Upper Saddle River, NJ: Prentice Hall, 2009), p. 262.

34. "100 Leading National Advertisers," *Advertising Age*, June 25, 2007, accessed at http://adage.com/article?article_id=118648.

35. Quotes from Stephen Cole, "Value of the Brand," *CA Magazine*, May 2005, pp. 39–40; and Lawrence A. Crosby and

Sheree L. Johnson, "Experience Required," *Marketing Management*, July/August 2007, pp. 21–27.

36. See Kevin Lane Keller, *Strategic Brand Management* (Upper Saddle River, NJ: Prentice Hall, 2008), Chapter 10.

37. "Fact Sheet," *DFAIT*, November 25, 2008, accessed at www.international.gc.ca/trade-agreements-accords-commerciaux/agr-acc/colombia-colombie/facts-fiches-services.aspx?lang=en, June 2009; "Special Feature – Service Sector," *The Economy 2009*, accessed at www.economics.gov.nl.ca/E2009/servicesector.pdf, June 2009.

38. Adapted from information in Leonard Berry and Neeli Bendapudi, "Clueing in Customers," *Harvard Business Review*, February 2003, pp. 100–106; with information accessed at www.mayoclinic.org, August 2008. See also Leonard L Berry and Kent D. Selman, "Building a Strong Services Brand: Lessons from Mayo Clinic," *Business Horizons*, May–June 2007, pp. 199–209.

39. See James L. Heskett, W. Earl Sasser Jr., and Leonard A. Schlesinger, *The Service Profit Chain: How Leading Companies Link Profit and Growth to Loyalty, Satisfaction, and Value* (New York: Free Press, 1997); Heskett, Sasser, and Schlesinger, *The Value Profit Chain: Treat Employees Like Customers and Customers Like Employees* (New York: Free Press, 2003); and John F. Milliman, Jeffrey M. Ferguson, and Andrew J. Czaplewski, "Breaking the Cycle," *Marketing Management*, March–April 2008, pp. 14–17.

40. William C. Johnson and Larry G. Chiagouris, "So Happy Together," *Marketing Management*, March–April 2006, pp. 47–50.

41. Adapted from information in Jeffrey M. O'Brien, "A Perfect Season," *Fortune*, pp. 62–66.

42. Jeffrey M. O'Brien, "A Perfect Season," *Fortune*, p. 66.

43. See "Prescription Drug Trends," *Kaiser Family Foundation*, May 2007, accessed at www.kff.org/rxdrugs/3057.cfm; and "UPS Fact Sheet," accessed at http://pressroom.ups.com/mediakits/factsheet/0,2305,866,00.html, August 2008.

44. "Air Canada Lays Out Air Service Cut Plans," CTV News, July 5, 2008, accessed at www.ctv.ca/servlet/ArticleNews/story/CTVNews/20080705/air_canada_080705?s_name=&no_ads=, June 2009; Brian Hindo, "Satisfacton Not Guaranteed," *BusinessWeek*, June 19, 2006, pp. 32–36. See also Frances X. Frei, "Breaking the Trade-Off Between Efficiency and Service," *Harvard Business Review*, November 2006, pp. 93–99.

Chapter 10

1. Quotes and other information in this Apple story from Betsy Morris, "What Makes Apple Golden?" *Fortune*, March 17, 2008, pp. 68–74; Brent Schlender, "How Big Can Apple Get?" *Fortune*, February 21, 2005, pp. 67–76; "Apple," *BusinessWeek*, March 26, 2007, p. 84; "The World's Most Innovative Companies," *BusinessWeek*, May 14, 2007, p. 55; Adam L. Penenberg, "All Eyes on Apple," *Fast Company*, December 2007/January 2008, pp. 83+; and financial reports and other information accessed at www.apple.com, April 2008.

2. Calvin Hodock, "Winning the New-Products Game," *Advertising Age*, November 12, 2007, p. 35.

3. Information and examples from Robert M. McMath and Thom Forbes, *What Were They Thinking? Money-Saving, Time-Saving, Face-Saving Marketing Lessons You Can Learn from Products That Flopped* (New York: Times Business, 1999), various pages; Beatriz Cholo, "Living with Your 'Ex': A

Brand New World," *Brandweek*, December 5, 2005, p. 4; and www.arborstrategy.com/asg/newproductworks/about-newproductworks.html, accessed October 2008.

4. "IBM Taps Into Its Workers' Bright Ideas," *Irish Times*, October 27, 2006, p. 12; and Luke Collins, "Embedding Innovation into the Firm," *Research Technology Management*, March–April, 2007, pp. 5–6.

5. John Peppers and Martha Rogers, "The Buzz on Customer-Driven Innovation," *Sales & Marketing Management*, June 2007, p. 13.

6. See Rik Kirkland, "Cisco's Display of Strength," *Fortune*, November 12, 2007, pp. 90–100; and "Cisco on Cisco: Web 2.0 in the Enterprise," accessed at www.cisco.com, September 2008.

7. Based on material from Anna Fifield, "Samsung Sows for the Future with Its Garden of Delights," *Financial Times*, January 4, 2008, p. 13; and Peter Lewis, "A Perpetual Crisis Machine," *Fortune*, September 19, 2005, pp. 58–67. See also "Camp Samsung," *BusinessWeek Online*, July 3, 2006, accessed at www.businessweek.com.

8. Example from http://ideo.com-/portfolio/re.asp?x=19009472, accessed July 2008.

9. See Chris Reidy, "100,000 Heads Are Better Than One," *Boston Globe*, August 21, 2006, p. E1; and information from www.innocentive.com, accessed April 2008.

10. Cliff Saran, "Wake Up to the Dawn of Web 2.0," *Computer Weekly*, June 5, 2007.

11. Paul Gillin, "Get Customers Involved in Innovations," *BtoB*, March 12, 2007, p. 111. See also Patricia B. Seybold, *Outside Innovation: How Your Customers Will Co-Design Your Company's Future* (New York: Collins, 2006); and Patricia B. Seybold's blog at http://outsideinnovation.blogs.com, accessed April 2007.

12. Based on quotes and information from Robert D. Hof, "The Power of Us," *BusinessWeek*, June 20, 2005, pp. 74–82. See also Robert Weisman, "Firms Turn R&D on Its Head, Looking Outside for Ideas," *Boston Globe*, May 14, 2006, p. E1.

13. "Bill Invites Customers to Share Ideas and Original Video via Dell IdeaStorm and StudioDell," February 16, 2007, accessed at www.dell.com. See also www.ideastorm.com.

14. Information accessed online at www.avon.com, August 2008.

15. Quotes from Robert Gray, "Not Invented Here," *Marketing*, May 6, 2004, pp. 34–37; and Betsy Morris, "What Makes Apple Golden?" *Fortune*, March 17, 2008, pp. 68–74.

16. See George S. Day, "Is It Real? Can We Win? Is It Worth Doing?" *Harvard Business Review*, December 2007, pp. 110–120.

17. Information for this example obtained from www.teslamotors.com, accessed April 2008; and Alan Pierce, "Seeing Beyond Gasoline Powered Vehicles," *Tech Directions*, April 2008, pp. 10–11.

18. Examples adapted from those found in Carol Matlack, "The Vuitton Machine," *BusinessWeek*, March 22, 2004, pp. 98–102; and Linda Grant, "Gillette Knows Shaving—and How to Turn Out Hot New Products," *Fortune*, October 14, 1996, pp. 207–210. See also Anna Van Pragh, "One of These Bags Cost £23,000 . . . the Other a Snip at £116. Can You Tell the Difference?" *Daily Mail* (London), March 10, 2007.

19. "KFC Fires Up Grilled Chicken," March 23, 2008, accessed at www.money.cnn.com.

20. Jack Neff, "Is Testing the Answer?" *Advertising Age*, July 9, 2001, p. 13; and Dale Buss, "P&G's Rise," *Potentials*,

January 2003, pp. 26–30. For more on test marketing, see Philip Kotler and Kevin Lane Keller, *Marketing Management*, 13th ed. (Upper Saddle River, NJ: Prentice Hall, 2008), pp. 587–590.

21. Information on BehaviorScan accessed at http://us.infores.com/page/manufacturers/market_performance/behaviorscan_testing, August 2008.

22. Example developed from information found in Allison Enright, "Best Practices: Frito-Lay Gets Real Results from a Virtual World," *Marketing News*, December 15, 2006, p. 20; and "Decision Insight: SimuShop," accessed at www.decisioninsight.com, September 2008.

23. See Steve McClellan, "Unilever's Sunsilk Launch Goes Far beyond the Box," *Adweek*, August 21–28, 2006, p. 9.

24. Melita Kuburas, "KD Cracks the Lunchbox Crowd," *Media in Canada*, May 14, 2009, accessed at www.mediaincanada.com/articles/mic/20090514/kraftdinner.html; Kraft Canada website, www.kraftcanada.com, accessed May 2009.

25. See Beth Snyder Bulik, "$500 Million for Vista? Wow," *Advertising Age*, January 29, 2007, pp. 1, 30.

26. Robert G. Cooper, "Formula for Success," *Marketing Management*, March–April 2006, pp. 19–23; and Barry Jaruzelski and Kevin Dehoff, "The Global Innovation of 1000," *Strategy + Business*, Issue 49, fourth quarter, 2007, pp. 68–83.

27. Adapted from information in Barry Jaruzelski and Kevin Dehoff, "The Global Innovation of 1000," *Strategy + Business*, Issue 49, fourth quarter, 2007, pp. 68–83.

28. Lawrence A. Crosby and Sheree L. Johnson, "Customer-Centric Innovation," *Marketing Management*, March–April 2006, pp. 12–13.

29. Teressa Iezzi, "Innovate, But Do It for Customers," *Creativity*, September 2006, pp. 8–11.

30. Portions adapted from Chuck Salter, "Google: The Faces and Voices of the World's Most Innovative Company," *Fast Company*, March 2008, pp. 74–88.

31. Youngme Moon, "Break Free from the Product Life Cycle," *Harvard Business Review*, May 2005, pp. 87–94.

32. See Constantine von Hoffman, "Glad Gives Seal of Approval to Alternate Wrap Uses," *Brandweek*, November 27, 2006, p. 10; and www.1000uses.com, accessed September 2008.

33. For a more comprehensive discussion of marketing strategies over the course of the product life cycle, see Philip Kotler and Kevin Lane Keller, *Marketing Management*, 13th ed. (Upper Saddle River, NJ: Prentice Hall, 2008), pp. 278–290.

34. Example based on information provided by Nestlé Japan Ltd., May 2008; with additional information from http://en.wikipedia.org/wiki/Kit_Kat and the Japanese Wikipedia discussion of Kit Kat at http://ja.wikipedia.org, accessed November 2008.

35. Information accessed online at www.deutsche-bank.com, July 2008.

36. Information accessed online at www.interpublic.com and www.mccann.com, August 2008.

37. See "2007 Global Powers of Retailing," *Stores*, January 2007, accessed at www.stores.org; "Wal-Mart International Operations," accessed at www.walmartstores.com, April 2008; and information accessed at www.carrefour.com/english/groupecarrefour/profil.jsp, July 2008.

Chapter 11

1. Quotes and other information from Beth Snyder Bulik, "Kodak Develops New Model: Inexpensive Printer, Cheap Ink," *Advertising Age*, March 12, 2007, p. 4; Clive Akass, "Kodak Inkjets Shake Industry," *Personal Computer World*, April 2007, accessed at www.pcw.co.uk/personal-computer-world/news/2174253/kodak-halves-cost-photo-prints; David Pogue, "Paying More for a Printer but Less for Ink," *New York Times*, May 17, 2007, p. C1; Stephen H. Wildstrom, "Kodak Moments for Less," *BusinessWeek*, May 14, 2007, p. 24; William M. Bulkeley, "Kodak's Strategy for First Printer—Cheaper Cartridges," *Wall Street Journal*, February 6, 2007, p. B1; Keith J. Winstein, "Kodak Forecasts Increase in Revenue, Pinning Optimism on Inkjet Printers," *Wall Street Journal*, February 8, 2008, p. B4; "Consumer Launch Campaign of the Year 2008," *PRweek*, March 10, 2008, p. S11; and www.kodak.com, accessed September 2008.

2. George Mannes, "The Urge to Unbundle," *Fast Company*, February 27, 2005, pp. 23–24. See also Stuart Elliott, "Creative Spots, Courtesy of a Stalled Economy," *New York Times*, April 11, 2008.

3. Linda Tischler, "The Price Is Right," *Fast Company*, November 2003, pp. 83–91. See also Elizabeth A. Sullivan, "Value Pricing: Smart Marketers Know Cost-Plus Can Be Costly," January 15, 2008, p. 8.

4. For more on the importance of sound pricing strategy, see Thomas T. Nagle and John Hogan, *The Strategy and Tactics of Pricing: A Guide to Growing More Profitably* (Upper Saddle River, NJ: Prentice Hall, 2007), Chapter 1.

5. John Tayman, "The Six-Figure Steal," *Business 2.0*, June 2005, pp. 148–150; and 2008 Bentley Continental GT Speed, Wheels.ca, September 16, 2007, accessed at www.wheels.ca/article/31407, July 2009.

6. These and other examples are from Stuart Elliott, "Creative Spots, Courtesy of a Stalled Economy," *New York Times*, April 11, 2008; and www.vw.com/rabbit/en/us/#, accessed April 2008.

7. Example adapted from Anupam Mukerji, "Monsoon Marketing," *Fast Company*, April 2007, p. 22.

8. Elizabeth A. Sullivan, "Value Pricing: Smart Marketers Know Cost-Plus Can Be Costly," *Marketing News*, January 15, 2008, p. 8. See also Venkatesh Bala and Jason Green, "Charge What Your Products Are Worth," *Harvard Business Review*, September 2007, p. 22.

9. Here, accumulated production is drawn on a semilog scale so that equal distances represent the same percentage increase in output.

10. The arithmetic of markups and margins is discussed in Appendix 3: Marketing by the Numbers.

11. Joshua Rosenbaum, "Guitar Maker Looks for a New Key," *Wall Street Journal*, February 11, 1998, p. B1; and information accessed at www.gibson.com, September 2008.

12. See Thomas T. Nagle and John Hogan, *The Strategy and Tactics of Pricing: A Guide to Growing More Profitably* (Upper Saddle River, NJ: Prentice Hall, 2007), Chapter 7.

13. Andrew Willis, "My $36,000 Ferrari," *Globe and Mail*, November 5, 2007.

14. "Sleeman Hurt by Price War," *Marketing Magazine*, August 11, 2005; "Sleeman to Increase Marketing for Low-Price Brands," *Marketing Magazine*, October 31, 2005; and Sarah Dobson, "Sleeman Stays True to Premium Roots," *Marketing Magazine*, November 7, 2005.

15. See Robert J. Dolan, "Pricing: A Value-Based Approach," *Harvard Business School Publishing*, 9-500-071, November 3, 2003.

16. See Philip Kotler and Kevin Lane Keller, *Marketing Management*, 13th ed. (Upper Saddle River, NJ: Prentice Hall, 2008), pp. 383–384; and Chris Tribbey, "HDTV Prices Projected to Drop 15% in 2008," *Home Media Magazine*, January 20–January 26, 2008, p. 10.

17. Adapted from information found in Mei Fong, "IKEA Hits Home in China; The Swedish Design Giant, Unlike Other Retailers, Slashes Prices for the Chinese," *Wall Street Journal*, March 3, 2006, p. B1; and "IKEA to Open Three Stores in China in 2008," *Sinolcast China Business Daily News*, August 31, 2007, p. 1.

18. Information from "Pollution Prevention Success Stories: MacTara Limited," Environment Canada, accessed at www.atl.ec.gc.ca/epb/pollprev/mactara.html, July 2009; "MacTara Jobs May Be Safe After Deal with Creditors," CBC News, March 11, 2008, accessed at www.cbc.ca/canada/nova-scotia/story/2008/03/11/lumber-yard.html, July 2009; and Monique Chiasson, "Deal in the works for MacTara," *Truro Daily News*, March 13, 2008, accessed at www.atlanticfarmfocus.ca/index.cfm?sid=124503&sc=586, July 2009.

19. See Thomas T. Nagle and John Hogan, *The Strategy and Tactics of Pricing: A Guide to Growing More Profitably* (Upper Saddle River, NJ: Prentice Hall, 2007), pp. 244–247; Bram Foubert and Els Gijsbrechts, "Shopper Response to Bundle Promotions for Packaged Goods," *Journal of Marketing Research*, November 2007, pp. 647–662; Roger M. Heeler et al., "Bundles = Discount? Revisiting Complex Theories of Bundle Effects," *Journal of Product & Brand Management*, vol. 16, no. 7, 2007, pp. 492–500; and Timothy J. Gilbride et al, "Framing Effects in Mixed Price Bundling," *Marketing Letters*, June 2008, pp. 125–140.

20. See "Air Canada Company Description," Hoovers, www.hoovers.com/air-canada/—ID__157623—/free-co-profile.xhtml, accessed July 2009.

21. Based on information from Eric Anderson and Duncan Simester, "Mind Your Pricing Cues," *Harvard Business Review*, September 2003, pp. 96–103. See also Heyong Min Kim and Luke Kachersky, "Dimensions of Price Salience: A Conceptual Framework for Perceptions of Multi-Dimensional Prices," *Journal of Product & Brand Management*, 2006, vol. 15, no. 2, pp. 139–147; and Monika Kukar-Kinney et al, "Consumer Responses to Characteristics of Price-Matching Guarantees," *Journal of Retailing*, April 2007, p. 211.

22. For more discussion, see Manoj Thomas and Vicki Morvitz, "Penny Wise and Pound Foolish: The Double-Digit Effect in Price Cognition," *Journal of Consumer Research*, June 2005, pp. 54–64; Alex Mindlin, "For a Memorable Price, Trim Syllables," *New York Times*, August 14, 2006, accessed at www.nytimes.com; Christine Harris and Jeffery Bray, "Price Endings and Consumer Segmentation," *Journal of Product & Brand Management* vol. 16, no. 3, 2007, pp. 200–205; Wilson Rothman, "The Weird Science of Pricing" *Money*, April 2007, p. 127; and Keith S. Coulter and Robin A. Coulter, "Distortion of Price Discount Perceptions: The Right Digit of Fact," *Journal of Consumer Research*, August 2007, pp. 162–171.

23. Karyn McCormack, "Price War Leaves AMD Reeling," *BusinessWeek Online*, January 25, 2007, p. 4; and Chris Nuttall, "AMD Suffers Further Losses Amid Price War with Rival Intel," *Financial Times*, October 19, 2007, p. 18.

24. Example adapted from Louise Story, "Online Pitches Made Just for You," *New York Times*, March 6, 2008.

25. Based on information found in Bruce Einhorn, "Grudge Match in China," *BusinessWeek*, April 2, 2007, pp. 42–43; "Struggling Dell Enters Partnership," ChinaDaily.com.cn, September 25, 2007; and "Dell Continues to Expand Retail Presence in China," *Business Wire*, April 17, 2008.

26. Brent Jang, "Air Canada Off Bottle," *Globe and Mail*, April 20, 2006.

27. Example adapted from information found in Ellen Byron, "Fashion Victim: To Refurbish Its Image, Tiffany Risks Profits," *Wall Street Journal*, January 10, 2007, p. A1; and Aliza Rosenbaum and John Christy, "Financial Insight: Tiffany's Boutique Risk: By Breaking Mall Fast, High-End Exclusivity May Gain Touch of Common," *Wall Street Journal*, October 20, 2007, p. B14.

28. Jack Neff, "Viva Viva! K-C Boosts Brand's Marketing," *Advertising Age*, June 11, 2007, p. 4.

29. See the *Competition Act*, Sections 34–38, accessed at http://laws.justice.gc.ca/en/C-34.

30. For discussions of these issues, see Dhruv Grewel and Larry D. Compeau, "Pricing and Public Policy: A Research Agenda and Overview of Special Issues," *Journal of Public Policy and Marketing*, Spring 1999, pp. 3–10; and Michael V. Marn, Eric V. Roegner, and Craig C. Zawada, *The Price Advantage* (Hoboken, NJ: John Wiley & Sons, 2004), Appendix 2.

31. Jim Middlemiss, "Don't Get Caught Offside in Rule Changes," *Financial Post*, March 23, 2009.

32. Julie Jargon, "Retailers' Lawsuits Accuse Candy Makers of Fixing Prices," *Wall Street Journal*, April 1, 2008, p. B3; "Germany Raids Offices of Candy Makers," *Wall Street Journal*, February 12, 2008, p. A15; and Alia McMullen, "Chocolate Giants Sued for Collusion," *Financial Post*, February 19, 2008, p. FP1.

33. N. Craig Smith and John A. Quelch, *Ethics in Marketing* (Boston: Irwin, 1993), pp. 389–404.

Chapter 12

1. The "e" logo, Enterprise, and "We'll Pick You Up" are registered trademarks of Enterprise Rent-A-Car Company. Quotations and other information from "Enter Enterprise," *Business Travel News*, April 23, 2007; Carol J. Loomis, "The Big Surprise Is Enterprise," *Fortune*, July 24, 2006, p. 140; Carol J. Loomis, "Enterprise Pulls Up at the Airport," *Fortune*, July 23, 2007, p. 50; Darren Everson, "Car-Rental Companies Learn to Share," *Wall Street Journal*, February 7, 2008, p. D1; and www.hertz.com and http://aboutus.enterprise.com/press_room/fact_sheets.html, accessed October 2008.

2. Grand & Toy's website, www.grandandtoy.com, and a Canadian NewsWire press release at www.newswire.ca/en/releases/archive/October2009/28/c3443.html.

3. See "No Time to Rest for Goodyear," *Tire Business*, February 13, 2006, p. 8; Kevin Kelleher, "Giving Dealers a Raw Deal," *Business 2.0*, December 2004, pp. 82–84; Jim MacKinnon, "Goodyear Tire & Rubber Company," *Knight Ridder Tribune Business News*, April 8, 2007, p. 1; and Jim MacKinnon, "Goodyear Boasts of Bright Future," *McClatchy-Tribune Business News*, April 9, 2008.

4. Information accessed at www.kroger.com, www.safeway.com, and www.luxottica.com/english/profilo_aziendale/index_keyfacts.html, October 2008.

5. Adapted from information found in Kerry Capell, "Fashion Conquistador," *BusinessWeek*, September 4, 2006, pp. 38–39; Miguel Helft, "Fashion Fast Forward," *Business 2.0*, May 2002, p. 60; Kasra Ferdows, Michael A. Lewis, and Jose A. D. Machuca, "Rapid-Fire Fulfillment," *Harvard Business Review*, November 2004, pp. 104–110; Cecilie Rohwedder and Keith Johnson, "Pace-Setting Zara Seeks More Speed to Fight Its Rising Cheap-Chic Rivals," *Wall Street Journal*, February 20, 2008, p. B1; and the Inditext Press Kit, accessed at www.inditex.com/en/press/information/press_kit, October 2008.

6. Information from Industry Canada's franchising website, www.strategis.ic.gc.ca/ SSG/dm01179e.html, accessed August 2003; "Answers to the 21 Most Commonly Asked Questions about Franchising," International Franchise Association website, www.franchise.org, accessed July 2002; Canadian Franchise Directory, www.franchisedirectory.ca, accessed May 2006; and Canadian Franchise Association website, www.cfa.ca, accessed June 2009. Franchising facts from www.franchise.org/content.asp?contentid=379 and www.azfranchises.com/franchisefacts.htm, accessed July 2008.

7. Tony Martin, "Love Thy Franchisees," *Profit*, May 2008, p. 62; and information accessed at www.nursenextdoor.com, June 2009.

8. See Melinda Liu, "Just Beware of the White Lightning: Car Culture Is Booming in China," *Newsweek*, November 19, 2007, p. E24; and http://english.sinopec.com/about_sinopec/our_business/refining_selling/, accessed July 2008.

9. See Paolo Del Nibletto, "Dell Stuck in the Middle," *Computer Dealer News*, March 21, 2008, p. 12.

10. Quotes and information from Normandy Madden, "Two Chinas," *Advertising Age*, August 16, 2004, pp. 1, 22; Russell Flannery, "China: The Slow Boat," *Forbes*, April 12, 2004, p. 76; Jeff Berman, "U.S. Providers Say Logistics in China on the Right Track," *Logistics Management*, March 2007, p. 22; and Jamie Bolton, "China: The Infrastructure Imperative," *Logistics Management*, July 2007, p. 63.

11. Nanette Byrnes, "Avon Calls. China Opens the Door," *BusinessWeek Online*, February 28, 2006, p. 19; Mei Fong, "Avon's Calling, but China Opens Door Only a Crack," *Wall Street Journal*, February 26, 2007, p. B1; "Direct-Selling Giants to Dig Chinese Market," *SinoCast China Business Daily News*, August 3, 2007, p. 1; and "Cosmetic Changes in China Market," www.chinadaily.com.cn, October 11, 2007.

12. Jennifer Wells, "We Can Get It for You Wholesale," *Report on Business Magazine*, March 1995, pp. 52–62.

13. See Steven Burke, "Samsung Launches Revamped Partner Program." *CRN*, February 12, 2007, accessed at www.crn.com/it-channel/197005419; and "Program Details: Samsung Electronics America, IT Division," *VAR Business 2007 Partner Programs Guide*, accessed at www.crn.com/var/apps/2007/ppg/ppg_details.jhtml?c=54, July 2007.

14. Information from the Canadian Marketing Association website, www.thecma.org/PublicUploads/225849CodeofEthics08.pdf; and the American Marketing Association website, www.marketingpower.com, accessed June 2009.

15. Ari Natter, "Freight Costs Rising," *Traffic World*, April 14, 2008; Neil Shister, "Redesigned Supply Chain Positions Ford for Global Competition," *World Trade*, May 2005, pp. 20–26; and supply chain facts from www.cscmp.org/Website/AboutCSCMP/Media/FastFacts.asp, accessed July 2008.

16. Shlomo Maital, "The Last Frontier of Cost Reduction," *Across the Board*, February 1994, pp. 51–52; and information accessed at www.walmartstores.com, October 2008.

17. William Hoffman, "Supplying Sustainability," *Traffic World*, April 7, 2008.

18. "Wal-Mart Canada Plans Massive Grocery Distribution Centre in Balzac, Alberta," *Canadian Press*, May 12, 2009; Gail Braccidiferro, "One Town's Rejection Is Another's 'Let's Do Business,'" *New York Times*, June 15, 2003, p. 2; Dan Scheraga, "Wal-Smart," *Chain Store Age*, January 2006 supplement, pp. 16A–21A; and facts from www.walmart.ca, accessed June 2009.

19. Example adapted from Evan West, "These Robots Play Fetch," *Fast Company*, July/August 2007, pp. 49–50.

20. See "A Worldwide Look at RFID," *Supply Chain Management Review*, April 2007, pp. 48–55; Owen Davis, "Time to Roll with RFID," *Supply & Demand Chain Executive*, February–March 2007, p. 56; and "Wal-Mart Says Use RFID Tags or Pay Up," *Logistics Today*, March 2008, p. 4.

21. See Laurie Sullivan, "Hey, Wal-Mart, A New Case of Pampers Is on the Way," *InformationWeek*, January 23, 2006, p. 28; "Collaborative Supply Chain Practices and Evolving Technological Approaches," *Supply Chain Management*, May 2007, pp. 210–220; and Yuliang Yao and Martin Dresner, "The Inventory Value of Information Sharing, Continuous Replenishment, and Vendor-Managed Inventory," *Transportation Research*, May 2008, p. 361+.

22. See "The 2007 Supply & Demand Chain Executive 100," *Supply & Demand Chain Executive*, May 2007, accessed at www.sdcexec.com/print/Supply-and-Demand-Chain-Executive/2007-Supply-and-Demand-Chain-Executive-100/1$9672; and David Blanchard, "Sterling Commerce Shifts from EDI to the Supply Chain," *Supply Chain and Logistics*, December 2007, p. 50.

Chapter 13

1. Quotes and other information from "Costco's Louise Wendling Named 2009 Distinguished Canadian Retailer of the Year by the Retail Council of Canada," Press Release, *Canada NewsWire*, May 21, 2009; "Walmart Canada to Close Sam's Club Stores," CBC News, February 27, 2009, accessed at www.cbc.ca/money/story/2009/02/27/walmart-samsclub.html, June 2009; Lesley Chesterman, "Costco Chic?" *Montreal Gazette*, February 23, 2008, accessed at http://global.factiva.com.ezproxy.library.dal.ca/ha/default.aspx, June 2009; "Costco vs. Sam's Club," *Consumer Reports*, May 2007, pp. 16–19; Matthew Boyle, "Why Costco Is So Addictive," *Fortune*, October 25, 2006, pp. 126–132; Anthony Bianco, "Wal-Mart's Midlife Crisis," *BusinessWeek*, April 30, 2007, pp. 46–55; John Helyar, "The Only Company Wal-Mart Fears," *Fortune*, November 24, 2003, pp. 158–166; Reena Jana, "The Revenge of the Generic," *BusinessWeek*, December 27, 2006, accessed at www.businessweek.com/innovate/content/dec2006/id20061227_049239.htm; Pat Regnief, "Hunting Big Savings at Costco," *Money*, June 22, 2006; Andrew Bary, "Everybody's Store," *Barron's*, February 12, 2007, pp. 29–32; Merrill Markoe, "Life Lessons: Love for Sale?" *Real Simple*, January 2008, pp. 52–57; and information from www.costco.com, accessed November 2008.

2. Quotes from "Ogilvy Gets Activated," *MediaPost Publications*, January 8, 2007, accessed at http://publications.mediapost.com/index.cfm?fuseaction=Articles.showArticle&art_aid=53477; and "OgilvyAction Takes Regional Marketers to the Last Mile," January 23, 2008, accessed at www.entrepreneur.com/tradejournals/article/173710015.html. Retail sales statistics from "Annual Revision of Monthly Retail and Food Services: Sales and Inventories—January 1992–2007," U.S. Census Bureau,

March 2007, p. 3; and www.census.gov/mrts/www/mrts.html, accessed May 2008.

3. For more on shopper marketing, see Grocery Manufacturers Association and Deloitte Consulting, *Shopper Marketing: Capturing a Shopper's Mind, Heart, and Wallet*, 2007; Jack Neff, "What's in Store: The Rise of Shopper Marketing," *Advertising Age*, October 1, 2007, pp. 1, 42; and Bob Holston, "Avoid Shopper Marketing Pitfalls," *Advertising Age*, March 31, 2008, pp. 20–21.

4. Dana Flavelle, "Bonnie Brooks: Homecoming Queen," TheStar.com, June 7, 2009, accessed at www.thestar.com/news/insight/article/646819, July 2009; Marina Strauss, "The Pragmatic Fashionista: With a Focus on Newer Labels and Price, Bonnie Brooks Has Big Plans for the Bay," *Globe and Mail*, April 23, 2009, p. B1.

5. Jo-Ann Heslin, "Supermarkets—Are They on the Endangered Species List?" HealthNewsDigest.com, March 30, 2008, accessed at www.healthnewsdigest.com/news/Food_and_Nutrition_690/Supermarkets_—_Are_They_On_The_Endangered_Species_List.shtml.

6. Blanca Torres, "4th Quarter Profit Soars at Safeway," *Knight Ridder Tribune Business News*, February 23, 2007, p. 1; Justin Hibbard, "Put Your Money Where Your Mouth Is," *BusinessWeek*, September 18, 2007, pp. 61–63; and "Safeway Feels Impact of Generics," *Drug Store News*, March 3, 2008, pp. 4+.

7. "Loblaw Companies Ltd—Loblaw Encourages Customers to 'Buy Big and Save Big' with Club Pack® Items," *Market News Publishing*, May 21, 2009, accessed at http://global.factiva.com.ezproxy.library.dal.ca/ha/default.aspx, July 2009; Marina Strauss, "Loblaw Targets Better Days with More Staff," *Globe and Mail*, May 1, 2008.

8. Hugh Large, "Surviving in a Changing Convenience Market," ConvenienceStores.ca, accessed at www.conveniencestores.ca/index.php?option=com_content&task=view&id=136&Itemid=2, July 2009; "State of the Industry Report," Press Release, Canadian Convenience Stores Association, April 7, 2009; and "Convenience Store Industry Sales Top $569 Billion, NACS Reports," April 11, 2007, accessed at www.nacsonline.com.

9. Statistics based on information from "SN Top 75 2007," http://supermarketnews.com/profiles/top75, accessed June 2008; http://walmartstores.com/FactsNews/NewsRoom/6852.aspx, accessed June 2008; and "Industry Overview: Grocery Stores and Supermarkets," Hoover's Company Records, accessed at www.hoovers.com/grocery-stores-and-supermarkets/—ID__84—/free-ind-fr-profile-basic.xhtml, June 2008.

10. Elizabeth Woyke, "Buffett, the Wal-Mart Shopper," *BusinessWeek*, May 14, 2007, pp. 66–67.

11. Marina Strauss, "H&M's Next Move: Taking It to the Streets," *Globe and Mail*, May 23, 2009, B3; information from H&M Canada's website, www.hm.com/ca#/startns/, accessed July 2009.

12. See Talbot Boggs, "Would You Like Franchise with That?" *Canadian Retailer*, January–February 2007, www.retailcouncil.org/storeops/crarticles/crjanfeb07_franchisewiththat.pdf, accessed July 2009. Company information from www.mcdonalds.com/corp.html and www.subway.com/subwayroot/AboutSubway/index.aspx, September 2008.

13. Quotes from "Sears Rethinks Amidst Revenue Decline," *Brandweek*, March 17, 2008, p. 12; and Natalie Zmuda, "Sears Wants to Dust off Brand," *Advertising Age*, April 7, 2008, p. 8.

14. The Whole Foods example is based on quotes and information from Diane Brady, "Eating Too Fast at Whole Foods," *BusinessWeek*, October 24, 2005, pp. 82–84; Kim Wright Wiley, "Think Organic," *Sales & Marketing Management*, January–February 2007, pp. 54–59; "Whole Food Market, Inc.," *Hoover's Company Records*, May 1, 2008, p. 10952, p.1; and www.wholefoods.com, accessed September 2008.

15. Erdem Tulin, Ying Zhao, and Ana Valenzuela, "Performance of Store Brands: A Cross-Country Analysis of Consumer Store-Brand Preferences, Perceptions, and Risk," *Journal of Marketing Research*, 41(1), February 2004, pp. 86-100.

16. Adapted from information found in Katie Hafner, "Inside Apple Stores, a Certain Aura Enchants the Faithful," *New York Times*, December 27, 2007.

17. Information from www.harryrosen.com, accessed July 2009.

18. For definitions of these and other types of shopping centres, see *Dictionary of Marketing Terms*, American Marketing Association, accessed at www.marketingpower.com/mg-dictionary.php, September 2007.

19. Angela Kryhul, "Malls Get the 'Destination' Makeover," *Globe and Mail*, December 23, 2008, accessed at www.ellisdon.com/locations/toronto/toronto-news/?i=146, July 2009; Ryan Chittum, "Mall-Building Industry Takes Stock," *Wall Street Journal*, May 17, 2006, p. B7; Kelsey Volkmann, "Business Malls Evolving to Imitate Traditional Downtowns," *Associated Press*, January 31, 2007, p. 1; the International Council of Shopping Centers, "U.S. Mall Report," April 2007, accessed at www.icsc.org; and "Birth, Death, and Shopping," *The Economist*, December 22, 2007.

20. Information from Bayers Lake website, www.bayerslakepark.com, accessed July 2009; Dean Starkman, "The Mall, Without the Haul—'Lifestyle Centers' Slip Quietly into Upscale Areas, Mixing Cachet and 'Curb Appeal,'" *Wall Street Journal*, July 25, 2001, p. B1; Paul Grimaldi, "Shopping for a New Look: Lifestyle Centers Are Replacing Enclosed Malls," *Providence Journal (Rhode Island)*, April 29, 2007, p. F10; and Laura Klepacki, "Open-Air Shopping with the Works," *Chain Store Age*, March 2008, pp. 136+.

21. "Canadian Retail Trends for 2007," 2007 Global Powers of Retailing, Deloitte & Touche LLP (Canada), accessed at www.deloitte.com/dtt/article/0,1002,cid=150861,00.html, July 2009.

22. George J. Heller, "The Changing Canadian Retail Landscape," Speech published in *The Empire Club of Canada Speeches 2001–2002*, Edited by Edward P. Badovinac (Toronto: The Empire Club Foundation, 2002) pp. 527–539.

23. Mylene Mangalindan, "Surge Seen in U.S. Online Sales," *Globe and Mail*, April 8, 2008, p. B11; "E-commerce: Shopping on the Internet," *The Daily*, November 17, 2008.

24. Dana Flavelle, "Traditional Retailers Clicking on the Internet," TheStar.com, July 4, 2009, accessed at www.thestar.com/business/article/660774, July 2009; Nanette Byrnes, "More Clicks at the Bricks," *BusinessWeek*, December 17, 2007, pp. 50–51.

25. "Facts about America's Top 500 E-Retailers," Internet Retailer, accessed at www.internetretailer.com/top500/facts.asp, April 2008.

26. Information from London Drugs' website, www.londondrugs.com, accessed July 2009; Eve Lazarus, "London Drugs Puts Spa Right In Store," *Marketing Magazine*, November 18, 2005, accessed at www.marketingmag.ca/magazine/marketingdaily/article.jsp?content=20051120_170033_11348;

27. Sara Minoque, "Blurring the Boundaries," *Strategy Magazine*, June 30, 2003, p. 13.

27. "2007 Global Powers of Retailing," Deloitte & Touche LLP (Canada), accessed at www.deloitte.com/dtt/article/0,1002,cid=150861,00.html, July 2009.

28. See "The Fortune 500," *Fortune*, May 5, 2008, p. F1.

29. "The Canadian Retail Technology Survey: Summary," Industry Canada, accessed at www.retailinteractive.ca/SSG/ri00920e.html#shift, July 2009.

30. See "2008 Global Powers of Retailing," *Stores*, January 2008, accessed at www.nxtbook.com/nxtbooks/nrfe/stores-globalretail08.

31. "Top 250 Global Retailers," *Stores*, January 2008, accessed at www.nxtbook.com/nxtbooks/nrfe/stores-globalretail08; and information from www.walmartstores.com and www.carrefour.com, accessed April 2008.

32. Virtual Museum of Canada website, www.museevirtuel-virtualmuseum.ca/index-eng.jsp, accessed July 2009.

33. See www.acklandsgrainger.com, accessed July 2009; the *Grainger 2008 Fact Book* and other information accessed at www.grainger.com, September 2008.

34. See Dale Buss, "The New Deal," *Sales & Marketing Management*, June 2002, pp. 25–30; Colleen Gourley, "Redefining Distribution," *Warehousing Management*, October 2000, pp. 28–30; Steve Konicki and Eileen Colkin, "Attitude Adjustment," *InformationWeek*, March 25, 2002, pp. 20–22; Stewart Scharf, "Grainger: Tooled Up for Growth," *BusinessWeek Online*, April 25, 2006, p. 8; and John Nank, "W. W. Grainger Inc.: Industrial Strength," *Smart Business Chicago*, September 2007, p. 14.

35. Information from "About Us" and "Supply Management Online," accessed at www.mckesson.com, October 2008.

36. Facts accessed at www.supervalu.com, October 2008.

37. See www.mckesson.com/static_files/McKesson.com/CorpIR/PDF_Documents/2007%20Form%2010-K%20BM.pdf, p. 101, accessed October 2008.

38. Information sourced from Carole Pearson, "Grocery Slotting Fees Deprive Consumers and Manufacturers of Shelf-Respect," *Straight Goods*, March 19, 2009, accessed at www.straightgoods.com/item428.shtml, July 2009.

Chapter 14

1. Portions adapted from Jack Neff, "Digital Marketer of the Year: Unilever," *Advertising Age*, March 17, 2008, p. 50. See also Jack Neff, "K-C, Unilever Turn Down TV to Ramp Up ROI," *Advertising Age*, February 25, 2008, p. 1; and Stephanie Kang, "Media & Marketing: Hellmann's Spreads Message with Flay," *Wall Street Journal*, May 23, 2008, p. B9.

2. The first four of these definitions are adapted from Peter D. Bennett, *The AMA Dictionary of Marketing Terms*, 2nd ed. (New York: McGraw-Hill, 1995). Other definitions can be found at www.marketingpower.com/_layouts/Dictionary.aspx, accessed December 2008.

3. Bob Garfield, "The Chaos Scenario," *Advertising Age*, April 4, 2005, pp. 1, 57+; and Garfield, "The Chaos Scenario 2.0: The Post-Advertising Age," *Advertising Age*, March 26, 2007, pp. 1, 12–13.

4. Chase Squires and Dave Gussow, "The Ways in Which We Watch TV Are Changing Right Before Our Eyes,"

St. Petersburg Times, April 27, 2006; and Geoff Colvin, "TV Is Dying? Long Live TV!" *Fortune*, February 5, 2007, p. 43.

5. Bob Garfield, "The Chaos Scenario 2.0: The Post-Advertising Age," *Advertising Age*, March 26, 2007, pp. 1, 12–13.

6. Brian Steinberg and Suzanne Vranica, "As 30-Second Spot Fades, What Will Advertisers Do Next?" *Wall Street Journal*, January 3, 2006, p. A15; Warren Berger, "A Hard Sell," *Business 2.0*, May 2007, pp. 91–96; and Megan McIlroy, "Serving Other Media with TV Ups Appetite for Products," *Advertising Age*, June 2, 2008, accessed at http://adage.com/print?article_id127454.

7. TV advertising stats from Lisa Snedeker, "Ad Spending Goes Limp as 2007 Ends," *Media Life*, March 28, 2008, accessed at www.medialifemagazine.com/artman2/publish/Media_economy_57/Ad_spending_goes_limp_as_2007_ends.asp; quotes from Mike Shaw, "Direct Your Advertising Dollars Away from TV at Your Own Risk," *Advertising Age*, February 27, 2006, p. 29; and Bob Liodice, "TV Makes Strides While Marketers Experiment Widely," *Advertising Age*, March 24, 2008, pp. 16–17.

8. Adam Armbruster, "TV Central in Mixology of Multimedia," *TelevisionWeek*, March 3–March 10, 2008, p. 30; and Bob Liodice, "TV Makes Strides While Marketers Experiment Widely," *Advertising Age*, March 24, 2008, pp. 16–17.

9. Bob Garfield, "Lee Chow on What's Changed Since '1984,'" *Advertising Age*, June 11, 2007, p. 3.

10. Dan Hill, "CMOs, Win Big by Letting Emotions Drive Advertising," *Advertising Age*, August 27, 2007, p. 12.

11. "Brand Design: Cracking the Colour Code," *Marketing Week*, October 11, 2007, p. 28.

12. Jonah Bloom, "The Truth Is: Consumers Trust Fellow Buyers Before Marketers," *Advertising Age*, February 13, 2006, p. 25.

13. Linda Tischler, "What's the Buzz?" *Fast Company*, May 2004, p. 76; Matthew Creamer, "BzzAgent Seeks to Turn Word of Mouth into a Saleable Medium," *Advertising Age*, February 2006, p. 12; Lisa van der Pool, "Word of Mouth Marketing Takes Off," *Boston Business Journal*, November 24, 2007; "BzzAgent Reaches 34M Consumers," *Boston Business Journal*, December 17, 2007; and www.bzzagent.com, accessed October 2008.

14. See Mark Evans, "Can Cindy Klassen Save Manitoba Tel?" February 28, 2007, accessed at http://evans.blogware.com/blog/_archives/2006/2/28/1788317.html, April 2006; *Canadian Press*, "Olympic Hero Cindy Klassen Returns Home to Winnipeg," March 28, 2006, accessed at www.canada.com/globaltv/manitoba/story.html?id=1cdae7b5-5911-4abb-9b2b-877dfcd86d5e, April 2006; Paul Coro, "Nash Signs to Endorse Watches for His Charity," *The Arizona Republic*, February 19, 2007; and Joanna Pachner, "The Making of Mike Holmes," *Globe and Mail Report on Business*, June 3, 2009. See also Kate Fitzgerald, "Women's Golf Extends Its Footprint," *Advertising Age*, January 29, 2007, p. S4; Tim Arango, "Lebron, Inc.," *Fortune*, December 10, 2007, pp. 100–108; and "Athletes Help Brands Win Big," *Marketing News*, March 15, 2008, p. 17.

15. Andy Hoffman and Grand Robertson, "Beer Ad's Angry Scot Faces Porn Charges," *Globe and Mail*, February 16, 2006; and Oliver Moore, "Beer Icon's the Buzz of Bars," *Globe and Mail*, February 17, 2006.

16. Eugenia Levenson, "When Celebrity Endorsements Attack," *Fortune*, October 17, 2005, p. 42; Charlie Gillis, "Thee Shill of Victory," *Maclean's*, February 27, 2006, p. 40; and Cathy Yingling, "Beware the Lure of Celebrity Endorsers," *Advertising Age*, September 24, 2008, p. 19.

17. For more on advertising spending by company and industry, see http://adage.com/datacenter/datapopup.php?article_id=119881, accessed September 2008.

18. For more on setting promotion budgets, see W. Ronald Lane, Karen Whitehill King, and J. Thomas Russell, *Kleppner's Advertising Procedure*, 17th ed. (Upper Saddle River, NJ: Prentice Hall, 2008), Chapter 6.

19. Canadian Media Directors Council, *2008–2009 Media Digest*, p. 17; Brian Steinberg, "Super Bowl Busts Ratings Record on 'The Greatest Day Ever' for Fox," *Advertising Age*, February 11, 2008, p. 21; Jeff Klein, "Cup Finale on NBC Was Most Watched NHL Game in 36 Years," *The New York Times*, June 18, 2009; Sergio Ibarra, "Weekly Prime-Time Ratings—Week of Feb. 18–Feb. 24," *Television Week*, March 3, 2008, p. 34; "2.62 Million Watch American Idol Season 8 Finale," *Canada Channel*, May 23, 2009, accessed at www.channelcanada.com/article2957.html; Lisa de Moraes, "'Idol' Takes a Ratings Dip—Albeit a Slight One—in Season Opener," *Washington Post*, January 17, 2008, p. C7; and "American Idol Season 8 NOT the Lowest Rating," *Aceshowbiz*, May 22, 2009, accessed at www.aceshowbiz.com/news/view/00024452.html.

20. Roy Chitwood, "Making the Most out of Each Outside Sales Call," February 4, 2005, accessed at http://seattle.bizjournals.com/seattle/stories/2005/02/07/smallb3.html; and "The Cost of the Average Sales Call Today Is More Than $400," *Business Wire*, February 28, 2006.

21. Based on Matthew P. Gonring, "Putting Integrated Marketing Communications to Work Today," *Public Relations Quarterly*, Fall 1994, pp. 45–48. See also Philip Kotler and Kevin Lane Keller, *Marketing Management*, 13th ed. (Upper Saddle River, NJ: Prentice Hall, 2009), pp. 491–493.

22. For more on the legal aspects of promotion, see W. Ronald Lane, Karen Whitehill King, and J. Thomas Russell, *Kleppner's Advertising Procedure*, 17th ed. (Upper Saddle River, NJ: Prentice Hall, 2008), Chapter 25; and William L. Cron and Thomas E. DeCarlo, *Dalrymple's Sales Management*, 9th ed. (New York: Wiley, 2006), Chapter 10.

Chapter 15

1. Adapted from CASSIES 2005 Cases, "United Way: The Hand Campaign," accessed at www.cassies.ca/caselibrary, May 2006; Paul-Mark Rendon, "United Way Advertising Focuses on Long-Term Goals," *Marketing Daily*, September 30, 2005, accessed at www.marketingmag.ca; Annette Bourdeau, "Outstanding New Campaigns," *Strategy Magazine*, October 2005, p. 22; John Burghardt, "United Way Deserves an Exaggerated Hand," *Strategy Magazine*, December 1, 2003, p. 15; David Brown, "Publicis Sees the United Way," *Marketing*, June 11, 2007, p. 12; and information accessed at www.unitedwaytoronto.com.

2. Data on global advertising spending accessed at http://adage.com/datacenter/#top_marketers;_adspend_stats, September 2008; and Canadian Media Directors Council, 2008–2009 Media Digest, accessed at www.cmdc.ca/pfd/2008_09_Media_Digest.pdf, June 2009.

3. For more on advertising budgets, see Ronald Lane, Karen King, and Thomas Russell, *Kleppner's Advertising Procedure*, 17th ed. (Upper Saddle River, NJ: Prentice Hall, 2008), Chapter 6.

4. For more discussion, see John Consoli, "Heavy Lifting," *MediaWeek*, March 3, 2008.

5. Kristin Laird, "A Hands-Up Play for MINI," *Marketing Magazine*, June 19, 2009.

6. Canadian Media Directors Council, 2008–2009 Media Digest, accessed at www.cmdc.ca/pfd/2008_09_Media_Digest.pdf, June 2009; "Commercial Conundrum," Marketing Management, April 2006, p. 6; and "Number of Magazines by Category," accessed at www.magazine.org/editorial/editorial_trends_and_magazine_handbook/1145.cfm, April 2008.

7. Louise Story, "Anywhere the Eye Can See, It's Likely to See an Ad," *New York Times*, January 15, 2007, accessed at www.nytimes.com; and Matthew Creamer, "Caught in the Clutter Crossfire: Your Brand," *Advertising Age*, April 1, 2007, pp. 1, 35.

8. See http://adage.com/images/random/0907/2007_Ad_Age_TV_Price_Survey.pdf, accessed June 2008; Meg James and Maria Elena Fernandez, "Ad Buyers Hooked on 'Idol' Too," *Los Angeles Times*, January 13, 2008, p. 1; and Steve McClellan, "Super Bowl Spots Hit 3 Mil," *Adweek*, June 5, 2008, accessed at www.adweek.com.

9. Ken Krimstein, "Tips for the Ad World," *Forbes*, October 16, 2006, p. 34; and Bob Garfield, "The Chaos Scenario 2.0: The Post-Advertising Age," *Advertising Age*, March 26, 2007, pp. 1, 12–13.

10. John Consoli, "Broadcast, Cable Ad Clutter Continues to Rise," *MediaWeek*, May 4, 2006, accessed at www.mediaweek.com.

11. Ronald Grover, "The Sound of Many Hands Zapping," *BusinessWeek*, May 22, 2006, p. 38; Daisy Whitney, "DVR, Broadband Users Take Control," *Television Week*, October 29, 2007, p. 10; "Attack of the Pod People," Adweek.com, March 24, 2008; Jack Neff, "Study Finds Mixed DVR Effects," *Advertising Age*, March 24, 2008, p. 8; and Brian Morrissey, "Can Online Video Queue or DVR Cure DVR Commercial Skipping?" *Adweek*, May 8, 2008, accessed at www.adweek.com.

12. See Steve McKee, "Advertising: Less Is Much More," BusinessWeek Online, May 10, 2006, accessed at www.businessweek.com; and Stewart Elliott, "Now, the Clicking Is to Watch the Ads, Not Skip Them," *New York Times*, August 17, 2007, accessed at www.nytimes.com.

13. For this and other examples, see Wendy Tanaka, "D.I.Y Ads," *Red Herring*, January 29, 2007, accessed at www.redherring.com/Article.aspx?a=20955&hed=D.I.Y.+Ads; and Lee Gomes, "Tips from Web Greats on Becoming a Legend in Your Spare Time," *Wall Street Journal*, November 14, 2007, p. B1.

14. See Brian Steinberg, "Super Bowl Advertisers Hand Amateurs the Ball," *Wall Street Journal*, January 12, 2007, p. B1; "How All the Ads Ranked in USA Today's Super Bowl Ad Meter," *USA Today*, February 5, 2007, accessed at www.usatoday.com; "Fans Full 22-Year-Old Singer/Songwriter Kina Grannis Winner in Doritos Crash the Super Bowl Challenge," *PR Newswire*, February 3, 2008, and http://216.178.38.116/doritoscrashthesuperbowl, accessed June 2008.

15. Louise Story, "Can a Sandwich Be Slandered?" *New York Times*, January 29, 2008, accessed at www.nytimes.com.

16. Wendy Tanaka, "D.I.Y Ads," *Red Herring*, January 29, 2007, p. 3; and Laura Petrecca, "Madison Avenue Wants You! (Or at Least Your Videos)," *USA Today*, June 21, 2007, p. 1B.

17. Allison Enright, "Let Them Decide," *Marketing News*, June 1, 2006, pp. 10–11.

18. Ibid; and "Who's in Control?" *Advertising Age*, January 28, 2008, p. C1.

19. Stuart Elliot, "New Rules of Engagement," *New York Times*, March 21, 2006, p. C7; Abbey Klaassen, "New Wins Early Battle in Viewer-Engagement War," *Advertising Age*, March 20, 2006, p. 1; Mike DiFranza, "Rules of Engagement," *MediaWeek*, January 15, 2007, p. 9; Andrew Hampp, "Water Cooler," *Advertising Age*, April 16, 2007, p. 32; Megan McIlroy, "So Much for Engagement; Buys Are Still Based on Eyes," *Advertising Age*, January 14, 2008, p. 1; and Betsy Cummings, "Marketers Size Up New Metric System," *Brandweek*, April 6, 2008, accessed at www.brandweek.com.

20. For these and other examples and quotes, see Chris Walsh, "Ads on Board," *Rocky Mountain News*, February 27, 2007; David Kiley, "Rated M for Mad Ave," *BusinessWeek*, February 26, 2006, pp. 76–77; Cliff Peale, "Advertising Takes Many Forms," *Cincinnati Enquirer*, December 3, 2006, accessed at http://news.enquirer.com; Louise Story, "Anywhere the Eye Can See, It's Likely to See an Ad," *New York Times*, January 15, 2007, p. A12; and Adam Remson, "School Buses Latest Victim of Ad Creep," *Brandweek*, February 4, 2008, p. 4.

21. Adapted from information found in Claudia Wallis, "The Multitasking Generation," *Time*, March 27, 2006, accessed at www.time.com; Curtis L. Taylor, "Teens' Balancing Act: New Study Shows Young People Are Spending More Time Multitasking," *Knight Ridder Tribune Business News*, December 16, 2006, p. 1; John Harlow, "How We Squeeze 31 Hours into a Day," *Times (London)*, April 13, 2008, p. 8; and Tanya Irwin, "Study: Kids Are Master Multitaskers on TV, Web, Mobile," *MediaPost Publications*, March 10, 2008, accessed at www.mediapostpublications.com.

22. See "Pounds 10M Domino Effect Cheers Up Guinness," *Daily Record*, February 15, 2008; and Frank Ahrens, "$2 Million Airtime, $13 Ad," *Washington Post*, January 31, 2007, p. D1.

23. See Stuart Elliot, "How Effective Is This Ad, in Real Numbers? Beats Me," *New York Times*, July 20, 2005, p. C8; Jack Neff, "Half Your Advertising Isn't Wasted,—Just 37.3 Percent," *Advertising Age*, August 7, 2006, pp. 1, 32; Ben Richards and Faris Yakob, "The New Quid Pro Quo," *Adweek*, March 19, 2007, p. 17; and Kate Maddox, "ROI Takes Center Stage at CMO Summit," *BtoB*, February 11, 2008, p. 3.

24. David Tiltman, "Everything You Know Is Wrong," *Marketing*, June 13, 2008, pp. 28+.

25. Stuart Elliot, "How Effective Is This Ad, in Real Numbers? Beats Me," p. C8; and "Taking Measure of Which Metrics Matter," *BtoB*, May 5, 2008.

26. Information on advertising agency revenues from "Top 10 Worldwide Ad Agencies," *Advertising Age*, May 5, 2008, accessed at http://adage.com/datacenter/datapopup.php?article_id=126731; and "World's Top 50 Agency Companies," May 5, 2008, accessed at http://adage.com/datacenter/datapopup.php?article_id=126706.

27. Adapted from information in Geoffrey A. Fowler, Brian Steinberg, and Aaron O. Patrick, "Mac and PC's Overseas Adventures," *Wall Street Journal*, March 1, 2007, p. B1.

28. See Alexandra Jardine and Laurel Wentz, "It's a Fat World After All," *Advertising Age*, March 7, 2005, p. 3; George E. Belch and Michael A. Belch, *Advertising and Promotion* (New York: McGraw-Hill/Irwin, 2004), pp. 666–668; Jonathan Cheng, "China Demands Concrete Proof of Ads," *Wall Street Journal*, July 8, 2005, p. B1; Cris Prystay, "India's Brewers Cleverly Dodge Alcohol-Ad Ban," *Wall Street Journal*, June 15, 2005, p. B1; Dean Visser, "China Puts New Restrictions on Cell Phone, E-Mail Advertising," *Marketing News*, March 15, 2006, p. 23; Steve Inskeep, "Ban Thwarts

'Year of the Pig' Ads in China," National Public Radio, February 6, 2007; Maxine Frith, "It Worked in Canada to Ban Junk Food Ads and Now the Call Is on TV in Australia," *Sun Herald (Sydney)*, March 16, 2008, p. 14.

29. Adapted from Scott Cutlip, Allen Center, and Glen Broom, *Effective Public Relations*, 9th ed. (Upper Saddle River, NJ: Prentice Hall, 2006), Chapter 1.

30. See Jeff Manning and Kevin Lane Keller, "Got Advertising That Works?" *Marketing Management*, January–February 2004, pp. 16–20; Alice Z. Cuneo, "Now Even Cellphones Have Milk Mustaches," *Advertising Age*, February 26, 2007, p. 8; "Got Milk? Campaign Searches for America's First-Ever 'Chief Health Officer,'" *Business Wire*, May 6, 2008; and information from www.bodybymilk.com and www.whymilk.com, accessed September 2008.

31. "Consumer Launch Campaign of the Year 2008," *PRWeek*, March 6, 2008, accessed at www.prweekus.com/Consumer-Launch-Campaign-of-the-Year-2008/article/100570.

32. Al Ries and Laura Ries, "First Do Some Publicity," *Advertising Age*, February 8, 1999, p. 42. See also Al Ries and Laura Ries, *The Fall of Advertising and the Rise of PR* (New York: HarperBusiness, 2002). For points and counterpoints and discussions of the role of public relations, see O. Burtch Drake, "'Fall' of Advertising? I Differ," *Advertising Age*, January 13, 2003, p. 23; David Robinson. "Public Relations Comes of Age," *Business Horizons*, May–June 2006, pp. 247+; and Noelle Weaver, "Why Advertising and PR Can't Be Separated," *Advertising Age*, May 14, 2007, accessed at www.adage.com.

33. "Aveeno Case Study," accessed at www.ogilvypr.com/case-studies/aveeno.cfm, October 2008; and see www.youtube.com/watch?v=hfn8Dz_13Ms.

34. See "Butterball Turkey Talk-Line Fact Sheet," accessed at www.butterball.com, November 2008.

35. Paul Holmes, "Senior Marketers Are Sharply Divided about the Role of PR in the Overall Mix," *Advertising Age*, January 24, 2005, pp. C1–C2.

Chapter 16

1. Quotes and other information from "Fortune Ranks CDW First in Wholesalers: Electronics on America's Most Admired Company List," *Business Wire*, March 10, 2008; Jeff O'Heir, "Michael Krasny—IT Sales Innovator." *Computer Reseller News*, November 18, 2002; Ed Lawler, "Integrated Campaign Winner: CDW Computer Centers," *BtoB*, December 9, 2002, p. 20; Chuck Salter, "The Soft Sell," *Fast Company*, January 2005, pp. 72–73; Paolo Del Nibletto, "CDW Goes to Class," *Computer Dealer News*, May 25, 2007, p. 20; "CDW Corporation," *Hoover's Company Records*, May 1, 2008, p. 16199; and information from www.cdw.com, accessed September 2008, and www.cdw.ca, accessed June 2009.

2. Based on information in Jennifer J. Salopek, "Bye, Bye, Used Car Guy," *T+D*, April 2007, pp. 22–25. See also "Prepare to Win," *Selling Power*, April 2008, p. 27.

3. For more on "salesperson-owned loyalty," see Robert W. Palmatier et al. "Customer Loyalty to Whom? Managing the Benefits and Risks of Salesperson-Owned Loyalty," *Journal of Marketing Research*, May 2007, pp. 185–199.

4. This extract and strategies that follow are based on Philip Kotler, Neil Rackham, and Suj Krishnaswamy, "Ending the War Between Sales and Marketing," *Harvard Business Review*, July–August 2006, pp. 68–78. See also Timothy Smith, Srinath Gopalakrishna, and Rabikar Chatterjee, "A Three-Stage Model of Integrated Marketing Communications at the Marketing–Sales Interface," *Journal of Marketing Research*, November 2006, pp. 564–579; and Christian Homburg, Ove Jensen, and Harley Krohmer, "Configurations of Marketing and Sales: A Taxonomy," *Journal of Marketing*, March 2008, pp. 133–154.

5. See "Lear Corp. Honored by GM as Supplier of the Year," *St. Charles County Business Record*, May 10, 2006, p. 1; Andy Cohen, "Top of the Charts: Lear Corporation," *Sales & Marketing Management*, July 1998, p. 40; "Lear Corporation," *Hoover's Company Records*, June 15, 2008, p. 17213; and information from www.lear.com, accessed June 2008.

6. For more on this and other methods for determining sales force size, see Mark W. Johnston and Greg W. Marshall, *Sales Force Management*, 9th ed. (Boston: McGraw-Hill Irwin, 2009), pp. 152–156.

7. Theodore Kinni, "The Team Solution," *Selling Power*, April 2007, pp. 27–29.

8. Roy Chitwood, "Making the Most Out of Each Outside Sales Call," February 4, 2005, accessed at http://seattle.bizjournals.com/seattle/stories/2005/02/07/smallb3.html; and "The Cost of the Average Sales Call Today Is More Than $400," *Business Wire*, February 28, 2006.

9. Carol Krol, "Telemarketing Team Rings Up Sales for Avaya," *BtoB*, October 10, 2005, p. 34. For more on the Avaya's sales strategy, see Julia Chang, "On Top of the World," *Sales & Marketing Management*, January–February 2006, pp. 31–36.

10. See Martin Everett, "It's Jerry Hale on the Line," *Sales & Marketing Management*, December 1993, pp. 75–79. See also Irene Cherkassky, "Target Marketing," *BtoB*, October 2006, pp. 22–24.

11. Jennifer J. Salopek, "Bye, Bye, Used Car Guy," *T+D*, April 2007, pp. 22–25; and William F. Kendy, "No More Lone Rangers," *Selling Power*, April 2004, pp. 70–74. See also Michelle Nichols, "Pull Together—Or Fall Apart," *BusinessWeek Online*, December 2, 2005, accessed at www.businessweek.com; and Theodore Kinni, "The Team Solution," *Selling Power*, April 2007, pp. 27–29.

12. "Customer Business Development," accessed at www.pg.com/jobs/jobs_us/work_we_offer/advisor_overview.jhtml?sl=jobs_advisor_business_development, November 2008.

13. For more information and discussion, see Benson Smith, *Discover Your Strengths: How the World's Greatest Salespeople Develop Winning Careers* (New York: Warner Business Books, 2003); Kevin McDonald, "Therapist, Social Worker or Consultant?" *CRN*, December 2005–January 2006, p. 24; Tom Reilly, "Planning for Success," *Industrial Distribution*, May 2007, p. 25; Dave Kahle, "The Four Characteristics of Successful Salespeople," *Industrial Distribution*, April 2008, p. 54; and information from www.gallup.com/consulting/1477/Sales-Force-Effectiveness.aspx, accessed October 2008.

14. Geoffrey James, "The Return of Sales Training," *Selling Power*, May 2004, pp. 86–91. See also Rebecca Aronauer, "Tracking Your Investment," *Sales & Marketing Management*, October 2006, p. 13; Geoffrey James, "Training: A Wise Choice," *Selling Power*, January–February 2007, pp. 88–90; James, "Return on Your Sales Training Investment," *Selling Power*, October 2007, p. 102; and Ashraf M. Attia et al., "Global Sales Training: In Search of Antecedent, Mediating, and Consequence Variables," *Industrial Marketing Management*, April 2008, pp. 181+.

15. David Chelan, "Revving Up E-Learning to Drive Sales," *EContent*, March 2006, pp. 28–32. See also "E-Learning Evolves into Mature Training Tool," *T+D*, April 2006, p. 20;

Rebecca Aronauer, "The Classroom vs. E-Learning," *Sales & Marketing Management*, October 2006, p. 21; and Harry Sheff, "Agent Training Beyond the Classroom," *Call Center Magazine*, April 2007, p. 18.

16. From David Chelan, "Revving Up E-Learning to Drive Sales," *EContent*, March 2006, pp. 28–32; and "International Rectifier Drives Sales with Global E-Leaning Initiative," GeoLearning case study, accessed at www.geolearning.com/main/customers/ir.cfm, October 2008.

17. Joseph Kornak, "07 Compensation Survey: What's It All Worth?" *Sales & Marketing Management*, May 2007, pp. 28–39.

18. See Henry Canaday, "How to Increase the Time Reps Spend Selling," *Selling Power*, March 2005, p. 112; George Reinfeld, "8 Tips to Help Control the Hand of Time," *Printing News*, January 9, 2006, p. 10; David J. Cichelli, "Plugging Sales 'Time Leaks,'" *Sales & Marketing Management*, April 2006, p. 23; Rebecca Aronauer, "Time Well Spent," *Sales & Marketing Management*, January–February 2007, p. 7; and Dave Bradford, "Finding More Time for Selling," *Electrical Wholesaling*," April 2007, pp. 66–67.

19. See Gary H. Anthes, "Portal Powers GE Sales," *Computerworld*, June 2, 2003, pp. 31–32. See also Betsy Cummings, "Increasing Face Time," *Sales & Marketing Management*, January 2004, p. 12; David J. Cichelli, "Plugging Sales 'Time Leaks,'" *Sales & Marketing Management*, April 2006, p. 23; and Henry Canaday, "How to Boost Sales Productivity and Save Valuable Time," *Agency Sales*, November 2007, p. 20.

20. For extensive discussions of sales force automation, see the May 2005 issue of *Industrial Marketing Management*, which is devoted to the subject; Gary K. Hunter and William D. Perreault, "Making Sales Technology Effective," *Journal of Marketing*, January 2007, pp. 16–34; Mary M. Long, Thomas Tellefsen, and J. David Lichtenthal, "Internet Integration into the Industrial Selling Process: A Step-By-Step Approach," *Industrial Marketing Management*, July 2007, pp. 676–689; and Anupam Agarwal, "Bringing Science to Sales," *Customer Relationship Management*, March 2008, p. 16.

21. Based on information from Thomaselli, "Pharma Replacing Reps," *Advertising Age*, January 2005, p. 50; and Matthew Arnold, "Is There a Doctor on the Web?" *Medical Marketing and Media*, 2008, pp. 10–11. See also Mary M. Long, Thomas Tellefsen, and J. David Lichtenthal, "Internet Integration into the Industrial Selling Process: A Step-By-Step Approach," *Industrial Marketing Management*, July 2007, pp. 676–689.

22. Quotes from Bob Donath, "Delivering Value Starts with Proper Prospecting," *Marketing News*, November 10, 1997, p. 5; and Bill Brooks, "Power-Packed Prospecting Pointers," *Agency Sales*, March 2004, p. 37. See also Gerhard Gschwandtner, "The Basics of Successful Selling," *Selling Power*, 25th Anniversary Issue, 2007, pp. 22–26; and Maureen Hrehocik, "Why Prospecting Gets No Respect," *Sales & Marketing Management*, October 2007, p. 7.

23. Quotes in this paragraph from Lain Ehmann, "Prepare to Win," *Selling Power*, April 2008, pp. 27–29.

24. Adapted from Charlotte Huff, "EXTREME Makeover," *Workforce Management*, May 8, 2006, p. 1. See also "iLevel Performance Home Educates Homebuyers on What to Look For in a Home's Structural Framing," *PR Newswire*, April 29, 2008; and www.ilevel.com, accessed November 2008.

25. Phil Sasso, "Listening in for More Sales," *Professional Distributor*, December 2007, pp. 18–19. See also Gerhard Gschwandtner, "The Basics of Successful Selling," *Selling Power*, 25th Anniversary Issue, 2007, pp. 22–26; and Robert

L. Bailey, "Story of Two Salespeople," *Rough Notes*, April 2008, p. 142.

26. Betsy Cummings, "Listening for Deals," *Sales & Marketing Management*, August 2005, p. 8. See also Michele Marchetti, "Listen to Me!" *Sales and Marketing Management*, April 2007, p. 12.

27. Adapted from Izabella Iizuka, "Not Your Father's Presentation," *Sales & Marketing Management*, March/April 2008, pp. 33–35.

28. *Shopper-Centric Trade: The Future of Trade Promotion* (Wilton, CT: Cannondale Associates, October 2007), p. 15.

29. Quotes and other information from Alan J. Liddle, "Hardee's Connects with Mobile Device Users, Offer Discounts," *Nation's Restaurant News*, May 14, 2007, p. 16; Alice Z. Cuneo, "Package-Goods Giants Roll Out Mobile Coupons," *Advertising Age*, March 10, 2008, p. 3; Alex Palmer, "Cellular Savings," *Incentive*, April 2008, p. 69; and information from www.cellfire.com, accessed August 2008.

30. See "2007 Promotion Products Fact Sheet," at Promotion Products Association International website, www.ppai.org, accessed May 2008.

31. Adapted from information found in Betsey Spethmann, "Doritos Experiments with Sampling and Sweeps," *Promo*, June 19, 2007, accessed at http://promomagazine.com/contests/news/doritos_experiments_sampling_sweeps_061907.

32. "Exclusive PQ Media Research: Branded Entertainment Defies Slowing Economy," February 12, 2008, accessed at www.pqmedia.com/about-press-20080212-bemf.html.

33 See Marketing Advertising Association Worldwide website, www.maaw.org, accessed June 2009.

34. *Shopper-Centric Trade: The Future of Trade Promotion* (Wilton, CT: Cannondale Associates, October 2007), p. 15.

35. See the Consumer Electronics Association Press website, www.cesweb.org/press/default_flash.asp, accessed May 2008; and the BAUMA website, www.bauma.de, accessed October 2008.

Chapter 17

1. Quotes and other information from Terry Poulton, "February Web Rankings Released by comScore," *Media in Canada*, www.mediaincanada.com/articles/mic/20080328/comscore.html?word=amazon; Mark Brohan, "The Top 500 Guide," InternetRetailer.com, June 2009, accessed at www.internetretailer.com/article.asp?id=30594, July 2009; Dawn Kawamoto, "Amazon's Revenue Jumps, Beats Street Forecast," CNET News, January 29, 2009, accessed at http://news.cnet.com/8301-1023_3-10152828-93.html, July 2009; Josh Quittner, "The Charmed Life of Amazon's Jeff Bezos," CNNMoney.com, April 15, 2008, accessed at www.cnnmoney.com; Joe Nocera, "Putting Buyers First? What a Concept," *New York Times*, January 5, 2008; Jena McGregor, "Bezos: How Frugality Drives Innovation," *BusinessWeek*, April 28, 2008, p.64; and annual reports and other information found at www.amazon.com and www.amazon.ca, accessed July 2009.

2. Kristin Laird, "Globe and Mail Shifts Focus Online," *Marketing Daily*, January 9, 2009.

3. See "Figure 104: Comparative Development of Direct Marketing Expenditure Worldwide," in *International Direct Marketing*, Manfred Krafft, Jürgen Hesse, Jürgen Höfling,

Kay Peters, Diane Rinas, eds., (New York: Springer), p. 11, accessed at http://books.google.ca, July 2009.

4. Gregor Anton, "Internet Statistics Released by The Interactive Advertising Bureau of Canada," *Marketing Resource Centre*, June 16, 2009; "IAB Canada's 2008 Canadian Media Usage Trend Study," accessed at http://marketingworkshops.ca/wordpress/2009/06/16/internet-statistics-released-by-the-interactive-advertising-bureau-of-canada, July 2009.

5. Roy Chitwood, "Making the Most out of Each Outside Sales Call," February 4, 2005, accessed at http://seattle.bizjournals.com/seattle/stories/2005/02/07/smallb3.html; and "The Cost of the Average Sales Call Today Is More Than $400," *Business Wire*, February 28, 2006.

6. Tim Shepherd, "Holt Renfrew Invites Passersby to Smudge Up Its Windows," *Media in Canada*, July 15, 2009, accessed at www.mediaincanada.com/articles/mic/20090715/windowfx.html?word=blog, July 2009; and Melita Kiburas, "Canadian Opera Company Bows New Website," *Media in Canada*, June 25, 2009, accessed at www.mediaincanada.com/articles/mic/20090625/canadianopera.html?word=blog, July 2009.

7. "Cornerstone Releases 2008 Annual Seasonality Report on Canadian Direct Response Media," press release, May 11, 2009, accessed at www.cstonecanada.com, July 2009; "Cornerstone Selected as Exclusive List Manager for Yves Rocher Canadian Package Insert Program," press release, June 10, 2009, accessed at www.cstonecanada.com, July 2009.

8. Daniel Lyons, "Too Much Information," *Forbes*, December 13, 2004, p. 110; Mike Freeman, "Data Company Helps Wal-Mart, Casinos, Airlines Analyze Data," *Knight Ridder Business Tribune News*, February 24, 2006, p. 1; and Mary Hayes Weier, "HP Data Warehouse Lands in Wal-Mart's Shopping Cart," *InformationWeek*, August 6, 2007, p. 31.

9. Melita Kuburas, "Michelin Helps Road Trippers Get Rolling Online," *Media in Canada*, June 10, 2009, accessed at www.mediaincanada.com/articles/mic/20090610/michelin.html?word=database, July 2009.

10. David Ranii, "Compact Discs, DVDs Get More Use as Promotional Tool," *Knight Ridder Tribune Business News*, May 5, 2004, p. 1; "DVD & CD Serious Cardz Increase Response Rate Over 1000% Over Traditional Direct Marketing," *Market Wire*, January 10, 2007, p. 1; and Emily Maltby, "A Marketing Tool That Fits in Your Wallet," *FSB*, April 2007, p. 76.

11. Jack Neff, "P&G, Unilever Are Ready to Clutter," *Advertising Age*, June 11, 2007, p. 4.

12. Emily Bryson York, "This Isn't the Holiday Catalog You Remember," *Advertising Age*, October 29, 2007.

13. Ylan Q. Mui, "Paging Through the Holidays," *Washington Post*, December 1, 2007, p. D1.

14. Direct Marketing Association, "The Power of Direct Marketing: 2007–2008 Edition," June 2008.

15. "Global News Uncovers Serious Loophole in 'Do Not Call' List," January 14, 2009, accessed at www.globaltv.com/globaltv/ontario/story.html?id=1176350, July 2009; "Thousands Call to Complain about Do-Not-Call List," CBC News, accessed at www.cbc.ca/canada/story/2008/11/27/calling.html, July 2009; Michael Geist, "Tough Action Can Reverse Do-Not-Call Disaster," TheStar.com, accessed at www.thestar.com/sciencetech/article/580741, July 2009; "Off the Hook," *Marketing Management*, January–February 2008, p. 5; and www.donotcall.gov, accessed October 2008.

16. Ira Teinowitz, "'Do Not Call' Does Not Hurt Direct Marketing," *Advertising Age*, April 11, 2005, pp. 3, 95.

17. Ibid.

18. See Brian Steinberg, "Read This Now! But Wait! There's More! The Infomercial King Explains," *Wall Street Journal*, March 9, 2005, p. 1; and Natasha Singer, "Why Kids Have All the Acne," *New York Times*, October 18, 2007, p. G1.

19. Jack Neff, "What Procter & Gamble Learned from Veg-O-Matic," *Advertising Age*, April 10, 2006, pp. 1, 65; and Jack Neff, "P&G Turns Lights Out on DRTV Players," *Advertising Age*, March 19, 2007, p. 3.

20. Steve McLellan, "For a Whole New DRTV Experience, Call Now," *Adweek*, September 5, 2005, p. 10; Jack Neff, "What Procter & Gamble Learned from Veg-O-Matic," p. 1; and "Analysis: Can DRTV Really Build Brands Better than Image Ads?" *Precision Marketing*, February 9, 2007, p. 11.

21. "The Shopping Channel" LinkedIn page, accessed at www.linkedin.com/companies/the-shopping-channel; and information from www.TheShoppingChannel.com and http://shoptvcanada.com, accessed July 2009.

22. "Interactive: Ad Age Names Finalists," *Advertising Age*, February 27, 1995, pp. 12–14.

23. Hugo Miller, "Public Mobile, Wal-Mart in Talks on Canada Phone Plan (Update 3)," Bloomberg.com, July 9, 2009, accessed at www.bloomberg.com/apps/news?pid=20601205&sid=aZ4vQeIF7dww, July 2009; Stephanie Kang, "Consumers Come Calling, Literally, for the Holidays," *Wall Street Journal*, November 16, 2007, p. B5; Daniel B. Honigman, "On the Verge: Mobile Marketing Will Make Strides," *Marketing News*, January 15, 2008, pp. 18–21; and "Nielsen Says Mobile Ads Growing, Consumers Respond," *Reuters*, March 5, 2008, accessed at www.reuters.com.

24. Alice Z. Cuneo, "Scramble for Content Drives Mobile," *Advertising Age*, October 24, 2005, p. S6; "Where Are Those Mobile Ads?" *International Herald Tribune*, May 4, 2008; and CTIA: The Wireless Association, June 2008, accessed at www.ctia.org.

25. Alice Z. Cuneo, "So Just What Is Mobile Marketing?" *Advertising Age*, March 17, 2008, p. 36. The following example is adapted from Paul Davidson, "Ad Campaigns for Your Tiny Cellphone Screen Get Bigger," *USA Today*, August 9, 2006, accessed at www.usatoday.com/tech/wireless/2006-08-08-mobile-ads_x.htm.

26. For this and other examples, see Alice Z. Cuneo, "Marketers Get Serious About the Third Screen," *Advertising Age*, July 11, 2005, p. 6; Louise Story, "Madison Avenue Calling," *New York Times*, January 20, 2007, accessed at www.nytimes.com; and Stephanie Kang, "Retailers Come Calling, Literally, for the holidays," *Wall Street Journal*, November 30, 2007, p. B5.

27. See Paul Davidson, "Ad Campaigns for Your Tiny Cellphone Screen Get Bigger," *USA Today*, August 9, 2006, p. 2; Julie Schlosser, "Get Outta My Phone," *Fortune*, February 10, 2007, p. 20; Emily Burg, "Acceptance of Mobile Ads on the Rise," *MediaPost Publications*, March 16, 2007, accessed at http://publications.mediapost.com; Steve Miller and Mike Beirne, "The iPhone Effect," Adweek.com, April 28, 2008; and Spencer E. Ante, "The Call for a Wireless Bill of Rights," *BusinessWeek*, March 31, 2008, pp. 80–81.

28. Tim Shepherd, "Fido Embeds Twitter Feeds in Its Digital Ads," *Media in Canada*, June 24, 2009, accessed at www.mediaincanada.com/articles/mic/20090624/fidovideoegg.html?word=mobile%20phone, July 2009.

29. Amy Reusch, "BBM Explores Tech Trend Uptake among Canadians," *Media in Canada*, April 14, 2009, accessed at www.mediaincanada.com/articles/mic/20090414/mtm.html?word=podcast, July 2009.

30. Evie Nagy, "Podding Along," *Billboard*, May 10, 2008, p. 14.

31. For these and other examples, see Marija Djukic, "BMO Starts Podcast Dialogue with Students," *Media in Canada*, October 20, 2008, accessed at www.mediaincanada.com/articles/mic/20081030/bmo.html?word=podcast, July 2009; Kate Calder, "Hot Topic Cranks Its Music Biz," *Kidscreen*, May 2007, p. 22; and "Official Disneyland Resort Podcasts," accessed at http://disneyland.disney.go.com/disneyland, July 2008.

32. Shahnaz Mahmud, "Survey: Viewer Crave TV Ad Fusion," Adweek.com, January 25, 2008.

33. For these and other statistics on Internet usage see "Canada Internet Usage, Broadband and Telecommunications Reports," Internet World Stats, accessed at www.internetworldstats.com/am/ca.htm, July 2009; Wayne MacPhail, "Canadian Internet Usage Quiz—Surprise Answers Inside," rabble.ca, February 24, 2009, accessed at www.rabble.ca/columnists/canadian-internet-usage-quiz-surprise-answers-inside, July 2009; "Nielsen Online Reports Topline U.S. Data for April 2008," Nielsen/NetRatings, May 15, 2008, accessed at www.nielsen-netratings.com; and "Global Index Chart," www.nielsen-netratings.com/press.jsp?section=pr_netv&nav=3, accessed May 30, 2008.

34. See "America's Top Ten Retail Businesses," accessed at www.internetretailer.com/top500/list.asp, August 2008.

35. See Tom Sullivan, "A Lot More Than Paper Clips," *Barron's*, April 16, 2007, pp. 23–25; and information from www.officedepot.com, September 2008.

36. Statistics Canada, "E-commerce: Shopping on the Internet," *The Daily*, November 17, 2008; "Canada B2C E-Commerce, eMarketer, 2009, accessed at www.emarketer.com/Reports/All/Em_ecom_canada_b2c_jan07.aspx; "Online shopping jumped to $12.8B in 2007: StatsCan," CBCnews.ca, November 17, 2008, accessed at www.cbc.ca/consumer/story/2008/11/17/online-shopping.html, July 2009.

37. "Canada B2C E-Commerce," eMarketer, 2009, accessed at www.emarketer.com/Reports/All/Em_ecom_canada_b2c_jan07.aspx, July 2009.

38. Information for this example accessed at www.dell.com/html/us/segments/pub/premier/tutorial/users_guide.html, August 2008.

39. See "eBay Inc.," *Hoover's Company Records*, June 1, 2008, p. 56307; and facts from eBay annual reports and other information accessed at www.ebay.com, September 2008.

40. Beth Snyder Bulik, "Who Blogs?" *Advertising Age*, June 4, 2007, p. 20.

41. Adapted from "Max Colchester, "Nescafé Brews Buzz via Blogs," *Wall Street Journal*, November 23, 2007, p. B3.

42. See David Ward, "GM Blog Keeps Everyone Up to Speed," *PRWeek*, April 3, 2006, p. 7; "Welburn: Calm Down, Camaro Complainers," *Automotive News*, January 14, 2008, p. 42; and Michelle Martin, "GM Keeps Pace with Customers Through Blogs," *Crain's Detroit Business*, May 12, 2008, p. 35.

43. Pete Blackshaw, "Irrational Exuberance? I Hope We're Not Guilty," *Barcode Blog*, August 26, 2005, accessed at www.barcodefactory.com/wordpress/?p=72.

44. Laurie Peterson, "When It Comes to Blogs, It Pays to Listen," *MediaPost Publications*, September 29, 2006, accessed at www.publications.com; and Michael Bush, "Starbucks Gets Web 2.0 Religion, But Can It Convert Nonbelievers?" *Advertising Age*, March 24, 2008, p. 1.

45. Carolyn Kepcher, "Bad Service? Point, Click, Complain," *New York Daily News*, May 12, 2008; and Kermit Pattison, "Does a New Website Hold the Secret to Great Customer Service?" *Fast Company*, April 2008, accessed at www.fastcompany.com/articles/2008/04/interview-muller.html.

46. Adapted from Jack Neff, "Media Owners Take Heed: P&G's Staid Old Web Site Has You Licked," *Advertising Age*, December 4, 2007, pp. 1, 38.

47. Jeffrey F. Rayport and Bernard J. Jaworski, *e-Commerce* (New York: McGraw-Hill, 2001), p. 116. See also Goutam Chakraborty, "What Do Customers Consider Important in B2B Websites?" *Journal of Advertising*, March 2003, p. 50; and "Looks Are Everything," *Marketing Management*, March/April 2006, p. 7.

48. Jesse Kohl, "Online Advertising to Hit $1.5 billion: IAB Canada," July 4, 2008, *Media in Canada*, accessed at www.mediaincanada.com/articles/mic/20080704/iabcanada.html, July 2009.

49. Danielle Sacks, "Down the Rabbit Hole," *Fast Company*, November 2006, pp. 86–93.

50. Jonathan Paul, "Brillant! Hellmann's Serves Up Food for Thought," *Strategy Magazine*, July 2009, p. 7.

51. Chaddus Bruce, "Big Biz Biddies Up to Gen Y," *Wired*, December 20, 2006, accessed at www.wired.com; "Masterclass: The Revolution Masterclass on Social Networking Sites," *Revolution*, January 25, 2007, accessed at www.brandrepublic.com.

52. Jon Swartz, "Despite Filters, Tidal Wave of Spam Bears Down on e-Mailers," *USA Today*, November 23, 2008, p. 6B; "Spam Turns 30 and Never Looked Healthier," *TechWeb*, May 2, 2008; and Symantec, "The State of Spam," A Monthly Report—May 2008, accessed at www.symantec.com/business/theme.jsp?themeid=state_of_spam.

53. Adapted from Regina Brady, "Profitable E-Mail," *Target Marketing*, April 2007, pp. 21–22.

54. William Hupp, "E-Mail," *Advertising Age*, March 17, 2008, p. 48.

55. "Sweepstakes Groups Settles with States," *New York Times*, June 27, 2001, p. A14; "PCH Reaches $34 Million Sweepstakes Settlement with 26 States," *Direct Marketing*, September 2001, p. 6; and Steve Higgins, "Reader's Digest Will Pay Up in Connecticut Sweepstakes Settlement," *Knight Ridder Tribune Business News*, March 29, 2005, p. 1.

56. "Internet Fraud in Canada: Reports Predict an Ominous Rise in Online Crimes in Canada," *Fraud and Scam News*, April 23, 2008, accessed at www.419legal.org/blog/2008/04/23/internet-fraud-in-canada-reports-predict-an-ominous-rise-in-online-crimes-in-canada, July 2009.

57. "Canadians Keep Falling for Nigerian Letter Scams," PhoneBusters Press Release, July 3, 2009, accessed at www.phonebusters.com/english/legal_2009_jul3.html, July 2009; Jon Swartz, "Despite Filters, Tidal Wave of Spam Bears Down on e-Mailers," *USA Today*, November 23, 2008, p. 6B.

58. "Canadian Youth Rate Online Safety as a Top Concern, But Many Still Engage in Risky Online Behaviour, Report Finds," Microsoft Press Release, February 25, 2009, accessed at www.microsoft.com/canada/media/releases/2009_02_25.mspx, July 2009.

59. See "Consumer Security Fears Continue to Rise in Banking Industry," *Business Wire*, December 14, 2006; and Tom Wright, "Online Card Use Stirs Fears Despite Relatively Low Fraud," *Cards and Payments*, April 2007, p. 16.

60. "Net Threats," *Consumer Reports*, September 2007, p. 28. Excerpt adapted from Ben Elgin, "The Plot to Hijack Your Computer," *BusinessWeek*, July 17, 2006, p. 40. See also Joseph Menn, "Online Tunes are More Risky than Web Porn," *Los Angeles Times*, June 4, 2007, p. C3.

61. "Anti-Spam Laws in Canada," Email Marketing Reports, accessed at www.email-marketing-reports.com/canspam/Canada, July 2009; "Government of Canada Protects Canadians with the Electronic Commerce Protection Act," Industry Canada News Release, April 24, 2009, accessed at www.ic.gc.ca/eic/site/ic1.nsf/eng/04595.html, July 2009.

62. Information on TRUSTe accessed at www.truste.com, October 2008.

63. Ellen Roseman, "There's Nothing Positive for Consumers with Negative Option Billing," *Toronto Star*, April 26, 2009, accessed at www.thestar.com/specialsections/recession/article/624521, October 2009.

Chapter 18

1. Quotes and other information from Gene Marcial, "Nike: Set for Two Great Leaps," *BusinessWeek*, April 14, 2008, p. 78; Matt Woolsey, "Nike's Game Plan: Growth in China, India," *Forbes*, May 2, 2007, accessed at www.forbes.com; and annual reports and other sources at www.nikebiz.com, accessed October 2008.

2. Logitech annual report, accessed at http://ir.logitech.com/annuals.cfm, June 2008.

3. For more on Encyclopaedia Britannica's competitive positioning, see Paula Berinstein, "Wikipedia and Britannica: The Kid's All Right (And So's the Old Man)," *Searcher*, March 2006, pp. 16–27; "Encyclopedia Britannica, Inc.," *Hoover's Company Records*, May 1, 2008, p. 40871; and information at http://corporate.britannica.com, accessed October 2008.

4. Adapted from Taylor Clark, "Who's Afraid of the Big Bad Starbucks?" *The Week*, January 18, 2008, p. 46.

5. See Michael Porter, *Competitive Advantage: Creating and Sustaining Superior Performance* (New York: Free Press, 1998), Chapter 6.

6. Based on Devin Leonard, "The Player," *Fortune*, March 20, 2006, p. 54; "The Slow Death of Digital Rights," *The Economist*, October 13, 2007; and information from www.apple.com, accessed May 2008.

7. Adapted from information found in "Blue Ocean Strategy: Making the Competition Irrelevant," accessed at www.blueoceanstrategy.com/resources/press.php, June 2008; and W. Chan Kim and Renée Mauborgne, *Blue Ocean Strategy* (Boston: Harvard Business School Press, 2005).

8. The Stonyfield story is adapted from Margaret Menge, "Guerrilla Marketing Works for NH's Stonyfield Farms," *New Hampshire Union Leader*, November 7, 2005; with information from "From Seven Cows in a Leaky Barn to the World's Top Organic Yogurt Maker," *PR Newswire*, April 29, 2008; and www.stonyfield.com, accessed September 2008.

9. Michael E. Porter, *Competitive Strategy: Techniques for Analyzing Industries and Competitors* (New York: Free Press, 1980), Chapter 2; and Porter, "What Is Strategy?" *Harvard Business Review*, November–December 1996, pp. 61–78. See also Richard Allen and others, "A Comparison of Competitive Strategies in Japan and the United States," *S.A.M. Advanced Management Journal*, Winter 2006, pp. 24–36; and Stefan Stern, "May the Force Be with You and Your Plans for 2008," *Financial Times*, January 8, 2008, p. 14.

10. Philip Kotler and Kevin Lane Keller, *Marketing Management*, 12th ed. (Upper Saddle River, NJ: Prentice Hall, 2006), p. 243.

11. See Michael Treacy and Fred Wiersema, "Customer Intimacy and Other Value Disciplines," *Harvard Business Review*, January–February 1993, pp. 84–93; Treacy and Wiersema, *The Discipline of Market Leaders: Choose Your Customers, Narrow Your Focus, Dominate Your Market* (New York: Perseus Press, 1997); Wiersema, *Customer Intimacy: Pick Your Partners, Shape Your Culture, Win Together* (Santa Monica, CA: Knowledge Exchange, 1998); Wiersema, *Double-Digit Growth: How Great Companies Achieve It—No Matter What* (New York: Portfolio, 2003); and Edward M. Hindin, "Learning from Leaders: Questions to Ask and Rules to Follow," *Health Care Strategic Management*, August 2006, pp. 11–13.

12. For more discussion, see Philip Kotler and Kevin Lane Keller, *Marketing Management*, 13th ed. (Upper Saddle River, NJ: Prentice Hall, 2009), Chapter 11.

13. Based on information found in Andrew Adam Newman, "The Skinny on Males Dieting," *Adweek*, April 7–April 14, 2008, pp. 24–27; and information from www.nutrisystem.com, accessed September 2008.

14. Adapted from information found in Jack Neff, "Why Unilever Lost the Laundry War," *Advertising Age*, August 6, 2007, pp. 1, 25; and "Bidders Eye Unilever's US Detergent Arm," *Financial Times*, April 9, 2008, p. 24.

15. See "Consumers Can Get More Camera for Less Money," *USA Today*, January 30, 2008, p. 8B; and Betsy McKay, "Soft-Drink Sales Volume Slipped Faster Last Year," *Wall Street Journal*, March 13, 2008, p. B6.

16. "Fortune 500: Largest U.S. Corporations," *Fortune*, May 5, 2008, pp. F1–F2.

17. Adapted from David J. Bryce and Jeffrey H. Dyer, "Strategies to Crack Well-Guarded Markets," *Harvard Business Review*, May 2007, pp. 84–91.

18. Based on information from Janet Frankston Lorin, "Kosher Food Brand Is Branching Out," *Los Angeles Times*, December 11, 2006, p. C3; Stuart Elliott, "Manischewitz Wants to Move to a Mainstream Aisle," *New York Times*, July 7, 2006; "R.A.B. Food Group," *Hoover's Company Records*, May 15, 2008, p. 56134; and information from www.rabfoodgroup.com, accessed September 2008.

19. "Alberto Culver Company," *Hoover's Company Records*, May 15, 2008, p. 10048; Jim Kirk, "Company Finds Itself, Finds Success: Alberto-Culver Adopts Strategy of Knowing Its Strengths and Promoting Small Brands, Rather Than Tackling Giants," *Chicago Tribune*, January 22, 1998, p. B1; and information from www.alberto.com, accessed September 2008.

Chapter 19

1. Information provided by representatives of McCain Foods and the company's "Corporate Social Responsibility Report," accessed at www.mccain.com/company/socialresponsibility/Documents/McCain%20Foods.Global%20CSR%20Report.Fiscal%202009.pdf, October 2009; Richard Blackwell, "'Hollowing Out' Fears Unfounded, Report Says," *Globe and Mail*, September 18, 2008; "Still Growing Strong, McCain Celebrates 50 Years of Success,"

McCain Press Release, June 21, 2007; Gordon Pitts, "Once a Tortoise, McCain Foods Is Determined to Be the Hare," *Globe and Mail*, October 29, 2005, p. B12; Laura Ramsay, "Canada to Bombay: Want Fries with That?" *Globe and Mail*, June 1, 2006; Natalia Williams, "The McCain Makeover," *Strategy Magazine*, January 2005, p. 15; "GB Launches Awareness Campaign," *The Star*, Vol. 38(1), February 2006; "Canada Wins Cassie," *The Star*, Vol. 38(1), February 2006.

2. Data from Michael V. Copeland, "The Mighty Micro-Multinational," *Business 2.0*, July 28, 2006, accessed at http://cnnmoney.com; "Fortune 500," *Fortune*, May 5, 2008, pp. F1–F2; and "List of Countries by GDP," Wikipedia, accessed at http://en.wikipedia.org/wiki/List_of_countries_ by_GDP_%28nominal%29, July 2008.

3. "State of Trade and Investment Update 2009: Executive Summary," *Foreign Affairs and International Trade*, April 4, 2009, accessed at www.international.gc.ca/economist-economiste/performance/state-point/2009.aspx, July 2009; *Global Economic Prospects, 2007*, World Bank, June 3, 2005, accessed at www.worldbank.org; CIA, *The World Factbook*, accessed at https://www.cia.gov, June 2008; and Jonathan Lynn, "World Trade Growth to Slow Further This Year," *Reuters*, April 17, 2008, accessed at www.reuters.com/article/topNews/idUSL1692469520080417.

4. Andrew Chung, "The Unlikely Home of High-End Bikes," *Toronto Star*, May 18, 2008, accessed at http://veloptimum.net/velonouvelles/8/ART/5mai/TorontoStar18.html, July 2009; Sahm Adrangi, "Tiny Toronto Bike Firm Spins Success," *Globe and Mail*, July 26, 2003, pp. B1, B4; "The Amazing Race: Cervélo Cycles," *Profit Magazine*, May 2006; accessed at www.canadianbusiness.com/entrepreneur/managing/article.jsp;jsessionid=MHIPHDJKDHKC?content=20060404_153018_5420, June 2006.

5. Information from www.michelin.com/corporate and www.jnj.com, accessed October 2008.

6. Steve Hamm, "Borders Are So 20th Century," *BusinessWeek*, September 22, 2003, pp. 68–73; and "Otis Elevator Company," *Hoover's Company Records*, June 15, 2008, p. 56332.

7. Andrew Mayeda and Sheldon Alberts, "'Buy American' Clause Concerns Harper," *Financial Post*, January 29, 2009, accessed at www.canada.com/business/fp/story.html?id=1232625, July 2009.

8. "What Is the WTO?" accessed at www.wto.org/english/thewto_e/whatis_e/whatis_e.htm, September 2008.

9. See the WTO website, www.wto.org, accessed July 2009; and World Trade Organization, "10 Benefits of the WTO Trading System," accessed at www.wto.org/english/thewto_e/whatis_e/whatis_e.htm, September 2008; Peter Coy, "Why Free-Trade Talks Are in Free Fall," *BusinessWeek*, May 22, 2006, p. 44; and "EU Officials Still Hopes for Doha Meeting in May," *Journal of Commerce*, April 25, 2008.

10. "The EU at a Glance," accessed at http://europa.eu/abc/index-en.htm, September 2008.

11. "Economic and Monetary Union (EMU)," accessed at http://europa.eu/abc/12lessons/lesson_7/index_en.htm, September 2008.

12. See David J. Bailey, "Misperceiving Matters: Elite Ideas and the Failure of the European Constitution," *Comparative European Politics*, April 2008, pp. 33+; and CIA, *The World Factbook*, accessed at https://www.cia.gov, June 2008.

13. See Statistics Canada, "Imports, Exports and Trade Balance of Goods on a Balance-Of-Payments Basis, by Country or Country Grouping," June 10, 2009, accessed at www40.statcan.ca/l01/cst01/gblec02a-eng.htm, July 2009. Other statistics and information from CIA, *The World Factbook*, accessed at https://www.cia.gov, June 2008; and "NAFTA Analysis 2007" and "NAFTA—A Success for Trade," Office of the United States Trade Representative, October 2007, accessed at www.ustr.gov/Trade_Agreements/Regional/NAFTA/Section_Index.html.

14. "Trade Negotiations and Agreements (TNA)," Foreign Affairs and International Trade Canada, 2009, accessed at www.international.gc.ca/trade-agreements-accords-commerciaux/index.aspx, July 2009.

15. Adapted from information in Clay Chandler, "China Deluxe," *Fortune*, July 26, 2004, pp. 148–156; "Brand Strategy in China: Luxury Looks East," *Brand Strategy*, June 12, 2007, p. 56; and "More Academic Focus on Luxury Product Craze," Chinadaily.com.cn, January 22, 2008. Information on Canada's millionaires can be found in "Canada's Super-Rich," CBC News, March 6, 2008, accessed at www.cbc.ca/news/background/wealth, July 2009.

16. Wai-Chan Chan, Richard. C. Cheung, and Anne Tse, "How Half the World Shops: Apparel in Brazil, China, and India," *McKinsey Report*, December 28, 2007, accessed at www.mckinseyquarterly.com/Retail_Consumer_Goods/Sectors_Regions/How_half_the_world_shops_Apparel_in_Brazil_China_and_India_2075, July 2009.

17. "Trade Negotiations and Agreements (TNA)," Foreign Affairs and International Trade Canada, 2009, accessed at www.international.gc.ca/trade-agreements-accords-commerciaux/index.aspx, July 2009; "Canada-India Trade Relations to Intensify," News Release No. 61, Department of Foreign Affairs and International Trade, April 6, 2005.

18. See "Venezuelan Financial Analyst Says Inflation Could Spark Political Instability," *BBC Worldwide Monitoring*, January 24, 2008; and "Venezuela," accessed at www.buyusa.gov, May 2008.

19. Ricky Griffin and Michael Pustay, *International Business*, 5th ed. (Upper Saddle River, NJ: Prentice Hall, 2008), pp. 522–523.

20. For other examples, see Emma Hall, "Do You Know Your Rites? BBDO Does," *Advertising Age*, May 21, 2007, p. 22.

21. Jamie Bryan, "The Mintz Dynasty," *Fast Company*, April 2006, pp. 56–61; and Viji Sundaram, "Offensive Durga Display Dropped," *India-West*, February 2006, p. A1.

22. For other examples and discussion, see www.executiveplanet.com, accessed December 2008; *Dun & Bradstreet's Guide to Doing Business Around the World* (Upper Saddle River, NJ: Prentice Hall, 2000); Richard Pooley, "When Cultures Collide," *Management Services*, Spring 2005, pp. 28–31; Terri Morrison and Wayne A. Conaway, *Kiss, Bow, or Shake Hands* (Avon, MA: Adams Media, 2006); and Helen Deresky, *International Management*, 6th ed. (Upper Saddle River, NJ: Prentice Hall, 2008).

23. See "Life's Good Film Festival," LG Press Release, July 6, 2009; "Canadian Creativity Shines as LG Canada Contest Winners Announced," LG Press Release, July 3, 2009; "Advertising Story: Outdoor Ads," accessed at http://ca.lge.com/en/experience/advertising/ad_outdoor.jsp, July 2009; "Canada's Next Top Model Woos Media Shops in Bid to Case More Brands in Cycle 3," *Media in Canada*, January 15, 2009, accessed at www.mediaincanada.com/articles/mic/20090115/canadasnexttopmodel.html?word=LG%20Electronics, July 2009; Elizabeth Esfahani, "Thinking Locally, Succeeding Globally," *Business 2.0*,

December 2005, pp. 96–98, Evan Ramstas, "LG Electronics' Net Surges 91 Percent as Cell Phone Margins Improve," *Wall Street Journal*, January 25, 2006, p. B2; and information from www.lge.com, accessed October 2008.

24. Adapted from Mark Rice-Oxley, "In 2,000 Years, Will the World Remember Disney or Plato?" *Christian Science Monitor*, January 15, 2004, p. 16; Thomas L. Friedman, *The Lexus and the Olive Tree: Understanding Globalization* (New York: Anchor Books, 2000).

25. "Canada's Most Valuable Brands 2009," *Brand-Finance*, Spring 2009, accessed at www.brandfinance.com/Uploads/pdfs/BrandFinanceCanadaMostValuableBrands2009.pdf, July 2009.

26. Quotations from "Brand Canada," *Marketing Magazine*, February 23, 2009, accessed at www.marketingmag.ca/english/news/agency/article.jsp?content=20090313_103322_9828. See also Evan H. Potter, "Canada's Brand Vital in International Realm," *Ottawa Citizen*, June 30, 2009, accessed at www.ottawacitizen.com/Canada+brand+vital+international+realm/1747670/story.html, July 2009.

27. Portions adapted from information found in Mark Rice-Oxley, "In 2,000 Years, Will the World Remember Disney or Plato?" *Christian Science Monitor*, January 15, 2004, p. 16. See also Liz Robbins, "The NBA and China Hope They've Found the Next Yao," *New York Times*, June 25, 2007, accessed at www.nytimes.com; and Fara Warner, "Hidden Dragons," *Brandweek*, July 2, 2007, p. 18.

28. See Paulo Prada and Bruce Orwall, "A Certain 'Je Ne Sais Quoi' at Disney's New Park—Movie-Themed Site Near Paris Is Multilingual, Serves Wine—and Better Sausage Variety," *Wall Street Journal*, March 12, 2002, p. B1; and "Euro Disney S. C. A.," *Hoover's Company Records*, May 15, 2008, p. 42391. Hong Kong Disneyland faced similar problems, see Merissa Marr and Geoffrey A. Fowler, "Chinese Lessons for Disney," *Wall Street Journal*, June 12, 2006, p. B1; and Benjamin Scent, "Double-Digit Percentage Gain in Disneyland Attendance," *The Standard*, May 8, 2008.

29. Lisa LaMotta, "McDonald's Golden in International Markets," *Forbes*, February 8, 2008, accessed at www.forbes.com.

30. See Noreen O'Leary, "Bright Lights, Big Challenge," *Adweek*, January 15, 2007, pp. 22–28; and Dexter Roberts, "Scrambling to Bring Crest to the Masses," *BusinessWeek*, June 25, 2007, p. 72.

31. Adapted from information in the Vicky McCrorie, "Hershey: Hoping to Taste Success in India," *Food Business Review*, April 2007, accessed at www.food-business-review.com; and Jennifer Fishbein, "Chocolatiers Look to Asia for Growth," *BusinessWeek*, January 18, 2008, accessed at www.businessweek.com.

32. Bruce Einhorn and Nandini Lakshman, "PC Makers Are Racing to India," *BusinessWeek*, October 1, 2007, p. 48.

33. Quotes from Pankaj Ghemawat, "Regional Strategies for Global Leadership," *Harvard Business Review*, December 2005, pp. 97–108; and Ben Laurance, "Unilever Learns to Join the Dots," *Sunday Times*, March 18, 2007, p. B1. See also Ghemawat, "Managing Differences," *Harvard Business Review*, March 2007, pp. 59–68.

34. Warren J. Keegan, *Global Marketing Management*, 7th ed. (Upper Saddle River, NJ: Prentice Hall, 2002), pp. 346–351. See also Phillip Kotler and Kevin Lane Keller, *Marketing Management*, 13th ed. (Upper Saddle River, NJ: 2009), pp. 596–615.

35. Adapted from Jack Ewing, "First Mover in Mobile: How It's Selling Cell Phones to the Developing World," *BusinessWeek*, May 14, 2007, p. 60.

36. See Douglas McGray, "Translating Sony into English," *Fast Company*, January 2003, p. 38; James Coates, "Chicago Tribune Binary Beat Column," *Chicago Tribune*, January 9, 2005, p. 1; and information from http://vaio-online.sony.com/prod_info/vgn-u8g/index.html, accessed June 2008.

37. Adapted from Gordon Fairclough and Janet Adamy, "Sex, Skin, Fireworks, Licked Fingers—It's a Quarter Pounder Ad in China," *Wall Street Journal*, September 21, 2006, p. B1.

38. Kate MacArthur, "Coca-Cola Light Employs Local Edge," *Advertising Age*, August 21, 2000, pp. 18–19; "Case Studies: Coke Light Hottest Guy," *Advantage Marketing*, msn India, accessed at http://.advantage.msn.co.in, March 2004; and www.youtube.com/watch?v=Tu5dku6YkHA, accessed June 2008.

39. See Alicia Clegg, "One Ad One World?" *Marketing Week*, June 20, 2002, pp. 51–52; Ira Teinowitz, "International Advertising Code Revised," *Advertising Age*, January 23, 2006, p. 3; George E. Belch and Michael A. Belch, *Advertising and Promotion: An Integrated Marketing Communications Perspective*, 7th ed. (New York: McGraw Hill, 2007), Chapter 20; and Shintero Okazaki and Charles R. Taylor, "What Is SMS Advertising and Why Do Multinationals Adopt it?" *Journal of Business Research*, January 2008, pp. 4–12.

40. "Softwood Lumber Dispute," CBC News Online, August 23, 2006, accessed at www.cbc.ca/news/background/softwood_lumber, July 2009.

41. Adapted from Jack Ewing, "First Mover in Mobile: How It's Selling Cell Phones to the Developing World," *BusinessWeek*, May 14, 2007, p. 60.

42. See Leslie Chang, Chad Terhune, and Betsy McKay, "A Global Journal Report: Rural Thing—Coke's Big Gamble in Asia," *Wall Street Journal*, August 11, 2004, p. A1; and "Coca-Cola Rolls Out New Distribution Model with ZAP," accessed at www.zapworld.com/zap-coca-cola-truck, January 2008.

Appendix 3

1. This is derived by rearranging the following equation and solving for price: Percentage markup = (price – cost) ÷ price.

2. The equation is derived from the basic profit = total revenue – total cost equation. Profit is set to equal the return on investment times the investment (ROI × I), total revenue equals price times quantity (P × Q), and total costs equals quantity times unit cost (Q × UC): ROI × I = (P × Q) – (Q × UC). Solving for P gives P = ((ROI × I) ÷ Q) + UC.

3. The break-even volume equation can also be derived from the basic profit = total revenue – total cost equation. At the break-even point, profit is equal to zero, and it is best to separate fixed and variable costs: 0 = (P × Q) – TFC – (Q × UVC). Solving for Q gives Q = TFC ÷ (P – UVC).

4. As in the previous note, this equation is derived from the basic profit = total revenue – total cost equation. However, unlike the break-even calculation, in which profit was set to equal zero, we set the profit equal to the dollar profit goal: Dollar profit goal = (P × Q) – TFC – (Q × UVC). Solving for Q gives Q = (TFC + dollar profit goal) ÷ (P – UVC).

5. Again, using the basic profit equation, we set profit equal to ROI × I : ROI × I = (P × Q) − TFC − (Q × UVC). Solving for Q gives Q = (TFC + (ROI × I)) ÷ (P − UVC).

6. Again, using the basic profit equation, we set profit equal to 25% of sales, which is 0.25 × P × Q: 0.25 × P × Q = (P × Q) − TFC − (Q × UVC). Solving for Q gives Q = TFC ÷ (P − UVC − (0.25 × P)) or TFC ÷ ((0.75 × P) − UVC).

7. "US Television Households Increase 1.3% for 2007–2008," www.marketingcharts.com/television/us-television-households-increase-13-for-2007-2008-season-1385, accessed August 25, 2008.

8. "HDTV Penetration and Sales Figures," www.parksassociates.blogspot.com/2008/02/hdtv-penetration-and-sales-figures.html, accessed August 25, 2008.

9. "Broadband Internet to Reach 77 Percent of Households by 2012," www.tmcnet.com/voip/ip-communications/articles/35393-gartner-broadband-internet-reach-77-percent-households-2012.htm, accessed August 25, 2008.

10. Daisy Whitney, "'06 HDTV Sales to Outpace Analog," *Television Week*, October 31, 2005, pp. 19–24.

11. See Roger J. Best, *Market-Based Management*, 4th ed. (Upper Saddle River, NJ: Prentice Hall, 2005).

12. Total contribution can also be determined from the unit contribution and unit volume: Total contribution = unit contribution × unit sales. Total units sold were 297 619 units, which can be determined by dividing total sales by price per unit ($100 million ÷ $336). Total contribution = $70 contribution per unit × 297 619 units = $20 833 330 (difference due to rounding).

13. Recall that the contribution margin of 21% was based on variable costs representing 79% of sales. Therefore, if we do not know the price, we can set it equal to $1.00. If the price equals $1.00, 79 cents represents variable costs and 21 cents represents unit contribution. If the price is decreased by 10%, the new price is $0.90. However, variable costs do not change just because the price decreased, so the unit contribution and contribution margin decrease as follows:

	Old	New (reduced 10%)
Price	$1.00	$0.90
− Unit variable cost	$0.79	$0.79
= Unit contribution	$0.21	$0.11
Contribution margin	$0.21/$1.00 = 0.21 or 21%	$0.11/$0.90 = 0.12 or 12%

Appendix 4

1. See "Companies Give 'Web Search' a New Meaning," *CFO.com*, April 21, 2008, accessed at http://backwww.CFO.com.

Glossary

Action programs Action programs should be coordinated with the resources and activities of other departments, including production, finance, purchasing, and so on.

Adapted global marketing An international marketing strategy for adjusting the marketing strategy and mix elements to each international target market, bearing more costs but hoping for a larger market share and return.

Administered VMS A vertical marketing system that coordinates successive stages of production and distribution, not through common ownership or contractual ties, but through the size and power of one of the parties.

Adoption process The mental process through which an individual passes from first hearing about an innovation to final adoption.

Advertising Any paid form of nonpersonal presentation and promotion of ideas, goods, or services by an identified sponsor.

Advertising agency A marketing services firm that assists companies in planning, preparing, implementing, and evaluating all or portions of their advertising programs.

Advertising budget The dollars and other resources allocated to a product or company advertising program.

Advertising media The vehicles through which advertising messages are delivered to their intended audiences.

Advertising objective A specific communication *task* to be accomplished with a specific *target* audience during a specific period of *time*.

Advertising strategy The strategy by which the company accomplishes its advertising objectives. It consists of two major elements: creating advertising messages and selecting advertising media.

Affordable method Setting the promotion budget at the level management thinks the company can afford.

Age and life-cycle segmentation Dividing a market into different age and life-cycle groups.

Agent A wholesaler who represents buyers or sellers on a relatively permanent basis, performs only a few functions, and does not take title to goods.

Allowance Promotional money paid by manufacturers to retailers in return for an agreement to feature the manufacturer's products in some way.

Alternative evaluation The stage of the buyer decision process in which the consumer uses information to evaluate alternative brands in the choice set.

Approach The step in the selling process in which the salesperson meets the customer for the first time.

Attitude A person's consistently favourable or unfavourable evaluations, feelings, and tendencies toward an object or idea.

Baby boomers The 78 million people born during the baby boom following World War II and lasting until 1964.

Behavioural segmentation Dividing a market into groups based on consumer knowledge, attitudes, uses, or responses to a product.

Belief A descriptive thought that a person holds about something.

Benchmarking The process of comparing the company's products and processes to those of competitors or leading firms in other industries to identify "best practices" and find ways to improve quality and performance.

Benefit segmentation Dividing the market into groups according to the different benefits that consumers seek from the product.

Brand A name, term, sign, symbol, design, or combination of these that identifies the products or services of one seller or group of sellers and differentiates them from those of competitors.

Brand equity The differential effect that knowing the brand name has on customer response to the product or its marketing.

Brand extension Extending an existing brand name to new product categories.

Brand personality The specific mix of human traits that may be attributed to a particular brand.

Break-even analysis Analysis to determine the unit volume and dollar sales needed to be profitable given a particular price and cost structure.

Break-even price The price at which total revenue equals total cost and profit is zero.

Break-even pricing (target profit pricing) Setting price to break even on the costs of making and marketing a product, or setting price to make a target profit.

Broker A wholesaler who does not take title to goods and whose function is to bring buyers and sellers together and assist in negotiation.

Budgets Managers use budgets to project profitability and plan for each marketing program's expenditures, scheduling, and operations.

Business analysis A review of the sales, costs, and profit projections for a new product to find out whether these factors satisfy the company's objectives.

Business buyer behaviour The buying behaviour of the organizations that buy goods and services to use in the production of other products and services or to resell or rent to others at a profit.

Business buying process The decision process by which business buyers determine which products and services their organizations need to purchase, and then find, evaluate, and choose among alternative suppliers and brands.

Business portfolio The collection of businesses and products that make up the company.

Business product A product bought by individuals and organizations for further processing or for use in conducting business.

Business promotions Sales promotion tools used to generate business leads, stimulate purchases, reward customers, and motivate salespeople.

Business-to-business (B2B) online marketing Businesses using B2B websites, email, online catalogues, online trading networks, and other online resources to reach new business customers, serve current customers more effectively, and obtain buying efficiencies and better prices.

Business-to-consumer (B2C) online marketing Businesses selling goods and services online to final consumers.

Buyer-readiness stages The stages consumers normally pass through on their way to purchase, including awareness, knowledge, liking, preference, conviction, and purchase.

Buyers The people in the organization's buying centre who make an actual purchase.

Buying centre All the individuals and units that play a role in the purchase decision-making process.

Buzz marketing Cultivating opinion leaders and getting them to spread information about a product or service to others in their communities.

By-product pricing Setting a price for by-products to make the main product's price more competitive.

Cannibalization The situation in which one product sold by a company takes a portion of its sales from other company products.

Captive-product pricing Setting a price for products that must be used along with a main product, such as blades for a razor and film for a camera.

Catalogue marketing Direct marketing through print, video, or digital catalogues that are mailed to select customers, made available in stores, or presented online.

Category killer A giant specialty store that carries a very deep assortment of a particular line and is staffed by knowledgeable employees.

Causal research Marketing research to test hypotheses about cause-and-effect relationships.

Chain ratio method Estimating market demand by multiplying a base number by a chain of adjusting percentages.

Chain stores Two or more outlets that are commonly owned and controlled.

Channel conflict Disagreement among marketing channel members on goals and roles—who should do what and for what rewards.

Channel level A layer of intermediaries that perform some work in bringing the product and its ownership closer to the final buyer.

Channels and logistics review In this section of the marketing plan, marketers list the most important channels, provide an overview of each channel arrangement, and identify developing issues in channels and logistics.

Closing The step in the selling process in which the salesperson asks the customer for an order.

Co-branding The practice of using the established brand names of two different companies on the same product.

Cognitive dissonance Buyer discomfort caused by postpurchase conflict.

Commercial online databases Computerized collections of information available from online commercial sources or via the Internet.

Commercialization Introducing a new product into the market.

Communication adaptation A global communication strategy of fully adapting advertising messages to local markets.

Competitive advantage An advantage over competitors gained by offering greater customer value, either through lower prices or by providing more benefits that justify higher prices.

Competitive marketing strategies Strategies that strongly position the company against competitors and that give the company the strongest possible strategic advantage.

Competitive review The purpose of a competitive review in the marketing plan is to identify key competitors, describe their market positions, and briefly discuss their strategies.

Competitive-parity method Setting the promotion budget to match competitors' outlays.

Competitor analysis The process of identifying key competitors; assessing their objectives, strategies, strengths and weaknesses, and reaction patterns; and selecting which competitors to attack or avoid.

Competitor-centred company A company whose moves are mainly based on competitors' actions and reactions.

Complex buying behaviour Consumer buying behaviour in situations characterized by high consumer involvement in a purchase and significant perceived differences among brands.

Concentrated (niche) marketing A market-coverage strategy in which a firm goes after a large share of one or a few segments or niches.

Concept testing Testing new-product concepts with a group of target consumers to find out if the concepts have strong consumer appeal.

Consumer buyer behaviour The buying behaviour of final consumers— individuals and households that buy goods and services for personal consumption.

Consumer market All the individuals and households who buy or acquire goods and services for personal consumption.

Consumer product A product bought by a final consumer for personal consumption.

Consumer promotions Sales promotion tools used to boost short-term customer buying and involvement or to enhance long-term customer relationships.

Consumer-generated marketing Marketing messages, ads, and other brand exchanges created by consumers themselves—both invited and uninvited.

Consumer-oriented marketing The philosophy of sustainable marketing that holds that the company should view and organize its marketing activities from the consumer's point of view.

Consumer-to-business (C2B) online marketing Online exchanges in which consumers search out sellers, learn about their offers, and initiate purchases, sometimes even driving transaction terms.

Consumer-to-consumer (C2C) online marketing Online exchanges of goods and information between final consumers.

Consumerism An organized movement of citizens and government agencies to improve the rights and power of buyers in relation to sellers.

Contract manufacturing A joint venture in which a company contracts with manufacturers in a foreign market to produce its product or provide its service.

Contractual VMS A vertical marketing system in which independent firms at different levels of production and distribution join together through contracts to obtain more economies or sales impact than they could achieve alone.

Contribution margin The unit contribution divided by the selling price.

Controls Controls help management assess results after the plan is implemented, identify any problems or performance variations, and initiate corrective action.

Convenience product A consumer product that customers usually buy frequently, immediately, and with a minimum of comparison and buying effort.

Convenience store A small store located near a residential area that is open long hours seven days a week and carries a limited line of high-turnover convenience goods.

Conventional distribution channel A channel consisting of one or more independent producers, wholesalers, and retailers, each a separate business seeking to maximize its own profits even at the expense of profits for the system as a whole.

Corporate VMS A vertical marketing system that combines successive stages of production and distribution under single ownership—channel leadership is established through common ownership.

Corporate (or **brand**) **website.** A website designed to build customer goodwill, collect customer feedback, and supplement other sales channels, rather than to sell the company's products directly.

Cost-based pricing Setting prices based on the costs of producing, distributing, and selling the product plus a fair rate of return for effort and risk.

Cost-plus pricing Adding a standard markup to the cost of the product.

Countertrade International trade involving the direct or indirect exchange of goods for other goods instead of cash.

Creative concept The compelling "big idea" that will bring the advertising message strategy to life in a distinctive and memorable way.

Cultural environment Institutions and other forces that affect society's basic values, perceptions, preferences, and behaviours.

Culture The set of basic values, perceptions, wants, and behaviours learned by a member of society from family and other important institutions.

Current marketing situation In this section of the marketing plan, marketing managers discuss the overall market, identify the market segments that they will target, and provide information about the company's current situation.

Customer database An organized collection of comprehensive data about individual customers or prospects, including geographic, demographic, psychographic, and behavioural data.

Customer equity The total combined customer lifetime values of all of the company's customers.

Customer insights Fresh understandings of customers and the marketplace derived from marketing information that become the basis for creating customer value and relationships.

Customer lifetime value The value of the entire stream of purchases that the customer would make over a lifetime of patronage.

Customer relationship management (CRM) The overall process of building and maintaining profitable customer relationships by delivering superior customer value and satisfaction. Managing detailed information about individual customers and carefully managing customer "touchpoints" to maximize customer loyalty.

Customer sales force structure A sales force organization under which salespeople specialize in selling only to certain customers or industries.

Customer satisfaction The extent to which a product's perceived performance matches a buyer's expectations.

Customer value analysis Analysis conducted to determine what benefits target customers value and how they rate the relative value of various competitors' offers.

Customer-centred company A company that focuses on customer developments in designing its marketing strategies and on delivering superior value to its target customers.

Customer-centred new-product development New-product development that focuses on finding new ways to solve customer problems and create more customer-satisfying experiences.

Customer-perceived value The customer's evaluation of the difference between all the benefits and all the costs of a marketing offer relative to those of competing offers.

Customer-value marketing A principle of sustainable marketing that holds that a company should put most of its resources into customer value-building marketing investments.

Deciders People in the organization's buying centre who have formal or informal power to select or approve the final suppliers.

Decline stage The product life-cycle stage in which a product's sales decline.

Deficient products Products that have neither immediate appeal nor long-run benefits.

Demand curve A curve that shows the number of units the market will buy in a given time period, at different prices that might be charged.

Demands Human wants that are backed by buying power.

Demographic segmentation Dividing the market into groups based on variables such as age, gender, family size, family life cycle, income, occupation, education, religion, race, generation, and nationality.

Demography The study of human populations in terms of size, density, location, age, gender, race, occupation, and other statistics.

Department store A retail organization that carries a wide variety of product lines—each line is operated as a separate department managed by specialist buyers or merchandisers.

Derived demand Business demand that ultimately comes from (derives from) the demand for consumer goods.

Descriptive research Marketing research to better describe marketing problems, situations, or markets, such as the market potential for a product or the demographics and attitudes of consumers.

Desirable products Products that give both high immediate satisfaction and high long-run benefits.

Differentiated (segmented) marketing A market-coverage strategy in which a firm decides to target several market segments and designs separate offers for each.

Differentiation Actually differentiating the market offering to create superior customer value.

Direct investment Entering a foreign market by developing foreign-based assembly or manufacturing facilities.

Direct marketing Direct connections with carefully targeted individual consumers to both obtain an immediate response and cultivate lasting customer relationships—the use of direct mail, the telephone, direct-response television, email, the Internet, and other tools to communicate directly with specific consumers.

Direct marketing channel A marketing channel that has no intermediary levels.

Direct-mail marketing Direct marketing by sending an offer, announcement, reminder, or other item to a person at a particular physical or virtual address.

Direct-response television marketing Direct marketing via television, including direct-response television advertising (or infomercials) and home shopping channels.

Discount A straight reduction in price on purchases during a stated period of time.

Discount store A retail operation that sells standard merchandise at lower prices by accepting lower margins and selling at higher volume.

Disintermediation The cutting out of marketing channel intermediaries by product or service producers, or the displacement of traditional resellers by radical new types of intermediaries.

Dissonance-reducing buying behaviour Consumer buying behaviour in situations characterized by high involvement but few perceived differences among brands.

Distribution centre A large, highly automated warehouse designed to receive goods from various plants and suppliers, take orders, fill them efficiently, and deliver goods to customers as quickly as possible.

Diversification A strategy for company growth through starting up or acquiring businesses outside the company's current products and markets.

Downsizing Reducing the business portfolio by eliminating products of business units that are not profitable or that no longer fit the company's overall strategy.

Dynamic pricing Adjusting prices continually to meet the characteristics and needs of individual customers and situations.

Economic community A group of nations organized to work toward common goals in the regulation of international trade.

Economic environment Factors that affect consumer buying power and spending patterns.

Engel's laws Differences noted over a century ago by Ernst Engel in how people shift their spending across food, housing, transportation, health care, and other goods and services categories as family income rises.

Environmental sustainability A management approach that involves developing strategies that both sustain the environment and produce profits for the company.

Environmentalism An organized movement of concerned citizens and government agencies to protect and improve people's current and future living environment.

Eprocurement Purchasing through electronic connections between buyers and sellers—usually online.

Ethnographic research A form of observational research that involves sending trained observers to watch and interact with consumers in their "natural habitat."

Event marketing Creating a brand-marketing event or serving as a sole or participating sponsor of events created by others.

Exchange The act of obtaining a desired object from someone by offering something in return.

Exclusive distribution Giving a limited number of dealers the exclusive right to distribute the company's products in their territories.

Execution style The approach, style, tone, words, and format used for executing an advertising message.

Executive summary This section of the marketing plan summarizes the main goals, recommendations, and points as an overview for senior managers who will read and approve the marketing plan. A table of contents usually follows this section, for management convenience.

Experience curve (learning curve) The drop in the average per-unit production cost that comes with accumulated production experience.

Experimental research Gathering primary data by selecting matched groups of subjects, giving them different treatments, controlling other factors, and checking for differences in group responses.

Exploratory research Marketing research to gather preliminary information that will help define problems and suggest hypotheses.

Exporting Entering a foreign market by selling goods produced in the company's home country, often with little modification.

Factory outlet An off-price retailing operation that is owned and operated by a manufacturer and that normally carries the manufacturer's surplus, discontinued, or irregular goods.

Fixed costs (overhead) Costs that do not vary with production or sales level.

FOB-origin pricing A geographical pricing strategy in which goods are placed free on board a carrier; the customer pays the freight from the factory to the destination.

Focus group interviewing Personal interviewing that involves inviting six to ten people to gather for a few hours with a trained interviewer to talk about a product, service, or organization. The interviewer "focuses" the group discussion on important issues.

Follow-up The last step in the selling process in which the salesperson follows up after the sale to ensure customer satisfaction and repeat business.

Franchise A contractual association between a manufacturer, wholesaler, or service organization (a franchiser) and independent businesspeople (franchisees) who buy the right to own and operate one or more units in the franchise system.

Franchise organization A contractual vertical marketing system in which a channel member, called a franchiser, links several stages in the production–distribution process.

Gatekeepers People in the organization's buying centre who control the flow of information to others.

Gender segmentation Dividing a market into different groups based on gender.

General need description The stage in the business buying process in which the company describes the general characteristics and quantity of a needed item.

Generation X The 45 million people born between 1965 and 1976 in the "birth dearth" following the baby boom.

Geographic segmentation Dividing a market into different geographical units such as nations, provinces, regions, counties, cities, or neighbourhoods.

Geographical pricing Setting prices for customers located in different parts of the country or world.

Global firm A firm that, by operating in more than one country, gains R&D, production, marketing, and financial advantages in its costs and reputation that are not available to purely domestic competitors.

Good-value pricing Offering just the right combination of quality and good service at a fair price.

Government market Governmental units—federal, provincial, and municipal—that purchase or rent goods and services for carrying out the main functions of government.

Gross margin percentage The percentage of net sales remaining after cost of goods sold—calculated by dividing gross margin by net sales.

Group Two or more people who interact to accomplish individual or mutual goals.

Growth stage The product life-cycle stage in which a product's sales start climbing quickly.

Growth-share matrix A portfolio-planning method that evaluates a company's strategic business units in terms of its market growth rate and relative market share. SBUs are classified as stars, cash cows, question marks, or dogs.

Habitual buying behaviour Consumer buying behaviour in situations characterized by low-consumer involvement and few significantly perceived brand differences.

Handling objections The step in the selling process in which the salesperson seeks out, clarifies, and overcomes customer objections to buying.

Horizontal marketing system A channel arrangement in which two or more companies at one level join together to follow a new marketing opportunity.

Hybrid or **click-and-mortar companies** Traditional companies that have added online marketing to their operations.

Idea generation The systematic search for new-product ideas.

Idea screening Screening new-product ideas to spot good ideas and drop poor ones as soon as possible.

Income segmentation Dividing a market into different income groups.

Independent off-price retailer An off-price retailer that is either independently owned and run or is a division of a larger retail corporation.

Indirect marketing channel A marketing channel containing one or more intermediary levels.

Individual marketing Tailoring products and marketing programs to the needs and preferences of individual customers—also labelled "one-to-one marketing," "customized marketing," and "markets-of-one marketing."

Influencers People in an organization's buying centre who affect the buying decision; they often help define specifications and also provide information for evaluating alternatives.

Information search The stage of the buyer decision process in which the consumer is aroused to search for more information; the consumer may simply have heightened attention or may go into an active information search.

Innovative marketing A principle of sustainable marketing that requires that a company seek real product and marketing improvements.

Inside sales force Inside salespeople who conduct business from their offices via telephone, the Internet, or visits from prospective buyers.

Institutional market Schools, hospitals, nursing homes, prisons, and other institutions that provide goods and services to people in their care.

Integrated marketing communications (IMC) Carefully integrating and coordinating the company's many communications channels to deliver a clear, consistent, and compelling message about the organization and its products.

Intensive distribution Stocking the product in as many outlets as possible.

Interactive marketing Training service employees in the fine art of interacting with customers to satisfy their needs.

Intermarket segmentation Forming segments of consumers who have similar needs and buying behaviour even though they are located in different countries.

Intermodal transportation Combining two or more modes of transportation.

Internal databases Electronic collections of consumer and market information obtained from data sources within the company network.

Internal marketing Orienting and motivating customer-contact employees and supporting service people to work as a team to provide customer satisfaction.

Internet A vast public web of computer networks that connects users of all types all around the world to each other and to an amazingly large "information repository."

Introduction stage The product life-cycle stage in which the new product is first distributed and made available for purchase.

Inventory turnover rate (or **stockturn rate**) The number of times an inventory turns over or is sold during a specified time period (often one year)—calculated based on costs, selling price, or units.

Joint ownership A joint venture in which a company joins investors in a foreign market to create a local business in which the company shares joint ownership and control.

Joint venturing Entering foreign markets by joining with foreign companies to produce or market a product or service.

Learning Changes in an individual's behaviour arising from experience.

Licensing A method of entering a foreign market in which the company enters into an agreement with a licensee in the foreign market, offering the right to use a manufacturing process, trademark, patent, trade secret, or other item of value for a fee or royalty.

Lifestyle A person's pattern of living as expressed in his or her activities, interests, and opinions.

Line extension Extending an existing brand name to new forms, colours, sizes, ingredients, or flavours of an existing product category.

Local marketing Tailoring brands and promotions to the needs and wants of local customer groups—cities, neighbour-hoods, and even specific stores.

Macroenvironment The larger societal forces that affect the microenvironment—demographic, economic, natural, technological, political, and cultural forces.

Madison & Vine A term that has come to represent the merging of advertising and entertainment in an effort to break through the clutter and create new avenues for reaching consumers with more engaging messages.

Management contracting A joint venture in which the domestic firm supplies the management knowledge to a foreign company that supplies the capital; the domestic firm exports management services rather than products.

Manufacturers' sales branches and offices Wholesaling by sellers or buyers themselves rather than through independent wholesalers.

Market The set of all actual and potential buyers of a product or service.

Market challenger A runner-up firm that is fighting hard to increase its market share in an industry.

Market description Describing the targeted segments in detail provides context for the marketing strategies and detailed action programs discussed later in the marketing plan.

Market development A strategy for company growth by identifying and developing new market segments for current company products.

Market follower A runner-up firm that wants to hold its share in an industry without rocking the boat.

Market leader The firm in an industry with the largest market share.

Market nicher A firm that serves small segments that the other firms in an industry overlook or ignore.

Market offering Some combination of products, services, information, or experiences offered to a market to satisfy a need or want.

Market penetration A strategy for company growth by increasing sales of current products to current market segments without changing the product.

Market potential The upper limit of market demand.

Market segment A group of consumers who respond in a similar way to a given set of marketing efforts.

Market segmentation Dividing a market into distinct groups of buyers who have different needs, characteristics, or behaviours, and who might require separate products or marketing programs.

Market share Company sales divided by market sales.

Market targeting The process of evaluating each market segment's attractiveness and selecting one or more segments to enter.

Market-centred company (targeting) A company that pays balanced attention to both customers and competitors in designing its marketing strategies.

Market-penetration pricing Setting a low price for a new product to attract a large number of buyers and a large market share.

Market-skimming pricing Setting a high price for a new product to skim maximum revenues layer by layer from the segments willing to pay the high price; the company makes fewer but more profitable sales.

Marketing The process by which companies create value for customers and build strong customer relationships to capture value from customers in return.

Marketing channel (distribution channel) A set of interdependent organizations that help make a product or service available for use or consumption by the consumer or business user.

Marketing channel design Designing effective marketing channels by analyzing consumer needs, setting channel objectives, identifying major channel alternatives, and evaluating them.

Marketing channel management Selecting, managing, and motivating individual channel members and evaluating their performance over time.

Marketing concept The marketing management philosophy that holds that achieving organizational goals depends on knowing the needs and wants of target markets and delivering the desired satisfactions better than competitors do.

Marketing control The process of measuring and evaluating the results of marketing strategies and plans and taking corrective action to ensure that objectives are achieved.

Marketing environment The actors and forces outside marketing that affect marketing management's ability to build and maintain successful relationships with target customers.

Marketing implementation The process that turns marketing strategies and plans into marketing actions to accomplish strategic marketing objectives.

Marketing information system (MIS) People and procedures for assessing information needs, developing the needed information, and helping decision makers to use the information to generate and validate actionable customer and market insights.

Marketing intelligence The systematic collection and analysis of publicly available information about consumers, competitors, and developments in the marketing environment.

Marketing intermediaries Firms that help the company to promote, sell, and distribute its goods to final buyers.

Marketing logistics (physical distribution) Planning, implementing, and controlling the physical flow of materials, final goods, and related information from points of origin to points of consumption to meet customer requirements at a profit.

Marketing management The art and science of choosing target markets and building profitable relationships with them.

Marketing mix The set of controllable tactical marketing tools—product, price, place, and promotion—that the firm blends to produce the response it wants in the target market.

Marketing myopia The mistake of paying more attention to the specific products a company offers than to the benefits and experiences produced by these products.

Marketing organization The marketing department may be organized by function, by geography, by product, or by customer (or some combination).

Marketing research The systematic design, collection, analysis, and reporting of data relevant to a specific marketing situation facing an organization.

Marketing return on investment (or **marketing ROI**) A measure of the marketing productivity of a marketing investment—calculated by dividing net marketing contribution by marketing expenses.

Marketing return on sales (or **marketing ROS**) The percent of net sales attributable to the net marketing contribution—calculated by dividing net marketing contribution by net sales.

Marketing strategy The marketing logic by which the business unit hopes to create customer value and achieve profitable customer relationships.

Marketing strategy development Designing an initial marketing strategy for a new product based on the product concept.

Marketing tools These sections of the marketing plan summarize the broad logic that will guide decisions made about the marketing tools to be used during the period covered by the plan.

Marketing website A website that engages consumers in interactions that will move them closer to a direct purchase or other marketing outcome.

Markup The difference between a company's selling price for a product and its cost to manufacture or purchase it.

Markup chain The sequence of markups used by firms at each level in a channel.

Maturity stage The product life-cycle stage in which sales growth slows or levels off.

Maturity stage The product life-cycle stage in which sales growth slows or levels off.

Merchant wholesaler An independently owned business that takes title to the merchandise it handles.

Microenvironment The actors close to the company that affect its ability to serve its customers—the company, suppliers, marketing intermediaries, customer markets, competitors, and publics.

Micromarketing The practice of tailoring products and marketing programs to the needs and wants of specific individuals and local customer groups—includes local marketing and individual marketing.

Millennials (or **Generation Y**) The 83 million children of the baby boomers, born between 1977 and 2000.

Mission statement A statement of the organization's purpose—what it wants to accomplish in the larger environment.

Modified rebuy A business buying situation in which the buyer wants to modify product specifications, prices, terms, or suppliers.

Motive (drive) A need that is sufficiently pressing to direct the person to seek satisfaction of the need.

Multichannel distribution system A distribution system in which a single firm sets up two or more marketing channels to reach one or more customer segments.

Natural environment Natural resources that are needed as inputs by marketers or that are affected by marketing activities.

Need recognition The first stage of the buyer decision process, in which the consumer recognizes a problem or need.

Needs States of felt deprivation.

Net marketing contribution (NMC) A measure of marketing profitability that includes only components of profitability controlled by marketing.

Net profit percentage The percentage of each sales dollar going to profit—calculated by dividing net profits by net sales.

New product A good, service, or idea that is perceived by some potential customers as new.

New task A business buying situation in which the buyer purchases a product or service for the first time.

New-product development The development of original products, product improvements, product modifications, and new brands through the firm's own product-development efforts.

Nonpersonal communication channels Media that carry messages without personal contact or feedback, including major media, atmospheres, and events.

Objective-and-task method Developing the promotion budget by (1) defining specific objectives; (2) determining the tasks that must be performed to achieve these objectives; and (3) estimating the costs of performing these tasks. The sum of these costs is the proposed promotion budget.

Objectives and issues The company's objectives should be defined in specific terms so management can measure progress and plan corrective action if needed to stay on track. This section of the marketing plan describes any major issues that might affect the company's marketing strategy and implementation.

Observational research Gathering primary data by observing relevant people, actions, and situations.

Occasion segmentation Dividing the market into groups according to occasions when buyers get the idea to buy, actually make their purchase, or use the purchased item.

Off-price retailer A retailer that buys at less-than-regular wholesale prices and sells at less than retail. Examples are factory outlets, independents, and warehouse clubs.

Online advertising Advertising that appears while consumers are surfing the Web, including display ads, search-related ads, online classifieds, and other forms.

Online companies The so-called dot-coms, which operate only online without any brick-and-mortar market presence.

Online focus groups Gathering a small group of people online with a trained moderator to chat about a product, service, or organization and gain qualitative insights about consumer attitudes and behaviour.

Online marketing Company efforts to market products and services and build customer relationships over the Internet.

Online marketing research Collecting primary data online through Internet surveys, online focus groups, web-based experiments, or tracking consumers' online behaviour.

Online social networks Online social communities—blogs, social networking websites, or even virtual worlds—where people socialize or exchange information and opinions.

Operating expense percentage The portion of net sales going to operating expenses—calculated by dividing total expenses by net sales.

Operating ratios The ratios of selected operating statement items to net sales.

Opinion leader A person within a reference group who, because of special skills, knowledge, personality, or other characteristics, exerts social influence on others.

Opportunities Opportunities are external elements that the company may be able to exploit to its advantage.

Optional-product pricing The pricing of optional or accessory products along with a main product.

Order-routine specification The stage of the business buying process in which the buyer writes the final order with the chosen supplier(s), listing the technical specifications, quantity needed, expected time of delivery, return policies, and warranties.

Outside sales force Outside salespeople who travel to call on customers in the field.

Packaging The activities of designing and producing the container or wrapper for a product.

Partner relationship management Working closely with partners in other company departments and outside the company to jointly bring greater value to customers.

Percentage-of-sales method Setting the promotion budget at a certain percentage of current or forecasted sales or as a percentage of the unit sales price.

Perception The process by which people select, organize, and interpret information to form a meaningful picture of the world.

Performance review The stage of the business buying process in which the buyer assesses the performance of the supplier and decides to continue, modify, or drop the arrangement.

Personal communication channels Channels through which two or more people communicate directly with each other, including face to face, on the phone, through mail or email, or even through an Internet "chat."

Personal selling Personal interactions between a customer and the firm's sales force for the purpose of making sales and building customer relationships.

Personality The unique psychological characteristics that lead to relatively consistent and lasting responses to one's own environment.

Pleasing products Products that give high immediate satisfaction but may hurt consumers in the long run.

Political environment Laws, government agencies, and pressure groups that influence and limit various organizations and individuals in a given society.

Portfolio analysis The process by which management evaluates the products and businesses that make up the company.

Positioning Arranging for a product to occupy a clear, distinctive, and desirable place relative to competing products in the minds of target consumers.

Positioning statement A statement that summarizes company or brand positioning—it takes this form: *To (target segment and need) our (brand) is (concept) that (point-of-difference).*

Postpurchase behaviour The stage of the buyer decision process in which the consumers take further action after purchase, based on their satisfaction or dissatisfaction.

Preapproach The step in the selling process in which the salesperson learns as much as possible about a prospective customer before making a sales call.

Presentation The step in the selling process in which the salesperson tells the "value story" to the buyer, showing how the company's offer solves the customer's problems.

Price The amount of money charged for a product or service, or the sum of the values that customers exchange for the benefits of having or using the product or service.

Price elasticity A measure of the sensitivity of demand to changes in price.

Primary data Information collected for the specific purpose at hand.

Pro forma (or **projected**) **profit-and-loss statement** (or **income statement** or **operating statement**) A statement that shows projected revenues less budgeted expenses and estimates the projected net profit for an organization, product, or brand during a specific planning period, typically a year.

Problem recognition The first stage of the business buying process in which someone in the company recognizes a problem or need that can be met by acquiring a good or a service.

Product Anything that can be offered to a market for attention, acquisition, use, or consumption that might satisfy a want or need.

Product adaptation Adapting a product to meet local conditions or wants in foreign markets.

Product bundle pricing Combining several products and offering the bundle at a reduced price.

Product concept A detailed version of the new-product idea stated in meaningful consumer terms.

Product development A strategy for company growth by offering modified or new products to current market segments. Developing the product concept into a physical product to ensure that the product idea can be turned into a workable market offering.

Product invention Creating new products or services for foreign markets.

Product life cycle The course of a product's sales and profits over its lifetime. It involves five distinct stages: product development, introduction, growth, maturity, and decline.

Product line A group of products that are closely related because they function in a similar manner, are sold to the same customer groups, are marketed through the same types of outlets, or fall within given price ranges.

Product line pricing Setting the price steps between various products in a product line based on cost differences between the products, customer evaluations of different features, and competitors' prices.

Product mix (or **product portfolio**) The set of all product lines and items that a particular seller offers for sale.

Product position The way the product is defined by consumers on important attributes—the place the product occupies in consumers' minds relative to competing products.

Product quality The characteristics of a product or service that bear on its ability to satisfy stated or implied customer needs.

Product review The product review summarizes the main features for all of the company's products, organized by product line, type of customer, market, or order of product introduction.

Product sales force structure A sales force organization under which salespeople specialize in selling only a portion of the company's products or lines.

Product specification The stage of the business buying process in which the buying organization decides on and specifies the best technical product characteristics for a needed item.

Product/market expansion grid A portfolio-planning tool for identifying company growth opportunities through market penetration, market development, product development, or diversification.

Production concept The idea that consumers will favour products that are available and highly affordable and that the organization should therefore focus on improving production and distribution efficiency.

Profit-and-loss statement (or **income statement** or **operating statement**) A statement that shows actual revenues less expenses and net profit for an organization, product, or brand during a specific planning period, typically a year.

Promotion mix (marketing communications mix) The specific blend of advertising, sales promotion, public relations, personal selling, and direct-marketing tools that the company uses to persuasively communicate customer value and build customer relationships.

Promotional pricing Temporarily pricing products below the list price, and sometimes even below cost, to increase short-run sales.

Proposal solicitation The stage of the business buying process in which the buyer invites qualified suppliers to submit proposals.

Prospecting The step in the selling process in which the salesperson or company identifies qualified potential customers.

Psychographic segmentation Dividing a market into different groups based on social class, lifestyle, or personality characteristics.

Psychological pricing A pricing approach that considers the psychology of prices and not simply the economics; the price is used to say something about the product.

Public Any group that has an actual or potential interest in or impact on an organization's ability to achieve its objectives.

Public relations Building good relations with the company's various publics by obtaining favourable publicity, building up a good corporate image, and handling or heading off unfavourable rumours, stories, and events.

Pull strategy A promotion strategy that calls for spending a lot on advertising and consumer promotion to induce final consumers to buy the product, creating a demand vacuum that "pulls" the product through the channel.

Purchase decision The buyer's decision about which brand to purchase.

Push strategy A promotion strategy that calls for using the sales force and trade promotion to push the product through channels. The producer promotes the product to channel members who in turn promote it to final consumers.

Reference prices Prices that buyers carry in their minds and refer to when they look at a given product.

Relevant costs Costs that will occur in the future and that will vary across the alternatives being considered.

Retailer A business whose sales come primarily from retailing.

Retailing All activities involved in selling goods or services directly to final consumers for their personal, nonbusiness use.

Return on advertising investment The net return on advertising investment divided by the costs of the advertising investment.

Return on investment (ROI) A measure of managerial effectiveness and efficiency—net profit before taxes divided by total investment.

Return on investment (ROI) pricing (or **target-return pricing**) A cost-based pricing method that determines price based on a specified rate of return on investment.

Return on marketing investment (or **marketing ROI**) The net return from a marketing investment divided by the costs of the marketing investment.

Sales force management The analysis, planning, implementation, and control of sales force activities. It includes designing sales force strategy and structure and recruiting, selecting, training, supervising, compensating, and evaluating the firm's salespeople.

Sales promotion Short-term incentives to encourage the purchase or sale of a product or service.

Sales quota A standard that states the amount a salesperson should sell and how sales should be divided among the company's products.

Salesperson An individual representing a company to customers by performing one or more of the following activities: prospecting, communicating, selling, servicing, information gathering, and relationship building.

Salutary products Products that have low appeal but may benefit consumers in the long run.

Sample A segment of the population selected for marketing research to represent the population as a whole.

Secondary data Information that already exists somewhere, having been collected for another purpose.

Segmented pricing Selling a product or service at two or more prices, where the difference in prices is not based on differences in costs.

Selective distribution The use of more than one, but fewer than all, of the intermediaries who are willing to carry the company's products.

Selling concept The idea that consumers will not buy enough of the firm's products unless it undertakes a large-scale selling and promotion effort.

Selling process The steps that the salesperson follows when selling, which include prospecting and qualifying, preapproach, approach, presentation and demonstration, handling objections, closing, and follow-up.

Sense-of-mission marketing A principle of sustainable marketing that holds that a company should define its mission in broad social terms rather than narrow product terms.

Service Any activity or benefit that one party can offer to another that is essentially intangible and does not result in the ownership of anything.

Service inseparability A major characteristic of services—they are produced and consumed at the same time and cannot be separated from their providers.

Service intangibility A major characteristic of services—they cannot be seen, tasted, felt, heard, or smelled before they are bought.

Service perishability A major characteristic of services—they cannot be stored for later sale or use.

Service retailer A retailer whose product line is actually a service, including hotels, airlines, banks, colleges, and many others.

Service variability A major characteristic of services—their quality may vary greatly, depending on who provides them and when, where, and how.

Service–profit chain The chain that links service firm profits with employee and customer satisfaction.

Share of customer The portion of the customer's purchasing that a company gets in its product categories.

Shopping centre A group of retail businesses planned, developed, owned, and managed as a unit.

Shopping product A consumer product that the customer, in the process of selection and purchase, usually compares on such bases as suitability, quality, price, and style.

Social class Relatively permanent and ordered divisions in a society whose members share similar values, interests, and behaviours.

Social marketing The use of commercial marketing concepts and tools in programs designed to influence individuals' behaviour to improve their well-being and that of society.

Societal marketing A principle of sustainable marketing that holds that a company should make marketing decisions by considering consumers' wants, the company's requirements, consumers' long-run interests, and society's long-run interests.

Societal marketing concept The idea that a company's marketing decisions should consider consumers' wants, the company's requirements, consumers' long-run interests, and society's long-run interests.

Spam Unsolicited, unwanted commercial email messages.

Specialty product A consumer product with unique characteristics or brand identification for which a significant group of buyers is willing to make a special purchase effort.

Specialty store A retail store that carries a narrow product line with a deep assortment within that line.

Standardized global marketing An international marketing strategy for using basically the same marketing strategy and mix in all the company's international markets.

Store brand (or **private brand**) A brand created and owned by a reseller of a product or service.

Straight product extension Marketing a product in a foreign market without any change.

Straight rebuy A business buying situation in which the buyer routinely reorders something without any modifications.

Strategic group A group of firms in an industry following the same or a similar strategy.

Strategic planning The process of developing and maintaining a strategic fit between the organization's goals and capabilities and its changing marketing opportunities.

Strengths Strengths are internal capabilities that can help the company reach its objectives.

Subculture A group of people with shared value systems based on common life experiences and situations.

Supermarket A large, low-cost, low-margin, high-volume, self-service store that carries a wide variety of grocery and household products.

Superstore A store much larger than a regular supermarket that offers a large assortment of routinely purchased food products, nonfood items, and services.

Supplier development Systematic development of networks of supplier–partners to ensure an appropriate and dependable supply of products and materials for use in making products or reselling them to others.

Supplier search The stage of the business buying process in which the buyer tries to find the best vendors.

Supplier selection The stage of the business buying process in which the buyer reviews proposals and selects a supplier or suppliers.

Supply chain management Managing upstream and downstream value-added flows of materials, final goods, and related information among suppliers, the company, resellers, and final consumers.

Survey research Gathering primary data by asking people questions about their knowledge, attitudes, preferences, and buying behaviour.

Sustainable marketing Marketing that meets the present needs of consumers and businesses while also preserving or enhancing the ability of future generations to meet their needs.

SWOT analysis An overall evaluation of the company's strengths (S), weaknesses (W), opportunities (O), and threats (T).

Systems selling (or **solutions selling**) Buying a packaged solution to a problem from a single seller, thus avoiding all the separate decisions involved in a complex buying situation.

Target costing Pricing that starts with an ideal selling price, then targets costs that will ensure that the price is met.

Target market A set of buyers sharing common needs or characteristics that the company decides to serve.

Team selling Using teams of people from sales, marketing, engineering, finance, technical support, and even upper management to service large, complex accounts.

Team-based new-product development An approach to developing new products in which various company departments work closely together, overlapping the steps in the product development process to save time and increase effectiveness.

Technological environment Forces that create new technologies, creating new product and market opportunities.

Telephone marketing Using the telephone to sell directly to customers.

Territorial sales force structure A sales force organization that assigns each salesperson to an exclusive geographic territory in which that salesperson sells the company's full line.

Test marketing The stage of new-product development in which the product and marketing program are tested in realistic market settings.

Threats Current or emerging external elements that could potentially challenge the company's performance.

Total costs The sum of the fixed and variable costs for any given level of production.

Total market demand The total volume that would be bought by a defined consumer group in a defined geographic area in a defined time period in a defined marketing environment under a defined level and mix of industry marketing effort.

Trade promotions Sales promotion tools used to persuade resellers to carry a brand, give it shelf space, promote it in advertising, and push it to consumers.

Undifferentiated (mass) marketing A market-coverage strategy in which a firm decides to ignore market segment differences and go after the whole market with one offer.

Uniform-delivered pricing A geographical pricing strategy in which the company charges the same price plus freight to all customers, regardless of their location.

Unit contribution The amount that each unit contributes to covering fixed costs—the difference between price and variable costs.

Unsought product A consumer product that the consumer either does not know about or knows about but does not normally think of buying.

Users Members of the buying organization who will actually use the purchased product or service.

Value chain The series of departments that carry out value-creating activities to design, produce, market, deliver, and support a firm's products.

Value delivery network The network made up of the company, suppliers, distributors, and ultimately customers who "partner" with each other to improve the performance of the entire system in delivering customer value.

Value proposition The full positioning of a brand—the full mix of benefits upon which it is positioned.

Value-added pricing Attaching value-added features and services to differentiate a company's offers and charging higher prices.

Value-based pricing Setting price based on buyers' perceptions of value rather than on the seller's costs.

Variable costs Costs that vary directly with the level of production.

Variety-seeking buying behaviour Consumer buying behaviour in situations characterized by low consumer involvement but significant perceived brand differences.

Vertical marketing system (VMS) A distribution channel structure in which producers, wholesalers, and retailers act as a unified system. One channel member owns the others, has contracts with them, or has so much power that they all cooperate.

Viral marketing The Internet version of word-of-mouth marketing—websites, videos, email messages, or other marketing events that are so infectious that customers will want to pass them along to friends.

Wants The form human needs take as shaped by culture and individual personality.

Warehouse club An off-price retailer that sells a limited selection of brand-name grocery items, appliances, clothing, and a hodgepodge of other goods at deep discounts to members who pay annual membership fees.

Weaknesses Internal elements that may interfere with the company's ability to achieve its objectives.

Wheel-of-retailing concept A concept that states that new types of retailers usually begin as low-margin, low-price, low-status operations but later evolve into higher-priced, higher-service operations, eventually becoming like the conventional retailers they replaced.

Whole-channel view Designing international channels that take into account the entire global supply chain and marketing channel, forging an effective global value delivery network.

Wholesaler A firm engaged primarily in wholesaling activities.

Wholesaling All activities involved in selling goods and services to those buying for resale or business use.

Word-of-mouth influence Personal communication about a product between target buyers and neighbours, friends, family members, and associates.

Workload method An approach to determining sales force size based on the workload required and the time available for selling.

Zone pricing A geographical pricing strategy in which the company sets up two or more zones. All customers within a zone pay the same total price; the more distant the zone, the higher the price.

Name Index

Subject Index

Key terms and pages on which they're defined are indicated in bold.

Chapter 7

212 Stan Honda/AFP/Getty Images/Newscom. 213 Getty Images, Inc. 215 © 2008 Intel Corporation. All rights reserved. Photographer: Zach Gold. Used with permission. 216 Inter IKEA Systems B.V. 2009. 217 CCNMATTHEWS PHOTO/UPS Canada. 221 Courtesy of Cardinal Health. 222 © 2008 Peterbilt Motors Company. All rights reserved. Used with permission. 223 L.D. Gordon/Getty Images, Inc. 225 Copyright © 2007 Sharp Electronics Company. All rights reserved. Reprinted with permission. Photographer: Carl Zapp. 227 Courtesy of Magna. 228 © 2008 Sun Microsystems, Inc. All rights reserved. Used with permission. 229 RBC Financial Group. CHAPTER 8 238 Copyright © 2008 The Procter & Gamble Company. All rights reserved. Reprinted with permission. 239 Copyright © 2008 The Procter & Gamble Company. All rights reserved. Reprinted with permission. 244 © 2008 Daisy Rock Guitars. All rights reserved. Used with permission. 245 © 2008 The Ritz-Carlton Hotel Company, L.L.C. All rights reserved. Reprinted with the permission of The Ritz-Carlton Hotel Company, L.L.C. 246 PEEPS® and the PEEPS® chick shape are registered trademarks of Just Born, Inc., Bethlehem, PA, http://www.marshmallowpeeps.com/. 247 (top) © James Leynse/CORBIS All Rights Reserved. 247 (bottom) Courtesy of Environics Analytics. 248 © 2004 American Express Company. All Rights Reserved. Courtesy of Ogilvy & Mather. 249 The Canadian Press(Frank Gunn). 250 Courtesy of Anything Left Handed. All rights reserved. 252 NAUTICA and the sailing symbol are registered trademarks of Nautica Apparel, Inc. North Face is a registered trademark of North Face Apparel Corp. Riders and Lee are registered trademarks of The H.D. Lee Company, Inc. Wrangler and Rustler are registered trademarks of Wrangler. Lucy is a registered trademark of Lucy Activewear Inc. Reef is a registered trademark of South Cone. 7 for all mankind is a registered trademark of 7 for all mankind. All rights reserved. 253 Copyright © 2008 The Procter & Gamble Company. All rights reserved. Reprinted with permission. 255 © 2007 Zappos.com, Inc. 256 © 2008 MINI, a division of BMW of North America, LLC. All rights reserved. The MINI and BMW trademark, model names and logo are registered trademarks. Photo courtesy of Jim Sulley with Newscast and MINI. 258 © Bebeto Matthews/AP Wide World. 260 Copyright © 2008 Toyota Motor Sales. All rights reserved. Used with permission. 261 © 2008 Staples Inc. All rights reserved. Used with permission. 262 CCNMATTHEWS PHOTO/WestJet. 264 Courtesy of SC Johnson, A Family Company.

Chapter 9

275 Phil Date/Shutterstock. 277 Permission granted to uses Books and Beyond ad. Courtesy of The Alberta Library. 278 © Jim Craigmyle/ CORBIS All Rights Reserved. 280 © Scott Gries/Getty Images. 282 © 2007 OXO International Inc. All rights reserved. Used with permission. 283 Courtesy of H. J. Heinz Company. 284 Courtesy of Arthur's Fresh Co. - We Don't Dilute our Fruit! 285 (top) Courtesy of Pepsi-Cola North America, Inc. All rights reserved. 285 (bottom) © 2008 Hewlett-Packard Company. All rights reserved. Used with permission. 287 © 2008 Sony Electronics Inc. All rights reserved. Used with permission. 288 Chris Mueller/Redux Pictures. 289 © 2008 Research in Motion. All rights reserved. Used with permission. 291 Godiva Chocolatier. 293 Copyright © 2006 Costco Wholesale Corporation. All rights reserved. Reprinted with permission. 294 © 2007 Viacom International Inc. All rights reserved. Nickelodeon, SpongeBob SquarePants and all related titles, logos, and characters are registered trademarks of Viacom International Inc. Created by Stephen Hillenburg. 295 Jim Whitmer Photography. 296 © Disney Enterprises, Inc./Joe Raedle/Getty. 300 Robyn Twomey. 301 Copyright © 2008 British Airways Plc. All rights reserved. Reprinted with permission. 304 (top) David Butow/Corbis/SABA Press Photos, Inc.; (bottom) Alyson Aliano.

Chapter 10

312 © Cameron Spencer/Getty Images. 314 © Jeff Chiu/AP Wide World. 315 Courtesy of NewProductWorks, a division of GFK Strategic Innovation. Used with permission. 316 Ki Ho Park. 318 Rick Rappaport Photography. 319 © 2008 Tesla Motors. All rights reserved. Used with permission. 322 Brooks Kraft/Corbis Sygma. 323 © Darron Cummings/AP Wide World. 324 Copyright © 2008 Decision Insight. All rights reserved. Reprinted with permission. 325 Copyright © 2008 Microsoft Corporation. All rights reserved. Reprinted with permission. 327 Copyright © 2008 Trek Bicycle Corporation. All rights reserved. Reprinted with permission. 329 © Erin Siegal/Reuters. 331 TABASCO® is a registered trademark for sauces and other goods and services; TABASCO, the TABASCO bottle design and label designs are the exclusive property of McIlhenny Company, Avery Island, LA, USA 70513. www.TABASCO.com. 332 © 2008 Kraft Foods Inc. All rights reserved. Used with permission. 335 GLAD® PRESS'N SEAL® are registered trademarks of The Glad Products Company. Used with permission. 338 NESTLE and KIT KAT are registered trademarks of Société des Produits Nestlé S.A., Switzerland and are reproduced with the consent of the trademark owner.

Chapter 11

346 © 2008 Eastman Kodak Company. All rights reserved. Used with permission. 347 © 2008 Eastman Kodak Company. All rights reserved. Used with permission. 348 Getty Images, Inc. 351 AP Wide World Photos. 352 Raghu Rai. 357 © 2008 Titus Cycles. All rights reserved. Used with permission. 358 © The New York Times/Redux. 360 © 2008 Kohler Co. All rights reserved. Used with permission. 361 © 2004 Gibson Guitar Corp. All rights reserved. 364 © Romain Degoul/REA/Redux. 366 (top) Courtesy of Intuit Canada. 366 (bottom) © 2008 Six Flags Theme Parks Inc. All rights reserved. Used with permission. 368 Jim Whitmer Photography. 369 D. Young-Wolff/PhotoEdit Inc. 370 © Pedro Armestre/AFP/Getty Images. 372 (top left) David Zalubowski/AP Wide World Photos; (top right) AP Wide World Photos; (bottom left) AP Wide World Photos; (bottom right) David Zalubowski/AP Wide World Photos. 373 © Noah Berger/AP Wide World. 374 © 2008 Dell Inc. All rights reserved. 376 © Ric Francis/AP Wide World. 378 © 2008 The Procter & Gamble Company. All rights reserved. Used with permission.

Chapter 12

388 © 2008 Enterprise Rent-a-Car Company. All rights reserved. Used with permission. 389 © 2008 Enterprise Rent-a-Car Company. All rights reserved. Used with permission. 390 © Paul Sakuma/AP Wide World. 393 Courtesy Grand & Toy. 394 Joe Heiner. 396 Courtesy of Inditex. Reprinted with permission. 397 Courtesy of Nurse Next Door. 398 STR/AFP/Getty Images, Inc. AFP. 400 © 2008 Black & Decker, Inc. All rights reserved. Used with permission. 401 Reproduced by permission of Netflix, Inc.

Copyright © 2008 Netflix, Inc. All rights reserved. Photographer: Remy Haynes Photography. 404 © Ami Vitale/Getty Images. 405 © CHINA NEWSPHOTO/Reuters/ Corbis. 406 Copyright © 2008 Samsung Electronics America, Inc. All rights reserved. Reprinted with permission. 407 © David Boily/AFP/Getty Images. 411 Gene Helvig/Fine Image Photography. 412 Chris Crisman/Chris Crisman Photography. Used with permission.

Chapter 13

420 © Chris Mueller/Redux Stock. 422 © Carolyn Kaster/AP World Wide. 424 The Canadian Press(Nathan Denette). 425 (left) Courtesy OrangeTwice; (right) Ben Margot/AP Wide World Photos. 426 Courtesy Alimentation Couche-Tard Inc. 427 H&M Hennes & Mauritz Inc. 428 Gary Armstrong. 431 © Mark Peterson/Redux. 433 © Elise Amendola/AP Wide World. 434 Getty Images, Inc. 435 © 2008 Sony Electronics Inc. All rights reserved. Used with permission. 437 West Edmonton Mall. 440 AP Photo/Ric Feld. 442 Source: Virtual Musem of Canada (www.virtualmuseum.ca). Permission of the Canadian Heritage Information Network (CHIN), © CHIN 2009. 443 Courtesy of New Town Associates, LLC. 448 © 2008 McKesson Corporation. All rights reserved. Used with permission.

Chapter 14

454 © Chris Polk/Getty Images. 456 Copyright © 2008 Unilever PLC. All rights reserved. Reprinted with permission. 457 © moodboard/Corbis. 460 © Dominic Lipinski/PA Wire URN:5902155 (Press Association via AP Images). 465 Copyright © 2008 International Business Machines Corporation. All rights reserved. Reprinted with permission. Photographer: John Clang. 466 Courtesy of United Way of America. Used with permission. 467 © Molson Coors Brewing Company. 468 © Glow Images/Getty Images. 469 CPimages.ca/PHOTO/ Reebok Canada Inc. 472 © Thomas Northcut/Getty Images. 474 Tim Boyle/Getty Images, Inc. - Getty News. 477 Courtesy of RONA.

Chapter 15

485 Reprinted with kind permission of United Way Toronto. 488 Courtesy of Stokely-Van Camp, Inc. All rights reserved. 490 Bayerische Motoren Werke Aktiengesellschaft. 491 Courtesy of www.istockphoto.com. 492 Cover image of Madison & Vine, by Scott Donaton. © 2004 The McGraw-Hill Companies. Used with permission. 495 © 2008 Sanford, a Newell Rubbermaid Company. All rights reserved. Used with permission. 496 Advertisement provided courtesy of Frito-Lay, Inc. 498 Copyright © 2008 The Procter & Gamble Company. All rights reserved. Reprinted with permission. 499 Courtesy of Suncor Energy Inc. 501 Jupiter Images - FoodPix - Creatas - Brand X - Banana Stock– PictureQuest. 503 Copyright © 2008 The Procter & Gamble Company. All rights reserved. Reprinted with permission. 506 © Lucas Jackson/Reuters. 507 Courtesy of Johnson & Johnson. Used with permission.

Chapter 16

514 © 2008 CDW Corporation. All rights reserved. Used with permission. 515 © 2008 CDW Corporation. All rights reserved. Used with permission. 517 © Wong Maye-E/AP Wide World. 518 © Rob Melnychuk/Photodisc/Getty Images. 521 Getty Images, Inc. 522 © Paul Sakuma/AP Wide World. 525 Courtesy of Jennifer Hansen. Photographer: Linda Ford. Used with permission. 526 ©

2008 International Rectifier. All rights reserved. Used with permission.528 Jupiter Images - FoodPix - Creatas - Brand X - Banana Stock–PictureQuest. 532 (top) © 2008 Weyerhaeuser Company. All rights reserved. Reprinted with permission. 532 (bottom) Jon Feingersh/CORBIS/Jon Feingersh. 534 Lon C. Diehl/PhotoEdit Inc. 538 © 2008 Cellfire Inc. All Rights Reserved. Used with permission. 539 Courtesy of Perfetti Van Melle. 540 © 2008 CEA. All Rights Reserved. Used with permission.

Chapter 17

548 Stuart Isett. 550 © Amazon.com, Inc. or its affiliates. All Rights Reserved. Amazon, Amazon.com and the Amazon.com logo are registered trademarks of Amazon.com, Inc. or its affiliates. 551 © 2008 GEICO. All rights reserved. Used with permission. 553 David Cooper/GetStock.com. 554 (top left) © Gerard Guittot/REA/Redux; (top right) © Taxi/Getty Images. 554 (bottom) Courtesy Michelin North America. 557 Amanda Kamen. 559 The Shopping Channel website 2009. 560 Courtesy of The New York Times. 561 (top) Courtesy Fido. 561 (bottom) Julia Grossi/Corbis Zefa Collection. 563 Courtesy of Office Depot. 566 General Motors Corp. Used with permission, GM Media Archives. 568 Courtesy The Home Depot Canada. 569 (top) Courtesy of United Parcel Service of America, Inc. and Andy Azula. 569 (bottom) © Unilever Canada Inc. Reproduced with permission. 572 Courtesy of imeem, Inc. Used with permission. 574 © Copyright 2009, Her Majesty the Queen in Right of Canada as represented by the Royal Canadian Mounted Police.

Chapter 18

584 © Adrian Dennis/AFP/Getty Images. 585 © Adrian Dennis/AFP/Getty Images. 588 © 2008 Viking Range Corporation. All rights reserved. Used with permission. 591 Courtesy of Johnson & Johnson. Used with permission. 592 © Anita Bugge/WireImage/Getty Images. 593 © 2008 Stonyfield Farm, Inc. All rights reserved. Used with permission. 596 © 2008 The Ritz-Carlton Hotel Company, L.L.C. All rights reserved. Reprinted with the permission of The Ritz-Carlton Hotel Company, L.L.C. 599 Courtesy of Campbell Soup Company. Used with permission. 600 Amanda Kamen. 601 Richard Drew/AP Wide World Photos. 603 Courtesy of R.A.B. Food Group. LLC. Used with permission. 604 © 2008 Logitech Inc. All rights reserved. Used with permission.

Chapter 19

613 Courtesy McCain Foods Limited. 615 (bottom) © Guo Shiqiang/AP Wide World. 615 (top) Reprinted with permission of Cervélo. 617 (top) Corbis RF; (bottom) Courtesy of the WTO. 618 © European Community. 619 Richard Jones/Sinopix Photo Agency Limited. 621 Mike Clarke/Getty Images, Inc. AFP. 622 Tracey Foster/GetStock. 625 Richard Jones/Sinopix Photo Agency Limited. 627 YOSHIKAZU TSUNO/AFP/Getty Images, Inc. AFP. 628 © Arko Datta/Reuters. 631 Gary Armstrong. 633 © Tony Avelar/AP Wide World. 634 © Inter IKEA Systems B.V. 636 Panos Pictures. 637 BlackBerry®, RIM®, Research In Motion®, SureType®, SurePress™ and related trademarks, names and logos are the property of Research In Motion Limited and are registered and/or used in the US and countries around the world.

Appendix A3, A4 Courtesy ZENN Motor Company.